A History and Genealogy

of

CAPTAIN JOHN LOCKE

(1627–1696)

of

Portsmouth and Rye, New Hampshire

and
His Descendants

also of

NATHANIEL LOCKE
of Portsmouth

and a Short Account of the

History of the LOCKES in England

Arthur H. Locke, A.M.
#7816
Member of New Hampshire Historical Society

HERITAGE BOOKS
2011

HERITAGE BOOKS
AN IMPRINT OF HERITAGE BOOKS, INC.

Books, CDs, and more—Worldwide

For our listing of thousands of titles see our website
at
www.HeritageBooks.com

A Facsimile Reprint
Published 2011 by
HERITAGE BOOKS, INC.
Publishing Division
100 Railroad Ave. #104
Westminster, Maryland 21157

Originally published
Concord, New Hampshire
The Rumford Press
(c.1916)

Previously published in two volumes.

— Publisher's Notice —
In reprints such as this, it is often not possible to remove blemishes from the original. We feel the contents of this book warrant its reissue despite these blemishes and hope you will agree and read it with pleasure.

International Standard Book Numbers
Paperbound: 978-1-55613-889-8
Clothbound: 978-0-7884-8913-6

PREFACE

The Locke Genealogy, like most family histories, was first started out of a curiosity, which finally led to duty; curiosity to learn who and what was our family; duty to preserve that which was going so rapidly by the deaths of those older ones whose early days, sitting in the home circle, were filled with local and family events, which became memorized, and so were handed down to us. It was and is this class which has made genealogies possible, supplying us with facts not contained in the early meager town records, and happening before the present careless town statistics were inaugurated.

Thus the work was started in college days, and continued during a busy life, yet a life which gave me access to all the large libraries of the country, and its only drawback was lack of opportunity to travel and thus be able to solve some problems which no correspondence could accomplish. I could boast a few years ago that every genealogy or local history published up to that time and contained in the larger libraries had been carefully scrutinized, and this review of several thousand books has given me data concerning unknown Lockes which with index would fill fifty pages of this work; rather too much to incorporate here, though a few New Hampshire items are inserted in hopes that some may be recognized and properly connected before forgotten.

The Locke Family Association, even if in its twenty-five years of life has not realized its intention of greatly helping the writer, yet has been of the utmost importance in getting the Lockes together from all over the country, has advertised the fact that a genealogy was being prepared, and this alone puts the blame for any omissions or manifest errors on the Lockes themselves. Thousands of letters have gone out seeking information, and every effort has been made to keep the data as correct as conflicting town records, tombstone inscriptions, and imperfect memory would allow. In looking back I can see where other duties with consequent interruptions have marred the work somewhat, and fear of too bulky a volume caused me to sacrifice smoothness to brevity, but I have no apologies to offer under the circumstances. Much thought has been given to a permanent rag paper with the result of doubling the usual cost of the one item.

I am under great obligation to many people for their help in the work and trust the completion of it in their lifetime may be some recompense to them. "The Book of Lockes," by John G. Locke of Boston, 1853, has been of great assistance to me. Although almost wholly confined to the Massachusetts family, yet he collected and preserved much of interest to our family and in the later pages of this book I have copied *in toto* what he collected of our common Locke history in England.

All unknown items in my possession and all additions and corrections, which I trust may be sent to me, will in time be indexed and deposited with the New Hampshire Historical Society, Concord, N. H., for preservation and inspection.

Some of the oldest Lockes in my memory, now long departed, have been quite insistent that we were related to the famous John Locke, a very laudable ambition and tradition, but the English records are so very incomplete, that while some American families have tried to prove this idea, not much foundation exists at present for such pretence. A statement made a few years ago in England was: "It would take a regiment ten years to copy the church and town records."

I have made no distinction as to spelling Lock or Locke, and have used the latter entirely. I have no doubt those who spell their name Loch were originally of English descent, as those whom I have interviewed seem to think, but the line is far removed from any of the New England Lockes.

About the year 1726, the present town of Rye was set off from New Castle, Portsmouth and Hampton, nine tenths being from the first town. This will explain the apparent confusion of names.

I find Lockes among the earliest Dutch settlers of New York city, a family settled in New Jersey, one in Virginia, another in North Carolina, all quite as old in time of settlement as William of Massachusetts or John of New Hampshire. Some of our own missing branches lived in Chenango and Orleans Counties, New York, and Branch County, Michigan. Many other Lockes have settled in the country since 1800.

PREFACE v

To quote from "The Book of Lockes": "I do not offer you a history of high dignitaries in Church or State, or valiant warriors who have won renown at the head of armies. Mine is the history of the yeomanry and artisan; of those who have earned their bread on their farms and in their workshops by the sweat of their brow; and if they performed well their part in their station—however humble it may have been,—they are not to be despised, —but honored.

"I have labored to rescue from oblivion the names of those who have gone before us, to record their virtues, and to place landmarks where they resided; that those of us who are now on the stage, and those that come after us, may answer the question—Who was your father?"

ABBREVIATIONS

When no state is mentioned, New Hampshire is understood. The usual abbreviations: b., bapt., m., unm., d., signifying born, baptized, married, unmarried, died, are used throughout the book. The sign ? is used where doubt exists. Parenthesis ( ) are used where necessary also to distinguish maiden names.

ARRANGEMENT

Every descendant has an individual number beginning with Captain John, those having children have F before the number and this number, in heavy type in consecutive order, forms the heads for the succeeding generation.

Reversing the process, to find ancestors: having found the name in the index, take the heavy type number at head of that family and go back to that number, and so follow heads back to Captain John, who is **F. 1.**

ARTHUR H. LOCKE.

PORTSMOUTH, N. H.

IN MEMORY OF
CAPT. JOHN LOCKE
WHO CAME FROM ENGLAND TO THESE
SHORES ABOUT 1640
HE WAS KILLED BY THE INDIANS
AUG. 26, 1696 AT THE AGE OF 70 YRS.
WHILE REAPING IN HIS FIELD AT LOCKES
NECK THIS TOWN.

ADDRESS OF JUDGE JAMES W. LOCKE

On the Occasion of the Dedication Aug. 27, 1902, of the Monument Illustrated on the Opposite Page.

Ladies and Gentlemen, Members of the Locke Family Association:

More than two centuries ago, our common ancestor was snatched from life near this spot, by the hands of members of that race which before the march of civilization was slowly disappearing. The vigor and force with which he had been wont to protect his family and home, had called down upon him the antagonism of his enemies, and his bravery was now overcome by the cunning of the savage, and overwhelming numbers, and after a most gallant fight with the only instrument at hand, that not even a weapon of war but an emblem of peace, he yielded to the inevitable. If we are to credit the records, both written and traditional, we may believe that he had lived a life of energetic action and forcible achievement. Of toil and labor, of hardship, exposure and discomforts inseparable from the life of a first settler in a wild and savage country he had his share; but we may also believe that he had been, as a man, a leader among men, and left a name, that within the small circle in which he moved was not without honor. His life was a long and eventful one; he had reached his three score years and ten and had unquestionably seen the results of his labors commencing to turn the wilderness to a land of families and settled homes, in place of the wandering tribes of Red Men. His death was one of the many sacrifices which is continuously being demanded by the advance of races and the change of conditions, the advance of civilization and the establishment of new nations.

The contest waged with the original occupants of the soil was on each side but a strife for self preservation in which the weaker had to succumb and the stronger to succeed. But what the final result of these individual sacrifices has been in the great aggregate, the present condition of our nation clearly shows.

Little could Capt. John Locke perceive, think or even dream, two hundred and six years ago yesterday of the final result that was to flow from the efforts of himself and those like him in their efforts to make for themselves homes in the new world. How little could he conceive with even the dimmest imagining to what a grand result the little seed that he was planting was to grow. Yet it is to be believed that in everything he did his present duty to the best of his understanding and knowledge.

Let us imagine if we can the circumstances of that time; the, to him, eventful day, the surroundings of that tragic ending of the life of the old man upon whose head the snows of seventy winters then rested. Undoubtedly the sun shone with a splendor equal to that of to-day; the blue of the old ocean was as vivid, and the ripplings of its waves upon the pebbly beach as musical as at the present. But the shades of the primeval forests surrounded the little clearing where the small house and outbuildings were standing as sentries, and as an advanced guard to the coming civilization.

Vigorously the sickle was plied in the waving corn until the large boulder against which leaned the faithful musket was left at a distance, and in the joy and satisfaction of a well earned harvest the brightness of nature was only thought of and danger forgotten. But unnoticed and slowly and softly with the stealthy step of the beast of prey, dark forms came slowly gliding out from the forest shades and concealed behind the stumps and dead, although standing trees, got between him and his only weapon of defense, when, with a war-whoop, which even then sounded of victory, they rushed upon their victim.

The contest was too unequal; the strife determined from the beginning by a force too great to be overcome; and he who had fought his last fight and won his last battle, struggling to the last with his sickle's blade, yielded at length to the deadly arrow and tomahawk. But he had already done his work. He had acted well his part in planting the seed for a magnificent nation. If it is true that

"To the hero when his sword has won the battle for the free
Death's voice comes like a prophet's word
And in its hollow tones are heard,
The voice of millions yet to be:"

may we not believe in his last moments he felt that his life had not been in vain? and from his duties well done there might in the providence of an All-wise Ruler be fruits and rewards to the coming generations?

Could it be that there might have been with a prophetic glimpse a flash of coming events; of the heights of Bunker Hill and Ticonderoga, the sufferings of Valley Forge, the glories of Saratoga and Yorktown, of Gettysburg, of Vicksburg, of Lookout Mountain and Missionary Ridge, and later the swamps and mountains of the Philippines, in all of which his descendants would take up the life of the pioneer in carrying civilization into the new places of the earth, as they might have, might not his last moments have been like the glory of a setting sun after a day of clouds and darkness?

Here, therefore, come we to-day to dedicate to the memory of Capt. John Locke a humble token of our consideration and relationship. We attempt no grand or expensive column, no beautiful or ornate mausoleum, but a simple block as evidence of our appreciation of the fair record of a life of duty well performed and honorably ended; of a name which has been handed down to us unsullied by him who first bore it in this land. We are well aware that this simple tribute can add nothing to the memory of the departed or the value of his example.

The lives of his descendants have and will determine whether they have been true or recreant to the principles of right living, of honest, energetic action which made him favorably known among his neighbors and associates.

But may it, firmly fixed on its foundations as it is, be to us a suggestion that our lives and actions, examples and influences, do not cease with our parting breath but will live for the encouragement or regret of coming generations even as is now the memories of the life of our common ancestor an inspiration to higher living and nobler achievements!

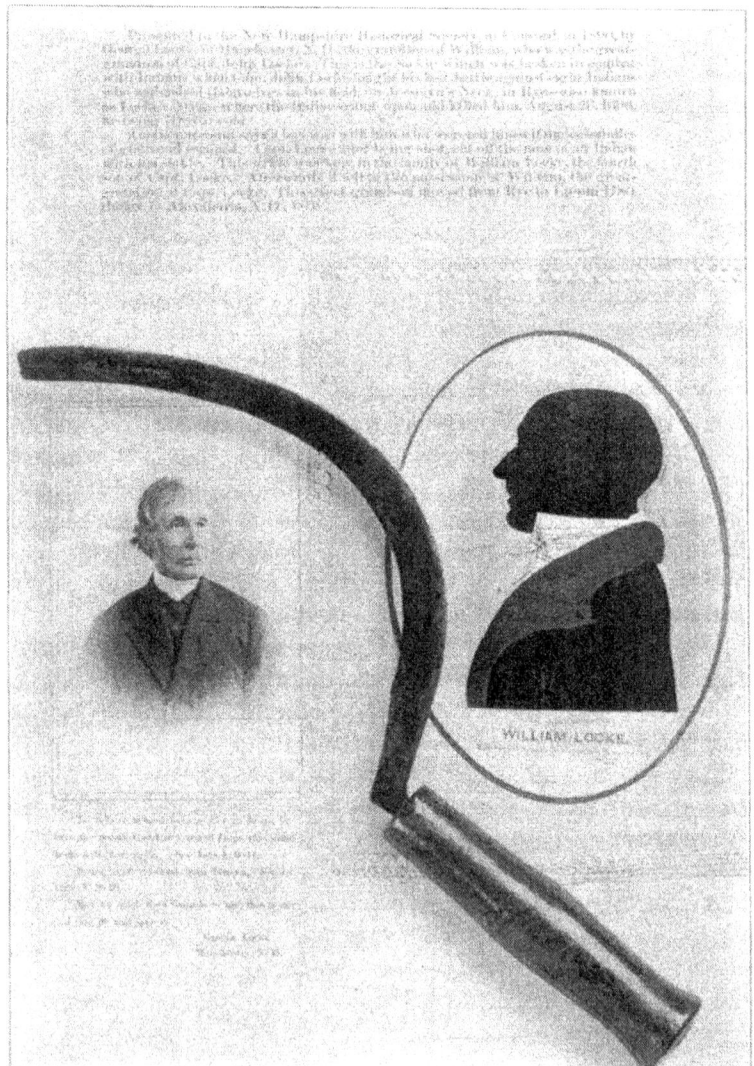

SKETCH OF CAPTAIN JOHN LOCKE

In writing the history of John Locke, the progenitor of the Lockes in New Hampshire, and some of the oldest families of that name in Rhode Island, New York, and Nova Scotia, we have some records, more tradition, and much circumstantial evidence. A most careful search of published English records gives us nothing more than that found in Savage's Genealogical Dictionary (an American work of inestimable value), and the London White Chapel Register. See History of English Lockes on later pages. This register shows us that Thomas Locke of London, married Christena French, July 26, 1624, and they had sons, John, baptized Sept. 16, 1627, and Nathaniel, baptized Nov. 11, 1629. Assuming that John and Nathaniel Locke of Portsmouth, N. H., were brothers, and taking into account their ages, we have no other recourse at present than to accept it as very probable that these were the sons of Thomas of London, recorded above. Possibly time will bring to light further proof or give us welcome facts on other lines.

In 1620, during the reign of James I, the religious and political persecutions drove the Puritans from England and forced them to find a home on foreign shores, and this emigration continued for a long period and in constantly increasing numbers. To stop this drain on his kingdom, Charles I ordered every person emigrating to take the oath of supremacy and allegiance, and this had two effects. One was, that all who took the oath were thus privileged in having their names, time of sailing, and, in many cases, their place of birth, age, and occupation, recorded in the office. On the other hand, hundreds refusing to sign away their independence were forced to sail surreptitiously leaving no trace behind, and so their first movement was recorded on American shores. Our own John Locke was undoubtedly one of the latter, and perhaps came to these shores in one of those hundred ships, which we are told touched the New England coast between Salem and Portland, in the years 1630–1640 and of which we have no record.

The family tradition from the very earliest times is that John

Locke came from Yorkshire, England, and settled in New Hampshire about the years 1638–1644; that "at first he settled in Dover where he owned a right of land"; that from thence he moved to Fort Point, New Castle, and about the year 1652 married Elizabeth the daughter of William Berry, who was probably the first settler in Hampton at a place called Sandy Beach, now in Rye. From New Castle Mr. Locke moved to Sagamore Creek where he lived until 1665, when he went to Hampton, now Rye, N. H. The early records of Dover have nothing to corroborate the above first statement. The Selectmen of Portsmouth, in 1652, started a new town record, copying only a few items from an older book covering the years 1623–1651, the oldest book of the colony, which is now lost, and so any possible clue that might interest us is forever gone.

The Portsmouth records do, however, mention him as follows: "And likewise John Locke is to have a house lott between John Jacksons and William Cotton's rails, the lott eight acres. At a town meeting held this first day of Januarie, 1656." At a meeting Jan. 22, 1660, "John Locke having eight acres, to have eight more"; and the same year there was laid out to him "eight acres from Stony Brooke towards John Jones, 24 pole wide and 40 pole back into the woods, upon a south west line." Tradition tells us that John Locke framed the first meeting house in Portsmouth, and probably the first in New Hampshire about 1645. The specifications read: "The meeting house to be made 40 ffeet square with 12 windowes well fitted, 3 substanciall doers and a complete pulpit." It was ordered built, Aug. 27, 1657, as given in "Historic Portsmouth." The date must be wrong as the seats were ordered in 1654. This church stood south of Pickering's Dam (now South Mill Bridge), at the junction of South and Marcy Streets, and was removed about 1750. It is barely possible that the town took the above means to pay this young man for his work by granting him the eight acres in the southern part of Portsmouth.

The first grant of eight acres in 1656 bears out the tradition of his living at Sagamore Creek, since it was very close to that locality, being in reality on the present Little Harbor road, on the side of hill just east of the new brick Memorial Church, and overlooking the city of Portsmouth, of which it is a part. See enclosed plan. Evidently he did not live here long, as shown by the following sale.

"Be it known unto all men by these presents that I, John Lock of Portsmouth, on Piscataqs river, Carpenter & Elizabeth my wife for and in consideration of the sum of Thirty two pounds 10 s. to us in hand before the engaging hereof, by James Drew of the same place marrynor, do . . . sell unto the said James Drew my new dwelling house . . . therewith eight acres of uplands on which the said house stands and is situate, and being between ye lands of John Jones on the West northly & ye lands of John Jackson on the East Southerly. Said lands of eight acres be it more or less was given & granted me the said Lock by the Town of Portsmouth, as may appear by the sd Towns grant & record of the bounds when it was laid out. All the said premises with the appurtenances of same which belonging to ye sd Locke & Elizabeth my wife . . . unto the sd Drew & his heirs etc. . . . furthermore whereas there is a piece of marsh in disspute between me the sd Jno Lock & Wm. Cotton; I ye sd Jno. Lock & Elizabeth my wife do include in the sd forementioned bargain, if either ye sd Lock or ye sd Drew can recourus of ye hand of the sd Cotton, & ye sd Lock do hereby promise to do all in my power for the attainment of the same etc. . . . , in witness thereof his hand & seal & deliver the 23 day of March 1660-61."

Jno X Lock
Elizabeth X Lock

I am convinced also that the grant of 1660 was near the first grant if not adjacent, and this he sold long after he went to Locke's Neck, Hampton, as shown by the sale to his late neighbor Cotton with whom he had the dispute over the marsh land.

"John Lock of Portsmouth, carpenter & wife Elizabeth, sold to William Cotton eight acres land to be layd out in Portsmouth, as appears in town book Sept. 8, 1674." John acknowledged the sale, March 26, 1675.

I should judge that this dispute over marsh land was not settled since it appears in John's estate in 1707, and again later according to these transfers. "Shadrack Walton of New Castle sold John Dennett of Portsmouth, 3 acres of salt marsh in Little Harbor bounded by Mark Hunking's marsh on the south side and Jno. Locke's on the north side, and by the main brook on the east side, dated; Dec. 12, 1693." This marsh was later transferred in August and November 1709; Jno. Lock's marsh being mentioned on the north side.

"Jno. Lock & Daniel Thomas having Edward Colcord committed to them for keeping & Letting him go in the night, are fined 2-6 apiece & are enjoyned to do their utmost to gott him again; if they do, are to be released from their fines otherwise to pay as above. 1662." Could it be possible that Edward bribed his jailors? At any rate there is no mention that they "gott" him.

At a town meeting in Portsmouth March 8, 1665-6, John Locke subscribed 5 shillings for the support of the minister, Mr. Moody. The town record also has in the same year:

"Capt. Locke was fined 5," whether shillings or pounds, or for what is not stated. Note the official record calls him Captain.

"The names of such who took the oath of fidelity ye 2nd. of Oct., 1666, upon ye Election of Military officers; Jno Lock." "A noate drawne on Hen. Dering, Constable, to pay Jno Lock 12 s: dated Oct. 26, 1671."

These items all go to show that while he was living at Joselyn's or Locke's Neck at this time, having moved there before 1665, he considered, and Portsmouth considered that he was within the latter's jurisdiction. Hampton took a different view of the matter and the town records show they acted accordingly.

"He sat down (squatted hence the word 'Squatter') on the public lands at Josselyn's Neck" and began clearing a farm without saying "by your leave," and as the inhabitants claimed the right of saying who should be citizens of the town, they chose a committee May 24, 1666, to pull up his fence and March 12, 1667, to warn him to desist from improving the town land and to notify him "that the town is displeased with his building there." Complaint was made against him as a "Trespasser" and he was warned to appear at the next meeting and give an account of himself. On the 8th of March 1667 the town voted: "Upon the motion of John Lock who desireth to yield himself to the town of Hampton as an inhabitant here amongst us, being already settled upon Josselyn's Neck in Hampton bounds, the town hath accepted of the said John Lock for an inhabitant accordingly." So John Locke from being the first squatter

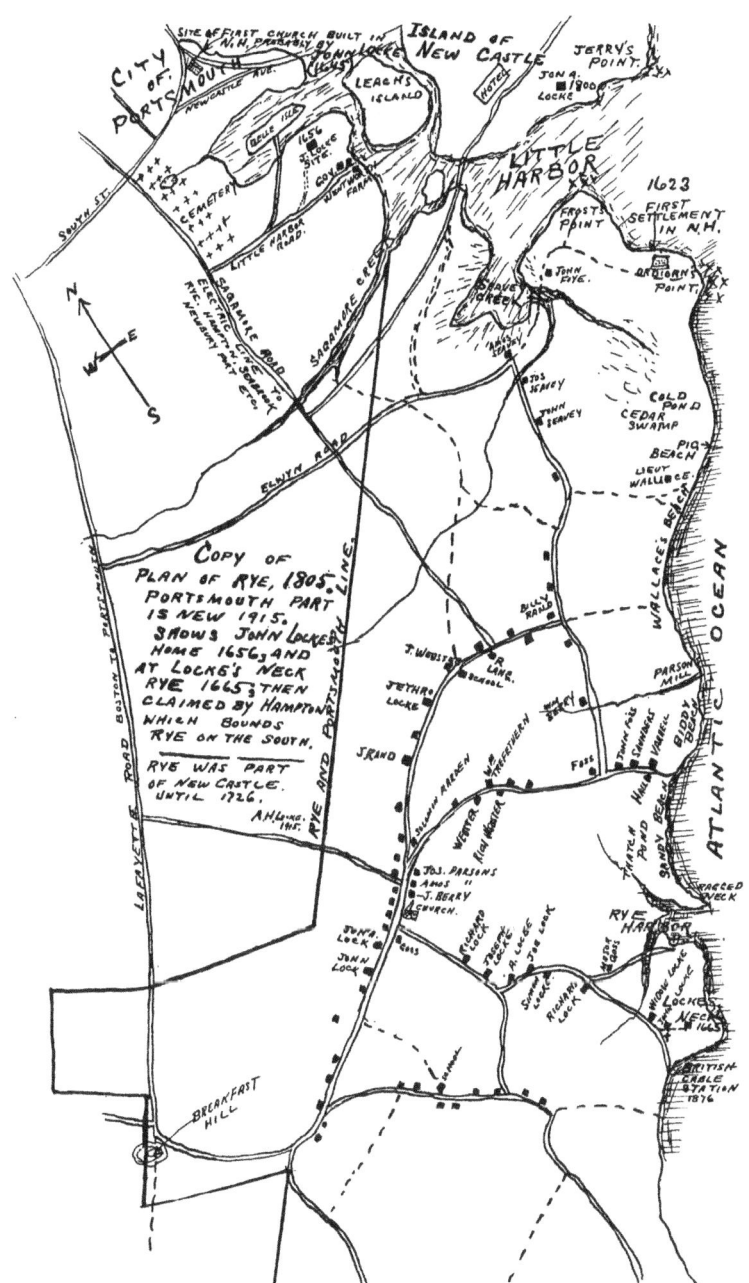

became an inhabitant of Hampton, now Rye, N. H., and here he continued to live until his death.

Joselyn's Neck became Locke's Neck and so continued for two hundred years, in fact today it is equally as well known as by the newer name Straw's Point, a name given because Governor Straw bought much of the land and erected many houses upon it.

These depositions of his neighbors are interesting as fixing his residence, and landmarks.

"The Deposition of George Hunt aged 35 years testifiethe and Saith that Living with John Lock of Hampton and that I being then a Servant with him, that I Did help fence the neck of Land called Joselyn's neck thirteen year agoe (1667), and did help fence the marsh belonging to the neck twelve year agoe and further saith not. Taken upon Oath Sept. 1st. 1680."

"Nathaniel Drake aged 68, and John Goss aged 46, and John Berry aged 43, "Testfiieth and saith that John Lock hath enjoyed ye neck of Land commonly called Josliens neck fifteen years or thereabouts peacably and had it in fence moste part if not all the time above said, and further we testify that the marsh in Contreversy between Francis Jinins and Said Lock is within said Lock's fence as above said which he made near fifteen years ago (1665). Taken under oath Sept. 8, 1680."

"John Brackett aged 39 years testifieth that fourteen or fifteen years ago (1665) I helped John Lock fence a corn field at a place called Joslien's neck and since I have seen a fence at the head of the neck where the cattle used to come over. Sworn to Sept. 7, 1680."

"John Lock aged about 75, and John Foss aged about 69, testifieth that they have known the great Pond in Rye known by name as Sandy Beach Pond to have been fenced and in possession of John Lock formerly of Hampton deceased and William Berry of Portsmouth, disceased, for 60 years (1668), and fence enclosed meadows all around on back side and ends running down to the sea, and has been possessed by their descendants since. Sworn to, Feb. 5, 1728-9."

In 1672 John Lock was a witness to a land claim of Nathaniel Wallis of Casco, Me. He served on the jury in Portsmouth, Nov. 6, 1683, in the trial, "Proprietor Mason versus Vaughan." (He perhaps heard there why the early colonial record was destroyed.)

Either John Locke Sr. or Jr. was a witness to Anthony Brackett's will in 1691, and Anthony was killed by Indians that same year. John Locke's province tax rate of 1693, was 3 pounds, charged to New Castle but paid in Hampton; his son John's tax was 2 pounds.

There seems to be some discrepancy in the date as to when John Locke died. According to Hampton records:

"John Locke Senior was killed by the Heathen in his lott at work upon August 26 1696." In the Rev. Huntington Porter's address delivered in Rye Jan. 1 1801, he says "In 1694 (it should be 1696), John Locke being at the Neck was ambushed and killed by the Indians as he was reaping grain in his field."

Undoubtedly the most reliable report is that contained in Reverend John Pike's Journals 1678 to 1709. Written by a divine living in those years, and shepherd of those early settlers, surely he could not be more than a day wrong as compared with the Hampton record. He writes: "Lieut. Lock was slain by the Indians at Sandy Beach, Aug. 25, 1696." It will be noted that this is the second time a title is given to John Locke, and this time by one who wrote advisedly.

The early writings of Rye and Hampton mention three garrison houses, one of which, called the Lock Garrison, was at Locke's Neck and existed as late as 1708, and we may presume that it was Locke's house, built strongly of timbers to repel the savages and in which his neighbors sought refuge during the several Indian assaults on these early settlers. It is also probable that having such a stronghold and being in charge or in command of it as owner, he very naturally acquired the title of Lieutenant or Captain as noted in two cases above, even though we do not know that he ever received such commission from the authorities themselves.

With only a difference of wording the histories and early writers have this to say of Captain Locke's death. He was noted for the daring and success with which he fought the Indians, foiling their many attempts to destroy the settlers, hence was correspondingly hated by them. On one of their raids from the east, landing on the coast near Locke's Neck, they concealed their canoes in the bushes and went inland to surprise their intended victims. Locke discovered the canoes and cut generous slashes in them where the cuts were not seen at first glance. The Indians returning from their murderous expedition, pushed off only to find themselves sinking, thereby losing nearly all their plunder, stores, and arms and making it necessary for them to escape overland, suffering many hardships and losing some of their band. Later, a party of eight came from the eastward with the express purpose of killing Locke and, surprising him as he was reaping grain in his field, mortally wounded him with his own gun, which he had left against a rock at some distance away. They then returned without doing further damage. One account says that when the Indians ran up to scalp Locke, the latter had strength enough left to cut off the nose of one with the sickle he had been using; which act was seen by one of his sons who had secreted himself in the grain.

Several anecdotes are told concerning this fact. One was that years after when friendship with the Indians was restored, the same son who saw his father killed, met an Indian minus a nose while both were out hunting, and who when questioned said "Old Locke cut it off." He explained that they tried to capture him alive as he was such a brave man, but he fought so they were compelled to kill and scalp him. Whereupon the son killed the Indian. Another account is that a grandson, named Berry, met at a Portsmouth tavern a noseless Indian, who, rendered talkative by liquor, boasted that he had killed a brave white man, "Old Captain Locke." Whereupon Berry waited outside, killed the Indian, and threw his body in a well, which well was filled up the next day. Jonathan Locke, born 1702, a grandson of Captain Locke, built a house at Rye Center, where the late Jonathan lived (the same site). Seeing an Indian one day a short distance away, he raised the window, propped it up with a book, and taking careful aim with his gun which rested on the window sill, shot the red man dead. When taken to task for killing an Indian in time of peace, he replied that the Indians killed his grandfather and he would kill one whenever he had the chance. Thus it seems that Captain Locke must have been sufficiently avenged, that is if the Indians held out.

John Locke left no will, but letters of administration were granted March 4, 1706, whereby John and Joseph, the oldest and youngest sons, were to settle the estate. An inventory made by James Rendle and William Seavey was returned as follows:

An Inventory Est. of John Lock deceased now under Adm. of John & Joseph Lock   May 19 1707.

on yoke of oxen	£8–00–00
two Cows	5–10–00
on yearling & Calf	1–03–00
eight Swine	5–10–00
to puter and Candl Stick	1–01–00
two Iron pots	0–16–00
two tramels on pare of pot hooks	0–08–00
on Spite & fire tongs & a small cops	0–07–00
4 chares	0–04–00
on bras kittel	0–09–00
on Sword	6–06–00
on frying pan	00–03–00
two Chests	09–00
to Earthen ware	03–00
to his Carpenters tules	12–00
on draft chain	06–00
feathers and two old coverleds	1–10–00
on bed & bedding	5–00–00
house & land & medow at gossling neck	25–00–00
two akers of salt marsh at little harbor	8–06–00
	64–07–00

The estate was divided among ten children as given below, the oldest, John, to receive a double portion, although he had already in 1677 been given one half of all his father's lands at Locke's Neck: John, Nathaniel, Edward, William, James, Joseph, Alice, Phenea (Tryphena), Rebecca, Mary. John and Joseph made return to court, May 4, 1708.

"As there was nothing taken out for the widdows thirds, by reason the Adms. did voluntarily promise and agree in open court to take care for the maintainance of the widdow; it is therefore ordered that the said Adms. take care to maintain the widdow during her natural life accordingly. Charles Storer. Recorder."

There can be no doubt that there was an Elizabeth in the above family, and Dr. John Locke born 1772, in a signed statement, names all the above children and Elizabeth also. Eleven children are also named by other old descendants. We can only suppose she died before 1708.

Those of us who recall the early years of our Locke Association will remember that a sword and sickle, claimed to have been used by our ancestor was presented to us and later placed in the keeping of the New Hampshire Historical Society. The fact that a sword is listed in his estate makes the above much more credible, particularly as it passed through only three hands. It is claimed that William Locke, 1677-1768, gave sword, gun, and sickle to his grandson, William, 1758-1828; from him these relics descended to his grandson George Locke, 1817-1903, who gave them to the Association. Excessive patriotism of the Locke boys July 4, 1840, caused the old gun to burst, and though its parts were treasured many years, they gradually disappeared.

That John Locke possessed a sword does not prove that he was an officer or that he was foolish enough to pursue savages with it. Rather let us suppose our ancestor was a man, brave as the Indians called him, such a one as would naturally take the leadership of settlers or scouts when after an enemy, and to whom they would look not as a superior officer but as a fellow settler, perhaps more daring than the rest.

Our progenitor's home at Locke's Neck was probably situated almost in the middle of the present road to the outer end of the point, and just beyond its junction with the road to Jenness Beach and the cable station. The only landmarks are the tansy and one upright stone gate post on the left, which at one time held a gate which gave entrance to the property. His remains, together with his kinsfolk, we must suppose rest in a little plot of land in the southeast corner of these two roads, where thirty-five graves, or rather rough stones may be counted. See the cross marked on the map. The oldest Rye people can tell nothing about this graveyard, except that many years ago a few, perhaps five shipwrecked people were buried there in the space nearest Jenness Beach.

Not being sure of John Locke's burial place, The Locke Association a few years ago erected in the Central Cemetery at Rye, a handsome granite monument to the memory of our ancestor. This association, further honors his memory by holding its annual meetings on the Wednesday nearest the 26th day of August, at Rye, N. H.

John Locke left little in financial estate, what he left was far more valuable. He left in a struggling settlement ten children from whom came at least forty-eight grandchildren. A score or more of his descendants inheriting his fighting spirit took part in the Indian Wars. At least a hundred fought in the War for Independence, and since that time thousands, whether they be governors of New Hampshire, lawyers of national reputation, the honest mechanics, or the humble tillers of the soil, claiming him as ancestor, have performed their little or much in making our country what it is today. Such an estate we claim has no esti mate in dollars and cents.

F1 Captain John Locke was probably baptized in London, England, Sept. 16, 1627, married about 1652, ELIZABETH, the daughter of William and Jane Berry, and was killed by the Indians Aug. 26, 1696, in Rye, N. H. Elizabeth the widow was living in 1708 when the estate was settled and the children given below shared in its distribution. Several old papers prepared by descendants born about 1735, give the entire family, and in the following order. As first names only were given it is impossible to determine whether the girls were married, or to whom married at that time (1708) but we know nearly all were.

Children of 2nd Gen.

F2 JOHN, b. 1654 (?), m. ELIZABETH BOLLES (Bowles).
3 ELIZABETH, b. ——, probably d. before estate was settled in 1708.
F4 NATHANIEL b, 1661 (?), m. 1688-9, DOROTHY BLAKE.
5 ALICE or ELSIE, b. ——, m. NEHEMIAH BERRY, March 14, 1714-5.
F6 EDWARD, b. ——, m. HANNAH JENNESS, in 1692.
F7 TRYPHENA, b. ——, m. JOHN WEBSTER, in 1693.
8 REBECCA, b. ——, living in 1708.
9 MARY, b. ——, m. WILLIAM HEPWORTH of Boston, Jan. 31, 1697.
F10 WILLIAM, b, Apl. 17, 1677, m. HANNAH KNOWLES, in 1699.
F11 JAMES, b. ——, m. HANNAH PHILBRICK, in 1713.
F12 JOSEPH, b. ——, m. SALOME WHITE.

THIRD GENERATION

F2 John Locke, b. 1654 (?), m. ELIZABETH BOLLES (now spelled Bowles) of Wells, Me., about 1677. York deeds say: "Joseph Bolles of Wells by deed Oct. 25, 1678, gives Elizabeth Locke ten acres of land at 3 mile brook, Wells," and by will dated Sept. 18, 1678, he gives dau. Elizabeth, ten pounds. A correspondent writes that he thinks this Elizabeth m. 2nd, WILLIAM PITMAN of Portsmouth. The Rye records say an Elizabeth Locke d. Nov. 12, 1734; and I think this is she. Were it Capt. John's widow, she would have been over 100 years old, and his dau. ELIZABETH must have died before 1708. This accounts for all of that name now known.

He was on jury duty in 1704, and scouts were posted June 5, 1705, as far as his house. About 1677 his father gave him half his right of land on Josling's Neck, and Feb. 3, 1707–8 this JOHN, JR., now Senior, gave his son JOHN, JR., half of all his rights at Josling's Neck in consideration that he pay a debt to Robert Eliot, and the other half on condition that he maintain his mother and pay his brother JETHRO 5 pounds. He bought land in Rye in 1728 at Locke's Neck, and sold all his lands to his son JOHN Dec. 18, 1733. He lived in Rye.

Children as far as known of 3rd Gen.

F13 JOHN, b. 1683, m. SARAH ———.
14 RICHARD, b. ———.
F15 JETHRO, b. ———, m. 1720, his cousin DOROTHY LOCKE, #18.
F16 (ELIZABETH (?) b. ———, m. Feb. 28, 1710-11, SAMUEL NEAL.)

F4 Nathaniel Locke, b. 1661 (?), m. in Hampton, Jan. 22, 1688-9, DOROTHY BLAKE, dau. of Jasper and Deborah (Dawlton), who was b. Sept. 17, 1668, d. Hampton, Sept. 28, 1737. He was called a planter of Hampton in 1727, when he made a deposition about land. He d. Nov. 12, 1734, in Hampton. Tradition says he had 19 children and lived where Mrs. Sarah F. Willcut now lives.

Children b. in Hampton, 3rd Gen.

17 JOHN, b. 1689, m. SARAH ———. Probably the first of that name in Rhode Island and of whom nothing more is known.

THIRD GENERATION

13

   18 DOROTHY. b. March 20, 1690, m. 1720, her cousin JETHRO LOCKE, (See F15).
   19 NATHANIEL, b. 1691, died young.
F20 TRYPHENA, b. 1692, m. JOHN KNOWLES, in 1713.
F21 ELIZABETH, b. 1694, m. THOMAS LEAVITT, in 1714.
F22 RACHEL, b. Dec. 12, 1695, m. WILLIAM MOULTON, in 1715.
F23 JOSEPH, b. 1697 (?), m. MERCY NIXON, in 1722.
F24 NATHANIEL, b. Oct. 20, 1699, m. 1st, ABIGAIL PRESCOTT, 1726; m. 2nd, MARY STUBBS.
F25 TIMOTHY, b. 1700 (?), m. MIRIAM BROOKE, in 1722.
F26 SAMUEL, b. 1701-2, m. JERUSHA SHAW, in 1729.
   27 DEBORAH, b. 1704 (?), m. WILLIAM BUCKINGHAM, Oct. 19, 1732. She, her infant child, brother NATHANIEL'S wife, and a Mrs. Noyes, were all lost in a vessel going from Falmouth, Me., to Cape Ann, in 1735.
F28 JONATHAN, b. Dec. 22, 1705, m. SARAH or MARY NORTON, 1729–30.
   29 ABIJAH, b. ——, went to Rhode Island, and nothing further is known of him.
   30 ALICE, b. ——, m. THOMAS EDMONDS, Feb. 22, 1721-22, in Greenland.
   31 MARY, of Dover, b. ——, m. GEORGE BANFIELD, of Portsmouth, May 25, 1727, by Rev. Wm. Allen.
   32 MEHITABLE, b. ——, m. Sept. 13, 1726, in Greenland by Rev. Wm. Allen to MOSES BLAKE, b. Apl. 22, 1707, son of Moses and Abigail (Smith); *children:* 33 DANIEL, b. 1727; 34 MOSES, b. 1730.

F6 Edward Locke, b. ——, m. in 1692, HANNAH JENNESS, dau. of Francis and Hannah (Swaine) of Hampton. She b. March 26, 1673. His name appears on petitions in the years 1721-6, and in the year 1701, his father-in-law conveys land at Sandy Beach Pond to Edward and wife Hannah, and after their decease to their son FRANCIS. Edward sells house, barn, and part of land at Sandy Beach Pond, July 17, 1738, to son THOMAS. He was a farmer in Rye, and died about 1739.

Children of 3rd Gen. all b. in Rye.

F35 FRANCIS, b. July 18, 1694, m. DELIVERANCE BROOKIN in 1716, and SARAH MOULTON in 1733.
F36 SAMUEL, b. Sept. 4, 1698, m. MARGARET WARD in 1725.
F37 EDWARD, b. May 28, 1701, m. HANNAH BLAKE in 1724.
F38 PRUDENCE, b. May 30, 1707, m. EBENEZER WARE in 1735, and ANDREW WEBSTER in 1742.
F39 JAMES, b. Oct. 4, 1709, m. MERCY FOSS, 1731.
F40 THOMAS, b. June 10, 1713, m. (ABIGAIL BERRY).
   41 (LYDIA, b. Oct. 29, 1726 (?).)
   42 A Son of Edward d. Kensington Jan. 12, 1747, age 37.

F7 Tryphena Locke, b. ——, m. in Haverhill, June 14, 1693, JOHN WEBSTER, son of Stephen and Hannah (Ayer). She d. March 6, 1729. He m. 2nd, JOANNA CALLUM. He b. in Haverhill, March 15, 1668, and d. there May 4, 1742. Only one of ten children is known.

Child of the 3rd Gen.

43 JUDITH WEBSTER, b. Haverhill, Sept. 1694, m. Jan. 9, 1718, PHILIP HAZELTON, son of John and Mary. He b. March 13, 1685, lived in Windham.

Had children of the 4th Gen. as follows:

44 JAMES, b. March 28, 1720, m. 1st, Nov. 13, 1741, ELIZABETH HUTCHINS, who d. July 12, 1750. He m. 2nd, Nov. 5, 1751, RUTH LADD. He had seven children in Haverhill.
45 TRYPHENA, b. March 3, 1722, m. NATHANIEL DUSTIN. Nine more children died young.

F10 Deacon William Locke, b. Hampton, Apl. 17, 1677, m. Nov. 23, 1699, HANNAH KNOWLES of Kingston, dau. of John and Jemima (Austin). She b. Hampton, Apl. 18, 1678, d. in Rye, Sept. 12, 1769, aged 91. He was on various petitions 1717–21–26; was a selectman in 1726, and called Lieut. William; was a moderator in 1743. He bought land on the way from Sandy Beach to Greenland, 1723–4, and gave it to his son JONATHAN in 1728. In 1723 he bought land at Portsmouth Plains. William, a shopkeeper of Portsmouth, bought land on northwest side of the road from "Ye Bank to Greenland." June 30, 1728, he bought land in Rye called "Ye Island of ye Pond once called Locke's Hole." He sold land in Rye in 1751, and died there Jan. 22, 1768, aged 91.

Children of the 3rd Gen.

F46 JONATHAN, b. March 15, 1702, m. SARAH HAINES, 1727.
F47 WILLIAM, b. ——, m. MIRIBAH PAGE, 1729, and ELIZABETH RAND, 1734.
F48 ABIGAIL, b. 1706, m. JOSES PHILBRICK, 1726–7.
49 HANNAH, b. ——, d. young.
F50 PATIENCE, b. 1711, m. NOAH MOULTON, 1749.
51 SARAH, b. ——, m. FRANCIS JENNESS of Barrington. He b. Dec. 30, 1699, son of Hezekiah and Ann (Folsom). Sarah had child of 4th Gen.: 52 ELIZABETH, b. Rye, Sept. 9, 1741.
F53 DEACON ELIJAH, b. ——, m. HULDAH PERKINS, 1739.
F54 ELISHA, bapt. 1719, m. Jan. 13, 1743, TRYPHENA MOULTON.
55 ELIPHALET, b. ——, d. May 1740.
F56 JEMIMA, b. Jan. 20, 1720, m. 1740, JOHN BLAKE.
F57 HANNAH, b. July 1, 1724, m. 1745, JEREMIAH BERRY.

THIRD GENERATION

F11 James Locke, b. ——, m. in Greenland by Rev. Wm. Allen Dec. 3, 1713, HANNAH PHILBRICK, probably a second wife, bapt. Oct. 31, 1697, dau. Thomas and Hannah (White). On July 17, 1712–3, there was allotted to him half of two shares in the 1st north division where his house stood in Hampton, at the north end. He bought land of H. Jenness Feb. 24, 1724–5, and sold land to John Locke in 1734. He sold land at Sandy Beach 1742–3; and in 1750 conveyed land to James and wife Sarah, who agree to keep their father for life.

Children of 3rd Gen., perhaps others unknown.

F58 JAMES, b. ——, m. SARAH REMICK, Oct. 25, 1720.
59 (MERIBAH, b. Apl. 23, 1719.) Rochester Hist. says dau. of James and Sarah. I place her as sister of James.

F12 Capt. Joseph Locke, b. ——, m. in Greenland by Rev. Wm. Allen, SALOME WHITE, dau. of William. She was bapt. Sept. 30, 1711, d ——. Both were received into the Greenland Church in 1718. May 13, 1713, he bought "one-fourth part of the meadow and upland fenced in at Sandy Point at a place called Dry Point." July 31, 1718, he bought rights in the town commons at New Castle, also in April 1720 and June 1723. Dec. 19, 1721, he bought land in Chester. Ensign Joseph bought land at Dry Point May 15, 1728. Jan. 7, 1730, he bought land in Rye. Nov. 17, 1722, he sold rights in Chester. Capt. Joseph bought land in Portsmouth Oct. 23, 1735. In 1739 he sold land at Dry Point and Sandy Beach Pond. Joseph, "Gent.," sold land to dau. Salomie & Jonathan Goss, Dec. 12, 1738. In 1763 he conveyed land to son JOSEPH and HANNAH his wife, and after their death to their two sons RICHARD and JOSHUA, 30 acres. He lived at Locke's Cove, was a selectman, 1726–39, and was called Captain and Ensign. 1730–42 was moderator, and town clerk in 1739. Wallace S. Goss now lives on the homestead. "Captain Joseph Locke, of Rye, Gent., for 10000 pounds do convey to my son JEREMIAH all my land 115 acres at (Locke's) Neck, one half grist Mill, tools, etc.; also Nimshi, a Molater boy until he is 30 years of age." Dated Feb. 15, 1763.

In "Col. Sherburne's Regiment, 9th Co.; Capt. Joseph Locke had 90 men, Aug. 6, 1740."

NIMSHI (Locke), the colored boy slave of Capt. Joseph Locke, certainly deserves mention. He enlisted and served under Capt. Joseph Parsons at Fort William and Mary, and was on Capt. Parsons' roll at Cambridge Nov. 22, 1775; mentioned as enlisted Dec. 6, 1775, at Cambridge; was paid Sept. 6, 1776, in Capt. Jona. Robins Co., and was killed in the war, where or when is unknown. Tradition says he was freed by Jeremiah before enlistment, so he fought and died as a free man.

Children 3rd Gen. all b. in Hampton.

F60 SALOME, b. Oct. 20, 1710, m. May 22, 1735, JONATHAN GOSS.
F61 JOSEPH, b. Apl. 27, 1716, m. 1st., HANNAH JENNESS, Dec. 4, 1739; m. 2nd, WIDOW MARY (YEATON) ORDIORNE.
F62 ELIZABETH, b. Dec. 1, 1718, m. Jan. 6, 1743, JUDE ALLEN.
F63 MARY, b. May 1, 1720, m. SOLOMON WHITE of New Castle.
F64 ANNIS, b. Mar. 25, 1723, m. Mar. 10, 1748, JOHN PERKINS.
F65 ABIGAIL, b. Nov. 6, 1725, m. Jan. 25, 1748, ROBINSON TREFETHERN.
F66 JEREMIAH, b. Aug. 1, 1728, m. 1st, Feb. 5, 1753, MARY ELKINS; m. 2nd, WIDOW MARY (BERRY) HAINES.

FOURTH GENERATION

F13 John Locke, b. 1683, m. Sarah ———. He, "a husbandman," bought land Dec. 28, 1733, on the road near Rye Meeting House. He sold land in Rye, Oct. 17, 1734; JOHN "a yeoman," bought land 1742. Received into Greenland Church 1723. Sarah and four children died in 1736 with throat distemper. He d. 1774-5.

Children of the 4th Gen. all b. in Rye.
67 JOHN, b. 1714, d. Jan. 26, 1717-8.
F68 RICHARD, b. July 28, 1720, m. ELIZABETH GARLAND of Rye.
69 MARY, b. Nov. 13, 1722, d. July 1736.
70 ABNER, bapt. 1723, d. Aug. 11, 1736.
71 TRYPHENA, bapt. 1723, d. Aug. 13, 1736.
72 JACOB, b. Nov. 12, 1727, d. Aug. 1736.
73 JOHN, b. ———, d. June 23, 1730.

F15 Jethro Locke, b. ———, m. Jan. 14, 1720, his cousin **Dorothy Locke** #18. She b. Mar. 20, 1690, d. ———. He bought land in Hampton, May 30, 1717, also some near Breakfast Hill, March 10, 1729-30; bought land between Breakfast Hill and Sandy Beach, in 1735, and sold land in 1735.

"Will of Jethro Locke in the parish of Rye to my well beloved son Jethro, all my whole estate of land and salt marsh lying and being in the parish of Rye aforesaid or in any other town parish or precinct whatsoever together with one Dwelling house and Barn chains and axes, one loom and tackling for weaving, one bed & bedclothes, one Gun, one Iron Kettle, one Pott together with all my wearing clothes.

I do give to my well beloved dau. Deority Locke 5 pounds currant Money of N. E., to be paid by my son Jethro when he comes of age & is entered in possession of my estate, 1 grt Pott, one little iron Kettle, 1 bed & bedclothes, one Chist, one Trunk & all other of my household furniture together with all Her mothers wearing clothes.

I do give and bequeth unto my well beloved brother John Locke 2 cows 1 year old 2 stears coming in four years old, one heifer coming in three years in Dea. Jennins pasture, 6 sheep one mair, 3 hoggs, 3 piggs, which he is to dispose of to the best advantage in order to pay the Doctors Funeral charges & all other nessary charges and if there is any money left over & above mentioned it is my will that it be equally divided and given to my children etc." Dated June 18, 1737.

Children of 4th Gen. b. in Rye.

74 DOROTHY, bapt. June 28, 1721, nothing further known.
75 SIMON, bapt. Dec. 29, 1723, died young.
F76 JETHRO, b. June 27, 1727, m. HANNAH RAND, Feb. 2, 1748.

F16 Elizabeth Locke, m. in Greenland by Rev. Wm. Allen, Feb. 28, 1710–11, SAMUEL NEAL, son of Samuel and Jane (Foss).

Children of 4th Gen.

One account says they had: 77 SAMUEL J. who had 3 chlldren, and 78 JOHN WALTER who had 7. Another party writes that Elizabeth had:
79 SAMUEL NEAL, m. Feb. 7, 1754, ELIZABETH HALEY, dau. of Andrew and Deborah Wilson of Haley's Island, Isle of Shoals, and they had:
80 SAMUEL, b. March 22, 1755; 81 ANDREW, b. Jan. 19, 1758; 82 JEREMIAH, b. Nov. 4, 1759; 83 JOSEPH, b. March 23, 1762, m. 1787, HANNAH SMITH, dau. of Jeremiah, b. March 27, 1771, d. March 24, 1851; he and his brother John went "into the wilderness" (Meredith), where he made his home of cut logs. He d. March 23, 1851; 84 JOHN, b. March 10, 1764; 85 ELIZABETH, b. May 29, 1768; 86 MARY, b. June 1, 1770; 87 SARAH, b. June 23, 1773; 88 ABIGAIL, b. Jan. 29, 1775; 89 DEBORAH, b. Jan. 22, 1778.

F20 Tryphena Locke, b. 1692, m. Dec. 31, 1713, JOHN KNOWLES, the son of John and Susannah. He was b. in Hampton, May 14, 1686, later lived in Rye and both belonged to the Greenland Church in 1719.

Children of 4th Gen.

90 JOHN, b. Oct. 12, 1716, m. Jan. 1, 1741, SARAH MOULTON. He lived in Chester and d. March 26, 1798. *Children:* 91 JOHN, b. 1743; 92 NATHAN, b. ——; 93 MARY; 94 SARAH, b. 1741; 95 TRYPHENA, b. 1745.
96 ABIGAIL, b. Sept. 17, 1717.
97 JAMES, b. Feb. 26, 1720, m. in Rye, Oct. 7, 1744, MARY LIBBEY, b. Nov. 4, 1722, dau. of Isaac and Mary (Farmer); m. 2nd, June 30, 1748, COMFORT WALLACE. They removed to Rochester in 1749. Had: 98 DANIEL, bapt. 1746; 99 MARY; 100 COMFORT, bapt. 1749.

FOURTH GENERATION

101 SUSANNA, b. 1726, m. July 18, 1745, SAMUEL BROWN, b. Nov. 20, 1720, d. 1804, son of Joseph and Elizabeth (Moulton), lived at Rye and Chester. Had: 102 MARY, b. Apl. 21, 1746; 103 JONATHAN, b. Sept. 15, 1747; 104 JOHN, b. Nov. 20, 1760, m. COMFORT JENNESS, d. Sept. 5, 1822. She d. Oct. 30, 1846; 105 DAVID, m. ELIZABETH NAY.

F21 Elizabeth Locke, b. 1694, m. Hampton Falls, Nov. 24, 1714, THOMAS LEAVITT, son of Aretus and Ruth (Sleeper). He b. Jan. 15, 1686; d. Nov. 16, 1761; was a farmer in Hampton. She d. Hampton Falls, July 11, 1776.

Children of 4th Gen. b. in Hampton.

106 MARY, b. Oct. 14, 1716.
107 JOHN, b. May 4, 1719, m. MARY TILTON; lived at Sargents Island and he was frozen to death Jan. 12, 1770.
F108 AMOS, b. Oct. 23, 1720, m. ELIZABETH VARRELL, Jan. 13, 1740.
109 JONATHAN, bapt. Aug. 11, 1723.
110 ANN, bapt. Aug. 6, 1727.
111 MARCIA, b. ——, m. —— HASKELL.
112 JOSEPH, b. Oct. 4, 1732, d. yng.
F113 BENJAMIN, b. 1732 a twin, m. ESTHER TOWLE, Dec. 6, 1753. ELIZABETH, bapt. Apl. 14, 1734.

F22 Rachel Locke, b. Dec. 12, 1695, m. in Hampton, March 6, 1715, WILLIAM MOULTON, b. Feb. 18, 1690, son of Josiah and Elizabeth (Worthington). She d. Jan. 20, 1774. He lived in Hampton and d. there Nov. 19, 1762. They lost five children with throat distemper.

Children of 4th Gen. b. in Hampton.

F114 WILLIAM, b. Apl. 15, 1716, m. ——.
115 RACHEL, b. Nov. 3, 1718, d. Sept. 6, 1736.
F116 JOSIAH, bapt. Dec. 4, 1720, m. 1st, HULDAH MARSTON; m. 2nd, ABIGAIL MARSTON.
117 NATHANIEL, bapt. Oct. 14, 1722; was unm. and drowned June 25, 1751.
118 ELIZABETH, bapt. Apl. 19, 1724; d. Sept. 5, 1736.
F119 THOMAS, bapt. Apl. 27, 1726, m. Aug. 1, 1750, HANNAH DOWNES.
120 ELISHA, bapt. July 14, 1728; d. Sept. 9, 1736.
121 LUCY, bapt. June 7, 1730, d. Feb. 21, 1736.
122 DOROTHY, b. Apl. 30, 1731, d. Sept. 8, 1736.
123 ANN, b. May 18, 1735, d. Sept. 2, 1736.
124 SIMON, b. May 29, 1737.

F23 Joseph Locke, b. Rye, 1697, m. MERCY NIXON in Block Island, Dec. 12, 1722; Thomas Rathbun, Feb. 20, 1730-1 gave land to "Marcy Lock, for the love and good will that I have unto her, whom I have brought up from her childhood." Block Island Records. Joseph Locke was made freeman in 1734, was "town sargent and constable" in 1737; was assessed for taxes from 1748 to 1773, between these dates he held many minor offices, but he and his wife are not mentioned after 1773. See note under Sylvanus D. Locke, F 1399.

Children of 4th Gen. b. in Block Island.

F125 NATHANIEL, b. Sept. 29, 1723, m. 1st, ANN ROSE; 2nd, TEMPERANCE ROSE.
126 MERCY, b. March 16, 1727.
F127 JOSEPH, b. ——, m. LUCY or ELIZABETH RATHBON.

F24 Capt. Nathaniel Locke, b. in Hampton, Oct. 20, 1699, m. 1st, Jan. 6, 1725–6, ABIGAIL PRESCOTT, the dau. of Jonathan and Elizabeth of Chichester; she was b. Mar. 23, 1703, and was drowned in 1735 on a vessel going from Falmouth to Cape Ann, Mass. He m. 2nd, MARY STUBBS of Cumberland, Me., the dau. of Richard and Rebecca. She b. July 10, 1718, d. Mar. 21, 1802. Nathaniel of Falmouth, Me., late of Hampton, sold Nov. 14, 1729, one original right of land in Chichester as one of the original proprietors. He and wife Mary were received in the Falmouth Church 1742. In 1775 Capt. Nathaniel Locke carried 14 cords of wood from Falmouth into Boston to relieve the distress of the port bill. He was sentinel in Capt. George Berry's Company, Falmouth, May 19, 1746–Jan. 19, 1747.

Children of the 4th Gen. First five b. in Hampton, the others in Falmouth.

128 JOHN, bapt. Nov. 29, 1727, died young.
F129 ELIZABETH, bapt. Oct. 27, 1728, m. JACOB CLIFFORD.
130 NATHANIEL, bapt. Dec. 1731, d. Dec. 8, 1758. Marriage intentions of NATHANIEL and MARY LOMBARD were published in Portland, Me., Oct. 31, 1756.
131 SON, or DAU., b. 1734, m. —— JEFFREYS, and settled in the "Provinces."
F132 SON, m. ——.
Second wife's children.
F133 JONATHAN, b. Jan. 23, 1739-40, m. SARAH DUNBAR of Hingham, Mass.
F134 JOHN, b. Aug. 23, 1742, m. SUSANNA (RING) YORK, of Falmouth, Me.

135 MARY, b. Dec. 7, 1744, m. ——— BARKER, and d. Nov. 15, 1780.
F136 REBECCA, b. Sept. 28, 1746, m. published to ELIJAH HUNNEWELL, Jan. 6, 1776.
F137 ABIJAH, b. Jan. 29, 1751, m. ——— Prince, 1793.
F138 DOROTHY, b. Oct. 10, 1755, m. NATHAN FARRAR of No. Yarmouth.
F139 JOSIAH, b. May 21, 1757, m. 1779, ELIZABETH GILPATRICK.

F25 Timothy Locke, b. in Hampton, 1700 (?), m. MIRIAM BROOKE of South Kingston, R. I., about 1722. He with his brothers JOSEPH, ABIJAH, and probably JOHN, went to Rhode Island about 1720 from Hampton. His grandson SAMUEL, b. 1790 says the above is true. In 1751 Timothy bought land at Point Judith Ponds, Kingston, R. I., and sold land in 1757. The General Assembly, Oct. 1776, made him First Lieut., of the 1st Battalion to be raised by the State. Oct. 12, 1776, he was recommended by Washington for the "New Establishment." May 1778, the General Assembly made Captain Timothy Lock one of the officers to command the State Militia. They reappointed him captain in July 1780, and he received pay for services in 1780. He died in So. Kingston, 1797 (?).

Children of 4th Gen. b. South Kingston, R. I.

140 TIMOTHY, b. and d. in So. Kingston, unm. in 1800. In 1779-84 he was Captain of 1st Co., 3rd Battalion R. I. troops.
F141 EDWARD, b. 1755 (?), m. MARY JECKWORTH, who d. before 1820.
F142 SAMUEL, b. So. Kingston, 1744 or 1764, m. ANN SEAGER. He m. 2nd, ANN (WILKINSON) VAN DERYER.
143 SUSANNA (?), who m. ——— TUCKER.
144 JEMIMA (?), who m. ——— BALLEAU. He d. before 1843; but they had a dau. 145, m. a MR. ——— BENNINGTON, of Phoenix, R. I., and one, 146 who m. a MR. ANTHONY of Providence, R. I.

F26 Samuel Locke, b. 1701-2, m. Dec. 11, 1729, JERUSHA SHAW, dau. of Joseph and Hannah (Johnson) of Hampton Falls. She b. Mar. 2, 1709, d. Nov. 4, 1780. He bought land in Hampton, Aug. 31, 1727; was a farmer there, also a selectman.

Children of 4th Gen. all b. in Hampton.

147 ESTHER, b. Oct. 5, 1730, d. Apl. 22, 1736.
F148 JONATHAN, b. Sept. 29, 1732, m. HANNAH FOGG, of Hampton.
149 NATHANIEL, b. 1735, d. May 3, 1736.
150 DEBORAH, bapt. May 5, 1737, d. May 26, 1737.
F151 CALEB, b. Aug. 12, 1738, m. Feb. 18, 1762, BETSEY DYER.
F152 SAMUEL, b. July 28, 1740, m. 1st, DEBORAH VEAZEY; 2nd, ESTHER DOW; 3rd, HANNAH MAGOON; 4th, SALLY ADAMS, or SALLY JAMES.

153 MIRIAM, b. June 16, 1743, m. Oct. 31, 1780, ELISHA MOULTON (# 364), who was b. Apl. 14, 1743. They had: 154 JONATHAN, bapt. Mar. 24, 1782.
155 JOSEPH, bapt. Aug. 18, 1745, d. Dec. 10, 1745.
156 MARY, b. Dec. 14, 1746, m. 1st, TRISTRAM REDMOND, son of Joseph and Hannah (Rawlings). He was b. Nov. 12, 1735, d. 1797. She m. 2nd, JOSEPH TOWLE, b. Dec. 28, 1730, d. Jan. 20, 1820, son of Joseph and Sarah (Dawlton). They lived at Little River, Hampton, where she d. Aug. 16, 1800: *Child:* 157 JONATHAN REDMOND, b. 1774, d. 1775.

F28 Jonathan Locke, b. Dec. 22, 1705, m. in Martha's Vineyard, Jan. 1, 1729-30, MARY or SARAH NORTON, dau. of Samuel, of Chilmark, Mass. He was in Newport, R. I., 1728, perhaps also in Attleboro, Mass. Tradition says his wife had a posthumus child only, who was brought up by his grandfather Norton. Tradition says Jonathan was killed by falling down a bank in Rye.

Child of the 4th Gen.

F158 JONATHAN, b. ——, m. ABIGAIL PERRY.
F159 SAMUEL LOCKE, b. ——, m. LUCY BILL. I do not propose to reject any tradition such as that JONATHAN LOCKE, b. 1705, had a posthumous child, JONATHAN, only, but I do feel warranted for several reasons in placing this Samuel as a possible son of Jonathan, rather than leave him among the unknowns. First, Jonathan was in or about Providence when "Samuel son of Jonathan" was born 1725-30. Second, Jonathan, Sr., had brothers of similar names to Samuel and his known descendants. Third, A Rhode Island Locke of our known branch writes that his mother used to visit a distant relative Mary Burt Locke or Mary Bird Locke as he recalls the name.

F35 Francis Locke, b. July 18, 1694, m. Jan. 24, 1716-7, DELIVERANCE BROOKIN; m. 2nd, March 11, 1733, SARAH MOULTON, dau. of Joseph and Bethia. She was b. Feb. 10, 1692. On Feb. 7, 1717, he sold one-half of a 50 acre grant near Breakfast Hill, sold land to brother THOMAS in 1739. In 1750, he sold land rights, formerly his wife Sarah's. He was a farmer in Rye; Captain of a company which served at Fort William and Mary July 2, 1746. On Dec. 4, 1750, he sold the homestead in Rye to his son FRANCIS, and probably died in 1754. Sarah, his widow, Sept. 4, 1760, sold to dau. PRUDENCE land and personal property.

Children of the 4th Gen. all b. in Rye.

160 HANNAH, b. Jan. 8, 1719, d. —— (?).
161 SARAH, b. Feb. 17, 1722, d. Kensington, Dec. 6, 1735.

F162 FRANCIS, b. June 27, 1724, m. 1st, SARAH PAGE. He m. 2nd, ELIZA-
BETH (PAGE (?)) BACHELDER.
163 DELIVERANCE, b. Aug. 16, 1726.
164 ELEANOR, b. March 16, 1728, m. Feb. 15, 1749, WILLIAM HAM, of Dover.
F165 LIEUT. EPHRAIM, b. Feb. 10, 1730, m. May 14, 1752, COMFORT DOWRST.
F166 PRUDENCE, b. March 20, 1732, m. Dec. 27, 1753, ISRAEL MARDEN.
167 ELIZABETH, b. May 2, 1735.
168 FRANCES, b. Oct. 12, 1737.

F36 Samuel Locke, b. Sept. 4, 1698, m. in Hampton Falls, Feb. 13, 1725, MARGARET WARD, dau. of Thomas and Sarah. She was b. July 2, 1705. There is record of at least twelve transactions wherein Samuel, a farmer of Kingston, buys or sells land there between the years 1722–5. He sold land to Edward Locke 1745. He bought land in Gilmanton in 1766, sold it in 1769. He probably was the Samuel who bought land in Canterbury in 1770. He died in 1770 (?).

Children of the 4th Gen. all b. in Kingston.

169 MARGARET, b. Nov. 20, 1726, m. ORLANDO CARTER, Apl. 1744–5.
170 SAMUEL, b. Apl. 22, 1728, d. Kingston, May 26, 1729.
171 ABIGAIL, b. Dec. 12, 1730, m. Hampton Falls, Apl. 8, 1752, JERE-
MIAH BLAKE, son of Joshua and Jemima. He was b. 1731, and m. 2nd, SARAH GOVE. Another account says Abigail d. unm. March 14, 1731.
172 HANNAH, b. Jan. 31, 1732, d. June 17, 1735.
173 WARD, bapt. 1734. The following shows how a young man of the olden times held property:
Power of Attorney at Court of Probate held in Portsmouth 26th Day July 1758 estate of Ward Lock late of Kensington in said Province Housewright was granted to Moses Shaw of Kens. aforesaid who gave bond.
Inventory of estate of Ward Lock late of Kensington Housewright deceased intestate as shown to us by Moses Shaw Adm. of said est. taken Oct. 8 1759.

The wearing apparel of said deceased	71–10–00
Powder Horn & Cartouch Box 25 Bible 50 Cash 378	381–15–00
A note payable by Moses Lock to said Adm for	133–10–00
1 do. Payable to said Adm by Jacob Thompson & Stephen Palmer on Int. from 19th. of June Last for	116–00–00
Joint Rule 30 Shave 50 Chest Lock 20	5–00–00
	£707–15–00

174 SARY, b. Aug. 15, 1736, d. Oct. 17, 1745.
F175 EDWARD, b. Dec. 18, 1741, m. ABIGAIL HAINES.
176 SAMUEL, b. Feb. 18, 1744.
F177 THOMAS, b. Jan. 1, 1746-7, m. ELIZABETH COLLINS.
178 SARA, b. Apl. 7, 1750.

F37 Edward Locke, b. May 28, 1701, m. in Hampton Falls, Dec. 17, 1724, HANNAH BLAKE, dau. of Moses and Abigail (Smith). She was b. Hampton, Dec. 18, 1704, d. Kensington Nov. 27, 1789. In 1723 he bought land, 44 acres bounded by Kingston line and Samuel Locke. Bought land in Kensington in 1729, also 1745, from Samuel. He sold land in Kensington, in 1753 and 1757. He died in Kensington Jan. 29, 1788.

Children of the 4th Gen. all b. in Kensington.

179 LYDIA, bapt. Dec. 22, 1725, d. Kensington, Nov. 17, 1735.
180 ABIGAIL, bapt. Apl. 12, 1730, d. Kensington, Dec. 18, 1735.
F181 MOSES, b. July 8, 1733. m. MARY ORGAN of York, Me.
F182 TIMOTHY BLAKE, b. Oct. 30, 1735, m. 1st, June 1, 1757, LYDIA DOW; m. 2nd, Jan. 22, 1781, PATIENCE PERKINS.
183 LYDIA, b. Apl. 5, 1738, m. July 7, 1759, BENJAMIN EASTMAN. She d. Seabrook, 1816.
F184 ABIGAIL, b. July 25, 1741, m. ONESEPHORUS PAGE.
185 EDWARD, b. March 6, 1744, (d. Feb. 7, 1747 (?)).
F186 HANNAH, b. Apl. 26, 1747, m. 1765, JEREMIAH DEARBORN.

F38 Prudence Locke, b. May 30, 1707, m. 1st, Apl. 3, 1735, EBENEZER WARE of Hampton Falls, son of Peter and Elizabeth (Wilson). He b. March 4, 1708. She m. 2nd, Dec. 29, 1743 ANDREW WEBSTER. On Feb. 24, 1741, the widow Prudence was appointed administratrix of the estate, and in 1750 the son NATHANIEL, b. 1736, was placed under the guardianship of his stepfather ANDREW WEBSTER.

Children of 4th Gen.

F187 NATHANIEL WEARE, b. July 8, 1736. Another account says Meshech Weare; possibly brothers, one of whom, probably Nathaniel, m. MEHITABLE WYMAN. At least Nathaniel had a son, 188 NATHANIEL, b. Hampton Falls, March 21, 1757, m. March 7, 1793, MARY LOCKE, b. Deerfield, Apl. 19, 1766.
188a PRUDENCE WEBSTER, b. Dec. 25, 1744.
188b ANDREW WEBSTER, b. Oct. 30, 1746.
188c EBENEZER WEBSTER, b. Hampton Falls, Oct. 22, 1749.
188d DANIEL WEBSTER, b. Feb. 12, 1751.

F39 James Locke, b. Oct. 4, 1709, m. March 2, 1731–2, MERCY FOSS of Barnstead. He bought 50 acres of land in Rochester 1732, and sold the same in 1733. "James, cordwainer and Mercy," sold land in Rochester 1737, also in 1763. One Adams is called the first settler of Barnstead, the reason being that he settled in the southern part, while James Locke settled in the remote northeast part a few years before. James served under Genl. Wolf at Quebec in 1759, and returning to his home in Rochester, again took up his routine of farming and hunting. On one of these trips he fell in with a hunter named Libbey, who lived on what is now New Durham Ridge. Libbey wanted a neighbor, even though he be five miles away, and showed Locke a clearing where Indians had apparently camped. This seemed a desirable location, as it was within a mile of a large tract of marsh land, and its hay would winter several cattle. Here he built his cabin and to it moved his family from Rochester about 1762. George L. Hall of Barnstead near the Strafford line lives on the site of this cabin. Locke and Libbey worked the marsh together, cutting and stacking the grass to be drawn in the winter on sleds by the elders or their sons. Moose fed on these stacks, and one winter three were shot; Indians also slept there but did no damage. James died on the home place about 1805, and was buried there. His wife was a large powerful woman.

Children of 4th Gen.

189 SUSANNAH, bapt. 1737, died young.
190 SUSANNAH, bapt. 1741, m. July 16, 1779, RICHARD HODGDON in Portsmouth.
F191 EDWARD, bapt. 1747, perhaps b. Hampton Falls, July 9, 1733.
192 MARY, bapt. 1750–1, m. Lebanon, Me., June 1, 1769, PHILIP DORE, son of Philip and Lydia (Mason).
F193 JAMES, b. 1752, m. 1778, MARY BEAN.
194 PRUDENCE, bapt. 1756, m. Jan. 27, 1780, at Belmont, SAMUEL AVERY, JR.
195 SARAH, b. Jan. 1, 1758, m. March 20, 1777, BENJ. DORE, son of Philip and Lydia (Mason). He b. Jan. 9, 1756. She d. May 19, 1850. *Child:* 196 MEHITABLE, b. Lebanon, Me., May 2, 1778, d. Newfields, Sept. 1865, m. LIEUT. JOSEPH MERROW, who d. May 15, 1856.
197 MEHITABLE, b. ——, m. JOHN GOODWIN of Kittery, Me., son of John and Keziah Tebbetts.

F40 Thomas Locke, b. in Hampton June 10, 1713, m.

(Abigail Berry, b. June 21, 1719, dau. of Ebenezer?). Thomas of Rye sold part of his father's estate in Rye 1739; he also sold land in Barrington that same year. In 1745 he sold 130 acres of land in Barrington, at which place he probably lived. He also lived in Rochester. He was probably a Louisburg soldier serving in Capt. Jonathan Prescott's Co. 1745.

Children of the 4th Gen.

198 BENJAMIN, bapt. Kensington, Aug. 25, 1745. He was probably in Capt. Parsons Co. in R. I. service 1777–8.
F199 LEVI, bapt. Kensington, Aug. 25, 1745, m. RACHEL FULLER.
F200 THOMAS, b. Bridgwater, Apl. 14, 1751, m. MARTHA WORTHEN.
F201 MARTHA, b. ——, m. JONATHAN INGALLS.

F46 Jonathan Locke, b. in Rye March 15, 1702, m. in Portsmouth, by Rev. Wm. Allen, March 2, 1727, SARAH HAINES, dau. of William and Mary (Lewis) of Greenland. She was b. Oct. 18, 1705, d. Oct. 1753. He bought 31 acres of land on the Sandy Beach Road in Rye 1723–4 and in 1735 bought 34 acres of land in New Castle (Part of Andrew Pepperell's land). In 1739 he sold land on the Greenland Road, again sold land in Chester 1758. In 1767 he gave son DAVID 35 acres of land in Rye provided he support his sister SARAH until her marriage. He gave common land to son JONATHAN in 1771. He lived in Rye and was a Representative to the General Assembly. At General Assembly Jan. 1744 he with two others were appointed a committee "to go to James Jeffreys, late Clerk of the Assembly and demand and bring back the books and files belonging to this house." He lived where Deacon Jonathan Locke now resides at Rye Centre, and died there Jan. 2, 1774. His wife and five children died of throat distemper in 1753.

Children of the 4th Gen. all b. in Rye.

202 SARAH, b. Jan. 3, 1728, d. Rye, Sept. 26, 1742.
F203 PATIENCE, b. Feb. 10, 1730, m. BENJAMIN WOODBRIDGE.
F204 JONATHAN, b. Jan. 29, 1732, m. June 8, 1758, ABIGAIL TOWLE.
205 MARY, b. Sept. 20, 1733, d. Oct. 11, 1753.
F206 DEACON DAVID, b. Aug. 24, 1735, m. 1st, HANNAH LOVERING, Feb. 9, 1758. He m. 2nd, March 24, 1809, WIDOW OLIVE (MARDEN) ELKINS.
F207 ABIGAIL, b. Sept. 5, 1736, m. Feb. 23, 1758, JAMES PERKINS.
F208 CAPT. WILLIAM, b. July 26, 1738, m. CHRISTENA PAINE.
209 MARGARET, b. July 20, 1740, d. 1753.
210 ABNER, b. July 31, 1742, d. Oct. 1753.

211 SARAH, b. Aug. 28, 1744, d. unm. in Rye, Dec. 31, 1796.
212 HANNAH, b. Dec. 18, 1746, d. Oct. 1753.
213 JOHN, b. Dec. 9, 1748, d. Oct. 1753.

F47 William Locke, b. in Rye, m. Jan. 7, or Feb. 17, 1729 MIRIBAH PAGE, dau. of Francis and Hannah (Nudd). She was b. Feb. 2, 1707, d. soon after marriage. He m. 2nd, Jan. 5, 1734 ELIZABETH RAND, who bore him 7 children. His name appears on Rye petitions 1724-5. He paid 1500 pounds Oct. 29, 1739, for "a tract of land in Two Mile Streak" at south end of Barrington near the Rochester and Dover line, and sold some of this to Thomas Locke the next day. Sold land in Barrington 1740-46-51. He sold 50 acres land in Epsom 1742. He received 21 pounds for work at Fort William and Henry in 1764. He was a mason by trade, and lived near Charles and Gilman Garland's place in Rye. I think he may have moved to Barrington 1745-50, as the Rye records contain no dates of his family after 1745.

Children of 4th Gen., five of whom were born in Rye.

214 MEREBETH, or MIRIBAH, b. Aug. 6, 1735.
F215 HANNAH, b. Feb. 18, 1737, m. DEACON REUBEN PHILBRICK # 226.
216 ELIZABETH, b. March 3, 1739-40.
F217 ABIGAIL, b. March 4, 1743, m. Sept. 18, 1764, JOSHUA FOSS.
F218 WILLIAM, b. Sept. 9, 1745, m. 1st, BETSEY BABB; m. 2nd, Apl. 20, 1802, MARY HAYES.
F219 SAMUEL, b. Aug. 14, 1748.
220 MARY, b. Apl. 6, 1751.

F48 Abigail Locke, b. in Rye 1706, m. Jan. 4, 1726-7, JOSES PHILBRICK, b. Nov. 5, 1703, son of Joseph and Tryphena (Marston). She d. Aug. 12, 1783. He was a blacksmith in Rye and Hampton, and d. March 24, 1757.

Children of the 4th Gen. b. in Rye.

F221 HANNAH, b. Apl. 24, 1729, m. REUBEN MOULTON of Hampton.
F222 TRYPHENA, b. Apl. 24, 1729, m. 1st, Jan. 29, 1760, JOHN SANDERS; m. 2nd, Apl. 16, 1780, JONATHAN BERRY.
F223 ABIGAIL, b. Nov. 11, 1730, m. Nov. 24, 1748, MARK RANDALL of Moultonboro.
F224 JOSEPH, b. Aug. 10, 1735, m. Dec. 2, 1760, ANN TOWLE.
225 SARAH, b. Nov. 9, 1732, m. 1760, ROBERT MOULTON. She d. in Gilmanton Aug. 10, 1823. They moved to Gilmanton in 1775, and had 11 children, 34 grandchildren, 60 great grandchildren.

226 REUBEN, b. Feb. 27, 1737, m. 1st, HANNAH LOCKE; 2nd, WIDOW MARY WEDGWOOD; 3rd, MARY (DAWLTON) JENNESS; 4th, MARY BECK. (See F215.)
F227 DANIEL, b. Feb. 2, 1740, m. ABIGAIL MARDEN.
F228 JONATHAN, b. Nov. 26, 1745, m. Dec. 8, 1768, MARY MARDEN.
229 MARY, b. Feb. 12, 1749, d. Nov. 15, 1834.

F50 Patience Locke, b. in Rye, 1711, m. Nov. 16, 1749, NOAH MOULTON, b. in Hampton, Feb. 23, 1705, son of Daniel and Mary; he lived in Rye, served under Captain Francis Locke at the Fort, 1746, and about 1770 removed to Lyman, at a place now known as Moulton's hill. She was received into the Greenland Church in 1719, and a Rye record says Patience Locke (not Moulton) d. May 11, 1755. Credit has been given to Patience Locke for the sterling qualities inherited by many of her descendants among this large and influential family. Noah had a nephew b. 1726, sometimes given as husband of Patience, but I think it is the older one.

Children of 4th Gen., the first five born in Rye.

230 SARAH, bapt. Apl. 14, 1751, m. —— McFARLANE, and had no children.
F231 JOB, b. 1752, m. ANNIE WAY of Lyman, and d. 1838.
231a MARY, b. 1754, was unmarried.
F232 JONATHAN, b. Feb. 8, 1757, m. MARTHA GIBSON, b. Jan. 16, 1772, d. in Lyman, Apl. 7 1842. He was a Revolutionary soldier, a farmer in Lyman and d. there July 12, 1846.
F233 NOAH, b. 1759, m. PRISCILLA BARRON, b. 1768, d. 1861. He d. 1850.
233a DANIEL, b. 1761, m. MILLICENT WHEELER, and d. 1836.
The following are also his children, but not in order. In fact some of these latter are said to be the oldest in the family.
F234 DAVID, b. 1763, m. SALLY KNAPP and d. 1841.
234a WILLIAM, b. ——, m. SARAH DICKINSON, and lived in New York State.
F235 JOHN, b. ——, m. POLLY SMITH, and lived in Lyman.
235a ABIGAIL, b. ——.
235b MARGARET, b. ——, m. —— POWERS, and lived in Hardwick, Vt.

F53 Deacon Elijah Locke, b. in Rye, m. in Rye, May 22, 1739, HULDAH PERKINS, dau. of James and Huldah (Robie), who was b. July 17, 1718. He bought land of his father in 1740, also 32 acres of the home place in 1740. Bought part of Locke's Neck from his father in 1747. He sold land in Rye 1752, and in Epsom Nov. 10, 1766. He lived at Knowles' Corner, Rye, near where Chas. and Gilman Garland now live. He may also have lived a few of his later years in Chichester. He died about 1782.

Children of the 4th Gen. all b. in Rye.

F236 HULDAH, b. Oct. 2, 1739, m. MOSES SEAVEY of Deerfield.
F237 MARTHA, b. Dec. 15, 1741, m. March 8, 1764, BICKFORD LANG.
F238 MARY, b. Nov. 25, 1744, m. June 7, 1765, ROBERT SAUNDERS.
239 ELIJAH, b. Sept. 29, 1746, d. Nov. 1, 1753.
240 ELIZABETH, b. Jan. 25, 1748, d. Aug. 30, 1753.
241 LEVI, b. Dec. 4, 1750, d. Nov. 14, 1753.
242 WILLIAM, b. Apl. 13, 1753, d. Dec. 1753.
F243 ELIJAH, b. Dec. 15, 1754, m. 1st, Nov. 21, 1776, ELIZABETH BROWN. He m. 2nd, MRS. NANCY (WATTS) FISHER.
F244 WILLIAM, b. June 16, 1758, m. Oct. 29, 1779, ABIGAIL SAUNDERS, # 714.
245 HANNAH, b. Feb. 2, 1761.

F54 Elisha Locke, bapt. 1719 in Rye, m. Jan. 13, 1743, TRYPHENA MOULTON, dau. of Daniel and Phoebe (Philbrick), who was b. Jan. 24, 1726. July 2, 1746, he served at Fort William and Mary at New Castle. Elisha of Rye bought land in Barrington Oct. 30, 1739, he and wife sold it in 1752. He, called a housewright, bought and sold land in Barrington 1752–5–6. Sold land in Rye 1755. He bought land in Chester in 1755–6, and sold it in 1764. Elisha of Chester bought land in Haverhill 1763 and Elisha a miller of Haverhill sold, in 1767 all his rights as charter member of Chester. He was a pioneer business man of Haverhill, N. H.

Children of the 4th Gen.

246 ELISHA, b. 1743, d. yng.   247 Daniel, b. 1745, d. yng.
F248 MARY S., b. 1747, m. JONATHAN LADD.
F249 SERGT. WILLIAM, b. 1753, m. TRYPHENA SAUNDERS.
F250 HANNAH, b. 1755, m. Dec. 3, 1772, JAMES LADD.
F251 CORPORAL ELISHA, b. 1760, m. MEHITABLE STICKNEY.
F252 DAVID, b. 1767 (?), m. 1st, 1787, ELIZABETH LELLINGHAM; 2nd, Nov. 6, 1809, RACHEL BRAINARD.

F56 Jemima Locke, b. in Rye Jan. 20, 1720, m. May 1740, JOHN BLAKE of Greenland, son of John and Mary (Dearborn). He was b. May 20, 1716.

Children of 4th Gen.

253 ELISHA, bapt. July 3, 1743.   255 MARY, b. Dec. 13, 1747.
254 JOHN, bapt. Nov. 3, 1745.   256 WILLIAM, m. BETSEY FOSTER.

F57 Hannah Locke, b. in Rye July 1, 1724, m. in Rye Oct. 3, 1745, JEREMIAH BERRY, b. 1724, son of William and Sarah (Hobbs). She d. July 1, 1770. He m. 2nd, Sept. 8, 1770, ELEANOR BRACKETT. He m. 3rd, DORA EMERSON. He was a corporal in Capt. Parsons Co. in the Revolution stationed at New Castle. Lived on the Eliza A. Walker farm.

Children of the 4th Gen. The first 10 are Hannah's.

257 SARAH, b. 1746.
F258 HANNAH, b. June 28, 1747, m. July 22, 1768, NATHANIEL MARDEN.
259 SARAH, b. July 6, 1749, m. AARON JENNESS, and had: 260 JEREMIAH; 261 WILLIAM; 262 AARON; 263 LEVI. Aaron, senior, was son of William Jenness who m. Sarah Locke in Greenland, Jan. 3, 1733-4, and had: 264 WILLIAM; 265 MOSES; 266 AARON and 267 DAVID. Sarah Locke is unknown.
F268 MARY, b. March 24, 1751, m. Jan. 15, 1774, SAM'L DOWST FOSS.
F269 WILLIAM, b. Apl. 12, 1752-3, m. 1st, Nov. 10, 1774, LOVE BRACKETT; 2nd, March 6, 1796, ELIZABETH WENDELL.
270 JEREMIAH, b. Apl. 2, 1755, m. FANNY HAYES.
271 JOSES, b. 1757, died young.
F272 LEVI, b. Feb. 29, 1760, m. Nov. 13, 1785, SARAH JENNESS.
273 PATIENCE, b. Feb. 13, 1762, m. JAMES SEAVEY, May 23, 1780 (?), who was bapt. 1754, lived in Rye, had no children and d. Apl. 1, 1829.
F274 SOLOMON, bapt. Nov. 17, 1765, m. Oct. 5, 1794, PATTY KATE.

Second wife's children.

F275 HANNAH, b. Aug. 21, 1773, m. Apl. 17, 1801, JAMES LOCKE. # 1086.
276 LYDIA, b. Nov. 27, 1777, m. Jan. 2, 1801, WILLIAM TREFETHERN, who was b. Apl. 24, 1775. Lydia d. June 20, 1820, and he m. 2nd, SUSAN PIPER in Feb. 1821. Lived in Rye, where he d. Oct. 5, 1853.

F58 James Locke, b. in Rye ———, m. by Rev. Wm. Allen of Greenland, Oct. 25, 1720, to SARAH REMICK of Kittery, Me., dau. of Joshua and Ann (Lancaster). She b. Aug. 27, 1696. In 1748 he gave his home and 60 acres at Dry Point to son JAMES, and in case of death without issue to son JOHN. James in 1750 makes agreement with son to keep him for life. James or son James sells land in Rye 1763. He lived at Rye, no doubt at Locke's Neck.

Children of the 4th Gen. all b. in Rye.

F277 SARAH, b. July 27, 1725, m. March 28, 1746, JOHN MARDEN.
278 ANNA, b. Oct. 10, 1726, d. Nov. 10, 1735.
F279 JAMES, b. June 30, 1729, m. June 14, 1750, SARAH LEAVITT.
280 ELIZABETH, b. Oct. 12, 1730.

FOURTH GENERATION

281 MARY, b. Jan. 21, 1732.
282 MIRIBAH or MEREBETH, b. Oct. 13, 1733.
283 LOVE or LYDIA (Ledy in Rye record), b. June 3, 1735.
284 JOHN, b. Oct. 3, 1737, d. in Revolutionary War.
285 ABIGAIL, b. March 25, 1741.

F60 Salome Locke, b. in Rye Oct. 20, 1710, m. in Rye May 22, 1735, JONATHAN GOSS, son of Richard and Martha. He was a weaver in Rye and bought land of Salome's father in 1738.

Children of the 4th Gen. b. in Rye.

286 RICHARD, b. Nov. 3, 1738, d. about 1768.
F287 SALOME, b. Feb. 22, 1741, m. MARK LANG.
F288 JONATHAN, b. 1743, m. Feb. 16, 1769, ELIZABETH BROWN.
289 JOSEPH, b. 1746.   290 ELIZABETH, b. 1749.

F61 Joseph Locke, b. in Rye Apl. 27, 1716, m. 1st in Rye Dec. 4, 1739, HANNAH JENNESS, dau. of Richard and Mary (Dow). She was b. July 4, 1714, d. ——. He m. 2nd, Apl. 20, 1768, MARY (YEATON) ODIORNE, widow of Nathaniel Odiorne; she was b. 1724, and d. Jan. 28, 1805. He sold Peter Garland "marsh land beginning at grey rock thence N. E. with the bridge that leads to the wharf and Dry Point on the S. W. Apl. 1, 1763." Also sold marsh land in 1770, "late my father's and grandfather's." Lived in Rye where John Oliver Locke resides and d. Apl. 22, 1790-1.

Children of the 4th Gen. all b. in Rye.

291 HANNAH, b. June 3, 1740.
    JOSEPH, bapt. Apl. 4, 1742, died young.
F292 RICHARD, b. Sept. 4, 1744, m. March, 1767, HULDAH HOBBS.
293 JOSEPH, bapt. July 21, 1751, died young.
F294 JOSHUA, b. Apl. 28, 1753-4, m. Jan. 18, 1776, CHARITY MARDEN.
295 MARY, bapt. Nov. 21, 1756, m. Feb. 7, 1782, LEVI TOWLE, son of
    Jonathan and Elizabeth (Jenness), who was b. 1757. They had
    one son: 296 DEARBORN TOWLE, b. 1783, m. RHODA HARVEY.
    Levi, m. 2nd, LUCY HOBBS; 3rd, PERNA JUDKINS, and had children
    by them.
By second wife.
F297 JOSEPH, b. 1768, m. 1st, Nov. 16, 1794, MARY BROWN. He m. 2nd,
    July 16, 1804, OLIVE FOSS.
298 BENJAMIN, b. 1770, died young.
F299 HANNAH, b. March 1773, m. Oct. 2, 1803, SAMUEL MOWE of Rye.
300 BENJAMIN, b. 1776, died young.

F62 Elizabeth Locke, b. in Hampton, Dec. 1, 1718, m. Jan. 6, 1743, JUDE ALLEN. He was b. 1714, d. Epsom, 1793. She d. before 1776, and he m. 2nd, 1776, DORCAS (MARDEN) MOWE and had : ELIZABETH LOCKE ALLEN, bapt. Apl. 19, 1778, m. Nov. 10, 1803, SIMON LOCKE, F340.

First wife's children of 4th Gen.

  301 NATHANIEL, bapt. July 12, 1747.
  302 JUDE, bapt. Sept. 18, 1743, d. 1751.
  303 JOSHUA, bapt. Aug. 9, 1761.
F304 SALOME, bapt. 1771 a twin, m. Feb. 4, 1779 JOHN BROWN. She d. 1852.   305 ——— (?) bapt. 1771 a twin.

F63 Mary Locke, b. in Hampton, May 1, 1720, m. in New Castle June 25, 1745, SOLOMON WHITE of New Castle. He was a deacon in N. C. 1768, and may have lived in Epping. Probably son of Nathan White of N. C. whose will was proved in 1747, mentions his wife Elizabeth and son Solomon.

Their children of the 4th Gen.

  306 JOSEPH, b. July 11, 1746.   307 NATHAN, b. Aug. 16, 1749.

F64 Annis Locke, b. in Hampton, March 25, 1723, m. March 10, 1748, JOHN PERKINS, son of James and Huldah (Robie). He was b. Jan. 8, 1723. He m. 2nd, ——— HOYT and had JAMES and MARY.

Children of the 4th Gen.

  308 LIEUT. JONATHAN, bapt. 1749, m. in Exeter, Apl. 1, 1778, ELIZABETH FOLSOM, dau. of Peter and Mary. He was an officer of the Rev.
  309 ANNA, b. ———, m. Nov. 20, 1772, ELIAS PHILBRICK, son of Caleb and Mary (Sherburne). He was b. Epping, Oct. 20, 1748, d. Meredith, 1804. They lived in Northwood in 1773, and had no children.
  310 JOHN, bapt. 1750, m. 1770, LUCY PRESCOTT, dau. of John and Hannah (Rundlett). He was a farmer in Meredith; had dau. 311 ANNIS PRESCOTT, m. JOHN SMITH of Meredith.
  312 JOSEPH, b. ———.   313 BENJAMIN, b. ———.

F65 Abigail Locke, b. in Hampton, Nov. 6, 1725; m. Jan. 25, 1748, ROBINSON TREFETHERN of New Castle. He was b. 1721, son of Henry and Mary. He lived at Rye Center and sold his place to Col. Benjamin Garland in 1756.

FOURTH GENERATION

Children of the 4th Gen.

314 MARY, b. Apl. 12, 1748, m. ———— MILLS, or MILLER.
F315 CAPTAIN WILLIAM, b. June 5, 1751, m. Jan. 27, 1774, ELIZABETH TUCKER.
316 ROBINSON, b. March 3, 1753, lost at sea.
317 ABIGAIL, b. Apl. 6, 1755, m. WILLIAM MORRISON of Portsmouth, Nov. 14, 1779, and had: 318 WM. ROGERS, b. 1781.
319 JOSEPH, b. Aug. 14, 1757, d. yng.
320 JOSEPH, b. March 5, 1759.
321 LUCRETIA, b. May 24, 1763.
322 SALOME, b. May 1, 1765, m. SAMUEL FOSS of Rye, son of Nathaniel and Mary (Tucker). He bapt. July 3, 1762. She d. Apl. 10, 1851. They had: 323 SUPPLY C. who married; and both he and wife were killed by the falling of a house in Dubuque, Iowa. Another son, 324 SAMUEL P., bapt. Dec. 22, 1799.
325 MARGARET, b. May 28, 1767.
326 HENRY, b. Aug. 16, 1769, m. ———— PARTRIDGE.

F66 Jeremiah Locke, b. in Hampton, Aug. 1, 1728, m. 1st, Feb. 5, 1753, MARY ELKINS, b. 1731, dau. of Henry and Catherine (Marston). He m. 2nd, in Greenland, May 28, 1761, MARY (BERRY) HAINES, widow of Joseph. From 1758 to 1763 he and wife Mary buy or sell twelve lots of land at Sandy Beach Pond and other places in Rye. In 1757 he bought land in Brentwood. 1763 he sold land in Kingston. He was on a Committee to build wharf at Sandy Beach, 1763. Petitioned for Newmarket Bridge 1755. He was inspector and director of Minute Men 1775–81. His will is dated May 10, 1794, and he died in Rye Jan. 28, 1795. Lived at the present Wallace Goss place.

License to Jeremiah Locke of Rye & Mary his wife to sell real estate of Joseph Hains late of Greenland of which they were Administrators Feb. 4, 1762 value £5290. Mary Haines Widow.

Children of 4th Gen. b. in Rye.

F327 JOSEPH, b. Oct. 23, 1753-4, m. June 25, 1778, MARTHA DOW, of Rye.
F328 MARY, b. May 25, 1755, m. March 21, 1775, SAMUEL JENNESS.

FIFTH GENERATION

F68 Richard Locke, born in Rye July 28, 1720, married ELIZABETH GARLAND of Rye, dau. of John and Elizabeth (Dearborn). She was born March 13, 1724. July 2, 1746, he served at Fort William and Mary, and took the oath of allegiance in 1776. Sold land in Rye 1767, that he bought of JAMES LOCKE, JR. He died May 15, or 22, 1804.

Children of the 5th Gen., b. in Rye.

F330 JOHN J., b. Oct. 19, 1746, m. 1st, 1769, SARAH JONES; m. 2nd, Aug. 18, 1796, THANKFUL BLAZO.
331 ABNER, b. May 13, 1748, died young.
F332 RICHARD, bapt. June 7, 1750, m. Nov. 2, 1769, SARAH PALMER.
333 JACOB, bapt. Feb. 23, 1752, died young.
F334 ABNER, bapt. March 26, 1754, d. in Rye Apl. 25, 1825.
F335 JACOB, bapt. Jan. 22, 1757, m. Jan. 4, 1778, MEHITABLE HIGGINS or HUGGINS.
336 TRYPHENA, b. June 1759, d. in Rye Aug. 3, 1830.
F337 JOB, bapt. Sept. 26, 1762, m. 1st, Nov. 10, 1785, HANNAH LANG, # 1075; m. 2nd, Dec. 8, 1806, ABIGAIL PHILBRICK, # 735; m. 3rd, Nov. 25, 1810, SARAH LOCKE, # 1085.
338 SARAH, bapt. Sept. 8, 1765, d. Feb. 8, 1803.
339 ELIZABETH, bapt. Apl. 10, 1768, probably died young.
F340 SIMON, bapt. Sept. 23, 1770, m. Feb. 14, 1792, ABIGAIL MACE. He m. 2nd, 1803, ELIZABETH L. ALLEN, F62.

F76 Jethro Locke, born in Rye June 27, 1727, married February 2, 1748, HANNAH RAND, dau. of Thomas and Hannah (Pray). She born May 28, 1729, died in Barrington, Feb. 15, 1831, aged 101. He was a farmer at Barrington and Rochester, and died Oct. 29, 1807. He bought land in Portsmouth 1759 and in Barrington Nov. 13, 1760; sold land in Rye 1753 and 1760 and sold land in Barrington 1762.

Children of 5th Gen.

341 HANNAH, b. 1748, m. Feb. 5, 1782, JOSHUA HAYES of Barrington, son of Robert, and they had five children.
F342 DOROTHY, b. 1750, m. July 19, 1771, ELIJAH OTIS.
F343 REV. SIMON, b. Sept. 20, 1752, m. in Barrington March 29, 1774, LYDIA FOSS.
344 MIRIBAH, b. 1756, m. in Rochester Aug. 22, 1780, MOSES BABB of Strafford.

FIFTH GENERATION 35

345 ELIZABETH, b. 1758-9, m. 1st, in Rochester, Sept. 18, 1778, JOHN BARBER of Barrington, m. 2nd, SAMUEL DROWN.
F346 JETHRO, b. Barrington March 6, 1764, m. ABIGAIL HOWARD, 1786.
F347 MARY, b. Apl. 25, 1760, m. SOLOMON GRAY.
348 LYDIA, b. ——. All had children save Lydia.

F108 Amos Leavitt, born in Rye Oct. 23, 1720, married Jan. 13, 1740, ELIZABETH VARRELL; he lived in Hampton and died June 26, 1808.

Children of the 5th Gen.

354 THOMAS, b. ——, m. ABIGAIL TUCK, July 2, 1772, dau. of John and Sarah (Godfrey). Abigail was b. Dec. 30, 1749. Had 6 children in Hampton.
355 MERCY, b. Feb. 10, 1756, m. AARON MERRILL Oct. 3, 1775. Had two children in Hampton. She d. Jan. 1, 1826.

F113 Benjamin Leavitt, born a twin, Oct. 4, 1732, married Dec. 6, 1753, ESTHER TOWLE, born Jan. 16, 1734, died in Hampton Falls, 1815, dau. of Philip and Lydia Dow. He lived at Hampton Falls and died March 14, 1805.

Children of 5th Gen.

356 JONATHAN, b. 1756, m. a MRS. WARD and settled in Eastport, Me.
357 REUBEN, b. ——, m. RUTH NORRIS.
358 BRACKETT, b. ——, m. MITTY PRESCOTT.
359 LYDIA, b. ——, m. JONATHAN LANE.
360 COMFORT, b. ——, m. MOSES NORRIS.
361 PATIENCE, b. ——, m. TRISTRAM CRAM.
All the above settled in Pittsfield.
362 THOMAS, b. 1774, m. HANNAH MELCHER, and he d. 1852.
363 BETSEY, b. 1777, m. OLIVER JONES of Canterbury.

F114 William Moulton, born in Rye Apl. 15, 1716, m. ——.

Children of the 5th Gen.

364 ELISHA, bapt. Apl. 17, 1743, m. Oct. 31, 1780, MIRIAM LOCKE # 153.
365 RACHEL, bapt. Sept. 2, 1744, m. JOHN PAGE (?).
366 INFANT, d. July 20, 1746.
367 MARY, bapt. Feb. 14, 1748, d. Sept. 19, 1756.
368 DOLLY, bapt. Apl. 8, 1750, m. Nov. 23, 1768, MOSES ELKINS, son of Jonathan and Elizabeth (Taylor). He b. Dec. 16, 1743. They had 6 children.
369 ELIZABETH, b. Oct. 29, 1752, d. unm. Apl. 1, 1832.
370 SARAH, b. Nov. 9, 1755.
371 WILLIAM, b. March 26, 1758, m. MOLLY PAGE, bapt. May 20, 1759, the dau. of Francis and Mary (Marston). He lived in No. Hampton, was a Revolutionary soldier, and d. March 18, 1851. They had: 372 DANIEL.

F116 Josiah Moulton, bapt. in Rye Dec. 4, 1720, married HULDAH MARSTON, Jan. 12, 1744, the dau. of Jeremiah and Mary (Smith). She born Dec. 2, 1725, died March 1, 1745. He married 2nd, ABIGAIL MARSTON, dau. of Lieut. Jonathan and Abigail. She born Oct. 29, 1721, died March 3, 1815. He was in the Revolution and died Apl. 29, 1784.

Children of the 5th Gen.
373 JOSIAH, b. Jan. 13, 1745, d. Oct. 3, 1754.
374 ABIGAIL, b. Dec. 28, 1746, d. Sept. 21, 1754.
375 HULDAH, b. Dec. 11, 1748, d. Sept. 28, 1754.
376 MARY, b. March 3, 1751, d. May 2, 1753.
377 MARY, b. Apl. 3, 1755, d. Oct. 16, 1759.
378 JOSIAH, b. Apl. 17, 1757, d. Nov. 22, 1759.

F119 Thomas Moulton, bapt. Apl. 27, 1726, married HANNAH DOWNES Aug. 1, 1750. She born at the Shoals. He lived at No. Hampton and Deerfield.

Children of the 5th Gen.
379 NATHANIEL, b. ——, was m. and lived "beyond the White Mountains."
380 JOHN M., b. Nov. 9, 1755, m. July 7, 1780, ANNA BROWN, who was b. Dec. 19, 1756, d. May 23, 1846. He was a Revolutionary soldier and d. Jan. 2, 1831. They had 8 children.
381 DAVID, lived Penobscot Co., Me.

F125 Nathaniel Locke, born in Rhode Island Sept. 29, 1723, married ANN ROSE, Jan. 30, 1745; he married 2nd, TEMPERANCE ROSE, Aug. 27, 1756. She born Aug. 27, 1734. In 1775 he moved to Chenango Co., N. Y., with all his family except JOHN and ABIJAH. The Hunnewell Genealogy says that Lyman Hunnewell and cousins Nathaniel and Amasa Locke came from Block Island, and settled in Oxford Co., N. Y. No Amasa Lock is recorded in Block Island records. Nathaniel paid his first tax in Block Island (New Shoreham) in 1744. In 1751 he received a gift of land from his father-in-law, Daniel Rose; was made a freeman in 1756 and from that year to 1775 was constable, tax collector, overseer of the poor, and harbor master many years.

Children of the 5th Gen., all b. at Block Island (New Shoreham).
382 JOHN, b. Nov. 6, 1746; was a sea captain, probably never married. He paid taxes 1756 and 1757; and in 1783 sold property bought of his father, does not appear again in the records until 1806 when the selectmen of Block Island made provision for the necessities of Captain John Lock of Sherburn, on the Island of Nantucket.

FIFTH GENERATION

He had a cancer on his face and died, cared for by Block Island about 1812–14; so said a resident who knew him.
383 DOROTHY, b. Feb. 16, 1748.
384 JESSE, b. Sept. 14, 1752, died young.
385 ABSOLOM, b. May 10, 1753. Was taxed in Block Island 1771, not later.
386 LEMAR or (TENNAH), b. Apl. 4, 1754.
387 ANNE, b. Jan. 12, 1757.
388 ABIJAH, b. May 10, 1759, m. WIDOW SALLY (DODGE) WILLIS, of Block Island. He was a Sea Captain and returned to Block Island in 1804, and by vote June 2, 1821, was provided with necessary food and clothing, but he did not die on the town says an old witness. He did leave a daughter, who by report was bound out when 3 or 4 years old.
390 RACHEL, b. March 4, 1760.
391 LEAH, b. Oct. 1, 1761.
392 TILPAH, or (ZILBAH), b. March 1, 1763.
393 BILBAH, or (BETHIA), b. Oct. 25, 1764.
394 NATHANIEL, b. Apl. 27, 1766.
F395 JESSE, b. Jan. 21, 1768.
396 TEMPERANCE, b. Feb. 12, 1770.
397 LYDIA, b. Nov. 27, 1772.
398 EMMONS, b. May 11, 1774.

F127 Joseph Locke, born 1734 (?), in Rhode Island, married 1756 (?) LUCY or ELIZABETH E. RATHBON, who was born in Exeter, R. I., 1735, the dau. of John. They both died about 1815. They moved from Block Island to So. Kingston, R. I., about 1750.

Children of the 5th Gen. b. in Rhode Island.
F399 REV. ELLIOTT HUNNEWELL, b. ——, m. MARY WEST.
400 BENJAMIN, b. ——, m. about 1791 DOROTHY WORDEN, b. in Westerly, R. I., Feb. 28, 1771, d. in Richmond, March 1802, dau. of John and Eliza (Babcock). He died about 1794.
401 SYLVESTER, b. ——.
402 JOSEPH, JR., b. ——, m. GIFFY SHERMAN.
F403 JOSHUA R., b. March 8, 1777, m. 1798, WAITY SHELDON.
404 JONATHAN, b. ——, m. MARY SWEET.
405 MOLLY, b. ——, not married.
406 NANCY, b. ——, m. DAVID BATES. *Children:* 407 MERCY L., b. in Boziah, Conn., Aug. 18, 1799, d. in Central Village, Conn., Apl. 26, 1866, m. Oct. 21, 1819, ALLEN CLEVELAND, who d. in Conn. Sept. 23, 1872, aged 77.
408 ELIZABETH, b. ——, d. 1815, m. MERCHANT BURROUGHS.
409 MERCY, b. ——, d. March 25, 1855, m. March 18, 1800, BLACKBURN F. AYLESWORTH, b. Oct. 8, 1776, son of Daniel and Ruth.

F129 Elizabeth Locke, bapt. Oct. 27, 1728; she was probably the Elizabeth who married JACOB CLIFFORD about 1755, and settled in Prospect, now Stockton Springs, Maine, in 1760. He was in the siege of Louisburg and was granted land in Standish, Me. He born Me. 1726, died 1790. She died in 1811.

Children of the 5th Gen., perhaps b. in Prospect, Me.

F410 JACOB, b. 1756, m. RACHEL R. WALKER about 1783.
411 ABIGAIL, b. 1758, m. ——— RUNNELLS.
412 MEHITABLE, b. 1760, m. ——— LANCASTER.
413 POLLY, b. 1762, m. ——— CUMMINGS.
414 BETSEY, b. 1764, m. ——— SPATWELL.
415 JOHN, b. 1766, unknown.
416 NATHANIEL, b. 1768, d. 1793.

F132 Locke, Son, married ———.

Child of the 5th Gen.

F417 ABIGAIL, b. 1750 (?), m. 1769, MOSES NOYES of Falmouth.

F133 Jonathan Locke, born Falmouth, Me., Jan. 23, 1739-40, married SARAH DUNBAR of Hingham, Mass. He was a shipmaster.

Children of the 5th Gen.

418 JONATHAN, b. 1772, m. Aug. 27, 1797, WIDOW HANNAH (TATE) HADDAWAY of Boston who lived as late as 1850. He was a Shipmaster, and was lost in the Mediterranean in 1804. Had no children.
419 LEAR, b. ———, m. SAMUEL BUCKMAN of Portland, Me. Lived in the Province of New Brunswick. Had a son: 420 E. T. BUCKMAN, New York City.

F134 John Locke, born in Falmouth, Me., Aug. 23, 1742, married SUSANNA (RING) YORK of Falmouth. She was the widow of Joseph York who died in 1760, having had six children by him. She born 1730, died Oct. 25, 1825, aged 95. John was a Mariner in Falmouth and died in 1810. She left 11 children, 89 grandchildren, 211 great-grandchildren, 14 great-great-grandchildren, a total of 325. Until she was 90 she rode several miles on horseback each Sunday to attend worship.

Children of 5th Gen. b. Falmouth.

F421 MARY, b. Apl. 15, 1767, m. 1st, NATHANIEL PRINCE; m. 2nd, JAMES NOYES.
F422 LUCY, b. ———, m. JOHN MASON of Falmouth, Me.
F423 EBENEZER, b. Sept. 8, 1774, m. 1st, Jan. 3, 1801, HANNAH TEWKSBURY; m. 2nd, 1828, WIDOW ANN POMEROY.

FIFTH GENERATION

F136 Rebecca Locke, born in Falmouth, Me., Sept. 28, 1746, marriage published Jan. 6, 1776, to ELIJAH HUNNEWELL of Windham, Me. He died there March 16, 1815. She died same place Feb. 12, 1830.

Children of 5th Gen., all b. Windham, Me.

424 SUSANNAH, b. Jan. 21, 1777, m. Dec. 30, 1799, EBENEZER HALL of Gorham, Me. Had one child, died an infant.
425 HANNAH, b. Jan. 29, 1778, m. Dec. 1, 1795, JONATHAN FOGG of Scarboro, probably no children.
426 MARY, b. Nov. 27, 1779, m. Feb. 5, 1803 JOHN SWEET of Windham. *Children:* 427 JOHN, died young; 428 CAROLINE; 429 JOHN; 430 MARY A., died young; 431 EMILY; 432 MARY A.; 433 NATHANIEL; 434 WILLIAM.
435 ANNA, b. March 23, 1781, m. March 1, 1807, PETER HALL; *Children:* 436 CHARLES; 437 GEORGE; 438 LOUISA; 439 MARY; 440 CAROLINE; 441 ELIZABETH.
442 WILLIAM, b. June 10, 1782, m. LUCY BARKER; removed to China, Me.
443 LUCY, b. Apl. 5, 1784, unmarried.
444 ZERUBBABEL, b. Nov. 6, 1785, m. June 2, 1815, ANNE MITCHELL of Gorham, Me.; *Children:* 445 ELIJAH, b. Feb. 28, 1816, d. Sept. 16, 1836, unm.; 446 EDWIN, b. May 18, 1820, m. May 27, 1845, MARGARET LOVETT. He d. Nov. 14, 1896, no children; 447 CHARLES H., b. March 3, 1827, m. June 16, 1852, JERUSHA W. SMALL of Westbrook, Me.
448 NATHANIEL, b. Jan. 15, 1788, lost at sea when a young man, unmarried.
449 PATIENCE, b. May 2, 1790, m. Jan. 31, 1810, JAMES POOL of Portland. *Children:* 450 ALBERT; 451 EDWARD; 452 CAROLINE; 453 MONROE; 454 LUCY.

F137 Abijah Locke, born in Falmouth, Me., Jan. 29, 1751, married ——— PRINCE, 1793. He was a shipmaster of Falmouth in the West India trade; helped build fort in Falmouth 1775. He died of Yellow fever in Trinidad Harbor, 1794.

Child of the 5th Gen., b. Falmouth.

F455 SUSANNA W., b. 1794, m. 1815, REUBEN NOYES of Falmouth.

F138 Dorothy Locke, born in Falmouth, Me., Oct. 10, 1755, married NATHAN FARRAR of No. Yarmouth, son of Zerubbabel and Hannah (Haswell). He settled in Yarmouth, thence moved to Lisbon, later to East Corinth, Me.

Children of 5th Gen., b. North Yarmouth, Me.

456 APHIA, d. in Falmouth of old age, unmarried.
457 HANNAH, d. unmarried.
458 SEWELL, b. Feb. 14, 1790, m. Jan. 29, 1816, his cousin ELIZA LOCKE. (See F473.)

459 JOHN, bapt. June, 1795, m. March 28, 1809, SOPHIA UNDERWOOD. He d. Dec. 13, 1856. They had in 6th Gen. b. North Yarmouth: 460 DOROTHY, b. Sept. 9, 1810, d. aged 1 year; 461 SOPHIA ANN, b. Nov. 27, 1812, d. July 1, 1815; 462 JOHN WILLIAM, b. Feb. 13, 1815; 463 DAVID U., b. Lisbon, Aug. 24, 1818, lived in Dexter, Me., 1902; 464 MARY YORK, b. Sept. 8, 1821, d. Oct. 26, 1857; 465 JOSEPH UNDERWOOD, b. May 22, 1828, d. Aug. 23, 1858; 466 SOPHIA S., b. Aug. 18, 1831, m. S. S. DEXTER, lived 1902, in Woodfords, Me.

F139 Josiah Locke, born in Falmouth, Me., May 21, 1757, married 1779, ELIZABETH GILPATRICK of Falmouth, who died Sept. 21, 1839. He was a farmer in Falmouth, helped on fort there 1775, and was in expedition to Penobscot 1779 and was corporal in Capt. Cobb's Co., 1779. He died Falmouth Apl. 12, 1841. Gilpatrick name was afterwards known as Patrick.

Children of the 5th Gen., all b. Falmouth.

F467 MARY, b. May 1, 1781, m. ELIAS MERRILL of Falmouth.
F468 DOROTHY, b. Dec. 13, 1783, m. ELIAS MERRILL.
469 LUCRETIA, b. May 19, 1786.
F470 NATHANIEL, b. Dec. 4, 1788, m. 1st, EUNICE STEVENS; m. 2nd, her sister, CHARLOTTE STEVENS.
471 DEBORAH, b. Jan. 4, 1791, d. unmarried Oct. 1879, in Falmouth, Me.
472 JOHN, b. May 5, 1793, d. unmarried 1808.
F473 ELIZA, b. July 10, 1795, m. SEWELL FARRAR # 458.
474 MATILDA, b. May 28, 1799, m. CAPTAIN EBEN PRINCE # 1286, of Portland, where they lived and their children were born. She d. 1841. *Children:* 475 EBENEZER FLOYD, b. 1820, d. 1841, no children; 476 MARY ELIZABETH, b. 1822, m. SAMUEL GATES of Auburn, Me., who d. 1858, and they had: 477 SAMUEL, b. 1851; 478 EDWARD PAYSON, b. 1824, m. and had son in Shelbyville, Ill.; 479 GEORGE W. PRINCE; 480 CHARLES PRINCE; 481 MATILDA LOCKE PRINCE; 482 JULIA PRINCE.
F483 ABIJAH, b. Sept. 8, 1801, m. Dec. 31, 1828, MARY HALL MORSE.
F484 MARY, b. Nov. 19, 1804, m. ABRAM MERRILL.
F485 JOANNA, b. Jan. 7, 1807, m. Sept. 13, 1835, EBENEZER LOCKE # 1297, b. Nov. 12, 1805, d. Nov. 21, 1844. She d. Portland, Me., May 23, 1899, aged 92.

F141 Edward Locke, born in So. Kingston, R. I., 1755 (?), married MARY JECKWORTH, who died before 1820. His brother deeded him land in So. Kingston, R. I., Dec., 1781. Probably died later than 1820.

Children of 5th Gen.

486 MIRIAM, b. ——, probably died young.
487 JEMIMA, b. ——, m. CAPT. BARLOW. *Children:* 488 MARY; 489 SARAH.

FIFTH GENERATION

490 NATHAN, b. ——, left home and never heard from.
F491 EDWARD, b. 1777, m. ELIZABETH WEBSTER. He died between 1828 and 1832.

F142 Samuel Locke, born in So. Kingston 1744 (?), married 1788-9 ANN SEAGER, (dau. of Samuel), a Captain and Colonel in the Revolution. She died in Warren, N. Y., March 13, 1808. He married 2nd, ANN (WILKINSON) VAN DERYER or VAN DEUSER, in Aurora, N. Y., 1812, and died there 1828.

Children of 5th Gen.

F492 SAMUEL, b. March 24, 1790, m. ANNA WENTWORTH.
F493 JONATHAN, b. of second wife, in Aurora, N. Y., Aug. 17, 1813, m. there 1834, ELSIE TRITTS.

F148 Jonathan Locke, born in Hampton Sept. 29, 1732, married HANNAH FOGG, of Hampton, Apl. 14, 1756, in Kensington; she born 1736, died June 10, 1819. He was a farmer in Hampton and died Jan. 27, 1800. He mentions land in Hampton and Deerfield in his will made 1799.

Children of 5th Gen., b. in Hampton.

494 HANNAH, b. Jan. 14, 1762, d. Feb. 14, 1789.
495 JONATHAN MOULTON, b. June 26, 1764, m. March 4, 1790, DEBORAH KNOWLES. He lived on the old homestead in Hampton and d. March 4, 1790.
F496 NATHANIEL, b. Aug. 26, 1766, m. March 18, 1792, LYDIA PAGE.
F497 MARY, b. May 24, 1770, m. 1st, Nov. 2, 1791, STEPHEN LOCKE # 500; m. 2nd, ROBERT HALEY.
498 MIRIAM, b. June 16, 1773, d. June 25, 1796, m. Oct. 22, 1794, DUDLEY LAMPREY son of Daniel and Elizabeth (Leavitt), he b. Apl. 13, 1771, d. Nov. 1853. Had no child by Miriam. He m. 2nd, ABIGAIL DRAKE.

F151 Caleb Locke, born in Hampton Aug. 12, 1738, married Feb. 18, 1762, BETSY DYER, dau. of Thomas and Elizabeth (Melcher) of Winter Harbor, Me. She born Apl. 15, 1744, died Dec. 17, 1825. Probably descended from Mary Dyer the Quakeress hanged in Boston June 1, 1660. From Hampton Caleb went to Winter Harbor, now Biddeford Pool, thence to Hollis, Me. He was a shoemaker and died Apl. 10, 1820.

Children of 5th Gen., b. in Hollis, Me.

F499 BETSEY, b. June 17, 1763, m. JOSEPH HOOPER.
500 STEPHEN, b. Feb. 2, 1765, m. his cousin MARY LOCKE. (See F497.)
F501 THOMAS D., b. June 13, 1768, m. ABIGAIL CHADBOURNE.
F502 TRISTRAM, b. Oct. 19, 1771, m. ELIZABETH LORD.

F503 CALEB, b. Dec. 7, 1773, m. March 17, 1802, SARAH FROST CLARKE.
504 JOSEPH, b. Jan. 1, 1779, he was a seaman and died unmarried at Matanzas, Cuba, Oct. 26, 1799.
F505 SAMUEL, b. Aug. 16, 1784, m. WIDOW ELIZABETH (STANWOOD) WAITE, Oct. 16, 1812.
F506 MARY, b. Aug. 12, 1787, m. JOHN BRADBURY.

F152 Samuel Locke, born in Hampton July 28, 1740, married 1st, Dec. 14, 1762, in Brentwood, DEBORAH VEAZEY, dau. of Benjamin and Deborah. She died Jan. 15, 1768. He married 2nd, Aug. 14, 1769, in Brentwood, ESTHER DOW. He married 3rd, Jan. 25, 1771, in Kensington, HANNAH MAGOON. He married 4th, July 16, 1797, in Kensington, SALLY JAMES. She died Apl. 1832. He lived at Brentwood and Raymond and died at Raymond, Oct. 22, 1818. He probably enlisted Hampton Falls Apl. 17, 1779–Dec. 1780, and was the Corporal Samuel of Dec. 1782.

Children of the 5th Gen.

F507 BETSEY, b. Oct. 2, 1763, m. 1st, Apl. 16, 1783, COFFIN PAGE; m. 2nd, his brother, NOAH PAGE, Jan. 13, 1806.
F508 BENJAMIN VEAZIE, b. Effingham, May 12, 1765, m. Nov. 27, 1790, OLIVE ROBINSON.
509 DEBORAH, b. Jan. 12, 1768, m. Nov. 26, 1789, ABRAHAM SMITH; he was b. in Poplin, Dec. 6, 1760, died in Bridgewater, March 16, 1852, where he settled, coming from Raymond. She died in Bridgewater, Sept. 12, 1848.
510 LUCY, the first of second wife's family, b. June 3, 1769, d. aged 14 days.
511 MIRIAM, b. Sept. 23, 1770, m. in Kingston, Apl. 5, 1809, CAPT. ELISHA HOOD, said to be both of Poplin.
512 LUCY, b. Oct. 29, 1771, m. in Kingston, Dec. 15, 1794, NICHOLAS MARSH, called both of Brentwood.
F513 JOHN WEARE, always went by name Weare, b. Dec. 26, 1773, m. Oct. 14, 1798, ANNA JAMES.
F514 SAMUEL, b. March 23, 1778, m. 1st, SALLY GOODWIN; m. 2nd, ABIAH HARDING.

F158 Dr. Jonathan Locke, born probably in Boston, 1726, married ABIGAIL PERRY, who was born March 16, 1726–7. He was a doctor in Boston, but in 1761 went to Shelburne Co., Nova Scotia, where he founded the town of Lockport, a thriving town ever since.

Children of 5th Gen., perhaps b. in Lockport, Nova Scotia.

515 SAMUEL, not m., probably lost at sea.
F516 JACOB, m. 1st, VISS VERNON; m. 2nd, MARGARET BARRY.

FIFTH GENERATION 43

517 MARY, no record.
518 ABIGAIL, no record.
F519 JONATHAN, b. 1758, m. MARY E. RYDER of Rhode Island.

F159 Samuel Locke, born ——, married LUCY BILL.
Child of 5th Gen.
F520 NATHANIEL, b. ——, of Newport, m. July 30, 1764, by Rev. Gardner Thurston, to MARY BURT.

F162 Francis Locke, born in Rye June 27, 1724, married 1st, Jan. 24, 1751, SARAH PAGE. He married 2nd, ELIZABETH (PAGE [?]) BACHELDER, at East Kingston, Dec. 31, 1761, who was born 1734, and died in Concord, Jan. 4, 1805. He signed the petition for the Newmarket bridge in 1755; sold land in Portsmouth Jan. and May 1759, and sold all his rights in Rumney, in 1767. He was a farmer and selectman in Epsom July 21, 1744, and died in Epsom. He was in Capt. Dearborn's Co., Stark's Reg., May 9, 1775, for 3 y. 6 m., and was paid for 103-8-6 miles travel.

Children of 5th Gen., b. in Rye.
521 SARAH FRANCES, b. Oct. 13, 1751, m. Dec. 24, 1769, JOSEPH SEAVEY, son of Henry J., and —— Smith, who was bapt. Oct. 7, 1744. *Children:* 522 ABRAHAM; 523 FRANCES; 524 EBENEZER; 525 JEREMIAH; 526 HANNAH.
527 DELIVERANCE, bapt. Apl. 11, 1754.
528 ELIZABETH, b. May 2, 1755, m. in Deerfield, July 11, 1775, SIMEON CASS of Epsom.
529 FRANCIS, b. Oct. 12, 1757, m. in Deerfield, Oct. 14, 1779, MOLLY SEAVEY. (Spelled Saven, Stevens.) He was in Capt. Dearborn's Co., Stark's Reg., July 8, 1775, and was paid for 103 miles travel. He was said to have been killed in the Revolutionary War.
F530 DEACON ABRAHAM, bapt. June 28, 1760, m. 1779, MARY SANBORN.
531 HANNAH, bapt. Jan. 9, 1763, m. in Deerfield, Jan. 13, 1779, BENJAMIN BICKFORD. He died before Aug. 1790, and she was living in 1803. *Children:* 532 SAMUEL, b. May 13, 1779, d. May 8, 1863; 533 BENJAMIN, b. Nov. 30, 1781; 534 THOMAS, b. Feb. 26, 1785, d. Sept. 9, 1865.

F165 Lieut. Ephraim Locke, born in Rye Feb. 10, 1730, married May 14, 1752, COMFORT DOWRST, born Aug. 21, 1731, at Rye, dau. of Ozem and Elizabeth (Seavey) of Epsom. He bought 50 acres of land in Epsom in 1747, and 40 acres more in 1756. He sold land there in 1762, and willed land there in 1763. He left Rye in 1767, was a moderator in Epsom 1773-5, made list of soldiers there Aug. 24, 1776. He represented the town in the Legislature, and was a Revolutionary soldier. He died March 7, 1798.

Children of 5th Gen., b. in Epsom.
- 535 ORSAM, he enlisted in Capt. B. Emery's Co., Apl. 1777, and was killed at Saratoga, N. Y., Sept. 19, 1777.
- 536 PRUDENCE, b. 1753.
- F537 FRANCIS, b. July 6, 1755, m. 1st, MARY ABIGAIL KATHERWOOD; m. 2nd, Dec. 2, 1819, OLIVE HAINES BICKFORD.
- 538 EPHRAIM, b. 1757.
- F539 ASA, b. 1763, m. in Epsom, March 4, 1784, WIDOW MARY (FLETCHER) (NASON) SHAW.
- F540 CAPT. SAMUEL (true name, CAPT. WM. SAMUEL), b. ——, m. 1785 MARY EVANS.
- 541 ESTHER, b. ——, m. ISAAC KNOWLES, b. 1751; son of Amos and Betsey (Palmer), and moved to Maine.
- 542 COMFORT, probably never married.
- F543 HANNAH, b. July 20, 1768, m. in Epsom, Feb. 9, 1792, AARON LAMPREY.
- F544 OLIVE, b. Epsom, 1772, m. March 8, 1795, PHILIP STEVENS.
- F545 BETSEY or MARTHA, b. 1773, m. 1st, Dec. 23, 1792, in Epsom, SAMUEL HUTCHINS; m. 2nd, Dec. 14, 1797, EDWARD THURSTON.

F166 Prudence Locke, born in Rye March 20, 1732, m. Dec. 27, 1753, ISRAEL MARDEN, son of Thomas and Mary (Smith). He had four children by a second wife.

Children of 5th Gen.
- 546 THOMAS, b. 1756.
- 547 SARAH, b. 1758, died young.
- 548 SARAH, b. 1761, m. —— MORRILL.
- F549 FRANCIS, b. 1763, m. SARAH LAMPREY.

F175 Edward Locke, born in Kingston Dec. 18, 1741, married ABIGAIL HAINES, dau. of John and Hannah (Wiggin). He was a Revolutionary soldier. Edward, a yeoman of Brentwood, bought 40 acres of land in Gilmanton 1764, and Edward a cordwainer of Toplin, bought land joining East Concord line in 1764, and sold it in 1765. He and his wife moved to Gilmanton in 1775, where they were baptized Aug. 15, 1775. Abigail lived later than 1810, and is buried two miles west of Farmington Village, N. H., on the road to New Durham Ridge. He joined the Baptist Church May 7, 1777, and was licensed to preach by that Church Dec. 4, 1779. In 1780 he became a preacher of the Freewill denomination, of which he was an originator. In company with Elder Tozar Lord of Barrington and John Shepherd, Esq., of Gilmanton, he is said to have spent a week in fasting and prayer locked in an unoccupied house, at the close of which they wrote down their views and ordained each other in the new denomination. He turned to Shakerism in 1782, with all his congregation. In 1792 he removed to Farmington, Me., and was the first settler in Chesterville, Me., where he started a church colony scheme, which failed, and the criticism caused him to leave the pastorate. He went milling in 1800, and died when absent from home, in Embden, Me., Feb. 1824. (See History of Gilmanton, page 215.) He possibly had more than these children given.

Children of 5th Gen.

550 REV. WARD, b. in Gilmanton 1784, m. BETSEY STEARNS, dau. of Josiah of Mt. Vernon, Me. They had one son in 6th Gen.: 551 HIRAM WARD, born 1819, who was a teacher in Mississippi in 1849, and then was lost track of. Ward Locke was ordained as Minister of the Frewill Baptist Church in 1813. Was a representative in the Maine Legislature in 1821, and d. Nov. 25, 1828. Betsey Stearns b. Dec. 13, 1793, m. 2nd, Dec. 27, 1829, SAMUEL CUSHMAN of New Gloucester, Me., and had 3 children.

552 JOHN, b. ——, no record.

F177 Thomas Locke, born in Kingston Jan. 1, 1746–7, married ELIZABETH COLLINS. She born May 31, 1743; died in Seabrook March 15, 1830, aged 86–9. He was a Justice of the Peace in Seabrook in 1776 and died there March 15, 1835.

Children of 5th Gen.

F553 MARY, b. Oct. 26, 1768, m. BENJAMIN PERKINS in 1789.
F554 SARAH, b. Oct. 31, 1773, m. CAPTAIN JOHN JANVRIN.
F555 SAMUEL, b. Feb. 16, 1776, m. Oct. 2, 1806, HANNAH LOCKE # 576.
556 JOHN, b. Sept. 8, 1785, m. Sept. 8, 1814, HANNAH FELCH, dau. of Nicholas and Sarah (Gove). She b. Oct. 1792, d. March 10, 1815. He m. 2nd, in Seabrook, Apl. 11, 1818, HANNAH ALLEN of Allenstown who was b. Oct. 13, 1784, d. Feb. 7, 1868. He d. Feb. 9, 1820. His widow m. JESSE HARRIMAN, in 1825, who d. March 28, 1872, aged 93. No issue from either marriage.

F181 Moses Locke, born in Kensington July 8, 1733, married in Kensington, March 12, 1755, MARY ORGAN of York, Me. Widow Mary paid taxes in Epsom 1804–10. He moved from Kensington to Epsom about 1768 and was taxed there as late as 1797. He served seven years in the Revolution, had been given up for dead, hence, when he returned his family did not recognize him. He enlisted in Capt. Dearborn's Co., Col. Stark's Reg. on May 9, 1775, and traveled 102 miles, but did not like this Company so enlisted 1776 for 6 years in the 1st N. H. Reg. Enlisted in Col. McClary's Reg. 1777 for 3 years. He was at Bunker Hill. A record says, "Moses of Kens. cordwainer, bought 50 acres of land in Epsom 1769."

Children of the 5th Gen., all b. in Epsom.

F557 MEHITABLE, b. Oct. 18, 1757, m. 1775, JOHN BLAKE.
F558 ANN (called SALLY), b. March 9, 1760, m. Nov. 24, 1785, JOHN GODFREY, JR.
F559 JONATHAN, b. in Kensington, Apl. 6, 1762, m. in Epsom, Feb. 6, 1785, ALICE (RUHUMA) PEARSONS.
F560 ANNAH (HANNAH), b. in Kensington, May 4, 1764, m. in Epsom, March 5, 1789, HON. JOSIAH SANBORN.
F561 MARY (RUHUMA), b. July 9, 1766, m. 1786 CALEB PEARSONS.
F562 ELIJAH, b. May 4, 1768, m. in Epsom, Oct. 28, 1792, LYDIA OSGOOD; m. 2nd, Aug. 12, 1816, WIDOW DOLLY (BACHELDER) BROWN.
F563 RICHARD, b. Sept. 20, 1770, m. Dec. 28, 1797, SARAH MOSES.
564 MOSES, b. March 13, 1773, d. unm. of yellow fever in the West Indies.
F565 JAMES MUNROE, b. March 4, 1776, m. in Epsom, Nov. 28, 1799, ABIGAIL SHERBURNE.

F182 Timothy Blake Locke, born in Kensington Oct. 30, or Nov. 8, 1735, married 1st, June 1, 1757, LYDIA Dow of Kensington; she born Oct. 27, 1734, died Aug. 28, 1780. He married 2nd, Jan. 22, 1781, PATIENCE PERKINS of Seabrook, who was born 1743, died June 18, 1816. "Tim Blake of Sandown, tanner," bought land in Kensington 1758 and 1764, and "Tim Blake, a trader," sold land there in 1764, and also sold land in So. Hampton in 1769. He was a prominent man of his time, living at Kensington and Seabrook. He was paid for service in Col. New's Co., July 10, 1776, was Sergt. of Capt. Rowe's Co. and discharged at Kensington at age of 39. His Revolutionary water bottle, engraved by stones giving dates of battles, etc., is held by descendants in Seabrook. He died in Seabrook, May 12, 1822.

Children of 5th Gen., most of whom b. in Seabrook.

F566 JOSIAH, b. Nov. 10, 1757, m. BETHIA BLANEY.
F567 SIMON, b. Aug. 13, 1759, m. MARY DOW.
F568 EDWARD, b. Dec. 15, 1760, m. Nov. 27, 1781, BETTY PERKINS.
F569 JAMES, b. Nov. 14, 1762, m. WIDOW TABITHA (EDWARDS) ORDIORNE, widow of John; m. 2nd, in Newburyport, Nov. 28, 1803, WIDOW SALLY (STICKNEY) DAWLTON, dau. of David. She b. 1769, d.

FIFTH GENERATION

Sept. 17, 1835. He was a Shipmaster of Salisbury, Mass., in 1803, later in Andover, Mass., was a tavern keeper and died there Apl. 20, 1845.

F570 JOHN, b. Feb. 29, 1764, m. in Concord Nov. 30, 1790, MOLLY SANBORN.
F571 BLAKE, b. Feb. 20, 1766, m. SALLY BROWN.
572 DAVID, b. June 27, 1768, d. unm. in South Carolina of smallpox March 10, 1790.
F573 LYDIA, b. Feb. 3, 1770, m. EDWARD GOVE.
F574 JOSEPH, b. Feb. 22, 1772, m. 1st, unknown; m. 2nd, Feb. 12, 1804, SARAH STANWOOD.
F575 JEREMIAH H., b. May 5, 1776, m. 1802, LOUISA SANBORN.
576 HANNAH, b. Apl. 23, 1783, m. Oct. 2, 1805, SAMUEL LOCKE. (See F #555.)
F577 BETSEY, b. Apl. 22, 1786, m. 1st, MOSES MERRILL; m. 2nd, THOMAS EATON.

F184 Abigail Locke, born in Kensington July 25, 1741, married ONESEPHORUS PAGE, son of Onesephorus and Patience. He born in East Kingston, Oct. 9, 1743, and moved to Deerfield in 1790.

Children of the 5th Gen., b. in So. Hampton.

F578 JANE, b. Sept. 3, 1763, m. Apl. 1, 1784, STEPHEN BACHELDER.
F579 MOSES, b. July 1, 1769, m. 1st, JOANNA BOHONON; m. 2nd, March 12, 1812, JUDITH BEAN.
580 MEHITABLE, b. Sept. 1, 1771, m. DEACON BENJAMIN HUNTOON. She d. Sept. 9, 1804.
F581 JOHN, b. June 10, 1773, m. Jan. 24, 1799, HANNAH BACHELDER.
582 ONESEPHORUS, b. ——, m. 1st, Sept. 6, 1807, RHODA SEARLES, dau. of Rev. Jonathan; m. 2nd, Feb. 19, 1811, DOLLY SARGENT of Boscawen.
583 BENJAMIN, b. July 10, 1778.
584 DAVID, b. Oct. 16, 1780, was a doctor in Meredith.
585 SAMUEL, b. July 24, 1782.

F186 Hannah Locke, born in Kensington Apl. 26, 1747, married in Kensington Oct. 30, 1765, JEREMIAH DEARBORN, son of Nathaniel and Mary (Batchelder). She died Oct. 18, 1820. He born Kensington Nov. 30, 1741; lived at Kensington then at Portsmouth where he died Apl. 18, 1816.

Children of 5th Gen., b. at Kensington.

586 SAMUEL, b. Jan. 15, 1767, m. JEMIMA BROWN, dau. of Stephen and Elizabeth (Nudd). She b. Feb. 11, 1774, d. Feb. 6, 1848. He lived in Kensington and d. March'8, 1847.
F587 HANNAH, b. July 23, 1768, m. July 28, 1793, ENOCH GOVE.
F588 ASA, b. Aug. 12, 1771, m. Jan. 1, 1798, RUHUMA CHOATE.

589 NATHANIEL, b. Nov. 5, 1774, m. Aug. 28, 1799, LUCY BLAKE, dau. of Hezekiah and Lucy (Prescott). She b. Oct. 17, 1779, d. July 2, 1824. He m. 2nd, ANNE (BREEDE) MUDGE, dau. of Aaron Breede and Sarah (Atwell). She b. Sept. 8, 1784, d. March 8, 1837. Nathaniel d. Jan. 18, 1852.
590 MARY, b. July 28, 1776, d. July 4, 1780.
F591 SARAH, b. July 24, 1778, m. March 7, 1800, JOSIAH TILTON.
592 MARY, b. July 19, 1781, m. May 25, 1828, CHARLES CHASE. She lived in Lynn, Mass., and d. Apl. 20, 1851.
593 JULIA, b. Jan. 16, 1792, m. Nov. 19, 1829, HENRY B. MULLEN of New Castle, lived in Lynn, and she d. Feb. 10, 1864.

F187 Nathaniel or Meshech Weare, born July 8, 1736, married MEHITABLE WYMAN.

Child of 5th Gen.

F594 NATHANIEL WEARE, b. March 21, 1757, m. March 7, 1793, MARY LOCKE (unknown).

F191 Edward Locke, bapt. in 1747 at Rye, and lived at Locke's Corner, Farmington. He may have had at least one son whose descent is given by tradition. Edward is said to have been with Washington at Valley Forge. John Knight and wife Temperance of Newington gave Edward Locke land in Rochester Dec. 4, 1769. This might be a gift to EDWARD, SR., or to EDWARD, JR., perhaps a son-in-law.

Child of the 5th Gen.

F595 Son, ——— LOCKE. First name unknown.

F193 James Locke, born 1752; married 1778, MARY BEAN, who was born 1758 and died 1844. He tried to enlist for the Revolution but was rejected by Capt. Norris, 1775. James and Mary went from Rye to North Barnstead, where he was one of the proprietors of Locke's Corner, 1768. When a lad of seventeen he worked in a grist mill in Rochester, and received one bushel of corn for five and one-half days work. Throwing his meal over his shoulder, he would leave for home Saturday noon following the spotted trees through the forest, arriving home at night, often so weary that he could scarcely walk. His fiancée being a Quakeress, he also became a Quaker, and after marriage bought wild land near what is now known as Locke's Corner, and converted it into a beautiful and productive farm, on which he passed a prosperous and contented life. He was selectman several years, and regarded by all as a man of honor. He died in Nov. 1833.

FIFTH GENERATION

Children of the 5th Gen., b. in Barnstead.
F596 JOHN, b. March 18, 1779, m. SALLY STANTON, Apl. 11, 1799.
F597 EDWARD, b. 1781, m. Oct. 3, 1805, ELIZABETH MEADER.
F598 JAMES, b. 1783, m. ABIGAIL NUTTER, Apl. 14, 1808.
F599 LOVIE, b. May 29, 1786, m. 1807, ELIPHALET NUTTER.
F600 ENOCH, b. 1790, m. SALLY BERRY of Strafford.

F199 Levi Locke, bapt. in Kensington Aug. 25, 1745; married RACHEL FULLER. Joseph Fuller of Rye and Joanna (Seavey) had a dau. Rachel born 1749, perhaps this one. He died, a young man in Sandown, Aug. 10, 1773. Rachel married 2nd, SHERBURNE SANBORN of Sandown and had seven children by him. She died June 16, 1837.

Children of the 5th Gen., b. in Sandown.
F601 ABIGAIL, b. June 29, 1768, m. JOSIAH FULLER.
F602 BENJAMIN, b. Apl. 10, 1770, m. March 17, 1796, HANNAH FAVOR. He m. 2nd, July 23, 1826, NANCY GURDY.
F603 RACHEL, b. Rye, Oct. 15, 1772, m. Nov. 30, 1793, ABRAHAM DOLOFF.

F200 Thomas Locke, born in Bridgewater Apl. 14, 1751, married MARTHA WORTHEN of Bridgewater. She born 1745, died in Stanstead, Can., March 17, 1826, probably was a sister of Lieut. Saml. Worthen. Thomas lived in Bristol from 1777 to 1782 when he removed to Stanstead, Can. Three children are said to be buried in Bristol. "Tom" was a great bear hunter, and one fall killed 16 bears on "Briar" Hill. He died in Stanstead, Can., Apl. 14, 1816.

Children of the 5th Gen., b. in Bristol or Bridgewater.
604 MOSES, b. May 3, 1773, m. MARGARET DURGAN. (A Margaret Dearborn b. July 12, 1782, dau. of Sherburne, m. a Moses Locke.)
605 SARAH, b. Jan. 28, 1776, m. ―――― CONVERSE, lived and died in Wilmot.
606 ABIGAIL, b. Sept. 22, 1778, m. in Lisbon Apl. 19, 1798, OBADIAH BELNAP of Concord who was b. in Lisbon, 1774, died in Canada 1834. She d. Apl. 3, 1861. They settled in Barnston, Canada, in 1807. *Children:* 607 MITCHELL, b. Jan. 21, 1800; 608 SALLY, b. Dec. 21, 1801, m. NICHOLAS DAVIS; 609 THOMAS, b. Aug. 10, 1803, m. SALLY DEARBORN; 610 WILLIAM, b. Sept. 20, 1805, m. ROXANNA TAYLOR; 611 MARTHA, b. Apl. 1807, m. JAMES FELDEN; 612 HANNAH, b. 1810, m. JOSEPH BAILEY.
F613 LEVI, b. Dec. 22, 1780, m. Sept. 30, 1804, SALLY CLEMENT.
614 WARD, b. Aug. 12, 1784.
615 MARY, b. March 28, 1787, m. LEVI HILL, son of Samuel and Patience (Meader) of Portsmouth.

F201 Martha Locke, born ——, married JONATHAN INGALLS. He was born in Sandown, 1750, died in Bridgewater, 1834. He was a son of Timothy, was in the Revolution and after Martha's death married 2nd, EDNA HASTINGS, in 1813.

Martha's Children of the 5th Gen.

616 SARAH, b. 1770, m. Jan. 8, 1789, HUBBARD DUDLEY.
617 JONATHAN, b. 1771-4, m. ABIGAIL CLEVELAND March 8, 1785. They moved to Canada about 1816. *Child:* 618 SALLY, b. 1793, d. 1867, m. JOHN BROWN, b. 1789, d. 1885, and they had 5 children.
619 JAMES, b. in New Hampton July 3, 1772, m. RUTH SLEEPER, and moved to Farnum's Corner, Canada.
620 DANIEL, b. June 6, 1784, m. 1st, POLLY DIAMOND; 2nd, EUNICE EVANS; moved to Berkshire, Vt.
621 SAMUEL, b. ——, m. MARGARET JACKMAN (?). He was living in Dunham, P. Q., in 1809, and western N. Y. 1818, an unlearned poet whose works were published at Angelica, N. Y., in 1825.
622 OLIVE, m. MR. RICHSON.
623 HANNAH, m. MR. WORTHEN.
624 MARY, m. MR. SANBORN.
625 DAU. m. WILLIAM GROSS.

F203 Patience Locke, born in Rye Feb. 10, 1730, married BENJAMIN WOODBRIDGE, son of Benj. and Mary (Osgood). He born Apl. 18, 1718, died in Milford, 1804. She died Feb. 4, 1756. They lived in Andover, Mass., and Milford, N. H. I am sure many descendants of this couple can be found in Andover, Mass., records, but time does not allow me to examine them.

Child of the 5th Gen.

F626 PATIENCE, b. Andover, Mass., Feb. 4, 1756, m. Dec. 17, 1789, her cousin, WOODBRIDGE GRAFTON.

F204 Jonathan Locke, born in Rye Jan. 29, 1732, married in Greenland June 8, 1758, ABIGAIL TOWLE. She born 1736, died March 22, 1817. He bought land in Rye in 1758 and lived there as a farmer. He was an inspector of "Minute Men" in Rye 1777. He gave each son a farm except HALL JACKSON, who chose money for an education. He died in Rye, Sept. 13, 1813.

He set out two elms in front of his home in Rye, now large and majestic. Soon after planting them he noticed a boy riding by on horseback break off a branch to whip his horse. The boy got the whipping, and years after the boy, now a very old man would go to that tree, tap it with his cane, and thank Locke for whipping him and so saving so fine a tree. He then would go

FIFTH GENERATION 51

to see his great-grandchildren and tell them about it. Another time, going to Portsmouth on horseback, he met a man whom he invited to share his horse. Coming to the tavern and knowing his companion's weakness, he called for a gill of rum, and dividing it he drank the other's health with the words, "Those who cannot govern themselves, must be governed."

Children of the 5th Gen., all b. in Rye.

F627 JONATHAN, b. Jan. 1, 1759, m. Nov. 23, 1785, OLIVE RAND.
628 ABNER, b. Oct. 30, 1760, enlisted Capt. Parsons Co. Aug. 14, 1777, was in New Jersey campaign and died at Valley Forge, Pa., Aug. 16, 1778, of camp fever.
629 MARY, b. July 21, 1763, d. 1826.
F630 ABIGAIL, b. July 21, 1764, m. March 18, 1785, JONATHAN JENNESS.
F631 JOHN, b. July 15, 1767, m. Sept. 30, 1787, ABIGAIL JENNESS.
F632 JOSEPH, b. March 21, 1770, m. ABIGAIL MARDEN Dec. 4, 1794.
633 DANIEL, b. Oct. 26, 1772, was a tailor and d. in Rye, Jan. 1, 1840, unmarried.
F634 JETHRO, b. June 29, 1775, m. Apl. 26, 1801, MARTHA WEBSTER.
F635 HALL JACKSON, b. 1777, m. 1st, Jan. 11, 1801, WIDOW ABIGAIL (UNDERWOOD) AMAZEEN; m. 2nd, Apl. 25, (30), 1834, MARGARY MANSON.

F206 Deacon David Locke, born in Rye Aug. 24, 1735, married 1st, ANNA LOVERING of Kensington, Feb. 9, 1758. She was dau. of John, and born March 11, 1739, O. S., died in Rye, Sept. 23, 1807. He married 2nd, March 24, 1809, WIDOW OLIVE (MARDEN) ELKINS, who was born Jan. 6, 1747, died Dec. 4, 1835. He hired soldiers in Rye 1781, for the Revolution, was selectman in Rye 1777–9, again 1783, and 1784; also moderator in 1785. He lived in Rye and Locke's Hill, Epsom, and died in Rye, June 3, 1810, leaving 13 children all married. Of 90 grandchildren, 77 were living, of 10 great-grandchildren, 8 were living. This family of 13 children were all singers, save one, and their voices when singing at home were often heard at the Centre Church one mile away.

Children of the 5th Gen., all b. in Rye.

F636 REUBEN, b. Apl. 26, 1758, m. in Epsom March 27, 1791, PHEBE CHAPMAN.
F637 SIMEON, b. March 21, 1760, m. in Epsom Jan. 29, 1784, ABIGAIL BLAKE.
F638 SARAH, b. Nov. 21, 1761, m. in Portsmouth Nov. 15, 1780, JOSHUA WEBSTER; m. 2nd, SOLOMON WATERHOUSE.
F639 MARY, b. May 7, 1763–4, m. in Hampton Nov. 3, 1785, JOSIAH B. SANBORN.
F640 DAVID, b. Nov. 24, 1765, m. May 31, 1789, ANNA TOWLE.

F641 JONATHAN, b. Feb. 19, 1768, m. 1st, Dec. 23, 1790, MISS LYDIA HALL; m. 2nd, Dec. 1826, MRS. HANNAH (TARLTON) BEALS.
F642 LEVI, b. Feb. 7, 1770, m. in Hampton Falls, Aug. 31, 1796, HANNAH PRESCOTT.
F643 REV. DR. JOHN, b. May 22, 1772, m. ABIGAIL DEARBORN of No. Hampton.
F644 ANNAH, b. March 27, 1774, m. Jan. 2, 1794, TIMOTHY PRESCOTT.
F645 DR. WILLIAM, b. Apl. 9, 1776, m. Oct. 23, 1800, ESTHER KNOWLES.
F646 ABIGAIL D., b. Nov. 20, 1778, m. Jan. 2, 1797, her second cousin, CAPT. BICKFORD LANG # 929.
F647 BENJAMIN, b. Dec. 28, 1780, m. Oct. 18, 1801, MISS PAMELIA CONNOR.
F648 NANCY, b. March 9, 1785, m. in Greenland Apl. 2, 1801, MORRIS LAMPREY.

F207 Abigail Locke, born in Rye Sept. 5, 1736, married Feb. 23, 1758, JAMES PERKINS, son of James and Huldah (Robie). He was born Jan. 5, 1735, died Nov. 2, 1805. She died in Rye, March 24, 1803. Her husband dug iron on the farm in Rye, and carried the same to Boston during the Revolution.

Children of the 5th Gen., b. in Rye.

649 MARY, b. Jan. 28, 1759, m. Apl. 1, 1777, NATHANIEL EMERY, son of Dr. Anthony and Abigail (Leavitt). He b. 1751, lived at Andover and Loudon.
F650 ABIGAIL, b. Oct. 10, 1760, m. Oct. 18, 1778, JOHN GARLAND.
F651 SARAH, b. Sept. 7, 1762, m. LIEUT. WILLIAM EMERY.
F652 JOHN, b. Nov. 7, 1764, m. Feb. 26, 1789, RUTH NUDD.
653 NANCY, b. March 12, 1767, m. March 4, 1787, JONATHAN SHERBURNE.
F654 JAMES, b. Apl. 20, 1769, m. Feb. 6, 1791, MARY PERKINS; m. 2nd, June 12, 1812, WIDOW MEHITABLE GARLAND.
F655 JONATHAN, b. Jan. 30, 1772, m. 1801, MARY LOCKE # 1139.
F656 JOSIAH, b. July 13, 1774, m. 1806, BETSEY BACHELDER.
657 HULDAH, b. Apl. 7, 1777, m. Sept. 8, 1799, NATHANIEL THURSTON, b. Jan. 17, 1755, d. Oct. 21, 1811, son of Daniel and Hannah (Parker). Huldah had: BENJ., b. 1800, d. 1801, and she d. Sept. 8, 1801. She was his third wife and he had four more after her.
658 HANNAH, b. May 9, 1780, m. Jan. 10, 1799, JOSEPH PARSONS of Rye, b. 1774; had no children. He m. 2nd, 1802, ELIZABETH MUNROE.

F208 Capt. William Locke, born in Rye July 26, 1738, married in Rye (KEZIAH) or CHRISTENA PAINE (Chester records say Rachel Payne), dau. of John and Sarah of Portsmouth. She born May 3, 1740, died 1800. He married 2nd, WIDOW MARY DUSTIN of Candia, Aug. 28, 1800, who died July 13, 1827 in Candia. He died in Chester, Nov. 16, 1825. His father bought land in Chester in 1761 and William settled on lot # 12; he built a sawmill there in 1780, which was burned

FIFTH GENERATION

March 27, 1796. Jan. 8, 1782, the General Assembly voted to see if the town would accept the plan of Government and William was appointed on a committee. In 1793 he was on a committee to settle a minister. He resigned a commission in the British Army and fought with the patriots at Bunker Hill. Wm. Locke and Simeon Berry came to Chester from Rye about the same time and later their fathers came the same road to visit them. Mr. Berry wore new sheep skin breeches and being caught in a shower they sagged to his calves whereupon he cut them off at the knee. Soon the sun came out and the breeches shrunk so that they were as much too short as they were before too long.

Children of the 5th Gen. b. in Chester.

F659 SARAH, b. Dec. 13, 1761, m. JOSEPH KNOWLES.
F660 JOHN, b. 1765, m. —— 20, 1793, ELEANOR TUCKER.
661 ABIGAIL, b. March 19, 1768, m. JAMES TUCKER, he b. Apl. 26, 1762. They lived at Chester and Andover. *Children:* 662 JAMES, b. Sept. 19, 1788, d. Sept. 19, 1846; 663 ABIGAIL, b. Oct. 30, 1795, d. June 8, 1828; 664 CYRENE, b. Sept. 26, 1805; 665 ELIZA A., b. May 30, 1808; six others died under 4 years of age.
F666 POLLY, b. Oct. 27, 1769, m. in 1783, CAPT. BENJAMIN TRUE.
F667 MARGARET, b. 1770, m. in Chester, Nov. 15, 1792, CAPT. WILLIAM MOORE.
668 WILLIAM (Chester records say bapt. Oct. 6, 1771). (Not recalled by descendants.)
669 DOLLY, b. June 9, 1780, m. 1st, in Chester, Dec. 31, 1801, JOSIAH MOORE of Chester, son of Charles and Mary (Whittier). He d. Feb. 16, 1821, aged 53; she m. 2nd, THOMAS SHANNON Dec. 31, 1826, son of Thomas and Mary of Isles of Shoals. He was b. in Hampstead in 1750 and had a first wife SALLY PILLSBURY. Dolly was living in 1868.
670 HANNAH, b. ——, was not married.

F215 **Hannah Locke,** born in Rye Feb. 18, 1737, married DEACON REUBEN PHILBRICK, who was born Feb. 27, 1737, in Rye. He married three times after her death. See #226.

Children of the 5th Gen. b. in Rye.

F671 REUBEN, b. Sept. 9, 1773, m. Sept. 4, 1794, BETSEY JENNESS.
2nd wife's children.
672 HANNAH, b. Jan. 7, 1776, m. Aug. 1, 1792, AMOS TOWLE, who was bapt. Sept. 8, 1764, d. Feb. 15, 1855. They had two children.
673 SALLY, b. Apl. 13, 1778, m. Dec. 8, 1801, LIEUT. JOSEPH JENNESS, son of Joseph and Mary (Dow). He b. Feb. 12, 1771, died a farmer in Rye Sept. 13, 1845. She d. Nov. 8, 1808. *Child:* 674 REUBEN, b. Dec. 2, 1807, m. MARY KNOWLES, whose daughter 675 SARAH, m. RICHARD L. LOCKE. See F6263.

676 JOSES, b. May 19, 1781, m. Nov. 3, 1803, POLLY PAGE; m. 2nd, Mrs. NANCY (JENNESS) WOODMAN, who was b. 1780, the dau. of Jonathan Jenness and Betsey (Rand), and d. May 2, 1860. *Children:* 677 REUBEN; 678 JOSEPH; 679 MARY.

F217 Abigail Locke, born in Rye March 4, 1743, married Sept. 18, 1764, JOSHUA FOSS, son of John. He born in Rye June 12, 1738.

Children of the 5th Gen.

680 WILLIAM, b. Oct. 15, 1765, no record.
681 ELIZABETH, b. Jan. 22, 1768, m. DAVID HATCH.
682 JOSHUA, b. March 14, 1770, m. ELIZABETH LOCKE, dau. of Simon of Hollis.
683 DAVID, b. Aug. 9, 1772, lived in Strafford.
F684 JOHN, b. Jan. 9, 1775, m. ELIZABETH TITCOMB.
685 JOB, b. March 22, 1777, m. 1st, a MARDEN; m. 2nd, WIDOW TILTON; lived in Dover.

F218 William Locke, born in Rye Sept. 9, 1745, married 1st, BETSEY BABB; married 2nd, in Barrington Apl. 20, 1802, MARY HAYES of Barrington. He bought land in Barrington of his father in 1767 and from the town in 1769. He lived in Barrington and his will is dated Apl. 18, 1826.

Children of the 5th Gen. b. in Barrington.

F686 HANNAH, b. Dec. 16, 1766, m. WINTHROP REYNOLDS.
F687 SAMUEL, b. March 16, 1768, m. March 1, 1792, LUCY CATE; m. 2nd, Mrs. TAMSEN HAYES, Jan. 27, 1801.
F688 JOHN, b. Sept. 17, 1769, m. Sept. 20, 1792, ABIGAIL PAGE; m. 2nd, Oct. 19, 1800, MERCY DAME, m. 3rd, WIDOW MARGARET PIERCE.
F689 MIRIBAH, b. Dec. 19, 1771, m. July 19, 1792, AMOS MAIN.
F690 MARY E., b. Aug. 2, 1773, m. 1798, ISAAC WOODMAN.
691 ELIZABETH, b. Apl. 26, 1775, d. Feb. 3, 1778.
692 WILLIAM, b. Jan. 23, 1777, d. Jan. 31, 1777.
F693 WILLIAM, b. Dec. 22, 1779, m. Feb. 21, 1802, SARAH HOITT.
F694 ELISHA, b. Oct. 26, 1780, m. Durham, Dec. 18, 1806, SOPHIA PINKHAM.
F695 BETSEY, b. Apl. 21, 1783, m. MOSES DEMERITT who was b. 1794.
F696 DOLLY, b. Aug. 11, 1784, m. Sept. 9, 1810, BARZILLA SHURTLEFF.
F697 ALICE, b. June 24, 1787, m. Feb. 16, 1812, SAMUEL DEMERITT.
698 ABIGAIL, b. Aug. 1, 1789, d. Apl. 24, 1790.
F699 BENJAMIN BABB, b. Sept. 20, 1792, m. Nov. 23, 1815, BETSEY HURD.

F219 Samuel Locke, born Aug. 14, 1748. Nothing further authentic is known of him, but at the request of a Locke I add the following: A Samuel Locke was impressed on the British Ship "Little Belt" from a "Market Town" in New England.

FIFTH GENERATION 55

He was at the siege of Londonderry, and was discharged from the English Navy in Nova Scotia in 1802 aged 54. His 1st wife is unknown; married 2nd, HANNAH WOOD. He is buried in the Churchyard at Digby, N. S. These Samuels may be identical.

Children of the 5th Gen. b. Nova Scotia, Canada.
(Great doubt of these descendants being from John Locke.)
700 ADNA, was a drummer in the English Army, was blown up with the Garrison with Major Drummond.
701 LOUIS, was a clarionet in the English Army.
702 MARTIN, married but no record.
2nd wife's child:
F703 WILLIAM, b. 1806, m. EMILY MARSHALL.
F704 JAMES ED., b. Frederick, N. B., July 1, 1807, m. 1835, MERCY MARSHALL.
705 FRANCIS, b. Weymouth, N. S., m. FANNY BERRY, lived at Bear River, N. S. She d. Apl. 29, 1880, he d. Aug. 9, 1883. Had 4 children, one 706 HARRIET ANN, m. WILBUR APT, had 12 children.
707 HENRY, went under alias HENRY GLASCOMB, was killed on a R. R. in N. B. in 1842.
708 ANN, m. WILLIAM HOPP of Weymouth, N. S.
709 HANNAH, m. JAMES LONGWORTH, of Digby, N. S.; had: 710 JOHN, m. LOUISA APT, lived in Medway, Mass.

F221 Hannah Philbrick, born in Rye Apl. 24, 1729, married Nov. 24, 1748, REUBEN MOULTON, born Jan. 4, 1729, son of Jonathan and Elizabeth (Lamprey). He married 2nd, MARGARET JONES.

Children of 5th Gen. b. in Rye.
711 JONATHAN, b. Oct. 27, 1749, d. March 24, 1767.
712 ELIZABETH, b. Feb. 8, 1751, m. NATHANIEL MARDEN.
713 LUCY, b. Aug. 4, 1757, m. PAGE PHILBRICK.

F222 Tryphena Philbrick, born in Rye Apl. 24, 1729, married Jan. 29, 1760, as his 2nd wife, JOHN SANDERS of Torbay, England, born 1720. He was lost in the big gale of 1770, and she married 2nd, Apl. 16, 1780, JONATHAN BERRY.

Children of 5th Gen. by Sanders.
714 ABIGAIL, b. Oct. 7, 1760, m. WILLIAM LOCKE Oct. 28, 1778, # F244.
715 WILLIAM, bapt. June 19, 1763.
716 SARAH, bapt. July 28, 1763, m. 1st, March 6, 1783, WILLIAM SANDERS; 2nd, JOSEPH VARRELL.
717 OLLY, b. 1766, m. WILLIAM TUCKER.

F223 Abigail Philbrick, born Nov. 11, 1730, died 1816; married Nov. 24, 1748, MARK RANDALL of Moultonborough, born in Rye, Oct. 25, 1726, son of Edward and Hannah.

Children of 5th Gen.

718 ABIGAIL, bapt. Dec. 5, 1749, m. GIDEON MARSHALL; lived at Hampton Falls.
719 JOSES, b. Apl. 11, 1751, m. ELIZABETH GALLOWAY; he died a prisoner in a Jersey prison ship; she m. 2nd, NOAH JENNESS; 3rd, THOMAS GOSS.
720 SALLY, b. Oct. 28, 1752, m. JOHN JENNESS.
721 ELIZABETH, b. Apl. 10, 1755, m. RICHARD WEBSTER.
722 MARK, b. June 18, 1757, m. ——— ———. Had: 723 MARK, m. AUGUSTA BERRY.
724 REUBEN, b. Feb. 9, 1760, m. SARAH YOUNG and had: 725 SARAH; 726 JOSES; 727 LEVI D.
728 JOHN, b. June 18, 1762, d. Oct. 19, 1781, in a Revolutionary prison.
729 DEBORAH, b. June 11, 1764, m. ABNER DOWNES. She d. June 1, 1803.
730 SAMUEL, b. July 3, 1767, m. ——— TIBBETTS and lived in Maine.
731 DANIEL, b. Oct. 26, 1769, m. ELIZABETH QUIMBY, and lived in Sandwich.
732 OLLY, b. Oct. 21, 1772, d. unmarried in Moultonborough.
733 HANNAH, b. Aug. 30, 1778, d. Sept. 6, 1778.

F224 Joseph Philbrick, born in Rye Aug. 10, 1735, married Dec. 2, 1760, ANN TOWLE. who was born March 28, 1741, died Sept. 11, 1788, dau. of Jonathan and Anna (Norton). He lived in Rye.

Children of the 5th Gen. b. in Rye.

734 JOSES, b. Sept. 12, 1761, m. July 7, 1782, SUSANNAH PITMAN, and had 10 children.
735 ABIGAIL, b. Sept. 28, 1768, m. Dec. 8, 1806, JOB LOCKE, bapt. 1762. (See F337.)
736 ANNA, b. Jan. 23, 1769, m. JOSIAH WEEKS of Greenland.
737 HANNAH, b. Dec. 12, 1770, d. unmarried 1831.
738 JONATHAN, b. Sept. 17, 1773, m. Oct. 22, 1795, SARAH MARDEN, and had 8 children.
739 DANIEL, b. Jan. 19, 1776, m. 1800, DOLLY GROVER.
740 LEVI, b. May 6, 1778, m. MARY NUDD.
741 JAMES, b. July 8, 1780, m. May 21, 1801, ABIGAIL PERVIERE, who d. Feb., 1862.
742 JOSEPH, b. June 14, 1783, died in Demerara, W. I.
743 SALLY, b. Aug. 30, 1788, m. SAMUEL MARDEN.

F227 Daniel Philbrick, born in Rye Feb. 2, 1740, married ABIGAIL MARDEN. He died in Rye Nov. 1780.

FIFTH GENERATION

Children of the 5th Gen. b. in Rye.
F744 MERCY, b. Jan. 8, 1763, m. MICHAEL DALTON.
745 SARAH, b. July 30, 1764, m. AMOS BROWN, son of Saml. and Eliza (Johnson); he bapt. Dec. 20, 1761.
F746 JOSES, b. July 1776, m. Jan. 12, 1790, SALLY SMITH.

F228 Jonathan Philbrick, born in Rye Nov. 26, 1745, married Dec. 8, 1768, MARY MARDEN. He was a blacksmith and died Apl. 1, 1822.

Children of the 5th Gen.
747 DANIEL, b. July 12, 1769, m. BETSEY WELLES.
748 JONATHAN, b. Sept. 29, 1772, m. June 1, 1797, SARAH WELLS of Epsom.
749 ABIGAIL, b. Oct. 30, 1776, m. JAMES CHAPMAN.
F750 EPHRAIM, b. Sept. 9, 1780, m. SALLY WEBSTER.
751 BETSEY, b. Nov. 2, 1783, m. Dec. 8, 1809, LIEUT. JOSEPH JENNESS.
F752 JOSEPH, b. May 1788, m. May 1810, BETSEY PAGE and had 8 children.

F231 Job Moulton, born 1752, married ANNIE WAY of Lyman, and died in 1838.

Children of 5th Gen.
753 ISAAC, b. ——, m. —— MINOT, had one son.
754 ALPHEUS, b. ——, m. SARAH A. PORTER, who had: 755 SETH; 756 LUTHERIA.
757 ALDEN, b. twin with last, d. unmarried.
758 PATIENCE, b. ——, m. SETH PADDLEFORD, and lived in Monroe.
759 NABBY, b. ——.
760 RUBY, b. ——, m. WILLIAM BARBER, who d. in Lyman 1858. *Children:* 761 MIRIAM; 762 JOHN; 763 NATHAN; 764 RUBY; 765 ISAAC; 766 LYDIA A.; 767 AUSTIN.
768 MINDWELL, b. ——.
769 MARTHA, b. ——, m. JONATHAN MOULTON, her cousin. *Children:* 770 CORDELIA; 771 ARVISTA; 772 FLORA J.; 773 CHARLES C.
774 MATILDA, b. ——, m. SOLOMON MINER. *Children:* 775 EPHRAIM; 776 ALDEN; 777 MARTHA; 778 JOHN; 779 ANN; 780 ISAAC; 781 WESLEY.
782 One DAUGHTER in this family, m. PHILIP PADDLEFORD of Monroe, and had: 783 MARY A.; 784 PHILIP; 785 COOMER. Another 786 DAU., m. a CARLETON of Littleton; and a third, m. —— KIMBALL.

F232 Jonathan Moulton, born Feb. 8, 1757, married MARTHA GIBSON, born Jan. 16, 1772, died in Lyman, Apl. 7, 1842. He was a Revolutionary soldier, a farmer in Lyman and died there July 12, 1846.

Children of 5th Gen.

787 JONATHAN, m. MARTHA MOULTON, his cousin #769.
788 SAMUEL, m. in Michigan and had four boys.
789 BETSEY, m. ADNA THORNTON, and lived in Lyman, he b. 1791, d. 1842. *Children:* 790 WILLIAM; 791 SIDNEY; 792 HANNAH; 793 MARTHA; 794 SARAH.
795 HANNAH, m. 1st, BENJAMIN PADDLEFORD, and had: 796 BYRON; 797 CLAYTON; 798 LADOSKA; 799 BENJAMIN A.; she m. 2nd, FREEMAN HINMAN of Monroe, and had: 800 FRANK.
801 ROXANNA, m. BARRON MOULTON, who died in St. Johnsbury, Vt., in 1874, aged 76. *Children:* 802 LOUISA; 803 SABRINA; 804 AUGUSTA; 805 JAMES; 806 BARRON C.; 807 PAULINE; 808 DR. ALZINA V.
809 GABRIEL, b. 1810, m. 1st, SOPHIA WALKER; m. 2nd, HANNAH HOSKINS, and died in Littleton, 1899. *Children:* 810 MOSES; 811 ANSEL; 812 ELLEN; 813 MINERVA; 814 LOUISE.
815 ANN, m. HEROD STEVENS, lived in Littleton. *Children:* 816 MURILLA; 817 JONATHAN; 818 CALISTA; 819 OLIVIA.
820 NATHAN, m. SUSAN WHEELOCK, lived in Littleton. *Children:* 821 MARTHA; 822 JANE; 823 JONATHAN.
824 SABRINA, m. 1st, JESSE BAILEY, lived in the west. *Children:* 825 FLAVIA; 826 ANGELETTA; 827 MELISSA; 828 LOWANA; 829 MARIETTA; 830 OLEVIA; 831 VIOLA; 832 SON.
833 FRANK, lived in Littleton aged 80, unmarried.

F233 Noah Moulton, born 1759, married PRISCILLA BARRON, born 1768, died 1861. He died 1850.

Children of 5th Gen.

834 PRISCILLA, m. LEVI PARKER, and lived in Wolcott, Vt.
835 JONATHAN, was m., went west and had a family.
836 DAVID, m. 1st, —— PARKER; 2nd, HARRIET ——.
837 SALLY, m. SEARLES EASTMAN. *Children:* 839 ORRIN; 840 PERSIS; 841 HULDAH; 842 PRISCILLA; 843 LURANCIA; 844 JOEL; 845 AUGUSTA.
846 MILLICENT, m. MOODY PARKER, of Wolcott, Vt.
847 FANNIE, m. ISAAC CLOUGH; lived in Lyman.
848 BARRON, m. ROXANNA MOULTON, a cousin.
849 WILLIAM, was m. twice and lived in New York.
850 JACOB, was m. had children in the west.
851 NOAH, b. 1803, d. 1893, m. 1st, 1830, RUTH COWAN, b. 1801, d. 1863; m. 2nd, MRS. MARILLA KEENEY. *Children:* 852 DARWIN; 853 ARMENIA; 854 BYRON; 855 HELEN; 856 JULIA; 857 ARBA.
858 SMITH, m. MARY CHARLES; lived in Barnet, Vt.
859 CHARLES, b. ——.
860 HULDAH, m. LARKIN HASTINGS. *Children:* 862 JENNETT; 863 LURANCY; 864 NOAH; 865 LUELLA; 866 SERAPHIM; 867 JONATHAN.
868 RINALDO, m. HARRIET KENT.
869 GRANDISON, m. 1st, NANCY BAILEY; m. 2nd, ELLEN ——; he lived in Wolcott, Vt., and had children.

FIFTH GENERATION

F234 David Moulton, born 1763, married SALLY KNAPP and died in 1841.

Children of 5th Gen.

870 REUBEN, m. SALLY COREY. *Child:* 871 REUBEN.
872 GEORGE, m. FANNIE CLOUGH.
873 JAMES MADISON, b. 1809, m. BETSEY TITUS, and d. 1865. *Children:* 874 JAMES M.; 875 GEORGE M.; 876 HERBERT; 877 JENIFER; 878 ELIZABETH; 879 FLORENCE; 880 DANIEL.
881 ALMIRA, m. ——— DODGE and lived in Lisbon.
882 JOANNA, m. ——— HIBBARD.
883 MARTHA, m. TIMOTHY CLOUGH, lived in Bath.
884 DAVID, b. ———. Another list adds these names to David's family: 885 BENJAMIN (?); 886 DANIEL (?); 887 ALBERT (?); 888 LUCY; 889 HULDA.

F235 John Moulton, born ———, married POLLY SMITH, and lived in Lyman.

Children of 5th Gen.

890 BETSEY, m. ——— Dow and lived in Lyman.
891 POLLY, m. DANIEL STICKNEY. *Children:* 892 MARY ANN; 893 ELIZA; 894 ENOS.
895 COL. JOHN, m. LUCY TITUS. *Children b. Lyman:* 896 CELESTA; 897 LOWELL; 898 MERRITT.
899 GUY, m. MARY MOORE and d. 1886 aged 93. *Children:* 900 ELSIE; 901 LUVIA A.
902 UNKNOWN, m. ——— KIMBALL and went west.
903 LOTTIE, m. DAVID CHILDS; had children in Barnet, Vt.
904 ETHAN, went to Maine.
905 MATILDA, m. ——— MILLEN and went west.
906 NOAH, b. 1792, d. 1864, m. SALLY FLOYD. *Children:* 907 ELLEN; 908 ELIZA; 909 WEBSTER; 910 JAMES; 911 MARY; 912 PHOEBE.
913 WEBSTER, lived in the west unmarried.

F236 Huldah Locke, born in Rye Oct. 2, 1739, married MOSES SEAVEY of Deerfield, son of Benjamin; he born 1734. They moved to Deerfield in 1762.

Children of the 5th Gen.

914 SAMUEL, b. 1762.
915 HULDAH, b. 1763.
F916 LEVI, b. Dec. 29, 1765, m. Nov. 25, 1790, HANNAH TILTON.
917 MOSES, b. 1767, m. RUTH TARLTON of New Castle.
918 ABIGAIL, b. 1770. One of these daus. m. GILBERT NEALLY of Exeter.
919 ANOTHER m. LEVI PHILBRICK who had a dau. m. JOHN C. FRENCH.
920 ELIJAH, b. 1774, m. in Deerfield March 3, 1803, LUCY BASSETT of Deerfield.
921 SARAH, prob. a granddau. m. TRUE CURRIER; he d. Sept. 28, 1866 aged 71-6-18. She d. Nov. 8, 1877, aged 83.
921a JONATHAN, b. ———.

F237 Martha Locke, born in Rye Dec. 15, 1741, married March 8, 1764, BICKFORD LANG who was a blacksmith, moved from Rye to Epsom. He was son of John and Sarah (Bickford) Lang, who lived in Portsmouth near the Mill Dam.

Children of the 5th Gen.

922 JOHN, b. Apl. 12, 1767, m. MERCY DRAKE of Effingham, lived at Limerick, Me. *Children:* 923 FRANCES, bapt. 1789; 924 HULDAH, bapt. 1793; 925 POLLY, bapt. 1795; 926 DATA, bapt. 1796.

F927 HANNAH, b. Sept. 16, 1769, m. DOWST RAND of Rye, b. June 24, 1764.

928 MARTHA, b. Feb. 15, 1772, m. 1st, JEREMIAH FOGG; 2nd, JOHN BACHELDER, of No. Hampton.

929 BICKFORD, b. Rye Oct. 30, 1774, m. 1797 ABIGAIL LOCKE (See F646.)

930 SARAH, b. Oct. 6, 1776, m. 1st, JONATHAN CROCKETT; 2nd, JOSIAH TUCK, his 3rd wife; Josiah, b. Hampton Apl. 19, 1773, son of Jonathan and Huldah (Moulton) and died in Effingham, Sept. 28, 1856. Probably no children.

931 WILLIAM, b. Apl. 21, 1782, d. 1783.

F238 Mary Locke, born in Rye Nov. 25, 1744, married June 7, 1765, ROBERT SAUNDERS, son of John and Mary (Berry) who was born July 3, 1743; buried in Effingham, N. H. She died 1840, aged 96.

Children of the 5th Gen.

F932 ROBERT, bapt. Oct. 12, 1766, m. MARY FOSS, b. Feb. 11, 1764.

933 MARY, bapt. Aug. 16, 1767, m. JOSEPH CHAPMAN.

934 ELIJAH, b. Aug. 20, 1769, m. Nov. 29, 1792, MERCY RAND, and had: 935 PATIENCE LOCKE, bapt. June 29, 1794.

936 JOHN, b. Apl. 10, 1774, m. ——— CHAPMAN.

937 NATHANIEL, b. Nov. 29, 1778, m. ——— GOSS.

938 WILLIAM, b. ———, m. ——— HALL.

F243 Elijah Locke, born Dec. 15, 1754, married 1st, Nov. 21, 1776, ELIZABETH BROWN of Rye, dau. of Col. Jonathan and Mary (Garland). She born June 21, 1755. He married 2nd, MRS. NANCY (WATTS) FISHER. He moved to Epsom in 1800, thence to Chichester. He was a soldier in the Revolution of the N. H. line, and was pensioned at $80 per year in 1818. He fell dead into the fireplace in Chichester Aug. 1, 1838.

Children of the 5th Gen. b. in Rye.

F939 ELIJAH, b. June 28, 1781-2, m. Jan. 15 (21), 1802, HANNAH SAUNDERS.

F940 MARY, b. 1784, m. Apl. 12, 1804, JOHN WALLIS of Epsom.

F941 LEVI, b. March 20, 1786, m. Aug. 15, 1805, RACHEL D. TOWLE.

FIFTH GENERATION 61

F244 William Locke, born in Rye June 16, 1758, married Oct. 29, 1779, ABIGAIL SAUNDERS # 714 of Epsom. She born Oct. 7, 1760, died in Alexandria, Oct. 23, 1828. He enlisted at age of 16 in the Revolution, under Genl. Sullivan, at Portsmouth. He moved from Rye to Epsom about 1790 and in 1811 moved to Alexandria where he died Apl. 9, 1828. He was a farmer and a blacksmith, and was disabled in the Revolution by fever, which settled in his legs, causing them to burst.

Children of the 5th Gen. b. in Epsom.

F942 JOHN, b. March 17, 1780, m. Sept. 1797, ABIGAIL LOCKE #1578;
· m. 2nd, MEHITABLE BICKFORD.
943 ABIGAIL, b. Sept. 3, 1781, m. JEREMIAH PAGE of Alexandria; she died in Epsom Nov. 5, 1847, had no child.
F944 HULDAH, b. Aug. 4, 1783, m. Sept. 1, 1799, JOHN PAGE.
F945 WILLIAM, b. Sept. 6, 1785, m. Dec. 25, 1808, MERCY SHAW.
F946 ELIZABETH, b. July 11, 1788, m. June 1813, JOHN LANGLEY.
F947 REUBEN, b. March 14, 1791, m. Sept. 10, 1815, JANE McMURPHY.

F248 Mary S. Locke, born 1747, married JONATHAN LADD of Haverhill, son of Jonathan and Mehitable (Roberts). He born Dec. 10, 1760, died March 11, 1833.

Children of the 5th Gen.

948 THEODOSIA, b. Feb. 15, 1786, m. ―――― SMITH, son of Rev. Daniel and Phebe (Chase).
F950 ELISHA L., b. Bradford, Vt., June 14, 1787, m. Jan. 1, 1822, ASENATH BACHELDER.
951 RUTH, b. July 4, 1789, m. July 6, 1849, JOHN BOISE.
952 ISAAC, b. July 6, 1792, m. NANCY RIGGS. He lived in Warren, Ohio, and d. Oct. 15, 1849. *Children:* 953 HENRY R., b. Oct. 13, 1822; 954 MARTHA J., b. June 1824; 955 ISAAC, b. 1826.
956 WILLIAM W., b. Nov. 25, 1794.
957 JAMES, b. Feb. 12, 1797.
958 TRYPHENA, b. March 11, 1803.

F249 Sergt. William Locke, born 1753, married TRYPHENA SAUNDERS. William of Bath, aged 22, enlisted June 24, 1776, in James Osgood's Co. He also served in Stark's Reg., Capt. Post's Co. He was a stone-cutter, hence got the nickname of "Picker" Locke, and was called a very peculiar man. He came to Rye (probably born there) "a lone man" and died there Apl. 19, 1828.

Children of the 5th Gen.

F959 JONATHAN, b. Nov. 6, 1797, m. Jan. 31, 1822, SOPHIA THURSTON.
F960 ABIGAIL, b. ――――, m. JOHN SAUNDERS.
F961 TRYPHENA, m. ISAAC WINTER.

F962 ADELINE, m. CORNELIUS RICE.
F963 NELSON HORATIO, m. 1st, AMANDA SQUIRES; 2nd, UNKNOWN; 3rd, —— PETTIBONE.

F250 Hannah Locke, born 1755, married Dec. 3, 1772, JAMES LADD of Haverhill, son of Jonathan and Mehitable (Rogers). He born Apl. 10, 1753, died Dec. 5, 1836. She died Nov. 7, 1841.

Children of the 5th Gen.

964 TRYPHENA, b. June 23, 1774, m. 1st, —— GOODWIN; 2nd, DAVID HEATH.
965 PHOEBE, b. Feb. 24, 1776, m. WILLIAM KELSEY.
966 ABIGAIL, b. Dec. 3, 1778, m. March 5, 1800, WILLIAM TARLTON.
967 SUSANNA, b. Feb. 1, 1780, m. Sept. 3, 1805, SIMEON OLMSTEAD.
968 THEODORA, b. Dec. 19, 1782, m. AMOS TARLTON.
969 JAMES, b. Apl. 6, 1784, was unmarried.
970 TIMOTHY, b. Sept. 18, 1786, m. ESTHER PILLSBURY; lived at Piermont. *Child:* 971 EMALINE, b. May 11, 1822, m. Dec. 11, 1847, JOHN HARTWELL.
972 ETHAN S., b. May 31, 1791, m. ROXANA DAVIS, who d. Nov. 3, 1879. He was an 1812 soldier, lived in Haverhill, and d. Dec. 24, 1879. *Children:* 973 ELIZA A., b. Sept. 1821, m. JAMES H. HARRIMAN; 974 CATHERINE, b. 1825, m. H. M. DUNBAR; 975 HORACE, unmarried; 976 CHARLES, unmarried.
977 SAMUEL, b. Aug. 25, 1793, m. Nov. 21, 1822, MARY D. MELVIN, who d. Jan. 26, 1875. He d. June 27, 1882. *Children:* 978 MARY H., b. Apl. 19, 1825, m. Oct. 31, 1849, GEORGE BARRY; 979 SAMUEL J., b. March 9, 1830; 980 ADALINE, b. June 13, 1834, d. Feb. 23, 1850.

F251 Corporal Elisha Locke, born 1760, married MEHITABLE STICKNEY, dau. of James and Eleanor (Wilson). She probably died 1810–20. He was in Simpson's Rangers 1776; in Stark's Reg., Capt. Post's Co., July 24—Sept. 25, 1777; was sergeant in Capt. Barrows' Co. 1779; and was paid for services, 1777 to Jan. 1778, and Apl. 9, 1782. He and his sons were instrumental in developing the town of Haverhill where he settled in 1776; thence moved to Monroe County, N. Y., in 1816. He was pensioned in 1841, and died in Monroe Co. Jan. 28, 1844.

Children of the 5th Gen. probably b. in Haverhill.

981 PHOEBE, b. 1790, d. 1809.
982 REV. WALLACE, b. 1792, m. ANNA ——, who was b. in Mass. 1790. He was a Methodist minister in Orleans Co., N. Y., 1851, and second minister of West Sweden Church. He had at least one son: 983 WILLIAM R., b. 1823, m. 1849-50, DIANTHA ——, who was b. in N. Y., 1831. Wm. was a farmer in Ridgway, Orleans Co., in 1850, but not in 1860.

FIFTH GENERATION

984 SUSAN, b. 1794, m. in Bath, Nov. 21, 1811, PETER EASTMAN, who was b. in Bath, Jan. 7, 1790, died about 1870 in Hartland Co., N. Y., where he settled in 1840. *Children:* 985 MARY, b. Bath Jan. 3, 1813, died New York Jan. 9, 1890; 986 DAVID, b. Nov. 16, 1814; was m. had a son, died young and he died in N. Y. Apl. 15, 1869; 987 A CHILD, b. 1816, died young. Probably five other children.

988 DAVID, b. 1796, m. (Coventry, Vt., record says MEHITABLE PATTEE Jan. 12, 1817). He lived in Cold Water, Mich.

989 DORATHY, b. 1798, d. 1816.

990 JONATHAN, b. 1800, d. 1829, had no family.

991 JOHNSON, b. 1802, m. 1st, MALINDA ———, who was born in N. Y. 1805; and 2nd, ANGELINE ——— (?) b. in N. Y. 1810. He was of Orleans Co., N. Y. (1850 census), and Kendall in 1860. *Children:* 992 WESLEY, b. 1837, a farmer in Kendall, N. Y., 1850–60; 993 SARAH, b. 1834.

F994 NATHAN, b. Apl. 4, 1804, m. March 2, 1828, ESTHER KITTREDGE.

F995 AMOS, b. 1806, m. SOPHIA ——— (?), who was b. in N. Y. State, 1811.

996 DUDLEY, b. Aug. 1, 1809, m. 1832, OLIVE STRONG, dau. of William and Abigail (Pratt), b. Verona, N. Y., Apl. 3, 1812. He lived in Sweden, N. Y., and in 1850 was worth $6,300, and d. June 16, 1868. They had at least one child: 997 ORETTA E., b. Aug. 5, 1834, m. Dec. 17, 1857, GEORGE W. SMITH of Ogden, N. Y. She d. Aug. 28, 1864. Smith was son of Dr. John B. and Elizabeth, and was Mail Agent on the N. Y. Central R. R. in 1871.

998 DOLLY (DORATHY), b. ———, m. JAMES PIERCE, and lived in Hartland, N. Y.

F252 David Locke, born 1767(?), married 1st, June 2, 1787, ELIZABETH LELLINGHAM, born in Germany, and died Dec. 18, 1808. He married 2nd, in Stewartstown, Nov. 6, 1809, RACHEL BRAINARD, dau. of Daniel B., born in Rumney, July 25, 1782, died in Ohio, July 23, 1849. David was one of the incorporators of Stewartstown in 1799, and settled on lot # 2 in 1800. He is said to have been a selectman in Cincinnati, Ohio, but died in Maidstone, Vt., Feb. 19, 1834.

Children of the 5th Gen. all but last three b. in Stewartstown.

999 JOHN, b. Feb. 4, 1788, d. Stewartstown, July 1, 1815.

1000 WILLIAM, b. Dec. 19, 1790; probably m. and had a family; lived in Ohio in 1851.

F1001 DAVID, b. Feb. 19, 1792, m. in Batavia, N. Y., 1816, MARY ESTERBROOK. He m. 2nd, 1841, SARAH J. LARRABEE.

1002 JAMES, b. June 11, 1794, lived at Mt. Healthy, Ohio, in 1851.

1003 HANNAH, b. March 4, 1796, d. in Stewartstown, Feb. 17, 1797.

1004 BETSEY, b. March 15, 1798, m. ——— YIRRILL, and had a family in Illinois.

1005 AMOS, b. Aug. 8, 1800, d. Aug. 31, 1816.

1006 JEREMIAH, b. Aug. 31, 1802, d. Oct. 15, 1807.

F1007 JOEL W., b. Jan. 6, 1804; m. Nov. 13, 1829, MARY C. CHANDLER.
1008 ELISHA, b. Sept. 19, 1806, lived in Ohio, in 1851, unmarried.
1009 LUCINDA, b. March 19, 1812, died unmarried in Cincinnati, aged 60–70.
F1010 JOHN F., b. 1815, m. LUCRETIA BUNDY (BRUNDY).
1011 BRAINARD, b. Sept. 13, 1822, died unmarried Cincinnati, July 23, 1844.
1012 MARY, b. May 21, 1825, lived in Cincinnati.

F258 Hannah Berry, born in Rye June 28, 1747, married July 22, 1768, NATHANIEL MARDEN. She died Apl. 11, 1773 and he married 2nd, May 29, 1777, ANNA TOWLE. He died Nov. 21, 1804.
Children of the 5th Gen.
1013 PRUDENCE P., b. Jan. 1, 1769, m. EBENEZER SEAVEY, b. 1765.
1014 KEZIAH, b. Feb. 22, 1770, not married but had : 1015 JOHN H. MARDEN who m. SARAH SEAVEY.

F268 Mary Berry, born in Rye, March 24, 1751, married Jan. 15, 1774, SAMUEL DOWST FOSS, who was born in 1754.
Children of the 5th Gen.
1016 WALLIS, b. Aug. 5, 1775, m. MARY LIBBEY.
1017 SAMUEL, b. July 4, 1777, m. ABIGAIL RHEID.
1018 HANNAH, b. 1779, died young.
1019 JEREMIAH B., b. 1780, d. 1794.
1020 POLLY, b. 1783, died young.
1021 MARY, b. Jan. 8, 1785, m. JOHN H. HAM of Portsmouth.
1022 JAMES S., b. Jan. 22, 1787, m. Sept. 1, 1816, SALLY HODGDON. He was in the 1812 War and had twelve children.
1023 PATIENCE, b. 1789, m. 1st, JAMES NEWTON; 2nd, JAMES BUTLER; 3rd, JOHN SMITH of Barrington.
1024 SARAH, bapt. July 3, 1791, m. SAMUEL RAND # 2539 born 1793.

F269 William Berry, born in Rye Apl. 12, 1752–3, married 1st, Nov. 10, 1774, LOVE BRACKETT, born Aug. 9, 1758, died Jan. 17, 1795, dau. of Samuel and Eleanor (Dow). He married 2nd, March 6, 1796, ELIZABETH WENDELL.
Children of the 5th Gen. b. in Rye.
1025 LYDIA, b. 1775, m. Jan. 20, 1801, WILLIAM TREFETHERN # 1110, b. Apl. 24, 1775, d. Oct. 4, 1853. She d. June 20, 1820.
1026 SAMUEL B., bapt. Apl. 14, 1777, m. Feb. 1798, ABIGAIL WEBSTER, b. 1777.
1027 HANNAH, bapt. March 25, 1781, m. Dec. 24, 1801, JOSIAH MARDEN, b. 1778.
1028 JEREMIAH, b. Dec. 16, 1783, m. June 22, 1808, SALLY FOSS.
1029 ELEANOR, b. Apl. 25, 1786, m. Feb. 18, 1808, JAMES LOCKE. (See F2779.)
1030 LOVE, b. May 17, 1788, m. June 26, 1806, EBEN MARDEN, b. Jan. 22, 1779, d. Dec. 5, 1862. She d. July 21, 1876.
1031 WILLIAM, b. Nov. 10, 1790.
1032 PATTY, b. July 21, 1792, m. March 22, 1809, JOB FOSS, b. 1785.

FIFTH GENERATION 65

Second wife's children:
1033 SARAH W., b. Jan. 12, 1797, d. May 13, 1877.
1034 DOLLY, b. May 1798, d. July 12, 1822.
1035 SARAH S., b. Sept. 3, 1799, m. Feb. 17, 1823, GILMAN DEARBORN # 1900, b. Apl. 10, 1799, d. Apl. 18, 1862.
1026 ELIZA, b. Dec. 1806, m. A. K. WARREN.

F272 Levi Berry, born in Rye Feb. 29, 1760, married Nov. 13, 1785, SARAH JENNESS, who was born May 11, 1763, died Sept. 6, 1857. He died Apl. 1, 1833; was a cordwainer.
Children of the 5th Gen. b. in Rye.
1037 MARY, b. Apl. 17, 1785, m. March 18, 1803, ALEXANDER SALTER, b. June 4, 1778. She d. March 13, 1810.
1038 SALLY, b. Feb. 8, 1787, m. Apl. 27, 1806, SIMON GOSS, b. 1771; no child.
F1039 JOSEPH J., b. May 17, 1789, m. 1st, 1812, BETSEY WEDGWOOD; 2nd, 1818, HANNAH LOCKE # 2055.
1040 HANNAH L., b. June 19, 1791, m. Jan. 29, 1810, JOSEPH TREFETHERN, b. Aug. 20, 1787, d. Feb. 10, 1859. (See F1124.)
1041 OLIVE, b. June 24, 1793, m. JOSEPH LOCKE. (See F1141.)
1042 BETSEY, b. March 24, 1797, m. Oct. 3, 1821, JOSEPH BERRY, b. Sept. 24, 1787.
1043 NANCY, b. March 4, 1801, m. May 22, 1825, WILLIAM VARRELL, b. May 1801, d. Dec. 2, 1884. She d. Feb. 19, 1881.
1044 LEVI, b. Sept. 19, 1804, d. Sept. 27, 1873; was a cripple.

F274 Solomon Berry, born in Rye, bapt. Nov. 17, 1765, married Oct. 5, 1794, PATTY KATE.
Children of the 5th Gen.
1045 BENJAMIN, m. —— BRASBRIDGE.
1046 LEVI, unmarried.
1047 BETSEY, m. ROBERT SPENCER.
1048 SARAH.
1049 LYDIA.
1050 BELINDA.
1051 THOMAS.
1052 MEHITABLE.
1053 KEZIAH, b. Dec. 3, 1815, m. PATRICK OWENS.

F275 Hannah Berry, born Aug. 21, 1773, died Jan. 10, 1810, married Apl. 17, 1801, **James H. Locke** # **1086**, born June 3, 1773, was a mariner in Rye, and died there Jan. 8, 1808.
Children of the 5th Gen.
F1054 JONATHAN HOBBS, b. Nov. 17, 1802, m. Sept. 17, 1831, IZETTA LEWIS.
F1055 ELEANOR DOW, b. May 11, 1806, m. May 21, 1826, JOSEPH RAND, JR.

F277 Sarah Locke, born July 27, 1725, married March 28, 1746, JOHN MARDEN, son of William.
Children of the 5th Gen.
1056 JOHN, b. Nov. 30, 1747, m. March 23, 1769, SARAH SAUNDERS, and lived in Epping. *Children:* 1057 JOHN; 1058 SAMUEL, b. 1775,

5

m. March 2, 1800, NANCY TREDWELL MARDEN; 1059 JAMES, b. ——, m. ———— LANGMAID; 1060 BENJAMIN; 1061 SARAH; 1062 OLIVE, m. ———— FRENCH; 1063 HANNAH, m. ————CATLIN. 1064 SARAH, m. March 17, 1772, SAMUEL KNOWLES; he b. Oct. 27, 1749.

F279 James Locke, born in Rye June 30, 1729, married June 14, 1750, SARAH LEAVITT, dau. Samuel and Ruth (Johnson). She born in Hampton Feb. 6, 1732. He resided at Rye, bought land there Aug. 26, 1757, and sold land Oct. 22, 1763. He took the Oath of Fidelity in 1776.

Children of the 5th Gen. b. in Rye.

1065 MOSES, b. 1751. 1066 RUTH, b. 1752, unmarried.
F1067 JAMES, b. 1753, m. Sept. 29, 1774, MARTHA SEAVEY.
1068 HANNAH, b. 1755.
F1069 JOHN, b. 1757, perhaps m. and d. 1787 (?).
1070 SARAH, b. 1759. 1071 SAMUEL, b. 1761.
F1072 ELIZABETH L., b. 1763, m. Feb. 2, 1804, JOSIAH HILL.

F287 Salome Goss, born in Rye Feb. 22, 1741, married MARK LANG, bapt. 1741, son of William and Elizabeth (Rand). He lived on the New Road in Portsmouth and died July 25, 1808.

Children of the 5th Gen. b. in Rye.

1073 ELIZABETH, b. 1761.
1074 ANNAH, bapt. 1763, m. Apl. 22, 1784, JOHN VARRELL bapt. 1759 d. Sept. 10, 1811, and had 5 children.
1075 HANNAH, bapt. 1765, m. Nov. 10, 1785, JOB LOCKE. (See F337.)
1076 MARK, b. 1768, d. 1845, m. Oct. 9, 1792 HANNAH MARDEN who d. Jan. 5, 1772, dau. Nathl. and Elizabeth (Moulton). Had: 1077 MARK, JR., who m. 1823, PATIENCE WENTWORTH.
1078 RICHARD, d. May 6, 1854, aged 76, m. Dec. 31, 1798, NANCY WALKER who d. Apl. 1860, aged 82; had 9 children. He served in the 1812 War.
1079 JONATHAN, b. 1773, m. and called a doctor. He died Jan. 8, 1806, had 4 children.
1080 WILLIAM, b. 1774, m. Nov. 13, 1794, BETSEY WALKER; he died May 3, 1831; had 10 children.

F288 Jonathan Goss, born in Rye 1743, married Feb. 16, 1769, ELIZABETH BROWN, dau. of Joseph and Abigail (Goss ?), who was born May 14, 1750, died June 7, 1830. She married 2nd, ALECK LEAR. Jonathan sailed in the Privateer "Portsmouth" under Capt. Sam Seavey, was captured and died of smallpox in Dartmoor prison.

Children of the 5th Gen. b. in Rye.

F1081 JONATHAN, b. Oct. 14, 1771, m. Jan. 10, 1796, PATTY DAVIDSON.
1082 JOSEPH, b. ——, m. March 6, 1791, SARAH SEAVEY, b. 1772, dau. Paul and Sarah (Willis). He was in the War of 1812; had 4 children.

FIFTH GENERATION

F292 Richard Locke, born in Rye Sept. 4, 1744, married March 1767, HULDAH HOBBS, dau. of Jonathan and Mary (Berry). She born Jan. 12, 1746, died Dec. 20, 1828. Sept. 5, 1757, he bought land in Rye; Aug. 30, 1769, he sold all rights in his father's and grandfather's estate in Rye to Benj. Garland. He enlisted as private in the 2nd N. H. Reg., May 29, 1775, and later in the 3rd; served almost continuously until Jan. 27, 1780, when he was discharged. He lived in Rye, but died in Northwood, Oct. 20, 1823.

Children of the 5th Gen. b. in Rye.
- 1083 HANNAH, b. 1767, died young.
- F1084 HANNAH J., b. May 22, 1769-70, m. 1796, JOHN MARSTON.
- 1085 SARAH, b. Feb. 29, 1771-2, m. Nov. 25, 1810, JOB LOCKE. (See F337.)
- 1086 JAMES H., b. June 3, 1773, m. Apl. 17, 1801, HANNAH BERRY. (See F275.)
- F1087 ASA, b. Aug. 14, 1775, m. Nov. 12, 1799, his cousin ELIZABETH J. HOBBS.
- 1088 JOSHUA, a twin, b. Aug. 14, 1775, died young.
- F1089 RICHARD, b. Oct. 5, 1779, m. 1st, March 19, 1807, SARAH WOODS; m. 2nd, Feb. 20, 1817, BETSEY TUCKER.

F294 Joshua Locke, born Apl. 28, 1753-4, married Jan. 18, 1776, CHARITY MARDEN, dau. of Benj. and Rachel (Dowst). She born March 29, 1760. (She married 2nd, PETER ACKERMAN, Oct. 19, 1797, and by him had: BENJAMIN, born 1800; married 1821, SALLY PHILBRICK. By a former marriage he had four children. Peter was crippled at Bemis Heights by a musket ball going in at the elbow and coming out at the shoulder Sept. 19, 1777. Was a Revolutionary pensioner, lived at Rye and in Grafton Co.) Joshua was at Cambridge in the Revolutionary War, was in Col. Poore's Co. at Crown Point July 8, 1776, in Capt. Calve's Co. Jan. 24, 1777, and was a corporal at New Castle Fort in 1777. He lived in Rye, and died before 1797.

Children of the 5th Gen.
- 1090 NABBY, b. ——, m. Apl. 8, 1812, JOEL FURBER of Farmington.
- F1091 POLLY, b. June 22, 1788, m. Nov. 5, 1805, JONATHAN BROWN, #1099.
- F1092 RACHEL, m. March 15, 1810, JOSEPH BROWN, #1100.

F297 Joseph Locke, born in Rye, 1768; married 1st, Nov. 16, 1794, MARY BROWN, dau. of Col. Jonathan and Mary (Garland), who was born Aug. 24, 1766, died Dec. 11, 1803. He married 2nd, July 16, 1804, OLIVE FOSS, who died March 5, 1825, aged 46. Joseph lived in Rye, was a moderator there in 1825, also a representative in 1825, and died March 3, 1841.

Children of the 5th Gen. b. in Rye.

F1093 JOHN, b. 1795, m. Jan. 15, 1815, MARY ANN RINDGE.
F1094 MARY B., b. Aug. 9, 1800, m. Nov. 19, 1826, JOHN W. P. LOCKE # 1168; m. 2nd, March 11, 1846, JESSE LOCKE. # 2928

F299 Hannah Locke, born in Rye March 1773, married Oct. 2, 1803, SAMUEL MOWE of Rye, born 1768, died March 2, 1841.

Children of the 5th Gen.

F1095 EPHRAIM, m. OLIVE COOMS; she m. 2nd, BENJAMIN MASON in 1840.
1096 SALLY, b. 1807, m. 1st, SAMUEL ALLEN; m. 2nd, JAMES H. LOCKE. (See F2800.)
F1097 SAMUEL P., m. Oct. 6, 1833, HARRIET MATHES.

F304 Salome Allen, bapt. 1771, died 1852, married Feb. 4, 1779, JOHN BROWN, born Nov. 13, 1759, son of Jonathan and Mary (Garland). He lived at Chester and Epsom and died Jan. 21, 1807.

Children of 5th Gen.

1098 JOHN, b. Aug. 14, ——, m. 1st, July 29, 1802, SARAH FOSS; m. 2nd, Apl. 28, 1807, NANCY JENNESS. He d. Dec. 10, 1854. Had 4 children.
1099 JONATHAN, b. June 1, 1782, m. Nov. 5, 1805, MARY LOCKE, b. June 22, 1788. (See F1091.)
1100 JOSEPH, b. Feb. 22, 1784, m. March 15, 1810, RACHEL LOCKE, sister of MARY, and lived at Epsom. (See F1092.)
1101 ELIZABETH, b. ——, m. JOSEPH YEATON and lived in Epsom.
1102 MARY, b. ——, m. CHARLES MILLS and lived in Concord.
1103 JEREMIAH, b. ——, m. MARY BALL, lived in Hampton Falls.
1104 SARAH, b. ——, m. —— BURNHAM, lived at Epsom.
1104a JAMES, b. Nov. 1789, m. Dec. 9, 1819, MARTHA WEBSTER; had 10 children.
1105 BENJAMIN, b. ——, m. March 31, 1817, JANE LOCKE, F2921, and they had: 1106 ESTHER, b. 1817, m. DANIEL RAND.
1107 ABIGAIL, b. March 12, 1802, m. JONATHAN PHILBRICK.
1108 JOSIAH, b. ——, m. MARY GARLAND; lived in Concord.
1109 WILLIAM, b. Aug. 14, 1796, m. LUCETTA GRAY, who d. May 11, 1875, aged 90.

F315 Captain William Trefethern, born in Rye, June 5, 1751, married Jan. 27, 1774, ELIZABETH TUCKER. She born Nov. 19, 1753, and died Feb. 12, 1837. He died June 17, 1825. He was in Capt. Parson's Co. in the Revolution.

FIFTH GENERATION

Children of the 5th Gen.
1110 WILLIAM, b. Apl. 24, 1775, m. 1st, Jan. 20, 1801, LYDIA BERRY # 1025, b. Nov. 27, 1777, d. June 20, 1820; m. 2nd, Feb. 1821, SUSANNA PIPER. He d. Oct. 5, 1853. *Children:* 1111 LEVI B.; 1112 BENJAMIN B.; 1113 WILLIAM; 1114 SABRINA; 1115 HANSON H.
1116 NATHANIEL, b. Oct. 27, 1777, d. June 11, 1784.
1117 ABIGAIL, b. Dec. 18, 1779, d. June 20, 1784.
1118 BETSEY, b. Dec. 2, 1782, d. unm. in Barnstead.
1119 NATHANIEL, b. Feb. 22, 1785, m. July 1, 1807, CHARLOTTE JEWELL, b. Sept. 1784, d. Dec. 20, 1868. He lived in Rye, and d. March 8, 1856. *Children:* 1120 CHARLES F.; 1121 FLORENCE; 1122 DANIEL J.; 1123 LOUVIA.
F1124 JOSEPH, b. Aug. 20, 1787, m. 1810, HANNAH BERRY # 1040.
1125 NANCY, bapt. Nov. 4, 1790, m . SAMUEL AYERS of Barnstead.
1126 POLLY, bapt. Aug. 27, 1792, m. GEORGE RANSTEAD.
1127 HENRY, b. Oct. 5, 1795, m. MARY BROWN, and he d. Sept. 8, 1828.
F1128 JOHN A., b. July 27, 1799, m. 1834, MARY LOCKE # 2061.
1129 SEBASTIAN J., b. Jan. 27, 1801, m. Nov. 1835, ELIZABETH LOCKE, # 2927, b. 1808, d. Dec. 29, 1854. He lived in Rye and Kansas and died Aug. 18, 1875. *Children:* 1130 HUBBARD; 1131 HANSON; 1132 ALFRED M., b. May 7, 1837; 1133 DAVID; 1134 ELLEN, b. Nov. 20, 1840, m. Apl. 20, 1862, GEORGE PERKINS; 1135 OCTAVIA, b. Nov. 17, 1847, m. May 11, 1864, —— DALRYMPLE, b. 1844; 1136 HANSON, b. Jan. 17, 1843, d. 1884.

F327 Joseph Locke, born Oct. 23, 1753-4, married June 25, 1778, MARTHA DOW of Rye, dau. of Henry and Martha (Perkins). She born Oct. 6, 1758, died Jan. 31, 1792. He enlisted March 11, 1777, in Capt. Bell's Co. and was reported missing from Capt. Hale's Co. 1778. He was a farmer at Locke's Neck, and died Apl. 22, 1790.

Children of the 5th Gen. brought up by grandfather.
F1137 JEREMIAH, b. Dec. 9, 1778, m. 1800, MEHITABLE RAND.
1138 HENRY, b. Aug. 25, 1780, died an infant.
1139 MARY, b. March (Apl.) 31, 1782, m. 1801, JONATHAN PERKINS # F655.
F1140 MERCY, b. Jan. 11, 1784, m. Nov. 12, 1801, SAMUEL MASON.
F1141 JOSEPH, b. March 4, 1787, m. Aug. 4, 1811, OLIVE BERRY # 1041.

F328 Mary Locke, born in Rye May 25, 1755, married March 21, 1775, SAMUEL JENNESS of Rye, born 1752, son of Samuel and Abigail (Garland). They lived at No. Hampton.

Children of the 5th Gen.
1142 JEREMIAH, b. 1776, m. MARY HOBBS; lived in No. Hampton.
F1143 POLLY, b. Rye, Jan. 3, 1778, m. JOHN BROWN.

SIXTH GENERATION

F330 John J. Locke, born in Rye, Oct. 19, 1746, married 1st, SARAH JONES, Sept. 29, 1769, who died Apl. 29, 1795. He married 2nd, Aug. 18, 1796, THANKFUL BLAZO who was his widow in 1801. He took the oath of allegiance in 1776, enlisted in Capt. Blodgett's Co. May 19, 1777. In his will dated Apl. 30, 1801, he mentions only his wife THANKFUL and son JEREMIAH. He lived in Rye and died May 5, 1801.

Children of the 6th Gen. b. in Rye.
1144 JOHN, bapt. 1770, died 1786.
F1145 JEREMIAH, b. 1771, m. Nov. 26, 1793, SUSAN RAND.
1146 RICHARD, b. 1773. 1147 MOLLY, twin, b. 1773.
1148 GEORGE WASHINGTON, b. 1777.
1149 JONATHAN, b. ———.

F332 Richard Locke, baptized June 7, 1750, married Nov. 2, 1769, SARAH PALMER. He enlisted in Capt. Parson's Co. Dec. 6, 1775; was a farmer in Rye and died there Dec. 26, 1827.

Children of the 6th Gen. b. in Rye.
1150 RICHARD, b. 1773, died young.
F1151 JOSEPH, b. 1775, m. 1st, May 13, 1794, LUCY MARDEN; m. 2nd, Sept. 11, 1814, WIDOW HANNAH (VITTUM) BERRY.

F334 Abner Locke, baptized March 26, 1754; a farmer on Locke's Road, Rye; died Apl. 25, 1825.

Adopted child of 6th Gen. b. in Rye, son of his sister Tryphena.
F1152 DEACON WILLIAM, b. 1801, m. 1st, July 31, 1825, ELIZABETH KNOWLES; he m. 2nd, MARY L. MARSTON.

F335 Jacob Locke, baptized Jan. 22, 1757, in Rye, married Jan. 4, 1778, MEHITABLE HIGGINS of Greenland who was born Feb. 10, 1758. He settled in Wakefield where his children were born, and died there Feb. 16, 1814, a farmer and tanner. Walpole, N. H., records say, "POLLY MUZZEY of Walpole married May 10, 1803, JACOB LOCKE." This is possibly a second wife but I doubt its being this Jacob. (There was an unknown Jacob Locke in Vermont.)

Children of the 6th Gen. b. in Wakefield.
F1153 NATHANIEL, b. Jan. 18, 1779, m. March 19, 1803, ABIGAIL PITMAN.
F1154 MARY, b. July 9, 1783, m. Sept. 16, 1802, MARK ALLEN.

SIXTH GENERATION 71

F1155 BETSEY, b. Dec. 3, 1787, m. JOSEPH PITMAN.
1156 SARAH, b. Sept. 3, 1792, m. Nov. 21, 1811, JAMES COOK of Wakefield. *Children:* 1157 JOSEPH; 1158 MEHITABLE.
1159 EMILY, b. Nov. 14, 1798, d. Aug. 19, 1800; a twin, JULEY, d. aged 12 days.
1160 JACOB, b. July 17, 1801, d. Feb. 16, 1814.
F1161 JOHN HIGGINS, b. Dec. 16, 1802, m. 1st, June 13, 1822, ELIZABETH FERNALD; m. 2nd, Nov. 8, 1827, SALLY DEARBORN; m. 3rd, ADALINE TIBBETTS; m. 4th, June 3, 1868, BETSEY D. GERRY.

F337 Job Locke, baptized in Rye, Sept. 26, 1762, married 1st, Nov. 10, 1785, HANNAH LANG # 1075. She was baptized in 1765, and died Jan. 29, 1806. He married 2nd, Dec. 8, 1806, ABIGAIL PHILBRICK, # 735, dau. of Joshua. She was born Sept. 28, 1768, died March 11, 1810. He married 3rd, Nov. 25, 1810, SARAH LOCKE, # 1085, who was born 1772, died Aug. 29, 1852. He was a farmer and fisherman in Rye and died July 20, 1849.
Children of the 6th Gen. b. in Rye.
1162 DANIEL, b. 1787, died young.
1163 POLLY, b. 1790, m. in Hampton, Nov. 7, 1815, JAMES BOWLEY of Stratham.
1164 SARAH W., b. 1791, d. Dec. 31, 1831.
F1165 HANNAH, b. 1793, m. WILLIAM B. RANDALL.
F1166 ELIZABETH G., b. 1797, m. 1st, Nov. 2, 1816, JOHN CASWELL; m. 2nd, WILLIAM S. RANDALL.
F1167 CAPTAIN JOB, b. 1799, m. HANNAH RANDALL.
1168 JOHN W. P., b. Apl. 1803, m. Nov. 19, 1826, MARY B. LOCKE, # F1094.
1169 ANNA, b. 1807, died young.

F340 Simon Locke, baptized in Rye, Sept. 23, 1770, married in Greenland, Feb. 14, 1792, ABIGAIL MACE, daughter of Ithamar. She was born 1776, died Feb. 18, 1803. He married 2nd, Nov. 10, 1803, ELIZABETH L. ALLEN, daughter of Jude. She was born Apl. 20, 1775, died Nov. 29, 1838. He was a farmer in Rye and died there July 31, 1863, aged 93.
Children of the 6th Gen. b. in Rye.
1170 MEHITABLE, b. June 1792, m. Jan. 29, 1824, DANIEL BURLEIGH of Lee, b. 1789, son of Josiah and Ruhuma (Marston). She adopted the children of her sister, SARAH F. (LOCKE) CASWELL, and lived in Stratham.
F1171 CAPTAIN RICHARD, b. 1794, m. Oct. 21, 1823, MARGARET WELCH.
F1172 SARAH FROST, b. 1796, m. June 13, 1819, EDWARD CASWELL.
1173 SIMON, b. 1797, d. Aug. 1, 1819.

F1174 WILLIAM, b. Dec. 1799, m. Nov. 6, 1825, CHARLOTTE H. WENTWORTH.
1175 ELIZABETH G., b. 1801, died young.
1176 RACHEL B., a twin, probably died young.
Second wife's children:
F1177 ABNER, b. May 6, 1804, m. 1st, MARY A. YOUNG; m. 2nd, EUNICE WALLIS.
1178 ABIGAIL MACE, b. 1805, m. brothers; 1st, April 15, 1824, ASA LOCKE, JR., # F2799; m. 2nd, 1863, LEMUEL LOCKE, # F2801.
F1179 JOHN LANGDON, b. Aug. 30, 1807, m. May 16, 1833, MARY RANDALL.
1180 THOMAS, b. 1808. 1181 ELIZABETH, b. 1811.
F1182 EDWIN, b. March 9, 1815, m. ADALINE SHEPPARD.
1183 ALFRED, born 1819.
1184 DAVID, b. ——, m. MARY A. TOWLE. He was killed at Chapins Farms, Va., Sept. 29, 1864.

F342 Dorothy Locke, born 1750, married July 19, 1771, ELIJAH OTIS of Barrington, son of Joshua and Jane (Hussey) of Dover. He was born June 10, 1749, served in the Revolution under Stark, lived at Rochester and Durham and died Apl. 8, 1838. She died in Rye in 1824.
* *Children of the 6th Gen. b. in Rochester.*
F1185 LEMUEL, b. Nov. 24, 1774, m. Nov. 9, 1796, LEAH PEARL.
1186 HANNAH, b. ——, m. JOHN GRAY. She had 10 children and died in Sheffield, Vt., June 1817.
1187 JANE, twin with Hannah, m. NATHANIEL HAM; had 5 children in Sheffield, Vt.
F1188 PAUL, b. March 28, 1777, m. July 5, 1798, MARY FOSS.
1189 JOHN, b. 1779, m. HANNAH HOWARD, who had 2 children and d. Dec. 31, 1825.
F1190 JETHRO, b. March 1, 1781, m. March 31, 1802, ESTHER HOWARD.
F1191 THOMAS, b. Feb. 9, 1783, m. March 26, 1811, POLLY LEE.
F1192 MICAJAH, b. Dec. 6, 1785, m. 1st, Jan. 23, 1806, HANNAH ALLARD, who d. in 1845; m. 2nd, POLLY BROCK.
F1193 JOSHUA, b. 1786, m. LOVIE ELKINS.
1194 ELIJAH, b. ——, m. May 13, 1811, JANE OTIS, dau. of Joshua. Elijah went to the 1812 War and was never heard from. (An Elijah Otis m. JANE MARDEN in Portsmouth, in 1815.)
F1195 WILLIAM, b. May 16, 1790, m. Nov. 4, 1814, HANNAH BOWLES.
1196 DOROTHY, b. March 2, 1792, m. Dec. 31, 1812, DEA. HENRY GRAY. See F1215.
F1197 SIMEON, b. ——, m. July 1, 1816, JOANNA WALLINGFORD of Alton.
1198 MARTHA, was drowned in Strafford, a young girl.

F343 Rev. Simon Locke, born in Rye, Sept. 20, 1752, married in Barrington March 29, 1774, LYDIA FOSS, who was born Dec. 19, 1752, died Nov. 11, 1855, aged 103. He was in

SIXTH GENERATION 73

Senter's expedition to Rhode Island, enlisted in Capt. Parsons' Co. Aug. 14, 1777; was a pensioner in 1831 at $20 per year. He was in Barrington until 1782 when he went through the wilderness on horseback to Lyman, Me., where he built a one windowed house. He preached in the Lyman and Hollis churches forty-nine years, baptized 1200 people, married 835 couples, officiated at 1325 funerals, and preached 9800 sermons. He died Sept. 1, 1831.

Children of the 6th Gen. b. in Barrington.
F1199 EPHRAIM, b. Feb. 18, 1775, m. Dec. 21, 1797, SARAH FOSS.
F1200 JESSE, b. Sept. 9, 1777, m. Jan. 9, 1799, HANNAH DANIELSON.
1201 JOSHUA, b. Dec. 11, 1779, d. Aug. 16, 1802.
F1202 SIMON, b. Feb. 3, 1786, m. 1st, Oct. 1806, MIRIAM DAY; m. 2nd, WIDOW MARY (HALEY) STAPLES, in 1833.
1203 ELIAKIN, b. Feb. 20, 1789, died an infant.
F1204 LYDIA, b. Jan. 10, 1792, m. Dec. 17, 1807, JOHN DENNETT.
F1205 HANNAH, b. May 16, 1794, m. Sept. 3, 1812, JOSHUA DENNETT.

F346 Jethro Locke, born in Barrington, March 6, 1764, married in Barrington Feb. 16, 1786, ABIGAIL HOWARD, who was born in Barrington Jan. 14, 1762, died in Barrington Apl. 5, 1829. He was a farmer in Barrington and died there March 30, 1814.

Children of the 6th Gen. b. in Barrington.
F1206 SIMON, b. Sept. 30, 1786, m. 1st, June 5, 1808, OLIVE CHADBOURNE; m. 2nd, March 15, 1853, SARAH RUNNELS.
F1207 HANNAH, b. May 16, 1789, m. Dec. 19, 1805, ELIAS VARNEY.
1208 ISAAC, b. Dec. 7, 1790, m. BETSEY HOWARD of Barrington. (Barrington records say he m. BETSEY PATRICK, Oct. 19, 1812.) He was a farmer in Strafford and d. Feb. 21, 1829.
1209 HOWARD, b. May 24, 1795, d. Feb. 4, 1808.
F1210 JETHRO, b. Nov. 14, 1796, m. 1st, Feb. 19, 1818, SUSAN CLARKE; m. 2nd, Nov. 14, 1839, MISS LYDIA HANSCOM.
F1211 NATHANIEL, b. March 20, 1799, m. Jan. 17, 1825, MARIA OTIS.
F1212 JOSHUA, b. Dec. 19, 1802, m. ABRA FURBUSH.
1213 ABIGAIL, b. Oct. 4, 1805, m. in Strafford, Oct. 8, 1824, SAMUEL SNELL of Barrington. She had an infant which died May 20, 1827, two days old, and she died seven days later.

F347 Mary Locke, born in Barrington, Apl. 25, 1760, married in Strafford, July 15, 1784, SOLOMON GRAY, who was born in Strafford, Apl. 21, 1760, was a farmer and died in Strafford March 7, 1824. She died Nov. 7, 1827.

Children of the 6th Gen. b. in Strafford.
F1214 SIMON, b. Apl. 14, 1785, m. PATTY PAGE.

F1215 HENRY, b. Apl. 12, 1786, m. 1st, Dec. 31, 1812, his cousin, DORATHY OTIS, # 1196; m. 2nd, JOANNA HALL, and m. 3rd ——— ———?
1216 BARBAR, b. Jan. 4, 1788, m. HANNAH GRAY; was a farmer in Strafford and had one dau.
F1217 MARY, b. Aug. 2, 1789, m. WILLIAM GRAY.
F1218 HANNAH, b. Jan. 16, 1791, m. ——— TRIPP.
F1219 SOLOMON, b. Sept. 7, 1792, m. CAROLINE WENDELL, Nov. 28, 1819.
1220 LYDIA, b. Jan. 29, 1795, d. about 1880, unmarried.
1221 ABIGAIL, b. June 15, 1796, m. Oct. 10, 1841, JOHN BUZZELL, b. Aug. 27, 1797, son of Moses and Sarah (Caverno). Lived in Strafford, had no children and she died about 1880.
F1222 WILLIAM, b. Feb. 19, 1798, m. MARY RAND, Nov. 30, 1819.
F1223 JETHRO, b. Oct. 21, 1799, m. LUCRETIA POTTLE.
1224 DORATHY, b. Aug. 4, 1801, m. JOHN DOWNING, lived in So. Berwick, Me., and she d. Sept. 15, 1878.
F1225 JOSEPH, b. Apl. 25, 1803, m. HANNAH GRAY.

F395 Jesse Locke, born in Block Island, R. I., Jan. 21, 1768. He settled in Oxford, Chenango County, N. Y., and after marriage in 1800 went to Cincinnatus, Cortland Co., N. Y. He surveyed Madison Co., N. Y., with five men in 1792, and received $2.00 per day; they received $5.00 per month. He was Sheriff of Chenango Co., 1801–05, Loan Commissioner 1808, and Representative to the New York Assembly, 1810. He was accidentally killed Nov. 15, 1813, at Cincinnatus, by the discharge of a gun held in the hands of a "fellow in an adjoining room."

Children of the 6th Gen. b. in Cincinnatus, N. Y.

F1226 JOHN, b. Nov. 20, 1791, m. BETSEY OLDS.
1226aSEBER, the 1840 census says he lived in Cincinnatus, N. Y., had a wife, one son and four daus.
1227 AMASA, b. ———.
1228 NATHANIEL, 1840 census gives two sons, one dau., in Cincinnatus.
1229 SALLY, b. ———. 1230 POLLY, b. ———.
F1231 JESSE, b. Apl. 3, 1804, m. May 13, 1824, LAURA REXFORD.

F399 Rev. Elliott Hunnewell Locke, born in So. Kingston, R. I., ———, married MARY WEST; was a highly esteemed Baptist minister in Exeter, R. I. He died Feb. 3, 1852.

Children of the 6th Gen. probably b. in Exeter, R. I.

1232 HANNAH, b. ———, m. HERMAN CLARK.
1233 SARAH, b. ———.
F1234 CHARLES B., b. May 15, 1787, m. ELIZABETH BRAMAN.
1235 STEPHEN, b. ———, not married.
1236 BENJAMIN, b. ———, m. HANNAH LEWIS of Exeter, R. I., b. Oct. 6, 1793, dau. of Benj. and Mary (Cleveland).
1237 MARY, b. ———, m. ALLEN PALMER.

SIXTH GENERATION

F403 Joshua R. Locke, born in So. Kingston, R. I., March 8, 1777, married 1798, WAITY SHELDON, born Oct. 13, 1783, died Apl. 25, 1870, daughter of James and Elizabeth. He lived in Richmond, and died Feb. 3, 1852.

Children of 6th Gen.

1238 JAMES, b. March 1800, died young.
F1239 JOSHUA R., b. Apl. 22, 1801, m. 1st, PHEBE BOSS, Feb. 1822; m. 2nd, Apl. 10, 1842, ABBIE BROWN.
1240 WAITY, b. July 18, 1804, m. 1st, Feb. 1822, NORRIS SMITH. *Children:* 1241 MEHITABLE; 1242 ELIZABETH,; m. 2nd, NATHAN KENYON, who d. Apl. 15, 1897, and by him had: 1243 JAMES; 1244 WAITY; 1245 PHEBE; and perhaps others.
1246 JOSEPH, b. ——, died young.
F1247 BENJAMIN, b. Sept. 30, 1807, m. Apl. 5, 1829, MARY H. TANNER.
F1248 REV. EZEKIEL JAMES, b. Nov. 27, 1809, m. Oct. 27, 1833, MRS. CHLOE WOODMANSEE.
1249 Two MARYS, who died young.
1250 MERCY J., b. March 24, 1812, d. Aug. 15, 1903, m. JAMES S. MOORE. *Children:* 1251 MARY; 1252 WAITY; 1253 HANNAH; 1254 BENJAMIN; 1255 FRANKLIN; 1256 LILLA ESTELLE.
F1257 STEPHEN, b. July 20, 1814, m. March 10, 1839, RHODA LEWIS.
1258 ELIZABETH S., b. Jan. 3, 1817, d. Feb. 24, 1900, m. Oct. 3, 1841, SIMEON C. JAMES, who d. Feb. 1895. *Children:* 1259 ROXY; 1260 LOVINA; 1261 WILLIAM; 1262 EDWIN.
F1263 WILLIAM J. S., b. Apl. 4, 1823, m. Apl. 24, 1843, CATHERINE STEADMAN.
1264 MARY A., b. March 20, 1828, m. GEORGE W. UNDERWOOD, and had a son and daughter.

F410 Jacob Clifford, born 1756, married about 1783 RACHEL R. WALKER, and died 1838. He served in the War of the Revolution.

Children of the 6th Gen. perhaps b. in Prospect, Me.

1265 JOHN, b. 1783, left home, never heard from.
1266 SALLY, b. 1785, m. —— LANCASTER.
1267 JACOB, b. 1787, m. 1st, a SAWYER; m. 2nd, a FELKER.
1268 RACHEL, b. 1790, unknown.
1269 NATHANIEL, b. 1792, d. 1793.
F1270 NATHANIEL, b. March 28, 1794, m. LUCY SMALL.
1271 WILLIAM, b. 1796, m. KATE PENDLETON.
1272 HENRY, b. 1798, d. 1819.
1273 EDWARD, b. 1801, d. 1825.
1274 ELIZABETH, b. 1803, m. an ELLENWOOD.
1275 HARRIET, b. 1803, twin, m. 1st, a PENDLETON; m. 2nd, a WOODMAN.

F417 Abigail Locke, born in Falmouth, Me. (1750 ?), married 1769, MOSES NOYES of Falmouth, son of Justice Josiah and

Mary (Lunt). He was in the Revolution, 1777, and then went to Pownal, Me., 1790. He was born in Portland, March 29, 1746, died 1831. One party writes that Abigail was Abigail Phinney; married 1st, a HUSTON; 2nd, a LOCKE; 3rd, MOSES NOYES. If so, it is a problem with no facts to guide us.

Children of the 6th Gen. probably b. in Falmouth, Me.

F1276 THOMAS, bapt. Nov. 5, 1769, m. 1793, BETSEY HAINES.
1277 EUNICE, bapt. Apl. 26, 1772, died young.
1278 MOSES, b. Nov. 15, 1775, m. ——. Had a son: 1279 MOSES, who m. RHODA MERRILL and they had 6 children; the latter MOSES d. May 15, 1868.
1280 JOHN, b. Oct. 27, 1778
F1281 NATHANIEL LOCKE, b. Apl. 3, 1780, m. 1801, DORCAS NOYES; m. 2nd, 1811, SOPHIA GOULD.
1282 DORCAS or EUNICE, b. Oct. 5, 1783, d. 1842.
1283 ABIGAIL, b. Feb. 7, 1785, m. 1810, SETH WINSHIP.
F1284 JAMES L., b. March 23, 1794, m. 1822, MARY CONNOR.

F421 Mary Locke, born in Falmouth, Me., Apl. 15, 1767, married 1st, NATHANIEL PRINCE, son of Sylvanus and Elizabeth (Johnson); married 2nd, JAMES NOYES. She died in Falmouth, June 4, 1854.

Children of the 6th Gen.

F1285 SYLVANUS, b. Feb. 26, 1789, m. 1st, MATILDA PRINCE; m. 2nd, ANN BLANCHARD, b. 1800; m. 3rd, EUNICE FERNALD; 4th, MARY MALCOLM.
1286 EBENEZER, b. Sept. 30, 1792, m. MATILDA LOCKE, # 474.
1287 REUBEN, b. Sept. 21, 1794, m. ELIZA MERRILL.
1288 OLIVE, b. Aug. 16, 1797, d. Yarmouth, Me., 1891, aged 94.
1289 SUSANNA, b. Dec. 16, 1799, m. —— MARSTON.
1290 MARY ANN, b. May 10, 1802, m. JONATHAN BRADFORD.

F422 Lucy Locke, born in Falmouth, Me., ——, married JOHN MASON of Falmouth, Me.

Children of the 6th Gen.

1291 REBECCA, b. ——, m. ROBERT MILLER.
F1292 MERCY, b. June 7, 1805, m. 1827, BENJAMIN F. MERRILL
1293 DAUGHTER, m. JAMES MITCHELL.
1294 DAUGHTER, m. AMOS GREENLEAF.

F423 Ebenezer Locke, born in Falmouth, Me., Sept. 8, 1774, married 1st, Jan. 3, 1801, HANNAH TEWKSBURY, who was born Nov. 29, 1780, died Oct. 15, 1825. Intention of 2nd marriage was published in Saco, June 28, 1828, to WIDOW ANN POMEROY, who died Apl. 14, 1845. (By Pomeroy she had: ANN; PHEBE;

SIXTH GENERATION

DEBORAH; JOSEPH.) Ebenezer was captain of a ship sailing from Portland, and died in Falmouth, Nov. 11, 1831.

Children of the 6th Gen. b. in Falmouth, Me.
1295 SUSANNA, b. July 11, 1802, d. 1826, unmarried.
1296 HANNAH, b. Sept. 24, 1803, m. late in life, CAPTAIN STURTEVANT. She d. in 1871; no children.
1297 EBENEZER, b. Nov. 12, 1805, m. Sept. 13, 1835, JOANNA LOCKE. (See F485.)
F1298 JOHN MASON, b. May 15, 1807, m. July 14, 1841, PHOEBE POMEROY.
1299 STEPHEN, b. March 9, 1809, d. Sept. 23, 1831, unmarried.
F1300 NATHANIEL C., b. March 8, 1812, m. March 18, 1847, SARAH A. CARLISLE.
1301 JOEL, b. Oct. 1, 1815; was married and settled in Connecticut where he was a hat maker; had no children and died about 1856.
F1302 MILES STANDISH, b. May 17, 1818, m. DEBORAH LOCKE NOYES, # 1309.
1303 LUCY N., b. Dec. 9, 1821, m. GEORGE TAYLOR of Portland, Me., had no children and she d. Aug. 18, 1843.
1304 ELIZABETH RING, b. July 19, 1824, d. Apl. 9, 1896, probably unmarried.

F455 Susanna W. Locke, born in Falmouth, Me., 1794, married in 1815, REUBEN NOYES of Falmouth, son of Samuel and Elizabeth (Barton). He was born in Falmouth, Aug. 15, 1789, was a farner there and died March 11, 1840. She died in 1866.

Children of the 6th Gen. b. in Falmouth, Me.
1305 SAMUEL M., b. Nov. 11, 1815, d. July 7, 1825.
1306 REUBEN M., b. Jan. 6, 1817, d. Oct. 27, 1833.
F1307 ELIZABETH S., b. Dec. 19, 1819, m. JOHN WOODBURY.
F1308 DORCAS A., b. June 1, 1821, m. ROBERT HUSTON.
1309 DEBORAH LOCKE, b. Apl. 8, 1823, m. MILES S. LOCKE. (See F1302.)
F1310 RUTH C., b. Nov. 7, 1824, m. GEORGE W. LEIGHTON.
1311 NATHANIEL, b. Aug. 14, 1826, d. a youth.
F1312 SARAH PRINCE, b. July 8, 1828, m. in 1848 AMOS LEIGHTON.
F1313 AMOS W , b. Apl. 12, 1830, m. 1863, GEORGIE MARSTON.
F1214 EUNICE B., b. July 6, 1832, m. RENSALAER GREELY.
F1315 JOHN E., b. Nov. 8, 1834, m. LAURINDA GREELY.
F1316 MARY ANN, b. Oct. 12, 1836, m. 1860, EDWARD NELSON GREELY.
F1317 REUBEN, b. July 11, 1839, m. 1862, LUCELIA BOWIE.

F467 Mary Locke, born in Falmouth, Me., May 1, 1781, married ELIAS MERRILL of Falmouth, and died in childbirth. He married for a second wife her sister **F468 Dorothy Locke,** born Dec. 13, 1783, died 1869. He was born in Falmouth, Dec. 31, 1777, lived in Falmouth and Augusta, lost his ship in the War of 1812 and died in 1859.

Children of 6th Gen.

1318 MARY ANN, b. ——, m. DOCTOR BOND and went West.
1319 RUTH R., b. 1805, d. 1831, m. 1824 JACOB HALEY, went from Webster, Me., to St. Stevens, N. B. *Children:* 1320 JACOB; 1321 MARY ANN; 1322 DOLLY; 1323 ISAAC M.
1324 GEORGE W., b. Falmouth, 1807, d. Havana, Cuba, 1828.
1325 LUCRETIA L., b. Falmouth, 1808, d. 1871, m. Webster, Me., 1837, SAMUEL LANE of Gardner. *Children:* 1326 MARY E.; 1327 SARAH L.; 1328 CHARLES D.; 1329 GEORGE FREDERICK.
1330 ISAAC D., b. in Falmouth, Dec. 16, 1810, d. in Bridgton, Mich., Dec. 14, 1883, m. 1844, AUGUSTA MCKENNEY of Greene, Me. He was in the lumber business in Maine in 1839, then went to Bridgton, Mich., one of four pioneers in 1845; was engaged in the lumber business until retirement, was highly respected and prominent in town affairs. *Children:* 1331 DAVIS PRINCE; 1332 JAMES M.; 1333 WINFIELD S.; 1334 EDWARD T.; 1335 AUGUSTA; 1336 DOLLY M.; 1337 FRANK M.
1338 ELIAS W., b. in Falmouth, Oct. 2, 1812, d. 1902, m. 1840, SARAH A. TITCOMB of Yarmouth, Me. Went to Muskegon, Mich., in the lumber business. *Children:* 1339 GEORGE WILLARD; 1340 ANNIE J.; 1341 ELLEN; 1342 MARY E.; 1343 ELIZA F.
F1344 CHARLES H., b. 1818, m. 1841, CHARITY TOTMAN.
1345 JOSIAH L., b. Saco, 1820, d. 1903, m. 1860, SARAH H. CHASE of Litchfield, Me. *Children:* 1346 CARRIE J.; 1347 LIZZIE M.; 1348 CHARLES O.; 1349 MABEL S.
1350. HANNAH ELIZABETH, b. 1827, m. Webster, 1855, DANIEL C. MITCHELL of Farmingdale, Me. Lived there, had no children.

F470 Nathaniel Locke, born in Falmouth, Me., Dec. 4, 1788, married 1st, July 5, 1816, EUNICE STEVENS of Haney, New Brunswick, born 1793, died Jan. 3, 1821; married 2nd, her sister, CHARLOTTE STEVENS. He was a mariner in early life, was captured by the English in the 1812 War and confined in a West India prison. After his release he settled in New Brunswick, where he engaged in the lumber business, and died March, 1870.

Children of 6th Gen. b. Alma, N. B.

1351 JOSIAH, b. ——, died young.
F1352 CHARLOTTE, b. Apl. 5, 1820, m. Dec. 28, 1843, ISAAC PULSIFER.
F1353 JOANNA, b. of 2nd wife, Oct. 1835, m. Dec. 1855, ALBERT FOSTER.

F473 Eliza Locke, born in Falmouth, Me., July 10, 1795, died Feb. 16, 1861, married Jan. 29, 1816, her cousin SEWELL FARRAR, born Feb. 14, 1790; settled and lived in Charlestown, Me., where he died May 13, 1845.

SIXTH GENERATION

Children of the 6th Gen. b. in Charlestown, Me.
F1354 JOHN, b. Aug. 17, 1817, m. SARAH A. KELSEY.
F1355 SEWELL, b. Sept. 4, 1819, m. 1st, MARY ROLLINS; m. 2nd, ELTHEA BAGLEY.
1356 ELIZABETH, b. Nov. 1, 1821, d. Feb. 24, 1886.
1357 EPHRAIM S., b. Oct. 27, 1823, d. California, in 1852.
1358 DEBORAH L., b. Aug. 27, 1825, d. Apl. 20, 1852.
.1359 JULIA ANN, b. Apl. 20, 1827, lived Portland, 1900.
1360 JOSIAH, b. Dec. 5, 1830, d. Lake View, Me., May 27, 1902.
1361 JOSHUA H., b. July 20, 1832, d. Jan. 8, 1872.
1362 DOROTHY, b. June 5, 1837, d. July 13, 1854.

F483 Abijah Locke, born in Falmouth, Me., Sept. 8, 1801, married Dec. 31, 1828, MARY HALL MORSE of Camden, Me., who died in Nebraska. He was a farmer in Falmouth until 1842, then went to Charlestown, Me.; in 1871 he moved to Iowa, from there he settled on a Government grant, and finally went to Arcata, California, in 1883 and died there Oct. 11, 1887.
Children of the 6th Gen. b. in Falmouth, Me.
F1363 JOHN MORSE, b. Jan. 1, 1830, m. Oct. 7, 1869, SARAH ELLEN FOSS.
F1364 ELIZABETH, b. Feb. 12, 1832, m. Dec. 8, 1853, DANIEL HERRICK.
1365 SARAH PORTER, b. March 20, 1834, lived Cal. unmarried.
1366 STEPHEN DECATUR, b. July 21, 1836, m. ANNA C. ROGERS in Dutch Flat, Cal., Oct. 27, 1863, lived at Raymond, Cal., and d. there March 7, 1909.
F1367 SUSANNA MARSTON, b. Apl. 21, 1839, m. 1867, BENJAMIN M. HARDY.
1368 JOSIAH, b. Apl. 5, 1841, m. in Yankee Settlement, Delaware Co., Iowa, March 4, 1869, ANNA L. BOARD. He went to Iowa in 1865, a farmer, then to Polk Co., Neb., then to Osceola, Neb., where he lived in 1899. Had no children. He enlisted Nov. 4, 1861, in 11th Maine Reg., Co. H, discharged Nov. 18, 1864. Was in battle of Newport News, Youngsville, Lees Mills, Siege of Yorktown, was taken sick and sent to hospital, returned in time for the Seven Days' battle, Williamsburg, White Oak Swamp, Malvern Hill, night march to Harrison Landing, and back to Yorktown; was sent to Beaumont, N. C., then to South Carolina, and to Florida; was at Morris Island, siege of Charlestown (N. C.), and in smaller skirmishes.
1369 DEBORAH, b. Charlestown, Me., March 8, 1843, d. Aug. 19, 1855.
F1370 ELEANOR HOSMER, b. June 22, 1846, m. 1869, WILLIAM LORD.
F1371 LEONARD MORSE, b. July 26, 1849, m. VIOLA LUCINDA CHASE, 1879.
1372 WILLIAM FLOYD, b. Aug. 8, 1852, d. unmarried in Lincoln, Neb., July 12, 1884.

F484 Mary Locke, born in Falmouth, Me., Nov. 19, 1804, married ABRAM MERRILL who was a tanner in Portland, Me.

Child of the 6th Gen. b. in Portland, Me.

1373 NATHANIEL LOCKE, b. 1828, m. PRUDENTIA D. WATERS of Johnson, Vt., dau. of Samuel. He went to Lowell, Mass., when a young man and lost his leg in the mill, then became a photographer in New Hampshire and Vermont. He died in 1888 at Johnson, Vt.
Child: 1374 MARY D. LOCKE MERRILL, who m. HAHNEMAN BEST, proprietor of the Quincy House, Enosburg Falls, Vt.

F485 Joanna Locke, born in Falmouth, Me., Jan. 7, 1807, married Sept. 13, 1835, **Ebenezer Locke,** # **1297,** born Nov. 12, 1805. She died in Portland, Me., May 23, 1899, aged 92. He went to sea at the age of 12 with his father, became captain of a merchantman, and died at Falmouth, Nov. 21, 1844.

Children of the 6th Gen. b. in Falmouth, Me.

1375 SUSAN MARY, b. Nov. 12, 1837, d. 1843.
F1376 JOEL TALBOT, b. Oct. 9, 1839, m. March 9, 1870, ELLEN REBECCA PIKE.
1377 MATILDA PRINCE, b. Sept. 6, 1842, d. Jan. 16, 1863.

F491 Edward Locke, born 1777, married ELIZABETH WEBSTER, who was born 1784, died 1852. He lived in Rhode Island and died between 1828 and 1832.

Children of the 6th Gen. b. in So. Kingston, R. I.

F1378 SALLY, b. 1799, m. Aug. 27, 1815, WILLIAM DYER.
1379 MARY, b. Aug. 13, 1800, m. 1st, ELIJAH GAVITT; m. 2nd, SYLVESTER W. COLVIN. She had no children and d. Oct. 16, 1882. Colvin married her sister MIRIAM, later.
F1380 REV. HENRY BROOKE, b. Nov. 5, 1803, m. Sept. 4, 1825, MARY ALLYN.
1381 DEBORAH, b. ——, m. JOHN PERRYMAN.
1382 HARRIET, b. ——, m. JAMES SWEET.
1383 ELIZABETH, b. ——, m. CHARLES FISKE.
F1384 ABBIE A., b. Jan. 12, 1812, m. Oct. 25, 1832, ALFRED L. FISKE.
1385 DELILA, b. ——, d. an infant.
F1386 NATHAN TUCKER, b. 1818, m. 1st, PHILENA LEACH; m. 2nd, HARRIET M. POTTER.
F1387 THOMAS WEBSTER, b. Sept. 24, 1819, m. July 18, 1841, HANNAH WOOD; m. 2nd, Sept. 1883, SUSAN CHAPPEL.
1388 MIRIAM, b. 1822, m. 1st, AUGUSTUS POTTER; m. 2nd, Sept. 13, 1883, SYLVESTER W. COLVIN, b. 1813; they lived at Sea Konk and Coventry, R. I. By Potter she had: 1389 CHARLES H. POTTER, b. River Point, R. I., 1865, m. in Providence, Sept. 15, 1892, IDA MATTERSON, b. 1873, dau. of Wm. H. and Esther.
1389 DELILA, b. 1826, m. 1st JONAH JEWETT, 2nd; m. 2nd, JOHN WATSON. She had no children, and d. Feb. 8, 1911.

F492 Samuel Locke, born in South Kingston, R. I., March 24, 1790, married in Columbia, N. Y., March 5, 1810, ANNA WENT-

SIXTH GENERATION 81

WORTH, who was born in Bennington, Vt., March 4, 1793, died in Richfield, N. Y., Nov. 8, 1868, the dau. of David W., a Revolutionary soldier, and Rebecca (Dyer). He died in Richfield Dec. 6, 1866.
Children of the 6th Gen. b. in Richfield, N. Y.
1390 NANCY, b. in Columbia, N. Y., March 29, 1811, d. in Richfield, May 9, 1882, unmarried.
F1391 REBECCA, b. Sept. 11, 1812, m. Feb. 28, 1832, DAVID AMES.
1391a JONATHAN, b. in Columbia, June 29, 1815, left home aged 16, never heard from.
F1392 DAVID, b. March 4, 1817, m. June 15, 1841, AURELIA P. CLARKE.
F1393 HARVEY D., b. Feb. 10, 1820, m. 1st, Aug. 24, 1851, MARY BROWN; m. 2nd, Dec. 4, 1860, SARAH E. DEWEL.
F1394 ABNER W., b. July 11, 1824, m. Nov. 22, 1859, MARIETTA BLISS.
F1395 CHRISTOPHER H., b. June 13, 1826, m. Oct. 24, 1854, MARY WARMOUTH.
1396 RHODA A., b. May 9, 1828, d. in Richfield, March 24, 1845.
1397 NORMAN V., b. Oct. 30, 1830, d. in Vandalia, Ill., Aug. 15, 1860, probably unmarried.
F1398 ANSLEY A., b. Feb. 14, 1832, m. Dec. 30, 1852, MARY E. GETMAN.
F1399 SYLVANUS DYER, b. Sept. 11, 1833, m. Aug. 13, 1861, ELLEN JOSEPHINE PARKER.

F493 Jonathan Locke, born of second wife, in Aurora, N. Y., Aug. 17, 1813, married there in 1834, ELSIE TRITTS of Aurora, born Sept. 21, 1811, died in Aurora, Dec. 21, 1881. He died in Aurora, Feb. 2, 1873. Perhaps also lived at Poplar Ridge, N. Y.
Children of the 6th Gen.
1400 ADELIA, b. Dec. 1, 1835.
1401 EDWARD A., b. Apl. 28, 1836, d. in Dover (state ?) May 10, 1879. He was married and was a marble worker.
1402 ABRAHAM W., b. July 25, 1838.
1403 ELIZA, b. Dec. 10, 1841, d. July 28, 1847.
F1404 AUGUSTUS B., b. Sept. 23, 1845, m. 1862, EMALINE A. HOAG; m. 2nd, May 1, 1879, HATTIE M. MOSHER.
1405 MARY E., b. Apl. 6, 1851, d. Sept. 8, 1851.

F496 Nathaniel Locke, born in Hampton, Aug. 26, 1766, married March 18, 1792, LYDIA PAGE, daughter of Dr. Samuel and Sarah (Sherburne). She was born Jan. 26, 1771, died May 23, 1864, aged 94. He lived and died on the old homestead in Hampton, Feb. 8, 1855.
Children of the 6th Gen. b. in Hampton.
F1406 HANNAH, b. Aug. 3, 1792, m. 1st, JOHN TOWLE; m. 2nd, WILLIAM NI(T)CHER of Maine.
F1407 JONATHAN MOULTON, b. 1794, m. Jan. 24, 1822, MARY ELKINS.

F1408 MIRIAM LAMPREY, b. March 13, 1796, m. May 3, 1816, JOSEPH PALMER.
F1409 SAMUEL, b. June 24, 1798, m. June 3, 1825, MARY B. DEARBORN.
F1410 SHERBURNE, b. 1800, m. Aug. 15, 1824, LOUISA LAMPREY.
F1411 MARY ANN, b. ——, m. REUBEN L. BROWN.
1412 NATHANIEL, b. Oct. 1803, d. May 27, 1810.
1413 SARAH, b. Dec. 12, 1806, d. Nov. 2, 1825, unmarried.
F1414 NATHANIEL S., b. Jan. 27, 1812, m. July 29, 1839, MARY LANE.
1415 LYDIA, b. Aug. 3, 1814, m. JOHN LAMPREY of North Hampton, son of John and Polly (Philbrick). Lydia d. March 1846, no children. He m. 2nd, MARY P. PHILBRICK, dau. of Joseph.

F497 Mary Locke, born in Hollis, Me., May 24, 1770, married 1st, Nov. 2, 1791, **Stephen Locke,** # 500, of Hollis, Me. He was born Feb. 2, 1765, died Dec. 21, 1812. She married 2nd, ROBERT HALEY, by whom she had no children and died in 1852.
Children of the 6th Gen. b. in Hollis, Me.
1416 CALEB, graduated from Bowdoin College in 1825, was a lawyer in Gardner, Me., and died there aged 35, not married.
F1417 HANNAH, b. ——, m. June 10, 1813, JOHN EMERY.
F1418 MIRIAM, b. ——, m. intentions published Sept. 7, 1816, to DANIEL S. HOOPER.

F499 Betsey Locke, born in Hollis, Me., June 17, 1763, married JOSEPH HOOPER, a farmer of Waterboro, Me.
Children of the 6th Gen. b. in Waterboro, Me.
1419 JOHN, b. ——.   1420 JOSEPH, b. ——.   1421 TRISTRAM, b. ——.
1422 WILLIAM, b. ——, d. aged 20.
1423 DAU., m. NATHAN CHADBOURNE.   1424 DAU., m. a GUPTIL.
1425 DAU., m. a JOHNSON.

F501 Thomas D. Locke, born in Hollis, Me., June 13, 1768, married ABIGAIL CHADBOURNE, who was born 1774, died in Hollis, Apl. 21, 1859. They joined the Hollis church. He was a farmer there, and died Oct. 9, 1854.
Children of the 6th Gen. b. in Hollis, Me.
F1426 JAPHETH CHADBOURNE, b. Aug. 16, 1795, m. Oct. 23, 1817, MARTHA BURBEEN SMITH.
1427 JONATHAN M., b. Apl. 17, 1798, m. MRS. LANE of Oldtown, Me. He was a mariner many years, also a farmer in Hollis, had no children, and d. Dec. 16, 1868.
F1428 JOSEPH L., b. March 13, 1801, m. 1st, Aug. 22, 1822, LILLIAS WOODMAN; m. 2nd, March 16, 1866, MARY A. KILGORE.
F1429 OLIVE C., b. Sept. 8, 1806, m. Jan. 20, 1826, RICHARD SMITH.
1430 MARY, b. June 13, 1814, d. Dec. 18, 1831, unmarried.
F1431 LUCY B., b. 1817, m. June 2, 1852, RICHARD SMITH.

SIXTH GENERATION

F502 Tristram Locke, born in Hollis, Me., Oct. 19, 1771, married ELIZABETH LORD of Gardner. (Maine Historical Record says, "Anna, daughter of James and Eliz. Lord.) They joined the Hollis Church, but he was a carpenter in Hallowell, and died June 2, 1832.

Children of the 6th Gen. probably b. in Hallowell, Me.
1432 ELIZABETH, b. Apl. 4, 1795, m. a GRAY, lived in Gardner, Me.
1433 TRISTRAM, b. June 3, 1798, was m., but no record.
1434 JOAN, b. Jan. 26, 1800, was m., but no record.
F1435 SAMUEL, b. Dec. 14, 1802, m. Jan. 7, 1827, JANETT M. LYMBURNER.
1436 MARY ANN, b. Apl. 8, 1807, was married ——.
1437 LUCY ANN, b. a twin.
1438 THOMAS L., b. March 11, 1810.
1439 AUGUSTINE, b. Dec. 6, 1811, died in youth.

F503 Caleb Locke, born in Hollis, Me., Dec. 7, 1773, married March 17, 1802, SARAH FROST CLARKE, daughter of Nathanial and Sarah Pepperell (Frost), who was born in Kittery, March 4, 1781, died Sept. 1, 1851. She was the 4th Gen. from Andrew Pepperell and 5th from Major Charles Frost of Kittery, killed by Indians July 4, 1697. He was one of the first townsmen of Hollis, where he lived as a farmer and died Aug. 9, 1857.

Children of the 6th Gen. b. in Hollis, Me.
F1440 SALLY FROST, b. Jan. 15, 1803, m. Oct. 14, 1825, MOSES SMITH.
F1441 SAMUEL, b. Apl. 11, 1804, m. 1st, Nov. 25, 1829, FANNY FOSS; m. 2nd, Apl. 30, 1837, RUTH SANDS.
F1442 NATHANIEL CLARKE, b. Nov. 9, 1808, m. 1st, Dec. 23, 1834, OLIVE GRANT; m. 2nd, Nov. 21, 1870, MRS. ELIZA HUNT CROCKETT FOGG.
F1443 STEPHEN, b. Jan. 17, 1816, m. Apl. 13, 1842, LUCINDA CLARKE.
1444 HANNAH CLARKE, b. Aug. 1, 1819, m. Jan. 28, 1850, as his 2nd wife, DANIEL W. SAWYER. She d. July 1, 1868; lived at Boothbay, Me., and Cleveland, Ohio. They had: 1444a ELLA M., 1853-55; 1444b FLORENCE M., 1857-83, unmarried.

F505 Samuel Locke, born in Hollis, Me., Aug. 16, 1784, married in Ipswich, Mass., Oct. 16, 1812, MRS. ELIZABETH (STANWOOD) WAITE, who was born in Ipswich, Sept. 29, 1781, died in Hallowell, Apl. 15, 1850. By her first husband she had EUNICE HALE WAITE, who married REV. SYLVANUS COBB. Samuel was a very able school teacher and mathematician, lived in Hallowell, Me., and died in Stillwater, Mich., Sept. 9, 1873.

Children of the 6th Gen. b. in Hallowell, Me.
F1445 ELIZABETH STANWOOD, b. Jan. 24, 1814, m. HENRY WING DECKER.
1446 HANNAH STANWOOD, b. Jan. 8, 1816, m. HARRISON SMITH of Hal-

lowell. She d. June 1856, and her son: 1447 HARRY, b. 1855, was adopted by his uncle, JOSEPH H. LOCKE.
F1448 SAMUEL EBENEZER, b. Jan. 18, 1818, m. 1844, HARRIET FLETCHER.
F1449 JOSEPH HALE, b. Apl. 7, 1820, m. 1845 MARTHA B. BRADFORD.
F1450 HOSEA BALLOU, b. July 12, 1822, m. 1844, ELIZABETH W. PILLSBURY.
F1451 ISAAC STANWOOD, b. July 28, 1824, m. 1849, LYDIA ALMIRA MORRIS.
1452 JOHN CALEB, b. Dec. 12, 1826, m. 1st, July 3, 1853, MARY PIERCE, who d. Nov. 24, 1857; m. 2nd, Apl. 2, 1866, ELLEN A. ALLEN. He was a Royal Arch Mason, a noted singer, and member of the Waltham Quartette. He had one dau, 1452a BELLE FLORENCE, b. Apl. 28, 1855. He died Apl. 28, 1879.

F506 Mary Locke, born in Hollis, Aug. 12, 1787, married JOHN BRADBURY, a farmer of Hollis, Me.

Children of 6th Gen. b. Hollis, Me.

1453 STEPHEN, died young.
F1454 BRICE B., b. Apl 19, 1810, d. June 1, 1892, m. Dec. 17, 1840, HANNAH LOCKE, b. 1814, # 3107; was a mason of Hollis, Me.
1455 SAMUEL; 1456 OLIVE; 1457 MIRIAM; 1458 JACOB; 1459 IVORY; 1460 CALEB, alive Biddeford, 1903; 1461 JOHN; 1462 WINTHROP; 1463 ELSIE; 1464 ELIZABETH; 1465 STEPHEN, alive 1903, Biddeford.

F507 Betsey Locke, born Oct. 2, 1763, married 1st, Apl. 16, 1783, COFFIN PAGE, who was baptized May 25, 1755, died July 12, 1801. She married 2nd, his brother NOAH PAGE, Jan. 13, 1806. He was baptized Sept. 21, 1766. They were sons of Francis and Mary (Marston) and lived in North Hampton.

Children of the 6th Gen. b. in North Hampton.

1466 REDMAN, bapt. Sept. 12, 1784. 1467 BENJAMIN, b. Sept. 12, 1792.
1468 COFFIN, b. 1795 (?), d. March 18, 1803.
1469 DAVID, b. 1797 (?), d. March 1803.
1470 SAMUEL, bapt. Aug. 1800, m. MARY GODFREY, b. May 1802, d. in Hampton Feb. 25, 1861, dau. of Jona. and Mary (Lane). *Children:* 1471 OLIVER, b. March 2, 1820, m. SUSAN ROWE of Seabrook, lived at Little River, and had 8 children; 1472 DAVID C. b. Jan. 4, 1822, m. Oct. 28, 1848, MARY F. CLARKE, b. Jan. 6, 1829. He was a cordwainer and had 9 children; 1473 MARY J., b. Oct. 15, 1824, m. Dec. 27, 1841, LOWELL S. MARDEN of Rye; they lived at Boston and Deerfield; 1474 SARAH A., b. July 20, 1826, d. March 23, 1875, m. July 4, 1843, JEREMIAH BROWN, b. Sept. 15, 1821, son of Simon and Ann (Sherburne). He was a carpenter, had 6 children, and later he m. MRS. MIRIAM PALMER DUNBAR.
1475 BETTY, b. Jan. 1802, d. March 15, 1803.
1476 STACY, b. 1807, d. in North Hampton, May 4, 1894. (Second husband's child.)
F1477 DEBORAH, m. JOHN T. DOW, and he m. 2nd, MRS. BETSEY NEWMAN.

SIXTH GENERATION

F508 Benjamin Veazie Locke, born in Effingham, N. H., May 12, 1765, married Nov. 27, 1790, OLIVE ROBINSON, daughter of Squire James, of Epping. She was born in 1772, died May 7, 1849. Olive married 2nd, OBADIAH FRENCH a Revolutionary soldier. Benjamin came from New Hampshire and settled on the wild lands of Mount Vernon, Me., as a farmer and there he died Jan. 18, 1810, being overcome by the cold.

Children of the 6th Gen. probably b. in Mt. Vernon, Me.

1478 SALLY R., b. July 28, 1792, m. Oct. 17, 1815, JAMES WHITTIER of Vienna, Me. She d. Sept. 1865. *Children:* 1479 MATILDA; 1480 OLIVE; 1481 PERLEY; 1482 SAMUEL. Mrs. Saml. Savage of No. Anson, Me., is a descendant of one of these.
1483 SAMUEL, b. June 21, 1794, d. March 15, 1799.
F1484 JAMES R., b. Aug. 21, 1796, m. HANNAH COLLEY.
1485 BETSEY R., b. Aug. 16, 1798, m. 1st. Oct. 23, 1816, WM. H. DICKEY of Exeter; m. 2nd, JESSE EMERSON of Salem, Mass. She died in Salem. *Children:* 1486 SYLVINA; 1487 OLIVE; 1488 WILLIAM.
F1489 COL. SAMUEL, b. Sept. 25, 1800, m. 1822, ABIGAIL W. COLLEY.
1490 OLIVE, b. Sept. 22, 1802, d. Aug. 22, 1805.
1491 SYLVINA R., b. Dec. 13, 1805, m. Nov. 24, 1825, SAMUEL MOORS of Vienna, Me. She d. Aug. 13, 1845. *Children*: 1492 ELIZABETH T., b. Redfield, Me., March 11, 1827, m. ——— ROBINSON, and d. Portsmouth, Apl. 27, 1893; 1493 CAROLINE; 1494 SYLVINA; 1495 DANIEL; 1496 TRUE; 1497 TIMOTHY; 1498 EVERARD.
1499 OLIVE, b. Jan. 28, 1808, m. March 27, 1827, JAMES M. ROBINSON, lived at Mt. Vernon, and she d. Feb. 8, 1866. *Children:* 1500 MARY; 1501 CHESSMAN; 1502 REV. JOHN, lived East Madison, Me.; 1503 ELIZABETH, m. ——— FAUNCH, lived Salem, Mass.; 1504 HARRIET; 1505 GEORGE; 1506 OSCAR; 1507 WINFIELD.

F513 John Weare Locke, always went by the name of Weare Locke, born Dec. 26, 1773, married Oct. 14, 1798, ANNA JAMES of Kensington. He was a farmer in Brentwood and Raymond, at which latter place he died March 11, 1825.

Children of the 6th Gen.

1508 HULDAH, b. Kensington, Oct. 16, 1798.
F1509 SAMUEL, b. Feb. 15, 1802, m. 1823, DOLLY ABBOTT.
F1510 SALLY, b. Feb. 17, 1809, m. July 4, 1825, JOHN POLLARD; m. 2nd, SEWELL ABBOTT.

F514 Samuel Locke, born March 23, 1778, married 1st, SALLY GOODWIN; married 2nd, ABIAH HARDING, who died Aug. 24, 1870. He went from New Hampshire to Athens, Me., was a farmer at Lord's Hill and died Oct. 16, 1865.

LOCKE GENEALOGY

Children of the 6th Gen. b. in Athens, Me.

1511 SALLY, b. 1801, m. LYMAN TURNER. She d. March 22, 1883. *Children:* 1512 SAMUEL L.; 1513 LEWIS; 1514 WARREN; 1515 LYDIA; 1516 DARIUS K.; 1517 BETSEY; 1518 SARAH; 1519 MARY A.; 1520 MARTHA.

F1521 ICHABOD, b. March 17, 1802, m. NANCY MOSES.
F1522 JOHN, b. 1804, m. MELINDA BROWN.
F1523 GEORGE, b. Nov. 24, 1805, m. MARGARET BRADBURY.
1524 DOW, b. ——, m. ELIZA DORE. He was a joiner in Mt. Vernon, Me., 1830. He m. several times, and moved west, perhaps to Wisconsin. Eliza divorced him and with her children lived in Memphis, Tenn., later in Ohio. *Children:* 1525 CHARLES; 1526 BELLE; 1527 ALMIRA; 1528 LOUISA.
1529 BETSEY, b. ——, m. 1st, WILLIAM R. KINGSLEY; m. 2nd, JAMES CILLEY. By Kingsley she had: 1530 ALBERT E.; 1531 WILLIAM; and 1532 SOPHIA M., b. Orono, Me., Feb. 2, 1834, m. a BOWMAN and d. Lancaster Sept. 19, 1895. Betsey and Cilley had: 1533 JAMES; 1534 SAMUEL; 1535 CHARLES.
1536 HANNAH, b. 1812, m. JEREMIAH KINGSLEY, had: HULDAH P.
F1537 LUCY, b. Dec. 31, 1816, m. 1837, REV. JESSE L. WILSON.
F1538 CHARLES, b. Apl. 2, 1819, m. 1842, DATE S. HALLET.
F1539 ALANSON, b. March 22, 1823, m. Sept. 14, 1845, MINA A. EMERY.

F516 Jacob Locke, married 1st, VISS VERNON; married 2nd, MARGARET BARRY.

Children of the 6th Gen. b. in Lockport, Nova Scotia.

F1540 JACOB, m. CATHERINE GUYOT.
F1541 EBENEZER, m. ELIZABETH BOWL.

F519 Jonathan Locke, born in 1758, married Mary E. Ryder of Rhode Island, who was born in 1762, died in 1844. He died 1852.

Children of the 6th Gen. b. in Lockport, Nova Scotia.
Average age of first five is 89 $^4/_5$ years.

F1542 JOHN, b. 1782, m. MARY HARLOW. He d. 1869.
F1543 SAMUEL, b. 1785, m. LETITIA MCKILLOP.
F1544 JAMES, b. 1786; d. 1872, m. FANNY STRICKLAND.
1545 PRISCILLA, b. 1789, d. unmarried 1885, aged 96.
F1546 ABIGAIL, b. 1802, m. Dec. 19, 1822, ENOS CHURCHILL.
1547 MARY, m. CAPTAIN GEORGE CANN of Yarmouth (N. S. ?). *Children:* 1548 SAMUEL; 1549 GEORGE; 1550 ELIZABETH; 1551 LETITIA; 1552 MAHALIA; 1553 MARY; 1554 THANKFUL; 1555 FANNIE.
1556 ELIZABETH, b. ——, m. in Falmouth, Feb. 16, 1816, CAPTAIN SAMUEL FARROW (Farrar ?) of No. Yarmouth, Me. *Children:* 1557 WASHBURN; 1558 JOHN; 1559 WILLIAM; 1560 MARY; 1561 SALOME; 1562 KEZIAH.

SIXTH GENERATION

F520 Nathaniel Locke of Newport, was married July 30, 1764, by Gardner Thurston, to MARY BURT.

Children of 6th Gen.
F1563 NATHANIEL, b. Feb. 19, 1778, m. REBECCA REED.
1564 SAMUEL, b. ——, killed in war (?).

F530 Deacon Abraham Locke, baptized June 28, 1760, married in Deerfield Apl. 6, 1779, MARY SANBORN, daughter of Reuben and Elizabeth (Ward) of Epsom. She was baptized Nov. 30, 1760. He lived in Epsom where his wife Mary administered his estate May 5, 1805. Aug. 17, 1805, his cousin SAMUEL was appointed guardian over his minor children as given below. The story is told that the good wife Mary was preparing bear meat for the family one day when a party of "bad looking" Indians appeared, and in order to propitiate them, she was compelled to cook the entire bear before they grunted their satisfaction and retired.

Children of the 6th Gen. b. in Epsom.
1565 SALLY, b. Apl. 10, 1780, m. in Epsom, Feb. 19, 1801, SAMUEL DAVIS.
   Children: 1566 SALLY, m. RICHARD CHESLEY and had 1567 SARAH, who m. HENRY SHERBURNE and went west.
1568 BETSEY, b. Jan. 2, 1782, m. JONATHAN EATON. *Child:* 1569 POLLY, b. Epsom, May 4, 1807, m. a TAYLOR, and she d. Laconia, Sept. 5, 1890.
1570 FRANCIS, b. Sept. 27, 1783.
F1571 REUBEN, b. May 18, 1785, m. 1805, MRS. SARAH (BROSIAS) DENNETT.
1572 NANCY, b. ——, m. ANDREW FISHER, who lived in Epsom and Chichester and was in the 1812 War. *Child:* 1573 HANNAH B., b. Epsom, 1830, m. a REYNOLDS, d. Concord Nov. 13, 1884. Nancy also had: 1574 a son in the Navy 1863.
1575 LYDIA, b. Jan. 27, 1787, m. in Weare, 1838, EPHRAIM DAVIS of Sunapee.
F1576 ABRAHAM, b. Jan. 2, 1789, m. KEZIAH ALLEN.
1577 MOSES, was m. but did not live with wife, and d. Apl. 27, 1861. I judge by the 1820 census that he had 1 son and 3 daus. but nothing is known of them.

F537 Francis Locke, born in Epsom, July 6, 1755, married 1st, MARY ABIGAIL KATHERWOOD; married 2nd, Dec. 2, 1819, OLIVE HAINES BICKFORD, who was born in Greenland and died in Allenstown, the daughter of John and Olive (Weeks). He lived in Epsom, was pensioned at $96 per year for service in the Revolutionary War, N. H. Continental Line, and died in 1835.

Children of the 6th Gen. b. in Epsom.

1578 ABIGAIL, b. Jan. 27, 1777, m. 1797, JOHN LOCKE # F942.
F1579 MARGARET, b. 1779, m. 1806, JONATHAN KNOWLES.
F1580 EPHRAIM, b. July 15, 1783, m. 1st, Nov. 25, 1807, DEBORAH WELLS; m. 2nd, Aug, 20, 1838, LYDIA (YEATON) CHESLEY; m. 3rd, Feb. 15, 1842, RHODA COLLINS.
F1581 POLLY, b. 1784, m. DANIEL PHILBRICK.
F1582 FRANCIS, b. June 26, 1791, m. 1st, MARY PHILBRICK; m. 2nd, Sept. 24, 1856, MRS. RHODA (COLLINS) LOCKE.
1583 COMFORT, b. ——, not m.   1584 MARTHA.

F539 Asa Locke, born in 1763, married in Epsom, March 4, 1784, MRS. MARY (FLETCHER) (NASON) SHAW of Vermont. She was born in 1758, died Feb. 12, 1844. He moved to St. Albans, to Richford and then to Springfield, Vt. He died in St. Albans Nov. 19, 1847.

Children of the 6th Gen. b. in Vermont.

F1585 RICHARD, b. Apl. 13, 1792, m. 1st, Jan. 22, 1817, MERCY MUNSON; m. 2nd, March 8, 1820, JULIA PARKER; m. 3rd, Oct. 1853, EVALINE G. FOOT.
F1586 WILLIAM M., b. 1793, m. ABIGAIL WITHEY.
F1587 VERANUS, b. July 15, 1800, m. 1825, STATIRA JENNE.
1588 LEVI, died young.
1589 SALLY, m. JOHN MUNSEL, lived in Sharon, Vt.; no children.
1590 LYDIA, m. WARREN KATHEN, lived in Plattsburg, Vt., had 2 sons, 1 daughter.
1591 NANCY, m. DANIEL KIRBY, emigrated to Ohio in an ox team, lived there several years, then came back to Canada; had 4 children.
1592 MARY, m. GEORGE RICHARDSON, had 5 children.

F540 Capt. Samuel Locke (true name, Wm. Samuel Locke), born ——, married in Epsom, Dec. 28, 1785, MARY EVANS of Epsom. He enlisted for the Revolutionary War in the First N. H. Regiment in 1776; again enlisted in Col. McClary's Co., 1777, for three years. He was so young when he enlisted and was so long away in the Yorktown campaign, that his people did not know him when he returned. He was guardian of his cousin Abraham's minor children in 1805. He kept a tavern in Dover and died about 1816. She had dower rights in his property in Epsom, Jan. 16, 1819.

Children of the 6th Gen. b. in Epsom.

1593 BETSEY, b. Jan. 3, 1786, m. ABEL BROWN, of Epsom, May 19, 1807 (or Nov. 27, 1806); had 2 sons died young.
1594 ELEANOR, b. Oct. 14, 1788, perhaps m. WINTHROP SMITH # 3979.
F1595 SAMUEL, b. Nov. 19, 1790, m. Feb. 28, 1809, LYDIA BUZZELL.

SIXTH GENERATION 89

F1596 DANIEL EVANS, b. Nov. 24, 1793, m. Jan. 19, 1819, ANN COLEMAN.
F1597 POLLY, b. Oct. 10, 1794, m. 1815, WEARE PRESCOTT.
1598 CHARLOTTE, m. in Epsom, May 6, 1817, EZEKIEL ELKINS of Gilford. *Children:* 1599 IRENE; 1600 BETSEY; 1601 ELIZA; 1602 HANNAH.
1603 RUHUMA P., m. in Deerfield, Dec. 10, 1818, JACOB WHIPPLE of Epsom.
1604 IRENE, m. Feb. 28, 1822, DR. JACOB WILLIAMS of Gilmanton, b. Groton, Mass. They lived in Kensington, 1845.
F1605 HANNAH MARY, m. July 2, 1820, DANIEL SMITH of Durham.
1606 COMFORT, not mentioned in father's will dated 1814 in which he leaves an estate of $4,636. (One daughter is said to have m. a SNOW.)

F543 Hannah Locke, born July 20, 1768, married in Epsom, Feb. 9, 1792, AARON LAMPREY, who was born in Concord, Aug. 29, 1766, died July 29, 1850. She died Aug. 9, 1835.
Children of the 6th Gen. b. in Epsom.
F1607 LEVI, b. Sept. 10, 1792, m. 1st, POLLY COOK; m. 2nd, Jan. 6, 1862, ELEANOR BUZZELL.
1608 HANNAH, b. March 7, 1794, m. JOHN PAGE of Epsom. He m. 1st, HULDAH LOCKE # 944, was a farmer in Epsom, had no children. Hannah died Aug. 20, 1877.
1609 AARON, b. Sept. 15, 1796, m. May 27, 1818, MARY JUDKINS of Epsom, b. 1807, d. Oct. 23, 1858; m. 2nd, MARY NICHOLS or PIERCE, b. 1806, d. Oct. 15, 1896. He lived at Candia and Concord and died July 2, 1882. *Children by 1st wife:* 1610 WARREN; 1611 MORRIS.
1612 DELIA B., b. June 2, 1798, d. Aug. 5, 1882, m. 1st, JAMES LITTLE and 2nd, a LITCHFIELD. Had a son: 1613 JAMES LITTLE, who had 1614 DELIA; and 1615 MARY C., who m. HENRY HUBBARD.
1616 EPHRAIM, b. May 27, 1800, m. BRIDGET PHELPS, who d. 1884. He was a farmer in Groveton, and d. Nov. 13, 1884. *Children:* 1617 DELIA C., b. Feb. 6, 1828; 1618 MARY B., b. Dec. 22, 1830; 1619 HENRY P., b. Nov. 3, 1832, Concord; 1620 MYRA B., b. Feb. 15, 1834; 1621 MORRIS L., b. Oct. 1, 1835; 1622 JOHN H., b. Jan. 5, 1837; 1623 MAITLAND C., b. Sept. 30, 1838, teacher Florida; 1624 AUSTIN L., b. Oct. 17, 1840, Concord; 1625 HORACE A., b. June 27, 1842; 1626 CYRIL, b. March 29, 1844; 1627 CLARENCE S., b. May 14, 1847.
F1628 ABEL, b. Aug. 3, 1802, m. 1st, Nov. 20, 1826, LYDIA A. CAMPBELL; m. 2nd, 1834, SUSAN P. WEBSTER; m. 3rd, Jan. 22, 1869, ELIZA P. COLBURN.
1629 JOHN LOCKE, b. July 31, 1804, m. MARY CAIN of Maine, b. 1811, d. Apl. 15, 1851. He d. Aug. 16, 1876. *Children:* 1630 HANNAH; 1631 ELIZABETH; 1632 LYDIA; 1633 DELIA, m. a DUDLEY, lived Montpelier, Vt.; 1634 DANIEL; 1635 STEVEN; 1636 JOHN; 1637 GEORGE.
1638 DANIEL, b. Dec. 29, 1806, d. Dec. 23, 1829, unm. Epsom.

1639 ELIZABETH, b. Oct. 18, 1809, d. March 14, 1832, unm.
1640 LYDIA, b. Oct. 24, 1811, m. SIMON DAVIS, lived in Concord, had no child and she d. May 5, 1874.
F1641 JUDITH, b. July 29, 1815, m. CHANDLER E. STEVENS # 1651.

F544 Olive Locke, born in Epsom, 1772, married March 8, 1795, PHILIP STEVENS, who was born 1773, died July 17, 1850. She died Aug. 8, 1845. They lived in Concord.

Children of the 6th Gen. b. in Epsom or Concord.

1642 JAMES, b. June 6, 1796, m. in C. Nov. 24, 1822, ISMENIA WASHER of C. He was a stone cutter in Quincy, Mass., and was killed there by an explosion.
1643 COMFORT, b. March 25, 1798, d. June 9, 1804.
1644 JANE M., b. March 6, 1800, m. in C. Sept. 22, 1834, THOMAS GRAHAM of Quincy, Mass. She d. 1876. *Children:* 1645 THOMAS and others.
1646 PHEBE, b. July 10, 1802, m. JOHN KELLEY. She d. 1851, had a son in C.
1647 DANIEL, b. May 29, 1804, d. June 10, 1804.
1648 DANIEL, b. Aug. 9, 1805, d. 1828, unm.
1649 MARY B., b. March 15, 1808, m. SMITH GLIDDEN, a farmer of Pembroke. He had no child by Mary, who d. P. Jan. 22, 1894.
1650 ABIGAIL, b. 1811, m. in Concord, Apl. 28, 1828, DAVID MORRISON of C., b. in Dunbarton, 1792, d. Sept. 14, 1860; was a stone cutter in Quincy, Mass. She d. Feb. 21, 1872.
1651 CHANDLER E., b. East Concord, May 12, 1812, m. Aug. 22, 1837, JUDITH LAMPREY (See F1641), his cousin. He d. in C. Oct. 18, 1898.
1652 COMFORT, b. 1815, m. JOHN SIMPSON of East Derry. *Children:* 1653 SUSAN; 1654 SARAH; 1655 MARY; 1656 WILLIAM; 1657 SAMUEL.

F545 Betsey or **Martha Locke,** born 1773, married 1st, Dec. 23, 1792, in Epsom, SAMUEL HUTCHINS. Hutchins married 2nd, a STEVENS and had: SUSAN; JUDITH; MATILDA; JASON. The record sent me says she married 2nd, Dec. 14, 1797, EDWARD THURSTON of Deerfield, though the children are all named Hutchins. She died in 1850.

Children of the 6th Gen. b. in Epsom.

1658 HANNAH, b. May 30, 1793. 1659 BETSEY, b. Aug. 26, 1796.
1660 SALLY SEAVEY, b. May 9, 1798.
1661 COMFORT LOCKE, b. June 23, 1800.
F1662 JOHN, b. March 17, 1802, m. Dec. 2, 1829, LUCY ANN MILLS.
F1663 MARGARET, b. May 29, 1806, m. LELAND THURSTON.

F549 Francis Marden, born 1763, married Sarah Lamprey. They lived on the Lafayette Road, Portsmouth.

SIXTH GENERATION 91

Children in the 6th Gen.
1664 JAMES, b. 1786, m. 1st, unknown; m. 2nd, MERCY PAGE; lived in Portsmouth, had 11 children.
1665 SIMON, bapt., Nov. 18, 1787.
1666 ISRAEL, bapt. Oct. 11, 1789, m. ——— NUDD and he d. June 11, 1865; lived in Portsmouth, had 5 children.
1667 THOMAS, b. ———, m. MARY LANG, b. Feb. 22, 1795; lived in Portsmouth, had 2 sons.
1668 FRANCIS, bapt. Aug. 3, 1794.
1669 JOSEPH, b. ———, m. ——— MARSTON.
1670 PATIENCE, b. Feb. 29, 1796, m. LEVI BERRY of Greenland, he b. March 26, 1792, d. Dec. 1867. She d. Feb. 1864.
1671 PRUDENCE, b. ———, m. CAPTAIN THOMAS.

F553 Mary Locke, born in Seabrook, Oct. 26, 1768, died Aug. 19, 1827, married 1789, BENJAMIN PERKINS of Seabrook.
Children of 6th Gen. b. in Seabrook.
F1673 SAMUEL, b. Oct. 13, 1790, m. 1817, MARY M. STOCKMAN.
1674 MARY, b. Apl. 6, 1793, d. Oct. 19, 1882, m. Apl. 1835, PEABODY ILSLEY of West Newbury, Mass., had no child.
F1675 SALLY, b. July 3, 1795, m. Apl. 5, 1827, ADONIRAM GEORGE.

F554 Sarah Locke, born in Seabrook, Oct. 31, 1773, died March 22, 1844, married Captain JOHN JANVRIN. He sailed from Italy for New York in 1812 and his ship was wrecked in a terrible storm. With a few of the crew he remained with the ship but they were never heard from afterward. The survivors of one of the long boats, after weeks of torture were picked up and told the story. He was son of John and descendant of John, who was born Island of Jersey July 8, 1707.
Children of 6th Gen.
F1676 BELINDA JANVRIN, b. Nov. 3, 1801, d. Dec. 10, 1872, m. EDMOND PILLING.
1677 DENIS, b. ———. 1678 JOHN.
1679 SALLY, b. ———, d. aged 2 years.
1680 OLIVE G.

F555 Samuel Locke, born in Seabrook, Feb. 16, 1776, married Oct. 2, 1806, HANNAH LOCKE # 576. She was born Apl. 23, 1783, died Seabrook, Nov. 11, 1863. He was a boat builder in Seabrook, and died Sept. 13, 1855.
Children of the 6th Gen. b. in Seabrook.
1681 HANNAH, b. July 19, 1807, m. Dec. 10, 1833, WILLIAM H. FITTS of Salisbury, Mass., b. 1804. Hannah had one dau: 1682 MARY L., b. Jan. 1, 1835, d. Jan. 11, 1854, and she d. May 25, 1872. He m. 2nd, LAURA DAY, and d. May 25, 1881.

F1683 NEWELL, b. May 18, 1809, m. Jan. 15, 1838, HANNAH TRUE.
1684 MARY, b. Apl. 29, 1811, m. in Salisbury, Mass., Nov. 15, 1831, ABRAM TRUE of Salisbury, son of Rev. Jabez, b. Sals., Sept. 17, 1804, d. Sals., May 17, 1839. She d. Jan. 29, 1888.
F1685 SALLY, b. May 17, 1813, m. Jan. 7, 1834, MOSES RIDGEWAY.

F557 Mehitable Locke, born in Epsom, Oct. 18, 1757, married in Deerfield, Nov. 30, 1775, JOHN BLAKE of Loudon.

Child of the 6th Gen.

1686 MEHITABLE BLAKE, b. ——, m. JACOB BACHELDOR. *Children:* 1687 ELVIRA, m. a KENNISTON; 1688 FLORENDA, m. DR. WOODMAN and lived in Stanstead, Can.; 1689 JOHN, was a farmer in Stanstead, Can.; 1690 A DAU. m. a MUDGET, in Loudon.

F558 Ann Locke (called **Sally**), born in Epsom, Feb. 13, or March 9, 1760, married Nov. 24, 1785, JOHN GODFREY, JR., of Northwood who died there Jan. 25, 1820.

Children of the 6th Gen.

1691 JOHN GODFREY, m. in Northwood, d. there, had *children*: 1692 MARY, m. a RICKER, and d. in Manchester, who had: 1693 EDWIN and 1694 MARILLA; 1695 MARILLA, m. a MITCHELL of Lincoln, Mass.; 1696 ELIZABETH, b. 1811, m. Sept. 1, 1845, JOHN CHANDLER, b. in Methuen, Mass., July 30, 1820, d. March 3, 1865, son of Dr. John and Priscilla (Kimball). She d. Bedford, Mass., 1845; 1697 HARRIET, b. July 3, 1817, m. BENJ. S. SANBORN and d. Sept. 27, 1855. He b. Aug. 19, 1820, lived Hampstead; m. 2nd, MARTHA HODGE of Manchester, and d. Jan. 20, 1860; 1698 SARAH, m. a GODFREY.

1699 MOSES GODFREY, m. —— WOODBURY, moved from Canada to California and had: 1700 JOHN, and four daus.

1701 ABIGAIL GODFREY, m. 1810, SAMUEL JAMES of Northwood, b. Apl. 24, 1788. *Children:* 1702 SAMUEL S., was a farmer in Northwood and had 3 boys and 3 girls; 1703 SHEPPARD; 1704 DAU., m. WOODBURY DURGIN of Northwood; 1705 SON or DAU. m. BACHELDER; 1706 MOSES, a farmer in Northwood.

1707 MARY ANN GODFREY, m. JOHN BACHELDER of Northwood, b. Apl. 14, 1784, son of Jethro and Deborah (Leavitt), lived in Vershire, Vt. *Children:* 1708 EMALINE, b. ——; 1709 ELIZA, b. ——; 1710 HANNAH, b. ——, m. 1st, Aug. 26, 1849, JAMES M. BEAN of Newport, Vt.; m. 2nd, J. PEABODY of Manchester; 1711 MARY A., b. ——; 1712 JOHN, b. ——, m. —— KNOWLES; 1713 HARRIET, b. ——, m. —— GILBERT of Hartford, Vt.; 1714 CHARLES, b. ——; 1715 HIRAM, b. ——, d. in Cal.; 1716 JOSEPH, b. ——, m. JANETTE GODFREY of Vershire, Vt.

F559 Jonathan Locke, born in Kensington, Apl 6, 1762, married in Epsom, Feb. 6, 1785, ALICE (RUHUMA) PEARSONS,

SIXTH GENERATION 93

who was born July 12, 1763, died Nov. 7, 1854. He was a farmer in Epsom, elisted in Scott's Company Revolutionary War, July 11, 1780, and died May 27, 1803.
Children of the 6th Gen. b. in Epsom.
F1717 NAOMI, b. Sept. 5, 1786, m. March 19, 1807, GREENLEAF BRACKETT.
 1718 FLORINDA, b. Nov. 9, 1788, d. Epsom Jan. 3, 1790.
 1719 FLORINDA, b. Jan. 18, 1791, m. Oct. 11, 1810, DAVID LOCKE (See F2095), b. Oct. 19, 1788, d. March 19, 1863. Lived in Lyman, and she d. Jan. 11, 1880.
 1720 JOHN, b. Oct. 18, 1793, d. in Boscawen, Aug. 12, 1872; was a West India sailor in early life, was eccentric, and never married.
F1721 DAVID, b. Jan. 19, 1796, m. Dec. 23, 1818, ELIZABETH S. CHASE.
F1722 REBECCA, b. Apl. 15, 1798, m. Dec. 31, 1818, ISAAC TOWLE.
F1723 MARY, b. Sept. 10, 1800, m. Feb. 19, 1822, JAMES WEEKS.

F560 Annah (Hannah) Locke, born in Kensington, May 4, 1764, married in Epsom, March 5, 1789, HON. JOSIAH SANBORN son of Eliphalet (born in 1730 in Rye), and Margaret (Wallace). He was born in Epsom, Oct. 4, 1763, died June 14, 1843. She died Aug. 18, 1838. Josiah was a selectman nineteen years, one year a representative and three years a state senator.
Children of the 6th Gen. b. in Epsom.
F1724 FREDERICK, b. Oct. 28, 1789, m. March 20, 1816, LUCY SARGENT.
F1725 JAMES, b. Nov. 14, 1791, m. 1st, Dec. 29, 1814, ABIGAIL PARSONS # 1749; m. 2nd, NANCY TOWLE.
 1726 NANCY, b. Nov. 28, 1793, d. 1877, m. 1st, JOHN PERKINS; m. 2nd, ANDREW NEALEY of Northwood. *Children:* 1727 SARAH PERKINS, m. WILLARD WILLIAMS, a tailor in Manchester; 1728 DAU. NEALEY, m. ———— SMART; and a DAU. 1729 NEALEY, m. ———— WILLIAMS.
 1730 RACHEL, b. Jan. 3, 1796, m. Epsom, JOHN LOCKE (See F2097), Oct. 30, 1822.
F1731 HANNAH, b. Feb. 8, 1798, m. Jan. 11, 1821, BENJAMIN M. TOWLE.
 1732 JOSIAH, b. May 5, 1800, m. MRS. HARRIET (CHESLEY) BEAN, b. May 18, 1800. Lived in Medford, Mass., and d. 1882; had son: 1733 JOHN F., b. 1827, m. LYDIA WENTWORTH.
 1734 ELIPHALET, b. 1802, died young; and SALLY, b. 1804, died young.

F561 Mary (Ruhuma) Locke, born in Epsom, July 9, 1766, married in Epsom, Feb. 11, 1786, CALEB PEARSONS of Chichester. They were in Epsom until 1790, then moved into Canada, and she was lost at sea coming from the Provinces.
Children of the 6th Gen.
 1735 CALEB, b. ———, m. ———, and lived in Chichester. *Children:* 1736 CALEB; 1737 ELLEN; 1738 JULIA A., m. HENRY CROSS; 1739 GEORGE FRANKLIN, m. ELLEN KEYSER; 1740 AUGUSTA, m.

OTIS CROSS of Bristol; 1741 WILLIE, m. ROXY DOLOFF and d. 1899; 1742 MARY, m. ――― RECKUM.
1743 MARY, m. ――― DAVIS, settled in Canada, and had: 1744 DAU., m. WILLARD CENTRE; 1745 WILLIAM; 1746 PARSONS D., lived Barnston, Can.
1747 RUHUMA, m. ――― CRAM of Pittsfield, had no child of age.
1748 SALLY, m. ――― SMART, went west; had 2 sons and 2 daughters.
1749 ABIGAIL, b. March 4, 1797, m. Dec. 29, 1814, her cousin, JAMES SANBORN. (See F1725.)

F562 Elijah Locke, born in Epsom, May 4, 1768, married in Epsom, Oct. 28, 1792, LYDIA OSGOOD, who died Feb. 16, 1816. He married 2nd, Aug. 12, 1816, WIDOW DOLLY (BACHELDER) BROWN, who was born in Loudon, March 23, 1783, died July 14, 1857. She was the daughter of Moses Bachelder and Mary (Brown). He was a tanner and farmer in Epsom and Loudon and died Feb. 9, 1859.

Children of the 6th Gen. b. in Loudon.

1750 OSGOOD, b. 1795, d. unm. in Boscawen 1870; was a farmer in Loudon.
1751 MARY, b. ―――, d. Aug. 26, 1842, m. in Canterbury, June 7, 1815, JACOB MATTHEWS of Franklin, b. Northwood. *Children:* 1752 LOUISA L., b. Loudon, Nov. 1, 1815, m. ――― WALKER, and d. Andover, March 28, 1894; 1753 LIZZIE, b. ―――, m. GEORGE B. TRUE of MANCHESTER, b. 1857, son of Geo. H. and Maria; had 3 children.
1754 MOSES, b. 1799, m. Apl. 4, 1822, HARRIET BACHELDER of Loudon, who d. there Apl. 13, 1871, dau. of Libbe and Love (Blaisdell). He was farmer in Loudon, had no child and d. July 6, 1858.
1755 ISAAC, was a wanderer, had no trade, and d. unm. in Franklin, aged 50.
1756 KATHERINE J., d. Feb. 3, 1811, aged 7 months and 20 days.
1757 ELIZA, b. ―――, m. JOEL ELLIOTT of Topsham, Vt.
1758 HARRIS B., b. May 26, 1819 (2nd wife's child), m. 1st, Dec. 29, 1840, MARY C. HERBERT of Mason; m. 2nd, 1846-7, SARAH R. ADAMS, b. Mason, Sept. 16, 1821, d. Aug. 16, 1894, dau. of Dea. Jonas and Sally (Wright). He was a farmer in Epsom, went west in 1850, and d. in Princeton, Ill., March 7, 1861. *Child by 2nd wife:* 1759 SARAH FRANCES, b. Mason, Apl. 3, 1849, lived unm. with Adams family, and d. Greenville, Jan. 13, 1898.
F1760 IRA A. C., b. March 23, 1822, m. Apl. 12, 1843, MEHITABLE J. BROWN.
F1761 ELIJAH TRUE, b. July 26, 1827, m. March 14, 1849, HARRIET J. ALLEN.

F563 Richard Locke, born in Epsom, Sept. 20, 1770, married Dec. 28, 1797, SARAH MOSES, daughter of Sylvanus and Miriam (Young) of Epsom. He was drowned while logging at Short Falls, Epsom. His widow married 2nd, a GIRARD of Montreal, Can., who took the whole family to Canada with him.

SIXTH GENERATION

Children of the 6th Gen.

1762 MOSES, b. ——, was educated in Montreal, married and went to New York to educate his children; was a sea captain out of New Y., later came back to Epsom.

1763 ANNA, b. ——, m. a doctor, lived Grand River above Montreal, and her mother lived with them.

F565 James Munroe Locke, born in Epsom, March 4, 1776, married in Epsom, Nov. 28, 1799, ABIGAIL SHERBURNE of Ports. She was born July 17, 1775, died Sept. 29, 1859. He had a good education, having studied with Rev. Wm. Hazeltine at Epsom. He visited England, taught school in Virginia, returned to Epsom and in 1800 moved to Stanstead, Canada, where he lived and raised his family. He was killed by a horse March 29, 1845.

Children of the 6th Gen. b. Stanstead, Canada.

1764 LOUISA, b. May 15, 1801, d. Oct. 12, 1818.
F1765 JAMES MUNROE, b. Oct. 15, 1804, m. 1829, SALLY CASS.
1766 MARIA O., b. Aug. 4, 1806, d. Columbia, Mich., m. 1830, IVES WALLINGFORD of Stanstead, Can., b. Apl. 9, 1809, son of David and Abigail (Stoker). He settled as a farmer in Mich., 1836; *Children:* 1767 GEORGE, lived in Cal.; 1768 CHARLES, was unm.; 1769 MARION, m. —— WOODRUFF, lived Columbia, Mich., and had 1770 GEORGE and 1771 FRED; 1772 ANN, m. (——) PERRY, had a dau. 1773 CAROLINE; 1774 JAMES, lived in Kansas.
F1775 REV. WILLIAM SHERBURNE, b. Aug. 28, 1808, m. Aug. 27, 1833, CAROLINE DAME TEBBETTS.
1776 EDWARD J., b. March 30, 1810, d. June 30, 1814.
F1777 FLORINDA, b. March 6, 1812, m. March 9, 1844, OSCAR WYMAN.
1778 ABIGAIL, b. Sept. 26, 1815, d. unm. Barnstead, 1848.
F1779 EMALINE, b. Apl. 27, 1818, m. May 30, 1842, CAPT. MOSES W. COPP.
1780 EDWARD J., b. May 1, 1820, d. unmarried in Magog, 1871.

F566 Josiah Locke, born Nov. 10, 1757, married Bethia, daughter of Judge Blaney. He was at Bunker Hill, having enlisted June 17, 1775; was a Corporal in the Rhode Island service 1777, was discharged Jan. 5, 1778; appears on Capt. Parsons' pay roll Sept. 8, 1777, and finally was drowned at Isles of Shoals, Sept. 23, 1816. His widow married 2nd, Nov. 4, 1832, REV. DANIEL GALE of Palmira, Me.

Children of the 6th Gen. b. in Kensington.

1781 LYDIA, b. Aug. 1, 1784, m. in Kensington Sept. 16, 1804, ISAAC BROWN, a sea captain of Newburyport, Mass. *Children:* 1782 JAMES, was a sea captain, m. had no children, d. Merrimac, Mass.; 1783 ELIZABETH, m. —— MOODY, and had: 1784 SARGENT and 1785 ISABELLE; 1786 MARY, m. ——; 1786a ISAAC, m., was a

sea captain, no child, d. at sea; 1787 JOHN, m. ——, 2 children and wife drowned at Yarmouth, Me.
F1788 EUNICE, b. Dec. 12, 1785, m. 1st, Oct. 14, 1808, DAVID GEORGE; m. 2nd, NATHAN SMITH; m. 3rd, STEPHEN LITTLEFIELD.
1789 SALLY, b. Apl. 6, 1786, died young.
1790 DAVID, b. Feb. 7, 1791, m. No. Hampton, Sept. 1, 1814, ELIZABETH SANBORN, b. July 4, 1789, dau. of James and Betty (Blake); had a dau: 1791 ELIZABETH, died young. He was a sea captain of Newburyport.
1792 RUTH, b. Dec. 24, 1793, died young.
F1793 ELIZABETH, b. March 22, 1795, m. Jan. 21, 1812, JONATHAN MORRISON.
F1794 DOROTHY (DOLLY), b. Oct. 9, 1797, m. Dec. 2, 1821, WILLIAM PALMER.
F1795 OLIVER PEABODY, b. March 6, 1800, m. Jan. 17, 1826, SARAH A. SANBORN.
F1796 SALLY DALTON, b. Dec. 18, 1802, m. Dec. 12, 1826, REV. ASA LAMSON.
F1797 SAMUEL, b. Oct. 31, 1806, m. May 20, 1835, EMILINA GUESDON.
F1798 JOHN DAWLTON, b. Jan. 12, 1809, m. May 17, 1830, JULIA A. GOFF.

F567 Simon Locke, born Aug. 13, 1759, married MARY DOW, who was born Apl. 19, 1770, died Nov. 11, 1856. He lived at Fogg's Corner, Hampton Falls, in 1800, two years later moved to Seabrook and died there Sept. 14, 1833 or 35. Mary Dow Locke was said to be the mother of 18 children and to be a pensioner of the War of Revolution.

Children of the 6th Gen. b. in Seabrook.

F1799 HUBBARD, b. 1802, m. Oct. 20, 1823, JENNIE DOW.
F1800 ELIZA, b. Nov. 12, 1805, m. Aug. 7, 1833, EDWARD GOVE.
1801 GILMAN, b. ——, enlisted in Navy and d. before the war.
F1802 LYDIA, b. ——, m. MESHACK or CALEB ROLLINS.
1803 MARY ANN, nothing known.
1804 PATIENCE, b. ——, m. No. Hampton, Jan. 15, 1818, BERLEY BARTLETT, had 2 sons.
1805 REBECCA, b. ——, m. EDWARD CLOUGH, a Quaker, who preached in Seab. *Children:* 1806 MARY, m. HIRAM JEFFERSON; and 1807 DAVID, died young.
1808 WILLIAM, died by accident aged 19.

F568 Edward Locke, born Dec. 15, 1760, married Nov. 27, 1781, BETTY PERKINS of Kensington, who was born Sept. 26, 1761; living in 1820. He lived in Kensington, was in New Hampshire Militia March 4, 1831, pensioned at $23.33 per year, Rockingham County. He died Aug. 18, 1834.

SIXTH GENERATION

Children of the 6th Gen. b. in Kensington.
F1809 LYDIA, b. Apl. 30, 1782, m. June 1800, MOSES PRESCOTT.
1810 BETTY, b. March 30, 1786, d. March 16, 1788.
1811 TIMOTHY, b. Sept. 11, 1789, d. Feb. 9, 1794.
1812 BETTY, b. June 1, 1794.
1813 LAVINIA, b. Sept. 24, 1801, m. Oct. 9, 1817, JOHN GILMAN of Exeter, lived in New York.
1814 TIMOTHY (probably).

F569 James Locke, born Nov. 14, 1762, married 1st, MRS. TABITHA (EDWARDS) (ORDIORNE); married 2nd, Nov. 28, 1803, MRS. SALLY (STICKNEY) (DAWLTON). He was a sea captain, later an inn keeper in Andover, Mass., and died Sept. 13, 1835.
Children of the 6th Gen. b. in Salisbury, Mass.
1815 DAVID, b. June 16, 1791, d. at sea Apl. 30, 1811.
1816 JAMES ORDIORNE, b. Feb. 22, 1796, was a sea captain and died by accident in Boston, Sept. 30, 1840.
1817 HIRAM, b. Dec. 12, 1800, died at sea Sept. 28, 1820.

F570 John Locke, born in Seabrook, Feb. 29, 1764, married in Concord, Nov. 30, 1790, MOLLY SANBORN of Seabrook, daughter of Dudley S. and Mary (Green). She was born in Hampton Falls, Sept. 23, 1767, died Oct. 7, 1844. He was a grocer in Seabrook and died Apl. 1, 1822.
Children of the 6th Gen. b. in Seabrook.
F1818 MARY, b. March 14, 1792, m. Feb. 14, 1814, ENOCH WINKLEY.
1819 JOHN, b. Nov. 22, 1793; was a merchant in Apalachicola, Fla., and d. there unmarried June 27, 1841.
F1820 CLARISSA, b. June 1, 1797, m. Oct. 15, 1818, RICHARD DODGE.
F1821 DUDLEY S., b. Jan. 19, 1800, m. 1832, CAROLINE W. NUDD.
F1822 SOPHRONIA, b. Apl. 8, 1805, m. Oct. 20, 1830, EDMUND NOYES CLARKE.
F1823 JAMES, b. Apl. 22, 1807, m. Jan. 11, 1841, HANNAH P. CHESLEY.
F1824 ADALINE, b. Feb. 17, 1811, m. Jan. 18, 1835, JOHN PHILBRICK.

F571 Blake Locke, born in Seabrook, Feb. 20, 1766, married SALLY BROWN, who was born in 1763, died in Seabrook, Apl. 19, 1827. He was in Capt. Jos. Nason's Company Sept. 12–29, 1814, and died of small pox in Seabrook June 4, 1840.
Children of the 6th Gen. b. Seabrook.
1825 SALLY LOCKE, b. 1792, m. Seab. Feb. 27, 1818, BENIAH TITCOMB of Seab., had 4 children. (A Beniah Titcomb of Derry, m. 1828, MARY E. STACY; also Beniah Titcomb of D. m. 1844, MARY J. MCMURPHY; possibly same man.)
F1826 NANCY, b. 1794, m. July 6, 1812, NATHANIEL GOVE.

F1827 BENJAMIN, b. 1795, m. MRS. MATILDA (JANVRIN) FELTCH.
1828 LOWELL, b. Kensington, March 2, 1798, m. SUSAN JANVRIN of Seabrook who d. when a young woman. He was a storekeeper in S. and "died out in a boat." They had no children so say the family. The census says Lowell Locke had one boy and one girl under ten years in 1820.

F573 Lydia Locke, born in Seabrook, Feb. 3, 1770, died in Seabrook Feb. 3, 1820, married EDWARD GOVE, born Seabrook, Jan. 25, 1771, son of Winthrop and Elizabeth (Ring). He married 2nd, WIDOW LOCKE BROWN, was a boat builder, and died in Seabrook Sept. 13, 1832.
Children of 6th Gen. b. in Seabrook.
1829 MARY, b. Sept. 16, 1798, d. 1872, m. NATHANIEL DOLE.
1830 ELIZA, b. March 3, 1801, d. 1841, m. BELCHER DOLE.
F1831 DAVID LOCKE, b. July 14, 1803, m. HARRIET LOWELL.

F574 Joseph Locke, born in Seabrook, Feb. 22, 1772, married 1st, unknown; married 2nd, Feb. 12, 1804, SARAH STANWOOD who was born Feb. 8, 1774, died March 17, 1851. He conveyed land to Danl. Thompson in 1823, lived in Sanbornton and died there Dec. 15, 1845.
Children of the 6th Gen. b. in Sanbornton.
1832 JOSEPH S., b. 1798, m. March 11, 1832, JANE H. CROSS, b. Northwood. He lived in Minnesota, died there June 22, 1875. *Children:* 1833 NELSON; 1834 HERBERT, who married.
1835 WILLIAM (a William b. Sanb., d. Pittsfield, Apl. 1, 1868, aged 57 years, 10 months, 14 days, m., a farmer, son of Joseph and Mary).
F1836 HIRAM D., m. 1st, HARRIET YOUNG; m. 2nd, unknown.
1837 PHILIP AUBIN, b. 1809, m. JULIA WEED of Troy, N. Y., b. Jan. 2, 1825, d. Sept. 14, 1893, at Troy where she had lived since 1861. He was in the wholesale fur trade in Boston, left much property and died in Lexington, Mass., Sept. 16, 1861.
F1838 MARY J., b. ——, m. Oct. 20, 1831, Capt. JOHN W. SANBORN.
1839 CAROLINE S., b. May 1807, m. in Lynn, Mass., Nov. 9, 1834, CALVIN NOURSE of Bedford, Mass., had one dau. and four sons.

F575 Jeremiah H. Locke, born in Seabrook, May 5, 1776, married 1802, LOUISA SANBORN of Seabrook, daughter of Dudley S. and Hannah (Hook). She was born in 1776, died 1855. He was a boat builder and mason in Seabrook and died there Dec. 18, 1818.
Children of the 6th Gen. b. in Seabrook.
F1840 CYNTHIA, b. Dec. 29, 1801,? m. Dec. 29, 1818 (Nov. 20, 1822), EDWARD D. GREELY.

Philip Aubin Locke 1837

LOCKE FAMILY REUNION, 1894

SIXTH GENERATION 99

F1841 CHARLES, b. 1810, m. 1st, ELIZA CHASE; m. 2nd, MRS. BETSEY (JANVRIN) SCRIBNER.
1842 LUCINDA, b. ——, m. THOMAS CHASE, bro. of Eliza.
F1843 JEREMIAH A., b. Apl. 1819, m. MRS. LUCINDA (GREEN) SANBORN.

F577 Betsey Locke, born in Seabrook, Apl. 22, 1786, married 1st, MOSES MERRILL; married 2nd, THOMAS EATON, a farmer in Salisbury, Mass. She died Sept. 4, 1864. Moses Merrill hung himself on the day his wife moved. (Evidently they had moving days then.)
Children of the 6th Gen. all Merrill's.
1864 MOSES, m. 1st, SOPHRONIA TUCKER of Salisbury, Mass.; m. 2nd, SARAH GRIFFIN. They had: 1865 LAVONIA, m. —— PRATT.
1866 JAMES, b. ——, m. DIANTHA FOOTE of Woburn, Mass.; had: 1867 JAMES MERRILL, who lives Boston.
1868 WINGATE, ran away, probably died at sea.
1869 JOSEPH, m. OCTAVIA FENDERSON of Saco, Me. *Children:* 1870 CLARENCE; 1871 LIZZIE, m. —— BENNETT; 1872 MARY I., m. LEONARD BROWN; 1873 CLARA.
1874 JOHN, m. SOPHIA GOODWIN of Amesbury, Mass. Had: 1875 MARIA, m. —— WALKER.
1876 CLARA, m. DARIUS MORSE of Salem, Mass. *Children:* 1877 WINGATE; 1878 EMMA.
1879 MARY, m. CHARLES MANSON of Salisbury, Mass.

F578 Jane Page, born in South Hampton, Sept. 3, 1763, married Apl. 1, 1784, STEPHEN BACHELDER, son of Stephen and Elizabeth (Tucker). He was born Feb. 12, 1760, died May 28, 1808. She died July 17, 1826. They lived in Deerfield.
Children of the 6th Gen. b. in Deerfield.
1880 STEPHEN, b. May 20, 1785, m. 1st, Dec. 8, 1808, BETSEY CRAM; m. 2nd, HANNAH MORRILL. He died in Ohio, June 1856.
F1881 PAGE, b. July 8, 1788, m. Feb. 28, 1811, BETSEY R. DARRAH.
1882 BETSEY, b. Apl. 15, 1790, d. unm. Aug. 30, 1860.
1883 NABBY, b. June 27, 1794, d. Apl. 27, 1843, m. JOSEPH E. BARTLETT of Deer.
F1884 JENNIE, b. Oct. 22, 1796, m. Feb. 20, 1822, JOSHUA LANE.
1885 JAMES, b. Sept. 22, 1799, m. SALLY MORRILL, and d. Manchester, Sept. 1876.
1886 DEBORAH, b. Dec. 14, 1801, d. Jan. 1808.

F579 Moses Page, born in South Hampton, July 1, 1769, married 1st, JOANNA BOHONON, born 1764, died Oct. 4, 1811, the daughter of Jacob; married 2nd, March 12, 1812, JUDITH BEAN, daughter of Phineas and Judith (Snow). She was born in Salisbury, Mass., March 21, 1786, died Aug. 31, 1869. He lived in Salisbury and died Nov. 12, 1835.

Children of the 6th Gen.

1887 MARY, b. March 8, 1813, m. Nov. 14, 1843, ISRAEL PALMER, of Garland, Me.
1888 JOHN B., b. Apl. 17, 1815, d. unm. Apl. 1851.
1889 DAVID, b. Dec. 7, 1816, m. 1850, ELIZABETH AKERMEN, lived in Alexandria.
1890 MOSES, b. Oct. 22, 1818, m. 1st, HANNAH WALKER; m. 2nd, MRS. ——— FOGG, 1838, and had 6 children in Garland, Me.
1891 JOSHUA B., b. Apl. 26, 1822, m. 1st, 1850, JANE PHELPS, who d. 1853, m. 2nd, MRS. THAIS TYLER, 1854, had 5 children.
1892 BENJAMIN F., b. May 24, 1825, m. 1st, Apl. 1848, HARRIET A. DANFORTH; had 2 children. She d. Sept. 2, 1851; m. 2nd, 1866, ELVIRA C. PEASLEE.

F581 John Page, born in South Hampton, June 10, 1773, married Jan. 24, 1799, HANNAH BACHELDER, daughter of Capt. Carter and Huldah (Moulton). She was born June 28, 1772, died Sept. 6, 1893. He was farmer, carpenter, and cooper, lived in Sanbornton and died June 9, 1852.

Children of the 6th Gen. b. in Sanbornton.

1893 JAMES, b. Jan. 15, 1800, m. ETMAR GREENLEAF, lived in Haverhill, and both died in Norwich, Conn.
1894 NANCY, b. Oct. 11, 1802, m. ISAAC V. GREENLEAF of Groton.
1895 CALVIN, b. Jan. 1, 1806, m. 1st, LUCY COLEMAN; m. 2nd ABIGAIL S. COLEMAN, and lived in Sanbornton.
1896 JOHN, b. Oct. 29, 1808, lived unmarried in Tilton.
1897 HANNAH, b. Oct. 2, 1814, lived unmarried in Sanbornton.
1898 WILLIAM B., b. July 14, 1818, d. July 22, 1820.

F587 Hannah Dearborn, born July 23, 1768, married July 28, 1795, ENOCH GOVE of Kensington, son of Obediah and Mary (Dow). He was born Aug. 10, 1764, died Dec. 3, 1828. She died July 2, 1842.

Child of the 6th Gen.

1899 HANNAH GOVE, m. EMERY BROWN; had ASA W. of Cincinnati, Ohio.

F588 Asa Dearborn, born Aug. 12, 1771, married Jan. 1, 1798, RUHUMA CHOATE, daughter of Simon, a Revolutionary soldier, and Ruth (Thompson). She was born in Salisbury, Sept. 19, 1773, died July 21, 1847. They lived in Kingston, Weare, Salisbury, Mass., Portsmouth, and he died in Boston, June 8, 1829.

Children of the 6th Gen. b. in Portsmouth.

1900 GILMAN, b. Apl. 10, 1799, d. Apl. 18, 1862, m. Feb. 17, 1823, SARAH S. BERRY, # 1035, of Rye, b. Sept. 4, 1801, d. May 13, 1877, lived in Ports., had no children but adopted a dau. of William?.

SIXTH GENERATION

F1901 FRANCES, b. May 19, 1801, m. 1823, ELDER MOSES HOWE.
1902 IRENA, b. Apl. 15, 1803, d. Aug. 15, 1870, m. 1st, Oct. 15, 1827, DANIEL WALDRON of Ports., b. May 4, 1798, d. Wakefield, Oct. 7, 1843; m. 2nd, Nov. 17, 1859, DR. GEORGE ODELL of Stratham, b. Apl. 13, 1793, d. July 23, 1873.
1903 RUHUMA, b. May 25, 1805, m. Dec. 13, 1827, JOHN KENT, b. Rochester, Oct. 13, 1799, d. Sept. 23, 1843; m. 2nd, JOSEPH A. WALKER, b. Ports., 1802, d. July 16, 1854. Had one son: 1904 JOHN H. KENT, b. Barnstead, Oct. 10, 1828, d. ———, m. ADELINE PENNIMAN, and had: 1905 HORACE P. KENT of Wollaston, Mass.
F1906 JULIA A., b. Nov. 27, 1806, m. Nov. 30, 1834, DAVISON WEBSTER.
1907 CATHERINE, b. Feb. 10, 1808, d. aged 14 days.
1908 MARY, b. Sept. 22, 1809, d. May 15, 1885, m. Oct. 10, 1844, JOHN H. CHAPMAN, b. July 18, 1803, lived in New Bedford, Mass., no children.
F1909 DANIEL G., b. Aug. 24, 1811, m. Apl. 23, 1851, LUCINDA BERGER.

F591 Sarah Dearborn, born July 24, 1778, married March 7, 1800, JOSIAH TILTON, son of Samuel and Deborah (Bachelder). He was born in Deerfield, Feb. 28, 1778, died Aug. 20, 1860. She died April 16, 1864.

Children of the 6th Gen.

1910 GEORGE P., b. Nov. 26, 1800, m. 1st, ELIZA DAKIN; m. 2nd, MARY TRASK.
1911 HARRIET, b. July 21, 1802, m. MARSHALL STAPLES, and had: 1912 SARAH T.
F1913 MARY J., b. Aug. 8, 1804, m. Jan. 8, 1833, BENJAMIN F. BUTLER.
1914 IRENE, b. March 23, 1806, d. Apl. 4, 1889, unmarried.
1915 SAMUEL, b. Dec. 15, 1807, m. 1st, HANNAH FULLER; m. 2nd, ELIZA PATCH, and had: 1916 ALICE.
1917 REV. ALBERT F., b. Oct. 16, 1809, m. REBECCA ELIZABETH MOOR, no children.
1918 SARAH TRUE, b. Nov. 10, 1811, d. Nov. 16, 1834.
1919 REV. JOSIAH H., b. Oct. 31, 1814, d. Apl. 24, 1905, m. 1st, MARY EMERY; m. 2nd, ELIZA EMERY; m. 3rd, WIDOW CAROLINE GRISWOLD.
F1920 REV. JEREMIAH, b. Sept. 16, 1816, m. 1st, ABBY S. FREEZE; m. 2nd, MARTHA JACKMAN.
1921 JULIA, b. Feb. 21, 1819, d. Oct. 12, 1860.
1922 ASA, a twin, died young.
1922a FRANCES, died young.

F594 Nathaniel Weare, born in Hampton Falls, March 21, 1757, married March 7, 1793, **Mary Locke,** born Deerfield, Apl. 19, 1766. He was town clerk of Deerfield from 1796–1826, and an extra good penman.

Children of 6th Gen. b. in Deerfield.
1923 CAROLINE WAINWRIGHT, b. Feb. 23, 1794, d. Apl, 17, 1799.
F1924 MESHECH, b. Feb. 18, 1795, m. June 8, 1820, MERIBAH GREEN.
1925 HANNAH REDFORD, b. Nov. 25, 1796, m. Feb. 1829, BAILEY TENNEY of Chester.
1926 CAROLINE W., b. Feb. 1, 1802, d. in Wisconsin, Jan. 29, 1887.

F595 —— Locke, son. Name unknown.
Child of 6th Gen.
F1930 JAMES LOCKE, b. 1800 (?), m. MARY TOWNSEND.

F596 John Locke, born in Barnstead, March 18, 1779, married in Barrington, SALLY STANTON, April 11, 1799. She died 1821. He was a cattle dealer, lived at Lockes Corner, Barnstead, and died March 16, 1853.
Children of the 6th Gen. b. in Barnstead.
1936 MARY B., b. Dec. 1799, d. June 1861, m. Apl. 17, 1817, JOSEPH DREW of Barnstead, who deserted his family. *Children:* 1937 CORTES, b. Oct. 1817, m. twice and had: 1938 FINANDO and 1939 CORTES; 1940 GEORGE, b. 1819, was a shoe manufacturer in Washington, D. C., and died in Georgetown, 1870; 1941 ASA, b. 1821, was a music teacher, d. in Concord, 1871.
F1942 ELIPHALET, b. July 9, 1801, m. Sept. 1820, SALLY STANTON.
F1943 TAMSON, b. Aug. 1804, m. Oct. 20, 1825, WILLIAM BERRY.
F1944 PHINEAS, b. July 11, 1806, m. Nov. 21 (27), 1830, MARY PINKHAM.
F1945 LOVIE, b. Dec. 1808, m. 1833, JOSEPH WENTWORTH PERKINS.
1946 JULIA, b. Oct. 9, 1810, d. Sept. 5, 1881.

F597 Edward Locke, born in Barnstead, 1781, married in Rochester, Oct. 3, 1805, ELIZABETH MEADER of Rochester, daughter of Nathl. and Mary. She was born July 6, 1781, died in Rochester, Apl. 19, 1852. All belonged to the Society of Friends. He died in Rochester, Nov. 4, 1853.
Children of the 6th Gen. probably b. in Barnstead.
1947 MARY, b. July 26, 1806, d. a widow Feb. 19, 1844, m. in Rochester, Sept. 19, 1827, OLIVER EVANS of Hiram, Me.; lived there. *Children:* 1948 CHARLES; 1949 IVORY.
F1950 ANNIE, b. Apl. 28, 1808, m. Oct. 4, 1832, AMOS VARNEY.
F1951 JAMES, b. Aug. 8, 1811, m. 1836, ELLEN C. KIMBALL.
1952 LOUISA, b. Feb. 26, 1810, d. Apl. 1, 1810.
1953 IVORY, b. Aug. 7, 1813, d. March 18, 1829.
F1954 CHARLOTTE, b. Oct. 8, 1815 or 17, m. 1st, Dec. 29, 1836, CHARLES P. KIMBALL; m. 2nd, 1871, JACOB B. SMITH.
F1955 SARAH W., b. March 10, 1818, m. June 13, 1837, OBADIAH VARNEY.
F1956 ELIZABETH, b. July 6, 1820, m. 1st, Sept. 2, 1841, LEWIS THOMPSON; m. 2nd, Nov. 20, 1864, ISRAEL DURGIN.
F1957 LYDIA M., b. Aug. 10, 1822, m. Feb. 2, 1842, STEPHEN M. GOVE.

SIXTH GENERATION

F598 James Locke, born in North Barnstead, 1783, married ABIGAIL NUTTER, Apl. 14, 1808 (Barnstead rec. 1807). She was born 1787, died 1869. He was selectman in Barnstead 1800–3, and died 1822.

Children of the 6th Gen.
F1958 SAMSON B., b. 1808, m. June 26, 1828, ESTHER NUTTER.
F1959 ENOCH, b. Aug. 21, 1811, m. Dec. 26, 1843, MARTHA B. LANE.
F1960 MARY ANN, b. 1817, m. June 3, 1838, JOHN HILL.

F599 Lovie Locke, born in North Barnstead, May 29, 1786, married 1807, ELIPHALET NUTTER, son of John, who was a Revolutionary soldier. He was born 1780, died 1855. She died 1861.

Children of the 6th Gen. b. in Barnstead.
1961 ELIZA, b. May 25, 1809, d. Concord, Jan. 3, 1890, m. ——— BUNKER.
1962 MARY, b. July 30, 1811.
1963 JOHN L., b. July 31, 1812.
1964 LUCINDA, b. July 17, 1816.
1965 ELIPHALET S., b. Nov. 26, 1819, d. Concord, Nov. 22, 1897, m. 1845, SYLVIA M. BLANCHARD of Lowell. At 18, he was a lieutenant of militia; was in business at Barnstead in 1844; 1855 was in Concord, then 5 years in N. Y., and 11 years in Lowell, holding positions in R. R. and other companies; had a dau.: 1966 ADA R., d. aged 17.
1967 LOVIE G., b. May 17, 1822, died young.
1968 NANCY, b. July 24, 1823.
1969 LOVIE, b. March 8, 1826.
1970 JAMES N., b. Dec. 30, 1828.
1971 MARY, b. Nov. 20, 1832.

F600 Enoch Locke, born in North Barnstead, 1790, married SALLY BERRY of Strafford, lived in Barnstead and died in 1872.

Children of the 6th Gen. b. in Barnstead.
1972 LUCY C., b. Sept. 11, 1815, d. in Barnstead, March 17, 1889, unm.
F1973 JACOB B., b. Jan. 15, 1818, m. 1840, PARMELIA H. DOW.
1974 JAMES, b. Sept. 30, 1820, m. Sept. 23, 1849, SARAH F. ELKINS; had no children. He was in business at Locke's Corner, North Barnstead and d. Nov. 17, 1879.

F601 Abigail Locke, born in Sandown, June 29, 1768, married JOSIAH FULLER. He came from Sandown to Bristol in 1812, thence to New Found Lake; was a carpenter and tailor and died about 1843.

Children of the 6th Gen. b. in Bristol.
1975 POLLY, b. March 21, 1791, m. ——— SMITH and lived in Boston.
1976 LEVI, b. Jan. 6, 1793, m. ———, lived and died in Exeter.
F1977 RACHEL, b. March 10, 1795, m. Nov. 12, 1812, NATHAN TIRRILL.

F1978 JOSIAH, b. 1802, m. 1st, MARY PIKE; m. 2nd, —— HUCKINS.
1979 CLARKE, b. 1808, m. COMFORT MOSES of Bridgewater, b. 1798, d. Apl. 27, 1875. He d. in Bridgewater May 4, 1875.
F1980 ABIGAIL, b. ——, m. THOMAS ROBERT EMMONS who m. 2nd, BETSEY WEBSTER in 1866.
1981 RUSSELL, died aged 14. 1982 DOROTHY, d. unmarried, insane.

F602 Benjamin Locke, born in Sandown, Apl. 10, 1770, married March 17, 1796, HANNAH FAVOR, daughter of Cutting. She was born in Hill, Aug. 6, 1776, died in Bristol, Nov. 15, 1825. He married 2nd, July 23, 1826, NANCY GURDY, daughter of Jacob. She was born March 11, 1788, died Apl. 15, 1866 (1878). He settled in Bristol in 1790, and died there Apl. 9, 1858. Benjamin lived with his uncle Thomas, built a house before marriage which was destroyed by fire in 1822 and, although poor, he rebuilt it. He was a man of character and influence. The whole family were Methodists and at revivals, his shouts could be heard a mile away.

Children of the 6th Gen. b. in Bristol.

F1983 FAVOR, b. Apl. 21, 1797, m. Jan. 30, 1821, SALLY C. DOLOFF, # 1997.
F1984 ROXY, b. Dec. 3, 1798, m. Dec. 2, 1819, LEVI DOLOFF, # 1996.
F1985 SHERBURNE, b. Apl. 10, 1801, m. Sept. 26, 1822, SALLY I. HILLS.
F1986 LEVINA, b. Jan. 29, 1805, m. Sept. 16, 1824, HENRY WELLS.
F1987 JOANNA, b. Apl. 6, 1807, m. March 13, 1826, JACOB WEBSTER.
1988 PHILENA F., b. March 1, 1809, d. Bristol May 20, 1898, m. May 20, 1857, TIMOTHY WIGGIN of Bridgewater, b. March 1, 1809. They had no children and he d. March 31, 1890.
F1989 BENJAMIN, b. Apl. 17, 1810, m. Apl. 18, 1835, HARRIET MASON.
F1990 HANNAH F., b. June 12, 1812, m. May 29, 1832, KIAH WELLS.
F1991 SALLY D., b. Sept. 4, 1814, m. June 28, 1837, WINTHROP R. FELLOWS.
F1992 LEVI, b. May 15, 1817, m. 1st, July 18, 1839, SUSAN GILMAN; m. 2nd Feb. 13, 1884, MRS. SARAH P. (CARTER) ROBINSON.
F1993 DOROTHY SARGENT, b. March 25, 1819, m. July 18, 1837, MITCHELL H. PAGE.
F1994 HARRIET, b. Jan. 14, 1822, m. Apl. 11, 1839, PHILIP S. DRAKE.
Second wife's child:
F1995 SUSAN D., b. Feb. 11, 1828, m. Dec. 12, 1850, MILO FELLOWS.

F603 Rachel Locke, born in Rye, Oct. 15, 1772, married in Chester, Nov. 30, 1793, ABRAHAM DOLOFF, of Rye or Sandown, son of Nicholas D. and Sally (Clough). He was born Aug. 27, 1768, died in Bristol, May 15, 1855, was a Methodist, farmer and carpenter, settling in Bristol in 1793. Rachel died Bristol, May 11, 1860.

SIXTH GENERATION

Children of the 6th Gen. b. in Bristol or Bridgewater.
1996 LEVI LOCKE, b. Nov. 9, 1795, m. Dec. 2, 1819, ROXY LOCKE. (See F1984.)
1997 SALLY CLOUGH, b. May 30, 1798, m. Jan. 30, 1821, FAVOR LOCKE. (See F1983.)
F1998 SUSAN SANBORN, b. Dec. 9, 1800, m. Nov. 9, 1819, SAMUEL BROWN.
1999 NICHOLAS BLAISDELL, b. Feb. 6, 1803, m. 1st, Jan. 29, 1851, MRS. HARRIET (MASON) LOCKE, b. July 22, 1814, d. Nov. 16, 1856; m. 2nd, RHODA ALDRICH, b. March 16, 1816, d. Bristol, Sept. 29, 1885, dau. of Doctor Aldrich; he was a lumber mfr. for 20 years in Bristol, d. in Woodstock, July 13, 1892. *Children:* 2000 MASON D., b. Franconia, Nov. 10, 1852, m. Dec. 14, 1876, EMMA E. HANSON, d. Bristol Hospital, March 12, 1902, lived in Lincoln and Woodstock; 2001 LOREN, b. Franconia, Dec. 17, 1854, lived in Franconia and died about 1900.
F2002 MARY, b. June 9, 1805, m. Dec. 15, 1825, JOSEPH R. MOORE.
2003 MARGARET SANBORN, b. Nov. 28, 1807, d. Aug. 17, 1868, m. Feb. 11, 1829, JONATHAN EMMONS, b. Jan. 25, 1802. He m. 2nd, MRS. SARAH EMERSON, was a farmer in Bristol, and d. Oct. 19, 1880. *Children:* 2004 LAVINIA; 2005 GILBERT B.; 2006 ALVIRA; 2007 CHARLES; These with two others died young; also, 2008 LEROY S., d. unm. 1864, aged 28; 2009 SYLVESTER, m. and d. aged 32; 2609a CHARLES G., b. Sept. 20, 1849; was clerk in Legislature, and law student, d. unm. N. Y. City, March 7, 1886.
F2010 ALMIRA SMITH, b. Dec. 14, 1810, m. Feb. 14, 1832, JOHN ROBY.
F2011 RACHEL LOCKE, b. Apl. 24, 1814, m. March 11, 1834, CALVIN SWEET.
F2012 ABRAM, b. March 20, 1818, m. Feb. 22 1838. LYDIA NELSON.

F613 Levi Locke, born in Bridgewater, Dec. 22, 1780, married Sept. 30, 1804, SALLY CLEMENT who was born in Penacook, Feb. 28, 1787, died Apl. 15, 1859. They settled in Barnston, Can., where he died June 8, 1837.

Children of 6th Gen. b. at Barnston, Canada.
F2013 BETSEY, b. Nov. 23, 1805, m. Feb. 23, 1823, JOHN M. MOSHER.
2014 SALLY, b. Dec. 1, 1807, d. March 28, 1811.
2015 ALMEDA, b. Sept. 23, 1809, d. Feb. 21, 1811.
2016 ALMEDA, b. Nov. 26, 1811, d. Jan. 16, 1814.
2017 LEVI, b. Jan. 19, 1814, d. unm. Feb. 23, 1843.
F2018 CHLOE, b. Jan. 16, 1816, m. Oct. 17, 1832, GUY ALDRICH.
2019 MITCHELL, b. May 26, 1818, d. Dec. 24, 1818.
F2020 LOUISA, b. Nov. 8, 1819, m. June 29, 1841, WILLIAM BURROUGHS.
F2021 AMANDA, b. Feb. 13, 1822, m. Aug. 25, 1846, THOMAS E. COOPER.
F2022 THOMAS, b. June 16, 1824, m. July 16, 1846, LYDIA EMERSON HOWARD.
2023 SALLY, b. Apl. 20, 1826, d. Jan. 15, 1855, m. May 31, 1853, WALTER S. BALDWIN, b. May 12, 1823; had: 2024 SARAH F., b. Jan. 8, 1855, d. Jan. 10, 1855.
2025 LUCY, b. May 27, 1829, d. Nov. 1906, m. 1st, March 13, 1856, JOHN SHERRAR, b. March 2, 1825, d. Apl. 3, 1861; had: 2026 WILLIAM

ELLSWORTH, b. Aug. 29, 1859, d. Apl. 12, 1897, m. Feb. 1, 1886, CLARA BELLE STEVENS, b. June 14, 1862. Lucy m. 2nd, March 26, 1872, ENOCH FOGG OSGOOD, b. July 21, 1822, d. Apl. 6, 1902. Two children died at birth.

F626 Patience Woodbridge, born in Andover, Mass., Feb. 4, 1756, married Dec. 17, 1789, her cousin WOODBRIDGE GRAFTON, son of Joseph and Elizabeth (Woodbridge). He was born Apl. 14, 1763; lived in Salem, Mass.

Children of the 6th Gen.
2027 GEORGE W., b. Dec. 31, 1790, drowned Patagonia, S. A.
2028 WILLIAM, b. Sept. 6, 1792, d. July 16, 1793.
2029 ANNA F., b. Jan. 15, 1794, d. July 10, 1869, m. Sept. 24, 1815, JOHN W. FENNO, and had 5 children.
2030 ELIZABETH W., b. Apl. 1, 1797, m. May 10, 1818, ROBERT BROCKHOUSE, and had 2 children.

F627 Jonathan Locke, born in Rye, Jan. 1, 1759, married Nov. 23, 1785, OLIVE RAND of New Castle, daughter of Nathaniel and Mary (Leavitt). She was born Apl. 5, 1762. He was in the Revolutionary War Capt. Parsons' Co. in the Expedition to Rhode Island, Aug. 4 to Aug. 27, 1778; also in Capt. Hall's Co., 1778. He was a farmer in Rye and about the year 1800 moved to the Island of New Castle where he was farmer, selectman, and constable 1801–22 and died there 1842. Soon after returning from the war, he planted the two large elm trees in front of the old parsonage near the library at Rye Center, which are now in good condition.

Children of the 6th Gen. B. in New Castle.
F2031 JONATHAN, bapt. Nov. 18, 1787, m. Dec. 24, 1812, MARY VENNARD; m. 2nd, Oct. 10, 1842, EUNICE QUINCY.
2032 WILLIAM, b. Feb. 10, 1788, d. Feb. 6, 1869, was a sailor and supposed to be the last survivor of the ship *Constitution* fight, and was given a Military Funeral.
F2033 NABBY, b. Dec. 27, 1789, m. Nov. 1, 1807 (Feb. 21, 1808), WILLIAM NEAL.
F2034 JOSEPH L., b. March 1792, m. Nov. 29, 1816, SALLIE L. WEDGWOOD.
2035 MICHAEL, b. 1794, d. unm. aged 20.
F2036 MARY OLIVE, b. Dec. 25, 1796, m. Nov. 25, 1821, ASA WATSON.
2037 SARAH A., b. 1799, died young.
F2038 JOHN, b. Aug. 10, 1800, m. 1st, Dec. 14, 1820, MARTHA RAND of Rye; m. 2nd, Oct. 13, 1847, MRS. ALMIRA (SHAW) LEAR.

F630 Abigail Locke, born in Rye, July 21, 1764, married March 18, 1785, JONATHAN JENNESS, son of Joseph and Mary

SIXTH GENERATION

(Dow). He was born July 25, 1760, was a farmer in Rye and died 1844 (?). She died May 24, 1844.
Children of the 6th Gen. b. in Rye.
2039 POLLY, b. May 15, 1785, d. Oct. 15, 1853, m. May 11, 1809, JAMES MARDEN, b. Apl. 21, 1784, d. Nov. 5, 1851; had: 2040 WILLIAM, b. Dec. 24, 1810, d. Jan. 15, 1883; m. 1832, LUCY ANN GARLAND, b. 1812, d. 1870.
2040aNABBY, b. May 9, 1789, d. July 10, 1789.
2041 JONATHAN, b. May 29, 1791, d. July 11, 1870, m. June 30, 1814, ABIGAIL JENNESS, b. 1791, d. Oct. 17, 1818; had: 2042 OLIVER PETER, d. Oct. 3, 1818.
2043 JOSEPH, b. July 27, 1795, d. March 16, 1873, m. Dec. 19, 1824, POLLY L. GARLAND, dau. of Peter and Mehitable (Seavey), b. Dec. 12, 1799, d. Aug. 13, 1877, had: 2044 URI HARVEY, b. July 10, 1827, m. 1st, May 25, 1851, MARTHA H. BROWN, b. Apl. 26, 1832; m. 2nd, Feb. 23, 1890, SARAH L. GARLAND, b. May 9, 1860.
2045 ABIGAIL L., b. Apl. 3, 1801, d. Apl. 1867, m. Dec. 31, 1826, JONATHAN PALMER, b. Feb. 20, 1800, d. Aug. 8, 1881; lived in Kensington.
2046 EMILY, b. March 24, 1807, d. Aug. 15, 1866, m. Nov. 29, 1835, SAMUEL H. RAND, b. Apl. 28, 1803, d. Jan. 5, 1876 son of Joseph and Olive (Marden); had: 2047 JONATHAN JENNESS, b. Dec. 14, 1838, m. June 11, 1865, MARTHA A. MARDEN, b. May 20, 1846.

F631 John Locke, born in Rye, July 15, 1767, married Sept. 30, 1787, ABIGAIL JENNESS of Rye, daughter of Samuel and Elizabeth (Shapleigh). She was born 1769, died July 4, 1812. He died March 27, 1814, a farmer in Rye.
Children of the 6th Gen. b. in Rye.
2047 ELIZABETH, b. Jan. 21, 1788, d. Aug. 27, 1812, m. May 2, 1811, as his 2nd wife, DAVID JENNESS, b. Jan. 12, 1782, d. Jan. 22, 1843, son of Nathaniel and Mary (Wedgwood); had no children. He married four times.
F2048 SAMUEL JENNESS, b. March 1, 1790, m. 1st, Dec. 21, 1817, POLLY W. WALDRON; m. 2nd, Apl. 24, 1834, ELIZABETH W. MARDEN.
F2049 ABIGAIL, b. Nov. 22, 1792, m. June 2, 1816, GEN'L THOMAS GOSS.
F2050 OLIVE SHAPLEIGH, b. May 11, 1795, m. March 8, 1817, WILLIAM BERRY.
F2051 JETHRO, b. Nov. 19, 1797, m. Sept. 3, 1826, MARTHA MASON, # 2883.
2052 JONATHAN, b. Apl. 9, 1800, d. unm. in Rye, June 14, 1826.
F2053 MARY, b. Feb. 11, 1803, m. CAPT. JOHN CLARKE.
F2054 ELVIN, b. March 29, 1809, m. Apl. 5, 1835, LOUISA BERRY, # 2747.

F632 Joseph Locke, born in Rye, March 21, 1770, married ABIGAIL MARDEN Dec. 4, 1794, daughter of Wm. and Hannah (Wallis). She was born March 31, 1776, died March 25, 1848. He was a farmer in Rye, and died Jan. 27, 1816, leaving an estate of $5,241.00.

Children of the 6th Gen. b. in Rye.

2055 HANNAH WALLIS, b. Feb. 7, 1795, m. 1818, JOSEPH J. BERRY. (See # 1039.)
F2056 ABIGAIL TOWLE, b. Feb. 8, 1797, m. (Town Records Apl. 14, 1815) Aug. 31, 1815, BENJAMIN BERRY.
F2057 SARAH ANN, b. Apl. 1, 1799, m. Feb. 1819, AMOS S. JENNESS.
F2058 PATTY, b. March 17, 1801, m. June 11, 1826, RUEL GARLAND, # 2247.
F2059 LUCRETIA, b. June 8, 1803, m. June 18, 1822, MOSES L. GARLAND.
F2060 JOSEPH, b. Nov. 30, 1806, m. 1st, Nov. 28, 1833, HANNAH KNOWLES; m. 2nd, Apl. 3, 1860, MRS. ESTHER (MARDEN) LEAVITT.
2061 MARY, b. Sept. 25, 1809, m. Nov. 20, 1834, JOHN A. TREFETHERN, # F1128.
2062 WILLIAM, b. Aug. 17, 1812, d. Jan. 26, 1816.
F2063 JONATHAN, b. Aug. 17, 1812, twin, m. 1st, Dec. 2, 1838, ALMIRA BROWN, # 2832; m. 2nd, Feb. 3, 1863, MARTHA FRENCH.
2064 JAMES WILLIAM, b. Oct. 1, 1816, d. in Portsmouth, March 26, 1871, m. NANCY DROWN, b. March 16, 1825, d., the wife of Moses Garland, in Portsmouth, June 11, 1904, James had 2 infants died a few months old. He was a carpenter in Lyman, Me.

F634 Jethro Locke, born in Rye, June 29, 1775, married Apl. 26, 1801, Martha Webster, daughter of John and Dorothy. She was born 1781, died May 2, 1856. He was a stone mason in Portsmouth and died Apl. 3, 1821.

Children of the 6th Gen. b. in Rye.

F2065 HIRAM, b. Feb. 28, 1802, m. Dec. 16, 1827, MARY B. DUNCAN.
2066 DANIEL TREADWELL, b. May 26, 1804, d. in Linden, Mich., July 13, 1886, m. late in life ELIZA STANTON, who died in Argentine, Mich. He was a tailor, had no children, but adopted a daughter.
2067 JOHN WEBSTER, b. Feb. 5, 1807, was unmarried, a farmer and shoemaker in Argentine, Mich.
F2068 DAVID J., b. May 25, 1810, m. Dec. 10, 1834, MARY E. GRANT.

F635 Hall Jackson Locke, born in Rye, 1777, married 1st, Jan. 11, 1801, WIDOW ABIGAIL (UNDERWOOD) AMAZEEN, who was born 1764, died Nov. 11, 1828; married 2nd, Apl. 25 (30), 1834, MARGARY NANSON of Kittery, Me. She died in Kittery, March 1, 1869. He served in New Castle as selectman, collector, constable, and surveyor, but particularly was he noted as a teacher in New Castle and Kittery, Me. He died May 25, 1836.

Children of the 6th Gen. b. in New Castle.

F2069 WILLIAM B. A., b. Dec. 22, 1801, m. Apl. 10, 1831, OLIVE G. FERNALD.
2070 FRANCES M., b. Sept. 2, 1807, d. in Portsmouth June 1, 1893, m. Portsmouth, Feb. 15, 1829, JONATHAN M. T. VENNARD of P., b. March 31, 1802, d. May 10, 1839. Had no children, kept store in New Castle.

SIXTH GENERATION

F2071 ARIADNE SHAPLEIGH, b. 1812, m. Apr. 5, 1835, ANDREW BELL VENNARD.
2072 JOHN, b. ——, died aged 21.
2073 ETHAN ALLEN (adopted), b. 1811, d. Matanzas, Cuba., Jan. 12, 1835, unmarried.

F636 Reuben Locke, born in Rye, Apl. 26, 1758, married in Epsom, March 27, 1791, PHEBE CHAPMAN, daughter of Simeon and Mary, of Epsom. She was born June 1, 1770, died 1837. He enlisted in Capt. Parsons' Co. July 4, 1777, was paid for Revolutionary War services Jan. 20, 1782, and Apl. 9, 1782. He settled in Corinth, Vt., in 1791 and with ten others organized the First Congregational Church in town. He died Aug. 14, 1824.

Children of the 6th Gen. b. in Corinth, Vt.

F2074 DAVID, b. July 2, 1791, m. 1816, OLIVE G. BICKFORD.
2075 MARY, b. March 13, 1793, d. 1846, m. 1812, JOSHUA NORTHEY, a farmer in Lisbon. *Children:* 2076 LANG, b. 1814; 2077 ABIGAIL, b. 1816; 2078 DAVID, b. 1819; 2079 MARY, b. 1821, m. ALDEN TRACY of Vermont and had: 2080 JOSEPH; 2081 JENNIE.
2082 ANNAH, b. Sept., 15, 1794 d. 1820, m. 1817, PETER MERRILL,
#2188, b. Jan. 1, 1792, d. Oct. 8, 1864; had one dau.: 2083 ANNA.
F2084 SARAH A., b. July 19, 1796, m. ELLIOTT TAPLIN.
2085 REUBEN, b. Apl. 4, 1798, d. C. Apl. 6, 1837, m. a French lady; no children.
F2086 CAPT. JOHN, b. Oct. 21, 1799, m. SARAH F. THURSTON.
F2087 HAYNES, b. Oct. 29, 1801, m. MARY MACFARLAND, 1830.
2088 NANCY, b. Feb. 15, 1804, d. Apl. 18, 1804.
F2089 BLAKE, b. Feb. 15, 1805, m. JANETTE WHITNEY LEVETT.
2090 ALICE, b. March 5, 1807, m. IRA D. RICHARDSON; no children.
2091 MARGARET, b. 1809, d. Pepperell, Mass., 1874, m. 1st, JOSEPH CHILDS; m. 2nd, JOSEPH SIMES. No children.
2092 WILLIAM, b. 1809, twin, d. unmarried 1890 (?), in the South.

F637 Simeon Locke, born in Rye, March 21, 1760, married in Epsom, Jan. 29, 1784, ABIGAIL BLAKE of Epsom, daughter of Samuel B. She was born Feb. 23, 1766, died July 13, 1839. He enlisted with his brother REUBEN in Capt. Parsons' Co. July 4, 1777, and was in the R. I. service.

In his day it was customary to cast oxen on their side when shoeing. Helping in this work when quite young he lost an eye by an ox throwing back his horn. He became an excellent marksman however, and enlisted in the Revolutionary war, July 4, 1777, and performed efficient service therein. At the close of the war in 1783 he went to Epsom, when bridle paths and blazed trees were the means of reaching many parts of the town. He first settled in a clearing located about half a mile west of the Sherburne road in the north part of the town. A few years later, he bought and moved upon the farm on the top of Locke's Hill, where he was joined in June 1792 by his brother DAVID, who settled on the next farm south, and in 1800 by his brother LEVI, who settled on the next farm north. The three brothers at this time, owned all the beautiful round-topped hill and much of the land in the adjoining valley. To the south of them stretched the valleys of the Suncook and Merrimack. In 1818 he removed to the intervale at East Concord where he died Aug. 12, 1839.

Children of the 6th Gen. b. in Epsom.

F2093 ANNA, b. Dec. 16, 1784, m. June 13, 1804, JOHN SANDERS.
F2094 SAMUEL BLAKE, b. Oct. 22, 1786, m. July 1, 1813, BETSEY PHILBRICK.
F2095 DAVID, b. Oct. 19, 1788, m. Oct. 11, 1810, FLORINDA LOCKE, # 1719.
F2096 SIMEON, b. Dec. 14, 1790, m. July 4, 1813, CLARISSA TASH.
F2097 JOHN, b. March 14, 1794, m. Oct. 30, 1822, RACHEL SANBORN, # 1730.
F2098 JOSIAH KNOWLES, b. Sept. 16, 1796, m. Concord, Oct. 12, 1820, LYDIA PHILBRICK.
2099 JAMES, b. Sept. 18, 1798, m. 1st, Nov. 23, 1826, CLARISSA WALLACE, b. in Deerfield, 1803, d. May 8, 1868; m. 2nd, June 13, 1869, PHEBE M. AMES of Canterbury, b. July 15, 1820, d. in Concord, July 24, 1885, dau. of Samuel and Myra (Ayers). He learned the blacksmith trade of his uncle, Genl. James Blake at Chichester; worked at Bangor, Me., and Deerfield, N. H. James Locke died at his home at East Concord Jan. 1, 1892. He was born on Locke's Hill in Epsom. In Dec. 1835 he moved upon the farm in the mountain district, East Concord, and occupied the same house until his death. He early acquired habits of industry and frugality, a sincere respect for labor and a wholesome contempt for pompous show. Though without children of his own, his interest in, and kindness to, children was a marked feature of his character. Many persons of mature years even now recall his kindness towards them as boys. The beauties of nature were a perpetual pleasure to him and impressed him with the wisdom of the Creator. He loved all animals, believing they, like men, were created for some good purpose. To the very last he kept well posted on current events, his interest in the world never flagging. although all these later years he expressed himself as "living on borrowed time."
F2100 SARAH BLAKE, b. March 28, 1801, m. Dec. 28, 1825, WILLIAM YEATON.
2101 REUBEN, b. Oct. 19, 1802, d. in Epsom, Sept. 13, 1806.
2102 JOSEPH, b. Dec. 7, 1804, d. Sept. 29, 1806.
F2103 ABIGAIL B., b. Jan. 19, 1809, m. Oct. 18, 1837, ROBERT SANDERS.

SIXTH GENERATION

F638 Sarah Locke, born in Rye, Nov. 21, 1761, married in Portsmouth, Nov. 15, 1780, JOSHUA WEBSTER, son of Josiah. He was born May 11, 1757, died May 16, 1805. She married 2nd, SOLOMON WATERHOUSE.

Children of the 6th Gen.

2104 MARY, b. Apl. 17, 1781, m. 1806, HENRY ELKINS of Rye, b. Apl. 23, 1775, son of Samuel and Olive (Marden). *Children:* 2105 SAMUEL, b. Apl. 8, 1809, m. MARY LORD, had 2 children and d. June 8, 1868; 2106 CATHERINE, b. 1813, d. Aug. 26, 1869, m. EDWARD WALCOTT; no children. He m. 2nd, WIDOW ABIGAIL (BROWN) MARDEN.

F2107 JOSIAH, b. Jan. 6, 1783, m. May 20, 1806, HANNAH GRANT.

2108 DAVID, b. Sept. 23, 1784, m. Feb. 1, 1809, EUNICE GERRISH NOWELL of York, Me., b. York, May 23, 1784. *Child:* 2109 DAVID LOCKE, b. Portsmouth, July 24, 1813, d. in Boston, Apl. 28, 1903. David learned a trade in Dover, and started business in Boston in 1855. *Children:* 2110 AUGUSTUS F. and 2111 ANDREW G., who were leather merchants in Boston.

F2112 SALLY, b. March 16, 1786. m. 1807, EPHRAIM PHILBRICK.

2113 JOHN, b. June 20, 1788.

2114 FANNY, b. March 26, 1790, d. in Boston, Oct. 16, 1805.

2115 NATHANIEL, b. March 4, 1793, died in New Orleans.

F2116 MARTHA, b. Apl. 10, 1795, m. Dec. 9, 1819, JAMES BROWN.

2117 LEVI L., b. March 24, 1797, m. ELIZABETH MACY.

F639 Mary Locke, born in Rye, May 7, 1763-4, married in Hampton, Nov. 3, 1785, JOSIAH B. SANBORN, son of Jeremiah and Betsey (Beverly). He was born in Deerfield July 4, 1762, was a farmer in Campton and died there July 21, 1835.

Children of the 6th Gen.

2118 ELIZABETH, b. Dec. 23, 1786, d. Sept. 14, 1846, m. March 1811, REV. BENJ. SARGENT of Pittsfield.

2119 NANCY, b. Feb. 1, 1789, m. JOSIAH EMERY of Dover, b. Jan. ?7, 1784, d. in Dover, July 1837, his 2nd wife; had no children.

2120 ANNAH, b. June 22, 1791, d. 1813, m. May 18, 1812, JONATHAN BATCHELDER of Loudon, b. Apl. 26, 1790, d. 1873, son of Abraham; was a prominent man in Loudon. He m. 2nd, Lois Wells.

F2121 POLLY L., b. Oct. 25, 1793, m. Nov. 1818, JOHN WHITEHOUSE.

F2122 JEREMIAH, b. Dec. 30, 1795, m. Aug. 10, 1826, CLARISSA SMITH.

2123 DAVID L., b. Chichester, Jan. 15, 1800, m. Dec. 1835, LYDIA T. TUFTS of Somerville, lived in Concord and Weare, had: 2124 MARY E., b. May 9, 1836.

2125 AMELIA, b. C. March 10, 1805, m. Dec. 1843, ROBERT WILSON of Loudonville, Ohio.

F2126 JOSEPH B., b. March 6, 1810, m. March 14, 1833, MARY J. SMITH.

F640 David Locke, born in Rye, Nov. 24, 1765, married May 31, 1789 ANNA TOWLE of Hampton. She was baptized Apl. 24, 1768, the daughter of Abraham and Abigail (Moulton), and died July 8, 1839. He was a farmer, moved from Rye to Locke's Hill, Epsom, and died there Apl. 2, 1856.

Children of 6th Gen. b. Locke's Hill, Epsom.
F2127 DEA. DAVID, b. May 23, 1790, m. 1819, POLLY CARLETON.
F2128 ABIGAIL, b. Apl. 26, 1796, m. JONATHAN GREEN.
F2129 NANCY, b. Aug. 9, 1801, m. Feb. 15, 1826, EBENEZER GOVE.
2130 JOHN, b. June 23, 1807, d. Dec. 30, 1807.

F641 Jonathan Locke, born in Portsmouth, Feb. 19, 1768, married 1st, Dec. 23, 1790, MISS LYDIA HALL of Portsmouth. She was born Apl. 1, 1772, died Sept. 15, 1825. He married 2nd, Dec. 1826, MRS. HANNAH (TARLTON) BEALS, daughter of Stillman and Martha (Manning) and the widow of Zachariah Beals, by whom she had: MARY BEALS, who married STACY LOCKE, # 2137. Hannah died in Salmon Falls in 1851. Jonathan was a blacksmith or shipsmith in Portsmouth and later kept a tavern and the jail in Dover. He died in Freedom June 1841.

Children of the 6th Gen. b. in Portsmouth or Dover.
2131 PEGGY HALL, b. P., Oct. 16, 1791, d. Dec. 14, 1808.
2132 DAVID, b. P., May 21, 1793, d. May 31, 1801.
2133 SAMUEL HALL, b. P., Oct. 9, 1794, was Captain of a ship and died at sea of ship fever, July 1817, unmarried.
2134 LYDIA H., b. Dec. 1, 1797, d. Oct. 17, 1798.
F2135 NANCY, b. Feb. 12, 1800, m. (Dover rec.) Nov. 6, 1817, or (Lee, rec.) March 6, 1817, JOSEPH WHITTIER.
F2136 JONATHAN, b. Sept. 20, 1802, m. Sept. 5, 1830, MRS. RUTH CURTIS.
F2137 STACY HALL, b. Aug. 22, 1808, m. July 22, 1832, his step-sister, MARY E. BEALS.
2138 LYDIA, b. Oct. 28, 1810, d. Aug. 4, 1811.
2139 EDWIN R., b. March 16, 1812, d. in Portsmouth, Oct. 28, 1867, m. P., Dec. 6, 1841, OLEVIA S. HALL, b. P., Aug. 26, 1813, d. P., on the Hall farm, Dec. 29, 1891, dau. of Samuel and Lucy Shores (Rogers). He was editor of the *New Hampshire Globe* of Dover, 1833-4. In 1841 was in Lincoln, Me.; 1849 went to Cal.; came back to Ports. where he was a painter; had no children.
2140 ALBERT, b. in Dover, Aug. 14, 1814, d. in Freedom, Feb. 28, 1884, m. 1st, Aug. 12, 1838, ABIGAIL D. JACOBS of Dover, b. D. 1814, d. F. Jan. 1, 1869, dau. of Lyford; m. 2nd, in F., July 4, 1873, RHODA A. PRAY, b. in Ossipee, 1839, dau. of Levi and Rhoda. He was in the milling business in Effingham Falls, and had no children.

SIXTH GENERATION

F642 Levi Locke, born in Rye, Feb. 7, 1770, married in Hampton Falls, Aug. 31, 1796, HANNAH PRESCOTT, daughter of James and Abigail (Lane). She was born in Hampton Falls, Oct. 18, 1776, died July 18, 1845. He was a farmer and moved from Rye to Epsom in 1780. "At the age of 72, he is a short old gent and seems to have the enterprise and industry of a man of 40. Says he could mow 6 acres of wheat, and this spring (1842) he did his own work, also helped plow his son's land." He died Sept. 23, 1850.

Children of 6th Gen. b. in Rye and Epsom.

F2141 SIMEON PRESCOTT, b. Rye, Jan. 14, 1799, m. 1st, June 9, 1835, SARAH B. CASS; m. 2nd, Nov. 24, 1864, EUNICE PRESCOTT.
F2142 BENJAMIN LOVERING, b. July 26, 1802, m. May 5, 1825, HANNAH P. MOSES.
2143 SON, b. Apl. 24, 1804, d. 1 day old.
2144 LUCY MARIA, b. Sept. 19, 1805, d. Sept. 15, 1806.
F2145 LUCY MARIA, b. July 11, 1807, m. Oct. 20, 1830, DANIEL TILTON.
2146 THOMAS D. MERRILL, b. Epsom, Oct. 29, 1808, d. Tyngsboro, Mass., June 17, 1897, m. 1st, Oct. 4, 1837, SARAH T. COCHRAN of Pembroke, b. 1811, d. Manchester, Oct. 22, 1844, dau. Samuel and Sally (Folsom); m. 2nd, MRS. EMALINE (PARKER) LEWIS, who d. Feb. 9, 1897.

In early life he was a teacher in Great Falls, and later a dry goods drummer. Had no children by legal wives, but did have a child by ELIZA CASS: 2147 ELMA J. LOCKE, who m. 1852, JOSIAH D. LANGLEY.

F2148 BETSEY, b. March 5, 1811, m. Feb. 2, 1831, JACOB TILTON.
F2149 ALMIRA, b. Aug. 1, 1814, m. Sept. 16, 1847, JOHN B. JOHNSON.
F2150 REV. JOSEPH J., b. Sept. 8, 1816, m. Nov. 1841, SARAH WEBSTER.

F643 Rev. Dr. John Locke, born in Rye, May 22, 1772, married ABIGAIL DEARBORN of North Hampton. He was a physician in Boston and Chelsea. Originally a Universalist, after going to Boston he became a Swedenborgian, and was the author of a book on that faith. He died in Chelsea Sept. 5, 1846.

Children of 6th Gen.

2151 HARRIET, b. July 16, 1801, d. Aug. 7, 1801.
2152 EMALINE, b. Oct. 30, 1802, d. Feb. 19, 1859, m. 1835, WILLIAM HAWSE, b. Sept. 5, 1808, d. Oct. 16, 1880; He m. 2nd, MARIANNA J. LOCKE, #5068. Emaline had 12 children, all died young except 3; 2153 ELLEN MATILDA, m. WILLIAM LOW, and had 3 children: 2154 WILLIAM H., m. MARY TURNER and had 2 children in California; 2155 MARY EMALINE lived Woburn, Mass.
2156 ELIZA, b. Sept. 21, 1804.
2157 LUCY ELWELL, b. June 29, 1806.

2158 MARY A., b. Apl. 15, 1810, d. May 1810.
2159 EDWARD, d. in So. Boston hospital 1860, unmarried.
Two others probably died young.

F644 Annah Locke, born in Rye, March 27, 1774, married Jan. 2, 1794, TIMOTHY PRESCOTT of Kensington, son of Jonathan and Rachel (Clifford). She died in Gilmanton, Nov. 23, 1857. He was born May 12, 1768, was a merchant in Chichester, moved to Gilmanton, Oct. 27, 1806; was a farmer, deputy sheriff, etc., and died Sept. 12, 1845.

Children of 6th Gen.
2160 MITTIE LOCKE, b. Apl. 5, 1795, d. Dec. 1874, m. 1st, DANIEL RUNDLETT; m. 2nd, June 21, 1823, DANIEL TILTON. *Children:* 2161 ELIZABETH A. RUNDLETT; 2162 NEWELL A. RUNDLETT; 2163 ARVILLA TILTON; 2164 MARY TILTON; 2165 GEORGE TILTON.
2166 NANCY, b. Aug. 31, 1797, d. Aug. 1866, m. Feb. 16, 1832, WILLIAM P. CLOUGH of Canterbury, b. Oct. 1802, son of Leavitt; was a farmer in C. *Children:* 2167 CORNELIA A., b. June 26, 1834, m. June 27, 1860, REV. HOWARD MOODY, b. York, Me., May 4, 1808; 2168 ANN M., b. May 20, 1838, d. July 13, 1840.
2169 JONATHAN, b. Aug. 14, 1800, d. May 23, 1881, m. Jan. 22, 1835, MIRANDA CLOUGH of Canterbury, b. Feb. 14, 1808. *Children:* 2170 MARTHA E., b. Oct. 24, 1835, d. Aug. 18, 1841; 2171 ELLEN M., b. Oct. 24, 1835, twin, m. Apl. 1864, EDWIN J. RUNDLETT; 2172 ANNA, b. Sept. 18, 1838, d. March 9, 1863, m. EDWIN J. RUNDLETT, Sept. 18, 1856; 2173 GEORGE N., b. Sept. 8, 1846.
2174 WOODBURY TIMOTHY, b. Apl. 5, 1803, d. March 14, 1871, m. Dec. 29, 1829, FRANCES E. BANKS, b. Nov. 10, 1809. *Children,* 2175 GEORGE B., b. Oct. 20, 1832; 2176 EDWIN A., b. Dec. 16, 1841.
2177 JULIA A., b. Jan. 8, 1805, m. Dec. 24, 1829, NICHOLAS S. GILMAN, b. Feb. 20, 1800, d. March 1875, son of Samuel. *Child:* 2178 FRANCES, b. June 9, 1832, m. March 11, 1852, CARLUS G. HATHORNE of Hopkinton, later a lawyer in Iowa.
2179 BENJAMIN L., b. Sept. 23, 1809.
2180 ALFRED, b. in Gilmanton, Apl. 28, 1812, d. Nov. 5, 1889, m. May 13, 1838, OCTAVIA BEAN, b. in Sandwich, Aug. 18, 1816, d. in Lynn, Jan. 30, 1900, dau. of Dea. Josiah, was a printer in Gil. *Children:* 2181 ELIZA A., b. June 5, 1843, m. —— MORRILL, lived Gil.; 2182 EMMA OCTAVE, b. Sept. 6, 1846, m. Sept. 19, 1865, STEPHEN H. DEARBORN, of Laconia; 2183 ALFRED IRVING, b. Dec. 18, 1847, d. Kittery, Me., Sept. 10, 1915; 2184 CLARA, b. Aug. 24, 1852, m. J. K. SOULE of Waterville, Me.; 2185 ANNIE A., b. Dec. 28, 1853.
2186 EDWIN R., b. Gilmanton Nov. 3, 1815, d. Sept. 12, 1884, m. 1st, Jan. 1843, ANNETTE E. TOWLE, b. Aug. 27, 1822, d. July 27, 1858, dau. of John of West Cambridge; m. 2nd, Oct. 8, 1863, MATILDA RUSSELL, b. Apl. 7, 1835, dau. of Philemon of Somerville, Mass. *Child:* 2187 EDWIN R., b. Oct. 12, 1864.

SIXTH GENERATION 115

F645 Doctor William Locke, born in Rye, Apl. 9, 1776, married Oct. 23, 1800, ESTHER KNOWLES of Epsom, daughter of Simeon of Pembroke. She was born in Lyman, Nov. 29, 1781, died in Irasburg, Vt., Jan. 3, 1874. He was a Thompsonian physician in Lyman, until 1824, then went to Irasburg, where he was a farmer and died there March 3, 1841.

Children of 6th Gen. b. in Lyman.

F2188 ANNA LOVERING, b. July 13, 1801, m. Jan. 21, 1823, PETER MERRILL, # 2082.
F2189 SIMON KNOWLES, b. Nov. 2, 1802, m. 1st, Oct. 2, 1833, PHEBE ABBOTT; m. 2nd, ——— Campbell.
F2190 SARAH KNOWLES, b. Jan. 8, 1804, m. Apl. 16, 1826, ALEX JAMESON.
F2191 NANCY, b. May 26, 1806, m. March 17, 1832, WILLIAM P. DODGE.
F2192 WILLIAM LOVERING, b. Jan. 18, 1808, m. Sept. 25, 1838, FANNY M. GIBBS.
2193 LYDIA, b. Aug. 9, 1810, m. JESSE BARROWS, b. New Hampshire. He was a farmer in Irasburg, Vt. (his mother ELIZABETH, aged 88, was living with him in 1850). *Children:* 2194 EVALINE, m. JOHN SWASEY, an Adventist; 2195 ESTHER, b. 1834, m. ——— HUTCHINS; 2196 ABIGAIL, b. 1836, m. ——— HUTCHINS; 2197 HAMLET, b. 1839, m. twice; 2198 WILLIAM, b. 1840, m. ELLEN GRAY of Coventry, Vt.; 2199 ELLEN, b. 1852, m. GEORGE ———.
F2200 JOHN, b. May 19, 1811, m. 1835, KEZIAH CHASE; m. 2nd (1841), EMALINE HOVEY.
2201 FLORENDA, b. in Lyman, Oct. 22, 1812, m. HILAS FORSAITH of Irasburg, Vt. *Children:* 2202 EDWIN; 2203 WILLIAM, m. CARRIE GOLDSMITH and had 2 children; 2204 EMALINE, m. GEORGE GOLDSMITH and had 6 children; 2205 DENNIS, m. CARRIE ———, had 2206 ARTHUR, and d. 1888, in Belvedere Hospital, N. Y.
2207 FINETTA, b. June 22, 1816, died young.
F2208 FILENDA, b. Apl. 7 (T. R. Oct. 7), 1818, m. Feb. 22, 1837, BENJAMIN F. HERBERT.
2209 EMALINE, b. Dec. 2, 1819, m. JOHN C. KELLUM, # 5019, a policeman of Boston, who m. 2nd, 1887 SARAH H. D. LOCKE. Emaline had: 2210 CAROLINE, d. aged 16 years; 2211 GEORGE, m., had 3 or 4 children in Boston; 2213 EUGENE, died young.
F2214 ALBION, b. Apl. 28, 1822, m. June 15, 1848, MARY A. LOCKE, # 5017.

F646 Abigail D. Locke, born in Rye, Nov. 20, 1778, married Jan. 2, 1797, her second cousin, CAPT. BICKFORD LANG, # 929, son of Bickford. He was born in Rye, Nov. 6, 1774, died in Huntington, Ohio, Apl. 5, 1861. He was a Lieutenant in N. H. State Militia in 1812 and a Captain in 1814, when he with 14 of his men volunteered for active service and he was placed in command at Fort Sullivan in Maine. In 1800 he moved to Epsom to a place called New Rye and in 1837 moved to Huntington, Ohio. She died Feb. 5, 1862.

Children of 6th Gen. b. in Epsom.

F2215 WILLIAM, b. June 20, 1797, m. 1st, ABRILLA SUEARENGEN; 2nd, SYBIL SQUIRE.
F2216 DAVID, b. Feb. 5, 1799, m. 1st, Feb. 26, 1826, LYDIA BABB; m. 2nd, May 27, 1836, LORENDA HITCHCOCK.
F2217 REUEL, b. March 28, 1801, m. Jan. 30, 1823, AMY HART.
F2218 JOHN LOCKE, b. May 29, 1803, m. March 27, 1828, SARAH G. WHITE.
F2219 SARAH MARTHA, b. June 17, 1805, m. 1828, SAMUEL MORRILL CHESLEY.
F2220 ANNA M., b. Nov. 6, 1807, m. 1st, 1824, DR. JAMES BABB; m. 2nd, Sept. 1858, CAPT. NATHANIEL KIMBALL.
F2221 LORENDA, b. May 2, 1810, m. Nov. 21, 1830, DANIEL K. PRESCOTT.
F2222 BICKFORD, b. March 27, 1812, m. Feb. 26, 1835, JANE BACHELDER CRAM.
2223 ABIGAIL L., b. Feb. 2, 1814, d. Oct. 4, 1886, m. 1841, MILTON BARKER of Oberlin, Ohio, d. Oberlin 1892; had: 2224 ALBION, died young; 2225 ARVILLA L., m. EDWIN D. LOWRY, b. Aug. 17, 1872.
2226 BENJAMIN L., b. Feb. 19, 1816, d. 1 day old.
F2227 BENJAMIN L., b. June 11, 1817, m. Apl. 26, 1847, HELEN M. THRALL.
F2228 JOSIAH CROSBY, b. Nov. 20, 1820, m. Oct. 5, 1841, HULDAH A. CHAPMAN.

F647 Benjamin Locke, born in Rye, Dec. 28, 1780, married Oct. 18, 1801, MISS PAMELIA CONNOR of Portsmouth. She died July 2, 1825, in Portsmouth. He was a shoemaker and carpenter in Portsmouth, later kept the jail in Dover and probably died there, the date being Jan. or July 8, 1816. He sold property in Portsmouth in 1810.

Children of 6th Gen. b. in Portsmouth.

F2229 MARY AUSTIN, b. May 5, 1802, m. Portsmouth, Apl. 15, 1823, SAMUEL B. LARKIN.
2230 ELIZABETH H., b. Feb. 6, 1804, m. ——— CHICK of Boston, had: 2231 HATTIE, who m. ——— DEERING.
2232 PAMELIA, b. Oct. 29, 1805, was insane from 1834 to death, Dec. 16, 1882; never married.
F2233 MARGARET ANN LOVERING, b. Sept. 8, 1807, m. 1833, EPHRAIM HARRIS.
2234 CHARLOTTE ANN, b. Nov. 26, 1809, d. Oct. 12, 1878, m. ——— LEWIS.
2235 BENJAMIN FRANKLIN, b. Feb. 29, 1812, lost at sea, a young unmarried man.
2236 LYDIA H., b. Jan. 28, 1815, m. ——— NEALLY, had 2 children.

F648 Nancy Locke, born in Rye, March 9, 1785, married in Greenland Apl. 2, 1801, MORRIS LAMPREY, son of Lieut. John and

SIXTH GENERATION

Molly (Marston). He was born June 28, 1778, was a farmer at Little River, North Hampton, and died there July 5, 1841. She died North Hampton, Oct. 17, 1853.

Children of 6th Gen. b. North Hampton.

F2237 DAVID M., b. Oct. 18, 1801, m. Apl. 5, 1825, SALLY STEARNS.
F2238 JOHN, b. Dec. 15, 1803, m. Nov. 16, 1828, MARY S. ROBINSON.
2239 MORRIS, b. March 17, 1806, d. in Candia, 1827.
F2240 URI, b. Feb. 23, 1809, m. May 31, 1831, SALLY MARSTON.
F2241 HEZEKIAH B., b. Nov. 12, 1812, m. Aug. 1833, MARY A. E. JENNESS.

F650 Abigail Perkins, born in Rye, Oct. 10, 1760, married Oct. 18, (1778) JOHN GARLAND, son of Col. Benj. and Sarah (Jenness). He was born Oct. 14, 1758, died March 24, 1844. He hauled powder taken from Fort Constitution by the Continentals to Newport, R. I. He was in the Revolution.

Children of 6th Gen. from Rye History.

F2242 JOHN, b. Nov. 23, 1776, m. Aug. 15, 1799, ELIZABETH PARSONS.
2243 THOMAS, b. March 3, 1779, unmarried.
2244 ABIGAIL, b. Aug. 14, 1782, d. Sept. 22, 1857, m. Aug. 11, 1803, JOHN W. PARSONS, b. Dec. 12, 1778, d. Sept. 18, 1849. He was a doctor in Rye and had 8 children. (See History of Rye.)
2245 JAMES, b. Nov. 15, 1784, d. unmarried, July 21, 1850.
2246 BENJAMIN, b. July 30, 1791, m. POLLY PHILBRICK, b. Oct. 24, 1794.
2247 RUEL, b. Dec. 31, 1798, d. Aug. 28, 1869, m. June 11, 1826, PATTY LOCKE (See F2058), d. Feb. 17, 1866. A blacksmith.

F651 Sarah Perkins, born in Rye, Sept. 7, 1762, married LIEUT. WILLIAM EMERY, son of Dr. Anthony. He was born July 16, 1759, died March 29, 1827. She died Dec. 18, 1835.

Children of 6th Gen.

2248 NABBY, b. July 12, 1785, d. March 21, 1865, m. DAVID NUDD, had 8 children.
2249 LIEUT. WILLARD EMERY, b. Oct. 28, 1788, d. May 15, 1836, m. Nov. 1, 1811, SALLY MORSE, who d. in Kensington, March 30, 1866, dau. of Benjamin and Anna (Hoar); had 8 children. She m. 2nd, July 15, 1844, EZRA CHASE. Willard's children were: 2250 ELIZA A.; 2251 HARRIET H.; 2252 ALBIN; 2253 DAVID and 2254 MARY, died young; 2255 MARY A.; 2256 SARAH D.; 2257 MARTHA V.; 2258 DAVID W., b. 1836, m. ABBIE T. SANDERSON, and had 2 children.
2259 ANTHONY, b. Feb. 6, 1789, d. Dec. 22, 1864, m. BETSEY TOWLE.
2260 POLLY, b. May 6, 1791, d. May 19, 1855, m. 1st, THOMAS D. MARSTON; m. 2nd, JOHN COTTON; m. 3rd, SAMUEL MONSON.
2261 SARAH, b. Sept. 29, 1799, d. July 15, 1880, m. EBENEZER LANE.

F652 John Perkins, born in Rye, Nov. 7, 1764, married Feb. 26, 1789, RUTH NUDD.

Children of 6th Gen.
2262 JAMES, b. 1790, m. HULDAH SEAVEY of Wolfeboro.
2263 JONATHAN, b. 1792, m. PHEBE ROBINSON.
2264 NANCY, b. 1795, m. SAMUEL NUDD.
2265 ELIAS, b. March 13, 1797, m. July 7, 1822, POLLY LANGDON, b. Jan. 21, 1804.

F654 James Perkins, born in Rye, Apl. 20, 1769, married 1st, Feb. 6, 1791, MARY PERKINS, born Dec. 23, 1770, died Jan. 7, 1810; married 2nd, June 12, 1812, WIDOW MEHITABLE GARLAND, born Feb. 19, 1775, died May 1850. He died May 2, 1852.

Children of 6th Gen.
2266 ABIGAIL, b. Sept. 3, 1791, m. March 1, 1810, SAMUEL W. JENNESS, b. June 17, 1787, d. March 2, 1875; had 7 children in Rye.
2267 POLLY, b. Sept. 26, 1793, m. Nov. 21, 1811, LEVI GARLAND, b. June 14, 1793, d. Dec. 11, 1863; had 8 children by 1st wife; m. 2nd, 1838, MARY WATSON.
2268 HANNAH, b. May 26, 1796, m. Apl. 6, 1820, DANIEL GOSS, and had 4 children. He had a former wife, SARAH MACE.
2269 JANE M., b. Aug. 29, 1798, m. Sept. 6, 1820, IRA BROWN, b. May 30, 1795, d. July 10, 1845; had 8 children.
2270 JAMES, b. May 23, 1801, d. Sept. 26, 1806.
2271 HULDAH, b. Feb. 12, 1804, d. Aug. 23, 1880, m. Jan. 7, 1822, JOSIAH JENNESS, b. Aug. 15, 1797, d. Apl. 12, 1876; had 2 children.
2272 ELIZA J., b. March 2, 1807, m. Nov. 23, 1826, JOHN LEAVITT; he m. 2nd, —— MORSE.
2273 JOHN, b. March 1, 1809, d. Feb. 3, 1816.
2274 DAVID, b. July 11, 1814, d. Nov. 3, 1816 (2nd wife's child).
2275 ABRAHAM, b. Jan. 13, 1818, m. Dec. 29, 1838, CHRISTENA PHILBRICK, b. Aug. 27, 1822, d. Nov. 13, 1885; had 6 children.

F655 Jonathan Perkins, born in Rye, Jan. 30, 1772, married 1801, MARY LOCKE, # 1139, born Apl. 30, 1782, died in 1852. He was a tailor in Epsom and died Aug. 13, 1809.

Children of 6th Gen.
F2276 EDWARD S., b. 1803, d. 1850, m. ALMEDA KNOX.
2277 JEREMIAH, b. 1806, lived unmarried in Chichester.
F2278 JAMES H., b. 1808, m. Ruth Glidden.

F656 Josiah Perkins, born in Rye, July 13, 1774, married 1806, BETSEY BACHELDER, born Sept. 13, 1785, the daughter of Josiah and Abigail (Cotton). Josiah was a tailor and farmer in Rye.

Children of the 6th Gen.
2279 JAMES; 2280 NANCY; 2281 LOUIS, m. —— MORRIS of Rye.

SIXTH GENERATION

F659 Sarah Locke, born in Chester, Dec. 13, 1761, married JOSEPH KNOWLES, who was born in Chester, Jan. 15, 1758, died in Northfield, Feb. 16, 1815. She died there Aug. 30, 1841.

Children of 6th Gen.

2282 WILLIAM b. Apl. 6, 1781, d. May 26, 1864, m. 1st, 1802, BETSEY CLEMENT of Haverhill, Mass., who died on her wedding day; m. 2nd, 1805, ZILPHA THORN, b. Jan. 11, 1782, d. Dec. 27, 1876; had dau.: 2283 m. —— CASS.
2283 JOSEPH, m. Apl. 28, 1805, HANNAH HAINES. In 1806 he went to Piermont, N. H., in 1836 to Hurricane, Ill. He died in 1840; had 3 or 4 children; one, 2284 MRS. HARRIET RICHMOND another, 2285 MRS. HANNAH BOOT of Fillmore, Ill.
2286 CHRISTIAN; 2287 SARAH, twins, b. Oct. 7, 1786.
2288 SALLY, b. in Salisbury, Apl. 11, 1789, d. Aug. 29, 1859, m. March 24, 1819, JOSIAH BACHELDER of Andover; had: 2289, WILLIAM A., father of 2290 ex.-Gov. N. J. Bachelder; 2291 MARTHA, m. J. H. ROWELL of Franklin; 2292 MARY, m. GEORGE E. EMERY of Andover.
2293 HANNAH, b. Feb. 9, 1792, m. STEPHEN HAINES of Vershire, and Exeter, Vt.
2294 JOHN, b. Oct. 10, 1794, d. May 29, 1853, lived on the homestead.
2295 POLLY, b. Aug. 6, 1797, m. JOSIAH WOODBURY of Northfield. (See Northfield History.)
2296 SON and DAU., twins, b. 1800.

F660 John Locke, born in Chester, 1765, married in Kingston, —— 20, 1793, ELEANOR TUCKER of Poplin, who died Feb. 16, 1821, age 53. He lived on the old homestead in Chester, rebuilt the sawmill in 1810, and added a grist mill in 1820. He died June 18, 1846.

Children of 6th Gen. b. in Chester.

2297 SARAH, b. ——, d. 1825, m. June 31, 1816, HENRY OSGOOD of Raymond, b. 1789, son of Timothy and Jennie (Dearborn); had 2 children who died young. He died in 1850.
F2298 ABIGAIL T., b. 1795, m. Apl. 17, 1815, CAPT. JOHN MOORE.
F2299 MARY or POLLY, b. ——, m. JOHN CURRIER.
F2300 WILLIAM, b. Apl. 28, 1797, m. RACHEL BLAKE, Dec. 30, 1821.
F2301 JAMES, b. July 11, 1801, m. 1st, 1826, JANE W. TAGGART; m. 2nd, Aug. 2, 1861, WIDOW HANNAH P. DODGE.
2302 JOHN, b. Aug. 26, 1805, d. in Raymond, Sept. 27, 1872, m. SUSAN DUDLEY of Raymond, b. R., March 3, 1805, d. R., Nov. 5, 1893, dau. of Thomas and Mary (Moody). He had no children, was selectman in 1841, in the Legislature 1856, and later postmaster of Chester. He and TRUE rebuilt the sawmill.
F2303 ELIZABETH, b. July 30, 1808, m. 1840, RANDOLPH PHELPS.
F2304 TRUE T., b. Aug. 26, 1810, m. 1st, Oct. 29, 1839, JOANNA M. TUCKER; m. 2nd, AMANDA SAWTELLE.

F666 Polly Locke, born in Chester, Oct. 27, 176(8?), married 1783, CAPT. BENJAMIN TRUE, son of Benjamin and Mehitable (Osgood). Polly died Nov. 13, 1846. Benjamin was born in Chester May 6, 1762, was in the Revolutionary War, settled in Chester and died Dec. 6, 1843.

Children of 6th Gen.

F2305 HANNAH, b. May 24, 1784, m. Nov. 21, 1802, ISAAC WORTHEN.
F2306 SARAH, b. Aug. 22, 1788, m. Apl. 9, 1808, SAMUEL POOR.
F2307 MARY, b. Aug. 10, 1791, m. 1st, JOSEPH NORRIS; m. 2nd, LEVI BLAKE.
2308 JUDITH, b. Nov. 3, 1796, m. July 1, 1817, JOSEPH STEVENSON, a farmer in Fremont; had: 2309 JOSEPH; 2310 ORRIN; 2311 LINDSEY.
F2312 OSGOOD, b. Dec. 25, 1799, m. BETSEY TRUE.
2313 ALMIRA, b. Jan. 5, 1804, m. July 24, 1845, DANIEL SANBORN of Chester, a farmer, had no children.
2314 LYDIA, b. May 27, 1806, d. Apl. 5, 1810.
F2315 WILLIAM STEPHEN, b. Jan. 16, 1808, m. Nov. 17, 1836, MARY PRESCOTT.

F667 Margaret Locke, born in Chester, 1770, married in Chester, Nov. 15, 1792, CAPT. WILLIAM MOORE of Raymond, son of James and Mary (Todd). He was born in Chester 1762, lived there a farmer and died Oct. 31, 1840. She died March 27, 1844.

Children of 6th Gen. b. in Chester.

2316 SALLY, b. ——, d. unmarried.
2317 JAMES, b. 1797, d. unmarried in 1857.
2318 CHARLOTTE, b. Oct. 18, 1800, d. in Chester, June 2, 1893, unmarried.
2319 MARYANNA, bapt. Sept. 15, 1802, m. CYRUS SANBORN.
2320 ROBERT, b. 1811, m. June 25, 1845, NANCY E. LOCKE, # 4950.
2321 MARY TODD, b. 1812, d. May 14, 1846.
F2322 RUFUS W., b. Apl. 21, 1814, m. 1st, Apl. 1849, SARAH NIGHTINGALE GREEN; m. 2nd, June 4, 1863, NANCY LARKIN.

F671 Reuben Philbrick, born Sept. 9, 1773, married Sept. 4, 1794, BETSEY JENNESS, daughter of Nathaniel and Mary (Tarlton). She was born 1777. He died June 12, 1831.

Children of the 6th Gen.

2323 REUBEN, bapt. June 25, 1795, died in West Indies.
2324 SARAH, b. Sept. 1804, d. June 23, 1888, m. JOSEPH BATCHELDER, who died in North Hampton, March 8, 1877; had: 2325 ANGELINE; 2326 CLARINDA; 2327 CLARINDA AMANDA, who m. ROBERT P. LOCKE, # F6265.

SIXTH GENERATION

F684 John Foss, born in Rye, Jan. 9, 1775, married Elizabeth TITCOMB, and lived in Chicago, Ill.

Children of 6th Gen.

2328 CAROLINE T., b. 1806, m. STEPHEN COFFIN, lived in Moultonborough.
2329 WILLIAM HAM, b. 1807, m. MARY DROWN.
2330 LUCINDA, m. HANSON CAVERLY, lived in Bennington.
2331 SAMUEL, m. ELIZA HEYWOOD, lived in Chicago.
2332 ABIGAIL, m. DR. BEEBE, lived in Wisconsin.
2333 ROBERT, m. HARRIET SPEAR, lived in Chicago.
2334 JOHN, m. 1st, LYDIA TROOP; m. 2nd, HANNAH ———, lived in Chicago.
2335 MARY, m. ——— APPLETON.

F686 Hannah Locke, born in Barrington, Dec. 16, 1766, married WINTHROP REYNOLDS of Dover, 1791, son of Joseph and Lydia. He was born in Durham, Feb. 28, 1754–5. She was his fourth wife and died in Barrington, Aug. 21, 1846.

Children of 6th Gen. b. in Barrington.

2336 WILLIAM, b. Sept. 23, 1792, d. Dec. 1813.
2337 WINTHROP, b. March 2, 1794, d. Aug. 7, 1849, m. Nov. 8, 1817, ELIZABETH C. JONES of Barrington; had 9 children.
2338 SAMUEL L., b. Sept. 16, 1795, d. 1848–9, m. 1820, ADALINE SMITH of Boston, who d. 1827; m. 2nd, ——— ——— in Georgia; had 1 child.
2339 GEORGE F., b. Jan. 26, 1797, d. 1798.
2340 GEORGE F., b. Oct. 9, 1799, m. 1825, ABIGAIL LOCKE, # 2368.
2341 JOB F., b. Feb. 19, 1801, d. March 22, 1853, m. 1st, Oct. 11, 1827, EUNICE JONES of Milton, Mass., b. July 12, 1798, d. Dec. 6, 1842; m. 2nd, Sept. 1, 1843, ANN TEBBETS of Brookfield. He was a farmer.
2342 JACOB, b. Apl. 8, 1803, d. Sept. 26, 1865, m. 1st, 1834, SARAH JONES of Boston; m. 2nd, MEHITABLE STEVENS, who d. 1856; was a blacksmith in Haverhill and had 4 children.
F2343 EPHRAIM F., b. Dec. 27, 1804, d. Aug. 15, 1851, m. Apl. 14, 1825, MARY PINKHAM LOCKE, # 2424.
2344 ELIZABETH L., b. March 12, 1807, d. May 1885, m. March 13, 1831, JOSEPH P. WEEKS, b. May 3, 1809, son of Elisha and Mary (Porter). A farmer and hatter of Strafford; had 3 children.

F687 Samuel Locke, born in Barrington, March 16, 1768, married 1st, March 1, 1792, LUCY CATE, born Apl. 5, 1764; married 2nd, MRS. TAMSEN HAYES Jan. 27, 1801, daughter of Wentworth and Mary (Main). She was born in Farmington, Apl. 11, 1772, died in Alton, March 15, 1843. He was a farmer in Barrington.

LOCKE GENEALOGY

Children of 6th Gen. b. in Barrington.

F2345 EBEN C., b. Nov. 15, 1792, m. 1st, Nov. 28, 1822, MARY M. HAM; m. 2nd, SUSAN DENNETT.

F2346 MARY B., b. Jan. 20, 1795, m. 1815, JOHN D. HUCKINS.

2347 LUCY, b. Apl. 5, 1797, d. Jan. 26, 1844, m. 1826, DAVID COLEBURN of Leominster, Mass., was a farmer in Northwood and went to Massachusetts in 1845; had: 2348 ELIZABETH, b. 1802, d. unm.; 2349 ELLEN, b. 1806, m. MILO CHAPIN of Barnstead.

F2350 BETSEY, b. Apl. 1, 1800, m. Apl. 20, 1826, ELIPHALET BERRY.

F2351 ABIGAIL P., b. Sept. 30, 1801 (2nd wife's child), m. July 4, 1824, MAJOR GORAM W. HOITT.

2352 JOHN W., b. Sept. 10, 1807, d. Oct. 18, 1808.

2353 IRA W., b. Dec. 17, 1809, d. Aug. 10, 1826.

F688 John Locke, born in Barrington, Sept. 17, 1769, married 1st, Sept. 20, 1792, ABIGAIL PAGE, born Aug. 24, 1770, died July 18, 1800; married 2nd, Oct. 19, 1800, MERCY DAME, born Aug. 8, 1768, died Apl. 22, 1822. He married 3rd, WIDOW MARGARET PIERCE, who died in Barrington March 8, 1842. He was called "Honest John the miller" and died in Barrington March 29, 1838.

Children of 6th Gen. b. in Barrington.

2354 SARAH, b. May 18, 1793, m. 1813, DANIEL PAGE, and had: 2355 JONATHAN, b. 1816, run away aged 16; 2356 DAVID W., b. July 3, 1818, m. and had 5 children; 2357 JOSEPH, b. 1823; 2358 BENJAMIN, b. Oct. 4, 1832, m. and had 4 children; 2359 EMILY, b. Aug. 6, 1834, m. WILLIAM SNELL and had 6 children.

F2360 DANIEL, b. Nov. 11, 1794, m. 1st, Apl. 15, 1819, SUSAN HAYES; m. 2nd, MRS. HANNAH (DONALDSON) FOSS; m. 3rd, 1838, MRS. MEHITABLE (BUNKER) HOLMES.

2361 WILLIAM, b. Jan. 6, 1798, d. in So. Boston, May 29, 1846, m. in Boston, 1823, JUDITH BISHOP, b. in Gloucester, July 6, 1800, d. in So. B., July 26, 1869. They had: 2362 SARAH E., b. Boston, March 29, 1825, d. So. B., March 4, 1848; 2363 MARY A., b. Jan. 19, 1827, lived unm. in So. Boston; 2364 JOHN B., b. Sept. 22, 1833, a carpenter, unm. in So. Boston.

F2365 ELIZABETH, b. Nov. 16, 1799, m. March 24, 1822, WILLIAM NUTTER.

2366 ABNER, b. Sept. 14, 1801, d. Nov. 21, 1801.

F2367 JOHN, b. Dec. 11, 1802, m. 1st, March 25, 1832, CATHARINE TUCKER; m. 2nd, Oct. 1850, MRS. HANNAH (HOYT) LOCKE.

2368 ABIGAIL, b. Apl. 13, 1804, d. in Victoria, Ill., Nov. 24, 1876, m. in Milton, Mass., March 22, 1825, GEORGE F. REYNOLDS, # 2340, b. Oct. 10, 1799, lived in Victoria and had: 2369 GEORGE W., b. July 15, 1826, m. Feb. 4, 1849, MARY C. HOTCHKISS, and they had: 2370 LOUIS M., b. Oct. 25, 1849; 2371 CHARLES C., b. Dec. 24, 1828; 2372 JOHN W., b. March 31, 1833; 2373 JULIA A., b. Oct. 15, 1836, m. THEODORE HAMMOND.

Rev. William Sherburne Locke F1775

William S. Locke F2977

Gardner Towle Locke F2806

Stephen Locke F1443

Hannah (Hoyt) Locke, 1807-1902 F2375

SIXTH GENERATION

F2374 ABNER D., b. Dec. 23, 1806, m. Feb. 23, 1826, REBECCA COFFIN.
F2375 SILAS, b. Nov. 17, 1809, m. May 14, 1840, HANNAH L. HOYT.
F2376 SAMPSON B., June 17, 1811, m. Dec. 25, 1836, SARAH CANNEY.
2377 MERCY D., b. March 29, 1813, d. Dec. 1836, m. 1835, JOHN O'BRIEN of Groveland, Ill., had no children.

F689 Miribah Locke, born in Barrington, Dec. 19, 1771, married July 19, 1792, AMOS MAIN of Rochester, son of Rev. Amos (or Josiah), descended from John Main, York, Me., 1618 (?), to whom a statue was erected in Rochester in 1896. Amos was born in Rochester March 7, 1770, lived near the Garrison House and died in Lowell, Mass. Miribah died in Rochester.

Children of 6th Gen.

F2378 DAVID, b. 1792, d. 1826, m. ESTHER NORWOOD.
2379 BETSEY, b. ——, m. JONATHAN HORNE of Rochester, a carpenter; had 10 children.
2380 WILLIAM, b. ——, m. SUSAN R. SPINNEY of Portsmouth, March 25, 1823, a brick mason; had 3 children.
2381 ABIGAIL, b. ——, m. DR. HEZEKIAH CROCKETT of Farmington; had: 2382 COL. JOHN; and another.
2383 POLLY, b. ——, m. DANIEL NUTE of Rochester, a blacksmith; had 5 children.
2384 CHILD, died young.
F2385 LYDIA, b. ——, m. STEPHEN YOUNG of Strafford.
2386 AMOS, b. ——, was unmarried, a farmer and mason.
2387 MIRIBAH ANN, b. ——, m. EDWARD F. WATSON of Nottingham, a carpenter and builder, who later went to Lowell; had 6 children.
2388 JACOB, b. ——, m. —— CUTTER of Portsmouth; was a brick mason, lieutenant in Civil War; had 5 children.

F690 Mary E. Locke, born in Barrington, Aug. 2, 1773, married in Barrington, 1798, ISAAC WOODMAN of Durham. He was born in Durham, Aug. 13, 1770, was a farmer in Woodstock, where he moved about 1807, and died there Oct. 27, 1832. She died in West Thornton, Aug. 19, 1860.

Children of 6th Gen. b. in Barrington and Woodstock.

F2389 ELIZABETH L., b. June 4, 1798, m. Aug. 4, 1825, REUBEN FOSS.
2390 CLARISSA, b. May 3, 1800, d. 1804.
F2391 ALEXANDER, b. Aug. 27, 1801, m. Feb. 21, 1830, PHOEBE S. WALLACE.
F2392 IRA, b. July 6, 1803, m. Oct. 26, 1826, EUNICE M. KIMBALL.
F2393 NATHANIEL, b. Dec. 15, 1804, m. May 22, 1827, BETSEY KIMBALL.
F2394 CAROLINE, b. Sept. 5, 1806, m. Sept. 4, 1831, JOSHUA CONNOR.
F2395 JOSEPH, b. May 31, 1809, m. Jan. 1, 1838, ELEANOR BARNARD.
2396 FREEMAN, b. March 19, 1812, d. in Thornton, Oct. 15, 1836, m. Sept. 13, 1834, —— ——; had no children.
F2397 MARY ANN, b. May 1, 1816, m. Oct. 12, 1834, PELATIAH RUSSELL.

2398 CHARLES, b. May 24, 1822, d. in Bridgewater, Nov. 11, 1899, m. in Campton, May 20, 1848, JEMIMA AVERY of C., b. there March 7, 1829, d. Bridgewater, March 3, 1897, dau. of Jacob and Jennie (Cook). He was a Justice of Peace 30 years, went to Bridgewater in 1865 and was a merchant there 16 years. *Children:* 2399 JACOB A.; 2400 LYMAN B.; 2401 CHARLES S., m. Dec. 3, 1894, MARTHA FRENCH, is a dentist in Ashland, and has: 2402 CHARLES, 2403 ROGER, and 2404 GEORGE; 2405 ADDIE C.; 2406 CORYDON E.; 2407 CORA M.; 2408 AUSTIN W.

F693 William Locke, born in Barrington, Dec. 22, 1779, married Feb. 21, 1802, SARAH HOITT of Northwood. She was born in Lee, March 9, 1781, the daughter of Stephen and Lydia (Buzzell), and died March 4, 1842. He was a shoemaker and tanner in Barrington but moved to Lee in 1817, built a house and went farming. There he died May 13, 1869.

Children of 6th Gen. b. in Barrington.

2409 JAMES CARR (an adopted son), b. May 12, 1803, d. in Northwood, March 19, 1846, m. Nov. 8, 1833, ELIZABETH H. HAYES of Barrington, dau. of Samuel and Hannah (Demeritt). He spent his boyhood on the farm, was educated at Wolf Academy, taught in Dover schools several years very successfully; was an esteemed citizen of Northwood. His widow m. 2nd, March 20, 1855, DUDLEY BLAKE; m. 3rd, DUDLEY HILL; had no children.

F2410 DANIEL PIPER, b. Sept. 25, 1804, m. HANNAH HOITT.

F2411 WILLIAM J., b. Dec. 25, 1805, m. May 2, 1829, SARAH B. DAME.

F2412 STEPHEN H., b. Aug. 30, 1807, m. 1st, Apl. 7, 1831, ABIGAIL WIGHT; m. 2nd, June 14, 1847, DEBORAH R. CHASE.

2413 JOHN BUZZELL, b. Dec. 6, 1808, d. in Lee, Dec. 2, 1861, m. Apl. 5, 1835, NANCY NEWHALL, b. in Saugus, Mass., 1815, d. in Lee, Sept. 9, 1864. Was a carpenter and builder in Boston and Cambridge. In 1849 he returned to Lee. *Children:* 2414 JOHN G. b. June 10, 1836, d. unm. Dec. 12, 1854; 2415 WILLIAM N., b. Jan. 28, 1842, d. unm. Nov. 26, 1865; 2416 CORNELIUS AUSTIN, b. in Lee, Oct. 12, 1844, d. unm. July 23, 1861; 2417 MARY M., b. May 9, 1849, d. unm. Jan. 7, 1868.

2418 BARZILLA SHURTLEFF, b. Jan. 13, 1811, died in Sacramento, Cal., Oct. 15, 1866, m. MARTHA SMITH of Newton, Me., who died in Colima, Mex., Apl. 16, 1844. He was a machinist and overseer of cotton mills in Lowell; went to Lima, Peru, also to Mexico to set up mills and teach milling. He was a '49er in California. He had: 2419 MARTHA J., b. in Lowell, Jan. 23, 1837, m. Nov. 8, 1871, JOHN H. MACE; no children; live in Boston.

F2420 SARAH HOITT, b. May 29, 1812, m. Feb. 19, 1839, DEARBORN B. MOSES.

F2421 BETSEY BABB, b. Apl. 3, 1816, m. Oct. 29, 1839, JACOB H. TILTON.

2422 INFANT, born and died the same day.

F2423 SAMUEL HOITT, b. Dec. 28, 1818, m. March 10, 1846, ELEANOR A. PAYSON.

SIXTH GENERATION

F694 Elisha Locke, born in Barrington, Oct. 26, 1780, married in Durham, Dec. 18, 1806, SOPHIA PINKHAM of Durham, born in Durham, Feb. 20, 1790, died Feb. 15, 1876. He was a stone cutter and farmer and died Dec. 15, 1854.

Children of 6th Gen.
2424 MARY P., b. Barr., Apl. 4, 1807, m. 1st, Apl. 14, 1825, EPHRAIM REYNOLDS, # 2343; m. 2nd, Apl. 3, 1859, W. H. DEARBORN.
F2425 BENJAMIN F., b. July 20, 1809, m. 1st, Aug. 16, 1835, MARY P. CORSER; m. 2nd, CHARLOTTE PARKER (or CURRIER).
F2426 ALFRED, b. Dec. 19, 1811, m. Aug. 5, 1834, MARY A. D. SEAVEY.
F2427 ELISHA, b. Nov. 18, 1814, m. Jan. 27, 1841, LAVINA FRENCH.
F2428 ELIZABETH P., b. Dec. 12, 1817, m. Oct. 7, 1840, AARON S. CRAWFORD.
F2429 JAMES M., b. July 1, 1823, m. Jan. 28, 1846, IZETTA PLUMMER.
F2430 LYMAN, b. Jan. 22, 1824, m. Dec. 26, 1842, SUSAN CATER.
F2431 HENRY W., b. Sept. 28, 1827, m. 1st, July 4, 1847, ELIZABETH A. WATERHOUSE; m. 2nd, Apl. 13, 1870, ANGELINA HAYES.
F2432 SARAH PINKHAM, b. Apl. 16, 1830, m. Nov. 12, 1848, HENRY LITTLEFIELD.
F2433 OLIVER BABB, b. Feb. 20, 1835, m. Jan. 23, 1858, MARTHA ANN FERNALD.

F695 Betsey Locke, born in Barrington, Apl. 21, 1783, married MOSES DEMERITT, who was born 1794, died in Northwood, Feb. 28, 1856. He was a blacksmith at Farmington.

Children of 6th Gen.
F2435 JACOB JAY, b. Feb. 15, 1806, m. 1st, Aug. 13, 1823, ELIZA EVANS; m. 2nd, Jan. 2, 1833, MARCIA HERBERT FERNALD.
2436 MOSES, not married.
2437 ALBERT COLUMBUS, b. ——, m. and had: 2438 EMMA J.; 2439 JULIA M.; 2440 AMANDA; 2441 ALBERT, who was a city official in Brooklyn, N. Y.
2442 ELI, b. ——, m. SARAH PUTNAM; had: 2443 JAMES; 2444 EMILY. Eli kept a store in East Saginaw, Mich., and died in DeWitt, N. Y.
F2446 MARY ANN, b. Aug, 20, 1811, m. HORATIO BABB.
2447 HANNAH, b. ——, not married.

F696 Dolly Locke, born in Barrington, Aug. 11, 1784, married in Franconia, Sept. 9, 1810, BARZILLA SHURTLEFF of Illinois. He was born in Carver, Mass., Dec. 22, 1780, died in Victoria, Ill., Knox Co., where he was a farmer for ten years, Feb. 26, 1855. She died Nov. 26, 1855.

Children of 6th Gen.
2448 BENJAMIN, b. Oct. 27, 1811, m. PRISCILLA B. BROWN. He was of the firm of Shurtleff & Cotrell, Boston.
2449 ELISHA LOCKE, b. Aug. 27, 1813, d. Sept. 19, 1816.

2450 WILLIAM LOCKE, b. Oct. 19, 1814, m. MARY WESTFALL.
2451 HENRY SARGENT, b. Feb. 27, 1816, m. EMALINE WILLIAMSON.
2452 SAMUEL ATWOOD, b. Oct. 28, 1819, m. MARGARET TAYLOR.
2453 ABIGAIL, b. July 15, 1821, d. in Leavenworth, Kans., 1885, m. in Victoria, Ill., June 15, 1840, DAVID STURTIVANT.
2454 CHARLES AUGUST, b. Dec. 16, 1822, m. HESTER ANN TAYLOR.

F697 Alice Locke, born in Barrington, June 24, 1787, married in Madbury, Feb. 16, 1812, SAMUEL DEMERITT of Rochester, son of Jonathan 1753, son of Ebenezer 1726, Son of Eli 1696. Samuel was born in Madbury, Sept. 30, 1789; was a blacksmith in Rochester and died June 30, 1856. Alice died Apl. 19, 1866.

Children of 6th Gen. b. in Rochester.

2455 NANCY F., and 2456 LUCY C., died infants.
2457 ALICE L.; 2458 SOPHIA L.; 2459 SAMUEL; all died young.
2460 ELIZABETH J., d. in Gonic, 1880, m. SAMUEL L. SHERMAN of Salem N. Y.
2461 MARIA B., d. 1880, m. NATHAN WILSON of Salem, N. Y.
F2462 MARY J., b. ——, m. 1st, OLIVER P. BURLEIGH; m. 2nd, JOHN H. GLASS.
2463 EMALINE L., b. ——, died in early life.
F2464 DEBORAH, b. ——, m. WILLIAM H. FELKER.

F699 Benjamin Babb Locke, born in Barrington, Sept. 20, 1792, married in Rochester Nov. 23, 1815, BETSEY HURD (Heard in rec.) of Rochester, born Nov. 18, 1795 (Barrington record Feb. 8), died in 1866. He was farmer in Barrington until 1839, then went to New Durham, and died in 1856.

Children of 6th Gen. b. in Barrington.

2465 ELISABETH B., b. Oct. 21, 1816.
F2466 ELISHA, b. Dec. 11, 1818, m. 1st, June 19, 1847, NANCY C. SPARE; m. 2nd, July 29, 1851, ANNA E. PERRY.
2467 WILLIAM H., b. Nov. 22, 1820, died in Wilmington, Ind., July 23, 1849, was a physician there.
2468 SARAH H., b. Sept. 20, 1822, d. ——.
2469 LUCY H., b. Feb. 5, 1825, d. Apl. 4, 1827.
2470 IRA W., b. June 6, 1827, d. July 4, 1837.
2471 TRISTRAM B., b. Dec. 18, 1829, d. March 19, 1832.
2472 DOROTHY S., b. June 19, 1832, m. DANIEL COLOMY, b. Feb. 19, 1830, son of Daniel and Alice (Runnels), was a shoemaker in Dover, and d. Jan. 28, 1875; had: 2473 EMMA.
F2474 BENJAMIN T., b. Sept. 9, 1835, m. May 24, 1860, AGNES LABOUNTY.
2475 CAROLINE H., b. July 25, 1838, m. Feb. 19, 1870, ROBERT M. VARNEY of Dover, b. 1824, son of Robert.

SIXTH GENERATION

F703 William Locke, born in New Brunswick, 1806, married EMILY MARSHALL, lived in Victoria, N. S., in 1830, and later in Greytown, N. S.
> *Children of 6th Gen. b. in Nova Scotia.*
> 2476 CYNTHIA L., b. ——, m. JAMES WHALEN, about 1873.
> 2477 HENRY ALLEN, b. ——, m. and had a daughter.
> 2478 WILLIAM, b. 1842, d. 1864 unmarried.
> SEVEN others died, each less than 21 years of age.

F704 James Ed. Locke, born in Frederick, N. B., July 1, 1807, married 1835, MERCY MARSHALL, born Apl. 5, 1819. They lived Grand Manan, N. B.
> *Children of the 6th Gen. b. in New Brunswick.*
> Two infants died young.
> 2480 MARY PRISCILLA, b. 1841, d. Bear River, N. S., March 26, 1873, m. 1864, DANIEL PARKER of Weymouth, N. S. *Children:* 2481 GIRL, died young; 2482 MARY A., b. 1866, m. GEORGE GREEN, of Grand Manan; 2483 WILLIAM H., b. 1868; 2484 DANIEL, b. 1871; 2485 CHARLES T., b. 1873, of Gloucester, Mass.
> 2486 WELLINGTON JACKSON, b. Feb. 22, 1844-6, m. Nov. 15, 1869, JULIETTA GREEN, b. June 11, 1855. *Children:* 2487 LAURA, b. Aug. 31, 1870; 2488 JAMES E., b. Aug. 27, 1874; 2489 THOMAS OSCAR, b. Jan. 27, 1880; 2490 SARAH, b. Nov. 12, 1883, d. June 9, 1884; 2491 ALTON, b. Oct. 15, 1884; 2492 REBECCA, b. Apl. 8, 1889.
> 2493 JOHN EZRA, b. June 25, 1847, m. Dec. 24, 1874, MRS. REBECCA R. PEABODY, b. in Middleton, Mass., Jan. 17, 1832; no children. She had two former husbands, JAMES KELLEY and —— MCINTIRE. John was a gardener in Danvers, Mass.

F744 Mercy Philbrick, born in Rye, Jan. 8, 1763, died Nov. 19, 1846, married MICHAEL DALTON, born Nov. 13, 1753, son of Benjamin and Mary (May). He was a fifer in Capt. Parsons' Co. and died Oct. 6, 1846.
> *Children of 6th Gen.*
> 2494 BENJAMIN, b. 1780, m. Dec. 3, 1805, SARAH GARLAND, b. ——, d. 1844, aged 64. He d. Sept. 10, 1861. Had five children, the last of whom, 2495 ANNA LEAVITT, b. Sept. 7, 1818, m. 1st, WILLIAM GARLAND; m. 2nd, GARDNER T. LOCKE, # F2806.
> 2496 ABIGAIL, b. Apl. 15, 1782, m. Feb. 12, 1799, MOSES SHAW, and d. March 1, 1869.
> 2497 DANIEL PHILBRICK, b. 1785, m. Oct. 2, 1809, PATTY BROWN, who d. July 8, 1854. He d. Sept. 13, 1842, had five children.
> 2498 MARY, b. 1792, m. Sept. 2, 1813, ALEXANDER BROWN.

F746 Joses Philbrick, born July 1766, married Jan. 12, 1790, SARAH SMITH. He died Dec. 21, 1842.

Children of 6th Gen.

2500 DANIEL, b. Apl. 13, 1790, m. PAMELIA GUNNISON, lived at Portsmouth and had six children.
2501 MARY, b. Feb. 5, 1792, m. RICHARD WEBSTER, lived in Epsom.
2502 SALLY or POLLY, b. Oct. 24, 1794, m. BENJAMIN GARLAND.
2503 DAVID, b. Oct. 3, 1796, m. SARAH LAMOS, lived in Portsmouth; had two children.
2504 THOMAS, b. July 29, 1799, m. CLARISSA SHAW, lived in Rye; had eight children.
2505 JOHN, b. Jan. 5, 1804, m. Dec. 25, 1831, SARAH BROWN, lived in Rye, and d. Sept. 12, 1877; had five children.
2507 ABIGAIL, b. Sept. 1, 1805, m. Sept. 8, 1824, SAMUEL PARSONS.
2508 WILLIAM, b. June 20, 1812, m. ABIGAIL WILLIAMS.

F750 Ephraim Philbrick, born Sept. 9, 1780, married SARAH WEBSTER. He lived at Rye, was Captain of Militia in 1811, and died Jan. 25, 1860.

Children of 6th Gen.

2510 JOSIAH W., b. Oct. 2, 1807, m. June 25, 1833, SARAH ANN BROWN, who d. Sept. 22, 1870. He d. Oct. 17, 1870; had three children.
2511 SARAH ANN, b. Nov. 7, 1811, m. July 7, 1835, DANIEL PHILBRICK.
2512 MOSES C., b. Apl. 6, 1813, m. SARAH A. GARLAND, who d. Sept. 28, 1898. He d. Apl. 8, 1875.
2513 JOHN C., b. Apl. 9, 1818, m. May 25, 1845, ELIZA JENNESS, who d. Sept. 18, 1893. He d. Jan. 15, 1869; had three children.
2514 CHRISTIANNA, b. Aug. 27, 1822, m. Dec. 1838, ABRAHAM PERKINS.

F752 Joseph Philbrick, born May 1788, married March 10, 1810, BETSEY PAGE. He died Apl. 12, 1879.

Children of 6th Gen. b. in Rye.

2515 SILAS, b. ——, m. MARIA GOODWIN.
2516 MARY, m. NEWELL PHILBRICK.
2517 OLIVE, m. Dec. 9, 1834, EDMON MASON of Hampton.
2518 ABIGAIL, m. JOHN W. MACE.
2519 ELIZABETH, b. ——, m. Nov. 9, 1839, LEVI MASON.
2520 MARTHA ANN, m. GEORGE NAY.
2521 SAMUEL BICKFORD, b. 1821, m. LYDIA MOULTON; had eleven children.
2522 DANIEL.

F916 Levi Seavey, born in Rye, Dec. 29, 1765, married Nov. 25, 1790, HANNAH TILTON, born 1770, died in Deerfield, Feb. 17, 1852. He was a farmer and surveyor in Deerfield 1796, and died Oct. 27, 1858.

SIXTH GENERATION

Children of 6th Gen. b. in Deerfield.
2523 JOSIAH, b. May 27, 1792, d. Aug. 22, 1849, m. LOVE BLAKE and she d. 1846.
2524 SARAH, b. Feb. 25, 1794, d. March 9, 1877.
2425 HULDAH, b. Apl. 11, 1796, d. Jan. 1882.
2426 HANNAH, b. July 30, 1798, d. ——.
2427 MOSES P., b. July 20, 1800, d. Sept. 5, 1879.
2428 BETSEY, b. Dec. 12, 1802, d. Feb. 23, 1877.
2429 POLLY, b. March 13, 1807, d. 1882.
2430 MERIBAH, b. May 1, 1809, d. July 22, 1850.
2431 FANNIE, b. Aug. 20, 1811, d. June 24, 1890, m. and had a son: 2532 REV. J. W. F. BARNES.

F927 Hannah Lang, born in Rye, Sept. 16, 1769, married DOWST RAND of Rye, born June 24, 1764, son of Saml. and Sarah (Dowst). She died May 16, 1860, aged 91. He was in the 1812 War, lived in Rye and died Jan. 12, 1847.

Children of 6th Gen. b. in Rye.
2533 BILLEY, bapt. Jan. 11, 1789, m. Feb. 28, 1811, CHARLOTTE BATCHELDER, b. Feb. 14, 1793, d. Sept. 15, 1873, dau. of John and Mary (Cotton). He d. Dec. 26, 1846, had: 2534 JAMES; 2535 WILLIAM; 2536 JOHN.
2537 PATTY L., b. Oct. 1791, m. 1st, Nov. 11, 1813, SIMEON DOW of Gilmanton, b. July 11, 1786; m. 2nd, GEORGE BRAGG.
2538 SAMUEL, b. 1793, m. SARAH FOSS, # 1024, bapt. July 3, 1791.
2539 BICKFORD L., b. Feb. 22, 1795, d. Ports., Dec. 22, 1860, m. 1st EUNICE CARTER; m. 2nd, MARTHA (PATTY) BACHELDER, b. Nov. 13, 1797; was an agent of the Eastern Stage Co., Salem to Portsmouth, 1840.
2540 SARAH, b. Nov. 14, 1797, d. Apl. 13, 1883, m. July 25, 1824, JAMES PERKINS of Hampton, b. July 16, 1792, d. Feb. 18, 1855, son of John and Joanna (Elkins), lived in Hampton; had five children.
2541 TRUNDY, bapt. June 1800, d. Dec. 12, 1877, m. ELIZABETH STEVENS of Brentwood; had four children.
2542 OLIVER, b. 1802, d. 1802.
2543 HANNAH, b. 1805, m. Portsmouth, June 23, 1830, SAMUEL ODIORNE, b. 1802; had: 2544 OLIVE; 2545 JOSEPH P.
2546 OLIVER P., b. 1807, m. June 1828, POLLY BEAN.

F932 Robert Saunders, baptized in Rye, Oct. 12, 1766, married MARY FOSS, born Feb. 11, 1764.

Children of 6th Gen.
2547 JOHN, m. —— BUZZELL. 2548 BETSEY.
2549 ROBERT, m. HULDAH PHILBRICK.
2550 JOB, b. 1792, lived at Derry and had two children.
2551 ELIJAH, b. ——, m. OLLY PHILBRICK.
2552 FREDERICK, b. July 1803, m. —— MANSON and d. Feb. 28, 1881.
2554 WILLIAM, m. —— WALLACE.

F939 Elijah Locke, born in Rye, June 28, 1781-2, married Jan. 15 (21), 1802, HANNAH SAUNDERS of Alexandria. She was born Jan. 4, 1780, died Aug. 12, 1865. He was a farmer in Alexandria, and died Aug. 12, 1864.

Children of 6th Gen.

2555 BETSEY, b. in Epsom, Dec. 11, 1802, d. 1860, m. WILLIAM M. AIKENS of Boston, b. Dec. 10, 1800, son of Andrew and Martha (McAlister). He m. 2nd, —— MASON of Boston and d. there Jan. 19, 1866. *Children:* 2556 HANNAH, m. —— BODFISH, lived in Waltham, Mass.; 2557 MARY; 2558 WILLIAM; 2559 FRED; all died young.

2560 SAMUEL, b. in Alexandria, June 22, 1805, d. in Concord, Apl. 25, 1885, m. MARY WALLACE, # 2565, of Alexandria, his cousin; was a farmer in Alex. and Concord; had child, b. 1829, d. 1831.

F2561 REUBEN, b. Jan. 29, 1809, m. Feb. 15, 1832, IRENE G. HEALEY.

2562 NANCY, b. in Alex., Dec. 15, 1811, d. in Hyde Park, March 1887, m. MARTIN H. WHICHER, b. June 10, 1808, son of Benjamin and Catherine (Cole). He was a business man of Boston and Hyde Park, died Aug. 24, 1875.

F2563 BENJAMIN, b. Aug. 15, 1817, m. EFFIE WALLACE, # 2566.

F2564 GEORGE, b. Oct. 18, 1820, m. March 7, 1844, ELIZABETH CHENEY.

F940 Mary Locke born in Rye, 1784, married Apl. 12, 1804, JOHN WALLIS of Epsom. She died Apl. 25, 1856. He was a farmer and trader in Epsom and Concord and married 2nd, SARAH TOWLE.

Children of 6th Gen.

2565 MARY E., b. in Moultonborough, Apl. 8, 1811, d. in Concord, Dec. 28, 1884, m. her cousin, SAMUEL LOCKE, # 2560.

2566 EFFIE, b. 1817, m. cousin, BENJAMIN LOCKE. (See F2563.)

2567 ELIZA, not married.

2568 MARTHA, m. DOCTOR JOHNSON; had: 2569 JAMES, in Concord. She d. Concord.

2570 ABBIE, m. a man from Chicago.

2571 SUSAN, d. in Concord, m. JOHN ELLIOTT, who d. 1888, had a child died young.

2572 ELIJAH.

F941 Levi Locke, born in Rye, March 20, 1786, married Aug. 15, 1805, RACHEL D. TOWLE. She was born in Epsom, June 5, 1786, died in Chichester, March 3, 1864. He was a farmer and carpenter in Chichester and died there Aug. 14, 1838.

Children of 6th Gen. b. Epsom or Chichester.

2573 STEPHEN, d. infant.

2574 STEPHEN M., b. March 29, 1807, m. Sept. 14, 1828, MRS. MARY (LANGLEY) HOOK, was a farmer in Chichester, had no children and d. Nov. 27, 1860.

SIXTH GENERATION

2575 SARAH J., b. Nov. 25, 1808, was deaf and dumb, d. unmarried in Concord, Sept. 18, 1892.
F2576 ELIZA, b. Jan. 10, 1812, m. Jan. 27, 1831, CHARLES G. HOOK.
2577 BRADBURY C., b. Nov. 12, 1813, m. July 4, 1853, SALLY GRIFFIN, had no children, was a farmer and died in Chichester, March 23, 1870. She m. 2nd, JOSEPH W. MOSES, b. 1843.
F2578 PARNA T., b. July 20, 1816, m. HENRY HOOK.
F2579 BENJAMIN MARDEN, b. June 14, 1819, m. Feb. 3, 1840, FRANCENA M. HOOK.
F2580 HULDAH P., b. Apl. 22, 1822, m. June 8, 1846, JAMES M. JONES.
F2581 LEVI, b. March 24, 1824, m. June 6, 1846, NANCY E. DURGIN.

F942 John Locke, born in Epsom, March 17, 1780, married Sept. 1797, **Abigail Locke,** # **1578** of Epsom. She was born Jan. 27, 1777, died May 3, 1809. He married 2nd, MEHITABLE BICKFORD of Epsom, born Aug. 15, 1783, died Aug. 23, 1842, daughter of Samuel. He was a stone cutter and blacksmith in Epsom. At birth he weighed only 4 pounds but in his prime he was a tall, muscular man weighing some 200 pounds. He died in Loudon, March 15, 1849.

Children of 6th Gen. all b. in Epsom except three.
F2582 WILLIAM, b. Dec. 24, 1799, m. LOUISA FERREN.
2583 PATTY or MARTHA, b. Nov. 25, 1801, d. unm. in Boston, Nov. 9, 1822.
2584 FRANCIS, b. Nov. 25, 1803, died in Boston, a carpenter, unmarried, Dec. 17, 1831.
2585 ABIGAIL, b. 1805, d. Jan. 27, 1805.
2586 CHILD, b. 1807, d. Apl. 7, 1809.
2587 NABBY, b. Aug. 28, 1810, d. Apl. 29, 1817; a twin died one day old.
F2588 JOHN, b. Jan. 10, 1812, m. Nov. 19, 1834, SARAH SANBORN.
2589 SAMUEL B., b. March 17, 1814, m. July 2, 1837, LUCIA R. SANBORN of Gilford, b. Nov. 5, 1813, d. Feb. 16, 1877. He was a painter in Loudon, and died in Centre Harbor, Oct. 16, 1877; had no children.
F2590 SALLY V., b. Feb. 12, 1816, m. Jan. 24, 1839, PETER C. SEAVEY.
F2591 GEORGE, twin, b. Feb. 12, 1816, m. July 31, 1845, SABRA KIMBALL.
F2592 BENJAMIN B., b. Sept. 5, 1818, m. JULIA M. CURRIER, Nov. 14, 1850.
F2593 ABIGAIL, b. Jan. 3, 1821, m. 1st, Apl. 4, 1842, REUBEN SANDERS, # 4895; m. 2nd, Sept. 25, 1878, WILLIAM K. HOLT.
F2594 MARTHA, b. July 5, 1823, m. 1st, June 20, 1844, PIERCE BICKFORD; m. 2nd, 1854, JOSEPH WOOD.

F944 Huldah Locke, born in Epsom, Aug. 4, 1783, married in Epsom, Sept. 1, 1799, JOHN PAGE of Epsom, a farmer. She died May 28, 1829.

Children of 6th Gen. b. in Epsom.

2595 HANNAH, b. Nov. 7, 1800, d. 1887, m. JOHN FOSS of Northwood. *Child:* 2596 HANNAH, b. 1826, m. MAYHEW KNOWLTON of Northwood Ridge, and they had: 2597 EVERETT K., m. IDA WEEKS.

2598 ABIGAIL, b. July 30, 1802, d. Oct. 5, 1870, m. LEVI BERRY. *Children:* 2599 GILMAN; 2600 HULDAH; 2601 JOHN; 2602 MARY ANN; 2603 ALICE; 2604 CHARLES; 2605 FREEMAN; 2606 LEVI, who lived in Northwood.

F2607 JAMES, b. June 3, 1804, m. 1st, 1829, DOROTHY SMITH; m. 2nd, 1835, BELINDA BERRY.

2608 BETSEY, b. March 29, 1806, d. Apl. 1876, m. SAMUEL BROWN of Epsom. *Children:* 2609 JAMES; 2610 THEODATE.

2611 JEREMIAH, b. May 23, 1808, m. CYNTHIA MARTIN of Northwood. *Children:* 2612 JOHN; 2613 RUTH; 2614 BELSEN; 2615 SARAH T.; and 2616 VENDESA.

2617 HULDAH, b. May 5, 1810, m. SAMUEL BACHELDER; no children.

2618 THEODATE H., b. Apl. 27, 1813, d. 1887, m. May 12, 1836, ASA JEWELL, b. Feb. 10, 1811, son of Asa and Sarah (Wiggin); lived Exeter. *Children:* 2619 MARY A., b. March 21, 1837, m. May 1885, GILMAN B. HOYT of Exeter; 2620 NELLIE F., b. Jan. 19, 1842; 2621 ADALAIDE F., b. June 17, 1847; 2622 ALBERT B., b. Apl. 28, 1850; 2623 OSCAR, b. Feb. 4, 1852; and a twin, 2624 FRANK O.

F2625 JOHN, b. June 11, 1816, m. MAHALA B. LANE.

2626 SARAH, b. March 29, 1818, d. Dec. 15, 1833.

2627 MARY, b. Apl. 16, 1822, d. Oct. 12, 1876, m. Sept. 29, 1840, DAVID C. FOGG of Lynn. *Children:* 2628 JOHN P., b. Nov. 18, 1842, m. 1870, CAROLINE E. CARR; 2629 EMMA H., b. Oct. 19, 1845, m. BYRON D. HOITT of Lynn; 2630 MARY E., b. Feb. 7, 1848, m. Sept. 20, 1882, CHARLES H. CAMPBELL; 2631 ELLEN M., b. Sept. 26, 1850, m. THOMAS CRIEL.

F945 William Locke, born in Epsom, Sept. 6, 1785, married Dec. 25, 1808, MERCY SHAW, born Epsom, March 8, 1791, died in Lowell, Mass., Jan. 23, 1869. He was a farmer in Alexandria and died in Epsom, Sept. 3, 1829.

Children of 6th Gen. b. in Alexandria.

F2632 WOODBURY, b. March 4, 1813, m. 1st, —— SMILEY; m. 2nd, EMALINE LORING.

F2633 MARY, b. Aug. 4, 1815, m. Sept. 26, 1832, NATHANIEL RAY.

2634 TIRZAH R., b. Apl. 6, 1818, d. in Lowell, Jan. 18, 1882, m. L., Feb. 14, 1842, DAVID GILMAN of Gilmanton. He was an engineer in Lowell and d. there March 21, 1898. *Children:* 2635 HORACE E., b. Lowell, Nov. 4, 1842, m. 1st, NELLIE HAPPINEY; m. 2nd, a WIDOW ——, no children; 2636 ALBERT F., b. L., Dec. 23, 1844, m. in Boston, LIZZIE HORTON, and d. Gilmanton, 1881; 2637 ABBIE T., b. Concord, June 24, 1849, m. Lowell, Apl. 25, 1898, C. FRANK DURRELL of Lowell, d. L., June 21, 1898; 2638 CHARLES, lives in Boston.

SIXTH GENERATION

2639 MARTHA D., b. Jan. 29, 1822, m. in Lowell, Apl. 6, 1843, EDWARD M. SARGENT, b. Littleton, Nov. 17, 1820. He was an expressman in Lowell. *Children:* 2640 ELLEN, b. Dec. 25, 1843; 2641 FRED M., b. March 8, 1849. Both lived Lowell, unm.

2642 HIRAM, b. Sept. 1, 1823; d. Sept. 3, 1823.

2643 HORACE B., b. Feb. 25, 1826, d. Dec. 2, 1897, m. Apl. 28, 1850, HARRIET E. GROW of Vershire, Vt., b. Aug. 14, 1833, dau. of Peter and Lydia (Shaw). He was station agent in Keuka, Fla., on Southern Fla. R. R. *Child:* 2644 CARRIE H., b. Oct. 4, 1860, m. Keuka, Apl. 19, 1891, JACOB M. LEEDY of So. Dakota, b. May 9, 1830, d. K., July 20, 1897, no children. He came to Keuka, bought a hotel and 40 acres of land, and was a man of great enterprise and influence.

F946 Elizabeth Locke, born in Epsom, July 11, 1788, married June, 1813, JOHN LANGLEY, born in Deerfield, Apl. 3, 1789, died Nov. 8, 1862. Elizabeth died in Chichester, Apl. 22, 1823. He married 2nd, in 1824, LOIS A. SALTER. He was a farmer in Chichester.

Children of 6th Gen. b. in Chichester.

2645 SAMUEL, b. Nov. 26, 1813, d. in 1890, m. ELIZABETH SANDS of Saco. He was a slipper maker of Chichester and Boston. *Children:* 2646 ANNIE; 2647 ELLA, who m. HENRY JOHNSON of Boston.

F2648 HANNAH S., b. July 18, 1815, m. 1837, STEPHEN WATSON.

2649 MOSES, b. March 24, 1817, d. unmarried 1839.

2650 ELIZABETH, b. Sept. 4, 1819, m. 1st, GEORGE TUCK of Cincinnati, had: 2651 EMMA, who d. aged 4; m. 2nd, CUMMINS BUTTERFIELD, and had child d. 4 weeks old; m. 3rd, WM. W. ROBERTS; m. 4th, W. W. TICE.

2652 JOHN, b. May 17, 1821, d. Oct. 19, 1898, m. 1st, JANE COLLEY; m. 2nd, CASSANDRA WOODMAN, lived in Hartford, Conn., had: 2653 CAPITOLA.

F2654 WILLIAM, b. Apl. 18, 1823, m. Jan. 15, 1853, ELIZA MCCRILLIS.

F947 Reuben Locke, born in Epsom, March 14, 1791, married Sept. 10, 1815, JANE MCMURPHY of Alexandria, who died Jan. 30, 1850. He was a farmer in Alexandria, and died May 25, 1864.

Children of 6th Gen. b. in Alexandria.

2655 JAMES C., b. Apl. 4, 1816, d. Sept. 28, 1817.

2656 JAMES C., b. Sept. 23, 1818, d. unmarried, a Boston fruit dealer, May 29, 1846.

2657 FORESTE M., b. Jan. 9, 1821, d. Nov. 2, 1836.

F2658 HARVEY, b. Nov. 11, 1824, m. Dec. 22, 1850, ANN C. TEWKSBURY.

2659 DAVID, b. Aug. 6, 1826, d. Feb. 26, 1849.

F2660 WARREN W., b. Feb. 29, 1829, m. 1st, July 14, 1852, LODOISKI GAGE; m. 2nd, Sept. 4, 1859, MINNIE J. POSTON.

2661 GEORGE K., b. July 4, 1831, d. unmarried Sept. 8, 1860. He was agent of a Packing Company and was drowned on Lake Michigan when the steamer *Lady Elgin* went down with 100 persons.

F950 Elisha L. Ladd, born in Bradford, Vt., June 14, 1787, married Jan. 1, 1822, ASENATH BACHELDER born 1791, died in Alabama, Sept. 17, 1863, daughter of Rev. Daniel and Phebe (Chase). He lived in Atlanta, Ga., and died in Ohio, Apl. 26, 1845.

Children of 6th Gen. b. in Ohio.

2662 DANIEL B., b. July 19, 1822, m. Apl. 30, 1846, LUCINDA E. WILLEY, b. Aug. 2, 1822, lived in Atlanta, Ga.; had no children.
2663 ROXANNA, b. Jan. 17, 1825, d. Dec. 13, 1832.
2664 PHEBE, b. Feb. 22, 1827, d. Jan. 13, 1833.
2665 ALONZO C., b. Jan. 30, 1831, died in California in 1873, m. 1st, Oct. 27, 1858, MARY E. LADD, who d. Jan. 12, 1865, dau. of H. H. Ladd; m. 2nd, March 4, 1868, LOUISA G. STEUBNER. *Children:*
2666 HATTIE M., b. Oct. 2, 1861, m. Jan. 10, 1885, A. L. DELKIN;
2667 FREDDIE, b. Dec. 20, 1868; 2668 NORA A., b. Apl. 11, 1870, d. Sept. 14, 1870.

F959 Jonathan Locke, born in Haverhill, N. H., Nov. 6, 1797, married Jan. 31, 1822, SOPHIA THURSTON, born in St. Albans, Vt., May 11, 1800, died in Brasher Falls, N. Y., Aug. 4, 1881. He was a very kind man, a cooper by trade, and one of the first settlers in Brasher Falls, N. Y., where he died Sept. 17, 1879.

Children of 6th Gen. b. in Brasher Falls, N. Y.

2669 EUNICE, b. Aug. 23, 1823, d. March 23, 1825.
2670 ABIGAIL WILKINS, b. Feb. 27, 1825, m. AMBROSE STARK. He m. 2nd, HELEN SCRIPTURE. By Abigail he had: 2671 JONATHAN, b. 1845, m. ―― HILL and had five children in Winthrop, N. Y.; 2672 JOSEPHINE, d. infant.
2673 HORATIO NELSON, b. Sept. 15, 1826, m. his cousin, CHRISTIANA SAUNDERS, # 2684. All children died young.
2674 CANDACE JANETTE, b. Nov. 17, 1828, d. Dec. 22, 1846.
2675 ELIJAH FREDERICK, b. Jan. 23, 1832, d. Apl. 1, 1853.
F2676 ELISHA FERDINAND, b. a twin, Jan. 23, 1832, m. 1855, HANNAH SPAULDING.
2677 HARRIET STEBBINS, b. Oct. 10, 1834, d. June 27, 1858, m. Apl. 1, 1854, MOODY M. SANBORN, b. in Massena, N. Y., Apl. 18, 1829. He m. 2nd, ELIZABETH SCRIPTURE. By Harriet he had: 2678 LAWRENCE AUGUSTUS, b. Sept. 28, 1854; 2679 WILLIS JOHN, b. Jan. 9, 1857, lives 1915, in Winthrop, N. Y.
2681 JONATHAN, JR., b. May 20, 1837, d. Oct. 29, 1837.

SIXTH GENERATION

F960 Abigail Locke, born ——, married JOHN SAUNDERS.
Children of 6th Gen.
2682 MELISSA, m. HERMAN HOLMES, had: 2683 LORINDA, m. —— LARKIN and had eight children in Winthrop, N. Y.
2684 CHRISTIANA, m. HORATIO N. LOCKE, #2673.
2685 MARIA, m. —— STARK; three of their children live in Winthrop.
2686 VICTORIA, m. —— SAUNDERS; several children live in Michigan.
2687 EMMA.
2688 CHARLOTTE.

F961 Tryphena Locke, married ISAAC WINTER.
Children of 6th Gen.
2689 ELIZABETH, m. —— SLOSSON. *Child:* 2690 HERBERT, who lives in Kansas.
2691 SOLOMON, lives in Baxter Springs, Kansas.
2692 SARAH, m. GEORGE FOLLET of Brushton, N. Y. *Children:* 2693 LEMUEL; 2694 ELVIRA, m. OTIS PECK and had a large family.
2695 MIRANDA, m. SAMUEL KIMBALL, of Brushton, N. Y., and had a large family.

F962 Adeline Locke, married CORNELIUS RICE.
Children of 6th Gen.
2696 HARVEY, m. —— THATCHER, and had three children.
2697 MARIA, m. 1st, —— DAVIS; m. 2nd, —— STEVENS; had a child by each husband.

F963 Nelson Horatio Locke, born 1800(?), married 1st, —— SQUIRES; married 2nd, unknown; married 3rd, —— PETTIBONE.
Children of 6th Gen.
2698 ANDREW JACKSON, was in the Civil War, m., died about 1906 and left two children: 2699 FRED; 2700 AGNES, who m. ALLISON FARNSWORTH.
2701 ADALINE, m. JOHN BROWN of Brushton, N. Y., died about 1874 and left five or six children.
2702 TRYPHENA, was living in 1915, unmarried, at No. Lawrence, N. Y.
2703 AMANDA, m. twice, the 2nd time in California.
2704 SALOME, m. HORACE SHATTUCK of Brasher Falls; had ten children.
2705 WALTER, went to Massachusetts, was never heard from.
2706 BYRON, m. WELTHA KELLOGG of Brasher Falls. *Children:* 2707 NANCY; 2708 WALTER; 2709 BENJAMIN.

F994 Nathan Locke, born Apl. 4, 1804, married March 2, 1828, ESTHER KITTREDGE, born July 22, 1804, died Aug. 1, 1855. He was Trustee of the Methodist Church in Sweden, N. Y., and was worth $6,875 in 1850. He died in Sweden, Nov. 18, 1858.

Children of 6th Gen. b. in Sweden, N. Y.

F2710 ALMIRA, b. Dec. 29, 1828, m. Jan. 20, 1847, DARWIN ROOT.
F2711 ELISHA, b. Dec. 11, 1830, m. March 15, 1857, SARAH WAY.
  2712 DARWIN, b. Oct. 9, 1837, d. in Sweden, May 10, 1862, m. Jan. 4, 1860, ALMIRA DOTY; had no family.
  2713 MARY A., b. May 10, 1840, d. Apl. 6, 1890, m. in Sweden, Jan. 30, 1867, WALTER D. DAVIS, a farmer in Sweden. *Children:* 2714 ADDIE E., b. Jan. 12, 1868; 2715 ALBERT H., b. Aug. 22, 1869; 2716 NATHAN L., b. Aug. 16, 1871.
  2717 ADALAIDE F., b. Sept. 29, 1844, m. in Sweden, Nov. 7, 1878, CHARLES J. WHITE, a farmer in Sweden. *Children:* 2718 LILLIAN S., b. July 16, 1881; 2719 HARRISON L., b. Oct. 17, 1888.
  2720 EZRA, b. July 13, 1850, d. May 16, 1874, unmarried.

F995 Amos Locke, born in New York State, in 1806, married SOPHIA ———, who was born in New York State in 1811. He no doubt lived in New York State until about 1838 when he went to Coldwater, Mich., as his family show there in the 1850 census.

Children of 6th Gen.

2721 ANDREW, b. N. Y. 1829.   2722 DUDLEY, b. N. Y. 1830.
2723 EMILY, b. N. Y. 1833.   2724 WILLIAM, b. N. Y. 1835.
2725 CHARLES, b. Mich. 1838.   2726 JAMES, b. Mich. 1842.
2727 SARAH, b. Mich. 1840.

F1001 David Locke, born in Stewartstown, Feb. 19, 1792, married in Batavia, N. Y., 1816, MARY ESTERBROOK, daughter of Nehemiah and Elizabeth (Slapp), who died 1839. He married 2nd, 1841, SARAH J. LARRABEE, who was living in 1893. He was a pensioner of the 1812 War, went to Batavia, N. Y., in 1813, was a farmer and millwright and died in 1878.

Children of 6th Gen. b. in Batavia, N. Y.

F2728 HARRIET, b. Aug. 26, 1818, m. THOMAS CHICK.
F2729 EDWIN, b. March 16, 1821, m. March 26, 1848, MARY CULL.
F2730 ELIZABETH, b. Oct. 16, 1824, m. March 8, 1849, B. FRANKLIN NORTON.
  2731 WALTER G., b. Dec. 20, 1830, m. Jan. 25, 1854, MARY CLARK, b. Jan. 17, 1821; was in the War in 1861, later was a painter in Batavia, N. Y. *Children:* 2732 ALTON, b. Feb. 4, 1856, lives a painter in Batavia; 2732a WALTER F., b. Jan. 25, 1859, d. July 10, 1866.
  2733 MARY ANN, b. ——, m. ORSON HARMON, lived in Ohio. *Children:* 2734 FRANK; 2735 CARRIE.
  2736 SARAH A., b. ——, died young.

F1007 Joel W. Locke, born in Stewartstown, Jan. 6, 1804, married Nov. 13, 1829, MARY C. CHANDLER, born in Connecticut, Nov. 22, 1807, died in Columbia, Aug. 13, 1878. He was a farmer in Columbia, and died there March 29, 1875.

SIXTH GENERATION 137

Children of the 6th Gen.
2737 MARY MALVINA, b. Nov. 12, 1830, d. Dec. 1834.
F2738 JOHN, b. Nov. 7, 1831, m. Oct. 9, 1864, LOVINA POTTER.
2739 JOEL ED., b. Dec. 1, 1834, died Dec. 1835.
2740 JOSEPH ED., b. Dec. 1, 1834, died June 1838.
2741 ALMIRA J., b. Oct. 9, 1836, m. Sept. 30, 1867, her cousin, JOHN A. HODGE, b. Oct. 8, 1842, a son of Stephen and Louisa (Chandler). At the age of 19 he enlisted for three years, returned and became a moulder, farmer and clerk; had no children.
2742 MARY M., b. Feb. 3, 1841, was an invalid six years and d. July 3, 1867, unmarried.

F1010 John F. Locke, born in (Cranson), Vt., July 4, 1815, married LUCRETIA BUNDY (BRUNDY), daughter of Jonathan and Fanny (Morgan). She was born in Columbia in 1827 and died there March 1873. He was in the Mexican War, was a carpenter and auctioneer in Columbia, where he died Feb. 3, 1888.

Children of 6th Gen. b. in Columbia.
F2743 FRED W., b. 1849, m. LUCY E. ROGERS.
2744 FRANK, b. ——, m. KATE PERKINS, who died without children. He is a physician in Berlin, 1892.
2745 PORTES L., b. Jan. 3, 1863, m. in Concord, Aug. 22, 1891, EMMA GERTRUDE GRACE, b. in Piermont, 1873, dau. Simon and Rhoda (Whittier). He built a pulp mill in Berlin in 1883, was a grocer in 1885, and a needle maker in Franklin, 1891. *Child:* 2746 MINNIE PERSIS, b. Apl. 1, 1898, in Franklin.

F1039 Joseph J. Berry, born in Rye, May 17, 1789, married 1st, in 1812, BETSEY WEDGWOOD; married 2nd, in 1818, **Hannah Locke,** # **2055,** born Feb. 7, 1795, died June 30, 1893, aged 98. He died June 12, 1868.

Children of 6th Gen. b. in Rye.
2747 LOUISA, b. May 24, 1813, m. Apl. 2, 1835, ELVIN LOCKE, # F2054.
2748 SARAH W., b. Apl. 26, 1815, d. Dec. 3, 1898, m. July 17, 1834, LEONARD B. FRYE, of Ports., b. 1810, d. Ports., Apl. 14, 1856.
Second wife's children:
2749 JOSEPH W., b. July 3, 1819, m. 1st, Nov. 24, 1854, PAMELIA A. LOCKE, # 2933, b. Oct. 14, 1827, d. Feb. 26, 1886; m. 2nd, June 1, 1893, HARRIET A. HODGDON, b. in Greenland, March 4, 1832, dau. of Phineas and Sarah (Hurd); had no children.
2750 ABIGAIL, b. May 16, 1823, d. Sept. 20, 1878, m. LANGLEY B. LEWIS of Portsmouth. He died in Vallejo, Cal., March 19, 1873. *Child:* 2751 ABBIE F., b. 1857, d. 1871.
2752 CHARLES W., b. Aug. 15, 1830, died in Seattle, Wash., unmarried Sept. 10, 1879.
2753 WOODBURY W., b. Aug. 19, 1834, m. Sept. 24, 1863, MARIA A. LOCKE, # F6271, b. Feb. 20, 1836. *Children:* 2754 CHARLES, b. Rye, Apl. 9,

1865; 2755 JOHN, b. Oct. 10, 1867, both carpenters in Rye; 2756 ERNEST, b. Dec. 7, 1871, d. May 15, 1872.
2757 OLIVER, b. Oct. 3, 1837, died June 30, 1842.

F1054 Jonathan Hobbs Locke, born in Rye, Nov. 17, 1802, married Sept. 17, 1831, IZETTA LEWIS of Kittery, Me., born June 23, 1811, died Aug. 13, 1867. He was in Capt. Dearborn's Co. May 25-July 6, 1814, was a farmer in Rye and Greenland and died Jan. 11, or Feb. 16, 1847.

Children of 6th Gen. b. in Rye.

2758 JOSEPH BERRY, b. Nov. 13, 1837, died in Ports., Sept. 28, 1904, m., in Kittery, Me., Feb. 13, 1859, SARAH A. MURDOCK, b. Ports., June 13, 1836, d. May 20, 1901. *Child:* 2759 JOSEPH W., b. Nov. 25, 1860, d. Dec. 26, 1860. Joseph was many years in the U. S. Navy, returned to Portsmouth and was an engineer until his death. June 7, 1863, his wife supposing him dead as reported, since nothing had been heard from him, married WILLIAM HUDSON of Brooklyn, N. Y., but in a few weeks Joseph appeared and the marriage was void.

2760 FIDELIA ANN, b. Aug. 17, 1843, d. Dec. 25, 1862, m. OLIVER HUTCHINS of Kittery, Me.

2761 JOHN Q., b. Apl. 9, 1847, was killed at the battle of Spottsylvania, May 17, 1864.

F1055 Eleanor Dow Locke, born in Rye, May 11, 1806, married May 21, 1826, JOSEPH RAND, JR., son of Joseph and Olive (Marden) of Rye, born Jan. 21, 1796, died Dec. 11, 1885; was a farmer, town clerk, etc., in Rye. She died Sept. 27, 1880.

Children of 6th Gen. b. in Rye.

2762 OLIVE W., b. Oct. 14, 1826, died unmarried in PORTSMOUTH, Apl. 29, 1914.

2762aHANNAH B., b. Apl 13, 1829, m. in Rye, Sept. 5, 1852, GEORGE C. MERRIAM, b. Ports., May 21, 1824, son of Oliver and Mehitable (Cook). He was a carpenter in Roxbury, Mass., and genealogist of his family, and died Dorchester, Mass., Sept. 26, 1898. She lives in Ports., 1915. *Children:* 2763 ELEANOR H., b. Ports., June 6, 1855, m. Apl. 29, 1878, HORACE A. PRESCOTT of Dorchester, no children; 2764 CORNELIA LOCKE, b. Charlestown, Mass., Apl. 12, 1862, d. Jan. 27, 1865.

2765 SYLVIA, b. Apl. 11, 1831, d. Sept. 23, 1831.

2766 JULIA ANN, b. Feb. 10, 1833, d. 1910, m. in Rye, May 24, 1868, HENRY BICKFORD of Deerfield, b. Dec. 5, 1809, d. Jan. 10, 1889. *Child:* 2767 ETHEL, b. May, 1874, m. 1st, FRANK PHILLIPS; m. 2nd, ALBERT RAND.

F2768 SARAH J., b. Feb. 6, 1835, m. March 1855, SAMUEL RAND.

2769 MARY EMMA, b. Jan. 4, 1838, d. in Waltham, Mass., March 17, 1881, m. Charlestown, Feb. 1862, FRANCIS BURGESS, a machinist of Waltham. *Children:* 2770 MARTHA R., b. Nov. 1862, d. 1865;

SIXTH GENERATION

2771 HENRY F., b. Dec. 1864, m. ELLA GREELEY, lives Waltham, and has child: 2772 MARY.
2773 SUSAN E., b. Aug. 22, 1841, d. Nov. 1893, m. FRANCIS BURGESS, May 16, 1882; no children.
2774 CYRUS J., b. May 19, 1845, d. March 16, 1848.
2775 SERENA M., b. June 25, 1847, d. unmarried Sept. 15, 1877.
2775 FLORENCE W., b. Oct. 27, 1850, m. Nov. 1, 1868, W. H. LOWD, b. in Greenland, died in Waltham. *Child:* 2776 HENRY, died young.

F1067 James Locke, born in Rye, 1753, married Sept. 29, 1774, MARTHA SEAVEY, daughter of William and Ruth (Moses). She was born Dec. 15, 1754, died Jan. 31, 1832. He petitioned to enlist in Capt. Nathl. Rand's Co., March 4, 1776; was a butcher in Portsmouth and died Dec. 8, 1831.

Children of 6th Gen. b. in Portsmouth.
F2778 SARAH, b. 1777, m. Sept. 30, 1792, AARON RIGGS.
F2779 JAMES, b. 1777, m. Feb. 18, 1808, ELEANOR BERRY, # 1029.
2780 AARON, b. ——, died unmarried.
F2781 JOHN, b. 1784, m. July 22, 1804, ABIGAIL GOODWIN.
F2782 MARTHA, b. July 27, 1792, m. March 11, 1809, SAMUEL RAND.
F2783 HANNAH, b. Nov. 18, 1795, m. SAMUEL RAND, Oct. 29, 1811.

F1069 John Locke, born in Rye, 1757. One account says he went to Nova Scotia and disappeared. Another possibility is that he may be the father of JOHN (son of John) who learned the tanner's trade with his uncle in Portsmouth.

Child of 6th Gen. b. in Rye, Portsmouth or Epsom.
F2784 JOHN, b. Dec. 15, 1785, m. May 3, 1809 (Epsom rec. Nov. 26, 1807), MARIA or MERCY RAND.

F1072 Elizabeth Locke, born in Rye, 1763, married Feb. 2, 1804, JOSIAH HILL of Epping, born in Chester, Oct. 30, 1758, died before June 20, 1827. She died Epping, Sept. 25, 1849, being the 3rd wife of Josiah. He bought a farm in Epping in 1788, and his descendants lived there until 1902 when they sold. A granddaughter says "Elizabeth Burleigh, born in Epping, probably not married, had a son IRA LOCKE. The same Elizabeth married 2nd, Josiah Hill."

Children of 6th Gen.
F2785 IRA LOCKE, b. Jan. 5, 1791, m. March 27, 1815, REBECCA PRESCOTT.
F2786 SAMUEL HILL, b. Jan. 5, 1805, m. June 6, 1823, MARY BURLEIGH.

F1081 Jonathan Goss, born in Rye, Oct. 14, 1771, married Jan. 10, 1796, PATTY DAVIDSON, born Sept. 19, 1777 daughter of William and Sally (Blake). He was in the 1812 War and died Aug. 30, 1851. She died May 21, 1843.

140   LOCKE GENEALOGY

Children of 6th Gen. b. in Rye.

2787 SARAH BLAKE, b. Sept. 19, 1797, m. Nov. 24, 1825, DANIEL LORD, b. Sept. 25, 1797, d. Dec. 13, 1882.
2788 WILLIAM DAVIDSON, b. July 30, 1801, m. DATA MASON of Hampton.

F1084 Hannah J. Locke, born in Rye, May 22, 1769-70, married in Greenland, Feb. 1, 1796, JOHN MARSTON, son of Paul S. and Catherine (Elkins), born 1771, died in Rye, July 19, 1815. She died Sept. 16, 1825.

Children of 6th Gen.

2789 CAROLINE ELKINS, b. Aug. 12, 1798, d. May 13, 1850, m. 1st, WILLIAM CASWELL, of Isle of Shoals. *Child:* 2790 JOHN W. S., drowned June 10, 1840, aged 7. William d. Nov. 2, 1836, aged 43. She m. 2nd, WILLIAM S. RANDALL.
2792 WILLARD S., b. July 1, 1802, d. Oct. 25, 1872, m. MARTHA D. BROWN, b. in No. Hampton, Aug. 15, 1801.
2793 JOHN, b. May 24, 1804, died on Marstons Island, Portsmouth, m. ———. *Child:* 2794 a son m. a HOLMES and lived in Rye.
2795 MARY, b. Dec. 29, 1806, died young.
2796 MARY, b. Dec. 5, 1808, died at Shoals, Nov. 12, 1834, m. ASA CASWELL, of the Shoals, brother of above William.
2797 HULDAH, b. Oct. 22, 1811, m. JOHN HAZELTON, b. Feb. 14, 1814, son of James and Susanna.

F1087 Asa Locke, born in Rye, Aug. 14, 1775, married Nov. 12, 1799, his cousin ELIZABETH J. HOBBS, daughter of James and Mary (Towle), born Sept. 4, 1780, died Dec. 1, 1845. He was a joiner in Rye and died May 23, 1857.

Children of 6th Gen. b. in Rye.

2798 SALLY H., b. Feb. 15, 1800, d. Aug. 12, 1825.
F2799 ASA, b. Oct. 18, 1801, m. Apl. 15, 1824, ABIGAIL MACE LOCKE, # 1178.
F2800 JAMES H., b. Nov. 27, 1804, m. Aug. 12, 1827, MRS. SARAH (MOWE) ALLEN, # 1096.
F2801 LEMUEL (B.), b. Nov. 19, 1806, m. 1st, ESTHER Y. REMICK, March 31, 1832; m. 2nd, May 19, 1845, BELINDA J. BUNKER; m. 3rd, ABIGAIL M. LOCKE, # 1178.
2802 PERNIA T., b. Dec. 27, 1808, d. Dec. 5, 1809.
2803 THOMAS L., b. 1810, d. Sept. 14, 1824.
F2804 JONATHAN DEARBORN, b. Apl. 11, 1811, m. Dec. 23, 1838, CAROLINE GOODWIN GARLAND.
2805 PERNIA T., b. June 16, 1813, d. Oct. 31, 1829.
F2806 GARDNER T., b. Feb. 8, 1816, m. 1st, Dec. 28, 1844, JULIA A. GARLAND, # 2242; m. 2nd, Jan. 3, 1876, MRS. ANN (DAWLTON) GARLAND.
2807 JOHN O., b. Dec. 3, 1821, d. Aug. 16, 1822.
2808 MARY E., b. March 2, 1824, d. Feb. 25, 1825.

SIXTH GENERATION 141

F1089 Richard Locke, born in Rye, Oct. 5, 1779, married 1st, March 19, 1807, SARAH WOODS, born June 16, 1789, died Oct. 22, 1815; married 2nd, Feb. 20, 1817, BETSEY TUCKER, b. May 6, 1798, died in Concord, Feb. 26, 1847. He was a farmer in Concord and died there July 4, 1840.

Children of 6th Gen. first five b. in Rye.

2809 WORTHY DEARBORN, b. July 20, 1807, drowned at Newburyport, unmarried, aged about 25. Lived at Epsom.
2810 JAMES H., b. July 25, 1809, died in Massachusetts, Dec. 16, 1826.
2811 GORDON H., b. July 21, 1811, died at sea, unmarried, a mariner.
2812 SHERIDAN P., b. Apl. 20, 1813, died in Massachusetts Aug. 20, 1848, m. in Dedham, Mass., Apl. 23, 1837, HANNAH FIELD. He was a painter in Quincy, Mass.
F2813 WILLIAM T., b. Oct. 12, 1817, m. 1st, May 29, 1838, SUSAN B. NICHOLS; m. 2nd, Aug. 2, 1846, SARAH A. C. EVANS; m. 3rd, March 9, 1848, LAVINA B. NEWTON.
F2814 SARAH W., b. July 18, 1820, m. May 26, 1844, FRANCIS LOCKE KNOWLES, # 3915.
F2815 OLIVER H., b. Jan. 1, 1823, m. Sept. 1, 1845, HARRIET SHAW.
F2816 ELIZABETH ANN, b. Jan. 16, 1825, m. July 29, 1845, SEWELL A. PERRY.
F2817 JAMES N., b. March 12, 1827, m. 1st, Feb. 24, 1850, MARY G. BROCKWAY; m. 2nd, MRS. SAWYER.
F2818 NEHEMIAH C., b. Feb. 16, 1829, m. 1st, Jan. 1, 1850-1, CLARINDA L. ELLIOTT; m. 2nd, EMALINE WARRING; m. 3rd SARAH E. GERRY, m. 4th, unknown.
2819 OLIVE T., b. in Epsom, July 5, 1831, d. in Lowell, May 29, 1875, m. in Lowell, July 4, 1850, ALLEN WALDO of Weare, b. W., Dec. 20, 1819, d. L., March 30, 1881, son of Allen and Nancy (Maxwell). He was a hotel keeper and grocer in Lowell and March 5, 1881, m. his sister-in-law, HULDAH LOCKE BUZZELL. *Child:* 2820 FRED F., b. in Lowell, May 10, 1851, d. in Providence, June 1, 1891, m. Dec. 27, 1876, IDA A. HICKS, b. in Tilton, June 21, 1854, and they had a son, 2821 ROLFE, b. 1878, d. 1879.
F2822 RICHARD DEARBORN, b. Feb. 2, 1834, m. Sept. 24, 1854, NANCY B. ROGERS.
2823 HULDAH H., b. Feb. 9, 1836, m. 1st, WILLIAM BUZZELL, a farmer in Chichester, whom she left and later m. 2nd, J. H. PEASE. By Buzzell she had, *Children:* 2824 CHARLES; 2825 CLARENCE; both lived in Chichester.
2826 MARY F., b. Sept. 9, 1839, d. in Epping, Apl. 5, 1875, m. JED RAND, a farmer in Epping. *Child:* 2827 ABBIE, b. ——, m. —— HAZEN.

F1091 Polly Locke, born in Rye, June 22, 1788, married Nov. 5, 1805, JONATHAN BROWN, son of John and Salome (Allen), born June 1, 1782, died in Rye, Sept. 18, 1831. She died Dec. 6, 1853.

Children of 6th Gen. b. in Rye.

F2828 MARY S., b. March 6, 1806; m. Nov. 27, 1825, EBEN L. ORDIORNE.
F2829 SALLY, b. March 29, 1808, m. Dec. 25, 1831, JOHN PHILBRICK.

2830 ALFRED, b. July 27, 1810, d. Sept. 23, 1810.
F2831 CLARISSA, b. Nov. 12, 1812, m. Aug. 4, 1836, NATHAN BROWN.
2832 ALMIRA, b. March 16, 1815, m. Dec. 2, 1838, JONATHAN LOCKE. (See F2063.)
2833 RHODA, b. Sept. 10, 1817, d. unmarried Nov. 16, 1839.
F2834 ARTEMESIA, b. Apl. 13, 1820, m. March 29, 1842, DANIEL MARDEN.
2835 ABIGAIL, b. July 16, 1824, m. Nov. 21, 1848, OLIVER BERRY of Greenland, b. Apl. 28, 1821, d. G., Apl. 16, 1902. He was a farmer in Greenland and m. 2nd, ELIZABETH HATCH; m. 3rd, in 1869, JENNIE COLE. *Child:* 2836 FANNIE, by 1st wife, died young.
F2837 ANGELINA, b. Jan. 3, 1826, m. June 5, 1849, JAMES'HENRY DOW.
2838 JONATHAN A., b. Apl. 3, 1830, d. Aug. 12, 1838.

F1092 Rachel Locke, married March 15, 1810, JOSEPH BROWN of Deerfield, son of John and Salome, born Feb. 22, 1784, lived at Deerfield and Epsom.

Children of 6th Gen.

2839 JOHN, b. Apl. 1812, d. July 23, 1887, m. ACHSAH TENNEY, lived in Concord.
2840 FREDERICK, b. ——, married and had one child.
2841 HARRIET, b. ——, d. June 6, 1869, m. WM. KENDRICK, lived in Deerfield; had no children.
F2842 MARY ANN, b. ——, m. May 10, 1843, WILLIAM P. LADD.
2843 JOSEPH P., b. ——, d. in 1881, m. REBECCA TAYLOR who d. in 1881; had three girls.
2844 ANGELINE, b. ——, m. DAVID YOUNG and had seven children.

F1093 John Locke, born in Rye, in 1795, married in New Durham, Jan. 15, 1815, MARY ANN RINDGE, born in Alton, 1800, died Jan. 10, 1840. He was a farmer in Rye and died June 10, 1843.

Children of 6th Gen. b. in Rye.

2845 JOHN R., b. 1818, d. unmarried Feb. 20, 1837.
2846 WOODBURY, b. 1827, d. unmarried Feb. 25, 1852.
F2847 OLIVER LUTHER, b. Feb. 1, 1833, m. Apl. 3, 1854, OLIVIA A. HODGDON.

F1094 Mary B. Locke, born in Rye, Aug. 9, 1800, married Nov. 19, 1826, **John W. P. Locke,** # 1168, born 1803, died a farmer in Rye, Apl. 25, 1841. She married 2nd, March 11, 1846, **Jesse Locke,** # 2928, born Feb. 1809. He was a sailor in Rye and died June 24, 1860. She died March 16, 1852.

Children of 6th Gen. b. in Rye.

F2848 ANN M., b. 1830, m. Nov. 12, 1852, OTIS GOSS.
F2849 HANNAH OLIVE, b. ——, m. 1st, Aug. 7, 1854, JOHN O. LANE; m. 2nd, JOHN W. M. RANDALL.
2850 JOHN W., son of Jesse, b. June 10, 1846, m. in No. Hampton, Dec. 27, 1872, SARAH H. RANDALL, # 2961, b. at Shoals in 1847, died

SIXTH GENERATION

Ports., July 2, 1876; was a farmer of Rye. *Child:* 2851 WILLIE H., b. Rye, June 26, 1873, m. June 13, 1905, MARY FRAULEY.

F1095 Ephraim Mowe, married OLIVE COOMS. She married 2nd, Dec. 12, 1840, BENJAMIN MASON.
Children of 6th Gen.
2852 MARY ANN, b. Apl. 24, 1824, d. Apl. 8, 1884, m. CALVIN GARLAND.
2853 ELIZABETH, b. 1826, died at town farm, Apl. 30, 1850.
2854 EPHRAIM, b. 1828, m. and lived in No. Hampton.
2855 JACOB, b. ——, went to war; missing.
2856 FRANCES, b. ——, d.

F1097 Samuel P. Mowe, born ——, married Oct. 6, 1833, HARRIET MATHES, born June 7, 1812.
Children of 6th Gen.
2857 HARRIET, b. Feb. 8, 1834, m. Oct. 1853, WESLEY JENNESS, b. Apl. 10, 1831.
2858 MARY, b. 1837, d. Dec. 5, 1885, m. 1874, GILMAN JOHNSON, b. 1843.
2859 JOHN, b. Dec. 19, 1843, m. Jan. 13, 1867, FLORA A. RANDALL, b. Aug. 22, 1849, dau. John C. and Mary (Caswell).

F1124 Joseph Trefethern, born in Rye, Aug. 20, 1787, married Jan. 29, 1810, HANNAH BERRY, # 1040, born June 19, 1791. He lived in Rye and died Feb. 10, 1859.
Children of 6th Gen. b. in Rye. (See Rye History.)
2860 SIMON GOSS, b. March 10, 1810, d. Sept. 8, 1861, m. Apl. 1, 1833, LOUISA TREFETHERN, who d. March 5, 1865.
2861 MARY, b. 1812, m. JAMES SEAVEY.
2862 JOSEPH PARSONS, b. June 12, 1814, d. Dec. 24, 1889, m. Apl. 6, 1837, OLIVIA B. MARDEN, who d. Apl. 14, 1889.
2863 JOHN ICHABOD, b. June 11, 1816, m. 1st, ELIZABETH MASON; m. 2nd, 1864, ADNA NUTTER.
2864 LEVI, b. 1818, m. MARTHA MOULTON, who died July 15, 1848.
2865 SAMUEL A., b. Apl. 3, 1822, m. July 1846, ELIZA ANN MARDEN, who died May 19, 1903.
2866 OLIVER, b. March 4, 1826, m. SARAH MOULTON, who d. Sept. 13, 1875.
2867 WILLIAM H. J., b. 1831, d. May 7, 1838.
2868 EMILY, m. 1st, CHARLES W. HALL; m. 2nd, ALFRED S. TRAFTON.
2869 SUPPLY F., b. July 12, 1833, m. June 18, 1862, MARY E. CLARK.
2870 ALBERT B., b. Apl. 13, 1835, m. 1st, EMILY SEAVEY; m. 2nd, Dec. 14, 1864, MARY ABBY RAND.
2871 SARAH E., b. March 24, 1838, m. WM. I. HOLMES.

F1128 John A. Trefethern, born in Rye, July 27, 1799, married Nov. 20, 1834, **Mary Locke,** # **2061,** born 1809, died Sept. 30, 1888. He lived in Rye and died Oct. 4, 1870.

Children of 6th Gen. b. in Rye.

2872 IZETTA M., b. May 31, 1835, m. Feb. 1, 1880, OREN DRAKE of Rye, b. Jan. 30, 1824, d. Dec. 25, 1898; was a farmer in Rye; no children.

F2873 DENNIS H., b. Oct. 21, 1837, m. Dec. 17, 1868, MRS. ELLA (SMILEY) MAXWELL.

F2874 MARTHA S., b. July 6, 1841, m. 1st, Jan. 1, 1864, WOODBURY GREEN; m. 2nd, STORER GATES.

2875 JOHN E., b. Dec. 16, 1843, was unmarried.

F1137 Jeremiah Locke, born in Barrington, Dec. 9, 1778, married Jan. 14, 1800, MEHITABLE RAND, daughter of Nathaniel and Mary (Lovett), born Dec. 10, 1770, died Nov. 1852. He was a farmer at Locke's Neck, Rye, and died Aug. 4, 1857.

Children of 6th Gen. b. in Rye.

2876 HENRY, b. Apl. 23, 1801, was a farmer in Lebanon, Me., and died there unmarried May 23, 1870.

F2877 MARY WHITE, b. Feb. 16, 1803, m. Sept. 1829, WILLIAM A. MENDALL.

F2878 APHIA RAND, b. March 13, 1806, m. June 2, 1835, THOMAS SHAPLEIGH.

F2879 HANNAH DOW, b. March 5, 1808, m. Dec. 20, 1837, LEWIS DEARBORN.

F2880 JEREMIAH, b. Apl. 9, 1811, m. March 1835, HANNAH A. YOUNG.

F2881 MARTHA RAND, b. March 4, 1814, m. Dec. 25, 1845, JOHN PAGE FARMER.

F1140 Mercy Locke, born in Barrington, Jan. 11, 1784, married Nov. 12, 1801, SAMUEL MASON of Ordiorne's Point, Rye, son of Daniel and Elizabeth (Norton). He was a seaman in Rye, was in the War of 1812, and died in 1837, aged 62. She died Jan. 9, 1874.

Children of 6th Gen. b. in Rye and Portsmouth.

2882 JOSEPH, b. ——, died young.

2883 MARTHA, b. Dec. 20, 1807, d. Nov. 5, 1889, m. Sept. 3, 1826, JETHRO LOCKE. (See F 2051.)

F2884 MARY, b. in Ports., 1808, m. Sept. 16, 1830, DANIEL A. ADWERS.

F2885 LORINDA, b. 1810, m. Aug. 30, 1835, GEORGE T. BALL.

2886 SAMUEL, b. ——, m. MARY MOORE of Portland; was in the dry goods business in Portsmouth and Portland. *Child:* 2887 FRANCES, m. —— COVELL and had: 2888 FANNIE m. —— BILLINGS of Boston.

F2889 ELIZABETH J., b. 1816, m. Sept. 7, 1834, JOSEPH M. EDMONDS.

F2890 ROBERT, b. ——, m. EMALINE H. EDMONDS.

F1141 Joseph Locke, born in Barrington(?), March 4, 1787, married Aug. 4, 1811, OLIVE BERRY, # 1041 born June 24, 1793, died March 13, 1859. He was a carpenter in Rye called "Jiner Joe," lived on the Locke Neck road and died Jan. 18, 1865.

SIXTH GENERATION

Children of 6th Gen. b. in Rye.

2891 MARY, b. Oct. 11, 1811, d. Jan. 21, 1812.
F2892 MARTHA DOW, b. Apl. 16, 1813, m. Aug. 28, 1836, ADAM KNOX.
F2893 JOHN NEWTON, b. Jan. 22, 1815, m. Oct. 20, 1839, HARRIET A. WEATHERBEE.
2894 SARAH GOSS, b. Apl. 19, 1817, died in Charlestown, Mass., Jan. 3, 1882, m. Sept. 20, 1836, JAMES C. DAVIS, who d. in Chas., Nov. 20, 1855; was a gunner in U. S. Navy; had: 2895 SARAH, 1837-1837.
2896 CHARLES MILLER, b. Aug. 9, 1819, died in Rye a seaman, unmarried, Aug. 27, 1846.
2897 JEREMIAH, b. Jan. 26, 1823, d. May 26, 1823.
2898 MARY PERKINS, b. Jan. 20, 1828, d. Aug. 12, 1870, m. Nov. 21, 1846, GEORGE W. KIMBALL, a butcher in Bedford, Mass., who died in 1875. *Children:* 2899 OLIVETTE D., b. Jan. 31, 1848, d. Aug. 9, 1857; 2900 EMILY J., Sept. 28, 1850, d. Oct. 17, 1852; 2901 CORA M., b. Feb. 18, 1865, d. June 1, 1867.
F2902 HANNAH SALTER, b. March 14, 1830, m. Jan. 15, 1851, RICHARD PIGOTT.
2903 LEVI BERRY, b. Dec. 27, 1831, d. Feb. 27, 1832.
2904 CAROLINE FREEMAN, b. Apl. 2, 1833, d. Apl. 8, 1882, m. Nov. 27, 1860, ALBERT S. BAKER, a machinist of Cambridge, Mass., who d. Sept. 15, 1895.
2905 JAMES DAVIS, b. Jan. 11, 1838, d. in Charlestown, Mass., Jan. 25, 1914, m. Sept. 12, 1869, MARIA HOLMES, b. May 9, 1844; was a mason in Boston. *Child.* 2906 EMMA M., b. Feb. 16, 1871, lives Charlestown.

F1143 Polly Jenness, born in Rye, Jan. 31, 1778, married JOHN BROWN, son of Simon, born in Chester, Sept. 7, 1775, lived in North Hampton, and died Aug. 23, 1825. She died July 20, 1868.

Children of 6th Gen. b. in North Hampton.

2908 ELIZA, b. 1799, m. 1st, JOSEPH WARD; 2nd, NATHANIEL BATCHELDER.
2909 MARY, b. 1802, d. unmarried in 1840.
2910 SIMON, b. Aug. 1804, m. EMILY, dau. of Nathaniel Drake.
2911 LEONARD, b. 1806, m. LUCY ANN HALLET, d. Oct. 1879; lived in N. Y.
2912 JENNESS, b. Feb. 1808, m. LYDIA WARD of Hampton. She d. Feb. 1876; lived at Newburyport.
2913 JOHN TRUEWORTHY, b. March 1818, m. MRS. ELIZA G. WEDGWOOD, who died June 1869; lived in N. Y.
2914 JEREMIAH, b. Sept. 18, 1810, m. ELIZABETH SANBORN, d. Feb. 12, 1875; lived in No. Hampton.
2915 ADELAIDE, b. 1816, m. ABRAHAM DRAKE; lived in No. Hampton.

SEVENTH GENERATION

F1145 Jeremiah Locke, born 1771, married Nov. 26, 1793, SUSAN RAND, daughter of Nathaniel and Mary (Leavitt). He was a farmer, lived at Locke's Neck, Rye, and died there Oct. 21, 1804. Susan was born Aug. 31, 1768, married 2nd, THOMAS BABB, and died June 24, 1842.

Children of 7th Gen. b. in Rye.

F2916 RICHARD RAND, b. July 16, 1794, m. Jan. 20, 1824, SARAH A. LEAVITT.
F2917 JOHN W., b. June 28, 1796, m. Oct. 27, 1816, MARY POWERS.
F2918 HAMILTON CUTTS, b. Dec. 28, 1798, m. MARY ANN RAND of Ports.
2919 IRA, b. 1802, d. Oct. 14, 1824.
F2920 JEREMIAH, b. May 15, 1804, m. Feb. 14, 1828, MARY WENTWORTH.

F1151 Joseph Locke, born 1775, married 1st, May 13, 1794, LUCY MARDEN, born Sept. 28, 1776, died May 19, 1813, the daughter of Nathaniel and Elizabeth (Moulton); married 2nd, Sept. 11, 1814, MRS. HANNAH (VITTUM) BERRY, born 1792, died Dec. 18, 1851. He was a farmer in Rye and died there Nov. 2, 1853.

Children of 7th Gen. b. in Rye.

F2921 JANE, b. 1796, m. 1st, March 31, 1817, BENJAMIN BROWN, # 1105; m. 2nd, 1819, JOHN RANDALL.
F2922 NATHANIEL, b. 1798, m. 1st, July 25, 1821, MARY WEED; m. 2nd, Nov. 2, 1866, MRS. SARAH VITTUM.
F2923 JOSEPH, b. 1800, m. 1832, LUCY BEEDE.
F2924 SARAH PALMER, b. Sept. 17, 1801, m. May 4, 1823, LEMUEL L. CASWELL.
F2925 LOCADA, b. Feb. 7, 1804, m. LEVI B. TREFETHERN.
2926 RICHARD, b. 1805, left Rye when young, went to Sandwich, later was recognized as proprietor of a tobacco store N. Y. City. Nothing further known.
2927 ELIZABETH, b. Apl. 20, 1808, m. Nov. 1835, SEBASTIAN TREFETHERN, # 1129.
2928 JESSE, b. Feb. 1809, m. March 11, 1846, MRS. MARY B. LOCKE. (See F1094.)
2929 JONATHAN MARDEN, b. Jan. 19, 1810, d. Ports., m. Ports., Nov. 28, 1841, MRS. ELIZABETH (TOWNSEND) COLLINS of Ports. He was a sailor 1851 Ports., 1854 Newburyport.
2930 HANNAH, b. 1812, died young.
2930a WILLIAM, b. 1815, went to sea, d. ——.
F2931 HANNAH B., b. Dec. 18, 1819, m. 1st, Nov. 16, 1837, STEPHEN FERGUSON; m. 2nd, JOSEPH HOLMES; m. 3rd, ANDREW HOLMES.
2932 JOHN QUINCY, b. 1826, died in Mexican War.

SEVENTH GENERATION

F1152 Deacon William Locke, born 1801 (was a son of Tryphena Locke by a Berry), married 1st, July 31, 1825, ELIZABETH KNOWLES, born in Candia, 1796, died in Rye, June 8, 1851. He married 2nd, MARY L. MARSTON, born 1802, daughter of Levi and Abigail, died Rye, June 29, 1873. He lived in Rye, and died Jan. 27, 1873.

Children of 7th Gen. b. in Rye.

2933 PAMELIA ANN, b. Oct. 14, 1827, d. Feb. 21, 1886, m. Nov. 24, 1854, JOSEPH W. BERRY, # 2749, of Rye, b. July 3, 1819; lived at Rye, no children. He d. July 8, 1906.

2934 WILLIAM HARVEY, b. Aug. 9, 1830, d. Rye, Feb. 19, 1887, m. June 25, 1852, MARIA S. NUDD, b. June 1833, d. Rye, Oct. 26, 1889, dau. of Stacy and Mary (Johnson) of No. Hampton; was a carpenter and farmer in Rye, had: 2935 WILLIS E., b. Oct. 7, 1855, d. Rye, Sept. 22, 1863.

F1153 Nathaniel Locke, born in Wakefield, Jan. 18, 1779, married March 19, 1803, ABIGAIL PITMAN, born in Somersworth, Aug. 18, 1776. He was a shoemaker in Wakefield.

Children of 7th Gen. b. in Wakefield.

2936 JEREMIAH, b. Dec. 11, 1803, m. ELIZABETH D. SEAVER, b. Roxbury, Mass., Aug. 12, 1801, dau. of John and Betsey (Dudley); lived in Stetson, Me., had dau.: 2937 ADALINE M., who d. Aug. 1870.

F2938 HAMILTON, b. Feb. 3, 1806, m. 1st, Dec. 7, 1829, SOPHRONIA D. FROST; m. 2nd, Oct. 4, 1850, DORCAS GUPTIL; m. 3rd, Feb. 9, 1873, MARY F. ABBOTT.

2939 JAMES M., b. Apl. 22, 1809, d. Rochester, Oct. 26, 1890, m. Wakefield, Feb. 9, 1834, SARAH T. FOX, b. Wolf., 1811, d. W., Aug. 25, 1897, dau. of Samuel and Patience (Gilman). He was a shoemaker and had no children.

2940 JACOB, b. Jan. 18, 1812 (Jan. 12, 1815 ?), d. Wakefield, March 9, 1895, m. SUSAN REMICK b. Rochester, 1813. (Her mother was a Hurd). He was a farmer in Wakefield, and childless. She died two hours after her husband, March 9, 1895.

2941 JULIA, b. Jan. 6, 1817, d. unmarried 1846.

2942 JOSEPH HARRISON, b. Aug. 8, 1826, d. unmarried 1847.

F1154 Mary Locke, born in Wakefield, July 9, 1783, married in Wakefield, Sept. 16, 1802, MARK ALLEN.

Children of 7th Gen.

2943 MARK. 2944 THIAL. 2945 GARLAND. 2946 LYMAN. 2947 MARY.

F1155 Betsey Locke, born in Wakefield, Dec. 3, 1787, married JOSEPH PITMAN, and lived in Somersworth. She died in 1882, aged 95.

Children of 7th Gen.
2948 JAMES C., b. Moultonborough, 1825, d. M., June 28, 1892, m. MARY E. SLAGER; was a farmer and carpenter.
2949 JACOB, L., b. 1838, m. Somersworth, Nov. 2, 1861, SARAH E. BODWELL, b. 1840.
2950 JOHN, b. ——, m. March 2, 1837, ANN GARLAND of Rochester, had son: 2951, JOHN of Somersworth.
2952 HANNAH L., m. Somersworth, March 4, 1841, WILLIAM RANDALL of Rye, # 2959; lived Somers.
2953 MARY A., m. Somers., Oct. 22, 1835, JOHN BRACKETT of Milton; lived Acton, Me.
2954 EMILY, m. —— WHITTIER of Acton, Me.
2955 ELIZABETH, probably unmarried.
2956 EVALINE.

F1161 John Higgins Locke, born in Wakefield, Dec. 16, 1802, married 1st, June 13, 1822, ELIZABETH FERNALD of Wakefield; married 2nd, Nov. 8, 1827, SALLY DEARBORN; married 3rd, ADALINE TIBBETTS; married 4th, June 3, 1868, BETSEY D. GERRY, born Wolfeboro, 1803, daughter of Robert Drew (her 3rd marriage). John was a shoemaker in Wolfeboro, and died there May 31, 1885.

Children of 7th Gen.
F2957 SARAH ELIZABETH, b. May 21, 1828, m. Nov. 26, 1849, THOMAS JEFFERSON TIBBETTS, JR.
2958 HARRIET AUGUSTA, b. June 6, 1831, d. Oct. 1850.

F1165 Hannah Locke, born in 1793, died Oct. 11, 1833, married WILLIAM B. RANDALL. He married 2nd, MARY DOWNES of the Shoals.

Children of 7th Gen.
2959 WILLIAM m. HANNAH PITMAN, # 2952, March 4, 1841. She m. 2nd, WILLIAM S. RANDALL, b. 1805.
2960 JOB LOCKE, d. Great Falls, unmarried.
By his 2nd wife Downes, he had: JAMES A.; JUDSON; MARY; WM. MUNROE; 2961 SARAH H., who m. 1872, JOHN WILKES LOCKE, # 2850, and d. July 2, 1876, aged 29.

F1166 Elizabeth G. Locke, born in 1797, married 1st, Nov. 2, 1816, JOHN CASWELL, born May 8, 1791, died Aug. 30, 1822; married 2nd, WILLIAM S. RANDALL, Dec. 11, 1827, born Nov. 15, 1805, son of Benjamin and Sarah (Sanders). She died on Star Island, Sept. 14, 1836.

Child of 7th Gen.
F2962 REBECCA, b. ——, m. NATHANIEL BERRY.

SEVENTH GENERATION

F1167 Captain Job Locke, born in 1799, married HANNAH RANDALL, daughter of Benjamin and Polly (Rugg), born March 6, 1801, died of cancer in Rye, Dec. 24, 1855. Job was captain of a coasting vessel and died July 1, 1852.

Children of 7th Gen. b. in Rye.
2963 CHARLES W., b. ——, died young.
F2964 CHARLES FRED, b. Aug. 25, 1826, m. Aug. 25, 1851, ELLEN H. LOCKE, # 5986.
2965 MARGARET ANN, b. 1828, d. Sept. 25, 1830.
2966 ELLEN M., b. May 14, 1830, d. unmarried May 22, 1855.
F2967 SARAH ANN, b. Jan. 6, 1833, m. June 2, 1854, WILLIAM DUDLEY VARRELL.
2968 GRANVILLE, b. 1835, d. unmarried Dec. 25, 1854.
2969 ANNA E., b. 1838, d. Nov. 12, 1860, m. Ports., Sept. 9, 1858, WILLIAM P. YOUNG; had a boy d. aged 2 years. He m. 2nd, CLEMENTINA VARRELL of Rye.
2970 JOHN W., b. 1844, d. May 14, 1848.

F1171 Captain Richard Locke, born in Rye in 1794, married Oct. 21, 1823, MARGARET WELCH of Chichester, born in Kittery, Me., 1796, died March 11, 1860. He went to Boston in 1811 to learn the blacksmith's trade, later was a sea captain and died in Chichester, March 21, 1864, having made his will ten days before.

Children of 7th Gen. b. in South Boston.
F2971 ABIGAIL M., b. Sept. 10, 1825, m. GEORGE BACHELDER.
F2972 WILLIAM F. (William T. in father's will), b. Dec. 26, 1826, m. Jan. 6, 1857, LOVINA S. LAKE.
F2973 MEHITABLE B., b. Apl. 16, 1836, m. May 4, 1856, ELIHU BROWN, # 4981.

F1172 Sarah Frost Locke, born in Rye in 1796, married June 13, 1819, EDWARD CASWELL, son of Samuel, born Sept. 14, 1797. He married 2nd, SALLY VARRELL, and died in Brentwood, in 1860.

Children of 7th Gen. b. in Rye.
F2974 DANIEL W. (CASWELL) BURLEIGH, b. Aug. 1830, m. MARGARET A. LOCKE, # 6029.
2975 SYLVESTER (CASWELL) BURLEIGH, b. ——, m. ABBIE LOCKE, # 6030.
Both these boys were adopted by their aunt, Mrs. Daniel Burleigh.

F1174 William Locke, born in Rye, Dec. 1799, married in South Boston, Nov. 6, 1825, CHARLOTTE H. WENTWORTH of Boston, born Nov. 6, 1800 (Feb. 18, 1801), died Corry, Pa., May 20, 1867, daughter of Benjamin and Abigail (Bennett). William died May 22, 1843.

Children of 7th Gen. b. in South Boston.
2976 CHARLES F., b. 1825, d. Dec. 16, 1827.
F2977 WILLIAM S., b. Sept. 17, 1826, m. Dec. 24, 1857, AUGUSTA ANN HENDERSON.
2978 CHARLOTTE ABIGAIL, b. Apl. 24, 1830, m. June 20, 1857, HENRY F. SHAW of Augusta, Me. Lived Boston Highlands, had no children.
2979 SARAH MEHITABLE, b. June 6, 1832, d. unmarried March 19, 1860.
2980 MARY FRANCES, b. Aug. 14, 1834, d. June 1873, m. July 1854, WILLIAM S. NUTTING, and had: 2981 WILLIAM P., b. June 6, 1855, m. ALMIRA PHILIPS and lived Youngsville, Pa.
2982 SUSAN P., b. 1840, d. Aug. 1840.

F1177 Abner Locke, born in Rye, May 6, 1804, married 1st, MARY A. YOUNG; married 2nd, EUNICE WALLIS of Ipswich, Mass., who was living in 1856. He was a chain maker in South Boston where he died in 1850.

Children of 7th Gen. b. in So. Boston.
2983 SON, b. ——, died young.
F2984 MARY ANN, b. Apl. 11, 1828, m. Nov. 2, 1851, SAMUEL H. BAKER.
2985 ELIZABETH, b. Dec. 29, 1829, m. JOSEPH BAKER.

F1179 John Langdon Locke, born Aug. 30, 1807, married May 16, 1833, MARY RANDALL, born Feb. 21, 1812, daughter of Benjamin and Polly (Rugg). He lived in Boston.

Children of 7th Gen. b. in Boston.
F2986 JOHN H., b. Rye, Aug. 1, 1835, m. June 30, 1859, EMMA J. JOHNSON.
2987 ALMER F., b. July 25, 1838, m. Oct. 14, 1863, MARY E. OSBORN of So. Boston, where he lived, had: 2988 EDWARD E., b. Oct. 12, 1864, d. Feb. 19, 1874; 2989 SOPHIA S., b. Jan. 24, 1870, d. Aug. 9, 1870; 2990 LIZZIE G., b. Sept. 1, 1872, d. Feb. 12, 1874; 2991 HERBERT S., b. Aug. 23, 1875.
2992 MARY SUSAN, b. Aug. 8, 1840, d. June 2, 1891, m. Apl. 24, 1873, HARVEY C. GIFFORD of So. Boston; lived there, had no children.
2993 MALVINA A., b. July 5, 1848, lived So. Boston, unmarried 1900.
2994 CLARENCE S., b. July 27, 1854, d. Sept. 1, 1855.

F1182 Edwin Locke, born March 9, 1815, married ADALINE SHEPPARD, born in Boston, Oct. 1, 1819, died in Boston, Dec. 16, 1882.

Children of 7th Gen. b. in Boston.
2995 ADALINE A., b. Oct. 1, 1843, d. Jan. 12, 1854.
2996 MARY C., b. Apl. 14, 1848, d. Sept. 17, 1860.
2997 EDWIN S., b. Oct. 18, 1852.
2998 ALFRED F., b. July 20, 1853, d. Dec. 17, 1853.
2999 DANIEL B., b. Nov. 17, 1855, d. Oct. 7, 1889, m. MARGARET MULLERY, b. May 10, 1857, d. Apl. 24, 1882, had: 3000 ARIADNE, b. Dec. 25, 1881; 3001 MARGARET; and at least one more.
3002 MARY C., b. Sept. 30, 1857, d. Sept. 30, 1858.
3003 ANNIE C., b. Aug. 14, 1860, d. Aug. 26, 1864.

SEVENTH GENERATION

F1185 Lemuel Otis, born Nov. 24, 1774, married Nov. 9, 1796, LEAH PEARL.

Children of 7th Gen.

3004 LUCY, b. Sept. 6, 1797, m. JEREMIAH RICKER of Farmington; no children.
3005 JEMIMA, b. May 12, 1801, m. Apl. 12, 1832, HOWARD L. OTIS, # 3021, of Rochester, b. Sept. 15, 1809.
3006 MELINDA, b. ——, m. 1834, JOHN PEARL of Rochester.
3007 CLARISSA, b. July 11, 1799.
3008 HANNAH.

F1188 Paul Otis, born March 28, 1777, married July 5, 1798, MARY FOSS, who died Jan. 10, 1837.

Children of 7th Gen.

3009 DOROTHY, m. JOHN GRAY of Rochester.
3010 LYDIA, died young.
3011 JOSEPH Y., m. JUDITH CHESLEY of Sheffield, Vt.
3012 THOMAS T., m. SARAH FOSS.
3013 MARTHA, m. JOHN SULLOWAY, lived Wheelock, Vt.
3014 HANNAH, died young.   3015 LYDIA, died young.
3016 HANNAH F., m. WILLARD NUTTER, who d. 1843, Rochester.
3017 HARRIET, m. JONATHAN CLARKE of Lawrence.

F1190 Jethro Otis, born March 1, 1781, married March 31, 1802, ESTHER HOWARD.

Children of 7th Gen.

3018 NEHEMIAH, died young.
3019 EPHRAIM, b. Nov. 9, 1805, m. Jan. 6, 1830, SARAH MENDUM of Kittery, Me. He was an armorer on U. S. Ship *Concord*, and had seven children.
3020 MARTHA, b. Dec. 7, 1807, m. 1st, June 16, 1831, JONATHAN HAM of Farmington; m. 2nd, 1845, LEWIS VARNEY; had children.
3021 HOWARD LOCKE, b. Sept. 15, 1809, m. Apl. 12, 1832, his cousin, JEMIMA OTIS, # 3005, and had four children.
3022 RUFUS, b. Sept. 15, 1811, m. Apl. 7, 1834, ADA PERKINS of Wakefield, and had six children.
3023 HANNAH, b. Sept. 23, 1813, m. 1839, LEWIS HAM, and had four children.
3024 WILLIAM P., b. Apl. 8, 1815, m. July 4, 1839, ELIZABETH JOHNSON, had four children.
3025 SON, died Mexican War, June 1, 1848.
3026 WILLARD, b. Apl. 8, 1818, m. 1841, ELIZABETH M. GOVE, had four children in Newburyport.
3027 SARAH, b. Apl. 30, 1820, m. ——— DOWNES, had four children in Newburyport.
3028 JAMES H., b. 1822, d. 1845.
3029 DOROTHY, b. Aug. 15, 1825, m. LEMUEL WILLEY of Dover.

F1191 Thomas Otis, born Feb. 9, 1783, married March 26, 1811, POLLY LEE, born July 29, 1789; lived in New Boston.
Children of 7th Gen.
3030 PETER, b. Apl. 26, 1812.
3031 MARY, b. Nov. 29, 1813, d. 1822.
3032 HANNAH, b. March 6, 1819, m. JAMES G. HOLDEN of Rollinsford.
3033 THOMAS, b. Feb. 20, 1821.
3034 MARY J., b. Jan. 24, 1824, m. HENRY F. STRAW.
3035 HARRIET N., b. May 15, 1826.
3036 WILLIAM L., b. Apl. 21, 1829.
3037 JAMES L., b. June 7, 1831.
3038 ELIZABETH, b. Nov. 5, 1834.

F1192 Micajah Otis, born Dec. 6, 1785, married 1st, Jan. 23, 1806, HANNAH ALLARD, who died in 1845; married 2nd, POLLY BROCK.
Children of 7th Gen.
3039 THOMAS J., b. Dec. 9, 1806, m. 1st, March 31, 1830, SUSAN NUTTER and had four children; m. 2nd, 1846, ALMIRA CANNEY and had two children.
3040 WILLIAM A., b. Nov. 6, 1809, m. Feb. 22, 1835, SARAH W. DELAND of Brookfield, and had eight children.

F1193 Joshua Otis, born in 1786, married LOVIE ELKINS. He died Aug. 1, 1826.
Children of 7th Gen.
3041 ELDREDGE, lived Boston.
3042 SON, d. 1826.
3043 MARY J.

F1195 William Otis, born May 16, 1790, married Nov. 4, 1814, HANNAH BOWLES.
Children of 7th Gen.
3044 MARY and 3045 ELIZABETH, twins, b. Aug. 31, 1818.
3046 WILLIAM and 3047 THERESA, twins, b. Aug. 31, 1821.

F1197 Simeon Otis, born ——, married July 1, 1816, JOANNA WALLINGFORD of Alton.
Children of 7th Gen.
3048 JONATHAN C.
3049 MARY.
3050 ELIZABETH P.
3051 MARTHA.

F1199 Ephraim Locke, born in Barrington, Feb. 18, 1775, married in Barrington, Dec. 21, 1797, his cousin, SARAH FOSS, daughter of Ephraim and Abigail (Daniels), born in Barrington,

SEVENTH GENERATION 153

Jan. 16, 1776, died in Brooklyn, N. Y., Aug. 6, 1857. Ephraim was in Hollis, Me., until 1802, then lived four years in Saco. From 1806 to 1829 he was a merchant in Boston, and from there moved to New York City where he died Aug. 2, 1832.

He wrote the following in his Bible: "The following is known of my ancestors, that two brothers came from England about 1625–30; one settled at Cape Ann the other at Rye, near Portsmouth, the latter being the grandfather of my grandfather; my ancestors before my grandfather all lived and died in Rye. My wife's grandfather, JOSHUA FOSS (b. 1709), who married LYDIA RAND, has informed me that his grandfather came to Boston as midshipman on a war ship about 1630, left the vessel and settled in Rye, having a large family. This Joshua lived to be 99 years old. When I was young he gave me much information in regard to the early settlers, hardships and perils of the Indians. He well remembered seeing the workmen in 1713 cutting the canal from the sea to let the salt water into the fresh pond in Rye (at Rye Harbor), by which a large tract of salt marsh was made. His wife, Lydia Rand, also descended from Rye people; her grandparents came over aged people about 1630, and they with her father's first wife and two children were killed by the Indians and were buried in one grave, now known to Rye people. Signed EPHRAIM LOCKE.

Children of 7th Gen.

3052 HORATIO, b. Hollis, Me., March 9, 1800, d. Calcutta, May 31, 1840, m. Hollis, Oct. 30, 1828, ELIZABETH THAYER of Boston, b. Sept. 3, 1800, d. Chelsea, Aug. 23, 1859, dau. of Cotton and Abigail (Treat). He was a merchant in Calcutta, had: 3053 HORATIO FRED, b. Oct. 12, 1833, d. Nov. 2, 1834; 3054 ELIZABETH, b. ——, d. Aug. 26, 1859.

3055 SOPHIA A., b. H., Oct. 10, 1801, d. unmarried, New York City.

3056 SARAH, b. H., June 10, 1802, m. Nov. 15, 1838, REV. HIRAM JELLIFF of Lithgow, N. Y. He was an Episcopal minister in White Plains in charge of a boys' school. *Children:* 3057 CHARLES EPHRAIM, m. JENNIE FAY; was a real estate man in Brooklyn, N. Y., and they had: 3058 EDNA; 3059 HOWARD; and 3060 ANN M. B., was unmarried; 3061 HORATIO F., who m. and had two children.

3062 MARY A., b. Saco, July 18, 1804, d. N. Y. City unmarried ——.

F3063 CHARLES E., b. Aug. 16, 1807, m. MARIA ——.

F3064 FREDERICK A., b. Feb. 28, 1810, m. June 9, 1842, SALLY ANN WILLIAMSON.

F1200 Jesse Locke, born Sept. 9, 1777, married Jan. 9, 1799, HANNAH DANIELSON, born Barrington, Dec. 18, 1778, died July 30, 1863. He was one of the first settlers of Biddeford, Me., later went to Hollis, Me. He died Oct. 4, 1859.

Children of 7th Gen.

F3065 HARRIET BYNAM, b. Dec. 11, 1799, m. 1820, ERASTUS GOULD.
F3066 ELIZA, b. Apl. 14, 1802, m. 1818, THOMAS DAY.
3066aHANNAH D., b. March 21, 1804, d. Oct. 24, 1804.
F3067 JOSHUA, b. Oct. 25, 1805, m. Sept. 15, 1860, JANE L. WADLEIGH.
3067aLYDIA E., b. Feb. 4, 1808, d. unmarried Aug. 9, 1860.
F3068 ROYAL P., b. Apl. 31, 1811, m. 1st, LYDIA HEWS, m. 2nd, ANNA H. JENKINS.
3069 CAROLINE H., b. Aug. 5, 1813, d. Dec. 28, 1864, m. SYLVANUS DEARBORN, b. May 1810, d. Dec. 1863; had dau.: 3070 KATHERINE, who was adopted by her uncle, Jesse Locke.
F3071 JESSE ALBERT, b. Apl. 2, 1818, m. Aug. 14, 1845, SARAH B. COOLEDGE.

F1202 Simon Locke, born Feb. 3, 1786, married 1st, Oct. 1806, MIRIAM DAY, who died Feb. 22, 1833, daughter of Ebenezer of Kennebunk, Me.; married 2nd, June 1, 1833, MRS. MARY HALEY STAPLES, born July 11, 1793, died Jan. 28, 1872. He was in Hollis, Me., in 1820, and died Aug. 10, 1869.

Children of 7th Gen.

3072 MARY, b. ——, d. Sanford, Me., m. GEORGE HILL, who d. Sanford, and had a son, 3073 PELETIAH, who lived in Elkhart, Ind.
F3073 JESSE F., b. June 21, 1810, m. 1st, MEHITABLE GREEN HILL; m. 2nd, MARY ANN GWYNNE.
F3074 HANNAH WAKEFIELD, b. June 1811, m. June 22, 1832, BENJAMIN F. DUDLEY.
3075 MIRIAM, b. ——, died young.
3076 MEHITABLE D., b. Biddeford, Me., Aug. 23, 1818, d. Tonawanda, N. Y., June 26, 1881, m. PELATIAH HILL in Biddeford, Oct. 29, 1837, who d. Tonawanda, Apl. 3, 1871. He was a grocer many years. Adopted a son, 3077 ALPHEUS MOORE.
3078 LYDIA, b. 1823, d. Cornish, Me., Apl. 1, 1913, m. 1st, ALEXANDER GRANT, an officer of the Rebellion; m. 2nd, THOMAS KIMBALL, b. Parsonfield, Me., Feb. 22, 1808, a farmer in Cornish, Me., and son of Ensign Kimball. Had grandsons: 3079 D. F. DREW; 3080 FRED DREW.
F3081 SIMON J., b. 1826, m. 1st, LYDIA TEBBETTS; m. 2nd, CORNELIA DANFORTH.

Second wife's child:

F3082 JOHN S., b. Jan. 25, 1836, m. May 26, 1869, MARCIA CLEAVES.

SEVENTH GENERATION

F1204 Lydia Locke, born Jan. 10, 1792, married Dec. 17, 1807, JOHN DENNETT.

Children of the 7th Gen.
3083 SALLY.
3084 HORACE, m. MALVINA ———, lived 68th St. N. Y. City.
3085 ELIZA.   3086 HANNAH.
3087 APHIA, m. ——— BURNS, lived Yonkers, N. Y., and d. Apl. 12, 1901.
3088 OREN, lived 68th St., N. Y. City, was connected with Knickerbocker Ice Co.
3089 JOHN Q. A.   3090 HENRY C.

F1205 Hannah Locke, born May 16, 1794, married Sept. 3, 1812, JOSHUA DENNETT who was born Feb. 12, 1791, a brother of above.

Children of 7th Gen.
3091 MARY.   3092 CHARLES.   3093 LYDIA A.
3094 HARRIET G., m. 1848, STEPHEN OTIS, who was b. Livingston, Apl. 20, 1823, son of David and Anna (Libbey); went to Cal. in 1849, lived there; had a son: 3095 FRANK OTIS, b. San Francisco, Nov. 18, 1852, m. Aug. 26, 1880, LUCRETIA L. MASTICK. He graduated Univ. of Cal., 1873, A.B., A.M., a lawyer, and had: 3096 EDWIN, b. 1881; 3097 HARROLD, b. 1883, d. 1887; 3098 STEPHEN, b. 1886.
3099 MARTHA.   3100 ALBERT.   3101 CYRUS.
3102 JOSHUA F. L.   3103 SIMON.

F1206 Simon Locke, born in Barrington, Sept. 30, 1786, married 1st, June 5, 1808, OLIVE CHADBOURNE of North Berwick, Me., born March 9, 1790, died in Somersworth, March 26, 1853. He married 2nd, March 15, 1853, SARAH RUNNELS, born in Berwick, Me., Feb. 1, 1784, daughter of Samuel and Mary (March). (Rochester records say Sarah married 1st, JOHN HANSON of Rochester, and 2nd, SIMON LOCKE, who died Apl. 7, 1854.) Simon was a farmer, shoemaker and grocer in Hollis, Me., moved to Somersworth in 1828, and died there Apl. 28, 1855.

Children of 7th Gen.
F3104 MARTHA ANN, b. May 7, 1809, m. BENJAMIN HORN.
F3105 HOWARD, b. Oct. 13, 1810, m. 1st, June 9, 1833, EUNICE WENTWORTH; m. 2nd, June 27, 1853, SUSAN W. WENTWORTH.
F3106 MARY ANN, b. Aug. 31, 1812, m. JOHN HUSSEY.
3107 HANNAH, b. Apl. 17, 1814, m. Dec. 17, 1840, BRICE B. BRADBURY. (See F1454.)
F3108 ABIGAIL, b. May 10, 1815, m. Oct. 10, 1839, WILLIAM HILL.
3109 THOMAS DENNETT, b. Hollis, Dec. 24, 1820, drowned, Apl. 28, 1830.

F3110 SARAH OLIVE DENNETT, b. Nov. 27, 1821, m. Apl. 14, 1850, BENJAMIN F. HILL.
3111 SIMON, b. July 5, 1822, d. Aug. 23, 1832.
F3112 ANN MARIA OTIS, b. June 10, 1824, m. Apl. 21, 1847, WILLIAM S. EMBRY.
F3113 THOMAS DENNETT, b. Jan. 23, 1832, m. June 19, 1850, SOPHIA S. CROSS.
There was in this family a noted female quartette of singers: MARY ANN, HANNAH, ABIGAIL, and ANN MARIA.

F1207 Hannah Locke, born in Barrington, May 16, 1789, married in Barrington, Dec. 19, 1805, ELIAS VARNEY, a Quaker. She died Aug. 1, 1830, and he married 2nd, LAVINIA HODGDON. He was a farmer in Barrington and died about 1865.

Children of 7th Gen. b. in Barrington.

3114 PARMELIA HODGDON, b. ——, died young.
3115 HANNAH, b. ——, m. SAMUEL FELKER of Rochester and had: 3116 FRANCIS; 3117 HANNAH.
3118 RUFUS, b. ——, m. —— Foss, lived Barrington.
3119 SOLOMON, b. ——, m. RACHEL FELKER, lived Barr., and had: 3120 MARION; 3121 ELLEN; 3122 FREEMAN.
3123 ROCKWELL, b. ——, m. lived Portsmouth, had: 3124 LAVINIA.
3125 SHUBEL, b. ——, d. unmarried in war.
3126 LAVINA, b. ——, m. MARTIN LORD.

F1210 Jethro Locke, born in Barrington, Nov. 14, 1796, married 1st, in Barrington, Feb. 19, 1818, SUSAN CLARKE of Barrington; married 2nd, Nov. 14, 1839, LYDIA HANSCOM of Strafford, who died about 1880. He moved from Barrington to Dover, and died about 1880. (One record says he married 2nd, a GILMAN.) He was a farmer and blacksmith.

Children of 7th Gen. b. in Barrington.

3127 ADALINE P., b. ——, d. Apl. 10, 1892, aged 73-6-27, m. HERBERT DOWNES, lived Pittsfield, and Center Barnstead, had: 3128 LAURA, is unmarried; 3129 HERBERT, is married; 3130 ALBERT, is unmarried. All live in Barnstead Center.
3131 BELINDA, b. May 29, 1829, d. Jan. 25, 1912, m. 1st, Dover, Nov. 26, 1850, LYSANDER B. WATSON, b. Durham, 1827; had: 3132 WALTER SCOTT, b. Sept. 11, 1851, is married; 3133 LYSANDER LOCKE, b. Dec. 1855, is married and lives in Lowell; 3134 ALPHA MARIA, b. 1857, is married; 3135 MALINDA ADELL, b. 1859, is married. Belinda, m. 2nd, CYRUS McCUMBER of Minn.
3137 WAINWRIGHT G., b. 1825, was a farmer in Barrington and Strafford, served in Co. F, 13th N. H. Inf., and d. from effect of wounds, unmarried.
3138 CALVIN, was in Civil War, and d. unmarried, from effect of wounds.

SEVENTH GENERATION

F1211 Nathaniel Locke, born in Barrington, March 20, 1799, married in Rochester, Jan. 17, 1825, MARIA OTIS of Barrington, born May 11, 1802, daughter of Job. He was a mason in Barrington and was buried in Dover.

Children of 7th Gen. b. in New Durham.

3139 SARAH ABIGAIL, b. Apl. 9, 1829, m. 1st, in Strafford, Oct. 8, 1854, CLEMENT B. FOSS; m. 2nd, JOHN T. HILL, of Dover, b. Northwood, had: 3140 EDITH HILL, d. Dover, Dec. 11, 1888, aged 16; 3141 VIENNA HILL, lives Greenwood, Mass.
F3142 MARIA MALVINA, b. July 2, 1832, m. Nov. 19, 1856, ENOCH T. FOSS.
F3143 CORDELIA JANE, b. Jan. 20, 1837, m. March 22, 1858, MARTIN VAN B. FELKER.
3144 VIENNA OLEVIA, b. Dec. 1840, d. June 12, 1868, m. Dover, March 9, 1865, JOHN T. HILL of Dover, b. 1840, son of John and Fanny. He was a grocer in Dover, had no children.

F1212 Joshua Locke, born in Barrington, Dec. 19, 1802, married ABRA FURBUSH of Lebanon, Me., who died June 22, 1858, aged 54-9. He was of Dover and Great Falls, enlisted in Capt. Stephen Woodman's Co. Apl. 6, 1847, for the Mexican War and died June 8, 1849.

Children of 7th Gen. b. in New Durham.

3145 JOSHUA SMITH, b. Dec. 1831, d. Dover, Feb. 25, 1878, m. HARRIET W. ———, b. Saco, 1827, was a cordwainer in Northwood, 1860, had: 3146 JOSHUA S., JR., b. 1859, d. Amesbury, Mass., Apl. 16, 1888, unmarried; had: second child, ———; 3147 HATTIE A., b. East Kingston, Aug. 28, 1866, died young.
F3148 WILLIAM HENRY, b. May 25, 1835, m. 1st, June 7, 1857, SARAH E. RUNNELS; m. 2nd, ——— GOLDSMITH.

F1214 Simon Gray, born April 14, 1785, married PATTY PAGE. He died Oct. 12, 1814.

Children of 7th Gen.

3149 JONATHAN C. 3150 ELIZABETH P. 3151 MARY. 3152 MARTHA.

F1215 Henry Gray, born Apl. 12, 1786, married 1st, Dec. 31, 1812, his cousin, DORATHY OTIS, #1196, born March 2, 1792, died Sept. 11, 1840, by whom he had 16 children. He married 2nd, JOANNA HALL, and married 3rd, unknown. He was a farmer in Strafford.

Children of 7th Gen.

3153 SIMEON L., m. HANNAH MITCHELL, and had: 3154 SOLOMON L.; 3155 BETSEY, m. JOHN TRICKEY; 3756 ABBY, m. JOHN PINKHAM; 3157 CAROLINE; 3158 HENRY.

3159 SOLOMON F., m. LAVINA PERKINS, and had: 3160 SARAH; 3161 HARRIET; 3162 JOHN H.; 3163 JOSEPH F.; 3164 ANGELINA; 3165 SARAH A.
3166 MARTHA P., m. WELLS PINKHAM, and had: 3167 MARY A.; 3168 WILLIAM H.; 3169 HENRY; 3170 CLARA.
3171 BETSEY Y., m. GEORGE PINKHAM, and had: 3172 EMILY JANE; 3173 GEORGE F.; 3174 HENRY G.; 3175 TWINS, died young.
3176 HANNAH J., m. STACY HALL, and had: 3177 SOLOMON H.; 3178 DOROTHY G.; 3179 OTIS M.; 3180 JOHN.
3181 WILLIAM H., m. 1st, CLARA WOODMAN; m. 2nd, SARAH CYM, and had: 3182 ELLA; 3183 ELIZABETH; 3184 CLARA; 3185 JOHN N.; 3186 HENRY P.
3187 OTIS M., probably unmarried.
3188 MARY ANN, m. 1st, ——— CHAMBERLAIN; m. 2nd, ——— CHESLEY, and had: 3189 CARRIE; 3190 HERBERT; 3191 JOSEPH.
3192 WENDEL S., m. HANNAH FOSS, and had: 3193 SARAH A.; 3194 IDA; 3195 BETSEY.
3196 DOROTHY C.   3197 JOSHUA B.   3198 LAVINIA A.
Second wife's children:
3199 GEORGE W.; and 3200 SARAH E., twins;
3201 SOLOMON H., and 3202 CHARLES W., twins.

F1217 Mary Gray, born Aug. 2, 1789, married WILLIAM GRAY and lived in Dover.

Children of 7th Gen.

3203 SIMON. 3204 HEZEKIAH. 3205 BARBER. 3206 STEPHEN. 3207 LUCY.
3208 SARAH A. 3209 WILLIAM. 3210 MARY. 3211 DOROTHY.

F1218 Hannah Gray, born Jan. 16, 1791, married a TRIPP and lived in Dover.

Children of 7th Gen.

3212 SOLOMON. 3213 MARY JANE, and three others.

F1219 Solomon Gray, born Sept. 7, 1792, married CAROLINE WENDELL, Nov. 28, 1819, and lived in Dover.

Children of 7th Gen.

3214 ABIGAIL. 3215 GEORGE. 3216 FRANCIS and 3217 SARAH, twins.
3218 SOPHIE. 3219 CHARLES.

F1222 William Gray, born Feb. 19, 1798, married Nov. 30, 1819, MARY RAND, born in Portsmouth, 1804, died in Portsmouth, Jan. 17, 1873, daughter of James and Sarah. He was a teamster in Portsmouth and died June 1881.

Children of 7th Gen. probably b. in Portsmouth.

3220 MARY F., b. ———, d. Amesbury, Mass., Oct. 26, 1895, m. 1st, WESLEY MOSES; m. 2nd, JAMES M. HAYNES, and had: 3221 CHARLES; 3222 HERBERT; 3223 IRVING.

SEVENTH GENERATION

3224 ZERVIAH M., b. 1821, d. unmarried in Portsmouth, Sept. 6, 1904.
3225 LEONARD S. R., d. Oct. 5, 1895, m. MARY A. DAVIS, lived in Dover and had: 3226 MARTHA L., m. GEORGE MURRAY; 3227 IDA S., m. ANSEL LIBBEY; 3228 LIZZIE; 3229 MARY.
3230 WILLIAM HENRY, m. Ports., Dec. 10, 1846, ELLEN S. LEACH. He was a painter in Portsmouth, and d. Feb. 20, 1883; had: 3231 WILLARD, m. 1st, ANNIE COPPS; m. 2nd, MINNIE FRIZZELL and had three sons: 3232 ELLA F., m. GEORGE SAWYER; 3233 IDA, m. CHARLES SANBORN; 3234 ANNIE, d. unmarried; 3235 ALICE, d. unmarried; 3236 HORACE, m. HATTIE PINDER, and had four children.
3237 SARAH, b. 1828, d. Nov. 4, 1865, m. 1st, JOSEPH GREEN, and had: 3238 FRED, who d. aged about 25; m. 2nd, ROBERT GREEN, a brother of Joseph's and had: 3239 JOSEPH; 3240 ELMER, both living in Portsmouth.
3241 ELIZA G., died young.
F3242 MARGARET P., b. Jan. 6, 1832, m. Aug. 12, 1855, GEORGE HUMPHREYS.
3243 JOSEPHINE S., b. 1836, d. 1907, m. GEORGE H. HAM, b. 1836, d. Feb. 26, 1896, lived in Portsmouth and had: 3244 EVA E.; 3245 ADDIE S., b. 1856, m. CHARLES WILLEY, and had two children: 3246 CHARLES W., m. CECELIA SALMON and had five children; 3247 LIZZIE, m. FRANK PARSONS and had two children.
3248 CHARLES A. C., b. ——, died young.
3249 CLARENCE S., m. LOUISA DEROCHEMONT, lived in Kingston and had: 3250 MABEL; 3251 SADIE; 3252 CHARLES; 3253 LEONORA; 3254 KATE, who m. —— KIMBALL.
3255 CHARLES A. C., b. 1841, d. May 24, 1909, m. 1st, June 9, 1868, ANNIE HAM, and had: 3256 ELLEN; 3257 RUTH. He m. 2nd, June 29, 1885, MARTHA P. PALMER of Machias, Me., and had: 3258 RALPH, a lawyer in Portsmouth.
3259 WALTER S., b. 1845, d. Jan. 10, 1898, m. MARY O. PRIME and had: 3260 WALTER; 3261 CHARLES W., b. 1866, m. SARAH ROBERTS, is manager of Consolidation Coal Co. in Portsmouth and has several children: 3262 GEORGE; 3263 EDWIN; 3264 SALLY; 3265 FRED.

F1223 Jethro Gray, born Oct. 21, 1799, married LUCRETIA POTTLE, and lived in Strafford.

Children of 7th Gen.
3266 MARY E. 3267 SAMUEL. 3268 MOWE. 3269 WENDELL.

F1225 Joseph Gray, born Apl. 25, 1803, married HANNAH GRAY, and lived in Northwood.

Children of 7th Gen.
3270 WILLIAM HENRY. 3271 OLIVER J.
3272 MARY A., m. —— ELKINS, and had: 3273 ELLA; 3274 JOHN; 3275 WALTER.

F1226 John Locke, born in Cincinnatus, N. Y., Nov. 20, 1791, married BETSEY OLDS, born Feb. 11, 1792, died June 3, 1875. He moved from Cincinnatus to Livonia, N. Y., in 1840 and died Aug. 16, 1857.

Children of 7th Gen. b. near Cincinnatus, N. Y.
3276 SOPHIA.   3277 LOUISA.   3278 JAMES.   3279. JESSE.
3280 MARIA.   3281 BETSEY.   3282 NANCY.
3283 JOHN, b. Oct. 1, 1827, was a storekeeper in Livonia, N. Y.
3284 HENRY, b. Feb. 1, 1830, lived in Livonia, N. Y.
3285 POLLY.

F1231 Jesse Locke, born in Cincinnatus, N. Y., Apl. 3, 1804, married May 13, 1824, LAURA REXFORD, daughter of William and Anna (Blanchard), born Hartford, Conn., Dec. 23, 1804, died Wellsboro, Pa., Dec. 2, 1874. He lived in Oxford, N. Y., and Cincinnatus, N. Y., in 1840, and died Tioga County, Pa., July 12, 1849.

Child of 7th Gen.
F3286 FANNIE M., b. Jan. 23, 1836, m. 1852, LORAN A. SEARS.

F1234 Charles B. Locke, born May 15, 1787, married ELIZABETH BRAMAN, born 1788. He lived in Exeter, R. I., and was a cordwainer there in 1850.

Children of 7th Gen.
3287 EDSON B., b. 1816, m. SARAH A. WILSON, was a stone cutter in Exeter, or Richmond, R. I.
3288 JAMES W., b. ——, m. Oct. 3, 1843, SARAH HOWARD, dau. of John, lived Warwick, R. I.
3289 ELIZA A., b. ——, m. Westerly, R. I., Apl. 9, 1843, ALFRED B. COREY of North Kingston, R. I.
3290 JOSEPH H., b. ——, m. March 28, 1846, SUSAN C. MARBLE, lived Richmond, R. I.

F1239 Joshua R. Locke, born Apl. 22, 1801, married 1st, PHEBE BOSS, Feb. 1822, daughter of Peter and Susanna; married 2nd, Apl. 10, 1842, ABBIE BROWN of South Kingston, R. I. They joined the South Kingston Church and he was a farmer in Richmond in 1850 but not in 1860. He died Dec. 25, 1869.

Children of 7th Gen.
3291 MARY, b. ——.   3292 JOSIAH, b. ——.
3293 REBECCA, b. ——.   3294 HENRY CLARKE, b. ——.

F1247 Benjamin Locke, born Sept. 30, 1807, married Apl. 5, 1829, MARY H. TANNER, who died June 21, 1885, daughter of Thomas B. and Hannah. He died July 23, 1890.

Almon A. Locke 3311

CHLOE WOODMANSEE LOCKE
Wife of Elder Ezekiel James Locke

ELDER EZEKIEL JAMES LOCKE

SEVENTH GENERATION

Children of 7th Gen. b. in Exeter, R. I.
3295 DANIEL, b. ——.
F3296 BENJAMIN, b. Oct. 13, 1831, m. Dec. 1859, PHEBE ANN PALMER.
F3297 DEACON THOMAS TANNER, b. May 15, 1834, m. March 11, 1860, SARAH M. CARTER.
3298 JOSHUA ROCHMAN, b. Apl. 4, 1836, m. Nov. 14, 1867, BELLE CASE GARDNER of No. Kingston, b. Feb. 10, 1834, d. Dec. 15, 1905. He lived in Exeter, and d. June 19, 1895, had: 3299 ROWLAND; 3300 CARRIE.
3301 MARY H., b. May 27, 1839, died young.
3302 MARY H., b. March 1, 1841, d. June 23, 1859.
3303 JOHN T., b. Dec. 8, 1845, m. Nov. 15, 1868, ANNA TILINGHAST, b. Sept. 4, 1851; lived in Exeter, a farmer, and had: 3304 MARY J.; 3305 CHARLES F.; 3306 AMELIA T.; 3307 ANNIE E.

F1248 Rev. Ezekiel James Locke, born Nov. 27, 1809, married Oct. 27, 1833, MRS. CHLOE WOODMANSEE, born in Richmond, Dec. 21, 1816, died Atlantic, Iowa, Feb. 8, 1899, daughter of John and Jerusha (Moors). He was pastor of Queens River Baptist Church, South Kingston, R. I., in 1843, and died in Iowa, Feb. 6, 1887, to which place he had moved in 1866.

Children of 7th Gen. b. in So. Kingston, R. I.
F3308 WATEANN, b. Apl. 19, 1835, m. May 15, 1859, GEORGE ABEL PEASE.
F3309 PARDON T., b. Oct. 10, 1839, m. 1st, Sept. 15, 1859, JENNIE ODER; m. 2nd, Nov. 1, 1888, JOSIE H. HUNDLEY.
3310 HANNAH WOODMANSEE, b. Apl. 2, 1842, m. June 1, 1886, WILLIAM B. WHITE of Los Angeles, Cal.; have no children.
3311 ALMON ANDREW, b. Apl. 11, 1844. He has been in the grain, piano and real estate business, now retired living unmarried in Fort Worth, Texas, interested in travel, engaged in anti-cruelty work, in humane education, and other efforts in behalf of the civil and moral welfare.
F3312 CHARLES HORACE, b. March 25, 1848, m. Feb. 24, 1874, HENRIETTA C. GARWOOD.
F3313 SARAH JANE, b. May 8, 1852, m. March 21, 1875, JOSEPH A. PARK.
F3314 JOHN EDWIN, b. June 21, 1855, m. Apl. 24, 1881, MARY L. BARNES. Two children died young.

F1257 Stephen Locke, born July 20, 1814, married in East Greenwich, R. I., March 10, 1839, RHODA LEWIS, born 1816. They were called "both of Exeter," but he lived in South Kingston, R. I., 1850.

Children of 7th Gen. perhaps b. in So. Kingston.
3315 RODY O., b. 1842.
3316 ELIZABETH R., b. 1844.
3317 MARY E., b. 1845.
3318 DANIEL, b. 1847.
3319 WATE E., b. 1849.
3320 EDWARD, b. ——.

F1263 William J. S. Locke, born Apl. 4, 1823, married Apl. 24, 1843, CATHERINE STEADMAN of South Kingston, born 1825, daughter of Henry. He lived in Richmond in 1860 and died Jan. 16, 1908.

Children of 7th Gen. b. in Richmond.

3321 ELMIRA C., b. ——.   3322 HENRY J. N., b. 1843.
3323 WILLIAM F., b. ——.   3324 WILLIAM EDWIN, b. ——.

F1270 Nathaniel Clifford, born March 28, 1794, married LUCY SMALL, daughter of Job the 6th, born 1768. She was born Jan. 7, 1799, died Jan. 7, 1862. Nathaniel was in the War of 1812, and died March 18, 1883.

Children of the 7th Gen.

3325 RACHEL, b. 1818, m. —— KEEN.
3326 WILLIAM H., b. 1820, d. 1840.
3327 NATHANIEL G., b. 1822, d. 1894, m. 1st, JANE FLETCHER; m. 2nd, MRS. SARAH RICH; was a sea captain.
3328 THOMAS P., b. 1824, m. 1st, DELIA WALKER; m. 2nd, RUTH (FLETCHER) ELLIS. He was a sea captain, d. 1903.
3329 ANDREW J., b. 1827, m. PHEBE TREAT; was a sea captain.
3330 SAMUEL J., b. 1829, m. PRUDENTIA KELLEY; was a sea captain.
3331 DAVID B., b. 1837, m. RUTH SLEEPER; was captain of a ship and both were lost at sea 1855 on their bridal trip.
3332 FREDERICK O., b. Prospect, Me., Jan. 4, 1835, d. June 26, 1868, m. KATHERINE M. FOX, b. Feb. 5, 1839, d. Apl. 24, 1865. He was in the Civil War, and was father of 3333 MRS. HELEN M. HARRIMAN, Milford, N. H.

F1276 Thomas Noyes, baptized Falmouth, Me., Nov. 5, 1769, married in 1793, BETSEY HAINES. He died May 27, 1821.

Children of 7th Gen.

3334 WILLIAM, b. Nov. 17, 1793, d. Nov. 14, 1840, m. ——.
3335 JOHN H., b. June 26, 1796, m. 1st, 1823, CHARLOTTE THOMPSON; m. 2nd, MRS. MARTHA A. HUMPHREY, who d. June 1, 1884.
3336 BETSEY, b. Oct. 19, 1799, m. PHINEAS SOULE.
3337 THOMAS, b. Pownal, Me., June 23, 1803, d. May 4, 1871, m. 1st, JOANNA SAWYER; m. 2nd, 1840, LUCRETIA LAWRENCE.
3338 GEORGE, b. June 16, 1806, m. 1st, 1843, CELESTIA WARREN; m. 2nd, 1854, ALMIRA ROYAL.
3339 MARY A., b. Aug. 15, 1809, m. NOAH HARRIS.

F1281 Nathaniel Locke Noyes, born Apl. 3, 1780, married 1st, in 1801, DORCAS NOYES; married 2nd, in 1811, SOPHIA GOULD.

Children of 7th Gen.

3340 ELIZA A., b. Aug. 13, 1802.
3341 SOPHIA, b. Nov. 12, 1803, m. JOHN CHANDLER.

SEVENTH GENERATION

3342 LENDAL, b. Dec. 4, 1805.
3343 ALEXANDER, b. Oct. 9, 1807, m. 1st, 1829, ALMIRA RICE; m. 2nd, MRS. —— HATCH.
3344 DORCAS, b. Aug. 9, 1813, m. JOSEPH D. WOOD.
3345 NATHANIEL, b. Cumberland, Me., Jan. 25, 1816, d. Sullivan, Me., Nov. 4, 1899, m. HARRIET WOOD and had ten children.

F1284 James L. Noyes, born March 23, 1794, married in 1822, MARY CONNOR. He died March 3, 1859.

Children of 7th Gen.

3346 MARY A. K., b. June 3, 1823, m. 1843, JOHN T. WINSLOW.
3347 JAMES, b. Jan. 18, 1830, d. 1888, m. 1874, ANNE M. COLLEY.
3348 HENRY M., b. March 6, 1837, m. 1858, MARY J. BRACKETT, had
3349 GERTRUDE, b. 1866, and three others.

F1285 Sylvanus Prince, born Feb. 26, 1789, married 1st, MATILDA PRINCE, born Dec. 31, 1792, died Nov. 18, 1834, daughter of Pyam and Martha (Leach); married 2nd, ANN BLANCHARD, born 1800, died Nov. 26, 1837; married 3rd, EUNICE FERNALD, who died in 1856; married 4th, MARY MALCOLM. He died June 1871.

Children of 7th Gen.

3350 MARTHA, b. Oct. 8, 1812, m. FRANCIS B. ROBIE of Gorham, Me.
3351 THOMAS R., b. ——, d. Healdsburg, Cal., Dec. 1862, m. ABIGAIL OAKS, dau. of Nathan, lived in Cal.
3352 MARY M., b. 1823, m. 1849, CAPT. JOSEPH BUCKNAM, and had:
3353 JOSEPH W. BUCKNAM, b. off Peru, July 30, 1854, first officer on bark *S. K. Lyman*, of Portland.
3354 WILLIAM L. M., b. ——, m. LUCY HARDING of Gorham, Me.; a machinist of Portland.
3355 FRANCES M., b. March 1833, m. 1850, DAVID RICHARDS, lives Auburn, Me.

F1292 Mercy Mason, born June 7, 1805, married Nov. 22, 1827, BENJAMIN F. MERRILL of Falmouth, Me.

Children of 7th Gen.

3356 MARY S., b. Aug. 6, 1828, d. July 7, 1845.
3357 WILLIAM F., b. March 21, 1831, m. LYDIA DURRELL.
3358 ALBION, b. Aug. 4, 1833, m. MARTHA T. MASON.
3359 RUFUS S., b. Jan. 16, 1837, m. SARAH ROBINSON.
3360 CHARLES D., b. Nov. 4, 1839, d. 1862.
3361 LUCY E., b. July 10, 1843, m. SAMUEL N. HUTCHINSON.
3362 HENRY M., b. Apl. 24, 1846, d. 1847.
3363 MERCY A., b. Sept. 12, 1848, d. infant.

F1298 John Mason Locke, born in Falmouth, Me., May 15, 1807, married July 14, 1841, his stepsister, PHOEBE POMEROY, of Portland, who died 1858. He was a mariner in early life, later a farmer, and died 1884.

Children of 7th Gen. all b. in Falmouth, Me.

F3364 CORDELIA POMEROY, b. Apl. 16, 1842, m. Apl. 12, 1866, CHARLES D. THOMPSON.

F3365 JOHN MASON, b. Apl. 22, 1844, m. 1880, NELLIE BRIDGES.

F3366 EDWARD HOWARD, b. Feb. 28, 1846, m. Sept. 29, 1873, CHESTINA FREEMAN.

F3367 STEPHEN BRAINARD, b. Aug. 25, 1848, m. Apl. 8, 1874, SUSAN JANE SARGENT.

3368 WARREN GILMAN, b. Jan. 29, 1851, d. 1890, m. 1870, LIZZIE MOORE of Tarrytown, N. Y. He was employed in several states in the South, had: 3369 HARRY, who d. an infant; another infant died with its mother.

F1300 Nathaniel C. Locke, born in Falmouth, Me., March 8, 1812, married March 18, 1847, SARAH A. CARLISLE, born Bristol, Me., Aug. 22, 1820, died March 1, 1880. In early life he was a school teacher, later a merchant. He was a prominent temperance worker, belonged to the Whig party, and held several town offices; died in Falmouth, Dec. 9, 1873.

Children of 7th Gen. b. in Falmouth.

F3370 GEORGE M., b. July 17, 1849, m. CLARA HASKELL.

3371 ORVILLE G., b. Sept. 2, 1856, d. Feb. 1876.

3372 A boy and a girl died infants.

F1302 Miles Standish Locke, born in Falmouth, Me., May 17, 1818, married DEBORAH LOCKE NOYES, # 1309, born Apl. 8, 1823, died Dec. 31, 1892. In early life he lived in Calais, Me., later in Falmouth, was a tinsmith and died Feb. 1, 1881.

Children of 7th Gen. b. in Falmouth.

F3373 LEONARD STANDISH, b. 1854, m. EMMA J. HINES.

3374 MARY ELLA, b. 1856, d. 1881, m. CHARLES BUCKNAM of Falmouth, and had: 3375 GEORGIE E., b. Aug. 1876, d. 1889; 3376 ETTA, b. 1879. He m. 2nd, her sister, LUCY TAYLOR LOCKE.

3378 HARRIET ROUNDY, b. 1858, d. Dec. 7, 1887, m. GEORGE BUCKNAM, and had three children.

3379 LUCY TAYLOR, b. 1861, d. 1891, m. CHARLES BUCKNAM, and had: 3380 EMMA.

F1307 Elizabeth S. Noyes, born in Falmouth, Me., Dec. 19, 1819, married JOHN WOODBURY of Cape Elizabeth, Me. He was a farmer in Cape Elizabeth many years, then went to West Falmouth.

SEVENTH GENERATION 165

Children of 7th Gen.
3381 EBENEZER, was engineer U. S. revenue cutter service.
3382 CHARLES E., d. Portland, Apl. 1899, no children.
3383 EMMA, lived Falmouth.

F1308 Dorcas A. Noyes, born in Falmouth, Me., June 1, 1821, married ROBERT HUSTON of Falmouth, who was a farmer and died there March 22, 1896. She died July 7, 1888.
Children of 7th Gen. b. in Falmouth.
3384 HARLAN PORTER, b. March 21, 1845.
3385 HENRY FRANCIS, a twin, d. infant.
3386 HELEN AMELIA, b. March 14, 1847, m. HORACE W. GREELEY, had no children; lived Portland.
3387 HENRIETTA, b. ——, d. aged 20.
3388 DORCAS ABBIE, b. June 21, 1855, lives Portland, unmarried.
3389 WILLIE, b. Aug. 6, 1860, d. 1862.
3390 TILLIE CROSBY, b. Sept. 26, 1863, m. GEORGE COLLEY of Portland.
3391 WALTER PHILIP, b. Feb. 14, 1865, lives Portland, unmarried.

F1310 Ruth C. Noyes, born in Falmouth, Me., Nov. 7, 1824, married GEORGE W. LEIGHTON of Falmouth, who was a farmer there. She died Apl. 5, 1877.
Children of 7th Gen.
3392 ABBIE S., b. Feb. 1853, d. July 1874.
3393 HERBERT G., b. Feb. 8, 1857, d. July 22, 1873.

F1312 Sarah Prince Noyes, born in Falmouth, Me., July 8, 1828, married in 1848, AMOS LEIGHTON, who was a farmer in Falmouth.
Children of 7th Gen.
3394 HOWARD, b. 1851, d. 1876, m. 1873, MARIE E. WYMAN of Portland; no children.
3395 EDWARD, b. 1867, d. Aug. 6, 1882.
3396 EDGAR, a twin, m. ——, lived Portland.

F1313 Amos W. Noyes, born in Falmouth, Me., Apl. 12, 1830, married 1863, GEORGIE MARSTON of Falmouth, where he was a farmer and died Sept. 3, 1887.
Children of 7th Gen.
3397 WILLIAM, b. Apl. 19, 1864.
3398 EDWARD K., b. Oct. 6, 1865.
3399 ARTHUR C., b. June 8, 1877, m. 1899, LILLIAN MCDONALD; had:
 3400 HELEN R., b. Apl. 25, 1900.
3401 REUBEN M., b. Apl. 26, 1873.

F1314 Eunice B. Noyes, born in Falmouth, Me., July 6, 1832, married RENSALAER GREELY of Portland, son of Thomas. He was in Co. C., 1st Me. Reg. during the Civil War, later in milk business in Portland, Me.

Children of 7th Gen.

3402 CORA, b. 1858, d. Jan. 8, 1862.
3403 ANNIE, b. March 30, 1864, m. DR. WALTER P. CLARKE of Worcester, Mass.
3404 FRANK B., b. Oct. 16, 1865, m. —— MERRILL, dau. of Capt. Merrill of S. S. *Portland.* Lived Cambridge, Mass.
3405 GEORGE E., b. June 24, 1875, m. ——; is shipping clerk, Portland.
3406 DAUGHTER, d. an infant.

F1315 John E. Noyes, born in Falmouth, Me., Nov. 8, 1834, married LAURINDA GREELY of Falmouth. He was in the milk business in Cambridge, Mass.

Child of 7th Gen.

3407 MINNIE ALICE, a Boston public school teacher.

F1316 Mary Ann Noyes, born in Falmouth, Me., Oct. 12, 1836, married 1860, EDWARD NELSON GREELY of Cumberland, Me., born there March 3, 1835, son of Edward. He is in the milk business.

Children of 7th Gen.

3408 ELMER G., b. Portland, March 4, 1869.
3409 FRED E., b. P., June 8, 1872.

F1317 Reuben Noyes, born in Falmouth, Me., July 11, 1839, married 1862, LUCELIA BOWIE of Falmouth. He was street commissioner of Portland, Me.

Children of 7th Gen. b. in Portland.

3410 JENNIE LLOYD, b. June 8, 1862, m. 1886, JAMES MCLANE.
3411 NELLIE SUSAN, b. Feb. 14, 1864, m. 1884, CHARLES MCLANE.

F1344 Charles H. Merrill, born in Saco, Me., in 1818, died aged 70 in Portland, married in 1841, CHARITY TOTMAN of Harpswell, Me. He went to Portland in 1865, was in the lumber business.

Children of 7th Gen.

3412 CHARLES E., b. ——, m. ——, lived Portland, had: SON.
3413 IDA M., b. ——, m. ORRIN HAWKES, a clothing dealer in Portland; had: 3414 ABBIE.
3415 VESTA M., lived Portland, unmarried.

SEVENTH GENERATION

F1352 Charlotte Locke, born in Alma, N. B., Apl. 5, 1820, died Feb. 5, 1888, married Dec. 28, 1843, ISAAC PULSIFER of Alma, who was a ship calker.

Children of 7th Gen. b. in Alma, N. B.

3416 EUNICE ANN, b. Nov. 20, 1844, m. CALEB DOWNING of Alma, a ship builder; had no children.
3417 CHARLOTTE ELIZABETH, b. Dec. 8, 1846, m. 1st, May 25, 1868, WILLIAM LAVERTY; m. 2nd, Jan. 8, 1880, WARD V. MILTON of Alma; no children.
3418 SUSAN MARY, b. ——, d. infant.
3419 NATHANIEL MERRILL, b. May 1849, d. Dec. 29, 1852.
3420 SUSAN ELLA, b. July 14, 1852, unmarried.
F3421 LUCINDA JANE, b. Dec. 7, 1854, m. July 16, 1883, JOHN N. CANNON.
F3422 EVA MARIA, b. March 18, 1856, m. Sept. 2, 1891, J. J. DOWNING.
F3423 LAURA ALICE, b. Sept. 10, 1858, m. Sept. 26, 1879, JOHN FLETCHER.
3424 ISAAC WITMAN, b. June 30, 1862, m. May 27, 1890, MRS. ELIZABETH CLARKE; had no children.

F1353 Joanna Locke, born in Alma, N. B., of 2nd wife, Oct. 1835, died Dec. 1865, married Dec. 1855, ALBERT FOSTER.

Children of 7th Gen. b. in Alma, N. B.

3425 NATHANIEL, b. Dec. 25, 1856, d. May 1865.
3426 JAMES CLARKE, b. Nov. 18, 1858, lived unmarried, La Conner, Wash.
3427 ANNA LAURA, b. Sept. 25, 1860, m. Aug. 1888, ALVIN A. BRAY, lived Mt. Vernon, Wash.; had no children and d. Apl. 1, 1915.
3428 CLARA AGNES, b. Nov. 20, 1862, m. July 18, 1895, THOMAS E. COLPITTS, had: 3429 MARION, b. Sept. 27, 1896.
3430 JOANNA, b. Dec. 6, 1864, d. 1865.

F1354 John Farrar, born in Charleston, Me., Aug. 17, 1817, married SARAH A. KELSEY, born Knox, Me., Oct. 15, 1823, died East Corinth, Me., Dec. 7, 1898. He died Feb. 12, 1898.

Children of 7th Gen.

3431 SEWELL FRANKLIN, m. ELLEN A. HAYES of Foxcroft, Me.
3432 FREDERICK, m. MABEL TALMAN of Glenburn, Me.
3433 JOSIAH, m. MELISSA TRIM of Charleston, Me., lived Corinth, Me.
3434 ABIJAH LOCKE.
3435 ALBERT, b. June 7, 1858, m. GRACE M. HATCH of Cambridgeport, Mass., lived in Corinth, Me.
3436 GEORGE ORA, m. CARRIE E. HONDLETTE, lived Corinth, Me.

F1355 Sewell Farrar, born in Charleston, Me., Sept. 4, 1819, married 1st, MARY ROLLINS of Charleston, Me.; married 2nd, ELTHEA BAGLEY. He died March 13, 1866.

Children of 7th Gen.
3437 MARY E., m. —— GILMAN, lived Union, Me.
3438 SEWELL MEDVILLE, m. ANNIE SCRIBNER of Charleston, Me.
3439 EUNICE, m. HENRY TURNER of Berwick, Me.
3440 CHARLES, m. NELLIE SAVAGE of Milo, Me.

F1363 John Morse Locke, born in Falmouth, Me., Jan. 1, 1830, married Oct. 7, 1869, SARAH ELLEN FOSS of Charleston, Me. He was a school teacher at age of 20, and the next year started for California by the Panama route, had a fever but arrived in California Aug. 1851. He was a miner, went to the Frazer River, B. C., in 1858, and nearly perished in a blizzard. He returned to California, enlisted March 19, 1863, in California Battalion of Cavalry, being attached to Co. M, 2nd Mass. He took part in all battles of Sheridan's campaign in the Shenandoah Valley under Genl. Merritt, was twice wounded, and was mustered out July 20, 1865. In 1868 he went to Iowa farming, then to South Dakota, and in 1893 removed to Seward, Ill., where he was living in 1899. He died in Rockford, Ill., Oct. 29, 1906.

Children of 7th Gen.
3441 RICHARD FOSS, b. Arcadia, Iowa, Apl. 13, 1876.
3442 SARAH ELIZABETH, b. Arcadia, Iowa, March 27, 1880.

F1364 Elizabeth Locke, born in Falmouth, Me., Feb. 12, 1832, married Charleston, Me., Dec. 8, 1853, DANIEL HERRICK, son of Daniel and Jerusha (Cole), born March 11, 1824, died a farmer in Charleston, in 1903. She died Bangor, Me., May 6, 1912.

Children of 7th Gen. b. in Charleston, Me.
F3443 JOHN LOCKE, b. Oct. 22, 1854, m. 1st, Nov. 16, 1880, FANNIE E. LAMSON; m. 2nd, FRANCES O. PLUMMER.
F3444 MARY JERUSHA, b. Nov. 22, 1855, m. Feb. 12, 1879, JOHN C. STONE.
3445 RODNEY IRVING, b. Oct. 6, 1857, unmarried.
3446 LINCOLN, b. Feb. 18, 1861, lived California, unmarried.
F3447 SUSIE MARIA, b. Feb. 6, 1871, m. Sept. 14, 1890, WALTER A. DANFORTH.
3448 DANIEL ABIJAH, b. Sept. 16, 1877, unmarried.

F1367 Susanna Marston Locke, born in Falmouth, Me., Apl. 21, 1839, married in Boston, Sept. 27, 1867, BENJAMIN M. HARDY of Rumney. Lived in Boston many years then went to Mt. Vernon, Wash., where he died June 27, 1902. He was born in Bridgewater, Sept. 8, 1838.

SEVENTH GENERATION

Children of 7th Gen.
3449 GEORGE F., b. Boston, Dec. 19, 1870. Lives Hamilton, Wash., unmarried.
3450 ELEANOR, b. Charleston, Me., Nov. 6, 1876, d. Shelburne, Mass., Sept. 3, 1877.
3451 LOUIS BENJAMIN, b. Shelburne, March 1, 1880. Lives Seattle, Wash., unmarried.

F1370 Eleanor Hosmer Locke, born in Charleston, Me., June 22, 1846, married in Clarence, Iowa, Sept. 27, 1869, WILLIAM LORD, born Freedom, N. H., Feb. 8, 1840. He settled first in Orleans Bar, Cal., was a merchant and miner, and lived in Arcata, Cal., 1899.

Children of 7th Gen.
F3452 OSCAR WILLIAM, b. Orleans Bar, Cal., Dec. 4, 1870, m. May 17, 1893, LOTTIE L. RIDDELL of Eureka, Cal.
3453 LOUIS MORSE, b. March 5, 1872, m. Nov. 16, 1898, ABBIE A. DOLL of Etna, Cal. Had: 3454 ALICE M.; 3455 CHARLES H.; 3456 KATHERINE E.
3457 CHARLES WM., b. Jan. 23, 1874, m. Eureka, Cal., June 29, 1904, ROSSINA HANSEN. Had: 3458 HAROLD W.; 3459 R. STANLEY.
3460 SARAH BETSEY, b. March 31, 1876, m. Eureka, Cal., Feb. 6, 1908, SAMUEL H. LYTEL.
3461 BENJAMIN HARDY, b. Arcata, Cal., June 2, 1879, m. Eureka, Cal. Dec. 10, 1908, LUCY E. HASKIN.
3462 FRANK DANFORTH, b. A., July 27, 1881, m. Los Angeles, Cal., Apl. 23, 1907, IRENE MCGUIG. He d. Knights' Ferry, Cal., Oct. 18, 1907. Had posthumous son: 3463 FRANK D. LORD.
3464 EDWARD LOCKE, b. A., March 4, 1884, m. Berkeley, Cal., June 23, 1914, LILLIAN G. THAXTER.

F1371 Leonard Morse Locke, born July 26, 1849, married in Osceola, Neb., Nov. 18, 1879, VIOLA LUCINDA CHASE, born Redfield, Wis., Oct. 22, 1860. They lived 1899, in Garfield, Whitman Co., Wash., and live in 1915, in Fairfield, Idaho.

Children of 7th Gen.
3465 BESSIE JANETTE, b. Wayland, Neb., Jan. 8, 1881, m. Jan. 1, 1900, WILLIS PEDEN; lived in Idaho 1902.
3466 LYDIA SUSANNA, b. Redfield, S. D., Sept. 18, 1882.
3467 WALTER NORMAN, b. Redfield, Nov. 14, 1884, farmer and machinist.
3468 TONY CHESTER, b. Redfield, Jan. 7, 1887. Gold hunter, Fairbanks, Alaska.
3469 SARAH ELEANOR, b. Redfield, Apl. 15, 1889.
3470 ROBERT EARL, b. Farmington, Wash., Oct. 13, 1891. U. S. Marine, Pekin, China, 1915.
3471 MARY BELL, b. Garfield, Wash., Apl 3, 1894.

3472 EDNA ULMER, b. Garfield, May 31, 1899.
3473 NELLIE, b. Nov. 18, 1892, d. Nov. 24, 1893.
3474 DAVID ABIJAH, b. Nov. 24, 1895.

F1376 Joel Talbot Locke, born in Falmouth, Me., Oct. 9, 1839, married Johnson, Vt., March 9, 1870, ELLEN REBECCA PIKE, born New Orleans, La., July 19, 1845, daughter of Luther and Ellen. He was a mariner from age 16-22, then was mining in California two years. He has been in the photograph business in New England many years, in 1899 being in Portland, Me., and died there Feb. 21, 1905.

Children of 7th Gen.

3475 ALICE PIKE, b. Falmouth, Me., Dec. 25, 1874, d. Dec. 11, 1875.
3476 AGNES ELIZABETH, b. Waterford, Vt., Sept. 6, 1876, is a bookkeeper.
3477 HAROLD STOUGHTON, b. Claremont, March 3, 1880, was telegrapher for Associated Press, on *Portland Evening Express*, d. Portland Aug. 4, 1901, of appendicitis.

F1378 Sally Locke, born 1799, married Aug. 27, 1815, WILLIAM DYER, born July 4, 1796, lived in Arctic, R. I., and died Feb. 2, 1874. She died Oct. 21, 1872.

Children of 7th Gen.

3478 SAMUEL, b. Apl. 15, 1819, m. LYDIA HILL. *Children:* 3479 SARAH ANN; 3480 MELISSA; 3481 GEORGE; 3482 SAMUEL.
3483 MARY A., b. Dec. 1, 1821, m. July 25, 1839, STEPHEN MATTESON. *Children:* 3484 MARY ANN, b. Feb. 3, 1851, m. Jan. 7, 1897, HIRAM GREEN, b. July 19, 1832; 3485 PHILIP H., b. Jan. 31, 1856, m. BELLE CUSHING, b. Feb. 14, 1856.
3486 PATIENCE T., b. Oct. 26, 1823, m. SAMUEL TILLINGHAST. They had: 3487 ABBIE; 3488 HANNAH.
3489 EDWARD T., b. Apl. 1, 1825, m. PHEBE PECKNAM. They had: 3490 JOHN; 3491 HENRY.
3492 GEORGE P., b. Apl. 27, 1827, m. LUCY WOODMANSEE.
3493 JOHN P., b. Oct. 16, 1829.
3494 HENRY A., b. Apl. 29, 1833, m. PHEBE LOCKE, # F3512.
3495 WARREN H., b. Jan. 19, 1835, m. MARY JOHNSON. They had: 3496 MARY; 3497 GEORGEANNA; 3498 HENRY; 3499 BETSEY; 3500 PHEBE.
3501 SARAH H., b. July 7, 1839, m. JAMES NYE. They had: 3502 HERBERT; 3503 LILLY; 3504 ANNIE.
3504a WILLIAM, b. Jan. 29, 1841.

F1380 Rev. Henry Brooke Locke, born in South Kingston, R. I., Nov. 5, 1803, married Sept. 4, 1825, MARY ALLYN, born May 15, 1808, died Crompton, R. I., June 3, 1887. He was received into the Coventry church in 1838, became a Baptist minister and died in Warwick. R. I.. Nov. 10. 1865.

SEVENTH GENERATION

Children of 7th Gen.
F3505 MARY ELIZABETH, b. Aug. 6, 1826, m. 1st, Jan. 26, 1846, JOSEPH HOXIE; m. 2nd, SOLOMON MATTESON.
F3506 WILLIAM H., b. Oct. 4, 1828, m. Nov. 8. 1848, SARAH F. GAFFETT.
F3507 EDWARD, b. Sept. 21, 1830, m. 1st, LOIS WATKINS; m. 2nd, 1852 MARY J. GAFFETT.
F3508 GEORGE H., b. Dec. 25, 1832, m. Nov. 30, 1851, LUCY GEER.
3509 JOHN F., b. March 2, 1839, m. June 28, 1861, MARY E. BELLINGTON; was a storekeeper in Appanaug, R. I.
3510 DEBORAH, b. May 5, 1834, m. JAMES BOWEN, b. 1832, d. Feb. 2, 1872, lived Quidnick, R. I., had: 3510a ANNA, who m. GEORGE ALLEN and d. Jan. 1897; 3510b ELLA.
F3511 ELIJAH FERGUSON, b. Feb. 15, 1837, m. 1st, July 30, 1866, HARRIET N. CARTER; m. 2nd, Sept. 7, 1894, L. ISABEL SPRAGUE.
F3512 PHEBE, b. June 22, 1841, m. HENRY ALONZO DYER, # 3494.
F3513 MOSHIER W., b. Sept. 8, 1843, m. Apl. 29, 1866, WAITY J. BROWN.
F3514 EUNICE J., b. Jan. 27, 1846, m. HENRY CORNELL.
3515 THOMAS Y., b. Nov. 23, 1849, m. Dec. 23, 1897, HANNAH T. LOCKWOOD; was an unordained preacher in Quidnick, R. I.

F1384 Abbie A. Locke, born in South Kingston, R. I., Jan. 12, 1812, married Oct. 25, 1832, ALFRED L. FISKE of Phenix, R. I., b. Dec. 4, 1807. He was a miller in Pawtucket, son of Charles, and died May 25, 1879. She died Apl. 25, 1895.

Children of 7th Gen.
3516 PHEBE, b. Aug. 29, 1839, died young.
3517 MARIA, b. Nov. 1, 1840, died young.
3518 ABBIE F., b. Jan. 7, 1842, died young.
3519 THOMAS W., b. Aug. 5, 1845, died young.
3520 MARY E., b. Apl. 13, 1847, m. Apl. 13, 1864, JOSEPH E. HOOD, b. Oct. 7, 1840, lived Pawtucket, R. I., and had two children.
3521 EDWARD, b. Apl 17, 1849, died in the war.
3522 JEREMIAH, b. Dec. 24, 1850, m. Apl. 27, 1879, MARY L. SMITH, b. Dec. 14, 1848; was a miller in Pawtucket.

F1386 Nathan Tucker Locke, born in South Kingston, R. I., 1818, married 1st, PHILENA LEACH; married 2nd, HARRIET M. POTTER, born 1833, died Sept. 26, 1866, daughter of Caleb. He died May 27, 1874.

Children of 7th Gen.
3523 EDWARD J., b. 1842, d. Nov. 1, 1887, m. ELIZABETH FENNES, and had: 3524 EDWARD J., b. Feb. 12, 1881.
3525 NATHAN T., b. 1848, d. May 23, 1886, m. MARY A. ———, was a cigar maker in Providence, and had: 3526 LENA M., d. Oct. 14, 1881, aged 3.

F1387 Thomas Webster Locke, born in South Kingston, R. I., Sept. 24, 1819, married 1st July 18, 1841, HANNAH A. WOOD, born 1823, died Oct. 6, 1882, daughter of Peleg; married 2nd, Sept. 1883, SUSAN CHAPPEL, born 1842, died Apl. 7, 1888. He was four years in the Civil War, lived in Phenix, R. I., and died there Sept. 30, 1907.

Children of 7th Gen.

3527 HANNAH FRANCES, b. May 1, 1843, m. Sept. 16, 1866, CHARLES P. CLARKE, b. Feb. 9, 1845, d. Phenix, R. I., Aug. 3, 1907. He was a Civil War veteran.

3528 WILLIAM THOMAS, b. July 9, 1848, d. Aug. 4, 1873.

3529 LUELLA MARIA, b. July 24, 1852, m. 1st, Feb. 23, 1871, NATHAN A. SISSON, b. 1843, d. Sept. 10, 1896; m. 2nd, July 29, 1899, EDWARD G. REED, b. 1840; lived Phenix, 1911.

3530 JULIAN WEBSTER, b. Apl. 18, 1858, m. 1st, Oct. 18, 1883, MABEL MILLER, b. 1863, d. Apl. 18, 1886; m. 2nd, Sept. 13, 1887, ELIZA J. WAITY; m. 3rd, Oct. 22, 1902, LOUISE McKILLOP, b. Apl. 6, 1873.

F1391 Rebecca Locke, born in Columbia, N. Y., Sept. 11, 1812, married in Richfield, N. Y., Feb. 28, 1832, DAVID AMES, born in Richfield, Aug. 25, 1812. She died there Feb. 12, 1871.

Children of 7th Gen. b. Richfield.

3531 An infant died young.

F3532 JAY W., b. Nov. 29, 1837, m. Oct. 3, 1865, ROSETTA STERNBERG.

3533 JEROME, b. May 19, 1839, m. R., Jan. 13, 1865, MARIETTA YOUNG; had no children.

3534 LOVICIA A., b. Aug. 8, 1846, m. Pittsfield, N. Y., Nov. 25, 1884, ANDREW J. PROSSER, who d. Pitts., Nov. 18, 1888; had no children.

3535 LUCIUS, b. July 27, 1850, d. R., July 18, 1887, m. July 1, 1879, ELLA J. VROOMAN, b. Rich., July 16, 1859, dau. of Nicholas.

3536 MARY Z., b. Dec. 21, 1853, m. R., Dec. 4, 1882, LUCIUS M. CLEMENS, b. Columbia, Nov. 18, 1850; had no children.

F1392 David Locke, born in Richfield, N. Y., March 4, 1817, married June 15, 1841, AURELIA P. CLARKE, born in Columbia, N. Y., Dec. 4, 1824. He died Dec. 29, 1893.

Children of 7th Gen.

F3537 LEWIS CLARKE, b. Jan. 15, 1845, m. Feb. 22, 1866, NANCY M. VANDERHEYDEN.

F3538 HENRY LAMOTT, b. Apl. 24, 1850, m. Oct. 16, 1872, THERESA E. TALBOT.

F1393 Harvey D. Locke, born in Richfield, N. Y., Feb. 10, 1820, married 1st, Aug. 24, 1851, MARY BROWN of Little Lakes, N. Y., born in Richfield, May 23, 1822, died in Wisconsin,

SEVENTH GENERATION

Jan. 15, 1858; married 2nd, at Palmyra, Wis., Dec. 4, 1860, SARAH E. DEWEL, born in Granville, N. Y., May 8, 1840. He died June 12, 1897.

Children of 7th Gen.
3539 GORDON ROMAYNE, b. Richfield, N. Y., June 26, 1852, d. March 30, 1853.
3540 RHODA ANN, b. Rich., Sept. 27, 1853, lived Delavan, Wis.
3541 MARY BROWN, b. R., Jan. 5, 1858, d. Nov. 12, 1861.
Second wife's children.
3542 JEROME DEFOREST, b. R., June 15, 1862, d. Rich., Feb. 2, 1882.
F3543 MARTHA ELIZA, b. Feb. 13, 1867, m. Nov. 28, 1884, ERNEST E. KNILANDS.
3544 ANN ELIZA, b. March 30, 1871, m. Delavan, Wis., Jan. 14, 1903, EARL L. SHEPARD, had: 3545 MABEL IVERNA, b. May 19, 1904.

F1394 Abner W. Locke, born in Richfield, N. Y., July 11, 1824, married in Richfield, Nov. 22, 1859, MARIETTA BLISS, born in Exeter, N. Y.

Children of 7th Gen.
3546 FRANKLIN DEWITT, b. Richfield, N. Y., Oct. 30, 1862, d. R., Oct. 10, 1863.
3547 FRANK L., b. Rich., Oct. 6, 1865. (Newmarket, N. H., Records say Frank L., a mill operator and Nellie A. Clarke, b. Glastonbury, Conn., had a dau., 3548 3rd child, b. July 10, 1905.)

F1395 Christopher H. Locke, born in Richfield, N. Y., June 13, 1826, married in Richfield, Oct. 24, 1854, MARY WARMOUTH, born in Columbia, June 7, 1825, died in Columbia, Nov. 24, 1892. He died in Columbia Feb. 20, 1890.

Children of 7th Gen.
3549 EUGENE OSCAR, b. Richfield, N. Y., Feb. 10, 1858.
3550 ANNA MAY, b. Rich., Apl. 22, 1867.

F1398 Ansley A. Locke, born in Richfield, N. Y., Feb. 14, 1832, married in Columbia, Dec. 30, 1852, MARY E. GETMAN, born in Warren, N. Y., Feb. 1, 1834, died in Richfield, Apl. 8, 1907. He was a carpenter and died in Oneonta, N. Y., Nov. 17, 1914.

Children of 7th Gen.
F3551 NORMAN REUBEN, b. July 5, 1854, m. July 7, 1883, JOSEPHINE BLASIER.
3552 WILLIAM DE ALTON, b. Palermo, Oct. 6, 1857, is a farmer, unmarried, lives Oneonta, N. Y., 1915.
F3553 FRANK W., b. July 10, 1859, m. Oct. 7, 1882, CARRIE BUCHANAN.
F3554 EDWIN ANSLEY, b. Feb. 7, 1863, m. May 10, 1886, LENNA BLASIER.

F3555 CLARA MAY, b. Aug. 11, 1865, m. July 30, 1884, EARL J. LOHNAS.
F3556 JOHN FRANCIS, b. March 27, 1869, m. Jan. 4, 1893, DELLA HERKIMER.
F3557 FRED GETMAN, b. March 20, 1871, m. March 23, 1897, NELLIE FLAKE.
F3558 NELLIE HAYES, b. Nov. 8, 1876, m. DAVID JONES.

F1399 Sylvanus Dyer Locke, born in Richfield, N. Y., Sept. 11, 1833, married in Johnston, Wis., Aug. 13, 1861, ELLEN JOSEPHINE PARKER, born in Vienna, N. Y., June 11, 1840, daughter of Hon. John and Almira (Wadhams). Mr. Locke obtained his education in the public schools of New York supplemented by three years diligent study in academies. Starting West in 1856, he was employed by the Wisconsin Central R. R. as chief draftsman, designing their various bridges and viaducts, but the panic of 1857 drove him into teaching as principal of a seminary in Columbus, Ky. In 1859 he entered the office of a law firm in Janesville, Wis., and while there saw the need of an automatic binding machine. He designed his first machine while in the employ of Walter A. Wood, and in 1873, after thirteen years of experimenting and the expenditure of $100,000 he sold the first self-binding harvester ever used by farmers. In the next twenty years 5,000,000 machines were made and sold.

A pioneer in the invention of this machine, he held over one hundred patents on it, and in other fields of mechanics and machines he held almost as many more. His life was an illustration of the possibilities offered to energy and perseverance, and an example to the young and honest poor of the land. In his own country he enjoyed the confidence and approbation of all, manifested by his election as a Republican to the legislature in 1883. After many years of retirement he died in Hoosick Falls, N. Y., Sept. 27 1896.

The Locke family is under particular obligation to this man, who at much expense and time in 1890 traveled to Block Island, R. I., and personally went over and copied every Locke item to be found there, and by these proved to his own satisfaction, and to mine that the Block Island Lockes were from Hampton, N. H., traditions so called, notwithstanding; also that there were no others there in early times. From records and from the testimony of three persons born about 1800 he disproved the idea that any Locke was in bondage, except the four-year-old

SEVENTH GENERATION

daughter of CAPTAIN ABIJAH LOCKE who was bound out. He shows conclusively that of the four brothers who are said to have left Hampton for Rhode Island, JOSEPH settled in Block Island, TIMOTHY settled in South Kingston, and of JOHN and ABIJAH nothing is known, except in a negative way; that is, the John and Abijah mentioned in Block Island records must have been younger men, sons of NATHANIEL, born 1723. I have given the gist of Mr. Locke's research, embraced in twenty-five pages of type-written matter, in the various proper places and headings, but space forbids its entire publication. We surely appreciate the painstaking work.

Children of 7th Gen.

3559 NORMAN WENTWORTH, b. Janesville, Wis., Apl. 22, 1863, d. Orford, N. H., Feb. 22, 1890, m. Hoosick Falls, N. Y., Feb. 13, 1889, HELEN SCOTT, b. Granville, N. Y. He was a farmer, and had: 3560 NORMAN W., b. Apl. 24, 1890.
3561 LILLA JOSEPHINE, b. Janesville, March 13, 1866.
3562 JOHN PARKER, b. Janesville, Aug. 15, 1869.
3563 SYLVANUS DYER, b. Hoosick Falls, N. Y., Apl. 6, 1871.

F1404 Augustus B. Locke, born in Aurora, N. Y., Sept. 23, 1845, married in Aurora, Nov. 6, 1862, EMALINE A. HOAG, who died Jan. 26, 1869; married 2nd, May 1, 1879, HATTIE M. MOSHER. He lived in Aurora in 1895.

Children of 7th Gen.

3564 JARVIS J., b. Aug. 22, 1863, m. Dec. 31, 1891, JOSIE L. SEARING, and had: 3565 CHARLES A., b. July 18, 1894.
3566 EMALINE A., b. July 29, 1867, d. Nov. 8, 1875.
Second wife's children:
3567 HENRY W., b. Feb. 27, 1880.
3568 MARY M., b. July 20, 1881.

F1406 Hannah Locke, born Aug. 3, 1792, married 1st, JOHN TOWLE of Saco, Me., born 1791, son of Joseph and Sarah (Marston). He was killed on the railroad at Berwick, Me., Dec. 1, 1857. She married 2nd, WILLIAM NI(T)CHER of Maine. She died in Effingham, Ill., Nov. 25, 1879.

Children of 7th Gen.

3569 ELBRIDGE P., a machinist in Dover.
3570 ROBERT. 3571 HORATIO. 3572 HALEY. 3573 WESLEY NICHER.

F1407 Jonathan Moulton Locke, born in 1794, married Jan. 24, 1822, MARY ELKINS of Hampton, daughter of Jeremiah and Mary (Bachelder), born 1796, died Dec. 20, 1876. Jonathan lived on the home place and died in Hampton, Dec. 19, 1832. After his death Mary married IRA PAGE and had three children.

Child of 7th Gen.

3574 JEREMIAH, b. Hampton, May 24, 1824, m. Jan. 14, 1853, MARY E. WEARE, b. Hamp., Apl. 7, 1831, d. Hamp., Feb. 22, 1911, dau. of Taylor and Mary (Redman); lived Hemp Plain Hill, Hampton, had: 3575 JONATHAN P., b. Dec. 4, 1854, d. Feb. 19, 1856; 3576 MARY EMMA, b. Hamp., Sept. 24, 1858, is a dressmaker in Hampton.

F1408 Miriam Lamprey Locke, born March 13, 1796, married May 3, 1816, JOSEPH PALMER of Hampton, son of Joseph P. and Deborah (Tuck), born Oct. 11, 1792, died in Hampton June 24, 1862. She died Jan. 14, 1886.

Children of 7th Gen.

3577 ALFRED SHERBURNE, b. Sept. 14, 1816, drowned Hampton, Oct. 30, 1876, unmarried.
3578 CATHERINE BROWN, b. July 3, 1819, m. Nov. 1841, GEORGE WARREN of Sacarappa, Me.
F3579 JOHN MOORE, b. Nov. 3, 1821, m. Nov. 1851, MARY H. LADD.
3580 SARAH SHERBURNE, b. Sept. 19, 1824, m. Apl. 4, 1848, NOAH JEWETT of Cornish, Me.
F3581 LYDIA ANN, b. March 15, 1830, m. Aug. 15, 1851, JOSEPH L. MARSTON.
3582 MIRIAM LOCKE, b. Feb. 11, 1832, d. July 10, 1891, m. 1st, Aug. 16, 1854, JEFFERSON C. DUNBAR, son of Loring and Ann (Nash), and had: 3583 FRANK C., died young; 3584 ANNIE M., b. March 16, 1860, m. JAMES W. BERRY; 3585 MINNIE D., died young; and 3586 JOSEPH L., b. Aug. 1869, d. Apl. 4, 1884. She m. 2nd, Dec. 10, 1879, JEREMIAH W. BROWN, b. Sept. 15, 1821, son of Simon and Ann (Bachelder). She had no children by Brown.
3590 MARY KNAPP, b. Apl. 22, 1834, d. Aug. 26, 1834.
3591 MARY KNAPP, b. March 15, 1836, d. Stratham, Feb. 1, 1904, m. Oct. 24, 1861, GEORGE W. DUNBAR, son of Loring and Ann (Nash), lived Portsmouth, and had: 3592 WILLIAM W.; 3593 NELLIE, m. GEORGE M. HALL of Stratham; 3594 HERBERT, b. Feb. 25, 1872.
3595 JOSEPH ELDREDGE, b. Jan. 16, 1839, d. unmarried in war, May 16, 1864.

F1409 Samuel Locke, born in Hampton, N. H., June 24, 1798, married in North Hampton, June 3, 1825, MARY B. DEARBORN of Hampton, daughter of Samuel and Mary (Brown), born in Hampton, Dec. 27, 1805, died Aug. 8, 1872. He was a farmer in North Hampton and died Aug. 7, 1843.

SEVENTH GENERATION

Children of 7th Gen.

3596 JOHN, b. No. Hampton, Aug. 20, 1826, was a farmer and d. No. Hamp., May 13, 1893, unmarried.

F3597 MORRIS, b. Nov. 29, 1828, m. Jan. 1, 1860, MARY E. DOW.

F3598 SARAH ANN, b. May 21, 1831, m. Apl. 8, 1857, BENJAMIN W. DOW.

3599 SAMUEL, b. No. Hampton, Oct. 20, 1833, d. San Francisco, July 18, 1898, m. ALICE ———, in Cal., Dec. 7, 1881; no children. He first went to New York, then to San Francisco, and was a miner in northern California. One winter a snow slide killed seven persons, and he was snowed in with his horse and dog for several weeks, but was finally rescued by men on snow shoes. He recovered and came East after thirty-five years' absence. An attack of grippe sent him back to southern California where he married and soon after died.

3600 ALMIRA, b. No. Hamp., July 3, 1838, d. Nov. 23, 1841.

F3601 LYDIA ALMIRA, b. Apl. 20, 1843, m. May 3, 1863, GEORGE W. KNOWLES.

F1410 Sherburne Locke, born in Hampton in 1800, married Aug. 15, 1824, LOUISA LAMPREY, daughter of Reuben and Polly (Marston), born May 22, 1804, died Feb. 26, 1841. He settled on part of the homestead in Hampton and died there Oct. 17, 1881.

Children of 7th Gen. b. in Hampton.

F3602 DAVID, b. Dec. 1, 1824, m. March 28, 1847, NANCY B. PHILBRICK.

3603 SARAH ANN, b. Oct. 20, 1827, d. unmarried, June 8, 1903.

3604 REUBEN L., b. Apl. 1, 1830, d. Aug. 24, 1898, m. 1858, MRS. SUSAN (MORSE) PEABODY of Bradford, Mass., b. Sept. 5, 1837, had; 3605 EVA CARRIE, b. Aug. 23, 1869, m. CHARLES JOHNSON of Boston, and they had: 3606 CHARLES MARC; 3607 NELLIE, d. 1894. Reuben was a carpenter in Bradford. He enlisted Oct. 1861 in Mass. 4th Battery, reenlisted and served until 1865.

F3605 JOHN SHERBURNE, b. July 22, 1831, m. July 9, 1865, EUNICE EATON.

3606 JONATHAN MARSTON, b. Sept. 14, 1833, m. Sept. 6, 1857, AUSTICE LANE of Haverhill, Mass., lived at Brighton and Malden, had no children, and d. 1911.

F3607 MARTHA SHERBURNE, b. July 27, 1835, m. Sept. 7, 1855, IRA J. TAYLOR.

F3608 MARY LOUISE, b. Apl. 16, 1837, m. 1st, Apl. 1862, EDWIN P. PEMBERTON; m. 2nd, OLIVER B. SHAW.

F3609 GEORGE WILLIAM, b. Dec. 26, 1839, m. June 29, 1861, MARTHA A. EATON.

F1411 Mary Ann Locke, born ———, married Feb. 16, 1832, REUBEN L. BROWN, born Jan. 7, 1807, died Feb. 7, 1900, son of David and Ruth (Lamprey). They lived at Little River, Hampton, and she died July 30, 1889.

Children of 7th Gen.

F3610 GEORGE DANA, b. Hampton, 1837, m. RHODA J. FOGG, dau. of David.

3611 JACOB EVERETT, b. No. Hampton, June 2, 1839, d. Concord, Feb. 20, 1908, m. ALMEDA BROWN, dau. of John; was a carpenter, and had: 3612 CARRIE E.

F1414 Nathaniel S. Locke, born in Hampton, Jan. 27, 1812, married July 29, 1839, MARY LANE, born in Hampton, Oct. 17, 1817, died March 7, 1901, daughter of Thomas and Nancy (Brown). He was in early life a Labrador fisherman, later a prosperous farmer, lived on homestead in Hampton and died in Oct. 1904.

Children of 7th Gen.

3613 MARY ROSANNA, b. Hampton, June 30, 1841, d. Apl. 22, 1842.

3614 ANN MARY, b. H., Nov. 22, 1843, d. June 19, 1845.

3615 SARAH, b. H., March 7, 1845, d. June 22, 1874, m. Aug. 30, 1862, SAMUEL JAMES PHILBRICK, b. Enfield, Oct. 29, 1838, d. Jan. 11, 1879, son of David and Betsey (Edwards). He was a farmer in Hampton, and had: 3617 FRANK F., b. May 21, 1863, d. Aug. 2, 1867; 3618 JAMES A., b. July 3, 1867, d. July 28, 1867.

3619 THOMAS L., b. H., Feb. 19, 1848, m. Hamp., Dec. 30, 1889, ANNABEL HOBBS, b. Hamp., Jan. 5, 1869, dau. of Edwin J. and Hannah (Felch). He was a farmer in Hampton, had: 3620 THOMAS L., b. Hamp., March 30, 1890, d. H., May 5, 1890. They separated in 1898.

F1417 Hannah Locke, born ——, married June 10, 1813, JOHN EMERY of Kennebunk Landing, Me., born Nov. 17, 1788, died Dec. 19, 1868, son of Thomas and Hannah (Harmon). He was a blacksmith in Kennebunk. She died May 29, 1849.

Children of 7th Gen. b. in Kennebunk, Me.

F3621 MARY L., b. Apl. 29, 1814, m. July 29, 1839, REV. EDWARD COOK, D.D.

3622 ELIZA ELLEN, b. Feb. 25, 1816, d. Neponset, Mass., Nov. 2, 1880, unmarried.

3623 HANNAH, b. Jan. 4, 1818, d. Feb. 17, 1818.

F3624 STEPHEN L., b. Sept. 26, 1819, m. CLARA GILMAN of Portland, Me.

F3625 HANNAH, b. Aug. 3, 1821, m. Sept. 4, 1845, JAMES NEAL.

3626 SUSAN H., b. Jan. 15, 1823, m. March 17, 1851, THOMAS J. HOBBS, b. Sept. 1821, and had: 3627 FRANK E., b. So. Berwick, Jan. 1855; 3628 GEORGE S., b. 1861, d. 1884.

3629 ABBY M., b. Nov. 17, 1824, m. Oct. 19, 1854, WILLIAM G. PERKINS, b. June 25, 1823, and had: 3629 WILLIE B., b. 1857, d. 1862; 3630 HARRY F., b. Sept. 18, 1865.

3631 JOHN W., b. March 16, 1827, d. March 14, 1832.

3632 CHARLES W., b. Apl. 12, 1829, unmarried.

SEVENTH GENERATION 179

F1418 Miriam Locke, born ——, marriage intentions published Sept. 7, 1816, to DANIEL S. HOOPER of Biddeford, Me., son of Benjamin, born 1778. He was a farmer in Biddeford, and died Sept. 23, 1871. She died June 23, 1865.

Children of 7th Gen. b. in Biddeford, Me.

3633 STEPHEN, b. Aug. 27, 1817, d. Oct. 29, 1858, m. Saco, Oct. 29, 1848, ELIZABETH DYER, had: 3634 THOMAS D., 1854–1855; 3635 STEPHEN, b. Oct. 29, 1858; 3636 JULIA A., m. JOEL BEAN of Saco, Aug. 10, 1907.
3637 JULIA ANN, b. Jan. 9, 1826, m. STILLMAN GURNEY of Saco.
3638 BENJAMIN HILL, b. March 5, 1828, d. Biddeford, Feb. 23, 1886, m. Feb. 2, 1860, ANN J. EMERY, dau. of Ralph and Happy (Goodman), b. July 2, 1829. He was a grocer in Bidd., had: 3639 SON, died young; 3640 ALICE M., b. May 9, 1864.
3641 MARY ELIZABETH, b. July 3, 1830, d. Sept. 4, 1851.
3642 CALEB, b. Jan. 20, 1833, m. —— HILL.
3643 DANIEL O. S., b. Sept. 17, 1840.

F1426 Japheth Chadbourne Locke, born in Hollis, Me., Aug. 16, 1795, married Oct. 23, 1817, MARTHA BURBEEN SMITH of Hollis, born Dec. 7, 1797, died Reidsville, N. C., Aug. 28, 1889. He lived in Hollis, and was a carpenter in Biddeford in 1870. In May 1871, he with thirteen descendants went to Reidsville, N. C., and settled on a plantation, where he died May 1, 1876.

Children of 7th Gen.

F3644 TIMOTHY H., b. Oct. 22, 1822, m. Jan. 28, 1844, ELIZABETH LARRABEE NOBLE.
3645 DAUGHTER, died young.
3646 MARY C., adopted, b. Oct. 11, 1822, d. 1851, m. Biddeford, WILLIAM MOORE, lived Bidd., had: 3647 WILLIAM, d. aged 2 years; 3648 EDWARD, died young.

F1428 Joseph L. Locke, born March 13, 1801, married 1st, Aug. 22, 1822, LILLIAS WOODMAN, born Sebago, Me., Aug. 5, 1800, daughter of Jeremiah and Anna (Watson), died Aug. 26, 1861; married 2nd, March 16, 1866, MARY A. KILGORE of Biddeford, who died May 3, 1881. He was a farmer in Hollis, and died Jan. 16, 1884.

Children of 7th Gen. b. in Hollis, Me.

F3650 THOMAS DYER, b. Dec. 16, 1822, m. 1st, ELIZA ROBERTS; m. 2nd, —— Dow; m. 3rd, —— SMITH.
F3651 ELIZABETH, b. Dec. 21, 1824, m. ELEAZOR TUCKER of Saco.
3652 MARY ELLEN, b. Dec. 11, 1836, d. Dec. 11, 1905, m. LEONARD BEAN, and had: 3653 ALBERT, m. EVA WATERHOUSE.

F3654 JOHN FAIRCHILD, b. Sept. 23, 1838, m. MARY E. BEACH.
3655 EPHRAIM.
Second wife's child:
3656 REVERE J., b. Oct. 23, 1867, d. Dec. 8, 1874.

F1429 Olive C. Locke, born Sept. 8, 1806, married Jan. 20, 1826, RICHARD SMITH of Hollis, Me. Olive died Sept. 12, 1851, and Smith married her sister, LUCY B. He was a mason in Hollis.
Children of 7th Gen.
3657 Several children died young.
3658 LEROY, was living 1850, aged 33.
3659 JEFFERSON, b. 1842, d. unmarried in war, aged-23.
3660 LUCY M., b. Hollis, Me., 1848, d. Jan. 21, 1877, m. ANDREW CHADBOURNE, of Waterboro, Me., and had one or two children.

F1431 Lucy B. Locke, born July 27, 1817, died Feb. 27, 1905, married June 2, 1852, RICHARD SMITH, born in 1802. He was a mason in Hollis, and died Nov. 17, 1869.
Children of 7th Gen. b. in Hollis, Me.
3661 ELLA M., b. Oct. 27, 1852, d. infant.
3662 EDWIN T., b. Jan 4, 1853, m. 1st, EMMA MOORE; m. 2nd, Feb. 10, 1888, SARAH R. (LANE) WENTWORTH; m. 3rd, ANNIE (HOPKINSON) MCKENNEY; m. 4th, Feb. 3, 1908, MRS. OLIVIA M. (STONE) MERRILL.
3663 JOSEPH L., b. Jan. 21, 1855, m. June 14, 1887, SUSIE R. BENSON of Saco, Me. He was a farmer in Hollis, d. March 6, 1906, adopted RUTH (PORTER).
F3664 ARTHUR L., b. Oct. 4, 1856, m. May 19, 1892, MARY E. RAND of Ripley. He is farmer and mason in Hollis, has two children.

F1435 Samuel Locke, born Dec. 14, 1802, married Jan. 7, 1827, JANETT M. LYMBURNER, daughter of Capt. John,. born March 29, 1799, died Aug. 12, 1869. He came to Belfast, Me., in 1825, one of the incorporators, in 1849 went to California by ship, and died in Belfast, Feb. 19, 1851, a few weeks after his return. He was a tailor and druggist.
Children of 7th Gen. b. in Belfast, Me.
F3665 SAMUEL WESLEY, b. Oct. 9, 1827, m. Nov. 20, 1853, AMELIA FRANCES J. WARDWELL.
F3666 MARGARET J. L., b. Nov. 4, 1829, m. DOMINICUS DEARBORN.
3667 REV. JOHN LYMBURNER, b. Belfast, July 6, 1832, d. Feb. 18, 1876, m. Oct. 30, 1865, HANNAH ROGERS HUNT, dau. of Simon. He early learned the jewelers trade in Belfast, came to Camden in 1854, and kept store there. In the sixties he went to Sanbornton Academy and after graduation entered the Eastern Conference, preached in several Massachusetts cities, but returned to Belfast,

SEVENTH GENERATION

where he died. He had excellent literary ability, and great interest in history, being the author of the History of Belfast, Me. He had one son: 3668 HERBERT HUNT, b. Aug. 2, 1872, who about 1900 went to Alaska unmarried, and was supposed to have been lost there.
3669 CHARLES AUGUSTINE, b. Feb. 19, 1834, d. Apl. 26, 1835.
F3670 HORATIO JOHNSON, b. Nov. 4, 1837, m. Apl. 24, 1863, ANNIE M. DYER.

F1440 Sally Frost Locke, born Jan. 15, 1803, married Oct. 14, 1825, MOSES SMITH of Hollis, Me., born June 21, 1799, died Jan. 20, 1852. She died Sept. 8, 1848.

Children of 7th Gen. b.

F3671 JULIA ANN, b. Jan. 1, 1827, m. Sept. 23, 1849, GEORGE LITTLEFIELD.
3672 SARAH FRANCIS, b. Oct. 20, 1829, d. Oct. 4, 1906, m. Jan. 29, 1865, CHARLES D. SCAMMON, b. Dec. 3, 1833.
3673 RUTH, b. Jan. 28, 1831, d. Nov. 23, 1832.
3674 STEPHEN LOCKE, b. Jan. 26, 1834, m. Dec. 28, 1856, LYDIA NASON GOULD, had: 3674a ADDIE; 3674b FRED.
3675 MOSES, b. July 30, 18(34), d. unmarried Nov. 4, 1857.

F1441 Samuel Locke, born Apl. 11, 1804, married 1st, Nov. 25, 1829, FANNY FOSS, born Jan. 29, 1809, died March 17, 1836, dau. of John and Ann; married 2nd, Apl. 30, 1837, RUTH SANDS, born March 15, 1805, died Nov. 22, 1884, dau. of Samuel and Mehitable. He lived in Hollis, was a farmer and died Oct. 22, 1886.

Children of 7th Gen. b. in Hollis, Me.

F3676 CALEB, b. Sept. 25, 1830, m. Aug. 21, 1850, MARY JANE ROBERTS,

F1442 Nathaniel Clarke Locke, born Nov. 9, 1808, married 1st, Dec. 23, 1834, OLIVE GRANT, born March 28, 1814, died Oct. 2, 1869; married 2nd, Nov. 21, 1870, MRS. ELIZA HUNT CROCKETT FOGG, who died Aug. 20, 1891. He was a farmer in Hollis, and died March 25, 1885.

Children of 7th Gen. b. Hollis, Me.

F3679 JOHN GOULD, b. Jan. 21, 1837, m. 1865, SARAH J. HARMON; m. 2nd, 1891, LUCY R. LIBBY.
3680 ABRA FRANCIS, b. Nov. 3, 1839, d. unmarried Nov. 29, 1860.
F3681 HANNAH ELIZABETH, b. Nov. 12, 1842, m. HENRY H. SAVAGE.
F3682 AMBROSE COLBY, b. Nov. 3, 1848, m. March 4, 1876, HATTIE ABBIE BURNHAM.

F1443 Stephen Locke, born Jan. 17, 1816, married Apl. 13, 1842, his cousin, LUCINDA CLARKE of Hollis, daughter of Charles, born Apl. 4, 1814, died in Biddeford, Aug. 19, 1889. He was a mason by trade, but taught school 28 seasons, and died Oct. 18, 1906.

Stephen Locke, born 1816, says: "I was sickly till about 16 years of age then strength came to me and at 25 I was as strong as anyone. Father raised everything we ate or wore right on the farm. He never bought a barrel of flour in his life. Now there is not an acre of wheat grown in the county. Our suits were homespun and a travelling tailor came around, cut, and made up the suits. Thus attired I added to my Hollis schooling a year in Kennebunk Academy. In 1835 I went to school in Kennebunk studying by the fireplace or by pitch pine knots; very trying to the face and eyes for one had to get near the light and heat. I taught school and studied winters from 1835 to 1865 and in the summers worked at my trade of mason and bricklayer, ten years being in Boston. My 40-75 pupils of ages 3-25 kept the fireplaces or stoves full of wood but many bitter cold days we spent there. However they plodded along and many of them won worthy places in life. In Boston we got $1.50 a day and paid $4.50-$5.00 for board. When we got $2.00 I thought I was rich. We started at work at 5 and ended at 7 to 7.30 or 12 hours a day. The rest of the time was ours and we had to sleep some. I early joined the Methodist church and the Masons. Save weak eyes and bodily weakness I am in good health due to correct and temperate habits."

Children of 7th Gen.

F3683 JOSEPH ALVAH, b. Dec. 25, 1842, m. Aug. 27, 1873, FLORENCE E. PERLEY.

3684 IRA STEPHEN, b. Biddeford, Me., Feb. 4, 1853, m. Sept. 3, 1889, ELLA PHEBE WRIGHT, b. Bangor, Feb. 12, 1849, dau. of Capt. William H. and Alvira H. (Dore). He graduated from Bowdoin College in 1874, studied law and began the practice of law with his brother in 1880 and continued in the firm until his brother's death. The shock of this on a not over strong constitution caused him to retire from business and resulted in his death in Portland, Jan. 28, 1910. He was a true Christian and a beloved, devoted and most useful member of the Methodist church. He was also a member of the various Masonic and Odd Fellows lodges; also of the Maine State Historical and Genealogical Societies. He will be long remembered by our association as one of its most zealous workers, having been its president several years.

F1445 Elizabeth Stanwood Locke, born in Hallowell, Me., Jan. 24, 1814, married HENRY WING DECKER, born in Gardner, Me., Sept. 6, 1810, died in Feather River, Cal., Aug. 29, 1850. He was son of Isaac and was a California pioneer sailing on a

Ira S. Locke 3684

WILLIAM YEATON F4960

SEVENTH GENERATION 183

brig out of Boston (the first one out), going round the Horn. She died in Hallowell, Apl. 1881.
Children of 7th Gen.
3685 SAMUEL LOCKE, b. Hallowell, Me., June 17, 1838, m. 1st, Sept. 1859, MARIA E. ALLEN of Chelsea, Mass., who d. Apl. 1865; m. 2nd, Oct. 19, 1869, MARY E. MASON of Newport, R. I., who d. June 9, 1891. He lived in Boston, and had: 3686 HENRY ALLEN, b. June 1861; 3687 WILLIAM WALLACE, b. June 1, 1871.
3688 HANNAH MARIA, b. Sept. 24, 1839, m. MANLIUS W. BOYD, who d. Winthrop, Me., June 28, 1897, had no children.
F3689 LIZZIE FRANCES, b. Sept. 25, 1843, m. Oct. 11, 1865, GEORGE WEBBER HUBBARD.

F1448 Samuel Ebenezer Locke, born in Hallowell, Me., Jan. 18, 1818, married Aug. 25, 1844, HARRIET FLETCHER, born in Washington, N. H., Apl. 4, 1819, died in Waltham, Mass., Nov. 16, 1901, daughter of Joshua and Eliza (Stevens). He lived in Waltham, Mass., and died there Nov. 25, 1902.
Children of 7th Gen.
F3690 ALONZO STEPHENS, b. Nov. 13, 1847, m. June 13, 1878, CLARA ISABEL PRATT.
3691 FRANK ERNEST, b. Sept. 12, 1856, d. March 25, 1866.

F1449 Joseph Hale Locke, born in Hallowell, Me., Apl. 7, 1820, married in Dedham, Mass., Aug. 24, 1845, MARTHA B. BRADFORD, born in Livermore, Me., Oct. 11, 1822, died in St. Cloud, Minn., Nov. 23, 1896, daughter of Dr. Benjamin and Patty (Bisbee). He was a farmer and prominent Mason and died in St. Cloud, Jan. 22, 1891. He lived in Clear Water, Minn.
Children of 7th Gen. both by Adoption.
3692 FANNIE W., b. Hallowell.
3693 HARRY S, b. Feb. 19, 1855, m. March 9, 1878, KATE C. MAXWELL, had a child: 3694 EVA.

F1450 Hosea Ballou Locke, born in Hallowell, Me., July 12, 1822, married Sept. 11, 1844, ELIZABETH W. PILLSBURY of Augusta, Me. He went to California in 1849 by way of Panama, returning, was a blacksmith in Waltham, Mass. He was a noted local singer and a member of the Waltham Quartette, a well-known musical and entertainment club. He died June 22, 1881.
Children of 7th Gen. b. in Waltham, Mass.
F3695 WILLIAM PILLSBURY, b. Sept. 23, 1845, m. Nov. 27, 1867, EMILY G. SHERMAN.
3696 ELIZABETH L., b. Feb. 19, 1855, m. Oct. 28, 1878, EDWARD BICKNELL.

3697 JOSEPH BRADFORD, b. Apl. 11, 1857, m. ETTA SKINNER of Milton, Mass., b. March 1857, d. Aug. 22, 1897, had: 3698 EDWARD B., b. Sept. 1, 1883.

F1451 Isaac Stanwood Locke, born in Hallowell, Me., July 28, 1824, married in Nashua, Feb. 4, 1849, LYDIA ALMIRA MORRIS, born in Lowell, died in San Francisco, Aug. 22, 1882. He was inspector of the Waltham School Department 1873, on Harbor Commission, San Francisco, 1876–80, Department of Internal Revenue Inspector 1880–84, Collector of Port under President Harrison, and until his death was in U. S. Marshal's Office. He was a Knights Templar Mason and died March 14, 1895, in San Francisco.

Children of 7th Gen. perhaps b. in Waltham, Mass.

3699 NATHAN STANWOOD, b. Nov. 19, 1856; San Francisco Post Office clerk since 1886.
F3700 RAYMOND MORRIS, b. Aug. 12, 1858, m. May 2, 1879, JANE WHITET.
F3701 HOLLIS MAINE, b. July 14, 1860, m. Jan. 23, 1886, NELLIE RYAN.
F3702 JAMES BROWN, b. Sept. 5, 1865, m. Nov. 24, 1890, ANNIE FEATHERSTONE.

F1454 Brice B. Bradbury, born Apl. 19, 1810, died June 1, 1892, married Dec. 17, 1840, HANNAH LOCKE, born 1814, # 3107. He was a mason of Hollis, Me.

Children of 7th Gen.

F3703 WINTHROP BRADBURY, b. Nov. 1, 1842, m. 1st, Jan. 13, 1864, MARY E. LEAVITT; m. 2nd, HATTIE PIKE.
3704 LUELLA, b. March 16, 1849, d. Dec. 8, 1863.

F1477 Deborah Page, married JOHN T. Dow, and he married 2nd, MRS. BETSEY NEWMAN.

Children of 7th Gen. b. in North Hampton.

3705 ELIZABETH E., b. Oct. 26, 1808, m. 1st, JOSEPH BRANSCOMB; m. 2nd, ——— SIMONDS; m. 3rd, CHANDLER SPINNEY.
3706 DANIEL W., b. Apl. 14, 1810, lost at sea.
3707 JOHN T., b. March 31, 1812, m. and settled in Newington.
3708 MARY ANN, b. Feb. 7, 1814, m. ASA PARSONS.
3709 SALLY G., b. Apl. 26, 1816, m. JOSEPH PURINGTON.
3710 MARTHA B., b. June 13, 1818, m. JOSEPH STONE.
He had five children by second wife, also.

F1484 James R. Locke, born in Mt. Vernon, Me., Aug. 21, 1796, married HANNAH COLLEY, born Apl. 29, 1796, died May 29, 1851, daughter of Rathiel. James was captain of a militia

SEVENTH GENERATION

company and a farmer in Mt. Vernon, Me. He died April 23, 1875.

Children of 7th Gen. b. in Mt. Vernon, Me.

F3711 JOSIAH ROBERT, b. Sept. 27, 1817, m. 1843, MARGARET A. STURTEVANT.
F3712 ADONIRAM JUDSON, b. May 27, 1819, m. Feb. 27, 1845, CAROLINE PETTINGILL.
F3713 JAMES GRAFTON, b. July 11, 1821, m. HANNAH CLARKE.
F3714 PERLEY WHITTIER, b. Sept. 19, 1826, m. Apl. 25, 1852, SARAH C. FISH.
3715 ARTHUR DRINKWATER, b. March 25, 1828, m. Jan. 1851, LOUISA NORCROSS. Was a shoemaker in Augusta, Me., and had son: 3716 ARTHUR HERBERT, b. Oct. 25, 1852, an Episcopal clergyman in Grand Rapids, 1899.
F3717 CHRISTENA ROBINSON, b. Aug. 16, 1831, m. Dec. 29, 1850, HENRY S. PARKER.
F3718 CHARLES AUGUSTINE, b. Apl 29, 1835, m. 1860, ELIZABETH R. ELLENWOOD.
F3719 LOVINA DUDLEY, b. Jan. 29, 1838, m. Dec. 25, 1859, GEORGE H. FAIRCHILD.
F3720 CAROLINE MATILDA, b. May 19, 1841, m. 1st, Aug. 5, 1859, GEORGE T. HERSEY; m. 2nd, July 10, 1878, THOMAS MYER.

F1489 Col. Samuel Locke, born in Mt. Vernon, Me., Sept. 25, 1800, married Nov. 14, 1822, ABIGAIL W. COLLEY, born July 29, 1798, died Jan. 25, 1879, daughter of Rathiel. He was Colonel of militia, was tanner, currier, and shoemaker, built a house in 1823, which he afterwards gave to his son and built another across the road at Locke's Corner, Mt. Vernon, Me., where he died Feb. 26, 1872.

Children of 7th Gen. b. in Mt. Vernon, Me.

3721 SAMUEL, b. Oct. 30, 1824, d. Nov. 14, 1845.
F3722 JOHN, b. Feb. 15, 1826, m. BETSEY P. STARIN of Mt. Vernon.
3723 STORER PIERCE, b. Oct. 22, 1827, d. Nov. 4, 1895, m. Feb. 22, 1883, CLARA A. NORTON, dau. of Russell; living in 1900 at Mt. V. He was a farmer and carriage maker.
3724 SARAH A., b. Apl. 12, 1830, d. Jan. 25, 1891, m. J. WOODMAN CRESSY of Salem, Mass.
F3725 COLUMBUS JUDSON, b. Apl. 13, 1832, m. May 1, 1853, RUTH HUSSEY WILLS.
3726 MARTHA A., b. July 10, 1837, d. Feb. 18, 1857.
3727 SEWARD DILL, b. Aug. 8, 1840, d. Feb. 8, 1857.
3728 BENJAMIN EMERY, b. Apl. 25, 1843, m. 1st, LIZZIE BEAN of Mt. Vernon, dau. of Jesse K.; m. 2nd, EDITH A. CHAMBERLAIN of Natick, Mass., and lived there. Had: 3729 AURILLA FRANCES, who m. June 26, 1911, ARTHUR R. TARBOX of Lynn, and they had: 3730 EMERY, b. July 17, 1914.

F1509 Samuel Locke, born in Brentwood, Feb. 15, 1802, married June 30, 1823, DOLLY ABBOTT of Fremont, born in 1805, died in Raymond, March 2, 1881. He was a farmer, moved from Brentwood to Raymond and died there Aug. 22, 1875.

Children of 7th Gen.

3731 ISAIAH WASHINGTON, b. Raymond, Aug. 1830, d. R., March 4, 1892, was a farmer there and unmarried.

3732 SAMUEL STILLMAN, b. Raymond, July 16, 1832, m. Aug. 13, 1877, ORRIE M. GORDON, b. Brentwood, 1861. She was divorced Apl. 1880, and later m. GEORGE MILES of Nottingham. He was a farmer, had no children, and d. Nov. 25, 1915.

F1510 Sally Locke, born in Brentwood, Feb. 17, 1809, married 1st, in Raymond, July 4, 1825, JOHN POLLARD, born in Chester; married 2nd, SEWELL ABBOTT.

Children of 7th Gen. all Pollards but the Last.

3733 HIRAM LOCKE, b. March 13, 1826, m. March 8, 1854, DIANNA BASFORD of Chester, lived Derry, 1902. Had: 3734 HATTIE, who m. ———— EVANS of East Derry.

F3735 CHARLES ALFRED, b. March 10, 1828, m. OLIVE DURGIN of Nottingham, lived Raymond, 1905.

3736 ROSANNA, b. Apl. 12, 1830, m. JAMES BROWN of Newton, had: 3737 JAMES; 3738 SARAH; 3739 BELLE.

3740 ISAAC A., b. May 17, 1832, m. ALMIRA BEAN of Fremont, and went West. A nephew says he m. ALMIRA DOW, and had: 3741 ADDISON, b. 1862.

3742 SARAH J., b. Oct. 20, 1834, unmarried.

3743 EMILY, b. Nov. 28, 1836, m. OSMOND P. WEBSTER of Kingston, lived No. Raymond, had: 3744 PORTER O., of Haverhill, Mass.; 3745 CARRIE; 3746 JENNIE, m. WALTER LANG of Kensington.

3747 LUCINDA, b. May 23, 1839, m. ———— COLLINS of Kingston.

3748 SEWELL ABBOTT, b. Raymond, Jan. 4, 1840, d. Jan. 30, 1869, m. ALICE M. TENNEY of So. Hampton, b. Apl. 3, 1846, dau. of Edmund and Joanna (Poore). They had: 3749 SEWELL E., b. Epping, Apl. 17, 1865; 3750 ARTHUR E., b. Chester, May 3, 1868.

F1521 Ichabod Locke, born in Athens, Me., March 17, 1802, married NANCY MOSES of Harmony, Me. He was a farmer in Wellington, Me., and died Sept. 5, 1859.

Children of 7th Gen. b. in Wellington, Me.

3751 CYRUS, b. Oct. 10, 1828, m. Nov. 1888, MARGARET MARY ROCHE, was a landscape gardener in Nahant, Mass.

3752 LEONARD, b. Dec. 2, 1831, d. Sept. 15, 1905, m. Oct. 14, 1858, MAHALA S. BURGESS, was a farmer in Cornville, Me.

3753 JANE, b. March 27, 1836, d. July 1, 1899, m. Nov. 1863, MATTHEW WING.

SEVENTH GENERATION

3754 ALANSON L., b. Apl. 10, 1839, m. 1st, ELIZABETH FOSS; m. 2nd, ——— ———, was a farmer and carpenter in Lewiston and Brunswick, Me.

F3755 SAMUEL O., b. Aug. 26, 1844, m. 1st, Aug. 1868, CORA A. PEASE; m. 2nd, Feb. 27, 1898, MRS. SARAH (FLANDERS) EVANS.

3756 LAVINIA, b. May 18, 1845, m. JEREMIAH GRANT of Wellington, had: 3757 FRAZIER J., b. ———, m. 1893, in Gorham, N. H.

F1522 John Locke, born in Athens, Me., in 1804, married MELINDA BROWN. He was a farmer in Athens, and died Feb. 2, 1878.

Children of 7th Gen. b. in Athens, Me.

3758 MELISSA, b. ———, m. JOHN GOULD.
3759 JOHN H., b. 1834, d. Sept. 16, 1863, m. JULIA BOSTON.
3760 ELLEN, b. Aug. 26, 1836, m. Aug. 27, 1857, JERE COOK of Newburyport, b. Sept. 22, 1830, son of Wm. and Mary (Davidson). He was a trader in Biddeford and Chelsea, had: 3761 JOHN L., b. 1865, d. 1865; 3762 EUGENIE E., b. 1866.
3763 ALMINA, b. ———, was married.
3764 MERILLA, b. ———, m. LOUIS PERCY.
3765 MALINDA, b. Athens, Jan. 17, 1845, m. March 10, 1866, WILLIAM COOK of Newburyport, b. Feb. 4, 1837, son of Wm. and Mary. He was a trader at Biddeford and Athens, and in 1872, went to Hallowell, had: 3766 VIOLA M., b. Aug. 30, 1869; 3767 MILLIE E., b. Apl. 28, 1871.
3768 ALICE, b. ———, was married.
F3769 DORCAS A., b. ———, m. 1848 JOHN H. HILL of Augusta.
3770 SARAH, b. ———, m. JOHN DUNN.

F1523 George Locke, born in Athens, Me., Nov. 24, 1805, married MARGARET BRADBURY, born in Athens, Apl. 22, 1807, daughter of Daniel and Mary (Wingate). He died Jan. 20, 1870.

Children of 7th Gen.

F3771 MARY, b. Aug. 22, 1828, m. 1st, Sept. 30, 1849, LEWIS F. LEIGHTON; m. 2nd, June 12, 1867, WILLIAM GARROTT.
3772 SUMNER, b. Dec. 22, 1829, d. Nov. 24, 1833.
3773 LEONARD, b. July 4, 1832, d. Nov. 24, 1883, m. DIANTHA EMERSON; was a farmer in Athens.
F3774 DANIEL B., b. Feb. 11, 1835, m. Jan. 21, 1855, AMY D. LADD.
3775 FLAVILLA, b. May 20, 1837, d. Sept. 20, 1885, m. JOSEPH MOODY, had: 3776 FRED; 3777 EDWIN; 3778 WILLARD.
F3779 ROSELLA, b. Feb. 7, 1839, m. Feb. 18, 1859, JOHN LADD.
3780 MARIA, b. March 22, 1841, m. JOHN COOKSON of Hartland, Me.
F3781 MARGARET, b. Nov. 8, 1844, m. Apl. 12, 1869, WILLIAM P. COFFIN.
3782 FRANCES, b. March 22, 1847, d. Aug. 30, 1848.
3783 ALBRO, b. Apl. 4, 1851, m. LIZZIE WEBB, was a shoe dealer in Haverhill, Mass., had: 3784 FRED; 3785 BERTHA; 3786 LIZZIE.
3787 FRED, b. July 27, 1849, d. Dec. 22, 1872.

F1537 Lucy Locke, born in Athens, Me., Dec. 31, 1816, married June 22, 1837, REV. JESSE L. WILSON, born Embdem, Me., Nov. 1, 1808, died No. Anson, Me., Nov. 30, 1891. She died March 12, 1898.

Children of 7th Gen.

3788 PHILANDA, b. Apl. 24, 1838, m. July 4, 1860, SEVILLA GETCHELL, a farmer in No. Anson, Me.
3789 FIDELIA, b. Aug. 6, 1841, d. Aug. 20, 1890, m. Jan. 8, 1866, SUMNER GETCHELL.
3790 ALANSON L., b. Oct. 10, 1844, d. Feb. 16, 1862.
3791 ALLEN, b. May 25, 1850, m. 1876, EMMA BRYANT, who d. July 20, 1881; was a tailor.
3792 SUMNER, b. June 20, 1854, m. 1878, GRACE CUTTER; was a watchmaker.
3793 CORA A., b. June 2, 1859, m. Feb. 29, 1891, ALFRED P. DRAPER, b. Aug. 8, 1861, son of James and Abbie (Hart). They lived in Wayland, Mass.

F1538 Charles Locke, born in Athens, Me., Apl. 2, 1819, married in 1842, THEODATE S. HALLET, of Belgrade, Me., who died Apl. 17, 1895. He lived in Sidney, Me., and died Sept. 7, 1897, in Oakland, Me.

Children of 7th Gen. b. in Sidney, Me.

3794 CHARLES S., b. Dec. 28, 1842, was in 24th Maine Reg., Co. D, and d. Bonnet Carre, La., June 2, 1863.
3795 MARTHA E., b. March 4, 1844, d. Dexter, Me., Apl. 29, 1871, m. 1862, ALONZO SHATTUCK, had: 3796 MARTHA; 3797 CHARLES S.; 3798 HERBERT E.; 3799 MILDRED M.
3800 ELLEN A., b. June 7, 1847, d. Gardner, Ill., Oct. 27, 1871, m. Apl. 9, 1866, FRED G. THOMPSON, b. Athens, March 29, 1845, son of Osgood. He was in Co. B, 7th Maine Reg., had: 3801 INEZ W., b. Gardiner, Me., Aug. 18, 1869, m. THOMAS LYNCH.
3802 MARSHALL A., b. Jan. 17, 1849, m. 1st, 1882, SYBIL SECARD, who d. 1884; m. 2nd, 1890, SUSIE E. HALL; was a shoemaker of Lynn and had: 3803 EVERETT H.
3804 EDNA ADELLE, b. Harmony, Me., June 23, 1860, m. 1879, FRANK R. HOUGHTON of Augusta, had: 3805 CARROLL L., b. Sept. 7, 1892.

F1539 Alanson Locke, born in Athens, Me., March 22, 1823, married Sept. 14, 1845, MINA A. EMERY, born July 3, 1829. He was a farmer at Athens, Me., and died Jan. 23, 1898.

Children of 7th Gen. b. in Athens, Me.

3806 FRANCES A., b. June 9, 1848, m. Oct. 4, 1868, MELVIN H. GIFFORD, a farmer in Athens, Me., had: 3807 ORAL M., an overseer in envelope factory, Worcester, Mass.

SEVENTH GENERATION

3808 ALMON E., b. March 29, 1851, m. Oct. 19, 1892, MARIA C. LORD. He was a farmer in Athens, Me., had: 3809 GARA C., a school teacher.
3810 EDWIN S., b. Apl. 28, 1855, m. June 23, 1884, MARY F. MAGOON. He was a farmer in Wainwright, Alberta Co., Can., had: 3811 EVERETT B.
3812 FLORA E., b. Jan. 6, 1861, m. Aug. 30, 1880, HORACE D. PATTERSON, a farmer and horse dealer in Athens, Me., had: 3813 LESTER L.
3814 MABEL, b. Oct. 6, 1865, m. 1st, Oct. 31, 1885, W. H. MCLAUGHLIN; m. 2nd, Sept. 6, 1899, J. WARREN DRAKE of Stoneham, Mass., b. Plymouth, Mass., 1863, son of John and Emalie D. (Pike); was a R. R. conductor, had: 3815 MARION E. L. MCLAUGHLIN, a typesetter in Boston.
3816 ETTA M., b. Apl. 16, 1868, m. Aug. 18, 1891, P. H. DUNNIGAN, a piano dealer in Rockland, Mass.

F1540 Jacob Locke, married CATHERINE GUYON.
Children of 7th Gen. b. in Lockport, N. S.
F3817 GUYON, b. ——, m. AGNES CUNNINGHAM.
3818 ABRAM, b. ——.
3819 EBENEZER, b. ——, m. FANNIE PYE, and had: 3820 LEONARD.
3821 VERNON, b. ——, m. SUSAN COLE, b. Jan. 31, 1828, dau. of Jeremiah and Dolly (Perkins); had no children. (See Maine Historical Coll., 3rd Series, Vol. II.)
3822 JAMES, b. ——.
F3823 CATHERINE, b. ——, m. DAVID SMITH.

F1541 Ebenezer Locke, married in Lockeport, N. S., ELIZABETH BOWL.
Children of 7th Gen. b. in Lockport, N. S.
F3824 JOHN, b. ——, m. NANCY HOLDEN.
F3825 JACOB, b. ——, m. MELINDA WILLIAMS.
3826 GEORGE, b. ——.   3827 WILLIAM, b. ——.
3828 JAMES, b. ——.   3829 SAMUEL, b. ——.
F3830 THOMAS, b. ——, m. ELIZABETH MCKAY.
3831 EBENEZER, b. ——, m. SARAH RYER, and had: 3832 ROBERT; 3833 GEORGE.

F1542 John Locke, born in Lockeport, N. S., 1782, married MARY HARLOW. He died in 1869, aged 87.
Children of 7th Gen. b. in Lockport, N. S.
F3834 SAMUEL BRADFORD, b. ——, m. PATIENCE CHURCHILL.
F3835 ENOS, b. ——, m. 1st, ELLEN LOCKE, # 3859; m. 2nd, JANE HARRIS.
3836 PATIENCE, b. ——, m. JOHN MCALPINE, had no children; m. 2nd, JOHN SHAW, and had: 3837 WILLIAM; m. 3rd, JOSEPH FISHER.
3738 JERUSHA, b. ——, m. ROBERT B. TODD, and had: 3839 ALICE; 3840 HELEN; 3841 LOUISE; 3842 ROBERT.

3843 JOHN, b. ——, m. ELLEN CHADSEY, was called Captain, and had:
    3844 MARY OLEVIA, m. DEACON WELSLEY J. GATES of Wilmot,
    N. S., son of Oldham Gates.
F3845 JONATHAN, b. ——, m. BETHIA LOCKE, # 3868.
3846 GEORGE JAMES, b. ——, m., was drowned at sea.
3847 JOSIAH.   3848 ELIZA.
3849 ALLEVIA, m. STEPHEN KEMPTON.
3850 PRISCILLA, m. ALEXANDER HAMMOND.
3851 MARY E., m. ALLEN KEMPTON.

F1543 Samuel Locke, born in Lockeport, N. S., in 1785, was a merchant and died in 1881, aged 96. He married LETITIA MCKILLOP, daughter of Shipmaster McKillop of Dublin.

Children of 7th Gen. b. in Lockport, N. S.

F3852 ELIZABETH, b. 1810, m. WILLIAM STALKER.
F3853 LETITIA, b. 1812, m. BRADFORD HARLOW.
F3854 ANN, b. 1814, m. LEWIS CHURCHILL, # 3878.
F3855 SAMUEL, b. 1817, m. ANNE CROWELL.
3856 ABIGAIL, b. 1820, m. BENNIAH SPINNEY; had no children.
F3857 JACOB, b. 1822, m. EMALINE JAMIESON.
F3858 MARY, b. 1825, m. GORDON BILL.
3859 ELLEN, b. ——, m. ENOS LOCKE (see F3835.)
3860 KATHARINE, b. ——, m. WYNNE JOHNSON, had: 3861 WYNNE, who
    m. MAUD LOCKE, # 6993; 3862 LEWIS; 3863 SAMUEL L.; 3864
    ELLEN; 3865 ANN.
F3866 JOHN, b. 1830, m. ELIZABETH CHURCHILL, # 3879.
F3867 COLIN CAMPBELL, b. 1831, m. Sept. 1858, AMELIA JANE SHEY.

F1544 James Locke, born in Lockeport, N. S., in 1786, died in 1872, aged 86, married FANNY STRICKLAND. He was a merchant in Lockport.

Children of 7th Gen. b. in Lockport, N. S.

3868 BETHIA, b. ——, m. 1st, GEORGE LONGHURST; m. 2nd, JONATHAN
    LOCKE (see F3845). Had: 3869 GEORGE; 3869a CATHERINE.
F3870 SARAH, b. ——, m. LYMAN CANN.
3871 JAMES, b. ——, m. PRISCILLA MCKENZIE, had: 3872 SARAH; 3873
    FANNIE.
3873a HENRY, b. ——.
F3874 ELIZABETH, b. ——, m. THOMAS DAME.
3875 MARY, b. ——, m. CHARLES BOUCHER, had: 3876 CHARLES H.;
    3877 MARY.

F1546 Abigail Locke, born in Lockeport, N. S., in 1802, died in 1886 aged 84, married Dec. 19, 1822, ENOS CHURCHILL, born in Ragged Island, N. S., Apl. 9, 1797.

SEVENTH GENERATION

Children of 7th Gen.
F3878 LEWIS P., b. Nov. 8, 1826, m. Lockeport, N. S., ANN LOCKE. (See F3854.)
3879 ELIZABETH, b. ——, m. JOHN LOCKE. (See F3866.)
3880 TRYPHENA, b. ——, m. ANDREW C. CONGDON.
3881 LOUISA.
3882 EMILY, b. ——, m. HENRY STUDELEY, M. D.
3883 CECELIA.   3884 AUGUSTA.   3885 PRISCILLA.

F1563 Nathaniel Locke, born in Newport, Feb. 19, 1778, married in Newport, REBECCA REED, born Jan. 22, 1779, died 1844, daughter of Eleazor and Elizabeth. He had a sloop and was called captain, and died in 1828.

Children of 7th Gen.
F3886 NATHANIEL LOCKE, 3rd, b. March 10, 1805, m. July 1, 1830, LYDIA STANLEY HOWARD.
3887 EDWARD MARSHALL, b. ——.
3888 BETSEY, b. ——.   3889 REBECCA, b. ——.
3890 SAMUEL, b. ——.   3891 JEREMIAH, b. ——.

F1571 Reuben Locke, born in Epsom, N. H., May 18, 1785, married in Portsmouth, July 31, 1805, MRS. SARAH (BROSIAS) DENNETT. Tradition says she was born on the ocean coming from Holland. He was a cabinet maker in Gilmanton.

Children of 7th Gen.
F3892 REUBEN, b. June 30, 1807, m. 1st, Nov. 13, 1828, ELIZA SHAW; m. 2nd, June 6, 1867, NELLIE VARNEY.
3893 SARAH, b. ——, m. JAMES MALONEY, had: 3894 DAU., m. DANIEL MAXFIELD; 2895 AMANDA, lived N. Y.; 3896 WILLIAM, lived Boston.
F3897 ABIGAIL, b. Sept. 12, 1810, m. JOHN ELLIOT TUCKER.
3898 CATHERINE, b. ——, m. BENJAMIN HOYT, lived Cambridge, Mass., had: 3899 JOSEPHINE, m. BENJAMIN HOYT; also 3900 two boys in Laconia.

F1576 Abraham Locke, born in Epsom, N. H., Jan. 2, 1789, married KEZIAH ALLEN, born in Brunswick, Me., died in Amesbury, Mass., daughter of Jeremiah and Nancy (Eliott). He was an Ensign in 1812 War, in Massachusetts Company, lived in Epsom or Gilmanton, built the first factory in Dover and worry over it caused him to become insane. He died in Ipswich about 1858.

Children of 7th Gen.
3901 NANCY, b. Hallowell, Me., m. Loudon, Oct. 29, 1834, CHARLES FRANCIS HUTCHINSON of Gilmanton, b. 1806, son of Jonathan, had: 3902 boy and 3903 girl by Nancy; he m. 2nd, ELIZA DOWNES, and d. Oct. 1869.
3904 FRANCIS, b. Hallowell (Concord record says Francis of C. m. Dec. 21, 1848, HELEN M. STORY). Divorced, had no children.

F3905 MARY JANE, b. March 25, 1817, m. 1837-8, ENOCH H. KIMBALL.
F3906 EUNICE, b. Gilmanton, m. GEORGE W. WHITTIER.
F3907 DRUSILLA, b. Dec. 23, 1821, m. WILLIAM PEASLEE.
F3908 HANNAH STEVENS, b. 1831, m. CHARLES H. CURRIER.
3909 CHARLOTTE ANN, b. Gilm., died young.
3910 BENJAMIN FRANKLIN, b. Gilmanton, 1833, m. Newton, Feb. 7, 1859, MRS. NELLIE C. (WEED) LOVEJOY, b. Vassalboro, Me., 1835, dau. of Benj. Weed. He enlisted July 1862, in Co. E, 17th Mass., later in 1st Mass. Heavy Artil., and died Newton, June 9, 1874, was a shoemaker, had a son died young.

F1579 Margaret Locke, born in Epsom, N. H., in 1779, married in 1806, JONATHAN KNOWLES. He was a farmer in Epsom, and married 2nd, a sister of Francis' wife.

Children of 7th Gen. b. in Epsom.

3911 JOSIAH, b. 1808, d. May 1, 1838, m. —— NUTTER and had two daus.
3912 SAMUEL, b. 1810, d. Barnstead, 1887.
3913 ESTHER, b. 1812, m. —— NUTTER.
3914 FRANCIS, b. 1814, died young.
3915 FRANCIS L., b. Oct. 12, 1816, m. 1844, SARAH W. LOCKE. (See F2814.)

F1580 Ephraim Locke, born in Epsom, N. H., July 15, 1783, married in Epsom, Nov. 25, 1807, DEBORAH WELLS, born in Allenstown, July 6, 1781, died in Epsom Apl. 3, 1831; married 2nd, Aug. 20, 1838, LYDIA (YEATON) CHESLEY of Nottingham; married 3rd, Feb. 15, 1842, RHODA COLLINS of Gilford, born 1799, died July 14, 1885, in Gilford. He was a deacon of the Free Will Baptist Church, a highly respected, talented and hospitable man, by occupation a farmer. He died in Epsom, Apl. 14, 1855.

Children of 7th Gen.

F3916 EPHRAIM, b. May 4, 1809, m. Jan. 19, 1835, SARAH CRAM DYER.
F3917 ELIZA T., b. May 30, 1811, m. Apl. 21, 1832, SAMUEL B. DYER.
F3918 MARY S., b. June 11, 1813, m. Dec. 1, 1836 (Jan. 21, 1837), CAPT. SAMUEL WELLS.
F3919 MARGARET K., b. Feb. 17, 1817, m. Apl. 8, 1841, ABRAM D. SWAIN.
3920 SILAS M., b. Epsom, March 26, 1820, d. Eps. unmarried Nov. 18, 1839.

F1581 Polly Locke, born in Epsom, 1784, married DANIEL PHILBRICK, a farmer in Epsom.

Children of 7th Gen. b. in Epsom.

3921 ABIGAIL, b. 1809, died young.
3922 RUTH, b. Nov. 22, 1811, m. LEVI MASON.
3923 MARY, b. Nov. 27, 1813, d. May 7, 1890, unmarried.

SEVENTH GENERATION 193

3924 ASENETH, b. Sept. 3, 1816, d. unmarried Epsom, May 2, 1890.
3925 ABIGAIL, b. Nov. 26, 1818, m. BENJAMIN SARGENT.
3926 BETSEY, b. Feb. 26, 1821, m. STEPHEN S. RING.
F3927 DAVID M., b. Aug. 26, 1823, m. SARAH STEARNS.
3928 ALMIRA, b. Nov. 6, 1825, m. GEORGE F. BUFFAM.

F1582 Francis Locke, born in Epsom, June 26, 1791, married 1st, MARY PHILBRICK, born in Epsom, 1792, died in Epsom, Aug. 25, 1856; married 2nd, in Belmont, Sept. 24, 1856, his brother's widow, RHODA (COLLINS) LOCKE (1799–1885), the daughter of Ezekiel and Mary (Boyd). Francis was a farmer in Epsom, and also at Johnson's Hill, and died in Epsom Dec. 31, 1869.
Children of 7th Gen. b. in Epsom.
3929 DANIEL PHILBRICK, b. Epsom, Jan. 29, 1815, d. Pittsfield, Apl. 22, 1893, m. 1st, May 31, 1840, ABIGAIL FOWLER, b. March 16, 1815, d. Epsom, Nov. 13, 1867, dau. of Winthrop and Abigail (Davis); m. 2nd, Gilford, LEAH E. PRESCOTT, b. Gilford, Oct. 1828, d. Pittsfield, Dec. 22, 1891, dau. of Samuel and Mary (Brown). He was a farmer in Pittsfield, no children.
3930 EMALINE, b. Feb. 12, 1821, d. Feb. 12, 1822.
3931 LOVIE CHASE, b. Aug. 11, 1822, d. Epsom, Aug. 4, 1861, unmarried.
F3932 ARTHUR CAVERNO, b. Oct. 15, 1824, m. Sept. 23, 1847, SALINA O. BICKFORD.
F3933 SARAH EMALINE, b. Nov. 11, 1826, m. Oct. 10, 1843, JOSEPH H. VEAZEY.

F1585 Richard Locke, born in Epping, N. H., Apl. 13, 1792, married 1st, Jan. 22, 1817, MERCY MUNSON, born Aug. 24, 1788, died Dec. 31, 1818, daughter of Jared and Bridget (Utley); married 2nd, March 8, 1820, JULIA PARKER, born 180(, died Feb. 1, 1853; married 3rd, Oct. 1853, EVALINE G. FO. `. b. 1799, died July 7, 1858. He was a trunk, harness and saddle maker in St. Albans, Vt., and died there May 13, 1873.
Children of 7th Gen. b. in St. Albans, Vt.
3934 FIDELIA E., b. Dec. 21, 1818, d. May 9, 1819.
3935 FIDELIA A., b. Sept. 14, 1821, d. Oct. 25, 1833.
3936 HENRY PARKER, b. June 14, 1824, d. Sept. 27, 1842.
F3937 WORTHINGTON SMITH, b. May 19, 1827, m. Dec. 31, 1849, SARAH E. HOBBS.
F3938 WILLIAM, b. June 13, 1834, m. Oct. 16, 1855, ELIZABETH McDONALD SMITH.
3939 JOHN SHAW, b. 1831, a harness maker, d. unmarried in Whitehouse, Pa.
F3940 HOMER FRANKLIN, b. Nov. 30, 1836, m. May 17, 1857, MINNIE M. G. VAN DE SANDE.

F1586 William M. Locke, born in 1793, married ABIGAIL WITHEY, born in 1796 in New York. They lived in Grand Rapids, Mich., also in Paris, Kent Co., Mich., 1850–70.

Children of 7th Gen. probably b. in Ohio.

3941 WILLIAM H., b. Ohio, 1829, lived in Grand Rapids.
3942 CHESTER H., b. Ohio, 1832, m. SARAH J. ———, b. 1840, had: 3943 EDWARD L., b. 1856; 3944 FRANCIS C., b. 1859.
3945 ORSON E., b. Ohio, 1835, m. LOVINIA ———, b. N. Y. 1836.
3946 LEVI, b. Michigan, 1852.
3947 CHARLES H., b. 1853.

F1587 Veranus Locke, born in Springfield, Vt. July 15, 1800, married in 1825, STATIRA JENNE, born 1804, died 1875, daughter of Frasien and Polly (Perkins). He was in the battle of Moores Corner, Vt., in 1837, moved from Dunham, P. Q., to Richford, Vt., in 1842; was a carpenter, "kind in word and deed." He died July 26, 1866.

Children of 7th Gen.

F3948 EDWARD S., b. 1827, m. 1862, ALMINA C. ROYCE.
3949 SALLY, b. 1831, m. JOSIAH WILLEY, son of John and Betsey (Sanborn), had: 3950 EDITH; 3951 WEALTHY; 3952 RUTH; 3953 JOHN V.; 3954 ALICE.
3955 MASON, b. 1834, d. 1836.
3956 RUTH A., b. 1837, m. SAMUEL O. LADD, 1867, had: 3957 CARTER V., b. 1869, d. 1870.

F1595 Samuel Locke, born in Epsom, N. H., Nov. 19, 1790, married Feb. 28, 1809, LYDIA BUZZELL, born in Epsom, May 28, 1798, died in Lowell, Mass., March 27, 1854, daughter of Robert E. and Lydia (Danielson). He was in Locke's Mills, Dover, and afterwards went to Lowell. He was in the War of 1812, was nicknamed Yankee Locke, and died in Lowell, Sept. 25, 1847.

Children of 7th Gen.

3958 GEORGE E., b. Epsom, May 31, 1810, d. Epsom, Nov. 21, 1814.
3959 ELIZA M., b. June 15, 1812, d. Dover, Sept. 7, 1835, m. JOHN WENTWORTH of Dover.
3960 HARRIET S., b. Sept. 18, 1814, d. Nov. 2, 1897, m. 1832, DR. IRA ALLEN of Boston, and had four children.
3961 GEORGE EVANS, b. Jan. 31, 1816, d. Lowell, Jan. 5, 1880, m. MISS KIMBALL of Methuen, Mass., who was left a widow, with no children. He was a celebrated comedian in his day, and was called "Yankee Locke." (See History of Lowell, Mass.)
3962 MARY ANN, b. June 4, 1819, d. Charlestown, Mass., July 20, 1889, was m. twice, and had one son.

F3963 WILLIAM MOODY, b. Aug. 18, 1821, m. Oct. 16, 1852, RHODA J. COLE.
3964 MARIA M., b. Nov. 4, 1823, d. March 30, 1840.
3965 LYDIA D., b. Jan. 4, 1827, d. July 4, 1829.
3966 JAMES JEWELL, b. Apl. 9, 1831, d. Lowell, Apl. 6, 1891, was m., and had: 3967 LIZZIE, who m. HARRY REED.

F1596 Daniel Evans Locke, born in Epsom, N. H., Nov. 24, 1793, married in Portsmouth, Jan. 19, 1819, ANN COLEMAN of Newington, born in Dover, July 19, 1797, died Jan. 4, 1869. He enlisted for 60 days in Capt. Godfrey's Company, Sept. 29, 1814; was a farmer in Epsom, Alton, and Gilford, where he died Oct. 22, 1873.

Children of 7th Gen.

3968 SAMUEL W., b. June 19, 1820, d. Dec. 1890, m. Sept. 17, 1848, his cousin, IRENE ELKINS.
3969 MARY A., b. Gilford, Dec. 14, 1821, d. Jan. 1883, m. GEORGE SLEEPER, b. Gilford, had: 3970 GEORGE L.; 3971 CHARLES A., b. Gilford, 1853, m. Nov. 1, 1878, LAURA A. LIVINGSTON of Lake Village, b. Manchester. He has a store in Gilford.
F3972 JOHN C., b. Jan. 9, 1824, m. Aug. 26, 1847, MARY J. ROBERTS.
3973 ELIZA B., b. Gilford, Jan. 2, 1833, d. Laconia, Aug. 13, 1899, m. Aug. 20, 1865, MORRIL AMES of Gilford, had: 3974 IDA, b. 1870, d. Gilford, Jan. 3, 1887.

F1597 Polly Locke, born in Epsom, Oct. 10, 1794, married in 1815, WEARE PRESCOTT of Deerfield. She died Oct. 14, 1854.

Children of 7th Gen.

3974 HANNAH, b. Aug. 12, 1816, m. 1854, JOHN C. WATSON, had four children.
3975 SAMUEL, b. May 20, 1818, m. 1850, MARY A. JONES, b. Dec. 13, 1826.
3976 MARY J., b. May 4, 1820, m. 1850, BENJAMIN D. HILL, had: 3977 MARY E., b. May 12, 1854, d. May 1, 1863.
3978 JACOB W , b. May 1, 1822, m. 1st, 1847, ABBIE J. HOBBS, b. June 14, 1820; m. 2nd, SARAH A. RING, b. Oct. 17, 1827.

F1605 Hannah Mary Locke, born in 1760, died Feb. 13, 1831, married Jan. 2, 1820, MAJOR DANIEL SMITH of Durham, born Oct. 5, 1760, son of Joseph and Deborah. He had a first wife, MARY GILMORE. He died March 8, 1836.

Child of 7th Gen.

F3979 WINTHROP SMITH, b. Jan. 13, 1789, d. Aug. 28, 1844, m. ELEANOR LOCKE, # 1594 (?). This Winthrop was not son of Hannah Mary Locke, but was prob. son of Daniel's first wife.

F1607 Levi Lamprey, born in Epsom, Sept. 10, 1792, married 1st, POLLY COOK, who died Apl. 8, 1861, aged 77; married 2nd, Jan. 6, 1862, ELEANOR BUZZELL, who died Sept. 19, 1884, aged 91. He lived in Wentworth, and died Apl. 14, 1872.

Children of 7th Gen.

3980 EPHRAIM O., b. Meredith, 1820, m. 1st, SARAH PATTEE, b. Nov. 13, 1814; m. 2nd, in Warner, Dec. 30, 1870, SARAH MERCHANT, b. Newbury, Vt., 1826, d. July 22, 1902; lived in Newbury, Vt.
3981 LAVINIA, b. ——, m. JOHN PATTEE.
3982 MAHALA, b. 1821, d. Feb. 15, 1856, m. EPHRAIM MORRILL.
3983 LEVI, JR., b. Sept. 13, 1825, d. Aug. 31, 1903, m. JERUSHA EMMONS of Bristol, b. Aug. 14, 1832, d. Apl. 24, 1898.

F1628 Abel Lamprey, born in Epsom, Aug. 3, 1802, married 1st, in Malden, Mass., Nov. 20, 1826, LYDIA A. CAMPBELL of Boston, born 1807, died at Wilton, July 17, 1834; married 2nd, in Wilton, 1834, SUSAN P. WEBSTER, born 1801, died in Concord, Sept. 20, 1868; married 3rd, in Concord, Jan. 22, 1869, ELIZA P. COLBURN, born 1819. He died in Warner, Nov. 19, 1889.

Children of 7th Gen.

3984 BENJAMIN H., b. Sept. 11, 1827, drowned Franklin June 14, 1848.
3985 JOHN E., b. Nov. 3, 1828, d. Apl. 17, 1885, m. Feb. 5, 1854, JULIA A. TRASK and had: 3986 FLORA L.
3987 ABBY N., b. Dec. 6, 1830, d. Nov. 19, 1858, m. March 1858, WILLIAM STEVENS.
3988 LYDIA ANN, b. Apl. 29, 1832, d. Aug. 26, 1858, m. Jan. 1852, ELLIS ROBINSON.
3989 JOSEPH W., b. July 11, 1833, m. Sept. 1860, ELIZA A. MERRILL, had: 3990 ABEL B.; 3991 JAMES M.
3992 ABEL, b. Jan. 15, 1835, m. Nov. 1854, S. EVALINE COOPER.
3993 LOIS JANE, b. Maine, Dec. 17, 1838, d. Concord, June 8, 1901, m. Nov. 5, 1854, JOSEPH O. TRASK, lived Concord, had: 3994 SUSIE M.

F1641 Judith Lamprey, born in Epsom, July 29, 1815, died in Concord, March 8, 1898, married Aug. 22, 1837, CHANDLER E. STEVENS, # 1651, born May 12, 1812. He was a stone cutter and died in Concord, Oct. 18, 1898.

Children of 7th Gen.

3995 JAMES H., b. May 31, 1838, m. 1st, ARTEMESIA BROWN, b. 1842, d. 1866; m. 2nd, MADGE RICHARDSON of Mt. Desert, Me. Lived Woburn, Mass., and by first wife had: 3996 SETH, died young; 3997 PERLEY, lived Boston; 3998 CLARA, m. ARTHUR W. GLIDDEN; 3999 ETTA, m. JOS. JENKINS.
4000 HANNAH E., b. Dec. 8, 1839, d. Nov. 14, 1861, m. ALBERT N. WARDE of Lowell, lives Concord. no children.

SEVENTH GENERATION

4001 MARY A., b. Nov. 14, 1842, d. July 25, 1871, m. JOHN E. WILLS, lived Lowell.
4002 JENNIE E. WILLS, b. Dec. 29, 1857, m. WILLIE F. LOCKE, # 5776, b. Jan. 6, 1856. Lived in Concord.

F1662 John Hutchins, born in Epsom, March 17, 1802, married Dec. 2, 1829, LUCY ANN MILLS, born Billerica, Mass., March 21, 1808, died Feb. 4, 1877. He lived in Concord and died June 10, 1888.

Children of 7th Gen.

4003 LUCY J., b. Aug. 30, 1830, m. May 28, 1851, HENRY FROST of Billerica, b. June 12, 1827, d. June 2, 1859, had: CHARLES H., b. 1859, d. 1864.
4003a JOHN E., b. Apl. 27, 1838, m. 1st, June 1, 1859, ESTHER E. EMERSON of Hopkinton, who d. Nov. 7, 1863; m. 2nd, AGNES SMITH of E. Concord, lived Concord, had: ii. FRED; iii. IRVING, died young, by 1st wife; then iv. MARY; v. NELLIE M.; vi. WILLIAM E.; vii. GEORGE H.; viii. JOHN ED.

F1663 Margaret Hutchins, born in Epsom, May 29, 1806, married in Boston, Apl. 22, 1827, LELAND THURSTON of Keene, born in Windham, Vt., May 29, 1803, son of John and Lydia (Ball); lived in Denver, Col., and died March, 1883. She died 1899 (?).

Children of 7th Gen.

4004 CHARLES C., b. Troy, N. Y., Jan. 13, 1828, m. CAROLINE HUMPHREY.
4005 EDWIN M., b. Troy, Apl. 12, 1830, m. May 26, 1850, HARRIET SCHUMAN and had two children.
4006 EMILY M., b. Troy, Aug. 24, 1832, m. March 3, 1850, JEREMIAH M. MORTON, a carpenter in Boulder, Col., has seven children.
4007 FRANK A., b. Keene, Oct. 9, 1834, m. ANNIE E. RAPELGE.
4008 MARTHA J., b. K. Feb. 3, 1837, m. CHARLES L. DALRYMPLE.
4009 MARY E., b. K. Aug. 20, 1839, d. 1889, m. Feb. 26, 1861, ISAAC N. MYERS, b. Lubec, Me., Aug. 29, 1834, a carpenter in Springfield, Mo., had six children.
4010 CATHERINE M., b. K., Nov. 6, 1841, m. Millburn, N. J., Apl. 20, 1872, CHARLES HENDERSON of Denver, Col.
4011 HENRY S., b. Boston, Aug. 10, 1844, m. Dec. 24, 1868, ELLA C. POPE of Springfield, Mo., b. Tenn., Feb. 21, 1847. He is a carpenter there, and has six children.
4012 JOSEPHINE, b. Boston, Apl 25, 1847, m. Winchester, N. Y., Nov. 29, 1866, HENRY C. PERKINS, b. Morrisville, Vt., Aug. 29, 1844. He is a salesman in Denver, Col., and has six children.

F1673 Samuel Perkins, born in Seabrook, Oct. 13, 1790, married June 22, 1817, MARY MOODY STOCKMAN of Salisbury, Mass., who died Aug. 28, 1878, aged 87. He was a boatbuilder in Seabrook, and died by accident, Feb. 14, 1860.

Children of 7th Gen. b. in Seabrook.
4013 LUCY S., b. July 20, 1818, m. May 21, 1844, ROBERT WILSON of Salem, Mass., had no children. He d. Sept. 30, 1844.
F4014 BENJAMIN, b. March 20, 1821, m. 1st, LUELLA GOVE; m. 2nd, June 25, 1856, JULIA MARIA HOBBS.
4015 SARAH MOODY, b. Dec. 9, 1831, m. March 22, 1880, MOSES B. SMALL of North Hampton.

F1675 Sally Perkins, born in Seabrook, July 3, 1795, married Apl. 5, 1827, ADONIRAM GEORGE of Hampton Falls.

Children of 7th Gen.
4017 MARY ELIZABETH, b. ——, d. same day.
4018 DAVID A., b. Jan. 11, 1828, m. MARY H. TYLER, had: 4019 SARAH P., b. Jan. 22, 1872, m. MIRON H. GOODWIN of Gorham, Me., and had: 4020 MADELINE P. GOODWIN.

F1676 Belinda Janvrin, born in Seabrook, Nov. 3, 1801, died Dec. 10, 1872, married EDMUND PILLING.

Children of 7th Gen.
4021 JOHN R.   4022 EDWARD A.   4023 GEORGE H.
4024 CHARLES A., b. ——, m. and lives No. Andover, Mass.
4025 LAURA A., b. ——, m. —— SMITH.

F1683 Newell Locke, born in Seabrook, N. H., May 18, 1809, married Jan. 15, 1838, HANNAH TRUE, daughter of Rev. Jabez and Ruth (Brown), born June 19, 1807, died Seabrook, Oct. 4, 1889. He was a boatbuilder in Seabrook where he died Oct. 24, 1888.

Children of 7th Gen. b. in Seabrook.
4028 JULIA D., b. Nov. 21, 1840, d. Seab., Oct. 30, 1848.
4029 EMILY W., b. May 5, 1844, d. Seab. 1910, unmarried. She inherited much property from her father, and left some $10,000, mostly to charity.

F1685 Sally Locke, born in Seabrook, May 17, 1813, married Jan. 7, 1834, MOSES RIDGEWAY of "out west," born Jan. 1800, died in Newmarket, Jan. 17, 1888. Sally died March 31, 1883.

Children of 7th Gen.
4030 JOSEPH, b. Feb. 17, 1835, m. 1870, MARY FOLLANSBEE, lived Haverhill, Mass.
4031 JAMES L., b. Apl. 30, 1837, d. aged 18.

SEVENTH GENERATION 199

4032 SARAH M., b. March 10, 1840, lived West Newbury, unmarried.
4033 MARY A., b. July 19, 1843, lived West Newbury, unmarried.
4034 MOSES M., b. Dec. 24, 1845, m. 1880, MARY HALE; had two daus.
4035 JANE E., b. Apl. 17, 1851, lived West Newbury, unmarried.

F1717 Naomi Locke, born in Epsom, Sept. 5, 1786, married in Epsom March 19, 1807, GREENLEAF BRACKETT of Epsom, born Aug. 9, 1785, son of Ebenezer and Mary (Rogers). Naomi died in Concord, Dec. 15, 1839. He married 2nd, SALLY MARDEN, was a farmer in Epsom and Concord and died Oct. 6, 1878.

Children of 7th Gen.

4036 JAMES, b. 1812, d. unmarried Jan. 2, 1842; an invalid all his life.
4037 JONATHAN, b. 1814, d. 1817.
4038 WILLIAM, b. 1816, d. Nov. 23, 1879, m. BETSEY MOREY, lived at Short Falls, a farmer, and had: 4039 CHARLES W. of Holliston, Mass.
4040 JOHN LOCKE, b. Oct. 1817, d. Nov. 26, 1901, m. 1st, MIRIAM L. LANE, who d. 1847; m. 2nd, 1847, PHEBE HEALD, had: 4041 LOUISA, b. 1860, d. 1870. He was a mason and contractor in southern cities in his younger days, then returned to Epsom and farmed on the old homestead.
4042 JONATHAN, b. 1818, died young.
F4043 ABIGAIL, b. Nov. 13, 1821, m. Feb. 27, 1850, BENJAMIN W. SMITH.
4044 ALICE L., b. Epsom, 1823, d. Epping, June 15, 1890, m. 1863, JACOB PRESCOTT, a farmer in Epping, had: 4045 ALICE, b. 1865; 4046 ALFRED J., b. ——, lived West Manchester.
4047 BETSEY, b. 1827, died young.
F4048 NAOMI, b. Sept. 14, 1828, m. Sept. 14, 1847, GEORGE B. MERRIAM.

F1721 David Locke, born in Epsom, Jan. 19, 1796, married in Epsom, Dec. 23, 1818, ELIZABETH S. CHASE of Pittsfield, daughter of Samuel, born in Pittsfield, May 11, 1796, died in Hopkinton, Aug. 20, 1867. He was a farmer in Epsom until 1831, then went to Hopkinton, and died July 13, 1883.

Children of 7th Gen. b. Epsom.

F4050 DRUSILLA SANBORN, b. Feb. 8, 1821, m. Feb. 25, 1841, GEORGE W. WOODBURY.
F4051 ALPHEUS CROSBY, b. Feb. 11, 1823, m. Apl. 19, 1847, HARRIET A. KIMBALL; m. 2nd, Apl. 23, 1856, LOUISA KIMBALL.
4052 MARY ELIZABETH, b. Dec. 6, 1824, d. Hopk., Aug. 24, 1840.
F4053 SARAH CHASE, b. May 1, 1827, m. Apl. 9, 1857, CHARLES C. DOWE.
F4054 MILTON PUTNAM, b. June 9, 1829, m. 1st, Jan. 23, 1854, SARAH C. BOUSLEY; m. 2nd, LYDIA ANN CURTIS.
4055 ANN MERRILL, b. Epsom, Dec. 3, 1831, d. Kensington, Dec. 25, 1870, m. Jan. 23, 1854, JOSEPH H. BOUSLEY, a carpenter of Salem, had: 4056 WILLIE, who died young.

F4057 SILAS MERRILL, b. Dec. 30, 1834, m. 1st, Sept. 30, 1856, LIZZIE T. KIMBALL; m. 2nd, March 29, 1900, LIZZIE A. MURCH.
4058 NATHAN SMITH, b. Hopkinton, Oct. 27, 1837, m. 1st, Lewiston, Me., May 1, 1858, LOVINA J. GRAFFAM, b. Lewiston, Oct. 27, 1837, d. March 10, 1863; m. 2nd, Appleton, Wis., Nov. 7, 1868, ABBIE G. WARE of Wis., b. March 29, 1841. He is real estate dealer in Antigo, Wis., no children.
F4059 NATHANIEL CHASE (twin), b. Oct. 27, 1837, m. Oct. 30, 1858, SOPHRONIA T. FRENCH.
F4060 GEORGE HENRY, b. Dec. 18, 1842, m. Dec. 6, 1876, MARY ANN WRIGHT.

F1722 Rebecca Locke, born in Epsom, Apl. 15, 1798, married in Epsom, Dec. 31, 1818, ISAAC TOWLE of Epsom, born Oct. 18, 1794. He was a farmer in Concord and Northboro, Mass., and died in Sutton, Vt., Jan. 14, 1884. She died March 16, 1879.

Children of 7th Gen.

4061 JAMES F., b. Aug. 28, 1820, d. Nov. 19, 1820.
4062 JAMES MOSES, b. Nov. 14, 1821, m. May 25, 1852, JANE MCCLURE, lived Somerville, Mass., had: 4063 FRANK.
F4064 HENRY E., b. Oct. 9, 1823, m. Jan. 10, 1849, MARY ANN MCCRILLIS.
F4065 HORACE E., b. Dec. 16, 1825, m. Apl. 8, 1852, SUSAN M. DAILY.
4066 RODNEY H., b. March 24, 1827, d. July 24, 1827.
4067 CHARLES, b. Sept. 23, 1828, d. Sept. 18, 1831.
F4068 ALMIRA J., b. Oct. 18, 1829, m. Oct. 21, 1852, CYRUS FRENCH.
4069 GEORGE, b. June 7, 1831, d. Nov. 26, 1836.
F4070 CHARLES A., b. June 14, 1833, m. Dec. 1, 1854, MARIA SKATES.
4071 MARY A., b. July 28, 1834, d. Oct. 8, 1834.
F4072 MARY A., b. Aug. 1, 1835, m. Nov. 15, 1860, REV. ROBERT FORD.
F4073 ALBERT, b. Jan. 8, 1837, m. March 12, 1862, ANNIE E. RYNES.
F4074 ELLEN M., b. Apl. 1, 1839, m. Feb. 11, 1863, WILLIAM B. FELLOWS.
4075 ELIZABETH S., b. Apl 25, 1840, d. Feb. 14, 1864, m. 1862, JOHN F. CHADWICK, lived No. Sutton.
4076 GEORGE, b. Dec. 17, 1841, m. Feb. 21, 1867, MARY J. MCFARLAND, lived Roslindale, Mass.
4077 WILLIAM P., b. Oct. 28, 1843, d. in war, July 13, 1863.

F1723 Mary Locke, born in Epsom, Sept. 10, 1800, married in Epsom, Feb. 19, 1822, JAMES WEEKS of Concord, born in Concord, Nov. 22, 1795, son of John and Susan (Abbott). He was a tanner and currier in Concord, later a farmer in Epsom, and died Nov. 2, 1865. She died Feb. 27, 1846. He married 2nd, HANNAH MCCRILLIS.

SEVENTH GENERATION

Children of 7th Gen.
4078 SUSAN M., b. July 29, 1823, d. unmarried Oct. 3, 1847, Concord.
4079 ABIGAIL, b. Apl. 2, 1824, m. Concord, June 10, 1845, HENRY E. PEASE of Troy, N. Y., had: 4080 MARY, d. infant; 4081 LUELLA, died young lady; 4082 JENNIE M., m. LYMAN D. DUDLEY; parents lived Concord.
4083 JONATHAN L. B., b. Sept. 12, 1826, m. Jan. 31 1850, CAROLINE R. GARVIN of Concord, b. Feb. 3, 1830, he lived in and was assessor of Concord, had: 4084 MARY C., b. Dec. 5, 1850, d. Oct. 3, 1865.
4085 JOSEPH A., b. Sept. 17, 1832, d. Oct. 1865, m. HATTIE EMERSON of Boston. He was a clerk in Ditson's music store, had: 4086 FRANK B., b. 1862, is Boston superintendent of John Hancock Life Ins. Co.
4087 LIZZIE C., b. Apl. 1834, m. J. GREEN JONES, an insurance agent in Boston, had: 4088 J. EDWAPD, b. 1858, insurance man.
4089 ANN M., b. July 1836, m. HENRY S. JONES of Hopkinton, a watchmaker in Boston, no children.
4090 MARTHA C., b. June 17, 1838, d. June 3, 1898, m. E. OSBORN CROWELL of Boston, no children. He is of firm T. Y. Crowell & Co., bookbinders.

F1724 Frederick Sanborn, born in Epsom, N. H., Oct. 28, 1789, married March 20, 1816, LUCY SARGENT of Pittsfield, born May 12, 1793, died June 16, 1863, daughter of Rev. Benjamin, a Revolutionary soldier. He was a deacon in Concord Church, a farmer and lumber dealer in Epsom and died May 9, 1881.

Children of 7th Gen.
4091 CATHERINE G., b. Dec. 6, 1817, d. Dec. 16, 1838, m. REV. JOHN BURDEN.
F4092 HENRY F., b. Feb. 26, 1819, m. EUNICE DAVIS.
4093 MARTHA E., b. June 19, 1821, m. Apl. 28, 1845, JOHN G. PEARSON of Concord.
4094 ANN, b. Apl. 30, 1825, m. HENRY D. SMITH of Worcester, later of Cambridge.
F4095 JOHN B., b. Dec. 6, 1826, m. 1st, March 17, 1857, CATHERINE HILL; m. 2nd, Nov. 27, 1865, ANNA E. NIXON; m. 3rd, Apl. 15, 1880, RACHEL RICE.

F1725 James Sanborn, born in Epsom, Nov. 14, 1791, married 1st, Dec. 29, 1814, ABIGAIL PARSONS, a cousin, born March 4, 1797, died June 18, 1833; married 2nd, NANCY TOWLE, born 1806, died May 23, 1871. He died in Concord, Feb. 23, 1870.

Children of 7th Gen.
4096 SON, b. 1815, d. 1815.
4097 CALVIN, b. Nov. 9, 1816, d. Aug. 10, 1875, m. CHARLOTTE HOYT of Barnstead, dau. of Benj. Had no children.

4098 SOPHIA A., b. Sept. 30, 1818, d. Aug. 1, 1856, unmarried.
4099 JAMES, b. March 2, 1821, d. Northwood, July 21, 1863, m. Sept. 19, 1847, SARAH ELIZABETH YEATON of Epsom, b. Nov. 23, 1823, d. Sept. 19, 1888; was a farmer in Northwood, had: 4100 two died young; 4101 SARAH F.; 4102 DR. FRED J. James served in Co. D, 15th N. H. Inf.
4103 CHARLES H., b. July 6, 1823, m. VIENNA PRESCOTT of Epsom, dau. of John; was a millwright and tavern keeper, Pittsfield.
4104 MARY P., b. May 17, 1826, m. CHARLES PERKINS of Chichester, who d. 1848; m. 2nd, ADONIRAM R. SEAVEY of Chelsea, Mass., who d. 1895.
4105 LEWIS D., b. Jan. 17, 1829, m. Oct. 25, 1853, MARY A. HOITT of Barnstead, b. May 22, 1838, d. March 23, 1892. He was a mechanic, Pittsfield and Boston, had: 4106 DR. GEORGE, lives Henniker.

F1731 Hannah Sanborn, born in Epsom, Feb. 8, 1798, died March 21, 1877, married Jan. 11, 1821, BENJAMIN M. TOWLE of Epsom, born Sept. 20, 1797. He was a farmer in Epsom and died Nov. 19, 1857.

Children of 7th Gen.

4107 SARAH H., b. Oct. 23, 1821, m. JOHN WALLACE, had: 4108 SARAH N.
4109 ELIZABETH, b. Oct. 27, 1823, d. Apl 5, 1835.
F4110 NANCY N., b. March 28, 1826, m. June 2, 1847, JOHN SHAW.
F4111 BENJAMIN, b. Nov. 2, 1828, m. 1st, May 1850, ELIZA H. HAM; m. 2nd, Feb. 11, 1862, HARRIET E. EDGERLY.
4112 CATHERINE, b. Oct. 6, 1832, d. July 31, 1840.
F4113 CLARA M., b. Dec. 2, 1834, m. Nov. 27, 1856, ALFRED E. AMBROSE.
F4114 REV. CHARLES A., b. June 20, 1837, m. 1st, Dec. 14, 1869, JENNIE LAY; m. 2nd, Aug. 30, 1894, ELLA REINKING.
4115 CATHERINE E., b. March 20, 1842, m. Nov. 1, 1870, JOHN H. DOLBEE, b. Feb. 8, 1839, a farmer in Short Falls; no children.

F1760 Ira A. C. Locke, born in Loudon, N. H., March 23, 1822, married in Concord, Apl. 12, 1843, MEHITABLE J. BROWN, born Concord, June 22, 1822, daughter of Eliphalet and Alice (Willey). He was a farmer in Loudon, and died June 25, 1881. She was living in 1912.

Children of 7th Gen.

F4116 LEROY LESLIE, b. June 9, 1845, m. 1st, Jan. 30, 1868, HANNAH EVES; m. 2nd, May 20, 1885, ABBIE W. PALMER.
4117 LOREN L., b. March 24, 1850, d. Aug. 25, 1852.
4118 ADA A. C., b. Nov. 8, 1860, m. Apl. 3, 1880, ELLERY D. HUNKINS of Concord, b. Landaff, 1855, son of Harry and Maria. He was a miller in Penacook, had: 4119 EVA, b. Concord, Feb. 20, 1882, d. Dec. 16, 1890; 4120 IRA A., b. March 20, 1887.

SEVENTH GENERATION

F1761 Elijah True Locke, born in Loudon, July 26, 1827, married in Nashua, March 14, 1849, HARRIET J. ALLEN, born in Cabot, Vt., Dec. 1, 1828, died in Boscawen, Apl. 16, 1889. daughter of Hart and Lucia (Goss). He was a watchman in Harris Mills, Penacook, many years and died in Boscawen, Sept. 7, 1893.

Children of 7th Gen.

4121 GEORGE S., b. June 18, 1850, m. June 7, 1874, ANNA PRESCOTT, b. Epsom, Feb. 25, 1851, dau. of William and Harriet C. (Marden); no children. He is manager of Penacook Saw Co.
F4122 LUCIA L., b. May 2, 1858, m. Apl. 28, 1877, JOHN R. HILL.
4123 ELLA E., b. Concord, Jan. 16, 1860, m. Oct. 1875, WILLIAM H. BONNEY, b. Manchester, Feb. 5, 1858, son of Hannibal and Ellen (Dill). He was a hotel keeper in Boscawen, and had: 4124 INEZ, b. Aug. 25, 1882, m. June 2, 1908, DR. MERLIN BLODGETT, who was accidentally shot while hunting Oct. 1911.

F1765 James Munroe Locke, born in Stanstead, Can., Oct. 15, 1804, married in 1829, SALLY CASS, born Jan. 27, 1805, died March 25, 1885, daughter of Theophilus. He was a farmer, a magistrate, prominent in public affairs, a member of the Methodist Church, and died at his home in Stanstead, Can., Feb. 2, 1862.

Children of 7th Gen.

F4125 JANE M., b. Oct. 11, 1830, m. Oct. 10, 1849, HIRAM R. BISHOP.
4126 LOUISA A., b. Nov. 18, 1832, d. Hatley, Can., Nov. 25, 1869, m. June 8, 1869, LEVI E. PARKER of Hatley, a merchant there; had no children.
F4127 FLORELLA A., b. Dec. 20, 1834, m. Oct. 21, 1858, JAMES K. CURRIER.
F4128 FREDERICK W., b. Jan. 14, 1837, m. Dec. 14, 1865, TIRZAH MARTIN.

F1775 Rev. William Sherburne Locke, born in Stanstead, Can., Aug. 28, 1808, married Aug. 27, 1833, CAROLINE DAME TEBBETTS of Kittery, born in Kittery, 1809, died in South Manchester, Feb. 14, 1893, daughter of William and Jerusha (Dame).

He attended the public school and at the age of seventeen was apprenticed to a tanner and currier. For four years he worked at this trade and in 1829 took charge of a tanning business in Barton, Vt. While there he was awakened to the importance of a spiritual life, was converted and joined the Methodist Church. He determined to engage as a teacher and preacher, and selling his business entered Brownington Academy in order to train for the ministry. Here his health broke down, but acting on his physician's advice he went to Hampton, for the sea air, where he studied at the academy, holding meetings at different houses. His first regular work was as assistant on the Northfield Circuit. At the next Conference he received a "local preacher's" license and took charge at East Kingston. It was about this time that he married.

For many years as a member of the New Hampshire and Vermont Conference, then one body, he labored throughout the southern sections of these states, meeting with great success. He gained many converts, built churches where there had been none and in the second Adventist excitement during the early forties, held his people true to their church with a firm hand, a level head and sympathetic heart. In the spring of 1847 upon the death of his father, he went back to Canada where he remained for six years on the old home farm, at the same time preaching at various vacant places.

After this he returned to Manchester, where he purchased a farm a short distance from the city. With the exception of the years from 1861–6, passed in Kittery, Me., Kingston, and Conway, the remainder of his life was spent there, where he died after a hale and happy old age, July 21, 1896. He was greatly interested in the organization of the Locke Association and was one of its most enthusiastic supporters. A more detailed account of his life may be found in Willey's "Book of Nutfield," Vol. I, Part 8, page 343.

Children of 7th Gen.

F4130 MARY F., b. Sept. 6, 1835, m. Dec. 25, 1856, CHARLES H. BARTLETT.
F4131 JAMES W., b. Oct. 30, 1837, m. Oct. 5, 1866, ALVINA C. NEAL.
4132 JOSEPH LITCHFIELD, b. Merrimack, Feb. 20, 1841, m. Oct. 1878, EMMA D. MITCHELL of Cincinnati, b. May 26, 1856. She m. 2nd, June 18, 1903, WILLIAM C. BROOKS, of San Jose, Cal. Joseph attended the public schools of Manchester and in 1862 graduated from the normal school in Bridgewater, Mass. The same day he enlisted in the 33rd Mass. Volunteers in which he served during the war, and was mustered out as 1st Lieutenant in 1865. He was a merchant and manufacturer in Cincinnati and Chicago, was a G. A. R. Post Commander and d. Chicago, July 15, 1899; had no children.
4133 CAROLINE, b. Feb. 11, 1844, d. Sept. 4, 1846.
4134 EMMA J., b. May 24, 1847, d. Jan. 6, 1858.
F4135 EUGENE O., b. Feb. 20, 1850, m. March 30, 1875, ROSETTA R. OTTO.
4136 SARAH IZETTA, b. Oct. 3, 1852, m. Oct. 25, 1904, THOMAS M. HENDERSON of Toronto, Can., where they reside. She was a public school teacher in Manchester several years.

F1777 Florinda Locke, born in Stanstead, Can., March 6, 1812, died March 19, 1879, married March 9, 1844, OSCAR WYMAN of Barnston, Can., born Sept. 29, 1820. He was a miller in Magog, P. Q., and died there of fever, Nov. 7, 1900.

Children of 7th Gen.

F4137 FLORA J., b. March 29, 1848, m. Oct. 25, 1865, ERNEST H. BULLARD.
4138 EVALINE L., b. July 31, 1851, m. Lenoxville, Quebec, Nov. 18, 1879, EDWARD O. PAIGE. He is a teamster in Springfield, Mass.; had no children.

F1779 Emaline Locke, born in Georgeville, Can., Apl. 27, 1818, died Dec. 26, 1887, married in Stanstead, May 30, 1842, CAPT. MOSES W. COPP, born in Georgewell, P. Q., Sept. 9, 1809, son of Richard and Mary. He was a merchant in Magog, P. Q., and was once very wealthy. He died Apl. 28, 1879. This was his 2nd wife.

Children of 7th Gen.

4139 JOSHUA W., b. June 6, 1843, unmarried, went to Florida.
F4140 RICHARD J., b. March 4, 1845, m. 1870, MALVINA SCHOOLCRAFT.
F4141 EMALINE LOUISE, b. July 1, 1847, m. Oct. 1867, ADDISON L. NOYES.
4142 ELLEN ROSE, b. June 5, 1850, d. Jan. 15, 1855.
4143 CHARLES F., b. May 24, 1853, m. Superior, Iowa, May 24, 1876, CLARA GEER, lived Superior and had: 4144 CARROLL G., b. 1877.
4145 WILLARD W., b. Jan. 25, 1856, m. ABBY STEVENS, and was divorced, had: 4146 EMELINE L. He was an insurance agent.
4147 FLORA ELLA, b. March 22, 1861, m. Sept. 21, 1885, L. SAMUEL FOURNIER, who was a grocer in Lowell and had: 4148 JAMES ALBERT, b. July 4, 1886.

F1788 Eunice Locke, born in Hampton Falls, N. H., Dec. 12, 1785, married Oct. 14, 1808, DAVID GEORGE of Kensington, who died in Seabrook; married 2nd, NATHAN SMITH, a farmer in Seabrook; married 3rd, STEPHEN LITTLEFIELD, born March 7, 1813, son of John and Judith (Prescott).

Children of 7th Gen., all Smiths.

4149 HARRIET, b. ——, d. N. Y., m. LUCIUS CHITTENDEN of N. Y., had: 4150 LUCIA, m. FRANK COLSON of London; 4151 BOY, d. infant; 4152 GRACE, died young.
4153 SARAH, b. ——, m. 1st, EDWARD PHILBRICK; m. 2nd, SAMUEL T. PAYSON, had: 4154 ANNA PHILBRICK, m. GEORGE JEFFREY, lives So. Orange, N. J., had two children; 4155 CLIFFORD PAYSON, lives Chicago.
4156 STEPHEN H., died young.
F4157 CAROLINE, b. June 5, 1834, m. 1849, AARON BANCROFT.

F1793 Elizabeth Locke, born in Kensington, N. H., March 22, 1795, died in Portsmouth, Apl. 26, 1876, married in Seabrook, Jan. 21, 1812, JONATHAN MORRISON, born Sanbornton, March 12, 1785, son of Jonathan and Esther (Perkins). He was a dealer in stoves and tinware in Sanbornton, Kensington and Portsmouth. He was an Orderly Sergeant in Bran's Co., 3rd Reg., 1814. Died in Portsmouth, Dec. 25, 1873.
Children of 7th Gen.
4158 AUGUSTUS, b. Kensington, Nov. 17, 1813, d. San Francisco, June 17, 1859, unmarried.
F4159 RUTH E., b. Sept. 25, 1817, m. June 30, 1841, GEORGE NOYES CARLTON.
F4160 MARY ESTHER, b. Ports., Dec. 7, 1822, d. Apl. 14, 1881, m. Ports., Aug. 24, 1848, G. N. CARLETON, her brother-in-law, who was in the Railroad advertising business in N. Y.
4161 HORACE, b. Ports., Dec. 15, 1826, d. unmarried, Dec. 22, 1869, in California Steam Nav. Co.

F1794 Dorothy (Dolly) Locke, born in Kensington, Oct. 9, 1797, died in Kensington, married in Hampton Falls, Dec. 2, 1821, WILLIAM PALMER, a farmer of Kensington who died there.
Children of 7th Gen.
4162 JOHN, b. ——, died young.
4163 ALBERT, b. ——, d. unmarried, New Bedford, Mass.
4164 MARY N., b. 1829, d. Kensington, May 20, 1899, m. 1st, —— BROWN of Kens., m. 2nd, —— ——; m. 3rd, ELLERY PALMER, lived Kens., had: 4165 MARTHA, m. —— PALMER, and had: 4166 MARY; 4167 DOROTHY; 4168 SON; 4169 AMY, who m. ARTHUR EVANS.
4170 ALMIRA, b. ——, m. —— Dow, and had: 4171 Two sons; 4172 JULIA L., m. and had: 4173 ANNIE.

F1795 Oliver Peabody Locke, born in Kensington, March 6, 1800, married in Kensington, Jan. 17, 1826, SARAH A. SANBORN of Gilmanton, born in Gilmanton, Dec. 8, 1805, died in Chelsea in 1873, daughter of Lieut. David and Hannah (Hook). He was a merchant at Long Wharf, Boston, and died Chelsea, 1871.
Children of 7th Gen.
4175 SARAH JANE, b. in Boston, Feb. 8, 1827, m. Dec. 1, 1846, REV. CHARLES WADSWORTH, D.D., of Litchfield, Conn., b. 1815, d. Apl. 1, 1882, son of Harry. She d. Phila. 1891, and had: 4176 CHARLES, who was pastor of Philadelphia Presby. Church 1903; 4177 WILLIAM SCOTT, an M.D. of Phila.; 4178 EDITH.
4179 MARY OLIVE, b. Nov. 25, 1829, m. Chelsea, Mass., Oct. 15, 1857, WILLIAM BROWN, lived Chelsea, had two sons.

SEVENTH GENERATION

4180 AUGUSTUS, b. Oct. 5, 1830, d. Oct. 15, 1831.
4181 OLIVER, b. Nov. 4, 1832, was a war veteran, m. and went West.
4182 AUGUSTUS, b. Apl. 4, 1835, d. Apl. 3, 1837.
F4183 CHARLOTTE AUGUSTA, b. Sept. 28, 1838, m. Aug. 31, 1864, HENRY S. MOODY.
4184 JACKSON, b. Boston, March 25, 1842, was a lawyer in Chelsea.
4185 PHEBE, b. Boston June 4, 1846, d. March 7, 1847.
4186 ANNA, b. Oct. 14, 1853, d. Nov. 28, 1853.

F1796 Sally Dalton Locke, born in Kensington, Dec. 18, 1802, died in Chicago, Oct. 25, 1888, married in Portsmouth, Dec. 12, 1826, REV. ASA LAMSON of New Boston. He was a minister, farmer, and kept the Mansion House, Andover, Mass., some years. He died in New Boston, Aug. 25, 1860.

Children of 7th Gen.

4187 JOHN DALTON, b. ——.
4188 GEORGE OSMAN, b. ——.
4189 MARTHA D., died young.
4190 MARTHA D., b. March 31, 1833, d. July 21, 1874, m. Feb. 27, 1856, REV. GABRIEL H. DE BEVOISE, b. Jan. 7, 1831, graduated from Williams College 1857, pastor at Keene, Walpole, Leominster, Andover, and other cities, had: 4191 JAMES, of Portland, Ore.
4192 SAMUEL LOCKE, b. July 1, 1835, d. unmarried, Sept. 22, 1910. He passed his last years at Pigeon Cove, Mass., where his lonely life may have made him peculiar, but he had such a kind heart and took so great an interest in life, that his many friends always clung to him.
4193 JOSEPH, b. ——, died young.
4194 SARAH, b. Nov. 1840, m. REV. EVARTS SCUDDER of Gt. Barrington, Mass., they had: 4195 CHARLES, who was a doctor, Beacon St., Boston.
4196 EMILINA B., b. Aug. 23, 1846, m. EVERITTE ST. JOHN, a R. R. man, lived Norfolk, Va., and Gt. Barrington, Mass.

F1797 Samuel Locke, born in Kensington, Oct. 31, 1806, married May 20, 1835, EMILINE GUESDON of New Orleans, born Apl. 9, 1818, died in New Orleans, June 8, 1891. He was a wholesale dealer in hardware of all kinds, was mayor of New Orleans and one of its most prominent, influential, public-spirited citizens; was a man of very large means, but his fortune was impaired by the Civil War. He and his brother, JOHN D., were in business together in Geneva, N. Y., in 1826–7, then separated, each to achieve his fortune, and both succeeded. Samuel lost a son in the war and died heart-broken at Andover, Mass., July 28, 1865.

Children of 7th Gen. b. in New Orleans.
F4197 EMILIE, b. Aug. 18, 1836, m. July 1, 1856, GUSTAVE A. BREAUX.
4198 JOHN OLIVER, b. Nov. 16, 1838, was a Confed. soldier, killed in Georgia, Jan. 12, 1864, unmarried.
4199 MARY BETHIA, b. Feb. 7, 1846, d. May 22, 1899, m. May 18, 1866, ALPHONZE MAUREAU, b. N. Y., d. Egypt, 1876. She was reared in France, had son: 4200 ALPHONZE L., b. N. O., March 28, 1869, now a Jesuit Priest.
F4201 SAMUEL EDWARD, b. March 9, 1847, m. Oct. 7, 1868, MARY OLEVIA ELLIS.
4202 JOSIAH, b. Oct. 14, 1848, d. infant.
4203 PHILIP, b. Oct. 25, 1850, d. infant.

F1798 John Dawlton Locke, born in Kensington, Jan. 12, 1809, married May 17, 1830, JULIA A. GOFF, born Gilbertville, N. Y., May 18, 1815, died Whitestone, Long Island, Apl. 6, 1870. He went to Meriden, Conn., in 1822, with some new clothes and 25 cents and there learned the tinware trade. He then with his brother, SAMUEL, went to Geneva, N. Y., 1826–7 and they were in business together, but decided to separate. He went to Whitestone in 1845 where he established the first japanned ware factory in the United States, was a large real estate owner, and became very rich. During the war he was in Europe educating his children and nephew, SAMUEL. He died in Whitestone, Nov. 28, 1883.

Children of 7th Gen.
4204 SAMUEL MORRIS, b. Geneva, N. Y., Oct. 1, 1831, d. N. Y. City, Feb. 26, 1876, m. San Francisco, Jan. 5, 1860, SARAH DEXTER of Bradford, Mass., b. Griggsville, Ill., Nov. 20, 1837. He was in mercantile business in San Francisco, but lived in N. Y. and became rich. He was buried in Woodlawn Cemetery. His widow, m. 1879, ROSWELL TUCKER in Philadelphia. Samuel had: 4205 JOHN DEXTER, b. San Francisco, Nov. 21, 1860.
F4206 JOHN JOSIAH, b. Jan. 18, 1834, m. 1st, CORNELIA ACKERLEY; m. 2nd, EMMA CUTHBERT.
4207 MARY AMELIA, b. N. Y. City, March 17, 1836, d. Nov. 15, 1838.
F4208 JULIA FRANCES, b. July 10, 1838, m. WILLIAM BLOODGOOD.
F4209 CHARLES ED., b. Jan. 4, 1842, m. EMILY MILBURN.
F4210 HENRY CLAY, b. Jan. 9, 1845, m. FANNIE DAVIS.
4211 EMMA CAROLINE, b. N. Y. City, May 25, 1847, m. ALBERT H. WELLS of Vt. He is a commercial traveler, Detroit, Mich., had: 4212 BEATRICE, b. Whitestone, L. I., Sept. 1883; 4213 DALTON, b. Whitestone, May 1878.
4214 FRANK MORTIMER, b. Whitestone, Aug. 27, 1849, m. Apl. 18, 1883, SARAH BISHOP of Brooklyn, cousin of Emily Milburn, b. Feb. 9, 1863, dau. of Joseph and Sarah (Dougan). He is a commercial agent in Brooklyn.

SEVENTH GENERATION 209

4215 FLORENCE A., b. Oct. 17, 1851, d. W., July 1, 1853.
4216 CLARENCE GALE, a twin, d. Feb. 2, 1853.
4217 AUBIN GALE, b. Whitestone, Sept. 25, 1855, m. Apl. 1884, ADA OARE, dau. of Joseph and ——— (Smith). He was in business in Chicago, and in 1900 was a traveling agent, Syracuse, N. Y., had: 4218 AUBIN G., JR., d. an infant; 4219 GLADYS, b. 1886.

F1799 Hubbard Locke, born in Seabrook in 1802, married Oct. 20, 1823, JENNIE DOW of Seabrook, born in 1797, died Oct. 23, 1870. He was a laborer in Seabrook and died Dec. 1875.

Children of 7th Gen. b. in Seabrook.

F4220 JAMES, b. Jan. 24, 1825, m. 1869, EDITH I. COGSWELL.
F4221 LYDIA, b. Feb. 26, 1826, m. Dec. 24, 1846, ELIHU DOW.
4222 WILLIAM, b. 1827, left home about 1848, m. an Irish girl, probably was in the Navy, and perhaps was in Co. K, 2nd N. H. Reg., June 1861.
F4223 MARY JANE, b. Feb. 22, 1829, m. Nov. 8, 1849, AMOS JENNESS.
4224 FANNY STOCKTON, b. ———, d. 1859, m. Seabrook, Nov. 1, 1855, HENRY F. BRAGG of Seab., b. 1834, d. Seab., 1906. He was a shoemaker in Seabrook, and m. 2nd, SARAH BROWN. Fanny had: 4225 EFFIE; 4226 EMMIE; 4227 FANNIE, all died young.
4228 ADALINE, b. 1832, d. 1889, m. ANDREW SAWYER of Lynn, a carriage maker. Had: 4229 JENNIE, who m. ——— JACQUES, a farmer of Newburyport; 4230 HUBBARD HERBERT, who m. MAGGIE ——— and was a carriage maker in Lynn, and five others died young.
4231 LUCY, b. ———, d. aged 21, unmarried.
4232 ABBIE LEAVITT, b. 1841, d. Wakefield, Mass., 1909, m. 1889, EDWARD PARK, a piano maker; had no children, lived Wakefield Junc., Mass.

F1800 Eliza Locke, born Nov. 12, 1805, died in Seabrook, Jan. 26, 1881, married in Seabrook, Aug. 7, 1833, EDWARD GOVE of Seabrook, born Feb. 25, 1801, died a farmer in Seabrook, June 21, 1853. He was the son of Levi.

Children of 7th Gen. b. in Seabrook.

4233 MARY, b. Feb. 25, 1834, m. GILMAN S. HOYT of West Amesbury, Mass., who d. 1910, leaving: 4234 CHARLES E., living Merrimack, Mass., 1910.
4235 EDWARD D., b. June 4, 1836, d. 1910, m. Seabrook, 1871, MARY JANVRIN of Seabrook, b. 1843, d. Oct. 14, 1873. He was a farmer in Seab., had no children and left some $15,000 to charity.
4236 CATHERINE, b. Sept. 9, 1840, d. July 30, 1878, m. DR. HAZEN S. DAVIS of Cambridge, Mass.; left no children.

F1802 Lydia Locke, born ——, married MESHACK or CALEB ROLLINS of Stratham, born in 1799, son of James and Abigail (Mason), lived Boston.

Children of 7th Gen. b. in Boston.
4237 DEARBORN W., b. 1808, died young.
4238 CAROLINE, b. 1810, m. 1824, D. DECOSTA, and had eleven children in Boston.
4239 ABIGAIL, b. 1812, d. unmarried 1836.
4240 BARTLETT, b. 1814, d. Chelsea, a mariner.
4241 LYDIA, b. 1816, d. 1851, m. LARKIN MOULTON of Manchester, had two children.
4242 MARY ANN, b. 1818, d. 1860, m. EDW. DANIELS of Charlestown, had nine children.
4243 DEARBORN W., b. 1823, d. Boston, July 16, 1851.
4244 WILLIAM, b. 1825, m. ELIZABETH PAGE of Bangor.
4245 BENJAMIN F., b. 1828, m. ELIZABETH F. POTTER of Boston, had:
    4246 ANNA, b. 1859, d. 1870.
4247 CHARLES, b. 1830, d. 1844.
4248 GEORGE W., b. 1832, m. ELIZABETH GAGE of Dover; had no children.
4250 WINSLOW L., b. 1834, m. MRS. MARY E. WILLARD of Boston; was a painter in B., had four children.
4251 WELLS W., b. 1836, m. 1st, FANNY SANCRI, who d. Boston, June 8, 1870; m. 2nd, Feb. 11, 1872, MRS. CAROLINE MOODY.
4252 ABBY, b. 1838, d. 1870, m. FREDERICK WILSON of Montreal.

F1809 Lydia Locke, born in Kensington, Apl. 30, 1782, died Nov. 1, 1839, married June 1800, MOSES PRESCOTT, born in Kensington, Sept. 25, 1780. He was a farmer in Deerfield, and died Nov. 2, 1855.

Children of 7th Gen.
F4254 GEORGE W., b. July 13, 1801, m. BETSEY SEAVEY, 1827.
F4255 HIRAM A., b. Feb. 1804, m. 1825 MIRIAM MURRAY.
4256 TIMOTHY L., b. June 1806, d. Feb. 17, 1811.
F4257 EDWARD P., b. Apl. 14, 1812, m. Oct. 31, 1835, REBECCA A. COLLIS.
4258 JOHN B., b. Aug. 7, 1816, m. 1838, RUTH RANDALL, lived Deerfield and Concord.

F1818 Mary Locke, born in Seabrook, March 14, 1792, died Sept. 6, 1855, married Feb. 14, 1814, ENOCH WINKLEY, a tanner of Amesbury, Mass., born 1783, died 1880.

Children of 7th Gen.
F4259 JOHN FRANCIS, b. June 20, 1815, m. 1840, SUSAN SHAW TODD.
F4260 SARAH LOCKE, b. March 27, 1816, d. June 19, 1869, m. Dec. 1845, AMOS BINNEY of Boston; had no children.
F4261 MARY SANBORN, b. Oct. 14, 1817, m. Dec. 1841, WILLIAM C. BARTON.

SEVENTH GENERATION

4262 FRANCIS JOHN, b. June 1830, d. 1864, m. 1st, MIRA ———; m. 2nd, ——— ———, had: 4263 GRACE, m. 1st, ——— WILSON, who d. Italy; m. 2nd, 1902, L. VAUGHAN CLARKE of N. Y. City; lived West 93rd St., and had two children.

F1820 Clarissa Locke, born in Seabrook, June 1, 1797, died in Hampton Falls, Jan. 14, 1854, married Oct. 15, 1818, RICHARD DODGE of Hampton Falls, born July 30, 1788, died May 14, 1864, son of Nathaniel and Sally. He was a farmer and miller in Hampton Falls, and owned several vessels in West India trade and Labrador fishing. He was a deacon of the Baptist Church, was highly esteemed and lived on the old homestead. He married 2nd, MARY W. TITCOMB of Newburyport.

Child of 7th Gen.
F4264 JOHN WILLIAM, b. March 25, 1819, m. Sept. 2, 1840, HARRIET P. DUNKLEE.

F1821 Dudley S. Locke, born in Seabrook, Jan. 19, 1800, married in 1832, CAROLINE W. NUDD of Hampton Beach, born in Hampton Apl. 9, 1808, died in Seabrook, Jan. 22, 1881, daughter of David and Abigail. He kept a hotel in Seabrook and died there May 12, 1884.

Children of 7th Gen.
F4265 JOHN D., b. Dec. 31, 1832, m. Aug. 22, 1854, MARTHA M. BROWN.
F4266 ABBOTT A., b. Aug. 8, 1838, m. Feb. 26, 1860, S. HELEN CHASE.

F1822 Sophronia Locke, born in Seabrook, Apl. 8, 1805, died in Valley Falls, R. I., Jan. 17, 1894, married Oct. 20, 1830, EDMUND NOYES CLARKE of Salisbury, Mass., born Sept. 16, 1803. He was a tanner in Amesbury, Mass., and a coal dealer in Valley Falls, where he died Nov. 7, 1880.

Children of 7th Gen.
F4267 JOHN L., b. July 21, 1831, m. May 4, 1853, CORDELIA A. TITUS.
F4268 ADALINE L., b. Apl. 26, 1834, m. Sept. 1, 1857, JACOB M. HASKELL.
4269 EDMUND, b. June 11, 1843, was unmarried.
4270 MARY SOPHIA, b. Salisbury, Dec. 12, 1845, m. Valley Falls, R. I., June 25, 1879, JAMES P. JOHNSON of Penn., b. Trenton, N. J., Jan. 15, 1846, son of Julius and Deborah, lived New London, Conn., had: 4271 EDMUND C., b. Valley Falls, Oct. 3, 1883.

F1823 James Locke, born in Seabrook, Apl. 22, 1807, married Jan. 11, 1841, HANNAH P. CHESLEY of Rye, born in Rye, Oct. 23, 1813, died Sept. 2, 1850. He was a merchant in Seabrook and Florida, and died in Seabrook, Feb. 27, 1866.

Children of 7th Gen. b. in Seabrook.
F4272 JOHN W., b. Oct. 4, 1841, m. Aug. 11, 1869, SARAH LIZZIE SOUTH-
WICK.
4273 MARY O., b. May 6, 1843, m. July 24, 1871, JOSEPH L. LEAVITT,
b. Hampton, Feb. 25, 1838, d. Exeter, Apl. 26, 1914, son of Thomas
and Mary (Marston). Kept Hampton Beach Hotel since 1872,
had: 4274 SON, died young; 4275 JAMES L., b. Apl. 14, 1876,
of Arlington, Mass.; 4276 GEORGE T. W., b. June 17, 1879, of
Milwaukee; 4277 MARY M., b. Nov. 27, 1881, of Arlington,
Mass.
4278 JAMES B., b. Seab., June 1845, d. unmarried Seab., Sept. 5, 1897.
A clerk.

F1824 Adaline Locke, born in Seabrook, Feb. 17, 1811, died in Seabrook, Jan. 10, 1894, married in Hampton Falls, Jan. 18, 1835, JOHN PHILBRICK of Seabrook, born Sept. 24, 1791, son of John and Louisa (Hoag). He was a farmer in Seabrook and died there Sept. 25, 1884.
Children of 7th Gen. b. in Seabrook.
4279 SARAH J., b. Feb. 7, 1836, m. Aug. 27, 1862, FRANCIS M. DODGE
of Wenham, Mass., had: 4280 ADALINE P., b. Aug. 7, 1866.
4281 MARY B., b. Sept. 12, 1840, d. Oct. 6, 1841.
4282 MARY EMMA, b. July 15, 1843, m. Sept. 13, 1866, HORACE A. GOD-
FREY of Hampton Falls, had: 4283 JOHN P., died young; 4283a
ALIDA, b. 1870; 4284 ADALINE, b. 1875; 4285 PERSIS E., b. 1880;
4286 SARAH P., b. 1882.
4287 JOHN THOMAS, b. Sept. 5, 1846, d. 1888, m. Jan. 30, 1873, MARY
R. SANBORN of Chicago, had: 4288 JOHN, b. May 1877.

F1826 Nancy Locke, born in Seabrook in 1794, died June 21, 1840, married in Seabrook, July 6, 1812, NATHANIEL GOVE of Seabrook, born Apl. 26, 1790. He was a shoemaker and boat builder in Seabrook and died Aug. 30, 1849.
Children of 7th Gen. b. in Seabrook.
4289 HIRAM, b. Nov. 23, 1812, d. unmarried March, 1852.
F4290 LOUIS, b. Feb. 19, 1814, m. 1st, LURANA BOYD; m. 2nd, HARRIET
BOYD.
4291 CLARISSA, b. Dec. 14, 1816, d. Aug. 6, 1826.
4292 LUELLA, b. Oct. 27, 1823, d. July 2, 1848, m. Oct. 20, 1846,
BENJAMIN PERKINS of Seab., had: 4293 SAMUEL LEWIS, died
young.
4294 EMILY, b. Feb. 27, 1824, d. Dec. 2, 1908, m. CHARLES SANBORN of
Seabrook, a fisherman and boat builder; had no children.
4295 NATHANIEL, b. Dec. 12, 1826, d. unmarried, March 4, 1852.
4296 CLARISSA A., b. Oct. 30, 1834, d. unmarried, Nov. 1852.

SEVENTH GENERATION

F1827 Benjamin Locke, born in Seabrook, 1795, married MRS. MATILDA (JANVRIN) FELTCH, born in Seabrook in 1804. He was a boat builder in Seabrook and died Nov. 11, 1835. She married 3rd, —— FOSTER of Virginia, and died May 9, 1856.

Children of 7th Gen. b. in Seabrook.

4297 JOHN, b. Jan. 4, 1827, d. Seabrook, May 25, 1888, m. 1st, Jan. 2, 1848, ARVILLA A. COLLINS of Seab., b. 1828, d. May 1, 1863, dau. of Lewis; m. 2nd, Oct. 8, 1864, in Seab., SARAH S. EATON, b. S., June 5, 1843, d. S., Jan. 21, 1872, dau. of Oliver and Merriam. He was a shoemaker in Seabrook and by Arvilla had: 4298 CLARENCE E., b. Dec. 30, 1861, d. Exeter, Oct. 23, 1890, probably m. —— YOUNG.

F4299 JEREMIAH F., b. Dec. 6, 1828, m. Apl. 24, 1851, HANNAH SMITH.

4300 SALLY, b. Aug. 24, 1831, m. Seab., Sept. 16, 1855, CHARLES L. BROWN of Seab., lived S., had no children.

F1831 David Locke Gove, born in Seabrook, July 14, 1803, married in Salisbury, Mass., March 2, 1824, HARRIET LOWELL, born May 4, 1805, died in Amesbury, Mass., July 4, 1895, daughter of Stephen and Ann (Stevens) of Salisbury. He died in Salisbury, June 11, 1853.

Children of 7th Gen. b. in Salisbury.

4301 FRANCIS M., b. Sept. 14, 1826, m. MARY E. FREEMAN of York, Me., who d. Salisbury, Mass., May 27, 1859, aged 31. He d. Salisbury, Nov. 7, 1861, had no children.

4302 EDWARD PAYSON, b. June 3, 1828, m. ELEANOR W. GROUT, of Amesbury, who d. May 12, 1880. He d. in Amesbury, Aug. 14, 1899, and left two daus.: 4303 ELLEN FRANCES, b. 1856, a public school teacher in Malden, 1915; 4304 SARAH L., b. 1860, living in Amesbury, 1915.

F1836 Hiram D. Locke, married 1st, HARRIET YOUNG, who died in 1853, daughter of Capt. Elisha of Provincetown, N. Y. Hiram went West with his brother JOSEPH and married 2nd out there. Meanwhile his daughter lived with her uncle PHILIP, who adopted her.

Child of 7th Gen.

F4305 VIOLA, b. Feb. 22, 1850, m. Nov. 12, 1872, SAMUEL Y. NASH.

F1838 Mary J. Locke, born ——, married Oct. 20, 1831, CAPT. JOHN W. SANBORN of Farmington, Me., born in Andover, (?), June 30, 1806, son of Richard and Phebe (Page). He settled first in Lynn, then in Chesterville, Me.

Children of 7th Gen.
4306 Two children, died young.
4307 JOHN FRANCIS, b. Sept. 19, 1834, was Sergt. 6th Mass. Reg., lived Lawrence, Mass.
4308 THOMAS W., b. Dec. 16, 1835, m. Sept. 1861, JENNIE DUNKLEY, lived Silver Creek, Minn.
4309 PHILIP A., b. Oct. 31, 1837, lived Chesterville, Me.
4310 CHARLES R., b. twin, 1837, lived California.
4311 DEARBORN C., b. Feb. 24, 1839.
4312 KENDALL, b. Feb. 7, 1841.

F1840 Cynthia Locke, born in Seabrook, Dec. 29, 1801, died March 25, 1875, married Dec. 29, 1818, EDWARD D. GREELY of Seabrook, born in Salisbury, Mass., Dec. 12, 1801, son of John and Abigail (Smith).
Children of 7th Gen. b. in Seabrook.
4313 DUDLEY, b. July 18, 1823, died young.
4314 ABIGAIL, b. Nov. 8, 1824, m. THOMAS MORRILL of Amesbury, Mass., and had: 4315 LIZZIE; 4316 FRANK.
4317 S. LUCINDA, b. Apl. 16, 1831, m. HENRY DUCKWORTH of Amesbury, Mass., and had: 4318 EDWARD.
4319 A. JEREMIAH, b. Jan. 16, 1834, was a carriage painter, was first Lieut., 17th Mass. Reg., Captain of 2nd Reg. Mass. Artillery, d. unmarried, at Harristown, Ill., Dec. 12, 1874.
F4320 JOHN D., b. Dec. 8, 1841, m. LUCINDA BROWN of Seabrook.

F1841 Charles Locke, born in Seabrook in 1810, married 1st, ELIZA CHASE of Seabrook; married 2nd, MRS. BETSEY (JANVRIN) SCRIBNER of Newmarket, born in Newburyport, in 1809, died in Seabrook Sept. 9, 1882, daughter of Joseph Janvrin. He was a boatbuilder and carpenter in Seabrook and died June 14, 1883.
Children of 7th Gen. b. in Seabrook.
4321 CHARLES T., b. March 1838, d. Seabrook, 1908, m. Seab., Dec. 24, 1890, MRS. H. W. (PUTNAM) BLANCHARD, b. Millbury, Mass., 1827, dau. of Jonathan and Harriet; was a caterer in California, had no children.
F4322 FRANK E., b. July 8, 1848, m. Sept. 3, 1871, BETSEY B. WALTON.

F1843 Jeremiah A. Locke, born in Seabrook, Apl. 1819, married March 16, 1851, MRS. LUCINDA (GREEN) SANBORN, born in Stanstead, Can., Apl. 29, 1826, died in 1914. He was a boat builder and carpenter in Seabrook and died May 5, 1893.

SEVENTH GENERATION 215

Children of 7th Gen. b. in Seabrook.

F4323 GEORGE G., b. Feb. 22, 1852, m. Seab., March 29, 1874, MIMA A. DOW.
F4324 ALVIN H., b. July 25, 1859, m. June 25, 1881, ALWILDA A. EATON.
4325 MARY L., b. May 27, 1865, m. 1st, Nov. 23, 1889, FRANK W. LITTLE, b. 1862, a salesman of Newbury, Mass., had: 4326 ALFRED, b. 1896. She m. 2nd, May 30, 1898, RICHARD RONAN of Newbury.

F1881 Page Bachelder, born in Deerfield, July 8, 1788, married Feb. 28, 1811, BETSEY B. DARRAH, born June 18, 1786, died Sept. 13, 1879. He was a farmer in Deerfield and died Nov. 11, 1859.

Children of 7th Gen. b. in Deerfield.

4327 DANIEL C., b. Oct. 3, 1811, m. 1st, MARY RANDALL; m. 2nd, ———.
4328 STEPHEN J., b. Sept. 4, 1813, m. SARAH A. HALE; had six children.
4329 JOHN B., b. Feb. 24, 1816, m. RHODA DURGAN; had two children.
4330 GEORGE C., b. Jan. 8, 1819, m. DORA J. FOLSOM and had five children.
4331 MOSES B., b. Apl. 15, 1821, d. Manchester, Sept. 22, 1845.
4332 DUDLEY T., b. July 7, 1824, m. Nov. 3, 1850, LETTICE B. CAMPBELL, b. Jan. 9, 1823, was a grocer in Newburyport.

F1884 Jennie Bachelder, born in Deerfield, Oct. 22, 1796, married Feb. 20, 1822, JOSHUA LANE.

Children of 7th Gen.

4333 ERASTUS, b. March 16, 1823, d. Aug. 21, 1823.
4334 MEHITABLE J., b. Aug. 11, 1824, m. Nov. 11, 1847, GEORGE P. JAMES, and had four children.
4335 THOMAS A., b. June 17, 1827, m. May 4, 1847, HANNAH M. SMITH, and had four children.
4336 ABIGAIL A., b. Feb. 8, 1831, d. Feb. 15, 1854.
4337 SARAH E., b. June 1, 1833, m. Sept. 16, 1855, GEORGE F. MOOR, and had two children.
4338 ADONIRAM J., b. Oct. 30, 1835, m. March 4, 1856, MIRA W. ALDRICH.

F1901 Frances Dearborn, born in Portsmouth, May 19, 1801, died in Cambridge, Mass., Jan. 21, 1876, married Sept. 11, 1823, ELDER MOSES HOWE, born Haverhill, Mass., Aug. 22, 1789, died Cambridge, June 25, 1881.

Children of 7th Gen.

4339 MOSES G., b. Aug. 14, 1826, m. 1st, LYDIA VARNUM; m. 2nd, MARY VARNUM; m. 3rd, ABBIE ———, lived Cambridge, Mass., had son: 4340 B. V. HOWE of Boston, optician.
4341 WILLIAM S., b. Nov. 9, 1831, d. New Bedford, May 22, 1860.
F4342 LYMAN B., b. Jan. 25, 1838, m. MARY L. PERRY.
4344 IRENA, b. ———, m. twice.

F1906 Julia A. Dearborn, born in Portsmouth, Nov. 27, 1806, died in Portsmouth, Oct. 14, 1882, married in Portsmouth, Nov. 30, 1834, DAVISON WEBSTER of Strafford, born Sept. 30, 1811. He was a teacher in Strafford, Boston and Portsmouth, and died Jan. 7, 1844.

Children of 7th Gen.

F4345 ANNETTE A., b. Dec. 21, 1835, m. Oct. 26, 1863, JOHN H. TOMLINSON.
F4346 MARY H. M., b. Jan. 7, 1838, m. May 22, 1865, LEANDER M. ORMSBY.
4347 HENRY C., b. Ports., Nov. 10, 1839, was Lieut. U. S. Navy, d. Plymouth, N. C., Sept. 23, 1862, unmarried.
F4348 FRANK D., b. Sept. 4, 1841, m. 1st, NELLIE ———; m. 2nd, MARY FIVE.
F4349 GEORGINE H., b. Aug. 10, 1843, m. Dec. 2, 1863, FRED F. MOSES.

F1909 Daniel G. Dearborn, born in Portsmouth, Aug. 24, 1811, died Dec. 6, 1887, married Apl. 23, 1851, LUCINDA BERGER, born July 21, 1829, lived Toledo, Ohio, and Oakland, Cal.

Children of 7th Gen.

4350 CHARLES W., b. Feb. 29, 1852, m. June 6, 1876, KITTY D. HALL, b. Feb. 27, 1857, lived Oakland, Cal.
4351 MARY E., b. June 5, 1854, m. CHARLES S. GOODMAN.
4352 SARAH D., b. June 6, 1857, m. SAMUEL J. MERRILL of Los Angeles, Cal.
4353 GILMAN W., b. Feb. 15, 1859, lived Oakland, Cal.
4354 DELIA T., b. Oct. 29, 1865.

F1913 Mary J. Tilton, born Aug. 8, 1804, died Aug. 4, 1878, married Jan. 8, 1833, BENJAMIN F. BUTLER, born May 10, 1810, died Nov. 7, 1896.

Children of 7th Gen.

4355 HORACE B., b. Ports., Nov. 26, 1833, d. E. Boston, Dec. 26, 1910, m. SARAH A. HAMILTON, and had: 4356 BLANCHE; 4357 MARY.
4358 GEORGE A., b. Boston, Jan. 15, 1836, d. Aug. 6, 1895, m. 1st, MRS. LUCY A. SAWYER; m. 2nd, MRS. ELLEN LOUD, had: 4359 GEORGE A.; 4360 HENRY F.; 4361 a daughter.
4362 EDWARD P., b. March 8, 1838, d. Nov. 3, 1905, m. MARTHA G. MCMULLEN, had: 4363 REV. FRANK E.; 4364 DR. JOHN E., of Boston.
4365 SARAH T., b. Aug. 6, 1840, m. Sept. 18, 1866, W. H. H. EMMONS, had: 4366 HARRY; 4367 EDITH; 4368 GRACE; 4369 JENNIE; 4370 PAUL D.
4371 BENJAMIN F., JR., b. Feb. 18, 1844, m. LOUISE ORDIORNE, had: 4372 HERBERT F.; 4373 HAROLD O.; 4374 NELLIE.
4375 MARY JANE, b. Oct. 14, 1846, m. Sept. 23, 1873, HENRY NEWCOMB, had: 4376 ALMIRA, lived West Medford, Mass.
4377 ELIZABETH F., b. July 7, 1849, is unmarried.

SEVENTH GENERATION

F1920 Rev. Jeremiah Tilton, born in Deerfield, Sept. 16, 1816, married 1st, ABBY S. FREEZE, born in 1818, died in 1858; married 2nd, MARTHA JACKMAN, born in 1822, died in 1894. He died in Littleton, Oct. 5, 1893.

Children of 7th Gen. first b. Deerfield, last b. Sanbornton.

4378 AUSTIN VALECOURT, b. July 26, 1841, m. MARTHA GOVE, and he d. Concord, 1885.
4379 ABBIE RUTHENA, b. Nov. 22, 1842, d. June 13, 1912, m. Sanbornton, Nov. 9, 1864, J. B. WADLEIGH, b. Apl. 25, 1829, and had: 4380 OSCAR S.; 4381 FRED T.; 4382 HELEN A.; 4383 INEZ H.
4384 SARAH TRUE, b. Feb. 10, 1844, d. Concord, Aug. 8, 1903, m. Milford, Dec. 25, 1866, CAPT. LYMAN JACKMAN, b. Aug. 15, 1837, d. in Concord, June 23, 1913, had: 4385 CHARLES L.; 4386 FREEMAN.
4387 SARAH FREEZE, b. Feb. 10, 1844, d. 1844, one of triplets.
4388 SARAH FRENCH, b. Feb. 10, 1844.
4389 HARRIET INEZ, b. Oct. 7, 1845, m. Milford, Dec. 7, 1869, JOHN A. OBER, b. Amherst, Oct. 4, 1845, d. Milford, Sept. 7, 1910.
4390 CAREY FULLER, b. Jan. 10, 1848, m. Concord, Jan. 6, 1869, HELEN S. BROWN, b. Dec. 18, 1846, d. Concord, March 21, 1913. He d. Concord, Nov. 11, 1875.
4391 OSCAR IRVING, b. Sept. 24, 1849, d. Feb. 23, 1864.
4392 ALBERT FREEMAN, b. Limerick, Me., May 18, 1851, m. 1st, 1874, ANNIE LOWE; m. 2nd, Apl 30, 1884, HATTIE FRENCH, b. Keene, Apl. 27, 1858, d. Peterborough, Oct. 26, 1886.
4393 JOSIAH O., b. Limerick, July 29, 1853, m. Oct. 31, 1894, FLORENCE STRATTON, b. Lexington, Mass., Oct. 15, 1868. He is a physician in Lexington, Mass.
4394 MARY ELIZA, b. Aug. 21, 1856, d. Aug. 19, 1890, unmarried.
4395 WILL FREEZE, b. June 2, 1858, m. Sept. 30, 1885, EMMA MESSERGER, b. Natick, Mass., March 25, 1857, and had: 4396 LOUISA M.
4397 ELLEN GRACE, b. Oct. 16, 1861, m. CHARLES CROCKETT, b. Sanbornton, 1860.
4398 ROYAL JEREMIAH, b. Oct. 25, 1863, d. unmarried Seattle, Wash., 1896.
4399 MARTHA LUCRETIA, b. Jan 27, 1866, is unmarried 1915.

F1924 Meshech Weare, born in Deerfield, Feb. 8, 1795, married June 8, 1820, MERIBAH GREEN, born Sept. 8, 1790, died Feb. 14, 1822. He was in the War of 1812 and after the death of his first wife, he went to Moreland, Vt., then an unbroken wilderness. He died May 5, 1874.

Children of 7th Gen.

4400 MESHECH GARDNER, b. Oct. 28, 1820, m. Oct. 6, 1842, ABIGAIL B. YOUNG, b. Feb. 5, 1824, and they had: 4401 ALBERT M., b. Nov. 26, 1846; 4402 CHARLES D., b. Feb. 16, 1848, lives in Gilmanton; 4403 FRANK J., b. March 19, 1856, d, June 18, 1881.
4404 MERIBAH G., b. Jan. 26, 1822, m. GEORGE F. BROWN of Deer., b. Nov. 20, 1822, d. Sept. 23, 1902.

F1930 James Locke, born in Sutton, Vt., about 1800, married MARY TOWNSEND, who died in 1886. He was an officer in N. H. State Militia in 1843.

Children of the 7th Gen.

4405 JACOB F., b. ——, m. CATHERINE NEWELL, lived Pillsbury, Minn., had: WINFIELD S.; WILLIAM P.

F4406 SIMON J., b. ——, m. MARIA BURNHAM.

4407 WILLIAM P., killed at Fredericksburg, Va., Dec. 13, 1862, unmarried.

4408 J. FRANK, b. Ossipee, Apl. 27, 1846, m. 1st, Wolfeboro, Sept. 8, 1870, MARIETTA REMICK, of Wolfboro, b. 1849, d. Jan. 26, 1873; m. 2nd, 1878, ANNA S. PEASE. He was said to be a colonel in war of Rebellion, was ordained a minister in South Berwick, Me., in 1870, settled in Burnhamville, Minn., in 1879, later about 1898 was in Long Prairie, Minn. He was also an M. D. and Judge, had: 4408a GRACE E., b. Apl. 17, 1872; 4408 b. Daughter.

4408c ARVILLA B., d. 1863.

4409 CHARLES A., probably d. unmarried at sea.

F1942 Eliphalet Locke, born in Barnstead, July 9, 1801, married Sept. 1820, SALLY STANTON, born in Strafford, 1799, died in Barnstead, Sept. 30, 1875, daughter of William. He was a farmer and carpenter in Barnstead and died May 7, 1871.

Children of 7th Gen.

F4410 MARY A., b. March 1, 1821, m. July 1839, WILLIAM H. RIXFORD.

4411 JOHN W. F., b. Oct. 6, 1838, was a lawyer, selectman, Barnstead, 1867-70, representative to legislature 1869-70, drowned Apl. 25, 1873, unmarried.

F1943 Tamson Locke, born in Barnstead, Aug., 1804, died July 8, 1871, married in Barnstead, Oct. 20, 1825, WILLIAM BERRY of Barnstead, born in 1799, son of John and Hannah (Garland). He was a farmer and state treasurer, and died in 1859.

Child of 7th Gen.

4412 SARAH F., b. Barnstead, 1830, m. 1855, JAMES R. BERRY of Strafford. He was a mason of Barrington, had: 4413 IDA, b. 1856; 4414 CLARA, b. 1859; 4415 ETTA, b. 1864; 4416 ELLA, b. 1870.

F1944 Phineas Locke, born in Barnstead, July 11, 1806, married Nov. 21 (27), 1830, MARY PINKHAM of Farmington, born in New Durham, May 2, 1811, died in Barnstead, Jan. 18, 1892. He was a farmer in New Durham, 1830-48, later in Barnstead, and died there July 7, 1880.

SEVENTH GENERATION

Children of 7th Gen.

4417 EDWARD J., b. New Durham, Apl. 23, 1832, d. July 30, 1908, m. Apl. 28, 1870, BETSEY NUTTER, was a farmer in North Barnstead, had: 4418 EDWIN N., b. July 26, 1872, a painter in Barns., unmarried.

4419 JULIA A., b. New Durham, Sept. 15, 1841, d. Aug. 19, 1881, m. Aug. 19, 1870, CHARLES TIBBETTS of Alton, had no children.

F4420 WILLIAM H., b. Jan. 12, 1847, m. May 1, 1869, LIZZIE S. PICKERING.

4421 SMITH W., b. Barnstead, Nov. 5, 1852, was a farmer in Barns., and d. unmarried Dec. 12, 1906.

F1945 Lovie Locke, born in Barnstead, Dec. 1808, died in Chichester, Apl. 15, 1849, married in New Durham, Nov. 28, 1833, JOSEPH WENTWORTH PERKINS of Exeter, born in Rochester, Apl. 1, 1809, died in Exeter, Apl. 23, 1884.

Children of 7th Gen.

4422 SALLIE, b. 1834, d. 1856, m. —— CANNEY.
4423 JOHN L., b. Exeter, Apl. 4, 1837, d. Concord, Oct. 26, 1908, m. June 18, 1860, SUSAN CARLETON of Epsom, dau. of George and Nancy (Tripp). He was a farmer in Hooksett, and had: 4424 NELLIE B., b. June 3, 1867, m. Jan. 14, 1892, SAMUEL B. FLANDERS of Pembroke, and they have: 4425 ETTA L., b. Dec. 28, 1892.
4426 EMMA, b. ——, m. JOSEPH D. YOUNG of New Durham, have no children.
4427 ADDIE S., b. Feb. 1841, d. Farmington, Jan. 13, 1893, m. DR. MARK WALKER of Barnstead, who d. 1879, had: 4428 ALBION N., b. June 1864; 4429 AGNES, b. May 1865.
4430 WILLIAM, b. ——, d. 1883, was m. in Mass., and had two daus.

F1950 Annie Locke, born in Barrington, Apl. 28, 1808, died Dec. 17, 1864, married in Rochester, Oct. 4, 1832, AMOS VARNEY, born Farmington, Jan. 20, 1805, son of Faustus and Hannah. He was a farmer in Farmington and died March 22, 1858.

Children of 7th Gen. b. in Madbury or Farmington.

4431 CHARLES E., b. Jan. 24, 1834, d. Jan. 15, 1835.
4432 EDWARD, b. Oct. 15, 1836, d. Jan. 25, 1838.
F4433 ALBERT, b. Aug. 8, 1838, m. Feb. 6, 1867, ANTOINETTE CROCKETT.
4434 LYDIA L., b. Aug. 14, 1840, m. Farmington, Nov. 17, 1876, JOHN F. SCRUTON, lived Farmington. (His 2nd marriage.) They had: 4435 EUNICE, who m. ALBERT MEADER; 4436 ARTHUR; 4437 ALICE.
4438 SARAH J., b. Apl. 6, 1843, d. March 18, 1844.

F1951 James Locke, born in Barrington, Aug. 8, 1811, married in 1836, ELLEN C. KIMBALL, born in Farmington, Oct. 1, 1819, d. Oct. 21, 1877, daughter of Solomon and Martha (Babb). He lived in Rochester and died Apl. 1879.

Children of 7th Gen. b. in Rochester.

4439 Two children died young.
F4440 EDWARD FRANKLIN, b. Aug. 4, 1842, m. Sept. 1, 1869, JULIA E. JANVRIN.
4441 CHARLES C., b. Sept. 15, 1846, died young man, unmarried.
4442 LIZZIE E., b. Apl. 24, 1854, m. 1st, Apl. 23, 1872, HENRY CLOUGH, who d. March 17, 1890; m. 2nd, Apl. 17, 1892, EDWIN FLANDERS, lived Gilmanton and Rockport, Mo. Had: 4443 NELLIE E., m. SUMNER J. GARDNER; 4444 AMY. Lizzie d. Belmont 1907.

F1954 Charlotte Locke, born in Barrington, Oct. 8, 1815, died Aug. 24, 1882, married 1st, Dec. 29, 1836, CHARLES P. KIMBALL of Rochester. He was a farmer in Dover, was highway surveyor and constable in Deerfield in 1835, and died at Hilton Head, S. C., Sept. 14, 1862. He was a son of Solomon and Martha (Babb). She married 2nd, in Farmington in 1871, JACOB B. SMITH, a farmer in Strafford.

Children of 7th Gen. all Kimballs.

4445 ELIZABETH M., b. Farmington, Nov. 3, 1838, d. Nov. 23, 1874, m. 1st, June 1, 1858, CHARLES R. THOMPKINS of Dover, who was in Co. K, 11th N. H. Vols. and d. Knoxville, Tenn., Nov. 6, 1863. She m. 2nd, EBEN PARSHLEY of Strafford, had: 4446 ISABEL THOMPKINS, b. Nov. 15, 1860, d. Oct. 12, 1881; 4447 HERMAN K. PARSHLEY, b. Sept. 3, 1866.
4448 EDWARD L., b. Apl. 25, 1840, m. Feb. 27, 1864, CLARA WALKER of Rochester. He is a shoe cutter in Roch., had: 4449 ETHLYN, b. July 10, 1866.
4450 MARY AUGUSTA, b. Aug. 14, 1842, m. 1st, LABAN MILES of Madbury; m. 2nd, Feb. 15, 1868, J. LEIGHTON DUNTLEY of Roch. They lived Medford, Mass., and had: 4451 ALICE G. MILES, b. June 15, 1864, d. Aug. 2, 1865; 4452 EDWARD L. MILES, b. Apl. 12, 1866; 4453 WILBUR L. DUNTLEY, b. Dec. 27, 1871.
4454 SARAH W., b. Apl. 7, 1845, d. Sept. 1873, m. 1st, CHARLES SMITH; m. 2nd, LEWIS DAVIS, and had: 4455 CARRIE K., b. March 21, 1866; 4456 CHARLOTTE, b. Jan. 1868.
4457 LYDIA J., b. Nov. 7, 1847, m. June 23, 1867, HENRY F. WALKER of Rochester, b. Strafford, June 25, 1845, had: 4458 LOTTIE P., b. March 3, 1863; 4459 GEORGE C. P., b. Feb. 2, 1872.
4460 ALICE N., b. 1850, d. 1856.
4461 CHARLES F., b. 1852, d. 1852.

SEVENTH GENERATION

F1955 Sarah W. Locke, born in Barrington, March 10, 1818, died Dec. 30, 1844, married June 13, 1837, OBADIAH VARNEY of Farmington, born in Barrington, Apl. 20, 1811. He was a stone cutter, lived in Rochester and Rockport, Mass., and died May 13, 1840.

Children of 7th Gen.

4462 BOY, died infant.
4463 LAVINIA V., b. Rochester, Oct. 1, 1839, m. Feb. 13, 1859, CYRUS LIBBY, b. Jan. 1, 1830, lived Waterboro, Me., had: 4464 CHARLES E., b. Feb. 13, 1861; 4465 SARAH W., b. Apl. 4, 1863; 4466 LAVINIA E., b. June 30, 1866; 4467 CYRUS O., b. Apl. 27, 1871.

F1956 Elizabeth Locke, born in Barrington, July 6, 1820, died Nov. 23, 1898, married 1st, Sept. 2, 1841, LEWIS THOMPSON, born Epsom, Sept. 23, 1819, died Epsom, Sept. 18, 1862, a farmer in Epsom; married 2nd, Nov. 20, 1864, ISRAEL DURGIN of Northwood, b. Oct. 20, 1797, a farmer in Northwood. He died Pittsfield, Dec. 12, 1880.

Children of 7th Gen., all Thompsons.

4468 LYDIA M., b. Nov. 21, 1843, m. Dec. 25, 1862, JOSEPH P. LOCKE, # 5062, b. June 30, 1842, lived Epsom.
4469 SARAH W., b. Dec. 27, 1845, m. Sept. 20, 1883, HENRY ARNETT, had no children.
4470 MARY A., b. Dec. 3, 1847, m. Nov. 22, 1871, WILBUR F. FERNALD, lived Dover and had: 4471 ERNEST W., b. May 16, 1875; 4472 RALPH S., b. July 25, 1883.
4473 HENRY F., b. July 31, 1852, d. May 1, 1867.
4474 LUCY L., b. Apl. 14, 1856, m. 1st, Nov. 17, 1883, GEORGE W. FRIEL and had: 4475 ARTHUR O., b. May 31, 1885; m. 2nd, 1900, in Warner, CHARLES A. BEAN. Lived Epsom.

F1957 Lydia M. Locke, born in Barrington, Aug. 10, 1822, died Sept. 12, 1852, married in Rochester, Feb. 2, 1842, STEPHEN M. GOVE of Seabrook, born Sept. 5, 1821, son of Edwin and Elizabeth (Morrill). He was a farmer in Seabrook, and died July 5, 1881.

Children of 7th Gen. b. in Seabrook.

4476 HENRY MCLAURIN, b. Feb. 24, 1845, has fruit store Waltham, Mass., is unmarried.
4477 MELVIN LAGRAND, b. Sept. 9, 1846, m. AGNES ———; a merchant Illyria, Ohio, had: 4478 FLORENCE, b. 1895.
4479 HORACE NEWTON, b. March 23, 1849, m. Oakdale, 1874, CATHERINE LAWTON. Live Oakdale, Neb., had: 4480 GERTRUDE B., b. Dec. 18, 1875.
4481 OTIS MEADER, b. May 3, 1851, m. Waltham, Mass., NELLIE M. LOVELL, b. Weston, Mass., March 17, 1843, d. Waltham, July 29, 1898; was a state senator, lived Waltham.

F1958 Samson B. Locke, born in Barnstead, in 1808, died in Barnstead, Oct. 18, 1882, married June 26, 1828, ESTHER NUTTER, who died Feb. 19, 1893.

Children of 7th Gen. b. in Barnstead.

4482 NANCY, b. Nov. 4, 1830, d. Alton, Dec. 5, 1888, m. JAMES KIMBALL, and had: 4483 AMANDA G.; 4484 LAURA, m. JOHN HILL; 4485 SETH H., m. MARY SHAW, lives So. Alton; 4486 IDA, m. FRANK NUTTER, lives Center Barnstead; 4487 MARTIN L.

4488 MARY ABIGAIL, b. 1832, m. Dec. 26, 1874, MARTIN V. B. LANG, b. 1837, d. Sept. 1899, son of John. Was in N. H. Legislature 1891–2; had no children.

4489 ELIZA J., b. 1834, m. Barns., Nov. 8, 1854, JOHN JACKSON LANG, had: 4490 GEORGE, m. CHARLOTTE DREW; 4491 HARRIE; 4492 WM. HENRY.

F4493 LYDIA A., b. 1835, m. ORRIN CHESLEY of Center Barns.

F4494 JAMES O., b. Dec. 24, 1837, m. June 30, 1867, MARY E. NUTTER.

F4495 JETHRO N., b. Apl. 17, 1840, m. Oct. 23, 1863, ELECTRA CHESLEY.

F1959 Enoch Locke, born in Concord, Aug. 21, 1811, died in Barnstead, June 11, 1896, married in Nottingham, Dec. 26, 1843, MARTHA B. LANE, born in Hampton, Dec. 12, 1812, died in Barnstead, Oct. 20, 1895, daughter of David and Sally (Brown). He was a farmer in Barnstead.

Children of 7th Gen. b. in Barnstead.

F4496 SARAH ELIZABETH, b. Feb. 6, 1846, m. March 2, 1872, GEORGE W. DUDLEY.

4497 MARTHA FRANCES, b. Aug. 19, 1848, m. Barns., March 2, 1872, CHARLES A. PERKINS, b. Pittsfield, 1847, son of David and Sally; lived Concord and Central Point, Oregon, had: 4498 JAMES LOCKE, b. Nov. 26, 1876, a doctor in Cranford, N. J.; 4499 ERNEST, b. June 21, 1879, a grocer in Roxbury, Mass.

4500 EMMA ELFREDA, b. May 31, 1850, m. Oct. 15, 1876, THOMAS MILTON BERRY of Concord, b. Pittsfield, 1849, son of John B. and Mary E. A grocer in Concord, had: 4501 MARTHA H., b. Apl. 16, 1877; 4502 MARY E., b. March 16, 1887, m. PHILIP BROWER, in electrical business, Concord.

4503 AUGUSTA APPLETON, b. March 16, 1853, m. Manchester, June 28, 1898, NATHANIEL SOUTHERD of Manchester, lived Concord.

4504 GEORGEANNA, b. Oct. 31, 1855, m. WILLIAM HAYES, a farmer of Alton Center.

F1960 Mary Ann Locke, born in 1817, died Apl. 5, 1885, married in Barnstead, June 3, 1838, JOHN HILL, born 1812, son of John and Laura (Kimball). He was a wheelwright in Barnstead, served in 15th N. H. Reg. and died on return from war in 1863.

Children of 7th Gen. b. in Barnstead.
F4505 ABBIE H., b. 1839, m. Sept. 1854, JOSEPH W. HOWARD.
  4506 ENOCH W., b. Apl. 1, 1848, m. Aug. 19, 1871, SUSAN BROWN; was a carpenter in Barnstead.
  4507 JOHN DANA, b. March 5, 1858, m. Oct. 5, 1882, GEORGIE SMITH, who d. Pittsfield, Nov. 1, 1897. Lived No. Barnstead, 1898.

F1973 Jacob B. Locke, born in Barnstead, Jan. 15, 1818, died Aug. 25, 1860, married in 1840, PARMELIA H. DOW, born in Barnstead, 1818, died in Barnstead, Feb. 15, 1875, daughter of Timothy. He was selectman 1849–50, representative to Legislature 1859–60, justice of peace, and conveyancer.

Children of 7th Gen. b. in Barnstead.
  4508 NELLIE S., b. Aug. 25, 1841, d. No. Barns., Feb. 3, 1913, unmarried.
  4509 JAMES C., b. Sept. 7, 1846, m. Barnstead, May 10, 1885, EMMA ROGERS, b. England, 1848. She was a teacher, dau. of William and Catherine. He was farmer in Barns. and had no children.
  4510 (Barns. town records give, SARAH A. E., b. Aug. 9, 1841.)

F1977 Rachel Fuller, born March 10, 1795, died March 31, 1871, married Nov. 12, 1812, NATHAN TIRRILL, who died in Hebron in 1835.

Children of 7th Gen.
  4511 WOOSTER, b. ——, m. JUDITH VEASEY, and had: 4512 CHARLES; 4513 MELISSA.
  4514 LODEMA, b. Nov. 9, 1813, d. June 22, 1883, m. July 4, 1836, AARON H. FOGG. Lived Bristol, had four children.
  4515 HAZEN, b. 1818, d. May 1901, m. ADELINE H. WISE; m. 2nd, ARVILLA VARNUM. Lived Mass. and had nine children.
  4516 RUSSELL P., b. March 30, 1830, m. Aug. 16, 1855, EMELINE FRETTS, b. Oct. 5, 1839, lived Hebron and had seven children.

F1978 Josiah Fuller, born in 1802, married 1st, Mary Pike of Sanbornton; married 2nd, —— HUCKINS, was a farmer in Bristol, and died March 2, 1849.

Children of 7th Gen.
  4517 MERRILL, b. ——.
  4518 JULIA ANN, b. Aug. 5, 1831, d. Boston, Sept. 24, 1888, m. Oct. 23, 1850, AMASA DREW, b. Dec. 20, 1822, son of Amos and Dorothy. He was gatekeeper and ticket agent East Boston Ferry, had four children.

F1980 Abigail Fuller, born ——, died Feb. 26, 1839, married THOMAS ROBERT EMMONS, May 28, 1822, born in Bristol, Oct. 28, 1803, son of Moses. He was a farmer in Bristol; married 2nd, BETSEY WEBSTER in 1866, and died Feb. 26, 1891.

Children of 7th Gen. b. in Bristol.

4519 DAMON Y., b. Nov. 24, 1822, m. Jan. 15, 1845, HULDAH A. CHANDLER, a farmer in Bristol, had no children.

4520 MOSES, b. Hebron, May 2, 1825, d. Bristol, Dec. 3, 1892, m. Dec. 1848, LUCY M. BOHONON. Was three years on whaler, was a stone mason, and had five children in Bristol.

4521 LYFORD, b. 1828, went whaling and was never heard from.

4522 DARIUS, m. KATE MAXWELL, and lived in Somerville, Mass.

4523 ROSE W., b. July 21, 1835, d. Bristol, Jan. 23, 1877, m. March 30, 1854, WILLIAM TODD, b. June 3, 1832. Had two children in So. Boston.

F1983 Favor Locke, born in Bristol, Apl. 21, 1797, married in Bristol, Jan. 30, 1821, SALLY C. DOLOFF, # 1997, born in Bridgewater, May 30, 1798, died in Bridgewater, May 29, 1894, daughter of Abram and Rachel (Locke). He was a farmer and church deacon in Bristol, and died July 10, 1882.

Children of 7th Gen. b. in Bristol.

F4524 JANE, b. Aug. 22, 1823, m. Dec. 26, 1843, JOHN F. CASS.

F4525 ORRIN, b. Jan. 13, 1826, m. Apl. 19, 1849, NANCY J. FAVOR.

4526 ABRAM DOLOFF, b. Bristol, May 21, 1828, d. Concord, June 24, 1910, m. Bristol, Jan. 16, 1853, SARAH A. SLEEPER, b. Bris., May 10, 1830, d. June 1, 1901, dau. of Daniel and Dorothy (Tilton); m. 2nd, Jan. 16, 1902, AUGUSTA A. LOCKE of Concord, # 8118. He had no children, was a retired laborer in Concord.

F4527 FAVOUR, b. July 5, 1831, m. Nov. 27, 1862, ADALINE W. THOMPSON.

F1984 Roxy Locke, born in Bristol, Dec. 3, 1798, died July 7, 1884, married in Bridgewater, Dec. 2, 1819, LEVI LOCKE DOLOFF, # 1996, born Nov. 9, 1795, son of Abram and Rachel (Locke), # 603, lived on the Hook farm in Bristol and died Apl. 6, 1880, a very prosperous farmer.

Children of 7th Gen.

4528 SON, d. Dec. 24, 1820.

4529 DAU., d. Apl. 28, 1825.

F4530 SOLON, b. Oct. 3, 1827, m. May 1, 1850, NANCY SYMONDS.

4531 HANNAH F., b. Bristol, Jan. 6, 1831, d. B., March 9, 1902, m. Dec. 3, 1850, ABNER FOWLER, b. Hill, March 7, 1827, d. March 31, 1889, son of Abraham. A farmer in Bristol, had no children.

F4532 ORRIN LOCKE, b. July 26, 1833, m. May 26, 1859, CLARINDA ELLIOT.

4533 GILBERT B., b. Bristol, Dec. 7, 1835, m. 1st, Apl. 22, 1857, MARGARET H. TILTON, b. Oct. 15, 1834, d. June 1, 1867; m. 2nd, July 1868, MARY E. VOSE, who d. Dec. 28, 1869; m. 3rd, May 7, 1870, MRS. EMILY (EATON) SPENCER, b. 1841. He was a farmer in Bridgewater, had: 4534 ABNER F., b. July 3, 1863; 4535 ANSELL G., b. Dec. 24, 1869, m. June 6, 1891, CARRIE B. CURRIER, b. 1872, who had: 4536 HELEN M., b. 1893; 4537 AGNES M., b. 1872, m. HARRIS W. HAMMOND.

SEVENTH GENERATION

F1985 Sherburne Locke, born in Bristol Apl. 10, 1801, married Sept. 26, 1822, SALLY I. HILLS, born in Northfield, Nov. 26, 1800, died in Cedar Falls, Iowa, March 19, 1863, daughter of Daniel and Hannah (Young). He was a stone cutter in Iowa, and died Faribault, Minn., Nov. 23, 1873, or (March 1874).

Children of 7th Gen.

4538 HANNAH FAVOR, b. Bristol, June 26, 1826, m. May 7, 1854, SAMUEL LITTLE, who d. at Austin, Minn., Nov. 23, 1881. She lived there 1898.
4539 SARAH JANE, b. Cayuga, N. Y., Feb. 15, 1833, m. Oct. 30, 1855, HENRY ROBERTS, b. England, July 19, 1832, lived Austin, Minn., had two daus. 1898.
F4540 LEVI D., b. March 23, 1835, m. June 8, 1863, ELIZABETH HODGES.
4541 BENJAMIN, b. ——, m. ——— ———, lived Des Moines, Iowa.

F1986 Levina Locke, born in Bristol, Jan. 29, 1805, died in Bristol, Apl 16, 1884, married Sept. 16, 1824, HENRY WELLS of Bristol, born in New Hampton, June 28, 1802, son of Peter. In 1830 he moved from Plymouth to Bristol, was a carpenter and selectman and died Apl. 26, 1883.

Children of 7th Gen.

4542 PETER, b. Bristol, Dec. 21, 1825, d. Oct. 1, 1844.
F4543 BENJAMIN LOCKE, b. Dec. 21, 1832, m. 1st, 1857, MARY SLEEPER; m. 2nd, Aug. 12, 1866, HANNAH ROLLINS.

F1987 Joanna Locke, born in Bristol, Apl. 6, 1807, died in Caledonia, Minn., Nov. 2, 1892, married in Bristol, March 13, 1826, JACOB WEBSTER, born in New Hampton, Aug. 29, 1805. He first went to New York, then in 1853 to Minnesota, where he was a farmer and carpenter and died Oct. 26, 1873.

Children of 7th Gen.

4544 HANNAH, b. Bristol, Oct. 25, 1826, d. Lowell, Sept. 19, 1842.
4545 ELIZABETH AMANDA, b. New Hampton, July 13, 1828, d. Caledonia, Minn., Feb. 15, 1855, m. WASHINGTON F. ROBINSON, who d. Redwood Falls, Minn.
4546 BENJAMIN BAILEY, b. Alexandria, Apl. 22, 1841, m. Dec. 25, 1864, SALLY A. WHEATON. Lived Caledonia, Minn., 1899.

F1989 Benjamin Locke, born in Bristol, Apl. 17, 1810, married Apl. 18, 1835, HARRIET MASON, born in Bristol, July 22, 1814, died in Bristol, Nov. 16, 1856. She married 2nd, NICHOLAS DOLOFF, # 1999. Benjamin was a farmer in Bristol, and died March 30, 1840.

Children of 7th Gen.
4547 MARY, b. Bristol, July 19, 1837, m. Oct. 11, 1855, THOMAS KNIGHT, b. Franconia, Sept. 28, 1828; lived St. Johnsbury, Vt., had: 4548 GRACE; and 4549 a boy, died young.
4550 ESTHER M., b. Bris., Apl 28, 1839, d. Boston, Dec. 9, 1880, m. Jan. 8, 1858, WARNER HUNTOON, had no children.

F1990 Hannah F. Locke, born in Bristol, June 12, 1812, died in Bristol, Apl. 21, 1894, married May 29, 1832, KIAH WELLS of Bristol, born in Plymouth, May 24, 1810, son of Peter and Hannah (Blake). He was a farmer, moved in 1847 from Plymouth to Bristol, and died May 31, 1888.

Children of 7th Gen. b. in Bristol.
F4551 JOHN WINTER, b. May 11, 1833, m. 1853, ROSE BOSWELL.
4552 CHARLES WESLEY, b. Sept. 30, 1837, m. 1st, July 2, 1856, SARAH C. FERRIN, b. Concord, July 13, 1835, d. Minonk, Ill., Sept. 27, 1858; m. 2nd, March 2, 1861, A. BURLEIGH, b. Sanbornton, March 16, 1834, d. Apl. 1, 1899; m. 3rd, Nov. 7, 1900, MRS. ALICE B. (DENNETT) JONES. He was a carpenter and builder in Sanbornton, and adopted 4553 CARRIE MAY, b. Jan. 24, 1867.
4554 AMANDA WEBSTER, b. May 27, 1849, m. Apl. 2, 1868, CHARLES FLANDERS, b. Chelsea, Vt., Dec. 4, 1845, son of James and Lucy, had: 4555 OWEN L., b. Bris. Dec. 17, 1869, lives Bristol. CHARLES, m. 2nd, in Boston and lived there.

F1991 Sally D. Locke, born in Bristol, Sept. 4, 1814, died in Bristol, Apl. 18, 1898, married June 28, 1837, WINTHROP R. FELLOWS, born in Bristol, Aug. 1, 1813, son of Jonathan. He was a farmer and died in Bristol Jan. 11, 1891.

Children of 7th Gen.
4556 WARREN GERRY, b. Wentworth, Apl. 22, 1838, d. Bristol, July 4, 1897, m. 1st, Feb. 1, 1864, CAROLINE L. NUTTING of Newport, who d. Jan. 2, 1891, aged 56-2-26; m. 2nd, Concord, June 25, 1894, MRS. MARY J. (TRAVIS) LEWIS, b. Goshen, Jan. 13, 1837. He was a salesman in Boston, had: 4557 JOSEPH W., b. Nov. 17, 1866, is manager of theatrical troupe.
4558 LORETTA, b. Aug. 26, 1847, m. 1st, Oct. 7, 1883, ELMER V. PIKE, b. 1847, d. March 27, 1894; m. 2nd, Aug. 9, 1897, GEORGE H. FOWLER, b. March 5, 1849. He is a druggist.
4559 JONATHAN ALVIN, b. Apl. 29, 1841, m. Apl. 18, 1865, LOUISE T. BANGS in Mass., b. March 3, 1847, dau. of William and Lois. He was a machinist, 1903, a fruit farmer in Meriden, Conn., had: 4560 FRED WINTHROP, b. Aug. 19, 1867, a clerk in New Haven.
4561 SMITH D., b. June 6, 1843, d. June 20, 1844.
4562 ALMA L., b. Feb. 22, 1858, d. Apl. 4, 1865.

SEVENTH GENERATION 227

F1992 Levi Locke, born in Bristol, May 15, 1817, married 1st, July 18, 1839, SUSAN GILMAN, born in Dorchester, Mass., Oct. 11, 1819, died in Bristol, Jan. 7, 1881; married 2nd, Feb. 13, 1884, MRS. SARAH P. (CARTER) ROBINSON of New Hampton, who died in Bristol, May 31, 1901, aged 79. Levi was in Legislature 1866-7, was a farmer and in the meat business in Bristol and died May 14, 1898.

Children of 7th Gen. b. in Bristol.

F4563 ROXY DOLOFF, b. Apl. 19, 1840, m. Nov. 2, 1862, GEORGE H. WHITE.
4564 ANNETTE, b. June 27, 1842, d. Lowell, Apl. 29, 1878, m. Apl. 23, 1861, ALONZO W. JEWETT, b. Wentworth, Sept. 27, 1839. He is in the ice and milk business, Laconia; m. 2nd, 1879, MRS. CELESTIA (DAVIS) ANGELL. Annette had: 4565 KATIE B., b. Bristol, June 5, 1866, d. Laconia, unmarried, Nov. 11, 1890; 4566 HENRY C., b. Bris., May 24, 1874, d. Lowell, June 22, 1875; 4567 ARTHUR ALONZO, b. Apl. 18, 1878.
4568 BENJAMIN, b. June 23, 1847, d. Stratham, Nov. 24, 1879, m. Alexandria March 3, 1869, MRS. NELLIE J. (PLACE) COLBATH of Alex., b. 1848, dau. of Smith C. and Nancy J.
F4569 LEVI M., b. Dec. 9, 1854, m. June 12, 1875, FANNIE M. SMITH.
4570 CHARLES E., b. July 5, 1858, a painter living 1915 in Bristol unmarried.

F1993 Dorothy Sargent Locke, born in Bristol, March 25, 1819, married July 18, 1837, MITCHELL H. PAGE, born in Ryegate, Vt., Apl. 11, 1810, son of John and Dorcas. He was a carpenter in Bristol, and died in Bristol Aug. 16, 1890. She died Dec. 9, 1907.

Children of 7th Gen.

4571 MARTIN VAN BUREN, b. Bristol, Jan. 15, 1838, m. 1st, KATHERINE HENDRICKS; m. 2nd, LAVINA THOMPSON, went to Eau Claire, Wis., 1856, had four children.
4572 LEVI LOCKE, b. Bristol, Sept. 6, 1839. He was in 7th N. H. Reg. and d. Fort Jefferson, Fla., March 21, 1862. He m. Dec. 1861, HANNAH W. DREW, b. Hebron, Apl. 8, 1845, dau. of Asa and Sarah (Wells) and she m. 2nd, LORENZO FLANDERS.
F4573 ELIZABETH A., b. May 21, 1841, m. 1860 HARVEY DREW.
4574 JOHN C., b. Groton, May 28, 1843, m. GEORGIANNA HALL, served in 7th N. H. Reg. and d. Fort Jefferson, Fla., Apl. 16, 1862.
4575 ANDREW J., b. Hebron, June 2, 1845, served 9th N. H. Reg., was captured Poplar Grove Church, Va., and confined in prison. He escaped, was recaptured and d. in prison, Salisbury, N. C., Dec. 25, 1864.
4576 NATHANIEL SPRINGER, b. Hebron, Sept. 6, 1846, m. July 4, 1866, MARY JANE HOLLON. He served in 6th and 9th N. H. Reg., lived Leominster, Mass., had: 4577 LILLIAN A., b. Apl. 15, 1867, m. 1st, Feb. 26, 1885, ARTHUR L. ADAMS; m. 2nd, Jan. 11, 1894, LEWIS O. HAWKINS, and has three children in Meredith.

4578 RUTH B., b. Hebron, Sept. 8, 1849, m. Nov. 22, 1866, JOHN SMITH.
4579 JAMES H., b. Bristol, May 8, 1851, d. Oct. 4, 1870.
F4580 LAVINA J., b. Sept. 20, 1854, m. 1st, Sept. 25, 1869, HENRY W. DRAKE,
4584; m. 2nd, Dec. 28, 1886, OSCAR F. MORSE.

F1994 Harriet Locke, born in Bristol, Jan. 14, 1822, married in Bristol, Apl. 11, 1839, PHILIP S. DRAKE, born in Bristol, Apl. 14, 1819, son of Jacob and Polly. He was a farmer and stone cutter in Bristol and died Sept. 15, 1882. She died June 15, 1904.

Children of 7th Gen. b. in Bristol.

4581 CHARLES NORTON, b. Sept. 30, 1839, d. Sept. 1, 1896, m. Sept. 9, 1862, HARRIET A. ROLLINS, b. Bristol, Sept. 9, 1842, d. B., March 18, 1900, dau. of Col. S. A. and Irene (Whipple). He was in the service, lost a leg at Gettysburg, was a wood worker in Bristol, had: 4582 DAU., b. Nov. 5, 1878, d. 12 days old; 4583 IRENE, b. May 8, 1870.
4584 HENRY WELLS, b. May 30, 1846, m. Sept. 25, 1869, LAVINA PAGE. # (See F4580.)
4585 ABRA ANN, b. Bristol, Jan. 13, 1851, d. Laconia, Sept. 4, 1892, m. Aug. 13, 1869, ANDREW F. NUDD of Canterbury, b. Loudon, 1849, a farmer.
4586 FRANK LAFOREST, b. Bristol, Jan. 10, 1855, m. Nov. 17, 1883, MARY ANN WEBSTER, lives Laconia.

F1995 Susan D. Locke, born in Bristol, Feb. 11, 1828, died in Bristol, Oct. 12, 1899, married Dec. 12, 1850, MILO FELLOWS, born July 23, 1821, son of Benjamin and Miriam. He was a farmer and stone cutter, and was tax collector 17 years. He died Sept. 13, 1908.

Children of 7th Gen. b. in Bristol.

4587 ALBERT RUSS, b. Sept. 8, 1851, m. EVELYN T. GRANT, b. Prospect, Me., Dec. 29, 1853, dau. of Timothy and Henrietta (Seavey). He is a doctor in Winterport, Me., and had: 4588 TIMOTHY GRANT, b. June 4, 1878.
4589 SMITH DRAKE, b. March 17, 1853, m. Bristol, Dec. 26, 1876, ETTA B. JEWETT, b. Bristol, Apl. 25, 1857, dau. of Jeremiah and Mary. He was a tinsmith in Bristol, in 1903 a florist in Saugus, Mass. Had no children.
4590 OSCAR FOWLER, b. Sept. 10, 1859, m. May 24, 1884, EVA MARIA FLING of Bristol, b. May 11, 1863, dau. of Lewis and Mary (Sleeper). He is a lawyer in Bucksport, Me., had: 4591 RAYMOND, b. Oct. 17, 1885; 4592 FRANK, b. Nov. 7, 1889.
4593 MILO A., b. Sept. 23, 1861, d. March 24, 1864.
4594 LESLIE H., b. Dec. 11, 1863, m. Nov. 23, 1892, ELIZABETH KEER. He is a florist, Hyde Park, Mass., no children.

SEVENTH GENERATION

4595 SUSIE M., b. Apl. 21, 1866, d. July 13, 1902, m. May 29, 1897, GEORGE JENKINS, a farmer in Bristol, b. 1824, d. Jan. 4, 1900.

4596 ALICE A., b. March 16, 1873, graduated Bucksport, Me., Sem., was assistant postmaster, Bristol, 1903.

F1998 Susan Sanborn Doloff, born in Bridgewater, Dec. 9, 1800, died in Bristol, March 14, 1879, married Nov. 9, 1819, SAMUEL BROWN, born Oct. 28, 1793. He was a farmer in Bridgewater, and died there Oct. 1868.

Children of 7th Gen. b. in Bridgewater.

4597 SOLOMON, b. June 28, 1823, d. Sept. 1862, m. 1847, MATILDA S. HUGHES, who d. March 1868. He was a physician in Philadelphia, and had three children.

4598 HORACE, b. Aug. 15, 1825, d. Bridg., July 23, 1874, m. June 23, 1847, MARY AUGUSTA FLETCHER, b. Groton, Oct. 25, 1828, dau. of Jesse and Patience (Hobart). A farmer in Bridgewater; had four children.

4599 LEVI D., b. Apl. 28, 1833, m. Oct. 11, 1855, ELIZA ANN PHINNEY, b. Sandwich, Mass., Oct. 30, 1829, d. Phila., Jan. 6, 1882, dau. of Jabez and Jane (Fisher). He was a merchant and banker in Phila., had one child.

4600 WARREN S., b. Sept. 11, 1839, m. Oct. 29, 1871, MRS. WILHEMINA (POPPLAR) GILMORE, b. West Brighton, N. Y., March 3, 1844. He served in 19th Mass. Infantry, was a farmer in Center Harbor, had three children.

F2002 Mary Doloff, born in Bridgewater, June 9, 1805, died in New Hampton, Feb. 15, 1887, married Dec. 15, 1825, JOSEPH R. MOORE, born in Goffstown, Jan. 16, 1800, son of Robert and Jenny (Rolfe). He had a sawmill in Bristol and died there Apl 30, 1880.

Children of 7th Gen. b. in Bristol.

4601 JANE ROLFE, b. Aug. 8, 1826, d. June 4, 1884, unmarried.

4602 JAMES G., b. Jan. 27, 1828, m. CHRISTENA C. SHIPMAN, b. Springfield, Vt., Sept. 25, 1836, d. Franconia, dau. of Rev. Isaiah. He was a mathematician, also a lumber and bobbin manufacturer in Franconia, and Lisbon.

4603 OVID D., b. Aug. 6, 1829, m. 1st, Aug. 28, 1854, HENRIETTA I. HOWLAND, b. Franconia, Aug. 31, 1832, d. F., March 20, 1871; m. 2nd, Feb. 1, 1877, HATTIE A. HOWLAND, b. Oct. 10, 1850. He is a wood pulp manufacturer in Lisbon, had: 4604 GENEVIEVE, m. 1886, WM. NELSON; 4605 FRED J., m. JENNIE HARRIS.

4606 RACHEL LOCKE, b. Aug. 1, 1831, m. Oct. 25, 1854, DENNISON TAFT of Montpelier, Vt., b. Barre, Vt., June 6, 1819, d. Mont., Sept. 22, 1897, lived Montpelier, and had: 4607 ALICE R.; 4608 EDNA M., m. CHARLES GAY.

4609 MARY, b. July 14, 1836, m. Dec. 22, 1862, JOHN DAILEY of Lebanon, Pa., b. Cornwall, Pa., July 7, 1832, d. Phila., Aug. 1897. She was a teacher, later a painter; had: 4610 GRACE; 4611 CLAUDE; 4612 LILLIAN; 4613 PAUL.

4614 SARAH C., b. Dec. 26, 1837, d. unmarried Feb. 8, 1873, school teacher in Penn.

4615 JOSEPHINE, b. May 22, 1841, d. N. Y., Aug. 28, 1874, m. Oct. 15, 1872, METHUSALAH DUBOIS of N. Y., b. 1827, son of Jacob and Rachel, was cashier in bank, had: 4616 RACHEL, b. Oct. 1873, is a Stenographer in Boston.

4617 JOSEPH W., a twin, d. Bristol, June 19, 1892, m. Nov. 8, 1863, HARRIET ELLEN FLANDERS of New Hampton, b. Apl. 9, 1844, dau. of John and Harriet (Kelley). Was baggage master New Hampton, had five children.

F2010 Almira Smith Doloff, born in Bridgewater, Dec. 14, 1810, died in New Hampton, Feb. 24, 1902, married Feb. 14, 1832, JOHN ROBY, born in Bridgewater, June 20, 1809, son of Lowell and Margaret (Kenniston). He was a farmer in Alexandria and 52 years in Bristol, and died Feb. 28, 1892.

Children of 7th Gen. b. in Bristol.

4618 GUSTAVUS, b. Dec. 1, 1832, m. Nov. 21, 1861, MARY M. HAYWOOD, b. Alexandria, March 1, 1842, d. Bristol, June 20, 1894, dau. of James. He was superintendent of paper mill, Bristol, 24 years, had two children.

4619 OLIVE, b. Feb. 8, 1835, d. B., June 21, 1856, m. May 28, 1855, AUGUSTUS J. FERRIN, b. Nov. 20, 1826, a farmer, had five children.

4620 SARAH M., b. Apl. 15, 1843, m. AUGUSTUS J. FERRIN, June 5, 1864.

4621 NICHOLAS D., b. Nov. 6, 1838, d. June 26, 1846.

4622 LIZZIE KATHLEEN, b. Apl. 11, 1863, m. Dec. 20, 1883, GEORGE H. ROBINSON, b. Allenstown, Dec. 8, 1851, lived New Hampton, was a brakeman 1903, had five children.

F2011 Rachel Locke Doloff, born in Bristol, Apl. 25, 1814, died in Bristol, Aug. 2, 1865, married March 11, 1834, CALVIN SWEET, born in Wentworth in 1812. He was a lumberman, a school teacher, a Republican and selectman in Bristol and died there Oct. 28, 1882.

Children of 7th Gen.

4623 SYLVANUS W., b. Wentworth, Dec. 4, 1834, d. Bristol, Apl. 23, 1900, m. Dec. 17, 1857, SUSAN A. BLODGETT, b. Kalamazoo, Mich., Nov. 9, 1837, dau. of William. He was farmer in Bristol, had: 4624 SARAH M., b. Apl. 27, 1861; 4625 Son died young.

4626 ORRISON, b. 1842, drowned May 1, 1847.

F2012 Abram Doloff, born in Bristol, March 20, 1818, married in Bristol, Feb. 22, 1838, LYDIA NELSON, born in Bristol, Dec. 4, 1818, died Dec. 20, 1900, daughter of Levi. He was a farmer and drover and had the first meat market in Bristol. He was a Methodist, a Republican, and died March 3, 1904.

Children of 7th Gen. b. in Bristol.

4627 ALMIRA SMITH, b. Dec. 12, 1838, m. Aug. 16, 1859, REV. GEORGE J. JUDKINS, b. Kingston, Dec. 21, 1830, d. Bristol 1914. A Methodist minister, graduated from Tilton Sem., now retired and a farmer in Bristol, had four children.
4628 OTIS A., b. Nov. 25, 1843, d. Sept. 13, 1845.
4629 EMMA H., b. Feb. 14, 1845, m. Sept. 15, 1867, CYRUS NEWELL CASS, b. Alexandria June 1845, son of Seth and Belinda (Ladd). Lived in Spangle, Wash. She lives in Bristol and is engaged in Lyceum work, had: 4630 HARLAND H., b. 1868.
4631 LYNTHIA N., b. Jan. 20, 1850, d. Nov. 16, 1855.
4632 HARLAN H., b. June 29, 1852, d. Oct. 5, 1855.
4633 VIOLA L., b. Jan. 3, 1854, d. Oct. 10, 1855.
4634 ALMA K., b. Apl. 8. 1858, d. June 16, 1875.
4635 ANNA M., b. twin, Apl. 8, 1858, d. June 1, 1885, m. Nov. 5, 1884, DR. IRVING T. DRAKE of Franklin, b. Pittsfield, 1857. No child by 1st wife. He m. 2nd, MARY AIKEN.

F2013 Betsey Locke, born in Barnston, Can., Nov. 23, 1805, died Dec. 24, 1831, married Feb. 23, 1823, JOHN M. MOSHER, born Nov. 19, 1802.

Children of 7th Gen.

4636 LEVI, b. ——.
4637 WILLIAM, b. May 22, 1824, m. NAOMI MOSHER, b. June 4, 1834, d. March 8, 1896. He d. Oct. 24, 1911.
4638 RICHARD, b. ——.
4639 JANE, b. March 1, 1830, m. Oct. 18, 1855, JOHN B. FRAPPIED, b. Sept. 17, 1835. She d. Jan. 4, 1899.

F2018 Chloe Locke, born in Barnston, Can., Jan. 16, 1816, died July 25, 1882, married Oct. 17, 1832, GUY ALDRICH, born in Barnston, Apl. 30, 1813, died Oct. 16, 1870.

Children of 7th Gen. b. in Stanstead, Can.

F4640 BEAZAR, b. Dec. 19, 1832, m. Jan. 11, 1854, LOVINIA HORN.
4641 BETSEY LASURA, b. June 21, 1835, d. July 19, 1915, m. Dec. 21, 1854, JOHN CORLISS, b. July 9, 1828, d. June 19, 1912.
F4642 MARY VENAN, b. March 17, 1837, m. Sept. 1, 1859, RUFUS HOSMER PAINE.
F4643 THOMAS LOCKE, b. Dec. 23, 1839, m. Jan. 27, 1866, EMMA JOANNE CADE.

F4644 LEVI LOCKE, b. Jan. 6, 1841, m. Jan. 29, 1864, AREANNAH AUGUSTA LEWIS.
F4645 TIMOTHY CHAUNCEY, b. Feb. 18, 1844, m. Apl. 19, 1873, FLORENCE SIBYL FLETCHER.
F4646 ADELBERT LESTER, b. Oct. 21, 1848, m. Feb. 18, 1868, CYNTHIA NEWELL VANCE.
4647 NORMAN EDWIN, b. Apl. 3, 1853, m. 1st, March 15, 1876, CARRIE DENNISON, who d. Oct. 7, 1882; m. 2nd, Dec. 29, 1885, MARY SUSAN GLOVER, b. Dec. 22, 1865, had: 4648 NORMAN E., b. 1880, d. 1880.
4649 GUY EDWIN, b. Oct. 4, 1854, m. March 20, 1879, DELLA ROSE DUKE, b. Nov. 17, 1858, d. Oct. 22, 1891.

F2020 Louisa Locke, born in Barnston, Can., Nov. 8, 1819, died June 7, 1895, married June 29, 1841, WILLIAM BURROUGHS, born June 6, 1820, died Dec. 10, 1899.

Children of 7th Gen.

4650 THOMAS, b. Aug. 17, 1842, m. Dec. 5, 1866, CLARINDA PAMELIA EMBURY, b. Dec. 19, 1841.
4651 ELLEN AUGUSTA, b. Jan. 8, 1846, d. Apl. 30, 1855.
4652 CHARLES HENRY, b. Dec. 22, 1852, m. May 4, 1875, DORA H. EMBURY, b. Sept. 1, 1852.
4653 JOHN, b. Feb. 8, 1858, m. Sept. 10, 1883, CHRISTINA EILERTSEN, b. Nov. 24, 1863; he d. Sept. 14, 1914.

F2021 Amanda Locke, born in Barnston, Can., Feb. 13, 1822, married Aug. 25, 1846, THOMAS E. COOPER, born May 29, 1822.

Children of 7th Gen.

4654 HENRY NELSON, b. Jan. 20, 1847, d. June 2, 1847.
4655 EDGAR FRANCIS, b. July 1, 1849.
4656 ERASTUS BYRON, b. Nov. 13, 1851, m. SUSIE HANSON, b. Aug. 11, 1861.
4657 CLARA ELLA, b. Aug. 18, 1857, m. Feb. 20, 1878, FRED WORTHINGTON, b. Apl. 20, 1852.
4658 ALICE EFFIE, b. May 31, 1860, d. Nov. 1908, m. 1st, WILLIAM J. CLINT, b. Jan. 15, 1857, d. Jan. 25, 1885; m. 2nd, Dec. 9, 1890, FRANK DAY WOODWORTH, b. July 8, 1854.

F2022 Thomas Locke, born in Barnston, Can., June 16, 1824, married July 16, 1846, LYDIA EMERSON HOWARD, born in Lisbon, Feb. 22, 1825, died May 8, 1896. He lived in Barnston and died Jan. 27, 1884.

Children of 7th Gen. b. in Barnston, Can.

F4659 CLARA ELLIS, b. Oct. 1, 1847, m. March 21, 1871, WILLIAM WILDER HEATH.
4660 ELLEN ELIZA, b. Sept. 14, 1856, d. unmarried Dec. 27, 1905.

SEVENTH GENERATION 233

4661 SARAH EMMA, b. Barnston, Can., a twin, Sept. 14, 1856, m. Dec. 14, 1880, CLARENCE LEON HILL, b. Concord, Oct. 29, 1852, d. Feb. 18, 1894.
F4662 LIZZIE ELLSWORTH, b. Nov. 30, 1859, m. Jan. 16, 1884, GEORGE THOMAS COOPER.
4663 LEVI FREDERICK, b. July 27, 1864, lives in Barnston, Can., unmarried 1915.

F2031 Jonathan Locke, baptized Nov. 18, 1787, died March 15, 1853, married Dec. 24, 1812, MARY VENNARD of New Castle; married 2nd, Oct. 10, 1842, EUNICE QUINCY, born Gardiner, Me. Was a farmer and mariner in New Castle, built the present John Locke house and is buried with twenty more Lockes in the orchard there. Eunice married 2nd, Apl. 25, 1854, WILLIAM NEAL.

Children of 7th Gen. b. in New Castle.

4664 GEORGE V., b. June 14, 1813, d. N. C., May 22, 1894, m. 1st, at N. C., Apl. 9, 1840, MEHITABLE LEAR, b. Aug. 28, 1806, d. N. C., Feb. 1, 1886; m. 2nd, March 17, 1887, MRS. HANNAH BELL (LEACH) WHITE, b. Apl. 2, 1819, d. June 1910, dau. of Charles and Margaret. He had no children, was a farmer and lived at the Cape, New Castle.
F4665 DOROTHY, b. Aug. 13, 1814, m. Apl. 7, 1837, HENRY TREDICK.
F4666 MARY, b. March 15, 1816, m. Aug. 19, 1837, WILLIAM LANGDON.
F4667 WOODBURY, b. 1817, m. June 16, 1852, JANE SMITH.
F4668 JOHN, b. Aug. 1822, m. in N. C., Oct. 7, 1849, SARAH TREFETHERN.
4669 NATHAN, b. and died young.
F4670 EMALINE, b. N. C., Aug. 8, 1826, m. JOHN GARDNER.
F4671 ELVIRA, b. ——, m. 1st, March 10, 1839, ALFRED TUCKER; m. 2nd, Jan. 1, 1874, JOHN H. WELLS.

F2033 Nabby Locke, born Dec. 27, 1789, died in New Castle July 15, 1849, married Nov. 1, 1807, WILLIAM NEAL of New Castle, born May 17, 1784. He was a farmer in New Castle; married 2nd, EUNICE (QUINCY) LOCKE, 1854, and died Oct. 31, 1871.

Children of 7th Gen. b. in New Castle.

F4672 JAMES, b. Nov. 14, 1808, m. June 20, 1831, MARGARET WHITE.
F4673 WILLIAM L., b. Jan. 27, 1811, m. 1st, ABIGAIL HARRET; m. 2nd, Nov. 7, 1847, SARAH ODIORNE WILLARD.
F4674 MARY B., b. March 22, 1816, m. Dec. 3, 1835, SAMUEL BATSON.
F4675 JOSEPH L., b. July 29, 1819, m. 1844, MARGARET CARD.
4676 FRANK W., b. Dec. 22, 1825, went to Cal. in 1849, returned, was a joiner, and d. in New Castle unmarried 1887.

F2034 Joseph L. Locke, born in Rye, March, 1792, died in Portsmouth, Sept. 6, 1858, married in North Hampton Nov. 29, 1816, SALLIE L. WEDGWOOD of Rye, born Sept. 24, 1797, died Nov. 30, 1879, daughter of Jonathan and Hannah (Moore). He was a politician, port surveyor, etc., of Portsmouth, and was in Capt. Marshall's Co., July 25, 1812.

Children of 7th Gen. b. in Rye.

    4677 THADDEUS, b. March 31, 1817; was in U. S. Navy and lost at sea at age of 22, unmarried.
  F4678 ADALINE P., b. Nov. 1819, m. HIRAM TREFETHERN.
  F4679 JOSEPH PRENTICE, b. 1820, m. FRANCES MANSON.
  F4680 OLIVE R., b. Feb. 19, 1823, m. Feb. 28, 1847, THOMAS H. PHILBRICK.
    4681 ELBRIDGE G., b. 1825, d. March 24, 1839.
  F4682 ANDREW J., b. Apl. 24, 1829, m. July 3, 1853, CAROLINE A. HAYES.
    4683 MARTIN VAN BUREN, b. 1832, was a printer in Boston, New York, and Concord, where he d. unmarried Aug. 21, 1871.
    4684 WILLIAM, b. 1834, d. unmarried July 1853.
  F4685 JOSEPH, b. Sept. 1836, m. June 24, 1859, HELEN A. WOODSUM.
    4686 ISAAC HILL, b. 1838, d. June 13, 1848.

F2036 Mary Olive Locke, born in Rye, Dec. 25, 1796, died in Portsmouth May 4, 1880, married in Portsmouth, Nov. 25, 1821, ASA WATSON of Lee, born May 16, 1797, died Salmon Falls, Aug. 1848. He was a hotel keeper in Portsmouth.

Children of 7th Gen.

    4687 HENRY N., b. New Castle, June 4, 1822, d. unmarried June 12, 1861.
    4688 MARY ANN, b. March 11, 1824, d. Sept. 23, 1824.
    4689 FRANKLIN B., b. May 22, 1825, d. March 24, 1826.
    4690 NORMAN, b. June 23, 1827, d. unmarried 1848.
    4691 BENJAMIN D., b. Feb. 22, 1829, d. Nov. 1862, m. 1855, MARY ANN MCMANUS of Boston, b. 1836, d. 1874, had no children.
    4692 ALBERT, b. Dec. 28, 1830, d. Dec. 1848.
    4693 HELEN L., b. Sept. 13, 1833, d. July 1, 1849.
  F4694 OLIVE N., b. March 15, 1835, m. 1852, GEORGE LORD.
    4695 ASA, b. Feb. 22, 1837, d. Oct. 29, 1839.
    4696 JOHN, b. twin with last, d. unmarried Feb. 27, 1872.

F2038 John Locke, born in New Castle, Aug. 10, 1800, died in New Castle, Feb. 20, 1864, married 1st, Dec. 14, 1820, MARTHA RAND of Rye, born May 28, 1801, died July 13, 1847, daughter of Daniel and Dorothy (Seavey); married 2nd, Oct. 13, 1847, MRS. ALMIRA (SHAW) LEAR, born Jan. 14, 1805, died in Portsmouth, March 19, 1885. He was a farmer and assessor in New Castle, at one time owned much property there, most

SEVENTH GENERATION

of the land in front of the Wentworth Hotel, land on which the Wendell House was built, also "Inland." An energetic man with quick wit who could hold a crowd at any time.

Children of 7th Gen. b. in New Castle.
F4697 MARY OLIVE, b. March 3, 1821, m. Oct. 18, 1839, NATHANIEL BATSON.
4698 AMOS SEAVEY, b. N. C., March 19, 1823, d. May 3, 1832.
F4699 MARTHA ANN, b. March 8, 1825, m. March 12, 1844, BENJAMIN J. BATSON.
F4700 ABRAM T., b. May 2, 1827, m. Feb. 3, 1850, JANE TUCKER.
F4701 JOHN LANGDON, b. Dec. 12, 1829, m. Aug. 2, 1852, SARAH JANE VENNARD.
F4702 ADALINE, b. Apl. 1, 1832, m. Nov. 20, 1855, DANIEL SMITH.
F4703 AMOS SEAVEY, b. Apl. 26, 1834, m. Jan. 7, 1861, MARTHA ANN SILVER.
F4704 OLIVER HORTON, b. July 19, 1836, m. March 7, 1857, ELIZA JANE BRACKETT.
4705 ALMIRA AMANDA, b. Sept. 8, 1838, d. Nov. 22, 1846.
4706 LOUISA, b. Sept. 1, 1840, d. Oct. 18, 1840.
F4707 CHRISTENA, b. Dec. 8, 1842, m. 1860, HENRY BACHELDER.
4708 JAMES RAND, b. N. C., Apl. 8, 1844, d. Aug. 23, 1844.

F2048 Samuel Jenness Locke, born in Rye, March 1, 1790, died March 29, 1861, married 1st, Dec. 21, 1817, POLLY WESTBROOK WALDRON, born Aug. 19, 1792, died Aug. 27, 1831, daughter of Jonathan B., and descendant of Major Waldron of Dover; married 2nd, Apl. 24, 1834, ELIZABETH W. MARDEN, born Nov. 6, 1795, died Sept. 20, 1877, daughter of Nathaniel. He was farmer, tanner, shoemaker; was captain in state militia, in Legislature 1859–60 and a very able, much respected citizen.

In May 1814, when the alarm was given that a British warship was about landing boats in Rye, Samuel J. Locke was one of the first to hear of it, and emulating Paul Revere he immediately jumped on a horse and roused the minute men throughout Greenland. Lieutenant Simon Goss who lived nearest the meeting house, had retired and in his haste to ring the bell put on his breeches hind part before in which condition he was found when the men assembled.

Children of 7th Gen. b. in Rye.
4709 JOHN W., b. March 25, 1819, d. May 19, 1819.
4710 ROBERT W., b. May 7, 1821, d. Aug. 30, 1825.
4711 ABIGAIL, b. Dec. 21, 1823, d. Jan. 18, 1824.
F4712 E. EMERETT, b. Rye, Apl. 1, 1826, m. May 21, 1848, NATHANIEL MARDEN.
4713 MARY O., b. May 1, 1828, d. Aug. 5, 1828.
4714 OLIVE W., b. July 31, 1830, d. Sept. 14, 1830.
F4715 JAMES H. (adopted son), b. June 15, 1830, m. Dec. 28, 1864, SARAH A. TREFETHERN.

F2049 Abigail Locke, born in Rye, Nov. 22, 1792, died Feb. 25, 1881, married June 2, 1816, GENL. THOMAS GOSS, born Sept. 6, 1768, died Oct. 7, 1857, son of Nathan and Sarah (Johnson). He married 1st, SARAH MARDEN, 1801, died 1815. He was a farmer and miller at original "Dry Point," Rye.
Child of 7th Gen.
4716 JOHN SHERIDAN, b. Rye, Oct. 26, 1817, d. Rye, March 12, 1903, m. Oct. 7, 1855, WIDOW SULA (LOCKE) FOSS, # F6257, b. Oct. 11, 1824, d. July 7, 1894. He was a farmer and prominent man in Rye, lived at the Harbor.

F2050 Olive Shapleigh Locke, born in Rye, May 11, 1795, died May 18, 1874, married March 8, 1817, WILLIAM BERRY of Newington, born June 8, 1796, died Sept. 14, 1867, son of Isaiah and Bathsheba (Shaw). He was a farmer in Newington.
Children of 7th Gen. b. in Rye.
F4717 MARY J., b. Aug. 25, 1818, m. June 8, 1837, JOHN L. PICKERING.
F4718 ELIZABETH A., b. June 3, 1821, m. Aug. 28, 1844, JOSEPH W. WHIDDEN.
4719 JOHN G., b. May 8, 1824, d. Montana, unmarried, Feb. 18, 1878, a Cal. '49er.
4720 CHARLES WM., b. Feb. 25, 1829, was m. 1860, had a son and a dau. in Montana and later lived in Cal. Was a '49er.
F4721 MARTHA O., b. Nov. 4, 1830, m. Nov. 13, 1868, ROBERT MANSON.

F2051 Jethro Locke, born in Rye, Nov. 19, 1797, died in Portsmouth, Sept. 23, 1848, married Sept. 3, 1826, MARTHA MASON, born in Rye, Dec. 20, 1807, died in Boston, Nov. 5, 1889. He was in Capt. Parsons' Co., 1812–14, moved to Portsmouth in 1835 where he was a tailor. He was employed at the Navy Yard many years.
Children of 7th Gen. b. in Rye.
4722 JOHN SEWELL, b. Nov. 20, 1827, d. Ports., unmarried, Dec. 11, 1855. Was a clerk in Portsmouth.
4723 CORNELIUS E., b. Apl. 27, 1830; under firm name of Locke & Hurd he was for 35 years engaged in produce business at Faneuil Hall Market, Boston; d. Boston, Aug. 26, 1906. Was a California '49er and never married.
4724 FIDELIA F., b. May 28, 1832, d. Brookline, Mass., Apl. 17, 1910, m. June 4, 1868, WEBSTER HURD of Boston, b. Newfield, Me., March 30, 1827, d. Boston, Apl. 17, 1890. For 35 years was in produce business in Boston. Had one son: 4725 JOHN C., b. 1872, d. March 20, 1892.
4726 EMILY M., b. June 29, 1834, d. unmarried, Boston, Apl. 20, 1906.

SEVENTH GENERATION

F2053 Mary Locke, born in Rye, Feb. 11, 1803, died Sept. 9, 1831, married CAPT. JOHN CLARKE, born Apl. 4, 1804, died Aug. 8, 1847, son of Andrew and Hannah (Remick). He married 2nd, ADALINE TUCKER, was a farmer in Rye.

Child of 7th Gen.

F4728 MOSES, b. Sept. 29, 1829, m. SUSAN A. TUCKER, Oct. 26, 1858.

F2054 Elvin Locke, born in Rye, March 29, 1809, died June 23, 1882, married in Rye, Apl. 5, 1835, LOUISA BERRY, born Rye, March 24, 1813, died Rye, Oct. 5, 1861, daughter of Joseph and Betsey. He was Lieutenant in the Rye Militia, a shoemaker and prosperous farmer at Rye Center. He held minor town offices, was of a quiet disposition and much respected.

Children of 7th Gen. b. in Rye.

F4729 JOHN ELVIN, b. Aug. 25, 1835, m. 1st, Jan. 7, 1862, SARAH HAYES; m. 2nd, March 6, 1879, her cousin, LAURA HAYES.
4730 MARY ELIZABETH, b. Aug. 25, 1840, lives Rye, unmarried.
F4731 OLIVER ELBRIDGE, b. July 24, 1842, m. Dec. 20, 1873, ARABELLA CLOUGH.
4732 CHARLES ALVAH, b. March 6, 1844, d. Rye, unmarried, Sept. 6, 1872.
F4733 SARA LOUISE, b. March 25, 1845, m. Dec. 20, 1872, CLARENCE MARSTON.
4734 SAMUEL JENNESS, b. Nov. 19, 1846. Employed on R. R. in Seattle; unmarried.
F4735 EMMA AMANDA, b. Nov. 29, 1848, m. March 3, 1875, OLIVER B. FOGG.
4736 ABBIE MERILLA, b. March 12, 1851, d. Rye, Nov. 15, 1861.

F2056 Abigail Towle Locke, born in Rye, Feb. 8, 1797, died in Farmington, Nov. 19, 1878, married Apl. 14, 1815, BENJAMIN BERRY of Farmington, born in Rye, May 25, 1791, died a farmer in Moultonborough Dec. 17, 1868, son of James and Hannah (Randall).

Children of 7th Gen.

4737 NATHANIEL HUBBARD, b. Rye, July 31, 1817, d. Farmington, Jan. 15, 1908, m. Sept. 29, 1850, OLIVE S. PLACE, b. June 15, 1820; was a shoe cutter in Farmington, had no children. She d. Farmington, Apl. 17, 1906.
4738 JOSEPH LOCKE, b. Jan. 17, 1819, d. unmarried Jan. 10, 1840.
F4739 BENJAMIN, b. July 4, 1823, m. 1st, May 31, 1846, ROSANNAH HANSON; m. 2nd, July 18, 1874, MRS. MARGARET (ROBERTSON) JEWELL.
F4740 WILLIAM L., b. Feb. 2, 1827, m. Sept. 25, 1852, CALISTA COLBATH.
F4741 JOHN M., b. Oct. 28, 1841, m. Sept. 14, 1866, LEAH H. ROBERTS.
F4742 SARAH ANN, b. Apl. 1, 1837, m. Feb. 4, 1867, AMOS STEARNS.

F2057 Sarah Ann Locke, born in Rye, Apl. 1, 1799, died in Rye, Dec. 17, 1889, married Feb. 1819, AMOS S. JENNESS, born Oct. 3, 1801, died March 30, 1886, son of Benjamin and Martha (Seavey). He was a farmer in Rye.
Children of 7th Gen. b. in Rye.
F4743 WILLIAM BENJAMIN, b. May 29, 1819, m. Dec. 25, 1844, MARY A. JENNESS.
4744 ABBY COFFIN, b. Sept. 10, 1821, d. No. Hampton, Nov. 10, 1910, m. 1st, E. Boston, Feb. 7, 1870, SIMON S. ODIORNE, b. Ports., d. May 4, 1881, son of George and Ruth (Kinnear); m. 2nd, No. Hampton, June 1887, CHRISTOPHER MOORE, who was a farmer in No. Hamp. and d. June 20, 1892; no children.
F4745 JOSEPH GILBERT, b. March 21, 1825, m. 1st, Apl. 18, 1857, ELVIRA LOCKE GARLAND, # 4747; m. 2nd, March 1889, MARY OLIVIA MOORE MARDEN.
F4746 MARTHA SEAVEY, b. Aug. 17, 1829, m. Jan. 23, 1851, ALBION D. PARSONS.

F2058 Patty Locke, born in Rye, March 17, 1801, died in Rye, Feb. 17, 1866, married June 11, 1826, RUEL GARLAND, born Dec. 31, 1798, died Aug. 28, 1869. He was a farmer and blacksmith in Rye, son of John and Abigail (Perkins).
Children of 7th Gen. b. in Rye.
4747 ELVIRA LOCKE, b. Oct. 23, 1827, m. Apl. 18, 1857, her cousin, JOSEPH G. JENNESS, # F4745.
4748 ABIGAIL PERKINS, b. Feb. 12, 1832, d. unmarried, Dec. 22, 1865.
F4749 JOSEPH WM. b. Sept. 4, 1836, m. Oct. 22, 1860, ANNIE D. DRAKE.
4750 THOMAS RUEL, b. Feb. 7, 1839, was accidentally shot Oct. 9, 1854.

F2059 Lucretia Locke, born in Rye, June 8, 1803, died there Dec. 22, 1869, married June 18, 1822, MOSES L. GARLAND, born March 21, 1801, son of Peter and Mehitable (Seavey). He married 2nd, Nov. 26, 1871, NANCY (DROWN) LOCKE. Was a farmer in Rye, and died in Portsmouth Aug. 24, 1890.
Children of 7th Gen. b. in Rye.
4751 CHARLES, b. Sept. 11, 1822, d. March 30, 1905, m. May 26, 1852, SOPHIA P. JENNESS, b. Aug. 6, 1826, d. Nov. 3, 1858, had: 4752 EMMA L., b. Rye, Apl. 22, 1855, lives in Rye, 1915; 4753 WALTER, b. Rye, Apl. 27, 1858, d. Dec. 22, 1860.
4754 GILMAN, b. Nov. 27, 1825, m. Sept. 26, 1851, MARTHA J. JENNESS, b. Oct. 13, 1828, d. Feb. 24, 1854. He was a farmer in Rye and had: 4755 MILLARD F., b. Palmyra, Ill., Feb. 10, 1852, d. Rye, Jan. 25, 1854.
4756 MARY ABBY, b. June 3, 1841, m. May 24, 1865, WARREN G. BROWN, b. 1836. He was a farmer in No. Hampton and d. 1872, had: 4757 HOWARD G., b. No. Hampton, Apl. 6, 1867.
4758 MALVINA G., b. Dec. 1, 1844, is unmarried, lives Rye.

RYE CENTER, LOOKING WEST, 1889

The house in the distant center is on the site of the Jonathan Locke house, 1720, and large farm still in the family

Jonathan Locke F2063, of Rye, 1812–1908,
Taken when 94

SEVENTH GENERATION

F2060 Joseph Locke, born in Rye, Nov. 30, 1806, died March 23, 1886, married 1st, Nov. 28, 1833, HANNAH KNOWLES, born in Rye, Nov. 12, 1808, died in Rye, Oct. 18, 1858; married 2nd, Apl. 3, 1860, WIDOW ESTHER (MARDEN) LEAVITT, born March 3, 1816. He was a farmer at Rye Center, in the Rye Militia, a selectman, town clerk, and a staunch Democrat.

Children of 7th Gen. b. in Rye.

4759 HORACE W., b. June 2, 1837, d. Jan. 2, 1839.
4760 SARAH A., b. March 2, 1840, d. March 22, 1858.
4761 ELIZABETH M., b. March 18, 1844, d. March 10, 1872, m. Jan. 12, 1867, TRUE W. JONES, b. Barrington, May 13, 1844, d. Manchester, Oct. 2, 1899, son of Thomas and Mary (Priest). He m. 2nd, PAULINE J. SHEA of Bath, Me., in 1873. He was in the brewing business with his brother FRANK and managed the brewery in Manchester. Elizabeth had: 4762 an infant died a month old.
4763 ADNA P., b. Feb. 16, 1848, d. Rye, unmarried, May 26, 1877.

F2063 Jonathan Locke, born in Rye, Aug. 17, 1812, a twin, died in Rye, Dec. 31, 1908, aged 96; married 1st, Dec. 2, 1838, ALMIRA BROWN, # 2832; married 2nd, Feb. 3, 1863, MARTHA FRENCH, born in Stratham, Sept. 14, 1814, died in Rye, Dec. 14, 1896, daughter of David and Clara (Wiggin). He was in the Rye Militia, a prosperous farmer at Rye Center, a deacon in the Congregational Church 50 years, of happy genial nature, helpful and benevolent in church work, and a highly respected man. Almira was born March 16, 1815, died Oct. 29, 1860.

Children of 7th Gen. b. in Rye.

4764 RHODA B., b. Jan. 30, 1840, d. March 9, 1842.
F4765 FREEMAN J., b. Oct. 7, 1843, m. Apl. 13, 1865, MARY A. OTIS.
F4766 EMMA A., b. Dec. 15, 1849, m. July 1870, CYRUS FOGG.
4767 HORACE A., b. March 26, 1854, lives unmarried on the old Locke place near Rye Center, and carries on the farm.
4768 ABBIE M., b. Oct. 1, 1856, d. Rye, Oct. 2, 1877.

F2065 Hiram Locke, born in Rye, Feb. 28, 1802, died Jan. 27, 1843, married in Portsmouth, Dec. 16, 1827, MARY B. DUNCAN of New Castle, born Apl. 10, 1807, died Jan. 5, 1893. She married 2nd, March 31, 1869, WILLIAM TREFETHERN of Kittery. In 1833 Hiram bought the Dr. Cutter house in Portsmouth and changed it into the National Hotel, afterwards managed the Franklin House, then the Eagle Coffee House in Concord. Returning to Portsmouth, he managed the Plains Tavern.

Children of 7th Gen.

4769 MARTHA A., b. July 19, 1828, d. Dec. 1909, m. Ports., Nov. 14, 1850, JOHN P. HART of Ports., b. Ports. Oct. 25, 1828, son of George and Abigail (Pitman). Had no children. He was cashier of the Rockingham National Bank for many years. He m. 2nd, CARRIE A. COCHRAN, Dec. 8, 1910.

F4770 ALMIRA H., b. Sept. 22, 1830, m. June 23, 1852, JAMES F. GREENLEAF.

4771 MARY FRANCES, b. Feb. 1834, d. unmarried, after many years of insanity, May 16, 1903.

4772 CAROLINE, died aged 2 years, 5 months.

4773 HIRAM CHRISTMAS, b. Concord, Dec. 25, 1836, d. Ports., July 26, 1913, m. May 23, 1861, ELLEN E. CLARKE, b. Ports., Sept. 4, 1840, d. July 19, 1911, dau. of Samuel and Abigail Foster). He was a prominent citizen of Ports., for many years had a fruit store on Market St. After retiring in 1900, he occupied many positions of trust in the city, was a veteran fireman, and member of Odd Fellows. His children were: 4774 ARTHUR E., b. 1865, d. Feb. 13, 1871; 4775 HELEN MAY, b. Ports., Oct. 5, 1868, d. unmarried Aug. 3, 1888; 4776 CORA L., b. May 9, 1875, d. Jan. 25, 1877.

4777 FLETCHER D., b. July 30, 1842, was a clerk in the Navy Yard during and after the war; d. Ports., March 13, 1874, unmarried.

F2068 David J. Locke, born in Rye, May 25, 1810. He was the agent of a sugar company and died of Cuban fever in Cuba, Aug. 30, 1840. He married in Portsmouth, Dec. 10, 1834, MARY E. GRANT of Portsmouth, born Nov. 26, 1817, daughter of Samuel and Elizabeth (Tarlton) of New Castle. She married 2nd, Feb. 19, 1851, GEORGE H. WILLIAMS, a cabinet maker of Amesbury, Mass. She lived her last 20 years and died in 1909 in Skamocawa, Wash.

Children of 7th Gen.

F4778 MARY ELLEN, b. Jan. 19, 1836, m. 1st, Jan. 16, 1855, JOSEPH RHODES; m. 2nd, March 21, 1870, JOHN MALONE.

F4779 ADELAIDE L., b. Dec. 29, 1838, m. March 18, 1856, ALBERT BENNETT.

F2069 William B. A. Locke, born in New Castle, Dec. 22, 1801, died Apl. 6, 1860, married in New Castle, Apl. 10, 1831, OLIVE C. FERNALD of Kittery, born June 30, 1808, died Nov. 30, 1874, daughter of Elihu and Hannah (Chandler).

Children of 7th Gen. b. in in Kittery, Me.

4780 ELIZA J., b. Dec. 25, 1831, d. unmarried in Kittery, June 2, 1903.

F4781 ETHAN ALLEN, b. June 12, 1834, m. Apl. 9, 1857, LYDIA PRYOR.

F4782 WILLIAM WARREN, b. June 7, 1836, m. Dec. 20, 1870, JENNIE F. FORD.

SEVENTH GENERATION 241

4783 ERASTUS B., b. KITTERY, July 19, 1839, lost at sea Aug. 26, 1873, m. 1st, Jan. 1862, ATLANTA GORDON of Kittery, who d. Jan. 24, 1871; m. 2nd, ANNIE AMEE of Kittery, had: 4784 CHARLES, b. July 3, 1863, d. June 13, 1876. He was a mariner of Kittery, Me.
4785 HANNAH ABBIE, b. Aug. 24, 1842, m. Nov. 21, 1861, ROBERT BRIAD, b. Kittery, March 9, 1832, d. Kittery 1890. He was a joiner in K.; had no child but adopted a niece.
4786 JOHN J., b. Kittery, June 16, 1845, d. Kittery, Jan. 20, 1912, m. Aug. 24, 1889, MARY ESTELLE WENTWORTH, b. Jan. 17, 1856, d. K. Dec. 30, 1904, dau. of Andrew P. and Sarah. He was a joiner in Kittery and had: 4787 ELMER, b. 1890, d. 1893.
4788 OLIVE F., b. Sept. 26, 1847, d. unmarried March 30, 1881, Kittery.
F4789 SARAH ELIZABETH, b. Jan. 26, 1850, m. Sept. 18, 1870, NATHANIEL BOWDEN.

F2071 Ariadne Shapleigh Locke, born in New Castle in 1812, died in 1909, married in Portsmouth, Apl. 5, 1835, ANDREW BELL VENNARD of Portsmouth, born in 1808, died in 1857.

Children of 7th Gen. b. in Portsmouth.

4790 ANDREW B., b. 1838, was a clerk in Ports., and d. unmarried Feb. 25, 1869.
4791 FANNIE ALLEN, b. 1838, d. unmarried Ports., Feb. 17, 1915.
4792 ABBIE UNDERWOOD, b. 1842, d. 1905, m. Ports., July 26, 1871, GERSHOM F. MELCHER, b. Exeter, 1831, d. Nov. 17, 1876, son of Daniel and Nancy. He was a jeweler in Portsmouth.
4793 WILLIAM LAWRENCE, b. 1843, d. 1893, m. GEORGEANNA MCKESSOM and was one of firm of McKessom and McKessom, N. Y. City.
4794 EMMA GREENLEAF, b. 1845, d. unmarried in Ports., 1906.
4795 HELEN BELL, b. 1849, d. Ports. unmarried, 1910.
4796 FRANKLIN P., b. 1851, d. 1854.

F2074 David Locke, born in Corinth, Vt., July 2, 1791, died in Corinth, March 17, 1849, married 1816, OLIVE G. BICKFORD of Corinth, born in Corinth, Sept. 1, 1797, died Feb. 2, 1886. He was a farmer in Corinth.

Children of 7th Gen. b. in Corinth, Vt.

4797 REUBEN, b. ——, died young.
F4798 REUBEN, b. Oct. 13, 1817, m. 1st, 1840, EMILY ROWELL; m. 2nd, Jan. 1, 1849, ANNA MERRILL, # 5096.
4799 JOHN, b. ——, died young.
F4800 JOHN BICKFORD, b. July 15, 1819, m. March 31, 1842, CAROLINE TAPLIN.
F4801 ALMEDA SILVER, b. March 17, 1821, m. March 10, 1840, EPHRAIM SMITH.

4802 ANNAH N., b. March 3, 1823, d. Newton Lower Falls, Mass., Oct. 8, 1860, m. 1844, JUDSON SMITH, b. Framingham, Mass., Feb. 25, 1821, d. Oct. 18, 1852; m. 2nd, CASSANDER S. FLAGG of Newton, Mass. By Mr. Smith she had: 4803 ADONIRAM, who was unmarried and died in the war from wounds; 4804 DAVID LOCKE, who m., and lived in the Soldiers' Home in California.

F4805 OLIVE G., b. 1824, m. Sept. 22, 1846, JOSHUA F. WOODMAN.

4806 MARY ANN, b. 1826, d. Feb. 6, 1884, m July 30, 1850, ALLEN RICHARDSON, b. Oct. 10, 1827, d. March 1893, had: 4807 ALLEN LOCKE, b. June 2, 1851, who was m. and d. July 18, 1913; 4808 FRANK, b. Jan. 15, 1853, d. Sept. 28, 1853.

4809 JULIA, b. 1828, d. 1844, unmarried.

4810 DAVID, b. 1829, d. 1845, unmarried.

4811 PHEBE, b. 1831, m. 1st, B. F. Garvey; m. 2nd, PHILANDER WOODBURY of Lawrence, Mass. Was a farmer in Leroy, Minn., in 1898.

F4812 BLAKE, b. March 27, 1833, m. MARY ANN McCRILLIS, Dec. 23, 1857.

F4813 JANETTE, b. 1833, m. Jan. 1, 1851, CHARLES FARWELL.

4814 MARTHA S., b. June 7, 1835, m. Worcester, Mass., Nov. 2, 1871, CHARLES FLAGG, b. Holden, Dec. 25, 1807, d. Sept. 2, 1893. He was in the Railroad business Holden, Mass.; had no children.

F4815 ANNIS T., b. Apl. 11, 1837, m. 1st, June 24, 1863, WILLARD JONES; m. 2nd, Nov. 25, 1880, NATHANIEL BRIGHAM.

4816 DEARBORN BICKFORD, b. Feb. 18, 1839, was a farmer in Topsham, Vt., and d. unmarried Sept. 9, 1898.

4817 CHARLES B., b. 1841, d. 1842.

F4818 SARAH F., b. Dec. 3, 1842, m. Dec. 31, 1860, HARRY EMERY.

F2084 Sarah Abigail Locke, born in Corinth, Vt., July 19, 1796, married ELLIOTT TAPLIN, lived in Corinth, Vt.

Children of 7th Gen.

4819 ELIZABETH, b. Sept. 21, 1819, m. LEIGHTON EASTMAN, lived in Michigan, and had: 4820 FRANCIS; 4821 ELIZABETH; 4822 EASTMAN; 4823 CLARENCE; 4824 ELLIOTT, b. 1840; 4825 EDWARD; 4826 SIDNEY; 4827 SARAH.

F4828 NATHAN, b. Dec. 9, 1820, m. June 10, 1845, CAROLINE BICKFORD.

F4829 LUCINDA, b. ——, m. 1847, REUBEN KIMBALL.

F4830 SOPHIA, m. 1845, ISSUE FORD.

4831 HARRIET K., m. HENRY KIMBALL and had: 4832 WILLIAM H., b. May 1862; 4833 MABEL S., b. 1864; 4834 MAUD A., b. 1867, d. 1870.

4835 MARY, m. May 1847, JOSEPH LAMSON, had no children.

4836 SUSAN, m. GEORGE WARREN of East Saginaw, Mich., and had: 4837 WILLIAM, b. 1862; 4838 GEORGE, b. 1864; and three died young.

4839 ALMIRA, b. ——.

4840 EMMA F., b. 1854,? m. Nov. 26, 1896, FRANK E. MAYALL.

SEVENTH GENERATION

F2086 Capt. John Locke, born in Corinth, Vt., Oct. 21, 1799, died June 20, 1878, married SARAH F. THURSTON of Corinth, born in Corinth, Apl. 25, 1808, died March 4, 1865, daughter of Moses and Betsey (Lovering). He was a farmer in Chelsea, Vt.

Children of 7th Gen.

4841 LUCY M., b. Corinth, Vt., Nov. 11, 1824, d. in Kansas, Nov. 8, 1903, m. WILLIAM CAVERLY of Wentworth, N. H., had no children.
F4842 NANCY M., b. Corinth, Vt., Feb. 27, 1827, m. LEVI GRANT.
F4843 JOHN L., b. Feb. 19, 1829, m. 1870, NANCY G. RICHARDSON.
4844 SUSAN C., b. Apl. 19, 1831, d. Worcester, Mass., May 16, 1905, m. 1860, ALPHEUS H. HEMINWAY of Worcester, Mass., and had: 4845 GEORGEANNA, b. 1862; 4846 EUGENIE, b. 1864; 4847 WALDO, b. 1866; 4848 CLARENCE C., Capt. of Worcester Fire Dept., has a son.
4849 CHARLES C., b. Nov. 26, 1832, d. Sept. 25, 1835.
F4850 DEWITT C., b. Dec. 26, 1834, m. 1860, MARGARET RICHARDSON; m. 2nd, BETTIE R. LEWIS.
F4851 CHARLES C., b. Jan. 11, 1837, m. Jan. 22, 1869, CAROLINE KIMBALL.
4852 VICTORIA R., b. Feb. 18, 1839, d. Dec. 11, 1870, m. Orford, Sept. 9, 1862, NATHANIEL R. SARGENT of Orford, b. May 2, 1824, son of Timothy and Eunice (Rogers). He m. 2nd, CHARLOTTE JEFFERS; was a painter in Concord and d. there, Nov. 27, 1893, had: 4853 MARY P., b. Aug. 10, 1865, lived Kansas City; 4854 NELLIE T., b. June 30, 1867, m. ROY ANDERSON of Holton, Kan.
4855 ELLIOTT S., b. Corinth, Vt., Jan. 3, 1841, m. 1866, NETTIE CANFIELD; was a farmer in Holton, Kan., and d. 1880, had: 4856 EUSTACE, b. 1867, m. and lives Wichita, Kan.; 4857 MUSIE, b. 1870, d. Kansas; m. ROBERT WHEELER, and had: 4858 EUSTACE ARMARILLA; and 4859 BERTHA TEXAS; 4860 CARRIE, b. 1872.
4861 HANNAH M., b. Oct. 21, 1842, m. March 21, 1866, AUGUSTUS E. CARR, b. March 21, 1832, who served 3 years in the 12th and 140th Mass. Reg. He was a grocer in Worcester, Mass., and d. March 14, 1886; no children.
4862 CARRIE A., b. July 18, 1844, m. Medford, Mass., JAMES P. RICH-ARDSON, who was postmaster, West Medford, Mass.; no children.
4863 SARAH JULIA, b. Feb. 12, 1846, d. unmarried.
4864 ANNA DIANTHA, b. Chelsea, Vt., Apl. 10, 1848, m. NATHANIEL T. CLARKE of Salem, Mass. She d. May 1906.
4865 DR. GEORGE EUGENE, b. Chelsea, Vt., Dec. 30, 1849, graduated in medicine 1880 has a large general practice in Holton, Kan., was coroner and member State Board of Health six years.
4865a HENRY EUSTACE, b. Dec. 22, 1851, d. Oct. 14, 1876; studied medicine but health failed before finishing his course.

F2087 Haynes Locke, born in Corinth, Vt., Oct. 29, 1801, married about 1830, MARY MACFARLAND of Hopkinton, Mass., born Nov. 1806, died Nov. 1, 1877. He died 1849.

Children of 7th Gen. b. in Corinth, Vt.

4866 RODNEY, b. Nov. 1832, d. Jan. 1886.
4867 ARVILLA, b. Feb. 1834, d. Feb. 7, 1911, m. 1st, 1859, WILLIAM MARTIN, who was killed in the Civil War; m. 2nd, 1879, GEORGE MCDONOUGH, who d. 1909. By Martin she had: 4868 ELLA J., b. June 1862, in Hopkinton, Mass., d. Oct. 5, 1910, m. 1884, WILLIAM L. MERRILL, b. 1862, in Hopkinton, is now, 1915, assistant superintendent in a Brockton shoe factory.
4869 JACKSON, b. Feb. 1842, died in the Civil War.
4870 WILLIAM, b. ——, died young.
4871 NANCY A., b. Nov. 14, 1844, d. 1908, m. 1867, ELIAS O. HODGE, b. Marlow, Oct. 1, 1838, who was a Civil War veteran, had: 4872 JESSIE E., b. Hopkinton, Mass., Jan. 1875, and lives, 1915, with her father in Detroit, Mich. ELIAS OBEDIAH REDDING was said to be husband of Nancy but it must be a mistake as given in Hopkinton Record.
4873 MARY, b. Feb. 1847, m. March 1870, HENRY ALEXIS WILLIAMS, b. Nov. 26, 1844, is a mechanical engineer in Worcester, Mass., 1915. They had: 4874 ERNEST M., b. Medway Mass., Dec. 1871, d. Sept. 1872; 4875 AVICE EDNA, b. June, 1880, m. June 1908, GILBERT R. KENT, b. Jan. 1880, in Quincy, Mass. He is a civil engineer, and had children born in West Haven Conn., 4876 AVICE EDNA, 2nd, b. Aug. 1910; 4877 JAMES D., b. Jan. 1915.
4878 SARAH, 4879 MINERVA, and 4880 DAVID died in childhood.

F2089 Blake Locke, born in Corinth, Vt., Feb. 15, 1805, married JANETTE WHITNEY LEVETT, born in 1806, died Dec. 29, 1863. They lived in Boston, and he died March 4, 1854.

Children of the 7th Gen.

4881 ALFRED, b. 1823.
4882 THEODORE LYMAN, b. 1825.
4883 HORACE BLAKE, b. 1827.
4884 JANETTE ELMIRA RICHARDSON, b. 1829.

All lived to be adults but never married.

4885 ABIGAIL.
4886 NANCY, b. ——.
4887 WILLIAM, b. ——.
4888 MARGARET, b. ——, m. JOSEPH CHILDS, lived in Corinth, Vt.
F4889 ALICE, b. ——, m. IRA D. RICHARDSON, lived Washington, Vt.
I feel sure the last three are not children of Blake but are his brothers and sisters.

F2093 Anna Locke, born in Epsom, Dec. 16, 1784, died Apl. 863. married June 13, 1804, in Epsom, JOHN SANDERS of

LOCKE FAMILY REUNION, 1892

Sons and Daughters of Samuel Blake Locke F2094 and Betsey (Philbrick) Locke Living in 1892

SEVENTH GENERATION

Epsom, born in Rye, May 20, 1781, died March 13, 1870, son of George, who descended from Christopher, emigrant from England before 1661. He was a farmer and plow maker, a very energetic man who lived in Epsom until 1835, then in East Concord.

Children of 7th Gen. b. in Epsom.

F4890 GEORGE, b. Dec. 7, 1804, m. MARY TWOMBLEY.
F4891 SIMEON L., b. March 15, 1806, m. Apl. 6, 1837, CAROLINE COLBY.
F4892 ABIGAIL LOCKE, b. Jan. 20, 1808, m. SHERBURN GREEN.
4893 NANCY, b. Apl. 16, 1809, d. Sept. 15, 1810.
F4893 JOHN, b. July 15, 1811, m. March 21, 1839, ANGENETTE LEAVITT.
F4894 NANCY, b. Nov. 29, 1812, m. Aug. 23, 1839, JOHN WALLACE.
4895 REUBEN, b. May 7, 1814, m. Apl. 4, 1842, ABIGAIL LOCKE, # F2593.
4896 JOSEPH L., b. June 1, 1815, m. Aug. 1, 1842, HARRIET B. POTTER of E. Concord, and he d. Nov. 14, 1872; had no children.
F4897 DAVID L., b. Feb. 26, 1817, m. Nov. 14, 1844, MARY A. CARR of Concord.
4898 SOLOMON C., b. Epsom, Dec. 5, 1818, m. May 30, 1847, THIRZA C. CORLISS of Alexandria. Was a farmer in E. Concord, had: 4899 EMMA, b. 1848, d. 1864, and he died Concord, June 10, 1895.

F2094 Samuel Blake Locke, born in Epsom, Oct. 22, 1786, died Aug. 12, 1866, married July 1, 1813, BETSEY PHILBRICK of Epsom, born in Pittsfield, Sept. 6, 1792, died in East Concord, Jan. 25, 1871. He owned land in Penacook in 1856, later was a farmer in East Concord.

Children of 7th Gen. b. in Concord.

4902 DAVID, b. Jan. 16, 1815, d. Concord, Aug. 24, 1834.
F4903 JOHN P., b. Jan. 27, 1817, m. June 13, 1840, SARAH CLOUGH OSBORN.
4904 SIMEON, b. March 7, 1819, went to Cal. 1849, returned and was editor of a paper in Rutland, Vt. He later was in business in Buffalo, N. Y., where he died of cholera, unmarried.
F4905 REUBEN B., b. March 23, 1821, m. Jan. 9, 1848, SARAH H. CASS.
4906 DANIEL P., b. May 7, 1823, was a farmer in Pittsfield and d. unmarried in E. Conc., Nov. 25, 1896.
F4907 SAMUEL M., b Nov. 30, 1825, m. Dec. 31, 1857, CHARLOTTE K. CLIFFORD.
F4908 ELIZABETH F., b. June 1828, m. 1st, May 4, 1853, R. HENRY DAVIS; m. 2nd, Apl. 3, 1867, AARON G. FARNUM.
F4909 MARY EMERY, b. Sept. 19, 1830, m. Sept. 18, 1851, WILLIAM T. CASS.
F4910 MARGARET AYER, b. Apl. 13, 1832, m. Nov. 11, 1852, DR. JAMES M. BISHOP.
F4911 SARAH A., b. March 31, 1835, m. Nov. 13, 1856, JOHN T. BACHELDER.

4912 ABBIE A., b. Apl. 18, 1837, d. unmarried March 12, 1857.
F4913 HELEN S., b. Sept. 7, 1841, m. Sept. 8, 1867, REV. NICHOLAS F. WHITTAKER.

F2095 David Locke, born in Epsom, Oct. 19, 1788, died March 19, 1863, married Oct. 11, 1810, FLORINDA LOCKE of Lyman, # 1719. He moved from Rye to Lyman in 1812 where he built a log house, and there raised a large family, all of whom became prominent in life.

Children of 7th Gen.

F4914 JOSEPH, b. Feb. 27, 1812, m. 1844, ARVILLA CARR.
F4915 JONATHAN, b. May 17, 1814, m. Feb. 23, 1837, SALLY COOK.
F4916 MARY A. MINOT, b. March 29, 1816, m. Dec. 7, 1839, STEPHEN FARNSWORTH.
F4917 ELBRIDGE GERRY, b. March 24, 1818, m. 1st, March 21, 1844, JANETTE A. DIXON; m. 2nd, March 15, 1874, AMANDA PANKEY.
F4918 FLORINDA, b. Apl. 21, 1820, m. Oct. 19, 1843, HENRY WALKER.
F4919 SIMON LOVERING, b. Sept. 6, 1822, m. March 3, 1847, HARRIET BAILEY.
F4920 DAVID MORRILL, b. Sept. 1, 1824, m. 1st, Sept. 1, 1853, MARY J. JAMESON, # 5117; m. 2nd, Sept. 9, 1893, JENNIE A. GILLETT.
4921 SILAS MERRILL, b. Lyman, Aug. 16, 1826, m. July 25, 1857, SABINA MOULTON, b. Dec. 2, 1823, d. May 4, 1896, dau. of Baron Moulton of St. Johnsbury, Vt. He d. San Francisco, Jan. 25, 1903. After receiving a common school education, he for a time worked in a flour mill in Dayton, N. Y. He sailed for California via Cape Horn from New York, Jan. 1, 1849, and was several months on the way—so long, in fact, that his brother DAVID who bade him good-bye in New York, came back to Lyman, taught school that winter, and started for California in the spring, going by the Panama route arriving there three days before his brother. The surprise of Silas at being welcomed by his brother whom he had left in New York can be imagined. He started mining with indifferent success, and then bought a well, where California market, the Wall street of San Francisco, now stands, and for many years controlled the water supply of the city, a far more profitable business than mining. By advice of General W. T. Sherman, then a Lieutenant stationed there, he invested his savings in land within the city limits, and this in later years made him an extensive dealer in real estate. An original "49er," he was one of the oldest members of the Society of California Pioneers.
F4922 ALICE PARSONS, b. Nov. 13, 1828, m. Jan. 6, 1855, HALE RIX.
F4923 JOSIAH HANNIBAL, b. June 7, 1831, m. Oct. 13, 1859, CARRIE MACOMBER.
F4924 ABIGAIL BLAKE, b. Sept. 15, 1834, m. 1st, June 13, 1854, LYMAN J. MCINDOE; m. 2nd, June 1, 1876, REV. FRANKLYN BUTLER.

SEVENTH GENERATION 247

F2096 Simeon Locke, Jr., born in Epsom, Dec. 14, 1790, died in Newfields, Aug. 27, 1882, married July 4, 1813, CLARISSA TASH, born Oct. 25, 1792, died May 2, 1871, daughter of Dea. John and Mary (Ham). He lived in Rye, Epsom, and Concord, learned the blacksmith's trade with his uncle, JONATHAN LOCKE, bought the Messer tavern in Newfields, where he settled. He left off the use of rum to which he was addicted, and in 1830 raised his blacksmith shop, the first building raised in town without rum.

Children of 7th Gen.

F4925 LYDIA HALL, b. March 5, 1814, m. Oct. 2, 1845, NATHANIEL FOLSOM KIMBALL.

F4926 JOHN TASH, b. March 21, 1816, m. 1st, Sept. 12, 1841, ROXBURY SPOFFORD SANBORN; m. 2nd, July 9, 1863, SARAH WALDRON TREADWELL.

F4927 SIMEON, b. Dec. 25, 1817, m. Feb. 28, 1842, NANCY NORRIS CLARKE.

F4928 JOSEPH HAM, b. May 15, 1819, m. May 26, 1842, NANCY R. KENT.

4929 CLARA JOSEPHINE, b. Feb. 14, 1821, d. Feb. 19, 1854, m. Epping, Nov. 5, 1844, EZEKIEL SANBORN of Epping, b. Sept. 7, 1820, son of Moses and Abigail (Prescott). Lived in So. Newmarket and had no children. He m. 2nd, SARAH E. PERKINS, and d. Sept. 17, 1878.

F4930 SAMUEL BLAKE, b. Sept. 30, 1822, m. Apl. 28, 1846, ANNA HOWARD DAVIS.

4931 A SON, b. Oct. 12, 1824, d. same day.

4932 ABIGAIL WHEELER, b. Newmarket, Oct. 12, 1824, twin with last, d. July 13, 1886, m. Newmarket, May 15, 1845, CHARLES O. CUMMINGS of Andover, Mass., b. June 29, 1818, son of Dea. Joseph and Mary. He was a farmer and keeper of the almshouse and d. Andover, Sept. 14, 1898, adopted: 4933 BLANCHE OSGOOD, b. June 1870.

F4934 GEORGE OLIVER, b. Sept. 19, 1826, m. Nov. 22, 1849, HARRIET T. LOCKE, # 4953.

4935 MARY OLEVIA, b. June 19, 1828, d. unmarried, Newmarket, Nov. 20, 1845.

4936 ELLEN AUGUSTA, b. So. Newmarket, March 29, 1830, d. March 22, 1893, m. 1st, Feb. 20, 1851, JOHN T. KENNARD, b. 1830, d. 1910, son of Jonas B. and they had: 4937 CHARLES C., b. 1853, d. Apl. 20, 1857; 4938 ELLA F., b. Feb. 28, 1857, d. March 5, 1857. Ellen, m. 2nd, Nov. 1, 1882, GREENLEAF CLARK FOWLER, b. So. Newmarket, Feb. 27, 1823, son of John C. and Mary (Nutter). He was of the 8th generation of the Fowler Family in this country. After his early schooling in Newfields he entered the employ of Concord and Portsmouth R. R., rising to the position of assistant roadmaster, and remained with this road 23 years. He was deeply interested in the Locke Genealogy as well as local matters.

He was one of Newfields' most respected citizens, and died there Dec. 1, 1902. His 1st wife was SARAH M. HALL.

F4940 EDWIN AUGUSTUS, b. a twin, March 29, 1830, m. Jan. 4, 1854, MARTHA A. SMITH.

4941 MARTHA ANNA, b. March 27, 1832, d. Jan. 23, 1857, m. WILLIAM MURRAY of Lawrence, Mass., his 2nd marriage, had: 4942 ADA, b. 1854, d. 1856.

4943 SARAH ANN, b. March 25, 1834, m. Jan. 2, 1854, EDWIN B. LOCKE, # F5048.

F2097 John Locke, born in Epsom, March 14, 1794, died Aug. 15, 1865, married in Epsom, Oct. 30, 1822, RACHEL SANBORN of Epsom, # 1730, born Jan. 6, 1796, died March 3, 1880. Owned land in Penacook in 1856. He was admitted to the Concord church in 1824. He worked in Boston and saved his money, returned and bought a farm in East Concord where he afterward lived.

Children of 7th Gen. b. in East Concord.

4944 ANN MARIA, b. May 5, 1824, d. Oct. 17, 1848, m. June 11, 1846, SAMUEL W. SMITH of Manchester, who was a carpenter in Lawrence, had no children.

4945 JOSIAH SANBORN, b. March 28, 1826, m. Concord, March 11, 1857, CLARA G. EMERY of Concord, b. Jan. 21, 1821, d. E. Conc., March 4, 1904, dau. of Isaac and Esther (Tay). Had no children. He is a farmer at East Concord Intervale, of musical ability and Democratic faith, has served his city as assessor, councilman and alderman.

F4946 MARGARET ANN, b. Feb. 22, 1828, m. March 16, 1853, JOHN W. THATCHER.

F4947 JAMES W., b. Dec. 31, 1831, m. June 21, 1859, MARIA D. JARVIS.

4948 JOHN PERKINS, b. Sept. 5, 1834, d. March 5, 1858.

F2098 Josiah Knowles Locke, born in Epsom, Sept. 16, 1796, died in Pembroke, Jan. 7, 1878, married in Concord, Oct. 12, 1820, LYDIA PHILBRICK of Concord, born Oct. 20, 1797, died in Pembroke, Sept. 17, 1892, daughter of Edward and Sally (Durgin). He was a farmer in Pembroke since 1852.

Children of 7th Gen.

4949 ANNA SANDERS, b. July 28, 1820, d. Aug. 20, 1820.

F4950 NANCY EDGERLY, b. Jan. 25, 1823, m. 1st, June 25, 1845, ROBERT MOORE (See F2320); m. 2nd, Feb. 10, 1885, ISAAC C. BOYCE.

4951 SARAH PHILBRICK, b. Aug. 21, 1824, d. Feb. 8, 1835.

4952 ABBIE BLAKE, b. Lyman, March 14, 1826, m. Concord, Jan. 7, 1846, SAMUEL WEBSTER of Dover, b. Derry, was a printer in Concord and Pembroke, had no children, and d. in California, Apl. 1882.

4953 HARRIET TITUS, b. Lyman, Apl. 14, 1827, m. Nov. 22, 1849, GEORGE O. LOCKE (See F4934), of Newmarket, b. Sept. 19, 1826, d. Oct. 27, 1913.
F4954 ANNAH SANDERS, b. May 22, 1828, m. 1st, March 30, 1848, MARSTON M. TALLANT; m. 2nd, GEORGE F. WHITTREDGE.
F4955 EDWARD PHILBRICK, b. Oct. 5, 1832, m. 1st, Jan. 9, 1854, MARTHA A. MARTIN; m. 2nd, Jan. 12, 1887, EMMA J. FOWLE.
F4956 MORRIS LAMPREY, b. Aug. 18, 1841, m. 1st, March 1861, MARY HINES; m. 2nd, ELIZA DIXON; m. 3rd, FLORA J. ELKINS.

F2100 Sarah Blake Locke, born in Epsom, March 29, 1801, died Apl. 21, 1875, married Dec. 28, 1825, WILLIAM YEATON of Pittsfield, born in Pittsfield, July 29, 1793, died a farmer in South Pittsfield, May 9, 1851.

Children of 7th Gen.

F4957 JOSEPH, b. July 13, 1826, m. 1st, 1849, ANNA GREEN; m. 2nd, FANNIE COLLINS.
F4958 SIMEON L., b. Nov. 13, 1828, m. 1856, MARY BROWN.
4959 WILLIAM A., b. Sept. 1832, d. July 30, 1833.
F4960 WILLIAM, b. July 30, 1836, m. May 23, 1867, JOSEPHINE C. DRAKE.

F2103 Abigail B. Locke, born in Epsom, Jan. 19, 1809, died March 24, 1885, married in Concord, Oct. 18, 1837, ROBERT SANDERS of Ossipee who was a farmer there.

Children of 7th Gen. b. in Ossipee.

4961 JOSEPH, b. ——, died young.
F4962 SIMEON LOCKE, b. Nov. 21, 1839, m. JENNIE C. BRACKETT, Nov. 25, 1864.
4963 WILLIAM C., b. July 28, 1842, m. Nov. 25, 1864, ORISSA BICKFORD FRENCH. He has been treasurer of State of Colorado. In 1900 he was in Mexico, had: 4964 CLARA L., b. Apl. 29, 1867; 4965 ORISSA F., b. Dec. 12, 1875.
4966 ABIGAIL L., b. July 15, 1845, d. May 5, 1895, m. Sept. 1865, BENJAMIN YOUNG.
4967 SARAH A., b. Oct. 12, 1850, d. unmarried Feb. 22, 1893.
4968 CLARA E., b. Feb. 15, 1855, m. Dec. 1881, CHARLES P. BREWER, a painter, lives Chelsea, Mass.

F2107 Josiah Webster, born Jan. 6, 1783, died in Portsmouth, Dec. 9, 1833, married in Portsmouth, May 20, 1806, HANNAH GRANT of Portsmouth who died in 1841.

Children of 7th Gen.

4969 SON, b. Oct. 2, 1807.
4970 FRANCES, b. 1806.
4971 SARAH ANN, b. July 22, 1809.

4972 ADELAIDE, b. Ports., Aug. 20, 1811, d. Oakland, Cal., Nov. 15, 1878, m. Ports., Sept. 8, 1831, SAMUEL SPARHAWK HORNY, b. Cambridge, March 16, 1804, d. Chicago, March 2, 1872, son of Thos. Jr., had: 4973 GEORGIANA S., b. Boston, May 6, 1834, m. Chicago, July 5, 1853, GEORGE WAITE DEERING, b. Portland, Aug. 5, 1829, d. Berlin Falls, May 5, 1890.

F2112 Sally Webster, born March 16, 1786, married in 1807, EPHRAIM PHILBRICK of Rye, born Sept. 9, 1779–80.

Children of 7th Gen. b. in Rye.

4974 JOSIAH, b. Oct. 2, 1807, d. Oct. 17, 1870, m. June 25, 1833, SARAH ANN BROWN, b. March 12, 1810, d. Sept. 22, 1870, dau. of Jonathan and Hannah (Drake).

4975 SARAH ANN, b Nov. 7, 1811, d. March 22, 1901, m. July 7, 1835 DANIEL PHILBRICK, b. June 10, 1805, d. March 11, 1882, son of Jonathan and Sarah (Marden); had five children.

4976 MOSES, b. Apl. 6, 1813, d. Apl. 8, 1875, m. Apl. 12, 1838, SARAH A. GARLAND, b. Apl. 15, 1817, d. Sept. 28, 1898, dau. of Levi and Polly (Perkins).

4977 ELIZABETH, b. March 5, 1816, died young.

4978 JOHN C., b. Apl. 9, 1818, d. Jan. 15, 1869, m. ELIZA JENNESS, b. Sept. 20, 1824, d. Sept. 18, 1893, dau. of Joseph and Huldah (Perkins).

4979 CHRISTENA, R., b. Aug. 27, 1822, d. Nov. 13, 1885, m. Dec. 29, 1838, ABRAHAM PERKINS, b. Jan. 13, 1818, d. Dec. 23, 1899, son of James and Mrs. Mehitable (Garland).

F2116 Martha Webster, born Apl. 10, 1795, married Dec. 9, 1819, JAMES BROWN, born Nov. 1789, son of John and Salome (Allen).

Children of 7th Gen. b. in Rye.

4980 ROSILLA, b. Dec. 7, 1819, d. unmarried Dec. 20, 1887.

4981 ELIHU, b. Apl. 6, 1822, m. May 4, 1856, MEHITABLE LOCKE, # F2973.

4982 JAMES, b. Jan. 15, 1824, d. July 11, 1880, m. Nov. 2, 1855, MARGARET VERCILDA GREEN, b. March 9, 1827, d. June 15, 1897, dau. of Charles and Mary (Lamper).

4983 WILLIAM, b. Nov. 21, 1825, d. June 29, 1887, m. Oct. 23, 1851, HENRIETTA DOWNS, b. Apl. 10, 1828, dau. of Samuel and Mrs. Betsey Tucker.

4984 EMELINE, b. June 4, 1827, d. Sept. 23, 1838.

4985 JOHN A., b. Nov. 20, 1828, d. Jan. 22, 1887.

4986 LEVI W., b. Sept. 7, 1830, m. Oct. 2, 1852, SARAH O. VARRELL, dau. of Capt. William and Nancy (Berry).

4987 ABIGAIL, b. Sept. 12, 1832, m. 1st, DAVID MARDEN, b. 1827, had no children; m. 2nd, EDWARD WALCOTT and had one dau.

4988 SARAH, b. Feb. 16, 1835, d. July 2, 1848.

4989 SOPHIA, b. June 21, 1841, fatally scalded, Oct. 27, 1842.

SEVENTH GENERATION   251

F2121 Polly L. Sanborn, born Oct. 25, 1793, died Nov. 9, 1828, married Nov. 1818, JOHN WHITEHOUSE of Pembroke, born June 21, 1779, died July 14, 1829.
Children of 7th Gen.
4990 SOLOMON, b. Sept. 1, 1818, m. Jan. 17, 1842, ELIZABETH J. DUDLEY. b. Jan. 2, 1821, had four children.
4991 MARY A., b. Dec. 7, 1819, d. Sept. 6, 1829.
4992 SARAH J., b. Dec. 27, 1821, d. Feb. 19, 1836.
4993 JOHN, b. Oct. 24, 1824, d. Feb. 6, 1825.

F2122 Jeremiah Sanborn, born in Chichester, Dec. 30, 1795, died Sept. 14, 1846, married Aug. 10, 1826, CLARISSA SMITH of New Hampton, born March 23, 1801, died July 1866. He was a carpenter in Loudonville, Ohio.
Children of 7th Gen.
4994 GILMAN S., b. Jan. 28, 1828, was unmarried, a carpenter, miner, and postmaster, at Yankee Jims, Cal.
4995 JEREMIAH L., b. Campton, Nov. 29, 1829, m. March 10, 1852, ANNA VAN HORN, lives Cal., had: 4996 HARVEY L., b. 1853; 4997 CLARISSA, b. 1860.
4998 JOSEPH H., b. Jan. 13, 1831, d. Ohio, Aug. 24, 1895, m. Nov. 15, 1864, CLARISSA S. HAVEN, was a coal dealer in Loudonville, O., and had: 4999 HAVEN L.; 5000 MARY A.; 5001 LAURA C.; 5002 GILMAN S.

F2126 Joseph B. Sanborn, born in Chichester, March 6, 1810, died March 8, 1882, married March 14, 1833, MARY J. SMITH of New Hampton, born Sept. 16, 1810, died March 19, 1870, daughter of Moses. He was a Captain of Infantry, and teacher in Loudonville, O.
Children of 7th Gen.
5003 GEORGE P., b. Dec. 30, 1833, d. Sept. 25, 1845.
5004 SUSAN S., b. Dec. 10, 1835, d. Oct. 22, 1894, m. March 15, 1860, WILLIAM MUMPER of Washington, O.
5005 CLARISSA J., b. March 24, 1838, m. Nov. 1, 1860, ISAAC WINANS of Galion, Ohio.
5006 SARAH L., b. May 25, 1840, m. ——— TAYLOR of Loudonville, O.
5007 JOSEPH G., b. Nov. 8, 1847, m. Nov. 1876, KATE E. DAY, dau. of Dr. Stephen, lived Wooster, O., had: 5008 JOSEPH S., 5009 MARY A.; 5010 MARTHA V; 5011 LLOYD D.
5012 CHARLES L., b. Dec. 28, 1850, m. 1st, Oct. 25, 1877, ADA J. ROSENSTEEL, b. Nov. 1, 1853, d. Nov. 28, 1878; m. 2nd, March 12, 1880, SARAH REINHART, b. July 25, 1846. He is superintendent of Western Elev. Mill Co., had: 5013 ADA M.; 5014 JANE L.; 5015 QUINCY L.; 5016 EMILY C.

F2127 Dea. David Locke, born on Locke's Hill, Epsom, May 23, 1790, died in Epsom, Jan. 29, 1872, married in Canaan, Nov. 28, 1819, POLLY CARLETON, born in Canaan, Feb. 12, 1798, died in Epsom, Sept. 24, 1867. He enlisted for 60 days Sept. 29, 1814; was a farmer in Epsom all his life.

Children of 7th Gen. b. in Epsom.

5017 MARY ANN, b. May 10, 1821, m. June 15, 1848, ALBION LOCKE. (See F2214.)

F5018 ELIZABETH P., b. Apl. 23, 1823, m. Apl. 15, 1846, JAMES D. PAGE.

5019 SARAH D., b. Oct. 18, 1824, m. Apl. 15, 1849, JOHN KELLUM of Boston, lived So. Boston, had: 5020 CHILD, died young; 5021 GEORGE D., lives Medford, Mass. He had previously m. Emaline Locke #2209.

F2128 Abigail Locke, born on Locke's Hill, Epsom, Apl. 26, 1796, married JONATHAN GREEN, born 1791. From Epsom he went to Australia and decided to settle there, but died at sea in 1835 on his way home to get his family

Children of 7th Gen.

5022 CLARISSA, b. 1817, m. March 26, 1849, SHERBURNE FIFIELD, b. 1817 in Vermont. He was a truckman.

5023 ANN, b. 1812 (?), m. MERRILL F. DOW, and had: 5024 CHARLES M., b. Oct. 26, 1848; was with Brooks Bros., Haverhill, Mass., 1898.

F2129 Nancy Locke, born on Locke's Hill, Epsom, Aug. 9, 1801, died Jan. 1, 1858, married Feb. 15, 1826, EBENEZER GOVE, of Kensington, born May 6, 1801, died in Epsom, June 5, 1843.

Children of 7th Gen.

5025 DAVID LOCKE, b. Aug. 4, 1833, was with Killren Bell Co., Texas, in 1900, d. unmarried Aug. 7, 1903.

F5026 SARAH ANN, b. Jan. 10, 1835, m. Dec. 22, 1858, JOSIAH S. CLIFFORD.

F2135 Nancy Locke, born in Portsmouth, Feb. 12, 1800, died Dec. 22, 1882, married (Dover rec.) Nov. 6, 1817, (Lee Rec.) March 6, 1817, JOSEPH WHITTIER of Dover, born in Dover, Dec. 10, 1793, son of Obadiah and Sarah (Austin). He lived in Dover, Great Falls, Philadelphia, and Joliet, Ill., where he died July 22, 1889.

Children of 7th Gen.

5027 SAMUEL H. L., b. Dover, Nov. 20, 1818, m. Dec. 24, 1844, JEMIMA HUNTRESS of Lincoln, Me., who d. Fredericton, N. B., Jan. 15, 1892. He lived there in 1899, had: 5028 dau., b. 1845.

F5028 JOSEPH A., b. July 6, 1820, m. ANGELINE BRADFORD.

SEVENTH GENERATION

5029 ADALINE M., b. Dover, Apl. 14, 1822, d. Joliet, Ill., Jan. 10, 1888, m. Jan. 5, 1846, ALBERT C. BUFFAM of Orono, Me., who d. there, Sept. 12, 1856, had a son: 5030 J. W. BUFFAM, lived 1898, Chicago.

5031 LYDIA A., b. Apl. 7, 1824, d. Aug. 8, 1825.

5032 LYDIA H., b. Gt. Falls, March 6, 1827, m. Apl. 19, 1847, PELEG T. JONES of Lincoln, Me. They lived Bangor and he d. there, Sept. 13, 1895, had: 5033 FREELAND; 5034 HARLOW; 5035 MARY.

5036 CHARLES E., b. Gt. Falls, Dec. 2, 1828, m. a Spanish lady and lived San Jose, Cal., 1898, had: 5037 NELLIE.

5038 ELIZA A., b. Gt. Falls, Jan. 19, 1834, m. July 28, 1852, REV. H. R. WALWORTH of Lincoln, Me., lived Preston, Md., 1898, had a son.

5039 NANCY E., b. Gt. Falls, Apl. 14, 1836, m. Sept. 8, 1875, JOHN N. SMITH, of Joliet, Ill., lived Santiago, Cal., 1898, no children.

5040 GEORGE, b. Gt. Falls, Nov. 27, 1839, m. Feb. 10, 1855, SARAH M. LINDSEY of Lincoln, Me. He lived in Joliet, Ill., and d. Nov. 18, 1889, had: 5041 EDGAR; 5042 ANGELINE; 5043 LUCY; 5044 CLAIRE.

F2136 Jonathan Locke, born Sept. 20, 1802, died in California, June 13, 1878, married Sept. 5, 1830, MRS. RUTH CURTIS of Dover. He was a blacksmith in Great Falls, went to California in 1849.

Children of 7th Gen.

5045 MARY ABBIE, b. ——, unmarried.

5046 LYDIA HALL, b. ——, m. ——— DRISCO of California.

5047 EDWARD A., b. 1837, m. intentions Somersworth, Jan. 1, 1867, to EMMA H. DANIELS of Gt. Falls. She was b. in 1839, and after his death married again. Edward was a stone cutter in Dover, had no children and d. Dover, May 10, 1878.

F2137 Stacy Hall Locke, born in Dover, Aug. 22, 1808, died in Wells, Me., May 7, 1886, married July 22, 1832, his stepsister, MARY E. BEALS, born Portsmouth, Dec. 17, 1811, died in Dover, Apl. 29, 1891, daughter of Zachariah and Hannah (Tarlton). He was in the lumber and hotel business in Dover.

Children of 7th Gen.

F5048 EDWIN BEAL, b. Nov. 8, 1833, m. Jan. 2, 1854, SARAH A. LOCKE, #4943.

5049 ELLEN MARY, b. Dover, Feb. 15, 1836, m. Sept. 26, 1861, DR. JERE G. HALL of Alfred, Me., b. Apl. 28, 1836, has practiced in Wells for more than 35 years. She had no children and d. Wells, Nov. 15, 1907.

5050 CHARLES STACY, b. Dover, Sept. 20, 1837, m. 1st, June 15, 1862, ABBIE A. WHITE of Charleston, Me., b. Dec. 4, 1835, d. July 6, 1870; m. 2nd, in Exeter, Aug. 16, 1881, NELLIE E. SMITH of So. Newmarket, b. Exeter, in 1844, dau. of Daniel and Elizabeth. She lives in Wells, Me. He was a machinist in Chicago and d. in

Wells, Me., June 1, 1911. By first wife had: 5051 MAMIE C., b. Watertown, Mass., Feb. 19, 1864, died aged 4 mos.; 5052 LOTTIE HALL, b. Watertown, Apl. 25, 1865, d. Chicago, July 15, 1888; 5053 ALBERT STACY, died aged 3 mos.

F5054 MARTHA ABBIE, b. Apl. 18, 1840, m. Oct. 30, 1862, NATHANIEL E. HANSON.

5055 HANNAH BEALS, b. Freedom, Dec. 9, 1843, unmarried, was a teacher in Chicago for 25 years, now 1915 is living in Wells, Me., as a retired pensioned teacher of Chicago.

F5056 NANCY WHITTIER, b. Dec. 31, 1846, m. Jan. 1, 1868, CHARLES O. POPE.

F5057 LYDIA HALL, b. March 10, 1850, m. Feb. 25, 1875, MITCHELL R. MUDIE.

F5058 MARY ELIZABETH, b. Aug. 23, 1853, m. Sept. 16, 1874, FRANK B. WILLIAMS.

F2141 Simeon Prescott Locke, born in Rye, Jan. 14, 1799, died in Epsom, March 29, 1887, married 1st, June 9, 1835, SARAH B. CASS of Epsom, born Sept. 9, 1807, died June 26, 1849; married 2nd, in Loudon, Nov. 24, 1864, EUNICE PRESCOTT, born in Pittsfield, Jan. 1811, died in Epsom, Feb. 26, 1887, daughter of Eben and Naomi (Brown). He was a prosperous farmer in Epsom. (Was he the Simeon Locke who married in Durham, May 2, 1855, LYDIA R. PENDEXTER?)

Children of 7th Gen.

F5059 MANDANA C., b. Nov. 8, 1835, m. 1st, Dec. 20, 1855, JOHN W. PAGE, # 5823; m. 2nd, Nov. 26, 1865, SAMUEL STANLEY.

F5060 DEXTER H., b. Nov. 26, 1838, m. 1st, Nov. 30, 1864, SARAH A. PAGE; m. 2nd, Dec. 14, 1893, MRS. MARY ANN (PALMER) HILL.

5061 HORACE M., b. Dec. 3, 1840, was killed by a wagon Dec. 15, 1865.

5062 JOSEPH P., b. Epsom, June 30, 1842, m. Pittsfield, Dec. 25, 1862, LYDIA THOMPSON, # 4468, b. Nov. 21, 1843, d. 1907. He was a farmer and shoemaker, had no children, and d. Epsom, Feb. 12, 1911.

F5063 ORILLA H., b. Sept. 19, 1845, m. Apl. 19, 1858, HENRY W. BICKFORD.

F2142 Benjamin Lovering Locke, born in Rye, July 26, 1802, died March 26, 1883, married in Epsom, May 5, 1825, HANNAH P. MOSES, born in Epsom, Sept. 25, 1804, died Jan. 26, 1885, daughter of James and Betsey (Chesley). He was Major-Genl. of 3rd N. H. Regiment; was member of N. H. Legislature, a farmer and innkeeper in Epsom.

Children of 7th Gen. b. in Epsom.

F5064 LUCINDA M., b. March 30, 1826, m. Oct. 30, 1850, WILLIAM MC-MURPHY.

5065 HENRIETTA C., b. May 5, 1828, d. Eps., Feb. 23, 1830.

SEVENTH GENERATION 255

5066 ALMIRA E., b. Jan. 11, 1830, d. Oct. 10, 1857, m. Epsom, June 9, 1852, JOSEPH G. WHIDDEN of Boston, b. Loudon, March 9, 1827, had no child by Almira. He lived in Boston, and m. 2nd, 1891, ABBIE FOWLER.
F5067 JAMES LOVERING, b. May 14, 1832, m. May 16, 1858, SARAH M. SWALLOW.
F5068 MARIANNA J., b. May 5, 1834, m. Dec. 25, 1859, WILLIAM HAWSE, #2152.
F5069 ANNIE LOVERING, b. Sept. 9. 1836, m. July 4, 1859, GEORGE W. LANE.
5070 DAUGHTER, b. and d. May 1, 1838.
5071 ADELA A., b. Sept. 4, 1840, m. Nov. 30, 1870, JOHN D. GALE of Boston, b. May 31, 1847, had no children, and she d. June 17, 1893.
5072 SARAH M., b. Dec. 28, 1843, d. unmarried, Epsom, Dec. 28, 1860.
5073 BENJAMIN, b. twin with last, d. Apl. 28, 1844.
5074 WILLIAM T. ESTES, b. July 5, 1850, d. Epsom, Jan. 12, 1861.

F2145 Lucy Maria Locke, born July 11, 1807, died Dec. 13, 1893, married Oct. 20, 1830, DANIEL TILTON of Deerfield, born in 1800. He was a farmer and builder in Deerfield, and died Oct. 1855.
Children of 7th Gen. b. in Deerfield.
5075 DANIEL P., b. Nov. 28, 1831, d. in war, unmarried, Sept. 18, 1865.
5076 ANNA M., b. May 6, 1833, m. June 6, 1865, L. D. NEWELL of Rhode Island. She had no children and d. in Boston, May 30, 1879.
5077 Four children died infants.
5078 ALDEN M., b. Oct. 7, 1838, m. CORNELIA WELCH of Deerfield, had:
5079 ISABELLA, who m. a ―――― TOWNSEND; and two who died infants.
5080 ANGELA F., b. May 1, 1840, m. June 6, 1865, EZRA H. HEYWOOD, who d. May 1893; had four children in Princeton, Mass.
5081 JOAN F., b. July 31, 1842, never married.
5082 JOSEPHINE S., b. March 29, 1844; lives in Boston, unmarried.

F2148 Betsey Locke, born March 5, 1811, died Nov. 17, 1894, married Feb. 2, 1831, JACOB TILTON, a trader and hotel keeper in Deerfield.
Children of 7th Gen. b. in Deerfield.
5083 JACOB LOCKE, b. May 15, 1831, drowned, 1849.
5084 ALVIN H., b. Nov. 1834, d. Ottumwa, Iowa, Apl. 16, 1857. Was G. M. W. of A. O. M.
5085 RINALDO L., b. Sept. 17, 1836, is a lawyer, m. Nov. 5, 1900, FLORENCE E. BAYTISS of Ottumwa, Iowa, had: 5086 RINALDO L., JR., b. Aug. 26, 1901; 5087 FLORENCE, b. 1903; 5088 RUTH, b. 1909.

F2149 Almira Locke, born in Epsom, Aug. 1, 1814, died in Tyngsboro, Mass., Dec. 2, 1897, married Sept. 16, 1847, JOHN B. JOHNSON, born in Amesbury, Mass., Apl. 22, 1816. He was a war veteran, an inventor and lived in Tyngsboro, Mass.
Children of 7th Gen.
5089 ARABELLA, b. Epsom, Sept. 29, 1848, m. Aug. 10, 1868, HENRY M. NICHOLS of Reed's Ferry, N. H., have no children.
5090 ALMIRA L., b. Manchester, June 2, 1851, unmarried.
5091 ORVILLE B., b. Manchester, Oct. 28, 1856, m. Jan. 31, 1895, EVA S. BURKE of St. Johnsbury, Vt. He is an electrician.

F2150 Rev. Joseph J. Locke, born in Epsom, Sept. 8, 1816, died Nov. 4, 1870, married Nov. 1841, SARAH WEBSTER of South Kingston, born in 1815.
Child of 7th Gen.
F5092 SARAH A., b. Nov. 23, 1850, m. HENRY L. HADCOCK.

F2188 Anna Lovering Locke, born in Lyman, July 13, 1801, died Dec. 27, 1843, married Jan. 21, 1823, PETER MERRILL of Lisbon, born Jan. 1, 1792, died in Columbus City, Iowa, Oct. 8, 1864, son of Peter. He lived in Iowa, was a worthy, upright Christian, beloved by all.
Children of 7th Gen. probably b. in Iowa.
5093 PETER, b. Nov. 29, 1823, m. March 4, 1849, MARION T. WORKS; lived at Cumberland, Wis., and had: 5094 ESTHER L., lived Cumberland 1898.
5095 WILLIAM LOVERING, b. Sept. 10, 1825, d. Apl. 17, 1845.
5096 ANNA LOVERING, b. July 24, 1827, m. Jan. 1, 1849, REUBEN LOCKE. (See F4798.)
5097 HARRIET, b. Aug. 31, 1828, m. Sept. 28, 1847, OREN H. BENNETT; lived at Waco, Mo., 1898.
5098 JOHN L., b. March 11, 1831, m. Oct. 15, 1855, ALICE M. HIGHT.
5099 SARAH J., b. Aug. 28, 1832, m. July 3, 1851, MARSHALL MAY and lived Monroe, S. D., 1898.
5100 GEORGE W., b. Nov. 10, 1835, m. ——— ——— and lived Columbus Junc., Iowa, and had nine children.
5101 SAMUEL, b. Jan. 31, 1838, killed in battle Atlanta, Ga., July 22, 1864.
5102 ESTHER L., b. May 15, 1840.
5103 ASA, b. Apl. 30, 1842, m. Jan. 1, 1870, LAURA A. JOHNSON; was cashier of Columbus City Bank, Iowa, 1898, had: 5104 RALPH L., b. March 15, 1876.

F2189 Simon Knowles Locke, born in Lyman, Nov. 2, 1802, died in 1884, married 1st, in Concord, Oct. 2, 1833, PHEBE ABBOTT of Irasburg, Vt., born March 16, 1806, died in Boston

SEVENTH GENERATION 257

1876, daughter of Nathan and Rhoda (Brickett) of Concord; married 2nd, ―――― CAMPBELL of Charleston, Vt. He was a farmer in Barton Landing, Vt.

Children of 7th Gen.
5105 SIMON NEWELL, b. Nov. 2, 1834, died young.
5106 WILLIAM A., b. Oct. 9, 1835, d. Aug. 27, 1847.
5107 DANA A., b. July 30, 1837, m. SARAH A. SNELL, Jan. 12, 1859, and lived Stanstead Plains, Irasburg, Barton Landing and Derby, Vt., had: 5108 Two girls died young; 5109 CLARA S. who lives Pottersville, Mich.
F5110 SARAH B., b. Sept. 6, 1839, m. Jan. 6, 1863, AZRO C. BRYANT.
5111 ALBERT N., b. Sept. 26, 1841, d. unmarried in the war, Jan. 1, 1862.
5112 EMILY F., b. Dec. 28, 1845, d. Aug. 27, 1847.
5113 REV. EDWIN S., b. Feb. 28, 1849, m. EMMA BARTLETT, had: 5114 ARTHUR, who was in a clothing store in Brockton, Mass., and two other living children. Edwin was a farmer in Barton Landing Vt., and d. there 1880. His widow m. 2nd, a druggist named TRACY.

F2190 Sarah Knowles Locke, born in Lyman, Jan. 8, 1804, died in Irasburg, Vt., May 20, 1863, married in Irasburg, Apl. 16, 1826, ALEX JAMESON, born in Dunbarton, Nov. 21, 1798, died a farmer in Irasburg, Oct. 3, 1871, son of Alex and Jennie (Brown), of Scotch Irish descent.

Children of 7th Gen. b. in Irasburg, Vt.
F5114 SARAH ANNE, b. May 10, 1827, m. Oct. 1849, DAVID WEBSTER.
F5115 WILLIAM LOVERING, b. May 12, 1828, m. Nov. 11, 1852, AURILLA CRANDALL.
F5116 CAROLINE, b. Oct. 18, 1829, m. March 16, 1856, WARNER STRONG.
5117 MARY JANE, b. June 11, 1831, m. Sept. 1, 1853, DAVID MORRILL LOCKE. (See F4920.)
F5118 HORACE DUNKEE, b. Feb. 13, 1833, m. Oct. 31, 1859, ANNIE MC-SLAUGHLIN.
F5119 ZUAR E., b. Jan. 5, 1835, m. June 25, 1860, MARY ELLEN WILCOX.
F5120 LAURA M., b. Sept. 25, 1836, m. Dec. 31, 1859, ISAAC M. DAKIN.
5121 LUCY E., b. May 21, 1838, d. May 7, 1843.
F5122 JULIA E., b. July 9, 1840, m. Aug. 10, 1860, CHARLES F. DEWEY.
F5123 LUCY A., b. Nov. 27, 1843, m. July 18, 1867, REV. ORANGE W. SCOTT.
5124 EMMA JANETTE, b. Oct. 10, 1848, m. May 1, 1878, REV. NATHAN C. ALGER, b. Lowell, May 14, 1847. He is a graduate of the Methodist Seminary in Tilton, has had churches in Bourne, Bridgewater, Mass., and other places. She is a writer and lecturer in the interest of missions.

17

F2191 Nancy Locke, born in Lyman, May 26, 1806, died in Irasburg, Vt., June 2, 1855, married March 17, 1832, WILLIAM P. DODGE, born in Lyme, March 16, 1812, died in Orleans, Vt., Sept. 24, 1881. He was a farmer in Irasburg.

Children of 7th Gen. b. in Irasburg, Vt.

F5125 JOHN L., b. Oct. 21, 1833, m. Oct. 15, 1861, SARAH J. MERRILL.
5126 GEORGE S., b. Aug. 3, 1838, m. Grace Church, N. Y., Jan. 7, 1869, VIRGINIA ROSE. He was a chief sutler in the army, said to have been the first man over at assault of Fort Fisher, was Minister to Berlin under Johnson, and later was a broker in San Francisco. He had no children, and died Oakland, Cal., Aug. 24, 1881. His widow remarried.
5127 EMALINE, b. Feb. 13, 1847, d. St. Cloud, Minn., Apl. 30, 1895, m. Jan. 30 1872, GEORGE E. CHURCHILL, b. Stowe, Vt., July 29, 1847, lived St. Cloud, and had a child died young.
5128 SALMON, b. Jan. 14, 1841, m. Nov. 29, 1871, ELMA O. TWOMBLY, b. Brownington, Vt., Sept. 16, 1848, living 1911, at Orleans, Vt. He lived St. Cloud, Mich., and d. Sept. 1, 1893, had: 5129 GLENN S., b. Jan. 13, 1873, is m.; 5129a MARY, b. Apl. 13, 1876, is m.; 5130 GRACE E., b. March 10, 1884.

F2192 William Lovering Locke, born in Lyman, Jan. 18, 1808, died in Irasburg, Vt., Feb. 26, 1888, married in Troy, Vt., Sept. 25, 1838, FANNY M. GIBBS, born in Pittsfield, Jan. 19, 1819, died Sept. 12, 1863, daughter of Thomas and Delia (Bisbee). He was a stock breeder and fruit raiser in Irasburg, Vt.

Child of 7th Gen.

F5131 WILLIAM LOVERING, b. May 25, 1841, m. June 1, 1862, AMELIA E. HILL.

F2200 John Locke, born in Irasburg, Vt., May 19, 1811, died in Albany, Vt., March 19, 1855, married 1835, KEZIAH CHASE of Rhode Island; married 2nd (1841), EMALINE HOVEY of Albany, who married 2nd, GEORGE HIDDEN of Craftsbury, Vt. John was deputy sheriff at St. Albans, Vt. Keziah died in 1856.

Children of 7th Gen.

5132 EMALINE, b. ——, died young.

Second wife's children:

F5133 SARAH APPLETON, b. July 2, 1842, m. 1863, GEORGE E. MAGUIRE.
5134 JOHN WILSON, b. ——, died young.
5135 JOHN NELSON, b. ——, died young.
5136 CHARLES, b. ——, died young.
F5137 WILLIAM LOVERING, b. Sept. 21, 1853, m. Sept. 2, 1880, BELLE A. FISHER.

SEVENTH GENERATION

F2208 Filenda Locke, born in Lyman, Apl. 7 (T. R. Oct. 7), 1818, died Apl. 7, 1880, married Feb. 22, 1837, BENJAMIN F. HERBERT, born in New Hampshire, Aug. 25, 1806, died a tanner in Coventry, Vt., Aug. 26, 1864.

Children of 7th Gen.

5138 AUGUSTUS F., b. 1840, d. 1843.
5139 EDNA, b. Nov. 7, 1844, m. 1st, Nov. 11, 1867, GEORGE COLES, who d. Apl. 1871; m. 2nd, Oct. 16, 1878, ELIJAH CUTLER.
5140 FINETTA M., b. Aug. 28, 1846, m. Feb. 24, 1870, DR. HENRY C. MATTHEWS, b. Apl. 3, 1844, son of Jonathan and Nancy (Bell); was a physician on Quincy St., Brooklyn, N. Y., many years, and died Clifton Springs, N. Y., Oct. 22, 1902. His widow lives in Brooklyn. They had: 5141 FLORENCE M., b. Oct. 1, 1871, d. Jan. 18, 1874; 5142 GRACE EDNA, b. Dec. 30, 1873; 5143 HERBERT B., b. March 18, 1876; 5144 EDITH, b. Apl. 13, 1881.
5145 CHARLES, b. Apl. 20, 1849, d. Dec. 15, 1880, m. Sept. 1876, JENNIE KIMBALL of Irasburg, Vt., dau. of Moody B. and Lucy Spencer (Nye). Had a dau.: 5146 CARLENA, b. Jan. 11, 1881.

F2214 Albion Locke, born in Lyman, Apl. 28, 1822, died in Epsom, Sept. 4, 1902, married June 15, 1848, MARY A. LOCKE, # 5017. He moved from Irasburg, Vt., to the lovely farm on Locke's Hill, Epsom, in 1848, and was a miller in 1870. She was born in Epsom, May 10, 1821, and died in Epsom, March 10, 1906.

Children of 7th Gen.

5147 FLORA ESTHER, b. Epsom, June 2, 1854, m. Sept. 8, 1875, EDWARD O. SANDERSON, b. May 18, 1836, son of Daniel and Elizabeth P. (Frost). He is in the dry goods business in Pittsfield, had: 5148 HELEN LOCKE SANDERSON, b. Pittsfield, May 20, 1880, m. Boston, May 3, 1905, JOHN E. MARSTON, b. Chichester, June 15, 1870, lived in Pittsfield, and had: 5149 JOHN BENNETT, b. July 23, 1908.
5150 ADA ELORIA, b. Epsom, Feb. 12, 1862, m. Epsom, Sept. 25, 1884, CHARLES E. CILLEY, b. Northfield, Sept. 17, 1861. He is a farmer and shoemaker in Epsom, had: 5151 HELEN MARIA, b. Epsom, May 20, 1896.

F2215 William Lang, born in Epsom, June 20, 1797, died Dec. 12, 1895, married 1st, ABRILLA SUEARENGEN; married 2nd, SYBIL SQUIRE, lived in Iowa.

Children of 7th Gen.

5152 NICHOLAS, who lives at Lamont, Iowa.
5153 WILLIAM, lives Menona, Iowa.
5154 ABIGAIL.
5155 JOHN, lives Wasigoa, Minn.

5156 NANCY, m. —— JOHNSON.
5157 DAVID.
5158 CHARLES, lives Chicago.
8159 SARAH, m. —— YOUNG, lives Chapman, Iowa.

F2216 David Lang, born in Epsom, Feb. 5, 1799, died July 7, 1883, married 1st, Feb. 26, 1826, LYDIA BABB, born Nov. 6, 1796, died Apl. 12, 1836; married 2nd, May 27, 1836, LORENDA HITCHCOCK.

Children of 7th Gen.

5160 JAMES A., b. March 30, 1824,? m. Dec. 12, 1848, BETSEY A. WILLIAMS.
5161 LYDIA A., b. Jan. 4, 1826,? d. Feb. 11, 1894, m. Jan. 4, 1871, HORATIO N. NORTON.
5162 JOHN B., b. Jan. 16, 1828, m. Oct. 14, 1856, RUTHIA BOON.
5163 LUCINDA H., b. Nov. 19, 1830, d. Apl. 20, 1866, m. Dec. 23, 1853, JAMES O. HUTCHINGS.
5164 MARY ELIZABETH, b. May 6, 1833, d. Dec. 25, 1870, m. March 17, 1862, HIRAM A. CLOSE.
5165 DAVID LOCKE, b. March 8, 1836, died young.

Children of second wife:

5166 ABIGAIL, b. May 5, 1837, died young.
5167 CHARLES B., b. Apl. 4, 1838, died young.
5168 ELLA ARABELLA, b. Apl. 24, 1839.
5169 EMMA AUGUSTA, b. June 23, 1842, m. Dec. 28, 1871, WHITMAN S. SMITH, who d. Feb. 12, 1881.
5170 HENRY B., b. Apl. 24, 1846, was in Co. H, 124th Ohio Vols. and d. Reseca, Ga., May 29, 1864.

F2217 Reuel Lang, born in Epsom, March 28, 1801, died Apl. 3, 1891, married Jan. 30, 1823, AMY HART and lived in Wellington, Ohio.

Children of 7th Gen. b. in Wellington, Ohio.

F5171 JOSIAH B., b. Jan. 11, 1824, m. July 17, 1845, LORENDA M. CHAPMAN.
5172 JESSE HART, b. Dec. 21, 1825, m. Jan. 1, 1848, MARY E. FITCH, and lived Oberlin, Ohio.
5173 CYRUS WELCOME, b. March 10, 1828, d. Franklin, Aug. 4, 1847.
5174 LOUISA MARIE, b. Dec. 5, 1831, m. March 20, 1850, PETER S.WRIGHT, had: 5175 CHARLES, b. and d. 1854; 5176 CHARLES, b. 1857, d. 1858; 5177 WILMOT, b. and d. 1860; 5178 GRACE L., b. July 12, 1867, m. UTLEY WEDGE.
5179 CHARLES REUEL, b. Feb. 23, 1834, d. Apl. 28, 1853.
F5180 ESTHER ABIGAIL, b. Apl. 13, 1838, m. Aug. 12, 1860, CHARLES W. HORR.
5181 OLIVE AMY, b. June 21, 1840, m. June 28, 1864, M. B. LUKENS.

SEVENTH GENERATION 261

5182 GEORGE LOCKE, b. Huntington, Ohio, Feb. 5, 1843, m. Amherst, O., Aug. 7, 1867, ELIZABETH VILES, dau. of William and Dorlisca. Served Co. G, 12th Wis. Vols., Sept. 14, 1861–May 1865. Was superintendent of telegraph on New York, New Haven & Hartford R. R. many years, and some ten years ago accepted the same position with the Texas Pacific R. R. with headquarters in Louisville, Ky., had: 5183 CLARA MAY, b. March 25, 1869; 5184 GEORGE REUEL, b. March 28, 1876, d. June 30, 1876.

5185 MERRILL WARNER, b. Nov. 29, 1845, m. 1st, Feb. 13, 1866, MARY L. COOK; m. 2nd, Sept. 24, 1875, CELESTIA M. ROOT, b. Jan. 30, 1843, had: 5186 BURTON H., b. Dec. 3, 1866; 5187 MYRNA L., b. Sept. 20, 1868.

F2218 John Locke Lang, born in Epsom, May 29, 1803, died Sept. 23, 1846, married March 27, 1828, SARAH G. WHITE, born Oct. 16, 1798, died Sept. 3, 1855, daughter of Major William and Sarah (Greeley). They lived in Ashland.

Children of 7th Gen.

5188 SARAH W., b. March 14, 1830, d. March 31, 1832.
F5189 SARAH MATILDA, b. June 5, 1833, m. May 16, 1855, SPENCER WRIGHT.
5190 JOHN W., b. Nov. 1, 1835, d. Feb. 20, 1859.
5191 MARTHA GRACE, b. Feb. 28, 1839, d. 1902, m. 1860, JOHN S. FLEEK, who d. 1883. They had: 5192 GRACE, who m. a MILLER.
5193 GEORGE WILLIAM, b. Dec. 6, 1840, d. Feb. 1883.

F2219 Sarah Martha Lang, born in Epsom, June 17, 1805, died in Concord, Sept. 30, 1886. married 1828, SAMUEL MORRILL CHESLEY of Epsom, lived in Wolfeboro and Concord, and he died Sept. 1891.

Children of 7th Gen.

5194 ESTHER BLAKE, b. Apl. 8, 1829, d. May 16, 1875.
5195 WILLIAM ORLANDO, b. Oct. 1, 1831, d. Feb. 1832.
5196 SARAH ELIZABETH, b. Epping, March 25, 1839, d. Concord, Oct. 23, 1897, m. Sept. 1866, ALVAH H. BICKFORD of Wolfeboro, had: 5197 HARRIE M., b. Dec. 18, 1878.
5198 ELGINA C., b. Feb. 14, 1841, m. Nov. 1859, NATHAN BROWN of Medford, Mass., lived West Medford and he d. there, 1892, had: 5199 FRANK M., b. Oct. 14, 1862, d. Feb. 22, 1873; 5200 PAUL F., b. Oct. 12, 1873.

F2220 Anna M. Lang, born in Epsom, Nov. 6, 1807, died Dec. 17, 1891, married 1st, in 1824, DR. JAMES BABB of Manchester, born March 12, 1800, died July 24, 1853; married 2nd, Sept. 1858, CAPT. NATHANIEL KIMBALL, born in Bradford, Mass., Apl. 28, 1780, died in Manchester, Jan. 17, 1869, son of Daniel and E. (Tenney). She was Kimball's 3rd wife.

Children of 7th Gen., all Babbs.
5201 FRANCENA M., b. 1825, d. 1825.
5202 EMELINE A., b. June 24, 1827, d. July 13, 1901.
5203 GEORGE ALANSON, b. Apl. 1829, d. Feb. 1831.
F5204 GEORGEANNA, b. March 4, 1831, buried in Manchester, June 30, 1910, m. Dec. 28, 1848, REV. JOHN W. RAY, b. Dec. 24, 1814. Lived Lake City, Minn., and he d. Apl. 12, 1901.
5205 MARY F., b. May 1833, d. June 1833.
5206 LEONORA, b. Nov. 2, 1835, m. 1st, GEORGE A. HASSAM; m. 2nd, 1868, EVERETT PARSONS, lived Rochester.
5207 JOHN, b. Feb. 10, 1837, was m. and lived Denver, Col.

F2221 Lorenda Lang, born in Epsom, May 2, 1810, died Jan. 22, 1889, married Nov. 21, 1830, DANIEL K. PRESCOTT, lived Marietta, Wis.

Children of 7th Gen.
5208 HENRY R., b. Nov. 30, 1831, d. Jan. 22, 1833.
5209 WALTER SCOTT, b. Aug. 8, 1833, d. Apl. 3, 1854.
5210 INCREASE S. D., b. July 22, 1835, m. July 4, 1865, FLORENCE A. BULLOCK.
5211 SARAH LOCKE, b. twin with last, d. Jan. 10, 1838.
5212 ELI STEADMAN, b. May 23, 1838, d. Jan. 10, 1862.
5213 DEWITT C., b. Feb. 25, 1841, m. July 30, 1862, SARAH HOLGATE.
5214 PRISCILLA W., b. Feb. 8, 1844, d. March 8, 1844.
5215 DANIEL K., b. Feb. 10, 1847, d. June 3, 1851.

F2222 Bickford Lang, born in Epsom, March 27, 1812, married in Deerfield, Feb. 26, 1835, JANE BACHELDER CRAM, born in Deerfield, died June 1, 1877, daughter of Jonathan and Rachel (Lane). In 1837 he moved to Deerfield working as a farmer and blacksmith. He was several years in Epsom, East Pembroke, and in 1853 bought a farm in Suncook. The same year he was in the Penacook saw works, and later manufactured wagon wheels in Thetford, Vt. He returned to Pembroke in 1860, four years later located in Franklin, and died Nov. 27, 1898.

Children of 7th Gen.
F5216 AMANDA J., b. Feb. 14, 1836, m. Oct. 8, 1854, BENJAMIN F. GAGE.
5217 SAMANTHA R., b. Deerfield, Apl. 15, 1839, d. East Pembroke, Feb. 1, 1865, m. Thetford, Vt., June 20, 1858, ISAAC G. RUSS of Pembroke, b. Boscawen, Sept. 2, 1836, son of John and Sophronia (Gage). Had no children. He afterwards m. —— STEVENS and again m. —— DICKEY.
F5218 JOHN ADAMS, b. Sept. 23, 1842, m. Jan. 24, 1866, CARRIE A. GLINES.

BICKFORD LANG F2222

SEVENTH GENERATION 263

F2227 Benjamin L. Lang, born in Epsom, June 11, 1817, died Apl. 5, 1885, married Apl. 26, 1847, HELEN M. THRALL of Ottumwa, Iowa.
Children of 7th Gen.
5219 EDWARD ROSS, b. Feb. 16, 1848, m. June 6, 1874, AGNES SMITH.
5220 HELEN T., b. Aug. 8, 1849, m. July 9, 1872, SAMUEL MAHEN.
5221 FRANK T., b. Nov. 20, 1853.
5222 FANNIE W., b. Nov. 26, 1857, d. Oct. 20, 1891, m. Apl. 30, 1878, EDWIN C. COFFIN.

F2228 Josiah Crosby Lang, born in Epsom, Nov. 20, 1820, married Oct. 5, 1841, HULDAH A. CHAPMAN, born June 18, 1817, died Sept. 8, 1872. He lived in Huntington and Wellington, Ohio. He was at first a carpenter, later a grocer and served as mayor of Wellington. He recruited a company and enlisted in 1861, assigned as quartermaster in Columbus, Ohio, was taken sick and died Nov. 17, 1861.
Children of 7th Gen. b. in Huntington, Ohio.
5223 ZILPHA A., b. June 30, 1842, m. Nov. 1860, HARVEY MARIETTA.
5224 AMORETT A., b. May 7, 1843, d. Nov. 25, 1861.
5225 SARONE M., b. Dec. 11, 1845, m. Dec. 29, 1869, ELI PEABODY, lives Toledo, Ohio.
5226 FRANCENAH M., b. Dec. 23, 1847, d. May 29, 1867.
5227 ALBION EARLE, b. Sept. 12, 1849, m. Nov. 4, 1885, MARY FOLGER PORTER, who was b. Aug. 12, 1854. Mr. Lang attended the schools at Wellington and about 1863 became telegraph operator on the old Mad River Railroad. Resigning in 1868, he entered the employ of the Western Union Service remaining with them until 1874, when he resigned to study law. In 1881 he with friends purchased a horse car line in Toledo and to this was added other lines until all came under one head. This company afterwards acquired all the electric lighting, gas, and heating companies, together with several inter-urban trolley lines, and for many years Mr. Lang was either general manager or president of these properties. In 1902 he retired, spent two years in travel and on his return built his permanent home in Cornish, N. H.
5228 LILLY G., b. Nov. 22, 1857.

F2229 Mary Austin Locke, born in Portsmouth, May 5, 1802, died Apl. 27, 1882, married in Portsmouth, Apl. 15, 1823, SAMUEL B. LARKIN, born in Portsmouth, May 16, 1799, son of Samuel and Ann. He was a farmer in East Concord and died Aug. 8, 1863.

Children of 7th Gen.
5229 BENJAMIN L., b. Dec. 27, 1824, d. San Jose, Cal., Nov. 13, 1900, m. his cousin, SARAH E. HALL, b. Boston, 1835, d. Feb. 23, 1875, dau. of B. and E. E. Hall. He was of Concord, but spent his last years in Cal.; they had: 5230 JOSEPHINE C., b. Dec. 16, 1869; 5231 MARY E., b. Sept. 1, 1871; both in Concord, 1916.
5232 DAU., b. ——, m. FRED KIMBALL, a lawyer in Chelsea.

F2233 Margaret Ann Lovering Locke, born Sept. 8, 1807, married in 1833, EPHRAIM HARRIS, born in Boston, Jan. 27, 1814, lived Shoemakertown, Penn., and he died there Dec. 28, 1867.

Children of 7th Gen.
5234 SAMUEL LOCKE, b. Boston, 1834, was m. and was financial agent of a coffee importing house in N. Y. City. Reverses in late life nearly wiped out a very large property. He had: 5235 WILLIAM H., who was interested with him. His wife d. 1902, and he d. Orange, N. J., Sept. 21, 1911.
F5236 MARY ELLEN, b. Boston, June 30, 1836, d. Jan. 30, 1892, m. Nov. 7, 1860, a cousin, WILLARD HARRIS NORRIS, b. Sutton, Vt., March 5, 1839, son of Welcome and Mary Walsh (Harris). He lived in Sutton eleven years, then moved to Glens Falls, N. Y., where for forty years he was a manufacturer of carriages.

F2237 David M. Lamprey, born in North Hampton, Oct. 18, 1801, died in St. Paul, Minn., Oct. 20, 1868, married Apl. 5, 1825, SALLY STEARNS of Deerfield, born March 21, 1805, died in Deerfield, June 15, 1851, daughter of John and Sarah (Lane). He was a farmer and called Lieutenant.

Children of 7th Gen.
F5237 NANCY C., b. May 11, 1826, m. 1848, REUBEN F. JAMES.
F5238 MORRIS J., b. Dec. 9, 1827, m. Sept. 1869, EVA GOODHUE.
F5239 SARAH S., b. March 20, 1829, m. Oct. 3, 1849, HORACE CARPENTER.
F5240 JOHN S., b. May 23, 1831, m. 1st, Jan. 1861, MARY G. HARDY; m. 2nd, Oct. 16, 1888, BARBARA (HARDY) WYMAN.
F5241 MARTHA F., b. Oct. 8, 1832, m. Apl. 23, 1851, WILLIAM E. HILTON.
F5242 MALVINA C., b. Nov. 10, 1834, m. Nov. 4, 1857, EDWARD STUDLEY.
F5243 WILLIAM B., b. Nov. 30, 1836, m. July 25, 1862, SARAH A. WHITTAKER.
F5244 DAVID C., b. Apl. 5, 1839, m. July 6, 1861, ANNA BELLE WHITE.
F5245 URI LOCKE, b. Apl. 7, 1842, m. Feb. 4, 1865, JEANNETTE ROBERTS.
5246 ALMON S., b. Deerfield, May 15, 1843, d. Sept. 19, 1844.
5247 ELSIE I., b. Deerfield, Dec. 18, 1845, m. 1st, March 10, 1866, JOHN B. LEBOSQUET, b. May 5, 1840, son of Rev. John and Martha (Farrington). He was a R. R. conductor and d. Concord, March 18, 1867; m. 2nd, Sept. 1869, HOBART W. STEVENS, b. Merrimack, Mass., Aug. 7, 1847, son of Samuel and Abigail (Goodhue). He was a carriage manufacturer, and d. Boston, Feb. 9, 1902.

SEVENTH GENERATION 265

5248 MARY A., b. Deerfield, March 31, 1849, d. Concord, May 19, 1885, m. Oct. 8, 1867, JAMES H. GOODRICH, b. Sept. 4, 1840, son of Joshua and Emily (Swett). He was a carriage painter and d. Concord, May 18, 1909, had: 5249 STANLEY F., b. Concord, Nov. 18, 1869; 5250 EMMA A., b. Dec. 15, 1874.

5251 ALBION, b. Deerfield, May 1, 1851, d. unmarried Merrimack, Mass., July 27, 1875.

F2238 John Lamprey, born in North Hampton, Dec. 15, 1803, died in Concord, July 30, 1873, married Nov. 16, 1828, MARY S. ROBINSON, born Feb. 6, 1810, died in North Hampton, Apl. 2, 1899, daughter of Jonathan and Dolly (Fowler). He was a farmer.

Children of 7th Gen.

5252 JONATHAN, b. Concord, Sept. 4, 1829, d. Apl. 3, 1830.
F5253 JOHN A., b. Sept. 17, 1831, m. June 6, 1857, SUSAN H. PAVITT.
5254 JONATHAN, b. No. Hampton, May 29, 1832, d. July 6, 1832.
5255 JONATHAN, b. No. Hampton, June 29, 1834, d. unmarried Aug. 14, 1860.
F5256 EDWIN M., b. Sept. 17, 1836, m. March 11, 1862, MARY E. BROWN.
5257 SIMON O., b. Jan. 27, 1839, m. Nov. 27, 1862, HANNAH M. GARLAND, b. Portsmouth, June 29, 1839, dau. Samuel and Hannah (Marston). He d. Dec. 13, 1912, a farmer in No. Hampton, had: 5258 HATTIE R., b. June 12, 1863; 5259 WILLIE O., b. Oct. 25, 1867; 5260 GRACE A., b. June 11, 1873.
F5261 CHARLES C., b. Apl. 9, 1841, m. 1864, ANN S. BROWN.
5262 MARY W., b. No. Hamp., Feb. 7, 1843, is a teacher in Cal. and unmarried.
5262a GEORGE H., b. No. Hamp., Aug. 25, 1845, is a farmer and unmarried.

F2240 Uri Lamprey, born in North Hampton, Feb. 23, 1809, died in Hampton, March 15, 1881, married May 31, 1831, SALLY MARSTON of Hampton, born July 11, 1811, died in Hampton, Nov. 20, 1906, daughter of Jonathan and Polly (Philbrick). He was a farmer in Hampton.

Children of 7th Gen. b. in Hampton.

5263 JONATHAN M., b. Aug. 20, 1831, d. Exeter Academy, Sept. 23, 1848.
F5263a CHARLES M., b. Jan. 29, 1833, m. Aug. 5, 1859, CATHERINE OSBORNE BACHELOTTE.
5263b SARAH M., b. Apl. 3, 1842, d. Haverhill, Mass., July 26, 1905, m. Dec. 1871, JOSEPH C. HARDY, son of Peter and Barbara (Shirley). He was a lieutenant in 1863, later in the coal business.

F2241 Hezekiah B. Lamprey, born in North Hampton, Nov. 12, 1812, died July 19, 1886, married Aug. 1833, MARY A. E. JENNESS of Rye, born March 13, 1817, died in North

Hampton, March 8, 1881, daughter of David and Sarah (Taylor. He was a farmer in North Hampton.

Children of 7th Gen. b. in North Hampton.

5264 SARAH M., b. Dec. 28, 1834, d. Hampton, Aug. 2, 1904, m. Dec. 5, 1855, JOHN J. LEAVITT, b. May 4, 1831, son of Moses and Mary (Blake). He was town clerk, county commissioner, and member of Legislature, d. Hampton, Oct. 2, 1881, had: 5265 ELLEN M., b. Aug. 18, 1858, d. May 23, 1864; 5266 ALICE E., b. Oct. 2, 1864, d. Nov. 10, 1885, m. Oct. 11, 1879, HENRY D. TAYLOR, a carpenter, b. March 1861, and had: 5267 NELLIE TAYLOR, b. 1880, d. 1882; 5268 MILDRED M. TAYLOR, b. 1882, m. DANIEL BROWN, 1896, and had 5269 ALICE BROWN, b. 1897; 5270 HENRY R. TAYLOR, b. 1883.

5271 MORRIS J., b. Oct. 19, 1837, m. June 1, 1863, CARRIE A. JOHNSON of Greenland, b. May 1836, and had: 5272 CARRIE B., b. March 25, 1867, an artist.

5273 NANCY E., b. June 11, 1842, d. Feb. 15, 1916, m. No. Hampton, March 15, 1865, HIRAM A. BROWN, son of Jacob and Dolly (Dearborn). He was a shoemaker, had: 5274 HARRY L. BROWN, b. May 8, 1874, was in Harvard College, 1892.

F5275 DAVID J., b. Sept. 17, 1844, m. Jan. 1, 1867, CLARA M. NUDD.

5276 IRVING H., b. Oct. 4, 1847, m. Oct. 23, 1872, ELLEN P. BATCHELDER, b. Feb. 11, 1848, dau. of Dea. Emery and Dorothy (Dearborn). He was a farmer in No. Hampton, and d. Apl. 27, 1905, had: 5277 ERNEST B., b. May 25, 1875; 3278 HARROLD I., b. June 30, 1881.

5279 A child was adopted by Hezekiah, as the one sending record says.

F2242 John Garland, born in Rye, Nov. 23, 1776, married Aug. 15, 1799, ELIZABETH PARSONS, born in 1776, died Feb. 20, 1843. He lived in Rye.

Children of 7th Gen. b. in Rye.

5280 MARY ANN, b. March 25, 1800.
5281 HANNAH PARSONS, b. Aug. 11, 1802, m. May 6, 1824, REED RAND of Ports.
5282 JOSEPH PARSONS, b. Dec. 20, 1804.
5283 OLIVER, b. Nov. 25, 1806.
5284 ABIGAIL, b. Jan. 13, 1809, d. Dec. 23, 1828.
5285 SAMUEL PARSONS, b. Apl. 30, 1811.
5286 JOHN CALVIN, b. Nov. 1813, d. Apl. 28, 1889.
5287 DAVID, b. March 1816.
5288 JULIA ANN, b. Nov. 4, 1821, d. July 14, 1873, m. GARDNER T. LOCKE. (See F2806.)

F2276 Edward S. Perkins, born in 1803, died in 1850, married ALMEDA KNOX.

SEVENTH GENERATION 267

Children of 7th Gen.
5289 JAMES K., b. 1823, m. FIDELIA GILSON and lived in Nashua, had:
5290 WILLIAM; 5291 ALICE; 5292 another.
5293 MARY A., b. 1825, d. infant.
5294 JONATHAN S., b. 1828, m. AMELIA GIBSON, lived Fitchburg, Mass., and had: 5295 FANNIE; 5296 HARRIE; 5297 HATTIE.
5298 EDWARD, b. 1830, m. Manchester, 1849, JANE HOOK, # 5751, lived Hubbardston, Mass., and had: 5299 WILLIAM, who m., was a trader in Nashua, and had : 5300 GEORGE; 5301 HARRY.
5302 OLIVE ANN, b. 1833.
5303 JEREMIAH, b. 1835.

F2278 James H. Perkins, born in 1808, died in 1841, married RUTH GLIDDEN.

Children of 7th Gen.
5304 CHARLES H., b. 1831, m. 1st, ADALINE TASKER; m. 2nd, ELIZA A. FARRINGTON, and had: 5305 FRANK P., d. aged one year; 5306 FRED, b. 1863, d. 1865; 5307 GRACE M., b. 1875.
5308 JAMES M., b. 1833, was m. but had no children.
5309 MARY C., b. 1835, d. 1847.
5310 MARTHA J., b. 1838, d. 1842.
5311 OLEVIA A., b. 1841, d. 1842.

F2298 Abigail T. Locke, born in Chester in 1795, died Nov. 16, 1875, married in Epping, Apl. 17, 1815, CAPT. JOHN MOORE of Raymond, born in Chester, Jan. 21, 1792, son of Robert. He was a farmer in Raymond and died Apl. 2, 1862.

Children of 7th Gen. b. in Raymond.
5312 LAVINIA, b. Apl. 26, 1817, d. unmarried.
5313 JOHN L., b. ——, d. unmarried.
5314 HENRY, b. Jan. 18, 1822, m. Oct. 16, 1851, LAURA HAZELTON, b. Feb. 22, 1820, d. Feb. 24, 1910, dau. of Thomas and Lucretia (Hills). He was a farmer in Chester, and d. Sept. 9, 1896, had: 5315 EMMA M., b. Oct. 13, 1852; 5316 EUGENE, b. Sept. 3, 1854, d. Sept. 14, 1865; 5317 LAURA K., b. Aug. 1, 1856, d. 1868; 5318 CHARLES H., b. June 24, 1862, d. 1865.
5319 ELLEN, b. ——, d. unmarried.
5320 WILLIAM J., b. Jan. 1, 1827, m. Haverhill, Mass., July 4, 1871, MARY ANN ROWELL, b. Sandown, 1852, dau. of Smith A. He was a box manufacturer, in Sandown or Fremont.
5321 MARY, b. May 23, 1829, m. —— SMITH of Winchendon, Mass., and d. 1904.
5322 MELVIN B., b. Nov. 16, 1830, d. a farmer in Raymond, June 24, 1904, unmarried.
5323 KATHERINE, b. ——, m. HENRY GRIFFITH, and lived out West.
5324 ELBRIDGE GERRY, b. Apl. 26, 1835, m. LUCY MILLER, dau. of Capt. Wm. P. and Abigail (Noyes). He was a Corporal in Co. G, 2nd

U. S. Sharpshooters, later was a carriage maker, but for 30 years was a florist in Milford, Mass., where he d. May 1, 1913.
5325 BENJAMIN FRANKLIN, b. Dec. 12, 1836, m. Oct. 23, 1889, MRS. ABBIE S. (WHITE) SANBORN. He lived in Raymond and d. there Feb. 25, 1910, leaving widow and children: 5326 GRACE, who m. ——— ST. JOHN; 5327 GEORGE; 5328 ETHEL; 5329 LUCY.

F2299 Mary or Polly Locke, born in Chester, ———, married JOHN CURRIER, a farmer of Sandown.

Children of 7th Gen.

F5330 MARY, b. ———, m. JOHN SCRIBNER and lived in Sandown, N. H.
5331 TIMOTHY, b. ———, lived in Sandown, unmarried.
5332 RUTH B., b. Sandown, 1827, d. unmarried in Sandown, June 7, 1896.
5333 SUSAN, b. ———, lived in Sandown, and died there unmarried.
5334 JOSHUA, b. June 1832, was a farmer in Sandown, and died there unmarried, Aug. 24, 1890.

F2300 William Locke, born in Chester, Apl. 28, 1797, married Dec. 30, 1821, RACHEL BLAKE, born in New Hampshire Feb. 10, 1799, died in Janesville, Wis., July 8, 1874. He went from New Hampshire to Monroe Co., N. Y., then to Janesville, where he died Sept. 5, 1872. He was a cooper.

Children of 7th Gen.

5335 ALBERT G., b. Chester, Nov. 17, 1822, m. FIDELIA JANE FLEMING and d. March 23, 1888, had: 5336 FRANK A., unmarried, and lives Wis.; 5337 WILLIAM F., who m. and had: 5338 TRUE; 5339 FRANK, lives Norman, Oklahoma, 1915.
5340 ADALINE, b. July 9, 1825, d. 1853, m. NOYES N. JACKMAN, lived in Janesville, Wis., had: 5341 STILLMAN; 5342 MARY; 5343 EDNA.
5344 WILLIAM, b. Feb. 18, 1828, not married.
5345 HELEN, b. Apl. 27, 1830, d. Oct. 1868, m. TRAYTON DANN, had: 5346 ESTHER J., who m. ——— LEACH, lives Beresford, S. D.; 5347 MATTIE, who m. T. F. MURRAY lives Cedar Falls, Iowa; 5348 a son.
5349 ESTHER D., b. May 16, 1832, d. Aug. 1857, m. JOHN MCMARTIN, no children.
5350 MARTIN, b. Sept. 26, 1834, m. JENNIE ———, was a cooper and carpenter in Janesville, Wis., had: 5351 CHARLES; 5352 WALTER or FRANK; 5353 ELEANOR, and several grandchildren. All supposed to be in Janesville, 1909.
5354 SUSAN, b. Oct. 4, 1836, not m., lived Edgarton, Wis., 1909.
5355 TRUE T., b. N. Y., March 15, 1842, m. 1876, LAVINIA B. GILL, lives Alameda, Cal., since 1860; had: 5356 WILLIAM TRUE, b. Aug. 13, 1878, m. 1904 EDA CLEAVES, b. 1880, and had: WM. MELVILLE, b. 1908, lives Alameda, Cal.; 5357 PEARL, b. 1883.
5358 ELEANOR, b. N. Y., May 22, 1839, m. JOSEPH GREEN, and had: 5359 MATTIE; 5360 LEWIS. Lives Wisconsin.
5361 JOHN, b. Wis., Oct. 17, 1844, unmarried, d. 1904.

SEVENTH GENERATION

F2301 James Locke, born in Chester, July 11, 1801, died in Chester, June 23, 1882, married 1st, 1826, JANE W. TAGGART, born in Chester, Sept. 30, 1804, died in Chester, June 6, 1856; married 2nd, Aug. 2, 1861, MRS. HANNAH P. DODGE who died in Raymond, May 25, 1889. He was a cooper in Merrimack, Mass., Brentwood, and Chester.

Children of 7th Gen.

F5362 JOSEPH RICHARDSON, b. July 11, 1827, m. 1852, LYDIA FRANCES ROBINSON.

5363 MARY E., b. Chester, Oct. 19, 1830, d. Amesbury, Mass., Dec. 23, 1912, m. HIRAM PORTER ROBINSON of Brentwood, b. B., Nov. 17, 1827, lived Amesbury, had no children.

F5364 HARRIET A., b. Jan. 24, 1836, m. Jan. 24, 1856, SEWELL WORTHLEY.

5365 JAMES TRUE, b. Chester, Jan. 2, 1838, m. May 24, 1860, MARY A. ROBINSON, b. Brentwood, June 30, 1840. He was agent of West Amesbury Mfg. Co., member of fire department, member of board of Registrars, chairman of selectmen. He d. July 6, 1909.

5366 WILLIAM MOORE, b. Chester, Nov. 20, 1843, was a corporal in Co. C, 6th N. H. Reg., took part in 18 battles, was wounded at Petersburg, d. at Washington, D. C., Aug. 28, 1865, and was buried in Arlington.

5367 ELEANOR J., b. Aug. 10, 1847, is unmarried, and a teacher in Chester and Marion, Mass.

F2303 Elizabeth Locke, born in Chester, July 30, 1808, died in Orangeport, N. Y., Nov. 26, 1888, married in 1840, RANDOLPH PHELPS of Orangeport, born in Hebron, Sept. 20, 1808. He was a farmer in Orangeport.

Children of 7th Gen.

5368 JANE, b. Lockport, N. Y., Sept. 28, 1842, m. HENRY HUBBS, b. Apl. 17, 1841. He kept the hotel "Temperance House" Niagara Falls, had no children.

5369 JOHN, b. ———, m. and lived Orangeport, N. Y., d. there, May 15, 1910, had: 5370 CHARLES; 5371 WILLIAM; 5372 HATTIE; 5373 JENNIE; 5374 EDMUND.

F2304 True T. Locke, born in Chester, Aug. 26, 1810, married Oct. 29, 1839, JOANNA M. TUCKER, born in Andover; married 2nd, AMANDA SAWTELLE, who died in Chester, 1857. He was a selectman of Chester in 1844. He rebuilt the sawmill adding a shingle mill in 1847, which was entirely destroyed by fire in 1857. He was postmaster of Newton, Mass., and died at Newton Highlands, Apl. 1895.

Children of 7th Gen.
5375 SUSAN J., b. ——, m. JOSEPH LAWRENCE, and had two children in Pepperell, Mass.
5376 CORA S., b. ——, m. EDWARD MULLEN of Boston.
5377 HELEN G., b. ——, m. ALMON TEWKSBURY, lived Newton, Mass., 1909.

F2305 Hannah True, born in Chester, May 21, 1784, died in Hatley, Can., Jan. 1, 1864, married Nov. 21, 1802, ISAAC WORTHEN, born Feb. 4, 1781. He lived in Chester, was in the 1812 War, moved to and died in Hatley, Can.
Children of 7th Gen.
5378 TRUE W., b. Chester, Apl. 1, 1804, m. Nov. 4, 1831-4, MINERVA MCCONNELL, lived Ayers Flat, P. Q., and had seven children.
5379 MATTHEW F., b. Chester, July 15, 1805, m. Lowell, Dec. 8, 1831, JANE G. RICHARDS, and d. Lowell, Sept. 2, 1862.
5380 SARAH T., b. Feb. 7, 1807, m. SETH TRUE of Chester, and d. Ascot, P. Q., Feb. 14, 1880.
5381 JOHN D., b. Salem, Mass., Jan. 10, 1810, not m., d. Hatley, P. Q.
5382 LYDIA W., b. Salem, Dec. 4, 1811, m. Raymond, Oct. 1835, ASA H. STEWART, and lives Tilton.
5383 MARY, b. Candia, Sept. 21, 1816, d. March 19, 1880, m. Hatley, Jan. 1847, JAMES TAYLOR.
5384 BETSEY N., b. Hatley, Nov. 21, 1821, d. May 21, 1899, m. May 1847, JOHN O. PARNELL.
5385 SANBORN, b. Canada, Oct. 7, 1824, m. Lowell, Oct. 7, 1846, LUCINDA S. TAYLOR, lived Estatoe, N. C., 1899.
5386 BELA L., b. Apl. 26, 1826, m. Jan. 1845, ESTHER ——, and d. in Cal.
5387 GILMAN C., b. Jan. 16, 1827, m. Nov. 16, 1848, LUCY FRENCH of Manchester, and d. March 9, 1880.

F2306 Sarah True, born in Chester, Aug. 22, 1788, died Sept. 30, 1859, married Apl. 9, 1808, SAMUEL POOR, born Aug. 3, 1785-6, died in Raymond, May 21, 1868.
Children of 7th Gen.
5388 JOHN L., b. Jan. 9, 1809, m. Candia, Dec. 19, 1833, SOPHIA SHANNON, lived Raymond.
5389 ALMIRA T., b. Nov. 9, 1811, d. N. Y., Feb. 6, 1884, m. Raymond, Jan. 24, 1832, EDMUND WHITTIER.
5390 JUDITH T., b. May 21, 1814, m. Candia, 1866, JONATHAN CURRIER, and lived Hampton.
5391 ASA K., b. March 24, 1818, m. in Raymond BETSEY TOWLE, lived Raymond.
5392 SAMUEL, b. Aug. 5, 1820, m. 1st, Feb. 17, 1847, ELIZABETH P. MURRAY; m. 2nd, Aug. 19, 1855, ANGELINE J. BROWN, lived in Hampton.
5393 WESLEY, b. Aug. 31, 1829, m. Haverhill, Mass., 1851, LYDIA S. RICHARDS, lived Raymond.

SEVENTH GENERATION

F2307 Mary True, born in Chester, Aug. 10, 1791, died in Epping, Nov. 24, 1857, married 1st, JOSEPH NORRIS, born in Epping, March 18, 1785, died Apl. 27, 1823; married 2nd, LEVI BLAKE, born ——, died in 1850.

Children of 7th Gen. b. in Epping.
5394 MARY R., b. May 2, 1819, d. unmarried Apl. 9, 1838.
5395 BENJAMIN T., b. June 24, 1821, m. June 24, 1851, HARRIET A. FALL.
5396 JOHN P., b. Nov. 26, 1822, m. CAROLINE BARTLETT, and d. Jan. 19, 1887.

F2312 Osgood True, born in Chester, Dec. 25, 1799, married BETSEY TRUE, born May 29, 1802, died Jan. 18, 1880.

Children of 7th Gen. b. in Chester.
5397 LUTHER, b. ——, m. LUCINDA ——.
5398 JANE R., b. 1832, m. Newburyport, Aug. 23, 1851, JOHN F. BROWN. lived in Haverhill, Mass.
5399 LUCY A., b. ——, m. JOHN GREEN, had: 5400 ARTHUR; 5401 FRANK, lived in Haverhill, Mass.
5402 HORACE E., b. Feb. 15, 1843, m. MATILDA PHILBRICK, lived Danville.

F2315 William Stephen True, born in Chester, Jan. 16, 1808, died in Chester, July 8, 1879, married in Chester, Nov. 17, 1836, MARY PRESCOTTT, born June 10, 1818, died Apl. 7, 1894.

Children of 7th Gen.
5403 MARY A., b. March 18, 1838, d. Wakefield, Mass., Sept. 24, 1889, m. REUBEN MITCHELL of Lynnfield, Mass., and lived Santiago, Cal.
5404 BENJAMIN F., b. March 23, 1840, m. ELLEN POOR, had: 5405 NELLIE; 5406 LIZZIE, who m. DR. GUPTILL of Raymond.
5407 SARAH P., b. Nov. 24, 1841, d. Montana, Apl. 26, 1891, m. CHARLES ABBOTT, and lived Portland, Ore.
5408 CHARLES F., b. Feb. 5, 1844, m. Dec. 25, 1871, SARAH PHILBRICK, b. Dec. 21, 1853, dau. of Edward and Sarah (Webster), lived Chester, and had: 5409 EDWARD C., b. March 14, 1883.
5410 ABBIE J., b. Apl. 8, 1846, m. EVERETT A. MORSE, lived Brentwood, and Wakefield, Mass.
5411 JOHN C., b. March 20, 1848, d. June 28, 1848.
5412 OLIVE L., b. Nov. 30, 1849, d. Chester, Sept. 21, 1867.
5413 WILLIAM E., b. Dec. 3, 1851, m. EMMA RAND, lived Sandown and d. Feb. 18, 1905.
5414 ELLEN A., b. Apl. 15, 1855, m. ENOCH JUDKINS of Kingston, lived Bradford, Mass.
5415 ADA I., b. Apl. 24, 1856, lived unmarried Bradford, Mass.
5416 Herbert A., b. July 4, 1857, d. Chester, Sept. 24, 1858.
5417 ARTHUR E., b. Nov. 11, 1859, m. 1st, ADA POOR of Tremont, and had: 5418 WILLIE; 5419 BERTHA, b. in Chester; m. 2nd, MATILDA TIBBETTS of Melrose, and had: 5420 MARY, in Leominster, Mass.

F2322 Rufus W. Moore, born in Chester, Apl. 21, 1814, died June 13, 1887, married 1st, Apl. 1849, SARAH NIGHTINGALE GREEN of Chester, born Oct. 20, 1825, died in Chester, Feb. 1, 1854; married 2nd, June 4, 1863, NANCY LARKIN, who died in Lee. He was a farmer in Chester.

Children of 7th Gen. b. in Chester.

5421 GEORGEANNA, b. Oct. 19, 1850, was unmarried.
5422 LURIETTA, b. Jan. 26, 1852, m. May 15, 1873, CLEMENT WELLS, b. Sandown, Oct. 20, 1852, son of Timothy and Lydia. He is a farmer in Chester, and had: 5423 CHARLES P.; 5424 SADIE; 5425 WILSON; 5426 ANNIE; 5427 NINA.
5428 CHARLES W., b. Sept. 12, 1853, d. Nov. 1, 1862.
5429 CHARLES W., b. Apl. 4, 1865, m. ——— GEORGE, lived Ayers Village, Mass.
5430 EUGENE L., b. Aug. 1874, m. ETTA ———, lived Lee.

F2343 Ephraim F. Reynolds, born in Barrington, Dec. 27, 1804, died Aug. 15, 1851, married Apl. 14, 1825, **Mary Pinkham Locke,** #2424, 1807–90.

Children of 7th Gen. b. in Barrington.

5431 HORACE, b. ———, m. 1st, MARY E. YOUNG of Madbury; m. 2nd, ——— ———, lived Alton Corner and had: 5432 MARY J.; 5433 GEORGE.
5434 SOPHIA L., b. Nov. 5, 1827, d. Farmington, Nov. 4, 1907, m. WILLIAM H. BABB, lived Gonic and had: 5435 IDA F.; 5436 FRED.
5437 LUCY L., b. 1830, d. Apl. 4, 1908, m. CHARLES RANDLETT of Durham, lived East Rochester, and had: 5438 FRANK; 5439 MARY A.
5440 JOHN W., b. Oct. 1834, was m. and d. Barrington, Apl. 1, 1896.
5441 WINTHROP, b. 1835, m. July 11, 1885, OLIVE BERRY of Barrington, who was b. 1835. He was a sailor in the Civil War, lived E. Barrington and had: 5442 MARY S., who m. WM. AUSTIN, and had: 5443 NELLIE AUSTIN.

F2345 Eben C. Locke, born in Barrington, Nov. 15, 1792, died in Barrington, Oct. 21, 1870, married Nov. 28, 1822, MARY M. HAM, a teacher, born Dec. 12, 1799, died in Barrington, July 1875, daughter of Israel and Mehitable (Hayes). He probably married as 1st wife, SUSAN DENNETT but children are by Mary. He was a farmer and bought "Beauty Hill," Barrington, in 1823 and spent his life on it.

Children of 7th Gen.

F5444 SAMUEL AUGUSTUS, b. July 13, 1823, m. Apl. 1, 1850, SOPHRONIA A. SHERBURNE.
F5445 CHARLES DENNETT, b. Sept. 18, 1825, m. May 12, 1853, ANN M. SWAIN.

SEVENTH GENERATION 273

5446 IRA W. R., b. Jan. 30, 1828, d. March 11, 1828.
F5447 ISRAEL HAM, b. March 9, 1829, m. ANNIE MCCHARLES.
F5448 IRA WASHINGTON, b. Aug. 16, 1831, m. May 27, 1869, MARY ABBIE BABB.
F5449 WILLIAM H., b. Jan. 15, 1836, m. 1st, Apl. 25, 1855, LAURA J. CLEAVES; m. 2nd, MARY O. TEBBETTS.

F2346 Mary B. Locke, born in Barrington, Jan. 20, 1795, died Dec. 10, 1871, married in 1815, JOHN D. HUCKINS, born in Madbury, was a farmer in, and died at Alton.

Children of 7th Gen.

F5450 LUCY C., b. March 3, 1816, m. 1847, DURRELL S. CHAMBERLAIN.
5451 HANNAH, b. Apl 12, 1818, m. 1842, DR. RUFUS PEARL, and d. 1847. A note says all died young.
5452 ANDREW, b. Madbury, Apl. 19, 1820, m. 1845, MARIA J. CHAMBERLAIN, was a farmer in Alton and d. there, Oct. 6, 1894, had: 5453 MARIA, b. Sept. 1848; 5454 SYLVESTER, b. March 1852; 5455 ALICE R., b. 1861.
F5456 MARY E., b. 1827, m. 1853, JOSEPH E. BERRY.
F5457 JOHN I., b. Jan. 15, 1829, m. Nov. 6, 1853, ABBIE W. WHITEHOUSE.

F2350 Betsey Locke, born in Barrington, Apl. 1, 1800, died Jan. 11, 1877, married in Farmington, Apl. 20, 1826 ELIPHALET BERRY, born in Strafford, Dec. 7, 1798. He moved from Strafford to Barnstead in 1827, was farmer and traveling tailor, going from house to house to make the garments, and died Dec. 13, 1859.

Children of 7th Gen. b. in Barnstead.

5458 ELIZA A., b. Feb. 10, 1828, d. unmarried Dec. 10, 1854.
F5459 IRA L., b. 1830, m. 1854, LAVINA E. DREW.
5460 LUCY L., b. 1832, d. unmarried May 25, 1856.
5461 WILLIAM H., b. 1839, m. 1862 (?), JOSEPHINE EVANS of Pittsfield, dau. of William. He was in the 12th N. H. Vols., was wounded and died at Chancellorsville, May 18, 1863; had no children. His widow m. 2nd, GEORGE CARVER of Maryland.

F2351 Abigail P. Locke, born in Barrington, Sept. 30, 1801, died in Lee, Apl. 5, 1878, married in Barrington, July 4, 1824, MAJOR GORAM W. HOITT, of Lee, born in Northwood, March 5, 1804, son of Samuel and Bestey (Piper). He was a farmer in Lee and died Sept. 5, 1868. Lee Records give marriage as Aug. 13, 1824.

Children of 7th Gen. b. in Lee.

F5462 BETSEY J., b. Jan. 26, 1825, m. Jan. 1, 1861, ISAAC N. SAWYER.
5463 LUCY A., b. Oct. 2, 1826, d. unmarried Jan. 18, 1897.

18

F5464 SAMUEL L., b. Aug. 22, 1828, m. Apl. 12, 1849, ANN J. HADLEY.
5465 MARY A., b. June 16, 1831, was unmarried, a teacher in Lee 1898.
5466 IRA GUSTAVE, b. Lee, July 23, 1833, m. March 12, 1865, JULIA B. BURRELL of Roxbury, dau. of Capt. Benj. H. and Harriet (Morse). He graduated from Dartmouth in 1860, was superintendent of instruction in California for 5 years, lived Millbury, Cal., had: 5467 RALPH H., b. San Francisco, Feb. 4, 1872; 5468 GLADYS, b. San Francisco, Feb. 21, 1877.
5469 LEANDER M., b. Oct. 7, 1835, d. unmarried Oct. 23, 1859.
F5470 GEORGEANNA O., b. Nov. 4, 1837, m. June 5, 1866, IVORY J. CHAMBERLAIN.
5471 SYLVIA, b. Jan. 13, 1840, d. Aug. 15, 1841.
5472 ALBERTON G., b. July 14, 1842, m. Dec. 24, 1876, ALICE B. GRIGGS of Woodstock, Vt., b. Charlestown, Apl. 30, 1860, dau. of Elmason and Miriam (Royce). Lived at Woodstock, 1898, and had: 5473 IDA B., b. Wood., July 21, 1878; 5474 ALBERTON P., b. Wood., May 8, 1880.
F5475 BELLE S., b. Nov. 2, 1844, m. Dec. 5, 1867, HAMILTON A. MATHES.

F2360 Daniel Locke, born in Barrington, Nov. 11, 1794, died in East Boston, June 23, 1872, married 1st, Apl. 15, 1819, SUSAN HAYES of Barrington, born Dec. 3, 1792, died Dec. 18, 1825; married 2nd, MRS. HANNAH (DONALDSON) FOSS, born in Lyman, Me., in 1800, died Oct. 19, 1835; married 3rd, in Boston, 1838, MRS. MEHITABLE (BUNKER) HOLMES, born in Durham, died Jan. 1881, in Lawrence, Mass. He was a farmer and stone cutter.

Children of 7th Gen.

5476 JOSEPH PAGE, b. Barrington, Oct. 13, 1819, killed by a carriage Feb. 10, 1828.
5477 GEORGE W., b. Barr., Jan. 16, 1821, d. March 31, 1839.
5478 JOHN A., b. Dec. 23, 1822, m. Apl. 28, 1849, NANCY GOODWIN of Boston, b. Hiram, Me., Jan 16, 1829, and had: 5479 GARAPHALIA, b. 1850, d. 1853. He was a stone cutter and d. Somerville, Mass., Jan. 29, 1882.
F5480 DANIEL P., b. Aug. 5, 1824, m. Feb. 18, 1846, NANCY MOSIER.

Children of second wife:

5481 CHARLES D., b. Augusta, Me., Feb. 11, 1827, m. a Spanish lady, had four children, and was last heard of in Panama.
5482 ABIGAIL S., b. Augusta, Oct. 4, 1829, m. 1st, ——— SMITH, who lived only 6 months after marriage; m. 2nd, WILLIAM C. FULLER of Hallowell, Me. He was a blacksmith and had no children. She d. July 1854.
F5483 JOSEPH H., b. Oct. 24, 1831, m. Jan. 12, 1854, CATHARINE L. CRANSTON.

Child of third wife:

F5484 SARAH H., b. Jan. 24, 1839, m. JAMES WADDINGTON.

SEVENTH GENERATION

F2365 Elizabeth Locke, born in Barrington, Nov. 16, 1799, died in Rochester, Dec. 14, 1858, married in Rochester, March 24, 1822, WILLIAM NUTTER of Barrington, a farmer. He married 2nd, MRS. E. BICKFORD of Great Falls, and died Jan. 1, 1875.

Children of 7th Gen.

5485 JOHN L., b. Rochester, Apl. 3, 1823, died same day.
5486 ABIGAIL P., b. Farmington, Jan. 13, 1824, m. 1844, ASA DAME, had: 5487 GEORGE, who died in the war in 1861 and she d. Jan. 23, 1847.
5488 JERRY N., b. Farm., Jan. 17, 1826, m. a widow in Nashville, Tenn., in 1850 and later a 2nd wife; was a shoemaker in Delaware, Ind., and had: 5489 child by 2nd wife.
5490 SARAH O., b. Farm., Oct. 18, 1827, m. Feb. 15, 1847, JOHN BROWN, who d. Apl. 20, 1875. She d. Rochester, May 1, 1887, had no children.
F5491 JOHN H., b. Dec. 24, 1829, m. ALMIRA L. DAME.
5492 WILLIAM, b. Hallowell, Me., Dec. 16, 1832, d. unmarried Rochester, Apl. 4, 1875.
5493 IRA, b. Argyle, Me., Apl. 8, 1836, d. Rochester, June 28, 1840.
5494 DANIEL C., b. Farmington, June 15, 1840, d. Apl. 21, 1844.
5495 HUNKING C., b. July 31, 1843, d. Roch., June 16, 1850.
5496 MARY E., b. Farmington, Oct. 22, 1846, m. Milton, Jan. 1, 1869, WILLIAM H. WATSON. He was three years in the war, was wounded at Cold Harbor, and later was civil engineer and lawyer, had:
5497 WILLIAM H., b. Apl. 22, 1877.

F2367 John Locke, born in Barrington, Dec. 11, 1802, died in Henry, Ill., Sept. 1, 1878, married in New York, March 25, 1832, CATHARINE TUCKER, born in Boston July 18, 1808, died in New York, Aug. 22, 1848; married 2nd, in New York, Oct. 1850, MRS. HANNAH (HOYT) LOCKE, his brother's widow. He was a carpenter in New York City until 1851, then went to Henry, Ill. Father, sons JAMES and CHARLES H., and nephew SILAS LOCKE took up land in the Sioux Reservation May 22, 1868, and endured great privations from poor crops and Indian troubles.

Children of 7th Gen. b. in New York City.

F5498 JOHN W., b. Jan. 25, 1833, m. Oct. 16, 1856, ADELAIDE S. COOK.
5499 GEORGE HENRY, b. Oct. 24, 1834, d. Feb. 26, 1835.
5500 CHARLES HENRY, b. Apl. 25, 1836, m. Henry, Ill., Dec. 28, 1860, AMELIA S. CAMP, b. Apl. 27, 1837, d. May 29, 1862; had twins who died young. He m. 2nd, Sept. 10, 1865, CATHERINE E. BARGE of Penridge, Ill., b. Penn., May 19, 1839. He was a farmer, Justice of the peace since 1883 at St. James, Minn., where he d. Aug. 4, 1904.

5502 GEORGE W., b. Feb. 27, 1838, d. unmarried Henry, Ill., May 25, 1863.
5503 SARAH ELIZABETH, b. Jan. 29, 1841, d. Sept. 4, 1853.
F5504 CATHERINE E., b. Sept. 13, 1843, m. Sept. 18, 1866, CAPT. JAMES G. HULL.
F5505 JAMES THEODORE, b. May 10, 1846, m. 1st, Dec. 7, 1879, MISSOURI FALLS; m. 2nd, Apl. 11, 1891, EDNA L. BULLIS.
5506 FRANK A., died young, was son of 2nd wife.

F2374 Abner D. Locke, born in Barrington, Dec. 23, 1806, died in Barrington, Feb. 10, 1867, married Feb. 23, 1826, REBECCA COFFIN, born in Dover, in 1807, daughter of Stephen. He was a farmer in Dover.

Children of 7th Gen.

5507 LYDIA, b. 1827, m. JOHN W. REYNOLDS, b. Dover. They lived in the West and were divorced. She d. Jan. 1905, Victoria, B. C.
F5508 JOHN W., b. Nov. 17, 1828, m. 1st, Sept. 20, 1857, SARAH A. HOWE; m. 2nd, Dec. 24, 1894, MRS. MARTHA (WEST) HALL.
5509 CATHERINE, b. Barrington, m. DR. WILLIAM PADELFORD of N. Y. or Phila.
5509a SOPHRONIA, b. 1834, m. SAMUEL WIGGIN, who was a grocer in Dover and d. Biddeford, Me. She then went West.
5510 ALPHONZO, b. Dover, 1839, m., went West, and d. in California, had: 5511 EDITH; 5512 GEORGE.
5513 SARAH, b. 1841, m. JOHN WM. REYNOLDS, and went West, had: 5514 ANNA.
5515 STEPHEN, b. ——, m., was a farmer in Galesburg, Ill., but letters are returned.

F2375 Silas Locke, born in Barrington, Nov. 17, 1809, died in Henry, Ill., Feb. 2, 1849, married Snatchwine, N. Y., May 14, 1840, HANNAH L. HOYT, born in Remsen, N. Y., Feb. 5, 1807, died Feb. 16, 1902. He was a farmer in Henry, Ill.

Children of 7th Gen.

F5516 GEORGE MUNROE, b. Apl. 20, 1841, m. Oct. 10, 1867, SAMANTHA E. KITTRIDGE; m. 2nd, Feb. 14, 1903, MRS. MARY L. (BLOOD) HILDEBRANT.
F5517 SILAS HOYT, b. Sept. 12, 1842, m. March 29, 1874, CAROLINE BARGE.
5518 WASHINGTON B., b. Henry, Ill., May 24, 1844, died young.
F5519 MERCY VICTORIA, b. Apl. 9, 1846, m. Feb. 7, 1865, EUGENE HUTCHINS.

F2376 Sampson B. Locke, born in Barrington, June 17, 1811, died July 31, 1863, married in Barrington, Dec. 25, 1836, SARAH CANNEY of Madbury, born in Madbury, Feb. 8, 1809, died in Barrington, Sept. 23, 1879. He was a farmer in Barrington.

G. Monroe Locke F5516

Mercy (Locke) Hutchins F5519

SEVENTH GENERATION 277

Children of 7th Gen. b. in Barrington.

5520 FRANKLIN, b. July 20, 1838, d. Apl. 30, 1839.
F5521 CLARA JANE, b. May 8, 1840, m. Dec. 2, 1869, JOSEPH W. FRYE.
5522 LUCY CATHERINE, b. July 20, 1842, d. Dover unmarried Sept. 26, 1895.
F5523 SARAH E., b. Sept. 1, 1844, m. 1st, March 26, 1863, GEORGE W. RICHARDSON; m. 2nd, Nov. 14, 1874, SAMUEL HENDERSON.
5524 MERCY ABBIE, b. March 15, 1847, m. in Dover, Feb. 22, 1880, HOWARTH HARGRAVES, b. Lancashire, England, a mill operator, had no children.
5525 DARIUS W., b. May 3, 1849, is unmarried, a farmer in Barrington.
F5526 MARY F. E., b. Sept. 19, 1852, m. Jan. 13, 1870, GEORGE G. CLARKE.

F2378 David Main, born in 1792, died in 1826, married ESTHER NORWOOD of Rockport, Mass., born in 1790, died in 1832. He was a farmer in Rockport, Mass.

Children of 7th Gen.

5527 CHARLES, b. March 3, 1817, d. Ports., Jan. 15, 1906, m. 1846, MARY NORTON, b. May 11, 1811, d. Dec. 4, 1894, dau. of William and Betsey (Lamprey), of Portsmouth. He was a contractor during the war, supplying harnesses, etc., to the army and that with other interests in the West made him a multi-millionaire, having a home in Cal. and Ports. He had: 5528 CHARLES, d. unmarried, age 26; 5529 FLORA B., b. May 1848, d. Oct. 12, 1914, m. CHARLES MCDERMOTT, a capitalist of Oakland, Cal. They had: 5530 two sons and two daus.
F5531 GEORGE, b. Nov. 23, 1819, m. ELLEN MARIA PRESTON.
5532 MIRIBAH A., b. ——, m. —— HOOD, a sea captain, had no children.
5533 ELIZABETH, b. ——, m. COL. JOHN CROCKETT, who d. Rochester, Nov. 30, 1915, aged 92, had: 5534 Infant, died young; 5535 JONATHAN HORNE; 5536 DANIEL, who lives in Lowell; 5537 GEORGE, who lives in Lawrence.

F2385 Lydia Main, born ——, married Stephen Young of Strafford, a farmer in Rochester, and a "Pizen" Democrat.

Children of 7th Gen.

5538 GEORGE, m. and d. in Lowell, Mass., had: 5539 CHARLES of LOWELL; 5540 FLORENCE of Lowell; 5541 GEORGE of Rochester.
5542 LEVIT, m. and d. Lowell, Mass.
5543 FREEMAN, was unmarried, d. Strafford.
5544 CHARLES, m. —— SWASEY of Strafford, had: 5545 Dau.; 5546 GEORGE; both of Exeter where he lived.
5547 MARY ANN, was m.

F2389 Elizabeth L. Woodman, born in Barrington, June 4, 1798, died in Campton, July 1, 1859, married in Thornton, Aug. 4, 1825, REUBEN FOSS of Thornton, born in Thornton, Aug. 17, 1801. He was a shoemaker and died in Thornton, Sept. 14, 1864.

Children of 7th Gen. b. in Campton.

5548 CARLENDA JANE, b. June 6, 1827, m. Campton, Aug. 10, 1852, SAMUEL R. CHASE of Campton, b. Jan. 11, 1821, lived and d. Rumney, Aug. 27, 1900. She was living 1903.

5549 CLARISSA ANN, b. Feb. 26, ——, m. Laconia, Aug. 17, 1869, SAMUEL EASTER of Lowell, b. Canada, May 2, 1829, employed on R. R. in Lowell and d. there Dec. 24, 1883. She d. Lowell, Apl. 30, 1883.

F2391 Alexander Woodman, born in Barrington, Aug. 27, 1801, died in Plainfield, Vt., June 11, 1882, married in Thornton Feb. 21, 1830, PHOEBE S. WALLACE of Thornton, born in Thornton, March 8, 1801, died in Plainfield, Sept. 30, 1880. He was a farmer in Woodsville.

Children of 7th Gen. b. in Thornton.

5551 HANNAH, b. ——, probably died young.

5552 JAMES, b. ——, probably died young.

5553 HANNAH, b. ——, d. Woodsville, 1876, m. HENRY HOLT of Woodsville, where he was a farmer and d. 1872.

5554 AUGUSTA, b. June 11, 1844, d. Plainfield, Vt., Sept. 6, 1893, m. in Woodsville, ALBERT E. SNOW, b. Clinton, Me., 1846, a druggist, Plainfield, Vt., 1902.

F2392 Ira Woodman, born in Barrington, July 6, 1803, died in Appleton, Iowa, July 17, 1880, married in Rumney Oct. 26, 1826, EUNICE M. KIMBALL of Rumney, born in Rumney, Aug. 2, 1807, died in Warrensville, Ill., Jan. 27, 1865, where he was a farmer.

Children of 7th Gen.

5555 MIRETTA C., b. Rumney, May 22, 1827, d. Warrensville, Ill., Sept. 15, 1861, m. Chicago, Oct. 10, 1847, MALANTON FERRY.

5556 GEORGE E., b. Rumney, Oct. 13, 1828, m. Aurora, Ill., Nov. 20, 1856, LAURA THOMPSON, who d. before 1903. He d. Maxwell, Iowa, Nov. 20, 1888.

5557 EUNICE ANN, b. Boston, March 26, 1831, d. Aurora, Ill., m. Warrensville, HENRY STOLK of Aurora, where he was a farmer.

5558 HARRIET E., b. Boston, July 25, 1834, d. Jan. 30, 1854.

5559 FREEMAN I., b. Warrensville, June 21, 1838, m. Aurora, Ill., Feb. 20, 1859, LUCY HOLLISTER.

5560 MARY M., b. Warrensville, Jan. 20, 1841, m. Aurora, Ill., Jan. 20, 1864, ELISHA WARNE, a farmer; both living in 1902 at Elburn, Ill.

5561 JOSEPH A., b. June 1, 1846, d. Oct. 13, 1848.

F2393 Nathaniel Woodman, born in Barrington, Dec. 15, 1804, died in Woodsville, July 4, 1880, married in Rumney, May 22, 1827, BETSEY KIMBALL of Rumney, born in Rumney, Apl. 17, 1806, died in Woodsville, Sept. 22, 1875. He was a farmer and shoemaker in Woodsville.
Children of 7th Gen. b. in Thornton.
5562 BETSEY JANE, b. Apl. 30, 1830, d. Feb. 12, 1875, m. MARTIN CHAMBERLAIN, a farmer in Bath.
5563 EMILY CAROLINE, b. Apl. 8, 1831, d. Aug. 20, 1889, m. ALDEN MARTIN, a farmer in Bath.
5564 KIMBALL F., b. July 8, 1833, m. 1st, SUSAN HUTCHINS; m. 2nd, LYDIA BURBANK.
5565 LYMAN, b. Aug. 2, 1835, m. 1st, MARY JUDD; m. 2nd, MARY BERRY; is a mechanic in Laconia.
5566 MARTHA ANN, b. Dec. 14, 1845, d. Woodsville, Dec. 20, 1882, m. JOHN DAVIS, a hotel keeper in Woodsville.

F2394 Caroline Woodman, born in Barrington, Sept. 5, 1806, died in West Thornton, March 26, 1875, married in Quincy, Mass., Sept. 4, 1831, JOSHUA CONNOR of Quincy.
Children of 7th Gen. b. in Boston.
5567 MARY ELIZABETH, b. March 22, 1832, m. Thornton, Dec. 25, 1849, SAMUEL CONNOR of Thornton, b. Dover. He was a farmer in Thornton.
5568 CAROLINE, b. March 13, 1834, d. Boston, June 14, 1834.
5569 EMELINE, b. twin, March 13, 1834, d. May 20, 1834.
5570 HARRIET B., b. March 25, 1835, d. Woodstock, Vt., Feb. 15, 1875, m. West Thornton, Nov. 24, 1857, ISAAC FOX of Woodstock, b. W., March 2, 1831. He is a surveyor in No. Woodstock, Vt.

F2395 Joseph Woodman, born in Woodstock, May 31, 1809, died in Garden Grove, Cal., June 25, 1896, married in Woodstock, Jan. 1, 1838, ELEANOR BARNARD of Woodstock, born in Thornton, Nov. 19, 1815. He was a farmer in Elburn, Ill., and Garden Grove, Cal.
Children of 7th Gen. b. in Woodstock, Vt.
5571 FREEMAN, b. Dec. 21, 1838, m. Aurora, Ill., Feb. 13, 1864, ALICE E. BARTHOLOMEW of Aurora, b. Dresden, N. Y., Jan. 5, 1845, d. Evanston, Ill., July 25, 1899; was a war veteran and milk shipper in Elburn, Ill.
5572 JULIET, b. June 12, 1843, m. Sycamore, Ill., Sept. 15, 1859, JOSEPH GREY of Elburn, Ill., b. New Brunswick, Apl. 21, 1830; was a farmer in Elburn and d. there Sept. 16, 1901.
5573 REV. IRA, b. twin, June 12, 1843, m. Campton, Ill., DELLA HAWLEY, lived Ramona, Cal., and d. there March 1902.

5574 JOHN, b. Apl. 9, 1845, was a war veteran and d. Elburn, March 5, 1866.
5575 SARAH ELIZABETH, b. Feb. 28, 1848, m. Virgil, Ill., March 25, 1867, SIMON EURET CHAFFEE, b. Nov. 21, 1845, a milk shipper in Campton, Ill.
5576 JOSEPH GARDNER, b. Virgil, Ill., June 3, 1854, m. at Davis Junction, March 12, 1879, ALICE DAVIS of Davis Junc. He is grain inspector in Chicago.

F2397 Mary Ann Woodman, born in Woodstock, Vt., May 1, 1816, married Oct. 12, 1834, PELATIAH RUSSELL of Woodstock, born Oct. 12, 1813. He was a glove manufacturer, and died in Plymouth, Feb. 12, 1892.

Children of 7th Gen. b. in Thornton or Woodstock, Vt.

5577 CHARLOTTE MCQUESTON, b. Jan. 13, 1836, d. Tilton, Dec. 17, 1896, m. Thornton, Oct. 1857, CHARLES W. MORRISON of Tilton, b. Sanbornton, July 15, 1833. He was a spinner in Tilton and d. Concord, June 3, 1889, had: 5578 FREDERICK; 5579 FRANK; 5580 ANNA; 5581 WILLIS.
5582 MAY MELISSA, b. March 21, 1837, d. Campton, March 9, 1875, m. 1st, Feb. 1858, GILBERT DEARBORN of Plymouth, b. Aug. 26, 1835, d. in U. S. Service at Mechanicksville, Ky., Sept. 5, 1863. She m. 2nd, ALBERT SILVER of Campton, b. Apl. 28, 1813, had: 5583 MARY E.; 5584 NELLIE M.
5585 JOHN MARSHALL, b. Sept. 5, 1839, m. Thornton, Sept. 5, 1867, ELIZABETH HOMER of Thornton, b. Ellsworth, June 5, 1843, d. Campton, 1876. He was a wheelwright and mail carrier in Plymouth, had: 5586 CLARENCE; 5587 CLARA.
5588 WILLIAM ALONZO, b. Jan. 5, 1841, m. Aug. 1871, LAVINA WEST of Geneva, Ill. He is a war veteran and mail carrier in David City, Neb., had: 5589 MORRIS S.; 5590 MAUD; 5591 MABEL.
5592 ELIZABETH JANE, b. Dec. 1, 1843, m. Thornton, Sept. 1861, SHUBAEL SANBORN of Thornton, b. Holderness, Feb. 10, 1836. He was a farmer in Rising City, Neb., had: 5593 ELLEN S.; 5594 JOSEPHINE; 5595 NINA.
5596 CAROLINE, b. July 24, 1845, is a dressmaker in N. Y. City, 1902, unmarried.
5597 ELLEN, b. Jan. 25, 1847, m. Plymouth, Jan. 9, 1872, JOHN H. PLUMMER of Campton, b. C., Sept. 7, 1846. He was a farmer, kept livery stable in Campton, and d. Wentworth, July 8, 1891, had: 5598 RALPH; 5599 CARRIE L.
5600 EMILY, b. May 29, 1849, d. Plymouth, July 23, 1873, m. Plymouth, Nov. 1872, GILL FLETCHER DEARBORN, b. P., Jan. 18, 1851, lives Plymouth, has no children.
5601 ARMENA HELENA, b. Sept. 27, 1850, d. Campton, Sept. 10, 1878, m. Plymouth, Feb. 1, 1872, ALBERT J. ELIOTT, b. Camp., Dec. 2, 1850. He is a deer skin tanner in Campton, had: 5602 LILA, who m. RAYMOND EVERETT.

SEVENTH GENERATION

5603 FRANK PELATIAH, b. March 7, 1852, m. Toledo, O., Sept. 3, 1872, CARRIE E. BATEMAN of Toledo. He is a cloth dyer, had: 5604 ALICE ADALAIDE.
5605 HATTIE CORA, b. June 3, 1855, m. Plymouth, Feb. 26, 1881, JASON F. DRAPER of Plymouth, b. Lowell, Mass., Oct. 10, 1850. He is Supt. of Schools, San Jose, Cal., had: 5606 MARIE; 5607 MURIEL; 5608 MARGURITE; 5609 JASON R.
5610 FLORENCE MABEL, b. July 10, 1857, m. N. Y. City, May 10, 1893, THOMAS F. GLYNN of Plymouth, b. Ply., Dec. 1837. They have no children. He is a retired sporting goods mfgr. in Plymouth, 1902.
5611 CLARENCE DUDLEY, b. Sept. 19, 1859, d. Thornton, Feb. 12, 1864.
5612 KATE ETHEL, b. May 9, 1862, m. 1st, in Plymouth, Dec. 7, 1880, MARCUS L. EMMONS of Bristol, b. Feb. 1847. He was a glove mfgr. in Plymouth and d. July 5, 1891; m. 2nd, N. Y. City, May 10, 1893, DR. CHARLES R. GOULD of Tilton, b. Hillsborough, Dec. 28, 1841, lives in Tilton, has no children.

F2410 Daniel Piper Locke, born in Barrington, Sept. 25, 1804, died Sept. 3, 1840, married HANNAH HOITT who after his death married J. C. CARTER.

Children of 7th Gen.

F5613 JAMES C., b. Sept. 6, 1836, m. Sept. 6, 1858, LOANNA A. NEALLEY.
F5614 OREN D., b. —— , m. SARAH C. PIERCE.
F5615 CARRIE SWEET, m. Sept. 4, 1859, DAVID C. PRESCOTT.

F2411 William J. Locke, born in Barrington, Dec. 25, 1805, died in Lee, Dec. 27, 1840, married May 2, 1829, SARAH B. DAME of Lee, born March 21, 1811, died in Lee, Feb. 28, 1860, daughter of Israel and Hannah. He was a blacksmith in Lee. Lee and Barrington records conflict many times. Lee records say that Sarah married Feb. 25, 1830. Somersworth, says William married BETSEY GREEN.)

Children of 7th Gen. b. in Lee.

F5616 MARY ANN, b. June 27, 1830, m. 1st, March 21, 1846, JOEL JUDKINS; m. 2nd, Dec. 1872, NATHAN MARSH.
5617 ABIGAIL D., b. July 12, 1833, d. March 29, 1843.
F5618 BETSEY J., b. Nov. 4, 1835, m. Dec. 8, 1858, WILLARD H. DAMREN.
5619 LYDIA A., b. Lee, Sept. 10, 1836, m. Aug. 4, 1857, CAPTAIN TYLER P. COLEMAN, and both parents and one child were lost at sea June 4, 1862, on a voyage from the West Indies, had: 5620 WILLIAM J. COLEMAN, b. So. Berwick, Me., (Oct. 13, 1854,) a shoemaker in Derry 1898; 5621 ELLA M., b. Lowell, Aug. 24, 1858, was lost at sea June 4, 1862.
F5622 MARIA H., b. Dec. 26, 1838, m. 1st, July 14, 1856, CHARLES L. FOOTE; m. 2nd, Dec. 6, 1866, LEVI HOWARD.
5623 WILLIAM H., b. Oct. 1840, d. March, 1841.

F2412 Stephen H. Locke, born in Barrington, Aug. 30, 1807, died in Nottingham, Oct. 10, 1882, married Apl. 7, 1831, ABIGAIL WIGHT of Dedham, Mass., born Oct. 13, 1810, died Jan. 3, 1847, daughter of Andrew and Margaret (Corbet); married 2nd, in Deerfield, June 14, 1847, DEBORAH R. CHASE of Deerfield, born in Meredith, lived in Derry in 1904. He lived in Roxbury, Mass., several years.

Children of 7th Gen.

5624 CHARLES H., b. Dedham, Mass., Apl. 27, 1833, d. Nov. 3, 1837.
F5625 SARAH M., b. July 24, 1837, m. May 8, 1859, WILLIAM WALLACE.
5626 BETSEY JANE, b. Boston, May 27, 1842, d. July 22, 1864.
F5627 ANDREW WIGHT, b. Nov. 23, 1844, m. Feb. 5, 1868, MRS. SARAH G. WALLACE.
F5628 ABBIE A., b. Jan. 13, 1847, m. June 1, 1875, JOHN H. MOORE.
5629 2nd wife had child, Oct. 21, 1848, d infant.
F5630 JOSEPHINE R., b. Feb. 5, 1850, m. 1st, May 19, 1863, GEORGE W. LUCY; m. 2nd, JAMES P. GRIFFIN.
F5631 HERBERT L., b. May 8, 1852, m. Oct. 5, 1881, ELIZA VICKERS.
F5632 ORAH H., b. Nov. 30, 1854, m. 1st, Jan. 4, 1882, FRANK L. THOMPSON; m. 2nd, June 11, 1887, GEORGE H. ELLIOT.
5633 ANGELINE M., b. Nottingham, Apl. 29, 1857, d. Manchester, 1891, m. Dec. 25, 1873, JOHN F. DEARBORN, and had: 5634 NATHAN E., b. May 19, 1877, d. March 27, 1886.
5635 ALBERT A., b. Nott., Feb. 14, 1859, d. there June 1, 1865.
5636 GEORGETTA, b. Nott., March 6, 1862, prob. d. July 16, 1865.

F2420 Sarah Hoitt Locke, born in Barrington, May 29, 1812, died in Epsom, Sept. 5, 1886, married Feb. 19, 1839, DEARBORN B. MOSES, born in Epsom, Aug. 3, 1805, died, a farmer of Epsom, Aug. 23, 1881, son of Mark and Betsey (Cate).

Child of 7th Gen.

F5637 SARAH LOCKE, b. Nov. 25, 1841, m. June 19, 1869, JAMES H. TRIPP.

F2421 Betsey Babb Locke, born in Barrington, Apl. 3, 1816, died in Epping, July 25, 1891, married in Durham, Oct. 29, 1839, JACOB H. TILTON, born in Epping, June 11, 1806, died, a farmer of Epping, Apl. 13, 1892.

Children of 7th Gen. b. in Epping.

5638 MARY ELIZABETH, b. June 28, 1840, m. Epping, March 31, 1863, DAVID H. BOYNTON of Lowell, b. L., Aug. 26, 1835. He was a farmer in Merrimack until 1895, then removed to Epping, had no children.

SEVENTH GENERATION

5639 GEORGE WASHINGTON, b. Oct. 28, 1841, m. Merrimack, Jan, 1, 1873, J. AUGUSTA THYNG, b. Epping, Dec. 11, 1853; was a merchant, deputy sheriff of Rock. Co. many years, selectman and postmaster of Epping, had: 5640 RENA MAY, b. Epping, Dec. 24, 1875, m. Epping, June 8, 1898, FRANK N. HALL, who is an electrician in Enfield.

5641 WILLIAM HENRY, b. June 11, 1844, m. Concord, Jan. 1, 1867, ALFARETTA A. BOODY, b. Epping, Aug. 21, 1849, was a farmer and mechanic in Epping, had: 5642 JOHN JACOB TILTON, b. Epping, Feb. 14, 1868, m. Gorham, Me., Oct. 12, 1895, STELLA STOKES, b. Gorham, June 17, 1872, d. Epping, July 31, 1898. He graduated from Phillips Ex. Acad. 1886, lives Epping, 1915.

F5643 SARAH MARIA, b. twin, June 11, 1844, m. FRANK A. MILES.

5644 ANN DEBORAH, b. Dec. 23, 1846, d. Epping, Feb. 25, 1853.

5645 ELLEN JANE, b. Dec. 16, 1849. d. unmarried Lowell, June 10, 1869.

5646 JANE ELLEN, b. twin, Dec. 16, 1849, d. July 28, 1891, m. in Epping JOHN S. OSGOOD, b. Epping, July 3, 1843, a mechanic in Epping, had: 5647 MAY E., b. Aug. 18, 1880, a school teacher.

F2423 Samuel Hoitt Locke, born in Lee, Dec. 28, 1818, died in Cambridge, Feb. 29, 1852, married March 10, 1846, ELEANOR A. PAYSON of Cambridge, born March 4, 1824, died in South Boston, Nov. 1903. He was a carpenter in Boston and Cambridge, Mass.

Children of 7th Gen.

5648 EDGAR H., b. Cambridge, Mass., Jan. 23, 1847, m. Nov. 7, 1866, SARAH J. SPROUL, b. Aug. 12, 1847, d. Apl. 28, 1904; is a salesman in No. Cambridge, 1900.

5649 SAMUEL ELLIS, b. Cambridge, Mass., Apl. 28, 1850, m. Feb. 10, 1874, MRS. EMMA COLLINS, and had: 5650 ELLA MABEL, b. June 5, 1875.

F2425 Benjamin F. Locke, born in Barrington, July 20, 1809, died in 1871, married in Boscawen, Aug. 16, 1835, MARY P. CORSER of Boscawen, born in 1810, died in Boscawen, May 30, 1836; married 2nd, CHARLOTTE PARKER (or Currier?), born in Massachusetts, in 1810, died Aug. 9, 1889, daughter of Nathaniel and Lydia (Hayes). He was a merchant in Lowell in 1835 and in Manchester, on city council in 1854.

Children of 7th Gen.

5651 BENJAMIN F., b. July 1835, d. Dec. 25, 1836.

5652 MARY A., b. 1837, was unmarried. (A Mary Locke, dau. of Benj. m. Manchester, Feb. 6, 1865, JAMES O. HARRIMAN.)

5653 RODOLPHUS M., b. Lowell, July 17, 1839, m. ABIGAIL BLAKE, b. Haverhill, Feb. 22, 1844, d. Hill, May 26, 1911, dau. of James and Eliza D. He was a farmer and storekeeper in Manchester, and d. Apl. 6, 1833, had one: 5654 Child.
5655 CHARLOTTE A., b. 1843, d. unmarried Nov. 3, 1865, lived Manchester.
5656 HELEN M., b. 1849, died young.
5657 MARTHA M., b. 1863, died young.
5658 MARTHA J., b. 1865, m. ALONZO C. FRENCH, son of Moses of Manchester, lived at Burnside, Ky., and had: 5659 MABEL, b. 1881.
5660 HELEN M., b. twin, 1865, lived unmarried, with her sister in Ky.
5661 EMMA G., b. 1869, m. FRANKLIN B. FRENCH, son of Moses of Manchester, lived there and had: 5662 BERTHA M., b. 1889.

F2426 Alfred Locke, born in Woodstock, Dec. 19, 1811, died in Rochester, Apl. 8, 1892, married in Rochester, Aug. 5, 1834, MARY A. D. SEAVEY of Rochester, born in Barnstead, Oct. 9, 1811, died March 4, 1871. He was a farmer and stone mason in Rochester.

Children of 7th Gen.

F5663 SAMUEL S., b. Dec. 25, 1834, m. 1st, LYDIA A. SAVORY; m. 2nd, Oct. 11, 1885, ELIZABETH FAIRCLOTH MAHONEY.
5664 CHARLES A., b. Rochester, Feb. 25, 1837, m. Somersworth, June 23, 1860, MARY W. PERKINS, b. 1840. He enlisted in the Navy in 1862 and served three years, was a saloonkeeper and d. Somersworth, Sept. 30, 1881, had: 5665 WILLIAM H., b. Dec. 27, 1860, d. Dec. 1, 1863; 5666 CHARLES A., b. Nov. 9, 1876, d. Jan. 1, 1877.
F5667 GEORGE FRANCIS, b. March 8, 1841, m. Nov. 20, 1859, LYDIA F. CATER.
F5668 SERGEANT ELISHA E., b. Jan. 17, 1843, m. May 5, 1862, LUCY M. SMALLCON.
5669 ALFRED HERMAN, b. Oct. 7, 1845, d. unmarried March 1, 1875, a farmer in Barrington.
F5670 IRVING C., b. Oct. 23, 1846, m. March 22, 1877, ABBIE L. YOUNG.
F5671 ALPHONZO B., b. Apl. 10, 1849, m. Dec. 27, 1870, MARY A. WATERHOUSE.
5672 JOSEPH T., b. Dover, June 22, 1851, m. 1st, Rochester, Dec. 15, 1875, LYDIA E. TASKER, dau. of Eben, b. Jackson, Oct. 31, 1852, d. Berwick, Me., Sept. 28, 1877; m. 2nd, Rochester, Dec. 4, 1879, MRS. ROSE B. PERKINS, b. Gt. Falls, 1855, dau. of William W. and Abigail. He was a B. & M. R. R. employee in Lowell, later was a harness maker in Milton, had no children.
5673 MARY A., b. Feb. 7, 1854, m. Rochester, Dec. 22, 1888, WILLIAM S. AYERS, b. 1847, d. Jan. 11, 1901, and she d. childless Jan. 21, 1900.

F2427 Elisha Locke, born in Barrington, Nov. 18, 1814, died in Barrington, Oct. 29, 1886, married in Barrington, Jan. 27, 1841, LAVINA FRENCH of Northwood, born in Barrington, Feb.

SEVENTH GENERATION   285

28, 1811, died in Barrington, Nov. 8, 1890, daughter of Daniel and Mary (Tuck) of Eliot, Me. He was a farmer and lumber dealer in Barrington.

Children of 7th Gen, b. in Barrington.
5674 NAHUM FRANCIS, b. 1843, d. Apl. 14, 1846.
5675 MARY S., b. 1846, d. 1846, aged 3 months.
5676 MARY F., b. 1847, m. AUGUSTINE YOUNG, but they separated within a month. She lives with her brother.
5677 ELISHA JUDSON, b. Nov. 10, 1851, is unmarried, and a farmer on the old homestead in Barrington.

F2428 Elizabeth P. Locke, born in Barrington, Dec. 12, 1817, died Sept. 1, 1893, married in Barrington, Oct. 7, 1840, AARON S. CRAWFORD, a dentist of Salem, N. Y., born June 19, 1809, died May 21, 1867.

Children of 7th Gen.
5678 SARAH J., b. Lowell, Mass., Oct. 22, 1841.
5679 MARION F., b. Oct. 24, 1843, m. Oct. 31, 1894, LIZZIE A. COPELAND, b. in Salem, Mass., where he is an expressman.

F2429 James M. Locke, born in Barrington, July 1, 1823, died Nov. 19, 1853, married in Wolfeboro, Jan. 28, 1846, IZETTA PLUMMER of Wolfeboro, who died 1904 (?). He was a farmer and was killed by falling from a team.

Children of 7th Gen. b. in Barrington.
5680 GEORGE, b. July 4, 1850, d. 1852.
5681 FRANCENA M., b. 1847, m. 1st, Dec. 7, 1865, J. FRANK DAVIS of Milton, b. 1842, and had: 5682 GEORGE DAVIS, now a shoemaker in Milton, who m. and lost his wife; also, 5683 CLEORA A. DAVIS, who m. FRANK CORNER, and d. May 30, 1905, aged 31. Francena m. 2nd, May 24, 1875, MARK F. COOK of Brookfield; m. 3rd, WILLIAM F. JOHNSON, a tanner and farmer in Wolfeboro.

F2430 Lyman Locke, born in New Durham, Jan. 22, 1824(?), died in Barrington, Oct. 29, 1876, married in Barrington, Dec. 26, 1842, SUSAN CATER of Barrington, who died in Barrington, July 6, 1901, aged 81. He was a carpenter and selectman in Rochester, 1854–6. Lyman Locke G. A. R. Post, Rochester, is named for him. He enlisted in Co. G, 8th N. H. Reg., was made 2nd Lieut. in 1861, 1st Lieut. in 1863. He became Captain, was wounded the same year, and was discharged on account of wounds 1864.

Children of 7th Gen.

5682 LEVI W., b. Apl. 12, 1843, d. Feb. 4, 1846.

F5683 JAMES M., b. Nov. 8, 1844, m. Jan. 26, 1867, CORDELIA GRAY.

F5684 MARY E., b. Jan. 13, 1847, m. CHARLES F. MONTGOMERY.

5685 ANN ISABEL, b. Aug. 30, 1848, m. Rochester, March 30, 1874, J. E. V. THOMPSON of Barrington, b. Tamworth, 1841, son of Isaac and Lucy. He is a farmer in Barrington, had no children.

5686 IDA MAY, b. Barrington, June 30, 1857, m. Aug. 5, 1880, WALTER BUZZELL, b. Barr., May 28, 1855. He is a farmer in Barrington, and had: 5687 ANGIE, b. Dec. 23, 1883, is a school teacher, unmarried in Barrington.

5688 EMMA SOPHIA, b. Barrington, Nov. 11, 1858, d. there, Sept. 26, 1864.

F2431 Henry W. Locke, born in Barrington, Sept. 28, 1827, died in Barrington, March 20, 1895, married 1st, July 4, 1847, ELIZABETH A. WATERHOUSE of Gonic, died May 1855, daughter of Nicholas V. and Susan (Chesley-Place); married 2nd, Apl. 13, 1870, ANGELINA HAYES of Rochester, born March 26, 1839, daughter of Watson and Joan (Winkley). He received his early education in this native town, supplemented by several terms at Gilmanton Academy, the tuition for which he earned in the Gonic mills. Continuing at work in the mill and for his father-in-law until 1855, he moved to Sauk Rapids, Minn., remaining there for two years. The death of his wife ended his western plans and he soon returned to Gonic where he began the grocery business and continued until the war broke out. When President Lincoln called for 75,000 men he began enlisting men for the 3rd N. H. Reg. but unable to get an expected appointment in this Reg. he started enlisting the 4th Reg., 32 men of which went from Rochester. Starting as private in this Reg. Sept. 16, 1861, he was promoted rapidly until made a Captain in the Commissary Dept. in 1864, where he made good until discharged Nov. 27, 1865, as Brevet Major U. S. Vols. He was the pioneer brick manufacturer of Gonic, starting in 1866 and made brick and lumber for 20 years. From 1886 to his death he was engaged in farming in Barrington. He was a man of marked ability in divers ways, generous and impulsive in his actions, called "a tip top officer" and liked by the soldiers. He did much for the future of Gonic. He was postmaster of Rochester in 1861. In 1865 he was Post Commissary in Brownsville, Tenn., and resigned Nov. 1865. He was presented with a sword by the citizens of Rochester, and a G. A. R. Post has been named after him.

SEVENTH GENERATION

Children of 7th Gen.
F5689 FANNIE C., b. 1848, m. GEORGE H. JOHNSON of Boston.
Adopted children, three girls:
5690 NELLIE A. or HELEN C. RILEY, who m. in New York City, Apl. 12, 1899, ERNEST J. STONE of Montclair, N. J. and had: 5691 ROBERT.
5691 FLORA B. GROVER, who m. IRVING JOHNSON.
5692 MADGE HANNA, who m. EBEN LOCKE, # 8631.

F2432 Sarah Pinkham Locke, born in Barrington, Apl. 16, 1830, died Feb. 11, 1905, married Nov. 12, 1848, HENRY LITTLEFIELD of Wells, Me., born in Wells, Apl. 1, 1818, died in Dover, Aug. 25, 1898. He was for 50 years in the tinsmith, stove and hardware business in Dover, was in the Fire Department, an Odd Fellow, a Republican, and a genial, kind-hearted man.
Children of 7th Gen. b. in Dover.
5693 GEORGE O., b. Oct. 21, 1849, d. Oct. 22, 1853.
5694 FRANK O., b. Aug. 17, 1851, is a salesman in Boston, unmarried.
5695 FANNIE B., b. June 6, 1856, m. Apl. 21, 1881, H. F. TRIPP of Dover, and had: 5696 GRACE, b. Dover, May 1, 1882.

F2433 Oliver Babb Locke, born in Barrington, Feb. 20, 1835, died in Haverhill, Mass., Apl. 11, 1911, married Jan. 23, 1858, MARTHA ANN FERNALD of Barrington, born in Barrington, Feb. 14, 1839, died in Dover, July 1902, daughter of Wm. K. and Martha. He was a farmer in Dover.
Children of 7th Gen. First two b. in Barrington, the others in Dover.
5697 JAMES WESLEY, b. Aug. 4, 1858, m. Dover, Apl. 15, 1882, ELLEN C. THAYER of Brockton, Mass., b. Hanover, Mass., 1854, dau. of Henry and Mary; have no children. He is a carpenter in Dover and Farmington.
F5698 FANNIE AUGUSTA, b. Sept. 13, 1859, m. 1st, March 16, 1878 KING YOUNG; m. 2nd, Jan. 3, 1897, CHARLES GROVER.
5698aWILLIAM ELLSWORTH, b. Dec. 1, 1861, d. Dover, Nov. 13, 1864.
F5699 OLIVER ALBION, b. Jan. 1, 1863, m. Oct. 9, 1889, MARY E. FLAGG.
F5700 SARAH ELIZABETH, b. Apl. 29, 1865, m. May 18, 1881, SAMUEL M. P. DEMERITT.
5701 WILLIAM BERT, b. Sept. 23, 1868, m. Boston, 1906, ANNA R. BALCH. had a child d. an infant. He is a shoe cutter in Haverhill, Mass.
5702 HARRIE FRANCISCO, b. May 30, 1870, m. JOSEPHINE TRASK of Farmington who d. Haverhill, Mass., May 12, 1909. He was a shoemaker and farmer in Dover and died without children May 11, 1910.
5703 LEROY MARCELLUS, b. May 19, 1872, m. Dover, Nov. 29, 1894, ANAGUSTA STERLING of Dover, b. 1876, dau. of Sumner H. and Eliza (Chadwick). Was a farmer and shoemaker in Dover and Lynn and had at least: 5704 EVELYN L., b. Dover, Jan. 7, 1900.

5705 EDWIN FERNALD, b. Sept. 30, 1873, m. Feb. 21, 1895, MARY E.
CAREY of Haverhill, Mass., b. there 1871. He is a shoemaker in
Haverhill, Mass., and had: 5706 ALICE F., b. Dover, Apl. 18, 1896.
5707 FRANK WALKER, b. July 3, 1876, is unmarried and overseer in Portsmouth shoe shop.
5708 CHARLES ELLSWORTH, b. Apl. 19, 1878, is in United Shoe Company's office in Haverhill, Mass., unmarried.

F2435 Jacob Jay Demeritt, born Feb. 15, 1806, died Dec. 12, 1863, married Aug. 13, 1823, ELIZA EVANS, born June 13, 1809, died June 1, 1831; married 2nd, Jan. 2, 1833, MARCIA HERBERT FERNALD, born June 29, 1810, died Feb. 15, 1855. He lived in Dover.

Children of 7th Gen.

5709 LYDIA M., b. Sept. 14, 1829, d. June 15, 1837.
Second wife's children:
5710 ELIZABETH E., b. Aug. 3, 1834, d. June 13, 1837.
5711 SEORIUM, b. Dec. 24, 1837, m. in Lynn, Apl. 6, 1860, EMILY A. PERKINS, b. 1842, d. Aug. 18, 1862; m. 2nd, Dover, Apl. 4, 1867, FANNIE A. JOY, b. May 16, 1846, d. March 1906.
5712 JAMES HERBERT, b. Sept. 5, 1840, m. Aug. 13, 1862, FANNIE OSGOOD, of No. Berwick, Me., lives Dover.
5713 FRANCENA, b. Apl. 13, 1843, d. Sept. 17, 1845.
5714 ORLANDO, b. July 22, 1844, m. Dover, June 21, 1865, JENNIE B. HARTFORD and had a 5715 dau. in Dover. He d. Kansas City, Sept. 14, 1899.
5716 MARCIA ELIZABETH, b. March 3, 1847, d. Aug. 12, 1847.

F2446 Mary Ann Demeritt, born in Farmington, Aug. 20, 1811, died in Cattaraugus, N. Y., Dec. 8, 1886, married HORATIO BABB, born in Barrington, May 19, 1812, son of Thomas and Abigail. He was station agent on the Erie R. R. from the time the road was built until his death in Cattaraugus, Nov. 12, 1871.

Children of 7th Gen.

5717 ALBERT, b. Canisteo, 1849, an expert telegrapher, later in life a successful broker in Peoria, Ill. He was a thoughtful considerate brother, a 32d degree Mason, d. Cattaraugus, N. Y., Apl. 2, 1908, unmarried.
5718 M. ELIZABETH, was unmarried.
5719 H. SUSAN, was unmarried.
5720 BELLE, b. ——, m. —— HERRICK.
5721 THOMAS H., b. ——, lived Chicago.

F2462 Mary J. Demeritt, born ——, died in Dover, Jan. 1875, married 1st, Apl. 17, 1841, OLIVER P. BURLEIGH, born Apl. 10, 1815, died Nov. 8, 1848, son of Josiah and Margaret (Newcomb). She lived at Dover, and married 2nd, JOHN S. GLASS.

SEVENTH GENERATION

Children of 7th Gen.

5722 JOSIAH, b. Dover, Feb. 2, 1842, lived Dover.
5723 CHARLES H., b. Aug. 16, 1843, m. Feb. 21, 1867, DORA J. THOMPSON of Franklin, b. Hill, Aug. 17, 1845, dau. of Joseph and Sarah (Heath). He is overseer in Cocheco Mills, Dover, and has two children.
5724 SAMUEL D., b. Aug. 20, 1848, m. CLARA A. STILES of Dover, who was b. June 1, 1847. He is a mill employee in Dover, and has: 5725 HARRIE.

F2464 Deborah Demeritt, born ——, died Apl. 1904, married WILLIAM H. FELKER of Gonic.

Children of 7th Gen.

5726 HENRY FELKER, b. ——, lives Gonic, an ex-Mayor of Rochester.
5727 SAMUEL D. FELKER, b. ——, a lawyer in Rochester and Governor of New Hampshire, 1912-14.
5728 CHARLES FELKER, b. ——, died young.
5729 ALICE FELKER, m. ——, CHARLES BICKFORD.

F2466 Elisha Locke, born in Barrington, Dec. 11, 1818, married 1st, in Canton, Mass., June 19, 1847, NANCY C. SPARE of Canton, born in Cincinnati, O.; married 2nd, July 29, 1851, ANNA E. PERRY, a music teacher, born Dec. 22, 1831. They lived in Cincinnati, and he died Carroll, Iowa, July 15, 1903.

Children of 7th Gen.

5730 CHARLES FRANKLIN, b. June 4, 1853, m. May 25, 1881, ELLA BLONG. He was a physician and surgeon, had no children and d. Sept. 16, 1896.
5731 ELIZABETH, b. June 16, 1855, d. Sept. 15, 1857.
5732 LUA CATHERINE, b. Sept. 28, 1859, m. May 25, 1886, GEORGE L. SHERMAN, D.D.S., lived Carroll, Carroll Co., Iowa, and had: 5733 STANTON LOCKE SHERMAN, b. 1887.
5733 WILLIAM STANTON, b. Aug. 7, 1865, m. Sept. 30, 1896, EMMA S. WELLS, was a dentist in Cincinnati, had: 5734 WALTER WELLS LOCKE, b. Jan. 18, 1898, d. June 20, 1906.
5735 WALTER MORRISON, b. Aug. 26, 1868, m. June 29, 1898, MARGARET J. WHEELER, was a lawyer. She d. Oct. 21, 1912. Had: 5736 CHARLES W. LOCKE, Aug. 31, 1899.

F2474 Benjamin T. Locke, born in Barrington, Sept. 9, 1835, married in New Durham, May 24, 1860, AGNES LABOUNTY, born in Canada in 1838, daughter of John and Julia. He enlisted in Co. L, 1st Reg. Cavalry, was captured and spent six weeks in Libbey Prison. He returned home but soon re-enlisted and went with Sheridan as Sergeant of Cavalry. He was shot from ambush and fell dead from his horse at Kearneysville, Va.,

Aug. 24, 1864. When at home he was a farmer in New Durham. His widow married 2nd, Dec. 2, 1865, EDMUND ROBERTS of Farmington, born 1832.

Child of 7th Gen.

5737 WILLIAM H., b. New Durham, Oct. 22, 1861.

F2561 Reuben Locke, born in Alexandria, Jan. 29, 1809, died in Alexandria, Sept. 1, 1860, married Feb. 15, 1832, IRENE G. HEALEY, born in Raymond, Jan. 28, 1809, died in Alexandria, Oct. 22, 1882. He was a farmer in Alexandria.

Children of 7th Gen. b. in Alexandria.

5738 LUTHER, b. Aug. 28, 1832, d. March 10, 1833.
F5739 ISAAC HEALEY, b. July 7, 1834, m. June 30, 1867, MRS. ELLEN J. (CLARK) CROCKER.
F5740 BETSEY AIKEN, b. March 28, 1836, m. Oct. 26, 1854, FREEMAN E. BERRY.
5741 IRENA J., b. Oct. 19, 1839, d. Alex., unmarried Apl. 21, 1859.
F5742 LYMAN, b. Nov. 28, 1841, m. 1st, March 22, 1863, MARY AUGUSTA CLARKE; m. 2nd, Dec. 10, 1872, NELLIE V. HUNT.
5743 GEORGE M., b. Aug. 3, 1844, was in Co. G, 18th N. H. Vols., 1864; was in the real estate business in Stockton, Cal., and d. Jan. 1899, unmarried.
5744 CHARLES HENRY, b. Aug. 6, 1849, is unmarried. Has been for many years in the Maine lumber camps.

F2563 Benjamin Locke, born in Epsom, Aug. 15, 1817, married EFFIE WALLACE, # 2566, born in Epsom, Sept. 1817, died in Concord, March 11, 1887, daughter of Elijah and Polly. He was a stone cutter in Concord, but went to California in 1849, and was never heard from afterward.

Children of 7th Gen.

5745 MARY FRANCES, b. Concord, 1835, m. 1867, LEWIS C. CARTER, b. 1832, a harness maker in Concord; had no children.
5746 CAROLINE C., b. Concord, Oct. 6, 1839, m. Concord, Sept. 25, 1854, JABEZ S. STETSON of Concord, a shoemaker. She d. Concord, May 21, 1883, had: 5747 BRADFORD STETSON, b. 1856, now a cigar maker.
5748 JAMES A., b. 1843, probably died young.

F2564 George Locke, born in Epsom, Oct. 18, 1820, died Feb. 20, 1883, married March 7, 1844, ELIZABETH CHENEY, born in Bristol, July 23, 1812, died in Alexandria, Jan. 30, 1890, daughter of David and Anna. He was educated in the schools of Alexandria, was a farmer, a Democrat, and one of the leading men of the town.

SEVENTH GENERATION

Children of 7th Gen.

5749 MARY ANN, b. Alexandria, Apl. 23, 1845, d. unmarried March 16, 1869.

5750 EDMUND WEBSTER, b. Alexandria, Feb. 15, 1847, m. March 31, 1870, SUSAN WEBBER SMITH of Orange, b. 1845, dau. of Ransom R. and Mary (Coleburn). He was a prosperous and leading farmer in Alexandria, was road surveyor and on the school board, and d. Nov. 30, 1892.

F2576 Eliza Locke, born in Epsom, Jan. 10, 1812, died in Hubbardston, Mass., Apl. 1, 1886, married in Chichester, Jan. 26, 1831, CHARLES G. HOOK of Concord.

Children of 7th Gen.

5751 JANE HOOK, m. EDWARD PERKINS, # 5298, d. 1830, and lived Hubbardston, Mass., 1898.

5752 HENRY HOOK, m. twice and lived Colorado.

5753 GEORGE HOOK, m. SOPHIA HOWE of Bradford, lived Chichester.

5754 ELBRIDGE HOOK, d. 1898, m. and lived in Lynn.

5755 MARY F. HOOK, m. B. F. COBB, lived Boston.

5756 SARAH HOOK, was a teacher in Concord and d. aged 24, unmarried.

5757 SAMUEL HOOK, m. ——— POLLARD, lived Wendell, Mass., 1898.

F2578 Parna T. Locke, born in Epsom, July 20, 1816, died in Chichester, Dec. 26, 1873, married HENRY HOOK, born in 1802, who was a farmer in Chichester.

Children of 7th Gen.

5758 HARRISON HOOK, b. 1840, m. and lived California.

5759 ALONZO HOOK, b. 1843, m. Jan. 1, 1886, IDA MARY COLBY of Concord, lived in Chichester, and had: 5760 JUSTIN. Alonzo d. March 15, 1899.

5761 MELISSA HOOK, b. 1844, d. aged 18.

5762 SAMUEL HOOK, b. 1846.

5763 MICHAEL HOOK, b. 1848, d. aged 16.

5764 RACHEL HOOK, b. 1849, m. GEORGE LEAVITT, lived Pittsfield.

5765 LEVI HOOK, was unmarried, a veteran of 1861 war.

5766 GEORGEANNA HOOK, m. JAMES HARRIS, lived Lynn.

5767 SIMEON HOOK, d. aged 21.

5768 EDWIN, b. ———, was unmarried, lived California.

F2579 Benjamin Marden Locke, born in Chichester, June 14, 1819, died in Concord, Jan. 19, 1892, married in Concord, Feb. 3, 1840, FRANCENA M. HOOK, born in Chichester, Oct. 14, 1824, died in Concord, March 16, 1897, daughter of H. W. and Lucy (Watts). He was car inspector on the Northern N. H. R. R. in Concord for 39 years.

Children of 7th Gen.

F5769 FRANK HARTWELL, b. June 1, 1841, m. Apl. 2, 1862, SARAH J. FOLLANSBEE.

5770 CHARLES H., b. Concord, Apl. 1, 1843, d. 1859.

F5771 CYRUS MUNROE, b. Feb. 9, 1845, m. MARTHA AMELIA CHADWICK.

F2580 Huldah P. Locke, born in Chichester, Apl. 22, 1822, died March 17, 1899, married in Manchester, June 8, 1846, JAMES M. JONES, born Oct. 28, 1820, son of John and Hannah (Davis). He was a farmer and teamster in Concord.

Children of 7th Gen.

F5772 EMMA L., b. Dec. 3, 1853, m. Dec. 31, 1874, LEWIS T. EMERY.

5773 ALICE M., b. Nov. 17, 1857, m. Dec. 30, 1884, WILLIAM M. KIMBALL, b. Aug. 5, 1854, son of William and Rose (Swinburn). Employed on Worcester R. R., had no children.

F2581 Levi Locke, born in Chichester, March 24, 1824, died in Concord, Jan. 30, 1892, married in Lowell, June 6, 1846, NANCY E. DURGIN, born in Concord, Aug. 22, 1828, died in Concord, Apl. 26, 1909, daughter of John H. and Susan (Goodwin). He was in the coal, wood, and ice business in Manchester and Concord.

Children of 7th Gen.

F5774 JOHN SHERBURNE, b. March 12, 1848, m. Oct. 13, 1867, CHARLOTTE A. FOSTER.

F5775 GEORGE SCOTT, b. Dec. 18, 1849, m. Sept. 23, 1873, BELLE MARSHALL.

F5776 WILLIAM F., b. Jan. 6, 1856, m. 1st, JENNIE STEVENS, #4002, Feb. 11, 1879; m. 2nd, ——— SMITH; m. 3rd, ——— ———, a Western woman.

5777 IDA F., b. Concord, Sept. 6, 1858, d. Jan. 6, 1860.

5778 CHARLES H., b. Concord, Oct. 22, 1860, m. Concord, Oct. 5, 1881, ALICE E. STRONG of Mass., dau. of Fred W. He was a letter carrier in Boston, 1898. She b. 1861.

5779 FRED LEVI, b. Concord, May 29, 1866, m. MRS. MAY LISKLEY, lived in Woburn, Mass., had no children, and d. Sept. 30, 1897.

F2582 William Locke, born in Epsom, Dec. 24, 1799, married LOUISA FERREN, born Nov. 12, 1811, died March 18, 1843. He was a carpenter and farmer in Alexandria, a justice of peace, held several town offices, and was representative in Legislature. He died in Alexandria Nov. 15, 1848.

Children of 7th Gen. b. in Alexandria.

5780 MARCIA S., b. Nov. 25, 1830, m. PRESTON K. ROBINSON, a farmer in West Fairlee, Vt., had no children and she d. there Dec. 19, 1898.

F5781 HARRIET F., b. March 8, 1832, m. 1st, 1851, JOHN P. PHENIX; m. 2nd, JOHN H. WHALEN.

SEVENTH GENERATION 293

F5782 ADALINE K., b. Aug. 19, 1833, m. Sept. 3, 1852, HENRY C. MORSE.
5783 ANN MARIA, b. Feb. 23, 1835, d. May 28, 1865.
5784 CHARLES, b. Oct. 16, 1836, enlisted 1864 in Co. G, 2nd Mass. H. Art. also Co. F, 17th Mass. Inf., died Newburne, N. C., March 26, 1865.
5785 MARY J., b. March 4, 1839, d. Jan. 29, 1840.
5786 ABBIE CAROL, b. Sept. 1, 1840, m. Nov. 13, 1865, STEPHEN E. MORSE.
5787 FRANCES L., b. Aug. 6, 1842, d. March 11, 1843.

F2588 John Locke, born in Epsom, Jan. 10, 1812, died in Center Harbor, Apl. 26, 1887, married in Chichester, Nov. 19, 1834, SARAH SANBORN, born in Gilford, June 2, 1810, died in Moultonborough, Jan. 29, 1888, daughter of Sewell and ——— (Marden). He was a painter, lived some years in Central City, Iowa, then returned, and lived in Loudon, N. H.

Children of 7th Gen. probably b. in Loudon.

5788 EMERY B., b. Apl. 7, 1834, d. March 18, 1838.
5789 FRANCIS, b. July 24, 1835, d. Nov. 1, 1839.
F5790 CHARLES A., b. Aug. 29, 1837, m. June 10, 1865, LOTTIE M. FELLOWS; m. 2nd, Apl. 1867, MAY FELLOWS.
5791 MARIA M., b. Oct. 11, 1839, d. Oct. 24, 1839.
F5792 JOHN EMERY, b. Dec. 9, 1840, m. June 25, 1865, SUSAN M. FRENCH.
5793 MARY S., b. Apl. 1, 1843, living Santa Clara, Cal., 1914, m. 1st, ——— HATCH; m. 2nd, MICHAEL EGAN; m. 3rd, THOMAS N. GARVEY; had no children.
F5794 FRANK, b. March 10, 1846, m. June 23, 1874, EMMA HATCH.
5795 ABBIE A., b. Nov. 12, 1848, m. Aug. 11, 1869, JAMES L. CLARKE and lived San Jose, Cal., had: 5796 FRANK L., b. Jan. 26, 1870; 5797 JESSIE M., b. Dec. 23, 1880, m. ——— TILE.

F2590 Sally V. Locke, born in Alexandria, Feb. 12, 1816, died Dec. 29, 1898, married Jan. 24, 1839, PETER C. SEAVEY (who had a first wife, LYDIA ALLEN, married 1836, died 1838). He lived in Chichester, was a drum major in the Civil War. He left Sally, going to Canada where he married again about 1864, and died there 1896.

Children of 7th Gen. b. in Epsom.

F5798 SARAH J. M., b. Aug. 18, 1840, m. Feb. 3, 1858, NATHAN MARDEN.
F5799 ALONZO E., b. June 18, 1843, m. Apl. 19, 1864, FRANCES E. MEADER.
5800 JOHN L., b. Aug. 27, 1847, d. Nov. 26, 1861.
5801 GEORGE L., b. March 2, 1849, m. 1869, ALICE MCNEIL.
5802 LYMAN W., b. Nov. 19, 1857, m. June 1878, LIZZIE MARTIN, and he d. Feb. 26, 1884.
5803 ALICE S., b. Oct. 19, 1859, d. June 21, 1869.

F2591 George Locke, twin, born in Alexandria, Feb. 12, 1816, married in Concord, July 31, 1845, SABRA KIMBALL, born in East Concord, Oct. 21, 1817, died in Manchester, Jan. 2, 1892, daughter of Moses and Cynthia (Eastman). At the age of ten he began working for neighbor farmers, and in 1839 he started in the painting business. From 1846–9 he was engaged in painting Phillips Andover Academy buildings and from 1868–78 was employed by the Manchester mills as painter; retiring from active work about 1890. During his entire life he was a most devout Christian, doing an immense amount of lay work among the sick and old. In 1890 the compiler and Mr. Locke got into communication in regard to holding annual meetings of the Locke's, and with his leisure, he was able to interest people, so that the meetings became a reality. His age, knowledge of the older Lockes, together with considerable material of his own ancestors, has been of great help to the compiler of this genealogy. He died in Manchester, Sept. 25, 1903.

Children of 7th Gen. b. in Loudon.

5804 CHRISTENA, b. July 29, 1846, d. Aug. 27, 1846.
5805 CLARA F., b. Nov. 22, 1847, d. May 20, 1848.
5806 SARAH FRANCES, b. Apl. 10, 1850, lives unmarried in Manchester, a teacher.
5807 LUELLA S., b. July 13, 1853, lives unmarried in Manchester, a teacher.
F5808 CLARA PRESCOTT (adopted), b. March 25, 1848, m. Apl. 28, 1870, WILLIAM H. CROWTHER.

F2592 Benjamin B. Locke, born in Epsom, Sept. 5, 1818, married Nov. 14, 1850 in Lawrence, Mass., JULIA M. CURRIER of Sandwich, born in Sandwich, Feb. 10, 1829, died in Laconia, Oct. 19, 1900, daughter of Benjamin and Ruhuma (Jewell). He was a painter in Center Sandwich and died there Dec. 2, 1886.

Children of 7th Gen.

F5809 ORRA ANN, b. May 28, 1852, m. Feb. 19, 1874, CHARLES R. FELLOWS.
F5810 ELSIE EVELINE, b. May 14, 1854, m. May 14, 1873, FRED L. SMITH.
F5811 ADA FLORENCE, b. Aug. 1, 1857, m. Nov. 26, 1879, SAMUEL E. CLIFFORD.
5812 JULIA E., b. Sandwich, March 24, 1862, d. Dec. 9, 1886, m. June, 1886, REV. JOSEPH H. TROW of the Methodist, N. H., Conference.

F2593 Abigail Locke, born in Epsom, Jan. 3, 1821, died in Concord, Apl. 10, 1908, married 1st, Apl. 4, 1842, REUBEN SANDERS, # 4895, a farmer in Concord, born May 7, 1814, died Oct. 6, 1876; married 2nd, Sept. 25, 1878, WILLIAM K. HOLT, born in 1810, died Dec. 13, 1883. He had a sawmill and was a lumber dealer in East Concord.

Children of 7th Gen.
F5813 LUELLA C., b. Feb. 26, 1843, m. May 1, 1864, WALTER B. MAYNARD.
5814 CLARA A., b. Jan. 14, 1845, m. Apl. 4, 1867, ELBRIDGE EMERY of East Concord, b. Aug. 18, 1845, son of Timothy and Comfort (Potter). They lived E. Concord, have no children.
5815 ALICE J., b. Oct. 5, 1847, d. Sept. 4, 1856.

F2594 Martha Locke, born in Epsom, July 5, 1823, died Sept. 9, 1881, married 1st, June 20, 1844, PIERCE BICKFORD, who was fatally injured in 1852 while firing a salute on the nomination of President Pierce. She married 2nd, in Loudon in 1854, JOSEPH WOOD, who was in the shoe business in Chichester.

Children of 7th Gen.
5816 LAURA E., b. Aug. 7, 1845, d. 1903, m. 1st, JAMES MUNSEY; m. 2nd, R. M. FOOT, had no children.
5817 REBECCA, b. 1847, d. 1847.
F5818 CHARLES P., b. Nov. 15, 1850, m. Feb. 23, 1873, MARGARET COURSEY.
5819 ——— WOOD, b. 1856, d. 1856.
5820 JOHN L. WOOD, b. 1858, was a farmer in Epsom, 1902.

F2607 James Page, born June 3, 1804, married 1st, in 1829, DOROTHY SMITH, died Sept. 28, 1834; married 2nd, 1835, BELINDA BERRY, died June 1882.

Children of 7th Gen.
5821 CATHERINE, b. July 30, 1830, m. M. RAND of Northwood.
5822 JAMES, b. Feb. 10, 1832, d. Iowa, Oct. 29, 1879, m. 1st, NANCY WHITE; m. 2nd, BERTHA TAPPAN.
5823 JOHN, b. Sept. 10, 1833, m. Dec. 20, 1855, MANDANA C. LOCKE. (See F5059.)
5824 MARTHA, b. Nov. 3, 1836, m. JEFFERSON H. JEWELL, b. 1835, son of Francis and Betsey (Sherman). He was naval officer in Boston, had no children.
5825 GEORGE W., b. June 1, 1838, d. June 15, 1888, was m. and had children in Central City, Iowa.
5826 SARAH E., b. Dec. 18, 1839, m. 1st, Jan. 7, 1859, DR. AARON P. MITCHELL, who d. July 22, 1863; m. 2nd, Apl. 9, 1866, ISRAEL F. MITCHELL, who d. Sept. 9, 1874, had: 5827 AARON MITCHELL, b. Dec. 29, 1859; 5828 MARY E. MITCHELL, b. Apl. 1, 1862, m. EDWIN M. SAWYER, and had: 5829 JAY M. SAWYER, b. 1884; 5830 ZORA V. SAWYER, b. 1887; 5831 ROY M. SAWYER, b. 1892;

5832 C. C. MITCHELL, b. Jan. 20, 1869, d. Aug. 12, 1876; 5833 MARTHA J. MITCHELL, b. June 20, 1872, m. May 22, 1890, GAIL J. FOLSTON, and had: 5834 MITCHELL FOLSTON, b. 1895, at Wahoo, Neb.

5835 MARY F., b. Oct. 30, 1841, m. Apl. 27, 1857, JAMES OUTING, and had: 5836 GEORGEANNA OUTING, b. March 2, 1856, m. Nov.·9, 1876, CYRUS FISHER, and had: 5837 LEO Z. FISHER, b. 1878; 5838 EDNA L. FISHER, b. 1883; 5839 FOSTER E. OUTING, b. Jan. 16, 1862, m. Jan. 24, 1883, IDA V. WEEKS, and lives Central City, Iowa.

5840 ABBIE C., b. Feb. 8, 1844, m. ―――― HUTCHINS, a farmer.

5841 MUNROE L., b. Apl. 9, 1846, m. Oct. 21, 1867, IZETTA H. MITCHELL, b. Apl. 1845, lived Central City, Iowa, and had: 5842 ELLEN M., b. Dec. 22, 1870, m. June 18, 1892, GEORGE F. S. LARY, lived Haverhill, Mass.; 5843 LULU I., b. Oct. 10, 1872; 5844 ASA M., b. July 15, 1874; 5845 MINNIE H., b. Apl. 25, 1878; 5846 ROY L., b. Aug. 28, 1881; 5847 GLEN D., b. Feb. 14, 1883.

F2625 John Page, born June 11, 1816, died Feb. 1874, married MAHALA B. LANE of Pittsfield, born Aug. 6, 1822, daughter of John and Abigail (Cram). He was a tanner in Epsom and Central City, Iowa.

Children of 7th Gen.

5848 MARTIN B., b. June 30, 1840, m. SARAH E. SWITZER, and had: 5849 LILLIE, b. Nov. 23, 1862; 5850 HARRY, b. Feb. 14, 1864; 5851 BLANCHE, b. July 17, 1867; 5852 ROSE, b. March 12, 1869; 5853 ALBERT, b. June 12, 1872; 5854 CLARENCE, b. Nov. 9, 1874; 5855 EDNA, b. July 22, 1878; 5856 CHARLES, b. Oct. 8, 1880.

5857 HORACE L., b. March 2, 1843, m. JENNIE BOWEN and had: 5858 MAY, b. 1876, d. 1876; 5859 CARRIE, b. 1881; 5860 WILLIAM, b. 1885.

5861 WILLIAM HENRY, b. Apl. 23, 1845, d. Nov. 28, 1849.

5862 D. FRANK, b. March 26, 1847.

5863 MARY E., b. Dec. 7, 1849, m. JOHN C. SWITZER, and had: 5864 RAY, b. 1872; 5865 EVA C., b. 1874.

5866 ELLEN A., b. Aug. 26, 1852, m. ARTHUR HEDGES, and had: 5867 ROSS, b. 1875; 5868 GEORGE, b. 1876; 5869 SARAH A., b. 1878, d. 1880; 5870 MABEL T., b. 1881; 5871 ARTHUR, b. 1882; 5872 EFFIE, b. 1885, d. 1887.

F2632 Woodbury Locke, born in Alexandria, March 4, 1813, died Jan. 1883, married 1st, ―――― SMILEY; married 2nd, EMALINE LORING of Boston. He was a cloth cutter in Boston and lived Somerville.

Child of 7th Gen. b. First Wife.

5873 JENNIE LOCKE, b. Somerville, Mass., 1863, d. Sept. 24, 1897, m. WALTER E. BLAKE, baggage master at Concord, had: 5874 EASTMAN L., b. Apl. 11, 1897.

SEVENTH GENERATION

F2633 Mary Locke, born in Alexandria, Aug. 4, 1815, died Feb. 24, 1883, married in Alexandria, Sept. 26, 1832, NATHANIEL RAY, born in Meredith, Aug. 24, 1810, died in New Hampton, Oct. 2, 1871, son of Nathaniel and Sarah (Bickford). He was a farmer, carpenter and wheelwright in Alexandria.

Children of 7th Gen.

5874 HIRAM M., b. Apl. 28, 1833, d. Laconia, July 16, 1900, m. MARY J. COLBURN, lived New Hampton and Laconia; was a wheelwright, a Baptist, an Odd Fellow, left widow and two daughters.
5875 ERVILLE B., b. Rumney, Jan. 12, 1836, m. HIRAM R. DAVIS, b. Hillsborough. He was a shoemaker in Henniker, and had:
5876 HATTIE E. DAVIS, b. Washington, 1870, m. Sept. 15, 1888, ATER S. DREW of Henniker, b. Farmington, 1861, son of William and Charlotte (Babb); a shoemaker.
5877 NORMAN J., b. March 3, 1838, m. ADDIE W. HINES and d. June 16, 1863, in the war.
5878 WILLIAM, b. May 23, 1840, d. Feb. 5, 1841.
5879 ORREN C., b. July 22, 1842, m. NELLIE FRANK.
5880 MARY A., b. Dec. 21, 1844.
5881 EMMA E., b. Sept. 21, 1847, d. May 10, 1854.
5882 JENNIE T., b. Jan. 23, 1851, d. March 21, 1881.
5883 EUGENE E., b. Dec. 24, 1854, d. Aug. 13, 1856.

F2648 Hannah S. Langley, born July 18, 1815, died in Chichester, Dec. 15, 1894, married in 1837, STEPHEN WATSON, born in 1807. He was a farmer in Chichester and died there Feb. 11, 1857.

Children of 7th Gen.

5884 ALMIRA S., b. Feb. 19, 1839, m. CHARLES TUCKER, a farmer in Colebrook, and had: 5885 FANNIE J.; 5886 ANNIE W.; 5887 CLARA C.
5888 ELIZABETH L., b. Aug. 17, 1841, m. June 5, 1862, GEORGE O. KIMBALL, b. Feb. 21, 1842, son of Oren. He was a shoemaker lived in Loudon, had no children, and d. Oct. 14, 1864. She perhaps m. 2nd, E. HIGHT of Manchester.
5889 HANNAH A., b. March 16, 1843, d. unmarried, 1863.
5890 DANIEL L., b. Nov. 2, 1845, d. 1856.
5891 ABBIE J., b. Dec. 25, 1847, m. 1870, FRANK TOWLE, a farmer in Chichester, and had two children.
5892 HANNAH L., b. Dec. 24, 1849, d. May 31, 1881, m. JOHN J. BELL.
5893 AZILLA C., b. June 3, 1853, m. Manchester, 1870, SAMUEL D. SHERBURNE, a shoemaker of Mass., and had : 5894 STEPHEN W., b. 1873.
5895 ZUELLA C., a twin, b. June 3, 1853, d. Feb. 19, 1879.
5896 MARY P., b. Oct. 6, 1855, lived Chichester, and d. June 17, 1878.

F2654 William Langley, born Apl. 18, 1823, married Jan. 15, 1853, ELIZA MCCRILLIS of Skowhegan, Me., and lived in Strafford.

Children of 7th Gen. probably b. in Strafford.

5897 EMERETT E., b. Dec. 23, 1853, m. Jan. 14, 1876, JAMES O. SANBORN, b. June 2, 1851, son of Albert and Almira; a R. R. employee, lives Marblehead, Mass., and had: 5898 BERT W.; 5899 BERTHA W.; 5900 VERNON A.

5901 WILLIAM H., b. March 4, 1860, m. ADDIE A. BRACKETT, lived at Skowhegan, Me., and had: 5902 WILLIAM LANGLEY, JR.

5903 GRATIA, b. Aug. 3, 1862, m. CYRUS MORSE of Exeter.

5904 JOHN W., b. Feb. 10, 1866, m. LELIA SANBORN, had a shoe shop in Derry and d. Apl. 10, 1896.

5905 SHERMAN F., b. March 19, 1873, d. unmarried May 26, 1895.

5906 MINERVA L., b. Dec. 8, 1874, d. May 26, 1897, m. EVERETT SINCLAIR, lived in Marblehead and had: 5907 WILLIAM; 5908 RALPH.

F2658 Harvey Locke, born in Alexandria, Nov. 11, 1824, died in Kingston, July 23, 1908, married Dec. 22, 1850, ANN C. TEWKSBURY, born July 11, 1833. He was a farmer in Alexandria and Kingston.

Children of 7th Gen.

F5909 LOUIS CRISTIE, b. Jan. 31, 1855, m. July 24, 1882, MARY A. PIERCE.

5910 LOUELLA JANE, b. Alexandria, Sept. 19, 1857, m. E. Kingston, June 29, 1893, ORTWELL H. STONE of Worcester, b. Machias, Me., 1866, son of Francis and Sarah (Taylor). She was a teacher, and he a jeweler in Pittsfield.

F5911 HARVEY BELNAP, b. May 25, 1860, m. Dec. 24, 1887, RUTH HATCH.

F5912 WARREN, b. Dec. 2, 1868, m. July 2, 1892, LIZZIE M. MERCER.

F2660 Warren W. Locke, born in Alexandria, Feb. 29, 1829, died in Logan, Ohio, Aug. 5, 1876, married 1st, July 14, 1852, LODOISKI GAGE of Lancaster, N. Y., born in 1828, died July 5, 1856; married 2nd, Sept. 4, 1859, MINNIE J. POSTON of Nelson, Ohio, daughter of W. W. and Mary E. (Drew), born Aug. 16, 1843. He was in dry goods business in Logan, was part builder of the Marietta and Cincinnati R. R., and also the New York and Erie R. R.

Children of 7th Gen.

5913 Child by first wife died young.

5914 GEORGE P., b. Logan, O., June 26, 1861, m. Baltimore, Ohio, Nov. 19, 1885, DORA C. LUCKEY, b. 1862, dau. of Walter W. and Annie. He was a merchant, but is now owner of Wichita, Kan., *Daily Beacon.*

5915 IDA P. L., b. Logan, Ohio, June 4, 1870, m. Chicago, Dec. 29, 1892, DR. ELIJAH P. NOEL, of Portsmouth, Ohio, b. there, Dec. 1, 1860, lived Chicago, 1900.

5916 MINNIE W., b. Logan, March 10, 1872, d. July 30, 1876.

SEVENTH GENERATION

F2676 Elisha Ferdinand Locke, called Dan, born in Brasher Falls, N. Y., a twin, Jan. 23, 1832, died Jan. 22, 1874, married in 1855, HANNAH SPAULDING, born in Potsdam, N. Y., daughter of Dr. Thomas. His father nicknamed him "Dan the Dancer." He was a cooper in Brasher Falls, N. Y.

Children of 7th Gen. b. in Brasher Falls, N. Y.

F5917 QUEEN GENEVA, b. Feb. 10, 1857, m. Jan. 3, 1879, EDWIN GOODWIN MORSE.
F5918 CANDACE JENNETTE, b. May 3, 1860, m. 1878, CHARLES MOODY.
5919 ADA CHESTINA, b. Dec. 9, 1862, m. May 11, 1895, GEORGE STEVENS LITTLE, b. Atkinson, Aug. 11, 1855, a shoe machine operator in Bradford, Mass. They have no children.
5920 EMILY, b. Feb. 11, 1864.
5921 SOPHIA, b. Aug. 1865.
5922 JONATHAN, b. Apl. 9, 1867; has a child: 5923 JONATHAN, in Massena, N. Y.
5924 CHARLES ELDAD, b. Jan. 19, 1870, m. ——, no children.
5925 BENJAMIN, b. ——, m. ——, no children.
5926 THOMAS JEFFERSON, b. July 1872, m. ——, had: 5927 child in the West.
5928 WILLIAM A., b. Apl. 30, (1874), m. Nov. 15, 1886 (?), GERTRUDE E. DODGE, lived Massena, N. Y., and had: 5929 ALETHA ALMA, b. March 14, 1889.
5930 FRANCIS E.

F2710 Almira Locke, born in New York, Dec. 29, 1828, died Dec. 1853, married Jan. 20, 1847, DARWIN ROOT, born Sept. 13, 1827, son of Aaron and Salenda (Phelps). He died in Brockport, N. Y., Feb. 8, 1854.

Child of 7th Gen.

5931 ADELLE ROOT, b. May 15, 1849, m. Dec. 5, 1867, RUFUS H. ROOT, b. July 5, 1846, son of Henry and Sybil (Saulsbury). They lived in Brockport, N. Y., and had: 5932 KATE A., b. Dec. 21, 1868, m. May 1890, ALBERT BURCH; 5933 HENRY, b. Oct. 29, 1873, d. Aug. 13, 1891.

F2711 Elisha Locke, born in New York, Dec. 11, 1830, married in Sweden, N. Y., May 15, 1857, SARAH WAY, who died May 31, 1897. He lived in Sweden and died there June 20, 1876.

Children of 7th Gen. b. in Sweden, N. Y.

F5934 EUGENE D., b. June 27, 1858, a farmer in Brockport, N. Y., 1898, m. ——.
F5935 DR. CLAYTON W., b. Jan. 24, 1862, m. 1st, Nov. 5, 1889, EDITH M. BUTTS; m. 2nd, July 10, 1895, MARY L. CONAN.
F5936 GEORGE E., b. Aug. 15, 1866, m. Feb. 25, 1891, MARY E. COVELL.
5937 HATTIE A., b. Sept. 25, 1873, d. May 5, 1904.

F2728 Harriet Locke, born in Batavia, N. Y., Aug. 26, **1818,** died March 27, 1881, married THOMAS CHICK, born **Nov. 9,** 1804, died Aug. 12, 1867. They lived in Batavia, N. Y.

Children of 7th Gen. b. in Batavia, N. Y.

5938 SARAH E., b. June 2, 1839, lived unmarried in Buffalo, N. Y.
5939 MARY J., b. June 24, 1844, d. Aug. 10, 1890, m. Dec. 31, 1863, JAMES B. HOLRIDGE, b. 1837, lived in Buffalo, and d. Sept. 29, 1864.
5940 GEORGE G., b. March 7, 1847, m. Aug. 18, 1881, ELLA CASH, b. May 19, 1847, d. March 18, 1915. He was a farmer in Byron, N. Y., no children.
5941 JAMES BYRON, b. June 17, 1849, d. Feb. 1914, m. Nov. 5, **1870,** LIZZIE TANNER, b. Nov. 8, 1851, had no children; kept a restaurant in Batavia, N. Y. She d. March 1914.
5942 HARRIET, b. Apl. 8, 1856, m. Aug. 18, 1880, WILLIAM WATSON, b. July 14, 1857, d. Nov. 17, 1908, a jeweler in Buffalo, and had:
5943 JOSEPH, b. July 4, 1882.

F2729 Edwin Locke, born in Batavia, March 16, **1821, died** Apl. 5, 1898, married March 26, 1848, MARY CULL, born Jan. 16, 1831. He was 49 years on the old homestead in **Batavia,** N. Y. She died Sept. 19, 1906.

Children of 7th Gen. b. in Batavia, N. Y.

F5944 DAVID, b. Dec. 31, 1848, m. Dec. 27, 1870, ELLEN E. HINMAN.
F5945 WILLIAM H., b. July 24, 1850, m. Sept. 27, 1879, HARRIET E. HEDGES.
F5946 JENNIE E., b. Aug. 16, 1852, m. May 23, 1878, ALBERT G. SHERMAN.
F5947 EDWIN S., b. March 16, 1854, m. May, 1880, MARY H. DAILEY.

F2730 Elizabeth Locke, born in Batavia, N.Y., Oct. 16, **1824,** died May 5, 1896, married March 8, 1849, B. FRANKLIN NORTON, who lived in Bethany, N. Y., and died there Aug. 23, 1887.

Children of 7th Gen. b. in Bethany, N. Y.

5948 CHARLES A., b. March 1, 1845? m. Dec. 16, 1873, KATE A. NORTON, b. Apl. 23, 1853, d. March 17, 1894. He was a farmer in Bethany and had: 5949 EDNA, b. Oct. 9, 1874; 5950 SARAH, b. Dec. 24, **1876;** 5951 HERBERT, b. Jan. 27, 1879.
5952 WALTER F., b. Jan. 3, 1851, m. Jan. 23, 1872, MATTIE J. WOOD, b. Sept. 29, 1852; a farmer in Bethany, had no children.
5953 FRED L., b. Jan. 7, 1854, m. May 19, 1875, HARRIET STEWART, b. Oct. 11, 1857, d. Feb. 1, 1889. He was a farmer in **Bethany,** and d. Aug. 15, 1886, had: 5954 MAUDE, b. March 13, **1882.**
5955 WILLIAM, b. Dec. 4, 1862, d. Aug. 19, 1867.

F2738 John Locke, born in Colebrook, Nov. 7, 1831, married Oct. 9, 1864, LOVINA POTTER, born in Stark, Nov. 9, **1840,** died in Northumberland, Jan. 20, 1911, daughter of Justice **and** Elizabeth (Mills). He was a farmer in Columbia.

SEVENTH GENERATION

Children of 7th Gen.

5956 HERBERT P., b. Columbia, Aug. 6, 1867, m. WINNIE CHILDS, b. Waterville, Me., March 14, 1880, d. Northumberland, June 29, 1913. He was a teacher and farmer in Colebrook, had three children.

5957 CORA BELLE, b. Columbia, June 19, 1870, m. Northumberland, Sept. 6, 1900, GEORGE E. ALLEN of Maidstone, Vt.

F2743 Fred W. Locke, born in Northumberland, in 1849, died in Niagara, N. C., Jan. 3, 1912, married LUCY E. ROGERS, born in Clinton, 1855. He was a carpenter and mill owner in Groveton, also lived in Dorchester, Mass.

Children of 7th Gen.

5958 FANNIE, b. Colebrook, Aug. 29, 1874, m. May 25, 1899, AUGUSTUS E. HAM.
5959 MITTIE, b. ——.
5960 JOHN, b. Groveton, Apl. 22, 1893 (5th child).

F2768 Sarah J. Rand, born in Rye, Feb. 6, 1835, married in Rye, March 1855, SAMUEL RAND, born June 10, 1810, died Jan. 24, 1880, lived North Hampton. She died North Hampton Nov. 29, 1904.

Children of 7th Gen. b. in Rye.

5961 BERTHA, b. June 30, 1856, m. CHRISTOPHER SMART of Ports., and they had: 5962 CHRISTOPHER, Jr.; 5963 BEATRICE; 5964 ROLAND.
5965 MINA, b. Dec. 16, 1858, m. ALBERT MITCHELL of No. Hampton.
5966 ADA P., b. 1863, died young.
5967 EMMA, b. 1863, died young.
5968 MARY, b. Aug. 2, 1865, living 1895.
5969 ALICE, b. 1865, twin, died young.
5970 EDITH, b. July 1872, m. —— KNOWLES.

F2778 Sarah Locke, born in 1777, married Sept. 30, 1792, AARON RIGGS.

Children of 7th Gen.

5971 PATIENCE, b. ——, m. BENJAMIN TREFETHERN, and had family in Lynn, Mass.
5972 COMFORT, twin with last, m. EDWIN SHERBURNE and lived in Portsmouth and New York, had: 5972a LEWIS SHERBURNE.
5973 AARON LOCKE, b. ——, m. MARTHA S. LOCKE, # 5984, b. Apl. 5, 1819, d. Nov. 19, 1890, had no children, was a blacksmith, Rye.
5974 ANGELINE, b. ——, was unmarried.
F5975 MARTHA, b. ——, m. 1st, —— KNIGHT; m. 2nd, ISAAC PAINE of Vershire, Vt.
5976 SARAH. 5977 CHARLES. 5978 MARY, lived Cal., 1892.

F2779 James Locke, born in Portsmouth, 1777, married Feb. 18, 1808, ELEANOR BERRY, # 1029, died June 25, 1849, aged 70. James was a butcher, lived at the gravel pit in Portsmouth and died in Rye, Nov. 14, 1858, aged 81.

Children of 7th Gen.

5979 WILLIAM, b. 1811, d. 1815.
5980 ADALINE, b. June 10, 1813, d. Minn., Aug. 13, 1870, m. JOEL N. Foss, son of Benj. and Dorcas (Shapleigh), b. Dec. 7, 1821. They lived in Minnesota and had: 5981 ALMIRA P., b. May 26, 1850.
5982 ELEANOR, b. 1813.
5983 JAMES M., b. 1815, d. 1819.
5984 MARTHA S., b. Apl. 5, 18.9, d. Nov. 19, 1890, m. AARON L. RIGGS, # 5973, her cousin; He was a blacksmith in Rye, no children.
F5985 JAMES J., b. Sept. 12, 1821, m. March 4, 1847, MRS. JANE H.(BUNKER) FRISBEE.
5986 ELLEN H., b. Apl. 22, 1830, m. CHARLES F. LOCKE, # F2964.

F2781 John Locke, born in Portsmouth in 1784, married in Portsmouth, July 22, 1804, ABIGAIL GOODWIN, born in 1788, died March 14, 1851. They lived at the South End, Portsmouth. He was a boss painter at the Navy Yard, and died Apl. 10, 1850.

Children of 7th Gen. b. in Portsmouth.

F5987 SOPHIA, b. Nov. 1, 1805, m. Apl. 5, 1830, JOSHUA BAZIN.
F5988 JAMES M., b. 1808, m. ELIZABETH BAILEY.
F5989 ABIGAIL, b. 1811, m. Feb. 12, 1837, EZEKIEL FITZGERALD.
F5990 JOHN S., b. ——, m. Aug. 18, 1839, ANN M. LORD.
5991 MARTHA R., b. 1812, d. unmarried Buffalo, N. Y., Jan. 27, 1891.
F5992 HANNAH R., b. ——, m. Nov. 10, 1831, WILLIAM P. GOOKIN.
5993 SUSAN DWIGHT, b. 1819, d. Sept. 23, 1821.
5994 IZETTE A., a twin, b. 1819, d. Sept. 22, 1821.

F2782–F2783 Martha Locke, born in Portsmouth, July 27, 1792, died in Portsmouth, March 10, 1810, married in Portsmouth, March 11, 1809, SAMUEL RAND, born in Rye, March 2, 1783, son of Joshua and Ruth (Seavey). He was a painter in Portsmouth and married 2nd, his wife's sister, **Hannah Locke,** Oct. 29, 1811, and died in Portsmouth, March 17, 1822. Hannah, born Nov. 18, 1795, died Jan. 1882, in Portsmouth, married SAMUEL RAND.

Children of 7th Gen. b. in Portsmouth.

The first child only was Martha's, the others were Hannah's.

F5995 AARON LOCKE, b. Jan. 29, 1810, m. Apl. 29, 1834, MARGARET G. FROST.
5996 ALBERT GALLATIN, b. Apl. 24, 1813, d. unmarried, a painter in Ports., March 15, 1855.

SEVENTH GENERATION 303

5997 RUTH SEAVEY, b. Dec. 27, 1815, d. unmarried Ports., Dec. 1, 1895.
5998 JOSHUA JAMES, b. May 15, 1817, d. unmarried, Ports., a painter, 1843.
F5999 SAMUEL STREETER, b. June 1, 1819, m. June 1, 1848, Lucinda W. BROWN; m. 2nd, May 22, 1866, MARY BROWN.
F6000 MARTHA SARAH HANNAH, b. May 15, 1821, m. July 12, 1840, EDWARD N. ANDERSON.

F2784 John Locke, born Dec. 15, 1785, died in Franklin, July 15, 1865, married May 3, 1809 (Epsom.rec. Nov. 26, 1807), MARIA or MERCY RAND, born in Epsom, May 3, 1787-8, died Sept. 12, 1873-5. He learned a tanner's trade in Portsmouth with a Locke uncle, and later was a shoemaker in Epsom and Franklin.

Children of 7th Gen.

F6001 HARRIET, b. Nov. 13, 1809, m. Aug. 1833, DANA LYON.
6002 JOHN B., b. March 7, 1811, m. 1st, unknown; m. 2nd, MRS. HANCOCK; had three children in Libertyville, Ill., one being: 6003 LUCY ANN, who m. ———— —— ————.
F6004 CATHERINE, b. March 18, 1812, m. 1840, PETER BROGAN.
6005 MARY, b. May 19, 1813 m. Franklin, June 18, 1855, JONATHAN TAYLOR, b. 1803, d. Franklin, Apl. 27, 1893, had no children.
6006 MAHALEY, b. Sept. 5, 1814, d. Jan. 17, 1829.
6007 ROSANA, b. Hill, Feb. 29, 1816, d. Franklin, unmarried Oct. 24, 1892.
6008 RHODA, b. twin 1816, d. 1816.
F6009 HORACE, b. June 9, 1819, m. 1st, 1847, SARAH A. SHORT; m. 2nd 1851, ELIZABETH M. SPOFFORD DEARBORN.
6010 RHODA, b. July 6, 1820, d. 1822.
6011 EMILY, b. Salisbury, Apl. 17, 1823. Feb. 26, 1867, she was made guardian of nephew HORACE, and the paper reads that JOHN, SR., was of Rye and MARIA was of Epsom. She d. Franklin, unmarried Feb. 23, 1888.
F6012 CHARLES, b. Apl. 20, 1824, m. 1845, SARAH WEEKS.
F6013 ALBERT, b. Dec. 10, 1827, m. 1858, ANNIE SMITH.
F6014 GEORGE W., b. June 13, 1830, m. LOUISA ABBOTT.

F2785 Ira Locke, born in Deerfield, Jan. 5, 1791, died in Deerfield, Nov. 6, 1880, married in Epping, March 27, 1815, REBECCA PRESCOTT, born in Epping, Dec. 26, 1788, died in Deerfield, July 16, 1873, daughter of Jonathan and Hannah (Hayes). He was a farmer in Deerfield.

Children of 7th Gen.

6015 GEORGE H., b. Aug. 18, 1815, m. 1st, June 21, 1841, CAROLINE NIGHTINGALE, b. Quincy, Mass., Feb. 29, 1820, d. Aug. 14, 1843; m. 2nd, Nov. 22, 1846, her sister, EMALINE NIGHTINGALE, b. Aug. 24, 1822.
F6016 ARVILLA P., b. Apl. 29, 1817, m. Nov. 14, 1839, HILLARD SMITH.
6017 LUCY ANN, b. May 8, 1824, m. May 6, 1847, JOHN CRANE.

F2786 Samuel Hill, born in Epping, Jan. 5, 1805, died Nov. 23, 1853, married in Lee, June 6, 1823, MARY BURLEIGH, born in Lee, Dec. 13, 1803, died in Epping, Oct. 7, 1880, daughter of Samuel and Abigail. They lived in Epping.

Children of 7th Gen. b. in Epsom.

6018 MARTHA J., b. Oct. 25, 1824, m. in Epsom, Dec. 18, 1854, ISAAC S. BROWN of Exeter, had: 6019 MARY E., b. 1856. He b. Hampton Falls, d. Portland, Me., Jan. 30, 1886.
6020 ELIZABETH ANN, b. Dec. 25, 1826.
6021 JOSIAH E., b. July 29, 1829, d. Oct. 10, 1831.
6022 SUSAN A., b. Nov. 3, 1832, m. in Epsom, Oct. 10, 1871, BENJAMIN J. WHITE, b. New Castle, 1826, had: 6023 GRACE, died young; 6024 SAMUEL H.
6024aBURLEIGH F., b. Feb. 6, 1844, m. Apl. 25, 1894, ELORA (TRUE) PECKER, of Raymond, b. Chester, Sept. 15, 1849.

F2799 Asa Locke, born in Rye, Oct. 18, 1801, died Nov. 1, 1863, married Apl. 15, 1824, **Abigail Mace Locke,** born 1805, died June 15, 1882. He was a joiner in Rye.

Children of 7th Gen. b. in Rye.

6025 MARY E., b. March 2, 1824?, d. Feb. 26, 1825.
F6026 SARAH H. LOCKE, b. Aug. 3, 1825, m. Jan. 20, 1848, JOSEPH DUNBAR.
6027 THOMAS L., b. 1826, was unmarried, and drowned fishing, June 1848.
F6028 JOHN O., b. June 16, 1829, m. 1st, Feb. 29, 1864, ANN M. TARLTON; m. 2nd, Feb. 19, 1867, JOSEPHINE TREFETHERN.
6029 MARGARET A., b. July 23, 1833, m. Dec. 28, 1852, DANIEL W. CASWELL BURLEIGH, # F2974.
6030 ABBIE, b. Oct. 1840, d. July 1, 1876, m. SYLVESTER CASWELL BURLEIGH, # 2975.

F2800 James H. Locke, born in Rye, Nov. 27, 1804, died in Rye, Oct. 4, 1886, married Aug. 12, 1827, MRS. SARAH (MOWE) ALLEN, born in Rye, 1807, died in Rye, Feb. 7, 1857. He was a farmer and mariner in Rye. She married 1st, SAMUEL ALLEN, Apl. 8, 1824, and had: SAMUEL ALLEN, born 1824, died 1848.

Children of 7th Gen. b. in Rye.

6031 LEVI DEARBORN, b. Jan. 18, 1829, was a fisherman at Rye Harbor, and d. unmarried in Rye, May 13, 1902.
F6032 HANNAH E., b. Sept. 18, 1831, m. 1st, Aug. 20, 1864, CAPT. BENJAMIN W. MARDEN; m. 2nd, June 28, 1883, GILMAN VARRELL.
F6033 JAMES G., b. March 29, 1834, m. Dec. 6, 1865, ANGELINA DOCKUM.
6034 MARY J., b. Feb. 1, 1839, was a mill operator and d. unmarried in Ports. Feb. 18, 1867.

SEVENTH GENERATION

F2801 Lemuel B. Locke, born in Rye, Nov. 19, 1806, died in Rye, Aug. 25, 1897, married 1st, ESTHER Y. REMICK, daughter of Isaac and Lydia (Varrell), May 31, 1832, born Feb. 1811, died in Rye, Aug. 21, 1838; married 2nd, in Barnstead, May 19, 1845, BELINDA J. BUNKER, born Apl. 8, 1802, died in Rye, Aug. 25, 1863, daughter of Lemuel and Sally (Towle); married 3rd, **Abigail Mace Locke,** born 1805, died 1882. He was a farmer in Rye.

Children of 7th Gen. b. in Rye.

6035 DANIEL L. (named ASA), b. June 22, 1834, was Captain in 14th Mass. Reg., 1862, later a shoemaker, d. unmarried in Exeter, June 3, 1900.
6036 ISAAC M., b. twin, 1834, m. Rye, March 11, 1865, JENNIE E. WILLIAMS of Lyme, b.1838, d. Rye, Feb. 6, 1869. He was a shoemaker, d. Rye, July 22, 1867, had: 6037 WILLIE I., b. March 21, 1865, d. Aug. 20, 1870.
F6038 ELIZABETH G., b. Sept. 14, 1832, m. Sept. 15, 1855, SAMUEL JACKSON JONES.

F2804 Jonathan Dearborn Locke, born in Rye, Apl. 11, 1811, died in Rye, Oct. 16, 1885, married in Rye, Dec. 23, 1838, CAROLINE GOODWIN GARLAND, born in Rye, Sept. 10, 1816, died in Rye, Sept. 7, 1902, daughter of Lieut. Amos G. and Olive (Jenness). He was a farmer and mariner in Rye.

Children of 7th Gen. b. in Rye.

F6039 AMOS GARLAND, b. June 13, 1840, m. Nov. 9, 1875, NANCY A. HELM.
F6040 CARRIE NEWELL, b. Apl. 8, 1849, m. Sept. 25, 1878, AZRO WILLIS.
F6041 LAURA GOODWIN, b. Dec. 22, 1851, m. May 12, 1875, CHARLES H. HILL.
6042 GEORGEANNA, b. Rye, Jan. 20, 1854, m. Rye, Nov. 26, 1876, MELVIN HUTCHINS, b. York, Me., Apl. 29, 1850. He is a telegrapher, had no children.

F2806 Gardner Towle Locke, born in Rye, Feb. 8, 1816, died in Rye, Feb. 13, 1901, married 1st, Dec. 28, 1844, JULIA A. GARLAND, # 5288, born Nov. 4, 1821, died July 14, 1873; married 2nd, Jan. 3, 1876, MRS. ANN (DAWLTON) GARLAND, born Sept. 7, 1818, divorced Feb. 1880, died Dec. 25, 1902, daughter of Benjamin and Sarah (Garland). He was a prosperous farmer in Rye on Locke's Neck road, was a custom house officer, held many town offices, was a prominent Democrat, and much sought after for advice.

Children of 7th Gen. b. in Rye.
F6043 AUGUSTUS W., b. Feb. 26, 1846, m. Feb. 23, 1876, MARTHA P. PERKINS.
F6044 DAVID PARSONS, b. Apl. 28, 1850, m. Feb. 12, 1877, ANN GOLDING.
6045 FRANK B., b. Rye, March 28, 1857, is a civil engineer on State St., Boston.

F2813 William Tucker Locke, born in Rye, Oct. 12, 1817, died in Concord, Sept. 17, 1889, married 1st, May 29, 1838, SUSAN B. NICHOLS, born in Meredith, March 15, 1817, died Nov. 8, 1845; married 2nd, Aug. 2, 1846, SARAH A. C. EVANS of Hills Corner, born Feb. 2, 1828, died Apl. 16, 1847; married 3rd, in Concord, March 9, 1848, LAVINA B. NEWTON of Cornish, born in Meredith, Feb. 22, 1810, died Sept. 14, 1890. He was a stable keeper, city surveyor, and policeman, in Concord many years, also was in Co. G, 16th N. H. Reg.
Children of 7th Gen. b. in Concord.
F6046 WILLIAM D., b. Nov. 18, 1838, m. 1st, MAGGIE MAHLERVIN; m. 2nd, March 7, 1886, MINNIE G. HALL.
6047 SUSAN F., b. Feb. 16, 1840, d. Aug. 7, 1840.
6048 SARAH F. C., b. of second wife, Aug. 1, 1847? d. same day.
6049 ELLEN F., b. of third wife, Dec. 5, 1852, m. in Concord, Nov. 28, 1872, HENRY G. BUZZELL, b. Andover, Mass., July 25, 1848, son of Gilbert H. and Nancy (Jones). He is a carpenter in Concord. No children.

F2814 Sarah W. Locke, born July 18, 1820, died in Chichester, Oct. 26, 1900, married May 26, 1844, FRANCIS LOCKE KNOWLES, # 3915, born Oct. 12, 1817. He was a painter in Chichester.
Children of 7th Gen.
6050 CHARLES M., b. Jan. 9, 1846, m. 1867, ETTA ORDWAY, lived in Chichester and had: 6051 GEORGE.
6052 GEORGE F., b. March 5, 1848, m. 1st, 1872, MARY MULLEN; m. 2nd, 1883, LILLIAN BARRETT. He lived in Chichester and had: 6053 EDWIN F., b. 1887.
F6054 ELLA D., b. March 27, 1850, m. 1st, Nov. 3, 1864, GEORGE H. LEAR; m. 2nd, May 15, 1872, EDWIN H. BLOOD.
F6055 NELLIE E., b. Nov. 28, 1859, m. Sept. 18, 1880, JOHN W. TALBERT.

F2815 Oliver H. Locke, born in Northwood, Jan. 1, 1823, died in Lisbon, May 29, 1888, married in Canterbury, Sept. 1, 1845, HARRIET SHAW, born in Canterbury in 1825. He was in 15th N. H. Infantry, was a farmer and teamster in Littleton and Lisbon.

SEVENTH GENERATION

Children of 7th Gen.

F6056 CHARLES H., b. 1847, m. Jan. 26, 1867, SARAH E. CLARK.
F6057 SARAH A., b. June 15, 1850, m. 1st, WILLARD ORDWAY; m. 2nd, Apl. 23, 1892, JOHN KILLAM.
6058 HATTIE, b. Apl. 17, 1856, d. Apl. 12, 1896, m. JOHN HAZEN WILLIAMS (son of Jacob), b. Bath, Nov. 18, 1843; had a dau: 6059 DORA, b. March 31, 1880, in Lyman.
6060 ROSE, b. ——.
6061 NELLIE, b. Canterbury, Oct. 29, 1862, d. May 11, 1880, m. Aug. 4, 1879, LUTHER RICHARDSON, b. Lisbon, Oct. 18, 1850, son of James; was a farmer in Lisbon, had no children.
6062 FLORA ELIZABETH, b. Canterbury 1863, m. in Lisbon, May 6, 1882, WILLIAM L. WEBSTER, b. Lyman 1862.
6063 OLIVER, b. 1866.
F6064 HORACE, b. 1869, m. July 23, 1888, ALICE HAINES; m. 2nd, July 27, 1894, ETTA L. LITTLE.

F2816 Elizabeth Ann Locke, born Jan. 16, 1825, died in 1905, married July 29, 1845, SEWELL A. PERRY of Concord, born July 6, 1821, son of Varnum and Dorothy (French). He was a harness maker on the Plains and died Aug. 23, 1895.

Children of 7th Gen.

6065 GEORGE V., b. Dec. 10, 1849, m. 1872, MARY WELCH, who had: 6066 WILLIAM; 6067 GEORGE, who m. ADDIE ROLLINS; 6068 MAUD, who m. PETER RENIE.
6069 ELIZABETH A., b. Feb. 1, 1848, m. June 9, 1879, CHARLES E. FENNER, b. Dec. 8, 1833, dealer in boots and shoes in Boston, had no children.
F6070 ANNETTE, b. Feb. 7, 1846, m. 1863, ARUM P. SMITH.

F2817 James N. Locke, born in Suncook, March 12, 1827, died at Epping Corner, Aug. 31, 1893, married 1st, in Pembroke, Feb. 24, 1850, MARY G. BROCKWAY, who died in Epping, March 5, 1879, aged 47, daughter of Brooks and Julia; married 2nd, MRS. SAWYER (who was a widow before). He enlisted in Co. A, 11th N. H. Reg., was a stone cutter and iron moulder in Epping.

Children of 7th Gen.

6071 CHARLES, b. ——, was unmarried and killed in a mill in Epping, 1880, aged 18–20.
6072 ORIGINAL G., b. 1852.
6073 EMMA, b. Epping Dec. 12, 1856, m. MARK FOSS of Epping Corner, and d. 1903; had children.

F2818 Nehemiah C. Locke, born in Epsom, Feb. 16, 1829, died in Chichester, Dec. 6, 1888, married 1st, Jan. 1, 1850–1, CLARINDA L. ELLIOTT of Northwood; married 2nd, EMALINE

WARRING; married 3rd, SARAH E. GERRY, born 1853 (she perhaps married 1889, JOHN W. FULLER of Stewartstown). He was a farmer in Northfield and Chichester.

Children of 7th Gen.

F6074 FRANK A., b. 1873, m. July 2, 1898, IDA B. GRAY.
F6075 WALTER M., b. Nov. 10, 1876, m. May 31, 1900, MRS. EFFIE BRYANT.
6076 SARAH, b. Oct. 20, 1878.
6077 ABBIE, b. ——, m. —— WELCH.
6078 ELIZABETH, b. 1880, m. 1st, Dec. 16, 1893, EDWARD F. KING, a shoemaker who was b. Boston 1873; m. 2nd, Aug. 31, 1895, WILLIAM DUPLAISE, a teamster of Chichester, b. Canada, 1875; m. 3rd, FRANK WELLS.

F2822 Richard Dearborn Locke, born in Canterbury, Feb. 2, 1834, died in Tilton, Jan. 26, 1863, married Sept. 24, 1854, NANCY B. ROGERS, born in Loudon in 1836. He was a farmer at Hill's Corner, Canterbury. Nancy, married 2nd, 1864, EZRA CHASE and had four children by him.

Children of 7th Gen.

F6079 CHARLES A., b. Aug. 23, 1852,? m. Jan. 18, 1879, ELLEN HATTIE MILLS.
F6080 FRED A., b. 1859, m. May 25, 1882, LORETTA JENNIE FOOTE.
6081 JOSEPHINE L., b. March 31, 1863, m. 1st, July 1881, FRED HILLSGROVE, b. June 3, 1857, d. Feb. 10, 1884, had 6082 SUSIE, b. July 7, 1881; m. 2nd, —— HACKETT and lived Hopkinton.

F2828 Mary S. Brown, born March 6, 1806, died Dec. 15, 1859, married Nov. 27, 1825, EBENEZER L. ODIORNE born Apl. 16, 1800, died a farmer in Rye, Nov. 17, 1865.

Children of 7th Gen. b. in Rye.

6082 JONATHAN, b. March 26, 1826, d. May 24, 1859 unmarried.
6083 MARY A., b. June 23, 1828, d. unmarried, Oct. 6, 1857.
6084 MOSES H., b. May 22, 1830, was m. and d. in Black Hills, Dakota.
6085 EBENEZER, b. Feb. 11, 1834, d. unmarried Oct. 28, 1864, at Odiornes Point.
6086 CHARLES A., b. March 31, 1836, d. Lynn Mass. Nov. 5, 1915, m. March 26, 1864, ANZOLETTA A. BELL of New Castle, b. July 19, 1838, d. Nov. 25, 1914, had: 6087 RALPH, b. July 9, 1875, m. WINNIFRED S. BARTER, b. Apl. 1, 1875.
6088 CLARA E., b. Aug. 24, 1841, d. in Conn., Oct. 7, 1875, m. 1862, HOWARD RAND of Rye b. Sept. 25, 1840, had: 6089 FRANK; 6090 MARY. He m. 2nd, LOUISA MARDEN, #6112.
6091 CYNTHIA ANN, b. May 17, 1847, m. Jan. 9, 1872, DANIEL W. PHILBRICK, b. May 29, 1844, a farmer in Rye, had: 6092 ALFRED; 6093 IRVING; 6094 EMILY; 6095 CARRIE.
6096 LEVI W., b. June 7, 1832, d. July 31, 1838.

SEVENTH GENERATION 309

F2829 Sally Brown, born March 29, 1808, died Oct. 19, 1895, married Dec. 25, 1831, JOHN PHILBRICK, born Jan. 5, 1804, died a farmer in Rye, Sept. 12, 1877.

Children of 7th Gen.
6097 ANN M., b. 1830,? d. unmarried 1850.
6098 CAROLINE, b. ——, d. unmarried aged 16.
6099 MARY A., b. Sept. 1843, m. JAMES A. RAND of Ports. He m. 2nd, CLARA DOW, # 6118, lives Ports.
6100 JOHN W., b. ——, was unmarried.

F2831 Clarissa Brown, born Nov. 12, 1812, died May 23, 1858, married Aug. 4, 1836, NATHAN BROWN of North Hampton, born March 20, 1814, died May 1, 1898. He was a farmer there and married 2nd, ELIZABETH JENNESS.

Children of 7th Gen.
6101 VALERIA, b. June 17, 1838, m. JOHN W. BERRY of Greenland, b. Dec. 7, 1833, lived Malden and d. there, May 16, 1904. He was son of Jefferson and Letitia (Seavey), and had: 6102 LIZZIE; 6103 ALBERT, engineer Malden.
6104 MARTHA, b. Aug. 12, 1844, m. CHARLES BATCHELDER, b. March 18, 1843, lived No. Hampton, and had: 6105 CLARA B.; 6106 GEORGE ALPHONZO; 6107 MARTHA L.; 6108 BESSIE L., who m. R. JENNESS LOCKE; 6109 DORA C.; 6110 CHARLES LEVI.

F2834 Artemesia Brown, born Apl. 13, 1820, died Aug. 5, 1860, married March 29, 1842, DANIEL MARDEN, born June 14, 1812, died March 4, 1860, son of Levi and Patience. He was a farmer in Rye.

Children of 7th Gen. b. in Rye.
6111 SARAH ANGELETTE, b. Nov. 6, 1844; d. unmarried March 29, 1864.
6112 LOUISA N., b. Nov. 22, 1846, m. June 1, 1879, HOWARD RAND of Rye, b. Sept. 25, 1840, son of Elvin and Martha (Willey).
6113 DANIEL OTIS, b. May 2, 1849, d. unmarried Dec. 31, 1874.
6114 SAMUEL WOODBURY, b. Apl. 9, 1851, lives Rye, a farmer.
6115 ARTEMESIA, b. Apl. 2, 1854, d. May 21, 1864.
6116 CHARLES E., b. Apl. 21, 1855, d. May 16, 1867.
6117 DAU., died young.

F2837 Angelina Brown, born Jan. 3, 1826, died Apl. 9, 1871, married June 5, 1849, JAMES HENRY DOW, born Oct. 23, 1825, died Jan. 20, 1864, son of James and Data (Drake). He was a farmer in Rye.

Children of 7th Gen. b. in Rye.
6118 CLARA MARIA, b. Apl. 5, 1850, m. Nov. 4, 1869, JAMES A. RAND, son of James and Abigail (Berry); lives in Portsmouth and had: 6119 CHARLES; 6120 BLANCHE.

6121 CHARLES H., b. Jan. 22, 1852, d. 1852.
6122 HARRIET OLEVIA, b. twin 1852, d. Sept. 6, 1853.
6123 ELLA F., b. Sept. 12, 1853, d. Feb. 28, 1864.
6124 CHARLES H., b. July 31, 1854, d. March 18, 1869.
6125 FLORA B., b. Jan. 15, 1860, m. Oct. 21, 1896, ARTHUR H. BALLARD of Worcester, Mass. He is a banker there and had: 6126 IRENA, b. Dec. 25, 1898.

F2842 Mary Ann Brown, born ——, died June 23, 1867, married May 10, 1843, WILLIAM P. LADD, born in Deerfield, May 21, 1821, son of Eleazor and Betsey (Rollins).
Children of 7th Gen.
6127 GEORGE P., b. May 18, 1844, m. May 12, 1880, MINNIE STANTON.
6128 JAMES W., b. Nov. 28, 1845, d. Feb. 24, 1846.
6129 EMILY A., b. May 1, 1847, m. Oct. 9, 1869, JOSEPH T. ROLLINS.
6130 WILLIAM H., b. Dec. 20, 1849.
6131 MARY A., b. Oct. 6, 1851, m. Nov. 11, 1877, JAMES DOE.
6132 CAROLINE, b. Feb. 10, 1852.
7133 OLIVE, b. ——, died young.
6134 ELEANOR, b. Sept. 17, 1855, d. Feb. 4, 1873.
6135 HATTIE J., b. Dec. 2, 1856.
6136 ELEAZOR P., b. Feb. 21, 1858.
6137 LOUIS, b. Feb. 20, 1860.
6138 FREEMAN, b. Dec. 5, 1861.
6139 CHARLES G., b. Apl. 4, 1862.

F2847 Oliver Luther Locke, born in Rye, Feb. 1, 1833, died March 17, 1876, married in Exeter, Apl. 3, 1854, OLIVIA A. HODGDON, born in Greenland, Oct. 14, 1839, died in Portsmouth, July 31, 1889, daughter of Alex and Sarah A. (Walker). He was a carpenter in Rye.
Children of 7th Gen.
F6140 BELLE RINDGE, b. Sept. 27, 1856, m. March 25, 1884, CHARLES E. WALKER.
6141 FRED, b. July 27, 1859, lives in Boston, unmarried, in the electric light business.
6142 EMMA, b. May 1864, m. Sept. 27, 1910, MARK NICKERSON of Madison.
6143 MARCIA W., b. JULY 1866, lives unmarried, in Ports. Has for several years been the chief assistant of her brother-in-law, Mr. Walker.
6144 CLARENCE E., b. Rye, Aug. 22, 1868, d. Sept. 25, 1914.

F2848 Ann M. Locke, born in Rye, in 1830, died Feb. 9, 1867, married Nov. 12, 1852, OTIS GOSS, born in 1827. He was a farmer in Rye, and died June 3, 1909.
Children of 7th Gen. b. in Rye.
6145 ELZADA, b. Oct. 10, 1853, d. unmarried in Rye, Nov. 24, 1904.
6146 ISABELLA, b. July 3, 1855, lives in Rye unmarried.
F6147 OLIVE ANN, b. May 10, 1858, m. Nov. 20, 1878, J. ARTHUR BROWN.

SEVENTH GENERATION

F2849 Hannah Olive Locke, born ——, died July 30, 1858, married 1st, Aug. 7, 1854, JOHN O. LANE of Portsmouth, born June 6, 1828, died Aug. 12, 1854, son of Solomon and Eliza; married 2nd, JOHN W. M. RANDALL, born March 1828, died Apl. 8, 1862. She was his 3rd wife.

Children of 7th Gen. in b. Rye.

6148 BELLE LANE, b. Oct. 9, 1854, m. March 19, 1877, D. WOODBURY DAWLTON of Rye, b. May 21, 1849, son of Daniel and Martha (Brown). Has no children and lives in Rye.
6149 WILLIE RANDALL, b. July 26, 1861? m. Oct. 16, 1899, MRS. JESSIE LEAR, who d. in Rye, Apl. 30, 1901, had: 6150 GLADYS M., b. Oct. 19, 1900.

F2873 Dennis H. Trefethern, born Oct. 31, 1837, married in Portsmouth, Dec. 17, 1868, MRS. ELLA (SMILEY) MAXWELL, born in Benton, Me., March 27, 1842, died in Portsmouth, Sept. 7, 1908. A mason in Portsmouth.

Children of 7th Gen. b. in Portsmouth.

6151 MARCELLUS W., b. Oct. 12, 1869, d. May 29, 1873.
6152 AUSTIN W., b. Jan. 28, 1872, m. Apl. 7, 1894, MARY L. GILBERT, of Ports. He is a mason in Ports., and had: 6153 HARROLD; 6154 RUTH; 6155 GRACE; 6156 GLADDYS; and others.
6157 NELLIE C., b. Oct. 6, 1877, m. 1st, Nov. 28, 1900, GEORGE R. NEWICK, a brewer of Ports., b. 1877, d. Aug. 1, 1902, had: 6158 DOROTHY E., b. Oct. 6, 1902; m. 2nd, J. NORRIS PARKER, son of John and Elizabeth (Legg).

F2874 Martha S. Trefethern, born July 6, 1841, married 1st, Jan. 1, 1864, WOODBURY GREEN, born Oct. 9, 1836, died in Rye, Sept. 20, 1864; married 2nd, STORER GATES, born 1843, died July 14, 1892. A hostler in Portsmouth for Frank Jones.

Children of 7th Gen., all by Gates.

6159 CHARLES, b. July 1868, m. 1892, SUSIE GOODMAN of Milwaukee. He d. Feb. 14, 1901, had: 6163 RUBY, b. 1893.
6160 FRANK L., b. June 6, 1870, was a shoemaker in Ports. and d. March 13, 1895.
6161 WOODBURY C., b. Feb. 29, 1872, m. Feb. 12, 1898, LIZZIE T. PERKINS, b. Maine 1876, dau. of John and Flora. He was a shoemaker and d. Oct. 20, 1913.
6162 JAMES L., b. Apl. 25, 1874, d. Jan. 3, 1875.

F2877 Mary White Locke, born in Rye, Feb. 16, 1803, died in Boston, Nov. 4, 1881, married in Great Falls, Sept. 1829, WILLIAM A. MENDALL, a hotel keeper of Great Falls. He died 1860.

Children of 7th Gen. b. in Somerville, Mass.

6164 WILLIAM HENRY, b. March 22, 1832, m. 1st, March 22, 1855, ELIZABETH KENNARD of Eliot, Me. She d. March 1883, was dau. of Joseph; m. 2nd, March 22, 1885, ABBIE HAMMOND. He was an electrician in Newton, Mass., and d. June 1897, had son by first wife: 6165 WILLIAM, b. 1870, d. 1897.

F6166 GRANVILLE S., b. Oct. 1834, m. Oct. 1857, SOPHIA McMANN.

6167 MARTHA A., b. 1836, d. unmarried in Somerville, Feb. 8, 1858.

F2878 Aphia Rand Locke, born in Barrington, March 13, 1806, died in Melrose, Dec. 23, 1893, married in Somersworth, June 2, 1835, THOMAS SHAPLEIGH, born in Eliot, Me., Dec. 21, 1800, died in Somersworth, Oct. 10, 1857. He was a dry goods dealer in Great Falls.

Children of 7th Gen.

F6168 WILLIAM AUGUSTUS, b. Sept. 14, 1836, m. Sept. 18, 1872, ELLEN PICKERING.

6169 THOMAS E., b. Somersworth, 1838, d. 1842.

6170 JAMES A., b. S., 1840, d. 1842.

F6171 FRANCES APHIA, b. Dec. 21, 1843, m. 1st, March 10, 1864, RICHARD LINDSAY; m. 2nd, Nov. 1, 1875, ZIMRI HAYWOOD.

6172 ISABEL B., b. Nov. 19, 1846, m. Boston Apl. 25, 1877, LLEWELLEN MARR, b. Bath, Me., June 21, 1832, d. Boston, May 18, 1899, had: 6173 LLEWELLEN M., b. March 4, 1878, m. Oct. 15, 1902, ETHEL W. GIBBS, and they have: 6174 VIRGINIA, b. 1903.

F2879 Hannah Dow Locke, born in Rye, March 5, 1808, died in Malden, Mass., Aug. 27, 1891, married in Somersworth, Dec. 20, 1837, LEWIS DEARBORN of Great Falls, who was a photographer in Great Falls, and died in Boston 1870.

Children of 7th Gen.

6175 HELEN MARIA, b. Somersworth, May 30, 1839, m. Oct. 4, 1866, GEORGE EVERETT and she d. Malden, Mass., June 30, 1900. He was a bookkeeper in Malden and had: 6176 EDWIN, b. Boston, Apl. 6, 1869, now an artist; 6177 HELEN MATTIE, b. Dec. 27, 1871.

6178 MARTHA HAVEN, b. Somersworth, Oct. 4, 1851, m. July 27, 1885, GEORGE LAMBAUGH, a commission merchant of Malden, Mass.

F2880 Jeremiah Locke, born in Rye, Apl. 9, 1811, died in Portsmouth, Feb. 21, 1899, married March 1835, HANNAH A. YOUNG of North Berwick, born in Berwick, Oct. 1815, died in Portsmouth, May 7, 1870, daughter of John and Mary (Hanscom). He was a policeman and overseer of cotton mills in Portsmouth.

SEVENTH GENERATION 313

Children of 7th Gen.

F6179 MARY MEHITABLE, b. July 6, 1837, m. Dec. 24, 1854, ORWIN GRIFFIN.
F6180 JOHN HARRISON, b. July 29, 1841, m. Jan. 7, 1864, SARAH L. WEBSTER.
6181 JOSEPH JEFFERSON, b. Nov. 24, 1843, enlisted Co. K., 12th Me. Reg., and was killed at Port Hudson, May 25, 1863, unmarried.
6182 GEORGE EDWARD, b. Aug. 9, 1845, d. Ports., Dec. 10, 1870, unmarried, carpenter in Ports.
6182 ARABELLA AUGUSTA, b. Aug. 10, 1847, m. Ports., Nov. 28, 1866, BENJAMIN F. WINN of Wells, Me., b. Apl. 18, 1834. He was a joiner at the Navy Yard, lived in Portsmouth and died March 31, 1916, had: child 6183 d. infant; 6184 LOUIS F., b. Oct. 16, 1875, d. Nov. 29, 1896.
6185 MARTHA HELEN, b. Aug. 1849, d. an infant.
6186 MARTHA E., b. Oct. 1852, d. March 10, 1857.
F6187 FLORA ALBERTHA, b. Feb. 14, 1856, m. Nov. 29, 1877, GEORGE H. DENNETT.
F6188 EMMA ENDORA, b. March 20, 1858, m. Oct. 14, 1891, WILLIAM WARD BAILEY.
F6189 WINFIELD SCOTT, b. March 8, 1861, m. Dec. 1, 1886, CARRIE A. EDSON.

F2881 Martha Rand Locke, born in Barrington, March 4, 1814, died in Minnesota, Jan. 28, 1903, married in Somersworth, Dec. 25, 1845, JOHN PAGE FARMER of Boscawen, born Sept. 24, 1823, son of John and Sally (Gerrish). He is a farmer in Ada, Minn.

Children of 7th Gen. b. in Boscawen.

6190 JOHN Q., b. Feb. 23, 1848, d. Bosc., May 8, 1857.
6191 MARTHA J., b. June 17, 1851, d. Bosc., March 10, 1857.
F6192 MARY WHITE, b. March 22, 1853, m. Sept. 24, 1879, CHARLES R. ANDREWS.
6193 CHARLES RUSSELL, b. March 11, 1855, is a farmer in Ada, Minn., unmarried.

F2884 Mary Mason, born in Portsmouth in 1808, died May 24, 1882, married Sept. 16, 1830, DANIEL A. ADWERS of Portsmouth. He was a seaman born in Portsmouth in 1802, died Apl. 29, 1864, son of John and Sarah.

Children of 7th Gen.

6194 GEORGE M., b. Ports., was m. and had: 6195 HERBERT; 6196 CLARENCE.
6197 ANN LOUISA, b. Ports., Oct. 8, 1836, d. Apl. 23, 1892, m. FREEMAN BURLEIGH of Stratham, b. Dec. 15, 1835, son of Josiah and Theo (Piper). Was a farmer and town clerk of Stratham, had: 6198 GEORGE F., b. Feb. 22, 1869; 6199 EDITH L., b. Nov. 12, 1871; 6200 RALPH M., b. Sept. 25, 1877.
6201 HORACE F., b. ——, m. —— WINSLOW of Roxbury, Mass., had no children.

F2885 Lorinda Mason, born in 1810, died ——, married Aug. 30, 1835, GEORGE T. BALL, a sea captain of Portsmouth.
Children of 7th Gen. perhaps b. in Portsmouth.
6202 GEORGETTA, b. ——, m. HORACE F. ROBINSON of Boston, both d. before 1894.
6203 GRANVILLE, b. ——, m. —— LORD of Exeter, had no children.
6204 FRANK, b. ——, d. ——, unmarried.
6205 ARTHUR, b. ——, m. —— —— of East Boston and had: 6206 EDITH.

F2889 Elizabeth J. Mason, born in 1816, died Oct. 31, 1905, married Sept. 7, 1834, JOSEPH M. EDMONDS of Portsmouth, born 1814, died Sept 3, 1872. He was deputy collector in Portsmouth many years, son of Benjamin and Hannah.
Children of 7th Gen b. in Portsmouth.
6207 ANNIE E., b. Sept. 14, 1835, m. A.D. WALDRON of Chicago, a coal merchant, and they had: 6208 WILLIAM; 6209 EDNA.
6210 FRANCES A., b. Jan. 16, 1838, d. Camden, Me., Aug. 18, 1912, m. June 6, 1866, JOSEPH B. STEARNS of Boston, b. Wells, Me., Feb. 28, 1831. He was an electrician of Boston, son of Edwin and Elizabeth (Barker), d. Camden, Me., 1895, and had: 6211 EDWARD S. of Thomaston, Me.; 6212 HARRY W. of Camden, Me.
6213 CHARLES H., b. ——, m. MARY SHUTE of Boston and had: 6214 WILLIAM; 6215 SARAH ELIZABETH, m. —— WOODSWORTH of Boston; 5216 CHARLES; 6217 FRANK.
6218 JOSEPH M., b. ——, m. LUCY PARKER, had no child.

F2890 Robert Mason, born ——, married EMALINE H. EDMONDS of Portsmouth. He was a ship calker.
Children of 7th Gen.
6219 ROBERT D., b. ——, m. —— PICKETT of Boston, was a shoe dealer in Lawrence, Kan., and had: 6220 FRED; 6221 ALICE; 6222 WILLIAM; 6223 MARY; 6224 EMMA.
6225 MARIA, b. ——, m. MANLY SHERBURNE of E. Boston, was a shoe dealer in Dennison, Texas, and had: 6226 WILLIAM; 6227 FRED; 6228 VIOLA; 6229 LILLIAN; 6230 ELIZABETH; 6231 ROBERT.

F2892 Martha Dow Locke, born in Rye, Apl. 16, 1813, married Aug. 28, 1836, ADAM KNOX of Boston, who was a nurse. She died March 28, 1854.
Children of 7th Gen.
6232 MARY E., b. Sept. 14, 1837, m. May 1, 1862, CHARLES F. HALL and had: 6233 GEORGE P., b. May 28, 1863, m. Oct. 1, 1891, LIZZIE LEAVITT, lived in Boston.
6234 GEORGE H., b. Aug. 15, 1839, m. Sept. 1, 1862, MARY ADAMS.

SEVENTH GENERATION 315

6235 CHARLES H., b. March 14, 1841, m. 1867, MARTHA WALTON, lived in Maine.
6236 JOSEPH L., b. Feb. 11, 1844, m. Jan. 9, 1867, INEZ V. BACOCK and lived in Boston.
6237 JAMES A., b. Aug. 18, 1849, m. 1876, THERESA MOWRY, lived in Conn.

F2893 John Newton Locke, born in Rye, Jan. 22, 1815, died in Warren, R. I., Aug. 30, 1863, married in Providence, Oct. 20, 1839, HARRIET A. WEATHERBEE. He was a carpenter.
Children of 7th Gen.
6238 CHARLES N., b. Providence, R. I., July 15, 1840, m. —— ——, lived in Bristol, R. I.
6239 MARY A., b. Providence, Apl. 2, 1842, d. ——, m. SETH JAMES.
6240 CELIA A., b. Rehoboth, Mass., Dec. 28, 1844, m. CHARLES H. BULLOCK, lived in Bristol.
6241 ELLEN M., b. Rehoboth, May 8, 1847, d. ——, m. ROBERT H. BULLOCK of Bristol. She may have been the Ellen who m. JOSEPH MCGRATH in Providence, May 8, 1889.
6242 JOHN H., b. Rehoboth, Jan. 25, 1850, m. —— ——, d. ——.
6243 SARAH W., b. Reh., Feb. 23, 1853, d. 1853.
6244 LYDIA T., b. Sept. 10, 1854, d. 1858.
6245 PHEBE C., b. Swanzey, Dec. 9, 1856, d. 1859.
F6246 WILLIAM A., b. Apl. 25, 1859, m. Apl. 13, 1882, MARY I. POTTS.
6247 JAMES N., b. Warren, June 23, 1861, m. —— ——, lived in Nantucket, Mass.
6248 ADALAIDE F., b. Warren, Feb. 22, 1864, m. S. C. BAGLEY of Boston.

F2902 Hannah Salter Locke, born in Rye March 14, 1830, died June 21, 1898, married Jan. 15, 1851, RICHARD PIGOTT, born in Boston. He was a morocco finisher in East Boston and Charlestown, and died Sept. 30, 1872.
Children of 7th Gen.
F6249 RICHARD, b. Aug. 25, 1852, m. 1st, Aug. 25, 1874, ELIZA J. LOVELL; m. 2nd, Nov. 25, 1886, AUGUSTA DICKERSON.
6250 ALFRED H., b. July 17, 1854, d. Apl. 28, 1872.
6251 CHARLES, b. Sept. 12, 1857, d. same day.
6252 JOHN J., b. Feb. 2, 1861, m. Feb, 1, 1894, MARTHA V. RYDER, lived in Cambridge, Mass.
6253 CARRIE M., b. Jan. 22, 1865, lived unmarried in E. Boston.
6254 JAMES A., b. a twin, d. March 1866.
6255 OLIVETTE T., b. Chatham, Mass., Apl. 28, 1867, m. July 29, 1896, LOREN CHARLES LEIGHTON, b. 1867, son of Charles and Anna (Whitehouse), a farmer in Middleton, Mass.

EIGHTH GENERATION

F2916 Richard Rand Locke, born in Rye, July 16, 1794, died in Rye, Jan. 20, 1877, married Jan. 20, 1824, SARAH A. LEAVITT, born in North Hampton, Jan. 20, 1800, died in Rye, May 14, 1870, daughter of Ebenezer and Sarah (Jewell). He was in Captain Neal's Co., Portsmouth, July 7, 1812, was in Privateer *Portsmouth* in the 1812 War, was captured and confined a prisoner in Halifax and Dartmoor one year and nine months. He represented Rye in the N. H. Legislature in 1837, was moderator in 1850, was called Captain, and lived a farmer near Locke's Neck.

Children of 8th Gen. b. in Rye.

F6257 SULA ANN, b. Oct. 11, 1824, m. 1st, Aug. 10, 1845, SAMUEL W. FOSS, b. 1818, d. Apl. 13, 1849; m. 2nd, Oct. 7, 1855, JOHN SHERIDAN GOSS, # 4716.

F6258 S. EMALINE, b. Oct. 16, 1826, m. Oct. 15, 1848, WOODBURY LEVI JENNESS.

F6259 A. MARIA, b. June 18, 1829, m. Apl. 28, 1850, DEWITT C. JEWELL.

F6260 RICHARD L., b. Oct. 26, 1831, m. Nov. 15, 1859, SARAH P. JENNESS, # 675.

F6261 HARRIET J., b. Jan. 15, 1835, m. Oct. 17, 1858, RICHARD PICKERING GOSS.

F6262 ALBERT CARR, b. June 22, 1837, m. July 9, 1868, ELIZA E. VARREL.

F2917 John W. Locke, born in Rye, June 28, 1796, died in Rye, Jan. 10, 1868, married Oct. 27, 1816, MARY POWERS, daughter of Robert and Betsey (Shapleigh), born in Rye, Apl. 1796, died in Rye, Jan. 18, 1869. He was a farmer in Rye.

Children of 8th Gen. b. in Rye.

6263 SUSAN, b. Feb. 22, 1817, d. July 17, 1842, m. in Boston, Feb. 28, 1836, TIMOTHY C. KNOWLTON of Boston, b. in Hardwick, Mass., Aug. 14, 1810, son of Israel and Abigail (Carter), and d. Boston, July 9, 1869, had: 6264 MARY E., b. Dec. 20, 1834? was unmarried.

F6265 ROBERT P., b. Sept. 30, 1819, m. 1851, CLARINDA A. BACHELDER, # 2327.

6266 SARAH ELIZABETH, b. Aug. 1822, d. unmarried, Portsmouth, Nov. 26, 1911.

6267 LAURA AUGUSTA, b. Feb. 1, 1825, d. Jan. 19, 1908, m. Sept. 8, 1843, her brother-in-law, TIMOTHY C. KNOWLTON, and they had: 6268 SUSAN A., b. Jan. 9, 1847, m. 1880, ARTHUR GOSS, and had: 6269 ERNEST, 1881-1882.

F6270 CALVIN, b. June 1830, m. FRANCES PRIEST.

6271 MARIA ADALINE, b. Feb. 20, 1836, m. Rye, Sept. 24, 1863, WOODBURY BERRY, # 2753, b. Aug. 19, 1834. She d. Rye Oct. 18, 1915.

F2918 Hamilton Cutts Locke, born in Rye, Dec. 28, 1798, died in Portsmouth, June 14, 1860, married in Portsmouth, Jan. 2, 1825, MARY ANN RAND of Portsmouth, born in Rye, Aug. 26, 1805, died in Portsmouth, March 19, 1901, daughter of David S. and Polly (Salter). He was a tavern keeper in Rye and Portsmouth.

Children of 8th Gen. b. in Rye or Portsmouth.

6272 APHIA ANN, b. May 13, 1827, m. Portsmouth, Dec. 24, 1850, EDWIN P. MARDEN. He was a carpenter in Manchester, had no children and d. June 1903.
6273 MARY WHITE, b. Nov. 29, 1828, d. unmarried Portsmouth, Oct. 9, 1876.
F6274 MARTHA SARAH, b. Dec. 19, 1830, m. Nov. 6, 1853, JOHN T. LARRABEE.
F6275 WILLIAM WATSON, b. Apl. 7, 1833, m. Nov. 18, 1857, ANNIE M. FERNALD.
6276 CYRUS HAMILTON, b. June 29, 1835, d. Apl. 29, 1850.
F6277 SUSAN OLEVIA, b. Nov. 25, 1837, m. Oct. 12, 1856, CHARLES B. GREEN.
F6278 JAMES IRVING, b. Dec. 28, 1839, m. Oct. 23, 1867, LAURA A. KELLY.
6279 EDWIN WALLACE, b. Portsmouth, Dec. 22, 1842, m. Apl. 27, 1866, JENNIE KYLE, # 6288, b. Scotland, Apl. 6, 1845, d. Roslindale, Mass., Aug. 19, 1912. He was in U. S. Navy, later a jeweller in N. Y. City, had no children, and d. N. Y. Apl. 23, 1869.
6280 FRANCES ELLEN, b. Jan. 27, 1845, m. Portsmouth, June 27, 1869, WILLIAM A. HANSCOM of Haverhill, Mass., b. Apl. 1840, lived in Haverhill and Portsmouth, where he d. Feb. 7, 1886. She is living in Portsmouth 1916.

F2920 Jeremiah Locke, born in Rye, May 15, 1804, died in Madbury, May, 7, 1850, married Feb. 14, 1828, MARY WENTWORTH, born Nov. 7, 1807, died Aug. 17, 1848, daughter of George and Sarah (Lord) of Barrington. He was a farmer in Madbury and Dover.

Children of 8th Gen. b. in Dover.

F6281 IRA A., b. Sept. 5, 1828, m. Nov. 11, 1849, LYDIA V. CHURCH.
6282 MARK W., b. Apl. 25, 1830, lost at sea 1847.
6283 SUSAN J., b. July 29, 1832, d. unmarried Apl. 30, 1850.
F6284 ELIZABETH A., b. July 27, 1834, m. Oct. 15, 1859, HIRAM S. GOODELL.
F6285 ANDREW JACKSON, b. Sept. 29, 1836, m. March 9, 1858, SARAH A. SMITH.
6286 OLIVER BABB, b. Oct. 7, 1838, m. Somersworth, Dec. 6, 1862, MARY ABBIE HURD of Milton, b. Exeter 1837, dau. of William C. and Caroline. This was Mary's third marriage. Oliver was a machinist in Haverhill, Mass., and d. Tamworth, 1881. No children.

6287 JAMES WENTWORTH, b. Sept. 20, 1840, was in U. S. Navy on Gunboat *Vicksburg*, also in Co. D, 1st. R. I. L. Art. 1861–64 He d. unmarried at Soldiers' Home, Togus, Me.

F6288 JEREMIAH YOUNG, b. Aug. 27, 1842, m. Dec. 26, 1869, MRS. JENNIE (KYLE) LOCKE, # 6278.

6289 MARGARET A., b. Aug. 15, 1846, d. four days later.

F2921 Jane Locke, born in Rye, in 1796, died at Isles of Shoals, married 1st, March 31, 1817, BENJAMIN BROWN; married 2nd, 1819, JOHN RANDALL, born in Rye, July 1, 1795, a fisherman at the Shoals.

Children of 8th Gen. all Randalls, except the First.

F6290 ESTHER BROWN, b. 1817, d. Concord, July 20, 1887, m. 1st, DANIEL RAND; m. 2nd, MATTHEW D. ANNIS.

F6291 JOSEPH, b. ——, m. ARIADNE CASWELL.

6292 JOHN, d. unmarried aged 25.

F6293 RICHARD L., b. Dec. 23, 1823, m. Dec. 26, 1847, MARY A. CASWELL, # 6312.

F6294 LUCY JANE, b. June 1821, m. May 1844, RICHARD HALEY.

F6295 CATHERINE, b. ——, m. JAMES BURNES of Vermont.

6296 HANNAH, b. ——, m. 1st, FABIAS BECKER of the Shoals as his 2nd wife and they had: 6297 ANNIE; 6298 MARY; 6299 EVA; 6300 NELLIE; 6300a WILLIAM. She m. 2nd, JOHN RANDALL of Portsmouth. Hannah d. Ports. Jun 22, 1879.

F6301 ELIZA J., b. 1833, m. Oct. 11, 1848, DANIEL H. HALEY.

F2922 Nathaniel Locke, born in Rye in 1798, died in Meredith, married 1st, July 25, 1821, MARY WEED of Sandwich; married 2nd, Nov. 2, 1866, MRS. SARAH VITTUM, born in Gilmanton in 1801. He was a farmer in Sandwich and Tamworth.

Children of 8th Gen. b. in Sandwich.

6302 ELISHA, b. 1823, was in Concord; worked in Sandwich 1843, went to California 1849 and d. about 1850.

6303 ADALINE M., b. ——, m. 1st, in Sandwich, Jan. 1, 1845, HORACE FRANK BEAN of Boston, who lived in Tamworth and then went West. She m. 2nd, WILLIAM AMES.

F2923 Joseph Locke, born in Rye in 1800, married in 1832, LUCY BEEDE, born in 1810, who was alive in 1850. He was a stage driver from Rye to Portsmouth, and in 1838–9 moved to Charleston, Vt. In early forties they went to Mass., where she worked in a factory. He went to the lumber camps as a trader, and there disappeared.

Children of 8th Gen.

F6304 ELISHA BEEDE, b. Sept. 14, 1834, m. LUVIA CUTTER KNIGHT.

F6305 JOSEPH MARDEN, b. July 18, 1839, m. Oct. 30, 1859, HARRIET E. SWEET.

F2924 Sarah Palmer Locke, born in Rye, Sept. 17, 1801, died in Portsmouth, Oct. 26, 1881, married May 4, 1823, LEMUEL LAFAYETTE CASWELL, of Gosport, born at the Shoals, Nov. 1, 1796, died at the Shoals, Nov. 12, 1861, son of John. They lived at the Shoals.

Children of 8th Gen. b. Isles of Shoals.

6306 JOHN, b. Jan. 10, 1824, d. Jan. 4, 1906, m. 1st, ANNIE J. RANDALL, and had: 6307 EVALINE E., b. May 1853, drowned Sept. 1864. He m. 2nd, July 4, 1856, EMALINE B. ROBINSON, b. Apl. 20, 1840, d. Portsmouth, Jan. 12, 1915.

6308 LEMUEL LAFAYETTE, b. Oct. 3, 1825, d. Lynn, Oct. 5, 1907, m. LYDIA FELTCH of Seabrook, who d. Lynn 1904. He had a grocery store in Lynn, and had: 6309 HERBERT, m. and had: 6310 HORTENSE; 6311 EUGENE, m. and d. Lynn, 1898; 6311a JOHN, was in the Insurance business in the West and had two children.

6312 MARY ADA, b. Nov. 13, 1828, m. Dec. 26, 1847, RICHARD L. RANDALL, # F6293.

F6313 LOUISA BLAISDELL, b. Jan. 29, 1831, m. May 28, 1848, GEORGE W. RANDALL.

6314 HANNAH MARIA, b. Oct. 5, 1834, d. Ports., Dec. 8, 1909, m. 1st, May 4, 1855, ALBERT FAILES; m. 2nd, DANIEL H. HALEY, b. Nov. 5, 1824, d. Aug. 1, 1898. Lived in Portsmouth. By Failes she had: 6315 LIZZIE F., b. Newton Upper Falls, May 28, 1859, m. THOMAS SCHOOLS of Milton, Mass., and had: 6316 FRANCIS.

6317 PERRY ALFRED, b. Jan. 19, 1841, d. Portsmouth, Feb. 5, 1893, m. Jan. 19, 1869, EMMA SNOW and had: 6318 ALICE B., b. July 1870, m. 1897, CHARLES CARROLL, a grocer of Portsmouth and d. Feb. 1915; 6319 FREEMAN, b. Feb. 2, 1879, m. MRS. LILLIAN (WRIGHT) WARD of Ports.

F2925 Locada Locke, born in Rye, Feb. 7, 1804, died Apl. 27, 1851, married LEVI B. TREFETHERN, born in Rye, Oct. 21, 1801, died in Kittery, Me., Oct. 5, 1858, son of William and Lizzie. He was a boss teamster on the Navy Yard, had a 2nd wife, HARRIET KEEN, and lived in Kittery. She was brought up by William Marden of Rye.

Children of 8th Gen. b. in Kittery, Me.

6320 MARY JANE, b. Sept. 28, 1826, d. Fairhaven, Conn., May 12, 1877, m. in Kittery, WILLIAM HOFF, a boatswain in U. S. Navy, and had: 6321 MARY L., b. Aug. 22, 1848, m. ALFRED WALKER of Fairhaven, Conn., and had: 6322 JOHN.

F6324 JAMES O., b. Aug. 10, 1830, m. 1st., Nov. 29, 1855, JOANNA M. LAWRY; m. 2nd, June 15, 1864, ISABELLA C. KIMBALL.

6325 EMILY A., b. Nov. 3, 1832, d. Oct. 15, 1855 m. Oct. 1854, MARCUS CLARK of Boston, was a cabinet maker, lived in Wankon, Iowa. Child: 6326 EMMA, b. Oct. 15, 1855, m. ——— SHATTUCK; lived

Wankon, Iowa. Had: 6327 CHARLES; 6328 CARRIE, who m. JAMES OTIS of Kittery.

6329 LEWIS W., b. Feb. 8, 1837, d. in Kittery, unmarried, Nov. 5, 1866.

6330 FRANCES L., b. Dec. 5, 1841, m. in Kittery, NATHAN H. JUNKINS, a carpenter in U. S. Navy, lives in Kittery.

F6331 CHARLES W., b. Jan. 9, 1846, m. June 21, 1871, EMMA LOUISE WITHERELL.

F2931 Hannah B. Locke, born in Rye, Dec. 18, 1819, died in Boston, March 15, 1897, married 1st, in Portsmouth, Nov. 16, 1837, STEPHEN FERGUSON, who was a meat dealer in Portsmouth, born 1821, died Apl. 2, 1871?; married 2nd, JOSEPH HOLMES, born Dec. 26, 1815, a furniture dealer in Portsmouth, died Dec. 27, 1869; married 3rd, ANDREW HOLMES (cousin of Joseph), who died in Seabrook in 1879, aged 60. He was a butcher in Portsmouth.

Holmes Children of 8th Gen.

F6339 MUNROE, b. Ports. ——, m. Boston, Jan. 5, 1864, LAURA F. FARNUM.

6340 MARY ANN, b. ——, m. 1st, JAMES H. K. DOWNES, b. 1842, d. Sept. 1871; m. 2nd, E. D. WHITCOMB, b. 1841, d. Feb. 25, 1897.

6341 NELLIE, b. ——, d. 1876, m. WILLIAM CHANDLER of Portsmouth.

6342 FREDDIE, b. June 18, 1854, d. Sept. 12, 1854.

F2938 Hamilton Locke, born in Wakefield, Feb. 3, 1806, died in 1884, married 1st, Dec. 7, 1829, SOPHRONIA D. FROST of Wolfeboro, married 2nd, Oct. 4, 1850 DORCAS GUPTIL of Wolfeboro, born in BERWICK, 1813, died Jan. 31, 1872, daughter of William and Dorcas; married 3rd, in Wolfeboro, Feb. 9, 1873, MARY F. ABBOTT, born in Ossipee, 1840, daughter of James and Mary (Fall). She married 2nd, Jan. 7, 1890, SIMEON COLE.

Children of 8th Gen. b. in Wolfeboro.

6343 ALBA, b. 1854, d. Wolf., Sept. 1869, son of Dorcas.

6344 DORA BELLE, b. Feb. 24, 1875, m. Aug. 4, 1896, GEORGE D. HARRIMAN of Warner, b. 1852, son of Joel and Ann (Jacobs).

6345 DAUGHTER, b. Wolf., Aug. 1, 1877.

F2957 Sarah Elizabeth Locke, born in Wolfeboro, May 21, 1828, married Nov. 26, 1849, THOMAS JEFFERSON TIBBETTS, Jr. both of Wolfeboro.

Children of 8th Gen.

6346 MEHITABLE, b. July 26, 1850, m. CHARLES F. BURKE, a farmer of Milton.

6347 MARY E., b. July 23, 1852, d. July 3, 1914, m. 1st, LAFAYETTE CANNEY; m. 2nd, Nov. 16, 1891, JESSE F. PAGE, son of Jesse, a farmer of Alton.

EIGHTH GENERATION

6348 AUGUSTA, b. July 12, 1853, d. Jan. 8, 1910, m. WINTHROP PIKE, a railroad engineer.
6349 THOMAS, b. Sept. 1, 1858, m. ETTA HAMILTON.
6350 ORA, b. Oct. 1, 1861, m. Nov. 1879, DANIEL TUTTLE, a farmer.
6351 HERBERT, b. July 15, 1864, m. Jan. 1890, ADA SMITH.
6352 INFANT.
6353 IDA B., b. Sept. 12, 1871, m. Nov. 28, 1889, CHARLES E. VARNEY, b. Apl. 4, 1867, a carpenter in Wolfeboro.

F2962 Rebecca Caswell, married NATHANIEL BERRY, born June 8, 1808. They lived at Isles of Shoals.

Children of 8th Gen.

6354 ANN, m. JOHN CHADBOURNE, had children.
6355 WILLIAM C., m. SALLY A. CASWELL, had children.
6356 NATHANIEL, m. JESSIE HANSON, had several children.
6357 JOHN W., m. LAURA WILSON; had two children.
6358 DRUCILLA, b Jan. 2, 1838, d. Sept. 15, 1910, m. Dec. 11, 1861, DANIEL CLARKE, b. Jan. 23, 1831, d. Ports., Feb. 27, 1914, had: 6359 ELMER; 6360 HERMAN and several others.
6361 JUDITH, unmarried.
6362 HARRISON, b. June 27, 1840, m. ANNA BAKER.
6363 LORENZO D., m. and had a family.
6364 EDWIN, m. ANNIE M. GOVE.
6365 WINFIELD S.
6366 MILLARD F., m. twice, had no children.
6367 CORDELIA F.

F2964 Charles Fred Locke, born in Rye, Aug. 25, 1826, died in Somerville, Mass., Dec. 20, 1895, married Aug. 25, 1851, **Ellen H. Locke,** # 5986, born Apl. 22, 1830. He was a mason in Portsmouth and Somerville, but retired several years before his death.

Children of 8th Gen. b. in Portsmouth.

6368 EMMA J., b. May 24, 1852, d. 1856.
6369 CHARLES GRANVILLE, b. March 22, 1854, m. June 14, 1876, ESTELLE ORDIORNE of Ports., b. March 22, 1859, dau. of Eben and Emily (Grant). He was a mason in Bradford, Mass., and d. Somerville, Mass., Oct. 12, 1910; had: 6370 EMMA J., b. May 14, 1877, d. Sept. 4, 1897; 6371 CHARLES F., b. 1895, d. Aug. 3, 1896.
6372 NELLIE A. M., b. Nov. 2, 1857, m. Feb. 22, 1888, WILLIAM H. CARLETON, who d. Somerville, Mass., about 1897.
6373 ALBERT JONES, b. Aug. 22, 1870, m. 1st, Dec. 8, 1888, CARRIE E. ROBINSON, who d. with her child, June 1, 1890; m. 2nd, Aug. 5, 1890, BESSIE A. FRAZIER, b. Oct. 15, 1868. He d. Somerville, Oct. 10, 1907.

F2967 Sarah Ann Locke, born in Rye, Jan. 6, 1833, died June 17, 1897, married June 2 1854, WILLIAM DUDLEY VARRELL of Portsmouth, son of William and Nancy (Berry), born July 2, 1830, died in Portsmouth Sept. 20, 1905. He was boss carpenter at Jones' brewery many years.

Children of 8th Gen. b. in Portsmouth.

6374 ANNIE M., b. July 20, 1857. Living Ports. 1916.
6375 IDA, b. June 20, 1861. Living Ports. 1916.
6376 CHARLES D., b. Dec. 7, 1865, m. 1st, Dec. 7, 1887, ELLA MARSHALL, b. 1863, divorced; m. 2nd, Dec. 12, 1894, LENA A. WOOD, b. Portsmouth, 1875, dau. of Nathan and Lydia. He is a carpenter, has been chief engineer of fire department, etc., in Portsmouth.
6377 J. MORRISON, b. Aug. 23, 1870, m. Jan. 1, 1890, ESTELLE DENAVARRO of Boston, b. 1869. He is a carpenter in Ports, had, 6378 MERTON W., b. Apl. 20, 1903; 6379 SADIE, b. Nov. 29, 1892; 6379a WILLIAM, m. Boston, Dec. 20, 1915, JENNIE A. KERLEY of Ports.
6380 WILLIE, b. Oct. 1874, d. Nov. 30, 1874.

F2971 Abigail M. Locke, born Sept. 10, 1825, died Jan. 15, 1888, married GEORGE BACHELDER, born in Chichester, Aug. 13, 1822, died Apl. 3, 1848, son of Jonathan and Nancy. He was a farmer in Concord.

Children of 8th Gen. b. in Concord.

6381 ABBIE A., b. July 16, 1847, d. July 28, 1847.
6382 GEORGE E., b. Oct. 8, 1848, m. MARY K. EMERSON and had nine children.

F2972 William Fred Locke, (William T. in father's will) born in South Boston, Dec. 26, 1826, died Jan. 11, 1870, married Jan. 6, 1857, LOVINA S. LAKE of Chichester, born Sept. 1836, daughter of John and Sarah (Moses). She married 2nd, ——— WALKER and died Nov. 16, 1904.

Children of 8th Gen.

6383 CLARENCE RICHARD, b. Chichester, Oct. 6, 1857, m. Pembroke, Oct. 12, 1887, ANNIE B. WHITTEMORE, b. Pembroke, Apl. 15, 1859, dau. of Aaron and Ariana (Brewster). She was a teacher. He is a grocer in So. Boston, 1915, had: 6384 LOVINA M., b. Aug. 10, 1890; 6385 RICHARD B., b. June 25, 1897, both living So. Boston, 1915.
6386 ANNIE FLORENCE, b. So. Boston, Apl. 19, 1865, m. Jan. 19, 1887, AUGUSTUS W. PERCIVAL of Orleans, Mass., lives Waltham, has no children.

F2973 Mehitable B. Locke, born in Boston, Apl. 16, 1836, died Jan. 17, 1888, married May 4, 1856, ELIHU BROWN, # 4981, of Rye, born May 6, 1822, died Feb. 12, 1859. He was a farmer in Rye.

EIGHTH GENERATION 323

Child of 8th Gen. b. in Rye.
F6387 ETTA M., b. Jan. 25, 1857, m. Sept. 1, 1881, FRANK PEARSON.

F2974 Daniel W. (Caswell) Burleigh, born Aug. 1830, married **Margaret A. Locke**, # 6029.
Children of 8th Gen. b. in Lee.
6388 LILLIAN, b. Dec. 12, 1853, d. Feb. 5, 1855.
6389 DANIEL L., b. Dec. 12, 1856, m. Sept. 1882, MRS. ELIZABETH (DOW) YORK of Lee. He was a farmer in Durham and Lee 1907 and had: 6390 FRANK S., b. Nov. 1883; 6391 BLANCHE S., b. Apl. 1885.
6392 ELLA R., b. Apl. 27, 1859, d. Jan. 19, 1881.
6393 SARAH A., b. March 26, 1861, d. Jan. 17, 1881.
6394 WOODBURY, b. July 23, 1863, m. 1888, ROSE HARDY of Newburyport, who d. Dec. 16, 1895. He is a sawmill worker, had: 6395 WILBUR L., b. Dec. 10, 1889; 6396 HATTIE E., b. Jan. 26, 1891; 6397 ROSE C., b. Dec. 7, 1895.

F2977 William S. Locke, born in South Boston, Sept. 17, 1826, died in South Boston, March 17, 1903, married Dec. 24, 1857, AUGUSTA ANN HENDERSON, who died Dec. 31, 1904, aged 77-11. He was a California pioneer of 1849, returned and was a plumber in South Boston. He is well remembered as one of our most zealous workers in the early reunions of the Lockes.
Children of 8th Gen. b. in South Boston.
6398 WILLIAM S., b. Apl. 23, 1861, m. Sept. 8, 1891, SOPHIA JOS. LAVERY.
6399 SARAH MARIA, b. March 10, 1862, m. Nov. 24, 1885, ELMER E. GRAVES and had: 6400 LESTER L., b. Feb. 13, 1887; 6401 GERTRUDE A., b. Jan. 17, 1891; 6401a WALTER E., b. July 4, 1893.
6402 MARY PHOSA, b. 1866, d. June 7, 1866.
6403 LIZZIE AUGUSTA, b. So. Boston, Apl. 9, 1871.

F2984 Mary Ann Locke, born in Boston Apl. 11, 1828, died in Ipswich, Mass., Jan. 6, 1892, married in South Boston, Nov. 2, 1851, SAMUEL H. BAKER of South Boston born in Ipswich, Aug. 2, 1823. He was a pattern maker in B. &. M. R. R. employ and lived at Ipswich.
Children of 8th Gen. b. in Ipswich, Mass.
6404 EDITH L., b. 1867, d. Ipswich, 1896.
6405 HERBERT, b. Apl. 17, 1871, d. Ipswich, June 18, 1872.
6406 WILLIAM A., b ——, m. Medford, Mass., Dec. 14, 1898, CARRIE DOWNES, b. Illinois, May 18, 1860. He has a store in Medford, no children.

F2985 Elizabeth Locke, born in Boston, Dec. 29, 1829, died Jan. 16, 1876, married JOSEPH BAKER, born in Ipswich, July 1825. He was janitor of the South Boston Library. These were both sons of Samuel and Susan (Holmes).

Children of 8th Gen.

6407 WALTER A., b. Apl. 9, 1854, m. MRS. CARRIE L. MERRITT, b. May 18, 1860. He was surveyor in Dakota, later a Methodist minister.
6408 WILLIAM A., b. Oct. 12, 1856, d. Feb. 28, 1858.
6409 EDWARD M., b. Oct. 12, 1858, d. May 28, 1895.
6410 EDITH M., b. July 14, 1861, d. May 20, 1863.
6411 ALFRED, b. June 14, 1864, a morocco worker, Peabody, Mass.

F2986 John H. Locke, born in Rye, Aug. 1, 1835, married June 30, 1859, EMMA J. JOHNSON of South Boston, born Sept. 26, 1836. He was bookeeper in the First National Bank, South Boston.

Children of 8th Gen.

6412 EMMA J., b. July 30, 1860.
6413 MINNIE L., b. Dec. 3, 1861, m. So. Boston, 1880, WILLIAM STEADMAN, who is a blacksmith in Lynn, and had five children.
6414 ADDIE W., b. June 14, 1864.
6415 LILLIAN G., b. Jan. 29, 1869, m. Jan. 17, 1892, FRANK CORNELL, lives in So. Boston, and had: 6416 FRANK D., b. 1892; 6417 WILMER F., b. 1893, d. Feb. 15, 1894.
6418 JOHN H., b. July 3, 1874, d. age 2 days.

F3063 Dr. Charles E. Locke, born in Boston, Aug. 16, 1807, married MARIA ———. He was a doctor in New York City and died there.

Children of 8th Gen.

6419 MARY F., b. May 14, 1837, d. Bound Brook, N. J., m. JOHN KELLY, and lived Bound Brook.
6420 SARAH E., b. March 29, 1842, was m., lived and d. in Bound Brook.
6421 CHARLES, b. May 23, 1844, lived Bound Brook, a farmer, unmarried.
6422 EPHRAIM, b. May 23, 1844, twin, died young.

F3064 Frederick A. Locke, born in Boston, Feb. 28, 1810, married June 9, 1842, SALLY ANN WILLIAMSON of Newburgh, N. Y. He was cashier of the Merchants and Traders Bank, New York City, until 1890, when he retired. He lived in Rahway, N. J., as late as 1899.

Children of 8th Gen. b. in New York City.

6423 ANN T. B., b. July 31, 1843, m. THOMAS BINNS, b. England, lived in Bayonne, N. J., and had: 6424 SARAH A.; 6425 WARREN J.; 6426 EDITH; 6427 HESTER.

EIGHTH GENERATION

F6428 FREDERICK A., b. Dec. 9, 1848, m. Dec. 20, 1875, MARY A. ROBINSON.
6429 WILLIAM HENRY, b. Sept. 15, 1851, m. Bound Brook, LOUISE ———,
lived in Brooklyn, N. Y., and had: 6430 FRED; 6431 ROY.

F3065 Harriet Bynam Locke, born Dec. 11, 1799, died Jan. 18, 1876, married in 1820, ERASTUS GOULD born May 9, 1797, died Jan. 31, 1829.
Children of 8th Gen.
6432 ROYAL C., b. Sept. 5, 1821, d. Feb. 25, 1897, m. HELEN M. AVERY, and had: 6433 FRED E., b. Sept. 4, 1853; 6434 ERNEST G., who lived Kansas City, 1898.
6435 ERASTUS E., b. May 2, 1823, m. Nov. 6, 1848, MARY E. RANDALL (?), b. June 14, 1827. He lived Portland, d. May 4, 1859. Had: 6436 CAROLINE E., b. May 25, 1850, lived in Portland; 6437 GEORGE F., b. July 21, 1855, is a lawyer and police court judge, Portland; 6438 EMMA, b. Sept. 6, 1857, lives Portland.
6439 CAROLINE L., b. July 23, 1825, d. Dec. 28, 1840.
F6440 JESSE LOCKE, b. Nov. 2, 1827, m. 1st, SARAH JOHNSON; m. 2nd, M. F. J. WEDGWOOD.

F3066 Eliza Locke, born Apl. 14, 1802, died 1901, married 1818, THOMAS DAY, born March 20, 1792. He was a farmer in Biddeford, Me.
Children of 8th Gen. b. in Biddeford, Me.
6441 MEHITABLE, b. Apl. 20, 1820, m. COL. JOHN GOODWIN, who d. 1897, had: 6442 CLARA, who m. GEORGE STAPLES, and had a dau.; 6443 OCTAVIUS, who was m. and had a son; 6444 FRANK, not m.
6445 ALBERT, b. May 13, 1822, d. June 15, 1859, m. ADALINE PERKINS, had: 6446 EMMA; 6447 CLARENCE.
6448 FREDERICK A., b. March 29, 1830, lived unmarried Biddeford.
6449 MELVILLE C., b. June 2, 1839, m. MARY GARRISON, who d. a few months after m. He is a lawyer in Wall St., N. Y. City, no children.

F3067 Joshua Locke, born in Limerick, Me., Oct. 25, 1805, married Sept. 15, 1860, JANE L. WADLEIGH, born June 10, 1826, lived in Saco, 1908, daughter of Moses and Sarah. He was a traveler for forty-five years, during twenty-five of which he was in the U. S. Navy. He was three years in the Holy Land, a number of years with Dr. Livingstone in Africa, served through the Mexican War. Late in life he returned and settled down as a farmer in Buxton, Me., where he died Apl. 2, 1886.
Child of 8th Gen.
6450 SADIE, b. Buxton, Me., Sept. 12, 1862, m. Oct. 15, 1880, ALPHONZO WINGATE, b. Buxton, 1847. He is a machinist in Saco, Me., had: 6451 ARTHUR L., b. Jan. 21, 1882; 6452 ALBERT L., b. May 4, 1883.

F3068 Royal Putnam Locke, born in Biddeford, Apl. 31, 1811, died Oct. 24, 1864, married 1st, LYDIA HEWS, who died Oct. 1834; married 2nd, ANNA H. JENKINS of Hudson, N. Y. He started for California in 1849 but stopped at Milwaukee and engaged in business. In 1851 he again started for California, wintered in Salt Lake City, and arrived at his destination in 1852.

Children of 8th Gen.

6453 HARRIET BACON, b. 1850, d. 1908, m. JAMES ALGER, son of Rev. Dr. Alger. Had one dau.; 6454 ANNA, m. 1st. ———— ————; m. 2nd, ———— RICHARDSON, who is a bank officer in Brookline, Mass. Had several children.

6455 JOSIAH EVERETT, b. Castleton, N. Y., Dec. 15, 1859, m. 1879, FRANCES MAY CARPENTER, was divorced 1893; m. 2nd, 1895, MARY JANE (GREGORY) MARSHALL. He is proprietor of St. Charles Hotel, San Francisco, and had: 6456 FRANK, died young; 6457 ROYAL WILLIAM, who m. and had three girls.

F3071 Jesse Albert Locke, born Apl. 2, 1818, died Aug. 20, 1884, married Aug. 14, 1845, SARAH B. COOLEDGE, born Jan. 20, 1824, daughter of John and Mary, and grand-daughter of Joseph Cooledge who was killed at Lexington, Apl. 19, 1775. He lived in Limerick, Me., for some time and fifteen years in Portland. He then moved to Boston where he served several terms in the Legislature, and finally went to New York City, where he was a promoter of several enterprises.

Children of 8th Gen.

6458 JOHN FRANCIS, b. Newton, Mass., March 24, 1848, lived Calais, Me.

6459 EDWARD C., b. Aug. 20, 1850, in the publishing business, New Rochelle N. Y.

6460 GEORGE A., b. Apl. 22, 1853, d. May 22, 1859.

6461 EDGAR T., b. June 27, 1855, d. Oct. 16, 1880.

6462 JESSE ALBERT, b. May 12, 1859, m. Oct. 10, 1894, CAROLINE T. HECKER of N. Y., b. Apl. 24, 1859, dau. of George V. Hecker (the flour king) and Josephine (Wentworth), also niece of Father Isaac Hecker, Founder of the Jesuit Order in U. S. Mr. Locke was educated for the Episcopal ministry but ingaged in literary work in N. Y. City, had son: 6463 CYRIL WENTWORTH, b. Feb. 13, 1896, d. July 13, 1902.

6464 MELVILLE H., b. Oct. 26, 1860, d. March 25, 1867.

6465 JUSTUS VINTON, b. March 2, 1864, m. Chicago, Nov. 11, 1907, MRS. ELIZABETH (DOTY) COYNE. He is a manufacturer of carriages and automobile bodies in New Rochelle, N. Y., and lives in N. Y. City. He adopted: 6466 SARAH ELIZABETH COYNE, b. 1898, dau. of Edward P. Coyne.

6467 KATHERINE DEARBORN (an adopted niece), b. Apl. 23, 1850, # 3070.

EIGHTH GENERATION

F3073 Jesse F. Locke, born June 21, 1810, married 1st, Dec. 4, 1837, MEHITABLE GREEN HILL, born Apl. 16, 1816, died in Tonawanda, N. Y., Sept. 18, 1852, daughter of Charles and Martha (Green). He married 2nd, May 12, 1859, MARY ANN GWYNNE, born Aug. 11, 1834. He was a physician in Tonawanda, where he died March 12, 1861.

Children of 8th Gen. b. in Tonawanda, N. Y.

6468 ALBION VAN, b. Sept. 9, 1838.
F6469 MIRIAM DAY, b. Dec. 14, 1839, m. July 26, 1865, CAPT. LAVANT RANSOM.
6470 LUCY D., b. Sept. 28, 1844, d. Dec. 6, 1844.
6471 OCTAVIUS MASON, b. July 27, 1846, d. Sept. 17, 1847.
F6472 PAMELIA PRENTISS, b. Feb. 22, 1848, m. May 26, 1864, ANDREW J. HAUGHTON, M.D.
6473 JESSE FAYETTE, b. May 24, 1850, sailed in 1874 for Calcutta, India, and only one letter, dated that same year ever came from him.

F3074 Hannah Wakefield Locke, born June 1811, died 1889, married June 22, 1832, BENJAMIN F. DUDLEY, born Dec. 7, 1792, son of Trueworthy and Sarah (Stevens). He was a merchant in Kennebunkport, Me., and died July 10, 1869.

Children of 8th Gen.

6474 CLARISSA H., died young.   6475 CLARISSA H., died young.
6476 DANIEL W., died young.
6477 HELEN S., b. Sept. 1840, m. June 1, 1854, CAPT. IVORY GOODWIN of Boston: had: 6478 LEONORA L., b. ——, m. 1882, WILLIAM N. HUGHES.
6479 DANIEL W., b. Apl. 1842, m. HATTIE THOMPSON of Boston, was a sea captain in China trade.
6480 ISABELLA, b. 1845, d. 1892, m. EPHRAIM DRESSER of Chelsea, Mass.
6481 FRED, b. ——, died young.
6482 JAMES S., b. 1849, m. —— GOVE of Biddeford, Me., a druggist in Boston.

F3081 Simon J. Locke, born in Biddeford, Me., in 1826, married 1st, LYDIA TEBBETTS; married 2nd, at Pekin, N. Y., CORNELIA DANFORTH, who died in Tonawanda, N. Y. He was a poet, philosopher and druggist at Tonawanda, where he died May 13, 1864.

Children of 8th Gen.

6483 JESSE ALBERT, b. ——, d. Buffalo, N. Y., Dec. 13, 1897, m. July 11, 1888, BETSEY MEHITABLE RANSOM, who m. 2nd, HARRY KOLSETH.
6484 ALPHONZO, drowned 1865.

F3082 John S. Locke, born Jan. 25, 1836, married May 26, 1869, MARCIA CLEAVES, born March 13, 1838. He was an author, a historical writer, lived in Biddeford, Me., and died about 1900.

Child of 8th Gen.

6485 ALMIRA DUMMER, b. Apl. 6, 1871, m. GEORGE W. MCARTHUR of Biddeford, Me.

F3104 Martha Ann Locke, born in Barrington, May 7, 1809, married Nov. 1, 1829, BENJAMIN HORN, born Nov. 23, 1806, died Jan. 25, 1888, son of Jeremiah and Abigail (Tebbetts), and descendant of William of Dover 1655. He was a farmer in Rochester.

Children of 8th Gen.

6486 CAMELA, b. June 4, 1831, d. July 25, 1887, m. GERSHOM A. HORNE, a farmer in Rochester, had no children.

F6487 SIMON LOCKE, b. Apl. 3, 1835, m. Feb. 9, 1858, LYDIA PARSONS.

6488 BENJAMIN F., b. May 2, 1843, d. Dec. 27, 1889, m. Nov. 29, 1867, SARAH JENNIE MESERVE, who m. 2nd, EVERETT BLAISDELL. She had: 6489 WILLIAM ——— (?) by one of these husbands, who m. and d. in Boston.

F3105 Howard Locke, born in Barrington, Oct. 13, 1810, died in Somersworth, Dec. 12, 1889, married 1st, June 9, 1833, EUNICE T. WENTWORTH of Lebanon Me., born Feb. 20, 1813, died Oct. 8, 1852, daughter of Nathan and Lydia (Whitehouse); married 2nd, June 27, 1853, SUSAN W. WENTWORTH, niece of first wife, born Berwick, March 16, 1826, died Somersworth, Apl. 30, 1882, daughter of Andrew and Mehitable (Gordon). He was a grocer.

Children of 8th Gen. b. in Somersworth.

6489 MARTHA and six other children by first wife died young.

6490 EDWIN HOWARD, b. Oct. 3, 1844, m. 1869, ANNA HOWARD. He was in the Navy 1862-67, on ships *Ohio, Macedonia, Vandalia*, etc.; had no children and d. March 25, 1875.

F6491 JAMES ALBERT, b. Feb. 8, 1847, m. July 3, 1869, SUSAN AGNES HAMILTON.

F6492 CHARLES HENRY, b. Dec. 31, 1849, m. Nov. 24, 1876, HENRIETTA WILLETTE BLAISDELL.

F6493 EUNICE BELLE, b. March 26, 1854, m. Oct. 20, 1880. ALTON E. HERSOM.

F3106 Mary Ann Locke, born in Barrington, Aug. 31, 1812, died in Berwick, March 31, 1901, married JOHN HUSSEY, born in Acton, Me., May 5, 1810, died in Somersworth, Sept. 30, 1892, son of Richard and Alice (Thompson). They lived in Exeter, Me.

EIGHTH GENERATION

Children of 8th Gen. b. in Somersworth.

6494 OLIVE, b. Feb. 28, 1836, d. Oct. 17, 1857, m. DUDLEY GILMAN of Acton, Me., b. March 5, 1828, had no children; m. 2nd, LYDIA HUSSEY, and d. Dec. 9, 1893.

F6495 HOWARD E., b. Jan. 28, 1838, m. JULIA PERKINS.

F6496 MARY ELLEN, b. Aug. 3, 1839, m. JOHN G. ROBINSON.

F6497 JOHN S., b. Oct. 23, 1841, m. MARY E. BOYLE.

6498 ANN M., b. May 10, 1844, d. June 5, 1874, m. Oct. 20, 1865, PERKINS T. MOTT of Somersworth, b. Aug. 12, 1837, no children.

6499 HARRIET, b. Aug. 5, 1847, d. July 7, 1848.

6500 CHARLES M., b. Dec. 23, 1849, m. May 13, 1874, CLARA L. KELLEY of So. Boston, b. 1853, dau. of Freeman and Thirza. He was a pattern maker, had no children, and d. Aug. 5, 1891.

F6501 FREEMAN A., b. Jan. 23, 1852, m. Oct. 23, 1878, CELIA A. E. FALL.

6502 ETTA G., b. June 7, 1856, m. 1st, CHARLES MARVIN HODGDON; m. 2nd, ——— WORCESTER, whom she divorced.

F3108 Abigail Locke, born in Barrington, May 10, 1815, died in Somersworth, Aug. 10, 1897, married in Somersworth, Oct. 10, 1839, WILLIAM HILL, born in Strafford, died in Somersworth, May 1, 1893, aged 78-2-7, son of William and Polly (Clark). He was an undertaker in Somersworth.

Children of 8th Gen.

6503 ANDREW S., b. Somersworth, 1844, m. 1st, ——— ———; m. 2nd, 1868, ——— CHAPMAN; m. 3rd, in Great Falls, Aug. 19, 1876, FANNIE A. SMITH of Charlestown, Me., b. 1848, dau. of William and Phebe. He had no children, was a grocer, later a druggist in Somersworth.

6504 MARTHA, b. ——, m. JAMES EDWARD FRENCH of Moultonborough, had no children. He was collector of customs in Portsmouth, a politician and business man.

F3110 Sarah Olive Dennett Locke, born in Hollis, Me., Nov. 27, 1821, died Jan. 21, 1871, married in Somersworth, Apl. 14, 1850, BENJAMIN F. HILL, a carpenter in Somersworth, born in Strafford 1820.

Children of 8th Gen. b. in Somersworth.

6506 OLIVE A., b. Aug. 2, 1853, d. aged 6 months.

6507 SARAH OLIVE, b. March 13, 1855, m. Sept. 1895, JAMES B. HOUSTON of Dover, had no children. He is overseer of Beech's Soap Works, Dover.

6508 FRED B., b. May 22, 1857, m. 1885, WINNIE A. STANTON of N. Y. whose mother was a Locke. He is a railroad carpenter in Boston, had: 6509 SARAH MINERVA, b. Feb. 18, 1888.

6510 ARIANNA, b. Dec. 28, 1860, unmarried, was a kindergarten teacher in New Bedford, Mass., and Dover.

6511 GEORGE F., b. Dec. 5, 1862, m. Nov. 24, 1892, GRACE H. EMERY of Somersworth, b. 1868; He is paymaster of Dover Machine Co., had: 6512 DOROTHY L., b. 1893; 6513 CHILD, b. 1895; 6514 BENJAMIN F., b. 1896.

F3112 Ann Maria Otis Locke, born in Hollis, Me., Jan. 10, 1824, married in Somersworth, Apl. 21, 1847, WILLIAM S. EMERY, born in Limington, Me., June 21, 1819, died in Somersworth, June 23, 1876. He was a contractor in Somersworth.

Children of 8th Gen. b. in Somersworth.

6514 GEORGE ALBA, b. July 24, 1848, is unmarried and blind, keeps a store in Somersworth.
F6515 ABBIE, b. March 28, 1851, m. Oct. 28, 1874, EVERETT JEWETT STEVENS.

F3113 Thomas Dennett Locke, born in Somersworth, Jan. 23, 1832, died in Dover, June 27, 1893, married in Somersworth, June 19, 1850, SOPHIA S. CROSS of Hiram, Me., died 1880 in Dover, daughter of Rev. Aaron and Miriam (Lowell). He had an eating house in Great Falls in 1870, was a carpenter and horseman, owner of famous horse "Black Harry Clay."

Children of 8th Gen. b. in Great Falls.

6516 OLIVE, b. ——, d. aged 1 year.
F6517 OLIVE MARION, b. Oct. 19, 1851, m. Nov. 9, 1872, LEONARD A. MERRILL.
F6518 HANNAH BELL, b. Aug. 28, 1852, m. May 1, 1875, GEORGE H. FLINT.

F3142 Maria Malvina Locke, born in New Durham, July 2, 1832, married in Strafford, Nov. 19, 1856, ENOCH T. FOSS of Strafford. He died in Dover Oct. 20, 1876, a farmer.

Child of 8th Gen.

6519 ELMER M., b. Dover, 1870, d. Sept. 1898, m. there, Feb. 12, 1894, MARTHA J. SPURLING, b. Dover, 1873, lived in Dover.

F3143 Cordelia Jane Locke, born in New Durham, Jan. 20, 1837, married March 22, 1858, MARTIN VAN B. FELKER of Rochester, born Feb. 17, 1833. He was a farmer in Madbury, and died in Dover, Jan. 20, 1908.

Children of 8th Gen. b. in Barrington.

6520 GEORGE W., b 1857? d. Oct. 8, 1863.
6521 HENRY L., b. Jan. 20, 1859, m. March 22, 1893, ADDIE F. GARLAND, b. Dover, 1864, had: 6522 CLARENCE G., b. March 7, 1898; 6523 ELMER L., b. Dec. 30, 1900.
6524 ELLERY M., b. Feb. 5, 1868, m. Dover, May 7, 1890, ELIZABETH PAINE, b. Moultonborough, Dec. 30, 1861. He is a belt maker in Dover.
6525 SARAH M., b. Sept. 22, 1871, m. FRED W. LEIGH of Dover who d. Feb. 3, 1896, had; 6526 MARION F., b. May 25, 1890.

EIGHTH GENERATION 331

F3148 William Henry Locke, born in New Durham, May 25, 1835, died in Amesbury, buried in Dover, May 20, 1896, m. 1st, June 7, 1857, SARAH E. RUNNELS, born in Newmarket, Feb. 23, 1836, died May 24, 1856; m. 2nd, —————— GOLDSMITH of Lowell. Sarah was daughter of Daniel and Sarah (Watson). William was overseer in Woolen Mill, Amesbury.

Children of 8th Gen.

6527 WALTER H., b. Northwood, March 16, 1858, d. Aug. 16, 1858.
6528 GEORGE E., b. Northwood, Aug. 16, 1860.
6529 WILLIAM H., b. E. Kingston, Apl. 17, 1863.
6530 FLORA or CORA B., b. E. Kingston, Oct. 1, 1866.

F3242 Margaret P. Gray, born in Portsmouth, Jan. 6, 1832, died in Portsmouth Jan. 3, 1916, married Aug. 12, 1855, GEORGE HUMPHREYS, born Dec. 26, 1829. He was a skilled ship and house joiner and died in Portsmouth, Dec. 20, 1902.

Children of 8th Gen. b. in Portsmouth.

6531 CORA M., b. Oct. 12, 1856, died young.
6532 CHARLES W., b. Jan. 12, 1859, m. Sept. 29, 1890, LYDIA A. SHANNON, and had: 6533 JUNE M.; 6534 STEWART S.; 6535 JULIA L.; 6536 CORA M.; 6537 CECIL.
6538 J. STEWART, b. Jan. 26, 1861, d. 1868.
6539 ADEL CLIFTON, b. July 26, 1863, died young.
6540 CLIFTON S., b. Aug. 29, 1869. He graduated Dartmouth 1890, is a civil Engineer in Madison Me., m. Apl. 20, 1894, GRACE A. COLLIS, of Portsmouth; they had: 6541 MILDRED J., b. Apl. 9, 1895; 6542 GRACE S., b. Oct. 30, 1896; 6543 PHILIP C., b. Sept. 3, 1898.
6544 GEORGE CLINTON, b. Sept. 14, 1871, m. Apl. 17, 1901, MABEL A. WALDRON.

F3286 Fannie M. Locke, born in Cortland, N. Y., Jan. 23, 1836, married in Wellsboro, Pa., 1852, LORAN A. SEARS, born in Webster, Mass., Feb. 11, 1832, son of Larned B. and Hannah (Rockford). They lived in Wellsboro, Pa.

Children of 8th Gen. b. in Wellsboro, Pa.

6546 FRANKLIN A., b. March 15, 1854, m. Weston, N. Y., 1881, CORA HEALD, who d. Apl. 1886, a merchant.
6547 WALTER J., b. March 10, 1856, a captain in U. S. Navy.
6548 WILLIAM G., b. Aug. 16, 1858, m. 1884, MINNIE LEWIS, is a merchant in Gaines, Pa.
6549 LORA A., b. March 7, 1862, d. Aug. 28, 1863.
6550 EDWIN L., b. Apl. 20, 1864.
6551 LEROY B., b. June 26, 1866.
6552 LOVISA G., b. Apl. 11, 1869.

F3296 Benjamin Locke, born Oct. 13, 1831, married Dec. 1859, PHEBE ANN PALMER, born June 2, 1835, died Jan. 17, 1910. He lived in Exeter, R. I.

Children of 8th Gen.
6553 BENJAMIN C., b. ——, m. CARRIE F. EDWARDS, later was divorced, had: 6554 WILLIAM H.
6555 MARY F., b. ——.

F3297 Thomas Tanner Locke, born May 15, 1834, married March 11, 1860, SARAH M. CATER, born June 22, 1843. He was a deacon in, and published the history of, Queens River Church, 1883; lived in Usquepaug, R. I.

Children of 8th Gen.
6556 NELLIE B., b. June 5, 1862, m. June 27, 1881, CHARLES D. KENYON, b. July 28, 1861, had: 6557 THOMAS H.; 6558 CHARLES C.; 6559 ARCHIBALD B.
6560 HATTIE L., b. Nov. 13, 1864, d. Apl. 5, 1890, m. Nov. 16, 1886, JAMES A. BURDICK, had: 6561 GERTRUDE A.; 6562 JAMES L.

F3308 Wateann Locke, born in South Kingston, R. I., Apl. 19, 1835, died in Nebraska, married May 15, 1859, GEORGE ABEL PEASE, born in Oak Orchard, N. Y., June 18, 1830, died in Fairburg, Neb., March 4, 1889. He was a Calvanist Baptist minister, ordained Nov. 1856. His first pastorate was in Berlin, Ill.

Children of 8th Gen.
6563 GEORGE ALMON, b. Aug. 10, 1861, d. March 2, 1869.
6564 MINNIE MARION, b. Oct. 21, 1863.
6565 WINNIE WINSOME, b. twin with last, d. May 31, 1880.
6566 AUTUMN VINE, b. Sept. 14, 1866, m. Nov. 19, 1894, SARAH ELIZABETH BROWN.
6567 ALICE CARY, b. Aug. 31, 1871, m. Oct. 14, 1896, CHARLES HESS GROSS.
6568 CICADA LILY, b. Nov. 13, 1874, d. 1875.

F3309 Pardon T. Locke, born in So. Kingston, R. I., Oct. 10, 1839, married 1st, in Berlin, Ill., Sept. 15, 1859, JENNIE ODER, born in Indiana, Aug. 20, 1841, died July 13, 1887; married 2nd, Nov. 1, 1888, JOSIE H. HUNDLEY. He lives in Springfield, Mo., in 1915.

Children of 8th Gen.
6569 CHARLES EDWIN, b. Sept. 23, 1861, was principal of school in Tama, Iowa, but is unknown there in 1915.
6570 ARTHUR ROSS, b. July 21, 1864, d. ——.
6571 MARION B., b. Jan. 10, 1866.

EIGHTH GENERATION

6572 FLORENCE JUNE, b. June 24, 1867.
6573 LILLIAN MAY, b. Sept. 18, 1869.
6574 ALMON FRANCIS, b. Apl. 2, 1871.
6575 NELLIE E., b. June 27, 1873.
6576 FREDDIE, b. ——, died young.
6577 CLARENCE P., b. June 11, 1884.
6578 MELVIN TREMAINE (child of 2nd wife), b. ——, d. Aug. 15, 1893.
6579 WALTER EUGENE, b. Oct. 10, 1895.

F3312 Charles Horace Locke, born in So. Kingston, R. I., March 25, 1848, died in Monrovia, Cal., July 2, 1898, married in Stonington, Ill., Feb. 24, 1874, HENRIETTA C. GARWOOD, born in Stonington, Jan. 17, 1855. They went to California in 1887, and lived in Monrovia.

Children of 8th Gen.
6580 BERTHA E., b. Cass County, Iowa, March 4, 1875.
6581 ARTHUR AUSTIN, b. Cass County, Nov. 18, 1884.
6582 CORENA STEWART, b. Cal., Sept. 1, 1896.

F3313 Sarah Jane Locke, born in So. Kingston, R. I. May 8, 1852, married in Atlantic, Iowa, March 21, 1875, JOSEPH A. PARK, born in New Jersey, Feb. 20, 1851. They live in Cucamonga, Cal., 1915.

Children of 8th Gen.
6583 JOHN ALMON, b. Jan. 26, 1876, d. Aug. 5, 1876.
6584 ROY CLIFTON, b. May 10, 1878, d. May 14, 1895.
6585 HERMAN EARL, b. Dec. 9, 1881.
6586 WATIE LILLIAN, b. Oct. 25, 1883, d. Feb. 6, 1889.
6587 CHLOE EDITH, b. Sept. 5, 1887.
6588 CLARE P., b. twin with last, d. same day.

F3314 John Edwin Locke, born in So. Kingston R. I., June 21, 1855, died Dec. 1, 1897, married Apl. 24, 1881, MARY L. BARNES, daughter of Calvin W. and Harriet. He was a farmer in Atlantic, Iowa.

Children of 8th Gen. b. in Atlantic, Iowa.
6589 MARY ESTELLA, b. Apl. 20, 1882, m. Dec. 30, 1903, ROBERT WALTER ALLEN, had: 6590 GERTRUDE E., b. Feb. 15, 1910, d. Feb. 24, 1912; 6591 MARY V., b. Aug. 31, 1913, lived Atlantic, Iowa.
6592 EFFIE BLANCHE, b. Jan. 11, 1885, m. Dec. 9, 1909, JOHN ANDREW HANCOX.
6593 JESSIE EDNA, b. Dec. 10, 1887, m. Aug. 30, 1911, MATT H. SMILEY, a farmer in Malcom, Iowa, had: 6594 ROBERT, b. Dec. 14, 1912; 6595 MARY L., b. Jan. 3, 1915.
6596 INEZ ROBERTA, b. June 4, 1897, d. Jan. 20, 1906.

F3364 Cordelia Pomeroy Locke, born in Falmouth, Me., Apl. 16, 1842, married Apl. 12, 1866, CHARLES D. THOMPSON of Sweden, Me. He died in Portland, Dec. 17, 1902. They lived in Yarmouth, Me.

Children of 8th Gen.

6597 CHARLES E., b. Provincetown, Mass., March 29, 1867, m. CORA THOMAS of Portland. He is traveling salesman, home in Portland.
6598 STEPHEN C., b. Provincetown, July 18, 1869, unmarried, a baker in Yarmouth, Me.
6599 PHOEBE M., b. Portland, June 8, 1871, d. Dec. 15, 1875.
6600 CHESTINA W., b. Portland, July 29, 1872, m. ELMER E. LOWELL of Portland, had: 6601 PHILIP E., b. Oct. 15, 1896; 6602 MARION R., b. Apl. 3, 1897, d. June 26, 1898.
6603 BERTHA L., b. Jan. 7, 1875, d. Oct. 15, 1894.
6604 FREDDIE, b. June 13, 1877, d. infant.
6605 HAROLD, b. May 19, 1879, d. infant.
6606 FLORENCE L., b. Portland, Nov. 29, 1880.
6607 NELLIE E., b. Oct. 8, 1884.

F3365 John Mason Locke, born in Falmouth, Me., Apl. 22, 1844, married 1880, NELLIE BRIDGES of Freeport, Me., born in Lincoln, 1861. He was a blacksmith at Freeport.

Children of 8th Gen. b. in Freeport, Me.

6608 PHOEBE MAY, b. Oct. 9, 1881, m. Portsmouth, June 5, 1899, EMERY DENNISON of Brunswick, Me., b. 1876, a shoemaker, son of John and Lucia.
6609 ELIZABETH, b. 1887.

F3366 Edward Howard Locke, born in Falmouth Me., Feb. 28, 1846, married Sept. 29, 1873, CHESTINA FREEMAN of Provincetown, Mass., daughter of John and Mary. He is of the firm "Locke and York" carriage mfrs., Portland.

Children of 8th Gen. b. in Portland, Me.

6610 WALTER IRVING, b. March 2, 1875, m. Dec. 1, 1898, ALMA LEVIN, dau. of Henry of Portland. He is ticket agent, Casco Bay Steamboat Co., in Portland.
6611 MILDRED HOWARD, b. May 23, 1878.
6612 MAE EDNA, b. Oct. 13, 1879, m. Oct. 22, 1902, GEORGE HENRY SPRAGUE of Fitchburg, Mass.

F3367 Stephen Brainard Locke, born in Falmouth, Me., Aug. 25, 1848, married Apl. 8, 1874, SUSAN JANE SARGENT of Falmouth. He is a sail maker in Portland.

Children of 8th Gen. b. in Portland, Me.
6613 HARRY WARREN, b. Dec. 19, 1874, was a music teacher and organist, Portland.
6614 ELMER GEORGE, b. Sept. 8, 1882.
6615 LESTER SARGENT, b. June 2, 1884, d. 1886.

F3370 George M. Locke, born in Falmouth, Me., July 17, 1849, married CLARA HASKELL of Portland, who died Sept. 20, 1897. He went to sea in early life, became master in 1876 and commanded six different ships, the last being the *Clara E. Randall* on which he was killed in Matanzas Harbor, Cuba, by a falling boom, Feb. 1, 1895. A well known and greatly respected man.
Children of 8th Gen.
6616 EDITH C., b. 1876, buried at sea, 1878.
6617 ALICE, b. 1885, lived Portland, 1899.

F3373 Leonard Standish Locke, born in Falmouth, Me., 1854, married EMMA J. HINES of Falmouth. He was a tinsmith in Windsor, Vt.
Children of 8th Gen.
6618 MILDRED EARLE, b. March 1873, m. WILFRED ROBINSON of Windsor, Vt., and had two children.
6619 RICHARD STANDISH, b. Lewiston, Nov. 1879.

F3421 Lucinda Jane Pulsifer, born in Alma N. B., Dec. 7, 1854, died July 1889, married July 16, 1883, JOHN N. CANNON.
Children of 8th Gen. b. in Riverside, N. B.
6620 WARD, b. May 1884, d. July 1886.
6621 LOTTIE BEATRICE, b. March 27, 1886.
6622 AMANDA MAY, b. Feb. 14, 1888.
6623 JOHN WHITMAN, b. June 27, 1889.

F3422 Eva Maria Pulsifer, born in Alma, N. B., March 18, 1856, married Sept. 2, 1891, J. J. DOWNING.
Children of 8th Gen. b. in Riverside, N. B.
6624 PAUL ARDINE, b. Dec. 13, 1892.
6625 PERCY GEORGE, b. March 15, 1894.

F3423 Laura Alice Pulsifer, born in Alma, N. B., Sept., 10 1858, married Sept. 26, 1879, JOHN FLETCHER.
Children of 8th Gen. b. in Alma, N. B.
6626 THOMAS TALBOT, b. Aug. 15, 1880.
6627 MABEL J., b. May 13, 1882.
6628 CLARA B., b. July 22, 1885.
6629 PERCEY W., b. March 16, 1889.
6630 JOHN C., b. March 2, 1891.
6631 ALICE L., b. July 24, 1897.

F3443 John Locke Herrick, born in Charlestown, Me., Oct. 22, 1854, married 1st, Nov. 16, 1880 in Boston, FANNIE F. LAMSON, who died Sept. 13, 1894; married 2nd, FRANCES O. PLUMMER, born in Dexter, Me., July 6, 1875.
Children of 8th Gen. b. in Charlestown, Me.
6632 JOHN H., b. Sept. 2, 1881.
6633 RODNEY L., b. Oct. 22, 1892.
6634 GLADYS (2nd wife's child), b. Oct. 10, 1897.

F3444 Mary Jerusha Herrick, born in Charlestown, Me., Nov. 22, 1855, married in Charlestown, Mass.,? Feb. 12, 1879, JOHN C. STONE of Brownfield, Me.
Children of 8th Gen. b. in Charlestown, Mass. (?)
6635 MARION E., b. Feb. 12, 1881.
6636 ELEANOR, b. March 8, 1893.

F3447 Susie Maria Herrick, born in Charlestown, Me., Feb. 6, 1871, married Sept. 14, 1890, WALTER A. DANFORTH. They lived in Bangor, Me., in 1915.
Children of 8th Gen. b. in Boyd Lake, Me.
6637 EARL H., b. Oct. 12, 1891.
6638 HELEN L., b. Oct. 5, 1892.

F3452 Oscar William Lord, born in Orleans Bar, Cal., Dec. 4, 1870, married May 17, 1893, LOTTIE L. RIDDELL of Eureka, Cal.
Children of 8th Gen. in Eureka, Cal.
6639 CLARENCE W., b. July 23, 1894.   6641 RUTH.
6640 MIRIAM R., b. July 7, 1898.   6642 ELEANOR, who died young.

F3505 Mary Elizabeth Locke, born in South Kingston, R. I. Aug. 6, 1826, died March 19, 1888, married 1st, Jan. 26, 1846, JOSEPH HOXIE, born Aug. 17, 1822, died Nov. 26, 1857; married 2nd, SOLOMON MATTESON, born West Greenwich, R. I., Aug. 15, 1818, died May 29, 1894.
Children of 8th Gen. All by Hoxie.
6643 MARY E., b. Dec. 15, 1847, m. HERBERT ANDREWS, b. July 13, 1851, lived at Blackrock, R. I.
6644 ABBIE T., b. May 17, 1848, m. Sept. 1869, GEORGE P. DYER, b. Aug. 14, 1845, and lived Phenix, R. I.
6645 JOSEPH H., b. Apl. 21, 1850, m. Jan. 17, 1871, PHEBE E. CARDER, b. Jan. 11, 1853, lived Phenix.
6646 WILLARD, b. 1852, d. 1852.
6647 WARREN L., b. March 31, 1853, m. Jan. 21, 1871, ELLA WHITMAN, b. May 1855, had: 6648 WINNIFRED; 6649 ABBIE C., lived Phenix, R. I.

EIGHTH GENERATION 337

6650 ELIZABETH M., b. May 24, 1855, d. March 1900, m. June 21, 1871,
GEORGE P. PERCE, b. May 1848, had: 6651 WILLARD; 6652 CARRIE.
6653 M. EMMA, b. July 6, 1857, m. BENJAMIN BATES, had: 6654 BERTHA E.

F3506 William H. Locke, born in South Kingston, R. I., Oct. 4, 1828, married Nov. 8, 1848, SARAH H. GAFFETT of Charlestown, R. I., born in Charlestown, Apl. 30, 1830, died in Rutland, Iowa, Jan. 11, 1899. He lived in Rutland, Iowa. He was a school teacher and a retired contractor, served four years in the Civil War, discharged 1864 as captain. In 1865 he moved from Rhode Island to Iowa.

Children of 8th Gen.

6655 WILLIAM H., b. Dec. 25, 1852, m. March 10, 1882, CARRIE McKITRICK, b. Nov. 10, 1862. He was a contractor in Rutland Iowa, had: 6656 MAURICE H.
6657 WALTER E., b. Warwick, R. I., Dec. 28, 1854, m. Nov. 12, 1884, SADIE FAIRBANKS, b. Oct. 10, 1860, lived Mankato, Minn., and was salesman for Fairbanks Scales Co.
F6658 ARDELLE MARY, b. July 15, 1860, m. Feb. 28, 1884, R. C. BAIR.
6659 BYRON H., b. Humboldt, Iowa, May 10, 1867, m. June 10, 1887, CAROLINE SHERMAN, and had: 6660 HAZEL; 6661 BYRON H.; 6662 INEZ; 6663 MUSIE. Farmer Rutland, Iowa.
6664 ALLA BELLE, b. ——, died young.

F3507 Edward Locke, born in South Kingston, R. I., Sept. 21, 1830, died in Apponaug, R. I., Oct. 23, 1906, married 1st, LOUIS WATKINS; married 2nd, 1852, MARY J. GAFFETT, born July 6, 1832, died Aug. 27, 1906. They lived Apponaug, R. I.

Children of 8th Gen.

6665 MARY S., b. ——, died young.
6666 CHARLES BYRON, b. July 17, 1854, m. EDNA SALOME BATES, had: 6667 BYRON H., b. Feb. 8, 1880.
6668 ATWELL EDWARD, b. Nov. 23, 1856, has a store and fish market at Apponaug, R. I.
6669 MARY SUSAN, b. Aug. 5, 1859, d. Feb. 24, 1883.
6670 ADA JENNIE, b. March 31, 1868, lives Apponaug.
6671 FANNIE BEWETTE, b. Sept. 6, 1869, m. —— ——, lives Apponaug, and had: 6672 ELBREDA GOLDIE LOCKE ——, b. Nov. 15, 1894.
6673 LILLA, b. ——, died young.

F3508 George H. Locke, born in South Kingston, R. I., Dec. 25, 1832, married Nov. 30, 1851, LUCY GEER, born Jan. 5, 1835.

Child of 8th Gen.

6674 GEORGE F., b. Jan. 21, 1852, m. Nov. 9, 1875, ESTHER J. COVILL, b. Feb. 11, 1849. They lived at Putnam, Conn.

F3511 Elijah Ferguson Locke, born in South Kingston, R. I., Feb. 15, 1837, married 1st, July 30, 1866, HARRIET N. CARTER of Warwick, who died Jan. 19, 1890; m. 2nd, Sept. 7, 1894, L. ISABEL SPRAGUE of Warwick. He was a fisherman in Natick, R. I.

Children of 8th Gen.

6675 MINNIE A., b. Dec. 21, 1868, m. 1st, June 15, 1885, JAMES A. BROWN of Warwick, R. I., who d. Dec. 11, 1891, had: 6676 HATTIE M., b. Aug. 11, 1885; 6677 JAMES L., b. Sept. 1889, d. Nov. 1891. Minnie A. m. 2nd, March 4, 1895, EUGENE A. DYER of Coventry, R. I., and they had: 6679 LILLIAN J., b. Nov. 30, 1896; 6680 HARROLD E., b. Sept. 27, 1899.

6681 HENRY B., b. Feb. 19, 1870, d. Sept. 7, 1870.

Second wife's children:

6682 NETTIE M., b. July 8, 1895.   6683 EDITH J., b. Nov. 5, 1896.

F3512 Phebe Locke, born June 22, 1841, married Henry ALONZO DYER, a cousin, born Apl. 29, 1833. They lived in Apponaug.

Children of 8th Gen.

6684 ROLAND B., b. Dec. 11, 1859, m. June 30, 1881, ELLA A. SLOCUM, b. Nov. 15, 1855, lived in Anthony, R. I.

6685 WILBUR E., b. Dec. 17, 1861, m. Aug. 24, 1889, JENNIE WILSON, b. Sept. 10, 1859.

6686 EUGENE A., b. Oct. 6, 1866.

6687 MINNIE LOCKE, b. ——.

6688 WALTER L., b. Apl. 26, 1870, d. Jan. 10, 1891.

6689 MABEL, b. Jan. 14, 1872, m. HENRY JOHNSON.

6690 ELIZABETH, b. May 27, 1875, m. FRED HARRINGTON.

F3513 Moshier W. Locke, born in Warwick, R. I., Sept. 8, 1843, died in Apponaug, Nov. 20, 1906, married Apl. 29, 1866, WAITY J. BROWN, born Apl. 7, 1849. He was a fisherman at Apponaug.

Children of 8th Gen. b. in Warwick, R. I.

6691 EVA M., b. Sept. 4, 1867, m. Apl. 22, 1903, CHESTER ALLEN, b. Aug. 31, 1872.

6692 ISADORA N., b. Jan. 16, 1870, m. June 22, 1887, CHARLES S. GODFREY, b. Jan. 5, 1857, and had: 6693 JOSHUA S., b. July 7, 1888, and he had son: 6694 JOSHUA, b. 1914; 6695 SARAH R., b. Sept. 18, 1896. They all lived in Apponaug, R. I.

6696 HENRY N., b. Sept. 20, 1871.

F3514 Eunice J. Locke, born in Apponaug, R I.., Jan. 27, 1846, married HENRY CORNELL of Attleboro, Mass., born in 1842. They lived in North Attleboro, Mass.

EIGHTH GENERATION 339

Children of 8th Gen.
6697 HENRY B., b. June 3, 1869, m. Sept. 6, 1897, FLORENCE UNDERWOOD, b. Sept. 1875.
6698 ORIN, b. Aug. 2, 1875. 6699 ARTHUR, b. July 7, 1880.

F3532 Jay W. Ames, born in Richfield, N. Y., Nov. 29, 1837, married in Richfield, Oct. 3, 1865, ROSETTA STERNBURG, born in Richfield, Dec. 6, 1847, daughter of Peter.
Children of 8th Gen. b. in Richfield, N. Y.
6700 SPENCER A., b. July 3, 1866.
6701 LULU, b. Apl. 16, 1875, d. June 28, 1887.
6702 LILA, b. May 12, 1888.

F3537 Lewis Clarke Locke, born in Columbia, N. Y., Jan. 15, 1845, married in Richfield, N. Y., Feb. 22, 1866, NANCY M. VANDERHEYDEN, who was born in Troy, June 23, 1850.
Children of 8th Gen. b. in Richfield, N. Y.
6703 SARAH, b. Apl. 23, 1867.
6704 GRACE AMELIA, b. Aug. 24, 1876.
6705 CLARA LOUISE, b. March 24, 1886.
6706 MILDRED JULIA, b. May 16, 1889.

F3538 Henry Lamott Locke, born in Richfield, N. Y., Apl. 24, 1850, married Oct. 16, 1872, in Edmeston, N. Y., THERESA E. TALBOT, born in Edmeston, Aug. 29, 1853.
Children of 8th Gen. b. in Edmeston, N. Y.
6707 LEE WINFRED, b. Sept. 6, 1875.
6708 LOUIS WARD, b. Feb. 24, 1882.

F3543 Martha Eliza Locke, born in Richfield, N. Y., Feb. 13, 1867, married in Whitewater, Wis., Nov. 28, 1884, ERNEST E. KNILANDS, born in Richfield, Sept. 16, 1861.
Children of 8th Gen.
6709 ROBERT DANIEL, b. Richmond, Ill., Feb. 13, 1886.
6710 GRACE MAY, b. Darien, Wis., July 17, 1887, d. Nov. 29, 1887.
6711 RUBY ANN, b. Oct. 20, 1888, m. Ridgefield, Ill., Feb. 20, 1907, WILLIAM ORMSBY, and had: 6712 HAROLD EUGENE, b. Apl. 11, 1908.
6713 RHODA GERTRUDE, b. Jan. 18, 1890, m. Ridgefield, Dec. 2, 1912, CHARLES H. ORMSBY, and had: dau. died at birth.
6714 RALPH HENRY, b. Delavan, Wis., Apl. 20, 1891, d. Oct. 6, 1891.
6715 HENRY R., b. July 21, 1892, d. July 13, 1895.
6716 DONALD E., b. Hebron, Ill., Jan. 21, 1897, d. Nov. 22, 1911.

F3551 Norman Reuben Locke, born in Palermo, N. Y., July 5, 1854, married in Canaseraga, N. Y., July 7, 1883, JOSEPHINE BLASIER. He is a grocery clerk in Utica, N. Y.

Child of 8th Gen.
6717 CLIFTON, b. Richfield, N. Y., June 7, 1885, m. Canastota, N. Y., March 18, 1907, WINNIFRED WARDSWELL. He is a meat cutter in Utica, N. Y., had: 6718 WARDSWELL CLIFTON, b. June 29, 1910, d. March 19, 1913; 6719 NORMAN ALDRICH, b. Utica, Sept. 21, 1912.

F3553 Frank W. Locke, born in Palermo, N. Y., July 10, 1859, married Oct. 7, 1882, CARRIE BUCHANAN. He is a carpenter in Herkimer, N. Y.

Children of 8th Gen.
6720 HENRY, b. Richfield, N. Y., Jan. 23, 1883, lives Herkimer, N. Y., 1915.
6721 FLORENCE, b. May 14, 1891, m. J. G. BUSHNELL, a civil engineer of Herkimer.

F3554 Edwin Ansley Locke, born in Palermo, N. Y., Feb. 7, 1863, married in Richfield, May 10, 1886, LENNA BLASIER. He is a mail-carrier Canastota, N. Y.

Children of 8th Gen.
F6722 BENJAMIN HARRISON, b. Sept. 2, 1887, m. Oct. 5, 1907, MARY MATILDA KIMBALL.
6723 EDWIN NORMAN, b. Canastota, May 14, 1898, a student in Canastota High School 1915.

F3555 Clara May Locke, born in Richfield, Aug. 11, 1865, married in Richfield, July 30, 1884, EARL J. LOHNAS. He is a grocer in West Winfield, N. Y.

Child of 8th Gen. b. in Richfield, N. Y.
6724 LYMAN EARL, b. July 15, 1885, m. Jan. 7, 1910, BERTHA DAVIS. He is a grocer, with his father in West Winfield, N. Y., had: 6725 CHARLOTTE, b. Apl. 19, 1911; 6726 JOHN DAVIS, b. March 10, 1914.

F3556 John Francis Locke, born in Richfield, N. Y., March 27, 1869, married Jan. 4, 1893, DELLA HERKIMER, a descendant of Gen. Nicholas Herkimer. He is a carpenter and builder in Herkimer.

Children of 8th Gen. b. in Herkimer.
6727 STANLEY SYLVANUS, b. March 5, 1899.
6728 MARY ELIZABETH, b. Nov. 15, 1908.

F3557 Fred Getman Locke, born in Richfield, March 20, 1871, married March 23, 1897, NELLIE FLAKE. He is a farmer in Oneonta, N. Y.

EIGHTH GENERATION 341

Children of 8th Gen.
6729 SOPHIA, b. July 28, 1901.
6730 MARY ELIZABETH, b. Sept. 7, 1903.
6731 NORMAN A., b. Oct. 26, 1904.

F3558 Nellie Hayes Locke, born in Richfield, N. Y., Nov. 8, 1876, married DAVID JONES. He is a farmer in West Edmeston, N. Y.

Children of 8th Gen.
6732 CHARLES SYLVANUS, b. Richfield, N. Y., May 17, 1897.
6733 FRED ANSLEY, b. West Winfield, N. Y., July 29, 1898.
6734 PEARL ELIZABETH, b. Bridgewater, Nov. 4, 1899.
6735 MARY ANN, b. Bridgewater, N. Y., Feb. 22, 1901.
6736 RAYMOND DAVID, b. March 12, 1902, died young.
6737 RAYMOND DAVID, b. West Edmeston, Apl. 19, 1908.
6738 DELLA IRENE, b. Brookfield, N. Y., Apl. 20, 1910.
6739 GERALD ALEXANDER, b. Brookfield, Apl. 1, 1914.

F3579 John Moore Palmer, born Nov. 3, 1821, married Nov. 1851, MARY H. LADD of Piermont, daughter of Timothy.

Children of 8th Gen.
6740 ROBERT N., b. 1852, d. 1852.
6741 MARIA L., b. ——, m. JOSEPH GOODWIN of Londonderry.
6742 NELSON H., b. Aug. 30, 1855, m. LORETTA GEORGE.
6743 ANNIE M., b. May 15, 1859, m. EMMONS BROWN, son of Trueworthy, and had: 6744 WILLIAM E., m. GERTRUDE WENSLEY; 6745 ELIZABETH M., m. CHARLES W. TAYLOR, # 6791; 6746 IRA NELSON, m. SARAH J. MORRISON, and had: 6747 HELEN.
6748 JOHN, b. Nov. 30, 1860, d. Dec. 3, 1860.
6749 ADDIE J., b. July 26, 1862, m. URI A. LANE.

F3581 Lydia A. Palmer, born March 15, 1830, married Aug. 15, 1851, JOSEPH L. MARSTON, born 1829, son of Thomas and Mary (Bailey). They lived in North Hampton.

Children of 8th Gen. b. in North Hampton.
6750 CHARLES H., b. March 10, 1852.
6751 ELLA M., b. Nov. 19, 1855. 6752 EDWIN E., b. Oct. 8, 1857.

F3597 Morris Locke, born in North Hampton, Nov. 29, 1828, married in Exeter, Jan. 1, 1860, MARY E. Dow of Exeter, born in Lowell, Oct. 12, 1840. He was a farmer and carpenter in North Hampton. She died in North Hampton, Jan. 21, 1916.

Children of 8th Gen. b. in North Hampton.
F6753 ALBERT EVERETT, b. Sept. 16, 1860, m. Apl. 4, 1883, SUSIE A. BERRY.
F6754 WARREN ELLSWORTH, b. Apl. 3, 1863, m. Jan. 24, 1883, LILLA M. HEATH.

6755 EMMA ELIZABETH, b. July 22, 1867, m. No. Hampton, Jan. 10, 1889, JOHN W. BERRY, b. Dec. 5, 1867, son of Joseph E., and Annie (Loud). He is a carpenter in No. Hampton, had: 6756 LEON MERRILL, b. No. Hampton, July 2, 1889; m. Oct. 31, 1909, EMMA A. TOURTILLOTT, b. Somerville, Mass., Sept. 14, 1890, dau. of George A.; 6757 MARION EMMA, b. No. Hampton May 28, 1901.
6758 ELLEN SARAH, b. Exeter, Apl. 12, 1868, m. No. Hampton, Dec. 25, 1890, ANTHONY W. FRIZZELL, b. Chatham, Mass., Aug. 24, 1866. He is a cooper in Portsmouth, had: 6759 WARREN LOCKE, b. Portsmouth, Dec. 10, 1891.
F6760 SPERRY HERMAN, b. Jan. 22, 1873, m. Sept. 24, 1902, VERA CAROLINE NASH; m, 2nd Mrs. Rosina ———?

F3598 Sarah Ann Locke, born in North Hampton, May 21, 1831, married in Rye, Apl. 8, 1857, BENJAMIN W. Dow, born in Exeter, Sept. 24, 1826. He was a farmer in Exeter and died there July 16, 1909.

Children of 8th Gen. b. in Exeter.

6761 JOSEPHINE PLUMMER, b. Oct. 1, 1867, unmarried, a school teacher in Exeter.
6762 CHARLES HOWARD, b. Dec. 24, 1869, m. 1st, Sept. 23, 1896, MARY FULTON, b. July 12, 1869, d. West Somerville, Mass., Nov. 30, 1897, had: 6763 CHARLES H., 1897-1898. He is a lawyer in Boston; m. 2nd, June 22, 1905, INA F. CAPEN, b. July 18, 1879, dau. of Herbert H. and Edith (Parkhurst), and had: 6764 DORIS, 1907; 6765 RICHARD C., 1911-1912; 6766 BENJAMIN C., b. 1913.

F3601 Lydia Almira Locke, born in North Hampton, Apl. 20, 1843, married in Greenland, May 3, 1863, GEORGE W. KNOWLES of North Hampton, born in Stratham, July, 4, 1842, son of David S. and Eleanor (Leavitt). He was a carpenter in Exeter and North Hampton.

Child of 8th Gen. b. in North Hampton.

6767 HERBERT SHERBURNE, b. Oct. 9, 1866, m. No. Hampton, Dec. 9, 1896, EDITH B. RAND, b. No. Hampton, July 1, 1872. He is a farmer in No. Hampton, had: 6768 MARLAND DENZIL, b. June 13, 1900.

F3602 David Locke, born in Hampton, Dec. 1, 1824, died in Hampton, July 27, 1904, married in Hampton, March 28, 1847, NANCY B. PHILBRICK, born in Hampton, Sept. 19, 1829, died in Hampton, Aug. 20, 1887, daughter of Joseph and Betsey (Palmer). He was a carpenter on the Nook Road, Hampton.

EIGHTH GENERATION 343

Children of 8th Gen. b. in Hampton.
F6769 ELIZABETH ELLEN, b. Aug. 5, 1847, m. June 17, 1866, JOSEPH W. MACE.
6770 JOSEPH LEWIS, b. Oct. 13, 1850, m. 1st, Dec. 24, 1881, CLARA F. SPINNEY, b. So. Eliot, Me., July 1853, d. Hampton, Aug. 9, 1891, dau. of Nathaniel and Caroline (Leach); m. 2nd, July 6, 1892, MRS. EMILY H. (BURTON) CARRIGEN, b. Jan. 4, 1845, Dedham, Mass., d. Nov. 27, 1915. He is a carpenter in Hampton.
6771 CHARLES W., b. Hampton, Dec. 20, 1855, m. No. Hampton, Dec. 9, 1882, MARY A. PAGE, b. No. Hampton, 1863; A farmer in Hampton, had: 6772 MELVIN P., b. Dec. 27, 1892.
6773 ANNA L., b. Dec. 24, 1859, d. Hampton, Nov. 23, 1864.

F3605 John Sherburne Locke, born in Hampton, July 22, 1831, married July 9, 1865, EUNICE EATON of Salisbury, Mass., born 1845, daughter of Winthrop and Hannah. He served in 1864 on U. S. Ship *Vandalia*, was a farmer, lived next the old homestead in Hampton and died Dec. 19, 1906.

Children of 8th Gen. b. in Hampton.
6774 ABBIE FLORENCE, b. May 22, 1868, m. Nov. 12, 1884, FRANK COLLINS, b. Aug. 19, 1866. Lives Amesbury, Mass., had: 6775 FRANK L.; 6776 ARTHUR B.; 6777 JOSEPH, who died young.
6778 ALICE GERTRUDE, b. Oct. 28, 1870, lives Hampton.
6779 LEANDER MOORE, b. Sept. 17, 1871, d. Sept. 6, 1872.
6780 MABEL YOUNG, b. Feb. 7, 1875, m. Salem, Mass., Dec. 26, 1892, JOHNSON E. LANGILLE of Ossipee, who d. Apl. 23, 1908, had: 6781 JOHN SHERBURNE, b. No. Wakefield, Feb. 4, 1894; 6782 AVIS M., b. No. Wakefield, Sept. 7, 1895; 6783 MARY ELLEN, b. Everett, Mass., Feb. 8, 1897.

F3607 Martha Sherburne Locke, born in Hampton, July 27, 1835, married in Hampton, Sept. 7, 1855, IRA J. TAYLOR of North Hampton, a farmer there.

Children of 8th Gen. b. in North Hampton.
6784 EDWARD J., b. ——, m. 1st, NELLIE BACHELDER of Rye; m. 2nd, EVA DALTON of No. Hampton. He is a carpenter and had by 1st wife: 6785 EDWIN S.
6786 GEORGE E., b. ——, m. SOPHIA MARSTON of No. Hampton. He is a farmer in No. Hampton, has no children.
6787 SARAH E., b. ——, m. CHARLES PHILBRICK of No. Hampton, a tinsmith there, had: 6788 EARL H.; 6789 WILMAR LOUISE; 6790 EVELYN ARLINE.
6791 CHARLES W., b. Dec. 28, 1875, m. June 24, 1903, ELIZABETH M. BROWN, # 6745, lives No. Hampton.

F3608 Mary Louise Locke, born in Hampton, Apl. 16, 1837, married 1st, Apl. 1862, EDWIN P. PEMBERTON of Bradford, born Oct. 3, 1835, died Dec. 28, 1866, son of Jonathan K. and Mary (Payson); married 2nd, OLIVER B. SHAW of Sonoma, Cal., where he is in the fruit business.

Children of 8th Gen.

6793 ANNIE H. PEMBERTON, b. ——.
6794 HERBERT GOSS SHAW, b. March 23, 1874, m. ALICE KING WELLER. He is a surgeon in the U. S. Army, had: 6795 HERBERT WELLER, b. Dec. 16, 1902.
6796 HARRIE B. SHAW, b. Apl. 16, 1877, m. ETTA McGIMSEY, had: 6797 MARGARET LOUISE, b. Sept. 12, 1907.

F3609 George William Locke, born in Hampton, Dec. 26, 1839, married in Salisbury, Mass., June 29, 1861, MARTHA A. EATON of Seabrook, born there in 1843. He was a shoemaker in Seabrook.

Children of 8th Gen. b. in Seabrook.

6798 LESTER HERBERT, b. Dec. 11, 1863, d. unmarried, Nov. 16, 1910.
6799 HARRIET NEWELL, b. Oct. 10, 1864, d. Oct. 26, 1868.
6800 HARRIET NEWELL, b. Jan. 26, 1869, d. Feb. 4, 1869.
6801 HARRIET NEWELL, b. Sept. 9, 1870, m. Dec. 25, 1894, ADNA P. EATON, b. Seabrook, 1867, d. Sept. 1910, son of Samuel and Abigail. Lived in Lynn, Mass., no children.
6802 MARY JANE, b. Dec. 18, 1874, a school teacher.
6803 KATE LOU, b. Jan. 16, 1881, a teacher, Newton Upper Falls, Mass.

F3610 George Dana Brown, born Feb. 7, 1834, married RHODA M. FOGG, born Feb. 5, 1837, daughter of David and Elizabeth (Marston).

Children of 8th Gen.

6804 GEORGE A., b. ——.
6805 FREDERICK A., b. Nov. 5, 1857, m. 1st, Dec. 22, 1881, LUCY YOUNG, b. Feb. 7, 1862, d. Aug. 4, 1884, dau. of Enoch and Lucy (Cook); m. 2nd, Oct. 5, 1890, LIZZIE KNOWLES, b. Oct. 6, 1871, dau. of Charles N. and Ann (Garland) had: 6806 BESSIE; 6806a OSCAR; 6807 JOSEPHINE; 6808 ABBOT.
6809 FRANK P., b. JUNE 30, 1863, m. 1st, Sept. 13, 1883, CLARA B. BACHELDER, b. July 19, 1864, d. Dec. 12, 1886, dau. of Charles, had: 6810 LAURA. He m. 2nd, March 1893, EVA M. HORNE, b. Jan. 10, 1874, and had; 6811 HELEN.

F3621 Mary L. Emery, born in Kennebunk, Me., Apl. 29, 1814, married July 29, 1839, REV. EDWARD COOK, D. D.

Children of 8th Gen.
6812 JOSE, b. Kennebunk, Sept. 12, 1840.
6813 WILBUR F., b. Pennington, N. J., Feb. 17, 1842, d. Oct. 31, 1842.
6814 MARY E., b. July 21, 1845, m. ROBERT WRIGHT.

F3624 Stephen L. Emery, born Sept. 26, 1819, married CLARA GILMAN of Portland, Me.
Children of 8th Gen.
6815 ELLEN F., b. Charlestown, Mass., Dec. 15, 1849.
6816 CLARA MARCIA, b. Boston, Oct. 3, 1852, m. Dec. 23, 1873, CHARLES DUNBAR.

F3625 Hannah Emery, born Aug. 3, 1821, married Sept. 4, 1845, JAMES NEAL, born July 3, 1817.
Children of 8th Gen. b in North Berwick, Me.
6817 CHARLES E., b. Nov. 11, 1847, m. Dec. 10, 1873, ROSELLE BAKER and d. Jan. 25, 1877.
6818 CLARA A., b. Apl. 2, 1851, m. in Neponset, Mass., July 16, 1885, GEORGE E. CURRY.

F3644 Timothy H. Locke, born in Hollis, Me., Oct. 22, 1822, died in Reidsville, N. C., Apl. 20, 1891, married in Alfred, Me., Jan. 28, 1844, ELIZABETH LARRABEE NOBLE of Newfield, Me., born in Alfred, Feb. 2, 1824. He left Biddeford with the rest of his family and settled in Reidsville, N. C., where he was a carpenter. She died in Kittery, Me., Apl. 1, 1915.
Children of 8th Gen.
F6819 MARTHA E., b. Nov. 2, 1844, m. Jan. 25, 1865, HENRY G. MOORE.
F6820 WILLIAM F. FARRINGTON, b. Jan. 2, 1848, m. Nov. 2, 1867, GEORGEANNA WARD.
F6821 HELEN FRANCES, b. June 22, 1851, m. Jan. 3, 1869, ISAAC H. M. PRAY.

F3650 Thomas Dyer Locke, born in Hollis, Me., Dec. 16, 1822, married 1st, ELIZA ROBERTS, of Lyman, Me.; married 2nd, ——— Dow of Biddeford; married 3rd, ——— SMITH. He was a mason in Biddeford, Me., and died Oct. 9, 1854.
Children of 8th Gen.
F6822 JOSEPH WILBUR, b. Biddeford, m. STELLA C. RICHARDSON.
6823 DAUGHTER, b. ———.

F3651 Elizabeth Locke, born in Hollis, Me., Dec. 21, 1824, married ELEAZOR TUCKER of Saco.
Children of 8th Gen.
6824 MARY ELIZABETH, b. ———, m. 1st, ——— Foss; m. 2nd, ——— HILL.
6825 DAUGHTER, who m. and went West.
6826 DAUGHTER, b. ———.

F3654 John Fairchild Locke, born Sept. 23, 1838, died Aug. 27, 1900, married July 25, 1864, MARY E. BEACH, daughter of Augustus, born Aug. 20, 1843, died May 9, 1914. Farmer in Saco.

Children of 8th Gen.

6827 JOSEPH AUGUSTUS, b. Sept. 29, 1866, is m. and lives Edmonton, Alberta Province, Canada.
6828 LILLIAS, b. Dec. 10, 1868, m. Nov. 17, 1887, FRED J. STEWART, had: 6828a IDA MARIAN, b. May 22, 1893, m. July 31, 1912, LEROY SMITH and had: 6828b BERNICE SMITH, b. July 25, 1913; 6828c EDRIC F., b. Aug. 13, 1895; 6828d ROWLAND A., b. Dec. 8, 1898.
6829 HARRY C., b. ——, d. Apl. 2, 1874, aged 2 mos.

F3664 Arthur L. Smith, married 1892, Mary E. Rand.

Children of 8th Gen.

6830 LUCY GERTRUDE.   6830b EDWIN.
6830a REVERE J.   6830c WINONA MARY.

F3665 Samuel Wesley Locke, born in Belfast, Me., Oct. 9, 1827, died Feb. 7, 1857, married Nov. 20, 1853, AMELIA FRANCES J. WARDWELL, who after his death married DR. CALVIN MOORE of San Francisco.

Children of 8th Gen.

6831 CHARLES WESLEY, b. Dec. 24, 1854, is m. and is Methodist minister at Los Angeles, Cal.
6832 ANNIE MARIA, b. Nov. 22, 1856, m. —— JOHNSON.

F3666 Margaret J. L. Locke, born in Belfast, Me., Nov. 4, 1829, died July 13, 1858, married DOMINICUS DEARBORN of Saco.

Child of 8th Gen.

6833 JOHN B., b. Saco, Me., 1849, m. Ossipee, Oct. 15, 1894, MARY G. WATSON, b. Wakefield, 1854, dau. of Isaac and Etta (Fare). He is a carpenter in Ossipee.

F3670 Horatio Johnson Locke, born in Belfast, Me., Nov. 4, 1837, married Apl. 24, 1863, ANNIE M. DYER, born Sept. 24, 1839. He was a jeweler in Belfast and foreman of the fire engine company.

Children of 8th Gen.

6834 ELEANOR JENNET, b. March 14, 1865, d. Sept. 30, 1865.
6835 SAMUEL MERRILL RAY, b. Sept. 18, 1866, m. June 7, 1897, ETHEL WINSLOW KNOWLTON, b. 1873, d. Feb. 22, 1912, dau. of Frank B. He is a jeweler in Belfast, Me.

EIGHTH GENERATION 347

F3671 Julia Ann Smith, born Jan. 1, 1827, married Sept. 23, 1849, GEORGE LITTLEFIELD, and she died March 5, 1893.
Child of 8th Gen.
6836 BYRON, married LILLA HAYES and had: 6836i CHARLES; 6836ii EMMA; 6836iii CLINTON.

F3676 Caleb Locke, born Sept. 25, 1830, married Aug. 21, 1850, MARY JANE ROBERTS, born Aug. 28, 1835, daughter of Lewis and Susan. He was a farmer and brick mason in Hollis and died March 14, 1891.
Child of 8th Gen.
F6837 CHARLES F., b. Aug. 11, 1854, m. May 23, 1880, NELLIE A. STUART.

F3679 John Gould Locke, born in Hollis, Me., Jan. 21, 1837, married Jan. 10, 1865, MISS SARAH JANE HARMON, born Nov. 30, 1835, died Oct. 22, 1888, the daughter of Henry and Martha (Fenderson). Mr. Harmon was a prominent citizen, and for many years was chairman of the board of selectmen of Buxton, Me. Mr. Locke moved to Buxton, Me., in 1869, purchasing the Henry Harmon farm, which he actively carried on until a few years of his death and made it one of the best in town. He was a prominent citizen in Buxton, serving many years as selectman, and tax collector, was also a director of the Buxton and Hollis Savings Bank, also a Master Mason. He died Nov. 4, 1911. Mr. Locke married for his second wife MISS LUCY R. LIBBY of Buxton, Sept. 20, 1891.
Children of 8th Gen.
6838 HERMAN H., b. Hollis, Oct. 24, 1865, educated in Buxton public schools, and graduated in 1884, from the Gorham high school. He taught school in Buxton, was member of the school board, superintendent of schools, and chairman of board of selectmen. Dec. 27, 1906, he m. MISS ANNIE M. HILL, dau. of Samuel and Annie (Libby), b. Dec. 29, 1875, one of the oldest and most highly respected families in Buxton. He lives on the old homestead near Bar Mills, Me.
6838i ALBION B., b. Hollis, May 1, 1867, d. Apl. 7, 1868.
6838ii FANNIE E., b. Buxton, Feb. 27, 1869, graduated from the Gorham high school, and was a public school teacher, m. Aug. 6, 1900, ADELBERT A. PORTER, of Castle Hill, Me., b. Apl. 30, 1869, had: 6838iii ALTA E., b. Sept. 14, 1901; 6838iv VERNA M., b. Nov. 27, 1902.
6838v MARTHA OLIVE, b. Buxton, Aug. 29, 1870, also a graduate of the Gorham high school and a teacher, m. Apl. 5, 1899, WILLIS E.

PORTER of Castle Hill, b. Aug. 11, 1870; had one son: 6838vi HERMAN JOHN, b. Apl. 27, 1901. She d. Sept. 30, 1915. The above Porter brothers have been engaged in a prosperous grain business in Skowhegan, Me., for the past sixteen years.

6838vii EVELINA, b. in Buxton, July 7, 1873, d. Aug. 23, 1881.

F3681 Hannah Elizabeth Locke, born Nov. 12, 1842, married HENRY H. SAVAGE, who died in California.

Children of 8th Gen.

6839 HARRY, b. ——, m., had two children and lived Cleveland, Ohio.
6839aKIRK, m. and lived in Turtle Creek, Pa.

F3682 Ambrose Colby Locke, born Nov. 3, 1848, married March 4, 1876, HATTIE ABBIE BURNHAM, born June 4, 1855, daughter of Moses and Almira. He was a teacher now a farmer in Hollis, Me.

Children of 8th Gen. b. in Hollis.

6840 EDITH M., b. March 17, 1878, m. Dec. 5, 1900, LUCIEN L. CLARK, b. Aug. 8, 1876, now a lumberman and farmer in Hollis, had: 6840i KENNETH LOCKE, Oct. 7, 1902; 6840ii BEATRICE, b. June 6, 1905; 6840iii LAUREN FRANKLIN, b. June 13, 1907; 6840iv HARVEY AMBROSE, b. Sept. 1, 1910; 6840v NORMAN ELTON, b. July 11, 1915.
6840vi EVERETT, b. March 12, 1882, lives in HOLLIS, Me.

F3683 Joseph Alvah Locke, born in Hollis, Me., Dec. 25, 1842, married in Portland, Aug. 27, 1873, FLORENCE E. PERLEY, born Sept. 27, 1854, daughter of Joseph and Ruth (Merrill).

Hon. Joseph A. Locke, one of the best beloved citizens of Portland, Me., died at his home April 21, 1904, the result of overwork. Born in Hollis, he moved in childhood to Biddeford where he fitted for college, graduating from Bowdoin in 1865 with high honors, being salutatorian of his class. After graduation he taught a few years in the Portland high school in charge of Greek, Latin and chemistry, meanwhile pursuing his law studies. He was admitted to practice in 1868 and settled in Portland, where he had a large practice. In 1880 his brother joined him under the name of Locke & Locke. Mr. Locke was frequently honored with official positions, in all of which he acquitted himself with great credit. He was elected to the Legislature in 1877–1878, serving on the Judiciary Committee each time. In the 1879 election he was the only Republican representative out of five elected from Portland. He was nominated by his party for speaker but was defeated by combination of Democrats and

Greenbackers. The next year he was elected to the state senate and chosen president of the same, which act was repeated in 1881. He was then elected twice on the governor's council. In Free Masonry he achieved the highest rank, being elected in 1884 in Detroit, sovereign grand inspector of the 33rd degree of Scottish Rite Masonry and, had he lived a few months longer, he would have been elected captain-general of the Grand Commandery of Knights Templar of the United States, in all cases going through the regular offices. He was a leading active member of the Methodist Church, and a member of Maine Historical and Genealogical societies, etc. The city and state has lost a man exemplary in every condition of life.

Children of 8th Gen. b. in Portland, Me.
6841 HARROLD, b. June 24, 1874, d. Sept. 5, 1874.
6842 GRACE PERLEY, b. Oct. 21, 1875, graduated A. B., Bryn Mawr College, 1898, A. M. 1899.
6842aALFRED, b. Apl. 9, 1878, d. Portland, Aug. 27, 1880.
6843 JOHN RICHARDS, b. July 10, 1880, Harvard College, 1901, A. M. 1902, Law school 1905.
6844 ALLEN STEPHEN, b. June 7, 1885, Harvard graduate.
6845 JOSEPH ALVAH, b. Jan. 3, 1889.

F3689 Lizzie Frances Decker, born in Hallowell, Me., Sept. 25, 1843, married Oct. 11, 1865, GEORGE WEBBER HUBBARD, born Sept. 18, 1842. They lived in Worcester, Mass.

Children of 8th Gen.
6846 GEORGE WALTER, b. Nov. 8, 1868, m. Nov. 7, 1893, ALMA L. COLLINS, b. Hammonton, N. J., Nov. 20, 1868, had: 6846a DORIS A., b. Feb. 28, 1895.
6847 LOTTIE MARIA, b. Nov. 8, 1872.
6848 ADDIE ESTEY, b. Nov. 30, 1874.

F3690 Alonzo Stephens Locke, born in Waltham, Mass., Nov. 13, 1847, married in Waltham, June 13, 1878, CLARA ISABEL PRATT of Waltham, born in North Chelmsford, Feb. 14, 1849, died Oct. 26, 1902, daughter of William and Letitia M. He attended the schools of Waltham, and graduating from the high school he supplemented this with a short course of two years at the Institute of Technology. His father was superintendent of the gas company up to 1874, and Alonzo assisted him in his spare time. He afterwards entered the employ of the American Watch Company in the Nashua department, and continued in their employ until failing health prevented further labor. He was a member of long standing in the Universalist Church, and for many years was its parish clerk, his resignation being accepted only when the performance of the duties became impossible. He was an enthusiastic member of the Masonic fraternity, joining Monitor Lodge in 1869, going through the various chairs until he became Master in 1892. He also was a member of the other Masonic bodies including Gethsemane Commandery, Knights Templar. He held the office of secretary in Monitor Lodge some fourteen years—a man of the most exemplary habits, always cheerful, and of the strictest integrity, making many friends and losing none. After a prolonged illness, caused by a paralytic shock following an accident, he passed into the eternal life Sunday afternoon Dec. 27, 1914.

Child of 8th Gen.
6849 ERNEST LINWQOD, b. Waltham, Mass., June 6, 1882, m. Dec. 31, 1906, LUCIA J. SWIFT of Waltham had: 6850 LINWOOD IRVING, b. Apl. 8, 1909.

F3695 William Pillsbury Locke, born in Waltham, Mass., Sept. 23, 1845, married Nov. 27, 1867, EMILY G. SHERMAN of Sudbury, Mass.

Children of 8th Gen.
6851 MAY EVELYN, b. May 16, 1871, lives unmarried in Waltham, Mass.
6852 JAMES PILLSBURY, b. Sept. 22, 1876, m. Oct. 7, 1903, ALICE S. GIBSON of Croton Falls, N. Y., had: 6853 AGNES DALE, b. July 19, 1904; 6854 WILLIAM PILLSBURY, b. Sept. 5, 1906.

F3700 Raymond Morris Locke, born Aug. 12, 1858, married May 2, 1879, JANE WHITET. He has been a San Francisco post office clerk since Sept. 1884.

Children of 8th Gen. b. in San Francisco, Cal.
6855 MAUD EMERSON, b. Feb. 17, 1880.
6856 ALMIRA LYDIA, b. July 12, 1883.
6857 ANDREW ROBERTSON, b. Aug. 15, 1886.
6858 HOLLIS MAINE, b. Jan. 20, 1890.
6859 CARROL DEWEY, b. May 10, 1896.

F3701 Hollis Maine Locke, born July 14, 1860, married Jan. 23, 1886, NELLIE RYAN. He has been a San Francisco post office clerk since May 1890.

Children of 8th Gen.
6860 FRANK STANWOOD, b. Sept. 15, 1887.
6861 RAYMOND F. TAYLOR, b. Apl. 5, 1892.

EIGHTH GENERATION 351

F3702 James Brown Locke, born Sept. 5, 1865, married Nov. 24, 1890, ANNIE FEATHERSTONE. He has been agent of Southern Pacific R. R. in several cities, and in 1900 was in San Leandro, Cal.

Children of 8th Gen.
6862 MATTHEW JAMES, b. July 13, 1892.
6863 GEORGE STANWOOD, b. Sept. 28, 1893.

F3703 Winthrop Bradbury, born Nov. 1, 1842, married 1st, Jan. 13, 1864, MARY E. LEAVITT, born 1846. They were divorced. He married 2nd, HATTIE PIKE. He lived in Hollis, Me.

Children of 8th Gen. b. Hollis, Me.
6864 WALTER E., b. July 23, 1864, m. ABBIE F. MESERVE, b. Aug. 20, 1868. He is a farmer in Hollis, Me., had: 6865 BLANCHE M., b. Jan. 22, 1892, d. Jan. 31, 1892; 6866 CHESTER E., b. Apl. 9, 1895, d. same day.
6867 HARRY A., b. Nov. 20, 1865, m. June 15, 1889, LOUISA B. GUILFORD, b. Feb. 5, 1871. He is a farmer in Hollis, Me., had: 6868 BRICE A., b.Nov. 16, 1889; 6869 RETA H., b. Feb. 19, 1897; 6870 a DAUGHTER.

F3711 Josiah Robert Locke, born in Mount Vernon, Me., Sept. 27, 1817, married in 1842, MARGARET A. STURTEVANT, born in Waterville, Me., Dec. 15, 1823, died in Buffalo, N. Y., Apl. 5, 1887. He was a carriage maker, and went to California in 1856 where he afterward lived. He first came East in 1898.

Children of 8th Gen.
6871 CHARLES LLEWELLYN, b. Waterville, Me., Feb. 3, 1843, m. about 1875, LIZZIE ———, had no children. He d. N. Y. City, Apl. 6, 1892.
6872 ABBIE ANNA, b. Calais, Me., June 7, 1848, m. Buffalo, N. Y., Aug. 18, 1881, JAMES BENNETT STONE, b. Boonetown, N. J., Nov. 8, 1844, lives Worcester, Mass., had: 6873 JAMES L., b. St. Louis, June 9, 1882; 6874 FREDERICK L., b. St. Louis, Feb. 7, 1884; 6875 MARGARET, b. Worcester, Aug. 23, 1891.

F3712 Adoniram Judson Locke, born in Mount Vernon, Me., May 27, 1819, died in Boston, Feb. 23, 1885, married in Boston, Feb. 27, 1845, CAROLINE PETTINGILL, born in Andover, Mass., Jan. 25, 1827, daughter of Merrill. In early life a carriage maker, in 1866 he was a dentist in Portland, Me.

Children of 8th Gen.
6876 FREDERICK AUGUSTUS, b. E. Boston, Aug. 18, 1847, m. Sept. 27, 1869, MARY LOUISE BUTTERFIELD, b. Bradford, Mass., Jan. 25, 1841, d. Boston, June 16, 1890, dau. of Charles and Louisa. He adopted one child 6877 CHARLES B. ———, who proved an ingrate, and disappeared. Frederick is a dentist on Boylston St., Boston, but lives in Quincy, as is the case of his brother following.
6878 EDWIN MERRILL, b. Augusta, Me., Aug. 31, 1848, m. Skowhegan, Me., EMMA M. KING.

F3713 James Grafton Locke, born in Mount Vernon, Me., July 11, 1821, died in Boston, Jan. 28, 1889, married HANNAH CLARKE, born in Topsham, Me., Dec. 20, 1823. He was a carriage and piano maker in Boston.

Children of 8th Gen.
6879 EMMA FRANCES, b. Worcester, Mass., Feb. 21, 1851, m. Boston, March 27, 1883, FRANK R. RICE of St. Louis, a tobacco dealer.
6880 ADA C., b. New Bedford, Mass., June 18, 1852, m. June 18, 1884, FRANK CROGMAN who is in the roofing business, Brighton, Mass.
6881 WALTER E., b. Portland, Me., May 25, 1861, is a musician in Boston.

F3714 Perley Whittier Locke, born in Mount Vernon, Me., Sept. 19, 1826, married in Reidfield, Me., Apl. 25, 1852, SARAH C. FISH, born in Starks, Me., July 16, 1828. He was the oldest citizen of Stark, in 1909, to which place he moved in 1852. He is a Democrat, a granger, and a highly respected man.

Children of 8th Gen.
F6882 JAMES ANDREW, b. Nov. 29, 1852, m. Dec. 23, 1875, MARY A. OLIVER.
F6883 CHARLES H., b. March 23, 1856, m. Sept. 8, 1883, LILLA H. OLIVER.
F6884 HANNAH CAROLINE, b. Aug. 9, 1858, m. Dec. 16, 1876, RUFUS JENNINGS.
6885 LUTHER P., b. Jan. 9, 1863, d. Jan. 28, 1863.
F6886 EUGENE PARKER, b. Nov. 11, 1864, m. July 3, 1887, CORA M. LEEMAN.

F3717 Christena Robinson Locke, born in Mount Vernon, Aug. 16, 1831, married Dec. 29, 1850, HENRY S. PARKER, born in Camden, Me., Nov. 28, 1829, died in Belfast, June 14, 1880. He was engaged in stage and livery business in Fitchburg, Mass.

Children of 8th Gen.
6887 EVA A., b. Augusta, Me., Nov. 29, 1851, d. Belfast, July 13, 1854.
6888 WALTER EUGENE, b. Belfast, Me., June 14, 1855, m. Auburndale, Mass., Oct. 31, 1884, GERTRUDE BENYON, who d. Kansas City, May 21, 1894. He is a real estate broker in St. Louis, had: 6889 HAROLD P., b. Sept. 12, 1887.

EIGHTH GENERATION

F3718 Charles Augustine Locke, born in Mount Vernon, Apl. 29, 1835, died in Swansville, Me., Dec. 6, 1872, married in Winterport, 1860, ELIZABETH R. ELLENWOOD, born Dec. 15, 1834, died in Swansville, Feb. 21, 1882. He was a farmer, painter and music teacher in Swansville.

Children of 8th Gen. b. in Swansville, Me.

6890 SADIE MAUDE, b. Jan. 4, 1867, m. Worcester, Mass., Nov. 19, 1890, FRANK E. BOUKER, b. Wilmington, Vt., May 18, 1856, has a book and stationery store, Fitchburg, Mass.
6891 CHARLES ARTHUR, b. Oct. 22, 1871, is in the soap business in N. Y.

F3719 Lovina Dudley Locke, born in Mount Vernon, Me., Jan. 29, 1838, died in Boston, Dec. 19, 1881, married in Belfast, Dec. 25, 1859, GEORGE H. FAIRFIELD, born in Waterville, Me., Oct. 24, 1837. He was a printer on the *Boston Journal* 1898.

Child of 8th Gen. b. in Belfast, Me.

6892 MABEL P., b. Feb. 3, 1864, m. Boston, Feb. 28, 1887, SAMUEL B. CROGMAN, JR., b. Boston, Dec. 14, 1856. He has a hotel in Ashland, Mass., had: 6893 MARY L., b. St. Johnsbury, Vt., Nov. 29, 1887; 6894 LILA F., b. Aug. 1, 1889.

F3720 Caroline Matilda Locke, born in Mount Vernon, Me., May 19, 1841, died in Bangor, July 28, 1880, married 1st, Aug. 5, 1859, GEORGE T. HERSEY, born Feb. 14, 1828, died in Bangor, May 10, 1874. He was a plumber. She married 2nd, July 10, 1878, THOMAS MYER, born July 31, 1830, a painter in Bangor, 1898.

Children of 8th Gen. b. in Bangor, Me.

6893 GRACE P., b. Dec. 23, 1861, m. Boston, Feb. 8, 1882, JOSEPH A. THOMPSON, b. Bangor, Feb. 20, 1854. He is a grocer in Bangor, had: 6894 ARTHUR A., b. Bangor, Nov. 28, 1882.
6895 THOMAS MYER, b. July 8, 1880.

F3722 John Locke, born in Mount Vernon, Me., Feb. 15, 1826, married BETSEY P. STARIN of Mount Vernon, who died July 22, 1905, the daughter of John. He died Nov. 3, 1903.

Child of 8th Gen.

6896 LELA S., b. ——, m. —— HUSSEY, and they had: 6897 JOHN FRED, m. June 24, 1912, in Salem, Mass., DORA M. VICKAH of Salem. He was called "of Augusta."

F3725 Columbus Judson Locke, born in Mount Vernon, Me., Apl. 13, 1832, died May 8, 1890, married May 1, 1853, RUTH HUSSEY WILLS of Vienna, born June 10, 1837, died Jan. 11,

1862, daughter of John. At the age of 16 he went to Natick, Mass., as a shoemaker, later returned and was a tanner and currier at Mount Vernon, Me. He was called Jud C. Locke.

Children of 8th Gen. b. in Mount Vernon, Me.
6898 WILLIS J., b. May 10, 1854, drove a shoe wagon through the country many years, later manufactured shoes in Mount Vernon, probably unmarried.
6899 ADDIE R. T., b. July 25, 1861, d. Milton, July 27, 1890, m. No. Shapleigh, Me., Nov. 24, 1887, FRANK N. CROCKETT of Milton, b. Nov. 7, 1867, son of Nathaniel and Dorcas E. (Welch). He m. 2nd, 1894, LIZZIE E. DONAHUE.

F3735 Charles Alfred Pollard, born March 10, 1828, married Feb. 8, 1847, OLIVE J. DURGIN of Nottingham, born Sept. 30, 1831, died Feb. 10, 1908. He lived in Raymond and died Nov. 14, 1907.

Children of 8th Gen.
6900 CHARLES ALFRED, JR., b. May 5, 1848, d. July 28, 1885, m. LYDIA ANN GOTHAM of Epping, had: 6901 ABBIE MAY.
6902 JOHN DYER, b. July 20, 1851, d. Apl. 14, 1914, m. ——— ———, had: 6903 LILLIAN G., m. Nov. 11, 1903, WILLIS B. GILES.
6904 ARVILLA ANNA, b. Dec. 3, 1854, m. Sept. 2, 1880, REV. THOMAS RICHARD ROWE of Providence, R. I., who d. Sept. 26, 1910, had one son: 6905 LEWIS EARLE, b. June 19, 1892.
F6906 LEWIS OSMOND, b. Dec. 13, 1860, m. Apl. 3, 1884, JESSIE MAY HAZELTON.
6907 GEORGE ADDISON, b. July 20, 1863, m. MARY B. ———, had: 6908 MYRTLE OLIVE, b. Apl. 30, 1895; 6909 DAUGHTER, b. Sept. 11, 1897, d. Oct. 26, 1897; 6910 BERNICE MAY, b. March 22, 1900, d. July 11, 1902.
6911 HIRAM LOCKE b. Nov. 19, 1867, d. aged 20 months.

F3755 Samuel O. Locke, born in Wellington, Me., Aug. 26, 1844, married 1st, Aug. 1868, CORA A. PEASE of Wellington, born Jan. 14, 1852, died Jan. 11, 1896; married 2nd, Feb. 27, 1898, MRS. SARAH (FLANDERS) EVANS of Cornville, born Oct. 6, 1842. He was a farmer and drover in Cornville, 1898.

Children of 8th Gen. b. in Cornville, Me.
6912 EDDA C., b. ———, living in Newtonville, Mass., 1904.
6913 CHAUNCEY E., b. ———, living 1904.
6914 CHESTER A., b. ———, living 1904.

F3769 Dorcas A. Locke, born ———, died Sept. 1899, married 1848 JOHN H. HILL of Augusta, Me.

Child of 8th Gen. b. in Mount Vernon, Me.
6915 JOHN FRANKLIN, b. 1854, m. Dover, Dec. 11, 1891, MRS. ELVIRA NEWBEGIN of Biddeford, b. Parsonsville, Me., 1844; lived in Biddeford.

F3771 Mary Locke, born Aug. 22, 1828, married 1st, Sept. 30, 1849, LEWIS F. LEIGHTON; married 2nd, June 12, 1867, WILLIAM GARROTT, who lived in Athens, Me.
Children of 8th Gen. b. in Athens, Me.
6916 ALMEDA, b. May 28, 1850, d. May 5, 1872, m. SEPT. 20, 1867, ASA JUDKINS.
6917 AUGUSTA C., b. June 7, 1852, m. Sept. 10, 1869, ALPHONZO COOKSON.
6918 FLAVILLA, b. Dec. 7, 1853, d. Sept. 8, 1855.
6919 FLAVILLA, b. Aug. 18, 1855, d. May 25, 1876.
6920 CHARLES, b. Oct. 10, 1857, d. Sept. 5, 1859.
6921 LEWIS E., b. Aug. 12, 1858, m. Aug. 8, 1883, LILLA KNIGHTS.
6922 KATY M., b. Aug. 4, 1868, m. Nov. 18, 1888, ELIPHALET COOLEY.
6923 CONY W. b. May 29, 1870, m. Apl. 19, 1898, MARGARET COFFIN, #6935, b. March 20, 1876.

F3774 Daniel B. Locke, born Feb. 11, 1835, died Nov. 28, 1904, married Jan. 21, 1855, AMY D. LADD of Starks, Me., born March 29, 1836, daughter of John and Mehitable (Quimby). He was a merchant of Skowhegan, Me. She died Jan. 7, 1913.
Children of 8th Gen. b. in Skowhegan, Me.
6924 NELLIE A., b. Oct. 25, 1865, d. Oct. 30, 1911, m. July 1, 1891, WILMOT B. WHITTIER, a dealer in live stock, Skowhegan.
6925 FRANKLIN P., b. May 3, 1867, d. Apl. 5, 1868.
6926 DANIEL, b. Nov. 4, 1870, d. Sept. 4, 1876.

F3779 Rosella Locke, born Feb. 7, 1839, married Feb. 18, 1859, JOHN LADD of Starks, born May 13, 1832, died Dec. 31, 1888, son of John and Mehitable. She was living in Starks, 1906.
Children of 8th Gen. b. in Starks, Me.
6927 EDWIN F., b. Dec. 13, 1859, m. Aug. 16, 1893, RIZPAH W. SPRAGUE.
6928 CORA B., b. July 18, 1861, m. June 20, 1885, CEPHAS R. MOORE.
6929 FRANKLIN P., b. Oct. 13, 1865, m. Oct. 16, 1886, IDRIS F. WILLIAMS.
6930 WILLIE L., b. Aug. 12, 1867, d. Apl. 17, 1868.
6931 HERBERT W., b. Sept. 30, 1870, m. Jan. 18, 1893, CARRIE GILMAN.
6932 CLARA M., b. Dec. 25, 1873.
6933 FOREST D., b. Nov. 28, 1880, d. Sept. 1, 1883.

F3781 Margaret Locke, born Nov. 8, 1844, married Apl. 12, 1869, WILLIAM P. COFFIN, born Dec. 6, 1823, died March 28, 1880, son of William and Margaret (Plummer). She was his 2nd wife. They lived in Winthrop, Me.

Children of 8th Gen. b. in Winthrop, Me.
6934 GEORGE, b. Jan. 19, 1871, m. Jan. 21, 1896, ALICE PERCY. He is bookkeeper in Hammond Beef Co., N. Y. City.
6935 MARGARET, b. March 20, 1876, m. Apl. 19, 1898, CONY W. GARROTT, # 6923, b. 1870.
6935aSTELLA, b. Aug. 24, 1877.

F3811 Guyon Locke, born in Lockeport, N. S., married AGNES CUNNINGHAM. Her father was killed by pirates.
Children of 8th Gen. b. in Lockeport, N. S.
6936 JACOB, b. ——, m. CATHERINE RINGER, had: 6937 HATTIE.
6938 ADRE, b. ——, m. JAMES MAXWELL.
6939 MARY ANN, b. ——, d. unmarried.
6940 MARIA, b. ——, m. —— LLOYD.
6941 AGNES, b. ——, m. 1st, —— TRYDER; m. 2nd, GEORGE HOLDEN.

F3823 Catherine Locke, born in Lockeport, N. S., married DAVID SMITH.
Children of 8th Gen.
6942 JACOB. 6943 DAVID. 6944 ALEXANDER. 6945 VERNON. 6946 CATHERINE. 6947 ELIZA. 6948 SUSAN.

F3824 John Locke, born in Lockeport, N. S., married NANCY HOLDEN.
Children of 8th Gen. b. in Lockeport, N. S.
F6949 BARRY, b. ——, m. CATHERINE MCKAY.
F6950 GEORGE, b. ——, m. JERUSHA THORNBURNE.
6951 JOHN, b. ——, m. MARY MAHONEY, no children.
6952 SAMUEL, b. ——, died unmarried.
6953 COLIN, b. ——, m. ESSIE ABBOTT, no children.
6954 JACOB, b. ——, d. unmarried.
6955 MARY, b. ——, m. JOHN ANDERSON, had: 6956 FREDERICK.

F3825 Jacob Locke, born in Lockeport, N. S., ——, married MELINDA WILLIAMS.
Children of 8th Gen. b. in Lockeport, N. S.
6957 GEORGE, b. ——, d. unmarried.
6958 ALBERT, b. ——, m. SARAH LLOYD, had: 6959 WILLIAM; 6960 FRANK.
6961 JAMES, b. ——, m. ELIZABETH LLOYD.
6962 EBENEZER, b. ——, m. CAROLINE HEWITT.
F6963 JOHN b. ——, m. LETTIE HARDING.
6964 BETHIA, b. ——, m. —— STERLING.
6965 OLIVIA, b. ——, m. WALT DUNN.

F3830 Thomas Locke, born in Lockeport, N. S., married ELIZABETH MCKAY. He was a mason in Lockeport.

EIGHTH GENERATION

Children of 8th Gen. b. in Lockeport, N. S.

6966 WILLIAM; 6967 SAMUEL; 6968 ANDREW; all three d. unmarried.
6969 HIRAM, b. 1860, m. Rollingsford, Sept. 15, 1888, JULIA B. HOAR, b. Princeton, Me., 1859. He is a moulder Rollingsford, no children.
6970 JUDSON; 6971 INA; 6972 ANCIL; 6973 DAVID, all four died young.
6974 IRENE, b. ——, m. JACOB L. SMITH.
6975 MARTHA, b. ——, m. THOMAS RYAN.
6976 JANE, b. ——, died young.

F3834 Samuel Bradford Locke, born in Lockeport, N. S., married PATIENCE CHURCHILL.

Children of 8th Gen. b. in Lockeport, N. S.

6977 WINSLOW, b. ——.
F6978 HOWARD, b. ——, m. SARAH BILL, # 7036. Lived Lockeport, N. S.
6979 EDWIN, b. ——.
F6980 PIERS, b. ——, m. MARY ALLEN.
F6981 AUSTIN, b. ——, m. ALICE TODD.
6982 MARY, b. ——.
6983 AUGUSTA, b. ——, m. WILLIAM MUIR.

F3835 Enos Locke, born in Lockeport, N. S., married 1st, ELLEN LOCKE, # 3859; married 2nd, JANE HARRIS. He was a ship owner and West India trader in Lockeport.

Children of 8th Gen. b. in Lockeport, N. S.

6984 GEORGE, b. ——, m. MARGARET LLOYD.
F6985 CHURCHILL, b. ——, m. Nov. 29, 1882, ELLEN A. MORTON.
F6986 ALLEN K., b. ——, m. ANNIE PHILIPS.
6987 JERUSHA T., b. ——, m. June 15, 1881, LAWRENCE EATON, b. March 23, 1846, son of Leonard and Elizabeth. He was a farmer in Lower Canard, Cornwallis, N. S., and had: 6988 JONATHAN L., b. Dec. 25, 1882; 6989 JENNIE, b. Feb. 26, 1884.
F6990 ELLINOR, b. ——, m. June 12, 1872, ALLEN T. FREEMAN.

F3845 Jonathan Locke, born in Lockeport, N. S., married BETHIA LOCKE, # 3868. He was a captain in West India trade, and lived in Lockeport, N. S.

Children of 8th Gen. b. in Lockeport, N. S.

6991 IDA, b. ——, lived unmarried in Lockeport.
6992 MARY, b. ——, m. FREAK RAND, and lived in Cornwallis, N. S.
6993 MAUD, b. ——, m. WYNNE JOHNSON, # 3861, who is a boot and shoe dealer in Lockeport.
6994 ELIZABETH, b. ——, m. DR. TERRY LOCKWOOD, and lives Lockeport, 1899, had no children.

F3852 Elizabeth Locke, born in 1810, in Lockeport, N. S., married WILLIAM STALKER.

Children of 8th Gen. b. in Lockeport, N. S.
6995 GEORGE. 6996 WILLIAM. 6997 CHARLOTTE. 6998 SUSAN. 6999 ELIZABETH. 7000 MARY E. 7001 LETITIA. 7002 FANNIE.

F3853 Letitia Locke, born in 1812, married in Lockeport, N. S., BRADFORD HARLOW.
Children of 8th Gen. b. in Lockeport, N. S.
7003 ARABELLA. 7004 LETITIA. 7005 ANNIE. 7006 EDWARD. 7007 MARY.

F3854 Ann Locke, born in Lockeport, N. S., 1814, married LEWIS CHURCHILL. (See F3878 for comparison.)
Children of 8th Gen. b. Lockeport.
7008 HENRY, b. ——.
7009 FRANK, b. ——, m. MINNIE CRONON. He is a clerk in Lockeport, N. S., 1899.
7010 JOHN, b. ——, m. —— ——, is a physician in Woods Harbor, N. S.
7011 ENOS, b. ——, m. HELEN TODD.
7012 JOSEPHINE, b. ——, d. 1890, unmarried.
7013 TRYPHENA, b. ——, d. unmarried 1897.

F3855 Samuel Locke, born in Lockeport, N. S., 1817, married ANNE CROWELL. He was a captain in the West India Trade.
Children of 8th Gen. b. in Lockeport, N. S.
F7014 JOHN, b. ——, m. ELLEN TOWNER.
F7015 HENRY, b. ——, m. LOUISA CONDON.
F7016 FRANK, b. ——, m. 1st, LOUISA KEMPTON; m. 2nd, EMMA McMILLEN.
F7017 EDWIN, b. ——, m. SOPHIA SNOW.
7018 ALBERT, b. ——, was unmarried; had a grocery store in Lockeport.
7019 ELIZABETH, b. ——, m. ROBERT EAKINS, lived Yarmouth, N. S., and had: 7020 NELLIE; 7021 JEAN.
F7022 ELLEN, b. Apl. 7, 1847, m. Jan. 1, 1869, AMASA FISKE.
7023 LETITIA, b. ——, m. THOMAS BROWN, a silversmith in Boston, Mass.

F3857 Jacob Locke, born in Lockeport, N. S., 1822, married EMALINE JAMIESON, daughter of Dr. Jamieson.
Children of 8th Gen. b. in Lockeport, N. S.
F7024 MARION, b. ——, m. GEORGE JAMIESON.
7025 JENNET, b. ——, m. WILLIAM BROWN.
7026 MARGARET, b. ——, m. DR. HARTLEY JACQUES, who was a Halifax Oil Co. salesman in 1899; had several children.
7027 SOPHIA, b. ——, m. —— WETMORE.
7028 HARRIET, b. ——, m. FRANK SHATFORD.
7029 BERTHA, b. ——, is unmarried.
7030 FREDERICK DON, b. ——, is unmarried.

EIGHTH GENERATION

F3858 Mary Locke, born in Lockeport, N. S., in 1825, married GORDON BILL.

Children of 8th Gen. b. in Lockeport, N. S.

7031 JOSEPH, b. ——, m. ANNA HAMMOND.
7032 CALEB, b. ——, m. CAROLINE BRADLEY.
7033 CHARLES, b. ——.
7034 JOHN, b. ——, m. ANNA S. MCKENZIE, had one child died young.
7035 HENRY, b. ——, d. aged 11.
7036 SARAH, b. ——, m. HOWARD LOCKE, # 6978.
7037 ANNE, b. ——, m. WILLIAM BENT.
7038 ELIZABETH, b. ——, d. aged 16.

F3866 John Locke, born in Lockeport, N. S., in 1830, married ELIZABETH CHURCHILL, # 3878.

Children of 8th Gen. b. in Lockeport, N. S.

7039 CLIFFORD, b. ——, m. MARGARET D. CLELAND, was a merchant in Lockeport and had: 7040 VICTOR, perhaps others.
7041 STANLEY, b. Lockeport, 1857, m. Goffstown, Sept, 19, 1883, SARAH SEETON, b. Mighers Grant, N. S.,1859, dau. of Andrew and Matilda. He was a merchant and had: 7042 RUSSEL; 7043 META; 7044 HAROLD.
7045 GEORGEANNA, b. ——. 7046 ABBIE, b. ——.

F3867 Colin Campbell Locke, born in Lockeport, N. S., 1831, married 1858, AMELIA JANE SHEY of French descent, original name Ducheyne. He was a West India trader, justice of peace and later farmer and stock raiser, in Falmouth, N. S., and died July 31, 1908.

Children of 8th Gen.

7047 LAURA CHRISTINE, b. Oct. 16, 1860, m. 1884, CLARENCE HOYT DIMOCK, son of Edward, lived at Windsor, N. S.
F7048 AMANDA MURIEL, b. 1861, m. 1888, COLIN CAMPBELL KAY.
7049 EUGENE MASTERS, b. Nov. 22, 1862, unmarried 1898.
F7050 JONATHAN, b. Sept. 13, 1864, m. 1892, BRENT ROBINSON.
7051 MILWARD, b. June 17, 1866, d. unmarried Feb. 8, 1907.
7052 EVANGELINE, b. May 27, 1869, m. 1892, EDWARD NORMAN DIMOCK, son of Edward of Windsor, N. S., no children.
7053 AUSTIN PERCIVAL, b. March 4, 1871, m. 1895, MARY SMITH BROWN of Boston, had no children.
F7054 MABEL JEAN, b. Aug. 11, 1872, m. 1894, GEORGE JOHN TROOP, JR.
F7055 FLORENCE M., b. Sept. 15, 1874, m. 1896, HENRY MARTIN BRADFORD.
7056 COLIN CAMPBELL STALKER, b. March 13, 1878, m. MARGARET ROBINSON of San Antonio, Texas, had no children.
7057 SARAH ELIZABETH, b. March 30, 1880, unmarried 1898.

F3870 Sarah Locke, born in Lockeport, N. S., married LYMAN CANN.
Children of 8th Gen.
7058 JAMES. 7059 ARCHIBALD. 7060 WINSLOW. 7061 ADALINE. 7062 LILLIAN. 7063 EVA. 7064 FRANCIS.

F3874 Elizabeth Locke, born in Lockeport, N. S., married. THOMAS DAME.
Children of 8th Gen.
7065 PETER. 7066 JAMES. 7067 LEON. 7068 FANNIE. 7069 ATTILA. 7070 MARY. 7071 ZEBIAH. 7072 OSCAR. 7073 INA.

F3878 Lewis P. Churchill, born Nov. 8, 1826, married in Lockeport, N. S., ANN LOCKE. (See F3854 for comparison of record.)
Children of 8th Gen. Probably b. in Lockeport, N. S.
7074 ENOS, b. Sept. 6, 1852.   7079 LEWIS, b. March 2, 1863.
7075 TRYPHENIA, b. Oct. 5, 1854.   7080 HENRY, b. Apl. 7, 1865.
7076 EDMUND, b. Aug. 7, 1856.   7081 FRANK, b. Jan. 14, 1867.
7077 FLORENCE, b. Sept. 11, 1858. 7082 JOHN, b. Jan. 1, 1869.
7078 ARCHIBALD, b. Dec. 9, 1860. 7083 JOSEPHINE, b. Sept. 15, 1871.

F3886 Nathaniel Locke 3rd, born in Newport, R. I., March 10, 1805, married July 1, 1830, LYDIA STANLEY HOWARD, born in Newport, June 9, 1808, died Apl. 3, 1854. He was a cooper in Newport and died Oct. 5, 1845.
Children of 8th Gen.
7084 NATHANIEL 4TH, b. ———.
7085 EDWARD C., b. ———, m. MRS. ELIZABETH G. PARKER, dau. of Elijah, in Newport, Dec. 29, 1841.
7086 WILLIAM HOWARD, b. ———.
F7087 EMMA AUGUSTA, b. March 4, 1837, m. Jan. 6, 1859, DUTEE WILCOX.
7088 LYDIA ANN, b. ———, m. HEZEKIAH D. TENNER, Apl. 16, 1864.

F3892 Reuben Locke, born in Epsom, June 30, 1807, married 1st, Nov. 13, 1828, ELIZA SHAW, born in Hampton, Oct. 10, 1801, died in Concord, March 13, 1867; married 2nd, in Concord, June 6, 1867, NELLIE VARNEY of Dover, born in Dover, 1848. He was a painter in Loudon, 1868, went to Ansonia, Conn., returned to Loudon in 1891, where he died Dec. 14, 1895.
Children of 8th Gen.
7089 ABIGAIL J. SHAW, b. Apl. 16, 1832, d. Dec. 6, 1832.
F7090 CHARLES HENRY, b. Apl. 8, 1833, m. March 4, 1855, SARAH A. WILLOUGHBY.
7091 MARY ELIZABETH, b. Loudon, June 23, 1834, d. May 14, 1839.

EIGHTH GENERATION 361

F7092 ANDREW DIAMOND, b. Sept. 7, 1835, m. AMANDA M. (SANBORN) COOK, Jan. 1, 1857.
7093 HIRAM ELLIOTT, b. Gilmanton, Nov. 11, 1836, m. Nov. 25, 1864, ABBIE M. LEIGHTON, b. Strafford, June 9, 1838, dau. of John and Sarah. He was in Co. E, 13th N. H. Reg., serving three years, later was a carriage painter in Pittsfield, had no children.
7094 THEOPHILUS SHAW, b. Gilm., Apl. 25, 1838, d. May 20, 1839.
7095 JAMES JONES, b. Gilm., Oct. 22, 1839; enlisted in Co. B, 3rd N. H. Reg., was unmarried and a farmer; killed at Morris Island, S. C., July 10, 1863.
F7096 ELBRIDGE GERRY, b. Apl. 30, 1841, m. Apl. 20, 1867, SARAH C. REED.
F7097 MARY ELIZABETH, b. Aug. 15, 1842, m. March 4, 1861, JAMES ASA JONES.
F7098 SARAH ABBIE, b. Dec. 20, 1845, m. 1st, May 30, 1863, HENRY N. BLANCHARD; m. 2nd, Feb. 18, 1867, GEORGE WORTHINGTON.

F3897 Abigail Locke, born in Gilmanton, Sept. 12, 1810, died in Lynn, Sept. 2, 1904, married JOHN ELLIOT TUCKER of Newburyport. He was a shoemaker in Lynn.

Children of 8th Gen.

7099 ABIGAIL, b. ——, m. WILLIAM PERKINS.
7100 SARAH, b. ——, m. 1st, GEORGE GILBERT of Boston; m. 2nd, WARREN GORDON, and had: 7101 CHARLES W.
7102 ISABELLA L. D., b. Newburyport, Mass., Apl. 7, 1836, m. 1st. ALBERT MERRILL; m. 2nd, Boston, May 15, 1865, WILLIAM HARRY PERLEY, b. Jan. 26, 1836, d. Jan. 16, 1899, son of John. She lived Saugus, Mass., 1906.
7103 HANNAH L., b. ——, m. —— HORTON; and had: 7104 LIZZIE D., b. 1871, d. at the Shakers, Canterbury, 1906; 7105 HARRY, b. ——, killed on the railroad 1903.
7106 DANA, b. ——, not married. 7107 LIZZIE, b. ——, d. aged 18.

F3905 Mary Jane Locke, born in Gilmanton, March 25, 1817, died Nov. 14, 1858, married 1837–8, ENOCH H. KIMBALL of Warner, born in Warner, Jan. 10, 1809, died in Groveland, Mass., Dec. 23, 1874, son of Asa and Phebe (Carlton). He was a farmer on the old homestead, Groveland, Mass.

Children of 8th Gen.

7108 MARY A., b. So. Hampton, Nov. 12, 1838, m. Jan. 3, 1860, ALBERT P. HOVEY of Boxford, Mass., b. Nov. 23, 1828. He was a carpenter in West Boxford, Mass., 1897, had no children.
7109 ASA HOWARD, b. Groveland, Mass., Feb. 23, 1840, enlisted 12th Mass. Reg. and d. a prisoner at Richmond, March 25, 1864.
7110 LOUISA H., b. July 16, 1842, d. Bradford, Mass., June 3, 1859.
7111 CHARLOTTE A., b. Feb. 9, 1844, d. Westfield, Mass., unmarried Oct. 18, 1878.
7112 HANNAH JANE, b. Nov. 22, 1846, d. Dec. 14, 1858.

7113 CHARLES W., b. Pelham, Vt., Apl. 13, 1849, d. Groveland, Nov. 23, 1858.
7114 ELMER ALLEN, b. Groveland, Dec. 31, 1851, m. ADALINE WOOD, b. 1853. They had three children and were divorced.
7115 FRANCIS LOCKE, b, May 4, 1854, m. MARY ———, lived Sodis, Mich., a farmer.
7116 BENJAMIN F., b. ———.
7117 HENRY ALBERT, b. May 12, 1858, m. June 27, 1887, JENNIE PETERS of Morris, N. Y. They were divorced. He was a travelling actor.

F3906 Eunice Locke, born in Gilmanton, married GEORGE W. WHITTIER of Danbury, born in Kingston.

Children of 8th Gen.

7118 GEORGE W., b. Danville, 1840, m. June 21, 1867, MARTHA J. HAINES of Penacook, b. Pen. 1846; lived East Kingston, 1899.
7119 CHARLES HENRY, b. Danville, May 12, 1850, m. LILLA HANNAH PAGE, b. Mechanics Falls, Me., June 12, 1856, dau. of John O. and Harriet. He was a shoemaker and barber in Hampstead, had: 7120 LOTTIE, b. 1884, m. GEORGE WORTHEN; 7122 GRACE E., b. 1887; 7123 LEWIS B., b. 1889; 7124 JACOB H., b. 1902.
7125 Another son and another daughter.

F3907 Drusilla Locke, born in Gilmanton, Dec. 23, 1821, died a widow, in Fremont, March 25, 1895, married WILLIAM PEASLEE of Newton, Mass., born in Kingston.

Children of 8th Gen.

7126 CHARLOTTE ANN, b. ———.
7127 ALBERT, b. ———, m. ——— WHITTIER, was an evangelist.
7128 MELVIN, b. Newton, 1866, m. June 16, 1900, LILLIAN DAVIS WARNER of Newton, b. N. Y. City, 1870, his 2nd marriage.

F3908 Hannah Stevens Locke, born in Gilmanton, 1831, died in Boscawen, Feb. 4, 1897, married CHARLES H. CURRIER of Boscawen.

Children of 8th Gen.

7129 IDA, b. ———, m. ——— PROVO, lived West Concord.
7130 MATTIE, b. ———, m. ——— ———, lived West Concord.
7131 CHARLES, b. ———. 7132 FRANK, b. ———.

F3916 Ephraim Locke, born in Epsom, May 4, 1809, died in Epsom, Aug. 12, 1892, married in Epsom, Jan. 19, 1835, SARAH CRAM DYER, born in Nottingham, Oct. 18, 1805, died in Suncook, Jan. 10, 1884, daughter of Rev. Samuel B. and Abigail (Fogg). She was a highly esteemed Christian lady. He was a farmer, took a business course in North Hampton Academy, went to

Suncook in 1874, and then back to Epsom in 1890. He was respected by the townsmen, having been elected representative, town treasurer, and selectman several years.

Children of 8th Gen. b. in Epsom.

F7133 ANN LYDIA, b. July 28, 1839, m. May 16, 1860, WINTHROP FOWLER.

7134 RUHUMA JANE, b. Aug. 12, 1841, d. Epsom, Feb. 1, 1915, m. Epsom, Jan. 15, 1868, JAMES W. FOWLER, b. Pembroke, Dec. 10, 1844, son of Samuel and Elvira (Crichett). They lived in Epsom, were Grangers and members of Free Will Baptist Church, had no children.

F3917 Eliza T. Locke, born in Epsom, May 30, 1811, died in Hillsdale, Mich., Nov. 24, 1891, married Apl. 21, 1832, SAMUEL B. DYER of Ohio, born Apl. 13, 1808. They lived in Hillsdale, and he died there Feb. 9, 1897.

Children of 8th Gen.

7135 JENNIE, b. Abbaville, O., July 12, 1838, m. June 8, 1869, SYLVESTER F. DWIGHT, b. Woodhill, N. Y., March 27, 1836, son of Sylvester and Elizabeth (Stewart). Lives in Hillsdale, Mich., 1898. No children.

7136 ADDIE, b. Medina, O., Dec. 15, 1845, d. Washington, D. C., Sept. 3, 1887, m. Oct. 28, 1874, JOHN EASTWOOD, b. Aug. 29, 1841, d. Hillsdale, Mich., Apl. 4, 1889, had no children.

F3918 Mary S. Locke, born in Epsom, June 11, 1813, died March 11, 1882, married Dec. 1, 1836 (Jan. 21, 1837), CAPT. SAMUEL WELLS, of Epsom, born in Allenstown, Sept. 11, 1801. They lived in Pittsfield, and he died in Epsom.

Children of 8th Gen.

7137 SARAH A., b. Oct. 17, 1837, m. May 29, 1869, FRANK P. RICHER, b. Alton, July 15, 1847, lived in Epsom 1898, no children.

F7138 MARY E., b. Aug. 14, 1845, m. Oct. 8, 1863, JAMES S. STRAW.

F3919 Margaret K. Locke, born in Epsom, Feb. 17, 1817, married Apl. 8, 1841, ABRAM D. SWAIN, of Chichester, and lived in Michigan.

Children of 8th Gen.

7139 SILAS L., b. Aug. 12, 1846, d. Epsom, Aug. 28, 1846.

7140 SILAS L., b. Epsom, Feb. 19, 1848, lived unmarried Roselawn, Indiana.

7141 DAUGHTER, b. Apl. 5, 1842, d. same day.

7142 ARETUS D., b. Spencer, O., Dec. 5, 1856, m. Nov. 8, 1876, JESSE F. BURNHAM, b. Biddeford, Me., Apl. 8, 1855; lives Morocco, Ind., had: 7143 CARL F., b. June 27, 1878, d. July 20, 1896; 7144 LESLIE R., b. Feb. 2, 1881, d. March 26, 1885.

F3927 David M. Philbrick, born in Epsom, Aug. 26, 1823, married SARAH STEARNS.

Children of 8th Gen.
7145 CLARA J., b. ——, m. FRANK BUFFAM.
7146 DANIEL, b. Aug. 12, 1854.
7147 DAVID, b. Feb. 14, 1857, died young.
7148 MARY A., b. Sept. 29, 1858, m. GEORGE GILES.
7149 JOHN S., b. Sept. 26, 1860, m. ELIZA PHILBRICK.
7150 SUSAN, b. June 24, 1864, m. WILLIAM A. EDMONDS.
7151 GEORGE H., b. March 3, 1865.
7152 AUGUSTUS T., b. Apl. 7, 1867.

F3932 Arthur Caverno Locke, born in Epsom, Oct. 15, 1824, died in Epsom, May 10, 1884, married in Epsom, Sept. 23, 1847, SALINA O. BICKFORD, born in Epsom, 1830, died in Epsom, June 16, 1877, daughter of Nathan and Eliza. He was 1st Lieut. Co., E, 11th N. H. Reg. in 1862, was promoted to captain and was wounded Sept. 1864.

Children of 8th Gen. b. in Epsom.
7153 TRUMAN RANSOM, b. March 20, 1848, was unmarried, a merchant and d. in Leadville, Col., Oct. 6, 1878.
7154 FRANK I., b. Nov. 3, 1850, is unmarried, and a shoe dealer.
7155 SARAH, b. Nov. 23, 1853, died young.
7156 DANIEL LINCOLN, b. Apl. 23, 1860, m. Chichester, Oct. 1, 1884, LIZZIE L. HOIT of Epsom, b. Weare, 1863, dau. of Horace and Betsey (Gove). He was a doctor and d. N. H. Asylum, Aug. 28, 1889, had son: 7157 WILLIAM L., b. Oct. 2, 1888. His widow m. 2nd, DR. FRANK EATON of East Weare, 1891.

F3933 Sarah Emaline Locke, born in Epsom, Nov. 11, 1826, married Oct. 10, 1843, Joseph H. VEAZEY, born 1821, son of Benning and Jennette (Tilton). They lived in Epsom. She died Sept. 16, 1908.

Child of 8th Gen.
7158 MARY T., b. Sept. 25, 1864, m. J. A. TOWLE, and lived Chelsea, Mass.

F3937 Worthington Smith Locke, born in St. Albans, Vt., May 19, 1827, married Dec. 31, 1849, SARAH E. HOBBS of Camden, Me., born in Camden, May 25, 1822. He was in the dry goods business in Portland but spent his last years in Pittston, Pa., where he died June 1908. She died Pittston, Sept. 12, 1892.

Children of 8th Gen. b. in Boston.
7159 JULIA E., b. Sept. 26, 1852, d. Boston, Sept. 26, 1911, m. JUDD HEWITT, lived in Pittston, Pa., and had: 7160 CURTIS; 7161 WORTHINGTON.

EIGHTH GENERATION 365

7162 PHILIP AUBIN, b. Dec. 20, 1855, m. MARY EMMA MCSPARREN, lived 1915, Erie Pa., no children.
7163 INFANT, died young.

F3938 William Locke, born in St. Albans, Vt. June 13, 1834, died Feb. 22, 1890, married Oct. 16, 1855, ELIZABETH MCDONALD SMITH of Boston, born in North Enosburg, Vt., Feb. 24, 1835, daughter of William and Nancy (Cutler). He was in the clothing business in St. Albans, Vt.
Children of 8th Gen.
7164 JOHN FRANCIS, b. Jan. 23, 1858, in 1908 was in clothing business, unmarried, in St. Albans, Vt.
7165 ALTON, b. Bangor, Me., July 3, 1859, d. infant.
7166 LOUIS, b. March 1861, d. infant.

F3940 Homer F. Locke, born in St. Albans, Vt., Nov. 30, 1836, died in New York City, Jan. 24, 1901, married in Portland, Me., May 17, 1857, MINNIE M. G. VAN DE SANDE, born June 2, 1838, daughter of Daniel F. G. and Mary (Froelich). He was in the dry goods business in Portland in 1866, later was in the woolen business on Leonard St., New York City, with a home on West 145th St.
Children of 8th Gen.
7167 ALICE JULIA, b. Portland, Me., Nov. 1, 1858, m. SAMUEL BENNETT, probably later than 1898 when she was in Paris, France, with her mother. In 1915 she was "of St. Louis."
7168 WORTHINGTON, b. Portland, Nov. 4, 1863, m. Sept. 1, 1897, MRS. IDA (NOYES) FAVOR, lived Portland, Me.
7169 RICHARD VAN DE SANDE, b. Lawrence, Mass., Sept. 26, 1876, m. MISS JESSICA DENMEAD, had: 7170 MARGARET, b. 1904; 7171 HOMER F., b. 1905.

F3948 Edward S. Locke, born 1827, married 1862, ALMINA C. ROYCE, born June 16, 1839, died 1893, daughter of Caleb and Amanda (Flint). He was a tanner in Richford, Vt., in 1898.
Children of 8th Gen.
7172 EVELYN A., b. 1865, m. ——— BEDELL, lived Richford, Vt., 1898.
7173 LUCIA M., b. 1875, lived Richford, unmarried 1898.

F3963 William Moody Locke, born in Epsom, Aug. 18, 1821, died in Lowell, Apl. 2, 1898, married Oct. 16, 1852, RHODA J. COLE. He was in the war of 1847 in private service.

Children of 8th Gen.

7174 LYDIA M., b. June 30, 1853, lived 1898, Lowell, Mass.

7175 ROWENA, b. Nov. 5, 1857, m. March 16, 1881, ARTHUR W. WHITNEY of Haverhill, b. Jan. 16, 1858, son of George R. and Pauline (Hillard). They lived in Lowell.

F3972 John C. Locke, born in Alton, Jan. 9, 1824, died in Gilford, May 12, 1890, married in Belmont, Aug. 26, 1847, MARY J. ROBERTS, born in Gilford, June 15, 1826. He was a farmer in Gilford.

Child of 8th Gen.

7176 CORA E., b. Gilford, Dec. 6, 1858, m. March 31, 1883, OTIS G. ROBERTS, b. Meredith, a farmer in Gilford, had: 7177 CLINTON L., b. Sept. 5, 1884; 7178 CHARLES O., b. Dec. 29, 1887; 7179 HOWARD A., b. Aug. 7, 1896.

F3979 Winthrop Smith, born Jan. 13, 1789, died Aug. 28, 1844, married June 11, 1820, **Eleanor Locke,** # 1594, born Oct. 17, 1788, died Feb. 14, 1866. This Winthrop was not son of HANNAH MARY LOCKE, but was probably son of Daniel's 1st wife. He was called major, inherited the old homestead and was a man of great worth and highly respected.

Children of 8th Gen.

7180 MARY JOANNA, b. March 26, 1821, m. May 29, 1839, DR. ALONZO BICKFORD.

7181 MAJOR DANIEL, b. Jan. 27, 1823, m. Nov. 30, 1843, MARTHA A. PAGE, and had: 7182 MARTHA; 7183 ELLEN; 7184 WINTHROP; 7185 MARY; 7186 ISABEL.

F7187 JOSEPH, b. Apl. 17, 1826, m. Dec. 25, 1850, MARY E. NUTE.

F4014 Benjamin Perkins, born March 20, 1821, married 1st, LUELLA GOVE of Seabrook, who died July 9, 1848, and by her had: Samuel Lewis, died July 30, 1848, aged 21 days. He married 2nd, June 25, 1856, JULIA MARIA HOBBS, born Nov. 3, 1835. He lived in Seabrook.

Children of 8th Gen.

7188 ANNIE M., b. July 27, 1857, lives unmarried in Seabrook.

F7189 SAMUEL F., b. June 25, 1859, m. Feb. 16, 1882, MARY L. WALTON.

F4043 Abigail Brackett, born in Epsom, Nov. 13, 1821, died in Brattleboro, Vt., May 13, 1888, married in Epsom, Feb. 27, 1850, BENJAMIN W. SMITH, born in Sharon, Me., Dec. 29, 1815, died in Richmond, Jan. 4, 1871. They settled in Farmington, Me.

EIGHTH GENERATION 367

Children of 8th Gen. b. in Farmington, Me.
7190 CHARLES G., b. May 22, 1853, d. Hinsdale, July 19, 1882.
7191 ALICE B., b. May 19, 1855, d. Brattleboro, Vt., Aug. 22, 1889, m. Hinsdale, June 7, 1887, LUTHER C. STEBBINS, had: 7192 HAROLD E., b. Vt., Aug. 18, 1889.
7193 MELLEN K., b. Sept. 10, 1857, m. Camden, N. J., July 17, 1882, MAY L. ADAIR.
7194 LOUISA L., b. Marlborough, Oct. 19, 1861, lived Middleton, Conn., 1902.

F4048 Naomi Brackett, born in Epsom, Sept. 14, 1828, died Jan. 24, 1871, married in Epsom, Sept. 14, 1847, GEORGE B. MERRIAM of Lowell. They lived in Lowell and Epsom.

Children of 8th Gen.
7195 FRANK B., b. Oct. 1, 1848, left home, never heard from.
7196 ADA EVELYN, b. May 23, 1851, d. unmarried Nov. 4, 1887.
F7197 MARY ISADORE, b. Sept. 11, 1853, m. Oct. 5, 1879, HERMAN D. HAZEN.

F4050 Drusilla Sanborn Locke, born in Epsom, Feb. 8, 1821, died in Salem, Mass., May 1, 1890, married in Weare, Feb. 25, 1841, GEORGE W. WOODBURY, born Aug. 31, 1815; died Jan. 23, 1887. They lived in Weare.

Children of 8th Gen.
7198 JOHN A., b. Oct. 12, 1856, m. Weare, HATTIE FLANDERS. He was a farmer in No. Weare, had: 7199 EDITH; 7200 NATHANIEL.
7201 GEORGEANNA, b. ——, m. ORRIN COLBY, lived in Hill 1911.

F4051 Alpheus Crosby Locke, born in Epsom, Feb. 11, 1823, married in Hopkinton, Apl. 19, 1847, HARRIET A. KIMBALL, born March 25, 1822, died in Lewiston, Me., Apl. 30, 1853; married 2nd, Apl. 23, 1856, LOUISA KIMBALL, born March 14, 1823, both daughters of Daniel and Asenath (Herrick). He left Lewiston in 1865, was four years in Pembroke and two in Tennessee, then took final residence in Salem, Mass., where he died Aug. 28, 1908.

Children of 8th Gen. b. in Lewiston, Me.
7202 EDWIN H., b. Apl. 23, 1851, m. 1st, Jan. 8, 1870, CELIA A. WIGGIN of Henniker, b. Dec. 20, 1849, d. Salem, Mass., Nov. 17, 1873; m. 2nd, Feb. 6, 1875, HENRIETTA C. TILTON of Pittsfield, b. Jan. 6, 1856. He was a machinist, had no children and d. in Salem, Feb. 17, 1884.
7203 HARRIET A., b. Jan. 27, 1855; was living 1911, unmarried in Watertown, Mass.
7204 ELIZABETH E., (dau. of 2nd wife), b. Oct. 23, 1857, m. Aug. 5, 1914, JAMES ALBERT SANBORN, and they live in Salem.

F4053 Sarah Chase Locke, born in Epsom, May 1, 1827 died in Kensington, Feb. 13, 1911, married in Weare, Apl. 9, 1857, CHARLES C. DOWE of Kensington, born in Kensington, Nov. 16, 1827, died there a farmer Sept. 26, 1885.

Children of 8th Gen. b. in Kensington.

F7205 FRED HOWARD, b. June 26, 1858, m. Sept. 13, 1879, CLARA I. AUSTIN.
7206 HENRY SEWELL, b. Jan. 2, 1862, m. 1st, Dec. 24, 1885, ADDIE F. JANVRIN of Hampton Falls, who d. Dorchester, Mass., March 7, 1911; m. 2nd, Jan. 1, 1913, IMOGENE BOYD DOW. He is an employee of Swift & Co., Denver, Col.
F7207 WILLIAM NEWELL, b. Jan. 2, 1862, m. Dec. 9, 1884, HATTIE BROWN WEARE.
F7208 MINNIE ELIZABETH, b. Nov. 8, 1865, m. June 27, 1887, CLARENCE EUGENE JANVRIN.
7209 NELLIE MARGARET, b. twin, Nov. 8, 1865, drowned at Hampton Beach, July 4, 1898, m. Kensington, July 4, 1885, WILBUR K. PARKER, lived in Kens., had no children.

F4054 Milton Putnam Locke, born in Epsom, June 9, 1829, married Jan. 23, 1854, SARAH C. BOUSLEY of Salem, born Dec. 27, 1832, died Feb. 28, 1867; married 2nd, in Salem, May 31, 1873, LYDIA ANN CURTIS, born in Lowell, May 26, 1851. He was of firm Locke & Locke, stair builders, Salem, Mass. and died July 20, 1914.

Children of 8th Gen. b. in Salem. Mass.

7210 SILAS MERRILL, b. Dec. 3, 1854, m. Salem, March 18, 1890, MRS. ALICE (HOOD) STODDER of Salem, b. Dec. 22, 1850, d. Boxford, Mass., Dec. 28, 1913. He is a carpenter in Salem and Boxford and has no children.
F7211 CHARLES WARREN, b. Nov. 23, 1856, m. Oct. 6, 1881, ELIZABETH B. EDWARDS.
F7212 FRANK ELMER, b. June 16, 1860, m. Apl. 28, 1886, FLORENCE M. STODDARD.
F7213 ALBERT EDWARD, b. Aug. 2, 1862, m. 1st, June 2, 1886, ELIZABETH M. HARDY; m. 2nd, Apl. 20, 1892, ANNIE M. HILL.
7214 LILLIE BEECHER, b. Jan. 25, 1865, lives unmarried Kensington.
(*Children of 2nd wife.*)
7215 JANETTE WARREN, b. Apl. 14, 1875, m. Salem, May 10, 1899, CHARLES H. PERRY of Salem, a graduate of Brooklyn Polytechnic Institute. and they had: 7216 HAROLD, b. 1901.
7217 HOWARD MILTON, b. Feb. 20, 1879, graduated from Brooklyn Polytechnic Institute.
7218 ALFRED CURTIS, b. Aug. 31, 1889.

F4057 Silas Merrill Locke, born in Hopkinton, Dec. 30, 1834, died Dec. 13, 1907, in Mechanics Falls, Me., married 1st, in Hopkinton, Sept. 30, 1856, LIZZIE T. KIMBALL, born in Hop-

kinton, Sept. 30, 1832, died in Roxbury, Me.; married 2nd, in Hebron, Me., March 29, 1900, LIZZIE A. MURCH, born 1860. He lived in Salem, Mass., and Hebron, Me., and was a carpenter.
Children of 8th Gen.
7220 CHARLES F., b. Roxbury, Mass., Aug. 10, 1863, d. Rox., Feb. 7, 1878.
7221 CARRIE, b. May 10, 1866, m. May 6, 1891, REV. DANVILLE GAMMON, of the Free Will Baptist Church, had no children.

F4059 Nathaniel Chase Locke, born in Hopkinton, Oct. 27, 1837 twin, died July 29, 1914, married in Salem, Oct. 30, 1858, SOPHRONIA T. FELCH, born in Francestown, March 1, 1837. He was inventor and manufacturer of the Locke Steam Regulator, with machine shops in Salem.
Children of 8th Gen. b. in Salem, Mass.
7222 ALBERT NATHAN, b. Nov. 4, 1865, m. Salem, Apl. 28, 1896, ALICE GRISWOLD of Salem, b. Sept. 29, 1875. They live in Salem, have no children, and he manufactures the Locke Steam Regulator an machine supplies.
7223 SARAH ABBIE, b. Aug. 14, 1873, m. Salem, Dec. 6, 1899, CHARLES A. ARCHER of Salem, b. Apl. 24, 1876. He was an alderman of Salem 1904, d. Oct. 6, 1911, had: 7224 PHOEBE WALDO, b. Nov. 7, 1902; 7225 JOHN B., b. Dec. 13, 1908.

F4060 George Henry Locke, born in Hopkinton, Dec. 18, 1842, died in Hopkinton, May 24, 1911, married in Weare, Dec. 6, 1876, MARY ANN WRIGHT, born in Hopkinton, March 27, 1842. He was a farmer in Hopkinton and later an engineer.
Children of 8th Gen. b. in Hopkinton.
7226 ANNIE ELIZABETH, b. Aug. 5, 1878, m. Weare, CHARLES FAVOR, a farmer in East Weare; had two girls.
7227 JAMES WRIGHT, b. July 12, 1881, an unmarried farmer in Hopkinton, 1908.
7228 CHARLES EDWIN (Eddie C.), b. Aug. 28, 1883, m. MINNIE C. FLANDERS, is a driver in Hopkinton, had: 7229 RUTH C.

F4064 Henry E. Towle, born Oct. 9, 1823, married Jan. 10, 1849, MARY ANN MCCRILLIS, and lived in Boston.
Children of 8th Gen.
7230 GEORGE. 7231 DAVID. 7232 EDGAR.

F4065 Horace E. Towle, born Dec. 16, 1825, married Apl. 8, 1852, SUSAN M. DAILY, and lived in Dedham, Mass.
Children of 8th Gen.
7233 ELLA. 7234 COLLIS. 7235 HATTIE. 7236 SUSIE. 7237 HERBERT. 7238 LIZZIE.
24

F4068 Almira J. Towle, born Oct. 18, 1829, married Oct. 21, 1852, CYRUS FRENCH, and lived in Sutton.
Children of 8th Gen.
7239 JENNIE F.   7240 ANDREW C.   7241 LIZZIE M.   7242 ETTA C.

F4070 Charles A. Towle, born June 14, 1833, died Aug. 18, 1870, married Dec. 1, 1854, MARIA SKATES of Ossipee, born in Ossipee, died Portsmouth June 7, 1912, aged 82. He was a merchant in Boston.
Children of 8th Gen.
7243 FRANK A., b. ——, m. ANNIE L. WEEKS of Boston, had: 7244 CHARLES A.; 7245 DANIEL.
7246 WILLIE, b. ——.
7247 FRED S., b. ——, m. MARTHA H. PERRY of Boston. He is a physician in Portsmouth, had: 7248 CHARLES A., who m. MARION ROBY.
7249 CHARLES F., b. 1856, d. Dec. 1, 1914, was a theatrical manager.

F4072 Mary A. Towle, born in Epsom, Aug. 1, 1835, married Nov. 15, 1850, REV. ROBERT FORD and lived in Center Harbor, Danbury and Campton.
Children of 8th Gen.
7250 ALICE R.   7251 ARTHUR R.   7252 IDA.   7253 CHARLES.

F4073 Albert Towle, born Jan. 8, 1837, married March 12, 1862, ANNIE E. RYNES in Boston.
Children of 8th Gen.
7254 ANNIE.   7255 WILLIE.   7256 MABEL, m. W. E. CLARKE and lives in Dorchester, Mass.

F4074 Ellen M.. Towle, born Apl. 1, 1839, married Feb. 11, 1863, WILLIAM B. FELLOWS, and lived in Wilmot Flat, N. H.
Children of 8th Gen.
7257 ANNA.   7258 WILLIE.   7259 JENNIE.   7260 INA.

F4092 Henry F. Sanborn, born Feb. 26, 1819, died March 27, 1897 married in Princeton, Mass., May 31, 1843, EUNICE DAVIS, born June 21, 1819. He was a farmer in Princeton.
Children of 8th Gen.
7261 WALTER H., b. Oct. 19, 1845, m. EMILY F. BRUCE of Milford, Nov. 10, 1874. He graduated from Dartmouth College 1867, is a Doctor of Laws, judge of U. S. Circuit Court, and lives in St. Paul, Minn. He has four children.
7262 EDWARD P., b. May 19, 1853, m. Nov. 21, 1884, SUSAN DANA of St. Paul, b. Apl. 24, 1861, graduated Dartmouth, 1876; a lawyer and leading Mason of St. Paul; has no children.
7263 HARRIET A., b. June 16, 1854, m. Dec. 28, 1882, DR. WILLIAM B. COGSWELL of Strafford, Conn.

EIGHTH GENERATION 371

F4095 John B. Sanborn, born in Epsom, Dec. 5, 1826, married 1st, March 17, 1857, CATHERINE HILL of Newton, N. J., who died Nov. 16, 1860; married 2nd, Nov. 27, 1865, ANNA E. NIXON of Bridgeton, who died June 25, 1878; married, 3rd, Apl. 15, 1880, RACHEL RICE of St. Paul. He was a lawyer in Concord in 1854, and later in St. Paul, was brevetted Major-General U. S. Vols.

Children of 8th Gen.
7264 HARRIET F., b. June 4, 1858, d. 1880.
7265 JOHN, b. 1860, d. 1860. 7266 LUCY S., b. July 4, 1881.
7267 JOHN B., b. Nov. 9, 1883. 7268 RACHEL R., b. July 27, 1888.
7269 FREDERICK, b. Dec. 11, 1892.

F4110 Nancy N. Towle, born March 28, 1826, died Dec. 5, 1895, married June 2, 1847, JOHN SHAW of Chichester, born Jan. 8, 1825.

Children of 8th Gen.
7270 ANNIE A., b. Feb. 7, 1854, m. Dec. 1882, GEORGE C. TOWLE, had: 7271 GRACE S., b. 1883; 7272 MABEL N., b. 1889.
7273 CHARLES J., b. Jan. 14, 1858, m. Apl. 23, 1883, FANNIE OXFORD, who d. Jan. 15, 1896, had: 7274 GERTRUDE, 1886; 7275 MARY S., b. 1888; 7276 KATHERINE, b. 1889.

F4111 Benjamin Towle, born Nov. 2, 1828, died May 19, 1887, married May 1850, ELIZA H. HAM, born Nov. 28, 1830, died Sept. 12, 1861, married 2nd, Feb. 11, 1862, HARRIET E. EDGERLY.

Children of 8th Gen.
7277 GEORGE B., b. Jan. 9, 1851, d. Feb. 9, 1851.
7278 HARRIE F., b. May 20, 1852, m. ANNIE M. SPROUL.
7279 ANNIE E., b. Apl. 9, 1857, m. J. R. SMITH.
7280 BENJAMIN M., (*Second wife's child:*) b. Nov. 21, 1862, m. Feb. 2, 1887, ANNIE CILLEY and had: 7281 HELEN, b. 1889.
7282 HARRIET S., b. Sept. 5, 1867, m. FRED W. DUDLEY and lived in Hollis.

F4113 Clara M. Towle, born in Epsom, Dec. 2, 1834, married Nov. 27, 1856, ALFRED E. AMBROSE.

Children of 8th Gen.
7284 FRED M., b. Sept. 17, 1857, m. June 30, 1883, MARY COOK, had: 7285 CLARA E., b. 1884; 7286 CORA A., b. 1885; 7287 NATHANIEL, b. 1888; 7288 FRED K., b. 1890; 7289 HELEN, b. 1892; 7290 MARGARET b. 1894.
7291 CORA B., b. Aug. 2, 1861, m. June 30, 1885, ALBERT SANBORN, had: 7292 LENA, b. 1886; 7293 CLARA, b. 1890.
7294 DAVID A., b. Aug. 31, 1867.

F4114 Rev. Charles A. Towle, born June 20, 1827, married 1st, Dec. 14, 1869, JENNIE LAY who died May 8, 1881; married 2nd, Aug. 30, 1894, ELLA REINKING, born July 1856. He fitted at Pembroke Academy, graduated from Dartmouth in 1864, taught in Mt. Vernon, Andover, and Chicago, then took a seminary course in 1869. He had parishes in Chicago and Iowa and was with Congregational S. S. Publication Co. 12 years. He served in the war in Bank's Expedition, and was Sergt. of Co. D. 15th. N. H. Reg.

Children of 8th Gen.

7295 NELSON L., b. Sept. 19, 1870.
7296 MARIETTA, b. March 27, 1872, d. March 18, 1896, m. June 21, 1894, ARTHUR W. BARTLETT, had: 7297 EMMA, b. 1895.
7298 RALPH E., b. Apl. 5, 1875. 7299 NELLIE S., b. June 16, 1877.
7300 CHARLES A., b. Apl. 29, 1881.

F4116 Leroy Leslie Locke, born in Loudon, June 9, 1845, died in Loudon, March 5, 1911, married 1st, Jan. 30, 1868, HANNAH EVES of Concord, born in Jersey City, was divorced Apl. 1884, and she married, 1890, JOHN SARGENT. He married 2nd, May 20, 1885, in Concord, ABBIE W. PALMER, born in Boston, March 5, 1868, daughter of W. H. and E. M. of Boston. He was a farmer and engineer in East Concord. He was called also Royal Locke.

Children of 8th Gen. b. East Concord.

7301 FRANK L., b. March 25, 1869, m. 1st, NELLIE ABBOTT; m. 2nd, Oct. 29, 1892, MAUDE L. PIPER of Concord, b. Concord, 1871, dau. of H. L. and Mattie (Walker). He is a carpenter in Concord, had: 7302 IVY ANNA, b. Loudon, 1891, d. Oct. 14, 1891; 7303 MINTA ANINA, b. Nov. 7, 1896; 7303a BURNESS P., b. Aug. 5, 1893.
7304 HENRY E., b. Sept. 24, 1870, m. Warren, Apl. 20, 1897, MRS. MEANIE (WHICHER) COLBY ELLIOTT, b. Warren, Oct. 23, 1868, (her 2nd mg.) dau. of Henry Whicher and Hattie (Caswell). He is a lumberman in Warren.
7305 IRA J., b. July 19, 1873, m. Dec. 7, 1891, NETTIE M. LECOY, b. Northfield, Vt., 1874, dau. of Frank G. and Delia (Shortelle) of Canada. By trade he is an axle maker, but has done much lay preaching, had a dau: 7306 b. June 18, 1892.
7307 MARY A., b. June 6, 1875, m. Concord, May 14, 1891, NATT L. SWAIN of Concord, b. Warren, 1872, son of Foote and Sarah (Caswell), a R. R. employee in Warren, had: 7308 HERBERT L., b. Oct. 27, 1891, d. June 6, 1894.
7309 ALBERT TRUE, b. Dec. 23, 1882, m. 1st, —— ——; m. 2nd, Sept. 1, 1908, EVA L. ROBINSON, b. Pembroke, 1883, dau. of Augustus and J. Cornelia (Norcross). Is a car inspector in Concord.

EIGHTH GENERATION 373

Second wife's children:
7310 GEORGE W., b. March 20, 1886.
7311 ROY LOREN, b. Sept. 1, 1888, m. Jan. 4, 1909, BLANCHE E. BUZZELL, b. Concord, 1887, dau. of Henry and Addie.
7312 LEAMAN LESTER, b. June 24, 1890.
7313 SCOTT PALMER, b. Feb. 12, 1893, m. Laconia, July 24, 1911, ROSA EMMA CLEVETT of Laconia, b. 1894, dau. of Henry and Lena (Herbert). He is a machinist in Concord. Had: 7314 SCOTT PERRY, d. March 7, 1912, aged 1 day.
7315 SELDEN BARNEY, b. May 25, 1894, m. Concord, June 18, 1911, EVA ALICE KINNEY, b. Mattapoisett, Mass., 1892, dau. of Alonzo and Annie (Palmer). He was a R. R. man and later a silversmith in Concord, had: 7316 LOUIS ALDEN, b. Sept. 30, 1912; 7317 EARL RUSSELL, b. Dec. 15, 1914.
7318 CLARENCE EDWARD, b. June 29, 1899.

F4122 Lucia L. Locke, born in Loudon, May 2, 1858, married in Penacook, Apl. 28, 1877, JOHN R. HILL, born in Eliot, Me., Nov. 25, 1839, died in Penacook, Apl. 19, 1911, son of John and Eliza (Freeman). He was a War veteran, a cooper and farmer in Penacook.

Children of 8th Gen.
7319 MARY E., b. Aug. 15, 1878, m. Concord, Oct. 18, 1897, ARTHUR L. CLARKE of So. Berwick, Me., b. Nov. 1, 1871, son of John H. and Lucy (Gould). They live in Attleboro, Mass.
7320 JOHN T., b. Jan. 16, 1882, lives in Penacook with his mother.

F4125 Jane M. Locke, born in Stanstead, Can., Oct. 11, 1830, died Apl. 16, 1901, married Oct. 10, 1849, HIRAM R. BISHOP, born in Stanstead, Can., May 22, 1830. He was a woodenware manufacturer in East Somerville, Mass., where he died Feb. 10, 1888.

Child of 8th Gen.
7321 AGNES, b. Jan. 17, 1850, m. 1876, CORNELIUS W. WARNER of Eaton, Canada, b. 1852, lived East Somerville, Mass.

F4127 Florella A. Locke, born in Stanstead, Can., Dec. 20, 1834, married in Stanstead, Oct. 21, 1858, JAMES K. CURRIER, born in Oxford, March 11, 1834. He was a farmer in River Falls, Wis., and died Dec. 21, 1901. She died in River Falls, Dec. 24, 1904.

Children of 8th Gen. b. Clifton, Wisconsin.
F7322 JAMES FREDERICK, b. Feb. 13, 1859, m. June 24, 1885, ABBIE M. PARKER.
F7323 MARY LOUISE, b. Dec. 6, 1861, m. Nov. 15, 1883, VICTOR E. BAILEY.

7324 LILLIAN J., b. Sept. 2, 1868, unmarried, is assistant librarian of State Normal School, River Falls, Wis.

7325 HARRY LOCKE, b. Jan. 29, 1875, graduated River Falls Normal School 1893, and was a senior in University of Minn., when he organized a company of university students as 13th Minnesota Volunteers. They went to Manila where he d. Sept. 19, 1898, an exemplary youth.

F4128 Frederick W. Locke, born Jan. 14, 1837, in Stanstead, Can., died in Stanstead, March 1, 1886, married Dec. 14, 1865, TIRZAH MARTIN, born Aug. 27, 1841. He graduated from McGill College and was a farmer in Stanstead. His widow removed to Waterbury, Conn., in 1899.

Children of 8th Gen. b. Stanstead, Canada.

7326 IRVING JAMES, b. Oct. 14, 1866, d. Garden City, Kan., Dec. 2, 1884; and was a student of Richmond College at time of death.

F7327 LILLIAN F., b. Aug. 24, 1868, m. Oct. 8, 1892, HORACE STEERE.

7328 GENEVA M., b. June 30, 1870, m. Sept. 19, 1893, ROBERT JOHNSTON, b. Montreal, March 28, 1866, lived Sherbrook, P. Q., had three children who died young, and 7329 WALTER LOCKE, b. Apl. 5, 1904.

7330 ALICE E., b. Oct. 14, 1876, m. REV. ARCHIBALD A. LANCASTER, a Congregational minister of Middlebury, Vt. Had: 7331 ALICE CHRISTINE, b. Feb. 4, 1909; 7332 JAMES LOCKE, b. May 1, 1914.

7333 LOUISE A., b. Dec. 16, 1879, m. CHARLES R. VAILL, had: 7334 DEBORAH LOCKE b. Feb. 1, 1904; 7335 JOHN LOCKE, b. Dec. 12, 1907; 7336 FREDERICK WILLIAM, b. Nov. 9, 1910.

7337 JESSIE C., b. May 14, 1885, graduate of Mt. Holyoke College and later a high school teacher in New Britain, Conn.

F4130 Mary F. Locke, born in Chichester, Sept. 6, 1835, died Aug. 24, 1906, married Dec. 25, 1856, CHARLES H. BARTLETT of Kittery, Me., born Oct. 1833, lived in Kittery. He was employed on the Navy Yard and died Jan. 12, 1914.

Children of 8th Gen. b. Kittery, Me.

7338 JAMES T., b. Apl. 18, 1858, d. 1863.

7339 IDA, b. 1860, d. 1863.   7340 ALFRED, b. 1864, d. 1870.

7341 CHARLES CARROLL, b. Feb. 5, 1868, m. Kendall, Ill., Oct. 16, 1901, IVAH SIMONS, b. May 9, 1878, dau. of John R. and Susannah (Minkley). He is a lawyer in Chicago, has been an active worker and President of the Locke Association, has a dau: 7342 HELEN, b. Aug. 30, 1904.

7343 RUTH AMES (adopted), b. Nov. 1, 1886.

Eugene Olin Locke F4135

JUDGE JAMES W. LOCKE F4131

EIGHTH GENERATION

F4131 Judge James William Locke, born in Wilmington, Vt., Oct. 30, 1837, married Oct. 5, 1866, ALVINA C. NEAL in Kittery, Me., born Sept. 19, 1841, died in Jacksonville, Fla., Feb. 3, 1905, daughter of John and Ann M. (Badger).

He received a good education in the public schools of Manchester, N. H., and at the Wesleyan Academy at Stanstead, Canada. He began public life in teaching in the schools of Manchester, at the same time studying law in the office of Hon. William Stark. At the outbreak of the war he was appointed paymaster's clerk in the U. S. Navy and in 1863 was transferred to the Naval Station at Key West, Fla. Mustered out at the close of the war, he remained there and entered upon the practice of his profession. He was at various times County Superintendent of Education, Clerk of U. S. Courts, and U. S. Commissioner; in 1868 he was appointed judge for Monroe Co. and in 1870 was elected as state senator. He was appointed U. S. Judge for the Southern District of Florida on Feb. 1st, 1872, being recommended for such appointment by every member of the bar of the district without regard to political affiliations and continued to make his home in Key West. For several years he sat upon the bench of the Circuit Court of Appeals at New Orleans, La., until in 1894 the extension of his district and the duties of the court required the removal of his residence to Jacksonville, where he has since resided. On the 4th of July, 1912, he retired by resignation, having passed the age of seventy and served more than forty years upon the federal bench. Judge Locke is quite as well known in Portsmouth and Kittery, Me., where he spends his summers as in the South. He has served as President of the Locke Association many times and needless to say, is one of its most enthusiastic members.

Children of 8th Gen. living in Jacksonville, Fla., 1916.
7344 ANNIE M., b. Jan. 12, 1870.
7345 CARRIE, b. Aug. 12, 1871.
7346 ALISON N., b. Dec. 8, 1877.
7347 LILLIAN, d. an infant.

F4135 Eugene Olin Locke, born in Stanstead, Canada, Feb. 20, 1850, married March 30, 1875, ROSETTA R. OTTO, born March 24, 1854. He graduated from Dartmouth College in the class of 1870, and afterward studied law in the office of John B. Clarke, of Manchester. He accepted the position of principal of the High

School in Key West, Fla., and at the termination of this engagement commenced the practice of law in that city. In 1872 he was appointed Clerk of the U. S. Court and U. S. Commissioner, which positions he held until Jan. 1st, 1914, when, having resigned such office, he entered upon the practice of law in Jacksonville, Fla. He has been a prominent Mason and served as Grand Master of the I. O. O. F.

Children of 8th Gen.
7348 WILLIAM JOSEPH. b. May 1, 1876, m. July 1914, MARY FLINTER.
7349 FLORENCE ELIZABETH, b. March 13, 1883, m. N. Y. City, June 24, 1907, JOHN PELOSI LEWIS, b. March 1, 1883, had: 7351 EUGENE LOCKE, b. Jacksonville, Fla., May 24, 1908; 7352 VIVIAN, b. June 4, 1910.
7353 MARY, b. 1891, d. 1891.

F4137 Flora J. Wyman, born March 29, 1848, married Oct. 25, 1865, ERNEST H. BULLARD, born Feb. 4, 1846, died in Montreal, Nov. 23, 1901. He was overseer of the Dominion Cotton Mills, Springfield, Mass.

Children of 8th Gen.
7354 FREDERICK E., b. Oct. 21, 1866, m. June 1, 1893, ELMA E. TILSON. He is an overseer in a cotton mill in Magog, P. Q. Had: 7355 MARLE F., b. June 30, 1894; 7356 ORAL E., b. Nov. 28, 1896, d. Aug. 21, 1897.
F7357 HOMER E., b. Nov. 18, 1869, m. Nov. 14, 1888, EMMA M. HARDY.
7358 DAUGHTER, b. Nov. 13, 1871, d. Nov. 16, 1871.
7359 CHARLES H., b. Oct. 13, 1873, d. Feb. 10, 1875.

F4140 Richard J. Copp, born March 4, 1845, died 1901, married 1870, MALVINA SCHOOLCRAFT. He was a teamster in Magog, P. Q.

Children of 8th Gen. b. Magog, P. Q.
7360 ORAL A., b. Feb. 8, 1871, m. MYSTIC BUZZELL.
7361 ELLEN ETTA, b. Oct. 15, 1873, m. EDWARD REXFORD, had: 7362 EMMA L.
7363 WALTER FRED, b. Oct. 15, 1875.
7364 ANNIE EMMA, b. March 29, 1876, m. HARRY ———.
7365 EDITH M., b. Oct. 27, 1878, m. JOHN HOPKINS, lived Dover, had: two children.
7366 HATTIE B., b. March 27, 1880. 7367 MOSES W., b. March 25, 1882.
7368 JAMES W., b. Jan. 19, 1885.

F4141 Emaline Louise Copp, born July 1, 1847, died in East Boston, Apl. 14, 1893, married Oct., 1867, Magog, P. Q., ADDISON L. NOYES, born in Hartley, Can., 1828, died 1901. He had a livery stable East Boston.

Children of 8th Gen.
7369 SARAH BERTHA, b. Dec. 13, 1869, m. 1st, Nov. 19, 1890, HENRY HORTON, b. 1862, a merchant, had son: 7370 HENRY O., b. May 28, 1893. She m. 2nd, Dec. 22, 1896, FRANK W. THAYER, a lawyer of Boston, had a daughter.
7371 CHARLES ADDISON, b. 1876, m. L. THAYER, is a dentist in Chicago.

F4157 Caroline Smith, born June 5, 1834, married 1849, AARON BANCROFT of South Amesbury, born Feb., 1827. He is a broker in New York City, lives in Brooklyn.

Children of 8th Gen.
7372 CORNELIA, b. Apl. 3, 1851, m. Dec. 15, 1875, IRVING P. BENNETT, lived in Brooklyn, N. Y., had no children.
7373 CARRIE, b. Oct. 11, 1853, m. Feb. 12, 1894, C. B. FRENCH of Boston.
7374 GEORGE, b. Newburyport, Oct. 13, 1861, unmarried.

F4159 Ruth E. Morrison, born in Portsmouth, Sept. 25, 1817, died in Portsmouth, March 3, 1842, married in Portsmouth, June 30, 1841, GEORGE NOYES CARLTON of New York, born in Reading, Mass., June 11, 1816. He married 2nd, in Portsmouth, Aug. 24, 1848, his wife's sister, F4160 MARY ESTHER MORRISON, born in Portsmouth, Dec. 7, 1822, died Apl. 14, 1881. He was in the railroad advertising business in New York and died in Victoria, B. C., Oct. 11, 1890.

Children of 8th Gen. b. Portsmouth.
7375 GEORGE A., b. March 1, 1842, m. ——— ———, and lived Victoria, B. C.

Second wife's children:
7376 MARY ELIZABETH, b. Apl. 22, 1849, m. REV. JONATHAN ED. BELL, in 1870, a Presbyterian minister.
7377 HORACE M., b. Oct. 10, 1850, m. Oct. 12, 1874, CARRIE L. WENDELKEN. He is an advertising agent, Beekman St., N. Y. City.
7378 FREDERICK WILLIAM, b. Feb. 2, 1852, m. Jan. 25, 1881, EDNA C. BYRNE of Berkeley, Cal.
7379 EMILIE JOSEPHINE, b. Oct. 30, 1854.
7380 CORNELIA ADAMS, b. Jan. 31, 1857, m. Brooklyn, May 1, 1888, STEPHEN HOPKINS, b. Sept. 25, 1854, lived Buffalo, N. Y., had: 7381 HELEN, b. Apl. 20, 1889.
7382 CHARLES BURROUGHS, b. July 11, 1859.
7383 ISABELLE A., b. Oct. 6, 1864, d. Memphis, Tenn., May 17, 1865.

F4183 Charlotte Augusta Locke, born in Boston, Sept. 28, 1838, married Aug. 31, 1864, HENRY S. MOODY, born in Georgetown, Mass., Apl. 19, 1836, died in Council Bluffs, Iowa, Sept. 17, 1904.

Children of 8th Gen.
7384 GEORGE LOCKE, b. Georgetown, Mass., July 1, 1865, d. Nashville, Tenn., Apl. 20, 1889.
7385 FRANK, b. Omaha, Neb., Oct. 31, 1868, d. Oma. July 9, 1869.
7386 CHARLES WADSWORTH, b. Oma., Nov. 25, 1871.
7387 RALPH WALDO, b. Oma, Aug. 1, 1874.
7388 ALBERT M., b. Oma, Oct. 25, 1877.

F4197 Emilie Locke, born in New Orleans, Aug. 18, 1836, died May 26, 1872, married July 1, 1856, GUSTAVE A. BREAUX formerly of Paris, France, a lawyer in New Orleans. He was a Colonel in the Confederate Army, and Judge of Supreme Court at New Orleans.

Children of 8th Gen. b. New Orleans.
F7389 EMALINA MODESTE, b. June 11, 1857, m. Apl. 24, 1878, CHARLES THURSTON BALLARD.
F7390 SAMUEL LOCKE, b. Feb. 13, 1860, m. 1st, Apl. 5, 1885, NINA WILLIAMS; m. 2nd, Apl. 19, 1894, NINA ROGERS.
7391 GUSTAVE A., JR., b. Oct. 23, 1870, m. Oct. 25, 1899, EDNA ROWELL of Washington, D. C.

F4201 Samuel Edward Locke, born in New Orleans, March 9, 1847, died in Chattanooga, Tenn., July 24, 1874, married in Paris, France, Oct. 7, 1868, MARY OLEVIA ELLIS of Paris, daughter of Charles of Yorkshire, Eng. They lived in New Orleans, and after his death she made her home in Paris.

Children of 8th Gen.
7392 KATHERINE MARY, b. New Orleans, Oct. 6, 1869, d. Cornell Heights, N. Y., March 20, 1910, m. Germantown, Penn., Dec. 18, 1889, WATERMAN T. HEWETT, an editor of McMillens German publications, and Professor of German at Cornell University. She was educated in music at Paris, was of literary mind, editor of Freytag's Novels. Had child; 7393 GLADYS MATILDA, b. Sept. 14, 1890, d. Dec. 7, 1904.
7394 EMILIE OLIVIA, b. New Orleans, Aug. 16, 1871, m. 1900, WILLIAM STRUNK, JR., Professor of English at Cornell, had: 7395 WILLIAM OLIVER, b. March 4, 1901; 7396 EDWIN HART, b. March 14, 1903; 7397 KATHERINE MARY (Twin), b. March 14, 1903.
7398 EDWARD OLIVER, b. Paris, Dec. 17, 1874, d. Paris, Feb. 12, 1876.

F4206 John Josiah Locke, born in Geneva, N. Y., Jan. 18, 1834, died in New York City, Aug. 1877, married 1st, CORNELIA ACKERLEY of Geneva, married 2nd, EMMA CUTHBERT of Brooklyn, daughter of George. He was a merchant in New York City.

Children of 8th Gen.
7399 CARRIE, b. ——, d. infant.   7401 CARRIE, b. ——.
7400 CHILD, died young.   7402 EDNA, b. ——.

EIGHTH GENERATION 379

F4208 Julia Frances Locke, born in New York City, July 10, 1838, died in Whitestone, Long Island, Apl. 17, 1863, married WILLIAM BLOODGOOD of Flushing, who was a merchant there.
Child of 8th Gen.
7403 JULIA ESTHER, b. Sept. 1858, m. May 5, 1881, MAX A. SCHMEIWINT of Springfield, Mass. Had: 7404 HAROLD, b. 1882; 7405 SELMA, b. 1883; 7406 HANS, b. 1885.

F4209 Charles Ed. Locke, born in New York City, Jan. 4, 1842, died Dec. 8, 1896, married EMILY MILBURN of Brooklyn, daughter of John and Ann. He was a merchant in Brooklyn. She was living in 1898.
Children of 8th Gen. b. Kansas City.
7407 FLORENCE, b. Aug. 1868, was a school teacher in Brooklyn.
7408 EDWARD, b. Apl. 1877, lived Brooklyn, was in Spanish War.

F4210 Henry Clay Locke, born in Brooklyn, Jan. 9, 1845, died in Whitestone, Long Island, June 2, 1875, married FANNIE DAVIS of Lawrence, Kan. He was a merchant in Kansas. She married 2nd, —— DAVIDSON of Jamestown, Dakota.
Children of 8th Gen. b. Lawrence, Kansas.
7409 MABEL V., b. 1871, m. 1887, THEODORE AMIDOWN, b. July 27, 1864, lived Jamestown, Dakota, had: 7410 DORCAS; 7411 LESTER and two others.
7412 CLARENCE, b. 1874, was unmarried in San Frisco, 1899.

F4220 James Locke, born in Seabrook, Jan. 24, 1825, died in Boston, 1903, married in Seabrook, 1869, EDITH I. COGSWELL, born 1844, daughter of John and Mary (Darling). They lived in Boston and Seabrook.
Children of 8th Gen.
7413 STEWART ASHTON, b. No. Hampton, Dec. 8, 1870, was a hotel clerk in Philadelphia, enlisted in Spanish War and lost a leg in the service.
7414 CORA BELLE, b. twin, Dec. 8, 1870, d. June 22, 1871.
7415 JAMES LOWELL, b. Aug. 17, 1875, lived Boston 1914, is married.
7416 EDITH M., b. March 17, 1877, d. Boston, was m., name unknown.
7417 JOHN H., b. Nov. 20, 1880, d. July 20, 1881.

F4221 Lydia Locke, born in Seabrook, Feb. 26, 1826, died in Seabrook, 1902, married in Seabrook, Dec. 24, 1846, ELIHU DOW of Seabrook, born 1825, died Aug. 26, 1907.
Children of 8th Gen. b. Seabrook.
7418 CHARLES, b. ——, d. aged 19.
7419 LUCY, b. ——, m. EDWARD ADAMS of New York, who was in the shoe business, had: 7420 QUINCY; 7421 CLAUDE; 7422 ELIHU; 7423 CHARLES; and 7424 GERTRUDE who m. —— EVANS.
7425 RHODA or ROSA, b. ——, d. Seabrook, unmarried, aged 30.

F4223 Mary Jane Locke, born in Seabrook, Feb. 22, 1829, married in Rye, Nov. 8, 1849, AMOS JENNESS of Rye, born in Rye, Aug. 1, 1819. He was a farmer in Rye, and died in Concord, June 1, 1902, son of Richard and Caroline.

Children of 8th Gen. b. Rye.

7426 ELIZA PERKINS, b. March 20, 1851, m. 1st, RICHARD FOGG; m. 2nd, WOODBURY PHILBRICK; m. 3rd, JAMES BARTON.
7427 FRANK P., b. Sept. 1852, m. CAROLINE POLK of So. Carolina, had eight children and he d. 1890.
7428 ISABELLE, b. Dec. 15, 1857, d. July 14, 1909, m. Dec. 23, 1885, EDWIN WALKER, b. Jan. 31, 1855, son of ALBERT. They were divorced but had: 7429 FANNIE G., b. 1888; 7430 Jesse M., b. 1889.
7431 ABBOT C., b. 1861, d. June 18, 1863.

F4254 George W. Prescott, born July 13, 1801, died Apl. 12, 1869, married Sept. 1827, BETSEY SEAVEY of Deerfield.

Children of 8th Gen.

7432 GEORGE P., b. Dec. 1829, d. Oct. 1834.
7433 GEORGE P., b. March 3, 1835.   7434 SYLVESTER, b. Jan. 25, 1838.

F4255 Hiram A. Prescott, born Feb. 1804, died in Lowell, Jan. 14, 1841, married 1825, MIRIAM MURRAY, daughter of William. They lived in Haverhill, Mass.

Children of 8th Gen.

7435 LYDIA B., b. June 1829.   7436 WILLIAM A., b. June 1831.
7437 ALSOA, b. 1837, died young.

F4257 Edward P. Prescott, born in Deerfield, Apl. 14, 1812, died Apl. 17, 1889, married Oct. 31, 1835, REBECCA A. COLLIS of Deerfield born Feb. 28, 1814. He was a merchant of Deerfield.

Children of 8th Gen.

7438 SARAH R., b. July 1, 1837.
7439 SUSAN A., b. March 26, 1842.
7440 CLARA O., b. ——, died young.
7441 CLARA O., b. ——.

F4259 John Francis Winkley, born June 20, 1815, died Jan. 1852, married 1840, SUSAN SHAW TODD born Dec. 15, 1816.

Children of 8th Gen.

7442 JOHN F., b. 1845, d. 1845.
7443 MARY MARGARET, b. Sept. 24, 1842, m. Sept. 17, 1868, WILLIAM SIMPSON DEVAN of New Orleans, who d. Oct. 28, 1901; had five children. Lived in Los Angeles.
7444 SUSAN MARIA, b. June 10, 1847, m. Nov. 6, 1876, HENRY WEBSTER PARKER, b. Sept. 7, 1822, had: 7445 DONALD B., b. Apl. 21, 1879.

EIGHTH GENERATION 381

F4261 Mary Sanborn Winkley, born Oct. 14, 1817, died June 30, 1901, married Dec. 1841, WILLIAM C. BARTON of Salem, Mass., born Jan. 15, 1813, died Oct. 19, 1872. They lived West 10th St., New York City.
Children of 8th Gen.
7446 SARAH WINKLEY, b. 1843.
7447 FRANCIS WINKLEY, b. May 31, 1851, m. Las Vega, New Mexico, Nov. 17, 1881, VIOLA BELLE COWAN, b. Nov. 1, 1856, had seven children.
7448 MARY, b. ——, lived N. Y. City, 1905.
7449 DUDLEY LOCKE, and other children.

F4264 John William Dodge, born March 25, 1819, died in Franklin, June 3, 1875, married Sept. 2, 1840, HARRIET P. DUNKlEE of Concord, died in Hampton Falls, Sept. 1, 1903. He graduated from Brown University in 1839, was cashier of Weare Bank, and U. S. Consul, St. George, Newfoundland. From 1867 to 1875 he was Manager of Mt. Washington Railroad, leased the Summit House and the Hamilton Hotel, Bermuda.
Children of 8th Gen.
7450 MARY D., b. Oct. 24, 1841, m. Jan. 1, 1867, WALTER AIKEN, b. Dracut, Mass., Oct. 5, 1831, son of Herrick and Ann (Bradley). He m. 1st, SUSAN COLBY of Warner, lived in Franklin Falls, and d. Nov. 1, 1893.
7451 CLARISSA L., b. Aug. 16, 1843, m. PROF. CHARLES R. BROWN, had: 7452 SAMUEL E.
7453 RICHARD F., b. Feb. 2, 1847, d. Feb. 7, 1861.
7454 SUSAN C., b. Nov. 17, 1849, d. July 16, 1859.
7455 HARRIET, b. June 22, 1853, m. GEORGE C. HEALEY, son of Wells W., had: 7456 FRANCES, b. July 4, 1886.
7457 JESSIE B., b. Sept. 10, 1855, d. Hampton Falls, Jan. 26, 1900.
7458 HELEN S., b. Nov. 3, 1860, d. May 23, 1863.
7459 ARTHUR M., b. July 19, 1862,
7460 MARGARET D., b. Nov. 23, 1864, m. CHARLES L. WHITE, had: 7461 JESSIE D.; 7462 HARRIET; 7463 KATHERINE.

F4265 John D. Locke, born in Seabrook, Dec. 31, 1832, died in Seabrook, Feb. 26, 1902, married in Hampton, Aug. 22, 1854, MARTHA M. BROWN of Seabrook, born Sept. 13, 1832, died in Seabrook, Apl. 13, 1908. He was a farmer, grocer and postmaster of Seabrook many years.
Adopted child of 8th Gen.
7464 BERTHA M. (LEACH), b. East Weare, March 2, 1872, m. Seabrook, Aug. 28, 1893, EDWIN DAMON, b. Pembroke, Mass., 1872, son of Barley D., and Louisa M., lived Lancaster, had son.

F4266 Abbott A. Locke, born in Mass., Aug. 8, 1838, died ——, married in Amesbury, Mass., Feb. 26, 1860, S. HELEN CHASE of Seabrook, born Sept. 6, 1840, divorced Oct. 1887, daughter of David and Sally. He was a grocer in Seabrook many years.

Child of 8th Gen.

7465 H. GERTRUDE, b. Seabrook, Oct. 15, 1860, m. Seabrook, Sept. 27, 1885, ALFRED N. BECKMAN of Seabrook, b. Nov. 24, 1861, lived Everett, Mass., and had: 7466 CAROLINE L., b. Dec. 14, 1886.

F4267 John L. Clarke, born July 21, 1831, in Salisbury, Mass., died in Valley Falls, R. I., Feb. 26, 1876, married May 4, 1853, CORDELIA A. TITUS of Valley Falls.

Children of 8th. Gen. b. Valley Falls, R. I.

F7466 JOHN F., b. Feb. 7, 1854, m. June 19, 1877, CARRIE JENKS.
7467 LUCY S., b. Dec. 27, 1856, m. Nov. 1, 1874, ANDREW CURRIER of Valley Falls. Had: 7468 CARRIE C., b. June 25, 1875; 7469 ANDREW R., b. Sept. 1876.

F4268 Adaline L. Clarke, born in Salisbury, Mass., Apl. 26, 1834, married in Pawtucket, R. I., Sept. 1, 1857, JACOB M. HASKELL of Boston. He is of the firm of wholesale grocers, Haskell, Adams & Co.

Children of 8th Gen.

7470 WALDO C., b. Pawtucket, R. I., June 6, 1858, is unmarried.
7471 EDMUND N., b. Boston, Feb. 27, 1862.
7472 JACOB P., b. Boston, Feb. 26, 1869, d. Nov. 11, 1873.
7473 ADDIE M., b. Boston, Feb. 27, 1875.

F4272 John W. Locke, born in Seabrook, Oct. 4, 1841, died in Seabrook, May 12, 1903, married Aug. 11, 1869, SARAH LIZZIE SOUTHWICK, born in Peabody, Mass., Oct. 1, 1849. He was Sergeant 1863–66, in Co. D. 14th N. H. Regiment. Was a grocer in Seabrook. She married 2nd, in Peabody, 1910, FRANK LARRABEE.

Children of 8th Gen.

7474 RINDA C., b. Seabrook, 1870, m. Seab. Jan. 30, 1890, GEORGE E. FELCH of Seabrook, b. 1866, son of George E. and Josephine. He is a carpenter in Seabrook, had: 7475 JOHN W. L., b. Jan. 18, 1891.
F7476 JIM E., b. Sept. 6, 1877, m. Nov. 11, 1897, IDA S. MILLER.

F4290 Louis Gove, born in Seabrook, Feb. 19, 1814, died Sept. 9, 1864, married 1st, LURANA BOYD of Seabrook who died July 3, 1841; married 2nd, HARRIET BOYD of Seabrook who died 1851; lived Seabrook.

EIGHTH GENERATION

Children of 8th Gen.
F7477 NANCY L., b. Dec. 18, 1840, m. CHARLES PERKINS.
7478 LOUIS F., b. Oct. 5, 1846, m. June, 1870, ADELAIDE AUGUSTA ROWE of Seabrook, had: 7479 ELLEN, b. Nov. 15, 1873, m. HORACE BRAGG, and had: 7480 ARTHUR; 7481 ARCHIE; 7482 ROWLAND.
7483 HIRAM TUNE, b. Oct. 6, 1848, m. Feb. 22, 1870, FANNY S. EATON of Seabrook.
7484 EMILY, b. July 9, 1850, d. Jan. 1908, m. AMOS DOW, lived in Newburyport, and had: 7485 CHARLES; 7486 EMILY.

F4299 Jeremiah F. Locke, born in Seabrook, Jan. 6, 1828, died in Seabrook, Jan. 11, 1901, married Apl. 24, 1851, HANNAH SMITH of Salisbury, Mass., born in Salisbury, Aug. 7, 1830, died in Seabrook, Apl. 2, 1905. He was a farmer and shoemaker in Seabrook.

Children of 8th Gen. b. Seabrook.
7487 JOHN S., b. Aug. 13, 1853, d. Seab. July 12, 1855.
7488 JOHN B., b. July 20, 1856, was a farmer and stablekeeper in Seabrook and d. there, unmarried July 17, 1896.
7489 ANNIE M. (HANNAH E. town rec.) b. Sept. 18, 1858, d. unmarried, in Seabrook, May 10, 1914.
7490 SON, b. March 8, 1861, (died young?).

F4305 Viola Locke, born Feb. 20, 1850, died in Boston, Jan. 29, 1902, married Nov. 12, 1872, SAMUEL YOUNG NASH, born Jan. 9, 1845. He is with firm, Carter, Rice and Co., Boston. She was adopted by her uncle Philip Locke, # 1837.

Children of 8th Gen. b. Boston.
7491 JULIA L., b. Dec. 26, 1873, m. Brookline, Mass., Feb. 1, 1913, WILLIAM GUILD HOWARD, Harvard College 1891, now Assistant Prof. of German in Harvard.
7492 MABEL W., b. May 3, 1876, d. Aug. 29, 1877.
7493 ETHEL YOUNG, b. Dec. 17, 1878.
7494 SAMUEL AUBIN, b. Apl. 24, 1883.

F4320 John D. Greeley, born Dec. 8, 1841, married LUCINDA BROWN of Seabrook.

Children of 8th Gen.
7495 CHARLES, b. ——, m. LILLIAN BOYD of Hampton.
7496 ALBERT, b. ——, m. —— PITCHWORTH of Amesbury.
7497 SARAH, b. ——, m. SEWELL NOYES.
7498 FRANK, b. ——, was drowned.
7499 THOMAS, b. ——, never married.

F4322 Frank E. Locke, born in Seabrook, July 8, 1848, married Sept. 3, 1871, BETSEY B. WALTON, born in Seabrook, Oct. 25, 1853, daughter of William and Sally (Chase). He was a carpenter and clerk in Seabrook.

Children of 8th Gen. b. Seabrook.

7500 CHARLES W., b. March 19, 1873, m. HELEN SEARS, lives in Seabrook, is a shoemaker.
7501 MINNIE E., b. Jan. 29, 1880, m. WILLIAM A. GILMORE of Haverhill, Mass. They separated but had: 7502 SON, b. 1897, d. 1897; 7503 CLAUDE RAYMOND, b. 1903; 7504 RALPH LOCKE, b. 1906.
7505 FRANK, b. May 24, 1887, d. June 21, 1897.

F4323 George G. Locke, born in Seabrook, Feb. 22, 1852, married in Seabrook, March 29, 1874, MIMA A. Dow of Seabrook, born in Seabrook, Feb. 22, 1852, died in Seabrook, Oct. 3, 1909, daughter of TRISTRAM. He was a shoemaker in Seabrook.

Children of 8th Gen. b. Seabrook.

7506 ELENORE L., b. Feb. 26, 1875, d. Seab., Apl. 19, 1880.
7507 LAURA J., b. Apl. 9, 1877, d. Apl. 23, 1880.
7508 INEZ A., b. Nov. 22, 1884, m. GEORGE EASTMAN of Kensington, and had three children.
7509 MARY L., b. Oct. 22, 1889, m. HAROLD FELCH of Seabrook, had two children.
7510 LUELLA, b. Dec. 22, 1892, married, lives Seabrook.

F4324 Alvin H. Locke, born in Seabrook, July 25, 1859, married in Seabrook, June 25, 1881? ALWILDA A. EATON of Seabrook, born in Seabrook, Feb. 28, 1861, died in Seabrook, Nov. 20, 1913, daughter of Thomas and Betsey (Brown). He was a blacksmith and shoemaker in Seabrook.

Children of 8th Gen. b. Seabrook.

F7511 WILLIE M., b. May 5, 1878, m. Sept. 19, 1899, BERTHA ROWE.
7512 CLARENCE A., b. Feb. 1880, m. MILDRED E. ROWE of Seabrook, b. 1882. He is a shoemaker in Seab., has: 7813 EVERETT; 7514 ALFRED, b. Nov. 28, 1911.
7515 CHARLES T., b. June 6, 1888, d. June 1, 1890.
7516 JERE A., b. Apl. 10, 1890, d. Aug. 2, 1890.
7517 FRANK L., b. Sept. 19, 1891, d. 1891.

F4342 Lyman B. Howe, born in Manchester, Jan. 25, 1838, died in Hanover, Sept. 15, 1893, married MARY L. PERRY. He graduated at Dartmouth, in 1860, and was a doctor in Hanover.

Children of 8th Gen. b. Hanover.

7518 GERTRUDE F., b. Dec. 22, 1867, m. July 19, 1892, FRED L. ALLEN, had: 7519 ANNETTA.
7520 MAE L., b. Sept. 18, 1869.

EIGHTH GENERATION

F4345 Annette A. Webster, born in Strafford, Dec. 21, 1835, died in Chicago, March 4, 1911, married in East Boston, Oct. 26, 1863, JOHN H. TOMLINSON of East Boston, born in Granville, N. S., Nov. 5, 1827, died in Chicago, March 21, 1911. They lived in Chicago.

Children of 8th Gen. b. Chicago.

7521 ANNETTE B., b. June 16, 1866, d. Nov. 25, 1870.
7522 HENRY W., b. Aug. 31, 1869, m. Chicago, March 30, 1911, CAROLINE S. MERRIMAN, b. Chicago, May 16, 1871. He graduated Ithaca University 1895, is an architect in Chicago in 1915.

F4346 Mary H. M. Webster, born in Portsmouth, Jan. 7, 1838, died in Tremont, Neb., July 17, 1893, married in New Bedford, Mass., May 22, 1865, LEANDER M. ORMSBY, born Jan. 8, 1835, died Feb. 17, 1904. He married 2nd, Oct. 18, 1897, at Omaha, Neb., HELEN E. LEACH, of Greenville, Penn.

Children of 8th Gen., all by first wife.

7523 ALICE H., b. Hermitage, Penn., Apl. 25, 1866, m. Apl. 26, 1892, GEORGE F. STILPHEN, b. Swanton, Vt., Nov. 16, 1861; lives in Casper, Wyo.
7524 JAMES WILLIAMSON (MAJOR ORMSBY), b. June 27, 1869, m. July 24, 1895, JESSIE ANNA FINK, has: three boys and one girl, lives in Casper, Wyo.
7525 EDITH, b. Dec. 12, 1871, m. Sept. 8, 1901, ANDREW F. HOFF of Des Moines, Iowa, b. Sept. 3, 1858.
7526 FREDDIE, d. aged 1 year.
7527 GEORGINE W., b. Dec. 29, 1877, d. Feb. 16, 1891.

F4348 Frank D. Webster, born in Portsmouth, Sept. 4, 1841, married 1st, NELLIE ———, of Greenland; married 2nd, MARY FIVE of Philadelphia. He was Captain in U. S. Marine Corps.

Children of 8th Gen.

7528 DAUGHTER died young.
7529 RACHEL, b. ——, m. July 12, 1893, ARTHUR WILZIN.

F4349 Georgine H. Webster, born in Wakefield, Aug. 10, 1843, died Jan. 16, 1913, married in New Bedford, Mass., Dec. 2, 1863, FRED F. MOSES, born in Portsmouth, Dec. 21, 1839, died in Portsmouth, March 20, 1908, son of Samuel. He was a store keeper in Portsmouth.

Children of 8th Gen. b. in Portsmouth.

7530 FRANK W., b. March 16, 1865, m. SADIE HOLMES, had: 7531 GEORGINE, b. June 26, 1889; 7532 DEARBORN, 1891–1912; and 7533 BEATRICE O., b. June 18, 1893. He d. March 2, 1895.

7534 GEORGINE W., b. Dec. 7, 1870, m. Jan. 20, 1892, THOMAS FLANNIGAN, and had: 7535 BARBARA H., b. Feb. 16, 1896.
7536 HELEN F., b. Nov. 20, 1875, d. Feb. 21, 1880.
7537 JULIA, b. May 15, 1880, m. 1st, July 4, 1906, DR. HARRY P. CHASE of Exeter, b. May 14, 1871, d. July 9, 1909, son of Samuel and Mary (Kuse); m. 2nd, in Casper, Wyo., Apl. 27, 1913, GEORGE F. STILPHEN, b. Nov. 16, 1861.

F4406 Simon J. Locke, born ——, married MARIA BURNHAM, lives in Buxton, Me., 1898.

Children of 8th Gen.

7538 EUGENIA.
7539 FANNIE E., b. Buxton, Me., 1868, m. WILLIAM HILL, b. 1869, had six children in Rochester.
7540 LUCILLA. 7541 HATTIE. 7542 ARVILLA.

F4410 Mary A. Locke, born in Strafford, March 1, 1821, died in Hillsboro, July 21, 1896, married July, 1839, WILLIAM H. RIXFORD, who was a builder and died July 1891.

Child of 8th Gen. b. in Barnstead.

7543 EDNA E., b. March 5, 1850, m. 1st, JOSEPH SMART of Concord, who d. 1874; m. 2nd, 1880, PROF. ISAAC COPP, had son and daughter.

F4420 William H. Locke, born in New Durham, Jan. 12, 1847, married in Pittsfield, May 1, 1869, LIZZIE S. PICKERING, born in Barnstead, 1848, daughter of Caleb S. He is a farmer and shoemaker in Pittsfield.

Children of 8th Gen. b. in Barnstead.

7544 FRANK A., b. 1871, m. Farmington, Aug. 16, 1893, ANNIE L. DIXON, b. Lebanon, Me., 1871, dau. of Stephen and Alice; is a shoemaker in Barnstead.
7545 ROSA M., b. July 16, 1874, m. Dec. 25, 1894, ALDEN A. MORRILL of Pittsfield, b. 1874, son of Clarence and Lizzie (Lane).
7546 JOHN W., b. 1875, m. Pittsfield, May 10, 1894, 1st, to MAUDE B. GREEN, b. Pittsfield, 1876, dau. of Sherburne and Celia (Proctor), had: 7547 NELLIE B., b. July 6, 1894. MAUDE was divorced and m. 2nd, —— BRUNELL. John W., m. 2nd, MRS. IDA L. (HALL) PARSHLEY, in Nashua, Dec. 8, 1913, b. 1873, dau. of James A. Hall and Annie A. (Warren). He was a shoemaker.
7548 WAYLAND, b. Nov. 23, 1879.

F4433 Albert Varney, born in Madbury, Aug. 8, 1838, married in Farmington, Feb. 6, 1867, ANTOINETTE CROCKETT born June 6, 1847, died Apl. 24, 1912. He was a farmer in Madbury.

EIGHTH GENERATION

Children of 8th Gen. b. in Madbury.

7549 ANNIE A., b. May 20, 1868, is a teacher.
7550 ELVIN K., b. July 13, 1870, m. Lynn, Mass., Oct. 7, 1896, CLARA B. HILL, b. Apl. 25, 1868, had: 7551 GLADYS H., b. May 16, 1898; 7552 VIOLA G., b. May 14, 1910.
7553 EFFIE L., b. Sept. 20, 1874, is a teacher in Dover.

F4440 Edward Franklin Locke, born in Rochester, Aug. 4, 1842, married in Somersworth, Sept. 1, 1869, JULIA E. JANVRIN, born in Great Falls, 1843, daughter of Rufus and Fidelia. He was a teacher in Rockport, Mo. He has taught 40 years in High and Grammar Schools, three years of which was in New Castle, N. H.

Children of 8th Gen.

7554 ROSCOE J., b. June 16, 1877, m. 1904, LAURA EWOLDT. He has been a lawyer in Primghar, Iowa, since 1899, before that was prosecuting attorney of O'Brien County, Iowa for ten years. Children: 7555 MARION; 7556 MARCELLA; 7557 RUTH.
7558 FRANK R., b. Aug. 4, 1880, m. 1903, RULENNA SLEMP. He is a successful farmer in Iowa. Children: 7559 PEARL; 7560 ELLA; 7561 BEULAH; 7562 IDA; 7563 JAMES F., died young.
7564 JAMES R., b. Feb. 3, 1884, m. 1910, LOTTIE MADDEN. He graduated from University of Iowa City, has practiced law since 1908 at Lenox, Iowa.
7565 GOLDWIN, b. ——, died young.
7566 JOSEPH THURLOW, b. ——, died young.
7567 EDWARD, b. ——, died young.

F4493 Lydia A. Locke, born in Barnstead, 1835, married ORRIN F. CHESLEY, born in Durham, Feb. 23, 1835, died 1907. He was son of Jefferson, and lived in Barnstead.

Children of 8th Gen. b. in Barnstead.

7568 HERBERT L., b. July 10, 1853, m. 1st, IDA PICKERING of Barnstead; m. 2nd, ANNIE AYERS; and had: 7569 LILLIAN, who m. GEORGE FIFIELD, and 7570 GROVER C.
7571 MARY A., b. Nov. 7, 1854, m. March 18, 1872, FRANK SEAWARD, had: 7572 HARRY, and 7573 ALICE.

F4494 James O. Locke, born in Barnstead, Dec. 24, 1837, married June 30, 1867, MARY E. NUTTER, born in Roxbury, Mass. A farmer in Barnstead.

Child of 8th Gen.

F7574 GEORGE E., b. Sept. 9, 1872, m. Sept. 16, 1897, MABEL L. KELLY.

F4495 Jethro N. Locke, born in Barnstead, Apl. 17, 1840, married in Wolfeboro, Oct. 23, 1863, ELECTRA CHELSEY, born in Barnstead, Aug. 10, 1844, daughter of Jefferson. A farmer in Barnstead.

Children of 8th Gen. b. in Barnstead.

7574a LILLIE M., b. Oct. 8, 1865, m. Jan. 27, 1889, ALDEN DIAZ, b. Montpelier, Vt., 1853, son of John and Sarah; lives in Mechanic, Me., and has three children.

7575 EDITH F., b. Jan. 12, 1878. 7576 SON, a twin, b. Jan. 12, 1878.

F4496 Sarah Elizabeth Locke, born in Barnstead, Feb. 6, 1846, married March 2, 1872, GEORGE W. DUDLEY of Concord, born in Barnstead, Oct. 7, 1844, son of William and Harriet. He had a meat market in Concord.

Children of 8th Gen. b. in Concord.

7577 FRED W., b. Aug. 27, 1873, m. Concord, Nov. 28, 1895, SARAH H. CLARKE, dau. of Charles W. and Clara F. (Brown). He is in the insurance business Concord.
7578 CARRIE A., b. June 23, 1875, m. in Concord, BENJAMIN ORR, a plumber of Concord. She is a Vassar College graduate and has:
7579 DUDLEY W.
7580 ARTHUR D., b. May 21, 1879, m. Syracuse, N. Y., GERTRUDE WOODHULL of Syracuse. He is in Electrical Business there.

F4505 Abbie H. Hill, born in Barnstead, 1839, married Sept., 1854, JOSEPH W. HOWARD, a farmer in Alton in 1898.

Children of 8th Gen.

7581 SIDNEY W., b. Apl 1, 1856, was married.
7582 MARY ANN, b. 1858, d. Apl. 1896, m. HENRY SMITH and had two daus.
7583 ETOLA A., b. ——, m. HARTLEY PAGE of Pittsfield, who d. 1896, had two daus.
7584 FRANK, b. ——, was married twice.
7585 FRED, b. ——, was married twice.

F4524 Jane Locke, born in Bristol, Aug. 22, 1823, died in Bristol, Sept. 10, 1890, married Dec. 26, 1843, JOHN F. CASS, born Nov. 29, 1818, son of Daniel and Lydia (Clay). He was a farmer in Bridgewater and Bristol and died June 6, 1876. He was a deacon in the Congregational Church.

Children of 8th Gen. b. in Bristol.

F7586 ELLEN JANE, b. Nov. 26, 1845, m. May 27, 1865, HENRY GRIFFITH.
7587 JULIA A., b. March 9, 1849, m. Sept. 1, 1866, SIMON HENRY CROSS, b. May 21, 1844. He was in 12th. N. H. Reg., later was a farmer in Bristol.
7588 GEORGE F., b. July 4, 1851, m. Apl. 13, 1871, ELLEN E. KEEZER of Groton, Mass., b. Apl. 9, 1852, dau. of George F. He is overseer in woolen mill, Bristol.
F7589 SARAH AUGUSTA, b. Dec. 30, 1855, m. OTIS F. CROSS.
7590 WILLIAM F., b. July 5, 1857, m. May 1, 1880, ROXY DOLOFF of Bristol, # 7602 b. Franklin, 1859. He d. Apl. 3, 1881.

7591 MARY M., b. June 16, 1861, m. Dec. 22, 1885, EDWARD F. PECKHAM, b. July 21, 1862, son of Rev. Cyrus, lives in Providence, R. I., and had: 7592 EARL W., b. 1886.

F4525 Orrin Locke, born in Bristol, Jan. 13, 1826, died in Bristol, Feb. 5, 1898, married in Bristol, NANCY J. FAVOR Apl. 19, 1849, born in Hill, Feb. 26, 1825, died in Bristol, May 15, 1900, daughter of Dr. Daniel and Polly (Sleeper). He was a carpenter and had a paper mill in Bristol.

Children of 8th Gen. b. in Bristol.

F7593 MARY ANN, b. Sept. 21, 1850, m. Feb. 12, 1869, BURLEY M. AMES.
7594 SARAH, b. Dec. 31, 1857, m. 1st, Bristol, Feb. 19, 1884, DR. HADLEY B. FOWLER, b. Bridgewater, 1826, son of Blake and Ruth (Sleeper). He was Surgeon U. S. Army, 1863, and d. Bristol, Jan. 11, 1893. Had no children. She m. 2nd, GEORGE HODGDON of Grinnell, Iowa.

F4527 Favour Locke, born in Bristol, July 5, 1831, died in Alexandria, May 27, 1909, married Nov. 27, 1862, ADALINE W. THOMPSON, born in Andover, June 11, 1838, died in Bedford, Oct. 22, 1913, daughter of Andrew E. and Elizabeth (Perkins). He was a farmer and shoemaker in Bristol and Alexandria.

Child of 8th Gen.

F7595 ADA MARIE, b. Aug. 13, 1869, m. Jan. 1, 1891, REV. FRANCIS D. GEORGE.

F4530 Solon Doloff, born in Bridgewater, Oct. 3, 1827, died in Bristol, Oct. 28, 1903, married May 1, 1850, NANCY SYMONDS, born in Alexandria, March 1, 1829, daughter of Daniel and Martha. He was selectman, had a meat market and was a prominent man in Bristol.

Children of 8th Gen. b. in Bristol.

7596 WILBUR, b. Apl. 1, 1854, d. Dec. 24, 1854.
7597 IDA MAY, b. Oct. 3, 1856, m. March 1, 1879, FRED A. WHITTEMORE of Bridgewater, a Dartmouth graduate, and a farmer in Whitinsville, Mass. Had: 7598 WILFRED; 7599 LULA M.; 7600 LENA; 7601 FRED D.; and two daus., who died young.
7602 ROXY MAUD, b. Jan. 5, 1859, m. 1st, May 1, 1880, WILLIAM F. CASS # 7590 a business man of Bristol, b. July 5, 1857, d. Apl. 5, 1881; m. 2nd, Nov. 18, 1893, as his 3rd wife, CHARLES H. DICKINSON, b. Apl. 7, 1844, a store-keeper of Bristol.
7603 LEVI MANSON, b. Sept. 24, 1860, m. Nov. 14, 1894, MARY R. WORTHLEY, b. Nov. 15, 1867, dau. of Daniel. He is a milk man in Arlington, Mass.

7604 FRANK DANIEL, b. Sept. 7, 1862, m. Feb. 9, 1889, NELLIE F. JOHNSON, b. Bristol, Feb. 2, 1863, dau. of Levi. He is a farmer in Bristol, had: 7605 FRANK, b. 1892.

7606 LOUIS SOLON, b. Aug. 8, 1870, m. Newport, May 1, 1897, MINNIE O'BRIEN of Newport, b. 1871, dau. of John. He is in meat business.

F4532 Orrin Locke Doloff, born in Bristol, July 26, 1833, married May 26, 1859, CLARINDA ELLIOT, born in Rumney, Sept. 5, 1839, daughter of Daniel and Dorcas (Baker). He was a farmer in Bridgewater.

Children of 8th Gen. b. in Bridgewater.

7607 ALBA O., b. March 10, 1860, m. 1st, NELLIE VOSE of Alexandria, b. Apl. 17, 1856, d. Dec. 10, 1886, dau. of John and Emily (Heywood) m. 2nd, Jan. 12, 1889, JENNIE M. DEWAR of Manchester, b. Jan. 3, 1865. He is a letter carrier, Manchester.

7608 MYRA ETTA, b. Apl. 7, 1864, m. Dec. 25, 1882, FRANK H. ELLIOTT, lives Concord, had: 7609 CLARICE, b. 1888.

7610 MABEL M., b. Nov. 1, 1868, m. Sept. 15, 1897, HARRY P. HATHORNE of E. Boston, a book-keeper.

7611 MAUD M., b. a twin, Nov. 1, 1868, is a milliner.

F4540 Levi D. Locke, born in Chateaugay, N. Y., March 23 1835, died in Des Moines, Iowa, Apl. 3, 1892, married June 8 1863 ELIZABETH HODGES, born Aug. 2, 1841, daughter of Andrew They lived in Des Moines, Iowa in 1893.

Children of 8th Gen.

7612 WILFRED D., b. Cedar Falls, Iowa, March 4, 1865, m. Jan. 30, 1891 MARY MCLEON. He is a traveling agent, lives Des Moines, Iowa

7613 FRED LEROY, b. C. Falls, March 27, 1868, d. Des Moines, May 10 1891.

7614 JOHN E., b. C. Falls, Apl. 23, 1870.

7615 WALTER A., b. Des Moines, Aug. 23, 1875, is an electrician there.

7616 CARL, b. Des Moines, March 14, 1881, d. Apl. 14, 1890.

F4543 Benjamin Locke Wells, born in Bristol, Dec. 21 1832, married 1st 1857, MARY SLEEPER who died June 22, 1861 daughter of Leavitt; married 2nd, Aug. 12, 1866, HANNAH ROL LINS of Andover, born in Andover Oct. 14, 1841, daughter o Uriah. He lived in Bristol, was a carpenter, joiner and deale in building supplies.

Children of 8th Gen.

7617 ALBRO, b. Bristol, July 26, 1860, m. Sept. 15, 1885, HARRIET A ROBIE b. Bristol, May 12, 1867, dau. of George. He is a carpente and had: 7618 MARY BERNICE, b. July 17, 1886; 7619 HARR· DANIEL, b. Apl. 6, 1888; 7620 SARAH ELIZABETH, b. June 21, 1895

7621 ELLEN C., b. Apl. 3, 1870, m. Aug. 15, 1894, CHARLES A. GEORGE, b. Bristol Oct. 10, 1867, a lumber manufacturer, had: 7622 MARGARET, b. July 25, 1896; 7623 OLIVE A., b. Apl. 14, 1900, d. Sept. 7, 1900.

F4551 John Winter Wells, born in Bristol, May 11, 1833, married 1853, ROSE BOSWELL, daughter of Stephen and Harriet, born Sept. 6, 1833, died in Laconia, Sept. 6, 1897. He has been on the police force in Bristol and Laconia.

Children of 8th Gen.

7624 HENRY C., b. Feb. 24, 1856, m. 1st, 1884, IRENE PIPER, b. June 1, 1852, d. May 1, 1894, dau. of Oliver; m. 2nd, MRS. F. J. GEORGE, May 30, 1895. He has been a doctor in Laconia since 1879, no children.

7625 HOWARD ELGIN, b. Nov. 24, 1869, m. June 21, 1893, LILLIAN W. SIMONDS, dau. of Albert, b. Dec. 15, 1870. He is a farmer in Alexandria, had: 7626 DAU., b. 1896; 7627 RICHARD H., b. 1897.

F4563 Roxy Doloff Locke, born in Bristol, Apl. 19, 1840, died in Bristol, Aug. 27, 1898, married Nov. 2, 1862, GEORGE H. WHITE, born in Bristol, Nov. 13, 1841, son of Warren and Abigail (Danforth). He was a tanner and furrier, Bristol.

Children of 8th Gen. b. in Bristol.

7628 ANNETTE MAY, b. May 22, 1863, m. Oct. 23, 1884, WALTER F. PRINCE, b. Amherst, June 10, 1861, son of Francis L.; lived Princeton, N. J., 1900.

7629 WARREN, b. Apl. 1, 1867, m. Apl. 8, 1891, CATHERINE BURNS of Lowell. He is a pattern maker and draftsman, Winchester, Mass., 1903.

7630 HENRY GROVE, b. July 21, 1870, d. Apl. 24, 1871.

7631 FREDERICK GEORGE, b. May 2, 1872, is a draftsman, 1903, unmarried.

7631a WALTER HENRY, b. July 29, 1883.

F4569 Levi M. Locke, born in Bristol, Dec. 9, 1854, married in Bristol, June 12, 1875, FANNIE M. SMITH, born in East Haverhill, Apl. 8, 1858, daughter of Henry A. and ——— (Pike). He was a farmer and butcher in Lebanon.

Children of 8th Gen.

7632 ETHEL MAUDE, b. Bristol, Nov. 13, 1877, m. Oct. 14, 1906, JOSEPH C. SMITH of Lebanon, had: 7633 ANNETTE, b. Lebanon, June 2, 1914.

7634 HAZEL MARIA, b. E. Weymouth, Mass., Aug. 12, 1892, m. Apl. 12, 1914, JOSEPH YOUNG CHENEY of Orlando, Fla. They live in Orlando.

F4573 Elizabeth A. Page, born in Hebron, May 21, 1841, died in Alexandria, March 23, 1888, married 1860, HARVEY DREW, born Sept. 2, 1835, died in Alexandria, Aug. 5, 1895, son of Asa and Sarah (Wells); married 2nd, MRS. RUHUMA ALEXANDER. He was a blacksmith in Alexandria.

Children of 8th Gen.

7635 ELMER ELSWORTH, b. Dec. 17, 1861, m. ALBERTA AVERY of Plymouth.—He has been a policeman in Somerville, Mass., since 1895.

7636 NELLIE EVA, b. Bridgewater, May 7, 1865, m. Jan. 1, 1880, EDWIN W. FARNUM of Laconia, had: 7637 JAMES P., b. 1885; 7638 HARRY G., b. 1890; 7639 HELEN M., b. 1894.

7640 PERLEY ASA, b. Jan. 14, 1867, m. DELIA M. EMERY, dau. of Peter, b. July 15, 1869. They live in Cornish, had: 7641 FRANKLIN P., b. 1886; 7642 CLARENCE C., b. 1888.

7643 ETHEL DOLLIE, b. Sept. 14, 1882, lives Alexandria.

F4580 Lavina J. Page, born in Bristol, Sept. 20, 1854, married 1st, Sept. 25, 1869, HENRY W. DRAKE # 4584, born May 30, 1846, and was divorced; married 2nd, Dec. 28, 1886, OSCAR F. MORSE, born in Hebron, June 12, 1826. He was a brakeman and later a conductor; was for 41 years an Express Agent and retired on a pension.

Children of 8th Gen.

7644 MINNIE E., b. Oct. 8, 1870, m. Feb. 3, 1895, FRANK E. KEEZAR, b. Apl. 2, 1864, son of George and Mary.

7645 CHARLES M., b. Apl. 6, 1873, m. Sept. 1895, IDA M. LUKES.

F4640 Beazar Aldrich, born in Barnston, Can., Dec. 19, 1832, died in Stanstead, Can., Jan. 20, 1908, married Jan. 11, 1854, LOVINIA HORN, born in Barnston, Aug. 31, 1833, died June 6, 1914.

Children of 8th Gen. b. in Barnston, Canada.

7647 OZRO BURNHAM, b. March 21, 1857, buried in Langdon, Jan. 29, 1914, m. Nekoma, Dak., MRS. FRANCES STRUPP, and had: 7648 FRANCIS WILLIAM, b. June 7, 1908; 7649 HAROLD; 7650 ALICE MAE.

7652 FRANCES LESTER, b. Jan. 6, 1859.

7653 CHLOE ANN LUCY, b. March 4, 1861, m. May 2, 1894, CHARLES COLONEL ELLSWORTH DEMICK, b. Barnston, Oct. 3, 1864, and had: 7654 ROSE WINNIFRED, b. Dec. 27, 1895; 7655 LEO FRANCES, b. March 19, 1899.

7656 ROSA LYDIA, b. June 6, 1865, d. Dec. 1870.

7657 TIMOTHY HARLEY, b. May 7, 1871, m. Barnston, March 11, 1903, LUCY A. ALDRICH of London, Eng., who d. Beebe, Can., June 20, 1910, had: 7658 REGINALD EDWIN, b. Beebe, July 3, 1905.

EIGHTH GENERATION

F4642 Mary Venan Aldrich, born in Stanstead, Can., March 17, 1837, died in Suncook, Dec. 11, 1905, married Sept. 1, 1859, RUFUS HOSMER PAINE, born in Pembroke, Apl. 8, 1836, lived in Suncook, where he died June 12, 1911.

Children of 8th Gen. b. in Suncook.

7659 JESSE RUFUS, b. July 12, 1860, m. June 27, 1885, HATTIE LULA TENNANT, b. Allenstown, May 11, 1866, and had: 7660 HOWARD TENNANT, b. Suncook, Aug. 25, 1893; 7661 HILMA, b. June 3, 1898, d. June 2, 1899; 7662 MARION SHIRLY, b. Apl. 23, 1903.
7663 ELIZABETH ANN, b. Oct. 4, 1861.
7664 MARY NELLIE, b. July 12, 1864, d. March 19, 1894.
7665 CLARA LOCKE, b. May 3, 1869, d. Nov. 28, 1872.
7666 CLARA LOCKE, b. May 3, 1875, d. Aug. 25, 1875.

F4643 Thomas Locke Aldrich, born in Stanstead, Can., Dec. 23, 1839, married Jan. 27, 1866, EMMA JOANNE CADE, born Dec. 27, 1850, died Nov. 7, 1909. He lived in Barnet, Vt., and died June 5, 1908.

Children of 8th Gen. b. in Barnet, Vt.

7667 EMMA GERTRUDE, b. Barnet, Apl. 12, 1867, m. Nov. 9, 1886, CHARLES BUTLER CARR, b. July 6, 1865, and had children born in St. Johnsbury; 7669 MARTIN THOMAS, b. Jan. 17, 1888, m. Nov. 1915, RUBY MC MANN; 7670 THEODORE ALDRICH, b. March 6, 1893, and 7671 RUTH, b. Dec. 21, 1894.
7672 MARY VENAN, b. Feb. 13, 1869, m. March 20, 1887, EDGAR WALTER UNDERWOOD, b. Feb. 7, 1868, d. June 19, 1913, and they had in St. Johnsbury, Vt.: 7673 LULA BRITTANI, b. Sept. 20, 1887, d. Feb. 18, 1888; 7674 CLARENCE PATTERSON, b. Sept. 9, 1888, d. June 11, 1889; and 7675 HARRY ALDRICH, b. Apl. 17, 1897.
7676 CLARA LOCKE, b. Oct. 15, 1872, d. Jan. 11, 1885.

F4644 Levi Locke Aldrich, born in Stanstead, Can., Jan. 6, 1841, married in Manchester, Jan. 29, 1864, AREANNAH AUGUSTA LEWIS, born in Pembroke, Apl. 27, 1843, died Jan. 31, 1914, daughter of Joseph and Mary (Lear). He d. Sept. 26, 1910.

Children of 8th Gen. b. in Manchester.

7677 FREDDIE GUY, b. Feb. 14, 1874, d. Jan. 8, 1876.
7678 FRANK LEVI, b. May 1, 1875.

F4645 Timothy Chauncey Aldrich, born in Stanstead, Can., Feb. 18, 1844, died in La Canada, Col., Jan. 8, 1886, married Apl. 19, 1873, FLORENCE SIBYL FLETCHER, born Apl. 19, 1852. She married 2nd, Jan. 1, 1899, FRANK EUGENE CAMP.

Children of 8th Gen.

7679 TIMOTHY WESLEY RUSH, b. Barnston, Can., March 8, 1874, m. Oct. 4, 1904, HENRIETTA MAUDE ULIGGETT, b. Sherbrooke, Can., Oct. 6, 1873, and had: 7680 IRENE HENRIETTA, b. St. Johnsbury, Vt., May 19, 1906, 7681 STEPHEN RUSH, b. March 28, 1908.

7682 MARY, b. July 27, 1876, d. July 27, 1878.

7683 BETSEY MARY, b. Apl. 19, 1880.

F4646 Adelbert Lester Aldrich, born in Stanstead, Can., Oct. 21, 1848, died June 27, 1910, married Feb. 18, 1868, CYNTHIA NEWELL VANCE, born Feb. 28, 1848, at W. Burke, Vt.

Children of 8th Gen.

7684 ALICE GERTRUDE, b. W. Burke, Vt., Sept. 24, 1869, m. Dec. 31, 1888, OLIVER E. ROUNDY, b. Sutton, Vt. Had: 7685 ONA MAY, b. July 25, 1894, m. Nov. 26, 1913, PHILIP SHUFELT RUBLEE, b. May 29, 1891, and had: 7686 ALICE LOUISE, b. Oct. 19, 1914.

F4659 Clara Ellis Locke, born in Barnston, Can., Oct. 1, 1847, died Aug. 11, 1912, married March 21, 1871, WILLIAM WILDER HEATH, born in Barnston, Can., June 6, 1842.

Children of 8th Gen.

7687 SARA LYDIA, b. Barnston, Can., Jan. 5, 1873, m. Jan. 11, 1905, LAMBERT ASA HASTINGS, b. Barnston, Nov. 2, 1871, d. Sept. 21, 1911, had: 7688 MEREDITH HEATH, b. Stanstead, Can., June 4, 1907.

F7689 JOHN LOCKE, b. Jan. 11, 1876, m. Dec. 22, 1897, WINNIE MARY HILL.

7690 MARY LIZZIE, b. Apl. 24, 1883, d. Feb. 18, 1912.

F4662 Lizzie Ellsworth Locke, born in Barnston, Can., Nov. 30, 1859, died Oct. 26, 1908, married Jan. 16, 1884, GEORGE THOMAS COOPER, born in Barnston, Can., Jan. 16, 1842, died March 9, 1899.

Children of 8th Gen. b. in Barnston, Can.

7691 THOMAS LOCKE, b. Oct. 14, 1886, m. March 31, 1915, ANNIE MAY CALDWELL, b. Ottawa, Ill., July 23, 1890.

7692 ARTHUR HOWARD, b. Nov. 17, 1888.

7693 HAROLD GEORGE, b. Stanstead, Can., Nov. 9, 1890.

7694 RALPH CARROLL, b. Stanstead, Can., Nov. 24, 1893.

7695 STANLEY MORTON, b. Stanstead, Can., July 24, 1896.

F4665 Dorothy Locke, born in New Castle, Aug. 13, 1814, died there, Dec. 16, 1894, married in Portsmouth, Apl. 7, 1837, HENRY TREDICK of New Castle, born March 1, 1811, died in New Castle, Aug. 26, 1896, son of Wm. and Ruth (Tarlton). He was a fisherman in New Castle.

EIGHTH GENERATION 395

Children of 8th Gen. b. in New Castle.
7696 MARY ANN, b. Sept. 4, 1838, died young.
7697 GEORGE L., b. Sept. 24, 1839, d. unmarried, 1873.
7698 HENRY, b. Oct. 17, 1841, died young.
7699 ETHAN A., b. Dec. 18, 1843, d. unmarried, Oct. 10, 1889.
7700 EMMA, b. Apl. 27, 1847, lived unmarried in New Castle.
F7701 JOHN L., b. Dec. 13, 1854, m. Nov. 1, 1886, JULIA FORD.

F4666 Mary Locke, born in New Castle, March 15, 1816, died Oct. 3, 1875, m. Aug. 19, 1837, WILLIAM LANGDON of Portsmouth, born in Portsmouth, Feb. 10, 1818, died Aug. 19, 1872, son of William and Hannah. He was a farmer in Portsmouth.

Children of 8th Gen. b. in Portsmouth.
7702 MARY ANN, b. 1838, d. Apl. 6, 1880, m. 1857, ALFRED MARDEN, had:
  7703 HERMAN, who m. ISABELLE HALEY and had four children.
7704 WOODBURY T., b. May 9, 1839, m. Nov. 29, 1868, in Boston, ABBIE S. BRIGGS of So. Boston, b. 1849. He went to Boston 1865, was a machinist and for 35 years was foreman of a sugar refinery; had two children. He d. Boston, 1900.
7705 EMALINE B., b. 1841, d. Jan. 31, 1872, m. LEONARD BURROWS of So. Boston, had no children and he d. 1874.
7706 ANDREW J., b. June 28, 1843, m. June 28, 1867, MARY A. LANE, b. England, Dec. 28, 1847, had five children in Portsmouth.
7707 LAVINIA H., b. 1845.
7708 JOHN W., b. 1846, m. May 8, 1872, MRS. ELLEN F. KENNISTON of Portsmouth, b. 1847. He d. 1892.
7709 MAJOR SAMUEL, b. ——, m. Nov. 25, 1873, FRANCES E. BEALS, who d. Nov. 8, 1910, had: 7710 DAISY, d. Jan. 10, 1888, aged 10 years. He is a painter in Portsmouth.

F4667 Woodbury Locke, born in New Castle, 1817, died in Portsmouth, May 13, 1881, married June 16, 1852, JANE SMITH, born June 8, 1836, died in Boston, July 8, 1896, daughter of George and Sophia. He was a stable keeper in Portsmouth.

Children of 8th Gen.
7711 CHARLES W., b. 1853, d. Nov. 12, 1858.
F7712 HELEN W., b. Jan. 23, 1860, m. June 7, 1883, JAMES D. P. WINGATE.

F4668 John Locke, born Aug. 1822, died in New Castle, May 17, 1899, married in New Castle, Oct. 7, 1849, SARAH TREFETHERN, born in New Castle, Sept. 25, 1829, died in New Castle, July 13, 1912. He lived on the old Locke place, near the site of an older Locke house, and farmed when not working at his trade as a stone mason. He rebuilt Whales Back Lighthouse many years ago.

Children of 8th Gen. b. in New Castle.

7713 MARY K., b. March 7, 1850, d. 1903, m. Jan. 2, 1872, STEPHEN H. FLANDERS of New Castle, b. Alton, 1845, d. 1916, son of Dyer and Serene. He was a policeman in Pembroke, had: 7714 CLYDE, b. March 24, 1874, was a teacher in Manchester many years and d. New Castle, Dec. 18, 1914; also an infant, b. 1893, d. 1893.

7715 FRANKLIN P., b. Sept. 13, 1851, was a storekeeper in New Castle, and d. there Jan. 18, 1910, unmarried.

7716 IDA, b. Jan. 1, 1855, lives unmarried in New Castle.

F4670 Emaline Locke, born in New Castle, Aug. 8, 1826, died in Portsmouth, March 22, 1897, married Apl. 29, 1849, JOHN GARDNER of Portsmouth, born Oct. 16, 1817, died in Portsmouth, Dec. 12, 1894. He was a machinist at the Navy Yard and in Portsmouth.

Children of 8th Gen.

7717 ELLEN W., b. Nov. 21, 1849, d. Portsmouth, March 16, 1911, m. June 6, 1872, GEORGE ROSE, b. Oct. 12, 1849. He is janitor of U. S. Post Office, had: 7718 SON, b. 1873, died young; 7719 GEORGIE, b. Portsmouth, Feb. 21, 1875, m. June, 12, 1895, ARTHUR RUTLEDGE, b. Sept. 15, 1871, a U. S. Income Tax Agent, and they have: 7720 BRADLEY L., b. Oct. 14, 1896; 7721 FRANK, b. May 5, 1877, a machinist at Portsmouth Navy Yard.

7722 GEORGE, b. Apl. 15, 1851, d. Apl. 19, 1877.

7723 ANNAH, b. Dec. 8, 1855, d. Portsmouth, March 23, 1915, m. 1st, Apl. 24, 1882, LEVI MARDEN, b. Ports. May 6, 1851, d. May 6, 1889; m. 2nd, Oct. 5, 1898, GARDNER GREENLEAF, b. Apl. 24, 1831, a painter in Portsmouth who d. May 15, 1903.

F4671 Elvira Locke, born in New Castle, Aug. 12, 1819, died in Portsmouth, Dec. 6, 1882, married 1st, March 10, 1839, ALFRED TUCKER of Portsmouth, born 1810, died March 7, 1871; married 2nd, Jan. 1, 1874, JOHN H. WELLS born in Sandown, 1823, died in Portsmouth, son of John and Mary Wells, had for 1st wife SARAH HAMMOND.

Children of 8th Gen. b. in Portsmouth.

7724 ALFRED, b. 1839, d. Oct. 4, 1839.

F7725 CHARLES SAMUEL, b. Dec. 11, 1842, m. NELLIE HUBBARD.

7726 GEORGE ALBERT, b. Aug. 13, 1844, d. Sept. 29, 1865.

7727 JAMES E., b. Oct. 1, 1846, m. Dec. 26, 1872, MRS. EMMA C. (WATKINS) COOK, b. Feb. 4, 1849. He was a machinist in Portsmouth, had: IDA M., b. Sept. 21, 1873, m. B. FRANK GARDNER, a mason of Portsmouth.

7728 ADDIE A., b. Aug. 2, 1849, d. Sept. 10, 1863.

7729 FRANKLIN P., b. Apl. 15, 1852, an Adams Express Agent, Providence, R. I.

EIGHTH GENERATION

F4672 James Neal, born in New Castle, Nov. 14, 1808, died in New Castle, Apl. 1, 1833, married in New Castle, June 20, 1831, MARGARET WHITE, daughter of Nathaniel. She married 2nd, JOSEPH WHITE. James was a fisherman in New Castle. Margaret died in 1836.

Child of 8th Gen. b. in New Castle.

F7730 JAMES, b. Apl. 1, 1833, m. 1st, Oct. 1856, LUCY A. GREEN, m. 2nd, LIZZIE GALUSHA.

F4673 William L. Neal, born in New Castle, Jan. 27, 1811, died in New Castle, Sept. 19, 1895, married 1st, ABIGAIL HARRET, born Jan. 6, 1808, daughter of Charles and Abigail; married 2nd, Nov. 7, 1847, SARAH ODIORNE WILLARD of Kittery, Me., born Sept. 4, 1808. He was a mariner of New Castle.

Children of 8th Gen. b. in New Castle.

7731 CATHERINE HARRET, b. Dec. 22, 1837, d. Aug. 1869, m. 1859, FRANK DANA.
F7732 OLIVE LOCKE, b. Oct. 27, 1842, m. Jan. 30, 1864, FRANCIS W. DANA.
7733 MARY A. T., b. June 11, 1840, d. July 11, 1869, m. Dec. 22, 1863, JOSEPH AYERS.

Second wife's child:

7734 SARAH FRANKLIN, b. ——, m. Nov. 27, 1873, JAMES CUSHING LITTLEFIELD, and lived in Everett, Mass., had: 7735 OLIVE DANA, b. ——, m. H. E. SAXTON.

F4674 Mary B. Neal, born in New Castle, March 22, 1816, died Sept. 23, 895, married in Portsmouth, Dec. 3, 1835, SAMUEL BATSON, born Dec. 22, 1813. He was a mariner and was lost at sea March 28, 1860. (Brother of Nathaniel, # 4697.)

Children of 8th Gen. b. in New Castle.

7736 SAMUEL, b. Nov. 1, 1836, m. CHARLOTTE TARLTON, lived in Chelsea, and had: 7738 ALMER.
F7739 MARY ANN, b. Nov. 2, 1836, m. Nov. 1, 1853, ELIAS TARLTON.
7740 ABIGAIL N., b. July 15, 1842, m. GEORGE NEALLY and lived Charlestown, Mass. Had: 7741 FRANK and 7742 FRED, died young; 7743 WILLIE, b. 1870.
7744 IRVING W., b. June 2, 1845, d. Aug. 2, 1845.
F7745 CLARENDA, b. Sept. 17, 1846, m. 1st, FRANK WEST; m. 2nd, Nov. 25, 1866, CHARLES PETTIGREW.
F7746 HARRIET H., b. May 6, 1849, m. THOMAS HEYWOOD.
7747 SARAH L., b. Nov. 2, 1851, m. JOHN COLBETH of Farmington, had a daughter died young. They lived Australia.
7748 ANNIE, b. July 4, 1854, d. Sept. 28, 1854.
7749 FANNIE, b. twin, July 4, 1854, m. FORREST WEDGWOOD, a barber of Farmington, had no children.

7750 THOMAS E. O., b. Sept. 14, 1855, m. EDNA CLOUTMAN, was a mason in Haverhill, Mass., no children.
7751 WASHINGTON I., b. Dec. 25, 1859, died young.

F4675 Joseph L. Neal, born in New Castle, July 29, 1819, died 1859, married 1844, MARGARET CARD, who died 1861. He was a joiner in New Castle.

Children of 8th Gen. b. in New Castle.
7752 ABIGAIL, b. ——, m. CUSHING HATCH, had: 7753 EDWARD; 7754 NELLIE.
7755 MARY, b. ——, was m. and had two children.

F4678 Adaline P. Locke, born in Rye, Nov. 1819, died in Charlestown, Mass., July 26, 1861 married in Rye, Oct. 19, 1839, HIRAM TREFETHERN, born in New Castle, 1815, died June 2, 1904. He was a sea captain of Rye.

Children of 8th Gen.
7756 FRANCES EMILY, b. New Castle, Aug. 1, 1840, lives, unmarried, in Ports., 1916.
7757 THADDEUS, b. 1842, d. Charlestown, Mass., May 13, 1860.
7758 ADA, b. PORTSMOUTH, 1845, d. 1848.
F7759 ANDREW J., b. 1852, m. 1870, ISABELLE TOWNSEND.

F4679 Joseph Prentice Locke, born in Rye, 1820, died in Kittery, 1885, married FRANCIS MANSON, born 1830. He was keeper of Whales Back Light and had a grocery store in Portsmouth. He was quite a politician in his day. His widow married 2nd, EPHRAIM PETTIGREW of Kittery, March 9, 1893.

Child of 8th Gen.
F7760 FRANKLIN D., b. Portsmouth, 1865, m. NELLIE J. BOUCHER.

F4680 Olive R. Locke, born in Rye, Feb. 19, 1823, died in Portsmouth, March 4, 1897, married Feb. 28, 1847, THOMAS H. PHILBRICK, born March 30, 1822, died Oct. 13, 1879, son of James and Abigail (Pervier). He was a farmer in Rye.

Children of 8th Gen b. in Rye.
7761 CHARLOTTE A., b. 1849, d. Aug. 10, 1863.
F7762 EMMA O., b. Nov. 20, 1851, m. Jan. 3, 1869, JACOB A. MOULTON.
F7763 WILLIAM I., b. Nov. 13, 1855, m. 1st, Oct. 22, 1874, ARVILLA S. JUNKINS m. 2nd, July 29, 1882, LIZZIE BREED.
F7764 HERBERT E., b. June 28, 1858, m. Dec. 1880, IDA F. MARDEN.
F7765 IDA F., b. Oct. 30, 1863, m. June 19, 1884, GEORGE FRED BREED.

EIGHTH GENERATION 399

F4682 Andrew J. Locke, born in Rye, Apl. 4, 1829, died in Pawtucket, R. I., Oct. 18, 1905, married July 3, 1853, CAROLINE A. HAYES, born May 22, 1835, died Feb. 15, 1901. He was a mason, and in early life laid the granite quay walls at the Navy Yard, which even now, 70 years later, are considered particularly fine jobs. He lived later in Charlestown and Chelsea, Mass.
Children of 8th Gen.
7766 LOIS M., b. Aug. 15, 1855, m. Portsmouth, Apl. 23, 1873, COMMANDER WILLIAM I. MOORE of U. S. Navy, b. in Wheeling, W. Virginia, June 12, 1844, son of John and Sarah. She d. in Boston Aug. 14, 1915. William I. Moore was appointed to the Naval Academy from Virginia and entered the same, Apl. 14, 1862, at Newport, R. I., and graduated four years later. He was advanced through the various grades to Commander in 1899, was retired and d. Feb. 19, 1916. Had: 7767 CHARLES WILLIAM, b. Portsmouth, Dec. 7, 1873, d. Chester, Pa., Apl. 18, 1892, while a student of Penn. Military Academy.
7768 WILLIE A., b. July 21, 1865, d. Ports., Feb. 18, 1866.
7769 KATHERINE B., b. July 13, 1869, lived Brookline, Mass.
7770 PHILIP A., b. Portsmouth, Aug. 27, 1875, lived Chelsea, Mass.

F4685 Joseph Locke, born in Rye, Sept. 1836, died in Rye, May 1, 1902, married June 24, 1859, HELEN A. WOODSUM of Saco, born 1841, died March 9, 1888, daughter of John and Sarah. He kept a store in Portsmouth.
Children of 8th Gen. b. in Portsmouth.
F7773 THADDEUS W., b. Oct. 21, 1861, m. 1st, FLORA COBB; m. 2nd, Oct. 19, 1888, KATHERINE J. SULLIVAN; m. 3rd, ELLEN E. MARTIN.
7774 ELBRIDGE, b. Rye, Aug. 22, 1863, d. Aug. 18, 1864.
7775 MARTIN V. B., b. Dec. 11, 1864, m. Dover, June 8, 1886, KATHERINE A. CONNORS, b. Manchester, 1866, dau. of William and Mary. Has no children and lives in Manchester. By trade a moulder.
F7776 CLARA, b. Apl. 30, 1866, m. May 25, 1885, THOMAS G. B. MOULTON.
7777 HELEN, b. Dec. 5, 1868, m. 1st, June 27, 1886, WILLIAM HARTSHORN, b. Portsmouth, 1864, d. Apl. 10, 1889, son of Harry; m. 2nd, Sept. 29, 1892, WILLIAM DIXON, lives in Chicago, adopted 7778 NINA (CHASE).
7779 MARCELLUS, b. March 28, 1871, d. Aug. 22, 1871.
F7780 FREDERICK G., b. Nov. 26, 1873, m. July 22, 1893, FANNIE MARTIN.
7781 ERNEST L., b. July 22, 1876, d. Feb. 25, 1878.
7782 HOWARD, b. July 6, 1880, d. March 13, 1884.

F4694 Olive N. Watson, born in Portsmouth, March 15, 1835, died July 24, 1886, married 1852, GEORGE W. LORD of Portsmouth, born in Kittery, Me., Nov. 4, 1832, son of Moses. He was forty-two years in wholesale liquor business in Portsmouth; married 2nd, MARGARET MCMANUS and died in Portsmouth, Oct. 25, 1910. She died in Portsmouth, Aug. 19, 1915.

Children of 8th Gen. b. in Portsmouth.

F7785 NORMAN W., b. 1852, m. Nov. 8, 1872, MARY ANN TOWNSEND.
F7786 ANNA, b. Apl. 1854, m. 1st, May 9, 1872, LIEUTENANT THOMAS P. MOONEY; m. 2nd, EDWIN D. ACKERMAN; m. 3rd, VALENTINE HETT.

F4697 Mary Olive Locke, born in New Castle, March 3, 1821, died in Danvers, Mass., Apr. 28, 1901, married Oct. 18, 1839, NATHANIEL BATSON, born in New Castle, Aug. 3, 1811, died in Danvers, Dec. 27, 1898. In his early years he was a Labrador fisherman, later on moving to Danvers, he became a shoemaker, saved his money and enjoyed many years of retirement. He was a brother of 4674.

Children of 8th Gen. b. in New Castle.

F7787 HORACE W., b. Nov. 4, 1840, m. July 3, 1867, ELLEN TARLTON.
F7788 LEWIS C., b. Dec. 22, 1842, m. 1st, Oct. 21, 1873, ADA KENT, m. 2nd, July 22, 1899, MRS. CAROLINE COLE.
7789 ESTHER R., b. March 10, 1846, m. Sept. 18, 1866, NATHAN PATTERSON of Essex, Mass., b. 1843, a grocer in Danvers. He died there, May 8, 1872, had: 7790 LEWIS, b. March 8, 1868, a printer in N. Y. City; and 7791 FRED, b. July 11, 1870, a clerk in Danvers post office.
F7792 ANNIE, b. June 23, 1850, m. Sept. 10, 1874, JACOB MARSTON.
7793 LIZZIE, b. Sept. 21, 1853, for several years was a successful necktie manufacturer in Danvers, now living unmarried and retired in Danvers.
7794 NELLIE, b. Apl. 17, 1858, d. with her child, July 15, 1886, m. July 28, 1880, JOSH ARMITAGE, b. 1858. He was a shoe agent and m. 2nd, GERTRUDE TIBBETTS.

F4699 Martha Ann Locke, born in New Castle, March 8, 1825, died Apl. 19, 1877, married March 12, 1844, BENJAMIN J. BATSON of New Castle, born in Maine, June 12, 1811. He was a sea captain in New Castle and died May 9, 1883. He was son of Benjamin.

Children of 8th Gen. b. New Castle.

F7795 ELIZABETH, b. Nov. 9, 1845, m. Dec. 28, 1865, DANIEL S. YOUNG.
F7796 BENJAMIN JENKINS, b. Aug. 13, 1849, m. July 2, 1880, ELIZABETH IRENE HAMMOND.
7797 JOHN, b. Oct. 8, 1851, d. 1853.
7798 ADDIE CLIFTON, b. June 12, 1854, m. Portsmouth, July 31, 1877, PASCHAL M. SPINNEY, b. Eliot, Me., May 29, 1850, son of Jeremiah and Caroline (Staples). He was many years in the tinware business, now an invalid; had two infants d. a few days old.

EIGHTH GENERATION 401

F7799 JESSIE FREMONT, b. Nov. 10, 1856, m. N. C., Dec. 11, 1881, CHARLES
BENJ. AMAZEEN.
7800 MYRA BICKFORD, b. June 12, 1860, m. Manchester, Feb. 22, 1881,
J. Q. A. MARTIN, b. New Castle, Dec. 8, 1856, son of Chandler and
Harriet (Vennard). He was a painter in Manchester and d. N. C.,
Jan. 13, 1892, had one boy 7801 d. infant.

F4700 Abram Trefethern Locke, born in New Castle, May 2, 1827, married in Greenland, Feb. 3, 1850, JANE TUCKER of Portsmouth, born Oct. 14, 1830, daughter of John and Elizabeth (Lombard). He was a ship caulker, worked at the Navy Yard, owned his home on South St., Portsmouth and died there Apl. 28, 1876, in the prime of life. She died in Lawrence, Mass., June 8, 1915.

Children of 8th Gen. b. in Portsmouth.
F7802 LANGDON ELVIN, b. July 1, 1851, m. Jan. 3, 1876, IDA LANE.
F7803 WILBUR JESSE, b. Dec. 10, 1853, m. Dec. 10, 1883, ANNA TROW.
7804 MUNROE GORDON, b. March 23, 1856, m. 1st, 1877, ALICE BAKER of
Danvers, who d. 1898; m. 2nd, Apl. 27, 1898, MARY DAWLTON of
Lawrence, b. 1860. He had one son who died an infant. He was
a foreman for his brother many years and is now retired.
7805 MELVIN, b. Jan. 2, 1858, d. 1860.

F4701 John Langdon Locke, born in New Castle, Dec. 12, 1829, died Jan. 15, 1869, married Aug. 2, 1852, SARAH JANE VENNARD of New Castle, born Aug. 12, 1832, died in Danvers, Feb. 2, 1908, daughter of Capt. John. He was a shoemaker in Danvers.

Children of 8th Gen.
7806 NORMAN, b. Sept. 17, 1853, d. Danvers, Nov. 1, 1869.
7807 HERBERT L., b. Apl. 8, 1857, d. Dec. 1, 1858.
7808 ARTHUR LANGDON, b. Apl. 15, 1860, d. New Castle, Aug. 20, 1861.
7809 HERMAN VENNARD, b. Sept. 15, 1862, d. Aug. 16, 1863.

F4702 Adaline Locke, born in New Castle, Apl. 1, 1832, married Nov. 20, 1855, DANIEL SMITH of Canterbury, born in Concord, July 23, 1831, son of Zebulon and Hannah C. (Sargent). He had a meat market in Penacook many years and retired a few years ago. This couple, living quietly in 1915, after 70 years in Penacook, have by that life earned the highest esteem of the community. She died in Penacook, Jan. 15, 1916.

Children of 8th Gen. b. in Penacook.
7810 FRED, b. Oct. 18, 1856, was with his father in the meat market, died,
unmarried, Apl. 21, 1890.
7811 EVERETT, b. Feb. 1, 1860, was a joiner in Penacook, died unmarried,
Apl. 6, 1898.

F4703 Amos Seavey Locke, born in New Castle, Apl. 26, 1834, died in Concord, Aug. 11, 1912, married Jan. 7, 1861, MARTHA ANN SILVER, born Aug. 29, 1843, daughter of William and Mary. He served in the Navy during the Civil War and was in the assault on Fort Fisher. In early life he was a farmer and shoemaker, but the most of his life was spent in Concord, employed as tool maker by the granite firms. He was a deep reader, a ready talker and ever prepared for an argument.

Children of 8th Gen. b. in Concord.
F7812 ANNIE J., b. Dec. 12, 1862, m. March 31, 1880, ALBERT G. SMITH.
F7813 LILLIAN A., b. Jan. 4, 1872, m. 1894, FRED R. ROACH.

F4704 Oliver Horton Locke, born in New Castle, July 19, 1836, married in Portsmouth, March 7, 1857, ELIZA JANE BRACKETT, born in Portsmouth, Jan. 13, 1838, the daughter of Thomas and Jane (Walden), a descendant of Anthony Brackett of Rye and Portland, Me. At 15 he was shoemaking, and a year later went to Farmington as foreman of a shop. Returning to Portsmouth, he learned the house joiners trade, became a builder and continued as such the rest of his life except the last six years when he was incapacitated. He enlisted Nov. 20, 1862, and was carpenter's mate on the ship "Colorado" until his discharge Feb. 10, 1864. Lack of schooling was rapidly overcome by constant reading and study, so that in mature years he was able to hold his own with those of higher education, was an able talker, and one whose advice and sound judgment was eagerly sought and followed. He was a Master Mason, served the Odd Fellows 35 years as secretary, was long a member of the Fire company and the Mechanics Association of which he was several times President. A strong Republican, he served his party in conventions, and his city as Councilman and in other minor offices, although being elected from a strong Democratic ward. A lover of children, he had their respect and was held in the highest estimation by all adults. He died March 28, 1906.

Children of 8th Gen. b. in Portsmouth.
F7814 AMOS REVILO, b. May 26, 1858, m. 1st, Nov. 9, 1885, ELLA T. CURTIS; m. 2nd, Oct. 16, 1900, FLORENCE A. MCLEAN.
7815 LAURA ANNA, b. June 15, 1860, d. Sept. 6, 1871.
7816 ARTHUR HORTON, b. Apl. 3, 1866, m. in Penacook, Sept. 2, 1896, MABEL LILLIAN SYMONDS, b. Concord, July 21, 1870, daughter of Joseph E. and Sarah F. A. (Little). See History of Hancock, also Little Genealogy. He graduated from Dartmouth in 1890 and

Oliver H. Locke F4704

Arthur H. Locke 7816

EIGHTH GENERATION 403

received the degree of A.M. in 1893, was appointed draftsman in the U. S. Navy Department in 1891, and served as such for twelve years in several naval stations including two years in Washington. In 1903 he took charge of the Brick manufacturing plant of the York Harbor Brick Co., at York, Me., as Treasurer and Manager, with his home in Portsmouth. He has been alderman and councilman at large, declined mayoralty nomination, and has served in other places of trust and honor, one of which was seven years on the School Board. He is a member of the various Masonic bodies including De Witt Clinton Commandery of Knights Templar, and several local clubs. He is now serving his third year as Warden of St. John's Episcopal Church. It is quite possible that this genealogy would never have been completed, or at least not for many years, without the great assistance of Mrs. Locke. She has shared my labors in all the large libraries, has read all the proof with me, in every way has been my encourager and co-worker and is surely an equal sharer in any credit which this book merits. She is an active church worker, prominent in all women's efforts for the betterment of the race and city, and has served in various official capacities in the Woman's Club, Civic Club and Girls' Club of Portsmouth.

7817 VERNON BRACKETT, b. March 31, 1872, d. Dec. 14, 1873.
7818 GRACE HARTEAU, b. July 27, 1874, a girl of marked promise, d. Feb. 24, 1884.

F4707 Christena Locke, born in New Castle, Dec. 8, 1842, died in Danvers, Oct. 14, 1872, married in 1860 HENRY BACHELDER of Wenham, born in Wenham, 1841. He was an ice dealer in Danvers, Mass., died Feb. 3, 1915, leaving a fortune to his second wife and nothing to his daughters.

Children of 8th Gen. b. in Danvers, Mass.

F7819 ADDIE, b. Nov. 15, 1864, m. 1880 GEORGE REED.
F7820 HATTIE, b. Apl. 6, 1867, m. 1st, 1884, CHARLES FARNEST; m. 2nd, 1895, FRED ROUSER.

F4712 Elizabeth Emerett Locke, born in Rye, Apl. 1, 1826, died in Rye, May 25, 1909, married May 21, 1848, NATHANIEL MARDEN of Rye, born Feb. 20, 1817, died March 9, 1891, son of Reuben. He was a carpenter and farmer in Rye, was town clerk twelve years and held other town offices.

Children of 8th Gen. b. in Rye.

F7821 POLLY W., b. July 7, 1848, m. Sept. 29, 1869, GEORGE G. WHITE.
7822 CLARA OLIVE, b. Jan. 27, 1850, m. Jan. 15, 1879, CHARLES A. WALKER, b. Rye, June 22, 1837, a farmer in Rye, no child. He d. Dec. 14, 1909.
7823 ERVEN W., b. Nov. 21, 1852, d. unmarried, Rye, March 26, 1905.

7824 SAMUEL ANSON, b. March 3, 1854, unmarried.
7825 HOLLIS N., b. May 23, 1856, m. Rye, Dec. 28, 1883, CARRY M. FOSS, b. Rye, Feb. 28, 1860, dau. of John O. and Mary (Green). He is a carpenter in Rye, no children.
F7826 ELVIRA GARLAND, b. Nov. 8, 1857, m. May 29, 1879, WALTER E. LOCKE # 9329.
7827 FRED H., b. Dec. 20, 1859, d. Stoughton, Mass., unmarried, May 11, 1893.
7828 WILLIE P., b. Dec. 14, 1861, d. March 3, 1869.
F7829 EMERETT ELIZABETH, b. Oct. 6, 1863, m. Sept. 25, 1888, EDWARD E. RAMSDELL.
7830 ABBIE A., b. June 10, 1866.

F4715 James H. Locke (adopted son) born in Rye, June 15, 1830, married in Portsmouth, Dec. 28, 1864, SARAH A. TREFETHERN of Kittery, Me., born in Kittery, Dec. 11, 1831, daughter of Capt. Wm. M. and Sarah B. He was a carpenter and joiner in Kittery but for several years past had been retired, yet in good active health. He and his wife have been deeply interested in the Locke Association since its beginning. He died in Portsmouth, Jan. 6, 1916.

Child of 8th Gen.
7831 ANNIE J. (adopted) b. Jan. 28, 1878, m. Kittery, Me., Jan. 8, 1902, EDWIN E. BOWDEN # 7950 and had: SADIE L., b. Jan. 8, 1903.

F4717 Mary J. Berry, born in Rye, Aug. 25, 1818, died in Dover, Nov. 13, 1908, married June 8, 1837, JOHN L. PICKERING, born Jan. 9, 1811, died May 19, 1884 He was a farmer in Newington.

Children of 8th Gen. b. in Newington.
7832 MANDANA, b. March 7, 1839, d. in Dover, March 15, 1916, m. Dec. 9, 1879, GEORGE B. FOSS of Portsmouth, b. Jan. 8, 1836. He was a machinist in Dover, and d. March 16, 1893.
7833 ANNIE OLEVIA, b. Apl. 4, 1841, d. May 28, 1845.
7834 PHILENA, b. Apl. 29, 1843, d. March 28, 1914, m. Dover, Apl. 21, 1886, ANDREW HANSON of Dover, b. Madbury, Apl. 22, 1824. He was a farmer in early life and d. Dover, Apl. 1, 1901, no children.
7835 CHARLES, b. March 8, 1845, d. Aug. 29, 1865.
7836 WILLIAM, b. Feb. 23, 1847, d. Dec. 17, 1861.
7837 JOHN, b. July 17, 1851, d. Aug. 18, 1854.
F7838 MARY, b. May 19, 1849, m. Dec. 2, 1876, BENJAMIN W. PINKHAM.
F7839 OLIVE MARIA, b. Dec. 12, 1853, m. Aug. 27, 1879, JOHN RANKIN.
F7840 JAMES K., b. June 9, 1856, m. Oct. 6, 1883, JENNIE LAKE.
7841 JOHN GILMAN, b. Feb. 25, 1859, died young.
F7842 ELEANOR ANNIE, b. May 27, 1861, m. Oct. 23, 1883, HERBERT D. CAVERLY.

EIGHTH GENERATION 405

F4718 Elizabeth A. Berry, born in Rye, June 3, 1821, died Feb. 21, 1910, married in Newington Aug. 28, 1844, JOSEPH W. WHIDDEN, born 1818, died in Newington, Oct. 24, 1875. He was a farmer on Lafayette Road, Portsmouth.
Children of 8th Gen.
7843 CHARLES G., b. Portsmouth, July 7, 1845, d. May 27, 1868.
7844 MARY O., b. Aug. 28, 1848, m. Newington, Dec. 13, 1868, WILLIAM C. LAWS, who is a farmer, has three children. She d. Feb. 16, 1916.
7845 ELDORA A., b. Jan. 15, 1850, d. Jan. 18, 1881, m. Dec. 25, 1879, HENRY A. SURLES, a laborer in Kittery, Me., no children.
7846 JOSEPH W. M., b. Newington, June 16, 1853, m. 1st, SARAH E. PICKERING, m. 2nd, MRS. EMILY COLE. He is a farmer in Newington, no children.
7847 FRANK L., b. Jan. 17, 1855, m. June 26, 1890, MARION C. MARDEN. He is a farmer in Newington.
7848 CARRIE E., b. Nov. 4, 1860.
7849 IRA W., b. Jan. 19, 1862, m. Jan. 7, 1889, NELLIE P. PEARSON, is a clerk in Portsmouth, has two children.
7850 EDITH M., b. Apl. 16, 1866, m. Jan. 20, 1886, DANIEL WESLEY BADGER an Ex-Mayor and milk dealer of Portsmouth, have eight children.

F4721 Martha O. Berry, born in Rye, Nov. 4, 1830, died Feb. 11, 1876, married Nov. 13, 1858, ROBERT MANSON, born July 18, 1819. He was a farmer in Greenland and died in 1895.
Children of 8th Gen. b. in Greenland.
7851 EMMA, b. Nov. 1859, d. Rye, June 9, 1899, m. MORRIS J. GARLAND of Rye, b. Apl. 30, 1858, son of Rufus and Semira (Jenness) had:
7852 HAROLD, b. June 9, 1888.
7853 ETTA, b. ——, d. aged 7 years.

F4728 Moses Clarke, born in Rye, Sept. 29, 1829, married SUSAN A. TUCKER, Oct. 26, 1858, born in Rye, Apl. 28, 1829, died in Rye, March 15, 1905, daughter of Michael and Elizabeth (Moses). He was a farmer at Rye Harbor and died March 27, 1906.
Children of 8th Gen. b. in Rye.
7854 EMMONS B., b. March 6, 1860, is a mason in Rye, unmarried.
7855 MARCIA B., b. Oct. 23, 1863, m. Aug. 6, 1884, EDWIN H. DRAKE, b. Sept. 5, 1861, a farmer in Rye, son of Charles T. and Helen (Weeks).
7856 MARIETTA, b. Sept. 27, 1866, d. Jan. 27, 1887.
7857 CHARLES W., b. Jan. 13, 1870, d. Jan. 13, 1888.

F4729 John Elvin Locke, born in Rye, Aug. 25, 1835, married 1st, in Somersworth, Jan. 7, 1862, SARAH HAYES, born in

Milton, June 3, 1837, died in Portsmouth, Oct. 19, 1877, daughter of Ephraim and Rosamond (Dame); married 2nd, March 6, 1879, her cousin, LAURA A. HAYES, born Apl. 30, 1853. He was for many years in charge of the B. & M. R. R. wharves in Portsmouth, only retiring a few years ago. While in Portsmouth he was an active, influential citizen, holding several city offices including that of Alderman, and also was representative in the Legislature. He now, 1916, lives retired in Rye. He is an Odd Fellow and Mason.

Children of 8th Gen.

7858 WILLIAM M., b. May 23, 1862, was in leather business in Milton, d. unmarried there Sept. 24, 1906.

7859 MARY E., b. Dec. 28, 1863, d. aged 11 weeks.

7860 IDA L., b. Milton, May 29, 1865, d. Portsmouth, June 20, 1895, m. Ports., Dec. 12, 1888, HERBERT F. RAY, b. Hartford, Vt., Apl. 29, 1862, son of Benjamin F. and Sarah. He was an apothecary.

7861 CHARLES ELVIN, b. Portsmouth, Aug. 29, 1874, m. in Canada, June 30, 1903, MRS. LOUISE (OKE) STEWART of Canada, b. Sept. 12, 1866, dau. of James and Mary Elizabeth of Exeter, Ontario, Canada. He received the degree of B. S. from Technology, was an alderman of Portsmouth, and Knight Templar Mason. Later he removed to Boston where he is Professor of Mining Engineering and Metallurgy in the Mass. Institute of Technology. He has been for several years President of the Locke Association.

7862 HENRY HERBERT, b. Ports., Aug. 13, 1877, d. Greensboro, Ga., March 9, 1902, was a clerk and unmarried.

F4731 Oliver Elbridge Locke, born in Rye, July 24, 1842, married Dec. 20, 1873, ARABELLE CLOUGH of Rye, born in Rye, Feb. 3, 1852, daughter of Nathan and Abigail (Marden). He served on U. S. Ship Richmond in 1861, and was employed on the Navy Yard many years; lives at Portsmouth. She died Aug. 19, 1915 in Portsmouth.

Children of 8th Gen.

7863 HELEN CLOUGH, b. Portsmouth, Aug. 31, 1878, m. Bangor, Me., Oct. 17, 1903, HARRY LEGRAND HILTON of Chicago, b. July 13, 1876. He is a clerk on U. S. Navy Yard and lives in Ports.

7864 ELIZABETH DELANEY, b. Ports. Dec. 17, 1885, m. Ports. Sept. 10, 1910, HORACE ANDREW MASSEY, JR., b. Nov. 4, 1888, lives Sacramento, Cal., had: 7865 VIVIAN ISABELLE, b. July 23, 1911.

F4733 Sarah Louise Locke, born in Rye, March 25, 1845, married in Exeter, Dec. 20, 1872, CLARENCE MARSTON of Exeter, born there Feb. 11, 1850, died in Boston, Jan. 6, 1904. He was a painter and paper hanger in Exeter.

John Elvin Locke F4729

Prof. Charles Elvin Locke 7861

EIGHTH GENERATION 407

Child of 8th Gen.
7866 EDITH L., b. Exeter, Nov. 4, 1877, m. Feb. 1899, BENJAMIN ROCK, a teamster of Exeter, had: 7867 CLARA HELEN, b. June 6, 1900; 7868 IDA M. L., b. July 19, 1902, d. Feb. 1903; 7869 GRACE C., b. March 25, 1904.

F4735 Emma Amanda Locke, born in Rye, Nov. 29, 1848, married in Manchester, March 3, 1875, OLIVER B. FOGG, born in North Hampton, Nov. 19, 1848, son of Eben and Lydia (Dawlton). He is a farmer in North Hampton.

Children of 8th Gen.
7870 ELVIN LOCKE, b. Rye, June 30, 1875, lives in Portsmouth.
7871 GERTRUDE LOUISE, b. No. Hampton, Sept. 23, 1880, m. 1st, Oct. 21, 1903, ARTHUR L. YOUNG, son of Abbott L. They were divorced 1910 and she m. 2nd, Feb. 21, 1912, ARTHUR L. JENNESS, b. June 18, 1882, son of Dana and Clara J. (Garland).

F4739 Benjamin Berry, born in Moultonborough, July 4, 1823, died in Bangor, Feb. 13, 1904, married 1st, May 31, 1846, ROSANNAH HANSON, born in Gardner, Me., Feb. 7, 1829, died Jan. 13, 1871; married 2nd, July 18, 1874, MRS. MARGARET (ROBERTSON) JEWELL. He was a sail maker in Bangor, Me.

Children of 8th Gen.
7872 ROSA F., b. Bangor, Me., Oct. 16, 1848, d. Sept. 19, 1867.
7872a FRANK B., b. Feb. 26, 1853, d. Apl. 12, 1854.
7873 HATTIE ALICE, b. March 22, 1855, m. Farmington, May 19, 1885, WILLIAM H. GOODWIN, live in E. Boston, no children.
7874 LOTTIE M. J., b. Nov. 4, 1856, m. June 11, 1890, STACY L. ROGERS, live in Bangor, no children.
7875 LIZZIE M., b. Apl. 26, 1859, m. CHANNING WOOD, live in No. Cambridge.
7876 BENJAMIN, b. May 19, 1862, d. May 8, 1864.
7877 ARTHUR RUSSELL, b. Oct. 17, 1866, m. Jan. 29, 1891, CORA E. LANE, moved from Farmington, to Poughkeepsie, N. Y., 1898.
7878 MINNIE M., b. Dec. 15, 1869.
Second wife's children:
7879 ROSA B., b. Feb. 17, 1876, d. 1903, m. Apl. 30, 1900, BURTON R. STARE.
7880 BENJAMIN R., b. May 14, 1878. 7881 Two children, died infants.

F4740 William Berry, born in Moultonborough, Feb. 2, 1827, died in Farmington, June 25, 1890, married Sept. 25, 1852, CALISTA COLBATH of Farmington, born March 31, 1834. He was a shoe cutter in Farmington.

Children of 8th Gen. b. in Farmington.

7882 WILLIAM L., b. Dec. 3, 1854, is a bookkeeper in Dover.
7883 CHARLIE, b. Jan. 7, 1860, d. Oct. 23, 1862.
7884 FRED S., b. July 13, 1865, m. March 30, 1898, MRS. FOSTINA S. STRATTON, b. 1865. Graduated Dartmouth 1888, was a Civil Engineer in Concord.

F4741 John M. Berry, born in Moultonborough, Oct. 28, 1841, married Sept. 14, 1866, LEAH H. ROBERTS, daughter of Nathaniel and Tryphena (Thurston), born in Farmington, Sept. 10, 1848. He was a shoe cutter in Farmington and Haverhill, Mass. and died in Malden, Mass., Feb. 5, 1915.

Children of 8th Gen. b. in Moultonborough.

7885 ELLA GERTRUDE, b. May 26, 1867, died infant.
7886 AGNES LEAR, b. May 7, 1869, now a teacher in Boston.
7887 WINNIFRED HELEN, b. Feb. 5, 1871, m. Haverhill, Mass., Dec. 3, 1903, DR. WILLIAM W. LOUGEE, lives in Malden, Mass., had: 7888 RICHARD, b. 1905; 7889 LAWRENCE, b. 1906.
7890 JOHN ROBERT, b. Apl. 22, 1873, m. Concord, Dec. 3, 1900, FLORENCE ROGERS. They live in Boston. A travelling man.
7891 GEORGE FOSDICK, b. Oct. 26, 1878, m. Bar Harbor, Me., Feb. 8, 1913, LOUISE NEWMAN. He is a travelling man of Portland, Me.
7892 CLIFTON EUGENE, b. July 3, 1881, lives Chicago.
7893 HENRY C., b. Sept. 2, 1883, lives Philadelphia.

F4742 Sarah Ann Berry, born in Moultonborough, Apl. 1, 1837, married Feb. 4, 1867, AMOS STEARNS, born Nov. 29, 1828. He was a farmer in Waltham, Mass., and died Dec. 28, 1896.

Children of 8th Gen.

7894 WILLIAM BENJ., b. Nov. 27, 1867.
7895 ROSA FRANCES, b. June 11, 1869, m. Dec. 20, 1898, FRANCIS H. FOSTER of Gloucester, Mass., b. Oct. 7, 1866. He is in laundry business in Somerville, Mass., had: 7896 HOMANS S., b. Apl. 24, 1906.
7897 LIZZIE LUNETTE, b. March 31, 1874.
7898 NATH. AMOS, b. Oct. 20, 1877.

F4743 William Benjamin Jenness, born in Rye, May 29, 1819, died Dec. 31, 1906, married in Rye, Dec. 25, 1844, MARY A. JENNESS, born in Rye, June 3, 1826, died in Brentwood, July 24, 1900, daughter of Capt. Samuel and Clarissa. He was a farmer in Brentwood.

Children of 8th Gen. b. in Rye.

7900 CLARA ANN, b. June 17, 1845, d. Apl. 27, 1909, m. 1st, Aug. 3, 1866, CLARENCE MASON of Portsmouth; they were divorced; m. 2nd, June 17, 1886, JOHN SIMMONS, b. Fall River, Aug. 8, 1844. He was a piano maker, lived Brentwood and d. there, Nov. 11, 1907.

Martha (Locke) Hart 4769

Hannah B. Locke 5055

Jennie (Locke) Bishop F4125

Fidelia (Locke) Hurd 4724

Mrs. Martha Seavey (Jenness) Parsons F4746

EIGHTH GENERATION

7901 LEWIS WENTWORTH, b. June 7, 1848, d. Brentwood, Apl. 12, 1880, unmarried.

7902 FLORA MAY, b. Nov. 5, 1858, m. July 25, 1875, SAMUEL B. PIKE of Epping, b. Jan. 23, 1856, had: 7903 ALBA G., b. Nov. 1, 1895, m. JENNIE DOW; 7904 LOUIS ROBERT, b. Aug. 16, 1887, m. Oct. 14, 1910, SADIE KELLEY, b. 1890, lives Nashua. He is a R. R. brakeman.

F4745 Joseph Gilbert Jenness, born in Rye, March 21, 1825, married 1st, Apl. 18, 1857, ELVIRA LOCKE GARLAND # 4747, a cousin, born Oct. 23, 1827, died Oct. 13, 1864; married 2nd, March 1889, MRS. MARY OLIVIA MOORE MARDEN, born in North Hampton, June 15, 1847. He was a farmer in Rye and died there Aug. 14, 1906.

Children of 8th Gen.

7905 GEORGE M., b. Jan. 28, 1864, d. unmarried, July 16, 1884.

Second wife's child:

7906 JOSEPHINE G., b. Aug. 14, 1889, m. June 21, 1911, SAMUEL W. KIRKWOOD, son of Daniel and Mary A. (Huse), had: 7907 BARBARA M., b. 1912; 7908 EULA M.

F4746 Martha Seavey Jenness, born in Rye, Aug. 17, 1829, married in Rye, Jan. 23, 1851, ALBION D. PARSONS, born in Rye, Feb. 17, 1829, died in Rye, Sept. 15, 1890, son of Col. Thomas and Eliza (Brown). He was a farmer in Rye. She was one of the oldest and most beloved members of the Locke Association, and died July 4, 1915.

Children of 8th Gen. b. in Rye.

7909 FRANK EDWARD, b. June 17, 1851, m. Nov. 18, 1880, SARA HUBBARD of Holden, Mass., but was divorced. He is an electric car starter, Boston.

7910 EVALINE, b. Nov. 4, 1856, d. Nov. 5, 1856.

7911 DANIEL JENNESS, b. Oct. 26, 1857, m. in Newburyport, Mass., Oct. 30, 1889, ANNIE M. LEAVITT, b. Stratham, Oct. 8, 1861, dau. of James. He is a prominent farmer in Rye. Had son 7912 NORMAN LEAVITT, b. July 19, 1892, d. in Rye, May 21, 1915.

F7913 THOMAS WENTWORTH, b. Nov. 6, 1861, m. Nov. 9, 1892, MARTHA KATE LOCKE # 7923.

7914 ELIZA ANNA, b. Feb. 11, 1864, m. Oct. 23, 1890, RALPH MARDEN, b. Boston, Oct. 1, 1859, son of Daniel and Clara J. (Philbrick). She is matron of an Old Ladies Home in N. Y. City.

7915 CLARA ELLEN, b. Sept. 24, 1868, lives in Rye, unmarried. She is particularly interested in Rye History and Genealogy, and to her the writer is under the greatest obligation for continuous assistance. She has been Clerk of the Locke Association since its beginning.

F4749 Joseph Wm. Garland, born in Rye, Sept. 4, 1836, married Oct. 22, 1860, Annie D. Drake, born Sept. 26, 1840. He was a shoemaker in Exeter.

Children of 8th Gen. b. in Rye.

7916 John Orris, b. March 26, 1861, m. Jan. 16, 1889, Emma French of Stratham, dau. of David and Irene (Jewell). He is a shoemaker in Exeter.

7917 Elvira Jenness, b. Nov. 19, 1868, d. Aug. 18, 1872, Rye.

7918 James Weston, b. March 17, 1871, m. Sept. 20, 1893, Edna M. Chesley of Farmington, b. Jan. 1871, had: 7919 Norman, b. 1898, d. 1899; they were divorced.

7920 Ruel W., b. Dec. 11, 1877, d. Dec. 25, 1877.

F4765 Freeman J. Locke, born in Rye, Oct. 7, 1843, died in Rye, Feb. 10, 1904, married in Newmarket, Apl. 13, 1865, Mary A. Otis, born in Newmarket, Nov. 14, 1844, died in Rye, May 7, 1910, daughter of Simon and Maria (Wiggin). He was one of our most zealous workers for the Locke Reunions and even in his last years, while suffering intensely from rheumatism, he would go down to meet his old friends and see that all plans were carried out. In early life he was a blacksmith, but later was a farmer in Rye, on the old farm.

Children of 8th Gen. b. in Newmarket.

7921 Ethel M., b. Apl. 9, 1867, m. June 16, 1888, George A. Batchelder, b. No. Hampton, Sept. 13, 1866, lives there, had: 7922 Bartlett A., b. Jan. 30, 1901. He drives the auto stage to Rye Beach.

7923 Martha Kate, b. Oct. 31, 1868, m. Nov. 9, 1892, Thomas W. Parsons, # F7913.

F4766 Emma A. Locke, born in Rye, Dec. 15, 1849, married July 1870, Cyrus Fogg, a farmer of North Hampton, where he died Sept. 26, 1912.

Children of 8th Gen. b. in Rye.

7924 Bertha Emma, b. Sept. 26, 1871, m. Apl. 25, 1894, Irving W. Marston, b. Hampton, Nov. 6, 1872, son of David and Lucretia (Blake), has no children. He has a restaurant in Hampton.

7925 Abbie M., b. Aug. 23, 1879, living unmarried, 1905.

F4770 Almira H. Locke, born Sept. 22, 1830, died Oct. 5, 1900, married in Portsmouth, June 23, 1852, James F. Greenleaf, born Apl. 24, 1826, son of Abner and Miriam (Bell). He was a joiner in Beverly, Mass., and died Feb. 20, 1902.

EIGHTH GENERATION 411

Children of 8th Gen. b. in Portsmouth.
F7926 JAMES A., b. Feb. 19, 1856, m. 1st, Nov. 6, 1876, JENNIE E. SNYDER;
   m. 2nd, Sept. 15, 1880, S. JENNIE HATFIELD.
7927 ALMIRA B., b. Jan. 29, 1864, m. Nov. 13, 1882, ARTHUR C. WALLACE,
   b. Aug. 14, 1863. He is in shoe business, Beverly, Mass. Had:
   7928 JOSEPH A., b. May 23, 1884; 7929 HENRY A., b. Feb. 10, 1889;
   7930 MARION G., b. March 29, 1895, d. Oct. 3, 1895.
7931 FRANK M., b. Dec. 10, 1859, m. July 12, 1881, JULIA HARRIE of
   Huntingdon, Pa. He is Genl. Freight Agent H. & B. T. M. R. R.
   at Huntingdon, has no children.
7932 FREDERICK, b. July 2, 1865, d. July 24, 1865.

F4778 Mary Ellen Locke, born in Portsmouth, Jan. 19, 1836, married 1st, in Danvers, Mass., Jan. 16, 1855, JOSEPH RHODES, born in England, 1824, died in Portsmouth, Feb. 13, 1866; married 2nd, in Portsmouth, March 21, 1870, JOHN MALONE, born in Ireland, Feb. 25, 1825. He was a marine in the U. S. Navy many years, later settled on Government Land in Minnesota, and died at the Soldiers Home in Minnesota, Aug. 6, 1892.

Children of 8th Gen.
7933 ALICE L., b. Moosup, Conn., Nov. 5, 1855, d. Sept. 23, 1856.
7934 JAMES WEBSTER, b. Danvers, Dec. 22, 1859, d. Sept. 1, 1860.
7935 DAVID LOCKE, b. twin, Dec. 22, 1859, lives Alexandria, Minn.
7936 LOUISE MALONE, b. Portsmouth, July 3, 1871, m. Oct. 7, 1892, REV.
   LENO P. NEWELL, lived Ashtabula, No. Dakota; had: 7937 ESTHER
   E., b. 1893; 7938 GRACE E., b. 1895; 7939 RUTH E., b. 1897.
7940 ADA E. MALONE, b. Ports. Feb. 18, 1875.

F4779 Adelaide L. Locke, born in Portsmouth, Dec. 29, 1838, died in Dallas, Texas, Feb. 16, 1898, married in Plainfield, Conn., March 18, 1856, ALBERT BENNETT of Connecticut, born 1835, died in Denver, Col., Nov. 13, 1873.

Children of 8th Gen. b. in Plainfield, Conn.
7941 FLORENCE W., b. Jan. 13, 1857, d. Jan. 28, 1857.
7942 ALBERT L., b. Aug. 4, 1860, m. Chicago, Sept. 7, 1893, BONNIE
   BARRY. They live in Dallas, Texas, had: 7943 WINNIFRED, b.
   Dec. 30, 1894; 7944 BARRY, b. Apl. 20, 1897; 7945 BERNICE, a
   twin, d. May 21, 1898.

F4781 Ethan Allen Locke, born in Kittery, Me., June 12, 1834, died in Kittery, Nov. 19, 1912, married Apl. 9, 1857, LYDIA PRYOR, born Aug. 8, 1833. He conveyed land on Seavey's Island to the U. S. Government for a Navy Yard in 1866, later lived in Kittery. He was a sea captain.

Child of 8th Gen.
F7946 WILLIAM C., b. March 6, 1858, m. Nov. 12, 1881, CARRIE J. PAUL.

F4782 William Warren Locke, born in Kittery, Me., June 7, 1836, married Dec. 20, 1870, JENNIE F. FORD, born in North Berwick, Me., July 8, 1850. He has for many years occupied the position of foreman joiner at the Navy Yard and is called the most expert workman ever in that position, and even now at 80 years is at his daily work. He is a member of the Knights Templar Masons and several other orders.

Children of 8th Gen b. in Kittery, Me.

7947 GEORGE A., b. Sept. 28, 1871, d. Kittery, Dec. 14, 1895, unmarried.
7948 FRED FORD, b. Apl. 22, 1875, graduated Dartmouth College 1899, was a teacher, now 1916 is a clerk at the Navy Yard.

F4789 Sarah Elizabeth Locke, born in Kittery, Me., Jan. 26, 1850, married in Portsmouth, Sept. 18, 1870, NATHANIEL BOWDEN of York, Me., born Apl. 9, 1846. He is a laborer living in Kittery.

Children of 8th Gen. b. in Kittery, Me.

7949 ABBIE M., b. June 6, 1872, unmarried in 1899.
7950 EDWIN E., b. Sept. 18, 1874, m. Kittery, Jan. 8, 1902, ANNIE JANETTE LOCKE # 7831. He is a joiner in the Boat Shop, Kittery Navy Yard. Had: 7951 SADIE LOCKE, b. Jan. 8, 1903.
7952 FLORENCE C., b. July 11, 1880.
7953 MARION F., b. Feb. 2, 1882.

F4798 Reuben Locke, born in Corinth, Vt., Oct. 13, 1817, died in Canada, July 4, 1854, married 1st, 1840, EMILY ROWELL; married 2nd, Jan. 1, 1849, ANNA MERRILL # 5096. He was a merchant in Montreal.

Children of 8th Gen.

7954 MARY, b. 1842, d. Montreal, 1854.
7955 ALICE, b. 1844, d. Montreal, 1854.
7956 HELEN, b. ——, m. THOMAS BRIGHAM of Boston.

F4800 John Bickford Locke, born in Corinth, Vt., July 15, 1819, died Oct. 6, 1901 aged 82, married March 31, 1842, CAROLINE TAPLIN of Fairfield, Vt., born May 12, 1822, died July 23, 1898, daughter of Joseph and Sarah (Robie). He was a farmer, lumberman, and a justice of the peace and lived at Waits River, Vt.

Children of 8th Gen. b. in Corinth, Vt.

7957 JOSEPH TAPLIN, b. Nov. 16, 1843, d. Dec. 7, 1843.
F7958 JULIA ANN, b. May 8, 1845, m. March 1, 1866, ORRIN HUTCHINSON.
7959 HELEN CAROLINE, b. July 2, 1846, d. May 18, 1886, m. Oct. 23, 1876, ALVAH M. CARPENTER, b. Corinth, Jan. 17, 1841, son of Dr. Alvah and Ann (Cook). He was constable, Dept. Sheriff of Orange County, Vt., eighteen years, Sheriff two years, Collector for twelve years. Died Bradford, Vt., 1912.

EIGHTH GENERATION

7960 EMMA SOPHIA, b. Oct. 22, 1847, d. July 2, 1887, m. 1868, LOREN K. RICHARDSON, son of James and Almira (Kimball). He is a farmer and justice of peace, in Corinth, Vt. Had: 7961 BYRON, b. ——, died young; 7962 MARY E., b. ——, died young; 7963 WADE H., b. ——, died young; 7964 FRED R., b. ——, is a farmer in Corinth.

F7965 SPAULDING FLINT, b. July 20, 1849, m. 1st, June 17, 1879, ELIZA A. STANDLICK; m. 2nd, MRS. NANCY (NUTT) FOLSOM.

7966 JOHN FRANKLIN, b. Feb. 7, 1853, d. Apr. 20, 1854.

F7967 HARMOND JOHN, b. June 12, 1855, m. 1st, Apr. 17, 1884, MARY E. BERRY, m. 2nd, Sept. 18, 1898, CARRIE SAWYER.

F7968 DAVID BYRON, b. Oct. 4, 1857, m. 1st, 1881, NELLIE WINCH; m. 2nd, MINNIE CHURCHILL.

7969 DR. WILLIAM ELROY, b. March 8, 1860, m. Nov. 27, 1884, LENA A. CLARK of Barton Landing, b. Nov. 12, 1865, dau. of John and Martha (Sanborn). Graduated from Bradford Academy, Hahnemann Medical College 1884, he practices medicine in Cookville and Corinth, Vt.

F4801 Almeda Silver Locke, born in Corinth, Vt., March 17, 1821, died Oct. 9, 1852, married in South Framingham, Mass., March 10, 1840, EPHRAIM SMITH, a farmer there, born Dover, March 19, 1809, died Aug. 16, 1859.

Children of 8th Gen. b. in So. Framingham, Mass.

7971 ALMEDA, b. Sept. 2, 1841, m. in Washington, Vt., March 9, 1863, LYMAN PEPPER, b. Nov. 1, 1822, d. Jan. 4, 1905. She is living in Wellesley, Mass., 1915, has no children.

7972 ANN MARIA, b. Nov. 9, 1842, d. Nov. 21, 1851.

F7973 ELLEN FRANCES, b. Apl. 27, 1844, m. March 19, 1863, ALFRED EVERETT BEMIS.

7974 HARRIET ATLANTA, b. Jan. 21, 1846, d. Nov. 23, 1885, m. July 12, 1874, THOMAS HAYDEN, b. Sept. 7, 1848, d. May 2, 1895. They had: 7975 LAURA ATTLEA, b. Aug. 17, 1875, d. May 19, 1877; 7976 MINNIE E., b. Apl 8, 1877; 7977 ERNEST E., b. Aug. 9, 1878.

7978 EPHRAIM EMERY, b. Sept. 17, 1847, d. at LeRoy, Minn., July 11, 1874.

F7979 MARY ELIZABETH, b. June 18, 1849, m. Sept. 13, 1865, ALMON INGRAM.

7980 HENRY, b. July 31, 1852, d. Sept. 21, 1852.

F4805 Olive G. Locke, born 1824, died Jan. 13, 1915, married Sept. 22, 1846, JOSHUA F. WOODMAN, born Nov. 2, 1821, died 1907?, son of Peter and Mary. He was a farmer in Topsham, Vt.

Children of 8th Gen. b. in Topsham, Vt.

F7981 BETSEY S., b. March 20, 1848, m. 1868, M. A. CUNNINGHAM.

7982 PHEBE L., b. 1865, d. 1892, m. July, 1885, G. W. MCDUFFIE.

7983 JENNIE L., b. 1867, m. Jan. 3, 1894, G. W. MCDUFFIE.

F4812 Blake Locke, born March 27, 1833, married Dec. 23, 1857, MARY ANN MCCRILLIS of Corinth, Vt., born June 9, 1840, in Corinth, daughter of Evans and Annette (Bickford). He is farming on the old farm in Corinth, Vt.

Children of 8th Gen. b. in Corinth, Vt.
7984 MABEL, b. Aug. 19, 1859, d. Oct. 23, 1860.
7985 NETTIE ELLA, b. Oct. 2, 1863, d. June 10, 1874.
7986 IRA, b. July 6, 1874, d. July 6, 1874.
7987 WILLIE, b. twin, July 5, 1874, d. July 28, 1874.

F4813 Janette Locke, born 1833, died Nov. 18, 1912, married in Nashville, Mass., Jan. 1, 1851, CHARLES FARWELL, a comb manufacturer of Cambridge, Mass.

Children of 8th Gen. b. in Cambridge, Mass.
F7988 DEWITT, b. Aug. 29, 1852, m. HANNAH MOORE.
7989 JENNIE PHEBE, b. Apl. 21, 1861, m. Oct. 10, 1894, DAVID LOCHLIN WATSON of Cambridge, Mass., b. June 5, 1860. They live in Cambridge where he has a provision store, and have son: 7990 CHARLES BURNETT, b. Oct. 13, 1895.

F4815 Annise T. Locke, born in Corinth, Vt., Apl. 11, 1837, died in Worcester, Mass., Dec. 19, 1912, married 1st, June 24, 1863, WILLARD JONES, born in Winchester, Mass., May 15, 1824, died Aug. 17, 1874, an iron founder; married 2nd, in Worcester, Nov. 25, 1880, NATHANIEL BRIGHAM, born Feb. 28, 1829. He is a retired shell worker, lives in Worcester, Mass.

Child of 8th Gen.
7991 MINNIE L. JONES (adopted), b. Worcester, Mass., Feb. 18, 1871, m. HARRISON P. EDDY, June 1, 1892, b. Millbury, Mass., Apl. 29, 1870. Graduated from Worcester Polytec. 1891, was Supt. of City Sewers. Had: 7992 WILLARD T., b. March 11, 1893; 7993 HARRISON P., b. Feb. 17, 1895; 7994 RANDOLPH L., b. Dec. 15, 1898; 7994a CHARLOTTE F., b. July 4, 1903.

F4818 Sarah F. Locke, born Dec. 3, 1842, died Nov. 6, 1898, married Dec. 31, 1860, HARRY EMERY, son of Caleb and Eliza (Pepper). He was a farmer in Topsham, Vt., and was born Sept. 2, 1839, died June 2, 1907.

Children of 8th Gen.
7995 MARY C., b. May 1, 1862, m. Sept. 8, 1886, H. C. MARTIN, lives Waits River, Vt., no children.
7996 CLAYTON LEWIS, b. March 23, 1864, m. 1892, ANNIE TRANTER, lives Worcester, Mass.
7997 CLINTON LOCKE, b. twin, March 23, 1864, d. 1866.

EIGHTH GENERATION

7998 CLINTON LOCKE, b. July 11, 1867, m. 1891, JOSEPHINE TRAFTON of Worcester, had: 7999 MABEL, b. 1893.
8000 ABBIE JANE, b. June 18, 1870, d. May 24, 1891, m. 1889, WILLIAM BEEDE of Barre, Vt., had: 8001 HARRY, b. July 2, 1889, is m. and lives in Lynn.
8002 FRANK L., b. Dec. 20, 1872, d. March 19, 1879.
8003 WILLARD J., b. Feb. 11, 1877, d. Jan. 7, 1882.
8004 ANNIS J., b. July 21, 1879, d. March 10, 1880.
8005 ANNA LOCKE, b. twin, July 21, 1879, d. Springfield, Mass., March 12, 1915, m. July 1, 1896, HOMER CARL HUNTOON, b. Topsham, Vt., July 12, 1869. They lived in Springfield, and he d. East Orange, Vt., Feb. 20, 1903. Had: 8006 JAMES C., b. 1897; 8007 FRANK RAY, b. ——.

F4828 Nathan Taplin, born Dec. 9, 1820, married June 10, 1845, CAROLINE BICKFORD.

Children of 8th Gen.

8008 ELLIOTT C., b. March 31, 1847, m. Feb. 24, 1868, ALICE V. RANDALL, lives in Bradford, Vt., had: 8009 CARRIE A., b. Feb 24, 1870; 8010 HELEN L., b. June 6, 1872; 8011 ETHEL K., b. Aug. 15, 1882.
8012 CHARLES B., b. Oct. 2, 1851, m. June 7, 1882, EMMA M. CAMPBELL, lives Washington, Vt., had: 8013 FLORENCE, b. 1890.
8014 CARRIE M., b. June 13, 1855, m. 1882, JOSEPH H. CARTER, had: 8015 NATHAN F., b. Aug. 15, 1883; 8016 LIZZIE U., b. Feb. 14, 1885; 8017 EARL E. b. Feb. 24, 1888; 8019 JESSIE B., b. Dec. 1, 1890; 8020 RALPH W., b. Sept. 17, 1893; 8021 EARLE F., b. Aug. 28, 1895; 8022 NED H., b. June 29, 1897.
8023 JAMES O., b. Aug. 4, 1861.
8024 ADDIE B., b. Dec. 3, 1862, m. 1885, GEORGE C. BUTLER, had: 8025 MAUDE, b. 1887; 8026 LAURA, b. 1889; 8027 RUDOLPH, b. 1890; 8028 NATIE, b. 1891; 8029 KENNETH, b. 1892.
8030 SARAH, b. 1863, m. Feb. 12, 1882, THOMAS THURBER of Montpelier, Vt., had: 8031 MAUDE A., b. 1883; 8032 FRANK T., b. 1892, d. 1893.

F4829 Lucinda Taplin, born ——, married 1847, REUBEN KIMBALL.

Children of 8th Gen.

8033 HATTIE S., b. 1850, d. 1880.
8034 F. ELIZABETH, b. 1852, m. JOHN L. EASTMAN, had: 8035 NATHAN, b. 1881; 8036 CHILD, b. 1883, d. 1883; 8037 GRACE, b. 1885; 8038 DORA, b. 1887.
8039 EMMA, b. 1854.
8040 ELLA F., b. 1856, m. ARTHUR WADE.
8041 WILLIE G., b. 1858, m. Oct. 9, 1894, RETA F. CRISTIE.
8042 REUBEN H., b. 1860, m. Oct. 15, 1895, NELLIE STANLEY, had: 8043 MARY, b. Apl. 1898.

F4830 Sophia Taplin, married in Boston, 1845, ISSUE FORD.
Children of 8th Gen.
8044 JOSIE L., b. 1864, m. May 1881, CHARLES UNDERWOOD, had: 8045 FRED V., b. 1883.
8046 FRED, b. ——.

F4842 Nancy M. Locke, born in Corinth, Vt., Feb. 27, 1827, died May 7, 1912, married LEVI GRANT of Washington, Vt., and lived at Orange, Vt. He was born 1821, died June 21, 1907.
Children of 8th Gen.
8047 MARIE E., b. March 14, 1848.
8048 SARAH E., b. Feb. 4, 1851, d. Sept. 4, 1853.
8049 HENRY L., b. Feb. 27, 1855, d. 1914, m. 1879, IDA BRAMAN, had: 8050 FRED L., b. 1882; 8051 VERNIE R., b. Apl. 1884.
8052 VICTOR A., b. ——, m. FREDA GLADDING, lives at Bethel, Vt., had: 8053 RICHARD G., b. 1886; 8054 VICTOR, b. 1888, d. 1889; 8055 LUCILLE, b. 1892, is in Wellesley, 1915.
8056 ARTHUR J., b. March 20, 1868, m. 1890, CARRIE YEARTAW, had: 8057 IRENE, b. 1891.

F4843 John L. Locke, born in Corinth, Vt., Feb. 19, 1829, married 1870, NANCY G. RICHARDSON who was born 1848. He was a farmer in Holton, Kans., and died Aug. 17, 1904 in Colorado.
Children of 8th Gen.
8058 J. W. LAMSON (called LANSA W. LOCKE), b. 1873, is m. has four children, and is a successful rancher, with many cattle and horses at Woodland Park, Col.
8059 HANNAH FLORENCE, b. 1878, m. —— GREEN, has several children, one named 8060 GEORGIA, lives Kansas City, 1915.

F4850 Dewitt C. Locke, born in Corinth, Vt., Dec. 26, 1834, married 1st, 1860, MARGARET L. RICHARDSON, born 1841, died Aug. 1872, married 2nd, BETTIE R. LEWIS, who was born 1855. He was a farmer in Holton, Jackson Co., Kan., and died March 19, 1894.
Children of 8th Gen.
8061 WILLIAM E., b. Aug. 13, 1868, m. Denver, Col., Sept. 8, 1897, CARRIE E. COFFINE, had no children. He was a farmer and in the coal and feed business. Later was in tobacco trade until he was accidentally shot in Denver, May 10, 1909.
8062 LIZZIE M., b. Sept. 25, 1870, m. Holton, Kansas, Aug. 8, 1894, JOHN N. WILKERSON, a grocer in San Diego, Cal., had: 8063 COYLE N. b. Jan. 4, 1896, m. San Diego, Jan. 6, 1914, EDWARD N. STEELE, and had: 8064 LAURA MAY, b. Nov. 6, 1914.
8065 ELLIOTT T., b. ——. 8066 EUSTACE, b. ——. 8067 HATTIE, b. ——.
Second wife's children:
8068 EFFIE B., b. Aug. 13, 1877, m. GORDON G. EVERHART.

EIGHTH GENERATION 417

8069 CLARA J., b. Dec. 9, 1880, d. Chicago 1911, m. in Chicago, O. CORNAL, and left one son.
8070 NONA L., b. Nov. 1886, m. ——— LOWES, lived Kansas City.

F4851 Charles C. Locke, born in Corinth, Vt., Jan. 11, 1837, married Jan. 22, 1869, CAROLINE KIMBALL, born in Vershire, Vt., March 17, 1845, daughter of Stephen and Mary (Little). He was a farmer in Chelsea, Vt., and died ——— 1896. She married 2nd ———.

Children of 8th Gen.

8071 NELLIE S., b. Apl. 19, 1872, m. ——— LUCAS of Chelsea, Vt., was living there 1915.
8072 FRED, b. 1874. 8073 CHARLES K., b. Sept. 25, 1876, d. 1890.

F4889 Alice Locke, born ———, married IRA D. RICHARDSON and lived at Washington, Vt.

Children of 8th Gen.

8074 HAINES LOCKE, b. ———, m. ——— ———, lives N. Y. City.
8075 JERUSHA, b. ———, m. BENJAMIN LUTHER, had: 8076 MARTIN; 8077 FLORA; 8078 CORA; 8079 JAMES.

F4890 George Sanders, born in Epsom, Dec. 7, 1804, married MARY TWOMBLY of Barrington, born May 19, 1802, died Dec. 29, 1884. He was a farmer in Epsom and died Dec. 28, 1886.

Children of 8th Gen.

8080 GEORGE, b. Nov. 6, 1832, m. NANCY A. WHITE, of Antrim, had no children and he d. Jan. 30, 1897.
F8081 MARY, b. twin, Nov. 6, 1832, m. NATHANIEL TWOMBLY.
8082 JOHN, b. June 22, 1844, d. July 22, 1865.

F4891 Simeon L. Sanders, born in Epsom, March 15, 1806, married in Concord, Apl. 6, 1837, CAROLINE COLBY of Concord, who died 1888. He died Aug. 1885.

Children of 8th Gen.

8083 SARAH J., b. ———, m. WILLIAM STRAW, had: 8084 CARRIE, who m. ——— CASS; 8085 MARY, who m. ——— KENDALL.
8086 AUGUSTA, b. ———, m. ——— CHAPMAN, had no children.
8087 MARY A., b. ———, was unmarried.

F4892 Abigail Locke Sanders, born Jan. 20, 1808, married SHERBURN GREEN of Pittsfield, a farmer there. She died Aug., 1884.

Children of 8th Gen. b. in Pittsfield.

8088 BENJAMIN, b. ——, m. SUSAN JOHNSON of Hooksett, had: 8089 EDWARD, unmarried; 8090 SABRINA who m. —— BUTTERFIELD.

8091 JOHN S., b. ——, m. MARIA FLANDERS of Henniker, lived Short Falls, and had: 8092 EMMA, m. CHARLES S. PIPER; 8093 ANNIE, m. 1st, —— KYLE; m. 2nd —— WELLS, and lives Epsom; 8094 ARTHUR m. —— ——; 8095 HELEN.

8096 MELVINA, b. ——, m. —— CURRIER, no children.

8097 MELINDA, b. ——, m. GEORGE WEEKS.

8098 JAMES, b. ——, lives Concord, unmarried.

8099 EDWIN, b. Nov. 17, 1838, graduated Dartmouth 1863; enlisted, March 1, 1863, disc. June 10, 1865, Lieut. 9th N. H. Reg. He was a lawyer of Yankton, So. Dakota, and d. unmarried, March 31, 1900.

8100 MELISSA, b. ——, m. JOHN MORDOUGH of Chicago, had: 8101a ADDIE, who m. —— CLEVELAND and lived Mexico.

8101 LUCY, m. JAMES PADDOCK and d. Concord, Oct. 24, 1913, had: 8102 GERTRUDE, d. age 15; 8103 two others died young and 8104 LUCY.

8105 ALONZO, b. ——, m. RUTH MITCHELL of Hooksett, lives Chicago, no children.

F4893 John Sanders, born July 15, 1811, married in Concord, March 21, 1839, ANGENETTE LEAVITT of Concord. He was a farmer in Concord and died Feb. 28, 1885.

Children of 8th Gen. b. in Concord.

8106 MARY, b. March 1840, m. GEORGE T. ABBOTT of Concord, had several children.

8107 WALTER, b. June 1841, m. twice, lived So. Boston, and had children.

8108 GEORGEANNA, b. July 1843, m. SETH POTTER, had: 8109 AMY; and 8110 SAMUEL, both m.

8111 JOSEPH, was m., lived Somerville, Mass.

8112 HENRY, b. Nov. 1847, was m., lived Concord.

8113 CHARLES, b. ——, m. CLARA HODGE, had no children.

F4894 Nancy Sanders, born Nov. 29, 1812, married Aug. 23, 1839, JOHN WALLACE of Epsom, born Nov. 29, 1812. He was a farmer in Epsom and died Aug. 1, 1852.

Children of 8th Gen. b. in Epsom.

8114 MARY, b. ——, unmarried. 8115 ELIZA, b. ——, unmarried.

8116 ABBIE, b. ——, m. JAMES MCALLISTER, Feb. 24, 1877, had: 8116a EDITH, a teacher in Chicago.

F4897 David Locke Sanders, born Feb. 26, 1817, married Nov. 14, 1844, MARY A. CARR, born Aug. 14, 1819, in Dorchester, died Oct. 1, 1890. He was a farmer in West Concord, and died Jan. 5, 1906.

EIGHTH GENERATION 419

Children of 8th Gen. b. in Concord.

8117 CHARLES HENRY, b. March 5, 1846, m. Oct. 11, 1871, MARY A. DOW, b. in Fall River, Mass., May 19, 1846, d. Jan. 9, 1908. He is a machinist, lives in Concord, had: i CHARLES E., b. Apl. 9, 1873, d. July 27, 1877; ii GERTRUDE M., b. Aug. 27, 1874, d. May 3, 1876; iii ELLA P., b. March 31, 1876, d. Aug. 2, 1876; iv HERBERT M., b. July 23, 1877, a bookkeeper in Concord, m. June 24, 1914, SARAH G. TAYLOR; v IRENE, b. Oct. 9, 1880, m. June 4, 1902, HAROLD S. NELSON and had: vi MAURICE S. NELSON, b. May 7, 1903.

8117a JAMES HAMLINE, b. Feb. 10, 1850, m. Jan. 11, 1872, CLARA M. WOODWARD, b. in Hanover, March 21, 1854. He is a carriage painter in Concord, had: vii JAMES A., b. Nov. 24, 1872, d. Jan. 28, 1874; viii IDA M., b. May 26, 1876, m. Sept. 9, 1914, STEPHEN FOSTER and lives in Keene; ix DAVID H., b. Dec. 9, 1878, d. Feb. 20, 1880; x FRANK D., b. June 22, 1881, d. Nov. 9, 1883; xi MABEL L., b. Dec. 15, 1883, m. Apl. 26, 1911, ROYAL D. HOLDEN and had: xii JOHN S. HOLDEN, b. Feb. 29, 1912 in Concord; xiii HORACE W., b. Oct. 1, 1890, m. Apl. 15, 1914, PANSY I. TUCKER, he is a letter carrier in Concord, and had: xiv DORIS, b. July 17, 1915, d. same day.

F4903 John P. Locke, born in East Concord, Jan. 27, 1817, married June 13, 1840, SARAH CLOUGH OSBORN, born in Loudon, March 30, 1814, died in Concord, July 19, 1894, daughter of Joshua and Hannah (Clough). He was a farmer in East Concord, and died Sept. 12, 1899. He was a Democrat, lived in Ward 2 of Concord, fifty years, was selectman, alderman and member of Legislature in 1881, also member of Rumford Grange.

Children of 8th Gen. b. in Concord.

8118 ANN AUGUSTA, b. Dec. 4, 1840, m. Jan. 16, 1902, ABRAM D. LOCKE # F4526.
F8119 SARAH JANE, b. March 15, 1842, m. Nov. 14, 1865, JOHN B. BAKER.
8120 CLARA ELLA, b. Dec. 14, 1847, d. Apl. 4, 1877.

F4905 Reuben B. Locke, born in Concord, March 23, 1821, married Jan. 9, 1848, SARAH H. CASS, born in Andover, Aug. 25, 1828, died in Methuen, Mass., Feb. 14, 1912, daughter of Benjamin and Sarah (True). He was a farmer in Bristol and Tilton where he died Feb. 3, 1903. He learned the blacksmiths trade and followed the same in Alexandria, Bristol and Concord several years; later was in the grain business in Bristol, and in 1884 bought a farm in Tilton. He was a Democrat and for 55 years was a member of the M. E. Church.

Children of 8th Gen.

8121 MARTHA E., b. Alexandria, Oct. 14, 1848, d. Concord, Dec. 5, 1865.
8122 HANNAH LAVINA, b. Bristol, May 5, 1851, d. Plymouth, May 31, 1857.
8123 FRANCIS ASBURY, b. Concord, March 3, 1855, d. C. Feb. 7, 1866.
8124 HELEN SARAH, b. Concord, Jan. 10, 1859, d. Bristol, Jan. 10, 1877.
F8125 REV. GEORGE REUBEN, b. Jan. 1, 1864, m. June 23, 1887, FANNIE S. GORDON.
F8126 REV. WILLIAM BENJAMIN, b. Oct. 10, 1867, m. Aug. 16, 1893, MARY FRANCES ROWELL.

F4907 Samuel M. Locke, born in Concord, Nov. 30, 1825, married in E. Concord, Dec. 31, 1857, CHARLOTTE K. CLIFFORD of East Concord, born July 12, 1834, died in East Concord, June 8, 1914. He was a farmer on the Intervale, East Concord and died Nov. 25, 1912.

Children of 8th Gen. b. in East Concord.

8127 ABBIE M., b. Oct. 17, 1858, m. June 26, 1901, JAMES H. HUSSEY, b. Barrington, Feb. 18, 1853, lived East Concord; his second wife.
8128 LOTTIE A., b. July 10, 1865, lives E. Concord, unmarried.

F4908 Elizabeth F. Locke, born June 1828, married 1st, in Concord, May 4, 1853, R. HENRY DAVIS of Bristol, born July 24, 1824, died May 24, 1864; married 2nd, Apl. 3, 1867, AARON G. FARNUM of Gloucester, Mass., born Oct. 23, 1827, died Jan. 17, 1892. She died in East Concord, July 22, 1910.

Children of 8th Gen.

8129 MARY HELEN DAVIS, b. May 7, 1854, m. June 1, 1876, JAMES ALLEN, a letter carrier of Gloucester, Mass., b. Dec. 27, 1853, had: 8130 MAUDE, b. Oct. 23, 1876; 8131 MARY E., b. Nov. 13, 1877.
8132 ALICE FARNUM, b. ——, d. July 16, 1868, age 4 weeks.

F4909 Mary Emery Locke, born in Concord, Sept. 19, 1830, married in Concord, Sept. 18, 1851, WILLIAM T. CASS of Plymouth, born Feb. 7, 1826, son of Benjamin and Sarah (True). He was President of the Citizens National Bank, Tilton and died May 26, 1907.

Children of 8th Gen. b. in Tilton.

8133 ALFRED L., b. Oct. 28, 1860, d. Sept. 1, 1862.
8134 MARY A., b. March 5, 1863, m. Oct. 29, 1889, ABEL W. REYNOLDS of West Somerville, Mass., b. May 21, 1863, a banker in Boston, had: 8135 MARGARET, b. Sept. 23, 1890.
8136 ARTHUR T., b. Apl. 9, 1865, m. May 16, 1894, MARY W. PACKARD of So. Boston, dau. of Doctor ——. He is Cashier of Tilton National Bank, had: 8137 KINGMAN P., b. Sept. 1, 1895; 8138 WILLIAM T., b. May 1, 1899; 8139 DAUGHTER.
8140 WILLIAM D., b. Jan. 27, 1872, d. May 7, 1879.

F4910 Margaret Ayer Locke, born in Concord, Apl. 13, 1832, married Nov. 11, 1852, DR. JAMES M. BISHOP of Bristol, born in Hanover, May 14, 1821, son of John and Abigail (Parker). He lived in Hanover and Bristol, where he practised and died in Stamford, Conn., June 16, 1891.

Children of 8th Gen. b. in Bristol.
8141 MARY ABBIE, b. Aug. 11, 1854, a music teacher in Lynn, Mass.
8142 DANIEL LOCKE, b. May 15, 1856, d. Aug. 25, 1856, Bristol.
8143 LIZZIE BELLE, b. Aug. 27, 1857, m. Lynn, Aug. 23, 1893, EDWIN H. JOHNSON of Lynn, who d. Lynn, March 22, 1894. She was a graduate of Tilton Seminary, 1878, lived in Lynn and had: 8144 MARGARET, b. and d. July 22, 1894.
8145 DR. CHANNING, b. July 26, 1864, m. Lebanon, May 15, 1893, LENA B. CRAGIN, b. Lebanon, Dec. 24, 1867, dau. of Richard and Nancy (Emery). He is a graduate of Tilton Seminary, Brown Medical College 1889, is a doctor in Bristol, no children.

F4911 Sarah A. Locke, born in Concord, March 31, 1835, married Nov. 13, 1856, JOHN T. BACHELDER of Concord, born in Chichester, July 28, 1833, lived in East Concord.

Children of 8th Gen. b. in Concord.
8146 CHARLES H., b. July 5, 1858, unmarried, 1898.
F8147 SAMUEL L., b. May 22, 1863, m. Oct. 17, 1888, SARAH E. HUTCHINS.
8148 CHILD, died young.
8149 HELEN A., b. Feb. 3, 1874, unmarried, 1900.
8150 BESSIE M., b. Feb. 8, 1877.

F4913 Helen S. Locke, born Sept. 7, 1841, married Sept. 8, 1867, REV. NICHOLAS F. WHITTAKER of Hyde Park, Mass., born in Boston, Apl. 10, 1840, son of Edgar and Catherine (Holland). He was a Methodist minister in Chelsea, Lynn, and Lowell.

Children of 8th Gen.
8152 EDGAR S., b. June 3, 1870, m. EDITH ———, lived in Portland, Me., had: 8153 HOWARD, and another son.
8154 ETHEL, b. Sept. 10, 1882, d. July 29, 1885.

F4914 Joseph Locke, born in Lyman, Feb. 27, 1812, married in 1844, ARVILLA CARR of Haverhill, N. H. He lived in Titusville, Penn. and died July 6, 1877.

Children of 8th Gen. b. in Haverhill.
F8155 NANCY ALICE, b. Aug. 16, 1847, m. Apl. 8, 1865, THEODORE M. SHEARER.
F8156 HENRY WALKER, b. May 6, 1849, m. 1st, 1869, AMANDA LUTZ; m. 2nd, 1886, CLARA ALEXANDER.

8157 JOHN CARR, b. Feb. 11, 1852, a machinist, interested in the oil business, died unmarried in Harmony, Pa., June 1893.
8158 MORRIL SILAS, b. Aug. 20, 1854, m. Pleasantville, Pa., Nov. 7, 1876, SUSAN F. PARKER of Titusville. He was a machinist in Bradford, Pa., in 1897; was 1913, in Bridgeport, Ill; adopted, 8159 EMERY ALLEN, b. 1888.
8160 JOSEPH HANNIBAL, b. May 20, 1856, m. Lima, Ohio, July 26, 1888, SARAH DITSON. He was a machinist in the oil business at Robinson, Ill., where he d. June 1, 1907; had no children.
F8161 WILLIAM HALE, b. Aug. 17, 1858, m. July 13, 1891, ELIZABETH BOYD.

F4915 Jonathan Locke, born in Lyman, May 17, 1814, married in Deerfield, Feb. 23, 1837, SALLY COOK of Epping, born Apl. 24, 1814, died 1893?. In 1849 he moved from New Hampshire to Titusville, Pa., under a five year contract to put in and operate four saw mills and one grist mill on the Oil Creek River. He later erected two mills in California. At the solicitation of the Pennsylvania company he returned to Titusville, when the first original Drake Oil Well was drilled, in 1859, and leasing some machine shops, commenced the manufacture of tools for drilling oil wells, making the first set ever made in the oil region. He continued with this business many years, closing a useful career at Bradford, Pa., Jan. 20, 1894, aged 81.

Children of 8th Gen.

8162 FLORINDA, b. Feb. 16, 1838, d. Lyman, Dec. 9, 1854.
F8163 SARAH, b. Apl. 23, 1839, m. July 2, 1857, STEPHEN LOGAN.
F8164 HENRY HARRISON, b. Dec. 21, 1840, m. Sept. 26, 1866, MARTHA H. WADE.
F8165 MARTHA HELEN, b. Apl. 25, 1842, m. 1st, July 28, 1859, SAMUEL PARTRIDGE; m. 2nd, July 3, 1860, HENRY C. CARPENTER.
F8166 JONATHAN MORRILL, b. Feb. 15, 1844, m. Sept. 26, 1867, ELLEN A. FOSTER.
F8167 STEPHEN FARNSWORTH, b. March 9, 1846, m. March 5, 1869, MARY E. ASHLEY.
8168 MARY KEZIAH, b. Bradleyvale, Pa., Apl. 15, 1848, d. Nov. 1, 1850.
F8169 MARY K., b. Dec. 5, 1850, m. Sept. 29, 1870, BENJAMIN S. TRUXAL.
F8170 HANNIBAL ORLANDO, b. July 2, 1856, m. July 18, 1876, ELLA A. CLARK.

F4916 Mary A. Minot Locke, born in Lyman, March 29, 1816, married in Lyman, Dec. 7, 1839, STEPHEN FARNSWORTH, who was born Sept. 1, 1816. They lived in Haverhill where she died Apl. 29, 1848. He died in Felton, Cal., March 31, 1891. He was a farmer in Haverhill and East Barton, Vt., and had four wives.

EIGHTH GENERATION 423

Children of 8th Gen. b. in Haverhill.

F8171 DAVID LOVERING, b. Nov. 15, 1838,? m. Dec. 26, 1866, FRANCES P. CLOUGH.
F8172 ANN, b. Feb. 8, 1840, m. SAMUEL MAGOON.
F8173 ELBRIDGE G., b. March 13, 1842, m. 1st, LOUISE SOMERS, m. 2nd, Apl. 7, 1896, FRANCES G. CARR.
F8174 FLORINDA LOVERING, b. March 25, 1844, m. Nov. 2, 1867, JOB C. BARTLETT.
F8175 ORRIN EDWARD, b. Nov. 27, 1846, m. June 18, 1873, CATHERINE MARGARET PRAY.

F4917 Elbridge Gerry Locke, born in Lyman, March 24, 1818, married 1st, March 21, 1844, JANETTE A. DIXON, born in Ryegate, Vt., July 8, 1821, died Feb. 3, 1867; married 2nd, March 15, 1874, AMANDA PANKEY. He was a sawyer, lived in Dalton, and died Nov. 9, 1879.

Children of 8th Gen., all by first wife.

F8176 JANETTE D., b. Apl. 21, 1845, m. 1st, June 6, 1863, ORRIN E. CALKINS; m. 2nd, Nov. 16, 1869, HARRISON CASS.
8177 DAVID E., b. Dalton, N. H., Dec. 6, 1846, m. New York, Feb. 10, 1870, FLORENCE M. SIMMONS, b. N. Y., Sept. 4, 1850. He was a machinist in Titusville, Pa., had no children.
8178 MARY A., b. Feb. 23, 1849, d. Aug. 12, 1849.
F8179 ROBERT DICKSON, b. Aug. 26, 1850, m. July 12, 1884, FANNIE J. ALLISON.
F8180 ALICE I., b. July 13, 1852, m. July 9, 1874, WILLIAM WALLACE.
8181 FLORINDA J., b. June 17, 1856, m. Jan. 5, 1881, ALFRED PADEN who d. 1914, lived in Berkeley, Cal., had: 8182 GUY; 8183 AGNES, b. Oct. 1881.
8184 ANNETTE M., b. Nov. 28, 1858, d. Jan. 9, 1861.
8185 SARAH E. A., b. Titusville, Pa., Apl. 23, 1861, m. Cal., March 18, 1885, MILLARD FILLMORE NEFF, b. Cal. Jan. 24, 1860, lived at Fallbrook, Cal., had: 8186 CLARENCE WILSON, b. March 18, 1886; 8187 EDITH EUNICE, b. Nov. 28, 1887; 8188 ELBRIDGE GERRY, b. Dec. 9, 1893.

F4918 Florinda Locke, born in Lyman, Apl. 21, 1820, married Oct. 19, 1843, HENRY WALKER, a prominent citizen of Peacham, Vt., who died Sept. 28, 1872, aged 55. Since 1873 she lived in Windsor, Vt., an active member of the Congregational Church, and died Jan. 7, 1905. He was a manufacturer and at one time, editor of a paper.

Children of 8th Gen.

8190 FRANK J., b. Sept. 21, 1847, m. July 4, 1883, MARY J. JONES, b. June 12, 1862, lived Hanford, Cal., was Dept. Sheriff; later lived Los Angeles, Cal., where he d. Feb. 11, 1915, had: 8191 IRVING, b. March 17, 1888; 8192 WESTON, b. Aug. 1890; 8193 FRANK, b. 1892; 8194 HERBERT.

8195 HENRY G., b. July 13, 1852, d. Cal., Apl. 8, 1883.
F8196 ELIZABETH ABBIE, b. Aug. 12, 1854, m. Dec. 1, 1874, CHARLES J. WESTON.
8197 EMMA EDNA, b. Aug. 25, 1858, d. Windsor, Vt., unmarried, Nov. 13, 1911.

F4919 Simeon Lovering Locke, born in Lyman, Sept. 6, 1822, married in Lyman, March 3, 1847, HARRIET BAILEY, who was born in Lyman, June 12, 1828, died in Littleton, June 26, 1915, left three sons, one daughter, 19 grandchildren and 30 great-grandchildren. He was a farmer in Lyman and died Dec. 30, 1879.

Children of 8th Gen. b. in Lyman.

8198 MOSES B., b. July 29, 1848, d. Oct. 13, 1848.
F8199 ELEANOR H., b. July 29, 1850, m. Dec. 15, 1868, JOHN W. BAILEY.
F8200 FRANCISCO H., b. March 9, 1852, m. Feb. 17, 1872, PHEBE A. WETHERBEE.
F8201 SILAS MERRILL, b. June 16, 1854, m. Dec. 24, 1874, AMANDA M. WILLIAMS.
F8202 LYMAN J. M., b. March 19, 1860, m. Aug. 9, 1884, LETTIE BRADLEY.
8203 SIMEON GERRY, b. Jan. 20, 1862, m. March 1887, NELLIE M. BRADFORD, b. Barnet, Vt., 1866. He is a Rural Delivery carrier in Lisbon, had: 8204 MABEL BLANCHE, b. Georgetown, Mass., Nov. 1, 1890; 8205 GEORGE B., b. Lyman, Dec. 16, 1892, m. in Lisbon, June 21, 1916, AGNES M. HAMMOND.
8206 FLORA A., b. Apl. 13, 1863, m. Nov. 7, 1888, ALBERT E. STRAIN, b. Littleton July 8, 1868, son of CORNELIUS H. He is Deputy Sheriff, lives Littleton, had: 8207 ARTHUR L., b. Apl. 28, 1889; 8208 HAZEL, b. Sept. 3, 1897.

F4920 David Morrill Locke, born in Lyman, Sept. 1, 1824, married 1st, Sept. 1, 1853, MARY J. JAMESON # 5117 born June 11, 1831, died Sept. 2, 1881 in California; married 2nd, in Potsdam, N. Y., Sept. 9, 1893, JENNIE A. GILLETT, born in Brasher, N. Y., Apl. 30, 1860. She is living in California. Mary J. Jameson was a well known writer of early days whose pen name was "Mary Mountain." Going to California from New Hampshire in 1849, he established in San Francisco, a unique system by which he delivered water to house-holders in carts. He carried on this buisness until the first pipe line was established. He built the first toll bridge in California across the Stanislaus river at Knights' Ferry in 1853; and also built a flour mill which is still a landmark. In the early seventies he bought the St. Augustine rancho of 1200 acres in Scott's valley near Santa Cruz. He was living retired in Berkeley, Cal., where he died Oct. 27, 1908.

EIGHTH GENERATION 425

Children of 8th Gen.
8209 FINETTE CAROLYN, b. Knights' Ferry, Cal., Jan. 1, 1860, she graduated Santa Cruz High School and was in University of Cal. one year, m. Santa Cruz, Cal., Dec. 23, 1914, WILLIAM ARMSTRONG, b. Wis., 1847.
8210 ALEXANDER MORRILL, b. Irasburg, July 15, 1861, m. Nov. 28, 1887, MUSIDORA F. ROWANTREE, lives Berkeley, Cal., had: 8211 ALEXANDER R., b. Oct. 9, 1888; 8212 ERIC, b. July 1892; 8213 SARAH, b. 1894.

F4922 Alice Pearsons Locke, born in Lyman, Nov. 13, 1828, died in Alameda, Cal., Aug. 15, 1915, married Jan. 6, 1855, in San Francisco, HALE RIX, born in Stanstead, Can., June 8, 1828. He went to California in 1850, was mining law police judge for nine years and died Oct., 1900. He and Alice were acquainted in New Hampshire and this was renewed when she went to California with her brothers, and they were married there. "She was a woman of wide acquaintance, of most loving philanthropy, of disposition, sweet and noble, a faithful, self-sacrificing wife and mother."

Children of 8th Gen. b. in San Francisco.
8214 ANNIE R., b. Nov. 15, 1855, m. Nov. 28, 1891, PAUL MILITZ, b. Germany March 22, 1854. She was one of the first white children born in Cal. She became a Christian Scientist about 1886, a healer and preacher in N. Y., Denver and Chicago. In 1906, she traveled around the world and is now a lecturer on "New Thoughts," and editor of paper in Los Angeles called "Master Mind."
8215 ALICE F., b, Aug. 4, 1858, d. Jan. 6, 1862.
F8216 ABBIE L., b. Dec. 10, 1861, m. Feb. 10, 1887, FREDERICK MAURER, JR.
8217 HARRIET HALE, b. Nov. 10, 1863, is unmarried and head of "Home of Truth," Alameda, Cal.
8218 ELLA FRANCES, b. March 31, 1868, m. Feb. 5, 1888, MYRON B. HICKOK, b. Virginia City, Neb., Aug. 16, 1866. They were divorced 1892, and she became a Christian Scientist, and lives San Francisco, had: 8219 FRANK, b. Sept. 23, 1888, who later changed his name to FRANK HARRISON; 8220 EDNA, b. March 29, 1891, m. 1913, FRED R. JOHNSON and had: 8221 MARGARET F., b. 1914.
8222 EDWARD HALE, b. Dec. 15, 1871, m. 1902, EMMA WALKER NILES, lives San Francisco.

F4923 Josiah Hannibal Locke, born in Lyman, June 7, 1831, married Oct. 13, 1859, CARRIE MACOMBER, born in Bath, Me., Nov. 17, 1842. He also went to California and died in San Francisco, Apl. 7, 1904. She died in Purissima, Cal., July 25, 1914. He was superintendent of the largest flour mill in San Francisco and owned a large ranch at Purissima, Cal.

Children of 8th Gen.

8223 FLORINDA A., b. July 23, 1860, m. July 4, 1883, HORACE NELSON, who has a ranch at Purissima Cal., had: 8224 HANNIBAL LOCKE, b. Oct. 29, 1884.

8225 EMILY J., b. Oct. 25, 1862, m. Aug. 9, 1888, HENRY E. C. FEUNSIER, a civil engineer at Sonoma, Cal., had: 8226 RALPH E., b. June 1889.

8227 HORACE N., b. Nov. 10, 1864, lives in Purissima, Cal.

F4924 Abigail Blake Locke, born in Lyman, Sept. 15, 1834, married 1st, June 13, 1854, LYMAN J. McINDOE, born in Barnet, Vt., Jan. 17, 1819, died in Windsor, Dec. 23, 1873. She married 2nd, June 1, 1876, REV. FRANKLIN BUTLER, born in Essex, Vt., Oct. 3, 1814, died in Windsor, Vt., May 23, 1880.

John McIndoe came to America in 1784, settled at the head of McIndoe Falls, his son James lived on this farm until 1822, and Lyman was born there. He learned the printer's trade, became owner of the *Windsor, (Vt.) Journal,* the oldest weekly in Vermont, and this paper continued in his family down to Mr. Marsh O. Perkins, whose health compelled him to relinquish it. Abigail Blake, was educated in the Lyman schools, and in the famous academies at Peacham and Newbury, Vt. She was a teacher until marriage, and after the death of her husband, carried on the publication of the *Windsor Journal,* and later married Mr. Butler who was an editor of it. Her interest in education was shown by her financial assistance to many young people, enabling them to prepare for life's work. Her gifts to missionary and other philanthropic objects, were noble and generous yet without ostentation. Her motherhood ever contributed to the dignity, purity and beauty of the home circle and brought to her the unbounded affection of grandchildren and great-grandchildren. Possessed of a great heritage founded on the Christian's hope, she truly transmitted it enlarged and beautified to descendants, and to the community at large. She passed away in that hope Feb. 28, 1912.

Children of 8th Gen.

8228 LUCIA ABBIE, b. Newbury, Vt., March 12, 1856, d. Windsor, Nov. 3, 1864.

F8229 CLARA ALICE, b. Aug. 24, 1859, m. Dec. 31, 1878, MARSH O. PERKINS.

8230 ABBIE, b. Windsor, Feb. 2, 1868, d. March 17, 1868.

8231 FLORINDA, b. Windsor, July 9, 1869, m. Windsor, Oct. 11, 1893, ERNEST I. MORGAN, b. West Windsor, Vt., Oct. 30, 1870. He received his schooling in Windsor, Vt., graduated from University of Vermont in 1891 and then completed the three years' course of Boston University Law School in one year with the highest honors.

EIGHTH GENERATION

Located a short time in Gloucester, Mass., he then went to Worcester, Mass., where he rapidly rose to the office of Assistant Attorney General, only leaving that office because of poor health. He was known to his associates at the bar as one possessed of great legal ability and comprehension. Besides his love for his profession he took great interest in the study of history and natural history. He died in Worcester, Mass., Jan. 19, 1910, had: 8232 STUART CARLTON, b. Worcester, Nov. 5, 1900.

F4925 Lydia Hall Locke, born in Dover, March 5, 1814, died July 22, 1897, married in Newmarket, Oct. 2, 1845, NATHANIEL FOLSOM KIMBALL of Exeter, born in Exeter, June 21, 1806. They lived at South Newmarket and he died Apl. 26, 1894.

Children of 8th Gen.

8233 ORRIN TAPLIN, b. Sept., 1846, m. Nashua, Oct. 24, 1871, MARIA E. AYERS, b. Dorchester, Mass., 1847, dau. of John and Lucy. He d. Nov. 15, 1876, had: 8234 BLANCHE, b. 1873, d. 1878.
8235 EMILY A., b. July 22, 1849, m. Dec. 1, 1870, BENJAMIN B. TUTTLE, b. Apl. 27, 1847, lived in Andover, Mass.
8236 GEORGE PERKINS, b. June 7, 1851, unmarried 1898.

F4926 John Tash Locke, born in South Newmarket, March 21, 1816, married Sept. 12, 1841, ROXBURY SPOFFORD SANBORN, of Sandown, daughter of John and Mary, born May 19, 1817, died in South Newmarket, Feb. 19, 1861; married 2nd, July 9, 1863, SARAH WALDRON TREADWELL of Newmarket, born Oct. 13, 1818. He was a grocer and postmaster in South Newmarket 19 years and died there Feb. 26, 1864. Sarah his widow married 1867, ELDER JOHN F. ADAMS of Newfields.

Child of 8th Gen. by first wife.

8237 MARY OLIVIA, b. Nov. 7, 1849, m. 1st, July 1, 1869, CHARLES S. TILTON, who d. July 18, 1876; m. 2nd, Nov. 25, 1879, JAMES A. FOLSOM, b. March 13, 1845, son of Winthrop and Nancy (Tash). He is a real estate broker in Manchester, no children.

F4927 Simeon Locke, born in Newmarket, Dec. 25, 1817, married Feb. 28, 1842, NANCY NORRIS CLARKE of Epping. He was in the paper stock business in Boston 25 years, going west in 1862.

Children of 8th Gen.

8238 ORRIN ST. CLAIR, b. Aug. 18, 1842, d. Sept. 8, 1846.
8239 SARAH JOSEPHINE, b. June 17, 1847, d. Apl. 4, 1849.
8240 CHARLES E., b. Nov. 1849, d. Dec. 10, 1853.
8241 SARAH L., b. Nov. 1855, d. Apl. 6, 1857.
8242 WILLIAM E., b. ——, m. FANNIE BROOKS, was a carpenter in Malden, Mass., had: 8243 MAUDE A.; 8244 WINNIFRED.
8245 CHARLES K., b. ——, died young.

F4928 Joseph Ham Locke, born in Deerfield, May 15, 1819, married in Boston, May 26, 1842, NANCY R. KENT of Kent Hill, Me., born Dec. 31, 1822, daughter of D. and Mary (Warren), died in Terre Haute, Ind., Aug., 1882. He went from South Newmarket to Boston in 1837 and was in the junk business, later became interested in nine ships and lost $100,000 by the war. He went to Chicago in 1863, from there to Cincinnati, and finally to Terre Haute, where he was engaged in the paper stock business. He died at the latter place Jan. 16, 1879.

Children of 8th Gen.

F8246 JOSEPH HAM b. May 6, 1843, m. Sept. 23, 1868, G. EMMA GOODWIN.
8247 CHARLES E., b. Feb. 6, 1847, d. Apl. 11, 1847.
8248 LEANDER MORRISON, b. Melrose, Apl. 9, 1848, m. New Brunswick, N. J., June 4, 1884, ADELAIDE E. HOWE of N. Y. City, dau. of Thomas and Mary (Shaw). He was in the paper business, Terre Haute, Ind., 1875-8, later in flour mill business, and is now a grain and cotton broker in Danville, Ill. Had: 8249 CLARENCE HOWE, b. Sept. 2, 1885.
8250 MARY ALICE, b. Sept. 7, 1850, m. Terre Haute, Ind., Sept. 1870, THOMAS WARMSLEY, b. Philadelphia, Oct. 1843, lives Decatur, Ill. He is a traveling salesman, had: 8251 EMMA K., b. 1884, d. 1884.
8252 SIMEON, b. Charlestown, Mass., July 25, 1855, m. Terre Haute, Ind., March, 1895, ESTELLE HOWARD of Terre Haute. He is in the paper business in Terre Haute, had: 8253 HOWARD R., b. March 1896, in Terre Haute.

F4930 Samuel Blake Locke, born in Deerfield, Sept. 30, 1822, married Apl. 28, 1846, ANNA HOWARD DAVIS of Newmarket. He moved from Newmarket to Melrose, Mass., in 1845, later to Andover, died there Nov. 24, 1901. For forty years he had been a resident of Andover, but doing business in Boston, being engaged in the iron trade and coast shipping. For many years he owned the Somerville iron foundry. He was in the State Senate as a Democrat in 1886. For fifty years he was a member of a Boston Commandery of Knights Templar. He was known for his sympathetic nature, and was always ready to work for the best interests of the town.

Children of 8th Gen.

8254 ANNIE LOUISE, b. Malden, Mass., Aug. 12, 1847, a teacher, unmarried, in Andover, Mass.
8255 ABBIE CUMMINGS, b. ——, d. 1893, m. DENNIE THOMPSON, had: 8256 ELMER; 8257 PHIL SHERIDAN; 8258 CLARA; 8259 ROSAMOND.
F8260 CLARA TASH, b. Sept. 2, 1853, m. Oct. 29, 1885, FRANCIS JORDAN THOMSEN.

EIGHTH GENERATION

8261 FREDERICK D., b. Jan. 22, 1850, d. Feb. 6, 1850.
8262 SAMUEL DAVIS, b. ——.
8263 FLORENCE MADELINE, b. ——.
8264 MARION, b. ——, m. —— MORRISON.

F4934 George Oliver Locke, born in South Newmarket, Sept. 19, 1826, married in Pembroke, Nov. 22, 1849, **Harriet T. Locke** of Pembroke # 4953 born in Lyman, Apl. 14, 1827. He was a trustee of Pembroke Academy; a member of the N. H. Legislature, was tax collector and had a blacksmith shop in Suncook many years. He died there Oct. 27, 1913.

Children of 8th Gen. b. in Pembroke.

8265 JOSEPHINE S., b. Nov. 9, 1858, m. Jan. 3, 1880, IRA B. MOORE of Concord, who has a hardware store in Rochester, no child.
8266 SARAH A., b. June 25, 1861, m. Pembroke, Dec. 20, 1881, ALBERT R. CLOUGH of Dover. He is a traveling man from Manchester, had:
8267 DAISY M., b. Apl. 16, 1883, m. HARVEY D. BAILEY.

F4940 Edwin Augustus Locke, born a twin, at South Newmarket, March 29, 1830, married Jan. 4, 1854, MARTHA A. SMITH of Melrose, Mass. He was a carpenter and patternmaker in South Newmarket and died there Jan. 23, 1880. His widow married 2nd, JOHN FERNALD of Rochester and died June 1901.

Children of 8th Gen.

F8268 FRED AUGUSTUS, b. ——, m. LOTTIE DEXTER.
8269 CARRIE, b. ——, died young.

F4946 Margaret Ann Locke, born in East Concord, Feb. 22, 1828, died Feb. 1895, married March 16, 1853, JOHN W. THATCHER of Dorchester, Mass., who was a farmer in Littleton, Mass.

Children of 8th Gen.

8270 JOHN H., b. Apl. 8, 1854.
8271 CHILD, b. ——, d. 1856.
8272 JOSIAH P., b. Apl. 8, 1858, m. Jan. 1, 1884, MARY SANDERSON of Littleton, had: 8273 RUSSELL; 8274 MARGARET; 8275 RUTH, 8276 ANOTHER.
8277 GEORGE, b. Aug. 1860, m. Lunenberg, Mass., Apl. 28, 1889, LILLA M. LANE, lives Fitchburg, Mass.
8278 ELIZABETH, b. July 1863.

F4947 James W. Locke, born in East Concord, Dec. 31, 1831, married June 21, 1859, MARIA D. JARVIS of Concord, born Oct. 14, 1836. He was employed by Rich & Co., Boston, died and was buried in Concord, Sept. 8, 1909.

Children of 8th Gen.

8279 CARRIE MARIA, b. Oct. 3, 1860, m. Sept. 6, 1892, REV. EMERY L. BRADFORD, b. Naskeag, Me., 1859; he is a Congregationalist Minister in Boxford, Mass. Had: 8280 RUTH, b. Aug. 1, 1893, now 1915, in Wellesley College.

8281 ANNIE JARVIS, b. Feb. 5, 1863, a Stenographer in U. S. Court, Boston.

8282 EMMA PERKINS, b. Feb. 24, 1866, same occupation as last.

8283 ALICE FARNUM, b. May 16, 1868, d. June 29, 1868.

F4950 Nancy Edgerly Locke, born in Concord, Jan. 25, 1823, married 1st, in Concord, June 25, 1845, ROBERT MOORE # 2320 of Chester, born 1811, had a book store in Manchester and died May 26, 1882; married 2nd, Feb. 10, 1885, ISAAC C. BOYCE, born Dec. 1823, who was a farmer in Penacook and died there July 13, 1891. She is now living aged 93 in Penacook.

Children of 8th Gen.

8284 JOSIE ELSIE, b. Manchester, Oct. 20, 1847, d. Penacook, Apl. 15, 1915, m. Penacook, Nov. 10, 1870, WILLIAM W. ALLEN, b. Pen. Oct. 17, 1848, son of William H. and Hannah (Brown). He is a dry goods merchant in Penacook, had: 8285 GRACE, b. June 9, 1876; 8286 HARLEY W., b. 1879, died young.

8287 SARAH IMOGENE, b. Manchester, Sept. 30, 1852, m. Penacook, Nov. 18, 1872, ORVILLE UPTON of Concord, b. Contoocook, Sept. 14, 1848, lived in Concord, had: 8288 HARRY EDSON, b. Feb. 2, 1874, m. Oct. 1906, ALICIA DAVIS of Portland. He is a telegraph operator, lives Everett, Mass.

F4954 Annah Sanders Locke, born in Concord, May 22, 1828, died in Pembroke, Nov. 14, 1896, married 1st, March 30, 1848, MARSTON M. TALLANT, born in East Canterbury, June 6, 1824. He was a farmer in Concord and died Feb. 24, 1868. She married 2nd, GEORGE F. WHITTREDGE of Concord, a grocer who died there Sept. 22, 1891.

Children of 8th Gen., all by first husband.

8289 GEORGE M., b. June 9, 1850, m. March 1871, JOSIE GLIDDEN of Meredith who d. Duluth, Iowa, Aug. 24, 1901. He lived Concord and Iowa, had: 8290 ETHEL H., b. ——, m. ROBERT MARSHALL.

8291 MARTHA A., b. Jan. 25, 1852, d. Dec. 20, 1890, m. March 15, 1871, FRANK DOWST of Manchester, b. Dec. 1, 1855. He is a builder in Manchester, had: 8292 EDITH, b. 1874, d. 1885.

F8293 EDWIN FRANK, b. Dec. 2, 1855, m. Aug. 19, 1881, SUSIE DREW

F4955 Edward Philbrick Locke, born in Concord, Oct. 5, 1832, married 1st, Jan. 9, 1854, MARTHA A. MARTIN of Pembroke who died Aug. 1884, daughter of Moses and Rhoda (Hoitt);

married 2nd, Jan. 12, 1887, EMMA J. FOWLE of Pembroke, who was born Aug. 17, 1859. He formerly lived in Concord and Pembroke. He served 40 years on the Missouri Pacific R. R., was a well known and popular passenger conductor on the run Kansas City to Omaha. While assisting in attaching a car to his train, he slipped and lost one leg and a foot, living only 24 hours. He died in Kansas City, Dec. 24, 1900.

Child of 8th Gen. by Second wife.
8294 EMMA PEARL, born Feb. 1888.

F4956 Morris Lamprey Locke, born in Concord, Aug. 18, 1841, married 1st, March 1861, MARY HINES of Texas; married 2nd, ELIZA DIXON of Burlington, Iowa; married 3rd, FLORA J. ELKINS. He was a R. R. engineer in Minneapolis, and died May 1891.

Children of 8th Gen.
8295 ELLA, b. June 1862.
8296 MARY C., b. May 1863, m. ——— BUCHANAN of Chapel Hill, Texas.
8297 EDWARD P., b. Feb. 1865, lived Chapel Hill, Tex.
8298 MAUDE, b. ——., *By second wife:*

F4957 Joseph Yeaton, born July 13, 1826, married 1st, in 1849, ANNA GREEN of Seabrook; married 2nd, FANNIE COLLINS, born 1849, died Feb. 18, 1910, daughter of Thomas and Dorothy (Munsey). He died March 7, 1907, having lived in Seabrook and Pittsfield.

Children of 8th Gen.
8299 FRED, b. March 31, 1862, m. Aug. 4, 1915, ROSIE CUMMINGS.
8300 WILLIAM A., b. 1863, m. LOTTIE PALMER, children: 8301 CLARENCE P., b. July 3, 1892; 8302 HELEN D., b. Feb. 5, 1898, and another older than these.

F4958 Simeon L. Yeaton, born Nov. 13, 1828, married in 1856, MARY BROWN. He was a shoemaker in Plaistow.

Children of 8th Gen.
8304 ALICE L., and SARAH, both died young.
8305 S. ALBERT, b. Dec. 3, 1865, m. CORA MORSE, lives in Pittsfield, has: 8306 IVAN, b. 1894; 8307 CONRAD D., b. June 24, 1898.
8308 ELMER, b. ——, died young.

F4960 William Yeaton, born in Pittsfield, July 30, 1836, married May 23, 1867, JOSEPHINE C. DRAKE of Pittsfield, born Jan. 26, 1846, daughter of James S. and Susan F. (Young). He was educated in the public school of Pittsfield, graduating from the academy there, later teaching several years in Pittsfield,

Gilmanton and Hopkinton. After spending the year 1864 in Centralia, Ill., he returned and engaged in the insurance business in Pittsfield several years until appointed register of probate in Merrimack County, which position he held two years. He then became agent of the Detroit City Mills, in New Hampshire and Vermont, and established a large grain and flour business in Pittsfield. In 1881 he accepted the position of treasurer of the Farmington Savings Bank. In 1885 he was New England agent of the Dakota Farm Mortgage Co., with headquarters in Concord to which place he moved. After five years with this company he organized and was president of the American Trust Co., holding that position until its dissolution several years later. For some years and until his illness he was in the bond investment and real estate business. A prominent Democrat in town and state, he first represented Pittsfield in the legislature in 1867, when he acted as doorkeeper. Since that time he has been often honored by his party. He was a member of Mount Horeb Commandery of Knights Templar, a conscientious worker in St. Paul's Church, Concord, greatly interested in all educational matters. He was a man agreeable and beloved, one of the organizers of the Locke Association and to whom the compiler is under great obligation. He died in Concord after a long illness, Sunday, Feb. 14, 1914.

Children of 8th Gen.
8309 HELEN, b. May 25, 1869, d. Jan. 17, 1880.
8310 LILLIAN, b. Dec. 18, 1873, graduated Wellesley, 1897, now a teacher.
8311 GEORGE WILLIAM, b. Dec. 16, 1878, m. Medway, Mass., Oct. 30, 1907, EDNA BELLE ANDREWS, dau. of Robert; he graduated from Dartmouth Medical College 1902, is a physician in Medway, Mass. Had a son 8312 GEORGE WILLIAM, JR., b. Feb. 18, 1913.

F4962 Simeon Locke Sanders, born Nov. 21, 1839, married Nov. 28, 1864 JENNIE C. BRACKETT, and he died July 19, 1890.
Children of 8th Gen.
8312 WILLIAM BRACKETT, b. March 3, 1866, m. Aug. 26, 1889, ETTA TUTTLE, had: 8313 RENA M., b. 1891.
8314 ROBERT I., b. Oct. 7, 1869, d. Jan. 13, 1886.
8315 JOHN BRACKETT, b. Feb. 1, 1872.
8316 JOSIE B., b. Dec. 12, 1880.

F5018 Elizabeth P. Locke, born in Epsom, Apl. 23, 1823, died 1889, married in Epsom, Apl. 15, 1846, JAMES D. PAGE, born in Ryegate, Vt., 1819, lived in Epsom. He married again.

EIGHTH GENERATION 433

Children of 8th Gen.
8317 ALBION LOCKE, b. 1847, m. FLORA EVANS, lived in Pittsfield.
8318 CARRIE E., b. Penacook, March 1849, d. Epsom, Feb. 15, 1894, m. Epsom, 1869, ALONZO ELBRIDGE BACHELDER, lived Epsom.
8319 HARVEY, b. ——.

F5026 Sarah Ann Gove, born Jan. 10, 1835, married Dec. 22, 1858, JOSIAH S. CLIFFORD of Chichester, lived at Concord and Pittsfield.

Children of 8th Gen.
8320 GEORGIELLA, b. Feb. 18, 1861, d. March 21, 1866.
8321 FRED W., b. July 19, 1866.
8322 JOHN G., b. Sept. 5, 1868, m. ELLEN E. CROSS of Manchester, had: 8323 ROGER W., b. Sept. 6, 1891; 8324 ERNEST E., b. Sept. 26, 1896; 8325 RUTH ELIZABETH, b. Aug. 28, 1899.
8326 ELLEN E., b. March 7, 1869.   8327 ELLEN E., b. Sept. 11, 1870.
8328 ROGER N., b. Sept. 6, 1873.   8329 ERNEST G., b. Sept. 26, 1875.
8330 RUTH E., b. Aug. 28, 1880.

F5028 Joseph A. Whittier, born in Dover, July 6, 1820, married in Lincoln, Me., July 13, 1846, ANGELINE BRADFORD, who died in Saginaw, Mich., Nov. 9, 1889. He died in Saginaw, 1909.

Children of 8th Gen.
8331 HELEN L., b. Lincoln, Me., Sept. 1, 1847, m. A. S. MONTGOMERY of Saginaw, Mich.
8332 LUCY A., b. Feb. 6, 1849, d. Feb. 5, 1851.
8333 CHARLES A., b. July 13, 1850, m. 1st, L. E. LEITH of Saginaw, Mich.; m. 2nd, MRS. MARY E. WOOD of N. Y. City.
8334 JOSEPH B., b. Sept. 1, 1851, is unmarried.
8335 CAROLINE M., b. May 7, 1853, d. Sept. 6, 1853.
8336 SEWARD, b. Aug. 5, 1854, died same day.
8337 THOMAS P., b. March 17, 1859, m. 1st, LUCY E. LORD of Bangor, Me.; m. 2nd, MAUDE ROSS of Saginaw, Mich. Had: 8338 RUTH ANGELINE; 8339 ELIZABETH ROSS.

F5048 Edwin Beal Locke, born in South Berwick, Me., Nov. 8, 1833, married Jan. 2, 1854, **Sarah A. Locke,** # 4943 of Newmarket, born in South Newmarket, March 25, 1834, lived in Chicago, 1911. He was a machinist lived South Newmarket, Exeter, and Chicago where he died May 7, 1886.

Children of 8th Gen. b. in So. Newmarket.
8340 EMMA RUSSELL, b. Sept. 10, 1854, m. July 14, 1875, SOLON EUGENE AVERY of Chicago, b. Oct. 2, 1853, d. Aug. 25, 1882, had: 8341 WALTER CUMMINGS, b. Apl. 25, 1876, is m.; 8342 ROGER LOCKE, b. Aug. 12, 1881, who also is m.

8343 FRANK EDWIN, b. July 19, 1858, m. CLARA ELLA TALLMAN of Mich
igan b. July 14, 1866. He is a Notary in Chicago.
8344 CHARLES ALBERT, b. Dec. 9, 1861, m. JENNIE C. ———, in 1910, i
a storekeeper in Chicago.

F5054 Martha Abbie Locke, born in Effingham, Apl. 18
1840, married in Wells, Me., Oct. 30, 1862, NATHANIEL E. HAN
SON, born in Dover, Feb. 5, 1837, lived in Dover and diec
there, June 15, 1901. She lives in Dover, 1915.
Children of 8th Gen. b. in Dover.
8345 HARRY HALL, b. March 13, 1865, m. Guatemala, C. A., Jan. 17, 1897
CARMEN A. MATHERS, is a bank manager in Mexico City, had
8346 HARRY NATHANIEL; 8347 RICHARD LOCKE; 8348 ENRIQUI
N., b. Oct. 18, 1897.
8349 GRACE THOMPSON, b. Jan. 7, 1867, m. Dover, Sept. 2, 1891, J. E
VICKERY, b. Dover, July 4, 1866. He is a druggist in Dover, n
children.
8350 MARTHA AGNES, b. Dec. 16, 1869, d. Dover, Jan. 1, 1870.
8351 NATALIE, b. March 27, 1870, m. Oct. 18, 1893, EDWARD FRANCI
HASBROOK, of Chicago, a R. R. Purchasing agent, had children b
Chicago: 8352 ROBERT LOCKE, b. July 18, 1895; 8353 EDWAR:
FRANCIS, b. May 10, 1897; 8354 JOHN VAN AMBURG, b. Dec. 24
1898.
8354 ELLEN MAUD, b. Nov. 26, 1872, d. Nov. 24, 1876.
8355 STACY LOCKE, b. Oct. 18, 1874, is secretary in Dover factory.

F5056 Nancy Whittier Locke, born in Freedom, Dec. 31
1846, married Jan. 1, 1868, CHARLES O. POPE of Wells, Me., bori
March 11, 1841. They live in Wells where he has a hotel.
Children of 8th Gen. b. Wells, Me.
8356 MARY LOCKE, b. Jan. 4, 1869, m. Wells, Sept. 7, 1893, ALBERT CON
VERS PLACE, b. Oakland, Cal., a lumber dealer in Cambridge, Mass
had: 8357 RUSSELL P., b. Sept. 6, 1898.
8358 IRVING HALL, b. Sept. 23, 1872, d. Oct. 23, 1872.
8359 SON, b. May 25, 1874, d. same day.
8360 CHARLES EDWIN, b. March 20, 1878.

F5057 Lydia Hall Locke, born in Dover, March 10, 185c
married in Chicago, Feb. 25, 1875, MITCHELL R. MUDIE, of Scot
land, born in Glasgow, Jan. 1, 1848. They lived in Chicago an
he died in Wells, Me., Nov. 1, 1891. She lives in Chicago, 1915
Children of 8th Gen. b. in Chicago.
8361 MABEL LOCKE, b. May 2, 1876, d. Taunton, Mass., Feb. 20, 1911, n
Wells, Me., June 4, 1902, GEORGE ALBERT CUTTER, b. Vinelanc
Kan., Jan. 24, 1874. He was a Supt. in Taunton, Mass., had: 836
BARBARA DEERING, b. Nashua, Aug. 29, 1903; 8363 ELIZABET
MITCHELL, b. Newton, Mass., Aug. 30, 1905.
8364 EARL MACINTOSH, b. June 22, 1885, d. Aug. 14, 1895, Wells.

F5058 Mary Elizabeth Locke, born in Salmon Falls, Aug. 23, 1853, married in Dover, Sept. 16, 1874, FRANK B. WILLIAMS, born Aug. 22, 1850. They live in Dover, where he is a belt manufacturer of firm of I. B. Williams & Son.

Children of 8th Gen. b. in Dover.

8365 MARGUERITE LOUISE, b. June 4, 1884, m. Dover, June, 1909, PHILIP CARTER BROWN of Dover. He is Assistant Supt. of Belt Factory in Dover, had: 8366 MARY PHILLIS, b. Dover, July 20, 1910.

8367 DOROTHY LOCKE, b. Sept. 20, 1892, lives in Dover, unmarried.

F5059 Mandana C. Locke, born in Epsom, Nov. 8, 1835, married 1st, Dec. 20, 1855, JOHN W. PAGE # 5823, born Feb. 13, 1834, a shoemaker of Epsom; married 2nd, Nov. 26, 1865, SAMUEL STANLEY, born in Haverhill, July 8, 1833, a shoemaker in Epsom.

Children of 8th Gen. b. in Pittsfield.

8368 ARAMINTA A., b. Jan. 12, 1859, m. GEORGE WATSON.

8369 FRED A., b. Aug. 28, 1861, m. Epsom, Nov. 21, 1893, MRS. CLARA C. WOODMAN, b. Epsom, 1854, dau. of H. Bartlett and Abbie C. (Haynes). He is a farmer in Allenstown.

8370 HERBERT S., b. Nov. 27, 1873, m. Nov. 13, 1895, CARRIE G. KEYES of Rumney, dau. of Joseph C. and Almira C. (Willoughby). He is a farmer.

F5060 Dexter H. Locke, born in Pittsfield, Nov. 26, 1838, married 1st, Nov. 30, 1864, SARAH A. PAGE, born in Epsom, May 10, 1838, died in Pittsfield, May 12, 1890, daughter of Josiah and Hannah (Marston); married 2nd, in Ellsworth, Dec. 14, 1893, MRS. MARY ANN (PALMER) HILL (her 4th mg.), born 1838, died in Ellsworth, Aug. 16, 1900, daughter of Benjamin and Hannah (Avery). He was a farmer in Epsom and died in Pittsfield, May 31, 1895.

Children of 8th Gen.

8371 HORACE M., b. Epsom, March 7, 1868, m. CLARA BOWMAN, b. Sweden, 1864. He is a farmer in Pittsfield, had: 8372 DEXTER, b. Aug. 7, 1896, d. Aug. 17, 1896.

8373 GERTRUDE H., b. Epsom, Feb. 16, 1870, m. Pittsfield, Feb. 16, 1892, WALTER E. GOVE, b. 1866, son of Otis W. and Mary E. (Thompson). He is a shoemaker in Pittsfield.

8374 MARCUS K., b. Dec. 15, 1871, m. Apl. 13, 1902, MRS. MARY ETTA (COME) LABAENE, b. N. Y., 1868, d. Jan. 10, 1904, dau. of Peter and Mary (Walles). He is a farmer in Pittsfield.

F8375 SIMEON P., b. Sept. 4, 1874, m. Sept. 27, 1892, CORA D. MILLBURY.

8376 ARTHUR C., b. Epsom, Apl. 17, 1876, m. Epsom, July 29, 1911, CARRIE L. FRANCIES, b. 1866, dau. of George W. and Fannie (Jones) of Warner. He also m. MABEL WIGGIN, b. Brookfield, 1879, probably as first wife as he had: 8377 JAMES WILLIS, b. Wilton, July 15, 1899. He lived at Wilton, later at Wolfeboro.
8378 JAMES B., b. Pittsfield, June 22, 1878, d. Feb. 2, 1882.
8379 GEORGE OZRO, b. May 27, 1880, d. Pitts., June 18, 1884.
8380 MELICENT, b. Pittsfield, July 27, 1882, m. Pitts., Sept. 26, 1898, LEWIS E. GOVE of Concord, b. Pittsfield, 1878, son of Otis W., and Mary E. (Thompson). He is employed on B. & M. R. R. Concord.

F5063 Orrilla H. Locke, born in Epsom, Sept. 19, 1845, married Apl. 19, 1858, HENRY W. BICKFORD, born in Epsom, Feb. 23, 1830, son of William and Polly (Rand). He was a farmer in Epsom.

Children of 8th Gen.

8381 JAMES H., b. Pittsfield, Apl. 13, 1864, m. March 15, 1887, ELMA D. FISKE, b. 1862, dau. of James. He is a farmer in Campton, has no children.
8382 GEORGE P., b. Nov. 21, 1865, d. an infant.
8383 ANNIE B., b. Feb. 23, 1867, lives unmarried, in Epsom.
8384 ALICE P., b. Epsom June 4, 1868, m. Sept. 3, 1892, FRED C. GILES, b. Deerfield, 1871, son of Cyrus N. and Sarah (Rand). He is a clerk in Northwood, had: 8385 ARTHUR S.; 8386 LEONARD; 8387 LOREN C.
8388 CHARLES S., b. June 25, 1877.

F5064 Lucinda M. Locke, born in Epsom, March 30, 1826, married Oct. 3, 1850, WILLIAM MCMURPHY of Epsom, born Apl. 21, 1824. He was a farmer in Epsom and died 1900 (?).

Children of 8th Gen.

8389 EMMA, b. March 7, 1852, d. Dec. 31, 1860.
8390 MARY B., b. July 21, 1853, d. July 19, 1855.
F8391 ANNA, b. March 16, 1854, m. Nov. 26, 1878, FREEMAN R. NEVENS.
8392 MINOT, b. Sept. 17, 1857, d. Dec. 18, 1860.
8393 HATTIE, b. Epsom, Sept. 8, 1859, m. Sept. 5, 1883, FRED HOLDEN, b. Lynn, Feb. 28, 1860, lived there and had: 8394 ERNEST F., b. Aug. 25, 1885; 8395 ETHEL M., b. March 11, 1892; 8396 LILLA P., b. Sept. 2, 1895.
8397 CARRIE, b. Feb. 2, 1863, d. May 13, 1864.
8398 WILLIE, b. March 27, 1866, d. Sept. 24, 1881.

F5067 James Lovering Locke, born in Epsom, May 14, 1832, married May 16, 1858, SARAH M. SWALLOW of Dunstable, Mass., born Oct. 10, 1835. They live in Malden, Mass. She was daughter of John and Charlotte (McCutcheon). In early life he was in the hotel business in New Hampshire. He entered the employ of the Boston, Nashua and Lowell R. R. in 1862, as conductor, later was Station Master in Boston until 1872, when he assumed personal charge of the station restaurant and news stand and retired after thirty years service. He represented Ward 8 of Boston in the Legislature at three periods. In 1892 he removed to Malden where he built his present home.

Children of 8th Gen.

8400 ELMORE ESTES, b. Epsom, Oct. 29, 1860, m. Boston, Oct. 15, 1885, ALICE L. DEXTER, b. Boston, Jan. 6, 1863, dau. of Henry B. and Mary C. (White). He is President of the Locke Wood and Coal Co., Malden, Mass., has been Colonel on the Governor's Staff, had: 8401 MARION DEXTER, b. Malden, March 18, 1894, is a graduate of Wellesley College, 1915.

F8402 FRANK LOVERING, b. July 14, 1865, m. Jan. 16, 1901, MARY BROADHEAD KENDALL.

F8403 MABEL LOUISE, b. June 15, 1876, m. Nov. 28, 1900, GEORGE W. R. HARRIMAN.

F5068 Marianna J. Locke, born in Epsom, May 5, 1834, married Dec. 25, 1859, WILLIAM HAWSE of Chelsea, born Sept. 5, 1808. He was in the lumber business in Chelsea, and died Oct. 16, 1880. By a first wife, EMALINE LOCKE # 2152 he had 12 children.

Children of 8th Gen.

8404 HENRIETTA, b. Oct. 11, 1861, d. Apl. 11, 1887, m. Feb. 2, 1881, WILLIAM H. BUTMAN, who d. March 11, 1897, had: 8405 CARL H., b. Nov. 17, 1884.

8406 GEORGE E., b. Nov. 30, 1865, d. Sept. 5, 1875.

8407 CHARLES SUMNER, b. June 7, 1869, m. Dec. 15, 1897, FRANCES WILSON of Winchester, Mass., b. Jan. 26, 1871. She was a Smith College graduate. He graduated from Harvard, 1893, was two years in Harvard Medical School, Auditor 1899, of Harvard Dining Association. He lives in Cambridge.

F5069 Annie Lovering Locke, born in Epsom, Sept. 9, 1836, married July 4, 1859, GEORGE W. LANE of Chichester, born in Chichester, July 14, 1838, son of Isaiah and Abigail (Goss). He lived in Chichester, was a farmer, civil engineer, town clerk, moderator, a Republican and member of Constitutional Convention.

Children of 8th Gen. b. in Chichester.

8408 WALTER E., b. Feb. 19, 1860, d. Nov. 8, 1883.

8409 JOHN ALLISON, b. May 29, 1861, d. March 25, 1879.

8410 ALICE L., b. Dec. 6, 1862, m. 1898, EDGAR L. BURNHAM of Chichester.
8411 GEORGEANNA, b. Nov. 29, 1864.
8412 CLINTIE W., b. Sept. 4, 1867, m. Chichester, Sept. 4, 1896, FRANK L. SEAVEY, b. 1864, son of William A. and Abbie L. (Lane). He is a farmer in Epsom.
8413 ISAIAH LOVERING, b. May 26, 1871.
8414 ABBIE A., b. Feb. 19, 1877, m. May 21, 1902, ORRIN M. JAMES of Northwood Narrows.
8415 CARRIE M., b. May 7, 1881.

F5092 Sarah A. Locke, born in Barre, Mass., Nov. 23, 1850, married in Manchester-by-the-Sea, Mass., HENRY L. HADCOCK, born in Newport, Sept. 5, 1855. He is a druggist on Washington St., Roxbury, Mass. She died Apl., 1914.

Children of 8th Gen. b. in Roxbury, Mass.
8416 BEATRICE LOCKE, b. Dec. 29, 1878, is a teacher in Roxbury, and lives in Brookline with her nieces.
8417 EDWARD WEBSTER, b. May 1, 1881, m. Jan. 24, 1903, CERES HEYWOOD and d. Oct. 8, 1911, had: 8418 EDITHA, b. Aug. 16, 1905; 8419 CERES, b. March 23, 1907; 4820 THORA, b. Dec. 21, 1908.
8421 JOSEPHINE WRIGHT, b. July 30, 1884, m. June 29, 1910, WARREN D. SPENGLER, lives Hudson, Ohio, no children.
8422 HENRY FONDA, b. Nov. 13, 1885, d. July 30, 1896.

F5110 Sarah B. Locke, born Sept. 6, 1839, died in Coventry, Vt., Oct. 16, 1910, married Jan. 6, 1863, AZRO C. BRYANT, born Feb. 13, 1837. They lived in Coventry and he died Jan. 25, 1909. He was son of George O. and Sarah (Burton).

Children of 8th Gen.
8423 INA J., b. July 31, 1865, m. Jan. 1, 1897, LUKE S. EATON, son of Solomon and Annie D. (Kenney). They lived in Coventry, Vt., and had: 8424 MAURICE, b. Nov. 30, 1900; 8425 ANNA, b. Feb. 15, 1904; 8426 DONALD B., b. Jan. 26, 1908; and 8427 DOROTHY M., b. twin, Jan. 26, 1908.
8428 EMMA E., b. Apl. 6, 1868, d. Dec. 1886.

F5114 Sarah Anne Jameson, born May 10, 1827, died Oct. 29, 1851, married Oct., 1849, DAVID WEBSTER, born July 19, 1826.

Child of 8th Gen.
8429 ADA L., b. Oct. 16, 1850, m. Sept. 23, 1869, BYRON DE FOREST BROWN, b. Jan. 6, 1846, lived at Stockham, Neb., and had five children.

EIGHTH GENERATION

F5115 William Lovering Jameson, born in Irasburg, Vt. May 12, 1828, married Nov. 11, 1852, AURILLA CRANDALL, born in Albany, June 1, 1831, lived in Santa Cruz, Cal., where he died June 3, 1896.

Child of 8th Gen.

8430 HENRY A., b. Irasburg, Vt., Feb. 13, 1858, m. 1st Sept. 15, 1886, MARY E. THURBER; m. 2nd, ROSE M. SARPY. He had four children.

F5116 Caroline Jameson, born in Irasburg, Oct. 18, 1829, died May 24, 1862, married March 16, 1856, WARNER STRONG, born in Berlin, Vt., June 7, 1823. He lived in Berlin, Vt., and died March 8, 1890.

Child of 8th Gen.

8431 HORACE W., b. Feb. 27, 1857, m. Jan. 1, 1880, ELLA A. BROWN, had one child; lived West Berlin, Vt.

F5118 Horace Dunkee Jameson, born in Irasburg, Feb. 13, 1833, married Oct. 31, 1859, ANNIE MCSLAUGHLIN, born in Calais, Me., Dec. 19, 1843. He was a harness maker by trade but later was justice of peace, and President of a California Coal Mine Co. He died Nov. 10, 1882, and his widow married 2nd, ALLEN BARTLETT, and lived in California.

Children of 8th Gen.

8432 HERMAN A., b. Feb. 10, 1860, d. March 24, 1874.
8433 EMMA V., b. San Francisco, Feb. 14, 1870, m. Sept. 15, 1890, SMITH ANDERSON, b. Scotland, Apl. 11, 1861, lives Los Angeles, Cal., has two children.

F5119 Zuar E. Jameson, born in Irasburg, Jan. 5, 1835, married in Bristol, R. I., June 25, 1860, MARY ELLEN WILCOX, born in Bristol, Feb. 16, 1842. He was a farmer, writer for Agricultural papers, served in Legislature, was on State Board of Agriculture, and died in Irasburg, Vt., Jan. 4, 1886.

Children of 8th Gen. b. in Irasburg, Vt.

8434 ARTHUR LINCOLN, b. July 18, 1861, m. Jan. 12, 1886, FANNY WARD GLEN. He has a music store, was Park Commissioner, and Secretary of Savings and Loan Assoc., Ogdensburg, N. Y.
8435 GRACE WINNIFRED, b. Apl. 20, 1867, m. Woonsocket, R. I., Oct. 10, 1887, GEORGE ALBERT SMITH, b. Woonsocket, Dec. 23, 1863. They live there and he is Editor of *Evening Reporter,* had: 8436 HIRAM J., b. July 4, 1888; 8437 HARROLD LOCKE, b. Sept. 8, 1889; 8438 PRISCILLA DA COSTA, b. March 7, 1897.
8438 ISADORE DARLING, b. July 21, 1876, d. May 28, 1897.
8439 BESSIE ANTOINETTE, b. Feb. 13, 1878, d. Apl. 2, 1878.

F5120 Laura M. Jameson, born in Irasburg, Sept. 25, 1836, died in Berkeley, Cal., Aug. 22, 1893, married Dec. 31, 1859, ISAAC M. DAKIN, born in Lubec, Me., lived at Soquel, and Laurel Glen, Cal.

Children of 8th Gen.
8440 ROBERT HENRY, b. Apl. 24, 1863, lives California.
8441 ALICE LAURA, b. Sept. 15, 1864, m. Jan. 1, 1890, ARTHUR E. LOOMIS. She was a literary writer.
8442 WILBUR J., b. Nov. 10, 1860, m. Dec. 1, 1886, IRENE R. HILL.

F5122 Julia E. Jameson, born in Irasburg, July 9, 1840, died Apl. 24, 1885, married Aug. 10, 1860, CHARLES F. DEWEY, born in Berlin, Vt., March 27, 1836, son of William and Hannah (Hurlburt). He is a farmer and has served in the Legislature, etc.

Children of 8th Gen.
8443 NETTIE M., b. Jan. 10, 1864, d. Jan. 22, 1893, m. Nov. 6, 1886, MILTON D. DREW and lived Berlin, Vt. Had: 8444 LEWIS, b. Aug. 26, 1887; 8445 WILLIS, b. June 9, 1889; 8446 WILLIAM, b. Aug. 26, 1891.
8447 ELMER C., b. Sept. 24, 1866, m. Aug. 13, 1896, ALICE BERTHA COVELL, b. May 23, 1873, had: 8448 CHARLES S.

F5123 Lucy A. Jameson, born in Irasburg, Nov. 27, 1843, married in Newbury, Vt., July 18, 1867, REV. ORANGE W. SCOTT of Newbury, born Oct. 15, 1842. He is a Methodist minister, had churches in Norwich, Conn., Brockton, Mass., Malden and other cities.

Children of 8th Gen.
8449 EVERETT H., b. Aug. 15, 1858, m. Aug. 12, 1896, MINNIE E. GRANT. He graduated from Wesleyan Univ. 1891, is a teacher.
8450 GERTRUDE A., b. June 6, 1871, m. Oct. 14, 1896, ALBERT E. WAITE, a bookkeeper in N. E. Mills at Rockville, Conn.
8451 FLORENCE E., b. Oct. 13, 1876, is a teacher.
8452 ARTHUR O., b. Sept. 24, 1880.
8453 ALEC JAMESON, b. Dec. 10, 1882, d. 1891.

F5125 John L. Dodge, born in Irasburg, Oct. 21, 1833, married Oct. 15, 1861, SARAH J. MERRILL, born in Craftsbury, Vt., May 9, 1835, died in Irasburg, Oct. 16, 1910. He was a farmer in Barton Landing, and died in Irasburg, May 3, 1911.

Children of 8th Gen.
8454 IRENE L., b. Irasburg, Vt., July 26, 1868, d. Aug. 8, 1868.
8455 CARLOS A., b. March 31, 1872, m. ——— CLEVELAND and lived in Orleans, Vt.

EIGHTH GENERATION

F5131 William Lovering Locke, born in Irasburg, Vt., May 25, 1841, married in Irasburg, June 1, 1862, AMELIA E. HILL, born in Starksboro, Vt., Feb. 7, 1840, daughter of Perley and Mehitable (Brown). He was a farmer and fruit grower on the homestead in Irasburg, Vt.

Children of 8th Gen.

F8456 CHARLES CLARENCE, b. Nov. 16, 1863, m. Feb. 18, 1891, IDA L. GIFFEN.
8457 NETTIE MARIA, b. March 25, 1867, m. Irasburg, June 26, 1894, JOSEPH S. SCHOFIELD, b. Halifax, Feb. 26, 1864, son of Rev. William and Susanna (Ripley). He lived Lyndonville, Vt.
8458 NELLIE LOVERING, b. July 13, 1868, m. Irasburg, Vt., Dec. 23, 1896, BENJAMIN F. EATON, b. Irasburg, Sept. 21, 1868, son of Solomon and ——— (Kenny). Lived in Lebanon.
8459 GEORGE F., b. March 9, 1877, m. MAE CHENEY, lived in Orleans, Vt., and had three children.

F5133 Sarah Appleton Locke, born July 2, 1842, died in Paris, France, June 30, 1900, married Boston, 1863, GEORGE E. MAGUIRE of Randolph, Mass., born in Randolph, 1842, son of James and Mary (Burrell). He died 1885.

Children of 8th Gen.

8460 JAMES APPLETON, b. ———, m. MARIE BUCKNELL, lived in San Francisco and was divorced.
8461 GEORGE EDWARD, b. Boston, Apl. 18, 1867, lived San Francisco, d. Santa Barbara, Jan. 19, 1901, was m. Had: 8462 ARNOLD.
8463 BLANCHE, b. Jamaica Plains, m. July 24, 1890, FLETCHER F. RYER of San Francisco, had: 8464 FLETCHER F., JR., b. May 30, 1891, d. Oct. 9, 1891; 8465 DORIS F. b. Oct. 1893.

F5137 William Lovering Locke, born in Albany, Vt., Sept. 21, 1853, married in San Francisco, Sept. 2, 1880, BELLE A. FISHER of California, born Nov. 21, 1860, daughter of Charles A. and Mary. He was of firm "Locke and Pike Co.," San Francisco, 1898.

Children of 8th Gen. b. in San Francisco.

8466 FLORENCE, b. March 9, 1883. 8467 JOHN FISHER, b. Sept. 13, 1888.

F5171 Josiah B. Lang, born Jan. 11, 1824, married July 17, 1845, LORENDA M. CHAPMAN born June 24, 1824. They lived in Wellington and Cleveland, Ohio.

Children of 8th Gen.

8468 REUEL JESSE, b. Jan. 26, 1847, d. Oct. 8, 1853.
8469 EVA A., b. Nov. 21, 1852, m. GEORGE M. CODWELL.
8470 WATSON W., b. Apl. 24, 1863, m. 1883, ANNA ADAMS.
8471 CHARLES H., b. Cleveland, Oct. 13, 1864, m. Oct. 8, 1890, GRACE S. BLACK.

F5180 Esther Abigail Lang, born Apl. 13, 1838, married Aug. 12, 1860, CHARLES W. HORR, who died Oct. 3, 1894. They lived in Wellington, O.

Children of 8th Gen.

8472 NORTON TOWNSEND, b. Apl. 26, 1862, m. 1st, Sept. 6, 1884, MARGARET L. BARNARD; m. 2nd, Nov. 27, 1889, MARTHA UMBSTAETTER. He was a lawyer, served as President of Locke Association, and lived in Cleveland, Ohio, had: 8473 ELSA M., b. Oct. 8, 1885; 8474 AMY C., b. Aug. 9, 1891; 8475 EDWARD N., b. May 15, 1894; 8476 RUTH P., b. March 17, 1902.
8477 CHARLES WILLIAM, b. Oct. 6, 1866, m. MABEL HEBBARD.
8478 CLINTON LANG, b. Aug. 4, 1870, d. June 20, 1876.
8479 ALFRED REUEL, b. July 14, 1875.
8480 HARLEY MARTIS, b. Sept. 15, 1877.

F5189 Sarah Matilda Lang, born June 5, 1833, died May 17, 1905, married May 16, 1855, SPENCER WRIGHT, born Feb. 4, 1829, lived in Des Moines, Iowa, and he died Feb. 26, 1902. He was a merchant.

Children of 8th Gen. b. Des Moines, Iowa.

8481 JOHN L., b. Aug. 6, 1858, m. Oct. 15, 1885, ANNA CHAMBERS of Bogota, U. S. Columbia, had: 8482 SPENCER, b. 1893.
8483 CHARLES S., b. March 12, 1861, is a civil engineer in Kansas City.
8484 JESSIE, b. Jan. 12, 1864, m. Feb. 10, 1892, GEORGE J. ATKINS of Marietta, Pa., and had: 8485 SAMUEL, b. 1894.
8486 GRACE L., b. Feb. 18, 1867.
8487 HELEN, b. Nov. 18, 1871, m. 1893, EDWARD LEAVENWORTH.

F5204 Georgeanna Babb, born March 4, 1831, buried in Manchester, June 30, 1910, married Dec. 28, 1848, REV. JOHN W. RAY, born Dec. 24, 1814. They lived in Lake City, Minn., and he died Apl. 12, 1901.

Children of 8th Gen.

8488 JAMES S., b. Nov. 10, 1851, d. Aug. 11, 1853.
8489 LUCY H., b. July 16, 1853, m. Dec. 28, 1875, ERASTUS P. GATES, b. Apl. 16, 1850, d. Minn., Apl. 4, 1913, had: 8490 GEORGEANNA D., b. March 13, 1893, m. RAYMOND BOILEAU MIXSELL, A. M.; M. D.; F. R. G. S. of London, Eng., b. Jan. 23, 1882.
8491 GEORGE W., b. Apl. 25, 1860, d. Nov. 7, 1865.

F5216 Amanda J. Lang, born Feb. 14, 1836, died Oct. 7, 1867, married Oct. 8, 1854, BENJAMIN F. GAGE of Penacook, born in Boscawen, Nov. 7, 1827, son of Richard and Susanna (Chandler). He had saw works in Boscawen.

John A. Lang F5218

Reuel Lang F2217, Aged About 90

EIGHTH GENERATION 443

Children of 8th Gen.

8492 LIZZIE E., b. July 20, 1855, m. WILLIAM S. GEDDES of N. Y., lived at Beachmont, and Lynn, Mass.

8493 MADELLA J., b. Apl. 20, 1859, d. June 24, 1890, m. AMOS E. LOVERING.

F5218 John Adams Lang, born in Epping Centre, Sept. 23, 1842, married in Franklin, Jan. 24, 1866, CARRIE A. GLINES, born in Northfield, Dec. 26, 1842, He has been a machinist and blacksmith for 35 years, was at one time foreman of Walter Aiken's machine shop, Franklin, but now has his own shop on Dover St., Boston. He is a prominent Mason and a genial man to meet, being particularly interested in the Locke Association. Resides in Roslindale, Mass.

Children of 8th Gen.

8494 ELMER L., b. Franklin, Aug. 5, 1867, m. Strafford, England, Dec. 23, 1891, EMMA RICHARDS, b. England, Oct. 10, 1868. He is a machinist and manufacturer in Boston, home in Roslindale, Mass., had: 8495 HELEN M., b. 1894; 8495a RUTH R. b. July 16, 1905.

8496 JOHN B., b. Feb. 21, 1871, m. Nov. 9, 1897, ALICE M. COLBY of Franklin, b. Sept. 15, 1871. He is a foreman in a machine shop, and lives Cliftondale, Mass., had: 8496a ESTHER C. b. Beverly, Aug. 18, 1908.

8497 GEORGE H., b. Jan. 1, 1876, m. June 20, 1900, EDITH T. DRAKE, b. Franklin July 19, 1876. He is a machinist and manufacturer, lives Roslindale, Mass.

8498 HARROLD L., b. March 5, 1887, m. May 15, 1912, LILLIAN A. STANLEY, b. Dorchester, Dec. 25, 1889. He is a government chemist in Washington, had: 8498a JOHN S., b. Sept. 30, 1913; 8498b HAROLD B., b. Feb. 3, 1914.

8499 WALTER W., b. May 13, 1890, is a chemist, lives Roslindale.

F5236 Mary Ellen Harris, born in Boston, June 30, 1836, died Jan. 30, 1892, married Nov. 7, 1860, a cousin, WILLARD HARRIS NORRIS, born in Sutton, Vt., March 5, 1839, son of Welcome and Mary Walsh (Harris). He lived in Sutton eleven years, then moved to Glens Falls, N. Y., where for forty years he was a manufacturer of carriages.

Children of 8th Gen.

8500 ALLIE WILDE, b. Glens Falls, N. Y., Sept. 25, 1861, d. Aug. 1, 1891.

8501 EPHRAIM HARRIS, b. Shoemakertown, Pa., May 22, 1864, lived Atlanta, Ga.

8502 EPHRIETTA, b. twin, May 22, 1864, m. Jan. 3, 1895, HARRY STODDARD DODGE, b. Darien, Wis., Oct. 25, 1859; lived Glens Falls, N. Y.

8503 ALBERT LOCKE, b. Glens Falls, May 16, 1867, was a musician in Northampton, Mass.

8504 ARTHUR KRUM, b. twin, May 16, 1867, lived Brattleboro, Vt.

F5237 Nancy C. Lamprey, born in Concord, May 11, 1826, died in Haverhill, Mass., Apl. 25, 1902, married in Northwood, 1848, REUBEN F. JAMES, born in Deerfield, May 20, 1823, son of Ebenezer W., and Lucy (French). He was a farmer and died March 29, 1909.

Children of 8th Gen.

8505 HENRY C., b. Deerfield, Feb. 24, 1849, m. Oct. 1, 1874, FRANCES L. HAYNES, b. E. Limerick, Me., June 25, 1853, dau. of Francis G. and Harriet W. (Williams). He graduated from Harvard, 1871, admitted Minnesota bar 1874. Had: 8506 MARGARET, b. St. Paul, Oct. 26, 1875; 8507 CORNELIA, b. Nov. 17, 1876; 8508 HELEN, b. Sept. 19, 1878; 8509 ETHEL, b. May 15, 1881, d. Dec. 20, 1883; 8510 FRANCES, b. Feb. 6, 1885; 8511 HENRY, b. Newport, Minn., Dec. 6, 1888.

8512 LUCY C., b. Deerfield, Sept. 19, 1850, m. Sept. 10, 1879, FRANCIS B. C. CARLETON, b. Haverhill, Mass., Oct. 21, 1847, son of John and Mary (Chapman). He is a shoe manufacturer in Haverhill, Mass., had: 8513 RALPH H., b. June 28, 1880; 8514 HOMER J., b. Sept. 3, 1881; 8515 PAUL W., b. Apl. 10, 1883; 8516 HELEN F. b. Apl. 11, 1890; 8517 LUCY R., b. June 5, 1893, d. aged 3 days.

8518 FRANK M., b. Haverhill, Nov. 18, 1861, graduated from Institute of Technology 1888.

8519 LILLA J., b. Aug. 6, 1864, was a bookkeeper.

8520 MARGARET, m. Oct. 1, 1898, AARON M. BURT of Newport, Minn.

8521 CORNELIA, b. ——, m. June 25, 1901, WALTER B. CANNON.

F5238 Morris J. Lamprey, born in Concord, Dec. 9, 1827, married in Minnesota, Sept. 1869, EVA GOODHUE, born in St. Paul, July 4, 1851, daughter of James. He graduated from Dartmouth, 1851, was a lawyer in St. Paul, Minn., and died Apl. 9, 1879. She married 2nd, 1883, JASPER TARBOX.

Children of 8th Gen. b. in St. Paul, Minn.

8522 MARION C., b. Aug. 23, 1871, m. 1st March 19, 1893, KARL THIENES of Germany; m. 2nd, 1900, C. P. STERNSBEE, had: 8523 KARL A., b. Paris, 1894; 8524 DOROTHY.

8525 EVE L., b. Aug. 28, 1873, d. 1874.

8526 FLORENCE, b. Feb. 15, 1875, m. St. Paul, Nov. 16, 1897, GEORGE P. ROBBINS, b. March 16, 1869; live in St. Paul, have two children.

8527 RAY, b. July 19, 1876, m. Apl. 8, 1901, DR. ALBERT C. HEATH, son of Albert. They live in St. Paul, have two children.

8528 EVE, b. Oct. 31, 1877, d. Phila., Nov. 3, 1886.

F5239 Sarah S. Lamprey, born in North Hampton, March 20, 1829, died in Chichester, March 10, 1906, married in Deerfield, Oct. 3, 1849, HORACE CARPENTER, born in Chichester, Oct. 4, 1825, son of John T. and Lydia (Lane). He was a farmer and died Oct. 8, 1904.

EIGHTH GENERATION

Children of 8th Gen. b. in Chichester.

8529 CLARA S., b. Dec. 27, 1850, d. Merrimac, Apl. 1, 1893, m. Oct. 1, 1871, HORACE GOODHUE STEVENS, b. Jan. 4, 1844, son of Samuel and Abigail (Goodhue). He was a carriage mfg., and d. Deerfield, June 11, 1905. Had: 8530 BESSIE, b. July 11, 1877, d. Aug. 17, 1879; 8531 ROY, b. Merrimac, Mass., July 28, 1880.
8532 MORRIS, b. Sept. 21, 1853, d. Feb. 1862.
8533 BRYANT I., b. March 31, 1856, d. Feb. 1862.
8534 SADIE E., b. Feb. 24, 1861, m. Chicago, Oct. 25, 1885, ANDREW S. SMITH, b. Biddeford, Me., May 9, 1861, son of Sylvanus and Frances O. (Atkinson). He was a carpenter and had three children.
8535 EDDIE D., b. Jan. 11, 1863, d. Concord, Oct. 17, 1882.
8536 URI R., b. May 6, 1865.
8537 ALMOND S., b. Jan. 17, 1867, m. June 7, 1893, GERTRUDE M. POOR, b. Manchester, Aug. 20, 1869, dau. of Darwin and Carrie F. (Hadley), had: 8538 GEORGIA F., b. Nov. 12, 1894, and two others.
8539 JOHN T., b. Feb. 8, 1871, m. May 22, 1901, SUSIE M. WINN, dau. of William F. They lived in Manchester, had two children and he d. June 7, 1904.

F5240 John S. Lamprey, born in North Hampton, May 23, 1831, married 1st, in Haverhill, Mass., Jan. 1861, MARY G. HARDY, born in Chatham, Feb. 21, 1838, died in Boston, Nov. 27, 1881; married 2nd, Oct. 16, 1888, MRS. BARBARA (HARDY) WYMAN, born Oct. 22, 1849, daughters of Peter and Barbara (Shirley).

Children of 8th Gen. b. in Haverhill, Mass.

8540 FRED LOCKE, b. Aug. 28, 1861, d. Aug. 24, 1864.
8541 GEORGE, b. Aug. 25, 1865, d. Oct. 1865.
8542 EVA B., b. Feb. 8, 1867, unmarried, is a teacher.
8543 MAUD S., b. June 18, 1869, m. July 16, 1900, WALTER F. RICE, a teacher.
8544 JOHN H., b. Dec. 22, 1874, d. Boston, Nov. 22, 1881.
8545 URI H., b. Apl. 13, 1876, d. a student at Harvard, Apl. 15, 1897.

F5241 Martha F. Lamprey, born in North Hampton, Oct. 8, 1832, died in Haverhill, Mass., March 15, 1891, married Apl. 23, 1851, WILLIAM E. HILTON, born in Deerfield, Sept. 20, 1823, son of Winthrop and Mary (Tilton). He was a carpenter and died in Haverhill, Dec. 6, 1901.

Children of 8th Gen.

8546 MARTHA M., b. Deerfield, Oct. 28, 1852, d. Jan. 1853.
8547 MYRA B., b. Plaistow, Jan. 23, 1857, m. Haverhill, Mass., Oct. 21, 1880, FRANK P. STEVENS, b. Oct. 21, 1852, son of Enoch F. and Mary E. (Freeze). He is a shoemaker, had: 8548 STELLA A., b. March 23, 1883; 8549 CLINTON, b. June 15, 1889.
8550 NELLIE A., b. Haverhill, July 30, 1860, d. Sept. 2, 1877.

F5242 Malvina C. Lamprey, born in North Hampton, Nov. 10, 1834, married Nov. 4, 1857, EDWARD STUDLEY born in Cohasset, Mass., July 2, 1824, died in Concord, Feb. 10, 1883, son of Dawes and Betsey (Bates). He was a machinist.

Children of 8th Gen. b. in Concord.

8551 MAY L., b. Jan. 26, 1860, is unmarried, a bookkeeper in Concord.
8552 FRED M., b. Sept. 9, 1864, m. Dec. 10, 1891, LILLIAN J. LINDALL, b. Princeton, Ill., March 24, 1870, dau. of John C. Had two children.
8553 EDWARD S., b. Aug. 28, 1878, m. June 25, 1902, ALPHIA MCGOWAN, b. Dec. 12, 1879, had one child.

F5243 William B. Lamprey, born in Deerfield, Nov. 30, 1836, married in Haverhill, Mass., July 25, 1862, SARAH A. WHITTAKER, born in Haverhill, Sept. 1842, died in Haverhill, Jan. 6, 1892, daughter of James and Abigail (Emerson). He is a broker.

Children of 8th Gen. b. in Haverhill, Mass.

8554 FORREST C., b. Feb. 11, 1866, m. June 12, 1901, SUSIE B. WALKER. He is a storekeeper and has one child.
8555 WILLIAM E., b. Sept. 13, 1868, d. Andover Academy, Dec. 1, 1886.

F5244 David C. Lamprey, born in Deerfield, Apl. 5, 1839, died in Manchester, Sept. 22, 1907, married in Manchester, July 6, 1861, ANNA BELLE WHITE, born in Portsmouth, May 4, 1839, daughter of Wm. A., and Joan L. (Bell). He was a carpenter.

Children of 8th Gen. b. in Manchester.

8556 LIZZIE C., b. Apl. 26, 1862, m. Nov. 11, 1883, CLARENCE J. LEIGHTON, b. Gilmanton, March 9, 1855, son of Andrew S. and Sarah F. (Griffin). He is a shoemaker and had two children.
8557 ANNIE B., b. Jan. 23, 1865, d. May 1901, m. Nov. 29, 1888, WALTER L. CASWELL, son of Uriah and Hannah G. (Heath). He is a clerk and had: 8556 RALPH C., b. Boston, Jan. 22, 1891; 8557 HOWARD L., b. March 30, 1893; 8558 HELEN G., b. Feb. 24, 1895.
8559 MORRIS S., b. June 25, 1868, m. June 28, 1893, FANNIE A. BALCH, b. Manchester, May 19, 1867, dau. of Walter B. and Evelyn A. (Demeritt), had: 8560 LESLIE B., b. 1894, and three others.
8561 ETHEL G., b. Apl. 10, 1871, m. Oct. 31, 1892, CHARLES J. ADAMS, b. June 8, 1870, son of Joseph G. and Martha A. (Perry). He is a bookkeeper, had: 8562 HAZEL P., b. 1893, and another.
8563 DAVID C., b. Dec. 23, 1878, m. Jan. 2, 1907, MINERVA A. SIGNOR, who d. June 6, 1909.

F5245 Uri Locke Lamprey, born in Deerfield, Apl. 7, 1842, married in St. Paul, Minn., Feb. 4, 1865, JEANNETTE ROBERTS,

EIGHTH GENERATION 447

born in Prairie du Chien, Wis., June 18, 1845, daughter of Louis
and Mary (Turkin). He was a lawyer and died in St. Paul,
March 22, 1906.

Children of 8th Gen. b. in St. Paul, Minn.
8564 MIRIAM S., b. Dec. 28, 1867, d. Nov. 21, 1868.
8565 LOUIS R., b. July 20, 1872, d. Nov. 28, 1873.
8566 LILLIAN M., b. May 25, 1874, m. St. Paul, Oct. 4, 1898, DR. FRANCIS H. MURRAY, b. Nov. 29, 1873, lives in St. Paul, had: 8567 JEANETTE L.; 8568 URI L.; 8569 SON.
8570 JANETTE S., b. May 28, 1876, m. Nov. 28, 1894, EUGENE A. TOWLE, b. May 23, 1872, son of Patrick and Sarah (Hogan). He is a broker.
8571 ALMA I., b. Feb. 14, 1878, d. Jan. 10, 1883.
8572 ROSE MARIE, b. Dec. 4, 1879, d. Dec. 27, 1882.
8573 URI LOCKE, b. Nov. 13, 1882.
8574 ELSIE C., b. Oct. 6, 1884, m. Nov. 28, 1906, CHARLES T. REDFIELD.

F5253 John A. Lamprey, born Sept. 17, 1831, married in
Maryland, June 6, 1857, SUSAN H. PAVITT, born in Furlong,
Eng., Nov. 30, 1840, daughter of John and Sarah (Bond). He
was a farmer.

Children of 8th Gen.
8575 CLARENCE P., b. Wilmington, Del., Feb. 28, 1858, m. Dec. 17, 1891, JENNIE S. TYLER, b. Nov. 30, 1864, no children.
8576 EDGAR A., b. Maryland, July 11, 1862, m. Aug. 30, 1888, LUCY A. ARNOLD, b. Oct. 11, 1867; lived Southboro, Mass., had: 8577 FRANCIS H., b. June 29, 1890.
8578 NORVAL A., b. Nov. 2, 1864, m. Nov. 4, 1888, LILLIAN B. HYDE, b. June 29, 1865, had: 8579 RANDOLPH H, b. Southboro, Mass., Apl. 15, 1891; 8580 RACHEL H. and CLARENCE P., twins, b. Apl. 20, 1894.
8582 ZADIE M., b. Feb. 14, 1867, m. March 19, 1888, FRANK S. HANKINS, b. Apl. 8, 1859, a farmer, had: 8583 ESTHER M., b. Jan. 26, 1889; 8584 RALPH, b. May 10, 1892.
8585 WALLACE P., b. 1868, d. 1869.

F5256 Edwin M. Lamprey, born in North Hampton, Sept. 17,
1836, married March 11, 1862, MARY E. BROWN, born Sept. 8,
1840, daughter of Oliver and Elizabeth (Marston). He was a
farmer in North Hampton and died June 10, 1912. She died
June 26, 1903.

Children of 8th Gen. b. in No. Hampton.
8586 FANNIE M., b. May 20, 1863, m. CHARLES H. BRACKETT, 1886, b. Nov. 1, 1865, son of William H. and Henrietta (DeRochemont). He is a farmer and milk man, had: 8587 EDWIN L., b. Dec. 21, 1886, m. Exeter, Apl. 15, 1914, LOUISE S. HORTON, b. Feb. 29, 1888; 8588 CHARLES H., b. Sept. 10, 1889; 8589 WILLIAM H., b. Aug. 27, 1892; 8590 RALPH DeR., b. Oct. 3, 1893; 8591 ESTHER M., b. Oct. 22, 1895; 8592 CONSTANCE, b. July 23, 1899.

8593 MARY H., b. May 19, 1869.
8594 JENNIE R., b. Feb. 2, 1873, m. June 1, 1898, WILLIAM HAINES, a farmer in Greenland, who d. Apl. 24, 1904, had: 8595 NORMAN.

F5261 Charles C. Lamprey, born in North Hampton, Apl. 9, 1841, married 1864, ANN S. BROWN, daughter of Oliver, born in North Hampton, March 9, 1843. A very prosperous farmer and influential man in Portsmouth. He died May 2, 1911.

Children of 8th Gen.

8596 GEORGIE C., b. New Castle, Sept. 21, 1864, m. Dec. 25, 1888, LORING H. WORCESTER, a carpenter, had: 8597 LORA M., b. Feb. 1, 1890; 8598 GEORGE P., b. Oct. 8, 1891.
8599 EDITH, b. Sept. 30, 1865, m. Dec. 29, 1886, CYRUS FRINK, a farmer in Greenland, had: 8600 SIMES, b. Jan. 1, 1889; 8601 ANNIE S., b. Sept. 2, 1890; 8602 CHARLES, b. June 7, 1892.
8603 ANNIE L., b. Feb. 8, 1868, is a teacher, unmarried, lives Portsmouth.
8604 MORRIS L., b. Portsmouth, Oct. 11, 1871, d. Ports., Apl. 20, 1898.
8605 BLANCHE SADIE, b. March 4, 1875, m. March 31, 1902, HARRY L. BEACHAM, b. Tuftonboro, 1862, son of Richard. He was a stable and garage keeper in Portsmouth and died there March 2, 1913, had: 8606 SON.

F5263a Charles M. Lamprey, born in Hampton, Jan. 29, 1833, married in Georgia, Aug. 5, 1859, CATHERINE OSBORNE BACHELOTTE, born Dec. 17, 1838, daughter of John and ———— (Howell). He was a judge, and died in Hampton, Sept. 27, 1902.

Children of 8th Gen.

8607 CARRIE C., b. Sept. 18, 1860, m. Aug. 1883, RICHARD W. SHEA, a lawyer in Boston, had: 8608 WALTER, b. Dec. 11, 1884; 8609 HELEN L., b. Sept. 14, 1886; 8610 CATHERINE, b. July 1888.
8611 HOWELL M., b. Oct. 9, 1861, m. 1891, Mrs. MADELINE SYLVESTRE. He is a clerk in Hampton, no children.
8612 URI, b. May 25, 1880, lives in Hampton.

F5275 David J. Lamprey, born in North Hampton, Sept. 17, 1844, married Jan. 1, 1867, CLARA N. NUDD, born in Hampton, Oct. 4, 1846, daughter of Oliver and Sarah (Redman). He was a farmer in Hampton.

Children of 8th Gen. b. in Hampton.

8613 AUSTIN, b. Nov. 25, 1867, m. Jan. 20, 1904, JOSEPHINE H. DRAKE of No. Hampton, dau. of Freeman. They live at Little River.
8614 MARION A., b. Apl. 20, 1874, m. Nov. 10, 1896, CLARENCE N. DEARBORN, b. July 21, 1874, d. Hampton, Oct. 27, 1909, had: 8615 ELMORE, b. Jan. 2, 1898.
8616 WARREN CARLTON, b. Dec. 19, 1875, m. Hampton, Nov. 20, 1904, ANNIE P. DELANCEY, dau. of Curtis, lives Little Boars Head.

EIGHTH GENERATION

F5330 Mary Currier, born ——, married John Scribner and lived in Sandown, N. H.

Child of 8th Gen. b. in Fremont.

8617 MARY ELLEN, b. Jan. 13, 1853, m. FRED I. DROWNE, and had: 8618 CLARENCE IRVING, b. Sandown, May 25, 1875, m. MARIAN A. MERRICK and had: 8619 ALBERT IRVING, b. Sept. 5, 1909, 8620 RALPH CURRIER, b. Feb. 1, 1911. He is a farmer in Sandown, 1915.

F5362 Joseph Richardson Locke, born in Brentwood, July 11, 1827, married 1852, LYDIA FRANCES ROBINSON, born in Brentwood, Sept. 27, 1829. Graduated Kingston Academy, was a machinist, and made army wagons during the war in Amesbury under patents granted him, under firm name of Locke and Jewell. He was a member of the Board of Trade and a public spirited man. He died in Amesbury, Nov, 8, 1889.

Children of 8th Gen.

8620 ARTHUR TRUE, b. ——, m. NELLIE PHILBRICK of Amesbury, Mass. He is Assistant Supt. of Amesbury Carriage Co.

8621 JENNIE FRANCES, b. Brentwood (3rd child), Apl. 10, 1859, lives in Amesbury, unmarried.

F5364 Harriet A. Locke, born in Chester, Jan. 24, 1836, died Feb. 8, 1905, married in Manchester, Jan. 24, 1856, SEWELL WORTHLEY, born in Andover, Mass., June 24, 1836. They lived in Chester and Amesbury and he died in Chester, Feb. 16, 1903.

Children of 8th Gen.

8622 KATIE MEDORA, b. ——, died young.

8623 ALBERT LOCKE, b. Brentwood, Aug. 17, 1859, m. 1882, MARY MILLING of Holland. He is a painter in E. Boston, had: 8624 HARRIET L., b. Grand Rapids, Mich., Feb. 4, 1883; 8625 HENRY M., b. G. R., Apl. 6, 1887.

F5444 Samuel Augustus Locke, born in Barrington, July 13, 1823, married Apl. 1, 1850, in Barrington, SOPHRONIA A. SHERBURNE, born in Barrington, May 31, 1831. He was a farmer in East Barrington and died there, Feb. 6, 1885, she was living in 1911.

Children of 8th Gen. b. in Barrington.

8626 LUCY ELLEN, b. Sept. 23, 1851, d. Rochester, Apl. 7, 1901, m. RICHMOND CLARK of Rochester, had no children. He d. June 1901.

F8627 ELIZABETH SUSAN, b. Feb. 24, 1853, m. LEWIS N. SMITH.

8628 DANIEL SHERBURNE, b. Jan. 10, 1855, was a civil engineer, was unmarried, and disappeared in 1880 while in Luverne, Iowa.

8628a ADA, b. Dec. 29, 1857, d. Sept. 30, 1901, m. Oct. 5, 1899, EDWARD L. MILES, a teamster and farmer in Rochester. No children.

8629 EFFIE AUGUSTA, b. Nov. 19, 1861, m. Barr., Sept. 4, 1894, WILLIAM B. SWAIN, b. Barr., Aug. 23, 1861, son of Burnett. He is a farmer in East Barrington, had: 8630 WILLIAM SHERBURNE, b. Feb. 26, 1896.

8631 EBEN SAMUEL, b. Epsom, March 10, 1865, m. Aug. 21, 1913, MARGARET (HANNA) LOCKE # 5692 the adopted dau. of Major Henry W. Locke of Barr. He is a farmer in Barrington, no children.

8632 STANLEY ALWOOD, b. Aug. 30, 1877, m. 1st, in Lee, Jan. 8, 1898, ISABELLE THOMPSON, b. Lee, 1863, d. Nov. 15, 1902, dau. of Jonathan and Lucy (Moore); m. 2nd, Apl. 20, 1905, MRS. ISABELLE (BLACKBURN) CHESLEY of Barr., who had: 8633 STANLEY ELLSWORTH, b. June 3, 1906.

8634 AMY LUVERNE, b. May 26, 1883, m. Warren, Apl. 22, 1912, PERCY RAYMOND CROSBY of Wakefield, Mass. He is principal of Milford High School.

F5445 Charles Dennett Locke, born in Barrington, Sept. 18, 1825, married in Barrington, May 12, 1853, ANN M. SWAIN, born in Epping, died in Epping, March 29, 1900, aged 70-6. He was a farmer and died in Barrington, Nov. 12, 1895.

Child of 8th Gen.

8635 CORA A., b. 1856, d. Oct. 1888, m. Jan. 6, 1888, PETER LADD of Epping, lived in Epping, had no children.

F5447 Israel Ham Locke, born in Barrington, March 9, 1829, married ANNIE MCCHARLES of Cape Breton, N. S. He was a farmer and died in Madbury, July 1905.

Children of 8th Gen.

8636 EBEN SUTTON, b. Peabody, Mass., June 1875, d. Madbury, while a student, June 6, 1896.

8637 ANNIE, b. 1883, m. Somersworth, Nov. 28, 1901, ERNEST THOMPSON, b. Barrington, 1877, son of George and Lucy (Chesley). He is a dealer in autos in Medford, Mass.

F5448 Ira Washington Locke, born in Barrington, Aug. 16, 1831, married in Dover, May 27, 1869, MARY ABBIE BABB, born in Barrington, Sept. 5, 1846, died in Barrington, July 30, 1879, daughter of Joseph F. and Abigail (Kimball). He lived on the old homestead "Beauty Hill" Barrington.

Children of 8th Gen. b. in Barrington.

8638 NETTIE ESTELLE, b. Apl. 12, 1870, d. June 3, 1872.
8639 LEWIS I., b. Nov. 12, 1872, d. Apl. 10, 1873.
8640 EDNA FLORENCE, b. Oct. 30, 1874, lives East Barrington, 1915.
8641 MATTIE ETHELYN, b. Nov. 5, 1876, a school teacher in Barrington, 1915.

EIGHTH GENERATION 451

F5449 William H. Locke, born in Barrington, Jan. 15, 1836, married 1st, Apl. 25, 1855, LAURA J. CLEAVES of Great Falls, born in Boston, Apl. 25, 1836, died Apl. 30, 1871; married 2nd, MARY O. TEBBETTS of Springvale, Me., who was born there, 1836. He was a baker in Dover, 1860, and died July 1875.

Children of 8th Gen.

8642 ELLA JOSEPHINE, b. Somersworth, Jan. 2, 1856, m. Sept. 22, 1881, JAMES W. FARNSWORTH of Malden, b. May 15, 1855, son of Andrew, has no children; is manager of Bellows Falls Creamery.

8643 WILLIAM F., b. March 11, 1858, m. 1883, CARRIE THOMAS of Lynn, had no children, was a telegrapher and d. Apl. 7, 1884.

8644 BLANCHE L., b. Dec. 14, 1860, m. March 29, 1886, FREDERICK B. KING of Boston. They lived West Somerville, had: 8645 LEON H., b. Nov. 30, 1887, d. Jan. 6, 1888; 8646 HATTIE C., b. Feb. 24, 1889.

8647 HATTIE L., b. Dover, Dec. 25, 1862, d. Sept. 22, 1888, m. March 13, 1880, WILLIAM H. GOODWIN of Dover, no children.

8648 LILLIAN E., b. Nottingham, June 8, 1873.

F5450 Lucy C. Huckins, born in Alton, March 3, 1816, married 1847, DURRELL S. CHAMBERLAIN, and lived at Dexter, Me.

Children of 8th Gen.

8649 HENRY E., b. Nov. 20, 1847, m. SARAH TUCKER, b. 1846, had: 8650 STELLA C., b. Apl. 17, 1875, m. May 1893, HENRY C. KNOWLTON, of Alton; 8651 ARTHUR D., b. Nov. 20, 1876; 8652 LUCY H., b. March 28, 1880.

8653 IRA C , b. Apl. 29, 1852, m. May 1879, ELLA SEWARD, had: 8654 LENA, b. March 2, 1884.

8655 MARY E., b. Jan. 2, 1856, m. Nov. 18, 1889, FRANK FOSS, lives in Farmington.

F5456 Mary E. Huckins, born 1827, married 1853, JOSEPH E. BERRY, lived in Alton.

Child of 8th Gen.

8656 WILLIAM H., b. Aug. 1855, m. Nov. 10, 1876, MARTHA A. GARLAND, b. Nov. 10, 1851, dau. of Asa and Betsey (Chesley), lived No. Barnstead, had: 8657 MARY G., b. Oct. 16, 1881; 8658 PHILIP R., b. Oct. 14, 1885.

F5457 John I. Huckins, born Jan. 15, 1829, married Nov. 6, 1853, ABBIE W. WHITEHOUSE, of Somersworth, born Aug. 6, 1830, died Jan. 25, 1897. He was a farmer in Farmington.

Children of 8th Gen.

8659 MARY E., b. Nov. 10, 1854, d. Dec. 29, 1863.

8660 EDNA T., b. May 11, 1858, m. July 24, 1882, DANIEL BERRY, b. May 12, 1856, had: 8661 RALPH, b. June 28, 1883.

8662 JOHN A., b. Feb. 23, 1866, m. May 15, 1886, ETHEL M. SCRUTON of Strafford, b. May 15, 1869, had: 8663 EVERETT G., b. June 17, 1887; 8664 LAURA E., b. July 5, 1888; 8665 MARY A., b. 1889; 8666 ALDEN D., b. 1891; 8667 CHILD, b. Sept. 7, 1901.

8668 LAURA S., b. March 24, 1868, m. June 4, 1901, ALBERT SYZE of Yorktown, N. Y.

F5459 Ira L. Berry, born in Barnstead, 1830, married 1854, LAVINA E. DREW, born 1828, daughter of Joseph. He was a farmer in Alton, and died Feb. 28, 1892.

Children of 8th Gen.

8669 FRED E., b. Oct. 30, 1856, m. March 27, 1890, EDITH M. TABOR of Biddeford, b. March 27, 1870, dau. of Charles L., had: 8670 HELEN J., b. Jan. 15, 1891; 8671 GRACE E., b. Feb. 3, 1894; 8672 EDITH L., b. Sept. 27, 1896.

8673 LUCY A., b. Feb. 6, 1860, m. Sept. 7, 1887, DR. J. W. WHITNEY of Syracuse, N. Y., lived at Homer, N. Y., had: 8674 IRENE, b. Sept. 1888; 8675 GLADYS, b. Nov. 15, 1889; 8676 MARY, b. Apl. 9, 1892; 8677 HELEN, b. Aug. 5, 1894.

8678 MYRA E., b. Aug. 14, 1863, m. Oct. 18, 1882, EDWIN H. SHANNON of Gilmanton, who is a lawyer in Laconia, had: 8679 ELLA C., b. Jan. 9, 1886; 8680 MILDRED, b. June 9, 1889; 8681 EDWIN H., b. Nov. 9, 1897.

F5462 Betsey J. Hoitt, born in Lee, Jan. 26, 1825, married Jan. 1, 1861, ISAAC N. SAWYER of Salisbury, born in Salisbury, Apl. 5, 1811, son of Isaac F. and Rebecca (Pettingill). They lived in Salisbury and he died Nov. 26, 1894. A farmer.

Children of 8th Gen. b. in Salisbury.

8682 LEANDER N., b. Dec. 13, 1861, m. ELIZABETH B. ROGERS, dau. of Charles C. and Martha (Putney), lived in Durham, had: 8683 LUCY H., b. Oct. 21, 1891.

8684 GORHAM H., b. June 15, 1866, m. Feb. 20, 1891, ALICE M. LITTLE, dau. of Deacon Dearborn. He graduated Phillips Exeter Academy 1886, had: 8685 LESTER L., b. Aug. 16, 1893; 8686 CHARLES G., b. Oct. 20, 1895; 8687 WARREN D., b. Jan. 14, 1897; 8688 JOHN T., b. Aug. 22, 1900; 8689 EUGENE HOITT, b. June 24, 1904; 8690 LENA ALICE, b. Dec. 1, 1905, d. Apl. 4, 1906.

F5664 Samuel L. Hoitt, born in Lee, Aug. 22, 1828, married Apl. 12, 1849, ANN J. HADLEY of Portsmouth, daughter of Philip and Jane (Wallace). They lived in Marlboro, Mass., but she died in Port Jervis, N. Y.

Child of 8th Gen. b. in Manchester.

8692 EUGENE G., b. Apl. 12, 1850, m. Jan. 28, 1873, SARAH F. BARRET of Port Jervis, N. Y., b. Feb. 21, 1853, dau. of Dr. Simeon and Rachel H. (Leroy). He is a doctor in Marlboro, Mass., had: 8693 BLANCHE, b. 1875, d. 1894.

EIGHTH GENERATION 453

F5470 Georgeanna O. Hoitt, born in Lee, Nov. 4, 1837, married June 5, 1866, IVORY J. CHAMBERLAIN of Alton, born in Alton, July 16, 1837, son of George and Keziah (Jenkins). They lived in Durham in 1898.
Children of 8th Gen. b. in Boston.
8694 ABBIE F., b. Oct. 1, 1872, m. Sept. 1894, FREDERICK FULLER, a professor in Durham State College, had: 8695 MABEL L., b. 1896.
8696 GEORGE H., b. Dec. 25, 1875.

F5475 Belle S. Hoitt, born in Lee, Nov. 2, 1844, married in Durham, Dec. 5, 1867, HAMILTON A. MATHES, born in Durham, July 16, 1843, son of John and Pamelia. He was a brickmaker in Durham and prominent in all town affairs, and died Dec. 2, 1891.
Children of 8th Gen. b. in Durham.
8697 HAMILTON H., b. Jan. 10, 1872, d. Oct. 9, 1873.
8698 MARY ABBIE, b. Sept. 7, 1875, m. Durham, Oct. 2, 1901, FRED W. SMITH, b. Franklin, Dec. 8, 1874, a shoe drummer in Philadelphia, had: 8699 WILLIAM LEROY, b. Nov. 25, 1905; 8700 BELLE; 8701 DOROTHY.
8702 STANLEY LOCKE, b. Nov. 4, 1881, is a traveling salesman.
8703 ROY WENTWORTH, b. Dec. 15, 1883. Graduated Dartmouth Medical College 1906, now a doctor in Lynn.

F5480 Daniel P. Locke, born in Rochester, Aug. 5, 1824, married Feb. 18, 1846, NANCY MOSHIER of Rome, Me., born in Rome, July 17, 1814. He was a farmer in Augusta, Me., and died there July 27, 1852. His widow married 2nd, BENJAMIN AUSTIN of Augusta.
Children of 8th Gen. b. in Augusta, Me.
8704 SUSAN HELEN, b. Aug. 25, 1848, d. July 11, 1853.
F8705 DANIEL MOSHIER, b. July 12, 1850, m. Oct. 12, 1872, ELIZABETH M. BICKFORD.

F5483 Joseph H. Locke, born Oct. 24, 1831, married Jan. 12, 1854, CATHARINE L. CRANSTON, born in London, Eng., Dec. 25, 1835. He was a carpenter and stair builder in Somerville, Mass.
Children of 8th Gen.
8706 CHARLES H., b. East Boston, March 6, 1856, m. Sept. 13, 1877, EMMA FOGG of Chelsea. He was a carpenter and store fitter, had: 8707 MAUDE E., b. Oct. 15, 1878, and that year all went to California.
8708 JOSEPH A., b. E. Boston, March 24, 1858, m. Oct. 13, 1879, IDA R. BADCLIFF, b. Wakefield, Mass., Jan. 10, 1859. He is a sewing machine agent, has no children.

8709 EMMA J., b. May 18, 1862, m. WENDEL SCHNETZER, b. Germany, had:
    8710 IDA MAY, b. Sept. 28, 1883.
8711 JOHN ADAMS, b. Oct. 24, 1866, is a carpenter, unmarried.
8712 HANNAH F., b. Apl. 27, 1868, d. Aug. 12, 1868.

F5484 Sarah H. Locke, born Jan. 29, 1839, married James WADDINGTON of Lawrence, Mass., who died Feb. 3, 1871. She died June 1881.

Child of 8th Gen.

8713 ALICE M., b. Lawrence, Mass., Jan. 10, 1867, m. May 27, 1886, LAFORESTE TOZIER of Waterville, Me. Had a child, d. infant.

F5491 John H. Nutter, born in Farmington, Dec. 24, 1829, married ALMIRA L. DAME of Farmington. He was a shoemaker and died Sept. 8, 1883.

Children of 8th Gen. b. in Farmington.

8714 LAVINIA, b. Jan. 13, 1853.
8715 JULIA A., b. Nov. 7, 1854.
8716 SARAH E., b. March 13, 1857.
8717 ADA M., b. July 8, 1859, m. 1st, DOLBEE R. BLISS of Attleboro, Mass.; m. 2nd, Feb. 12, 1891, AMOS D. PALMER of Providence, son of Dr. Amos and Amelia. She was murdered in Prov. Feb. 12, 1899.
8718 CHARLES, b. ——, died young.   8720 CARRIE E., b. Dec. 19, 1868.
8719 JOHN H., b. June 20, 1866.   8721 DORA, b. March 16, 1872.

F5498 John W. Locke, born in New York City, Jan. 25, 1833, married in Brooklyn, Oct. 16, 1856, ADALAIDE S. COOK, born in Middleton, June 27, 1837. He was a carpenter in New York City, living in Brooklyn and was presented with a diamond medal for 26 years' continuous service in the 47th N. Y. State National Guards, by the Regiment. He died in Brooklyn, May 19, 1888.

Children of 8th Gen. b. in Brooklyn, N. Y.

8722 WILLIAM ARTHUR, b. Dec. 17, 1859, is Cashier of Eastern District Savings Bank, Brooklyn, N. Y. Not married.
8723 HERBERT EDGAR, b. March 8, 1864, is unmarried, lives in Brooklyn, and since 1884 has been Cashier of a Grain and Stock Commission House in N. Y. City.

F5504 Catherine E. Locke, born in New York City, Sept. 13, 1843, married Sept. 18, 1866, CAPT. JAMES G. HULL of Snatchwine, Ill., born in Essex, N. Y., Jan. 3, 1841. He was dealer in Agricultural implements and farm machinery at Danville, Ill., where she died Jan. 6, 1871.

Child of 8th Gen.

8724 EMMA A., b. St. James, Minn., May 25, 1868, m. 1892, EDWIN ELLIOTT, had: 8725 CHARLES H., b. March 8, 1893.

F5505 James Theodore Locke, born in New York City, May 10, 1846, married 1st, Dec. 7, 1879, MISSOURI FALLS, in South Branch, Minn., born in Indiana, Dec. 7, 1858, died in St. James, Minn., Sept. 28, 1886; married 2nd, Apl. 11, 1891, EDNA L. BULLIS, born Sept. 7, 1871. He was a farmer in Grantsburg, Wis.

Children of 8th Gen.

8726 EMMA H., b. St. James, Minn., March 15, 1881, d. St. James, July 16, 1905.
8727 JOHN ALONZO, b. Dec. 13, 1882, m. Sept. 24, 1907, EUGENIA LEE PULSIFFER, b. Sept. 5, 1883. He is interested in the Wenona Coal Co., Wenona, Ill., had: 8728 FRANCES ELLEN, b. Jan. 8, 1909; 8729 JOHN MONROE, b. May 5, 1914.
8730 JAMES HENRY, b. Oct. 26, 1884, m. May 22, 1912, CLARA STRUCK, b. Jan. 18, 1895. He is a farmer in Turtle River, Minn.

Second wife's children all living in Grantsburg, Wis.:

8731 LOLA G., b. Nov. 26, 1892.
8732 LOWELL GEORGE, a twin, b. Nov. 26, 1892.
8733 CHARLES WARREN, b. Jan. 12, 1900.
8734 FRANKLIN R., b. Apl. 5, 1903.

F5508 John W. Locke, born Nov. 17, 1828, married 1st, in Farmington, Sept. 20, 1854, SARAH A. HOWE, born in Barrington, May 2, 1836, daughter of Moses Dow and Betsey; married 2nd, in Strafford, Dec. 24, 1894, MRS. MARTHA (WEST) HALL, born in Barrington, 1830, daughter of Samuel and Sally. He was in Co. G. 8th N. H. Reg., was 4 years in a rebel prison, returned and was a farmer in Northwood and Bow Lake, Strafford.

Children of 8th Gen.

F8735 MARTHA J., b. Feb. 4, 1856, m. Nov. 15, 1875, GEORGE S. JACKSON.
8736 LUTHER F., b. July 19, 1857, d. Jan. 24, 1858.
8737 LAFAYETTE, b. July 20, 1860, m. May 3, 1891, EMMA CAVERLEY. He is a shoe laster in Strafford.
8738 JOHN F., b. Barrington, 1862, d. 1864.
8739 HENRY H., b. Strafford, Dec. 4, 1872, m. Strafford, Dec. 2, 1897, LIZZIE A. HOWARD, b. Barrington, 1881, dau. of John W. and Martha J., had: 8740 FLOSSIE MAY, b. Strafford, March 3, 1901; 8741 JAMES HENRY.
8742 Possibly there was an IDA in this family.

F5516 George Munroe Locke, born in Victoria, Ill., Apl. 20, 1841, married 1st, Oct. 10, 1867, SAMANTHA E. KITTREDGE, born June 22, 1850, died Nov. 29, 1901, daughter of Leonard; married 2nd, in Henry, Ill., Feb. 14, 1903, MRS. MARGARET L. (BLOOD) HILDEBRANT, born June 27, 1846, died in Florida, Nov. 27, 1912. He was in the real estate business, Henry, Ill.

Children of 8th Gen.

8743 CLARA VICTORIA, b. Snatchwine, Ill., Sept. 19, 1868, d. May 3, 1901, m. June 11, 1890, JAMES SPEERS, a farmer and stockman of Stark County, Ill., had: 8744 MIRIAM L., b. Jan. 13, 1895, d. next day.

8745 LEONARD S., b. Lawn Ridge, Ill., March 28, 1871, d. Oct. 30, 1872.

8746 GEORGE, b. Henry, Ill., July 22, 1874, died young.

8747 LATHA KITTREDGE, b. Apl. 16, 1876, m. Nov. 29, 1897, REV. JOHN F. NESBIT, a Presbyterian Minister, located at Morning Sun, and College Spring, Iowa; had: 8748 LEONARD LOCKE, b. Nov. 15, 1898.

8749 MIRIAM H., b. Lawn Ridge, Sept. 23, 1878, m. 1904, REV. PAUL L. CORBIN; both missionaries to Pekin, China.

8750 BESSIE E., b. Dec. 29, 1881, d. Sept. 22, 1886.

F5517 Silas Hoyt Locke, born in Victoria, Ill., Sept. 12, 1842, married in Long Lake, Minn., March 29, 1874, CAROLINE BARGE, born in Faye Town, Pa., March 19, 1841. He was a farmer on Sioux land in St. James, Minn., and died there May 23, 1881.

Child of 8th Gen.

8751 HANNAH E., b. Long Lake, Minn., Dec. 3, 1879, m. St. James, Minn., Dec. 24, 1899, JOSEPH WILTH, b. Chicago, Oct. 2, 1870, had: 8752 CARRIE A., b. So. Branch, Minn., Aug. 16, 1901; 8753 SILAS R., b. Long Lake, Minn., May 4, 1908.

F5519 Mercy Victoria Locke, born in Henry, Ill., Apl. 9, 1846, married in Henry, Feb. 7, 1865, EUGENE HUTCHINS, born in Cazenovia, N. Y., Sept. 12, 1841. He is in dry goods business, Henry, Ill.

Children of 8th Gen. b. in Henry, Ill.

8754 MARY ELLA, b. Oct. 17, 1867, m. Sept. 26, 1894, LEAVITT JENNESS of Rye, son of Harrison and Eliza, lived in Chicago, had: 8755 EUGENE b. Feb. 15, 1896; 8756 HUTCHINS L., b. Jan. 19, 1899.

8757 CLARA KATE, b. Jan. 25, 1870. 8758 JENNIE PRICE, b. Aug. 22, 1874.

8759 HORACE FRANK, b. Jan. 19, 1877.

F5521 Clara Jane Locke, born in Barrington, May 8, 1840, married in Dover, Dec. 2, 1869, JOSEPH W. FRYE, born in Eliot, Me., June 3, 1849, son of William and Hannah. He is a wheelwright in Dover.

EIGHTH GENERATION 457

Children of 8th Gen.
8760 ANGIE B., b. Kingston, Apl. 26, 1870, d. July 21, 1889.
8761 GEORGE E., b. June 3, 1872, m. in Dover, 1894, ——— ———?.
8762 IDA M., b. Sept. 29, 1874, d. Oct. 7, 1874.

F5523 Sarah E. Locke, born in Barrington, Sept. 1, 1844, married 1st, in Farmington, March 26, 1863, GEORGE W. RICHARDSON of Barrington, born 1842. They were divorced, and she married 2nd, Nov. 14, 1874, SAMUEL HENDERSON of Rochester, born in Eaton, Aug. 12, 1840, a farmer in Barrington.
Children of 8th Gen.
8763 FRANK L., b. Oct. 19, 1872.   8766 CARROLL C., b. Jan. 22, 1878.
8764 SAMUEL L., b. July 20, 1874.   8767 ALBA L., b. July 17, 1880.
8765 MARY E., b. Sept. 10, 1876.   8768 SARAH E., b. Nov. 22, 1885.

F5526 Mary F. E. Locke, born in Barrington, Sept. 19, 1852, married in Dover, Jan. 13, 1870, GEORGE G. CLARKE of Dover, born June 21, 1850, son of Greenleaf and Aphia (Johnson). He was a painter in Dover, and in Galveston, Texas, in 1894.
Children of 8th Gen. b. in Dover.
8769 GEORGE G., b. Nov. 4, 1874, m. Dover, Nov. 28, 1894, SABRINA F. DREW, b. 1876, dau. of Thomas and Amanda. He is a foundryman in Laconia.
8770 THATCHER R., b. June 7, 1881, m. Dover, Nov. 29, 1899, ADA B. PINKHAM of Dover, b. 1881, dau. of George and Belle of Lee. He is a laborer in Dover.

F5531 George Main, born Nov. 23, 1819, married ELLEN MARIA PRESTON of Boston, daughter of Eben, died 1906. He has just passed his 96th birthday in 1915, and is living with his daughter in Manchester.
Children of 8th Gen.
8771 ELIZABETH, b. ———, m. HENRY WEARE CLOUGH of Concord, had:
   8772 HARRY M., of Boston; 8773 CHARLES of Boston; 8774 MAUDE, d. aged 3.
8775 ESTHER A., b. ———.   8780 LYDIA, m. ——— HOLT of Manchester.
8776 GEORGE M.   8781 CHARLES, died young.
8777 MARY G., died young.   8782 FRANK A.
8778 CHARLES died young.   8783 EDWARD P.
8779 JAMES, died young.

F5613 James C. Locke, born in Northwood, Sept. 6, 1836, married Sept. 6, 1858, LOANNA A. NEALLEY of Northwood, born in Northwood, May 2, 1837, died in Northwood, June 7, 1913, daughter of John and Mary (Durgin). After his father's death he was adopted by his uncle. He was a farmer, and mill owner at Northwood Ridge, and died there May 11, 1909.

Child of 8th Gen.

8784 WALTER E., b. Northwood, Jan. 28, 1863, m. Northwood, Dec. 24, 1891, MRS. NELLIE L. (WOODMAN) GARDNER, b. Deerfield, March 28, 1867, dau. of James and Annie (Smith). He is in farming and lumbering business with his father in Northwood Ridge, had: 8785 MAUDE N., b. Northwood, Aug. 25, 1893, is an elocution teacher, unmarried, in Northwood.

F5614 Oren D. Locke (name changed to that of stepfather Carter) married SARAH C. PIERCE of E. Kingston and lived in Newton, Mass.

Children of 8th Gen.

8786 WILLIAM, b. ——. 8787 FRED, b. ——, was m.
8788 HARRY, b. ——, died young.
8789 BERT, b. ——, was in Brockton, Mass., 1906.

F5615 Carrie Sweet Locke, born ——, died July 27, 1868, married Sept. 4, 1859, DAVID C. PRESCOTT of Newton, born March 10, 1835, son of David and Nancy (Dow) of Kensington. He was in the Legislature in 1865–6, and is a shoemaker in Newton.

Children of 8th Gen.

8790 OSCAR C., b. June 19, 1860.
8791 ANNA F., b. Aug. 26, 1861, d. Sept. 29, 1863.
8792 FRANK M., b. Sept. 28, 1863, m. June 30, 1887, EMMA T. TAYLOR, lived Amesbury, Mass.
8793 CARRIE, b. ——.

F5616 Mary Ann Locke, born in Lee, June 27, 1830, died in Kingston, Nov. 27, 1889, married 1st, March 21, 1846, JOEL JUDKINS of Kingston, who was a currier of Kingston, and died from wounds received at South Mountain, Sept. 1862; married 2nd, Dec. 1872, NATHAN MARSH of Kingston, who was a blacksmith, had no children, and died Jan. 29, 1879.

Children of 8th Gen. b. in Kingston, all by Judkins.

8794 CHARLES S., b. Dec. 17, 1846, was m., and a blacksmith in Kingston, died there March 10, 1882.
8795 SULA S., b. May 24, 1847, m. DANIEL GILMAN of Brentwood.
8796 MOSES, b. Dec. 4, 1854, m. Nov. 10, 1877, HANNAH F. CHENEY of Kingston. He was a shoemaker in Kingston.
8797 HERBERT, b. Apl. 5, 1856, is m., a farmer in Lee.
8798 JOEL, b. March 28, 1858, is m., a shoemaker in Haverhill, N. H.

EIGHTH GENERATION 459

F5618 Betsey J. Locke, born in Lee, Nov. 4, 1835, married in Belgrade, Me., Dec. 8, 1858, WILLARD H. DAMREN, a farmer in Belgrade.

Children of 8th Gen. b. in Belgrade, Me.
8799 ELLEN J., b. Nov. 10, 1859, m. Sidney, Me., Nov. 7, 1881, HERBERT C. GILMORE, a farmer in Sidney.
8800 JOHN M., b. March 10, 1861, m. Belgrade, Oct. 29, 1891, CARRIE PAGE. He is a farmer in Mt. Vernon, Me.
8801 FRANK W., b. June 25, 1863, m. Augusta, Me., LORA GOODSELL. He is a farmer in Augusta.
8802 HERBERT M., b. Aug. 25, 1864, m. June 5, 1895, EMMA DUNN. He is a carpenter in Augusta.
8803 FRED P., b. Dec. 5, 1866, m. Augusta, 1895, MARY MAYO. He is a carpenter in Augusta.
8804 MAURICE, b. May 11, 1870, is a carpenter in Lawrence, Mass.
8805 GERTRUDE A., b. Aug. 24, 1877.
8806 NORMAN, b. May 10, 1880.

F5622 Maria H. Locke, born in Lee, Dec. 26, 1838, married 1st, in Salmon Falls, July 14, 1856, CHARLES L. FOOTE; married 2nd, Dec. 6, 1866, LEVI HOWARD, of Rochester, a carpenter in So. Berwick, 1898.

Children of 8th Gen. b. in Rochester.
8807 SARAH A. FOOTE, b. Sept. 24, 1857, d. May 1, 1882.
8808 ETTA G. HOWARD, b. June 5, 1868.
8809 ARTHUR D., b. May 21, 1870, m. Milo, Me., Nov. 3, 1890, EMMA WHITNEY. He is ticket agent and telegraph operator, Ipswich, Mass.
8810 ALBERT O., b. Gonic, Aug. 27, 1874, m. Oct. 30, 1897, LIZZIE OWEN of Portland. He is Associated Press telegraph operator, Lewiston, Me., had: 8810a MARION B., b. Lewiston, Me.; 8810b STANTON B., b. Newport, R. I.

F5625 Sarah M. Locke, born July 24, 1839, married May 8, 1859, WILLIAM WALLACE. He was a farmer in Manchester, born and died in Raymond.

Children of 8th Gen. b. in Raymond.
8811 ELLA E., b. July 14, 1862, m. THOMAS MATTHEWS, had: 8812 ELSIE S., b. June 16, 1888.
8813 CORA B., b. July 12, 1868.
8814 BLANCHE YOUNG, b. ——, m. 1899, FRED INGHAM.

F5621 Andrew Wright Locke, born in Lee, Nov. 23, 1844, married in Raymond, Feb. 5, 1868, MRS. SARAH G. WALLACE, born in Nottingham, May 13, 1843, daughter of Alexander and Sophia. He was in Co. B. 11th, Co. D. 8th, and Co. F., 5th Reg. N. H. Vols. 1866. He was a farmer in Epping.

Children of 8th Gen.
8815 MARY LIZZIE, b. Raymond, July 13, 1870, m. Epping, Nov. 11, 1903, CHARLES ARTHUR BARKER of Windham, lives in Hudson, Mass.
8816 ANNIE FLORENCE, b. Epping, July 14, 1881.

F5628 Abbie A. Locke, born in Deerfield, Jan. 13, 1847, married in Fremont, June 1, 1875, JOHN H. MOORE of Fremont, born in Lee, 1848, a farmer and shoemaker. She died in East Candia, Sept. 5, 1915.
Children of 8th Gen.
8817 LULU A., b. Fremont, Dec. 7, 1876.
8818 SARAH E., b. Fremont, June 14, 1880.
8819 FANNIE E., b. Raymond, March 2, 1882, m. D. P. LOVERING, lives Manchester.
8820 GEORGE H., b. Candia, Apl. 1, 1888, lived Charlestown, Mass.

F5630 Josephine R. Locke, born in Deerfield, Feb. 5, 1850, died Apl. 21, 1894, married 1st, May 19, 1863, GEORGE W. LUCY of Deerfield, born in Nottingham, a shoemaker there, died June 1, 1879; married 2nd, JAMES P. GRIFFIN.
Children of 8th Gen.
8821 GEORGE F., b. Nottingham, Apl. 3, 1864, is a carriage maker, Amesbury, Mass.
8822 J. PAGE, b. Sept. 2, 1866.
8823 ANNIE M., b. May 7, 1869.
8824 ORIN M., b. July 17, 1871.
8825 THOMAS R., b. Sept. 7, 1873.
Second husband's children:
8826 FANNIE F., b. Raymond, Apl. 14, 1882.
8827 LILLA M., b. Amesbury, Mass., Apl. 29, 1886.

F5631 Herbert L. Locke, born in Epping, May 8, 1852, married in Worcester, Mass., Oct. 5, 1881, ELIZA VICKERS, born in England, Feb. 14, 1853, died in Worcester. He was a baggageman in Worcester.
Children of 8th Gen.
8828 GEORGE E., b. Nottingham, Nov. 1882.
8829 GEORGELL, b. Nott., Jan. 16, 1883 (?), is a nun in Worcester, Mass.
8830 HERBERT H., b. Nott, Sept. 19, 1884.
8831 LOUISA D., b. Worcester, Mass., May 14, 1891.
8832 BYRON G., b. Worcester, Feb. 20, 1893, d. Manchester, July 13, 1893.

F5632 Orah H. Locke, born in Epping, Nov. 30, 1854, married 1st, Jan. 4, 1882, in Lee, FRANK L. THOMPSON, married 2nd, in Raymond, June 11, 1887, GEORGE H. ELLIOT, son of Freeman. He was a farmer in Derry.

EIGHTH GENERATION 461

Children of 8th Gen.
8833 GEORGIE R. LOCKE, b. Nottingham, July 16, 1871, m. June 9, 1895, GEORGE S. RYAN, b. Nova Scotia, 1865, son of Stephen and Margaret, had: 8834 CLYDE C., b. July 19, 1895.
8835 B. ALBERT, b. March 3, 1882.
8836 LEON H. ELLIOTT, b. July 13, 1892.

F5637 Sarah Locke Moses, born in Epsom, Nov. 25, 1841, married in Epsom, June 19, 1869, JAMES H. TRIPP, born in Epsom, June 15, 1849. He was a farmer in Epsom, and both are living in 1915.
Child of 8th Gen. b. in Epsom.
8837 WALTER H., b. Apl. 24, 1875, m. Oct. 12, 1898, ALICE M. FOWLER, had: 8838 HAROLD J., b. 1900; 8839 RUSSELL F.

F5643 Sarah Maria Tilton, born a twin, June 11, 1844, died in Epping, Nov. 13, 1891, married FRANK A. MILES, born in Epping, May 24, 1848, a farmer and shoemaker in Epping.
Children of 8th Gen. b. in Epping.
8840 NELLIE FRANCES, b. Oct. 17, 1873, d. Epping, unmarried, May 28, 1898.
8841 ANNIE TILTON, b. Feb. 5, 1877, lives Epping.
8842 LEWIS FRANK, b. July 21, 1882, m. Haverhill, Mass., Aug. 20, 1903, MYRTLE CATE, b. Epping, 1884, has a shoe shop in Haverhill.

F5663 Samuel S. Locke, born in Rochester, Dec. 25, 1834, married 1st, LYDIA A. SAVORY, born in Rochester, Feb. 9, 1837, died in Dover, June 29, 1883; married 2nd, in Dover, Oct. 11, 1885, ELIZABETH FAIRCLOTH MAHONEY, born in Portland, 1857, died in Dover, March 20, 1893, daughter of Timothy and Ann. He was a carpenter and machinist in Dover and died there Nov. 27, 1913.
Children of 8th Gen. b. in Rochester.
F8843 OSCAR ROCKWELL, b. Sept. 9, 1857, m. SARAH F. WINKLEY.
8844 WALTER ELVIN, b. May 21, 1859, m. Somersworth, Oct. 30, 1880, JENNIE ———, divorced in 1882; no children. He was a harness maker, d. Dover, Jan. 3, 1887.
8845 ADA BLANCHE, b. June 25, 1861, d. Dec. 26, 1895, m. CHARLES OTIS, lived in Dover, had no children.
8846 HARRY ARCHER, b. Feb. 11, 1864, m. LIZZIE NUTE, lived in Lynn and Madbury.
8847 ARTHUR LEON, b. Apl. 21, 1868, m. MARY WHEELER, b. Dover 1869, also said to have m. ELIZABETH CALVIN. He was a mechanic in Dover, probably had: 8848 WALTER; 8849 EDITH; 8850 ARTHUR, b. Oct. 4, 1894.

8851 ALBERT WILBUR, b. Aug. 9, 1871, m. MRS. ANNIE (NUTE) BRADEEN. He lived in Boston, had no children, and d. Dover, May 16, 1913.
8852 AUGUSTUS LINWOOD, b. Feb. 3, 1873, m. NELLIE ———, lived Hopkinton, Mass., no children.
8853 MARY ANN, b. July 29, 1876, d. Dover, Apl. 22, 1892.

By second wife:

8854 SAMUEL SEAVEY, b. Sept. 15, 1885, m. Barrington, Apl. 1, 1911, LIZZIE S. HART of Barr., b. Van Buren, Me., 1874, dau. of Albert and Madeline (Violette). He is a paper maker in Barrington, had no children.
8855 ESTHER ANNIE, b. June 24, 1887, m. ROY BRANDON, lives at Lards, British Columbia, had: 8856 MALCOLM; 8857 JAMES.

F5667 George Francis Locke, born in Barrington, March 8, 1841, married in Barrington, Nov. 20, 1859, LYDIA F. CATER, born in Barrington, June 6, 1844, daughter of Joseph and Hannah. He was sergeant Co. F. 13th. Reg. and was transferred to the Navy. He was a shoemaker and farmer in West Chelmsford, Mass., and died 1904.

Children of 8th Gen. b. in Barrington.

F8858 JOSEPH ALFRED, b. Nov. 17, 1860, m. Nov. 18, 1882, GERTRUDE M. PARKER.
F8859 GEORGIE ETTA, b. Dec. 1, 1862, m. Feb. 22, 1887, FRANK J. SPAULDING.
8860 ANNIE DORA, b. May 8, 1870, m. JAMES CLINGAN of Littleton, Mass., where they live and had: 8861 RUTH; 8862 ISABELLE, died young; 8863 GEORGE; and a fourth 8864 died young.
8865 CLARA BELLE, b. Nov. 13, 1872, m. July 1, 1891, MINOT A. BEAN, b. Jan. 20, 1870. He is station agent at Chelmsford, Mass., had: 8866 DOROTHY WEALTHY, b. Dec. 18, 1897; 8867 MILDRED LOCKE, b. Jan. 20, 1904.

F5668 Sergeant Elisha E. Locke, born Jan. 17, 1843, married May 5, 1862, LUCY M. SMALLCON, born in Barrington, Sept. 5, 1843. He was raised on a farm and early learned the habits of honesty, industry and steadfastness which still follow him. In 1862 he was largely instrumental in raising Company F. 13th Reg. but declined all commissions save Sergeant. His brothers George and Irving C., enlisted in the same company. Wounded in the left hand at Fredericksburg he was compelled to accept a discharge for disability March 19, 1863. Upon his return home he again took up the useful duties of civil life, where by honesty he has acquired a competency. Fair dealing and generosity have made him respected and honored by hosts of friends.

EIGHTH GENERATION 463

Children of 8th Gen.
8868 IRVING M., b. Barrington, Feb. 13, 1864, m. Barr., Feb. 1, 1897, LINNA M. BUZZELL, b. Barr., 1878, dau. of Samuel and Nellie (Hill). He is one of the stirring, thrifty New Englanders whose business instincts combined with foresight and sound judgment has even thus early in life brought well earned success. For several years he has been extensively engaged in the lumber business where by just dealings he has earned the esteem of all and is assured of an honorable future. *Children:* 8869 CLARENCE BRYON, b. Barr., March 10, 1898; 8870 EVA MAY, b. June 9, 1901.
8871 EVA T., b. Barr., March 26, 1873, d. July 19, 1884.

F5670 Irving C. Locke, born in Barrington, Oct. 23, 1846, married March 22, 1877, ABBIE L. YOUNG, born in Barrington, Aug. 26, 1856, died in Barrington, June 8, 1892, daughter of Ivory and Mary (Seavey). He enlisted in Co. F. 13th Reg. and was a corporal in 1864. He lives in South Barrington, a farmer.

Child of 8th Gen. b. in Barrington.
8872 BERNICE E., b. Oct. 30, 1885, m. ARCHIE COLBETH, had: 8873 BARBARA.

F5671 Alphonzo B. Locke, born in Barrington, Apl. 10, 1849, married in Dover, Dec. 27, 1870, MARY A. WATERHOUSE, born in Barrington, Aug. 12, 1851, died May 21, 1900, daughter of Alexander and Lucy (Cate). He is a farmer and dairyman living in Barrington.

Children of 8th Gen. b. in Barrington.
8873 EDITH L., b. Oct. 15, 1871.   8875 GERTRUDE, b. March 24, 1893.
8874 GEORGE W., b. Dec. 26, 1874.   8876 MILDRED, b. Nov. 11, 1895.
All living at home in Barrington.

F5683 James M. Locke, born in Barrington, Nov. 8, 1844, married Jan. 26, 1867, CORDELIA GRAY of Barrington, born there 1839, died there 1904. He is a farmer and owner of a sawmill in Barrington.

Child of 8th Gen.
8877 HENRY W., b. Barrington, July 12, 1869, m. Rochester, Aug. 23, 1893 HARRIET B. BERRY, b. Strafford, Nov. 3, 1870, dau. of Nahum L. and Mary J. (Scruton), of Rochester. She was a teacher. He is a farmer and lumberman in Barrington, no children.

F5684 Mary E. Locke, born in Barrington, Jan. 13, 1847, died in Strafford, Nov. 13, 1896, married CHARLES F. MONTGOMERY of Strafford, now a farmer in Barrington.

Children of 8th Gen. b. in Barrington.
8878 ANNIE, b. ———.   8879 GEORGIE, b. ———.   8880 ADDIE, b. ———.
8881 FANNIE, b. ———.

F5689 Fannie C. Locke, born 1848, married GEORGE H. JOHNSON of Boston.
> *Children of 8th Gen.*
> 8882 SUSAN W., b. ——, m. JAMES GRACE. 8883 HATTIE A., b. ——.

F5698 Fannie Augusta Locke, born in Barrington, Sept. 13, 1859, married 1st, in Barrington, March 16, 1878, KING YOUNG of Barrington, a farmer who died March 5, 1895; married 2nd, in Dover, Jan. 3, 1897, CHARLES GROVER of Sandown. He was a sawmill hand and died in Haverhill, Dec. 4, 1908.
> *Children of 8th Gen. b. in Barrington, all Youngs except the last two.*
> 8884 LEWIS EVERETT, b. Nov. 8, 1878, d. unmarried, July 28, 1900.
> 8885 CHARLES SUMNER, b. March 19, 1881, m. Jan. 1, 1904, MARY CRAIG of Andover. He is a shoemaker in Lynn.
> 8886 TWINS who died young.
> 8887 MERTIE ETHEL, b. Feb. 28, 1884, m. Aug. 29, 1901, WALTER HALL, a farmer of Barrington, had: 8888 ALMON; 8889 FRED; 8890 MILDRED.
> 8891 HERMAN EDGAR, b. Jan. 21, 1887, m. Dec. 25, 1905, STELLA BANKS of Haverhill. He is a farmer in Bradford, had: 8892 DORIS.
> 8893 FRED LOCKE, b. March 18, 1892, a shoemaker in Haverhill, Mass., unmarried.
> 8894 MARY GROVER and another child, died young.

F5699 Oliver Albion Locke, born in Dover, Jan. 1, 1863, married in Exeter Oct. 9, 1889, MARY E. FLAGG of Exeter, born 1861, died in Exeter, July 6, 1897, daughter of Isaac and Mary (Garland). He is a carpenter and lived in Dover, Exeter and Portsmouth.
> *Children of 8th Gen. b. in Exeter.*
> 8895 TWIN BOYS, b. May 1, 1890, died young.
> 8896 ISAAC WILLIAM, b. Aug. 8, 1891, is in a shoe office in Haverhill, Mass.
> 8897 HELEN ELIZABETH, b. Aug. 14, 1893, a nurse in Hanover Hospital.
> 8898 EMMA FLAGG, b. Jan. 22, 1895, d. Farmington, Sept. 23, 1907.

F5700 Sarah Elizabeth Locke, born in Dover, Apl. 29, 1865, married in Strafford, May 18, 1881, SAMUEL M. P. DEMERITT of Barrington, born in Barrington, March 23, 1856, son of Isaac and Tamson. He is a farmer in Barrington.
> *Children of 8th Gen. b. in Barrington.*
> 8900 JOHN WESLEY, b. Jan. 28, 1883, m. ALICE WHITEHOUSE. He is a farmer in Barrington, had: 8901 PHILIP O.; 8902 RUTH ELIZABETH 8903 HELEN ALICE.
> 8904 WALTER CLEVELAND, b. Nov. 15, 1884, m. MARGARET GALLANT of Jackson. He is a teamster in Barrington, had: 8905 FLORA W. 8906 EARL ISAAC; 8907 VICTOR SAMUEL; 8908 CATHLEEN.

8910 ANNAH FRANCES, b. March 1, 1886, lives in Farmington.
8911 RACHEL TAMSON, b. Oct. 1, 1887, a nurse in Manchester.
8912 MABEL A., b. July 24, 1894, a nurse in Barrington.
8913 FLORENCE E., b. March 3, 1898. 8915 MORRIS, b. May 6, 1908.
8914 NELSON, b. Apl. 3, 1904. 8916 ROSCOE, b. May 6, 1910.

F5739 Isaac Healey Locke (Town rec. James H.), born in Alexandria, July 7, 1834, married in Lyndeborough, June 30, 1867, MRS. ELLEN J. (CLARK) CROCKER of Halifax, Mass., born Apl. 12, 1834, in New Boston, died July 10, 1910. He was a gardener in Whitman, Mass.

Children of 8th Gen.
8917 JOSEPHINE RAYMOND, b. Apl. 8, 1869, lives in Whitman, Mass.
8918 JENNIE CLARKE, b. Apl. 2, 1871, d. Sept. 8, 1874.
8919 EDWIN ALLEN, b. Oct. 15, 1874. Graduated from a Medical School in Boston, is a doctor there 1915.
8920 RICHARD BALDWIN, b. ——, of Belmont, m. Dedham, Mass., Oct. 7, 1913, HELEN HUNT JOYCE, dau. of George F.

F5740 Betsey Aiken, born in Alexandria, March 28, 1836, married in Bristol, Oct. 26, 1854, FREEMAN E. BERRY, born in Alexandria, Oct. 7, 1831, son of Levi and Abigail. He was a farmer, moved from Alexandria to Bristol in 1890, and died there Jan. 3, 1902.

Child of 8th Gen.
F8921 MARTHA ETTA, b. Alexandria, May 24, 1856, m. Bristol, Dec. 24, 1873, REV. FRANK E. BRIGGS, b. Boscawen, Dec. 2, 1849, son of Sherman. He is a Free Will Baptist Minister at Washington, Vt.

F5742 Lyman Locke, born in Alexandria, Nov. 28, 1841, married 1st, March 22, 1863, MARY AUGUSTA CLARKE, born Oct. 12, 1843, died in Boston, Sept. 26, 1868; married 2nd, Dec. 10, 1872, NELLIE V. HUNT, who lived in California, 1900. He was a mason and contractor in South Boston and died at Martha's Vineyard, June 5, 1891.

Children of 8th Gen.
8922 FRED V., b. ——, 1874, m. —— ——, lives Los Angeles, Cal.
8923 EVA, b. Sept. 1, 1883.

F5769 Frank Hartwell Locke, born in Chichester, June 1, 1841, married Apl. 2, 1862, SARAH J. FOLLANSBEE, born June 3, 1840, died Feb. 12, 1904, daughter of David and Dolly (Prescott). He lived in Concord and was an engineer on the Northern N. H. R. R., later was Secretary of Concord Building and Loan Association. He died Jan. 28, 1904.

Children of 8th Gen. b. in Concord.

8924 JENNIE EVA, b. Dec. 12, 1864, m. 1st, Concord, Apl. 22, 1891, FRED B. GILE, b. Enfield, Apl. 23, 1864, son of John E. and Louisa (George). He was a tailor in Lebanon, and d. there Apl. 16, 1897; had son: 8925 JOHN A., b. Oct. 4, 1895. She probably m. 2nd, DAVID C. FOLLANSBEE, and was divorced, 1905, in Providence, R. I.

8926 HATTIE L., b. July 26, 1866, drowned E. Concord, Apl. 23, 1876.

F5771 Cyrus Munroe Locke, born in Chichester, Feb. 9, 1845, married MARTHA AMELIA CHADWICK, born in Randolph, Vt., July 6, 1847, daughter of Constantine and Martha (Gilson). He commenced railroading in 1862 on the Northern N. H. R. R., remained until 1876, when he settled in Toledo, Ohio. He was engineer on a passenger train on L. S. & M. S. R. R. for eleven years, running between Toledo and Cleveland.

Child of 8th Gen.

8927 IRVING BENJAMIN, b. West Lebanon, Sept. 13, 1868, is married.

F5772 Emma L. Jones, born in Concord, Dec. 3, 1853, married Dec. 31, 1874, LEWIS T. EMERY, born Nov. 2, 1848, a farmer in Concord.

Children of 8th Gen.

8928 BLANCHE, b. Nov. 11, 1881.   8929 INEZ J., b. Nov. 13, 1883.

F5774 John Sherburne Locke, born in Manchester, March 12, 1848, married in Franklin Oct. 13, 1867, CHARLOTTE A. FOSTER of Mt. Vernon, born there in 1849, daughter of C. J. Foster. He was in the wood and coal business in Concord, later went raising stock on a ranch in Huntington, Ore., where he was killed by a horse May 24, 1903.

Children of 8th Gen.

8930 HATTIE ARDELL, b. Concord, Feb. 20, 1875, m. lives in Oregon.
8931 JENNIE BLANCHE, b. Concord, July 20, 1880, d. Sept. 5, 1880.
8932 GROVER FRANK, b. Huntington, Oregon, March 4, 1889, lost in blizzard there Feb. 1902.

F5775 George Scott Locke, born in Chichester, Dec. 18, 1849, married in Lancaster, Sept. 23, 1873, BELLE MARSHALL, born in Lancaster, 1853, daughter of Anderson and Frances (Perkins). He was chief of police in Concord many years, and has been on State License Board since its creation.

Child of 8th Gen.

8933 GEORGE SCOTT, b. Lancaster, Apl. 29, 1875, m. Fort Davis, Texas, tc SARA FRANCES JANE. He was city Physician of Portsmouth 1901 then removed to Texas where he married and died Ft. Worth Texas, Nov. 4, 1910.

EIGHTH GENERATION 467

F5776 William F. Locke, born in Pembroke, Jan. 6, 1856, married 1st, JENNIE STEVENS, #4002, Feb. 11, 1879, who divorced him; married 2nd, —— SMITH, of the West; married 3rd, —— —— a Western woman. He lived in Denver, Col. 1898.
Children of 8th Gen.
8934 SHERBURNE C., b. Concord, Nov. 30, 1881, d. Nov. 12, 1886.
8935 CLARA V., b. Concord, Nov. 25, 1885, d. Nov. 20, 1886.

F5781 Harriet F. Locke, born in Alexandria, March 8, 1832, married 1st, 1851, JOHN P. PHENIX, born May 12, 1825, died in Boston, Apl. 15, 1864; married 2nd, JOHN H. WHALEN, son of John and Aseneth (Kenniston). They lived in Boston, where she died Sept. 19, 1882.
Children of 8th Gen. b. in Boston.
8936 MINA H., b. Oct. 2, 1853, m. Oct. 4, 1875, DAVID E. PARLIN of Boston, since a grocer in Lewiston, Me., had: 8937 MABEL A., b. Aug. 10, 1876; 8938 ALMA L., b. June 13, 1882.
8939 GEORGE H., b. Feb. 22, 1855, d. Jan. 20, 1856.

F5782 Adaline K. Locke, born in Alexandria, Aug. 19, 1833, married Sept. 3, 1852, HENRY C. MORSE of Loudon, born Aug. 23, 1830. He was a farmer and undertaker in Loudon and died in Loudon, Dec. 1, 1898. She died Dec. 30, 1885.
Children of 8th Gen. b. in Loudon.
8940 SARAH M., b. Sept. 16, 1854, d. Dec. 6, 1860.
8941 CORA J., b. Dec. 29, 1862, m. Loudon, June 10, 1891, JAMES B. BROWN, b. Loudon, March 4, 1857, son of Jere and Betsey (Arlin). He is a farmer in Loudon.

F5786 Abbie Carol Locke, born in Alexandria, Sept. 1, 1840, died Aug. 14, 1881, married Nov. 13, 1865, STEPHEN E. MORSE of Haverhill, Mass., who was in the lumber business in Newton, Mass., later in (Yoar?) Va.
Children of 8th Gen.
8942 CHARLES M., b. Jan. 23, 1871, lives in Virginia.
8943 STEPHEN HOWARD, b. March 24, 1873, m. 1898, —— ——, is a Railway Mail Clerk, Chicago.
8944 MARY L., b. Sept. 13, 1876, is a teacher.
8945 EDWARD P., b. Nov. 24, 1879.

F5790 Charles A. Locke, born in Concord, Aug. 29, 1837, married in Loudon, June 10, 1865, LOTTIE M. FELLOWS, born June 9, 1846, died Aug. 14, 1866; married 2nd, Apl. 1867, MAY

FELLOWS, daughters of S. B. and R. P. Fellows. He enlisted Apl. 22, 1861, in Co. E. 2nd. N. H. Reg., was made Corporal in 1861, wounded at Gettysburg 1863, was Sergeant 1864, Lieut. 1864. He lived in Central City, Iowa and was Provost Marshall in charge of prisoners, and was called Captain.

Children of 8th Gen.

8946 MABEL, b. July 25, 1866, m. Jan. 28, 1884, THOMAS C. BOND, a farmer in Central City, Iowa, had no children.
F8947 LOTTIE A., b. June 22, 1868, m. May 5, 1888, E. C. Pound.
F8948 WALTER, b. Dec. 24, 1869, m. Apl. 1, 1894, MAGGIE HAMBLIN.
8949 SARAH ESTELLE, b. Central City, May 20, 1872, d. Dec. 6, 1874.
8950 ELLA, b. Jan. 28, 1874, d. Feb. 21, 1874.
8951 MARY S., b. Nov. 23, 1878, is a housekeeper, Central City, Iowa.
8952 HATTIE F., b. June 19, 1881, is a teacher in Central City.

F5792 John Emery Locke, born Dec. 9, 1840, married June 25, 1865, SUSAN M. FRENCH of Leominster, Mass., born in Woonsocket, R. I., Dec. 1, 1843. He was in Co. E., Berdan's Sharpshooters, Sept. 9, 1861-1864, then Captain of Government Watch in Washington until the close of the war. He went to Iowa, was admitted to the Bar in 1874 and practised in Iowa and Missouri. Giving up the law in 1877, he returned to Moultonborough and Center Harbor, was a farmer and painter. He was in the Legislature, was postmaster of Center Harbor several years, and died there, Oct. 8, 1900.

Children of 8th Gen.

F8953 ALICE, b. July 1, 1870, m. June 7, 1893, ARTHUR F. TURNER.
8954 GRACE M., b. Norwalk, Conn., Sept. 19, 1876, d. Center Harbor, Jan. 8, 1900, m. Manchester, March 24, 1896, WALTER S. DURGIN, whom she divorced.

F5794 Frank Locke, born in Loudon, March 10, 1846, married June 23, 1874, EMMA HATCH, born in Bristol, June 30, 1857, daughter of William and Mary (Pierce). He was in 2nd Co. 5th Reg. H. Art. 1863 and was disabled in 1864. He lived in Central City, Iowa, and later engaged in real estate business in Boston, where he died Apl. 6, 1894.

Children of 8th Gen.

8955 EDWARD FRANK, b. Center Harbor, March 13, 1878, m. July 8, 1903, FLORENCE MORTON MACKINNON, b. Nov. 6, 1879; lived Revere, Mass., had: 8956 FRANK, b. Apl. 9, 1904.
F8957 MARSHALL ERNEST, b. Jan. 2, 1882, m. RACHEL MAE TAYLOR.

F5798 Sarah J. M. Seavey, born in Epsom, Aug. 18, 1840, died Feb. 1901, married Feb. 3, 1858, NATHAN MARDEN, and lived in Chichester.

Children of 8th Gen. b. in Chichester.

8958 JOHN H., b. Jan. 6, 1859, m. MARGARET ———, and had: 8959 HARRY, of La Crosse, Wis.; 8960 LOUISA.
8961 JAMES, b. Dec. 12, 1860.
8962 PETER L., b. Apl. 1862, m. Jan. 15, 1890, LIZZIE LANGLEY, lives in Oshkosh, Wis., had: 8963 LYMAN C.; 8964 NATHAN L.; 8965 JANE A.
8966 FREDERICK N., b. July 1864, m. had two children in Concord.
8967 WALTER, b. June 1866, m. ——— ———.
8968 SAMUEL C., b. 1868, m. had two children in Chichester.
8969 JENNIE BLANCHE, b. ———, m. WALTER ORDWAY of Loudon, lives in Concord, had: 8970 MARION J., b. Oct. 1, 1892; 8971 PERLEY W., b. Oct. 5, 1893; 8972 LENA G., b. Aug. 19, 1896.
8973 ORA, b. ———, m. ARTHUR KIRK; lives in Oshkosh, Wis., had: 8974 JESSIE B.; 8975 LUCY M.; 8976 BLANCHE; 8977 HAROLD.

F5799 Alonzo E. Seavey, born in Epsom, June 18, 1843, married in Chichester, Apl. 19, 1864, FRANCES E. MEADER. They lived in the Roxbury District, Boston, and he died July 12, 1879.

Children of 8th Gen.

F8978 GRACE A., b. Sept. 30, 1866, m. Nov. 28, 1889, ROBERT G. HARRIS.
8979 ERNEST A., b. Jan. 4, 1869, d. July 9, 1878.
8980 MARION, b. Nov. 27, 1871.

F5808 Clara Prescott (Adopted), born March 25, 1848, died in Manchester, June 14, 1914, married in Manchester, Apl. 28, 1870, WILLIAM H. CROWTHER of Penacook, born in England, Dec. 6, 1844. They lived in Penacook and Manchester.

Children of 8th Gen.

8981 WILLIAM A., b. Dec. 6, 1872.
8982 LILLIAN F., b. March 3, 1876.
8983 IDA MAY, b. Aug. 6, 1881, m. Manchester, Sept. 20, 1911, REV. ARTHUR E. GREGG of Milton, Mass., had: 8984 MARION A.; 8985 DONALD C.

F5809 Orra Ann Locke, born in Tamworth, May 28, 1852, married in Sandwich, Feb. 19, 1874, CHARLES R. FELLOWS, born in Sandwich, 1849. He was a farmer in Farnsworth and North Sandwich.

Children of 8th Gen.

8986 ARTHUR P., b. May 25, 1876.
8987 DAUGHTER, b. Oct. 2, 1877, d. aged 29 days.

F5810 Elsie Eveline Locke, born in Tamworth, May 14, 1854, married May 14, 1873, FRED L. SMITH, born Jan. 30, 1846. He was a machinist in Franklin Falls, lives West Hartford, Conn. in 1915.

Children of 8th Gen.
8988 SON, b. May 12, 1874, d. June 1, 1874.
8989 LENA FLORENCE, b. Aug. 3, 1875, m. Oct. 3, 1900, NELSON G. FORD, who is in the insurance business in Hartford, Conn., had: 8990 ELSIE E., b. Apl. 22, 1901.
8991 LELAND LEWIS, b. Jan. 24, 1877, m. Apl. 3, 1901, BERTHA GUILD, had: 8992 ELIZABETH, b. June 12, 1902.
8993 LEONA OLIVE, b. June 23, 1880.

F5811 Ada Florence Locke, born in Sandwich, Aug. 1, 1857, died in Franklin Falls, March 8, 1903, married in Sandwich, Nov. 26, 1879, SAMUEL E. CLIFFORD, born in Concord, 1840, son of Samuel and Mary. She was a school teacher, and he is a mechanic in Laconia.

Children of 8th Gen. b. in Concord.
8994 HARRY BENJAMIN, b. July 11, 1885.
8995 JULIA ESTELLE, b. Apl. 3, 1889.
8996 MARY KIMBALL, b. Feb. 10, 1891.

F5813 Luella C. Sanders, born Feb. 26, 1843, married May 1, 1864, WALTER B. MAYNARD of Loudon, born Apl. 26, 1840. They lived in Loudon.

Children of 8th Gen. b. in Loudon.
8997 FRANK W., b. March 4, 1866, m. Dec. 25, 1889, NANCY B. CATE. He was a carpenter in Loudon and d. there Sept. 12, 1896, had: 8998 WALTER E., b. March 19, 1892; 8999 JOHN W., b. Oct. 1, 1893; 9000 HATTIE E., b. July 22, 1895, d. Sept. 29, 1896.
9001 HARRY E., b. March 1, 1869, m. Jan. 4, 1898, MARY I. RAND of Concord, dau. of Charles J., b. 1875. He is a milkman of Loudon, had: 9002 DOROTHY E., b. Apl. 1, 1903.
9003 ROY F., b. Dec. 23, 1871, d. Apl. 22, 1877.
9004 GEORGE S., b. Oct. 20, 1874, m. ———— ————.
9005 WARREN F., b. May 25, 1880, d. Feb. 4, 1881.
9006 ROY W., b. Aug. 27, 1882.

F5818 Charles P. Bickford, born Nov. 15, 1850, married in Portsmouth, Feb. 25, 1873, MARGARET COURSEY, daughter of John of Erie, Pa. He was a hotel clerk in Portsmouth, 1873, went west and is now living in Erie, Penn.

EIGHTH GENERATION 471

Children of 8th Gen. b. in Erie, Pa.
9007 MARY, b. March 21, 1874, d. March 2, 1882.
F9008 MARGARET E., b. June 13, 1876, m. Feb. 27, 1906, JOSEPH D. BABO.
9009 ELLEN, b. Jan. 3, 1879, d. Feb. 21, 1885.
9010 DANIEL, b. Jan. 30, 1881.
9011 CLARA E., b. May 5, 1884, m. June 23, 1914, HARRY B. STRAW, son of Frank of Cambridge Springs, Pa.
9012 CHARLES FRANCIS, b. March 6, 1887, m. Detroit, July 23, 1910, MINNIE ADA CHIDESTER, b. Dec. 25, 1889, dau. of Dr. C. B., of Erie, Pa., had: 9013 GLADYS MARGUERITE, b. March 8, 1911; 9014 CHARLES 3RD, b. May 19, 1912, d. Aug. 11, 1912.
9015 JAMES P., b. Sept. 18, 1890, d. Apl. 21, 1894.

F5909 Louis Cristie Locke, born in Alexandria, Jan. 31, 1855, married July 24, 1882, MARY A. PIERCE, born in Massachusetts, 1865. He was in the meat business in Manchester and Hudson, Mass.

Children of 8th Gen.
9016 MABEL LOUISA, b. March 20, 1883.
9017 CHARLES, b. 1884, d. 1884.
9018 CLARENCE GAY, b. 1885, d. Manchester, June 18, 1885.
9019 GEORGE HARVEY, b. July 1887.

F5911 Harvey Belnap Locke, born in Alexandria, May 25, 1860, married in Westboro, Mass., Dec. 24, 1887, RUTH HATCH, born in Westboro, May 27, 1866, daughter of M. M. and Mary (Delano). He is a jeweler in Amesbury, Mass.

Children of 8th Gen.
9020 CHRISTENA B., b. Sept. 14, 1890.
9021 MARGARY P., b. Nov. 3, 1894.

F5912 Warren Locke, born in Alexandria, Dec. 2, 1868, married July 2, 1892, LIZZIE M. MERCER, born in Amesbury, Mass., 1870. He was a carpenter in Concord and East Kingston.

Child of 8th Gen.
9022 ANNIE E., b. Concord, Nov. 11, 1892.

F5917 Queen Geneva Locke, born in Brasher Falls, N. Y., Feb. 10, 1857, married there Jan. 3, 1879, EDWIN GOODWIN MORSE, born in Litchfield, Conn., March 19, 1852, son of Stephen. He was a carpenter and guide in Brasher Falls.

Children of 8th Gen. b. in Brasher Falls, N. Y.
9023 NELLIE ELIZABETH, b. Apl. 4, 1880, m. ―――― ROLFE.
9024 STEPHEN EDWARD, b. Oct. 22, 1882, d. Jan. 1883.
9025 EARL EDWARD, b. Nov. 30, 1888, d. Apl. 11, 1892.
9026 FANNIE GREEN, b. Jan. 16, 1891.
9027 ADA FRANCES, b. Dec. 14, 1894.

F5918 Candace Jennette Locke, born in Brasher Falls, N.Y., May 3, 1860, married in Brasher Falls, 1878, CHARLES MOODY, born Dec. 25, 1849. He is a farmer at Fort Jackson, N. Y.
Children of 8th Gen.
9028 ORPHA, b. 1879, m. May 19, 1897, CHARLES DELEMETER.
9029 FRED, b. 1880, d. Oct. 1892.
9030 FRANK, b. 1882, m. July 8, 1907, MAUDE JOCKE.
9031 GRACE, b. 1883, d. Dec. 1883. 9032 CLAYTON, b. 1884.
9033 BLANCHE, b. 1885, d. June 18, 1908, m. June 22, 1903, HENRY SNICKLES.
9034 MURLE, b. 1887, m. June 6, 1906, TOM BEMIS.
9035 JOSEPH, b. 1892. 9036 GLENN, b. 1896. 9037 DWIGHT, b. 1900.

F5934 Eugene D. Locke, born in Sweden, N. Y., June 27, 1858, married ——— ———.
Children of 8th Gen.
9038 E. DONALD, b. Nov. 15, 1908. 9040 LAURENCE, b. Sept. 27, 1913.
9039 ALLEN R., b. May 13, 1910.

F5935 Dr. Clayton W. Locke, born in Sweden, N. Y., Jan. 24, 1862, married Nov. 5, 1889, EDITH M. BUTTS; married 2nd, in Garretson, South Dakota, July 10, 1895, MARY L. CONAN. They lived in Garretson, 1898 and Lindsay, Cal., 1915.
Children of 8th Gen., by second wife.
9041 EDITH M., b. Apl. 24, 1896. 9042 LILLIAN S., b. Aug. 16, 1897.

F5936 George E. Locke, born in Sweden, N. Y., Aug. 15, 1866, married in Sweden, Feb. 25, 1891, MARY E. COVELL. He is a dentist in Brockport, N. Y.
Children of 8th Gen.
9043 MARION C., b. July 21, 1895. 9044 GILBERT E., b. Oct. 12, 1899.

F5944 David Locke, born in Batavia, N. Y., Dec. 31, 1848, married Dec. 27, 1870, ELLEN E. HINMAN of Batavia, born March 14, 1849, died May 30, 1913. He is in the tin and hardware business, Buffalo, N. Y.
Children of 8th Gen.
9045 WILLIAM H., b. Apl. 7, 1873.
9046 GEORGEANNA M., b. Jan. 10, 1878, m. Nov. 30, 1913, ALBERT DOLL.

F5945 William H. Locke, born in Batavia, N. Y., July 24, 1850, married Sept. 27, 1879, HARRIET E. HEDGES, born July 20, 1853, died March 21, 1908. He is of the firm of Boylan and Locke, Painters, Batavia, N. Y.
Child of 8th Gen.
9047 EDITH ISABEL (adopted), b. Dec. 23, 1891.

F5946 Jennie E. Locke, born in Batavia, N. Y., Aug. 16, 1852, married May 23, 1878, ALBERT G. SHERMAN, born Dec. 23, 1849, son of Orin and Caroline (Lathrop). He is a coal dealer on Main St., Buffalo.

Child of 8th Gen.
9048 FLORENCE LILLIAN (adopted), b. Aug. 10, 1888.

F5947 Edwin S. Locke, born in Batavia, N. Y., March 16, 1854, married in Newark, N. J., May 1880, MARY H. DAILEY, born Feb. 25, 1863, daughter of Peter and Alice (O'Rourke). He was a cloth cutter in New York City, lived in Brooklyn, and died there Nov. 1, 1913.

Children of 8th Gen. b. in Brooklyn.
9049 MALVINA A., b. June 16, 1881.
9050 GENEVIEVE E., b. Aug. 1, 1885.
9051 EDWIN S., b. Sept. 12, 1888.
9052 NATALIE, b. Dec. 20, 1890, d. May 17, 1891.
9053 GERTRUDE, b. March 3, 1892.
9054 GLADYS A., b. June 30, 1895.

F5975 Martha Riggs, born ——, married 1st, —— KNIGHT; married 2nd, ISAAC PAINE of Vershire, Vt., son of Jesse.

Children of 8th Gen.
9055 A DAUGHTER by first husband, died young.
9056 COL. MILTON K., was m., proprietor of Paine's Celery Compound.
9057 GEORGEANNA. 9058 ISAAC N. 9059 JESSE C. 9060 JOSEPH W.

F5985 James J. Locke, born in Portsmouth, Sept. 12, 1821, married March 4, 1847, MRS. JANE H. (BUNKER) FRISBEE, born in Kittery. He was a farmer in Rye and died there Feb. 10, 1871.

Children of 8th Gen. b. in Rye.
F9061 AARON R., b. Aug. 11, 1847, m. Apl. 24, 1871, FRANCINA M. RAND.
F9062 CLARA ELEANOR, b. Sept. 14, 1849, m. Aug. 6, 1872, JAMES I. WATSON.
9063 JOHN F., b. Apl. 14, 1851, m. Sept. 27, 1888, in Portsmouth, MARY E. WARD of Boston, b. Sept. 1, 1856, dau. of Edward and Julia (Grant). He was a carpenter in Rye, and d. May 4, 1904. His widow m. Sept. 29, 1909, WILLIAM W. ODIORNE of Rye.
F9064 ELSIE C., b. May 18, 1852, m. Aug. 7, 1870, CHRISTOPHER GRANT.
9065 MARTHA JANE, b. Jan. 27, 1855, d. Dec. 23, 1879, m. Portsmouth, Jan. 24, 1876, CHARLES E. HODGDON, b. Ports., Oct. 27, 1848, son of Benjamin and Hannah (Foster). He m. again and had children.
9066 MARY E., b. Feb. 29, 1857, d. Aug. 16, 1875.
9067 IDA GERTRUDE, b. May 29, 1859, d. June 16, 1876.

F5987 Sophia Locke, born Nov. 1, 1805, died Feb. 1882, married Apl. 5, 1830, JOSHUA BAZIN of Dover, born Nov. 1, 1800, son of John DeBazin. He was a tailor in Charlestown, Mass., and died Feb. 8, 1884.

Children of 8th Gen.

F9068 ABBIE S., b. March 16, 1832, m. Nov. 25, 1858, JAMES S. SPEAR.
9068a JOHN L., b. 1834, d. aged 9 mos.
F9069 SAVILLIAN E., b. Apl. 18, 1837, m. 1865, MARY E. WHITE.
F9070 SARAH W., b. Aug. 2, 1846, m. Apl. 1866, CHARLES L. ROBINSON.

F5988 James M. Locke, born in Portsmouth, 1808, married ELIZABETH BAILEY, who died in Portsmouth, Aug. 26, 1882, aged 75. He was a painter and later kept a grocery store in Portsmouth, and died May 23, 1887.

Children of 8th Gen. b. in Portsmouth.

9071 THOMAS KING, b. 1840, d. Apl. 17, 1841.
9072 THOMAS KING, b. May 1842, m. 1st, Portsmouth, July 11, 1871, SARAH MAY MENDUM, b. 1851 dau. of Charles H. They were divorced in 1887, and May 10, 1899, in Skowhegan, Me., he m. MYRTLE L. RICE. He was a prominent dry goods merchant in Portsmouth, now living, retired, in Concord.
9073 JOHN BAILEY, b. Feb. 28, 1848, m. June 2, 1888, MRS. RACHEL BIRDSALL, who d. Sept. 24, 1897. He has charge of a Dept. of Altmans, New York store.

F5989 Abigail Locke, born 1811, died 1891 (?), married in Portsmouth, Feb. 12, 1837, EZEKIEL FITZGERALD of Massillon, Ohio, son of Ezekiel and Margaret (Fernald). He was a '49er, and lived in Portsmouth and New York City.

Children of 8th Gen.

9074 JOHN L., b. ——, died young.
9075 REV. EZEKIEL, b. 1840, m. BELLE GRAHAM of Nova Scotia. He was in 47th Mass. Reg., had a family, separated from his wife, and later was in Mass. Soldiers Home.
9076 WILLIAM HENRY, b. New York, 1842, m. MARTHA HOLT, and had three children.
9077 LOUIS GOLDSBOROUGH, b. ——, died young.
9078 ARTHUR WARREN, b. 1847, was living West 1898.
9079 MARTHA ABBIE, b. 1849, m. JOSEPH DOW, lived in Worcester, Mass., and had nine children.
9080 GEORGEANNA, b. 1853, m. REV. JOSEPH K. MASON, had: 9081 HOPE; 9082 JOSEPH.
9083 MARIE, b. ——, d. aged 3 mos.

F5990 John S. Locke, born in Portsmouth, married in Portsmouth, Aug. 18, 1839, ANN M. LORD of Portsmouth, daughter of

EIGHTH GENERATION 475

Sampson B. He was a '49er, a master painter on Portsmouth Navy Yard, a painter and decorator in Boston. At one time he was Captain of Boston Police. He died about 1887.

Children of 8th Gen.
9084 AURELLA, b. 1846, d. Aug. 9, 1847.
9085 CHARLOTTE, b. ——, m. ALFRED HORTON, lived in Charlestown, Mass., and had: 9086 EUGENE.
9087 ALBERT, b. Charlestown, m. ADDIE PIERSON, and had: 9088 HARRY, b. 1875.

F5992 Hannah R. Locke, born in Portsmouth, married there, Nov. 10, 1831, WILLIAM P. GOOKIN of Portsmouth, son of Col. Samuel. He was a merchant tailor in Portsmouth, and perhaps married 2nd, ELIZABETH M. SMITH of Portsmouth, May 27, 1856.

Children of 8th Gen.
9089 CHILD, b. ——, died young.
9090 GEORGEANNA, b. Oct. 1832, m. HENRY DICKINSON, and had: 9091 HARRY.
9092 WILLIAM H., b. ——, was unmarried.
9093 CHARLES AUGUSTUS, b. ——, was unmarried.
9094 FREDERICK, b. ——, was unmarried.
9095 FRANK, b. ——, married, and lived in Cambridge 1898.
9096 JOHN S. b. ——, was unmarried.
9097 ALBERT, b. ——, d. aged 10 years.
9098 NELLIE, b. ——, d. Dakota, 1895, m. CHARLES TIDD, had: 9099 CHARLES.

F5995 Aaron Locke Rand, born in Portsmouth, Jan. 29, 1810, married in New Castle, Apl. 29, 1834, MARGARET G. FROST, born May 5, 1811, died Feb. 4, 1905, aged 93, daughter of Capt. John and Jane (White), one of 11 children. He was clerk in Col. Samuel Gookin's tailor and draper store and died in Portsmouth, July 6, 1882.

Children of 8th Gen. b. in Portsmouth.
9100 MARTHA HANNAH, b. Oct. 9, 1834, d. May 15, 1863.
9101 MARGARET JANE, b. Apl. 28, 1836, d. Aug. 16, 1854.
9102 MARY ANGELINE, b. May 3, 1838, d. Aug. 1841.
9103 SAMUEL ALBERT, b. Oct. 23, 1840, was a painter in Ports., where he died unmarried, respected by all, Apl. 1, 1914.
9104 GEORGETTE, b. July 17, 1844, d. Oct. 18, 1868.
9105 ABBIE SALTER, b. June 1846, d. March 1849.

F5999 Samuel Streeter Rand, born in Portsmouth, June 1, 1819, married in Lowell, June 1, 1848, LUCINDA W. BROWN of Claremont, born there March 6, 1819, died in Claremont Apl. 13,

1865; married 2nd, in Claremont, May 22, 1866, MARY BROWN, born in Claremont Nov. 6, 1824, died in Claremont, Apl. 14, 1892, daughter of Aaron and Anna (White). From Holderness, in 1852 he went to Claremont where for 30 years he was in the stove and tinware business. He died in Roslindale, Mass., Jan. 15, 1912.

Children of 8th Gen.

9106 EDGAR STREETER, b. Holderness, July 8, 1851, m. Claremont, Dec. 2, 1874, IDA J. BLOOD, b. March 15, 1854. He was a news dealer and had a fancy goods store in Claremont and d. Oct. 2, 1900, had: 9107 ARTHUR, b. June 13, 1880; 9108 ALBERT, b. Dec. 27, 1884; 9109 ROGER, b. Jan. 8, 1887.

9110 OSCAR BROWN, b.——, was in hardware business in Claremont.

9111 HATTIE L., b. Claremont, Nov. 18, 1855.

9112 FRED DeFORREST, b. Apl. 3, 1859, m. Concord, March 5, 1889, ALICE B. MORRILL, b. Jan. 25, 1863. He is a grocer in Roslindale, Mass., had: 9113 HAROLD, b. Feb. 9, 1891.

F6000 Martha Sarah Hannah Rand, born in Portsmouth, May 15, 1821, died there, Sept. 20, 1863, married in Portsmouth, July 12, 1840, EDWARD N. ANDERSON, born in Newburyport, Dec. 11, 1816. They lived in Portsmouth and Kittery, and he was mail agent for the Navy Yard and died at the Navy Yard, Dec. 21, 1874.

Children of 8th Gen. b. in Portsmouth.

9114 EDWARD EVERETT, b. Aug. 25, 1841, d. March 25, 1853.

9115 ANN SUSAN L., b. Oct. 26, 1843, d. May 20, 1848.

F9116 ELIZA SALTER, b. June 8, 1846, m. WILLIAM MARVIN.

9117 LUCY HANNAH, b. March 25, 1848, lives Portsmouth, unmarried, 1916.

9118 MARTHA EVERETT, b. Dec. 9, 1853, d. March 19, 1863.

9119 FANNIE EDWARD, b. Sept. 6, 1856, m. Apl. 15, 1896, WILLIAM H. ALLEN, b. N. Y., Apl. 24, 1837, son of William. He was a veteran of Civil War, a hack driver in Ports., and d. Feb. 5, 1908.

9120 WILLIAM HENRY, b. Aug. 29, 1858, m. Nov. 1881, IDA PICKERING of Ports. He was a policeman in Ports., had no children.

9121 FRANK CUTTER, b. Navy Yard, Oct. 15, 1860, d. Jan. 8, 1880.

9122 ABBIE HELEN, b. N. Yard, Dec. 15, 1862, d. Aug. 1865.

F6001 Harriet Locke, born Nov. 13, 1809, died May 31, 1889, married Aug. 1833, DANA LYON, born in Hubbardston Mass., June 11, 1801, son of Asa and Attara H. (Grimes). They lived in Hubbardston.

Children of 8th Gen.

F9123 EDWARD, b. June 10, 1835, m. 1856, MELISSA ABBOTT.
F9124 JOHN, b. Oct. 20, 1837, m. 1876, MARCIA HOLT.
9125 MARY, b. Feb. 11, 1839, m. 1862, FRANKLIN N. HANCOCK, had: 9126 MARY, b. 1872.

F6004 Catherine Locke, born in Hill, March 18, 1812, died in Lowell, Jan. 24, 1855, married in England, 1840, PETER BROGAN, born in Ireland, 1816. He was a mill hand in Lowell and died there Sept. 3, 1859.

Children of 8th Gen. b. in Lowell.

F9127 MARY E., b. Oct. 16, 1843, m. June 8, 1863, JAMES W. CASSIDY.
F9128 ANNIE, b. May 23, 1846, m. Nov. 26, 1868, JOHN GALLAGHER.
9129 CHARLES, b. Dec. 2, 1847, d. New Orleans, Aug. 4, 1863.
F9130 EMMA, b. June 7, 1854, m. Aug. 1875, JAMES L. KINSELA.

F6009 Horace Locke, born in Franklin, June 9, 1819, married 1st, 1847, SARAH A. SHORT; married 2nd, in Danville, 1851, ELIZABETH M. SPOFFORD DEARBORN, born in Danville, July 1826, died in Hampstead, Oct. 8, 1892, daughter of Leonard. He lived at Hampstead, and died in Winchester, Mass., probably before 1867.

Children of 8th Gen.

9131 HORACE W., b. Boston, June 10, 1849, m. in Franklin, May 10, 1883, MRS. MARGARET E. (HINKLEY) BERRY, b. Calais, Me., 1849, dau. of Charles G. Percy and Rose. She d. Franklin, May 22, 1914. He lived in Franklin and Haverhill, Mass.
9132 SARAH LIZZIE, b. Winchester, Mass., Jan. 19, 1854, m. Nov. 15, 1876, WILLIAM A. LITTLE, b. Hampstead, Jan. 7, 1851, son of Linus and Abiah (Tewksbury). He was a carpenter in Hampstead Center, had: 9133 HORACE WALTER, b. Nov. 2, 1878.
9134 FRANK A., b. Franklin, Jan. 10, 1855, m. Franklin, Dec. 31, 1874, ELLA M. ADAMS, b. 1855. He d. Bristol Oct. 30, 1883.
9135 ANNIE M., b. ——, was m.

F6012 Charles Locke, born Apl. 20, 1824, married in Lowell, 1845, SARAH WEEKS, who died Sept. 1907. He died Aug. 4, 1888.

Children of 8th Gen.

F9136 GEORGE H., b. Oct. 8, 1845, m. VIOLA WEEKS.
F9137 BRADLEY, b. Sept. 8, 1846, m. March 17, 1880, BINA WIGGIN.
F9138 ANN, b. March 24, 1849, m. JOSEPH STILLINGS.
F9139 SARAH J., b. Dec. 3, 1854, m. 1st, HARLTON STEVENS, 2nd, OZNO D. LOMBARD.

F6013 Albert Locke, born Dec. 10, 1827, married 1858, ANNIE SMITH. He was a piano maker.

Child of 8th Gen.

9140 ANNIE, b. 1859, m. C. FRANK OSMAN, M. D., lives in Dorchester Mass.

F6014 George W. Locke, born June 13, 1830, married LOUISA ABBOTT of Maine, born 1833. He was a very wealthy merchant of Sacramento, Cal., and was living in 1904.
Children of 8th Gen. b. in California.
9141 GEORGE, b. Cal., 1857, was m. had: 9142 GEORGE G. The father was in the carpet business in Sacramento, Cal.
9143 CARRIE, b. 1865, m. Sacramento, DR. C. NICHOLS at one time City Physician of Sacramento.

F6016 Arvilla P. Locke, born in Epping, Apl. 29, 1817, married Nov. 14, 1839, HILLARD SMITH, born Nov. 4, 1810, son of Josiah and Susan (Tucker), died Nov. 28, 1886. She lived on the old homestead from the age of six months to 1902, 85 years.
Children of 8th Gen. b. in Epping.
9144 CAROLINE O., b. May 15, 1844, d. Sept. 23, 1873, m. May 8, 1861, HOBART STEVENS.
9145 GEORGE A., b. Oct. 15, 1846, m. Sept. 28, 1873, ADDIE BROWN.
9146 EMMA F., b. Dec. 28, 1847, d. June 13, 1887, m. Nov. 14, 1864, WILLIAM H. BENNETT.
9147 CHARLES H., b. Nov. 7, 1850, m. Nov. 27, 1875, ETTA BROWN.
9148 FRANK P., b. Jan. 21, 1855, d. Nov. 6, 1858.
9149 IRA A., b. July 24, 1856.

F6026 Sarah H. Locke, born in Rye, Aug. 3, 1825, died in Brookline, Mass., Nov. 18, 1906, married Jan. 20, 1848, JOSEPH DUNBAR, born in Boston, July 23, 1823. He was Chief of Fire Dept., East Boston, and died in Brookline, Jan. 3, 1900.
Children of 8th Gen.
F9150 JOSEPHINE, b. Apl. 19, 1849, m. March 23, 1872, JOSEPH E. JENKINS.
9151 ADA, b. Nov. 1, 1851, m. Nov. 27, 1884, B. FRANK BARTLETT, had: 9152 DELLIE R.; 9153 HELEN D., died young; 9154 PERCY P.
9155 LILLIAN, b. Feb. 4, 1856, d. Jan. 3, 1915.
9156 THOMAS L., b. July 16, 1858, m. Oct. 12, 1881, HATTIE E. CHICK, lived in East Boston, had: 9157 WAYNE E., died young; 9158 FRANK B.; 9159 HARRY T.
9160 DELLIE, b. March 23, 1861.
9161 ASAETTE, b. Nov. 2, 1870, died young.
9162 URSALETTA, a twin, b. Nov. 2, 1870, lives E. Boston.
9163 ABBIE M., b. Jan. 8, 1875.

F6028 John O. Locke, born in Rye, June 16, 1829, married 1st, Feb. 29, 1864, ANN M. TARLTON, born in Rye, March 15, 1845, died March 16, 1865, had a child died aged one week; married 2nd, Feb. 19, 1867, JOSEPHINE TREFETHERN, born Nov. 29, 1845, died June 6, 1875. He was a fisherman in Rye and died Dec. 4, 1905.

EIGHTH GENERATION 479

Children of 8th Gen. b. in Rye.

F9164 CHARLES DUNBAR, b. Dec. 8, 1867, m. March 15, 1905, MABEL REMICK.

9165 ANNIE MARIA, b. Feb. 18, 1869, m. Rye, May 22, 1894, CHARLES O. ELLINGWOOD, b. New Brunswick, May 7, 1862, son of Giles and Almira (Bancroft). He is a surfman in Rye, U. S. Life Saving Service.

9166 GEORGE EVERETT, b. Apl. 4, 1871, is a farmer in Rye.

9167 JOHN A., b. Jan. 20, 1875, d. Pittsfield, Sept. 23, 1875.

F6032 Hannah E. Locke, born Sept. 18, 1831, died in Rye, Oct. 8, 1904, married 1st, Aug. 20, 1864, CAPT. BENJAMIN W. MARDEN, born July 27, 1800. He was a shoemaker in Rye, son of Samuel, and died Oct. 28, 1882. She married 2nd, June 28, 1883, GILMAN VARRELL, born Jan. 16, 1837, a farmer in Rye. He had a family by a former wife. Mr. Varrell died Jan. 12, 1905.

Children of 8th Gen. b. in Rye.

9168 SARAH J. LOCKE, b. Sept. 23, 1855, d. Rye, Aug. 23, 1879.

F9169 GEORGE A. LOCKE, b. June 14, 1858, m. 1st, May 7, 1886, CORA S. PLACE; m. 2nd, Jan. 22, 1892, MARGARET E. GILLIS.

9170 ELLA G. MARDEN, died young.

F6033 James G. Locke, born in Rye, March 29, 1834, married in Somersworth, Dec. 6, 1865, ANGELINA DOCKUM of South Berwick, born in Durham, July 11, 1845, died in Portsmouth, Oct. 3, 1910, daughter of Samuel and Sarah. He was an employee of the Jones Brewing Co. for 35 years, a respected and esteemed citizen, and died in Portsmouth, Sept. 5, 1899.

Child of 8th Gen. b. in Portsmouth.

9171 ANDREW G., b. July 2, 1868, m. Dover, Oct. 18, 1897, ELLA BERTHA HALEY of Dover, b. Rawdon, Nova Scotia, 1874, dau. of Samuel and Sarah. He is a blacksmith in Rye, had: 9172 EDISON GARDNER, b. Rye, Oct. 12, 1898.

F6038 Elizabeth G. Locke, born in Rye, Sept. 14, 1832, married Sept. 15, 1855, SAMUEL JACKSON JONES and lived in Rye and Exeter. She died in Exeter, Jan. 9, 1916.

Children of 8th Gen.

9173 LOREN MONTROSE, b. May 1856, m. FLORENCE FRENYEAR, and d. Exeter, Feb. 1902, had: 9174 FLORA LOCKE, b. 1896.

9175 SON, b. May 12, 1868, was married, is now dead.

F6039 Amos Garland Locke, born in Rye, June 13, 1840, married in Chicago, Nov. 9, 1875, NANCY A. HELM of Chicago, born in Wheeling, Ill., Sept. 8, 1845. He was a baker, had a restaurant in Freeport, Ill., and died in Clinton, Iowa, Aug. 25, 1905. He served two years in U. S. Navy, was member of G. A. R. Post at Clinton, and also a Master Mason.

Children of 8th Gen.
9176 ROY DEARBORN, b. Sept. 18, 1877, is a baker in Clinton, Iowa.
9177 BERT TUTTLE, b. Jan. 14, 1880, m. June 30, 1914, EDITH STAPLE of Bucyrus, Ohio; is a clerk in Chicago.
9178 PEARL BEATRICE, b. Jan. 6, 1882, m. Nov. 21, 1908, CHARLES CAMPBELL of Chicago, a stenographer in Chicago, had: 9779 HELEN LOUISE, b. Nov. 10, 1910.
9180 WAYNE FOSTER, b. Jan. 20, 1884, is a clerk.

F6040 Carrie Newell Locke, born in Rye, Apl. 8, 1849, died in Ramsey, Ill., Dec. 14, 1898, married in Chicago, Sept. 25, 1878, AZRO WILLIS of New York, born in Townline, N. Y. Sept. 29, 1829. He was in the lumber business and died in Ramsey, Ill., Apl. 2, 1899.

Children of 8th Gen. b. in Ramsey, Ill.
F9182 MINNIE LOCKE, b. Oct. 1879, m. Apl. 12 1899, FREDERICK MOODY STODDARD.
9183 LOCKE AZRO, b. July 31, 1884.
9184 FRANCES CARRIE, b. May 22, 1887.

F6041 Laura Goodwin Locke, born in Rye, Dec. 22, 1851, married in Rye, May 12, 1875, CHARLES H. HILL of Lowell, born in Lee, Feb. 28, 1851. He had a carriage shop in Lowell and died there Sept. 14, 1912.

Child of 8th Gen.
9185 HAZEN G., b. July 21, 1878, m. June 30, 1908, ALMA ABIGAIL NELSON. He is Assist. Paymaster of Merrimac Mfg. Co., Lowell, and had: 9186 ALMA G., b. Apl. 18, 1911; the mother dying the same day.

F6043 Augustus W. Locke, born in Rye, Feb. 26, 1846, married Feb. 23, 1876, MARTHA P. PERKINS, born March 2, 1848, daughter of Moses and Huldah (Johnson). He was educated in the schools of his native town, later graduating from the Institute of Technology as a civil engineer. He served in the Navy in 1862 for one and a half years, and was also employed in U. S. Coast Survey work. In 1869 he was appointed Assistant Engineer in the Construction of the Hoosac Tunnel, at that time a stupendous task, but from which he emerged with almost a national reputa-

CHILDREN OF AUGUSTUS W. AND MARTHA (PERKINS) LOCKE F6043
JULIA,   HARRIET,   AUGUSTUS,   EUGENIA

A. W. LOCKE F6043

EIGHTH GENERATION 481

tion. For eighteen years he was engaged in many engineering propositions, his last position being general manager of the Hoosac Tunnel, Troy and Greenfield Railroad, a position he held for seven years. He was honored by the Governor of Massachusetts by being named on many public commissions, the duties of which he always faithfully performed. He was an honest, upright, public spirited man and citizen, and his death from pneumonia May 14, 1893, was not only a shock to his family and friends, but a distinct loss to State and community.

Children of 8th Gen.

9187 EUGENIA, b. Aug. 14, 1879, graduated from Wellesley in 1903, and is now engaged by the Mass., State Board of Charity in its work in Boston.

9188 JAMES P., b. July 17, 1881, d. July 14, 1882.

9189 AUGUSTUS, b. Aug. 22, 1883, m. Dec. 18, 1915, HELEN A. LINCOLN, b. March 11, 1883, dau. of William E., and Caroline (Brett) of Brookline, Mass. He graduated from Harvard in 1904, and from the Scientific Dept., in 1913, as a mining geologist; is at present employed in Montana.

9190 JULIA G., b. July 20, 1887, graduated from Wellesley in 1909, at present working for the Associated Charities in their Boston work.

9191 HARRIET E., b. March 14, 1889, graduated from New Hampshire College in 1913, took a special course in Simmons College in 1914, now employed in charity work at the Boston Dispensary. The three above named ladies are well known to the Locke Association, noted for attractiveness and education as well as for their ability in all directions. The family picture is a decided addition to our book.

F6044 David Parsons Locke, born in Rye, Apl. 28, 1850, married Feb. 12, 1877, ANN GOLDING, born in Blosburg, Penn. He is a farmer, also a civil engineer in Rye.

Child of 8th Gen.

9192 BLANCHE, b. Rye, Aug. 6, 1878.

F6046 William D. Locke, born in Concord, Nov. 18, 1838, married MAGGIE MAHLERVIN, born in Germany, daughter of Jacob, and died in Concord, July 31, 1881, aged 33; married 2nd, in Boscawen, March 7, 1886, MINNIE G. HALL, born in Concord, Sept. 23, 1866, daughter of Lyman and Lorena. He was in Co. I 1st N. H. Vols., also in the 5th and 16th Regiments, and suffered seven months imprisonment. He was a farmer in East Concord and died there Dec. 25, 1898.

Child of 8th Gen.

9193 WILLIAM LYMAN, b. E. Concord, March 4, 1887, m. Concord, Dec. 21, 1912, ANNIE GRACE BLAISDELL of Meredith, b. Plymouth, 1891, dau. of Ira J. and Mary (Joyce). He is a boiler maker in Concord. She left him Feb. 1915.

F6054 Ella D. Knowles, born March 27, 1850, married 1st, Nov. 3, 1864, GEORGE H. LEAR, who died in 1869; married 2nd, May 15, 1872, EDWIN H. BLOOD and lived in Chichester.

Children of 8th Gen. b. in Chichester.

9194 ADA D., b. Jan. 14, 1866, d. 1893, m. CHARLES BUZZELL.
9195 GEORGEANNA, b. Oct. 18, 1867, m. JOSEPH MARSTON, had three children.
9196 LOUIS F. BLOOD, b. Aug. 14, 1875.
9197 RACHEL E., b. May 18, 1877, m. CHARLES E. MORRILL, had: 9198 CHARLES E., JR.
9199 SARAH, b. March 7, 1879, m. ERNEST HEATH.
9200 FLOSSIE E., b. Sept. 27, 1882, d. 1882.
9201 ALBERT H., b. Jan. 25, 1884. 9202 ADOLPH W., b. Apl. 14, 1887.

F6055 Nellie E. Knowles, born Nov. 28, 1859, married Sept. 18, 1880, JOHN W. TALBERT, who was a foreman in a Manchester shoeshop.

Children of 8th Gen.

9203 BLANCHE, b. July 24, 1883, m. June 26, 1907, EDDIE HARDY.
9204 SON, b. June 17, 1885, d. next day.
9205 GEORGIE, b. July 27, 1900, d. next day.

F6056 Charles H. Locke, born in Lisbon, 1847, married there, Jan. 26, 1867, SARAH E. CLARK of Lisbon, born in Haverhill, 1847, daughter of William B. of Vermont. He was a carpenter in Lisbon, Ossipee and Laconia. He enlisted Aug. 21, 1862, was a prisoner from Nov. 17, 1864, to May 1, 1865, and was mustered out June 21, 1865.

Children of 8th Gen.

9206 FRANK E., b. Bath, 1875, m. in Ossipee, March 31, 1900, MRS. ABBIE A. NUTE, b. 1868, in Ossipee, dau. of George W. and Sarah E. He was a laborer in Ossipee. His first, and her third marriage.
9207 DAU., b. Lisbon, Feb. 21, 1877.
9208 SON, b. Lisbon, Oct. 20, 1873.
9209 HOLLY E., b. Franconia, Feb. 24, 1879, d. Jan. 11, 1880.
9210 DAU., b. May 10, 1881.
9211 SON, b. Franconia, July 19, 1889.

F6057 Sarah A. Locke, born in Canterbury, June 15, 1850, married 1st, WILLARD ORDWAY, a carpenter; married 2nd, in

Hopkinton, Apl. 23, 1892, JOHN KILLAM, born in Nova Scotia, March 13, 1844, son of Mark and Mercy (Piper). He was a laborer in Warner, and had five children by a former wife.

Child of 8th Gen.
9212 GERTRUDE ORDWAY, b. 1869, m. Dec. 4, 1893, GEORGE H. CROSBY, b. 1870, a farmer in Gilford.

F6064 Horace Locke, born in Thornton, 1869, married 1st, in Waterford, Vt., July 23, 1888, ALICE HAINES, born in Whitefield, 1870, daughter of Emanuel, died Oct. 13, 1889; married 2nd, in Lyman, July 27, 1894, ETTA L. LITTLE, born in Lyman, 1868, daughter of Frank and ——— (Cram). He was a farmer in Lisbon.

Children of 8th Gen.
9213 HORACE O., b. July 1, 1888, d. Lyman, Oct. 3, 1892.
9214 NELLIE J., b. Lyman, Jan. 1892, d. Lyman, Oct. 9, 1894.
9215 SON (4th Child), b. Aug. 20, 1903.

F6070 Annette Perry, born Feb. 7, 1846, married 1863, ARUM P. SMITH.

Children of 8th Gen.
9216 HARRY S., b. June 26, 1864, m. MAY LIZZIE HODGDON of Pittsfield.
9217 FRED W., b. Aug. 18, 1866, m. ELIZA SHAW.
9218 GEORGE L., b. Feb. 21, 1868, m. ——— ———, of Nova Scotia.
9219 CORA B., b. Dec. 12, 1876, m. FRED CARLON.
9220 FRANK E., b. June 15, 1882.

F6074 Frank A. Locke, born in Henniker, 1873, married in Chichester, July 2, 1898, IDA B. GRAY, born in Jackson, 1880, daughter of C. M. and Hattie (Chester). He was a farmer in Pittsfield.

Child of 8th Gen.
9221 SON, b. Jackson, March 14, 1904.

F6075 Walter M. Locke, born in Pittsfield, Nov. 10, 1876, married in Northwood, May 31, 1900, MRS. EFFIE BRYANT, born in Northwood, 1874, daughter of William and Ella (Goodwin). He was a mill worker in Pittsfield.

Children of 8th Gen.
9222 DANIEL BRYANT, b. Deerfield, May 10, 1900.
9223 RUEL S., b. ———.

F6079 Charles A. Locke, born in Northwood, Aug. 23, 1852, married in Loudon, Jan. 18, 1879, ELLEN HATTIE MILLS, born in Concord, Nov. 26, 1859. He is a farmer on Concord Plains.

Children of 8th Gen. b. in Concord.

9224 WALTER A., b. June 12, 1879.
F9225 WARREN D., b. Sept. 14, 1880, m. HATTIE E. FAY.
F9226 CHARLES ELMER or ELMER D., b. Apl. 1, 1882, m. NELLIE C. PLUMMER.
9227 PERRY N., b. July 8, 1885, m. Oct. 26, 1909, GERTRUDE WING, b. Suncook, May 20, 1892, d. Apl. 9, 1912, dau. of Frank and Clara; had 3rd child, still born, March 31, 1912.
9228 EMMA J., b. Aug. 8, 1887, m. FRANK ALLEN FOOTE, a R. R. Brakeman, had: 9229 LEWIS CHARLES, b. Oct. 5, 1908.
9230 CHARLES, b. Oct. 21, 1889. (Concord reports.)
9231 JAMES, b. Oct. 21, 1890, d. Pembroke, Nov. 20, 1893.
9232 VANDER, b. ——, d. Pembroke, Dec. 28, 1893.
9233 ELZINA, b. March 14, 1894. 9234 HARRY, b. Dec. 26, 1895.

F6080 Fred A. Locke, born in Loudon, 1859, married in Concord, May 25, 1882, LORETTA JENNIE FOOTE, born in Concord, Oct. 25, 1862, daughter of Thomas J. and Sally B. (Green). He is a laborer at Hooksett.

Children of 8th Gen.

9235 ALZADA, b. 1883, m. Hooksett, Sept. 4, 1899, PHILIP E. CROCKER.
9236 BERT D., b. Concord, 1885, m. Lakeport, May 31, 1911, BERTHA E. DOWNES of Lyman, Me., b. So. Berwick, Me., 1894, dau. of William A. and Ella (Goodrich). He is a laborer in Laconia, had: 9237 FRED ALLEN, b. Dec. 5, 1911, d. Feb. 16, 1912.
9238 JOSEPHINE, b. Concord, Oct. 12, 1887.
9239 ELROY, b. 1889.
9240 LORETTA J. E., b. Hooksett, June 6, 1892.
9241 JULIUS FITZSIMMONS (8th child), b. Hooksett, March 5, 1897.

F6140 Belle Rindge Locke, born in Haverhill, Mass., Sept. 27, 1856, married March 25, 1883, CHARLES E. WALKER, born in Portsmouth, May 23, 1835, son of Charles and Sarah. He was one of Portsmouth's most prominent citizens, and a wealthy coal merchant, who died Feb. 23, 1908.

Children of 8th Gen. b. in Portsmouth.

9242 WILLIAM C., b. Apl. 28, 1884, d. next day.
9243 CHARLES H., b. Sept. 20, 1885, d. next day.
9244 CHARLES H., b. Aug. 19, 1886, a prominent merchant of Portsmouth, a club man and Knights Templar Mason.
9245 DAUGHTER, b. Sept. 7, 1888, d. Sept. 8, 1888.
9246 HELEN S., b. Sept. 7, 1888.

F6147 Olive Ann Goss, born in Rye, May 10, 1858, married in Nashua, Nov. 20, 1878, J. ARTHUR BROWN, born March 30, 1856, son of Charles and Mary (Drake). He is a farmer in Rye.

EIGHTH GENERATION

Children of 8th Gen. b. in Rye.
9247 CARROL WILDER, b. Sept. 24, 1879, is a civil engineer in Cleveland.
9248 BESSIE MARION, b. July 31, 1884.
9249 EDNA OLIVE, b. Oct. 24, 1886.
9250 CHARLES OTIS, b. Oct. 29, 1889, d. Feb. 17, 1892.
9251 ARTHUR LAWRENCE, b. Dec. 25, 1892.
9252 WILLIAM GOSS, b. Oct. 12, 1895.

F6166 Granville S. Mendel, born in Somerville, Mass., Oct. 1834, married Oct. 1857, SOPHIA MCMANN, who died in Boston, March 4, 1900. He was in the Boston Fire Alarm office and died May 1896.

Children of 8th Gen.
9253 MARTHA A., b. Dec. 8, 1858, m. 1880, FRANK GARVIN, had: 9254 ETHEL M., b. Sept. 5, 1884.
9255 LIZZIE B., b. Dec. 5, 1860, m. 1888, SAMUEL LINCOLN.
9256 FORD, b. March 14, 1871.

F6168 William Augustus Shapleigh, born in Hallowell, Me., Sept. 14, 1836, married in Portland, Sept. 18, 1872, ELLEN PICKERING. He died in Melrose, Mass., Sept. 7, 1900.

Children of 8th Gen.
9257 EFFIE L., b. Portland, Aug. 24, 1873, m. July 6, 1897, WALTER NORRIS, had: 9258 ELIZABETH; 9259 CATHERINE.
9260 ISABEL H., b. Exeter, Dec. 24, 1875, m. June, 14, 1899, WILLIAM COCHRANE, had: 9261 ELINOR.
9262 MARION, b. Melrose, May 30, 1880.
9263 HELEN A., b. Oct. 1888.
9264 WILLIAM P., b. Feb. 1890.

F6171 Frances Aphia Shapleigh, born in Somersworth, Dec. 21, 1843, married 1st, in Boston, March 10, 1864, RICHMOND LINDSAY, who died in 1869; married 2nd, in Boston, Nov. 1, 1875, ZIMRI HAYWOOD.

Children of 8th Gen.
9265 FREDERICK CUSHMAN, b. Brookline, Mass., March 15, 1867, d. Apl. 27, 1876.
9266 EDWIN PARKER, b. March 10, 1869, m. Boston, Dec. 2, 1895, AGNES SNOW. He is a paper mfgr. in Brookline.
By second husband:
9267 EFFIE HAYWOOD b. Boston, Oct. 14, 1878.

F6179 Mary Mehitable Locke, born in Barrington, July 6, 1837, married Dec. 24, 1854, ORWIN GRIFFIN of Lowell, born in Methuen, Mass., Apl. 8, 1833, son of Josiah and Lydia (Barker). He was employed as collector of the Portsmouth Gas Co. for 40 years, and died Aug. 30, 1915. She died Dec. 18, 1913.

Children of 8th Gen.

F9268 MARY WHITE, b. May 9, 1856, m. Nov. 29, 1876, FRED B. COLEMAN.
F9269 GEORGE ALBERT, b. March 12, 1858, m. Sept. 25, 1883, JULIA B. BRADFORD.
9270 LYMAN W., b. Sept. 30, 1860, m. June 3, 1885, ANNIE E. DODGE of Auburndale, Mass., b. Sept. 9, 1862. He is a druggist in Boston.
9271 JOSEPH F., b. Nov. 29, 1868, d. Jan. 15, 1871.
9272 ICHABOD GOODWIN, b. Sept. 5, 1870, m. Ports., Nov. 26, 1902, ADA TOPPAN LEAR of Ports. He is a Post Office clerk, had: 9273 HENRY D., b. March 9, 1904; 9274 ALBERT L., b. June 7, 1905.

F6180 John Harrison Locke, born in Barrington, July 29, 1841, married in Portsmouth, Jan. 7, 1864, SARAH L. WEBSTER of Rye, born June 5, 1845, died in Portsmouth, June 26, 1896, daughter of Mark R. and Mary (Lang). He enlisted in the Civil War and was wounded at Fredericksburg, Dec. 13, 1862, in nine places, returned home and was a clerk and surveyor of lumber at the Navy Yard for many years. He was appointed Postmaster of Portsmouth, but died just before taking the oath of office, June 15, 1889.

Children of 8th Gen. b. in Portsmouth.

9275 MARY ABBY, b. Oct. 7, 1864, d. unmarried, March 19, 1892.
9276 MATTIE BELLE, b. Jan. 2, 1867, m. Allston, Mass., Nov. 10, 1907, HERBERT D. COGSWELL, b. 1855. He was in the meat business and d. Allston, Mass., Nov. 23, 1907.
9277 JOHN WEBSTER, b. July 2, 1869, d. Feb. 28, 1870.
F9278 AUSTIN PIKE, b. March 23, 1871, m. Feb. 22, 1897, IMOGENE TEBBETTS.
9279 EMMA ALBERTA, b. Aug. 13, 1881.

F6187 Flora Albertha Locke, born in Portsmouth, Feb. 14, 1856, married there Nov. 29, 1877, GEORGE H. DENNETT of Portsmouth, born Oct. 6, 1855. He was a car inspector in Portsmouth.

Children of 8th Gen.

9280 BLANCHE EUDORA, b. Ports., Feb. 8, 1880, d. Feb. 19, 1892.
9281 GEORGE WINFIELD, b. Nashua, Jan. 31, 1884.
9282 PHILIP BOYD, b. Ports., March 21, 1896.

F6188 Emma Eldora Locke, born in Portsmouth, March 20, 1858, married Oct. 14, 1891, WILLIAM WARD BAILEY of Boston, born in Boston, Jan. 1851, son of Albert and Thirza. He was a bookkeeper in Dorchester, and died there Aug. 2, 1900.

Child of 8th Gen.

9283 EUDORA LOCKE, b. Apl. 21, 1897, d. Nov. 29, 1897.

EIGHTH GENERATION

F6189 Winfield Scott Locke, born in Portsmouth, March 8, 1861, married Dec. 1, 1886, CARRIE A. EDSON of Roxbury, Mass. He is a dry goods salesman in Boston.

Child of 8th Gen.

9284 GLADYS E., b. Oct. 12, 1887.

F6192 Mary White Farmer, born March 22, 1853, married Sept. 24, 1879, CHARLES R. ANDREWS of Cleveland. He is in the dry goods business in Ada, Minn.

Children of 8th Gen.

9285 WALLACE FARMER, b. July 20, 1880.
9286 HERBERT TENNEY, b. March 7, 1884.
9287 CHARLES RUSSELL, b. Nov. 19, 1886.
9288 HELEN MARTHA, b. May 20, 1891.

F6246 William A. Locke, born in Warren, R. I., Apl. 25, 1859, married in Providence, Apl. 13, 1882, MARY I. POTTS, and lived in Attleboro, Mass.

Children of 8th Gen.

9289 WILLIAM A., b. Providence, Aug. 21, 1882.
9290 CLARENCE M., b. June 17, 1891, d. June 29, 1891.
9291 GERTRUDE M., b. E. Providence, May 13, 1893.
9292 MADELINE B., b. Attleboro, Mass., June 20, 1897.

F6249 Richard Pigott, born Aug. 25, 1852, married 1st, Aug. 25, 1874, ELIZA J. LOVELL; married 2nd, Nov. 25, 1886, AUGUSTA DICKERSON, and lived in South Windham, Vt.

Children of 8th Gen.

9294 ALFRED H., b. Oct. 30, 1875, m. March 19, 1901, LILLIAN HATCH.
9295 CARRIE J., b. Dec. 15, 1878.
9296 CHARLOTTE, b. March 28, 1881, d. Aug. 8, 1881.
9297 CHARLOTTE, b. Aug. 6, 1893.
9298 OLIVETTE, b. Aug. 10, 1896.
9299 RICHARD, b. Apl. 11, 1899.

NINTH GENERATION

F6257 Sula Ann Locke, born in Rye, Oct. 11, 1824, died July 7, 1894, married 1st, Aug. 10, 1845, SAMUEL W. FOSS, born 1818, a machinist in Rye and died Apl. 13, 1849; married 2nd, Oct. 7, 1855, JOHN SHERIDAN GOSS # 4716 born Oct. 26, 1817. He was a farmer in Rye and died March 12, 1903.

Child of 9th Gen.

F9300 WALLACE S. GOSS, b. Dec. 20, 1856, m. 1st, May 21, 1880, SARAH E. CASWELL; m. 2nd, MRS. MARION C. (BENNETT) CONCONNAN, Oct. 20, 1909.

F6258 S. Emaline Locke, born in Rye, Oct. 16, 1826, died Feb. 1, 1890, married Oct. 15, 1848, WOODBURY LEVI JENNESS of Rye, born Apl. 24, 1824. He was a farmer in Rye, and died Jan. 9, 1852.

Children of 9th Gen.

9300aWALLACE A., b. 1849, d. Feb. 16, 1856.
9301 WOODBURY L., b. June 26, 1851, m. MARY D. POOL.

F6259 A. Maria Locke, born in Rye, June 18, 1829, died in Exeter, Feb. 28, 1911, married Apl. 28, 1850, DEWITT C. JEWELL, born Oct. 9, 1825, son of Levi and Hannah (Marston). He was a farmer in Stratham.

Children of 9th Gen. b. in Stratham.

9302 ERASTUS BLOOMER, b. Feb. 12, 1851, m. Kingston, 1875, ABBY DOW of No. Hampton. He is a miller in Stratham, had: 9303 ALICE, b. ——, m. J. LOUIS COE of Newfield; 9304 GEORGE; 9305 PERCY.
9306 FLORA ELIZA, b. July 5, 1864, m. Greenland, June 4, 1884, WILL HILLIARD of Kingston, who is a milkman there, had: 9307 MILDRED; 9308 LEON; 9309 RUSSELL; 9310 JOHN CLINTON.
9311 VIOLA ISABEL, b. Dec. 4, 1871, m. Oct. 13, 1898, GEORGE H. BOWLEY of Stratham, a farmer there, have no children.

F6260 Richard L. Locke, born in Rye, Oct. 26, 1831, married Nov. 15, 1859, SARAH P. JENNESS, born in Rye, Nov. 25, 1835, died Rye, Feb. 24, 1912, daughter of Reuben and Mary (Knowles). A carpenter in early life, he later became a hotel proprietor at Rye Beach.

Children of 9th Gen. b. in Rye.

F9312 RICHARD JENNESS, b. May 31, 1863, m. Feb. 23, 1898, BESSIE L. BACHELDER.
F9313 ANNIE L., b. Feb. 22, 1866, m. Apl. 11, 1894, LANGDON B. PARSONS.
9314 ARTHUR M., b. Oct. 2, 1868, d. Rye, March 11, 1887.

Harriet I. (Locke) and Richard Pickering Goss F6201

Locke Family Reunion, 1915

NINTH GENERATION

F6261 Harriet J. Locke, born in Rye, Jan. 15, 1835, married Oct. 17, 1858, RICHARD PICKERING GOSS of Rye, born in Rye, Sept. 5, 1833. He was a farmer in Rye and died June 3, 1914. He was son of Joseph Pickering and Mary (Goss) and took her name.

Children of 9th Gen. b. in Rye.

F9315 CLARENCE A., b. Feb. 11, 1860, m. 1st, MARY MACE, Jan. 23, 1876; m. 2nd, July 8, 1882, ELLA E. GARLAND, who d. June 10, 1916.
F9316 ESTELLE J., b. Aug. 6, 1861, m. Feb. 28, 1885, EDWARD P. PHILBRICK.
9317 ANNIE M., b. May 19, 1868, d. Oct. 9, 1877.
9318 GILMAN P., b. June 6, 1870, m. Rye, Nov. 3, 1910, LILLIAN G. MCGANTY, b. Nova Scotia, Dec. 1887. He is a farmer and teamster in Rye, had: 9319 RICHARD PICKERING GOSS, 2ND, b. Oct. 8, 1912; 9319a LAWRENCE E., b. Feb. 17, 1916.
9320 ERASTUS L., b. Aug. 3, 1872, is a bookkeeper and auctioneer in Somerville, Mass.
9321 WALTER W., b. Dec. 11, 1875, m. No. Hampton, Feb. 14, 1900, FRANCES B. KNOWLES, b. Feb. 6, 1877, d. No. Hampton, Oct. 22, 1911, daughter of Edwin and Cora (Page). He is a painter in No. Hampton, had: 9322 RICHARD I., b. Jan. 24, 1901.

F6262 Albert Carr Locke, born in Rye, June 22, 1837, married July 9, 1868, ELIZA E. VARRELL, born Jan. 1, 1844. He was a farmer near Locke's Neck, held several town offices, a selectman for twelve years, was greatly interested in the Locke Association and died in Rye, Oct. 30, 1913.

Children of 9th Gen. b. in Rye.

9323 EVERETT TRUE, b. Oct. 5, 1868.
9324 OLIVE ANN, b. Jan. 4, 1870.
9325 MABEL JENNESS, b. Nov. 12, 1872, d. July 30, 1891.
9326 ETHEL MAUDE, b. June 24, 1876, m. Rye, Feb. 23, 1899, WILLIAM C. GARLAND, b. Rye, Nov. 7, 1879, son of Charles and Eliza J. (Garland). He is a storekeeper in Rye, had: 9327 EDNA MAY, b. Rye, Sept. 20, 1899, and 9328 ELIZABETH, b. Jan. 5, 1911.

F6265 Robert P. Locke, born in Rye, Sept. 30, 1819, died in North Hampton, Oct. 11, 1909, married 1851, CLARINDA A. BACHELDER of North Hampton, born Dec. 30, 1829, died Oct. 16, 1881, daughter of Joseph and Sarah (Philbrick). He was a mason and farmer at Rye Beach.

Child of 9th Gen.

9329 WALTER E., b. Dec. 8, 1855, m. May 28, 1879, ELVIRA G. MARDEN, # F7826.

F6270 Calvin Locke, born June 1830, married Francis PRIEST, born March 1836. He died Jan. 30, 1866, and she went to Boston to live.

Children of 9th Gen.

9330 ELLA F., b. July 1859, m. J. E. EMERSON. They lived in Boston, where she died. No children.
9331 MARY A., b. Boston, 1862, m. FRANK JENNINGS of Farmington, Me., has a son.

F6274 Martha Sarah Locke, born Dec. 19, 1830, died in California, Dec. 24, 1914, married in Portsmouth, Nov. 6, 1853, JOHN F. LARRABEE, a harness maker of Portsmouth, who about 1890, removed to California.

Children of 9th Gen.

9333 JAMES H., b. Portsmouth, Nov. 2, 1854, d. St. Paul, Minn., Aug. 10, 1857.
9334 CHARLES F., b. June 1, 1856, m. Aug. 12, 1886, CLARA APPLETON, b. 1862. He was a watchman at the Court House, Riverside, Cal., had a son, 9335 JOHN L., b. May 10, 1889. They were divorced and she m. 2nd, March 4, 1894, FRANCIS E. VARNEY of Rochester.
9336 MARY E., b. St. Paul, Minn., Jan. 16, 1858, d. Portsmouth, Feb. 26, 1877, unmarried.
9337 EFFIE H., b. Nov. 25, 1860, d. 1863.
9338 EMMA F., b. Aug. 4, 1862, lives Corona, Cal., m. 1916, DR. FRANK B. MORRILL of Corona.
9339 JOHN E., b. Aug. 28, 1865, was m. twice, lives Pittsburg, Penn., connected with Westinghouse Machinery Co.
9340 ALBERT L., b. Aug. 31, 1867, d. 1867.
9341 ARTHUR, b. Dec. 20, 1872, is a harness maker in Corona, Cal., has a dau., 9342 FRANCES MARGARET, b. Oct. 13, 1910.

F6275 William Watson Locke, born Apl. 7, 1833, married in Portsmouth, Nov. 18, 1857, ANNIE M. FERNALD, of Portsmouth, born Sept. 1835, died in Beverly, Mass., Feb. 21, 1891. He served in the U. S. Navy 1862 to 1864, and died in Portsmouth, Sept. 5, 1868.

Children of 9th Gen. b. in Portsmouth.

9343 AUGUSTUS I., b. Dec. 30, 1857, d. Ports., Nov. 30, 1861.
9344 EFFIE H., b. 1859, d. Ports., July 24, 1860.
9345 ANNIE E., b. Dec. 10, 1859, died young.
9346 CARRIE WALLACE, b. July 17, 1861, m. Providence, R. I., Jan. 30, 1890, WALTER I. MURDOCK, b. July 7, 1853. He is a silversmith in Providence, no children.
9347 ANNIE L., b. May 31, 1867, m. March 1884, JOHN L. BERRY, a druggist of Beverly, Mass., had: 9348 RALPH C., b. Boston, Sept. 1884, d. Beverly, Jan. 1902.
9349 MARY A. R., b. twin, May 31, 1867, d. Ports., July 24, 1867.
9350 WILLIE, b. 1865, d. Apl. 1, 1865.

F6277 Susan Olevia Locke, born in Portsmouth, Nov. 25, 1837, died May 21, 1914, married in Portsmouth, Oct. 12, 1856, CHARLES B. GREEN, born in New Castle, Jan. 21, 1828. He was a carpenter in Portsmouth many years and died there, Sept. 9, 1888.

Children of 9th Gen. b. in Portsmouth.

9351 CHARLES E., b. July 20, 1857, m. Pittsfield, Nov. 24, 1887, SADIE V. KNOWLTON, b. 1860, her 2nd mg., dau. of George W. and Mary (Virgin). He is a shoe manufacturer in Manchester, had no children.

9352 FREDDIE A., b. Dec. 10, 1858, d. Dec. 26, 1861.

F6278 James Irving Locke, born in Portsmouth, Dec. 28, 1839, married in Portsmouth, Oct. 23, 1867, LAURA A. KELLY, born in Stratham, Oct. 5, 1845, died in Exeter, May 16, 1913, daughter of Joseph and Sarah (Burgess). He enlisted in 1861, was wounded at Cold Harbor, promoted to Lieutenant and Captain in 1865. Later he was a carpenter in Colorado, retiring to Exeter about 1900, and now lives with his sister, Mrs. Hanscom. "He has a war record to be proud of. For three months beginning Apl. 10, 1861, he was paid by the State, re-enlisted May 21, 1861 and served almost constantly until mustered out Dec. 19, 1865, a total service of four years and eight months. During this service he took part in twenty-two engagements, many of them being of the first importance and most noted of the war, yet was wounded only once. He is also noted as being the only Portsmouth man who enlisted as a private and came out as a captain. He is yet hale and hearty in his retirement."

Children of 9th Gen.

F9353 JAMES ADELBERT, b. July 11, 1872, m. UNA DEVERE HAZARD.

9354 WALTER IRVING, b. Providence, Feb. 7, 1875, m Haverhill, Mass., MRS. ALICE ABBOTT WALKER of Exeter. Was a printer in Loveland, Col., in 1913 was in Fitchburg, Mass.

F6281 Ira A. Locke, born in Dover, Sept. 5, 1828, married Nov. 11, 1849, LYDIA V. CHURCH of Madbury, born Oct. 13, 1833, daughter of Nathaniel. He was a farmer and machinist in Dover and Madbury, enlisted Co. K. 11th N. H. Reg. 1862, and died in 1908.

Children of 9th Gen.

F9355 GEORGE A., b. Nov. 28, 1850, m. Dec. 25, 1878, HATTIE J. SMITH.

F9356 ANN ELIZABETH, b. Aug. 19, 1852, m. 1st, Feb. 11, 1877, ISRAEL PIERCE CHURCH; m. 2nd, July 3, 1893, EDWIN J. ANDREWS.

9357 WILLIE C., b. March 16, 1856, d. March 5, 1861.
F9358 IDA B., b. May 10, 1858, m. March 9, 1879, ROSCOE S. OTIS.
F9359 FRED E., b. June 24, 1861, m. Nov. 27, 1889, MAY A. AMAZEEN.
9360 JAMES I., b. Madbury, Sept. 11, 1870, m. Sept. 10, 1892, ORA TOWLE of Haverhill, Mass., where he was a shoe laster.

F6284 Elizabeth A. Locke, born in Dover, July 27, 1834, married in Lawrence, Mass., Oct. 15, 1859, HIRAM S. GOODELL of Bradford, Mass. They live in Haverhill, Mass.

Children of 9th Gen. b. in Bradford, Mass.

9361 PERCY HOWARD, b. Sept. 5, 1860, is married.
9362 CHARLES WALTER, b. Jan. 9, 1862, lives in Haverhill, Mass., married.
9363 MABEL, b. May 28, 1864, lives Haverhill.
9364 FRANK ALLEN, b. Madbury, Apl. 1, 1867, m. ALICE WEST of Chester. They lived in Haverhill, where he d.
9365 CARRIE LOCKE, b. Aug. 30, 1870.
9366 HENRY OLIVER, b. Sept. 24, 1879, is now dead.

F6285 Andrew Jackson Locke, born in Dover, Sept. 29, 1836, married March 9, 1858, SARAH A. SMITH, born in Dover, Feb. 10, 1837, living in 1915. He was a farmer and plumber and lived in Portsmouth, Boston and Rochester. He died Oct. 22, 1874.

Children of 9th Gen. b. in Dover.

9367 CLARENCE E., b. July 12, 1859, m. Rochester, July 5, 1886, AUGUSTA W. PLUMMER, b. Milton, 1864, dau. of B. W. and Laura. He was a shoemaker in Rochester, had no children.
9368 LIZZIE B., b. Nov. 5, 1862, m. June 15, 1898, JOHN L. COPP, b. March 22, 1848. He is cashier of Rochester Loan and Trust Co.
9369 EFFIE A., b. Nov. 1, 1867, lives Rochester, unmarried 1915.

F6288 Jeremiah Young Locke, born in Dover, Aug. 27, 1842, married Dec. 26, 1869, MRS. JENNIE (KYLE) LOCKE, born Aug. 6, 1845, died Aug. 19, 1912. He served in 1862 in U. S. Navy on ships Ohio and Vicksburg. He died in Boston, Aug. 8, 1889.

Child of 9th Gen.

9370 GRACE MAY, b. July 27, 1877, m. Roslindale, Mass., Oct. 8, 1895, WILLIAM BAINES of Rosl., b. Dec. 14, 1872. Had: 9371 WILLIAM CHARLES, b. 1898, d. 1898.

F6290 Esther Brown, born in 1817, died in Concord, July 20, 1887, married 1st, DANIEL RAND, born in Rye, May 17, 1810. He was a carpenter in Concord and died there. She married 2nd, MATTHEW D. ANNIS of Warren.

NINTH GENERATION 493

Children of 9th Gen.
9372 DAVID, b. ——, m. ——. He was in Civil War serving in Cavalry and secret telegraph service, had son: 9373 PERCY.
9374 CLARENDA J., b. ——.
9375 JAMES C., b. 1846, entered the army at age of 18, and d. unmarried, aged 25.
F9376 CLARENDA J., b. Nov. 15, 1847, m. Oct. 17, 1865, JOHN DREW.
9377 JOHN W., b. ——, died young.
F9378 JOHN W., b. 1850, m. 1st, Nov. 26, 1872, EMMA WARD; m. 2nd, Nov. 26, 1890, IDA B. BROWN.

F6291 Joseph Randall, born ——, married ARIADNE CASWELL, dau. of William H.
Children of 9th Gen.
9380 ADRIANA or ADA was m. and lived in Mass.
9381 JOSEPH H., m. LIZZIE RAMSEY, lives in Rye, has no children.
9382 LAWRENCE, b. ——, died young.

F6293 Richard L. Randall, born in Rye, Dec. 23, 1823, married Dec. 26, 1847, MARY A. CASWELL # 6312, born Nov. 13, 1828, living in Portsmouth, 1916. He was in business in Portsmouth and died Feb. 29, 1892.
Children of 9th Gen. b. in Portsmouth.
9383 FRANCES A., b. Sept. 22, 1848, d. Nov. 28, 1867, m. ISAAC H. M. PRAY Nov. 29, 1866, b. Ports., Aug. 30, 1843. He is a carpenter in Kittery, Me. Had: 9384 ALICE B. who died young.
9385 FRANK B., b. Apl. 13, 1850, m. July 23, 1872, CLARA I. WILLIAMS who was divorced and m. 2nd, AUGUSTUS W. HODGDON of Portsmouth. Frank was Chief Engineer of the Revenue Cutter McCullough and dropped dead at the Battle of Manila Bay, May 1, 1898. He and Clara had a dau. 9386 LULU B. RANDALL, b. Nov. 3, 1883, who m. WILLIS KIMBALL, JR. of Concord.
F9387 IRA E., b. Jan. 31, 1854, m. July 12, 1876, ANNIE WILSON.
F9388 ADDIE, b. Sept. 2, 1858, m. Aug. 28, 1882, WILLIAM P. PICKETT.
F9389 JENNIE L., b. Feb. 2, 1861, m. Aug. 17, 1886, WALTER D. HARDY.
9390 EVA E., b. Aug. 23, 1864, lives at home in Portsmouth, unmarried.

F6294 Lucy Jane Randall, born at The Shoals, June 1821, died in Portsmouth, Apl. 29, 1911, married in Portsmouth, May 1844, RICHARD G. HALEY, born 1814, son of Samuel and Olive (Randall) of the Shoals. He was a fisherman and died in Portsmouth, 1870.
Children of 9th Gen. b. in Portsmouth.
9391 OTIS, b. 1844, d. Nov. 23, 1912, m. June 12, 1868, JULIA M. CHAUNCY of Kittery, Me., b. 1847, d. March 1911, had: 9392 GERTRUDE, who m. 1st, GEORGE CATLIN; 2nd, —— GILMORE; 9393 MILDRED, who m. RICHARD O'BRIEN; 9394 PERCY, who m. ANNIE HORN.

9395 JAMES M., b. July 23, 1846, m. July 3, 1866, HARRIET A. CLARK of Kittery, and had: 9396 HATTIE LILLIAN, b. 1867, m. FRED L. MARTIN; 9397 JAMES IRVING, b. 1872.
9398 JOSEPH B., b. July 24, 1849, m. LEONORA CASWELL, b. 1853, d. Feb. 1882, dau. of Lemuel and Henrietta (Garland,) and had: 9399 ALICE; 9400 GRACE.
9401 MARY L., b. Oct. 8, 1852, m. Jan. 27, 1872, WILLIAM H. PHINNEY, and had: 9402 LEROY.

F6295 Catherine Randall, married JAMES BURNES of Vermont.

Children of 9th Gen.

9403 CATHERINE, b. ——, m. —— JACOBS of Boston.
9404 JAMES, b. ——, was married.
9405 WILLIAM C., b. ——, m. ANNIE GREEN of Spencer, Mass.
9406 ROBERT I., was m., had an underwear factory in Worcester, Mass.
9407 MARY, b. twin ——, not married.

F6301 Eliza J. Randall, born in 1833, died in Portsmouth, Nov. 25, 1869, married at The Shoals, Oct. 11, 1848, DANIEL H. HALEY, born in Rye, Nov. 5, 1824, died in Portsmouth, Aug. 1, 1898, son of Samuel & Olivia (Randall).

Children of 9th Gen.

9408 ELLEN AMANDA, b. Shoals, March 18, 1849, m. WILLIS SAUNDERS, a fisherman of Gloucester, Mass., and had: 9409 BENJAMIN.
9410 MALINDA, b. Aug. 28, 1851, m. Sept. 13, 1868, JUDSON P. RANDALL, had five children.
9411 JOSIAH, b. March 18, 1853, m. LUELLA RANDALL, lived Portsmouth, had two children.
9412 EMMA, b. Dec. 1, 1855, d. Ports., Oct. 15, 1884, m. THOMAS JAMESON, had five children.
9413 WALTER, b. Oct. 8, 1858, lives unmarried in Portsmouth.
9414 WILLIE, b. July 1, 1859, d. Sept. 19, 1859.
9415 MARY, b. June 28, 1860, d. July 27, 1860.
9416 ISABEL, b. Oct. 30, 1862, m. HERMAN MARDEN, of Portsmouth, had three children.
9417 ANNIE, b. Aug. 30, 1864, d. Sept. 9, 1864.
9418 DANIEL, b. Aug. 6, 1866, d. Sept. 1, 1866.
9419 JENNIE OLEVIA, b. July 15, 1867, m. ALBERT STANLEY of Portsmouth, had three children.
9420 THOMAS, b. Oct. 8, 1869, d. Oct. 26, 1869.

F6304 Elisha Beede Locke, born in Sandwich, Sept. 14, 1834, married LUVIA CUTTER KNIGHT, born March 12, 1838, died Apl. 11, 1906. He died Feb. 11, 1906.

NINTH GENERATION

Children of 9th Gen.

F9421 ORRIN WILLEY, b. Apl. 24, 1859, m. 1st, May 19, 1886, LILLA LUELLA FAYER; m. 2nd, EDNA E. FAYER.

9422 JENNIE MARTHA, b. Dec. 1, 1860, was for 30 years a teacher, fifteen of which was in Barton, Vt., graded school. She m. 1st, July 11, 1907, CHARLES HENRY JONES, who d. March 15, 1909, leaving his estate for a Library at Orleans, Vt., after Jennie's death. She m. 2nd, July 6, 1914, GILBERT JOTHAM GROSS of Bennington, Vt. He has been a representative and State senator, lives Orleans.

F9423 BURT WALLACE, b. Oct. 7, 1874, m. Oct. 22, 1907, EVA AGNES MARTIN.

F6305 Joseph Marden Locke, born in Charlestown, Vt., July 18, 1839, married Oct. 30, 1859, HARRIET E. SWEET, born in Derby, Vt., Feb. 16, 1839, died Oct. 1912, daughter of John. He lived at Broome, Quebec.

Child of 9th Gen.

F9424 LILLAH B., b. May 14, 1866, m. Feb. 1888, JAMES M. STOWELL.

F6313 Louisa Blaisdell Caswell, born at The Shoals, Jan. 29, 1831, died in Portsmouth, Jan. 8, 1898, married May 28, 1848, GEORGE W. RANDALL.

Children of 9th Gen.

9425 MARY I., b. June 28, 1852, m. ―――― HORN of Rochester.

9426 LOUISA J., b. July 30, 1854, m. FRED HARRADEN; also, GEORGE PERKINS.

9427 WILLIAM C., b. Oct. 23, 1856, m. BESSIE BOARDMAN, had: 9428 LINCOLN; 9428a BOARDMAN.

9429 SARAH E., b. Nov. 11, 1858, m. FRANK BACHELDER.

9430 JOSEPH A., b. Oct. 11, 1860, was married.

9431 PARRY L., b. Feb. 21, 1864, married a Spanish woman in Brazil.

F6324 James O. Trefethern, born in Kittery, Aug. 10, 1830, married in Kittery, Me., Nov. 29, 1855, JOANNA M. LAWRY, born Apl. 18, 1835, died in Kittery, Apl. 19, 1863; married 2nd, June 15, 1864, ISABELLA C. KIMBALL, born Apl. 28, 1845. He was postmaster of Kittery.

Children of 9th Gen. b. in Kittery, Me.

9432 JOHN C., b. Nov. 29, 1864, m. ELLA PAUL of Kittery, lived in York, Me., had: 9433 JAMES; 9434 BEATRICE.

9435 FRANK L., b. Jan. 3, 1866, m. in York, Dec. 14, 1897, ABBIE HUTCHINS.

9436 CHARLES E., b. Apl. 4, 1868.

9437 FRED J., b. Sept. 10, 1871, m. Philadelphia, May 21, 1899, LAURA MCGRATH of Phila. He is an Apothecary in the U. S. Navy.

9438 GEORGE L., b. June 11, 1873.

F6331 Charles W. Trefethern, born in Kittery, Me., Jan. 9, 1846, married in Taunton, Mass., June 21, 1871, EMMA LOUISE WITHERELL, born Apl. 3, 1849. He is a machinist in Taunton.

Children of 9th Gen.

F9439 MABEL S., b. Aug. 9, 1872, m. June 19, 1899, GEORGE B. STACKPOLE.
9440 ETHEL M., b. July 15, 1886.

F6339 Munroe Holmes, born ——, married in Boston, Jan. 5, 1864, LAURA F. FARNUM of Bryants Pond, Me., who died in Hampton in 1902. He lived in Hampton and died July 25, 1903.

Children of 9th Gen. b. in Portsmouth.

9441 STELLA L., b. Apl. 2, 1866, m. Apl. 8, 1886, HENRY W. MASON, b. Aug. 26, 1858, son of Joseph. She is dead.
9442 JOSEPH F., b. Nov. 7, 1867.
9443 JAMES H., b. Sept. 6, 1870.
9444 ADA P., b. Feb. 11, 1874, d. ——.

F6387 Etta M. Brown, born in Rye, Jan. 25, 1857, married Sept. 1, 1881, FRANK PEARSON of Portsmouth.

Children of 9th Gen. b. in Portsmouth.

9445 CLARENCE, b. Jan. 27, 1882, m. June 26, 1912, MABELLE L. COLEMAN, b. 1886 in Newington, had: 9446 WILLIS C., b. Sept. 26, 1913; 9446a ELIZABETH M.
9447 ANNIE MAY, b. June 25, 1886, m. Ports., Nov. 29, 1906, WILBUR JAMES HALEY, had: 9448 CHARLES P., b. Nov. 17, 1914.
9449 IDA G., b. June 10, 1890, m. Aug. 22, 1908, THOMAS F. MCCAFFERY, had: 9450 RUTH P., b. Feb. 6, 1910.
9451 CHARLES, b. Aug. 26, 1898; 9452 FRED L., b. Oct. 13, 1901.

F6428 Frederick A. Locke, born in New York City, Dec. 9, 1848, married in New York, Dec. 20, 1875, MARY A. ROBINSON, born in Yorkshire, Eng., Sept. 19, 1849. He was a chemist in Brooklyn, N. Y.

Children of 9th Gen. b. in Brooklyn, N. Y.

9454 THOMAS B., b. May 13, 1877, d. Nov. 12, 1881.
9455 MARY E., b. Oct. 6, 1879.
9456 HELEN JOSEPHINE, b. March 20, 1881, d. Feb. 15, 1883.
9457 JESSIE B., b. Jan. 29, 1884. 9458 EDWARD S., b. Apl. 25, 1890.

F6440 Jesse Locke Gould, born in Portland, Nov. 2, 1827, married 1st, SARAH JOHNSON of Limerick, Me., born Sept. 7, 1828, died March 27, 1883; married 2nd, M. F. J. WEDGWOOD, born Apl. 7, 1832, lived in Limerick.

NINTH GENERATION

Children of 9th Gen.

9459 MELVILLE P., b. Aug. 16, 1856, m. Limerick, Me., NELLIE A. BROWN, b. Aug. 31, 1861, had: 9460 ELLA L., b. Nov. 13, 1886, d. Sept. 9, 1892; 9461 ARTHUR A., b. Feb. 19, 1891.
9462 HARRIET E., b. Oct. 23, 1859, m. WILLIAM P. MCMULLEN, lives Salem, Mass.
9463 ELLA E., b. Sept. 6, 1866, d. Dec. 20, 1873.

F6469 Miriam Day Locke, born in Tonawanda, N. Y., Dec. 14, 1839, died there, Nov. 13, 1894, married in Tonawanda, July 26, 1865, CAPT. LEVANT RANSOM, born in Clarence, N. Y., Jan. 21, 1825, died Nov. 1, 1911, son of Asa and Betsey (Clark).

Children of 9th Gen. b. in Grand Isle, N. Y.

9464 LEVANT, JR., b. May 20, 1866, m. May 29, 1895, SUSAN RACHEL O'DAY had: 9465 DANIEL, b. Aug. 23, 1902, d. Oct. 14, 1902.
9466 BETSEY MEHITABLE, b. Oct. 27, 1868, m. 1st, July 11, 1888, JESSE ALBERT LOCKE who d. Dec. 13, 1897; m. 2nd, March 20, 1902, HARRY L. KOLSETH, M. D., b. June 20, 1867, had: 9467 HAROLD RANSOM, b. March 13, 1903.
F9468 LELIA GOODWIN, b. May 6, 1871, m. July 8, 1889, JOSEPH B. BARNES.
9469 MAMIE BELL, b. Jan. 30, 1874, d. Aug. 30, 1882.
F9470 LUCIA EDWARDS, b. June 10, 1877, m. July 12, 1898, FREDERICK WILLIAM BYERS.
9471 CLARENCE LYMAN LOCKE, b. July 27, 1884, d. Sept. 9, 1910.

F6472 Pamelia Prentiss Locke, born Feb. 22, 1848, married May 26, 1864, ANDREW J. HAUGHTON, M. D., born Nov. 12, 1828, son of Hiram and Elizabeth (Potter) of Wilson, N. Y. He graduated from the Buffalo Medical School in 1862; served in the Civil War and died Jan. 25, 1890.

Children of 9th Gen.

F9472 JOSEPHINE, b. Apl. 20, 1865, m. Nov. 17, 1887, PERRY A. WILLBER.
F9473 CHARLES EDWIN, b. Dec. 10, 1866, m. Dec. 29, 1886, JENNIE ELIZABETH RIDGEWAY.
F9474 ANDREW J., b. Jan. 11, 1869, m. June 24, 1890, SURELDA A. WILLBER.
9475 GEORGE A., b. Oct. 25, 1870, d. July 20, 1899, was a high school teacher.
9476 JESSE P., b. May 18, 1872, m. Apl. 10, 1897, LAURA LACKEY. He was a lawyer in Vincennes, Ind., and d. Jan. 20, 1908.
9477 HIRAM R., b. Feb. 20, 1874. He and the next brother are ranchmen and sheep raisers in Big Horn Mountain, Wyo.
9478 FREDERICK LOCKE, b. Nov. 26, 1876, m. July 12, 1911, ESTELLA BOND, b. Sept. 18, 1879, had: 9479 FREDERICK, b. Feb. 27, 1914.

9480 NICHOLAS JOHN, b. Sept. 19, 1879, m. Oct. 2, 1907, BERTHA O. BEST, b. Dec. 8, 1884. He graduated from St. Louis College Physicians and Surgeons 1905, located at Greenup, Ill., had: 9481 NICHOLAS J., b. Apl. 11, 1911.
9482 LEWIS F., b. Aug. 26, 1881, is a lawyer in Tonapah, Nevada.
9483 JAMES W., b. Dec. 23, 1883, m. March 21, 1908, MARY ETHEL ALLEN, b. Aug. 1884. He is a Standard Oil employee at Evansville, Ind.

F6487 Simon Locke Horn, born Apl. 3, 1835, married Feb. 9, 1858, LYDIA PARSONS, born Nov. 22, 1834, a descendant of Cornet Joseph Parsons, Cape Ann, 1626. He was a farmer in Rochester, and died Dec. 4, 1904.

Children of 9th Gen. b. in Rochester.

9484 MARTHA A., b. Apl. 3, 1859, d. Apl. 4, 1900, m. Apl. 2, 1884, EUGENE A. WATSON, had: 9485 EMMA F., b. May 14, 1895.
9486 CHARLES HERBERT, b. Sept. 7, 1862, m. 1st, Dec. 24, 1884, GRACE I. PLUMMER and had: 9487 GUY H., b. Jan. 8, 1889, d. Jan. 30, 1889; 9488 RALPH D., b. June 3, 1898. He m. 2nd, Jan. 24, 1903, EDITH M. BERRY.
F9489 BERTHA L., b. Oct. 9, 1864, m. Jan. 18, 1888, JOHN A. ALLEN.
9490 ARTHUR T., b. Oct. 21, 1872, m. March 27, 1895, MARY I. KEIR and had: 9491 CHESTER A., b. Dec. 18, 1895.
9492 JOHN BRADBURY, b. July 19, 1874, m. Dec. 25, 1901, ETHEL M. ROBERTS, had: 9493 RUTH L., d. infant; 9494 RUTH F., b. May 6, 1906; 9495 JOHN B., b. Dec. 3, 1910.

F6491 James Albert Locke, born in Somersworth, Feb. 8, 1847, married in Somersworth, July 3, 1869, SUSAN AGNES HAMILTON, born in Waterboro, Me., 1847, daughter of Ivory and Belinda. He enlisted in the Navy when 15 and served 5 years. He held many offices in his native town, was State Senator and member of Constitutional Convention, was for 22 years yard Supt. of Great Falls Mfg. Co., upright and honorable in business, kind and affectionate in his family life.

Children of 9th Gen. b. in Somersworth.

9493 GUY HOWARD, b. Feb. 26, 1871, m. 1st, in Somersworth, June 7, 1899, MARY JANE MARCOTTE, b. Rochester, Jan. 25, 1874, d. Melrose, Mass., Apl. 13, 1905, dau. of Louis and Mary; m. 2nd, Melrose, Apl. 30, 1907, BLANCHE ROSS of Castine, Me. He graduated from Somersworth, High School, is now a Pullman conductor living at Melrose Highlands, Mass., had no children.
9494 ROY HAMILTON, b. Nov. 4, 1872, m. Somersworth, June 26, 1900, EMMA CHARLOTTE HATCH, b. Somersworth, May 27, 1873, dau. of Anderson and Sarah (Lord). He is in the ice business, had: 9495 SARAH AGNES, b. Amesbury, Mass., March 1, 1912.

9496 EDWIN CECIL, b. Dec. 28, 1876, m. Somerville, Mass., June 29, 1904, CLARA KATHERINE ZOELLER. He graduated from Somersworth High School and Bryant and Stratton's Business College, is now in the automobile business at Roslindale, Mass., had: 9497 STEPHANIE HAMILTON, b. Worcester, May 10, 1907.
9498 SUSAN AGNES, b. Jan. 27, 1882, was two years in Smith College, now a school teacher in Somersworth.
9499 ANNIE BELLE, b. Gt. Falls, Jan. 23, 1879, m. in Somersworth, July 2, 1906, JASON L. MERRILL of Waterville, Me., graduate of Mass. Institute Technology, now a chemist in Dept. of Agriculture, Washington, D. C., had: 9500 JAMES WILLIS, b. Nov. 3, 1910; 9501 RICHARD NATHAN, b. March 17, 1915.

F6492 Charles Henry Locke, born in Somersworth, Dec. 31, 1849, married Nov. 24, 1876, HENRIETTA WILLETTE BLAISDELL, born in Somersworth, 1859, died in Boston, Oct. 9, 1912, daughter of Uriah and Rebecca. He was a carpenter and grocer in Somersworth.

Children of 9th Gen. b. in Somersworth.

F9502 HOWARD ASHTON, b. May 15, 1877, m. July 22, 1896, LOTTIE A. WARREN.
9503 EUNICE EVELYN, b. Dec. 24, 1879, graduated from Somersworth High School 1897, m. Brockton, Mass., Oct. 3, 1909, E. GERRY BROWN, b. Charlestown, Mass., Oct. 8, 1886. They live in Brockton, had: 9504 FRANCES, b. May 8, 1910.
F9505 FLORENCE REBECCA, b. Sept. 12, 1883, m. Aug. 30, 1902, FRED WILMOT DYER.
9506 REBECCA, d. at birth.
9507 RACHEL BLAISDELL, b. Sept. 18, 1887, m. Sanford, Me., Nov. 19, 1912, JOSEPH FRED WILKENSON of Dover, lives in Dover. He is Chief Machinist's Mate, U. S. Navy.
9508 SON, b. Sept. 1890.
9509 CHRISTINE LOUISA, b. May 10, 1896.

F6493 Eunice Belle Locke, born in Somersworth, March 26, 1854, died in Somersworth, Sept. 14, 1911, married in Somersworth, Oct. 20, 1880, ALTON E. HERSOM, born in Berwick, Apl. 24, 1858, son of Lorenzo R. and Martha (Tibbetts). He was in the wool business in Somersworth and died Sept. 18, 1897. Eunice was graduate of Plymouth Normal School.

Child of 9th Gen.

9510 MARTHA ARLINE, b. So. Berwick, Me., July 27, 1881, m. 1914, JAMES E. FRENCH of Moultonboro. She was a high school graduate, and a teacher before marriage.

F6495 Howard E. Hussey, born Jan. 28, 1838, married JULIA PERKINS of Denmark, Me. He was an iron moulder in Somersworth and died Sept. 26, 1881.

Child of 9th Gen. b. in Somersworth.

F9511 RICHARD IRVING HUSSEY, b. Dec. 28, 1859, m. ANNIE GERRY of So. Berwick. He was a baker and d. July 12, 1887.

F6496 Mary Ellen Hussey, born Aug. 3, 1839, married JOHN G. ROBINSON of South Exeter, Me.

Child of 9th Gen. b. in Somersworth.

F9512 FRANK HUSSEY, b. Aug. 27, 1868, m. DORA D. AMAZEEN of Garland, Me. He is a farmer.

F6497 John S. Hussey, born in Somersworth, Oct. 23, 1841, married MARY E. BOYLE of Rochester, born March 1, 1844, died March 27, 1905. He was a patternmaker in Great Falls Mfg. Co. and died May 27, 1907.

Children of 9th Gen. b. in Somersworth.

9513 OLIVE A., b. March 1, 1861.
9514 CHARLES F., b. Sept. 7, 1867, m. CELIA PREBLE of York, Me. He is an optician in Portsmouth.
9515 JOHN E., b. ——, unmarried, is a machinist.
9516 ELMER E., b. Sept. 8, 1876, m. March 24, 1905, CECELIA BERNIER of Somersworth. He is a carpenter and had: 9517 MARY E., b. 1908; 9518 BEATRICE, b. 1912.

F6501 Freeman A. Hussey, born Jan. 23, 1852, married Oct. 23, 1878, CELIA A. E. FALL, born in Somersworth in 1855, daughter of Noah and Amanda.

Children of 9th Gen. b. in Somersworth.

9519 LEONA E., b. May 5, 1880, m. JORDAN S. SAVITHES of Lowell, Mass. He is in real estate and insurance business, Chicago, had: 9520 DOROTHEA, b. 1904.
9521 EDITH A., b. July 17, 1882, m. CHESTER R. ADAMS of Attleboro, Mass., where he is an Inspector of Telephones. No children.
9522 KIRKE H., b. March 28, 1884, d. Aug. 11, 1884.

F6502 Etta G. Hussey, born June 7, 1856, married 1st, CHARLES MARVIN HODGDON of Somersworth, a tanner; married 2nd, —— WORCESTER, whom she divorced.

Children of 9th Gen. b. in Somersworth.

9523 ALTON F., b. ——, is a carpenter in Lawrence, Mass.
9524 HARRY B., b. Dec. 19, 1876, m. SYLVIA MILLS of Somersworth, where he is a shoemaker, had: 9525 JOHN R. and 9526 CHARLES twins, b. 1901.

NINTH GENERATION

9527 RAYMOND C., b. Nov. 10, 1878, m. March 30, 1905, MABEL E. HUNTOON of Providence, b. Oct. 6, 1884. He was a machinist in Cranston, R. I., had: 9528 HOWARD R., b. 1906; 9529 DORIS E., b. 1911.
9530 WINNIE, b. Oct. 16, 1881, m. OLIFF DRAKE of Berwick. He is a salesman in Pittsburg, Mass., no children.
9531 JOHN, b. Oct. 16, 1883, m. Oct. 15, 1882, JULIA LEARY of Somersworth, where he is foreman in a bleachery; no children.
9532 GUY, b. ——, d. ——. 9533 MABEL, b. ——, d. ——.

F6515 Abbie Emery, born in Somersworth, March 28, 1851, married in Somersworth, Oct. 28, 1874, EVERETT JEWETT STEVENS of Dover, born in Ossipee, May 11, 1847, son of Major William and Mary. He is in the sandpaper business.

Children of 9th Gen. b. in Malden, Mass.

9534 GERTRUDE EMERY, b. May 18, 1877, m. Malden, Jan. 14, 1897, GEORGE C. DUTTON, b. Oct. 13, 1869, had: 9535 GERTRUDE, b. 1902.
9536 ALICE MADELINE, b. Jan. 18, 1880.
9537 HELEN MORETTE, b. May 19, 1893.

F6517 Olive Marion Locke, born in Somersworth, Oct. 19, 1851, married in Somersworth, Nov. 9, 1872, LEONARD A. MERRILL, born in Lisbon, Me., 1850. He is employed in Dover Print Works.

Children of 9th Gen. b. in Somersworth.

9538 SIMON LOCKE, b. ——, m. 1st, CARRIE HOYT, had: 9539 FRED, and was divorced. He m. 2nd, JENNIE HUSSEY and is employed on the railroad.
9540 OLIVE, b. Feb. 24, 1878, m. 1891, WILLIS J. FREEMAN of Dover, lives in Dover.
9541 MARILLA JANE, b. ——, d. ——.

F6518 Hannah Bell Locke, born in Somersworth, Aug. 28, 1852, married in Hollis Center, Me., May 1, 1875, GEORGE H. FLINT, born in Candia, Apl. 24, 1854. He was an expert machinist, employed at Portsmouth Navy Yard, later in Mass.

Children of 9th Gen.

9542 HATTIE LUELLA, b. Somersworth, Feb. 25, 1876, d. Jan. 10, 1894.
9543 GEORGE HENRY, b. Dover, Feb. 20, 1879, d. Sept. 27, 1880.
9544 MILDRED EDITH, b. Apl. 2, 1882, m. Jan. 4, 1905, JOHN CASWELL, b. Portsmouth, June 5, 1879, had: 9545 FORREST F., b. June 12, 1906, d. June 3, 1916; 9546 HENRIETTA HAZEL.
9547 THOMAS DENNETT, b. Dover, Dec. 5, 1885, is m., lives in Worcester, and had: 9548 GEORGE H. who d. Apl. 20, 1910.
9549 MARION REBECCA, b. Sept. 14, 1887, d. same day.
9550 WALTER HENRY, b. Portsmouth, July 12, 1890, d. Sept. 29, 1896.

F6658 Ardelle Mary Locke, born in Willimantic, Conn., July 15, 1860, married Feb. 28, 1884, R. C. BAIR, a cattle dealer in Rutland, Iowa.

Children of 9th Gen.

9551 NINA GERALDINE, b. ———.
9552 FEDORA C., b. ———.
9553 SADIE BELLE, b. ———.
9554 IONA B.
9555 MURRAY, or WALTER W.

F6722 Benjamin Harrison Locke, born in Richfield, N. Y., Sept. 2, 1887, married Oct. 5, 1907, MARY MATILDA KIMBALL. He is a machinist in Canastota, N. Y.

Children of 9th Gen.

9556 OLIVE MAE, b. July 31, 1908.
9557 AUDREY ELIZABETH, b. Dec. 7, 1910.
9558 BENJAMIN FREDERICK, b. Feb. 8, 1914.

F6753 Albert Everett Locke, born in North Hampton, Sept. 16, 1860, married in North Hampton, Apl. 4, 1883, SUSIE A. BERRY, born in Greenland, March 18, 1864. He is a blacksmith in North Hampton. She was daughter of Joseph E. and Annie (Loud.)

Children of 9th Gen. b. in No. Hampton.

9559 LILLA E., b. Aug. 27, 1883, d. Dec. 21, 1883.
9560 HAROLD RUSSELL, b. Aug. 20, 1888, worked for U. Shoe Machinery Co. and was killed at Beverly, Mass., Aug. 6, 1914, by an auto running into his motorcycle.
9561 NINA BERRY, b. Nov. 5, 1893.

F6754 Warren Ellsworth Locke, born in North Hampton, Apl. 3, 1863, married in Bristol, Jan. 24, 1883, LILLA M. HEATH, born 1865, daughter of Hiram and Dorcas (Whitemore). He is in the real estate business, West Somerville, Mass.

Children of 9th Gen.

9562 CLARENCE BLAINE, b. No. Hampton, Nov. 27, 1886.
9563 MARION HEATH, b. W. Somerville, Mass., Feb. 26, 1891, graduate of Wellesley College.

F6760 Sperry Herman Locke, born Jan. 22, 1873, married in Cherryfield, Me., Sept. 24, 1902, VERA CAROLINE NASH. She was born in Cherryfield, Aug. 22, 1880, daughter of Edward S. and Effie (Lord), and is teaching in Watertown, Mass., 1916, being divorced from Mr. Locke. He is a mine promoter. He married 2nd, in New York City, Sept. 20, 1915, MRS. ROSINA ———?

Children of 9th Gen. b. in Cherryfield, Me.

9564 ELIZABETH NASH, b. Aug. 3, 1903.
9565 EDWARD MORRIS, b. Sept. 23, 1905.

NINTH GENERATION 503

F6769 Elizabeth Ellen Locke, born in Hampton, Aug. 5, 1847, married June 17, 1866, JOSEPH W. MACE, born Apl. 7, 1839, son of Joseph and Elizabeth (Garland).
Children of 9th Gen.
F9566 MARY A., b. Feb. 1, 1867, m. June 6, 1886, JOHN W. GALE.
9567 CHARLES W., b. Aug. 30, 1878, d. Aug. 27, 1879.
9568 EDWIN W., b. March 29, 1882, d. Nov. 23, 1891.
9569 LEWIS L., b. May 26, 1884, m. Oct. 12, 1909, HELEN C. EDSON of Concord, had: 9570 MARGARET, b. July 5, 1910; 9571 ROBERT E., b. Aug. 12, 1913.

F6819 Martha E. Locke, born in Saco, Me., Nov. 2, 1844, married in Biddeford, Jan. 25, 1865, HENRY G. MOORE, born in Kennebunk, May 16, 1826. He was a California '49er, atter marriage went to California three years, thence to Biddeford until 1871, then moved to a plantation in Reidsville, N. C., where he died Jan. 28, 1896.
Children of 9th Gen.
F9572 MAUDE W., b. Jan. 10, 1867, m. Oct. 23, 1883, JAMES W. MCCARTHY.
F9573 HARRY LOCKE, b. Aug. 20, 1869, m. June 15, 1892, EMMA J. BROWN.

F6820 William F. Farrington Locke, born in Biddeford, Me., Jan. 2, 1848, married in Biddeford, Nov. 2, 1867, GEORGE-ANNA WARD of Biddeford who died in Lynn, 1887. He was a moulder in Biddeford and died in Danville, Va., March 20, 1886.
Children of 9th Gen.
9574 DAUGHTER died young.
9575 CHARLES HERBERT, b. Biddeford, Me., July 17, 1870, m. in Lynn, is a shoemaker there. Had: 9576 HERBERT.

F6821 Helen Frances Locke, born in Biddeford, June 22, 1851, married in Biddeford, Jan. 3, 1869, ISAAC H. M. PRAY, born in Portsmouth, Aug. 30, 1843. He is a joiner in Kittery, Me.
Children of 9th Gen.
9576aLUCIUS E., b. Biddeford, Oct. 23, 1870, d. May 29, 1872.
F9577 LIZZIE BRADBURY, b. Feb. 18, 1872, m. Sept. 9, 1891, CALVIN D. DUNBAR.
F9578 EVA ADELAIDE, b. Nov. 11, 1873, m. Oct. 3, 1894, FRED W. PRYOR.
9579 MARTHA FLORENCE, b. Reidsville, N. C., Jan. 9, 1876, m. Kittery, Me., Jan. 3, 1899 WILBUR F. STEPHENSON, b. Kittery, Oct. 6, 1870, son of Augustus. He was a carpenter in U. S. Navy, and d. Philippine Islands, Dec. 20, 1908, had: 9580 THOMAS PRAY, b. Oct 22, 1899.

9581 HELENA AUGUSTA, b. Nov. 15, 1878, m. Jan. 22, 1902, FRED E. DINSMORE, b. May 29, 1879, son of John R. and Abbie (Hanscom). He lives in Kittery, is an electrician on Navy Yard, had: 9582 DAU., b. July 24, 1904.
9583 MAUD ELLA, b. Kittery, Oct. 22, 1883, m. STEPHEN BOULTER of Kittery.
9584 FRED NOBLE, b. May 2, 1885, m. MARION THOMAS of Portsmouth, had: 9585 ESTELLE.
9586 ELMER ONSVILLE, b. Oct. 6, 1886, m. FRIEDA WETHERBEE of Bath, Me. He is a civil engineer in Melrose, Mass., had: 9587 SHIRLEY W.
9588 ETHEL MARION, b. Kittery, June 10, 1889, d. Oct. 4, 1891.

F6822 Joseph Wilbur Locke, born in Biddeford, Me., 1856, married STELLA C. RICHARDSON, born in Merrimac, Mass., 1862. He was a farmer in South Hampton, later in Newton, Mass.

Children of 9th Gen.

9589 ALPHONZO, b. March 1886, d. So. Hampton, Aug. 1, 1886.
9590 Two unknown.
9591 PEARL E., b. So. Hampton, Apl. 26, 1888.
9592 AUGUSTUS E., b. Newton, Mass., May 22, 1895.

F6837 Charles F. Locke, born in Hollis, Me., Aug. 11, 1854, married, May 23, 1880, NELLIE A. STUART, born Feb. 15, 1862, daughter of Roscoe G. and Miriam (Sanborn). He is a farmer and brick mason in Hollis.

Children of 9th Gen. b. in Hollis.

9592a DELLA O., b. Oct. 8, 1882, m. 1907, WILLIAM ROY DIXON, b. July 31, 1887, of Eliot, Me. He is a plumber employed on the Navy Yard, living in Portsmouth. Had: 9592b ELSIE B., b. Dec. 30, 1907.
9592c MILLARD C., b. Apl. 4, 1887, is field engineer of Michigan State Tel. Co., lives in Detroit.

F6882 James Andrew Locke, born in Stark, Me., Nov. 29, 1852, married Dec. 23, 1875, MARY A. OLIVER of Stark, daughter of Alexander and Julia A. He is a farmer in Stark.

Children of 9th Gen. b. in Stark, Me.

9593 CHILD, b. Feb. 1877, died young.
9594 JOHN FORREST, b. Jan. 14, 1879.
9595 ARTHUR H., b. Nov. 29, 1882.
9596 FLORENCE M., b. May 26, 1889.

F6883 Charles H. Locke, born in Stark, Me., March 23, 1856, married Sept. 8, 1883, LILLA H. OLIVER, daughter of John and Lavinia. He is a farmer in Stark.

NINTH GENERATION 505

Children of 9th Gen. b. in Stark, Me.
9597 BLANCHE L., b. Apl. 2, 1884, d. Feb. 13, 1894.
9598 CORA BELLE, b. March 9, 1887, m. Apl. 1909, VICTOR STAPLES of Kingfield, Me. He is connected with North Conway, N. H. Globe.

F6884 Hannah Caroline Locke, born in Stark, Me., Aug. 9, 1858, married Dec. 16, 1876, RUFUS JENNINGS of Industry, Me., son of Rufus and Hannah. He is a carpenter in Farmington, Me.

Children of 9th Gen. b. in Farmington, Me.
9599 GERTRUDE M., b. Sept. 13, 1877, m. Oct. 1895, J. ELMER WEYMOUTH, a carpenter in Farmington, Me.
9600 ALTON A., b. Feb. 19, 1892, d. Apl. 1, 1892.

F6886 Eugene Parker Locke, born in Stark, Me., Nov. 11, 1864, married July 3, 1887, CORA M. LEEMAN of New Sharon, Me., daughter of Charles and Mary. He is a mechanic in Farmington, Me.

Children of 9th Gen.
9601 EDITH M., b. Stark, Me., Jan. 13, 1888.
9602 CARLTON E., b. May 1890, d. March 1891.
9603 INFANT, b. 1898, d. 1898.

F6906 Lewis Osmond Pollard, born Dec. 13, 1860, married Apl. 3, 1884, JESSIE MAY HAZELTON.

Children of 9th Gen.
9604 ETHEL WINNIFRED, b. Aug. 27, 1889, m. HARRY PLANT of Providence R. I.
9605 FRANK LEWIS, b. June 15, 1891, m. ELLEN BELLEVANCE of Moosup, Can., and had: 9605a MARJORIE M., b. March 4, 1912.

F6949 Barry Locke, born in Lockeport, N. S., ——, married CATHERINE MCKAY.

Children of 9th Gen. b. in Lockeport, N. S.
9606 JOHN, b. ——. 9608 JOSEPHINE, b. ——.
9607 ANN, b. ——.

F6950 George Locke, born in Lockeport, N. S., ——, married JERUSHA THORNBURNE.

Children of 9th Gen. b. in Lockeport, N. S.
9609 FREDERICK, b. ——. 9611 LILLIAN, b. ——.
9610 WILLIAM, b. ——.

F6963 John Locke, born in Lockeport, N. S., married LETTIE HARDING.

Children of 9th Gen. b. in Lockeport, N. S.
9612 GEORGE, b. ——.
9613 HARRY, b. ——.
9614 ENOS, b. ——.
9615 LILLIAN, b. ——.
9616 ANN, b. ——.
9617 NELLIE, b. ——.

F6978 Howard Locke, born in Lockeport, N. S., ——, married SARAH BILL # 7036. Lived in Lockeport.

Children of 9th Gen. b. in Lockeport, N. S.
F9618 SIDNEY, b. 1861, m. JANETTE HAMMOND.
9619 GUERDON, b. ——.
9620 INGRAM, b. ——, is an M.D.
9621 CHARLES, b. ——.
9622 BRADFORD, b. ——.
9623 AUGUSTA, b. ——.
9624 FLORENCE, b. ——, died young.
9625 CORA, b. ——, died young.

F6980 Piers Locke, born in Lockeport, N. S., married MARY ALLEN.

Children of 9th Gen. b. in Lockeport, N. S.
9626 RALPH, b. ——.
9627 DAISY, b. ——.
9628 RUPERT, b. ——.
9629 MAGGIE, b. ——.
9630 WINNIE, b. ——.
9631 ALLEN, b. ——.
9632 JOSIE, b. ——.
9633 DOROTHY, b. ——.

F6981 Austin Locke, born in Lockeport, N. S., married ALICE TODD.

Children of 9th Gen. b. in Lockeport, N. S.
9634 THOMAS, b. ——.
9635 EDWIN, b. ——.
9636 HOWARD, b. ——.
9637 CYRIL, b. ——.

F6985 Churchill Locke, born in Lockeport, N. S., married Nov. 29, 1882, ELLEN A. MORTON, born Sept. 19, 1858, daughter of Charles E. and Salina (Freeman). They lived in Milton, Queens County, N. S.

Children of 9th Gen. b. in Lockeport, N. S.
9638 ENOS C., b. Oct. 30, 1883.
9639 EDITH, b. ——.
9640 ALENA, b. ——.

F6986 Allen K. Locke, born in Lockeport, N. S., married ANNIE PHILIPS.

Children of 9th Gen. b. in Lockeport, N. S.
9641 LILLIAN, b. ——.
9642 NELLIE, b. ——.
9643 BERTHA, b. ——, d. aged 5.
9644 JOSEPHINE, b. ——.
9645 LEWIS, b. ——, in 1899, was a Street R. R. employee, N. Y. City.
9646 WALTER, b. ——, in 1899 was in Boston.

NINTH GENERATION 507

F6990 Ellinor Locke, born in Lockeport, N. S., married June 12, 1872, ALLEN T. FREEMAN, born May 10, 1837, son of Allen and Mary (Bent). He was a lumber man in Milton, N. S.

Children of 9th Gen. b. in Lockeport, N. S.
9647 ELLEN, b. May 12, 1873.   9649 CHURCHILL L., b. Feb. 10, 1876.
9648 MARY B., b. Dec. 31, 1874.   9650 AUSTIN K., b. Jan. 2, 1878.

F7014 John Locke, born in Lockeport, N. S., married ELLEN TOWNER. He was Postmaster of Lockeport in 1899, and a West India trader.

Children of 9th Gen. b. in Lockeport, N. S.
9651 ARTHUR, b. ——, is m., a carpenter in Lockeport.
9652 MINNIE, b. ——, m. J. R. RUGGLES. She was a school teacher, he is a custom house officer Lockeport.
9653 EVA, b. ——.
9654 ELETIA, b. ——.

F7015 Henry Locke, born in Lockeport, N. S., married LOUISA CONDON and lived in Lockeport in 1899.

Children of 9th Gen. b. in Lockeport, N. S.
9655 WINNIE, b. ——.
9656 LOUIS, b. ——, in 1899 was in So. Africa.
9657 TRYPHENA, b. ——.

F7016 Frank Locke, born in Lockeport, N. S., married 1st, LOUISA KEMPTON; married 2nd, EMMA MCMILLEN. He was a dry goods merchant, Lockeport, in 1899.

Children of 9th Gen. b. in Lockeport, N. S.
9658 FREDERICK, b. ——, is a clerk in Lockeport.
9659 Two children by second wife.

F7017 Edwin Locke, born in Lockeport, N. S., married SOPHIA SNOW. He was in the clothing business, Lockeport in 1899.

Children of 9th Gen. b. in Lockeport, N. S.
9660 MURRAY, b. ——.   9662 ELLEN, b. ——.
9661 SAMUEL, b. ——.

F7022 Ellen Locke, born in Lockeport, N. S., Apl. 7, 1847, married Jan. 1, 1869, AMASA FISKE, born 1839. He was a merchant in Lockeport in 1899.

Children of 9th Gen. b. in Lockport, N. S.
9663 MARION, b. June 24, 1869, is in charge of W. U. Tel. Office, Lockeport, N. S.
9664 FRANK, b. Feb. 11, 1871, m. NELLIE SHINER, is a grocer, Charlestown, Mass.

9665 GRACE, b. Apl. 11, 1873.
9666 RALPH, b. July 6, 1875, d. aged 6.
9667 HARRY, b. Feb. 18, 1877, employed by C. L. Seabury Yacht Building Co., N. Y. City.
9668 EDWIN, b. Jan. 24, 1879.
9669 RUPERT, b. July 18, 1882.
9670 HELEN, b. Feb. 2, 1885.
9671 GLADYS, b. Jan. 15, 1887.
9672 JEAN, b. March 6, 1889.

F7024 Marion Locke, born —— in Lockeport, N. S., married GEORGE JAMIESON. He was a telegraph operator in Annapolis, N. S.

Children of 9th Gen.

9673 LEWIS, b. ——.
9674 GERTRUDE, b. ——.
9675 EDITH, b. ——, was in Boston, in 1899.
9676 PERCY, b. ——.
9677 DOUGLASS, b. ——.
9678 LENA, b. ——.

F7048 Amanda Muriel Locke, born Feb. 21, 1861, married, 1888, COLIN CAMPBELL KAY of New York, son of Daniel, and cousin of General Colin Campbell of Clydesdale, England.

Children of 9th Gen.

9679 COLIN CAMPBELL CLYDE, b. June 15, 1891, lives N. Y. City.
9680 DOUGLAS CLARENCE MORHAM, b. Sept. 12, 1895, d. at Bishops College School, Lenoxville, P. Q., March 15, 1913.

F7050 Jonathan Locke, born Sept. 13, 1864, married in 1892, BRENT ROBINSON of San Antonio, Texas.

Children of 9th Gen.

9681 ROGER, b. ——.
9682 JONATHAN, JR., b. ——.
9683 MIGNON, b. ——.
9684 COLIN CAMPBELL, b. ——.

F7054 Mabel Jean Locke, born Aug. 11, 1872, married in 1894, GEORGE JOHN TROOP, JR., of Halifax.

Children of 9th Gen.

9685 NORMAN EDWARD, b. ——.
9686 GEORGE JOHN, 3RD, b. ——, d. ——.
9687 MARGARET, b. ——.

F7055 Florence M. Locke, born Sept. 15, 1874, married in 1896, HENRY MARTIN BRADFORD, born in London, England. He received the degree of A.M. from St. Johns College, Cambridge, England and was once Head Master of Collegiate School in Halifax. He was a great grandson of Rev. Joseph Bradford, Secretary to Rev. John Wesley.

NINTH GENERATION

Children of 9th Gen.

9688 JOHN LOCKE, b. Apl. 1, 1897, employed by Royal Bank of Canada, at Windsor, N. S.
9689 ENA NOYES, b. Dec. 2, 1898, fatally burned, Aug. 21, 1904.
9690 MABEL JOYCE, b. March 21, 1905.

F7087 Emma Augusta Locke, born in Newport, R. I., March 4, 1837, married in Providence, R. I., Jan. 6, 1859, DUTEE WILCOX, born June 22, 1834.

Children of 9th Gen.

9691 EMMA LULU, b. Feb. 18, 1862, m. Oct. 19, 1880, GEORGE HARRISON FLINT of Providence, R. I., and had: 9692 HARVEY J., b. July 21, 1881; 9693 DUTEE W., b. Dec. 19, 1882; 9694 GEORGE H., b. July 17, 1888.
9695 GRACE MYRTLE, b. Feb. 17, 1866, m. in Providence, June 22, 1893, FREDERICK WM. DANFORTH of Buffalo, and had: 9696 EMMA L., b. Sept. 28, 1896; 9697 FREDERICK W., b. May 24, 1900.
9698 HOWARD D., b. Apl. 5, 1871, m. in Providence, Jan. 17, 1894, ANNA SPICER UTLEY, and had: 9699 MADELINE, b. Apl. 16, 1898.

F7090 Charles Henry Locke, born in Loudon, Apl. 8, 1833, married March 4, 1855, SARAH A. WILLOUGHBY, born in Holderness, Apl. 4, 1831, died in Lakeport, Oct. 31, 1902. He was a scene painter, principally of Biblical subjects, was a Minister in the Methodist Church, and lived in Lakeport. He enlisted in Co. F 12th N. H. Reg., was captured Nov. 17, 1864 and exchanged May 1865. He died in Lakeport, June 4, 1889.

Children of 9th Gen.

9700 CHARLES FREMONT, b. Gilford, June 28, 1856, m. in Gilford, Jan. 16, 1883, DELLA M. BEARD of Lake Village, b. Pembroke, May 12, 1858, dau. of Simon A. and Esther (Bagley). He was President of N. H. Soc. of Progress, a hardware merchant in Lakeport, tax collector and Sheriff of Belknap County. Had no children.
F9701 ALBERT VASCO, b. Feb. 5, 1862, m. June 30, 1885, LOTTIE M. BAILEY.
9702 JAMES B., b. Apl. 30, 1864, d. July 11, 1864.
9703 AI FORREST, b. March 10, 1868, m. Oct. 25, 1899, MRS. MABEL (EMORY) KIMBALL, b. Manchester, dau. of John D. and Susan A. He was a painter employed by B. & M. R. R. Concord, later was Foreman painter in Allegheny, Penn.

F7092 Andrew Diamond Locke, born in Gilmanton, Sept. 7, 1835, married in Loudon, Jan. 1, 1857, (the widow of Joel E. Cook) AMANDA M. (SANBORN) COOK, born in Loudon, Nov. 11, 1833, died in Pittsfield, Dec. 8, (1911?), daughter of Jeremiah and Ann. He was in Co. B 12th N. H. Reg., was wounded May 3, 1863, captured at Bermuda Hundred, Va., Nov. 17, 1864, and mustered out June 2, 1865. He lived at Loudon.

Children of 9th Gen.

9704 CHARLES A., b. Apl. 27, 1857, m. May 1879, LIZZIE DAVIS, b. March 2, 1861. (One record gives his wife as Lizzie Ingalls, dau. of Lovering.) He was a painter in Loudon and d. July 26, 1880; had no children. His widow m. 2nd, 1890, FRANK WELLS of Concord.

9705 FLORA E., b. Chichester, Oct. 6, 1858, d. Feb. 11, 1861.

9706 CLARA E., a twin, b. Oct. 6, 1858, d. Feb. 12, 1861.

F9707 IDA BELLE, b. Dec. 28, 1862, m. May 17, 1880, JEREMIAH L. FRENCH.

9708 JENNIE M., b. Gilmanton, March 20, 1865, d. Loudon, Nov. 6, 1895, m. Jan. 15, 1891, IRVING H. HATCH, b. Malden, Mass., 1850, son of Samuel and Sarah (Hanson). He is in the insurance business, had no children.

F9709 HENRY PEASLEE, b. Nov. 5, 1867, m. Apl. 4, 1886, JENNIE M. FOSS.

F9710 GEORGE ANDREW, b. Nov. 10, 1871, m. Dec. 28, 1893, DESDEMONA E. WOODS.

9711 MAMIE E., b. Loudon, June 15, 1876, m. 1st, OMAH YORK and was divorced. She m. 2nd, JOHN ABBOTT of Pittsfield, had: 9712 DORRIS MAE ABBOTT, b. June 8, 1911.

F7096 Elbridge Gerry Locke, born in Gilmanton, Apl. 30, 1841, married Apl. 20, 1867, SARAH C. REED, born in Prospect, Me., May 2, 1844, died in Lakeport, Dec. 24, 1905. He enlisted in Co. B 3rd N. H. Reg. He was a painter in Lakeport, where he died Aug. 2, 1887.

Children of 9th Gen. b. in Gilford.

9713 ARTHUR E., b. June 20, 1868, d. Apl. 4, 1871.

9714 ETHELYN R., b. March 6, 1874, d. Feb. 21, 1881.

9715 ELLA B., b. Sept. 21, 1877, d. March 10, 1881.

9716 GERRY REED, b. Dec. 28, 1885, was of Lakeport, later of Brockton, Mass., a traveling salesman.

F7097 Mary Elizabeth Locke, born in Gilmanton, Aug. 15, 1842, died in Meredith, Dec. 6, 1910, married March 4, 1861, JAMES ASA JONES, born in Gilmanton, May 17, 1824, son of James and Ruth (Hanson). They lived at Jones Mills, Gilmanton and he died March 17, 1901.

Children of 9th Gen. b. in Gilmanton.

9717 HAYDEN R., b. Dec. 30, 1861, d. June 6, 1864.

9718 ABBIE R., b. Jan. 11, 1862, d. May 16, 1864.

9719 ABBIE R., b. Feb. 12, 1865, d. Feb. 22, 1865.

9720 MYRA E., b. Feb. 1, 1866, m. Gilmanton, Jan. 4, 1888, SELDEN J. DAVIS, b. Springfield, 1864, son of Samuel and Edna A. (Pillsbury). He is a stagedriver in Gilmanton, had: 9721 EDNA ELIZABETH, b. Belmont, May 22, 1892; 9722 RUTH MARION, b. Aug. 24, 1894.

9723 ADDIE A., b. Dec. 15, 1867, m. Belmont, Sept. 8, 1888, JOHN C. BADGER of Belmont, b. Aug. 26, 1870, son of Joseph and Hannah (Ayer) and grandson of Governor Badger. He is a machinist by trade but has been a policeman in Manchester many years, had: 9724 ROLAND JAMES, b. Gilmanton, June 10, 1892.

NINTH GENERATION 511

9725 ALBERT H., b. Apl. 13, 1869, m. 1st, Feb. 18, 1894, JENNIE M. FLAN-
DERS who d. Dec. 28, 1902, dau. of Asahel G. and Lizzie; m. 2nd,
Sept. 24, 1904, LILLIAN E. BABBITT, b. Jamaica, Vt., dau. of John
and Ida M. He is a lumber dealer in Gilmanton, had: 9726 MARY
ELIZABETH, b. Belmont, May 23, 1906.
F9727 HARRIET F., b. Oct. 6, 1874, m. Nov. 10, 1894, FRANK A. CONVERSE.

F7098 Sarah Abbie Locke, born in Gilmanton, Dec. 20, 1845, married 1st, May 30, 1863, HENRY N. BLANCHARD of Wilton, whom she divorced; m. 2nd, Feb. 18, 1867, GEORGE WORTHINGTON of New Haven, Conn., born 1841, son of Thomas and Nancy (Hoyt). He was a carriage maker, lived in Concord, Ansonia, Conn., and Gilmanton, where he died May 31, 1898.

Children of 9th Gen. by Worthington.
9728 HARVEY J., b. Nov. 28, 1867, d. March 22, 1873.
9729 GEORGE T., b. Sept. 28, 1869, a bridge builder, lives Belmont.
9730 GRACE B., b. Aug. 3, 1878, lives Belmont.
9731 ETHEL M., b. July 18, 1883, lives Belmont.

F7133 Ann Lydia Locke, born in Epsom, July 28, 1839, died in Pembroke, Feb. 11, 1886, married in Epsom, May 16, 1860, WINTHROP FOWLER of Pembroke, born in Epsom, Jan. 20, 1827, son of Winthrop and Abigail (Davis). He lived in Pembroke; married 2nd, in 1890 OLIVE Z. HAINES, and died in Pembroke, Apl. 9, 1895.

Children of 9th Gen.
9732 MINOT L., b. Feb. 5, 1863, m. Sept. 23, 1895, MRS. MARY (BEATON) HARRISON of Greenville, b. 1863. He is a farmer in E. Pembroke, has no children.
9734 GEORGE W., b. Nov. 1, 1864, m. Jan. 17, 1888, ETTA BARTLETT, b. Suncook Feb. 11, 1862, dau. of John and Mary (Gordon). He graduated from Dartmouth, 1886, lives Pembroke, had: 9735 GEORGE S., b. Nov. 28, 1890.
9736 EDWARD M , b. Pembroke, Sept. 27, 1868, m. June 3, 1896, HARRIET A. EMERY, b. Suncook, June 20, 1867, dau. of J. N. and Martha E. (Hall). He lived at Suncook, had: 9737 MARTHA E., b. June 29, 1897.

F7138 Mary E. Wells, born Aug. 14, 1845, married Oct. 8, 1863, JAMES S. STRAW, born in Hill, July 15, 1842. They lived in Epsom.

Children of 9th Gen.
9739 ELLERY C., b. Apl. 10, 1866, m. Feb. 2, 1888, MAGGIE W. BERNARD, b. Prince Edward Island, Jan. 31, 1864, lives in Epsom, no children.
9740 LEOLA M., b. Sept. 27, 1867.

9741 LUCINDA S., b. Feb. 3, 1870, m. Oct. 16, 1894, GEORGE D. EMERSON, b. Alton, Feb. 18, 1872, lives Pittsfield, had: 9742 MILDRED E., b. Apl. 4, 1897.
9743 EDSON A., b. Apl. 24, 1872.
9744 OSCAR W., b. Apl. 26, 1878.

F7187 Joseph Smith, born Apl. 17, 1826, married Dec. 25, 1850, MARY E. NUTE, born 1831, daughter of Greenleaf and Sarah A. (Brock). He lived at Oyster River, Dover and died Nov. 25, 1871.

Children of 9th Gen. b. in Dover.

9745 IDA H., b. 1852, d. 1853.
9746 ADA BELLE, b. March 31, 1855, m. Apl. 15, 1886, DAVID FOSS, M.D., b. Aug. 30, 1837, lived Newburyport, and d. Dec. 2, 1911.
9747 FORREST S., b. June 30, 1857, m. Sept. 1, 1887, SARAH ADLA THOMPSON, b. Nov. 20, 1860.
F9748 WINNIFRED, b. June 1, 1861, m. Oct. 12, 1886, FREDERICK W. EMERY.

F7189 Samuel F. Perkins, born in Seabrook, June 25, 1859, married Feb. 16, 1882, MARY L. WALTON.

Children of 9th Gen.

9749 MARY ETHEL, b. May 22, 1883, m. ERNEST GOLDSMITH.
9750 BENJAMIN S., b. Apl. 23, 1886, m. CHRISTENA ROBINSON of Auburn, Me., had: 9751 SAMUEL L., b. Feb. 16, 1915, the 8th Gen. born on Perkins Land in Seabrook.
9752 SARAH M., b. Nov. 1, 1890, m. MARION PHELPS.
9753 CAROLYN, b. May 18, 1892.

F7197 Mary Isadore Merriam, born Sept. 11, 1853, married in Manchester, Oct. 5, 1879, HERMAN D. HAZEN of North Hebron, Vt. He was a cotton manufacturer in Manchester.

Children of 9th Gen.

9754 ROBERT DOUGLAS, b. Sept. 1, 1880, m. Sept. 8, 1900, MARY A. BAILEY of Lyme Center, had: 9755 SARAH LOUISE, b. Apl. 14, 1902.
9756 FREEMAN BRACKETT, b. Apl. 26, 1883.
9757 EDITH NAOMI, b. March 1, 1885, d. Aug. 19, 1885.
9758 BERNICE MERRIAM, b. Nov. 9, 1888.

F7205 Fred Howard Dow, born in Kensington, June 26, 1858, married in Kensington, Sept. 13, 1879, CLARA I. AUSTIN of Kensington. He was a shoecutter in Haverhill, Mass.

Children of 9th Gen.

9759 SARAH LOUISE, b. Kensington, Aug. 31, 1882, m. Ipswich, Mass., Apl. 26, 1905, CHESTER G. PERLEY, had: 9760 ELIZABETH, b. Feb. 15, 1906.
F9761 ETHEL AMANDA, b. Oct. 22, 1884, m. Oct. 26, 1904, OSCAR S. HUTCHINSON.

NINTH GENERATION 513

F7207 William Newell Dow, born twin, in Kensington, Jan. 2, 1862, married in Kensington, Dec. 9, 1884, HATTIE BROWN WEARE, born in Hampton Falls, Apl. 3, 1865, daughter of Jonathan and Irene S. (French). He is a shoemaker in Exeter, is a Prohibitionist and Adventist.
Children of 9th Gen.
9762 CHARLES FORREST, b. Kensington, Apl. 19, 1887, m. Merrimac, Mass., Oct. 17, 1910, VIOLA EMILY GROCUT.
9763 GEORGE WILLIAM, b. Jan. 19, 1889, d. March 10, 1891.
9764 HARVEY CHESTER, b. Exeter, June 10, 1893, d. Oct. 27, 1895.
9765 SADIE IRENA, b. Exeter, Sept. 14, 1895.
9766 CHESTER WEARE, b. Exeter, Aug. 23, 1897.
9767 NELLIE GERTRUDE, b. Kensington, Sept. 24, 1899.

F7208 Minnie Elizabeth Dow, born Nov. 8, 1865, married in Hampton Falls, June 27, 1887, CLARENCE EUGENE JANVRIN of Hampton Falls, who was in the meat business there and died July 3, 1913.
Child of 9th Gen.
9768 JAMES D. L., b. Sept. 25, 1889, m. Hampton Falls, Sept. 24, 1910, GLADYS LAWTON YOUNG, had: 9769 PHILIP E., b. Jan. 15, 1911; 9770 GORDON A., b. Sept. 24, 1912.

F7211 Charles Warren Locke, born in Salem, Mass., Nov. 23, 1856, married Oct. 6, 1881, ELIZABETH B. EDWARDS of Salem, born Feb. 28, 1857. He lives in Salem, and is employed as clerk in Atlas Webster Bank in Boston.
Children of 9th Gen. b. in Salem, Mass.
9771 MARY ELIZABETH, b. Aug. 12, 1882, m. AUGUSTUS DAIGNEAU, lived Salem.
9772 JOHN WARREN, b. Aug. 12, 1884, is a civil engineer in Texas.
9773 ALICE MERRILL, b. Dec. 14, 1887, is a teacher in Salem.

F7212 Frank Elmer Locke, born in Salem, Mass., June 16, 1860, married in Boston, Apl. 28, 1886, FLORENCE M. STODDARD of Boston, born Jan. 14, 1860. He is interested in real estate and insurance, Salem, Mass.
Children of 9th Gen.
F9774 HELEN FARRINGTON, b. March 28, 1887, m. EDWARD W. HALL.
9775 MARGARET b. Aug. 2, 1900.

F7213 Albert Edward Locke, born in Salem, Aug. 2, 1862, married 1st, in Hampton Falls, June 2, 1886, ELIZABETH M. HARDY of Hampton Falls, born June 13, 1863, died Feb. 2, 1890

33

married 2nd, Apl. 20, 1892, ANNIE M. HILL of York, Me. He is a stair builder in Salem. Elizabeth was a daughter of Charles A. and Abby.

Children of 9th Gen.
9775 EDNA, b. Salem, Nov. 26, 1893.
9776 MILTON HILL, b. June 30, 1895.
9777 ROGER PUTNAM, b. Dec. 14, 1904.

F7322 James Frederick Currier, born in River Falls, Wis., Feb. 13, 1859, married in Wisconsin, June 24, 1885, ABBIE M. PARKER, born Jan. 13, 1862. He was a farmer in South Dakota, later an orchardist in Saratoga, Cal.

Children of 9th Gen.
9778 FLORELLA G., b. River Falls, Wis., Apl. 13, 1886, lives Saratoga, Cal.
9779 RUTH L., b. Dec. 8, 1887, m. Saratoga, Cal., Sept. 12, 1913, PAUL W. MERRILL, lives Ann Arbor, Mich.
9780 DONALD LOCKE, b. Turton, S. D., Aug. 29, 1889, is a student at Leland Stanford University, Cal.
9781 FREDERICK M., b. July 26, 1891, is a mechanical engineer, San Francisco, Cal.
9782 GENEVA M., b. May 10, 1893, is a student at State Normal School and lives Saratoga, Cal.

F7323 Mary Louise Currier, born Dec. 6, 1861, married Nov. 15, 1883, VICTOR E. BAILEY of Prescott, Wis., born Aug. 17, 1859. He is a farmer in Prescott and River Falls, Wis.

Child of 9th Gen. b. in Prescott, Wis.
9783 FLOYD DOUGLAS, b. Apl. 18, 1887, m. Oct. 1, 1913, ALICE HUTCHINSON of River Falls, Wis. He is Plant Pathologist at State Agricultural College, Corvallis, Oregon, had son: 9784 WARREN H., b. Corvallis, July 28, 1914.

F7327 Lillian F. Locke, born in Stanstead, Can., Aug. 24, 1868, married Oct. 8, 1892, HORACE STEERE, born in Sherbrooke, Canada, Aug. 1, 1868, lived in Waterville, Conn.

Children of 9th Gen.
9785 G. IRVING, b. Sherbrook, Can., Aug. 9, 1893.
9786 LOUISA, b. Waterbury, Conn., June 8, 1896.
9787 MARTINA, b. Stanstead, Can. June 29, 1897.
9788 PAUL LOCKE, b. Sept. 5, 1900.
9789 HELEN, b. June 14, 1903.
9790 TIRZA WARNER, b. Nov. 29, 1904.

F7357 Homer E. Bullard, born Nov. 18, 1869, married Nov. 14, 1888, EMMA M. HARDY. He was an overseer in a Magog P. Q., cotton mill, and died there March 7, 1897. His widow remarried.

NINTH GENERATION

Children of 9th Gen.
9791 EVA G., b. June 10, 1889.
9792 CHARLES P., b. Oct. 28, 1890, d. May 10, 1901.
9793 ERNEST G., b. Oct. 4, 1893, d. July 28, 1894.
9794 ARTHUR L., b. May 18, 1896, d. Aug. 22, 1896.

F7389 Emalina Modeste Breaux, born in New Orleans, June 11, 1857, married in New Orleans, Apl. 24, 1878, CHARLES THURSTON BALLARD, born June 3, 1850. He is a flour manufacturer in St. Louis, Mo. Lives in Glen View, Ky.

Children of 9th Gen. b. in Louisville, Ky.
F9795 ABBY CHURCHILL, b. Feb. 16, 1879, m. June 1, 1899, JEFFERSON DAVIS STEWART.
9796 EMILIE LOCKE, b. Sept. 18, 1880, d. Dec. 10, 1886.
9797 MARY THURSTON, b. Nov. 25, 1882, d. Feb. 5, 1884.
9798 CHARLES M., b. Nov. 28, 1886.
9799 GUS BREAUX, b. Oct. 7, 1888, m. South Bend, Ind., Sept. 27, 1913, MARY JANE FISH, had: 9800 MARY JANE, b. March 13, 1915.
9801 FANNY THURSTON, b. Apl. 29, 1890, m. Glen View, Ky., Aug. 30, 1912, CHARLES HORNER.
9802 CHURCHILL, a twin, b. Apl. 29, 1890, d. Feb. 12, 1892.
9803 MINA, b. July 13, 1893, m. Glen View, Ky., June 6, 1914, WARNER LAVALLE JONES.

F7390 Samuel Locke Breaux, born in New Orleans, Feb. 13, 1860, married 1st, Apl. 5, 1885, NINA WILLIAMS, who died Nov. 13, 1892; married 2nd, Apl. 19, 1894, NINA ROGERS. He was an influential and highly respected citizen of New Orleans, a rice and cotton broker; has been president of the Board of Trade, and declined the mayoralty of the city.

Child of 9th Gen. b. in New Orleans.
9804 SAMUEL LOCKE BREAUX, 2ND, b. Apl. 21, 1886, m. ——— ———, had: 9805 NINA, b. June 5, 1910; 9806 EDNA GRACE, b. Sept. 25, 1912; 9807 MINA BALLARD, b. Jan. 3, 1915.

F7466 John F. Clarke, born in Valley Falls, N. Y., Feb. 7, 1854, married June 19, 1877, CARRIE JENKS of Pawtucket, R. I.

Children of 9th Gen.
9808 LUCY, b. Apl. 21, 1878.
9809 LOUISE, b. Apl. 14, 1882.
9810 CARMELLITA, b. Dec. 16, 1883.
9811 JOHN L., b. Aug. 2, 1887.
9812 WADE, b. July 15, 1891.

F7476 Jim E. Locke, born in Seabrook, Sept. 6, 1877, married in Hampton, Nov. 11, 1897, IDA S. MILLER, born in Lawrence, Mass., July 18, 1880, daughter of Charles R. and Elvira M. He was a grocer in Seabrook.

Children of 9th Gen. b. in Seabrook.
9813 SARAH ELIZABETH, b. Jan. 27, 1898, d. Jan. 5, 1899.
9814 MARY, b. March 3, 1900.
9815 ALBERTINA, b. March 1, 1903.
9816 JOHN W., b. Dec. 16, 1905.
9817 RINDA, b. July 5, 1906.
9818 OLIVE, b. Aug. 28, 1907.
9819 EDWIN FRANKLIN, b. Dec. 16, 1912.

F7477 Nancy L. Gove, born Dec. 18, 1840, died Oct. 1883, married CHARLES PERKINS of Hampton, and lived in Newburyport.

Children of 9th Gen.
9820 LILLIAN, b. ——, m. JAMES DOW.
9821 FLORA, b. ——, m. —— LOVELACE, had: 9822 VIOLET who m. —— CHICK; and 9823 FLORA.
9824 MYRTIE, b. ——.
9825 CLARA, b. ——.

F7511 Willie M. Locke, born in Seabrook, May 5, 1878, married in Seabrook, Sept. 19, 1899, BERTHA ROWE, born in Seabrook, 1881, daughter of Jeremiah and Mary L. He is a shoemaker in Seabrook.

Children of 9th Gen.
9827 CHARLES, b. Apl. 12, 1900.
9828 GLADYS B., b. Seabrook, March 27, 1904.
9829 MARY L., b.——.
9830 RAYMOND, b. ——.

F7574 George E. Locke, born in Barnstead, Sept. 9, 1872, married in Alton, Sept. 16, 1897, MABEL F. KELLY, born in Gilmanton, May 19, 1878, daughter of George F. and Frances H. He is a farmer and dealer in dressed lumber in North Barnstead.

Children of 9th Gen. b. in Barnstead.
9831 JAMES STERLING, b. July 16, 1898.
9832 MARJORIE, b. June 12, 1900.
9833 MARGARET, twin, b. June 12, 1900.

F7586 Ellen Jane Cass, born Nov. 26, 1845, died June 1, 1893, married May 27, 1865, HENRY GRIFFITH, born Sept. 1, 1844, a miller of Bristol. He married 2nd, MRS. MARY MARSHALL.

Children of 9th Gen. b. in Bristol.
9834 LINNIE M., b. July 9, 1867, m. Jan. 20, 1884, CLARENCE O. SMITH, b. Feb. 18, 1867. He was a blacksmith, had: 9835 ROY R., b. 1884.
9836 NORA VIOLA, b. Jan. 31, 1870, m. March 23, 1890, JOHN A. FAVOR, b. March 15, 1862. He is in the livery business, had: 9837 CORINNE, b. 1895.

NINTH GENERATION

F7589 Sarah Augusta Cass, born Dec. 30, 1855, married OTIS F. CROSS of Bristol, Nov. 2, 1872, born July 15, 1850. He was an operator in a woolen mill.

Children of 9th Gen.
9838 UNA ESTELLE, b. Aug. 13, 1873, m. Nov. 28, 1900, PROF. HENRY W. BROWN, Vice Pres. N. H. Literary Institute, She was teacher of music there. They had: 9839 MARION D., b. 1903.
9840 OTIS EARL, b. May 28, 1877.

F7593 Mary Ann Locke, born in Bristol, Sept. 21, 1850, married Feb. 12, 1869, BURLEY M. AMES, born March 8, 1848, son of James and Abigail (Bachelder). He was an ice dealer, paper maker, and Vice President of Bristol Bank.

Children of 9th Gen.
9841 ALETA ELFRA, b. Bristol, Feb. 27, 1872, m. May 30, 1888, NATHAN P. SMITH, b. Bridgewater, July 5, 1863, son of Phineas and S. (Covell). He is a farmer in Bridgewater, had: 9842 ABBIE SOPHRONIA, b. May 12, 1889.
9843 ETHEL WINNIFRED, b. Nov. 17, 1879, m. Jan. 19, 1895, CHARLES E. SPENCER, b. Plymouth, Sept. 20, 1865, son of Charles and Emily (Eaton). He is a teamster and farmer in Bristol and Bridgewater.

F7595 Ada Marie Locke, born in Bristol, Aug. 13, 1869, married in Bristol, Jan. 1, 1891, REV. FRANCIS D. GEORGE, born in New Sharon, Me., Feb. 7, 1857, son of David and Sarah L. (Webster). She was his second wife. He graduated from Bates College in 1878, has been located in Gardner, Me., Worcester, Mass., and Bedford.

Children of 9th Gen.
9844 EDITH ADALINE, b. Worcester, Oct. 23, 1891.
9845 HELEN LOUISE, b. Lowell, Dec. 28, 1892.
9846 FRANCES MARIE, b. Gardner, Me., Nov. 25, 1895.
9847 CAROLYN EMMA, b. Gardner, Apl. 21, 1899.
9848 LLOYD FAVOUR, b. Bedford, June 13, 1912.

F7689 John Locke Heath, born in Barnston, Can., Jan. 11, 1876, married Dec. 22, 1897, WINNIE MARY HILL, born in Barnston, June 21, 1873.

Children of 9th Gen.
9849 KATHLEEN LORRAINE, b. Barnston, Can., Sept. 16, 1899.
9850 MURIEL CLARE, b. Stanstead, Can., Oct. 25, 1904.
9851 MARY LIZZIE, b. Barnston.

F7701 John L. Tredick, born in New Castle, Dec. 13, 1854, married in Boston, Nov. 1, 1886, JULIA FORD of Portsmouth, born in Ireland, 1860. He was a shoemaker in New Castle and died there June 10, 1910.

Children of 9th Gen.
9852 ANN E., b. New Castle, June 9, 1887.
9853 GEORGE A., b. N. C. March 31, 1889.
9854 MARY, b. Aug. 16, 1892.
9855 AGNES, b. Portsmouth, Sept. 11, 1895.
9856 GERTRUDE C., b. March 3, 1897.

F7712 Helen W. Locke, born Jan. 23, 1860, married June 7, 1883, JAMES D. P. WINGATE of Exeter, born Apl. 2, 1855, son of Samuel and Orianna (Mitchell).

Children of 9th Gen. b. in Exeter.
9857 HELEN, b. May 25, 1885, m. May 19, 1908, CHESTER B. KELLEY of Winchester, Mass., son of Anthony.
9858 DOROTHY, b. Apl. 12, 1896.

F7725 Charles Samuel Tucker, born Dec. 11, 1842, married NELLIE HUBBARD, born in Portsmouth, July 12, 1843, died July 16, 1879, at South Framingham, Mass., where they lived. He died in Valley Falls, R. I., Dec. 1892.

Child of 9th Gen. b. in Portsmouth.
9859 EDITH VIOLA, b. Oct. 8, 1865, m. Framingham, Mass., Apl. 26, 1893, JAMES F. HIGGINS, b. Amesbury, June 27, 1866, now a drummer in Framingham, had: 9860 RUTH T., b. 1895; 9861 WILLIAM C., b. 1894.

F7730 James Neal, born Apl. 1, 1833, married 1st, Oct. 1856, LUCY A. GREEN, born in New Castle, May 16, 1835, died June 2, 1872; married 2nd, LIZZIE GALUSHA of Lynn, born Feb. 1857. He is a shoemaker in Lynn.

Children of 9th Gen. b. in Lynn.
9862 MARY B., b. July 5, 1857, m. Apl. 30, 1896, ALBERT W. HANSCOM of New Castle, b. Eliot, Me., July 24, 1842. She was his 3rd wife. He was a carpenter in N. C., had no children.
9863 CHARLIE M., b. 1863, d. aged 10 mos.
9864 ADDIE M., b. 1868, d. aged 2 mos.
9865 WALTER A., b. 1872, d. aged 8 weeks.
By second wife:
9866 WILLIE, b. Aug. 1882.
9867 EMMA, b. 1884.

F7732 Olive Locke Neal, born Oct. 27, 1842, married Jan. 30, 1864, FRANCIS W. DANA, lived in Everett, Mass.

Children of 9th Gen.
9868 SUSIE b. ——, m. WILLIAM MAYO, lives in Everett, Mass.
9869 FRANK, b. ——.   9971 ERNEST, b. ——.
9870 GEORGE, b. ——.   9872 ESTHER, b. ——.

9873 MAMIE, b. ——, m. ALVAH H. M. CURTIS, b. New Castle, Jan. 20, 1871, graduated Dartmouth College 1894, and for many years principal of a school in Manchester. 9874 Have twin sons, HERMAN and BALLARD.

F7739 Mary Ann Batson, born Nov. 2, 1836, died Dec. 1, 1898, married Nov. 1, 1853, ELIAS TARLTON, born Dec. 30, 1826. lived at New Castle.

Children of 9th Gen. b. in New Castle.

9875 FLORENCE E., b. Oct. 28, 1855, d. March 19, 1863.
9876 ELIAS, b. Dec. 26, 1856, m. Nov. 1, 1883, CARRIE POOLE, b. Shoals, 1863. He is in U. S. Life Saving Service, had: 9877 EVALINE L., b. 1882; 9878 ELIAS C., b. 1893.
9879 ABBIE C., b. June 5, 1858, d. Aug. 25, 1858.
9880 FRANCIS S., b. Sept. 5, 1861, d. Sept. 25, 1861.
9881 WILLIAM M., b. March 30, 1868, m. Aug. 2, 1890, CARRIE E. HALL of Portsmouth, b. 1873; in the express business in Portsmouth.

F7745 Clarenda Batson, born Sept. 17, 1846, died 1898, married 1st, FRANK WEST, a soldier at New Castle; married 2nd, Nov. 25, 1866, CHARLES PETTIGREW, born 1836.

Children of 9th Gen.

9882 FRANK H. WEST, b. Oct. 2, 1865, m. Aug. 26, 1895, ELIZABETH M. FOSTER, b. Portsmouth, 1868. He was a policeman in Portsmouth, had no children, and died June 9, 1916.
9883 LOULA PETTIGREW, b. ——, m. DR. ALBERT YORK.
9884 MARY B. PETTIGREW, b. ——, d. ——.

F7746 Harriet H. Batson, born May 6, 1849, died in Farmington, Oct. 4, 1877, married THOMAS HEYWOOD, a hotel keeper in Boston and New Castle, who for a second wife married DOLLY AMAZEEN.

Children of 9th Gen.

9885 IRVING, b. ——, m. JENNIE WILLIAMS of New Castle. He is a clerk at U. S. Navy Yard, had: 9886 GLADYS, m. July 24, 1909, QUENTIN J. BARKER son of Peter and Mary of Canada, and she had: MARY H. b. June 14, 1910; WILLIAM H. b. Sept. 30, 1914.
9887 EVA, b. ——, died young.

F7759 Andrew J. Trefethern, born 1852, married 1870, ISABELLE TOWNSEND of Portsmouth. He was a barber in Pawtucket, R. I. and died there Oct. 18, 1905.

Children of 9th Gen. as given me.

9888 BESSIE, b. ——, m. LEROY P. STONE, lives in Lakewood.
9889 FLORENCE, b. Portsmouth, Jan. 8, 1878, m. FRANK W. ELLIOTT, lives in Providence, R. I.

9890 THADDEUS, b. May 27, 1876, d. 1878.
9891 RAYMOND, b. ——.   9892 HELEN, b. ——.
9893 DAISY P., b. Aug. 23, 1872, d. 1873.

F7760 Franklin D. Locke, born in Portsmouth, 1865, married NELLIE J. BOUCHER, born in South Berwick in 1862. He was a shoemaker in Dover, Portsmouth and Rollingsford.

Children of 9th Gen.

9894 EVA STELLA, b. ROLLINGSFORD, Aug. 27, 1892, m. Portsmouth, Sept. 26, 1910, SYDNEY SULTZBACK, b. Philadelphia, 1887; a sailor in U. S. Navy.
9895 FRANCES ADALINE (3rd Child), b. Portsmouth, July 23, 1895.

F7762 Emma O. Philbrick, born in Rye, Nov. 20, 1851, married Jan. 3, 1869, JACOB A. MOULTON, born in 1841, a mason of North Hampton, who died Jan. 10, 1901. She died Oct. 24, 1915 in Rye.

Children of 9th Gen.

9896 EDITH, b. Dec. 3, 1870, m. Sept. 29, 1896, BYRON J. JENNESS of Portsmouth, b. Suncook, Feb. 16, 1870.
9897 ALBERT, b. June 22, 1872, d. June 19, 1873.
9898 HARRY T., b. July 25, 1873, m. Oct. 13, 1899 MABEL F. ABBOTT of Portsmouth, b. Aug. 8, 1880, had; 9899 LEORA I., b. May 12, 1903; 9900 DORIS J., b. March 6, 1908.
9901 PERCY A., b. July 23, 1886, m. Rye Beach, Oct. 1, 1914, ETHEL MAY SPAULDING of Rumney, dau. of Charles. He is Managing Editor Portsmouth *Times*.

F7763 William I. Philbrick, born in Rye, Nov. 13, 1855, married 1st, Oct. 22, 1874, ARVILLA S. JUNKINS of Kittery, Me. He was divorced and married 2nd, in Lynn, July 29, 1882, LIZZIE BREED, born Nov. 15, 1859. He was a shoemaker in Portsmouth.

Children of 9th Gen.

9902 WILLIAM R., b. Nov. 18, 1883.
9903 MADELINE O., b. June 17, 1885, m. June 17, 1910, FRED D. WHITTAKER of Worcester.
9904 SADIE E., b. Feb. 28, 1887, m. 1909, RAFAELE VICTOR VEGA of Havana, Cuba, had: SON.
9905 MARIAN C., b. Dec. 14, 1888, m. June 28, 1911, DOUGLAS LEIGHTON KEYS of San Francisco, had: 9906 CONSTANCE NADINE, b. March 29, 1912.

F7764 Herbert E. Philbrick, born in Rye, June 28, 1858, married Dec. 1880, IDA F. MARDEN, born Feb. 3, 1857, daughter of Charles and Mrs. Mary (Garland).

NINTH GENERATION 521

Children of 9th Gen.
9907 RAYMOND, b. Sept. 14, 1884, m. 1908, CECIL PREBLE of Providence, had: 9908 GERALDINE, b. June 10, 1910; 9909 KENNETH R., b. March 4, 1912.
9910 GUY, b. Aug. 9, 1889.
9911 MARGARITE, b. May 26, 1898.

F7765 Ida F. Philbrick, born in Rye, Oct. 30, 1863 married June 19, 1884, GEORGE FRED BREED, born in Lynn, July 31, 1856. He was a bookkeeper in Portsmouth and later in Brooklyn, N. Y. where he died Oct. 12, 1914.

Children of 9th Gen.
9912 BERNICE, b. March 15, 1885, m. Arlington, N. J., June 6, 1908, CHARLES N. STANLEY, b. Concord, now a salesman in N. Y. City, had: 9913 VIRGINIA B.; 9914 CHARLES NELSON.
9915 EDITH F., b. Dec. 17, 1888, m. Portsmouth, June 30, 1909, OLIVER B. KESSLER, had: 9916 VERNA, b. Feb. 1910.
9917 ETHEL I., b. Sept. 17, 1890.

F7773 Thaddeus W. Locke, born in Portsmouth, Oct. 21, 1861, married 1st, FLORA COBB of Portsmouth, who died; married 2nd, Oct. 19, 1888, KATHERINE J. SULLIVAN of Manchester and they were divorced in Jan. 1901. She married JAMES MARR. Thaddeus married, 3rd, ELLEN MARTIN born in Newfoundland 1883, and they were divorced in 1909, when she married SAMUEL C. MARSHALL, a Yeoman in U. S. Navy. She died May 11, 1916. Thaddeus was a barber in Portsmouth and died there Jan. 3, 1910.

Children of 9th Gen. by third wife.
9918 FLORA E., b. Aug. 18, 1903, in Portsmouth.
9918aHELEN, b. Oct. 3, 1904, d. infancy.
9918bTHADDEUS, b. Feb. 13, 1906, was adopted by party unknown.
9918cERNEST, b. Feb. 3, 1907.

F7776 Clara Locke, born in Portsmouth, Apl. 30, 1866, married May 25, 1885, THOMAS G. B. MOULTON, born 1860, son of Thomas. He had a first wife, EVA DREW, is now a teamster in Portsmouth.

Children of 9th Gen. b. in Portsmouth.
9919 THOMAS F., b. Apl. 24, 1886, m. 1909, ALICE MANNETT of Ports., is an electric car conductor, had: 9919a DORIS, b. 1910.
9920 CLARA M., b. Aug. 15, 1888, m. 1907, AUGUSTUS FINNIGAN, a clerk in Boston Post Office, had: 9920a ARTHUR A., b. 1908; 9920b FREDERICK, b. 1910.

F7780 Frederick G. Locke, born in Portsmouth, Nov. 26, 1873, married there July 22, 1893, FANNIE MARTIN of Newfoundland, b. Apl. 14, 1876, d. March 1915, the daughter of James and Martha. He is a shoemaker in Manchester.
  Children of 9th Gen. the first four b. in Portsmouth.
9921 HELEN EDWINIE, b. Feb. 2, 1894, m. 1909, GEORGE HANNON of Boston, had: 9921a GEORGE, b. Apl. 1910; 9921b ELEANOR, b. 1912.
9922 HOWARD JOSEPH, b. June 8, 1895, m. ——.
9922a CLARA AUGUSTA, b. Nov. 25, 1897, d. March 1916, Everett, Mass.
9922b MABEL PRISCILLA, b. Jan. 18, 1900.   9922d JENNIE, b. 1908.
9922c FRED, b. Exeter, Jan. 11, 1904.   9922e MARGIE, b. 1912.

F7785 Norman W. Lord, born 1852, married Nov. 8, 1872, MARY ANN TOWNSEND of Portsmouth, lived in Portsmouth and died Apl. 26, 1913.
  Children of 9th Gen.
9923 NORMAN, b. March 1873.
9924 GRACE A., b. July 25, 1875, m. July 4, 1895, FRED LEACH of Portsmouth, has a daughter.

F7786 Anna Lord, born Apl. 1854, married 1st, May 9, 1872, LIEUTENANT THOMAS P. MOONEY, U. S. Navy; married 2nd, EDWIN D. ACKERMAN, born 1855, died Apl. 3, 1882, an expressman; married 3rd, VALENTINE HETT.
  Children of 9th Gen. b. in Portsmouth.
9925 GEORGE (MOONEY) was brought up by his grandmother Lord and took her name.
9926 HARRY ACKERMAN, b. Sept. 28, 1875, d. Jan. 26, 1876.
9927 JAMES ARTHUR ACKERMAN, b. Feb. 18, 1878, m. Rye, March 4, 1899, ETTA F. COLBY of Boston, b. 1878. He is a R. R. Employee.
9928 FRED D. HETT, b. Dec. 22, 1885.
9929 MARION O., b. June 9, 1889.
9930 GRETCHEN A., b. Aug. 2, 1891, m. 1916, —— ——.

F7787 Horace W. Batson, born in New Castle, Nov. 4, 1840, married July 3, 1867, ELLEN TARLTON of New Castle, born Jan. 20, 1844. He enlisted Aug. 12, 1862 on U. S. Ship "Whitehead," was discharged Aug. 15, 1863. He was a shoe cutter in Boston and died in Allston, March 13, 1897.
  Children of 9th Gen. b. in Danvers, Mass.
9931 WALTER, b. July 20, 1872, is a consulting Electrical Engineer.
9932 ARTHUR, b. Nov. 30, 1874, m. ETHEL GODFREY. He is a commission merchant.
9933 ROLAND, b. Watertown, July 1, 1884, m. EMMA LITTLEFIELD. He is a gymnasium instructor.

NINTH GENERATION 523

F7788 Lewis C. Batson, born in New Castle, Dec. 22, 1842, married 1st, Oct. 21, 1873, ADA KENT of Worcester, Mass., born Oct. 26, 1855, died Dec. 1897; married 2nd, July 22, 1899, CAROLINE COLE. He was foreman in Pond's Machine shops in Plainfield, N. J., for 30 years. He retired, lived in Clinton, N. J., was Mayor in 1906, and died March 1916.
Child of 9th Gen.
9934 FRANK, b. Worcester, March 7, 1877, m. Nov. 18, 1914, HULDAH H. HOIRNER. He was in South America several years, now connected with National Cash Register Co., Dayton, Ohio, in the foreign department.

F7792 Annie Batson, born in New Castle, June 23, 1850, married Sept. 10, 1874, JACOB MARSTON, born in Parsonsville, Me., March 15, 1847, son of Jacob and Martha (Doe). He is in the express business in Danvers, Mass.
Children of 9th Gen. b. in Danvers, Mass.
9935 CHARLOTTE PAULINE, b. Dec. 5, 1881, m. Danvers, Oct. 21, 1911, JOHN HANCOCK DOWDELL, had: 9936 MURIEL C., b. May 21, 1913.
9937 GRACE BERNICE, b. Feb. 21, 1895, m in Danvers, June 3, 1916, DR. CLIFTON L. BUCK.

F7795 Elizabeth Batson, born in New Castle, Nov. 9, 1845, married in Portsmouth, Dec. 28, 1865, DANIEL S. YOUNG of Augusta, Me., born Dec. 7, 1840, son of Rev. David and Hannah (Hodgdon). He is a farmer and quarryman in Augusta, Me.
Children of 9th Gen.
9938 MELVIN STEWART, b. New Castle, May 7, 1866, d. Augusta, May 14, 1868.
9939 ANNIE ELIZABETH, b. Augusta, Me., March 15, 1868, m. Portsmouth, June 27, 1897, BENJAMIN F. LIBBEY of Saugus, Me., b. Canada, 1863, son of William P. and Elizabeth. Had: 9940 MAURICE Y., b. May 12, 1900, d ; 9941 DANIEL GILBERT, b. May 26, 1904; 9942 FLORENCE ELIZABETH, b. June 8, 1906. He is a baker in Gardner, Me.
9943 MAY HANNAH, b. Jan. 27, 1870, d. unmarried Feb. 13, 1893.
9944 DANIEL STEWART, b. May 16, 1872, d. Aug. 16, 1872.
9945 LESLIE STEWART, b. March 15, 1874, m. Oct. 25, 1899, ALICE M. ROBBINS, and had: 9946 MAYNARD R., b. Nov. 25, 1900; 9947 RAYMOND L., b. Jan. 14, 1903, d.; 9948 OLIVER P., b. Feb. 17, 1905; 9949 CARROLL E., b. May 22, 1906. He is a grocer in Augusta.
9950 FRANK OLIVER, b. Dec. 25, 1876, m. March 6, 1905, ADA M. TRASK. He is manager of a Lumber Co. in Eltopia, Wash., and had: 9951 FRANCIS, b. Dec. 4, 1906 who died.

9952 FLORENCE AUGUSTA, b. Apl. 16, 1879, m. July 18, 1907, FRANK B. FISH, manager of a Piano Company in Bangor, Me.
9953 ADDIE C. B., b. Oct. 28, 1881, d. unmarried 1901.
9954 MARGIE, b. twin, Oct. 28, 1881, died young.
9955 DANIEL STEWART, JR., b. June 4, 1884, m. March 5, 1902, MAUD F. WOODBURY. He is manager of a hardware company in Augusta, and had: 9956 IDA MURIEL, b. Oct. 10, 1903.

F7796 Benjamin Jenkins Batson, born in New Castle, Aug. 13, 1849, married Lowell, July 2, 1880, ELIZABETH IRENE HAMMOND of Princeton, Me., born Alexandria, Me., Oct. 7, 1855, died March 1913. He was a mason in Dorchester, Mass., and died there Apl. 21, 1915, buried in New Castle.

Children of 9th Gen.

9957 HATTIE HAMMOND, b. Lowell, Oct. 1, 1882, a successful teacher in Boston schools.
9958 BENJAMIN JENKINS, b. Haverhill, Mass., Aug. 31, 1884, m. Dorchester, Mass., June 1, 1914, EVA GERTRUDE VEASEY.

F7799 Jessie Fremont Batson, born in New Castle, Nov. 10, 1856, died in New Castle, June 19, 1899, married in New Castle, Dec. 11, 1881, CHARLES BENJ. AMAZEEN, born in New Castle, June 3, 1856, son of Benjamin. He is a moulder on Portsmouth Navy Yard and married 2nd, MARGIE HUTCHINGS.

Children of 9th Gen. b. in New Castle.

F9959 MARTHA ANN, b. July 3, 1882, m. CHESTER BECKER May 16, 1901.
9960 ORVILLE CHAPMAN, b. Jan. 16, 1884.

F7802 Langdon Elvin Locke, born in Portsmouth, July 1, 1851, married in Portsmouth, Jan. 3, 1876, IDA LANE of Portsmouth, born June 18, 1856, daughter of William F. and Ann (Shannon). Not satisfied with the outlook for success in Portsmouth, he very early went to Boston where he learned the mason's trade. At 24 he was in charge of the erection of one of the first big mills of Dover, at 27 was building the State Prison at Concord, and from that time until now he has kept on in the same line. Employing at times eleven hundred artizans and with building contracts of two and one half million dollars, he has erected many of the largest mills in Lawrence. He is a bank director, director in several Lawrence corporations, and owns much valuable property there. He is held in the highest esteem by the citizens but has declined all political favors. With very large means he might retire, but the habit of doing big things will

Langdon Elvin Locke F7802

not allow an active body and brain to become rusty, so his delight is still in action.

Child of 9th Gen.

F9961 FITZ HARRY, b. March 21, 1888, m. 1910, CLARA JOSEPHINE CRAWFORD.

F7803 Wilbur Jesse Locke, born in Portsmouth, Dec. 10, 1853, married Dec. 10, 1883, ANNA TROW of Sunapee, born Dec. 10, 1860. For many years he acted as foreman for his brother in his building operations in Lawrence, but is now incapacitated for work.

Children of 9th Gen. b. in Lawrence, Mass.

9962 LOUISE JANE, b. July 10, 1885, m. Methuen, Mass., June 6, 1911, LUTHER ROBBINS HARRIS. He is in the insurance business, with home in Lawrence; had: 9963 daughter, HONOR.
9964 WARREN A., b. March 4, 1887, d. March 8, 1887.
9965 WILBUR TROW, b. July 30, 1894, a student at Amherst College.

F7812 Annie J. Locke, born in Concord, Dec. 12, 1862, married March 31, 1880, ALBERT G. SMITH, born in Antrim, Dec. 18, 1858, son of David A. and Lydia (Gray). He was a printer on Concord *Monitor* many years, is now pressman in U. S. Government Printing Office, Washington, D. C.

Children of 9th Gen. b. in Concord.

9966 ARTHUR H. L., b. July 13, 1885, m. Jan. 7, 1914, MARTHA LOUISE BURNS, b. San Francisco, Aug. 14, 1893. He is a captain in U. S. Marine Corps, with home in Washington, D. C.
9967 EDWARD G., b. Nov. 6, 1892, d. Nov. 8, 1892.
9968 EDGAR F., twin, b. Nov. 6, 1892, d. Nov. 9, 1892.
9969 LILLIAN MARTHA, b. Jan. 4, 1899, in 1916 is a student at Washington College for girls.

F7813 Lillian A. Locke, born in Concord, Jan. 4, 1872, married 1894, FRED R. ROACH, born in Bennington, Vt., son of J. P. W. and Lucy M. (Martin). He was foreman painter in Concord, is now employed by B. and M. R. R. at Lowell.

Children of 9th Gen. b. in Concord.

9970 GLADYS MARIE, b. Aug. 15, 1895.
9971 WILLIAM AMOS, b. May 2, 1897, d. Nov. 4, 1897.
9972 BERTHA IRENE, b. June 9, 1898.
9973 ALBERT FRED, b. Feb. 14, 1900.
9974 ANNIE BELLE, b. Jan. 8, 1903.
9975 LOUISE MARGUERITE, b. Nov. 28, 1904.
9976 LUCY MARTIN, b. Oct. 25, 1906, d. Dec. 5, 1906.
9977 ARTHUR LOCKE, b. Nov. 22, 1907.
9978 MARTHA ADELE, b. Aug. 9, 1911.

F7814 Amos Revilo Locke, born in Portsmouth, May 26, 1858, married 1st, in Portsmouth, Nov. 9, 1885, ELLA T. CURTIS, daughter of Howard M. and Lucretia (Bickford) of New Castle. They were divorced and he married 2nd, in Portsmouth, Oct. 16, 1900, FLORENCE A. MCLEAN, born in Baddeck, N. S., June 15, 1873, daughter of Donald and Christena (McRae). After graduating from Portsmouth High School, he learned the machinist's trade in Worcester, Mass. He then served three years as Engineer's Yeoman on U. S. Ship "Vandalia." Returning home in 1889, he was appointed letter carrier in Portsmouth, and has served as such 27 years.

Children of 9th Gen.
9979 REVILO VERNON, b. New Castle, May 1, 1886, m. June 1915 in Arizona.
9980 EMERSON CURTIS, b. Portsmouth, Jan. 15, 1890, a pattern maker employed at U. S. Navy Yard. Lives in Portsmouth.

F7819 Addie Bachelder, born Nov. 15, 1864, married 1880 GEORGE REED, born in Peabody, Mass., 1860. He was a cotton mill operator.

Children of 9th Gen. b. in Danvers, Mass.
9981 HATTIE C., b. 1883, m. —— WILLARD, an engineer.
9982 ANNIE E., b. 1887, lives unmarried in Danvers.
9983 MARION L., b. 1894, is a bookkeeper in Danvers.

F7820 Hattie Bachelder, born Apl. 6, 1867, married 1st, 1884, CHARLES FARNEST, born in Peabody, 1864. He was a shoe cutter and died 1893. She married 2nd, 1895, FRED BOUSER, born 1860. He is in the milk business in Danvers.

Children of 9th Gen.
9984 MABEL A., b. 1885, m. HARRY INGRAHAM, who is in the leather business.
9985 AGNES J., b. 1887, lives unmarried in Danvers, Mass.
9986 HELEN L., b. 1891, a student in Danvers.
9987 BEATRICE BOUSER, b. 1897, attending school in Danvers.
9988 FRED BOUSER, b. ——, in Danvers school.

F7821 Polly W. Marden, born in Rye, July 7, 1848, married Sept. 29, 1869, GEORGE G. WHITE, born in Ossipee, Apl. 29, 1841, son of Parkman and Hannah (Libbey). He was a farmer and milkman at Rye Beach, and died Dec. 18, 1912.

Children of 9th Gen. b. in Rye.
9989 NELLIE M., b. March 20, 1870, m. GEORGE L. TREFETHEN of Kittery, Me.
9990 WILLIE M., b. Nov. 25, 1871.

NINTH GENERATION 527

9991 ROLLO S., b. Aug. 2, 1874, is a telephone inspector.
9992 ISABELLE T., b. Aug. 29, 1876, m. Oct. 15, 1894, THOMAS B. WHENAL of No. Hampton, b. Jan. 16, 1872, lives in No. Hampton, had: 9993 HARRY T., b. 1895; and 9994 HELEN, b. 1897.
9995 ABBOT H., b. Oct. 10, 1878, m. GERTRUDE C. PEEK of Rye, b. Sept. 19, 1883, dau. of Walter and Mary B. (Schile).
9996 ERVING G., b. Jan. 2, 1884, d. June 29, 1886.
9997 ADA E., b. Sept. 22, 1888, m. F. B. PATRICK of Melrose, Mass.

F7826 Elvira Garland Marden, born Nov. 8, 1857, married May 28, 1879, **Walter E. Locke,** # 9329, born Dec. 8, 1855.
Children of 9th Gen. on mother's side; and 10th on father's side.
9998 ELLA M., b. June 29, 1880.
9999 PERCY W., b. July 3, 1882.
F10000 BERTHA G., b. Apl. 1, 1888, m. Jan. 30, 1909, WILLIAM E. ELDRIDGE.
10001 MARY ADELAIDE, b. No. Hampton, Jan. 3, 1892.
10002 ANNIE EMERETT, b. N. Hampton, Feb. 18, 1894, m. Jan. 1915, WILFRED CURRIER, b. No. Adams, Mass.

F7829 Emerett Elizabeth Marden, born Oct. 6, 1863, married Sept. 25, 1888, EDWARD E. RAMSDELL, born Feb. 11, 1865, son of Edward and Annie (Littlefield).
Children of 9th Gen.
10003 BLAKE L., b. March 17, 1889.
10004 FRED M., b. Feb. 4, 1891.
10005 EDNA F., b. March 21, 1892, d. Aug. 20, 1893.
10006 RALPH ED., b. Feb. 3, 1898.

F7838 Mary Pickering, born May 19, 1849, married Dec. 2, 1876, BENJAMIN W. PINKHAM of Rochester, born June 21, 1844. He was a carpenter in Dover and died Feb. 6, 1908.
Child of 9th Gen.
10007 RUSSELL W., b. Sept. 11, 1877, m. HATTIE W. ――――, b. 1881, d. Dover, Nov. 1, 1907, had: 10008 EDWARD R., b. Nov. 3, 1905, and 10009 ELMER W., b. 1907.

F7839 Olive Maria Pickering, born in Newington, Dec. 12, 1853, married Aug. 27, 1879, JOHN RANKIN of Missoula, Montana, born Oct. 21, 1840. He was a ranch owner and died May 3, 1904.
Children of 9th Gen. b. in Missoula, Montana.
10010 JEANNETTE P., b. June 11, 1880, graduated from Montana University, is President of Montana Suffrage Association, 1915.
10011 PHILENA M., b. Oct. 6, 1881, d. Nov. 27, 1890.
10012 HARRIET L., b. Feb. 20, 1883, m. Missoula, Oct. 31, 1907, OSCAR ALFRED SEDMAN, lives in Missoula, had: 10013 MARY E., b. Sept. 15, 1908, also another girl.

10014 WELLINGTON D., b. Sept. 16, 1884, is married and a lawyer in Helena, Mont.
10015 MARY F., b. Aug. 30, 1888.
10016 GRACE E., b. Nov. 25, 1891. 10017 EDNA B., b. Oct. 21, 1893.

F7840 James K. Pickering, born in Newington, June 9, 1856, married Oct. 6, 1883, JENNIE LAKE, born March 17, 1859. He was superintendent of construction in Providence, R. I. In 1905 he went to California to construct some Panama Fair buildings and died as the result of a fall, Jan. 1914.
Children of 9th Gen.
10018 JAMES L., b. Aug. 4, 1884, d. Providence, R. I., Aug. 3, 1907, unmarried, lived in Somerville, Mass.
10019 HAROLD EDGAR, b. June 19, 1892, in 1911 was a photographer in Sacramento, Cal.

F7842 Eleanor Annie Pickering, born May 27, 1861, married Oct. 23, 1883, HERBERT D. CAVERLY of Dover, born Strafford, Oct. 23, 1859. He is a clerk in Providence, R. I.
Children of 9th Gen.
10020 BRAINARD EDWARD, b. Nov. 24, 1884, m. June 17, 1912, MARION C. AUSTIN.
10021 WALTER FRANKLIN, b. May 29, 1890.
10022 RUTH EVELYN, b. twin, May 29, 1890, m. (PROF. ERNEST REYNOLDS of Tennessee?).
10023 ROLAND GARDNER, b. May 21, 1894.

F7913 Thomas W. Parsons, born Nov. 6, 1861, married Nov. 9, 1892, **Martha Kate Locke,** # 7923, born Oct. 31, 1868. He is a business man of Portsmouth, lives in Rye.
Child of 9th Gen. b. in Rye.
10024 DOROTHY E., b. June 19, 1896, a student.

F7926 James A. Greenleaf, born in Portsmouth, Feb. 19, 1856, married 1st, in Pennsylvania, Nov. 6, 1876, JENNIE E. SNYDER, who died Apl. 1879; married 2nd, Sept. 15, 1880, S. JENNIE HATFIELD, born June 3, 1860. He is Assistant Superintendent of H. & B. T. M. R. R. at Huntingdon, Pa.
Children of 9th Gen. b. in Penn.
10025 JAMES A., b. Riddlesburg, Penn., Dec. 23, 1877, d. May 3, 1878.
10026 First child by second wife died young.
10027 ALBERT H., b. Feb. 17, 1883.
10028 JAMES F., b. Sept. 1, 1884.
10029 FRANK LOCKE, b. June 4, 1886.
10030 MYRA C., b. Jan. 29, 1888.
10031 MARY D., b. Sept. 17, 1889.

NINTH GENERATION 529

10032 GEORGE G., b. Apl. 1891, d. July 1891.
10033 HELEN M., b. Jan. 28, 1893.
10034 MARTHA J., b. Feb. 22, 1895.

F7946 William Cushman Locke, born in Kittery, Me., March 6, 1858, married Nov. 12, 1881, CARRIE J. PAUL of Kittery, Me., born May 10, 1858. He is Captain in charge of U. S. Navy Yard Ferry, Portsmouth.

Children of 9th Gen. b. in Kittery, Me.

10035 WILLARD C., b. Jan. 23, 1887, m. July 10, 1907, BESSIE E. WHITE-
HOUSE of Kittery, dau. of Edwin S. and M. B. (Seawards).
10036 FRANK CUSHMAN, b. May 26, 1889, m. Oct. 18, 1907, BERNICE IRISH,
b. Rockland, Me., Feb. 17, 1890, dau. of Judson C. Had: 10037
RALPH CUSHMAN, b. Kittery, Nov. 6, 1908. Purser on Alantic
Shore Line Ferry boat, lives Kittery.

F7958 Julia Ann Locke, born in Corinth, Vt., May 8, 1845, married March 1, 1866, ORRIN HUTCHINSON of East Orange, Vt., born May 25, 1838. He was a farmer in East Orange and died Jan. 1, 1900.

Children of 9th Gen. b. in East Orange, Vt.

10037 NELLIE C., b.——, d. Apl. 15, 1882, m. GEORGE MERRILL of Corinth,
Vt., Feb. 15, 1880, had: 10038 LEON H., b. Apl. 15, 1881 and lives
Bradford, Vt.
10039 WILLIAM O., b. Sept. 6, 1880, m. ILA M. DOWNING, June 7, 1906, b.
Washington, Sept. 7, 1883. He is a Doctor in Washington, Vt.,
and had 10040 NETA, b. June 9, 1910.

F7965 Spaulding Flint Locke, born in Corinth, Vt., July 20, 1849, married 1st, June 17, 1879, ELIZA A. STANDLICK, daughter of William and Elizabeth (Trelvar); married 2nd, MRS. NANCY (NUTT) FOLSOM. He is a merchant in Topsham, Vt., had been in the lumber business previously.

Children of 9th Gen. b. in Corinth, Vt.

10041 ERNEST S., b. Oct. 1881, m. ESTHER SANBORN. He is a teacher in
Waits River, Vt., had: 10042 RAYMOND.
10043 NELLIE E., b. —— 1883, m. HARRY MILES, lives Waits River, Vt.

F7967 Harmond John Locke, born in Corinth, Vt., June 12, 1855, married 1st, Apl. 17, 1884, MARY E. BERRY, born 1860, died March 20, 1895; married 2nd, Sept. 18, 1898, CARRIE SAWYER. He graduated from Dartmouth 1880, was a teacher in Kansas City.

Children of 9th Gen. b. in Kansas City, Mo.

10044 NETA GAIL, b. Apl. 17, 1885, lived Kansas City 1913, unmarried.
10045 JOHN BERRY, b. June 20, 1887.

F7968 David Byron Locke, born in Corinth, Vt., Oct. 4, 1857, married 1st, 1881, NELLIE WINCH; married 2nd, MINNIE CHURCHILL. He graduated from Dartmouth in 1880, was Superintendent of Schools, Winchendon, Mass. and Rutland, Vt.

Children of 9th Gen.

10046 WILLIE, b. —— 1881, d. ——. 10049 ALLEN W., b. 1896.
10047 ELIZABETH, b. 1883. 10050 RUTH, b. 1898.
10048 DAVID V., b. —— 1885.

F7973 Ellen Frances Smith, born in Framingham, Mass., Apl. 27, 1844, married March 19, 1863, in Southboro, ALFRED EVERETT BEMIS, born Sept. 29, 1842, died Dec 30, 1889. She died in Marlboro, Mass., Oct. 3, 1870.

Children of 9th Gen. b. in Southboro, Mass.

10051 NELLIE MARIA, b. Apl. 11, 1865, m. —— DENEISE, and lived only a few years after marriage.
10052 LIZZIE A., b. Marlboro, d. Aug. 23, 1868, aged 11 months.
10053 EMERY FRANKLIN, b. March 5, 1870, m. Nov. 3, 1901, CAROLINE E ERWING and had: 10054 LILLIAN ERWING, b. Marlboro, Dec. 20 1902; and 10055 HELEN FRANCES, b. Clinton, Mass., Nov. 20, 1907

F7979 Mary Elizabeth Smith, born in Framingham, Mass. June 18, 1849, married in Montpelier, Vt., Sept. 13, 1865 ALMON INGRAM of Washington, Vt., and lived at Wellesley Mass. He was Lieutenant in Co. G. 10th Vermont Reg., late detailed as Captain of Co. E.

Children of 9th Gen. b. in Marlboro, Mass.

10056 LESTER W., b. Apl. 1, 1871, m. Ashmont, Mass., June 29, 1904 CLARA ETTA RYDER, b. May 23, 1878. He is a lawyer of Boston and Belmont and had: 10057 RAYMOND WILBUR, b. Apl. 26, 1907 and 10058 WARREN RYDER, b. Sept. 8, 1915.
10059 VINTHIA ELIZABETH, b. March 2, 1874, m. at Wellesley, Mass., Feb 15, 1904, IRA HARMON MARSTON of Machias, Me., b. Marshfield Me., March 29, 1878, and had: 10060 ALMEDA VIOLET, b. at Welles ley, March 3, 1905.
10061 HAROLD GUY, b. March 16, 1887.
10062 ALMON, JR., b. Wellesley, March 17, 1892, m. at Jacksonville, Fla March 4, 1914, ULDINE SPENCER DERRIMAN.

F7981 Betsey S. Woodman, born March 20, 1848, marrie 1868, M. A. CUNNINGHAM.

Children of 9th Gen.

10063 WILLARD, b. Apl. 8, 1871, m. 1896, BESSIE FARNHAM, had: 1006 OLIVE, b. 1898.
10065 FRED O., b. Oct. 15, 1872, m. Dec. 25, 1895, MINNIE SHORTSHEAVI and had: 10066 LINNWOOD, b. 1897.
10067 GERTRUDE, b. Sept. 23, 1874, m. July 1892, ERNEST BATTIN and ha 10068 BERNICE, b. 1893, and 10069 ERWIN, b. 1896.

NINTH GENERATION 531

F7988 Dewitt Farwell, born Aug. 29, 1852, married HANNAH MOORE.
Children of 9th Gen.
10070 ALICE L., b. May 29, 1875.
10071 JENNIE, b. 1880, m. DAVID MARSTON, and had: 10072 CHARLES.

F8081 Mary Sanders, born twin, Nov. 6, 1832, married NATHANIEL TWOMBLEY of Barrington, born Jan. 1833. He was a farmer in Barrington and died Nov. 3, 1893.
Children of 9th Gen.
10073 MARY E., b. Aug. 13, 1857, d. Oct. 30, 1890.
10074 GEORGE W., b. Sept. 30, 1859, m. June 27, 1897, ——— ———. He is on Electric road, Boston.
10075 LAURA E., b. Nov. 27, 1861, m. ROYAL H. CLARKE of Barrington, and had: 10076 ARTHUR G., b. 1881, d. 1882, and 10077 FREDERICK K., b. 1883.
10078 ABBIE G., b. March 16, 1865, d. July 18, 1877.
10079 CHARLES E., b. Jan. 4, 1871, is a farmer in Barrington.

F8119 Sarah Jane Locke, born in Concord, March 15, 1842, married in Concord, Nov. 14, 1865, JOHN B. BAKER, son of Aaron W. and Nancy (Dustin). They lived at Bow Mills.
Children of 9th Gen. b. in Bow Mills.
10080 RUFUS H., b. March 16, 1870, m. Aug. 13, 1896, GRACE L. TUCK, b. Haverhill, dau. of John and Eliza (Bradley). They had: 10081 PERLEY DUSTIN, b. Bow, May 8, 1897, and 10082 BRADLEY LOCKE, b. July 22, 1899.
10083 JOHN PERLEY, b. Aug. 21, 1871, d. June 28, 1884.

F8125 Rev. George Reuben Locke, born in East Concord, Jan. 1, 1864; married in Landaff, June 23, 1887, FANNIE S. GORDON, born in Landaff, Jan. 15, 1864, daughter of Savory and Margaret A. He is a minister of the N. H. Methodist Church with appointments in various towns and cities.
Children of 9th Gen. b. in Tilton.
10084 MARGARET SARAH, b. Aug. 10, 1888.
10085 HELEN FRANCES, b. Apl. 8, 1893.

F8126 Rev. William Benjamin Locke, born in Bristol, Oct. 10, 1867, married in Merrimac, Mass., Aug. 16, 1893, MARY FRANCES ROWELL of Rumney, born in Merrimac, June 16, 1870, daughter of Charles and J. M. (Gile). Like his brother he is in the N. H. Methodist Conference.
Children of 9th Gen.
10086 JUDITH MAY, b. Seabrook, May 24, 1896.
10087 MILDRED S., b. Seabrook, June 10, 1897, d. Sept. 27, 1897.
10088 ——— dau., b. Newfields, June 15, 1901.

F8147 Samuel L. Batchelder, born in Concord, May 22, 1863, married Oct. 17, 1888, SARAH E. HUTCHINS, born in Concord, June 16, 1864, daughter of John C. and Caroline (Curtis). He is a clerk in East Concord.

Children of 9th Gen. b. in East Concord.
- 10089 JOHN H., b. Aug. 2, 1889.
- 10090 HENRY B., b. March 14, 1891.
- 10091 MARGARET, b. June 16, 1893, m. June 14, 1913, FRED THOMAS REED, b. 1890, a silversmith, son of Thomas and Daisy.

F8155 Nancy Alice Locke, born in Haverhill, Aug. 16, 1847, married in Titusville, Pa., Apl. 8, 1865, THEODORE M. SHEARER of Buffalo, born in Germany, Nov. 9, 1845, died 1912. She is living at Butler, Pa., 1915.

Children of 9th Gen. b. in Titusville, Penn.
- 10092 MARY A., b. Pithole, Pa., Feb. 13, 1866.
- 10093 GEORGE, b. Oct. 24, 1868, m. Limestone, Pa., July 11, 1887, EMMA K HOLLAR, b. Pittsburg, March 5, 1869. They had: 10094 CHARLOTTE, b. Bradford, Pa., June 4, 1888, d. Nov. 23, 1894; and 1009{ VALENTINE, b. Butler, Pa., Sept. 7, 1891, d. Nov. 23, 1894.
- 10096 THEODORE M., b. Shawbury, Pa., Oct. 20, 1870, m. New Martinsville Pa., Apl. 6, 1897, ELIZABETH MEEKER and had: 10097 MARGARE᠆ L., b. West Virginia, Feb. 20, 1898.
- 10098 CLARA LOUISE, b. May 28, 1874, m. June 14, 1906, GEORGE COPI STEWART of Butler, Pa.
- 10099 ALICE L., b. Aug. 15, 1876.
- 10100 LOUIS A., b. Bradford, Jan. 31, 1879.
- 10101 SUSAN, b. Bradford, Oct. 27, 1883.
- 10102 CHARLES H., b. Bradford, Sept. 22, 1886.
- 10103 GRACE D. a twin, b. Bradford, Sept. 22, 1886.
- 10104 ELIZABETH, b. Butler, Nov. 25, 1890.

F8156 Henry Walker Locke, born May 6, 1849, married 1st 1869, AMANDA LUTZ of Erie, Pa., born Nov. 14, 1850, died Nov 26, 1884; married 2nd, in Titusville, 1886, CLARA ALEXANDEF At age of 18 he located in Titusville, and as a machinist,manu factured and erected machines in the oil well field, where he ha an extensive acquaintance. He died at Bradford, Pa., Aug. 1(1913.

Children of 9th Gen.
- 10105 FLORA, b. Dec. 10, 1870, m. Butler, Pa., 1891, WARREN WHITE, an had: 10106 MALCOLM, b. Washington, Pa., Sept. 12, 1892; an 10107 WARREN, b. Garrett, Pa., 1894.
- 10108 HENRY, b. 1872, d. Petrolia, Pa., Nov. 1875.
- 10109 JAMES MORRILL, b. 1874, d. Titusville, 1874.

NINTH GENERATION 533

10110 ARVILLA, b, Petrolia, Feb. 14, 1876, m. 1896, at Sewickley, Pa., FRED
LEIDIEKER, and had: 10111 KARL G. b. Sept. 17, 1897.
10112 HENRY, b. Petrolia, 1879, d. Bradford, 1882.
10113 WILLIAM, b. Bradford, 1882.
By second wife:
10114 ORRIN, b. Butler 1888.
10115 DONNAN, b. 1891.

F8161 William Hale Locke, born in Haverhill, Aug. 17, 1858, married in Butler, Pa., July 13, 1891, ELIZABETH BOYD, born in Alleghany, Dec. 31, 1871. He is a machinist in the oil business at Robinson, Ohio, and Parkersburg, W. Va.
Children of 9th Gen.
10116 SARAH MILDRED, b. Harmony, Pa., Nov. 12, 1892.
10117 JOSEPH, b. Harmony, Oct. 18, 1893.
10118 HELEN, b. Tarentum, Pa., Nov. 10, 1895.
10119 ETHEL MARY, b. Wheeling, W. Va., Jan. 27, 1898.

F8163 Sarah Locke, born in Littleton, Apl. 23, 1839, married in Titusville, Pa., July 2, 1857, STEPHEN LOGAN of Riceville, Pa., born July 21, 1837, lived in Clay City, Ky.
Child of 9th Gen.
10120 HERMAN R., b. Apl. 5, 1858, m. Warren, Pa., May 21, 1879, SARAH E.
TRUBY, b. Leavenworth, Kans., July 10, 1859, and had: 10121
MARY OLIVE, b. Warren, May 15, 1880, and 10122 WILLIS JOHN,
b. Summit City, Apl. 8, 1882.

F8164 Henry Harrison Locke, born in Littleton, Dec. 21, 1840, married Sept. 26, 1866, MARTHA H. WADE, of Steuben, Pa., born Nov. 7, 1846, died in Bradford, Sept. 18, 1915. He succeeded his father in the manufacture of tools for oil well drilling and with the exception of service in the war has continued the same up to the present time in Bradford, Pa. He enlisted Sept. 6, 1861, under Capt. John Brown, Jr. (son of Ossowatomie Brown), and went to Kansas where he joined the 7th Kansas Cavalry. He reenlisted in 1864 and served until the regiment was mustered out, Nov. 12, 1865.
Children of 9th Gen. b. in Bradford.
10123 WARD LEON, b. March 24, 1870, d. March 27, 1870.
10124 GUY H. (adopted), b. March 15, 1878, m. June 24, 1903, ANNA
VANGALINE JORDAN. He is in business with his father, and
has children: 10125 GALE H., b. July 11, 1904; 10126 MARTHA
HELEN, b. March 7, 1907; 10127 RUTH ELIZABETH, b. Dec. 15,
1908.

F8165 Martha Helen Locke, born in Lyman, Apl. 25, 1842, married 1st, July 28, 1859, SAMUEL PARTRIDGE, born 1830, died Sept. 6, 1859; married 2nd, July 3, 1860, HENRY C. CARPENTER of Barnet, Vt. She died Apl. 7, 1863.

Children of 9th Gen. by Carpenter.

10128 EMMA FLORINDA, b. McClintocksville, Pa., Sept. 7, 1861, m. Titusville Sept. 21, 1879, LEVI L. STAGE of Titusville, b. Andover, O., Feb. 16, 1847, d. 1899. Had: 10129 LEROY L., b. Kane, Pa., Aug. 6, 1883; 10130 FLORA, b. Jan. 29, 1885; 10131 WALTER, b. Nov. 10, 1886.

10132 MARTHA HELEN, b. Rice Lake, March 21, 1863, m. HENRY C. MAPES.

F8166 Jonathan Morrill Locke, born in Lyman, Feb. 15, 1844, married in Titusville, Sept. 26, 1867, ELLEN A. FOSTER, born in Sheridan, N. Y., Sept. 26, 1847, living 1915. He was in the civil war and suffered eighteen months in a rebel prison. He was a machinist and station agent at Beldonville, Wis., and died in Ellsworth, Wis., Jan. 22, 1914.

Children of 9th Gen. b. in Titusville, Pa.

F10133 HARRY BERTON, b. Sept. 9, 1868, m. 1st, Nov. 27, 1890, ELLEN BARKER; m. 2nd, June 18, 1901, ELIZA ELLA TAYLOR.

F10134 EDNA AMY, b. Apl. 3, 1871, m. 1st, Nov. 24, 1887, CHARLES H. GOLDSMITH; m. 2nd, May 26, 1897, MILLARD FILLMORE REED.

F10135 SARAH CELESTIA (BIRDIE), b. June 7, 1874, m. Sept. 20, 1893, GEORGE BYRON REED.

10136 JONATHAN MORRILL, b. June 1, 1882, m. Aug. 19, 1903, MARTHA MASON, and had: 10137 IDA IRENE, b. June 8, 1905, and 10138 LORAINE LILLIAN, b. Sept. 1, 1912.

F8167 Stephen Farnsworth Locke, born in Lyman, March 9, 1846, married at Guys Mills, Pa., March 5, 1869, MARY E. ASHLEY, born at Guys Mills, Aug. 10, 1851. He was a machinist at Titusville, Pa.

Children of 9th Gen.

10139 MINA MAE, b. Pleasantville, Pa., Sept. 26, 1869, d. Titusville, Jan. 7, 1892, m. Dec. 24, 1890, WILLIAM O. CALKINS, # 10185, b. Feb. 15, 1865, lived Kennedy, N. Y. Had: 10140 CLAUDE EUGENE, b. Titusville, Dec. 19, 1891, is in U. S. Navy.

F10141 FRED EUGENE, b. Jan. 19, 1871, m. 1st, Aug. 12, 1891, MYRTLE VICTORIA KOUGH; m. 2nd, Oct. 12, 1899, MABEL LEONE YEARICK.

F10142 STEPHEN F., b. July 2, 1874, m. Apl. 27, 1897, FRANCES M. MURNING.

F10143 MAUDE ORA, b. July 20, 1876, m. July 20, 1892, JOSEPH NEWTON FULTON.

10144 GEORGE BARR, b. June 21, 1878, m. Aug. 23, 1899, FLORENCE M. MAYERS. He is a printer in Franklin, Pa., and had: 10145 GEORGE KENNETH, b. Dec. 5, 1903.

NINTH GENERATION 535

F10146 MARY ASHLEY, b. June 17, 1880, m. Dec. 5, 1903, GEORGE LANG.
F10147 MABEL EMMA, b. March 25, 1882, m. Apl. 1, 1899, JOSEPH C. CALDWELL.
10148 SARAH DAVIS, b. Apl. 21, 1884, m. Jan. 9, 1902, WILLIAM C. EICHER, who is a moulder in Greensburg, Pa., and had: 10149 ORA ARDARAY, b. Dec. 22, 1903, and 10150 EDITH MAY, b. Feb. 22, 1905.
F10151 HANNAH BIGELOW, b. Feb. 16, 1886, m. Jan. 28, 1903, OTTO RICKE.
F10152 LOUIS DUNMEYES, b. June 7, 1890, m. Apl. 14, 1910, ANNA JOHNSON.

F8169 Mary Keziah Locke, born in Titusville, Dec. 5, 1850, married in Pleasantville, Pa., Sept. 29, 1870, BENJAMIN S. TRUXAL of Pittsford, Pa., born in Armagh, Pa., March 22, 1842. He is a machinist in Chattanooga.
Child of 9th Gen. b. in Chattanooga.
10153 EVA SARAH, b. June 5, 1871, m. in Chat., Jan. 20, 1892, CARL T. PAINTER, b. Logansport, Pa., Nov. 12, 1865, and had: 10154 BENJAMIN F., b. June 23, 1893, and 10155 ROY, b. June 2, 1899.

F8170 Hannibal Orlando Locke, born in Titusville, Pa., July 2, 1856, married in Pleasantville, July 18, 1876, ELLA A. CLARK, born in Hydetown, Pa., May 11, 1860. He was a machinist in Bradford, Pa., where he died Dec. 7, 1902.
Children of 9th Gen.
10156 HARRY HARRISON, b. Pleasantville, Pa., Sept. 2, 1877, m. Limestone, N. Y., Sept. 15, 1895, LETTIE BARNUM, b. Bradford, Pa., July 15, 1879. He is a machinist in Bradford and had: 10157 MAY, b. Bradford, Sept. 26, 1896.
10158 JOHN L., b. Apl. 18, 1879, m. Limestone, N. Y., Apl. 12, 1899, DAISY MCKEOWN, b. Limestone, Oct. 6, 1880. He is a locomotive engineer in Bradford.
10159 EARL M., b. Sept. 30, 1881, is m. and a machinist in Bradford, Pa.
10160 LILLIAN, b. Apl. 24, 1887, m. ———— ————.
10161 ORA, b. Sept. 2, 1889, d. Bradford, Jan. 21, 1895.

F8171 David Lovering Farnsworth, born in Haverhill, Nov. 15, 1838, married Dec. 26, 1866, FRANCES P. CLOUGH, born March 9, 1850, died in San Francisco, Aug. 7, 1900. He lived in San Francisco, and died there Aug. 28, 1900.
Children of 9th Gen. b. in San Francisco.
10162 SILAS B., b. Feb. 28, 1868, lives San Francisco, unmarried.
10163 LOTTIE PAULINE, b. Jan. 28, 1871, m. Nov. 28, 1906, CHARLES A. ROSSIER of San Francisco.
10164 ADDIE L., b. March 6, 1876, d. Dec. 7, 1876.

F8172 Ann Farnsworth, born Feb. 8, 1840, died Aug. 1901, married SAMUEL MAGOON, born June 17, 1831, died Jan. 2, 1870.
Children of 9th Gen.
F10165 MARTHA E., b. Aug. 18, 1857, m. Feb. 16, 1879, WILLIAM H. HIGGINS.
   10166 CORA J., b. Feb. 28, 1860, d. Sept. 6, 1888, m. Dec. 25, 1885, GEORGE WAGNER, b. Aug. 1859, and had: 10167 FREDERICK G., b. Sept. 5, 1888.
   10168 OSCAR S., b. Sept. 28, 1862, m. Feb. 24, 1889, ALICE ANDREWS.
   10169 ORRIN E., twin, b. Sept. 28, 1862, m. June 1888, —— ——.

F8173 Elbridge G. Farnsworth, born March 13, 1842, married 1st, LOUISE SOMERS who died March 5, 1891; married 2nd, Apl. 7, 1896, FRANCES G. CARR of St. Johnsbury, Vt. He is a carpenter in East Barnet, Vt.
Children of 9th Gen. b. in East Barnet, Vt.
10170 ELBRIDGE G., b. March 14, 1870, d. Jan. 25, 1889.
10171 FANNIE LOUISE, b. Aug. 18, 1873, m. 1891, JAMES MOORE of East Barnet, Vt., and had three children.
10172 ROSS ELMER, b. Jan. 22, 1879, d. unmarried Westminster, Vt., Sept. 9, 1905.

F8174 Florinda Lovering Farnsworth, born March 25, 1844, married Nov. 2, 1867, JOSEPH C. BARTLETT, born 1831. He lived in Oakland, Cal., and died March 17, 1883.
Children of 9th Gen.
10173 ELMER H., b. Apl. 27, 1869, is unmarried.
10174 ADA B., b. March 7, 1875, m. WALTER LIPSETT. The husband, wife, and an infant 10175 FLORINDA were drowned in 1903 by a cloud burst in Heppner, Oregon.

F8175 Orrin Edward Farnsworth, born in Haverhill, Nov. 27, 1846, married in Portland, Ore., June 18, 1873, CATHERINE MARGARET PRAY, born in Lindley, Ohio, Feb. 4, 1849. He has a large wool ranch, and is a bank director and prominent man in Heppner, Oregon.
Children of 9th Gen. all but first b. in Morrow County, Ore.
10176 FRANK PRAY, b. Portland Ore., March 19, 1874, lives Heppner, Ore.
10177 LUCY HELEN, b. Oct. 12, 1875.
10178 EDWARD THOMAS, b. Nov. 21, 1876.
10179 FLORA MAY, b. May 12, 1878.
10180 MARY HANNAH, b. Feb. 2, 1880.
10181 EMMA ESTELLE, b. June 21, 1881.
10182 BLANCHE, b. Jan. 27, 1884, d. Nov. 19, 1889.
10183 KARL WILLIAM, b. March 21, 1886.
10184 HAROLD RAYMOND, b. Feb. 15, 1890, d. Apl. 14, 1891.

NINTH GENERATION

F8176 Janette D. Locke, born in Lyman, Apl. 21, 1845, died in Portland, Pa., Oct. 22, 1895, married 1st, June 6, 1863, ORRIN E. CALKINS, born in Richland, N. Y., March 23, 1839, died Feb. 9, 1865; married 2nd, Nov. 16, 1869, HARRISON CASS, born Nov. 27, 1842.

Children of 9th Gen.

10185 WILLIAM ORRIN CALKINS, b. Feb. 19, 1865, m. 1st, Dec. 24, 1890, MINA MAE LOCKE, # 10139, b. Sept. 26, 1869, d. Jan. 7, 1892, and had: 10186 CLAUDE E., b. 1891. William m. 2nd, ―――― CHASE and lived Titusville, Pa.

10188 THIRZA JANE CASS, b. Apl. 28, 1873, m. ROLLIN C. BENNETT, b. Clymer, N. Y., March 11, 1871, and had: 10189 MINA W., b. Portland, N. Y., Jan. 18, 1892; 10190 GUY R., b. June 1, 1893; 10191 CLYDE LOCKE, b. Jan. 8, 1895.

10192 DAVID E. CASS, b. May 12, 1881.

F8179 Robert Dickson Locke, born in Dalton, Aug. 26, 1850, married July 12, 1884, FANNIE J. ALLISON, born in New York City, July 22, 1865. He is a prosperous citizen of Titusville, Pa.

Children of 9th Gen. b. in Titusville, Pa.

10193 LUCILLE JANE, b. June 16, 1885, d. Jan. 16, 1887.
10194 LUCY ANN, b. Jan. 4, 1887, m. Titusville, Sept. 25, 1912, HENRY J. Z. WEYGARTT, a banker of Titusville, later of Hartford, Conn.
10195 ROBERT ALLISON, b. June 7, 1892.

F8180 Alice I. Locke, born July 13, 1852, died 1914, married July 9, 1874, WILLIAM WALLACE. They lived in San Luis Rey, Cal., and he died in 1893.

Children of 9th Gen. b. in San Luis Rey, Cal.

10196 WILLIAM LEE, b. Feb. 17, 1875.	10200 PEARL, b. 1886.
10197 ELBRIDGE H., b. March 24, 1876.	10201 ALICE.
10198 EDNA J., b. Dec 12, 1878.	10202 HUGH.
10199 ROBERT L., b. Apl. 19, 1880.	10203 ANNIE.

F8196 Elizabeth Abbie Walker, born Aug. 12, 1854, married Dec. 1, 1874, CHARLES J. WESTON, born Oct. 2, 1853, lived in Windsor, Vt. He died Feb. 5, 1884, she is living 1915.

Children of 9th Gen. b. in Windsor, Vt.

10204 ALICE E., b. July 1, 1876, m. Windsor, Jan. 1, 1898, WALTER W. BLANCHARD, a clerk in Windsor, and had: 10205 HILDA, b. Nov. 5, 1898; 10206 RALPH, b. Aug., 1900; 10207 EVANS H., b. March 5, 1905, d. Jan. 1, 1907.

10208 HENRY REUBEN, b. March 13, 1878, m. EMIR ROOT. He graduated from Dartmouth College 1900 and Medical College 1903, later entered the U. S. Army as Surgeon. *Children:* 10209 DORIS, b. ――――; and 10210 BARRETT LOCKE, b. Nov. 1906.

10211 CHARLES JOSEPH, b. March 31, 1883, graduated Dartmouth 1905, is a lawyer, unmarried in Springfield, Mass.

F8199 Eleanor H. Locke, born in Lyman, July 29, 1850, died in Haverhill, Jan. 18, 1898, married Dec. 15, 1868, JOHN W. BAILEY, born in Alexandria, son of John W. He was a blacksmith in Haverhill, was a war veteran.

Children of 9th Gen. b. in Haverhill.

10212 CLARENCE L., b. Nov. 11, 1869, m. Haverhill, Feb. 1, 1893, MAY A. SPOONER dau. of Alonzo and Mary (Bennett). He is a blacksmith in Woodsville and had: 10213 HAROLD ROY, b. Aug. 12, 1897; 10214 ELEANOR NETTIE, b. Oct. 5, 1898.

10215 ROY, b. July 1871, d. June 18, 1872.

10216 HARRIET B., b. Dec. 4, 1872, m. Dec. 6, 1893, WINFIELD KEYSER, a railroad employee and had: 10217 HAROLD and 10218 ROLAND, twins, b. and d. 1894; 10219 ROLAND, b. 1897; 10220 SON, b. 1898.

10221 BLANCHE F., b. June 30, 1877, d. Woodsville unmarried Jan. 1, 1898.

F8200 Francisco H. Locke, born in Lyman, March 9, 1852, married in Bath, Feb. 17, 1872, PHEBE A. WETHERBEE, born in Lisbon, 1848, daughter of Smith and Sally (Jesseman). He was a blacksmith in Oakland, Cal., and died there Oct. 3, 1906.

Children of 9th Gen. b. in Oakland, Cal.

10222 CARRIE A., b. July 24, 1875.

10223 SARAH HARRIET, b. March 15, 1878, m. Feb. 1897, —— REED, and had: 10224 FRANK WARREN, b. Aug. 24, 1898.

10225 ELSIE, b. Apl. 21, 1880, d. March 3, ——.

10226 ARTHUR L., b. June 4, 1881. 10228 ROY B., b. Jan. 19, 1886.

10227 FRANK W., b. Apl. 2, 1883.

F8201 Silas Merrill Locke, born in Lyman, June 16, 1854, married in Lyman, Dec. 24, 1874, AMANDA M. WILLIAMS, born in Littleton, Oct. 24, 1852, died in Lyman, Nov. 23, 1909. She was a school teacher, daughter of Franklin. He is a farmer in Lyman.

Children of 9th Gen. b. in Lyman.

F10229 HARVEY E., b. March 4, 1876, m. Dec. 24, 1895, ELLA M. SMITH.

10230 GRACE AMANDA, b. Aug. 13, 1878, m. Apl. 20, 1898, CARL MASON of Lyman, and has two children.

10231 SUSIE, b. June 24, 1886, m. JOSEPH RICHARDS.

10232 EARL S., b. Oct. 9, 1890, m. Landaff, Nov. 13, 1912, HELEN E. BURBANK, b. Landaff, 1893, dau. of Ezra C. and Mary (Flanders).

F8202 Lyman J. M. Locke, born in Lyman, March 19, 1860, married in Sheffield, Vt., Aug. 9, 1884, LETTIE BRADLEY, born in Sheffield, 1863. She was a teacher the daughter of Ward. He is a farmer in Lyman.

NINTH GENERATION 539

Children of 9th Gen. b. in Lyman.
10233 HARRIET WARD, b. March 21, 1887, m. May 1905, HARRY BLANCHARD of Woodsville, now of Lakeport.
10234 CLARA MCINDOE, b. Jan. 9, 1891, m. Lisbon, Apl. 29, 1910, QUO W. MUZZEY, and lives in Manchester.
10235 FLORINDA, b. Aug. 20, 1896.

F8216 Abbie L. Rix, born in San Francisco, Dec. 10, 1861, married Feb. 10, 1887, FRED MAURER, JR. They live in Alameda, Cal.

Children of 9th Gen. b. in Alameda, Cal.
10236 ALICE CLARA, b. Nov. 1887, m. DR. WILLIAM BAKER, and had: 10237 ELIZABETH and 10238 ROBERT.
10239 RIX, b. —— was a student in Stamford, Ohio, 1911.
10240 MILDRED, b. 1898.

F8229 Clara Alice McIndoe, born in Newbury, Vt., Aug. 24, 1859, married in Windsor, Vt., Dec. 31, 1878, MARSH O. PERKINS, born in Rutland, Feb. 7, 1849. He graduated from Middlebury College in 1870, and was principal of the Windsor, Vt., high school until 1880 when he became editor of the *Vermont Journal*, which he continued until 1905 when ill health compelled him to relinquish that office. From that date until recently he has been Town Librarian. Prominent in town affairs he served in all positions from moderator to state senator. He has been Colonel on the Governor's Staff, Presidential Elector and held many other places of trust and honor. He was one of the best known Masons of the state, having been presiding officer of all local bodies, also of the Grand Lodge, Grand Chapter, and Grand Commandery, Knights Templar, and was a 33rd, degree mason in the Scottish Rite Body. This exemplary man passed away Feb. 10, 1916, his funeral being attended by citizens, Masons and Odd Fellows from all over the state.

Children of 9th Gen. b. in Windsor, Vt.
10241 LOCKE MCINDOE, b. Nov. 20, 1879, m. Devils Lake, No. Dakota, Feb. 11, 1908, RUTH ROBERTS. He graduated from Dartmouth 1901 and from the Thayer School 1903, as a civil engineer. He is officially connected with the Northern Pacific R. R., his duties locating him in Minnesota, Montana and now in Washington. They have children: 10242 LOCKE MCINDOE, b. St. Paul, Minn., Oct. 11, 1910, 10243 DONALD, b. Tacoma, Wash., Feb. 25, 1912; 10244 MARSH OLIN, b. Dec. 30, 1915.
10245 GAIL GIDDINGS, b. Aug. 4, 1882, m. Oct. 25, 1905, FLOYD ORLIN HALE, b. Windsor, Vt., Apl. 13, 1882, son of Frank S. He graduated from

Dartmouth 1903, was Traffic Engineer Central Telegraph Co., Pittsburg, Pa., now Chief Engineer of South West Telephone Co., St. Louis, Mo. They have children: 10246 ELIZABETH PERKINS, b. Pittsburg, Oct. 12, 1907, and 10247 ROBERT LOCKE, b. Pittsburg, Aug. 13, 1909.

- 10248 MARGARET ELOISE, b. Sept. 9, 1889.
- 10249 MARION FLORINDA, twin, b. Sept. 9, 1889.
- 10250 HERBERT MARSH, b. Jan. 19, 1891, graduated from Dartmouth 1913, and from Thayer School as Civil Engineer 1915.
- 10251 KATHERINE LUCIA, b. May 24, 1898, was a member of the class of 1916, Windsor High School and d. March 20, 1916.

F8246 Joseph Ham Locke, born in Boston, May 6, 1843, married in Boston, Sept. 23, 1868, G. EMMA GOODWIN, born in Charlestown, Mass., Sept. 11, 1849, daughter of Henry P. and Mamie R. (Plummer). He is a wholesale paper dealer in Mobile, Ala.

Children of 9th Gen.

- F10252 ALICE MARION, b. May 3, 1869, m. Oct. 15, 1889, THOMAS D. NETTLES.
- F10253 EDITH JOSEPHINE, b. Feb. 12, 1871, m. Oct. 12, 1891, GEORGE T. BADEAU.
- 10254 HARRY GOODWIN, b. Mobile, May 13, 1875, m. Mobile, Jan. 5, 1891, CLARA CLARKE JACOBS of Mobile, b. Selma, Ala., Feb. 1879. He entered the U. S. Revenue Service in Nov. 1901, is now Chief Engineer, U. S. S. Bache.
- F10255 SIMEON YOUNG, b. Sept. 8, 1878, m. June 13, 1898, ANNA G. QUATTLEBAUM.

F8260 Clara Tash Locke, born Sept. 2, 1853, married Oct. 29, 1885, FRANCIS JORDON THOMPSON of Baltimore, who graduated from Phillips Andover Academy in 1871. She graduated from Abbott Academy 1872.

Children of 9th Gen.

- 10256 SAMUEL LOCKE, b. Aug. 25, 1886, m. Oct. 1909, ADELAIDE WILDE PORTER, and had: 10257 RICHARD, b. Dec. 1912.
- 10258 FRANCIS JORDAN, b. June 17, 1888.
- 10259 LAWRENCE, b. June 23, 1890, m. March 1909, GRACE FABER, and had: 10260 LAWRENCE, JR., b. Sept. 3, 1910. Father or son d. Sept. 4, 1910.
- 10261 AMY, b. Apl. 7, 1893.

F8268 Fred Augustus Locke, born ——, married LOTTIE DEXTER.

Children of 9th Gen.

- 10262 CARRIE, b. ——.
- 10263 WINNIFRED, b. ——.
- 10264 DAISY, b. ——.
- 10265 HARRISON, b. ——.
- 10266 FLORENCE, b. ——.

NINTH GENERATION

F8293 Edwin Frank Tallant, born Dec. 2, 1855, married Aug. 19, 1881, SUSIE DREW of Concord. He lived in St. Paul, Minn.

Children of 9th Gen. b. in Minnesota.
10267 MARSTIN EDGAR, b. Minneapolis, July 5, 1882, m. ADELAIDE PAARECH.
10268 WEBSTER, b. Minneapolis, Dec. 3, 1884, m. IRMA NYE.
10269 RUTH LYDIA, b. St. Paul, Apl. 15, 1886.
10270 MARY SUSAN, b. St. Paul, June 12, 1888, m. CHARLES M. KOPP.

F8375 Simeon P. Locke, born in Epsom, Sept. 4, 1874, married in Pembroke, Sept. 27, 1892, CORA D. MILLBURY, born in Nova Scotia, 1873, daughter of Charles and Lizzie. He is a farmer in Pittsfield.

Children of 9th Gen. b. in Pittsfield.
10271 CLARENCE, b. Jan. 21, 1896, d. Jan. 25, 1896.
10272 FRANK S., b. March 19, 1897, died young.
10273 GRACE, b. twin, March 19, 1897.
10274 MADELINE C., b. March 19, 1899, d. March 26, 1899.

F8391 Anna McMurphy, born in Concord, March 16, 1854, married Nov. 26, 1878, FREEMAN R. NEVENS, born in New Gloucester, Me., Sept. 16, 1849, lived at Milton, Mass.

Children of 9th Gen. b. in Milton, Mass.
10275 BERTHA M., b. May 12, 1880, d. June 18, 1882.
10276 CHARLES A., b. March 24, 1883, d. June 13, 1887.
10277 BLANCHE M., b. June 17, 1885.
10278 FLORENCE L., b. June 8, 1888.
10279 GEORGE A., b. Apl. 25, 1891.

F8402 Frank Lovering Locke, born in Boston, July 14, 1865, married Jan. 16, 1901, MARY BROADHEAD KENDALL, daughter of Charles B. and Anna (Pike) of Worcester, born in Newfields, N. H., Nov. 17, 1870. (She was granddaughter of James Pike, D. D. of Newfields, Member of Congress and Col. of 16th N. H. Vols., and great granddaughter of Rev. John Broadhead, D. D., member of Congress.) He was Colonel on Gov. Wolcott's Staff, and is Assistant Superintendent of the Boston Rubber Shoe Co. with factory at Malden. Has been President of the Locke Association.

Children of 9th Gen. b. in Malden, Mass.
10280 JOHN LOVERING, b. Sept. 11, 1902.
10281 ELEANOR BROADHEAD, b. March 11, 1904.
10282 FRANCIS KENDALL, b. Nov. 8, 1906, d. Nov. 18, 1906.

F8403 Mabel Louise Locke, born Boston, June 15, 1876, married Nov. 28, 1900, GEORGE W. R. HARRIMAN, born May 25, 1871, and lives in Malden.
Children of 9th Gen. b. in Malden, Mass.
10283 ROGER LOCKE, b. Jan. 19, 1902.
10284 CHARLOTTE, b. June 19, 1906.
10285 ELIZABETH, b. Sept. 20, 1911.

F8456 Charles Clarence Locke, born in Irasburg, Vt., Nov. 16, 1863, married in Newport, Vt., Feb. 18, 1891, IDA L. GIFFIN, born in Sheffield, Vt., daughter of Albert and Fannie (Colburn). He lived at St. Johnsbury, Vt.
Children of 9th Gen.
10286 GRACE WINNIFRED, b. Oct. 18, 1892, m. Feb. 22, 1915, OREM N. JENNE.
10287 WILLIAM GIFFIN, b. Nov. 10, 1894, m. Jan. 20, 1915, GLADYS M. REED.
10288 FLORENCE, b. May 25, 1898.

F8627 Elizabeth Susan Locke, born in Barrington, Feb. 24, 1853, married LEWIS N. SMITH of Barrington.
Children of 9th Gen. b. in Barrington.
10289 LILLIAN, b. ——.
10290 LEWIS L., b. ——, m. Sept. 3, 1903, ESTELLE B. DRYSDALE, who d. July 21, 1904, four days after birth of son 10291 LEWIS D. J.
10292 LAFOREST, b. ——, m. Aug. 26, 1912, VIRGINIA MERRITT, had: 10293 FRANCES V., b. Aug. 6, 1913.
10294 LOYD, b. ——. 10295 LYLE b. ——.

F8705 Daniel Moshier Locke, born in Augusta, Me., July 12, 1850, married in Augusta, Oct. 12, 1872, ELIZABETH M. BICKFORD, born in Belgrade, Me., Jan. 5, 1851. He is a painter in Augusta.
Children of 9th Gen.
10296 SUSAN NELLIE, b. Belgrade, Me., July 8, 1874.
10297 MATTIE THEODATE, b. Augusta, Me., Dec. 27, 1876.

F8735 Martha J. Locke, born in Strafford, Feb. 4, 1856, married in Dover, Nov. 15, 1875, GEORGE S. JACKSON, of Great Falls, born in Rangeley, Me., 1853. He is a farmer in Madison, Me.
Children of 9th Gen.
10298 LESLIE E., b. Strafford, July 27, 1876, m. May 24, 1896, LILLIAN M. EMERSON of Lakeport, b. Lyndonville, Vt., 1875, dau. of Ephraim W. and Lucinda (Mortimer). He is a salesman.
10299 IDA M., b. Aug. 16, 1880.
10300 GEORGE S., b. Sept. 25, 1887.
10301 MAMIE, b. June 18, 1888.
10302 DAU., b. Madison, Me., June 17, 1895.

NINTH GENERATION

F8843 Oscar Rockwell Locke, born in Rochester, Sept. 9, 1857, married SARAH F. WINKLEY, born in Strafford, 1863. He was a shoemaker in Haverhill, Mass., and died in Strafford, 1912.

Children of 9th Gen.
10303 ERNEST, b. Dover, Aug. 6, 1876, d. Dover, July 20, 1878.
10304 GRACE, b. ——, m. —— EASTMAN.
10305 SON, b. Dover, Feb. 15, 1887.
10306 SYDNEY, b. ——.

F8858 Joseph Alfred Locke, born in Barrington, Nov. 17, 1860, married Nov. 18, 1882, GERTRUDE M. PARKER. He is a blacksmith, employed on B. & M. R. R. at Lowell, Keene and Hudson.

Children of 9th Gen.
10307 MAUDE G., b. Feb. 13, 1885, lives unmarried in Nashua.
10308 BERTHA I., b. Dec. 4, 1886, m. GEORGE TAYLOR, lives in East Boston, had: 10309 MARJORIE; and 10310 EVERETT.
10311 CORNELIA F., b. Dec. 24, 1888, lives unmarried in Manchester.
10312 JOSEPH PARKER, b. Dec. 6, 1896, d. Apl. 8, 1898.

F8859 Georgie Etta Locke, born in Barrington, Dec. 1, 1862, married Feb. 22, 1887, FRANK J. SPAULDING, born in Chelmsford, Mass., May 1, 1851, son of Benjamin J. and Mary A. (Jenkins). He had a first wife, JULIA A. FLETCHER. They lived in Lowell.

Children of 9th Gen. b. in Lowell.
10313 JULIA E., b. May 5, 1888, m. HARLAN E. KNOWLTON.
10314 GEORGE CHESTER, b. Sept. 3, 1889, d. July 27, 1890.
10315 EARL EVERETT, b. Nov. 8, 1896.

F8921 Martha Etta Berry, born in Alexandria, May 24, 1856, married in Bristol, Dec. 24, 1873, REV. FRANK E. BRIGGS, born in Boscawen, Dec. 2, 1849, son of Sherman. He is a Free Will Baptist Minister at Washington, Vt.

Children of 9th Gen.
10316 EDWARD M., b. Alexandria, Oct. 23, 1878, was a teacher in New Hampton Institute, 1902.
10317 ENA, b. Nov. 18, 1883.
10318 BERNIECE, b. No. Berwick, Me., Apl. 28, 1888.

F8947 Lottie A. Locke, born in Manchester, June 22, 1868, died Sept. 1, 1894, married May 5, 1888, E. C. POUND of Ryan, Iowa.

Children of 9th Gen.

10319 GEORGE WESLEY, b. Apl. 30, 1889, is a farmer in Harrold, So. Dakota.
10320 ROY LEONARD, b. Dec. 25, 1891, is a bank cashier Mitchell, So. Dakota.
10321 OLIVE MABEL, b. June 2, 1892, is a house keeper Dalhart, Texas.
10322 LOTTIE MAY, b. March 4, 1894, is a music teacher Dalhart, Texas.

F8948 Walter Locke, born in Central City, Iowa, Dec. 24, 1869, married Apl. 1, 1894, MAGGIE HAMBLIN. He is a mechanic in Ryan, Iowa.

Children of 9th Gen. b. in Ryan, Iowa.

10323 RUSSELL Y., b. Jan. 4, 1895, is a farmer in Ryan.
10324 ETHEL, b. May 25, 1896, is a teacher in Ryan.
10325 CECIL, b. Oct. 3, 1898.   10326 RUTH, b. Sept. 3, 1900.
10327 MAGGIE, b. March 9, 1903.   10328 RAYMOND, b. Apl. 21, 1905.
10329 CLAIRE, b. June 15, 1907.   10330 HAROLD, b. Feb. 6, 1909.
10331 LILLIAN, b. Apl. 5, 1911, d. 1912.
10332 INA, b. May 21, 1913.

F8953 S. Alice Locke, born in Central City, Iowa, July 1, 1870, married June 7, 1893, ARTHUR F. TURNER, born in Chelsea, Mass., Sept. 28, 1869. He was a printer and letter carrier in Laconia.

Children of 9th Gen.

10333 HERBERT LOCKE, b. Jan. 27, 1894.
10334 ARTHUR RAY, b. Nov. 25, 1895.

F8957 Marshall Ernest Locke, born in Roxbury, Mass., Jan. 2, 1882, married RACHEL MAE TAYLOR, born in Aberdeenshire, Scotland, Jan. 6, 1885. He lived in Haverhill, N. H., afterwards in Melrose, Mass.

Children of 9th Gen. b. in No. Haverhill.

10335 MARSHALL ERNEST, JR., b. Oct. 27, 1905.
10336 PHYLLIS MAE, b. Sept. 29, 1907.
10337 MARJORIE EMMA, b. Sept. 7, 1909.

F8978 Grace A. Seavey, born in Pembroke, Sept. 30, 1866, married in Boston, Nov. 28, 1889, ROBERT G. HARRIS.

Children of 9th Gen.

10338 GRACE E., b. Feb. 19, 1891, m. 1908, LOUIS L. DIAMOND and had:
    10339 ROBERT L., b. 1912, and 10340 DONALD S., b. 1914. Live Seattle.
10341 ROBERT G., b. Feb. 9, 1892.

F9008 Margaret E. Bickford, born June 13, 1876, married Feb. 27, 1906, JOSEPH D. BABO, born Feb. 7, 1878.

NINTH GENERATION

Children of 9th Gen.

10342 BEATRICE, b. Dec. 22, 1906.   10345 BERNICE, b. June 14, 1911.
10343 MARGARET, b. Feb. 21, 1908.   10346 JAMES H., b. June 3, 1912.
10344 JOSEPH, b. Dec. 4, 1909.

F9061 Aaron R. Locke, born in Rye, Aug. 11, 1847, married in North Hampton, Apl. 24, 1871, FRANCINA M. RAND, born in Rye, Sept. 20, 1848, died in Rye, Jan. 13, 1901. He was a mason in Rye and died Jan. 12, 1888.

Child of 9th Gen. b. in Rye.

10347 ALVAH H., b. Feb. 14, 1874, m. 1st, in Rye, Feb. 4, 1893, EMMA L. SMART, b. Rye, June 21, 1876, d. with son, July 5, 1893, dau. of Samuel and Mary (Garland). He was a shoemaker, lived in Dover and m. a second wife there; m. 3rd, Aug. 4, 1914, NANCY SULLIVAN, b. 1884, in Hudson.

F9062 Clara Eleanor Locke, born in Rye, Sept. 14, 1849, died in Exeter, July 7, 1909, married in Exeter, Aug. 6, 1872, JAMES I. WATSON, born in South Berwick, Me., Oct. 12, 1851, son of Irving M. and Lucy. He was a painter and worked in Exeter shoeshop.

Children of 9th Gen. b. in Exeter.

10349 JOHN IRVING, b. Sept. 6, 1873, m. Rexton, N. B., March 22, 1905, ABBIE BELL who d. Jan. 1909, had: 10350 IRVING LOCKE, b. Exeter, July 1, 1906.
10351 BERTHA MAY, b. Dec. 17, 1874, d. Aug. 11, 1900, m. Nottingham, March 17, 1896, PERLEY H. WATSON, and had: 10352 LAURA P., b. June 17, 1897, d. Aug. 11, 1900; 10353 ELEANOR R., b. May 16, 1898; and 10354 LOIS ANNIE, b. Jan. 21, 1900.
10355 MARION SPARLING, b. Aug. 3, 1887, lives Exeter.

F9064 Elsie C. Locke, born in Rye, May 18, 1852, died Apl. 21, 1886, married Aug. 7, 1870, CHRISTOPHER GRANT, a farmer in Rye, who died Apl. 28, 1880.

Children of 9th Gen. b. in Rye.

10356 ELSIE J., b. Aug. 12, 1872, d. Dec. 2, 1875.
10357 CHARLES, b. Aug. 1877, m. Nov. 27, 1901, ELIZA A. WALKER, b. Jan. 1882, dau. of George and August (Page). He lives in Rye.

F9068 Abbie S. Bazin, born in Dover, March 16, 1832, married Nov. 25, 1858, JAMES S. SPEAR, born Nov. 9, 1837, son of James and Mary (Green). He lives in New York City, is Outside Superintendent of John's Asbestos Co.

Children of 9th Gen.

10358 ABBIE L. SPEAR, b. Apl. 14, 1859, m. Dec. 25, 1880, CHARLES H. CHURCH, a grocer of Melrose Highlands, Mass., son of Asa and Joan (Brown). They had: 10359 CLARA, b. 1881; 10360 LOTTIE G., b. Jan. 5, 1883; 10361 HERBERT E., b. Feb. 11, 1887; 10362 ETHEL M., b. Dec. 28, 1889; 10363 RUTH, b. Oct. 13, 1892.

10364 EMILY, b. March 9, 1861.
10365 ERVING L., b. Sept. 21, 1868.
10366 MARION G., b. Oct. 26, 1871.
10367 MABEL H., b. twin, Oct. 26, 1871.

F9069 Savillian E. Bazin, born Apl. 18, 1837, married 1865 MARY E. WHITE, born Feb. 17, 1841. He is a paper hanger in Roxbury, Mass.

Children of 9th Gen.

10368 FRANK W., b. Nov. 2, 1866.
10369 CHARLES E., b. Apl. 12, 1869.
10370 LILLIE M., b. March 18, 1872, d. July 1873.
10371 HARRY H., b. Feb. 23, 1876.
10372 TRUE L., b. May 22, 1880.

F9070 Sarah W. Bazin, born Aug. 2, 1846, married Apl. 1866, CHARLES L. ROBINSON, born Dec. 22, 1846. He is foreman in a furniture Manufacturing Company, Boston.

Children of 9th Gen.

10373 SADIE L., b. Jan. 9, 1867, d. 1868.
10374 CHARLES, b. June 2, 1871, m. Apl. 4, 1893, EMMA R. MAXWELL, b. June 22, 1874, and had: 10375 MILDRED E., b. Feb. 16, 1895 and 10376 EDITH M., b. May 13, 1896.
10377 ALICE E., b. July 18, 1877.
10378 SAMUEL B., b. twin, d. same day, July 18, 1877.

F9116 Eliza Salter Anderson, born June 8, 1846, married at Navy Yard, Portsmouth, WILLIAM MARVIN of Portsmouth, who was in business there, and now lives retired in New Castle.

Children of 9th Gen. b. in Portsmouth.

10379 RUTH ALICE, b. March 23, 1870, lives at New Castle.
10380 WILLIAM EDWARD, b. Jan. 1, 1872, m. SUSAN R. BENT and had four children. He is a lawyer in Portsmouth.
10381 OLIVER BELL, b. Oct. 16, 1880, m. Aug. 30, 1899, CORA I. WHEELER of Portsmouth. He is a clerk in Portsmouth, lives in New Castle and has two children.

F9123 Edward Lyon, born June 10, 1835, married 1856, MELISSA ABBOTT. He was in the dry goods business in Sacramento, Cal., and died there.

Child of 9th Gen. b. in Sacramento, Cal.

10382 HATTIE, b. 1857, m. 1882, WILLIAM GERBER of Sacramento, had: 10383 MELISSA, b. 1884; 10384 HARRIET, b. 1886, and others.

NINTH GENERATION

F9124 John Lyon, born Oct. 20, 1837, married 1876, MARCIA HOLT. He was a farmer in Franklin where he died.
Children of 9th Gen. b. in Franklin.
10385 HARRY, b. 1877.
10386 CARRIE, b. 1881, was m. and had a child in Franklin.
10387 EMMA, b. 1884.   10389 HARRIET, b. 1890.
10388 HERBERT, b. 1886.   10390 LOUISE, b. ——.

F9127 Mary E. Brogan, born in Lowell, Oct. 16, 1843, married in Lowell, June 8, 1862, JAMES W. CASSIDY, born in Ireland, Dec. 22, 1838, lived in Lowell.
Children of 9th Gen. b. in Dracut, Mass.
10391 KATE F., b. Sept. 29, 1863, m. Lowell, Aug. 25, 1895, PHILIP J. FARLEY, who is a lawyer in Cambridge, Mass. Had: 10392 PHILIP, b. 1896; and 10393 KATHARINE, b. 1897.
10394 GEORGE W., b. Feb. 14, 1866, is a drummer of Lowell.
10395 MARIETTA, b. Aug. 8, 1868, a teacher, d. in Lowell.
10396 FRANK, b. Oct. 26, 1870, d. July 14, 1871.
10397 MARGARET R., b. Aug. 2, 1872, Trust Co. bookkeeper.
10398 JAMES J., b. Lowell, Oct. 2, 1874, is a physician.
10399 AGNES L., b. Oct. 29, 1876, lives at home.
10400 ANNIE I., b. Nov. 7, 1878, is a teacher.
10401 LEO, b. May 3, 1881, d. 1881.
10402 LORETTA, b. twin May 3, 1881, d. 1881.
10403 PAUL A., b. May 7, 1883, is a clerk in Middlesex Bank.
10404 ALICE, b. Dec. 24, 1884, d. Aug. 25, 1885.

F9128 Annie Brogan, born May 23, 1846, died Feb. 2, 1888, married Nov. 26, 1868, JOHN GALLAGHER, born in Ireland, Dec. 25, 1838, lived in Lowell and died May 21, 1891.
Children of 9th Gen. b. in Lowell, Mass.
10405 CHARLES JULIAN, b. Dracut, Mass., Jan. 9, 1869, is a druggist in Lowell.
10406 FRANK, b. 1870, d. 1870.   10409 EDWARD, died young.
10407 EMMA G., b. May 2, 1871.   10410 GEORGE, died young.
10408 NELLIE, b. 1872, d. 1872.   10411 AUGUSTINE, d. Fall River.

F9130 Emma Brogan, born June 7, 1854, married in Lowell, Aug. 1875, JAMES L. KINSELA, born in Ireland, March 4, 1851, died in Lowell, July 24, 1891.
Children of 9th Gen. b. in Lowell.
10412 JOHN, b. May 31, 1876, d. Lowell, June 21, 1895.
10413 MAY A., b. July 22, 1878, is a bookkeeper.
10414 CHARLES, b. May 3, 1882, is a clerk.
10415 GEORGE, b. Jan. 3, 1885.
10416 LORETTA, b. Apl. 12, 1887, is a clerk.
10417 ARTHUR, b. May 18, 1889.

F9136 George H. Locke, born in Stetson, Me., Oct. 8, 1845, married VIOLA WEEKS. He was a carpenter, moved from Stetson to Bangor in 1896, and died June 10, 1913.
Child of 9th Gen.
10418 KATE, b. Lowell, Mass., Jan. 23, 1872, m. STILLMAN B. LAWRENCE, a caterer in Bangor, Me.

F9137 Bradley Locke, born Sept. 8, 1846, married March 17, 1880, BINA WIGGIN. She married 2nd, ——— STAPLES.
Child of 9th Gen.
10419 IRVING, b. ———, was married.

F9138 Ann Locke, born March 24, 1849, married JOSEPH STILLINGS, who lived in Lowell.
Children of 9th Gen. b. in Lowell, Mass.
10420 MEDORA, b. May 30, 1867, m. Nov. 24, 1887, HOWARD S. ADAMS, and lives in Chelmsford, Mass. Had: 10421 DONALD F.; 10422 ALLAN H.
10423 CHARLES, b. Jan. 26, 1872, m. FLORA MORAN.
10424 EUGENE, b. March 22, 1877, m. ANNIE DELMORE, and had: 10425 E. FORREST; 10426 KATHRYN E.; 10427 ARTHUR L.; 10428 RITA RUTH.
10429 JOSEPH, b. July 22, 1880, d. Aug. 1, 1881.

F9139 Sarah J. Locke, born Dec. 3, 1854, married 1st, in Lowell, HARLTON STEVENS; married 2nd, OZNO D. LOMBARD. She lived in West Somerville, Mass.
Child of 9th Gen.
10430 MAUDE E., b. Oct. 1, 1884, m. Oct. 1, 1912, HERBERT WARREN COX and lived in West Somerville, Mass.

F9150 Josephine Dunbar, born Apl. 19, 1849, married March 23, 1872, JOSEPH E. JENKINS who died in East Boston, Feb. 18, 1907. She died in Lee, Feb. 18, 1901.
Children of 9th Gen. b. in East Boston.
10431 ELLERY D., b. Dec. 18, 1872, m. Sept. 28, 1899, ALICE M. RICHARDS, had: 10432 WAYNE; 10433 RALPH; 10434 WOODRUFF LEE, died young.
10435 EVELYN, b. Nov. 26, 1877, m. Oct. 15, 1898, CHARLES WENTWORTH and had: 10436 VALERY.

F9164 Charles Dunbar Locke, born in Rye, Dec. 8, 1867 married March 15, 1905, MABEL REMICK, daughter of Albert and Anna (Mace). He is a carpenter in Rye.
Children of 9th Gen. b. in Rye.
10437 JOSEPHINE, b. —— 1905. 10439 DOROTHY, b. June 8, 1912.
10438 EVELYN, b. Aug. 8, 1907. 10440 ETHEL, b. Dec. 28, 1914.

NINTH GENERATION

F9169 George A. Locke, born in Rye, June 14, 1858, married 1st, in Jefferson, Me., May 7, 1886, CORA S. PLACE, divorced in Oct. 1891; married 2nd, Jan. 22, 1892, MARGARET E. GILLIS, born in Portland, Me., 1871, daughter of William and Marion. He was a surfman in the U. S. Life Saving Service at Rye, retired 1916 after 32 years service.
Children of 9th Gen. b. in Rye, living in Portsmouth.
10441 ANNIE M., b. Feb. 21, 1893.   10444 JOHN JOSEPH, b. June 7, 1899.
10442 SARAH ALLEN, b. Apl. 7, 1894.   10445 ETHEL T., b. Feb. 26, 1902.
10443 MARGARET, b. Sept. 11, 1896.   10446 ALICE M., b. Oct. 8, 1904.

F9182 Minnie Locke Willis, born in Ramsey, Ill., Oct. 1879, married in Ramsey, Apl. 12, 1899, FREDERICK MOODY STODDARD of Ramsey, born in Hillsboro, Ill., May 9, 1876. He is a drug clerk in Ramsey.
Children of 9th Gen. b. in Ramsey, Ill.
10448 WILLIS F., b. Jan. 16, 1900, is a drug clerk in Ramsey.
10449 CARRIE FRANCES, b. Jan. 1, 1901.
10450 CHARLES L., b. June 6, 1903, d. Feb. 20, 1908.
10451 HARRY G., b. Dec. 2, 1904.
10452 FRANK D., b. March 4, 1910.   10453 JOE M., b. Sept. 27, 1914.

F9225 Warren D. Locke, born in Concord, Sept. 14, 1880, married HATTIE E. FAY, born in Danbury, 1891.
Children of 9th Gen.
10454 CHARLES LOREN (4th child), b. Danbury, Aug. 2, 1911.
10455 EDGAR WARREN (5th), b. Concord, Sept. 2, 1913.

F9226 Charles Elmer or **Elmer D. Locke,** born Apl. 1, 1882, married NELLIE C. PLUMMER, born in Concord, 1888.
Children of 9th Gen.
10456 NELLIE IRENE, b. March 20, 1908.
10457 THELMA, b. March 10, 1909.
10458 PAULINE ELIZABETH, b. Oct. 2, 1911.
10459 RUTH E., b. Concord, Dec. 10, 1913.

F9268 Mary White Griffin, born May 9, 1856, died Portsmouth, June 8, 1913, married Nov. 29, 1876, FRED B. COLEMAN, born Portsmouth, Feb. 17, 1856, son of J. Wiley. He is a druggist in Portsmouth.
Children of 9th Gen. b. in Portsmouth.
10460 GERTRUDE M., b. March 5, 1879, d. Apl. 24, 1879.
10461 FLORENCE BELLE, b. March 25, 1880, m. Portsmouth, June 29, 1907, JAMES HORACE PEVERLY.
10462 FRED W., b. Dec. 15, 1883.
10463 RUTH A., b. June 19, 1893.   10464 LYMAN G., b. Oct. 5, 1898.

F9269 George Albert Griffin, born March 12, 1858, married Sept. 25, 1883, JULIA B. BRADFORD of Peabody, Mass., where he is a bookkeeper.

Children of 9th Gen. b. in Peabody, Mass.
10465 MILDRED AURORA, b. July 29, 1886.
10466 ORWIN BRADFORD, b. May 29, 1893.

F9278 Austin Pike Locke, born in Portsmouth, March 23, 1871, married in Wakefield, Feb. 22, 1897, IMOGENE TEBBETTS, born in Wakefield, 1871. He was a conductor in Allston, Mass., and died in Portsmouth, Feb. 7, 1903. She was a teacher, and married 2nd, Apl. 8, 1908, ORMOND D. JUNKINS.

Child of 9th Gen.
10467 BEATRICE TEBBETTS, b. Allston, Mass., Aug. 27, 1897.

The Locke Entertainers of 1915

UPPER PICTURES, LOCKE ENTERTAINERS, 1915
LOWER PICTURE, OLDER LOCKE SPECTATORS, ONE OF WHOM IS AGED 92

TENTH GENERATION

F9300 Wallace S. Goss, born in Rye, Dec. 20, 1856, married 1st, May 21, 1880, SARAH E. CASWELL, born in Rye, Apl. 6, 1862, died in Rye, Feb. 26, 1896, daughter of Samuel and Sarah; married 2nd, Oct. 20, 1909, MRS. MARION C. (BENNETT) CONCONNAN, born in Nova Scotia, 1872, daughter of John H. Bennett.

Children of 10th Gen. b. in Rye.

10470 JOHN STERLING, b. Dec. 17, 1880, drowned at Rye Harbor, July 11, 1903.
10471 MELVIN J., b. Oct. 14, 1882, m. Nov. 7, 1905, FLORENCE W. GARLAND, b. Nov. 12, 1881, dau. of Horace and Angenette. He is in a Lynn hardware store and they have in 11th. Gen. of children: 10472 STANLEY, b. Portsmouth, July 17, 1906; 10473 RICHARD, b. Concord, Jan. 8, 1912; 10474 RAYMOND L. b. May 1915.
10475 LEON W., b. Nov. 5, 1886, d. Taunton, Mass., Sept. 16, 1913.
10476 PHILIP N., b. Jan. 21, 1894, d. aged 7 mos.
10477 ELIZABETH A., b. Feb. 22, 1896.

F9312 Richard Jenness Locke, born in Rye, May 31, 1863, married in North Hampton, Feb. 23, 1898, BESSIE L. BACHELDER, born in North Hampton, 1874. He has a boarding house in Rye. She is the daughter of Charles and Martha (Brown).

Children of 10th. Gen. b. in Rye.

10478 RICHARD J., b. Apl. 3, 1903.
10479 EDWIN, J., b. Apl. 11, 1908.

F9313 Annie L. Locke, born Feb. 22, 1866, married Apl. 11, 1894, LANGDON B. PARSONS, born in Rye, Dec. 24, 1844, son of Thomas T. and Eliza (Brown). He lives in Rye.

Children of 10th Gen. b. in Rye.

10480 JOHN LANGDON, b. June 3, 1895, student Mass. Ins. of Technology.
10481 CORINNE BROWN, b. May 13, 1896, student Boston.

F9315 Clarence A. Goss, born Feb. 11, 1860, married 1st, Jan. 23, 1876, MARY MACE. They were divorced and he married 2nd, July 8, 1882, ELLA E. GARLAND, born Jan. 12, 1858, died June 11, 1916, daughter of Samuel and Eliza (Marston). He is a farmer in Rye.

Children of 10th Gen. b. in Rye.

10482 HARRIET D., b. June 1, 1888, m. June 1, 1910, ERNEST MOULTON of No. Hampton, and had: 10483 WILLIAM ALBERT, b. Rye, June 7, 1911.

10484 ANNIE M., b. Jan. 26, 1890.

F9316 Estelle J. Goss, born Aug. 16, 1861, married in Rye, Feb. 28, 1885, EDWARD P. PHILBRICK, born Dec. 5, 1856, son of Rufus and Hannah (Moshier). He is a janitor in Somerville, Mass.

Children of 10th Gen. b. in Rockport, Mass.

10485 NEAL BAILEY, b. Apl. 28, 1888, m. July 27, 1907, ANNIE R. JENNESS of Rye, where they reside. She was b. Jan. 20, 1885, dau. of Joseph Rand & Emily (Foss) but was adopted by a Jenness.

10486 HESTER, b. June 15, 1890, m. Sept. 15, 1915, ELIAS WILLIAM WENTZELL, b. Nova Scotia, Nov. 7, 1887, son of Elias. He is a salesman in Boston.

F9353 James Adelbert Locke, born July 11, 1872, married UNA DEVERE HAZARD of Providence, was a printer in Phoenix, Arizona, later (1913) in Pueblo, Col.

Children of 10th Gen.

10487 ALBERT J., b. Oct. 22, 1894.
10488 JAMES, b. ——.
10489 SON, b. Pueblo, Col. 1913.

F9355 George A. Locke, born in Madbury, Nov. 28, 1850, married in Lee, Dec. 25, 1878, HATTIE J. CHURCH, born in Dover, Aug. 20, 1860, died in Haverhill, Mass., Oct. 25, 1893, daughter of Samuel and Mary J. They lived in Dover.

Child of 10th Gen.

10490 EDITH M., b. March 23, 1880.

F9356 Ann Elizabeth Locke, born in Madbury, Aug. 19, 1852, married 1st, Feb. 11, 1877, ISRAEL PIERCE CHURCH of Madbury, born March 1, 1823, son of Benjamin and Abigail (Hall); married 2nd, July 3, 1893, EDWIN J. ANDREWS of Danville, P. Q., born 1862. He is a farmer in Durham.

Children of 10th Gen.

10491 JOHN E. CHURCH, b. Nov. 18, 1881, is in Albany, N. Y.
10492 EULAH G. ANDREWS, b. Durham, Apl. 13, 1896.

F9358 Ida B. Locke, born in Madbury, May 10, 1858, died Nov. 6, 1910, married in Lee, March 9, 1879, ROSCOE S. OTIS, a farmer of Durham.

TENTH GENERATION

Children of 10th Gen. b. in Durham.

10493 WINNIE F., b. May 3, 1881, m. 1901, PAUL W. WIGGIN and has four children in Newmarket.
10494 MAUDE E., b. Jan. 6, 1883, m. IRVING TOWLE, lives in Dover and has: 10495 KENNETH, b. Jan. 1914.
10496 CHARLES G., b. Oct. 11, 1886, d. May 23, 1899.
10497 LEON R., b. Jan. 28, 1890.
10498 LENA L., b. Dec. 13, 1890, m. JONES STEVENS of Newmarket.
10499 PAUL WESLEY, b. June 22, 1901.

F9359 Fred E. Locke, born June 24, 1861, married in Durham, Nov. 27, 1889, MAY A. AMAZEEN, born in Portsmouth, 1866, daughter of William H. and Mary. He was a farmer in Madbury, later a tinsmith in Haverhill, Mass.

Child of 10th Gen.

10500 HAROLD I., b. Madbury, Aug. 25, 1890, m. Nashua, Dec. 7, 1912, ESTHER M. BIXBY of Haverhill, Mass., b. Norway, Me., 1894, dau. of Wilbur F. and Lizzie E. (Dole). He is a shoemaker in Haverhill, Mass.

F9376 Clarenda J. Rand, born Nov. 16, 1847, married Oct. 17, 1865, JOHN DREW of Concord, born 1847, son of Moran. He lived in Concord and is now in Boston.

Children of 10th Gen.

10501 GRACE E., b. Nov. 26, 1866, m. Aug. 20, 1903, GEORGE W. ALGER, son of Charles J., of Vermont. He is a lawyer in N. Y. City, and has children.
10502 BESSIE R., b. Nov. 26, 1874, m. June 1, 1898 BENJAMIN H. CURRIER of Boston.

F9378 John W. Rand, born 1850, married 1st, Nov. 26, 1872, EMMA WARD of Penacook, born in Salem, 1855, died in Concord, Jan. 20, 1889, daughter of Thomas and Lydia (Gage); married 2nd, Nov. 26, 1890, IDA B. BROWN of Concord, born 1864, died 1915, daughter of Charles and Rebecca (Glines). He is a carpenter and farmer in Concord.

Child of 10th Gen. b. in Concord.

10503 EVA, b. 1885, m. Feb. 11, 1915, WALTER A. EMERY.

F9387 Ira E. Randall, born Jan. 31, 1854, married July 12, 1876, ANNIE WILSON.

Children of 10th Gen.

10504 ARTHUR E., b. Dec. 25, 1877.
10505 ELLA M., b. May 1, 1879, d. Portsmouth, 1903.

F9388 Addie Randall, born Sept. 2, 1858, married Aug. 28, 1882, WILLIAM P. PICKETT, born 1860, son of Charles and Sarah (Pettigrew). He was a prominent man in Portsmouth, a member of Odd Fellows and Masons, highly respected and well liked by all. He died Aug. 23, 1913.
Children of 10th Gen. b. in Portsmouth.
10506 MARIE, b. Jan. 28, 1884, m. ARTHUR E. McCLARY of Malone, N. Y. Aug. 24, 1909.
10507 CHARLES WALDO, b. May 6, 1885.

F9389 Jennie L. Randall, born Feb. 2, 1861, married Aug. 17, 1886, WALTER D. HARDY, son of Rev. Arthur C. and Elizabeth (Martins). They were divorced.
Child of 10th Gen.
10508 RICHARD, b. Sept. 6, 1887.

F9421 Orrin Willey Locke, born in Coventry, Vt., Apl. 24, 1859, married 1st, May 19, 1886, LILLA LUELLA FAYER, born Aug. 16, 1859, died Jan. 2, 1905; married 2nd, Feb. 15, 1906, her sister, EDNA E. FAYER, born May 7, 1853. He is a merchant in Barton Landing, Vt., a Sunday School Superintendent and has been a representative and senator in Legislature.
Child of 10th Gen. b. in Irasburg, Vt.
10509 CLYDE EARLE, b. Nov. 3, 1889, m. July 14, 1914, MURIEL PALMER of Wilder, Vt., He graduated from Dartmouth 1911, and is now a civil Engineer in Buffalo, N. Y.

F9423 Burt Wallace Locke, born in Barton Landing, Vt., Oct. 7, 1874, married Oct. 22, 1907, EVA AGNES MARTIN, born in East Bolton, Can., March 21, 1881, daughter of George A. of Lowell, Mass. He lives in Montpelier, Vt.
Children of 10th Gen.
10510 RALPH MARTIN, b. Apl. 17, 1909.
10511 FRANK KNIGHT, b. Aug. 24, 1911.
10512 KENNETH GILBERT, b. Oct. 28, 1913.

F9424 Lillah B. Locke, born in Brownington, Vt., May 14, 1866, died in Sutton, Quebec, June 9, 1910, married in Richford, Vt., Feb. 1888, JAMES M. STOWELL.
Children of 10th Gen.
10513 HOMER CEDRIC, b. Dec. 16, 1888, lives Sutton, Que.
10514 MYRTLE LILLIAN, b. Aug. 8, 1893.
10515 GLENNA MAY, b. Nov. 3, 1905.

TENTH GENERATION 555

F9439 Mabel S. Trefethern, born Aug. 9, 1872, married June 19, 1899, GEORGE B. STACKPOLE, born June 20, 1871, son of George W. of Maine. He lives in Taunton, Mass.
Children of 10th Gen. b. in Taunton, Mass.
10516 LOUISE E., b. Sept. 22, 1900.
10517 MARY G., b. Dec. 8, 1901.
10518 GEORGE TREFETHERN, b. Oct. 3, 1903.

F9468 Lelia Goodwin Ransom, born in Great Isle, N. Y., May 6, 1871, married July 8, 1889, JOSEPH B. BARNES.
Children of 10th Gen. b. in N. Y. State.
10519 JOSEPH. 10520 EDNA. 10521 RUTH. 10522 ROLLIN. 10523 RALPH, b. Dec. 1, 1893. 10524 JENNIE, b. Apl. 8, 1910.

F9470 Lucia Edwards Ransom, born June 10, 1877, married July 12, 1898, FREDERICK WILLIAM BYERS, born Jan. 13, 1874.
Children of 10th Gen. b. in N. Y. State.
10525 MIRIAM S., b. May 21, 1901.
10526 SELNA O., b. March 24, 1904, d. March 27, 1904.
10527 BEATRICE WINNIFRED, b. Jan. 10, 1907.

F9472 Josephine Haughton, born Apl. 20, 1865, married Nov. 17, 1887, PERRY A. WILLBER, born June 30, 1867. He was a school teacher and later County Commissioner, in Lawrence Co., Ill.
Children of 10th Gen. b. in Lawrence Co., Ill.
10528 ALICE H., b. July 8, 1889, is a high school teacher.
10529 KARL A., b. Aug. 15, 1890, m. June 11, 1914, AMY L. LOGSDON, b. July 17, 1893. They were both high school teachers.
10530 JOSEPHINE C., b. Apl. 10, 1892, a teacher in Bridgeport, Ill.
10531 PARMELIA F., b. March 22, 1894, a teacher in Centerville, Ill.
10532 GEORGE H., b. Sept. 14, 1896, is in High School.
10533 EDITH, b. July 29, 1898, is in High School.
10534 OKIE, b. March 16, 1901.
10535 BRYAN, b. Jan. 22, 1906.

F9473 Charles Edwin Haughton, born Dec. 10, 1866, married Dec. 29, 1886, JENNIE ELIZABETH RIDGEWAY, born March 9, 1868. He is a merchant in Oaktown, Ind.
Children of 10th Gen. b. in Oaktown, Ind.
10536 DEWEY, b. Feb. 7, 1888, a clerk in his father's store.
10537 MAYFAIR, b. July 29, 1900.
10538 HELEN GOULD, b. Sept. 4, 1903.

F9474 Andrew J. Haughton, born Jan. 11, 1869, married June 24, 1890, SURELDA A. WILLBER, born March 9, 1879. He is a carpenter and contractor, also alderman in Ravensville, Ill.

Child of 10th Gen. b. in Ravensville, Ill.
10539 EVALINE, b. Sept. 16, 1892, m. Sept. 20, 1909, ROSCOE JOHNSON, a farmer, and had: 10540 BYRON G., b. July 20, 1911; 10541 MARVIN O., b. Nov. 24, 1913.

F9489 Bertha L. Horn, born Oct. 9, 1864, married Jan. 18, 1888, JOHN A. ALLEN.

Children of 10th Gen.
10542 BESSIE L., b. Nov. 8, 1888, m. Sept. 23, 1914, LELAND H. GILE.
10543 MATTIE, b. Dec. 27, 1889, m. Oct. 28, 1914, WILLIS BLAISDELL.
10544 BERTHA, b. Sept. 4, 1893.

F9502 Howard Ashton Locke, born in Somersworth, May 15, 1877, married in Somersworth, July 22, 1896, LOTTIE A. WARREN, born in Prince Edward Island, Jan. 9, 1875, daughter of Wellington and Martha (Scott). He lives in Brockton, Mass.

Children of 10th Gen.
10545 MARGARET WARREN, b. Somersworth, July 3, 1899.
10546 CHARLES EVERETT, b. Somersworth, May 12, 1903.
10547 ETHEL MAE, b. Brockton, Mass., Dec. 22, 1914.

F9505 Florence Rebecca Locke, born in Somersworth, Sept. 12, 1883, married in Dover, Aug. 30, 1902, FRED WILMOT DYER, born in Dover, March 7, 1882. He is a painter in York Village, Me.

Children of 10th Gen.
10548 MADELINE EVELYN, b. Somersworth, May 4, 1905.
10549 THELMA ESTELLE, b. Brockton, Mass., Apl. 6, 1907.
10550 FRED WILMOT, JR., b. Brockton, June 3, 1909.
10551 GEORGE EVERETT, b. York Village, Me., Oct. 14, 1913, d. July 9, 1914.

F9511 Richard Irving Hussey, born Dec. 28, 1859, married ANNIE GERRY of South Berwick Me. He was a baker and died July 12, 1887.

Children of 10th Gen.
10552 ALSTON G., b. Jan. 24, 1886, d. Feb. 22, 1886.
10553 BERTHA L., b. July 23, 1884, m. July 23, 1906, GROVER C. HOYT, a reporter in Boston, and has: 10554 ESTHER M., b. June 9, 1907.

TENTH GENERATION 557

F9512 Frank Hussey, born Aug. 27, 1868, married DORA D. AMAZEEN of Garland Me. He is a farmer.
Children of 10th Gen.
10555 MARY E., b. ——, m. EDWIN WALKER of Exeter, Me., b. June 5, 1888.
10556 FANNY L., b. ——, m. PIERCE STRAW of Exeter, Me., b. Apl. 10, 1888.

F9566 Mary A. Mace, born Feb. 1, 1867, married June 6, 1886, JOHN W. GALE of Amesbury.
Children of 10th Gen.
10557 ANNA LOUISE, b. July 10, 1887, m. June 15, 1915, ——— ———.
10558 HARRIET ELLEN, b. Nov. 9, 1893.
10559 ROLAND ELVIN, b. Sept. 12, 1896.

F9572 Maude W. Moore, born in Brownsville, Cal., Jan. 10, 1867, married Oct. 23, 1883, JAMES W. MCCARTHY, a mechanic who died in Reidsville, N. C., Apl. 14, 1898.
Children of 10th Gen. b. in Reidsville, N. C.
10560 EVA E., b. Aug. 31, 1884.
10561 EUDORA H., b. Aug. 3, 1886.
10562 MAUDE E., b. Nov. 20, 1887.
10563 WILLIAM M., b. Oct. 29, 1890, d. 1896.
10564 JOHN W., b. Apl. 10, 1893, d. 1893.
10565 HENRY C., b. Nov. 10, 1896.

F9573 Harry Locke Moore, born in Biddeford, Me., Aug. 20, 1869, married June 15, 1892, EMMA J. BROWN of Thomasville, N. C.
Children of 10th Gen. b. in Reidsville, N. C.
10566 EMMA M., b. May 23, 1893.
10567 HARRIDEL L., b. Sept. 6, 1894.
10568 HENRY B., b. Nov. 19, 1897.

F9577 Lizzie Bradbury Pray, born in Reidsville, N. C., Feb. 18, 1872, married in Kittery, Me., Sept. 9, 1891, CALVIN D. DUNBAR, born in Bangor, Me., June 27, 1870. He is in the insurance business in Kittery.
Children of 10th Gen. b. in Kittery, Me.
10569 HELEN, b. March 7, 1893, m. Dec. 1, 1914, PAYMASTER GEORGE S. WOOD, U. S. N.
10570 NORMAN DEAN, b. Feb. 10, 1898.

F9578 Eva Adelaide Pray, born in Portsmouth, Nov. 11, 1873, married Oct. 3, 1894, FRED W. PRYOR of Melrose, Mass. He has a bicycle store in Hartford, Conn.
Children of 10th Gen. b. in Hartford, Conn.
10571 ARNOLD KENNETH, b. Nov. 27, 1895.
10572 EARL FRANCIS, b. Jan. 15, 1898.

F9618 Sidney Locke, born 1861, married JANETTE HAMMOND. He is in "Mens Furnishing" business, and was Municipal Councillor for Lockeport, N. S.
Children of 10th Gen. b. in Lockeport, Nova Scotia.
10573 RUBY, b. 1887. 10574 HOWARD, b. 1890. 10575 ERMINIE, b. 1893.
All three children were killed July 8, 1901.

F9701 Albert Vasco Locke, born in Lake Village, Feb. 5, 1862, married in Lake Village, June 30, 1885, LOTTIE M. BAILEY, born in Tilton, Oct. 16, 1866, daughter of Orrin D. and Sarah (Adams). A painter by trade, later was a dealer in shoes and rubbers, Brooklyn, N. Y., !n 1908.
Children of 10th Gen.
10574 HARRY FLETCHER, b. Jan. 23, 1886.
10575 EVELYN JENNIE, b. Gilford, Jan. 22, 1888.

F9407 Ida Belle Locke, born in Rochester, Dec. 28, 1862, married May 17, 1880, JEREMIAH L. FRENCH, born in Gilmanton, son of Sylvester. He was a farmer in Gilmanton, and later a carriage maker in Concord, 1907.
Children of 10th Gen. b. in Gilmanton.
10576 CHARLES A., b. Aug. 14, 1881, m. Nov. 1900 ——— ———, lived in Concord and had two children. Carriage maker, Concord.
10577 ALBERT, b. July 27, 1883, is m. lives Concord.
10578 HARRY A., b. Nov. 27, 1887, m. July 17, 1908, ELAINE DELIA CARROLL, b. 1892, lives in Concord.
10579 CARL F., b. Apl. 11, 1889.
10580 NEWMAN D., b. June 17, 1895.
10581 ROSE, b. ———.

F9709 Henry Peaslee Locke, born in Gilmanton, Nov. 5, 1867, married Apl. 4, 1886, JENNIE M. FOSS, born in Nottingham 1868, daughter of Edwin of Northwood. He is a carriage painter in Farmington and Northwood.
Children of 10th Gen.
10582 JESSIE MAY, b. Rochester, Feb. 21, 1888, m. ARTHUR COOPER of Nottingham, and had four children.
10583 LUELLA ANNA, b. New Durham, Apl. 24, 1890, d. Farmington, May 12, 1893.
10584 ROSCOE EDWIN, b. Farmington, July 15, 1897.

F9710 George Andrew Locke, born in Concord, Nov. 10, 1871, married in Webster, Dec. 28, 1893, DESDEMONA E. WOODS, born in Newbury, 1870, daughter of James F. and Eliza A. He

TENTH GENERATION 559

was a blacksmith in Webster several years, now is of Randolph, Vt.

Children of 10th Gen. b. in Webster.
10585 JENNIE M., b. Aug. 12, 1896.
10586 HIRAM ELIOT, b. March 18, 1899.
10587 OTIS LEON, b. Jan. 15, 1901. (4th Child).
10588 RAYMOND ELVIN, b. June 8, 1903.
10589 HENRY DODGE, b. Jan. 2, 1905.
10590 PEARL AGNES, b. Jan. 27, 1908.

F9727 Harriet F. Jones, born in Gilmanton, Oct. 6, 1874, died in Meredith, June 8, 1910, married Nov. 10, 1894, FRANK A. CONVERSE, born in Strafford, Conn., March 24, 1872, son of D. L. and Mary (Ledoit). He is a machinist by trade, lived at Gilmanton and Meredith, but since 1906 has been a B. & M. R. R. Clerk.

Children of 10th Gen.
10591 JAMES MILLARD, b. Belmont, Feb. 23, 1902.
10592 HAYDEN FRANK, b. July 5, 1903.
10593 RUDOLPH R., b. Northfield, Aug. 2, 1904.

F9748 Winnifred Smith, born June 1, 1861, married Oct. 12, 1886, FREDERICK W. EMERY of Somersworth, lived in Dorchester, Mass.

Children of 10th Gen.
10594 FORREST R., b. 1887, d. 1890.
10595 MARLON S., b. Nov. 24, 1891.
10596 FORREST S., b. June 2, 1894.

F9761 Ethel Amanda Dow, born in Salem, Mass., Oct. 22, 1884, married Haverhill, Mass., Oct. 26, 1904, OSCAR S. HUTCHINSON.

Children of 10th Gen.
10597 WINFIELD O., b. Aug. 14, 1905.
10598 HOWARD A., b. Oct. 10, 1906.
10599 CHARLES D., b. Nov. 9, 1907.
10600 LOUISA I., b. March 17, 1909.

F9774 Helen Farrington Locke, born in Salem, Mass., March 28, 1887, married EDWARD W. HALL of Peabody, who is in the B. &. M. R. R. freight office there.

Children of 10th Gen. b. in Peabody, Mass.
10601 RUTH F., b. Sept. 14, 1908.
10602 DONALD, F., b. Aug. 4, 1910.
10603 BARBARA, b. June 3, 1914.

F9795 Abby Churchill Ballard, born in Louisville Ky., Feb. 16, 1879, married there June 1, 1899, JEFFERSON DAVIS STEWART of Georgia.

Children of 10th Gen.
10604 ABBY BALLARD, b. Sept. 15, 1912.
10605 JEFFERSON D., JR., b. March 25, 1915.

F9959 Martha Ann Amazeen, born July 3, 1882, married CHESTER BECKER, May 16, 1901, of New Castle.

Children of 10th Gen. b. New Castle.
10606 FLOYD, b. Nov. 24, 1902, d. July 5, 1906.
10607 DOROTHY E., b. Jan. 29, 1905.
10608 HENRY, b. Jan. 8, 1907.

F9961 Fitz Harry Locke, born in Lawrence, March 21, 1888, married in Lawrence 1910, CLARA JOSEPHINE CRAWFORD, born in Lawrence, May 13, 1886, daughter of Dr. John W. and Carra R. (Marsh) of Lawrence. He is in the mill construction business with his father in Lawrence.

Children of 10th Gen. b. in Lawrence, Mass.
10609 SHIRLEY CARROLL, b. Aug. 29, 1910.
10610 MARGARET JUNE, b. June 24, 1912.
10611 LANGDON ELVYN, b. June 19, 1914, d. Oct. 1, 1914.
10612 SON.

F10000 Bertha G. Locke, born Apl. 1, 1888, married Jan. 30, 1909, WILLIAM E. ELDRIDGE, born in Nova Scotia, Oct. 22, 1881.

Children of 10th Gen.
10613 CHARLOTTE B., b. June 10, 1909.
10614 WILLIAM WALTER, b. Sept. 26, 1910.
10615 HARRY AUBREY, b. Jan. 5, 1915.

F10133 Harry Berton Locke, born Sept. 9, 1868, married 1st, Nov. 27, 1890, ELLEN BARKER, born in Rosendale, Wis., March 2, 1871, married 2nd, June 18, 1901, ELIZA ELLA TAYLOR. They live in Ellsworth, Wis.

Children of 10th Gen. b. in Beldenville, Pa.
10616 FRED EUGENE, b. June 21, 1892, lives in St. Paul, Minn.
10617 RALPH BARKER, b. March 12, 1896.

F10134 Edna Amy Locke, born Apl. 3, 1871, married 1st, Nov. 24, 1887, CHARLES H. GOLDSMITH, born in River Falls, Wis., May 12, 1868, died Sept. 1, 1895; married 2nd, May 26,

1897, MILLARD FILLMORE REED, born in Humphrey, N. Y., May 25, 1867. They live in Ellsworth, Wis.
Children of 10th Gen.
10618 BERNICE F. GOLDSMITH, b. Dec. 10, 1894.
10619 BIRDIE A. REED, b. July 15, 1898.
10620 ESTHER E. REED, b. March 31, 1902.
10621 EVERAL REED, b. Aug. 9, 1906.

F10135 Sarah Celestia (Birdie) Locke, born June 7, 1874, married in Hudson, Wis., Sept. 20, 1893, GEORGE BYRON REED, born in Humphrey, N. Y., May 26, 1868, lived in Beldenville, Pa., and later in Ellsworth, Wis.
Children of 10th Gen.
10622 CLYDE LOCKE, b. Beldenville, Pa., Feb. 26, 1895.
10623 EMMA IRIS, b. Beldenville, Pa., Feb. 14, 1897.
10624 EDWIN MORRIL, b. March 12, 1899.
10625 JOYCE AMY, b. Aug. 13, 1901.
10626 LENORE ELLEN, b. Sept. 20, 1903.

F10141 Fred Eugene Locke, born in Titusville, Pa., Jan. 19, 1871, married 1st, Aug. 12, 1891, MYRTLE VICTORIA KOUGH, born in Titusville, Oct. 26, 1875; married 2nd, Oct. 12, 1899, MABEL LEONE YEARICK. He is a bookkeeper in Titusville.
Children of 10th Gen. b. in Titusville, Pa.
10627 FLORENCE HAZEL, b. June 25, 1892, m. June 23, 1909, WILLIAM ANTILL, a laborer of Townville, Pa. They have in 11th Gen.: 10628 STEPHEN F., b. June 11, 1910; 10629 BLANCHE MARY, b. Nov. 10, 1912; and 10630 LOIS L., b. July 24, 1914.
10631 MAUDE MILDRED, b. July 24, 1895, m. Jan. 6, 1911, CARROLL J. BARKER, an oil well pumper of Kane, Pa. Have children in 11th Gen.: 10632 MARGARET L., b. Apl. 29, 1912; 10633 SARAH L., b. Feb. 1914.
By second wife:
10634 JONATHAN LLOYD, b. Jan. 21, 1901.
10635 EVE LEONE, b. Apl. 19, 1902.
10636 JOSEPH CARL, b. March 19, 1903.
10637 STEPHEN PAUL, b. twin, March 19, 1903.
10638 FRED E., JR., b. Nov. 5, 1905.
10639 CLAIRE BARTON, b. Feb. 6, 1907.
10640 THOMAS ASHLEY, b. May 26, 1910.
10641 MARY ELIZABETH, b. Oct. 5, 1912.

F10142 Stephen F. Locke, born in Titusville, Pa., July 2, 1874, married in Limestone, N. Y., Apl. 27, 1897, FRANCES M. MURNING, born in Randolph, N. Y., May 28, 1876. He is a moulder in Bradford, Pa.

Children of 10th Gen. b. in Bradford, Pa.
10642 ARTHUR FRANCIS, b. March 23, 1898.
10643 VIVIAN MARIE, b. Sept. 3, 1899.
10644 STEPHEN DONALD, b. Jan. 23, 1901.
10645 JAMES LAWRENCE, b. July 14, 1909.

F10143 Maude Ora Locke, born in Titusville, Pa., July 20, 1876, married July 20, 1892, JOSEPH NEWTON FULTON, born in Titusville, July 1, 1873. He is in the automobile business in Buffalo, N. Y.

Child of 10th Gen. b. in Titusville, Pa.
10646 CLARENCE DAVID, b. March 20, 1894, m. May 11, 1914, ANNA GEMMER. He and father have a garage in Buffalo, N. Y.

F10146 Mary Ashley Locke, born June 17, 1880, married Dec. 5, 1903, GEORGE LANG, who is an oil well worker in Shamrock, Oklahoma.

Children of 10th Gen.
10647 JOSEPHINE THELMA, b. Sept. 12, 1904.
10648 STEPHEN KENT, b. May 26, 1906.
10649 MARGUERITE, b. July 29, 1909.

F10147 Mabel Emma Locke, born March 25, 1882, married Apl. 1, 1899, JOSEPH C. CALDWELL, who is a hostler in Titusville, Pa.

Children of 10th Gen. b. in Titusville, Pa.
10650 JOSEPH FLOYD, b. Oct. 7, 1900.
10651 FLORENCE SARAH, b. May 7, 1902.
10652 PAUL LOCKE, b. July 19, 1904.
10653 LOIS LORETTA, b. Oct. 15, 1906.
10654 THIRZA MARION, b. June 25, 1911, d. same day.

F10151 Hannah Bigelow Locke, born Feb. 16, 1886, married Jan. 28, 1903, OTTO RICKE, who is a blacksmith in Titusville, Pa.

Children of 10th Gen. b. in Titusville Pa.
10655 OTTO MERLE, b. July 25, 1903.
10656 MINA JOSEPHINE, b. Apl. 15, 1907, d. Apl. 24, 1907.
10657 JONATHAN LOCKE, b. May 11, 1908, d. same day.
10658 MARY ALICE, b. Apl. 27, 1910.
10659 MARGARET LOIS, b. Dec. 24, 1912, d. Dec. 28, 1912.
10660 DONALD WILLIAM, b. Jan. 23, 1915.

F10152 Louis Dunmeyes Locke, born in Titusville, Pa., June 7, 1890, married Apl. 14, 1910, ANNA JOHNSON. He is a machinist in Buffalo, N. Y.

Children of 10th Gen.
10661 EVELYN GENEVIEVE, b. March 16, 1911.
10662 ESTHER GEORGEANNA, b. Feb. 22, 1913.
10663 ANNA LOUISE, b. Sept. 23, 1914.

F10165 Martha E. Magoon, born Aug. 18, 1857, married Feb. 16, 1879, WILLIAM H. HIGGINS.
Children of 10th Gen.
10664 ROSA BELLE, b. Aug. 19, 1881, m. Nov. 2, 1905, SHELDON S. SMITH of Boston.
10665 SAMUEL, b. 1883. 10666 STELLA, b. 1884.

F10229 Harvey E. Locke, born in Bath, March 4, 1876, married in Lyman, Dec. 24, 1895, ELLA M. SMITH of Bath, born in Lyman, 1877, daughter of William and Kate (Wright). He is a farmer in Lyman.
Children of 10th Gen.
10667 HARVEY MORRILL, b. Lyman, June 28, 1896.
10668 CARROLL, b. Bath, Aug. 26, 1897. (2nd child.)
10669 MAUDE MAY, b. March 25, 1901. (5th.)
10670 DAU., 6th child, b. Jan. 23, 1903.
10671 SON, 7th child, b. Apl. 16, 1904.
10672 SON, 8th child, b. Lyman, Nov. 19, 1905.

F10252 Alice Marion Locke, born in Mobile, Ala., May 3, 1869, married in Mobile, Oct. 15, 1889, THOMAS D. NETTLES, born in Alabama, July 7, 1859. He is local Manager of United Fruit Co. in Mobile.
Children of 10th Gen. b. in Mobile, Ala.
10673 THOMAS D., JR., b. May 5, 1892.
10674 JOSEPH LOCKE, b. Dec. 24, 1893.
10675 MARY EMMA, b. Dec. 17, 1895.
10676 HENRY GOODWIN, b. 1903.

F10253 Edith Josephine Locke, born Feb. 12, 1871, married in Mobile, Ala., Oct. 12, 1891, GEORGE T. BADEAU of New Orleans, born there, Feb. 1861. He is a commercial traveler in Memphis, Tenn.
Children of 10th Gen.
10677 GEORGE T., JR., b. New Orleans, Nov. 12, 1892.
10678 EDNA RUTH, b. New Orleans, Feb. 2, 1897.
10679 JOSEPH A., b. New Orleans, Aug. 13, 1899.
10680 EDWARD RAOUL, b. Hammond, La., May 15, 1901.
10681 JOHN E., b. ——.
10682 SIMEON LOCKE, b. ——.
10683 DAVID KENT, b. ——.
10684 MARY ALICE, b. ——.

F10255 Simeon Young Locke, born in Terre Haute, Ind., Sept. 8, 1878, married in New Orleans, June 13, 1898, ANNA G. QUATTLEBAUM, born in Mobile, May 29, 1881. He was in the wholesale paper business in Mobile and died Dec. 3, 1910.

Children of 10th Gen.

10685 First child died infant.
10686 ANNA GETZ, b. New Orleans, 1899.
10687 EDITH BADEAU, b. Mobile, 1901.
10688 ALICE MARION, b. ——.
10689 JOSEPH H., b. ——.

Nathaniel Locke of Portsmouth

Another Locke was in Portsmouth and vicinity, contemporary with John, as appears from the following deposition made May 10, 1810 by Jonathan and David Locke, and was perhaps a brother of Captain John Locke.

"This may certify to whom it may concern, that the following genealogy of the ancestors, in substance as followeth, hath been told unto us by our forefathers, the truth to which we attest, viz.: 1st. We say that Jonathan Palmer, deceased, was the son and lawful heir to Christopher Palmer and Elizabeth Palmer. 2nd., Christopher Palmer's wife Elizabeth, was daughter and lawful heir to William and Judith Berry. (A mistake, see record below). 3rd., William Berry's wife Judith was daughter and lawful heir to the Locke and his wife who came from England, said Locke's wife name before marriage was Hermins, and she brought with her into New England, a coat of arms so called, which referred to John Hermins. William Berry's wife Judith was daughter and lawful heir to Nathaniel Locke and his wife, whose name previous to marriage was Hermins."

The records of Portsmouth give the following items: "March 4 & 5, 1672, Nathaniel Locke did two days work on Highways at Great Island (New Castle) and Sept. 30, 1672, a noate was drawn on Henry Dering for Nathaniel Locke for six shillings". Another record is "At a meeting of the Selectmen this 5th., March 1674-5 upon motion made by Widow Locke to live in the school house on the Great Island in order to the teaching of children to read and sew, have granted her desire". Undoubtedly the widow of Nathaniel's as this name does not appear again except in John's family. Tradition says that the other Locke not John, left no sons, but is silent as to daughters.

A—**Nathaniel Locke,** married (in England, JUDITH) HERMINS.

Children, born in New Hampshire. 2nd Gen.

F. B. JUDITH LOCKE, b. May 16, 1656, married July 8, 1678, WILLIAM BERRY, son of John and Susannah (William was nephew of Elizabeth Berry, who m. Capt. John Locke).

SABINA LOCKE, called of Dover, m. Dec. 19, 1689, by Rev. John Pike, WILLIAM BERRY. (I place Sabina as a possible dau. of Nathaniel's because of her age, and because the family of John Locke is known.)

F. C. ELIZABETH LOCKE, b. (1674?), m. July 24, 1705, CHRISTOPHER PALMER, b. Feb. 12, 1687, son of Samuel and Ann. Such is town of Rye record.

F. B.—Judith Locke and WILLIAM BERRY had in 3rd generation.

ELIZABETH, b. March 16, 1680, died young.
F. D. NEHEMIAH, b. ——, m. SARAH ——.
ELIZABETH, b. New Castle, Oct. 15, 1686.
NATHANIEL, b. New Castle, Feb. 13, 1689.
F. E. STEPHEN, b. New Castle, Jan. 18, 1691, m. Jan. 4, 1716, ANNA PHILBRICK, dau. of Thomas.
F. F. WILLIAM, b. New Castle, Nov. 18, 1693, m. Dec. 21, 1721, SARAH LANE, who d. Jan. 3, 1776; he d. Oct. 8.
JEREMIAH, b. March 8, 1695, at N. C.
FREDERICK, b. N. C., Jan. 15, 1699.
ABIGAIL, b. N. C., March 15, 1700.
JANE, b. N. C., Jan. 26, 1702.

F. C.—Elizabeth Locke and CHRISTOPHER PALMER had in Rye of 3rd generation.

JONATHAN, b. May 16, 1707, died young.
JONATHAN, b. Apl. 28, 1710, m. May 20, 1746, ABIGAIL ROWE of Hampton.
WILLIAM, b. May 3, 1712, m. June 27, 1736, JANE FOSS, and had: JOSEPH, b. May 8, 1740, perhaps m. March 9, 1767, SARAH WILLEY; SARAH, b. 1742; JEREMY, b. 1745; WILLIAM, b. 1748.

F. D.—Nehemiah Berry and SARAH had in Rye of 4th generation.

SUSANNA, b. Aug. 23, 1725, m. NATHAN MARDEN.
JOHN, b. March 10, 1736, m. July 27, 1757, BETSEY YEATON.
F. G. JACOB, b. July 7, 1738, m. RACHEL RAND, d. Dec. 11, 1811, was a shoemaker.
HANNAH, b. Sept. 23, 1740.
NATHANIEL, bapt. June 1, 1746, d. unmarried Dec. 16, 1815.

F. E.—Stephen Berry and ANNA PHILBRICK had in 4th generation.

JOSEPH, b. March 11, 1717.
PHOEBE (or TRYPHENA), b. Sept. 3, 1719.
(TRYPHENA, bapt. Oct. 11, 1719.)
JUDITH, bapt. June 3, 1722.   EPHRAIM, b. Oct. 11, 1727.
STEPHEN, bapt. June 14, 1724.   JAMES, b. March 25, 1731.

F. F.—William Berry and SARAH LANE had in 4th generation.

> JEREMIAH, b. 1721, m. Oct. 3, 1741, HANNAH LOCKE, b. July 1, 1724. He m. 2nd, Sept. 8, 1770, MRS. ELEANOR BRACKETT; 3rd, DORA EMERSON. He lived in Rye, was Corporal in Capt. Parson's Co., Rev. War.
>
> MARY, bapt. March 10, 1723, m. March 28, 1745, JONATHAN HOBBS.

F. G.—Jacob Berry and RACHEL RAND had in 5th generation.

> ISAAC, b. Apl. 20, 1767, m. ——— TARLTON, d. of smallpox New Castle, where his dau. m. WM AMAZEEN.
>
> RICHARD, bapt. Apl. 26, 1772, m. March 30, 1805, OLIVE HOLMES dau. of William and Mary of Ports.
>
> SARAH, bapt. Nov. 30, 1777, m. THOMAS SLEEPER, and lived at Nottingham.

UNKNOWN LOCKES

Eliza A. Locke, m. Isaac F. Bacon, 1858, in Franklin.
Ann S. Locke, m. 1860, David F. Bacon of Franklin.
Sarah A. Locke, m. 1878, Wm. Dow of Concord.
Betsey Locke, m. 1858, Dover, Timothy son of Asa Dame.
Bird and Mary Locke, lived Orford, 1870.
Martha A. Locke, m. 1854, John Dow of Rye.
John Locke, d. 1807; Betsey Locke, d. 1800, Stewartstown.
Albert S. Locke, d. Stewartstown, 1887, aged 40.
Bertram G. Locke, b. Vt., m. 1870, Orford, Mary Cleasby.
Josiah J. Locke, m. Bathia Balch, 1787, Westmoreland.
Tamson D. Locke, son of John of Barrington, b. 1822.
Elias Varney Locke, m. 1838, Betsey Huntress of Strafford.
Sarah F. Locke, m. Wm. B. Davis of Pittsfield.
Widow Susan Locke, d. Laconia, 1888, aged 87.
John W. Locke, m. 1876, Franklin, Maria G. Stoughton.
James L. Locke, Manchester, m. 1858, S. M. Sullivan.
Sarah Locke, b. Dover, July 27, 1783.
James M. Locke, had son, b. Northwood, 1851.
Oliver Locke, had son, b. Northfield, 1854.
Stephen Locke, had dau., b. Epping, 1852.
John Locke, of Strafford, had dau., b. 1874, and son, b. 1873.
William Locke, East Kingston, had Flora B., b. 1866.
Locke, a Manchester druggist, had son, b. 1862.
C. A. Locke, Loudon, had dau. 1866.
William F. Locke, Barrington and Etta, had: Martie L., b. 1877.
Sarah F. (Pendergast) Locke, d. Farmington, 1884, aged 64.
Widow Lina B. Locke, d. Concord, 1890, aged 80.
Charles and Sarah Locke, had son, Holly, b. 1880, Franconia.
Ann Locke, d. 1871 Epsom; dau. of Simeon P.
Sarah Locke, d. Fremont 1891, aged 80.
James Locke, m. Elizabeth Pickering, Dover.
Sally Locke, Ports.,m. 1792, Jona. Briggs.
Peggy Locke, m. 1792, John Nelson, Portsmouth.
Nancy Locke, Dover, m. 1815, Josiah Akerman, Ports.
Frank A. Locke, d. 1883, aged 27, Bristol.
Charlotte Locke, d. Tilton, 1898, aged 69.
William Locke, m. Mrs. Nancy Judkins, 1845, Lee.
Henry Locke, Epping, m. 1837, Naomi E. Whicher.
William H. Locke, m. 1864, Exeter, Helen F. Eliot.
Joseph Locke son of John, d. Greenland, 1839, aged 15.
Hannah A. Locke, dau. of Isaac, d. Manchester, 1847, aged 18.
Mary H. Locke, d. Lynn 1871, a. 22, buried Seabrook.
Edward Locke, d. Ossipee, 1836, aged 28.
John H. Locke, lumberman, Lancaster 1873-1890.
Ira Locke, m. 1871, Littleton, Christie Bowman.
Elizabeth Locke, Seabrook, m. 1837, Samuel Harriman.
Hannah P. Locke, of Gilford, m. 1824, Richard Elkins.
Jennie Locke, of Warner, m. 1869, Walter S. Quimby.
Frances A. Locke, m. Concord, 1846, Amos A. Hawes.
Hannah Locke, Loudon, m. 1777, Joseph Gordon, Concord.
Nellie Locke, m. 1890, Dover, Edward Hanson.
Ira C. Locke, m. 1858, Abbie B. Libbey, Barrington.
Henry Locke, m. Carrie Varney, Barnstead.

UNKNOWN LOCKES

William Locke, m. 1740, Ports., Eunice Rice.
Linwood Locke of Dover.
John Locke, Rye; killed French & Indian War.
Margaret Locke, m. 1728, Richard Swain, Ports.
Nathaniel and Jonathan Locke taken prisoners, July 1758, while off Rye fishing.
Sarah Locke, Dover, m. 1810, John Smith.
Betsey Locke, Rochester, m. 1795, Timothy Dame.
Mercy Locke, m. 1753, Joseph Barbar, Barrington.
Meribah Locke, m. 1757, Thos. Babb, Barrington.
Chas. A. Locke, m. 1861, Eliz. McHurley, Loudon.
——— Locke, m. Newmkt. 1764, Sarah Sanborn.
Addie M. Locke, m. Almot Durgin, Freedom.
Myrtle A. Locke, m. 1895, Charles Sumner, Groveland.
Lockes in the Revolution whom I cannot place, name of town not necessarily his home.
James Locke, enlisted, Sept. 29, 1781, Ports.
Jonathan (of Haverhill), July 18, 1780, Ports.
Jonathan (Canaan), July 2, 1782, Ports.
Richard; Jan. 27, 1777, Col. Dearborn Co.
Sam; May 10, 1781, Col. Cillets Co.
Samuel; Feb. 15, 1781, (Exeter), Col. Livermore.
Henry; Sept. 13, 1778, at Bedford.
John; Sergt. went for Ipswich, 1781.
Jonathan; went for Deerfield, 1781.
Timothy, age 18, (Peterboro), July 24, 1779.
Timothy; July 9, 1778, from Sharon for Rhode Island Service.

Information about these unknowns or of any others should be sent to Arthur H. Locke, Portsmouth, N. H.

HISTORICAL ACCOUNT OF THE LOCKE FAMILY IN ENGLAND.
AND ORIGIN OF THE NAME AND ARMS.
From the "Gentleman's Magazine," Vol. 62, Part 2, page 798. 1792, and copied verbatim from Book of the Lockes, by John G. Locke 1852.
[The notes are by the author of the Book of the Lockes.]

MR. URBAN, *East Brent, Somersetshire, July 17.*

IN pursuance of the wishes of A. B. in p. 555, I here send you some account of the Locke family.

Tradition considers the name of Locke of Scotch extraction, originally spelt Loch; but, if so, it must have been in very early time; for when Alfred divided this kingdom into parishes, the dwelling of a great man, known by the name of Locke, was called after him Lockstown, or the Town of Locke. It adjoins East Brent whence I date this letter, and where the family at one time became numerous. At present it is called Lockston alias Loxton, the lordship of which belongs to the Marquis of Buckingham. The parish of Locking is distant two miles from Lockstown, and hath long since been divided; but a large farm of many hundreds per annum, called Lockinghead, together with the perpetuity of the living, belongs to the merchants of Bristol.

The Locke family in this neighborhood consider themselves as descended from a very ancient house, arguing that they gave name *to* the parishes where they lived, before the Conquest, and do not derive their name with a *De* from the parishes, as is very commonly the case.

However, I have not seen any account of this family before Robert Locke, whom we find to have been joined with Thomas de Saint Maur, as Vicecomes of Wiltshire, anno 1350. John Locke, sheriff of London, 1460, is the first in a pedigree in my possession. Thomas, his son, was a merchant in London, who died anno 1507, and by Joan his wife (who was the only daughter and heir of Mr. Wilcock of Rotheram in Yorkshire) left three sons, John, William, and Michael. John is said to have died without issue, and buried in Mercer's Chapel, 1519, with his arms (*a*) in the window, a proof the family bore arms before those granted by Queen Mary, 1555. William, married two wives; (*b*) first, Elizabeth, daughter and heir of Mr. Spencer, a citizen and fishmonger of London; secondly, Catharine, daughter of William, and sister and co-heir of Sir Thomas Cook, of Wiltshire, knight. Rose Locke, the only daughter by the second ventor was married to Anthony, son of Walter Hickman of Woodford, in Essex, Esq.; by whom she became ancestor to the baronets of that name, the late Lord Montjoy, the present Earl of Plymouth. Matthew Locke, the youngest son by the first ventor, had an only daughter Elizabeth, married to Richard Chandler of London, merchant, son of William Chandler of Little Walsingham, in Norfolk, Gent.; whose only daughter Elizabeth married Ferdinando Richardson (who died 1596), groom of the stole to Queen Elizabeth. The above William Locke, 25 Henry VIII. undertook to go over to Dunkirk, and pull down the pope's bull, which had been there posted up by way of a curse to the king and kingdom. For this exploit the king granted him a freehold of £100 per annum, dubbed him knight, and made him one of the gentlemen of his privy-chamber. Sir William lived to be an alderman of London, and was sheriff of the city in 1548. He died 1550, and by his first wife, left issue eight sons and daughters, exclusive of Matthew already mentioned. Of these elder branches of Sir William Locke's family we have in Somersetshire a very imperfect account. George Locke, of Tiverton, who was buried at St. Sidwell's in Exeter, anno 1586, was supposed to be one of the sons. And from another of them, Thomas Locke of Little Horsely, in Essex, is said to have been de-

---

(*a*) I am of opinion, after an examination of Stow's "Survey of London," that the "arms in the window" were those of Sir William Locke, who was buried in Mercer's Chapel in 1550; yet a doubt remains.
(*b*) He had four wives.

Page not indexed.

scended. He married Susannah, daughter of Sir William Welby, of Gedney, in Lincolnshire, Knight of the Bath, whose issue was an only daughter, Susannah, wife of the Rev. John Carse, D. D. She died Nov. 10, 1649. Perhaps from one of these sons descended the Rev. John Locke, Rector of Askerwell, in the County of Dorset, father to the Rev. William Locke, who died 1686, and who by a daughter of the Rev. Lyte Whynnel, clerk, became seized of the perpetuity of his father's living, which was by the Rev. William Locke, his son (who died May 8, 1722), sold to William Bennet of Norton Bavent in the County of Wilts, whose grandson is the present incumbent. It has been supposed that we are indebted to some part of Sir William Locke's family for two very respectable characters, in the persons of Sir John Locke, Knight, an East India director, who died 1746, and James Locke his brother, husband to the Turkey Company. I think you have told us in your Magazine, that a Mr. Oates, of Richmond in Surry, had one hundred and fifty thousand pounds in 1748, with a daughter of the latter; and a Mr. Rawlinson, of Wiltshire, is thought to have had some such sum with a daughter of the former, with whom he intermarried in 1740.

The Rev. Mr. Locke, of Newark upon Trent, the Lockes of Oxfordshire, Gloucestershire, Wiltshire, Essex, London, and Bristol, including the celebrated Miss Locke of poetical memory, (see p. 72 of your present volume,) can say whether they do or do not derive their descent from Sir William Locke, Knight, Alderman of London.

Michael Locke, younger brother (*a*) of Sir William, according to a pedigree now before me, was father amongst other children of Matthew Locke, who became seated at Pensford in Buckinghamshire, and had two sons, Richard and Christopher. The former was of Bedminster in the County of Somerset, and, dying 1617, left John Locke, his son, Mayor of Bristol 1641, father of another John Locke of Bristol, merchant, whose son, Samuel Locke, became a merchant in London, and of whose family and death I have not been able to procure any account. Christopher Locke, the youngest son, soon after Abbot Whiting's lands at East Brent were granted to the Whitmore family, was sent into that parish (which as I before observed adjoins to Lockstown), to divide the forfeited estates into farms; and having laid out a valuable farm for himself at a place called Pilrow, built a large house and became the stem of a very respectable family, whose baptisms, as by the parish register *penes me*, are as follows:

1. Christopher, bapt. March 25, 1593, father of another Christopher of Pilrow, William of South Brent, and John of Locke's Broad House, in the parish of Mark. This last Christopher had two daughters, Anne and Christian; the former married, first, Henry Symonds of South Brent, ancestor to the Symondses and Hardens; and, secondly, to Tory Tutton, great-grandfather of Isaac Phelps of South Brent, Esq. Christian intermarried with Robert Dod of Burnham, ancestor of the Dods of that parish. William of South Brent had one daughter, Mary, who married John Petheram, ancestor to the Petherams of this neighborhood. John of Locks Broad had but one daughter, Elizabeth, who married John Champion, and, by a female issue, became ancestor of the Guy family.

2. John Locke, baptized Aug. 1, 1595, was church-warden of the parish 1630, and upon our parish-book his name is signed as is represented in Plate II. (where the Locke arms are also engraved Fig. 4). He became a captain of foot in the civil wars of Charles the First, and was killed at Bristol in 1645. (*b*.) He had two sons, one of whom died in his minority; the other was the

---

(*a*) English antiquarians have supposed that the Michael Locke here spoken of was a *son* of Sir William and not his *brother*, and so I have represented him in the chart that follows this article; but I have strong suspicion that the statement in the text is true, and that Sir William had both a *brother* and a *son* named Michael. If I am right in my supposition, Matthew of Pensford, who is represented in the chart as the son of Michael, and *gr.* son of Sir William, was in fact the son of Michael and *nephew* of Sir William.

(*b*) That Capt. Locke was killed as above related, has been stated by several authors; but Lord King, in the life of John, the son of Capt. Locke, speaking of a letter written by John the son to his father, says "It is without date, but was probably written before 1660."

Page not indexed.

572 LOCKE GENEALOGY

judicious John Locke, the great metaphysician and philosopher; of whom hereafter.

3. Honour, bapt. August 21, 1597, and, intermarrying with Francis Shepard of Mark, became ancestor of the Shepards, Giles's, Giblets, Stars, Coomers, Counsels, and Smeaths in this part of Somersetshire.

4. Christian, bapt. July 3, 1601; of whom we have no farther account.

5. Lewis Locke, baptized 13th July 1606; was buried at Taunton Saint Mary Magdalen, March 27, 1692. By four wives he had thirty-five children, most of whom lived to be men and women; and what is more remarkable, his eldest son John, born 1625, was fifty-nine years of age, when his youngest son Christopher was born at Taunton, anno 1684. It is reported in the family that John had a great-grandson as old as his younger brother; which is, perhaps, the chief reason why this branch of the family cannot truly ascertain their respective degrees of kindred. It is, however, generally believed, that all the Lockes of Somersetshire and Devonshire derive themselves from this Lewis; but whether so or not, we know that Allen, one of the younger sons by the last wife, was father of another Allen who was father of the present Mr. Thomas Locke of Taunton, Maltster, who has six sons, three of whom are settled in London and three in Taunton, the youngest being a Master of Arts of the University of Oxford, also one daughter not yet married.

William Locke of Pitminster, near Taunton, was another son of Lewis by his fourth wife. He married Dorothy, daughter of Richard Cooksley of Dunstar, Gentleman, and died Jany. 25, 1719, aged 49. His only son Richard married Hannah, the only daughter of John Dod, of Burnham in the County of Somerset, Gentleman, and became an inhabitant of that parish. He died 1765, aged 59, leaving the present Richard Locke, Esq. of Highbridge House in Burnham, his son and heir. This last gentleman is well known in the literary line as an Antiquary and Agriculturist, he having in the course of forty years written many essays and short pieces, upon various subjects, in the different periodical publications of the day, some with, but more without his real signature. His two essays in the fifth volume of the Bath Agricultural Society's papers, (one on the improvement of meadow land; the other, an historical account of the flat part of Somersetshire, as it has been and still is capable of improvement), are originals in their kind. He has been announced in your present volume, (p. 241), as the original author of the History of Taunton; in which town he was not a resident, as there intimated, having always resided in Burnham where he was born. The ingenious Mr. Richard Locke, of Magdalen-Hall, Oxford, is his only son. The arms borne by this branch of the family are: Party per fesse, Azure and Or, a pale between three falcons indorsed, counterchanged. Crest: a falcon of the same with a padlock in its beak.

Another Richard Locke of Pitminster, above mentioned, was author of two mathematical tracts; one intitled, "An Essay on the Longitude," printed for Meadows and Ashby, in 1732; the other "The Circle Squared," printed for J. Wilford in 1734. I do not know whether he was a grandson or a great-grandson of Lewis; but he was uncle to the present John Locke, Esq. of Pitminster, whose only daughter and heir was lately married to Thomas Welman, Esq. near Taunton.

John Locke, Esq. the celebrated philosopher, was son of Captain Locke, already mentioned to have been killed at Bristol. He was born at Wrington (which is eight miles from East Brent), 29th August, 1632; and immediately upon the death of his father, was sent to Westminster School; whence he was removed to Christ-Church College, Oxford, in 1651; took his degree of Bachelor of Arts in 1655, and Master of Arts in 1658; became Secretary to Sir William Swan, an English Envoy to one of the foreign Courts in 1664; travelled with the Earl of Northumberland in 1668; began to write his essay on "Human Understanding" in 1670; made Fellow of the Royal Society in 1671; Secretary of the Presentations under Lord Chancellor Cowper in 1672; Secretary to a

Page not indexed.

Commission of Trade, in 1673; took the degree of Bachelor of Physick in 1674; travelled to France in 1675; became a courtier under the Earl of Shaftsbury in 1679; was prosecuted for libelling the Government in 1682; deprived of all preferments, even his student's place at Christ-Church College in 1683. By the application of William Penn to King James the Second, he might have received his pardon on pleading guilty, which he refused with this memorable saying, "He had committed no crime, and therefore should not plead guilty." In 1685 he fled to Holland, and was one of the Eighty-four persons demanded by King James of the State's General, which made him live in exile till 1687, when he constituted a weekly assembly at Amsterdam; amongst whom were Mr. Le Clerc, Mr. Limborch, &c. &c. In 1689 he returned to England, with the Princess of Orange; was made a Commissioner of Appeals in 1690; appointed one of the Commissioners of Trade and Plantations in 1695, which he resigned for want of health in 1700. He died at Oates, in the County of Essex, the country-seat of Sir Francis Masham, Bart., on the 28th of October, 1704. His works consist of twenty-two different publications, collected in three volumes folio.

I have never seen any account of this gentleman's marriage; neither do I know upon what ground Sir Peter King, Lord Chancellor of England, was considered his nephew, unless it was in consequence of becoming his heir. (a) Near fifty years since I heard one of the grandsons of Lewis Locke call the chancellor, son of a tallow-chandler in Exeter, and treat his name with some reproach, under the idea of having supplanted the Locke family in the affections of their relation; although this gentleman allowed he was not the heir, neither could he tell who was. Perhaps some of the female line of his father's elder brother.

That too much room for local matter may not be stolen in such an useful work as the Gentleman's Magazine, it became necessary to introduce within a narrow compass as much information as possible. It must therefore be expected that many younger branches of this respectable family are left unnoticed, and many proofs omitted, that might have been adduced; but if there be any imperfection or deficiency of importance in the present account, any person interested can, by a private correspondence or otherwise, have recourse to Mr. Locke, late Mayor of Oxford, Wadham Locke, Esq. of Devizes, Wilts, Thomas Locke, Esq. of the Herald's office, who is at present Norroy king-at-arms, or to any of the parties mentioned in this pedigree to be at present living."

H. F. Y.

"P. S. Having room, I ask Q, is the Rev. Dr. Locke of Norwich, and the Rev. William Locke, Rector of Burwell in Norfolk, mentioned in "Walker's Sufferings of the Clergy," p. 296, the same person, and how connected with this family?"

The following was from another correspondent:—

MR. URBAN, *August 22.*

"The inquiries of your correspondent A. B. (p. 555) as to the *family* of Mr. Locke, I am not furnished with materials to answer, but have no doubt, many of your readers have it in their power to give a very satisfactory answer to them. With respect to his *arms*, I can inform A. B. that he bore, or claimed to bear, Party per fesse Az. and Or, a pale counterchanged; on the three pieces of the first as many falcons (or hawks) volant of the second. At the same time it is proper to inform him that Edmonson, in his Alphabet of Arms, gives the following coat as granted to the name of Locke 5 July, 2 Philip and Mary, *viz.* Per fesse Az. and Or, a pale counterchanged, three hawks with wings indorsed of the last. Crest: a hawk with wings indorsed, holding in his beak a padlock, Or."

(a) Jerome King, father of Peter King, Lord High Chancellor, m. the sister of John Locke, the representative of whose family is now (1853) the Earl of Lovelace who m. Ada, the dau. of Lord Byron. Her early death was recently recorded in the newspapers.

Page not indexed.

As it respects the name of Locke and the Arms, my efforts in endeavoring to discover the origin have been of little avail. In the article on page 342, it is said that "Tradition considers the name of Locke of Scotch extraction originally spelt Loch, but if so, it must have been in early time; for when Alfred divided this kingdom [England] into parishes, the dwelling of a great man known by the name of Locke was called after him Lockstown or the Town of Locke." Again: "The Locke family consider themselves as descended from a very ancient house, arguing that they gave the name *to* the parishes where they lived, before the Conquest, and do not derive their name with a *De, from* the parishes, as is very commonly the case."

Surnames were not common in England until after the time of William the Conqueror, and the above statement may admit of some doubt, although the authority is allowed, by some of the most learned antiquarians in England, to be generally reliable. The English word *lock* is from the Anglo Saxon *loc* or *loce*, an enclosed place, the fastening of a door, a curl of hair; and the Danish word *lok* and the German *locke*, has the same general signification. The Welch word *llocc* is a sheep-cote, a fold, or close or narrow place, and the Gælic word *loch* means a lake, a bay, or arm of the sea, (that is, water confined or enclosed more or less). The Greek word for lake, in its radical sense, means a hole or other place that contains or holds. The original idea appears, then, in all these different languages, something that encloses or confines. But when and why it became a family name, must be left for others, more learned than the writer, to discover.

The Lockes in England are perhaps of a different origin from the Scotch Lochs, as the former in their bearings have the falcon and the padlock, while the latter have swans swimming in a lake. The orthography has ever been various. Some of the earliest records give us Locke, and somewhat later I find Loc, Lok, and Lock and Locke. Sir William's name is given Lock and Locke; his sons, Michael and John, who were both men of education, wrote it Lok, and the same variations are found through several centuries, showing most conclusively that the particular way which individuals may spell their names, is no proof that they are descendants from distinct families.

ARMS.

It is difficult, and in many cases impossible to determine when Arms were granted or for what cause, and the records of the Heralds' Visitations at London do not show the reasons for the particular bearings. In many instances the bearings were probably fanciful, either on the part of the person to whom they were granted, or that of the "Garter King of Arms," by whom they were granted. But in other cases the bearings had reference to the profession, occupation, or name itself, or to some exploit by which the person had made himself distinguished, some heroic deed of daring, as the capture of a castle or an enemy's ship. The reference to such acts would be shown more particularly in the Crests. The Heraldic books contain the description of eight Coats of Arms granted in England to the name of Lock and Locke, and one to that of Loch. Seven have the same principal bearings, three falcons, but somewhat differently arranged in the shield. This similarity shows that those to whom they were granted were all descendants from *one* original stock, the several arrangements with some slight additions designating different branches.

The Arms which I give stand first in Burke's General Armory, and no date being given, I presume they were those first granted, and probably to Sir William Locke, in the reign of Henry VIII. having reference to his exploit of going to Dunkirk in France, and tearing down the Pope's Bull of Excommunication against the King, a deed which at the present time would not be of much moment, but at that age when the Pope claimed great powers, and who was dreaded and feared by the people, it might require as much moral courage as to storm a castle. The cushion in the crest has reference probably to the

Page not indexed.

HISTORICAL ACCOUNT 575

Church, either Popish or Protestant, being symbolical thereof, and may be understood to mean, if it referred to the Popish, that he *tore it down*, or if to the Protestant, that he *supported* it. In the other crests, the *padlock* forms a part, and may have had a reference to the name, which was, in heraldry, called *"punning,"* and if, as stated above the arms which are here represented, are those that were first granted to the name of Locke, I think we may reasonably conclude that the padlock was an afterthought, and had no *original* connection with the name. That they are the oldest, in the absence of any date of their grant, the strongest evidence, according to the best authorities, is that the particular manner in which they are *"blazoned"* indicates more antiquity, than does the style of *blazonry* exhibited in the other Arms.

The following Arms are described by Burke and others:

Lock. (London.) Per fesse az. and or, in chief three falcons volant of the second. Crest—A hand ppr. holding up a cushion or. [See arms below.]

Lock. (Warnford, Co. Southampton.) (Rouge Dragon, Pursuivant of Arms, granted 1767.) Per fesse az. and or, a pale counterchanged; on the first three falcons rising of the second, collared gu. Crest—A falcon as in the arms, in the beak a padlock pendant sa.

Lock. (Mildenhall, Co. Suffolk; granted 8 Dec. 1770.) Per fesse az. and or, a pale counterchanged, on the first three falcons rising of the second, ducally crowned az. Crest—A falcon rising or, ducally crowned az. in the beak a padlock pendant sa.

Locke or Loke. Or, three pales az. on a chev. of the last a pair of wings conjoined of the first.

Lock. (Norbury Park, Co. Surrey.) Per fesse az. and or, a pale and three falcons, two and one with wings addorsed and belled, each holding in the beak a padlock, all counterchanged. Crest—A falcon as in the Arms.

Lock. Per fesse or and az. a pale counterchanged; three falcons volant of the first. Crest—A falcon with wings endorsed, holding in the mouth a padlock or.

Locke. (Granted 5 July, 2 Philip & Mary, and borne by *Wadham Locke*, of Ashton Gifford, Co. Wilts, Esq., son and heir of the late Wadham Locke, of Rowde Ford House, near Devizes, Esq., M. P.) Per fesse az. and or, a pale counterchanged; three hawks with wings endorsed of the last. Crest—A hawk with wings endorsed, holding in the beak a padlock or.

Locke or Loke. (London.) Or, on a chief az. three falcons jessed and belled or.

Loch. (Drylaw, Scotland.) Or a saltier engrailed sable, between two swans naiant, in fesse, each in water ppr.

According to the preceding article, the name of Locke was known in England in the time of King Alfred, about the year 880, when the place where a "great man" known by that name, "was called after him Lockstown, or the Town of Locke." As *greatness* would not be acquired in a day, it is presumable that the family had been known for a considerable period anterior to that time. The name does not stand out prominent in the early or more modern history of England, (excepting in the instance of JOHN, the great philosopher, who stands at the head of greatness and goodness in the ranks of the learned), however it often appears, and connected with events and individuals, which shows that they were of respectable standing. To gratify the curiosity of some, and for a future reference, should any one wish hereafter to make further researches

Page not indexed.

in England, I subjoin a few facts that have been collected, many of them being taken from documents published a few years since under the direction of the "Record Commissioners," by the Government of Great Britain, an incomplete copy having been given by said Government to the New England Historic-Genealogical Society. In many cases, the simple name only, and the date when recorded, is given. The different orthographies are seen.

1198. Eustace Loc.
1203. Ricardus Loc of Witteham, his wid. Letitia, living 1203, when she sues for right of dower.
1230. Johanna, wid. of William de Lok, who was son of Jordan Lok, to whom King John, in 1199, granted right to take tolls of ships on the Thames. William had son Thomas, under age in 1230.
1236. Thomas de Loch.
1250. Gilbert Locke, and William his son, of Co. of Lincoln.
1250. Ricardus Lok', Lucy his wf. and Mabillia her sister, of Co. of Oxford.
1291. Thomas Locke was of Merton.
1313. John Lok was of Scardiburg.
1350. Robert Locke was Vicecomes of Wiltshire.
1359. Berengarius Loc, of Narbonne, with John Bigot, of Biteria, were messengers sent by the States of Senescalcia Carcassiona to the King of France. Edward III. granted them protection in going and returning through and staying in his kingdom, and also to the 10 knights, horsemen and footmen, which composed their retinue.
1395. License was granted by Richard II. to William Lock and John Kenynghale, Scotch merchants, for exporting goods to Norway.
1412. Complaint was made to the King of England by William Locke and others, merchants of Lenn [Lynn] setting forth that notwithstanding that they had had rights granted them by the King of Norway, Dacia and Sweden, they had been robbed and ill-treated by the merchants of Hanse, and though the King of Sweden had imposed a fine of 1500 marks upon the aggressors, it had never been paid, and their troubles still continued; and that in 1409, a ship was freighted by William Locke and others, of Lenn, for Berne and Wysmer, and the captain of the ship was seized at Berne, and ordered to return to Lenn; and they claimed a redress for their great losses.

Sir William Locke was employed by Henry VIII., having the charge of his commercial affairs "both at home and abroad." In the Cottonian Library, London, are several manuscript letters from him to the King, and to Secretary Cromwell, dated at Antwerp, in 1533-4, 1535 and 1538, relating to some works carrying on at Calais, concerning negotiations with France and about the woollen trade. He was, says Collins, "Particularly employed by Queen Anne Bullen, [Boleyn] privately to gather the Epistles, Gospels and Psalms, from beyond sea, in which he ran great hazard, some having been secretly made away with, for attempting the same thing." He had four wives, (see the chart, p. 358-9,) and twenty or more children, many of which died young. The name of his first wife has been variously given by different writers; some say it was Alice Spence, and others Elizabeth Spencer. Anciently the names of Elizabeth and Alice were convertible, one for the other. The records of the Herald's office, which are the best authority, say that her name was Alice Spence.

In the Cottonian Library is also "a manuscript of many pages," dated 1577, written by "Michael Lok," in which he says he "is son of Sir Wm. Lok, Knight, Alderman of London, that he (Michael) was kept at schools of grammar in Eng. until he was 13, when he was sent over the seas to Flanders and France to learn their languages, and to know the world, since which time he has continued these 32 years to travel in body and mind, following his vocation in the trade of merchandize, passing through many countries, had the charge of and captain of a great ship of more than 1000 tons, three years in divers voyages; and that he has more than 200 sheets of manuscripts of his travels," which he wishes to publish.

Page not indexed.

HISTORICAL ACCOUNT 577

In Hakluyt's "Divers Voyages," pub. 1582, is a letter dated 1575, from James Alday to the "Worshipful Mr. Michael Locke, Agent in London for the Muscovie Co." Hakluyt's Voyages also contain a History of Sir Martin Frobishere's Voyage for the discovery of a passage towards Cathay, in 1574, written by Michael Locke, Locke himself being a great adventurer therein."

Hakluyt, in the introduction to his book, speaking of a passage to Cathay, says, "Secondly, that Master John Verazanus, which had been thrice on that coast, in an olde excellent mappe which he gave to King Henrie the eighth, and is yet in the custodie of master Locke," &c. Again. "The mappe is master Michael Locke's, a man for his knowledge in divers languages, and especially in cosmographie, able to do his country good, and worthy in my judgment for the manifolde good partes in him, of good reputation and better fortune." On this map is the following dedication:—"ELLUSTRI VIRO, DOMINO PHILIPPO SIDNAEO MACHAEL LOK CIVIS LONDINENSIS HANC CHARTAM DEDICABAT: 1582." (a)

In 1612, a book called "Peter Martyr de Novo Orbe," &c. &c. in eight decades, was pub. Three of the decades were translated from the Latin, by R. Eden and the others, "by the industrie and painfulle travaile of Mr. Lok."

5 July 1 and 2 of Philip and Mary Arms were granted or confirmed to Michael Locke.

John Locke, son of Sir William, was also a traveller; he made a voyage to Jerusalem in 1553, which is to be found in Hakluyt's Voyages. It contains a curious document in Latin, of which the following is a translation:

TO ALL AND EACH who may read the present letter, salutation in our LORD JESUS CHRIST. WE testify to you and to others whoever they may be, how an honorable man, JOHN LOK, the son of an honorable man, WILLIAM LOK, GOLDEN KNIGHT, visited in person the most holy places of the HOLY LAND, viz. the most holy sepulchre of our LORD JESUS CHRIST, from which on the third day he gloriously rose from the dead, the most holy Mount of CALVARY, on which, fastened to the cross, he deigned to die for us all; also, MOUNT SION, where he celebrated that wonderful Supper with his disciples, and where the HOLY SPIRIT, on the holy day of Pentecost, descended with fiery tongues on the same disciples; and OLIVET, the mountain whence he miraculously ascended into heaven; the tomb of the chaste VIRGIN MARY, situated in the midst of the valley of JEHOSAPHAT, and BETHANY also,—BETHLEHEM, the City of DAVID, in which he was born from the most pure VIRGIN MARY, and then was laid in a Manger—and besides other such places as well within as without the city of JERUSALEM, in the HOLY LAND OF JUDEA, as are customarily visited by modern travellers, he most devoutly visited, and in like manner worshipped. In attestation of which, I, brother ANTHONY, of BERGAMOS, of the order of younger brothers belonging to the regular attendance, Vicar, (perchance unworthy), of the Convent of MOUNT SION, in the province of the godlike SAINT ANTHONY, also by apostolical authority, a commissary and rector of other places in the HOLY LAND, have willed that this certificate should be confirmed by the greater seal of our office, and by our subscription.

Given at the most holy chamber of the LORD, on the often memorable MOUNT SION, in the year of our Lord one thousand five hundred and fifty-three, on the sixth day of the month of September.

BROTHER ANTHONY, AS ABOVE.

In 1554, "A voyage to Guinea was set out by Sir George Barne, Sir John Yorke, Thomas Locke [son of Sir William] Anthonie Hickman [who m. Rose, dau. of Sir William] and Edward Casteline, the Captain whereof was Mr. John Locke [son of Sir William]. It consisted of two ships of seven score tons each, and one of ninety tons." A history of this voyage is to be found in Hakluyt, by J. Locke.

Henry Lock, prob. gr. son of Sir William, was employed by Queen Elizabeth; letters of "instructions" to him in 1592 are in the Cottonian Library.

(a) Michael Lok, a citizen of London, dedicated this Chart to the illustrious Sir Philip Sidney: 1582.

Page not indexed.

37

Thomas Locke was connected with the Court of James I.

Thomas Locke, of Merton.—Lyson, in his Environs of London, says, that "Edward III. granted the Rectory of Merton belonging to a former Abbey of that name to Thomas Locke, about 1291." Here is an error, evidently, as the reign of Edward III. did not begin till 1327. Manning, in his History of the County of Surrey, within which is Merton, says of Merton Place, "Near the church is a large old mansion, which has been known from time immemorial by the name of Merton Place. In the year 1499, John Locke and Jane his wife, became possessed of it, [prob. by inheritance] in whose family it continued until the year 1646, when John, a remote descendant of John above, (and whose ancestors had in the meantime purchased the Impropriation of the Rectory in 7 of Edward VI.) conveyed it together with the Impropriation to Catherine, sometime wife of Rowland Wilson of the Parish, but late [wife] of John Highland, alderman of London."

From another source, not now recollected, I gather the following: "In the time of Henry VIII. the Locke family possessed the Estate of Merton Hall. Thomas Locke, Esq. was minister of Merton. In 7 of Edward VI. (1552–3) the King by his letters patent dated 14 March, in consideration of the sum of £359 granted unto Thomas Locke and Mary his wife forever, the Rectory of the Church of Merton with the appurtenances, late parcel of the possessions of the dissolved priory of Merton, to be holden of the King, his heirs and successors, as of his manor of East Greenwich, in free socage and not in chief. On 29 Oct. 1643, John Locke and Jane his wife mortgaged (and in 1646 conveyed the equity of redemption of) the Rectory with all the houses, &c. to Catherine Highlord, the wid. of John Highlord, an alderman of London."

There seems to be some discrepancy in the dates, which may possibly be reconciled in this way, viz. that a portion of the premises may have been granted in 1291, and the remainder at a subsequent period. I think it is evident that they belonged to the Lockes before 1552, as the second wife of Sir William Locke was buried there Oct. 14, 1537, and Sir William himself 1550. The fact that his wife was buried there, and the similarity of Christian names, leads me to suppose that Sir William was descended from the Thomas Locke who was at Merton, 1291.

Merton Place subsequently became the property of Lord Nelson, who bequeathed it to the lady of Sir William Hamilton. [See Lyson's Env'ns of London.]

Nicholas Lock, merchant, was the lessee in 1694, of the property now known as Chesterfield House, near Greenwich Park, which he held under the crown. Philip, Earl of Chesterfield, afterwards resided there. [Lyson's Environs of London.]

Zacharias Lok, Oct. 24, 1597, erected a monument in Christ's Church, Greenwich, to the memory of his wife Dorothy, who d. Feb. 24, 1596, the dau. of James Brampton, of Brampton, Norfolk. Henry, her son, was also buried beside her.

"In the Parish Church of St. Mary Bow, London, is a monument to John Locke one of the sheriffs of London, 1461." [See Stow's Survey of London.] He was gr. father of Sir William.

"In Mercer's Chapel, Cheapside, London, is a monument to John Locke, 1519." He was prob. bro. of Sir William; left no issue. [Same.]

In same Church is a Monument to Sir William himself, 1550; "with his Arms in the window." Both of these churches were destroyed in the great fire of 1666. [Same.]

Ann Locke, dau. of Thomas, m. John Page. A sarcophagus to his memory, in his pew in the Ch. at Harrow on the Hill, London. He has three hawks with wings endorsed for Locke in his arms." [Lyson.] No date.

Thomas Lock, of Gray's Inn, London, m. at Prestwold, in Leicestershire, Susannah, dau. of Sir William Welby, of Gedney, in the Co. of Lincoln, June 3, 1619. They had an only dau. [b. 1620, bap. at Merton?] who m. Rev. John Carse, D. D.

Page not indexed.

HISTORICAL ACCOUNT 579

Thomas Locke, Gent. of Rochester, in Kent Co. purchased of John and Robert Conny, the manor of Stockbury, in 1700. He d. Mh. 13, 1706, a. 42, and his wid. Prudentia, with her three sons and co-heirs, in *gavelkind*, Robert, Thomas and Henry, in 1723 sold the estate to Sir Roger Meredith, of Leeds Abbey, Gent. The above Thomas, Senr. was buried in Rochester Cathedral, and bore for his Arms—Parted per fesse azure and or, a pale counterchanged, three falcons volant of the 2d. [Hasted's History of Kent.]

In the Ch. at Askerswell is a monument to William Locke, Senr, Rector of that Ch.; b. Dec. 26, 1634, d. Ap. 22, 1686, and to his son William, Jr. Rector of Askerswell and Chilcomb, b. June 5, 1674, d. May 8, 1722; son and gr. son of the Rev. John Locke, of Askerswell.

Daniel Locke, Fellow of Trinity Coll d. 1754; his monument is on the west wall of the Chapel.

Elizabeth Judith, dau. of Robert Locke, of Dinton, in Wilts, m. Edward Ashby, who was b. 1690, and d. 1775; their son, Rev. George Ashby, B. D. and F. A. S. was Rector of Barrow, b. 1724, d. 1808; there is a monument to his memory in the Ch. at Barrow. [Gage's His. of Suffolk.]

William, son of Major William Locke, was buried at Southwark, Parish of St. George, Jany. 7, 1667.

In All Saints Ch. Tottenham, Lon. is a monument to the memories of Richard Chandler, Esq. 1602—Elizabeth, his wf. dau. and sole heir of Matthew Locke, 2d son of Sir Wm. Locke, 1622—Sir Ferdinand Heyborne, Gentleman of the Privy Chamber to Queen Elizabeth and James I. 1618—and Anne, his wf. dau. and heir of Richard Chandler, 1615.

Thomas Locke was Mayor of High Wycombe, in Bucks, in time of Charles I. [Lipscomb's His. of Bucks.]

Zachary Locke was mem. of Parliament for Southwark in 1700.

Mrs. Elizabeth Locke, an "Ancient Maid of Honor," d. Feb. 1710-11, a. 106.

Samuel Locke was one of the Commissioners of Lieutenancy, in London, 1707.

Matthew Locke, a native of Exeter, was an eminent English Composer of Music in Ordinary to Charles II. for whose public entry into London at the Restoration he furnished the Music. He is known as the first who ever published rules on thorough base in Eng. contained in a work, entitled "Melothesia." He acquired great reputation for the composition of the music for Shakespeare's and other tragedies, and subsequently was Organist for Queen Catherine II. of Portugal; and it is represented that he became a papist, of which there is some doubt. He d. 1677.

Queen Elizabeth, in 1573, granted her "dearly beloved Chaplain, Nicholas Locke, Master of Arts, and Rector of the Parishes of St. Mary Trimley, St. Martin, Trimley, and of Harksted, in Suffolk, license to remove and absent himself from any one of said Rectorships."

The following are abstracts of Wills, proved at the Prerogative Office in London: Richard Lock—will dated July 26, 1570, proved 1571, speaks of his father and mother of Westminster; no names given.

Henry Lok, no place mentioned; (undoubtedly son of Sir William,)—will dated Jany. 28, 1570, proved Oct. 31, 1571; wf. Anne, bro. Michael, Executor.

John Locke, of Bedminster, Co. of Somerset, sawyer—will dated June 4, 1575, proved 1576. Speaks of his wf., and child not born,—chil. Jane and Agnes—Margery Stokeman, his sister's dau.—bro. John, of Dondry, and chil. one named John,—bro. Richard, whom he requests to be "good to our bro. John."

Nicholas Lock, of South Brent, Somersetshire, husbandman—will proved 1581—has wife Margaret—son Lewis—son John Gillenge—daus. Agnes and Florence.

William Lock, of Northmoulton, Devonshire, husbandman—will dated May 20, 1590—had bro. John.

Jock Lock, of Northmoulton, husbandman—will dated Feb. 6, 1589, proved 1589—had wf. Alice—sons John, Jeffrey, Richard, and Alexander—daus. Jane, Grace, Maria, and Elizabeth the wf. of John Clement.

Page not indexed.

John Lock, of Brinsworth, in the Parish of Northmoulton—will dated Mh. 27, 1590—sons William and John—daus. (Johan?) Sybil and Mary.

John Lock, of Northmoulton—will dated June 1, 1593—wf. Ureth—sons Henry and John.

William Lock, of Northmoulton—will dated Sep. 20, 1594, witnessed by Philip Locke—wf. Alice—sons Thomas and William—daus. Margaret and Thomazine.

Matthew Lock, of Merton, Co. Surrey—will dated May 14, 1598—wf. Margaret—sons Robert, Thomas, Francis and William—daus. Mary, Elizabeth and Anne. To be buried at St. Thomas, of Acon or Acres, in the Mercer's Chapel, London, near his mother.

Zachary Lok—will dated Jany. 20, 1602—to be buried in Mercer's Chapel, near his gr. father Thomas, and his gr. father, Sir William Lok—gives to his father Michael, his seal of Arms—bros. Eleazer and Benjamin, bro. Jenny and his wf.—and bro. Sanson. Mistress Ursula Johnson, whom he intends to make his wife, Executrix.

Eleazer Lock—will dated Mh. 30, 1605—to be buried in the Church of All Hallows, Huntington—has bro. Benjamin—brother-in-law William Sanson—"brother Jenny and my sister"—speaks of his poor travelling brother.

Richard Lock, of the Cammandria, of Temple Combe, Co. Somerset—will dated Aug. 1, 1605—has chil. Richard Ryal, and William Lock—sisters Agnes and Ellen—bro. Edward and his two sons—brothers John Lock the elder, and John Lock the younger.

Benjamin Lock, of Bristol, merchant—will dated Jany. 6, 1605, proved 1611—being about to go beyond the seas—to be buried in Mercer's Chapel, London—father Michael—bro. Sanson—bro. Jenny—cousins Michael and Henry Lock.

William Lock, of Gerne Abbey, Dorsetshire, tanner—will dated Oct. 27, 1611—wf. Alice—sons Thomas, William and John—dau. Elizabeth—bro. Thomas Lock, of Brookhampton, and bro. Nicholas Lock, of Pensford.

John Lock, of Bristol, mariner—will dated Jany. 16, 1618—to be buried in the Ch. at Bedminster—wf. Anne—sons Edward and John—daus. Frances and Eleanor.

Roger Lock, of Bristol, merchant—will dated Aug. 27, 1610, aged 30—wf. Elizabeth—father and mother Andrews—son Richard—father Richard—bro. John—mentions Mathew Lock.

John Locke, of St. Martins, near Ludgate—will proved 1632—had no chil.—speaks of Sansford Peverill, in Devonshire, where he was born—had brothers Walter and Hugh—speaks of Thomas and William, sons of Nicholas Locke, deceased—nephew John, and nephew John the elder, to whom he gave £300. He was very wealthy, and gave £1000 to the Hospital in Bridewell, and to Christ Hospital in London, the maintenance of two poor chil. from the Parish of St. Michaels, Bassinghalls Church.

——— Lock, of Westminster, had no chil.—speaks of his bro. Nicholas, bro. Thomas, and his son Thomas—will proved between 1628 and 1635.

John Locke, of Lambeth, Co. Surrey—will proved June 27, 1595—had son and dau. names not given—wf. Sarah.

John Locke, of Oxsted, Co. Surrey—will proved Dec. 4, 1611—had wf. Elizabeth; son Thomas, daus. Agnes, Margaret and Mary—Thomas Lock, gent. Exec'r.

Francis Locke, of Martin, Co. Surrey, gent.—will dated Nov. 25, 1621; proved Dec. 14, 1621; wf. Ellen, and her three children Edward, John, and Miles Atlee, to have an estate in Dutchett in Buckinghamshire.

George Lock by will, when not known, gave interest of £20 for the poor of the parish of All Saints in Dorsetshire.

In the Gentlemen's Magazine, vol. 69, 1799, it is stated that about 1630 several persons of the name of Locke resided at Pool, in Somersetshire, who were chiefly commanders of merchant ships, and had landed property near Salisbury and Hindon, that in Particular Robert Locke was one of this family,

Page not indexed.

and gave precisely the same arms as John Locke; he lived at Berwick, St. Leonards, and Dinton, in Wiltshire, and d. 1706, and was buried at Dinton. This may have been the Capt. Robert Locke, commander of the ship Speedwell, of London, who in 1656, was prosecuted by the government of Massachusetts for having brought Quakers into the country, and was imprisoned in Boston. Oct. 14, 1656, he petitioned the Gen. Court that he may have a full hearing. I believe he was fined and forced to carry the Quakers back. [See Mass. Archives, vol. 10, pp. 235-237.] Capt. —— Locke was master of the ship Globe which sailed from Boston for London Dec. 1655, and Hull, in his diary under date of Aug. 1665, says "my returns likewise by Capt. Locke went saffe."

From the White Chapel Register, London.

Marriages. Robert Locke and Dorothy Hawkins, July 12, 1584.—Henry Lock and Rachel Hillinge, Jany. 29, 1589.—Thomas Lock and Elizabeth [Bud?] Feb. 5, 1609.—Thomas Lock and Christian French, July 26, 1624, [perhaps parents of John and Nathaniel Locke, of Hampton, N. H.]—John Lock and Jane Edwards, Nov. 3, 1625.

Baptisms. John Lock, son of James, Aug. 10, 1610.—Hannah Lock, dau. of Thomas, July 16, 1618.—Thomas Lock, son of John and Jane, May 14, 1626.—John Lock, son of Thomas and *Christopher* [Christian] Sep. 16, 1627, [perhaps John, of Hampton.]—John Lock, son of John and Jane, Mh. 11, 1629. —Nathaniel Lock, son of Thomas and Christian, Nov. 11, 1629, [perhaps Nathaniel of Portsmouth.]

Burials. John Locke, July 21, 1593.—Benjamin Locke, Dec. 16, 1609.— Susan Locke, May 29, 1622.—Robert Locke, Jany. 5, 1623.—Susan Locke, Mh. 15, 1626—Nicholas Locke, Mh. 15, 1626.—Thomas Locke, Aug. 14, 1628. —John Locke, Aug. 27, 1632.

From the Stepney Parish Records, London.

Baptisms. Christopher Locke, son of Robert, Oct. 21, 1576.—Mary Locke, dau. of John, Jany. 6, 1582.—Bridgett Locke, dau. of John, of Ratcliff, Sep. 30, 1593.—Mary Locke, dau. of John of Limehouse, sailor, Nov. 21, 1604.—William Lock, [William of Woburn] son of William and Elizabeth his wf. Dec. 20, 1628, 7 days old.—Rebecca Lock, dau. of John, of Limehouse, shipwright, and Judith his wf. May 6, 1629.

Burials. Elizabeth, wf. of William Locke, June 27, 1631.

From the Subsidy Rolls for Suffolk.

John Locke, of Lavenham, 1600.—Daniel Lock, of Laxfield, 1613.—John Locke, of Wattesfield, 1626.—Richard Locke, John and Robert, of Hinderelay, 1638.—Richard Locke, of Hunston, 1639.—Anthony Locke, Clerk of Knettishall [Knetshall?] 1639.—Daniel Locke, of Tressingfield, 1639.—John Locke, of Thelnethan, 1639.

JOHN LOCKE, "Gent."

The fame and character of JOHN LOCKE, commonly called "the great philosopher and metaphysician," are too well known to require a more extended notice. For nearly two centuries the whole civilized world has acknowledged him as one of its greatest luminaries. The names of Locke, Newton, and Bacon, have long been associated as standing at the head of those great minds, whose labors in science and literature have enlightened the world. Of Locke, it may be said that he was not great only in one particular branch of learning, for his mind was capable of grasping and mastering every thing. Metaphysics, religion, and the science of government were all handled by him equally well. Free from ambition (a) and the love of wealth, rocks on which so many have been shipwrecked, he lived a long life, honored by all, and left behind him a character on which no stain could be found. His private and his public life were both equally pure. In the political changes of the day, when kings were made and unmade, he suffered political persecution, and was obliged in 1682 with many others to quit his country for safety, and he was deprived of his privileges at Oxford College by the arbitrary command of the King, in defiance

(a) Under the first Charter of the Carolinas he was created a Landgrave, which title and power he declined.

Page not indexed.

of the rights of the College itself. After several years' absence, at the solicitation of William Penn, the King offered him a pardon, which was accompanied with gracious words of good will; but this he refused to accept, with this noble reply, that "he was ignorant of the crimes of which he had been declared guilty." At the revolution, however, he returned to England, and was honored by appointment to several offices, and he continued in office some years, and until his health became so impaired that he could not live in London only a few days at a time, when he sent in his resignation; on which the king sent for him, and proposed that he should retain his office and receive the emoluments, attending only occasionally, and leaving the duties to be performed by his deputies. Here again he exhibited the purity of his character by the memorable reply, "that he could not think of receiving pay for labor that he did not perform," (a) an example that is rarely followed in modern times, the practice being even in our republican country to receive all that can be obtained from the government.

All the English writers whose works I have consulted, seem to have been almost entirely ignorant of his pedigree. Even Lord King, his nephew, who was to a great extent educated by him, and who published an edition of his works, merely says that "He was the son of J. Locke, who was descended from the Lockes of Charter Court, in Dorsetshire. That his father, who was a Captain in the army of the Parliament, possessed a moderate landed property in Pensfold, [it should have been Pensford] and Bellerton, where he lived; that his fortune became so much impaired in the civil wars that he left a smaller estate to his son than he himself inherited." According to the Gent. Magazine, (see p. 344,) Capt. Locke was the son of Christopher, of Pilrow, in Somersetshire, but in the memoirs prefixed to the edition of the works of his son, pub. in London in 1801, it is said he was the son of Nicholas, of Suttenwick, in the parish of Chew-Magna, which is near Pensford, in Somersetshire. He was an Attorney, as well as a Captain, and officiated as "Steward or Court-keeper" to Col. Popham, who owned large possessions in the vicinity. Several authorities say that he was killed in battle, at or near Bristol, in 1645, and this seems to have been the prevailing opinion; but Lord King, in speaking of a letter written by John to his father, Capt. Locke, says, "It is without date, but was probably written before 1660." This remark would indicate that the father was living in 1660. Another writer says he was living at the restoration (1660), and was appointed Clerk of the Sewers. As the writer in the Gentleman's Magazine says he copies his pedigree from the record of the parish where Capt. Locke was a Church Warden, we must suppose his statement to be the most reliable, and if so, that he was the son of Christopher.

Equally contradictory are historians as to whom the wife of Capt. Locke was. Lord King, I think, does not name her. In the edition of Locke's works before named, published in 1801, in the memoir prefixed, it is said that Capt. Locke married Ann, the dau. of Edmund Keen or Ken, of Wrington; while on the other hand, the Rev. Joseph Hunter, in his article relating to the emigrants from Suffolk, (Eng.) to New England, which was pub. in the Mass. His. Society's Collections, says on the authority of Candler, a great antiquarian of England, and who left voluminous manuscripts, containing pedigrees of many families, that —— Bernard, who was the farmer of an estate of Custridge Hall, which he held of Lord Chief Justice Coke, married a dau. of Robert and Sibil Fisk, and that Bernard had a dau. who was the mother of John Locke Mr. Hunter is disposed to think Candler good authority, because Bernard was Candler's grand-uncle. Yet doubts may be entertained, for Mr. Hunter himself, who ranks high as a learned antiquarian, in this very article, makes a

(a) Mr. Locke was afterwards reproached for not having made interest for some of his friends to succeed to the office, or at least to inform them of his intended resignation of it "I know," said he, in answer to one of his relations who reproached him on this subject; "I know what you tell me very well, but that was the very reason why I would not communicate my intention to any one. I received my commission generously from the king himself, and to him I resolved to restore it, that he might have the pleasure of bestowing it on some man worthy of his bounty."

Page not indexed.

statement which shows that *he* is ignorant of what some of us even in New England have learned. He says "that little is known of Locke's father, but no one who has written on his life, has had the *slightest* knowledge of the mother." In contradiction of this statement, it is only necessary to refer to the memoir from which I have before quoted, prefixed to the edition of Locke's works, pub. 1801, where the writer knew, or pretended to know, that she was the dau. of Edmund Keen or Ken. I notice this that my readers may see how easy it is for writers to be mistaken, hoping that they will be charitable to the many errors that they may find in this unpretending volume.

I have before assumed that Candler was probably right, and that Locke's mother was a Bernard, and his statement seems to receive support from the association of the names of Matthew Barnard, (which I presume was only another way of spelling Bernard,) with the name of William Locke in Nicholas Davie's Will, on the presumption that there was a connection between William Locke and the family of John Locke.

The "progeny" of three of the sons of Robert Fisk, before named, emigrated to New England, as did several other puritan families with whom they were connected. So says Mr. Hunter on the authority of Candler, and goes on to say, as I have mentioned in another place, that "The mother of Locke must have been brought up among the more zealous puritans of the counties of Essex and Suffolk, (England), that she must have heard from her infancy stories of religious persecutions, that she must have seen near connections of her family leaving their native home, to find as they supposed, security and peace in a distant land; and the feelings thus engendered in her mind we may easily believe to have been communicated to her son, who in due time became the great defender of the principle of the utmost tolerance, in dealing with men in affairs of conscience and religious opinion."

The conflicting statements with regard to the family of the wife of Capt. Locke may be reconciled by supposing that he may have been twice married, a fact unknown to the different writers. It is to be hoped that these remarks may induce further inquiries, which may throw more light upon the subject.

All authorities agree that John Locke, the subject of this sketch, was born while the mother was from home in a small cottage in Wrington, in Somersetshire, Aug. 29, 1632. An exception to this, however, as to the date, is a most interesting article originally published in the London Athenæum, and which was afterwards copied into the Living Age, No. 341, p. 424, entitled, "The Grave of Locke." The date of his birth, taken from his tomb, is printed A. D. "1631." This may be a typographical error. Wrington is a small town not far from Bristol, and in the immediate vicinity of Pensford, Bedminster, Pilrow, and several other places where many of the Lockes resided.

Mr. Locke was never married, and after his retirement from public life he became the inmate of the family of Sir Francis and Lady Masham, at their seat at Oates, in Essex, and here he passed the remainder of an invalid life in the cultivation of his mind, and in the composition of many of his admirable works. Lady Masham, who was the dau. of the Rev. Dr. Ralph Cudworth, of Oxford, was a woman of a congenial mind, highly intellectual, and herself a writer. The friendship that existed between them, says one, "must have rested on similarity of tastes and feelings, and perfect confidence. The noble woman who administered to him his last consolation, was like himself calm and possessed, in that last scene which united the serenity of the antique sage with the pious resignation of the Christian saint. After passing without sleep the night which he had not expected to survive, he was taken out of bed and carried into his study, where he slept for some hours in his chair. On waking he desired to be dressed; and then heard Lady Masham read the Psalms, apparently with great attention, until perceiving his end to draw near, he stopped her, and expired a few minutes afterwards."

Thus ended the life of this eminent man, Oct. 27, 1704, a. 72. He was buried at the Church at High Laver, in Essex, near Oates, about 20 miles from London. Against the south wall of the Church is a square raised tomb covered

Page not indexed.

with a slab, on which is inscribed, "JOHN LOCKE, Ob. A. D. 1704." Above the tomb is a marble tablet bearing the Latin inscription written by himself. Here follows a translation:

"Stop, traveller! Near this place lieth John Locke. If you ask what kind of a man he was, he answers that he lived content with his own small fortune. Bred a scholar, he made his learning subservient only to the cause of truth. This thou will learn from his writings, which will show thee every thing else concerning him, with greater truth, than the suspected praises of an epitaph. His virtues, indeed, if he had any, were too little for him to propose as matter of praise to himself, or as an example to thee. Let his vices be buried together. As to an example of manners, if you seek that, you have it in the Gospel; of vices, I wish you may have one nowhere; if mortality, certainly, (and may it profit thee,) thou hast one here and every where."

I cannot close with any thing more beautiful than an extract from a Poem on the Progress of Science, delivered at Harvard College, Ap. 21, 1780, by the Hon. Samuel Dexter.

> "In Metaphysics, too, a LOCKE we find,
> Unfolding the recesses of the mind,
> Teaching mankind the great Creator's plan;
> Yet less admire the author than the man.
> Great in himself, he could with pleasure leave
> The tinsel'd greatness that a Court can give,
> Refuse a place—a pension, and retire,
> From glitt'ring pomp, to fan celestial fire."

Note.—The following items were omitted in their proper place.

James Loch was a merchant of Edinburg, m. Oct. 11, 1610, Margaret Barclay; his eldest son James of Drylaw, Scotland, Treasurer of Edinburg, b. Aug. 27, 1612, had James of Drylaw, b. May 2, 1650, who m. Isabel, dau. of Sir George Foulis, of Ravelston, and had George, of Drylaw, b. Mh. 28, 1678, who m. Jean, dau. of George Foulis, and had James, b. Aug. 16, 1693, who m. Frances, dau. of Hon. William Erskine, son of David, fourth Earl of Buchan.

John Lock, of Hollist. had dau. Mary, who m. Ogle Riggs, of Hollist house, who d. 1705, a. 69.

Mary Locke, of Martin, in Surrey, m. Edward Threle, of Loxwood.

Bridget Locke, of ffaucet, Eng.—Elizabeth Robinson, the wid. of Thomas Robinson, of Boston, (and formerly wf. of Richard Sherman of Boston, merchant, who d. 1660) d. at Boston 1666, left property which she had by Sherman to the children of her sister Bridget Locke of ffaucett, Eng.—to the daus. of Thomas Spaul or Spall of Boston, to her kindred John and Mary Greenleaf of Boston, to Samuel Demon (Damon) of Redding, and to John Brown, son of Edmund, of Dorchester.

SIR JOHN BRAMSTON.

The following, though in part a repetition of what has gone before, contains some additional facts, and is so interesting, as coming direct from Rose, the dau. of Sir William Locke, I cannot avoid the inclination to publish it.

It is from the Autobiography of Sir John Bramston, which was written between the years 1670 and 1699, but not published until 1845. Sir John Bramston was the gr. gr. gr. son of Sir William Locke. He was b. 1611, the son of Sir John Bramston, of Boreham, Knight, Lord Chief Justice of the King's Bench, who was b. May 18, 1577, and m. Bridget, dau. of Sir Thomas Moundeford, M. D. of London, who m. Mary, dau. of Richard Hill, mercer of London, who m. Elizabeth, the "20th" child of Sir William Locke.

"The said Thomas Moundeford married Mary Hill, one of the daus. of Richard Hill, of London, by Elizabeth Lock, the twentieth child of Sir William Lock, the famous citizen Alderman and Lord Maior (*a*) of London, of whome I think fitt here to insert the storie as I find it wreten by one of his daughters, Rose, married first to Anthony Hickman, merchant aduenturer, from whom is descended the now Earle of Plymouth, and soe is the alliance betweene our families, he beinge descended of one daughter, and myself from another of Sir William Lock, but his tytle to Lord Windsor came by a marriage in that familie; her second husband was Throgmorton of Brampton in Huntingdonsheire, esqueir. I find it in wast paper in her Bible, which hath binn carefully pre-

(*a*) It may be questionable whether Sir William Locke was ever Lord Mayor of London.

Page not indexed.

serued by the females in the familie acording to her order, and is now in the hands of my sister Lady Palmer, beinge giuen her by the aforementioned Mary, her and my Grandmother. The storie is (as I find it) thus: In the 25th yeare of King Henry the 8th, *that was* 1530, William Lock, citizen and Mercer of London, beinge in Dunkirke when a curse (interdiction, I suppose) was sett vp by the Pope's *messinger* or nuncio, against the King and Kingdom, in fauor and at the request of Queene Katharine, Mr. Lock beinge then there, he tooke it downe, (soe farr, sayes she, goes Hollinshead; but his daughter Rose adds) for which seruice the Kinge gaue him 100 pounds a yeare, and knighted him, and soe (says she) he was the first, that, beinge a Knight, was sheriff of London. He had alsoe the speciall fauor of the Kinge, to haue a key to his priuie chamber, to come to him when he would. The Kinge dined at his house, he being the King's mercer. . . . . . And she tells this storie, (I meane Rose that wrote the Memoires;) she says, that, in the tyme of her first husband, Anthony Hickman, after the death of Edward the Sixth, Queen Mary changinge the relligion, her husband and her elder brother Thomas Lock, beinge merchants and partners, they liued to geather and sheltred manie of the godlie preachers in theire house; but the Queene inioyninge all to come to mass, and persecutinge the refusers, they were forced to let them goe, giuing them monie; she mentions Hooper, Fox, Knox, and one Reinger, for which her husband and brother beinge questiond, before the commissioners, (she calls them high commissioners,) were committed close prisoners to the Fleete, and then shee tells how they gott out; . . . . after which she says her husband went to Antwerpe, tooke a house there at 40 pounds rent, sent for her, but she being with child could not goe, but went into Oxfordshire to a gentleman's house, but she names him not, but thincks the house was called Childwell, wher she was deliuered; names not the child, nor whether male or female; but says she went to Cranmer, Latimer, and Ridlie, prisoners then in Oxford, to know whether she might christen her child in the Popish manner. They answered her that baptisme was the least corrupted in that church, and therefore she might, but sayd she should haue gone away before, for the child was baptised by a Popish preist, but she says she put sugar instead of salt into the handkercher which was to be deliuered vnto the priest, after which she went to Antwerpe to her husband, left 2 houses of her husband's, well furnished, one in London, another at Rumford, taking noething but one feather bed, ... Whilst she was at Antwerpe she had another child, which with great care she procured to be baptised after the reformed manner by a Protestant minister, which was done thus: The fashion was to hange a peece of lawne out at the window where a child was to be baptised; and her house hauinge two dores into two streetes, she hunge lawne out at each dore, soe the neighbours of each side, thinckinge the child was carried out at the other dore, inquired no farther; the hasard she rann was great, for she sayes, that in the hatred which was borne by the townsmen to the Anabaptists, the magistrates used to come at midnight into houses where any children were suspected to be kept vnbaptised, and if they found any such they vsed to putt them into a sack and threw them into the sea and drowne them, which crueltie to auoid, she did, as is before sayd, hange out the lawne, and there beinge a secret congregation of Protestants in the Towne, she procured her child to be carried thither, where it was baptised, she not knowing who were godfathers or godmothers. She continued in Antwerpe to the death of Queene Mary; she died at Gainesborough 21 November 1613, in the 87th yeare of her age. And this is all I find of her in these memoires collected and made by her selfe and sister.

"Elisabeth Lock was the 20th child of Sir William Lock, which is testified by a note written by himselfe in the said Bible. She was borne in Milk Streete, London, the 3d day of August, 1535. She had 2 husbands, beinge first married to Richard Hill, with whome she liued 18 yeares, and had by him 13 childrenn; she continued a widow one yeare and a quarter, and then married [Nicholas] Bullingham, bishop of Worcester, and had one child by him. Hill died at Newington Greene, Sep. 1568; shee was very younge when she married Hill, for she was but 20 yeares old when she went with her husband into the Low Countries to Antwerpe; and yet she had then 4 children; she had fiue in Antwerpe. She hath not mentioned the names of all her children. What I find of them in that memoire is thus: her eldest daughter, Katharine Hill, was married to Dr. Goad; she was baptised 23 April, 1554; of her was borne Dr. Goad, one of the diunes sent by King James I. vnto the Synod of Dort. Martha, the 2nd daughter maried to Luke Smyth, Clerke; she was baptised 8th of September, 1560; she dyed at Worcester, 1593. Rowland, baptised 16th October, 1561. I thincke he had no issue male, but he had a daughter married to Mr. —— —— Munday. Mary, baptised 5th of June, 1562; she married Dr. Moundeford, from whome I am descended. Elizabeth, borne at Antwerpe the yeare before Queene Mary died, [1557]; she married with Edward Archbold, at Worcester. Otwell, borne alsoe at Antwerpe, the first yeare of Queene Elizabeth, [1558.] Ann, baptised 1566; married to Andros, I guess, parson of Chesterton. . . .

"I find Sir William Lock had a daughter married into Cornewell, for Otwell Hill went into Cornewell to his aunt, eldest sister to his mother; she is not named either by her husband's name or her owne Christen name, but I gues her husband's name was Cuswroth, for I remember one of that name that was clerke to my father, whome we called cousen."

Here ends the History of the Lockes in England. Many of the facts have a peculiar interest to those of the name in America, and go to show when the family was first known, and in what parts of the country they resided, and their occupation or profession. Like many of the early merchants of England, some of them were mariners, commanding their own ships and trading to different parts of the world. A thorough examination of the County and Town histories of England, which are very full of pedigrees, would undoubtedly give a vast number of additional particulars; and what appears in the preceding pages will be something of a guide as to where further information should be sought, and that was the principal object for inserting many of the items.

Page not indexed.

REFERENCE LIST, CONSULT NUMBERS, NOT PAGES.

Colonial Wars.

F12	F 50	7337	8449	9937	10236
F24	F 54	7392	8490	10039	10398
F35	F 68	7394	8505	10208	
F39	F129	7451	8518		
F40		7491	8545		**Lawyers.**
		7522	8694	3095	6437
		7564	9187	3258	6449

War of Revolution.

F12	308	7578	9189	3403	6762
F25	F315	F7595	9190	F3683	7261
F57	F327	7597	9191	3684	7262
F66	F330	7816	9498	F4095	7341
F68	F332	7861	9499	F4131	7369
F116	F342	7884	9563	4132	7554
F137	F343	7948	9680	F4135	7564
F139	371	7967	9734	4184	8098
140	380	F7968	9780	F4197	8231
F142	F410	7969	9838	F4342	8343
F152	F417	7991	9872	4408	8472
F162	F508	8055	9965	4411	8505
F165	529d	8098	9969	4590	8607
F175	535d	8143	10010	F4922	8678
F181	F537	8145	10208	5232	9476
F182	F540	F8229	10211	F5238	9482
F191	F559	8231	10239	F5245	10014
198	F566	8280	10241	F5262	10056
F201	F567	8310	10245	5496	10211
F204	F568	8401	10250	5509	10236
F206	F571	8407	10480	5727	10380
F207	F588	8407	10509	5735	10391
F208	F627			F5792	10501
F232	628d		**Doctors.**		
F243	F636	F158	7026		**Ministers.**
F244	F637	584	7055	F175	5038
F249	F650	1079	7156	550	F5123
F251	F651	F3063	7180	982	5124
F279	F666	3073	7247	F1248	F5204
284d	F667	3403	7263	F1380	5812
F288	719d	3882	7371	F1775	6407
F292	728d	3960	7537	F1796	6462
F294	Page 569	4236	7594	F1920	6834
		F4342	7624	3056	F7090
Army and Navy, Officers.		4393	7887	F3308	7221
		4408	7969	3515	7330
3381	9385	4587	8145	3667	7336
4347	9577	4597	8311	F3683	F7595
6547	9966	4635	8407	3716	7936
6794	10208	4865	8490	F4072	F8125
7766	10254	F4910	8527	4091	F8126
F7786	10569	5049	8566	F4114	8279
		5140	8673	4175	8747
College Graduates.		5451	8692	4176	8749
		5612	8703	4190	8749
3095	6540	5730	8010	4194	F8921
3684	6840	5733	8933	4200	8983
F3690	6842	5826	9140	4408	9075
4114	6843	5915	9143	4627	9080
F4128	6844	F5935	9338	F4913	
4132	7055	F5936	9466		
F4264	7215	6013	9480		**Governors.**
F4342	7217	F6472	9620	2290	5727
F5238	7261	6876	9746		
5466	7262	7010	9883	**Colonial General Assembly**	
F6043	7325			F46	

GEOGRAPHICAL INDEX

INDEX OF PLACES OUTSIDE OF NEW ENGLAND
RESIDENCES, RATHER THAN PLACES OF BIRTH OR DEATH

ALABAMA
  Mobile..................540, 563, 564
ALASKA.........................169, 181
ARIZONA
  Phoenix........................... 552
AUSTRALIA........................... 397
BRITISH COLUMBIA
  Lards............................. 462
  Victoria.......................... 377
CALIFORNIA........79, 79, 168, 214, 251, 253
                276, 277, 291, 351, 439
                     439, 440, 453
  Alameda.....................268, 425
  Arcata............................ 169
  Berkeley.....................423, 424
  Corona............................ 490
  Cucamonga......................... 333
  Eureka............................ 336
  Fallbrook......................... 423
  Hanford........................... 423
  Lindsay........................... 472
  Los Angeles........161, 346, 380, 423
                          425, 439, 465
  Monrovia.......................... 333
  Oakland.............216, 258, 277, 538
  Purissima......................... 425
  Ramona............................ 279
  Raymond............................ 79
  Sacramento.....124, 406, 478, 528, 546
  San Diego......................... 416
  San Francisco.............177, 184, 208
                246, 274, 325, 350, 379
                425, 425, 441, 514, 535
  San Jose................253, 281, 293
  San Leandro....................... 351
  San Luis Rey...................... 537
  Santa Clara....................... 293
  Santa Cruz........................ 424
  Santiago................253, 271, 514
  Stockton.......................... 290
  Sonoma........................344, 426
CANADA............................... 50
  Alberta.......................189, 346
  Barnston..............49, 94, 105, 232
                           392, 394, 517
  Hatley........................203, 270
  Magog.....................205, 205, 376
  Stanstead....49, 95, 214, 231, 374, 394
  Sutton............................ 554
  Toronto........................... 204
CHINA
  Pekin............................. 456
COLORADO......................249, 291
  Boulder........................... 197
  Denver...............197, 262, 368, 416
  Pueblo............................ 552
  Woodland Park..................... 416
DAKOTA, NORTH.................324, 475
  Ashtabula......................... 411
  Jamestown......................... 379

DAKOTA, SOUTH
  Beresford......................... 268
  Garretson......................... 472
  Harrold........................... 544
  Mitchell.......................... 544
  Munroe............................ 256
DISTRICT OF COLUMBIA
  Washington.................102, 525
FLORIDA
  Jacksonville..................375, 375
  Keuka............................. 133
  Orlando........................... 391
GEORGIA.......................121, 560
  Atlanta.......................134, 443
IDAHO
  Fairfield......................... 169
ILLINOIS............................. 63
  Aurora............................ 278
  Bridgeport........................ 422
  Campton........................... 279
  Centerville....................... 555
  Chicago.........121, 204, 253, 280, 288
                314, 372, 374, 377, 385, 418
                418, 433, 434, 434, 467, 480
  Danville......................428, 454
  Decatur........................... 428
  Elburn........................278, 279
  Freeport.......................... 480
  Galesburg......................... 276
  Greenup........................... 498
  Hebron............................ 339
  Henry..............275, 276, 456, 456
  Hurricane......................... 119
  Joliet............................ 253
  Knox County....................... 125
  Lawrence County................... 555
  Princeton.......................... 94
  Ramsey........................480, 549
  Robinson.......................... 422
  Rockford.......................... 108
  Shelbyville........................ 40
  Vandalia........................... 81
  Victoria.......................... 122
  Warrensville...................... 278
  Wenona............................ 455
INDIA............................... 327
INDIANA
  Delaware.......................... 275
  Elkhart........................... 154
  Evansville........................ 498
  Morocco........................... 363
  Oaktown........................... 555
  Ravensville....................... 556
  Roselawn.......................... 363
  Terre Haute....................... 428
  Vincennes......................... 497
  Wilmington........................ 126
IOWA...................79, 259, 372, 468
  Arcadia........................... 168
  Atlantic.......................... 333
  Carroll County.................... 289
  Cass County....................... 333

GEOGRAPHICAL INDEX

IOWA
Cedar Falls..................268, 390
Central City.......295, 296, 296, 468
Clinton.......................... 480
Columbus City................. 256
Council Bluffs................. 377
Des Moines.............225, 390, 442
Grinwell....................... 389
Lenox.......................... 387
Luverne........................ 449
Malcom......................... 333
Obrien County................. 387
Ottumwa....................... 255
Primghar....................... 387
Rowan.......................... 544
Rutland....................337, 502
Superior........................ 205
Tama........................... 332
Wankon......................319, 320

KANSAS........................... 135
Holton......................416, 243
Lawrence....................314, 379
Wichita.....................243, 298

KENTUCKY
Burnside....................... 284
Clay City....................... 533
Louisville....................260, 261
Glen View...................... 515

MARYLAND
Preston......................... 253

MEXICO
Mexico City.................... 434

MICHIGAN....................... 242
Argentine...................... 108
Bridgton........................ 78
Coldwater...................63, 136
Columbia........................ 95
Detroit.................208, 244, 504
Grand Rapids...............185, 194
Hillsdale....................... 363
Kent County.................... 194
Muskegon....................... 78
Pottersville.................... 257
Saginaw.................125, 242, 433
St. Cloud....................... 258
Sodis........................... 362
Stillwater....................... 83

MINNESOTA........................ 98
Ada........................313, 487
Alexandria...................... 411
Austin.......................... 225
Caledonia....................... 225
Clear Water.................... 183
Lake City...................262, 442
Leroy........................... 242
Mankato........................ 337
Minneapolis.................... 431
Pillsbury....................... 218
St. James...................275, 456
St. Paul.........370, 444, 446, 541, 560
Silver Creek.................... 214

MISSISSIPPI....................... 45
New Orleans....111, 207, 375, 378, 515

MISSOURI
Kansas City....243, 325, 417, 431, 529
Rockport...................220, 387
St. Louis.................352, 352, 515
Springfield..................... 197
Waco........................... 256

MONTANA......................... 236
Helena......................... 528
Missoula....................... 527

NEBRASKA
David City..................... 280
Fairburg 332
Omaha.......................... 378
Osceola........................ 79
Rising City.................... 280
Sioux Reservation.............. 275

NEBRASKA
Stockham...................... 438
Wahoo.......................... 296

NEVADA
Tonopah........................ 498

NEW BRUNSWICK.........38, 78, 335, 252
Alma........................... 167
Grand Manan.................. 127

NEW JERSEY
Bound Brook................... 324
Clinton........................ 523
Cranford....................... 222
Orange......................... 264
Rahway......................... 324

NEW YORK
Angelica........................ 50
Aurora...................41, 81, 175
Batavia.........63, 136, 300, 300, 472
Bethany........................ 300
Brasher Falls..........134, 299, 471
Brockport..................299, 472
Brooklyn.........125, 259, 325, 377
                379, 454, 473, 496, 558
Brushton....................... 135
Buffalo......245, 300, 327, 472, 554, 562
Canastota...................340, 502
Cattaraugus.................... 288
Chenango County............36, 74
Cincinnatus.................... 160
Columbia....................80, 172
Cortland County................ 74
Edmeston....................... 339
Flushing....................... 379
Fort Jackson................... 472
Glen Falls..................264, 443
Hartland County................ 63
Herkimer....................... 340
Homer.......................... 452
Hoosick Falls................... 174
Kendall........................ 63
Livonia........................ 160
Massena........................ 299
Munroe County................. 62
New Rochelle................... 326
New York..................353, 555
New York City.........38, 153, 155
                211, 275, 325, 326, 365
                378, 381, 409, 545, 553
Ogdensburg..................... 439
Oneonta....................173, 340
Orangeport..................... 269
Orleans County................. 62
Oxford County.................. 36
Poplar Ridge................... 81
Poughkeepsie................... 407
Richfield...........81, 172, 173, 339
Salem.......................... 126
Sweden..............63, 135, 299 472
Syracuse....................... 209
Tonawanda...................... 327
Utica.......................... 339
West Edmeston................. 341
West Winfield.................. 340
White Plains................... 153
Whitestone..................... 208
Winthrop...................134, 135
Yonkers........................ 155

NORTH CAROLINA
Estatoe........................ 270
Reidsville.........179, 345, 503, 557

NOVA SCOTIA
Annapolis...................... 508
Cornwallis..................... 357
Greytown....................... 127
Halifax........................ 508
Lockport......12, 55, 86, 189, 356, 357
                357, 506, 507, 558
Milton......................... 507
Ragged Island.................. 190

GEOGRAPHICAL INDEX

NOVA SCOTIA
  Windsor........................ 509
OHIO..................86, 100, 134, 251
  Cincinnati...............63, 204, 289
  Cleveland...........338, 348, 442, 485
  Dayton......................... 523
  Elyria......................... 221
  Hudson......................... 438
  Huntington.................115, 116
  Logan.......................... 298
  Loudonville.................... 251
  Robinson....................... 533
  Toledo................216, 281, 466
  Warren......................... 61
  Wellington............260, 263, 441
OKLAHOMA........................... 268
  Shamrock....................... 562
OREGON
  Central Point.................. 222
  Corvallis...................... 514
  Heppner........................ 536
  Huntington..................... 466
  Portland....................... 207
PANAMA............................. 274
PENNSYLVANIA
  Alleghany...................... 509
  Bradford............422, 532, 533, 561
  Butler......................... 532
  Erie......................365, 470
  Franklin....................... 534
  Gaines......................... 331
  Huntingdon.................411, 528
  Lebanon........................ 230
  Philadelphia..........229, 276, 453
  Pittsburg...................... 490
  Pittston....................... 364
  Pleasantville.................. 422
  Titusville....422, 423, 532, 534, 537, 561
  Tioga County................... 160
  Turtle Creek................... 348

PENNSYLVANIA
  Wellsboro...................... 331
SOUTH AFRICA....................... 507
TENNESSEE.......................... 528
  Memphis....................86, 563
TEXAS.............................. 513
  Chapel Hill.................... 431
  Dalhart........................ 544
  Dallas......................... 411
  Dennison....................... 314
  Forth Worth................161, 466
  San Antonio..........359, 359, 508
VIRGINIA........................... 467
WASHINGTON STATE................... 167
  Eltopia........................ 523
  Garfield....................... 169
  Mt. Vernon..................... 168
  Seattle...................169, 237
  Skamokawa...................... 240
  Tacoma......................... 539
WEST VIRGINIA
  Parkersburg.................... 533
WISCONSIN......................86, 102
  Antigo......................... 200
  Cumberland..................... 256
  Delavan........................ 173
  Eau Claire..................... 227
  Edgerton....................... 268
  Ellsworth.............534, 560, 561
  Grantsburg..................... 455
  Janesville............174, 268, 268
  Marietta....................... 262
  Milwaukee...................... 212
  Oshkosh........................ 469
  Palmyra........................ 173
  Prescott....................... 514
  River Falls.................... 373
WYOMING
  Casper......................... 385
  Big Horn Mountain.............. 497

Locke Reunion, 1916

INDEX OF NAMES

d signifies died young.

ABBOTT, Alice........................ 491
   Alice (Tenney)................... 186
   Arthur E......................... 186
   Charles.......................... 271
   Dolly............................. 85
   Dorris M......................... 510
   Essie............................ 356
   George T......................... 418
   James............................ 320
   John............................. 510
   Louisa........................... 303
   Mabel............................ 520
   Mamie (Locke-York).............. 510
   Mary F........................... 147
   Mary (Fall)...................... 320
   Mary (Sanders)................... 418
   Melissa.......................... 477
   Nathan........................... 257
   Nellie............................ 372
   Phebe............................ 115
   Rhoda (Brickett)................. 257
   Sally (Locke) Pollard.............. 85
   Sarah (True)..................... 271
   Sewell..................85, 186, 186
   Susan............................ 200
ACKERLY, Cornelia................... 208
ACKERMAN–AKERMAN.
   Anna (Lord-Mooney)............. 400
   Benjamin......................... 67
   Charity (Marden-Locke).......... 67
   Edwin............................ 400
   Elizabeth......................... 100
   Etta (Colby)..................... 522
   Harry............................ 522
   James A.......................... 522
   Josiah............................ 568
   Nancy (Locke).................... 568
   Peter............................. 67
   Sally (Philbrick).................. 67
ADAIR, May......................... 367
ADAMS, Mr............................ 25
   Allan H.......................... 548
   Anna............................. 441
   Arthur........................... 227
   Charles......................379, 446
   Chester.......................... 500
   Claude........................... 379
   Donald F......................... 548
   Gertrude......................... 379
   Edith (Hussey)................... 500
   Edward.......................... 379
   Elihu............................ 379
   Ella.............................. 477
   Ethel (Lamprey)................. 446
   Hazel............................ 446
   Howard S........................ 548
   Elder John F..................... 427
   Jonas, Deacon.................... 94
   Joseph........................... 446
   Lillian (Page).................... 227
   Lucy (Dow)...................... 379
   Martha (Perry).................. 446
   Mary............................. 314
   Medora (Stillings)............... 548
   Quincy........................... 379
   Sally.............................. 21

ADAMS, Sally (Wright)................ 94
   Sarah........................94, 558
   Sarah (Treadwell-Locke).......... 427
ADWERS, Ann L...................... 313
   Clarence......................... 313
   Daniel A......................... 144
   George M......................... 313
   Herbert.......................... 313
   Horace F......................... 313
   John............................. 313
   Mary (Mason).................... 144
   Sarah............................ 313
   (Winslow), Miss................. 313
AIKEN, Ann (Bradley)................ 381
   Herrick.......................... 381
   Mary............................. 231
   Mary (Dodge).................... 381
   Susan (Colby).................... 381
   Walter........................... 381
AIKENS, Andrew..................... 130
   Betsey (Locke)................... 130
   Fred d........................... 130
   Hannah.......................... 130
   Martha (McAlister).............. 130
   Mary d.......................... 130
   (Mason), Miss................... 130
   William......................130, 130
ALDRICH, Adelbert L................. 232
   Alice.........................392, 394
   Areanna (Lewis)................. 232
   Beazer........................... 231
   Betsey........................231, 394
   Carrie (Dennison)................ 232
   Chloe A. L....................... 392
   Chloe (Locke).................... 105
   Clara L. d....................... 393
   Cynthia (Vance)................. 232
   Della (Duke)..................... 232
   Dr............................... 105
   Emma (Cade).................... 231
   Emma G.......................... 393
   Florence (Fletcher).............. 232
   Frances L........................ 392
   Frances (Strupp), Mrs........... 392
   Francis.......................... 392
   Frank L.......................... 393
   Fred G. d....................... 393
   Guy..........................105, 232
   Harold........................... 392
   Henrietta (Uliggett)............. 394
   Irene H.......................... 394
   Levi L........................... 232
   Lovina (Horn)................... 231
   Lucy (Aldrich)................... 392
   Mary......................231, 394, 393
   Mary (Glover)................... 232
   Mira............................. 215
   Norman E....................232, 232
   Ozro B........................... 392
   Reginald E....................... 392
   Rhoda............................ 105
   Rose L. d........................ 392
   Stephen R........................ 394
   Thomas L........................ 231
   Timothy..................232, 392, 394
   William.......................... 392

INDEX OF NAMES

ALEXANDER, Clara................... 421
ALGER, Anna....................... 326
  Charles J....................... 553
  Emma (Jameson)................ 257
  George W....................... 553
  Grace (Drew).................... 553
  Harriet (Locke)................. 326
  James.......................... 326
  Nathan C., Rev................. 257
  Rev. Dr........................ 326
ALLARD, Hannah................... 72
ALLEN, Anna (Bowen).............. 171
  Annette....................... 384
  Bertha........................ 556
  Bertha (Horn).................. 498
  Bessie L....................... 556
  Chester....................... 338
  Cora (Locke)................... 301
  Dorcas (Marden-Mowe).......... 32
  Elizabeth L.................... 34
  Elizabeth Locke................ 32
  Elizabeth (Locke).............. 16
  Ellen A........................ 84
  Emery......................... 422
  Eva (Locke)................... 338
  Fannie (Anderson).............. 476
  Fred L......................... 384
  Garland....................... 147
  George.....................171, 301
  Gertrude....................... 333
  Gertrude (Howe)............... 384
  Grace.......................... 430
  Hannah....................... 45
  Hannah (Brown)................ 430
  Harley........................ 430
  Harriet J...................... 94
  Harriet (Locke)................ 194
  Hart.......................... 203
  Ira, Dr........................ 194
  James......................... 420
  Jeremiah...................... 191
  John.......................... 498
  Joshua........................ 32
  Josie (Moore).................. 430
  Jude 16, 71, 32
  Keziah........................ 87
  Lucia (Goss)................... 203
  Lydia......................... 293
  Lyman........................ 147
  Maria E....................... 183
  Mark......................70, 147
  Mary........147, 333, 357, 420, 498
  Mary (Davis).................. 420
  Mary E. (Locke)............... 333
  Mary (Locke).................. 70
  Mattie........................ 556
  Maude........................ 420
  Nancy (Eliott)................. 191
  Nathaniel..................... 32
  Robert W...................... 333
  Sally (Mowe)............68, 140, 304
  Salome..................32, 141, 250
  Samuel....................68, 304
  Thial.......................... 147
  William, Rev.................13, 15
  William............430, 430, 476, 476
ALLISON, Fannie.................... 423
ALLYN, Mary...................... 80
AMAZEEN, Abigail (Underwood)....... 51
  Benjamin...................... 524
  (Berry), Miss.................. 567
  Charles B...................... 401
  Dolly......................... 519
  Dora.......................... 500
  Jessie (Batson)................. 401
  Margie (Hutchins).............. 524
  Martha A...................... 524
  Mary......................... 553
  May........................... 492
  Orville C...................... 524

AMAZEEN, William...............553, 567
AMBROSE, Alfred E................. 202
  Clara......................... 371
  Clara (Towle).................. 202
  Cora.......................371, 371
  David......................... 371
  Fred.......................371, 371
  Helen......................... 371
  Margaret...................... 371
  Mary (Cook).................. 371
  Nathaniel..................... 371
AMEE, Annie...................... 241
AMES, Abigail (Bachelder).......... 517
  Adaline (Locke-Bean)........... 318
  Aleta E....................... 517
  Burley M...................... 389
  David......................... 81
  Eliza (Locke).................. 198
  Ella (Vrooman)................ 172
  Ethel W....................... 517
  Ida........................... 198
  James......................... 517
  Jay W......................... 172
  Jerome........................ 172
  Lila........................... 338
  Lovicia A...................... 172
  Lucius........................ 172
  Lulu d........................ 338
  Marietta (Young).............. 172
  Mary (Locke)................. 388
  Mary Z........................ 172
  Morrill........................ 198
  Myra (Ayers).................. 110
  Phebe M...................... 110
  Rebecca (Locke)............... 8
  Rosetta (Sternburg)............ 172
  Samuel........................ 110
  Spencer A..................... 338
  William....................... 31
AMIDOWN, Dorcas.................. 378
  Lester........................ 37
  Mabel (Locke)................. 37
  Theodore..................... 37
ANDERSON, Abbie d................ 47
  Ann d........................ 47
  Edward....................303, 47
  Eliza S........................ 47
  Emma (Jameson)............... 43
  Fannie E...................... 47
  Frank C d................... 47
  Frederick..................... 35
  Ida (Pickering)................ 47
  John.......................... 35
  Lucy H....................... 47
  Martha E. d.................. 47
  Martha (Rand)................ 30
  Mary (Locke)................. 35
  Nellie (Sargent)............... 24
  Roy........................... 24
  Smith......................... 43
  William H..................... 47
ANDREWS, Ann (Locke-Church)...... 49
  Alice......................... 55
  Charles R..................313, 48
  Edna......................... 43
  Edwin........................ 49
  Eulah......................... 55
  Helen M...................... 48
  Herbert....................336, 48
  Mary (Hoxie)................. 33
  Mary W. (Farmer)............. 31
  Robert........................ 43
  Wallace....................... 48
ANGELL, Celestia (Davis)........... 22
ANNIS, Esther (Brown-Rand)........ 31
  Matthew D................... 32
ANTHONY, Mr...................... 7
ANTILL, Blanche M................. 50
  Florence (Locke).............. 50
  Lois L........................ 50
  Stephen F..................... 50

INDEX OF NAMES

ANTILL, William 561
APPLETON, Mr. 121
   Clara 490
   Mary (Foss) 121
APT, Harriet A. (Locke) 55
   Louisa 55
   Wilbur 55
ARCHER, Charles 369
   John B. 369
   Phebe Waldo 369
   Sarah (Locke) 369
ARLIN, Betsey 467
ARMITAGE, Gertrude (Tibbetts) 400
   Joshua 400
   Nellie (Batson) 400
ARMSTRONG, Finette (Locke) 425
   William 425
ARNETT, Henry 221
   Sarah (Thompson) 221
ARNOLD, Lucy 447
ASHLEY, Mary 422
ATKINS, George 442
   Jessie (Wright) 442
   Samuel 442
ATKINSON, Frances 445
ATWELL, Sarah 48
AUSTIN, Benjamin 453
   Clara 368
   Jemima 14
   Marion 528
   Mary (Reynolds) 272
   Nancy (Moshier-Locke) 453
   Nellie 272
   Sarah 252
   William 272
AVERY, Alberta 392
   Emma (Locke) 433
   Hannah 435
   Helen 325
   Jacob 124
   Jemima 124
   Jennie (Cook) 124
   Prudence (Locke) 25
   Roger L. 433
   Samuel Jr. 25
   Solon E. 433
   Walter C 433
AYER, Hannah 14, 510
AYERS, Annie 387
   John 427
   Joseph 397
   Lucy 427
   Maria 427
   Mary (Locke) 284
   Mary (Neal) 397
   Myra 110
   Nancy (Trefethern) 69
   Samuel 69
   William 284
AYLESWORTH, BLACKBURN F. 37
   Daniel 37
   Mercy (Locke) 37
   Ruth 37
BABB, Abigail 288
   Abigail (Kimball) 450
   Albert 288
   Anna M. (Lang) 116
   Belle 288
   Betsey 27
   Charlotte 297
   Emeline A. 262
   Francena d. 262
   Fred 272
   George A. d. 262
   Georgeanna 262
   H. Susan 288
   Horatio 125
   Ida F. 272
   James, Dr. 116
   John 262

BABB, Joseph 450
   Leonora 262
   Lydia 116
   M. Elizabeth 288
   Martha 220, 220
   Mary 262, 273
   Mary A. (Demeritt) 125
   Meribah (Locke) 34, 569
   Moses 34
   Sophia (Reynolds) 272
   Susan (Rand-Locke) 146
   Thomas 146, 288, 288, 569
   William 272
BABBITT, Ida M. 511
   John 511
   Lillian 511
BABCOCK, Eliza 37
BABO, Beatrice 545
   Bernice 545
   James H. 545
   Joseph 471, 545
   Margaret 545
   Margaret (Bickford) 471
BACHELDER. BATCHELDER 92
   Abbie d. 322
   Abigail 517
   Abigail (Cotton) 118
   Abigail M. (Locke) 149
   Abraham 111
   Addie 403
   Alonzo E. 433
   Angelina 120
   Ann 176
   Annah (Sanborn) 111
   Asenath 61
   Bartlett A. 410
   Bessie 309, 421, 488
   Betsey 52, 99
   Betsey (Cram) 99
   Betsey B. (Darrah) 99
   Carrie (Page) 433
   Carter, Capt. 100
   Charles 92, 309, 309, 344, 421, 551
   Charlotte 129
   Christena (Locke) 235
   Clara 309, 344
   Clarinda 120, 316
   Daniel, Rev. 134
   Daniel C. 215
   Deborah 99, 101
   Deborah (Leavitt) 92
   Dolly 46
   Dora C. 309
   Dora (Folsom) 215
   Dorothy (Dearborn) 266
   Dudley T. 215
   Eliza 92
   Eliza (Brown-Ward) 145
   Elizabeth (Page) 23
   Elizabeth (Tucker) 99
   Ellen 266
   Elvira 92
   Emaline 92
   Emery Dea. 266
   Ethel (Locke) 410
   Florenda 92, 92
   Frank 495
   George 149, 215, 309, 322, 410
   Hannah 47, 92
   Hannah (Morrill) 99
   Harriet 92, 94
   Hattie 403
   Helen A. 421
   Henry 235, 532
   Hiram 92
   Huldah (Moulton) 100
   Huldah (Page) 132
   Jacob 92
   James 99
   Jane (Page) 47

INDEX OF NAMES

BACHELDER-BATCHELDER, Janette (Godfrey).......................... 92
  Jennie 99
  Jethro......................... 92
  John..............60, 92, 92, 92, 92
                  129, 215, 245, 532
  Jonathan...............111, 262, 322
  Joseph.................92, 120, 489
  Josiah....................118, 119
  (Knowles), Miss................. 92
  Lettice (Campbell)............... 215
  Libbe.......................... 94
  Lois (Wells).................... 111
  Love (Blaisdell)................. 94
  Margaret...................... 532
  Martha..................119, 129, 309
  Martha (Brown)............309, 551
  Martha (Lang-Fogg)............. 60
  Mary................47, 92, 119, 175
  Mary (Brown)................... 94
  Mary (Cotton).................. 129
  Mary (Emerson)................. 322
  Mary (Godfrey)................. 92
  Mary (Randall)................. 215
  Mehitable (Blake).............. 92
  Moses.......................94, 215
  Nabby......................... 99
  Nahum J. Gov.................. 119
  Nancy......................... 322
  Nathaniel..................... 145
  Nellie......................... 343
  Page.......................... 99
  Phebe (Chase) 134
  Rachel (Lane).................. 262
  Rhoda (Durgan)................. 215
  Sally (Knowles)................. 119
  Sally (Morrill).................. 99
  Samuel....................132, 421
  Sarah (Hale)................... 215
  Sarah (Hutchins)............... 421
  Sarah (Locke).................. 245
  Sarah (Philbrick)...........120, 489
  Sarah (Randall)................. 495
  Stephen...............47, 99, 99, 215
  William A..................... 119
BACHELOTTE, Catherine............... 265
  (Howell), Miss................. 448
  John.......................... 448
BACOCK, Inez....................... 315
BACON, Ann (Locke)................. 568
  David.......................... 568
  Eliza (Locke).................. 568
  Isaac.......................... 568
BADCLIFF, Ida...................... 453
BADEAU, David K.................... 563
  Edith (Locke).................. 540
  Edna R........................ 563
  Edward R...................... 563
  George.....................540, 563
  John E......................... 563
  Joseph A....................... 563
  Mary A........................ 563
  Simeon L...................... 563
BADGER, Addie (Jones).............. 510
  Ann M........................ 375
  Daniel W...................... 405
  Edith (Whidden)............... 405
  Governor...................... 510
  Hannah (Ayer)................. 510
  John C......................... 510
  Joseph........................ 510
  Roland J....................... 510
BAGLEY, Adalaide (Locke)........... 315
  Elthea......................... 79
  Esther........................ 509
  S. C........................... 315
BAILEY, Albert..................... 486
  Alice (Hutchinson)............. 514
  Angeletta..................... 58
  Blanche....................... 538

BAILEY, Clarence L.................. 5?
  Daisy (Clough)................. 4?
  Eleanor (Locke)................ 4?
  Eleanor N..................... 5?
  Elizabeth...................... 3(
  Emma (Locke).................. 3]
  Eudora d...................... 4?
  Flavia......................... ?
  Floyd D....................... 5]
  Hannah (Belnap)............... ?
  Harold R...................... 5?
  Harriet....................246, 5?
  Harvey........................ 4?
  Jesse.......................... ?
  John W...................424, 5?
  Joseph........................ ?
  Lottie......................... 5(
  Lowana....................... ?
  Marietta....................... ?
  Mary......................341, 5]
  Mary (Currier)................. 3?
  May (Spooner)................. 5?
  Melissa........................ ?
  Nancy......................... ?
  Olevia......................... ?
  Orrin.......................... 5?
  Roy d......................... 5?
  Sabrina (Moulton).............. ?
  Sarah (Adams)................. 5?
  Thirza......................... 4?
  Victor E....................... 3?
  Viola.......................... ?
  Warren H...................... 5?
  William W..................... 3?
BAINES, Grace (Locke).............. 4?
  William....................492, 4?
BAIR, Ardelle (Locke)............... 3?
  Fedora C...................... 5(
  Iona B......................... 5(
  Murray........................ 5(
  Nina G......................... 5(
  R. C........................... 3?
  Sadie B........................ 5(
  Walter W...................... 5(
BAKER, Aaron W................... 5?
  Albert S....................... 1?
  Alfred......................... 3?
  Alice.......................... 4(
  Alice (Maurer)................. 5?
  Anna.......................... 3?
  Bradley L..................... 5?
  Caroline F. (Locke)............ 1?
  Carrie (Downes)................ 3?
  Carrie (Merritt), Mrs.......... 3?
  Dorcas......................... 3?
  Edith.....................323, 3?
  Edward M...................... 3?
  Elizabeth...................... 5?
  Elizabeth (Locke).............. 1?
  Grace (Tuck).................. 5?
  Herbert d..................... 3?
  John......................419, 5?
  Joseph........................ 1?
  Mary A. (Locke)............... 1?
  Nancy (Dustin)................. 5?
  Perley D...................... 5?
  Robert........................ 5?
  Roselle........................ 3?
  Rufus H....................... 5?
  Samuel....................150, 3?
  Sarah J. (Locke).............. 4?
  Susan (Holmes)................ 3?
  Walter A...................... 3?
  William Dr.................... 5?
  William....................323, 3?
BALCH, Anna....................... 2?
  Bathia......................... 5?
  Evelyn (Demeritt).............. 4?
  Fannie........................ 4?
  Walter........................ 4?

INDEX OF NAMES

BALDWIN, Sally (Locke)............ 105
   Sarah F...................... 105
   Walter S..................... 105
BALL, Arthur..................... 314
   Edith....................... 314
   Frank....................... 314
   Georgetta.................... 314
   George T..................... 144
   Granville.................... 314
   (Lord), Miss................. 314
   Lorinda (Mason).............. 144
   Lydia....................... 197
   Mary........................ 68
BALLARD, Abby C................. 515
   Arthur H.................... 310
   Charles M.................... 515
   Charles Thurston.............. 378
   Churchill d.................. 515
   Emalina (Breaux)............. 378
   Emilie d.................... 515
   Fanny T..................... 515
   Flora (Dow)................. 310
   Gus Breaux................... 515
   Irena....................... 310
   Mina........................ 515
   Mary (Fish).................. 515
   Mary Jane.................... 515
   Mary T. d................... 515
BALLEAU, Mr..................... 21
   Jemima (Locke).............. 21
BANCROFT, Aaron.................. 205
   Almira...................... 479
   Caroline (Smith)............. 205
   Carrie...................... 377
   Cornelia.................... 377
   George...................... 377
BANFIELD, George................. 13
   Mary (Locke)................ 13
BANGS, Louise..................226, 226
   William..................... 226
BANKS, Frances E....*............ 114
   Stella...................... 464
BARBAR, BARBER.
   Austin...................... 57
   Elizabeth (Locke)............. 35
   Isaac....................... 57
   John........................35, 57
   Joseph...................... 569
   Lydia A..................... 57
   Mercy (Locke)............... 569
   Miriam...................... 57
   Nathan...................... 57
   Ruby........................ 57
   Ruby (Moulton).............. 57
   William..................... 57
BARGE, Caroline.................. 276
   Catherine................... 275
BARKER, ———.................. 21
   Abigail L. (Lang)............ 116
   Albion d.................... 116
   Arvilla L.................... 116
   Carrol J..,................. 561
   Charles A................... 460
   Elizabeth................... 314
   Ellen....................... 534
   Gladys (Heywood)............. 519
   Lucy........................ 39
   Lydia....................... 485
   Margaret L.................. 561
   Mary......................519, 519
   Mary (Locke)..............21, 460
   Maud (Locke)................ 561
   Milton...................... 116
   Peter....................... 519
   Quentin..................... 519
   Sarah L..................... 561
   William..................... 519
BARLOW, Capt.................... 40
   Jemima (Locke).............. 40
   Mary........................ 40

BARLOW, Sarah.................... 40
BARNARD, Eleanor................. 123
   Margaret.................... 442
BARNES, Calvin................... 333
   Edna........................ 555
   Fanny (Seavey).............. 129
   Harriet..................... 333
   J. W. F., Rev................ 129
   Jennie...................... 555
   Joseph...................497, 555
   Lelia (Ransom).............. 497
   Mary L...................... 161
   Ralph....................... 555
   Rollin...................... 555
   Ruth........................ 555
BARNUM, Lettie................... 535
BARRET, Lillian.................. 306
   Sarah....................... 452
   Simeon, Dr.................. 452
   Rachel (Leroy).............. 452
BARRON, Priscilla................ 28
BARROWS, Abigail................. 115
   Elizabeth................... 115
   Ellen....................... 115
   Ellen (Gray)................ 115
   Esther...................... 115
   Evaline..................... 115
   Hamlet...................... 115
   Jesse....................... 115
   Lydia (Locke)............... 115
   William..................... 115
BARRY, Bonnie.................... 411
   George...................... 62
   Margaret.................... 42
   Mary H. (Ladd)............. 62
BARTER, Wiinnifred............... 308
BARTLETT, Abbie (Haynes).......... 435
   Ada B....................... 536
   Ada (Dunbar)................ 478
   Alfred d.................... 374
   Allen....................... 439
   Annie (McSlaughlin-Jameson)..... 439
   Arthur...................... 372
   B. Frank.................... 478
   Berley...................... 96
   Caroline.................... 271
   Charles Carroll.............. 374
   Charles H................... 204
   Clara....................... 435
   Dellie...................... 478
   Elmer H..................... 536
   Emma.....................257, 372
   Etta........................ 511
   Florinda (Farnsworth).......... 423
   H........................... 435
   Helen....................374, 478
   Ida d....................... 374
   Ivah (Simone)............... 374
   James d..................... 374
   Job......................... 423
   John........................ 511
   Joseph E.................... 99
   Marietta (Towle)............. 372
   Mary (Gordon).............. 511
   Mary (Locke)................ 204
   Nabby (Bachelder)............ 99
   Patience (Locke)............. 96
   Percy....................... 478
   Ruth (Ames)................. 374
BARTHOLOMEW, Alice............... 279
BARTON, Dudley L................. 381
   Eliza (Jenness-Fogg-Philbrick)..... 380
   Elizabeth................... 77
   Francis W................... 381
   James....................... 380
   Mary........................ 381
   Mary (Winkley).............. 210
   Sarah W..................... 381
   Viola (Cowan)............... 381
   William..................... 210

INDEX OF NAMES

BASFORD, Dianna.................... 186
BATEMAN, Carrie.................... 281
BATES, Benjamin.................... 337
  Bertha........................... 337
  Betsey........................... 446
  David............................. 37
  Edna S........................... 337
  M. Emma (Hoxie)................ 337
  Mercy L........................... 37
  Nancy (Locke).................... 37
BATSON, Abigail.................... 397
  Ada (Kent)....................... 400
  Addie C.......................... 400
  Almer............................ 397
  Annie.......................397, 400
  Arthur........................... 522
  Benjamin..........235, 400, 400, 524
  Caroline (Cole), Mrs............. 400
  Charlotte (Tarlton).............. 397
  Clarenda......................... 397
  Edna (Cloutman)................. 398
  Elizabeth........................ 400
  Elizabeth (Hammond)............ 400
  Ellen (Tarlton).................. 400
  Emma (Littlefield)............... 522
  Esther R......................... 400
  Ethel (Godfrey).................. 522
  Eva (Veasey)..................... 524
  Fannie........................... 397
  Frank............................ 523
  Harriet H........................ 397
  Hattie H......................... 524
  Horace........................... 400
  Huldah (Hoiner)................. 523
  Irving d......................... 397
  Jessie F......................... 401
  John d........................... 400
  Lewis C.......................... 400
  Lizzie........................... 400
  Martha (Locke).................. 235
  Mary Ann......................... 397
  Mary (Neal)...................... 233
  Mary O. (Locke)................. 235
  Myra B........................... 401
  Nathaniel........................ 235
  Nellie........................... 400
  Roland........................... 522
  Samuel......................233, 397
  Sarah L.......................... 397
  Thomas E. O..................... 398
  Walter........................... 522
  Washington d.................... 398
BATTIN, Bernice.................... 530
  Ernest........................... 530
  Erwin............................ 530
  Gertrude (Cunningham).......... 530
BAYTISS, Florence.................. 255
BAZIN, Abbie S..................... 474
  Charles.......................... 546
  Frank W.......................... 546
  Harrie H......................... 546
  John d........................... 474
  Joshua........................... 302
  Lillie M.......................... 546
  Mary (White)..................... 474
  Sarah W.......................... 474
  Savillian E....................... 474
  Sophia (Locke).................. 302
  True L........................... 546
BEACH, Augustus................... 346
  Mary............................. 180
BEACHAM, Blanche (Lamprey)....... 448
  Harry L.......................... 448
  Richard.......................... 448
BEALS, Frances..................... 395
  Hannah (Tarlton)............52, 253
  Mary E........................... 112
  Zachariah..................112, 253
BEAN, Adaline (Locke)............. 318
  Albert........................... 179

BEAN, Almira....................... 186
  Clara (Locke).................... 462
  Charles A........................ 221
  Dorathy W....................... 462
  Eva (Waterhouse)............... 179
  Hannah (Bachelder)............. 92
  Harriet (Chesley), Mrs........... 93
  Horace F......................... 318
  James M.......................... 92
  Jesse K.......................... 182
  Joel............................. 179
  Josiah, Dea...................... 11·
  Judith........................... 4'
  Judith (Snow)................... 9
  Julia (Hooper)................... 179
  Leonard.......................... 179
  Lizzie........................... 18
  Lucy (Thompson-Friel).......... 22
  Mary............................. 2
  Mary (Locke).................... 179
  Mildred L........................ 46
  Minot............................ 46
  Octavia.......................... 11·
  Phineas.......................... 9
  Polly............................ 12
BEARD, Della....................... 50
  Esther (Bagley).................. 50
  Simon............................ 50
BEATON, Mary...................... 51
BECK, Mary......................... 2
BECKER, Annie..................... 31
  Chester.......................... 52
  Dorothy E....................... 56
  Eva.............................. 31
  Fabius........................... 31
  Floyd............................ 56
  Hannah (Randall)............... 31
  Henry............................ 56
  Martha (Batson)................ 52
  Mary............................. 31
  Nellie........................... 31
  William.......................... 31
BECKMAN, Alfred................... 38
  Caroline L....................... 38
  H. Gertie (Locke)............... 38
BEDELL, Mr........................ 36
  Evelyn (Locke).................. 36
BEEBE, Dr......................... 12
  Abigail (Foss)................... 12
BEEDE, Abbie (Emery)............. 41
  Harry............................ 41
  Lucy............................. 14
  William.......................... 41
BELL, Abbie....................... 54
  Anzoletta........................ 30
  Capt............................. 6
  Hannah (Watson)............... 29
  Joan............................. 44
  John J........................... 29
  Jonathan Ed. Rev................ 37
  Mary (Carlton).................. 37
  Miriam........................... 4
  Nancy............................ 2
BELLEVANCE, Ellen................. 50
BELLINGTON, Mary E............... 1'
BELNAP, Abigail (Locke)..........
  Hannah..........................
  Martha..........................
  Mitchell........................
  Obediah.........................
  Roxanna (Taylor)...............
  Sally............................
  Sally (Dearborn)...............
  Thomas..........................
  William.........................
BEMIS, Alfred E................... 4
  Caroline (Erwing)............... 5
  Ellen (Smith)................... 4
  Emery F......................... 5
  Helen F......................... 5

INDEX OF NAMES

Bemis, Lillian E. 530
   Lizzie d. 530
   Murle (Moody) 472
   Nellie 530
   Tom 472
Bennett, Mr. 99
   Abigail 149
   Adelaide (Locke) 240
   Albert 240, 411
   Alice (Locke) 365
   Barry 411
   Bernice d. 411
   Bonnie (Barry) 411
   Clyde L. 537
   Cornelia (Bancroft) 377
   Emma (Smith) 478
   Florence d. 411
   Guy R. 537
   Harriet (Merrill) 256
   Irving P. 377
   John H. 551
   Lizzie (Merrill) 99
   Marion 488
   Mary 538
   Mina W. 537
   Oren 256
   Rollin 537
   Samuel 365
   Thirza (Cass) 537
   William 478
   Winnifred 411
Bennington, Mr. 21
Benson, Susie R. 180
Bent, Anne (Bill) 359
   Mary 507
   Susan 546
   William 359
Benyon, Gertrude 352
Berger, Lucinda 101
Bernard, Maggie 511
Bernier, Cecelia 500
Berry, ———— 7
   Abigail 13, 137, 309, 465, 566
   Abigail (Brown) 142
   Abigail T. (Locke) 108
   Abigail (Page) 132
   Abigail (Webster) 64
   Agnes L. 408
   Albert 309
   Alice 132
   Alice (Locke) 11
   Ann 321
   Anna (Baker) 321
   Anna (Philbrick) 566
   Annie (Dunbar) 176
   Annie (Gove) 321
   Annie (Locke) 490
   Annie (Loud) 342, 502
   Arthur R. 407
   Augusta 56
   Bathsheba (Shaw) 236
   Benjamin 65, 108, 237, 407, 407
   Belinda 65, 132
   Betsey 65
   Betsey (Berry) 65
   Betsey (Locke) 122, 237, 290
   Betsey (Wedgwood) 65
   Betsey (Yeaton) 566
   (Brasbridge), Miss 65
   Calista (Colbath) 237
   Charles 132, 137, 408
   Charles W. 137, 236
   Clara 218
   Clifton E. 408
   Cora (Lane) 407
   Cordelia F. 321
   Daniel 451
   Dolly 65
   Dora (Emerson) 30, 567
   Drusilla 321

Berry, Ebenezer 26
   Edith 452, 498
   Edith (Tabor) 452
   Edna (Huckins) 451
   Edwin 321
   Eleanor 64, 139
   Eleanor (Brackett) 30, 567
   Eliphalet 122
   Eliza 65, 273
   Elizabeth 2, 11, 236, 566, 566
   Elizabeth (Hatch) 142
   Elizabeth (Wendell) 30
   Ella 218, 408
   Elsie (Locke) 11
   Emma (Locke) 222, 342
   Emma (Tourtillot) 342
   Ephraim 566
   Ernest d. 138
   Etta 218
   Fanny 55, 142
   Fanny (Hayes) 30
   Florence (Rogers) 408
   Frank d. 407
   Freeman 132, 290
   Fred 408, 452
   Frederick 566
   Fostina (Stratton), Mrs. 408
   George, Capt. 20
   George F. 408
   Gilman 132
   Grace 452
   Hannah 30, 30, 64, 65, 67, 69, 566
   Hannah (Garland) 218
   Hannah (Locke) 14, 65, 108, 567
   Hannah (Randall) 237
   Hannah (Vittum), Mrs. 70
   Harriet A. (Hodgdon) 137
   Harriet B. 463
   Harrison 321
   Hattie A. 407
   Helen 452
   Henry C. 408
   Huldah 132
   Ida 218
   Ira L. 273
   Isaac 567
   Isaiah 236
   Jacob 566
   James 176, 218, 237, 566
   Jane 11, 566
   Jefferson 309
   Jennie (Cole) 142
   Jeremiah 14, 30, 64, 566, 567
   Jessie (Hanson) 321
   John 5, 132, 138, 218, 222, 236
          237, 408, 490, 565, 566
   John W. 309, 321, 342
   Jonathan 27
   Joseph 65, 65, 108, 137, 147, 237
          237, 273, 342, 502, 566
   Josephine (Evans) 273
   Joses d. 30
   Judith 321, 566
   Judith (Locke) 565
   Keziah 65
   Laura (Wilson) 321
   Lavina (Drew) 273
   Leah (Roberts) 237
   Leon M. 342
   Letitia (Seavey) 309
   Levi 30, 65, 65, 91, 132, 132, 465
   Lizzie 309, 407
   Lorenzo 321
   Lottie M. 407
   Louisa 107, 137
   Louise (Newman) 408
   Love 64
   Love (Brackett) 30
   Lucy 273, 452
   Lydia 30, 64, 65, 69

INDEX OF NAMES

BERRY, Margaret (Hinkley), Mrs. 477
   Margaret (Robertson-Jewell) 237
   Maria A. (Locke) 137, 316
   Marion Emma 342
   Martha 222, 236, 465
   Martha (Garland) 451
   Mary 16, 30, 33, 60, 65, 67, 222
      222, 236, 279, 413, 451, 567
   Mary Ann 132
   Mary (Huckins) 273
   Mary (Scruton) 463
   Mehitable 65
   Millard F 321
   Minnie 407
   Myra E 452
   Nahum L 463
   Nancy 65, 250, 322
   Nathaniel 148, 237, 321, 566, 566
   Nehemiah 11, 566
   Olive 65, 69, 272
   Olive (Holmes) 567
   Olive S. (Locke) 107
   Olive (Place) 237
   Oliver 138, 142
   Pamelia (Locke) 137, 147
   Patience 30
   Patience (Marden) 91
   Patty 64
   Patty (Kate) 30
   Philip R 451
   Phoebe 566
   Rachel (Rand) 566
   Ralph 451, 490
   Rebecca (Caswell) 148
   Richard 567
   Rosa 407, 407
   Rosanna (Hanson) 237
   Sabina (Locke) 566
   Sally 49, 65
   Sally (Caswell) 321
   Sally (Foss) 64
   Samuel B 64
   Sarah 30, 30, 65, 65, 65
      100, 137, 237, 566, 567
   Sarah F. (Berry) 218
   Sarah (Hobbs) 30
   Sarah (Jenness) 30
   Sarah (Lane) 566
   Simeon 53
   Solomon 30
   Stephen 566, 566
   Susannah 565, 566
   Susie 341
   Tamson (Locke) 102
   (Tarlton), Miss 567
   Thomas 65, 222
   Tryphena 566
   Tryphena (Philbrick-Sanders) 27
   Valeria (Brown) 309
   William 2, 5, 11, 30, 30, 64, 102, 107
      237, 273, 321, 408, 451, 565, 566, 566
   Winfield S 321
   Winnifred H 408
   Woodbury 137, 316
BEST, Bertha 498
   Hanneman 80
   Mary D. L. (Merrill) 80
BEVERLY, Betsey 111
BICKFORD, Alice 436
   Alice (Felker) 289
   Alonzo, Dr 366
   Alvah 261
   Annette 414
   Annie B 436
   Benjamin 43, 43
   Caroline 242
   Charles 289, 295, 436, 471, 471
   Clara 471
   Daniel 471
   E., Mrs 275

BICKFORD, Eliza 364
   Elizabeth 453
   Ellen d 471
   Elma (Fiske) 436
   Ethel L 138
   George d 436
   Gladys 471
   Hannah (Locke) 43
   Harrie M 261
   Henry 138, 254
   James H 436, 471
   John 87
   Julia (Rand) 138
   Laura 295
   Lucretia 526
   Margaret 471
   Margaret (Coursey) 295
   Martha (Locke) 131
   Mary d 471
   Mary (Smith) 366
   Mehitabel 61
   Minnie (Chidester) 471
   Nathan 364
   Olive C 109
   Olive Haines 44
   Olive (Weeks) 87
   Crilla (Locke) 254
   Pierce 131
   Polly (Rand) 436
   Rebecca d 295
   Salina 193
   Samuel 43, 131
   Sarah 60, 297
   Sarah (Chesley) 261
   Thomas 43
   William 436
BICKNELL, Edward 183
   Elizabeth (Locke) 183
BILL, Anna (McKenzie) 359
   Anna (Hammond) 359
   Anne 359
   Caleb 359
   Caroline (Bradley) 359
   Charles 359
   Elizabeth d 359
   Gordon 190
   Henry d 359
   John 359
   Joseph 359
   Lucy 22
   Mary (Locke) 190
   Sarah 357, 359
BILLINGS, Mr 144
   Fannie (Covell) 144
BINNEY, Amos 210
   Sarah (Winkley) 210
BINNS, Ann (Locke) 324
   Edith 324
   Hester 324
   Sarah 324
   Thomas 324
   Warren 324
BIRD, Mary 22
BIRDSALL, Rachel, Mrs 474
BISBEE, Delia 258
   Patty 183
BISHOP, Abigail (Parker) 421
   Agnes 373
   Channing, Dr 421
   Daniel L. d 421
   Hiram R 203
   James M., Dr 245
   Jane (Locke) 203
   John 421
   Joseph 208
   Judith 122
   Lena (Cragin) 421
   Lizzie B 421
   Margaret (Locke) 245
   Mary A 421

INDEX OF NAMES

Bishop, Sarah 208
   Sarah (Dougan) 208
Bixby, Esther 553
   Lizzie (Dole) 553
   Wilbur F. 553
Black, Grace 441
Blackburn, Isabelle 450
Blaisdell, Annie 482
   Everett 328
   Henrietta 328
   Ira J. 482
   Love 94
   Mattie (Allen) 556
   Mary (Joyce) 482
   Rebecca 499
   Sarah (Meserve-Horn) 328
   Uriah 499
   Willis 556
Blake, Abigail 51, 284
   Abigail (Locke) 23
   Abigail (Smith) 13, 24
   Betsey (Foster) 29
   Betty 96
   Daniel 13
   Deborah (Dawlton) 12
   Dorothy 11
   Dudley 124
   Eastman L. 296
   Elisha 29
   Elizabeth (Hayes-Locke) 124
   Eliza D 284
   Hannah 13, 226
   Hezekiah 48
   James, Genl. 110
   James 284
   Jasper 12
   Jemima 23
   Jemima (Locke) 14
   Jennie (Locke) 296
   Jeremiah 23
   John 14, 29, 29, 46
   Joshua 23
   Levi 120
   Love 129
   Lucretia 410
   Lucy 48
   Lucy (Prescott) 48
   Mary 29, 266
   Mary (Dearborn) 29
   Mary (True-Norris) 120
   Mehitable 92
   Mehitable (Locke) 13, 46
   Moses 13, 13, 24
   Rachel 119
   Sally 139
   Samuel B. 109
   Sarah (Gove) 23
   Walter 290
   William 29
Blanchard, Alice (Weston) 537
   Ann 76
   Anna 160
   Evans d 537
   Harriet (Locke) 539
   Harry 539
   Henry N 361
   Hilda 537
   H. W. (Putnam), Mrs. 214
   Ralph 537
   Sarah (Locke) 361
   Sylvia M 103
   Walter 537
Blaney, Bethia 46
   Judge 95
Blasier, Josephine 173
   Lenna 173
Blazo, Thankful 34
Bliss, Ada (Nutter) 454
   Dolbee 454
   Marietta 81

Blodgett, Inez (Bonney) 203
   Merlin, Dr. 203
   Susan 230
   William 230
Blong, Ella 289
Blood, Adolph 482
   Albert H 482
   Edwin 306
   Ella (Knowles-Lear) 306
   Flossie d 482
   Ida 476
   Louis 482
   Mary 276
   Rachel E. 482
   Sarah 482
Bloodgood, Julia Esther 379
   Julia (Locke) 208
   William 208
Board, Anna L. 79
Boardman, Bessie 495
Bodfish, Mr. 130
   Hannah (Aikens) 130
Bodwell, Sarah E. 148
Bohonon, Jacob 99
   Joanna 47
   Lucy 224
Boise, John 61
   Ruth (Ladd) 61
Bond, Dr. 78
   Estella 497
   Mabel (Locke) 468
   Mary A. (Merrill) 78
   Sarah 447
   Thomas 468
Bonney, Ella (Locke) 203
   Ellen (Dill) 203
   Hannibal 203
   Inez 203
   William 203
Boody, Alfaretta 283
Boon, Ruthia 260
Boot, Mr. 119
   Hannah (Knowles) 119
Boss, Peter 160
   Phebe 75
   Susanna 160
Boston, Julia 187
Boswell, Harriet 391
   Rose 226
   Stephen 391
Boucher, Charles 190, 190
   Mary 190
   Mary (Locke) 190
   Nellie 398
Boulter, Maud (Gray) 504
   Stephen 504
Bouser, Beatrice 526
   Fred 403, 523
   Hattie (Bachelder-Farnest) 403
Bousley, Ann M. (Locke) 199
   Joseph 199
   Sarah 199
   Willie d 199
Bowden, Abbie 412
   Annie (Locke) 404, 412
   Edwin E. 404, 412
   Florence 412
   Marion 412
   Nathaniel 241
   Sadie 404, 412
   Sarah (Locke) 241
Bowen, Anna 171
   Deborah (Locke) 171
   Ella 171
   James 171
   Jennie 296
Bowie, Lucelia 77
Bowker, Frank 353
   Sadie (Locke) 353
Bowl, Elizabeth 86

BOWLES, Elizabeth..................11, 12
  Hannah............................ 72
  Joseph............................ 12
BOWLEY, George...................... 488
  James............................. 71
  Polly (Locke)..................... 71
  Viola (Jewell).................... 488
BOWMAN, Clara....................... 435
  Cristie........................... 568
  Mr................................ 86
  Sophia M. (Kingsley).............. 86
BOYCE, Isaac........................ 248
  Nancy (Locke-Moore).............. 248
BOYD, Elizabeth..................... 422
  Hannah (Decker).................. 183
  Harriet.......................... 212
  Lillian.......................... 383
  Lurana........................... 212
  Manlius W........................ 183
  Mary........................193, 329
BOYNTON, David H.................... 282
  Mary (Tilton).................... 282
BRACKETT, Abigail................... 199
  Addie............................ 298
  Alice............................ 199
  Anthony........................6, 402
  Betsey d......................... 199
  Betsey (Morey)................... 199
  Charles...............199, 447, 447
  Constance........................ 447
  Ebenezer......................... 199
  Edwin L.......................... 447
  Eleanor.......................30, 567
  Eleanor (Dow)..................... 64
  Eliza J.......................... 235
  Esther........................... 447
  Fannie (Lamprey)................. 441
  Greenleaf......................... 93
  Henrietta (DeRochemont).......... 447
  Louisa d......................... 199
  Louise (Horton).................. 447
  Love.............................. 30
  James d.......................... 199
  Jane (Walden).................... 402
  Jennie........................... 249
  John........................5, 148, 199
  Jonathan.....................199, 199
  Mary A. (Pitman)................. 148
  Mary J........................... 163
  Mary (Rogers).................... 199
  Miriam (Lane).................... 199
  Naomi............................ 199
  Naomi (Locke).................... 93
  Phebe (Heald).................... 199
  Ralph D.......................... 447
  Sally (Marden)................... 199
  Samuel............................ 64
  Thomas........................... 402
  William...................199, 447, 447
BRADBURY, Abbie (Meserve)........... 351
  Blanche d........................ 351
  Brice...................... 84, 155, 351
  Caleb............................. 84
  Chester d........................ 351
  Daniel........................... 187
  Elizabeth......................... 84
  Elsie............................. 84
  Jacob............................. 84
  Hannah (Locke)................84, 155
  Harry A.......................... 351
  Hattie (Pike).................... 184
  Ivory............................. 84
  John..........................42, 84
  Louisa (Guilford)................ 351
  Luella........................... 184
  Margaret.......................... 86
  Mary (Leavitt)................... 184
  Mary (Locke)..................... 42
  Mary (Wingate)................... 187
  Miriam............................ 84

BRADBURY, Olive...................... 84
  Reta H........................... 351
  Samuel............................ 84
  Stephen.......................84, 84
  Walter........................... 351
  Winthrop......................84, 184
BRADEEN, Annie (Nute)............... 462
BRADFORD, Angeline.................. 252
  Benjamin, Dr..................... 183
  Carrie (Locke)................... 430
  Emery, Rev....................... 430
  Ena N. d......................... 509
  Florence (Locke)................. 359
  Henry Martin..................... 359
  John L........................... 509
  Jonathan.......................... 76
  Joseph, Rev...................... 508
  Julia............................ 486
  Mabel J.......................... 509
  Martha B.......................... 84
  Mary Ann (Prince)................. 76
  Nellie........................... 424
  Patty (Bisbee)................... 183
  Ruth............................. 430
BRADLEY, Ann........................ 381
  Caroline......................... 359
  Eliza............................ 531
  Lettie........................... 424
  Ward............................. 538
BRAGG, Archie....................... 383
  Arthur........................... 383
  Effice d......................... 209
  Ellen (Gove)..................... 383
  Emma d........................... 209
  Fannie d......................... 209
  Fanny (Locke).................... 209
  George........................... 129
  Henry............................ 209
  Horace........................... 383
  Patty (Rand-Dow)................. 129
  Rowland.......................... 383
  Sarah (Brown).................... 209
BRAINARD, Daniel B................... 63
  Rachel............................ 29
BRAMAN, Elizabeth.................... 74
  Ida.............................. 416
BRANDON, Esther (Locke)............. 462
  James............................ 462
  Malcolm.......................... 462
  Roy.............................. 462
BRANSCOMB, Joseph................... 184
  Elizabeth (Dow).................. 184
BRASBRIDGE, Miss..................... 65
  Bray, Alvin A.................... 167
  Anna (Foster).................... 167
BREAUX, Edna G...................... 515
  Edna (Rowell).................... 378
  Emalina Modeste.................. 378
  Emilie (Locke)................... 208
  Gustave A.....................208, 378
  Mina B........................... 515
  Nina............................. 515
  Nina (Rogers).................... 378
  Nina (Williams).................. 378
  Samuel Locke.................378, 515
BREED. BREEDE, Aaron................. 48
  Anne.............................. 48
  Bernice.......................... 521
  Edith F.......................... 521
  Ethel I.......................... 521
  George F......................... 398
  Ida (Philbrick).................. 398
  Lizzie........................... 398
  Sarah (Atwell).................... 48
BRETT, Caroline..................... 481
BREWER, Charles..................... 249
  Clara (Sanders).................. 249
BREWSTER, Ariana.................... 322
BRIAD, Hannah (Locke)............... 241
  Robert........................... 241

INDEX OF NAMES 603

BRICKETT, Rhoda.................... 257
BRIDGES, Nellie 164
BRIGGS, Abbie....................... 395
  Berniece d..................... 543
  Edward M...................... 543
  Ena............................ 543
  Frank, Rev..................... 465
  Jonathan....................... 568
  Martha (Berry)................. 465
  Sally (Locke).................. 568
  Sherman...................465, 543
BRIGHAM, Annis (Locke-Jones)........ 242
  Helen (Locke).................. 412
  Nathaniel 242
  Thomas........................ 412
BROADHEAD, John, Rev................ 541
BROCK, Polly,....................... 72
  Sarah.......................... 512
BROCKHOUSE, Elizabeth W. (Grafton)... 106
  Robert......................... 106
BROCKWAY, Brooks.................... 307
  Julia.......................... 307
  Mary G......................... 141
BROGAN, Annie 477
  Catherine (Locke).............. 303
  Charles........................ 477
  Emma........................... 477
  Mary E......................... 477
  Peter.......................... 303
BROOKE. BROOKS.
  Emma (Mitchell-Locke).......... 204
  Fannie......................... 427
  Miriam......................... 13
  William........................ 204
BROOKIN, Deliverance................ 13
BROSIAS, Sarah...................... 87
BROWER, Mary E. (Berry)............. 222
  Philip......................... 222
BROWN, Mr........................... 206
  Aaron.......................... 476
  Abbie.......................... 75
  Abbot.......................... 344
  Abel........................... 88
  Abigail.............68, 111, 142, 250
  Abigail (Goss)................. 66
  Achsah (Tenney)................ 142
  Ada (Webster).................. 438
  Adaline (Locke)................ 135
  Addie.......................... 478
  Adelaide....................... 145
  Alexander...................... 127
  Alfred d....................... 142
  Alice.......................... 266
  Alice (Willey)................. 202
  Almeda (Brown)................. 178
  Almira................... 108, 142
  Amos........................... 57
  Angelina....................... 142
  Angeline....................142, 270
  Ann............................ 265
  Ann (Bachelder)................ 176
  Ann (Sherburne)................ 84
  Anna........................... 36
  Anna (White)................... 476
  Annie (Palmer)................. 341
  Artemesia..................142, 196
  Arthur L....................... 485
  Asa W.......................... 100
  Belle.......................... 186
  Benjamin....................68, 146
  Bessie....................344, 485
  Betsey......................... 384
  Betsey (Arlin)................. 467
  Betsey (Locke)................. 88
  Betsey (Page).................. 132
  Byron.......................... 438
  Carrie E....................... 178
  Carrol W....................... 485
  Charles........213, 381, 484, 485, 553
  Clara.......................... 388

BROWN, Clara (Bachelder)............ 344
  Clarissa (Brown)............... 142
  Clarissa (Dodge)............... 381
  Comfort (Jenness).............. 19
  Cora (Morse)................... 467
  Daniel......................... 266
  David......................19, 177
  Dolly (Bachelder).............. 46
  Dolly, (Dearborn).............. 266
  Edna O......................... 485
  E. Gerry....................... 499
  Elgina (Chesley)............... 261
  Elihu.....................149, 250
  Eliphalet...................... 202
  Eliza.................145, 409, 551
  Eliza (Johnson)................ 57
  Eliza (Phinney)................ 229
  Eliza G. (Wedgwood) Mrs........ 145
  Elizabeth....29, 31, 68, 84, 95, 343, 341
  Elizabeth (Jenness)............ 309
  Elizabeth (Marston)............ 447
  Elizabeth (Moulton)............ 19
  Elizabeth (Nay)................ 19
  Elizabeth (Nudd)............... 47
  Elizabeth (Sanborn)............ 145
  Ella........................... 439
  Emeline d...................... 250
  Emery.......................... 100
  Emily (Drake).................. 145
  Emma........................... 503
  Emmons......................... 341
  Esther.......................68, 318
  Etta......................323, 478
  Eunice (Locke)................. 499
  Eva (Horne).................... 344
  Frances........................ 499
  Frank......................261, 344
  Frederick..................142, 344
  George.................178, 217, 344
  Gertrude (Wensley)............. 341
  Hannah......................... 430
  Hannah (Drake)................. 250
  Hannah (Gove).................. 100
  Harriet........................ 142
  Harry.......................... 266
  Hattie M....................... 338
  Helen...................217, 341, 344
  Henrietta (Downs).............. 250
  Henry, Prof.................... 517
  Hiram.......................... 266
  Horace......................... 229
  Howard......................... 238
  Ida B.......................... 493
  Ira............................ 118
  Ira Nelson..................... 341
  Isaac..................95, 95, 304
  Jacob.......................... 266
  Jacob Everett.................. 178
  James.......68, 95, 111, 132, 186, 186
                    250, 467, 338, 338
  Jane (Locke)................68, 146
  Jane (True).................... 271
  Jane M. (Perkins).............. 118
  Jemima......................... 47
  Jenness........................ 145
  Jennet (Locke)................. 358
  Jennie......................... 257
  Jere........................... 467
  Jeremiah.............68, 84, 145, 176
  J. Arthur...................... 310
  John, Capt..................... 533
  Joan........................... 546
  John........19, 32, 50, 68, 69, 96
          135, 141, 142, 142, 145
          178, 250, 271, 275
  J. Jonathan........19, 67, 68, 142, 250
  Jonathan, Col............60, 67, 68
  Joseph.............19, 66, 67, 68, 142
  Josephine...................... 344
  Josiah......................... 68

INDEX OF NAMES

BROWN, Laura................... 344
   Leonard................99, 145
   Letitia (Locke).............. 358
   Levi......................229, 250
   Lizzie (Knowles).............. 344
   (Locke), Mrs.................. 89
   Lucetta (Gray)................ 68
   Lucinda..................214, 303
   Lucy A. (Hallett)............. 145
   Lucy (Young)................. 344
   Lydia (Locke)................. 95
   Lydia (Ward).................. 145
   Margaret (Green).............. 250
   Marguerite (Williams)......... 435
   Marion........................ 517
   Martha.....107, 140, 211, 309, 311, 551
   Martha (Hill)................. 304
   Martha (Webster)..........68, 111
   Mary.......19, 31, 68, 69, 81, 94, 95
      141, 142, 145, 176, 193, 249
      265, 303, 304, 359, 435
   Mary (Ball)................... 68
   Mary (Dalton)................. 127
   Mary (Drake).................. 484
   Mary (Fletcher)............... 229
   Mary (Garland).....60, 67, 68, 68, 238
   Mary A. (Locke)........68, 82, 206
   Mary I. (Merrill)............. 99
   Mary (Palmer)................. 206
   Matilda (Hughes).............. 229
   Mehitable.................94, 441
   Mehitable (Locke)........149, 250
   Melinda....................... 86
   Meribah (Weare).............. 217
   Mildred (Taylor)............. 266
   Minnie (Locke)............... 338
   Miriam (Palmer-Dunbar), Mrs..84, 176
   Nancy......................... 178
   Nancy (Jenness)............... 68
   Nancy (Lamprey).............. 266
   Nathan................142, 261, 309
   Naomi........................ 254
   Nellie........................ 497
   Olive (Goss)................. 310
   Oliver....................447, 448
   Oscar......................... 344
   Ossowatomie.................. 533
   Patty......................... 127
   Paul F........................ 261
   Philip C...................... 435
   Polly (Jenness)............... 69
   Polly (Locke)................. 67
   Priscilla B................... 125
   Rachel (Locke)..............67, 68
   Rebecca (Glines)............. 553
   Rebecca (Taylor)............. 142
   Reuben L...................... 82
   Rhoda......................... 142
   Rhoda (Fogg).................. 178
   Rosanna (Pollard)............. 186
   Rosilla....................... 250
   Ruth.......................... 198
   Ruth (Lamprey)............... 177
   Sally....................47, 141, 222
   Sally (Ingalls)............... 50
   Sally (Locke)................ 213
   Salome........................ 142
   Salome (Allen).........32, 141, 250
   Samuel..........19, 57, 105, 132, 381
   Sarah.68, 128, 128, 186, 209, 250, 250, 332
   Sarah (Foss).................. 68
   Sarah (Morrison)............. 341
   Sarah (Nutter)............... 275
   Sarah (Page).................. 84
   Sarah (Philbrick)............. 57
   Sarah (Varrell).............. 250
   Simon................145, 145, 176
   Solomon...................... 229
   Sophia d..................... 250
   Stephen....................... 47

BROWN, Susan.................. 223
   Susan S. (Doloff)............ 105
   Susanna (Knowles)............ 19
   Theodate..................... 132
   Thomas....................... 358
   Trueworthy................... 341
   Una (Cross).................. 517
   Valeria...................... 309
   Waity J...................... 171
   Warren...................229, 238
   Wilhemena (Popplar-Gilmore).... 229
   William.....68, 206, 250, 341, 358, 485
BRUCE, Emily.................. 370
BRUNDY, Lucretia............... 64
BRUNELL, Mr................... 386
   Maude (Green-Locke).......... 386
BRYANT, Azro.................. 257
   Effie, Mrs................... 308
   Ella (Goodwin)............... 483
   Emma.....................188, 438
   George O..................... 438
   Ina J........................ 438
   Sarah (Burton)............... 438
   Sarah (Locke)................ 257
   William...................... 483
BUCHANAN, Carrie.............. 173
   Mr........................... 431
   Mary (Locke)................. 431
BUCK, Clifton, Dr............. 523
   Grace (Marston).............. 523
BUCKINGHAM, Deborah (Locke).... 13
   William....................... 13
BUCKMAN, E. T.................. 38
   Lear (Locke).................. 38
   Samuel........................ 38
BUCKNAM, Charles..........164, 164
   Emma......................... 164
   Etta......................... 164
   George....................... 164
   Georgie E.................... 164
   Harriet (Locke).............. 164
   Joseph....................... 163
   Joseph Capt.................. 163
   Lucy (Locke)................. 164
   Mary (Locke)................. 164
   Mary (Prince)................ 163
BUCKNELL, Marie............... 441
BUFFAM, Adaline (Whittier).... 253
   Albert....................... 253
   Almira (Philbrick)........... 193
   Clara (Philbrick)............ 364
   Frank........................ 364
   George....................... 193
   J. W......................... 253
BULLARD, Arthur L............. 515
   Charles..................376, 515
   Elma (Tilson)................ 376
   Emma (Hardy)................ 376
   Ernest...................205, 515
   Eva G........................ 515
   Flora (Wyman)................ 205
   Frederick E.................. 376
   Homer E...................... 376
   Marle........................ 376
   Oral......................... 376
BULLIS, Edna.................. 276
BULLOCK, Celia (Locke)........ 315
   Charles...................... 315
   Ellen (Locke)................ 315
   Florence..................... 262
   Robert....................... 315
BUNDY, Jonathan............... 137
   Fanny (Morgan)............... 137
BUNKER, Belinda J............. 140
   Eliza (Nutter)............... 103
   Jane......................... 302
   Lemuel....................... 305
   Mehitable.................... 122
   Mr........................... 103
   Sally (Towle)................ 305

INDEX OF NAMES

BURBANK, Ezra C. 538
  Helen 538
  Lydia 279
  Mary (Flanders) 538
BURCH, Albert 299
  Kate (Root) 299
BURDEN, Catherine (Sanborn) 201
  John, Rev 201
BURDICK, Gertrude 332
  Hattie (Locke) 332
  James 332, 332
BURGESS, Ella (Greeley) 139
  Francis 138, 139
  Henry F 139
  Mahala S 186
  Mary 139
  Mary E. (Rand) 138
  Martha R. d 138
  Sarah 491
  Susan E. (Rand) 139
BURKE, Charles F 320
  Eva 256
  Mehitable (Tibbitts) 320
BURLEIGH, A 226
  Abbie (Locke) 149, 304
  Abigail 304
  Ann (Adwers) 313
  Blanche 323
  Charles H 289
  Clara (Stiles) 289
  Daniel 71, 323
  Daniel (Caswell) 149, 304
  Dora (Thompson) 289
  Edith 313
  Elizabeth 139
  Elizabeth (Dow-York), Mrs 323
  Ella R 323
  Frank S 323
  Freeman 313
  George 313
  Hattie 323
  Harrie 289
  Josiah 71, 288, 289, 313
  Lillian 323
  Margaret (Locke) 149, 304
  Margaret (Newcomb) 288
  Mary 139
  Mary J. (Demeritt) 126
  Mehitable (Locke) 71
  Oliver P 126
  Ralph 313
  Rose C 323
  Rose (Hardy) 323
  Ruhuma (Marston) 71
  Samuel 289, 304
  Sarah A 323
  Sylvester (Caswell) 149, 304
  Thos (Piper) 313
  Wilbur L 323
  Woodbury 323
BURNHAM, Mr 68
  Alice (Lane) 438
  Almira 348
  Edgar 438
  Hattie A 181
  Jesse 363
  Maria 218
  Moses 348
  Sarah (Brown) 68
BURNS, Annie (Green) 494
  Aphia (Dennett) 155
  Catherine 391, 494
  Catherine (Randall) 318
  James 318, 494
  Martha 525
  Mary 494
  Mr 155
  Robert I 494
  William C 494

BURRELL, Benjamin, Capt. 274
  Harriet (Morse) 274
  Julia 274
  Mary 441
BURROUGHS. BURROWS.
  Charles H 232
  Christena (Eilertsen) 232
  Clarinda (Embury) 232
  Dora (Embury) 232
  Elizabeth (Locke) 37
  Ellen d 232
  Emaline (Langdon) 395
  John 232
  Leonard 395
  Louisa (Locke) 105
  Merchant 37
  Thomas 232
  William 105
BURT, Aaron M 444
  Margaret (James) 444
  Mary 22, 43
BURTON, Emily, Mrs 343
  Sarah 438
BUSHNELL, Florence (Locke) 340
  J. G 340
BUTLER, Abbie (Taplin) 415
  Abigail (Locke-McIndoe) 246
  Benjamin F 101, 216
  Blanche 216
  Edward P 216
  Elizabeth 216
  Ellen (Loud), Mrs 216
  Frank E., Rev 216
  Franklin, Rev 246
  George 216, 216, 415
  Harold O 216
  Henry F 216
  Herbert F 216
  Horace 216
  James 64
  John E., Dr 216
  Kenneth 415
  Laura 415
  Louise (Ordiorne) 216
  Lucy (Sawyer), Mrs 216
  Martha (McMullen) 216
  Mary 216, 216
  Mary J. (Tilton) 101
  Maude 415
  Natie 415
  Nellie 216
  Patience (Foss-Newton) 64
  Rudolph 415
  Sarah (Hamilton) 216
  Sarah T 216
BUTMAN, Carl 437
  Henrietta (Hawse) 437
  William 437
BUTTERFIELD, Mr 418
  Charles 352
  Cummins 133
  Elizabeth (Langley-Tuck) 133
  Louisa 352
  Mary 352
  Sabrina (Green) 418
BUTTS, Edith 299
BUZZELL, Miss 129
  Abigail (Gray) 74
  Ada (Lear) 482
  Addie 373
  Angie 286
  Blanche 373
  Charles 141, 482
  Clarence 141
  Eleanor 89
  Ellen (Locke) 306
  Gilbert H 306
  Henry 306, 373
  Huldah H. (Locke) 141, 141
  Ida (Locke) 286

INDEX OF NAMES

BUZZELL, John 74
    Linna 463
    Lydia 88, 124
    Lydia (Danielson) 194
    Moses 74
    Mystic 376
    Nancy (Jones) 306
    Nellie (Hill) 463
    Oral (Copp) 376
    Robert 194
    Samuel 463
    Sarah (Caverno) 74
    Walter 286
    William 141
BYERS, Beatrice W 555
    Frederick 497
    Lucia (Ransom) 497
    Miriam S 555
    Selna O. d 555
BYRNE, Edna 377
CADE, Emma 231
CAIN, Mary 89
CALDWELL, Annie 394
    Florence S 562
    Joseph 535, 562
    Lois L 562
    Mabel (Locke) 535
    Paul L 562
    Thirza M 562
CALKINS, Claude E 534, 537
    Janette (Locke) 423
    Mina (Locke) 534, 537
    (Chase), Miss 537
    Orrin 423
    William 534, 537
CALLUM, Joanna 14
CALVIN, Elizabeth 461
CAMP, Amelia 275
    Florence (Fletcher-Aldrich) .. 393
    Frank E 393
CAMPBELL, Miss 115
    Charles 132, 480
    Colin, Genl 508
    Emma 415
    Helen L 480
    Lettice 215
    Lydia A 89
    Mary E. (Fogg) 132
    Pearl (Locke) 480
CANFIELD, Nettie 243
CANN, Adaline 360
    Archibald 360
    Elizabeth 86
    Eva 360
    Fannie 86
    Francis 360
    George, Capt 86, 86
    James 360
    Letitia 86
    Lillian 360
    Lyman 190
    Mahalia 86
    Mary 86
    Mary (Locke) 86
    Samuel 86
    Sarah (Locke) 190
    Thankful 86
    Winslow 360
CANNEY, Almira 152
    Lafayette 320
    Mary (Tibbitts) 320
    Mr 219
    Sally (Perkins) 219
    Sarah 123
CANNON, Amanda M 335
    Cornelia (James) 444
    John 167, 335
    Lottie B 335
    Lucinda J. (Pulsifer) 167
    Walter 444

CANNON, Ward 335
CAPEN, Edith (Parkhurst) 342
    Herbert 342
    Ida F 342
CARD, Margaret 233
CARDER, Phebe 336
CAREY, Mary 288
CARLETON, Mr 57
    Carrie (Wendelken) 377
    Cornelia Adams 377
    Charles Burroughs 377
    Edna (Byrne) 377
    Emilie Jos 377
    Francis 444
    Frederick W 377
    George 206, 219, 377
    Helen 444
    Homer 444
    Horace 377
    Isabella d 377
    John 444
    Lucy d 444
    Lucy (James) 444
    Mary (Chapman) 444
    Mary Elizabeth 377
    Mary (Morrison) 206
    (Moulton), Miss 57
    Nancy (Tripp) 219
    Nellie (Locke) 321
    Paul 444
    Phebe 361
    Polly 112
    Ralph 444
    Ruth (Morrison) 206
    Susan 219
    William 321
CARLISLE, Sarah A 77
CARLON, Fred 483
    Cora (Smith) 483
CARPENTER, Almond S 445
    Alvah, Dr 412, 412
    Ann (Cook) 412
    Bryant d 445
    Clara S 445
    Eddie 445
    Emma F 534
    Frances 326
    Georgia 445
    Gertrude (Poor) 445
    Helen (Locke) 412
    Henry 422
    Horace 264
    Lydia (Lane) 444
    Martha H 534
    Martha (Locke-Partridge) 422
    Morris d 445
    John T 444, 445
    Sadie E 445
    Sarah (Lamprey) 264
    Susie (Winn) 445
    Uri R 445
CARR, Arvilla 246
    Augustus 243
    Caroline E 132
    Charles B 393
    Emma (Aldrich) 393
    Frances 423
    Hannah (Locke) 243
    Martin T 393
    Mary 245
    Ruby (McMann) 393
    Ruth 393
    Theodore A 393
CARRIGEN, Emily (Burton) 343
CARROLL, Alice (Caswell) 319
    Charles 319
    Elaine D 558
CARTER, Abigail 316
    Bert 458
    Carrie (Taplin) 415

INDEX OF NAMES

CARTER, Earl..................415, 415
   Eunice........................ 129
   Fred.......................... 458
   Hannah (Hoitt-Locke)........... 281
   Harriet N..................... 171
   Harry d....................... 458
   J. C.......................... 281
   Jessie........................ 415
   Joseph H...................... 415
   Lewis......................... 290
   Lizzie........................ 415
   Margaret (Locke).............. 23
   Mary (Locke).................. 290
   Nathan........................ 415
   Ned........................... 415
   Orlando....................... 23
   Ralph......................... 415
   Sarah.....................104, 161
   William....................... 458
CARVER, George.................... 273
   Josie (Evans-Berry)........... 273
CASH, Ella........................ 300
CASS, Mr......................119, 417
   Alfred d...................... 420
   Arthur T...................... 420
   Belinda (Ladd)................ 231
   Benjamin..................419, 420
   Carrie (Straw)................ 417
   Cyrus N....................... 231
   Daniel........................ 388
   David......................... 537
   Eliza......................... 113
   Elizabeth (Locke)............. 43
   Ellen J....................... 388
   Ellen (Keezer)................ 388
   Emma (Doloff)................. 231
   George F...................... 388
   Harland....................... 231
   Harrison...................... 423
   Jane (Locke).................. 224
   Janette (Locke-Calkins)....... 423
   John F........................ 224
   Julia......................... 388
   Kingman....................... 420
   Lydia (Clay).................. 388
   Mary......................389, 420
   Mary E. (Locke)............... 245
   Mary (Packard)................ 420
   (Knowles) Miss................ 119
   Roxy (Doloff).............388, 389
   Sally......................... 95
   Sarah..................113, 245, 388
   Sarah (True)..............419, 420
   Seth.......................... 231
   Simeon........................ 43
   Theophilus.................... 203
   Thirza J...................... 537
   William........245, 388, 389, 420, 420
CASSIDY, Agnes L.................. 547
   Alice......................... 547
   Annie I....................... 547
   Frank d....................... 547
   George W...................... 547
   James, Dr..................477, 547
   Kate F........................ 547
   Leo d......................... 547
   Loretta d..................... 547
   Margaret R.................... 547
   Marietta...................... 547
   Mary (Brogan)................. 477
   Paul A........................ 547
CASWELL, Alice B.................. 319
   Annie (Lamprey)............... 446
   Annie (Randall)............... 319
   Ariadne....................... 318
   Asa........................... 140
   Caroline E. (Marston)......... 140
   Daniel........................ 149
   Edward........................ 71
   Elizabeth G. (Locke).......... 71

CASWELL, Emaline (Robinson)....... 319
   Emma (Snow)................... 319
   Eugene........................ 319
   Evaline d..................... 319
   Forrest F..................... 501
   Freeman....................... 319
   Hannah Maria.................. 319
   Hannah (Heath)................ 446
   Hattie........................ 372
   Helen......................... 446
   Henrietta..................... 501
   Henrietta (Garland)........... 494
   Herbert....................... 319
   Hortense...................... 319
   Howard........................ 446
   John.......71, 140, 319, 319, 319, 501
   Lemuel L..................146, 494
   Lemuel Lafayette.............. 319
   Leonora....................... 494
   Lillian (Wright-Ward), Mrs.... 319
   Louisa B...................... 319
   Lydia (Feltch)................ 319
   Mary......................143, 318, 319
   Mary (Marston)................ 140
   Mildred (Flint)............... 501
   Perry Alfred.................. 319
   Ralph......................... 446
   Rebecca....................... 148
   Sally......................... 321
   Sally (Varrell)............... 149
   Samuel....................149, 551
   Sarah..................372, 488, 551
   Sarah (Locke).............71, 146
   Sylvester..................... 149
   Uriah......................... 446
   Walter........................ 446
   William...................140, 140, 493
CATE, Betsey...................... 282
   Lucy.......................54, 463
   Myrtle........................ 461
   Nancy......................... 470
CATER, Hannah..................... 462
   Joseph........................ 462
   Lydia......................... 284
   Susan......................... 125
CATLIN, George.................... 493
   Gertrude (Haley).............. 493
   Hannah (Marden)............... 66
   Mr............................ 66
CAVERLY, Brainard E............... 528
   Eleanor (Pickering)........... 404
   Emma.......................... 455
   Hanson........................ 121
   Herbert....................... 404
   Lucinda (Foss)................ 121
   Lucy (Locke).................. 243
   Marion (Austin)............... 528
   Roland C...................... 528
   Ruth E........................ 528
   Walter F...................... 528
   William....................... 243
CAVERNO, Sarah.................... 74
CENTRE (Davis), Miss.............. 94
   Willard....................... 94
CHADBOURNE, Abigail............... 41
   Andrew........................ 180
   Ann (Berry)................... 321
   John.......................... 321
   Lucy (Smith).................. 180
   (Hooper), Miss................ 82
   Nathan........................ 82
   Olive......................... 73
CHADSEY, Ellen.................... 190
CHADWICK, Constantine............. 466
   Eliza......................... 287
   Elizabeth (Towle)............. 200
   Martha A...................... 292
   Martha (Gilson)............... 466
   John F........................ 200
CHAFFEE, Sarah (Woodman)......... 280

INDEX OF NAMES

CHAFFEE, Simon E................ 280
CHAMBERLAIN, Mr................ 158
  Abbie F....................... 453
  Arthur........................ 451
  Betsey (Woodman)............. 279
  Carrie........................ 158
  Durrell....................... 273
  Edith......................... 185
  Ella (Seward)................. 451
  George....................453, 453
  Georgie (Hoitt)............... 274
  Henry E....................... 451
  Herbert....................... 158
  Ira........................... 451
  Ivory......................... 274
  Joseph........................ 158
  Keziah (Jenkins).............. 453
  Lena.......................... 451
  Lucy.......................... 451
  Lucy (Huckins)................ 273
  Maria......................... 273
  Martin........................ 279
  Mary A. (Gray)................ 158
  Mary E........................ 451
  Sarah (Tucker)................ 451
  Stella C...................... 451
CHAMBERS, Anna................... 442
CHANDLER, Elizabeth (Godfrey).... 92
  Hannah........................ 240
  Huldah........................ 224
  John, Dr...................... 92
  · John.....................92, 162
  Louisa........................ 137
  Mary C........................ 64
  Nellie (Holmes)............... 320
  Priscilla (Kimball)........... 92
  Susanna....................... 442
  Sophia (Noyes)................ 162
  William....................... 320
CHAPIN, Ellen (Coleburn)......... 122
  Milo.......................... 122
CHAPMAN, Miss!................60, 329
  Mr............................ 417
  Abigail (Philbrick)........... 57
  Augusta (Sanders)............. 417
  Huldah A...................... 116
  James......................... 57
  John H........................ 101
  Joseph........................ 60
  Lorenda....................... 260
  Mary......................109, 444
  Mary (Dearborn)............... 101
  Mary (Saunders)............... 60
  Phebe......................... 51
  Simeon........................ 109
CHAPPEL, Susan................... 80
CHARLES, Mary.................... 58
CHASE, Miss...................... 537
  Carlenda (Foss)............... 278
  Charles....................... 48
  David......................... 382
  Deborah R..................... 124
  Eliza......................... 99
  Elizabeth S................... 93
  Ezra......................117, 308
  Harry P., Dr.................. 386
  S. Helen...................... 211
  Keziah........................ 115
  Lucinda (Locke)............... 99
  Mary (Dearborn)............... 48
  Mary (Kuse)................... 386
  Nancy (Rogers-Locke).......... 308
  Nina.......................... 399
  Phebe......................61, 134
  Sally.....................382, 384
  Sally (Morse-Emery)........... 117
  Samuel................199, 278, 386
  Sarah H....................... 78
  Thomas........................ 99
  Viola L....................... 79

CHAUNCY, Julia................... 493
CHENEY, Anna..................... 290
  David......................... 290
  Elizabeth..................... 130
  Hannah........................ 458
  Hazel M. (Locke).............. 391
  Joseph Y...................... 391
  Mae........................... 441
CHESLEY, Mr...................... 158
  Annie (Ayers)................. 387
  Betsey....................254, 451
  Edna.......................... 410
  Electra....................... 222
  Elgina C...................... 261
  Esther B...................... 261
  Grover C...................... 387
  Hannah P...................... 97
  Harriet....................... 93
  Herbert....................... 387
  Ida (Pickering)............... 387
  Isabelle, (Blackburn) Mrs.,... 150
  Jefferson.................387, 387
  Judith........................ 151
  Lillian....................... 387
  Lucy.......................... 450
  Lydia (Locke)................. 222
  Lydia (Yeaton), Mrs........... 88
  Mary.......................... 387
  Mary (Gray-Chamberlain)....... 158
  Orrin......................... 222
  Richard....................... 87
  Sally (Davis)................. 87
  Sarah......................87, 261
  Sarah M. (Lang)............... 116
  Samuel M...................... 116
  Susan......................... 286
  William d..................... 261
CHESTER, Hattie.................. 483
CHICK, Mr....................116, 516
  Elizabeth H. (Locke).......... 116
  Ella (Cash)................... 300
  George G...................... 300
  Harriet....................... 300
  Harriet (Locke)............... 136
  Hattie....................116, 478
  James B....................... 300
  Lizzie (Tanner)............... 300
  Mary.......................... 300
  Sarah......................... 300
  Thomas........................ 136
  Violet (Lovelace)............. 516
CHIDESTER, Minnie................ 471
  C. B., Dr..................... 471
CHILDS, David.................... 59
  Joseph....................109, 244
  Lottie (Moulton).............. 59
  Margaret (Locke)..........109, 244
  Winnie........................ 301
CHITTENDEN, Grace d.............. 205
  Harriet (Smith)............... 205
  Lucia......................... 205
  Lucius........................ 205
CHOATE, Ruhuma................... 47
  Ruth (Thompson)............... 100
  Simon......................... 100
CHURCH, Abbie (Spear)............ 546
  Abigail (Hall)................ 552
  Ann (Locke)................... 491
  Asa........................... 546
  Benjamin...................... 552
  Charles H..................... 546
  Clara......................... 546
  Ethel M....................... 546
  Herbert E..................... 546
  Israel P...................... 491
  Joan (Brown).................. 546
  John E........................ 552
  Lottie G...................... 546
  Lydia......................... 317
  Mary J........................ 552

INDEX OF NAMES 609

CHURCH, Nathaniel............... 491
  Ruth......................... 546
  Samuel....................... 552
CHURCHILL, Abigail (Locke)........ 86
  Ann Locke................190, 191
  Archibald..................... 360
  Augusta...................... 191
  Cecelia....................... 191
  Edmund...................... 360
  Elizabeth.................190, 191
  Emaline (Dodge).............. 258
  Emily........................ 191
  Enos...................86, 358, 360
  Florence...................... 360
  Frank....................358, 360
  George....................... 258
  Helen (Todd)................. 358
  Henry....................358, 360
  John, Dr..................358, 360
  Josephine.................358, 360
  Lewis................190, 191, 360
  Louisa....................... 191
  Minnie (Cronon).............. 358
  Patience..................... 189
  Priscilla...................... 191
  Tryphena..............191, 358, 360
  Winnie...................... 413
CILLEY, Ada (Locke)............... 259
  Annie....................... 371
  Betsey (Locke-Kingsley)........ 86
  Charles..................... 86, 259
  Helen M..................... 259
  James...................... 86, 86
  Samuel....................... 86
CLARKE, Abbie (Locke)............ 293
  Abigail (Foster).............. 240
  Ada (Pinkham)............... 457
  Adaline L.................... 211
  Adaline (Tucker)............. 237
  Andrew...................... 237
  Anna (Locke)................ 243
  Annie (Greeley).............. 166
  Aphia (Johnson).............. 457
  Arthur...................373, 531
  Aurelia P..................... 81
  Beatrice..................... 348
  Betsey....................... 497
  Carmellita................... 515
  Carrie (Jenks)................ 382
  Charles............172, 181, 388, 405
  Clara (Brown)................ 388
  Cordelia (Titus).............. 211
  Daniel....................... 321
  Drusilla (Berry).............. 321
  Edith (Locke)................ 348
  Edmund...................97, 211
  Elizabeth, Mrs................ 167
  Ella......................... 422
  Ellen....................240, 290
  Elmer....................... 321
  Emily (Trefethern)............ 319
  Emma....................... 319
  Emmons B................... 405
  Frank....................... 293
  Frederick.................... 531
  George...................277, 457
  Grace (Winkley-Wilson)....... 211
  Greenleaf.................... 457
  Hannah...................... 185
  Hannah (Locke)............74, 172
  Hannah (Remick)............. 237
  Harriet...................... 494
  Harriet (Otis)................ 151
  Harvey A.................... 348
  Herman...................74, 321
  James L..................... 293
  Jessie M..................... 293
  John, Capt................... 107
  John...........211, 373, 382, 413, 515
  Jonathan.................... 151

CLARKE, Kenneth................. 348
  Laura (Twombley)............. 531
  Lena........................ 413
  Loren F...................... 348
  Louise....................... 515
  Lucian....................... 348
  Lucinda...................... 83
  Lucy....................382, 515
  Lucy (Gould)................. 373
  Lucy (Locke)................. 449
  L. Vaughan.................. 211
  Mabel (Towle)................ 370
  Marcia....................... 405
  Marcus...................... 319
  Marietta d................... 405
  Martha (Sanborn)............. 413
  Mary...........84, 136, 143, 211, 290
  Mary (Hill).................. 373
  Mary (Locke).............107, 277
  Moses....................... 237
  Nancy N..................... 247
  Nathaniel.................83, 243
  Nellie....................... 173
  Norman E.................... 348
  Polly........................ 329
  Richmond.................... 449
  Royal H...................... 531
  Sabrina (Drew)............... 457
  Samuel...................... 240
  Sarah....................307, 388
  Sarah Frost.................. 42
  Sarah P. (Frost).............. 83
  Sophronia (Locke)............ 97
  Susan....................... 73
  Susan (Tucker)............... 237
  Thatcher R................... 457
  Wade........................ 515
  Walter P., Dr................. 166
  W. E........................ 370
  William...................... 482
CLAY, Lydia...................... 388
CLEASBY, Mary.................... 568
CLEAVES, Eda..................... 268
  Laura....................... 273
  Marcia...................... 154
CLELAND, Margaret D.............. 359
  Lucius M.................... 172
  Mary (Ames)................. 172
CLEMENT, Betsey.................. 119
  Sally........................ 49
CLEVELAND, Abigail............... 50
  Addie (Mordough)............ 418
  Allen........................ 37
  Mary........................ 74
  Mercy L. (Bates)............. 37
  Miss........................ 440
  Mr.......................... 418
CLEVDTT, Henry................... 373
  Lena (Herbert)............... 373
  Rose........................ 373
CLIFFORD, Abigail................. 38
  Ada (Locke)................. 294
  Andrew J.................... 162
  Betsey....................... 38
  Charlotte.................... 245
  David B..................... 162
  Delia (Walker)............... 162
  Edward...................... 75
  Elizabeth.................... 75
  Elizabeth (Locke)............. 20
  Ellen....................433, 433
  Ellen (Cross)................ 433
  Ernest...................433, 433
  (Felker), Miss............... 75
  Fred........................ 433
  Frederick O.................. 162
  Georgiella................... 433
  Harriet...................... 75
  Harry B..................... 470
  Helen M..................... 162

INDEX OF NAMES

CLIFFORD, Henry 75
  Jacob 20, 38, 75
  Jane (Fletcher) 162
  John 38, 75, 433
  Josiah 252
  Julia E. 470
  Kate (Pendleton) 75
  Katherine (Fox) 162
  Lucy (Small) 75
  Mary 470, 470
  Mehitable 38
  Nathaniel 38, 75, 162
  Phebe (Treat) 162
  Polly 38
  Prudentia (Kelley) 162
  Rachel 75, 114, 162
  Rachel R. (Walker) 38
  Roger 433, 433
  Ruth (Fletcher-Ellis) 162
  Ruth E. 433, 433
  Ruth (Sleeper) 162
  Sally 75
  Samuel 162, 294, 470
  Sarah (Gove) 252
  Sarah (Rich), Mrs. 162
  (Sawyer), Miss 75
  Thomas P. 162
  William 75, 162
CLINGAN, Annie (Locke) 462
  George 462
  Isabelle 462
  James 462
  Ruth 462
CLINT, Alice (Cooper) 232
  William 232
CLOSE, Hiram 260
  Mary (Lang) 260
CLOUGH, Abigail (Marden) 406
  Albert 429
  Amy 220
  Ann M. 114
  Arabella 237
  Charles 457
  Cornelia A. 114
  Daisy 429
  David 96
  Edward 96
  Elizabeth (Main) 457
  Fannie 59
  Fannie (Moulton) 58
  Frances 423
  Hannah 419
  Harry M. 457
  Henry 220, 457
  Isaac 58
  Leavitt 114
  Lizzie (Locke) 220
  Martha (Moulton) 59
  Mary 96
  Maude d. 457
  Miranda 114
  Nancy (Prescott) 114
  Nathan 406
  Nellie E. 220
  Rebecca (Locke) 96
  Sally 104
  Sarah (Locke) 429
  Timothy 59
  William P. 114
CLOUTMAN, Edna 398
COBB, B. F. 291
  Captain 40
  Eunice H. (Waite) 83
  Flora 399
  Mary (Hook) 291
  Sylvanus, Rev. 83
COCHRAN, Carrie 240
  Elinor 485
  Isabel (Shapleigh) 485
  Sally (Folsom) 113

COCHRAN, Samuel 113
  Sarah T. 113
  William 485
CODWELL, George 441
  Eva 441
COE, Alice (Jewell) 488
  J. L. 488
COFFIN, Alice (Percy) 356
  Caroline T. (Foss) 121
  Carrie 416
  Edwin 263
  Fannie (Lang) 263
  George 356
  Margaret 355, 356
  Margaret (Locke) 187
  Margaret (Plummer) 355
  Rebecca 123
  Stella 356
  Stephen 121, 276
  William 187, 355
COGSWELL, Edith 209
  Harriet (Sanborn) 370
  Herbert 486
  John 379
  Mary (Darling) 379
  Mattie (Locke) 486
  William, Dr. 370
COLBATH, Calista 237
  Nellie (Place) 227
COLBERT, John 397
  Sarah (Batson) 397
COLBETH, Archie 463
  Barbara 463
  Bernice (Locke) 463
COLBURN. COLEBURN.
  David 122
  Elizabeth 122
  Eliza P. 89
  Ellen 122
  Fannie 542
  Lucy (Locke) 122
  Mary 291, 297
COLBY, Alice 443
  Caroline 245
  Etta 522
  Georgeanna (Woodbury) 367
  Ida 291
  Meanie (Whicher), Mrs. 372
  Orrin 367
  Susan 381
COLCORD, Edward 4
COLE, Caroline, Mrs. 400
  Catherine 130
  Dolly (Perkins) 189
  Emily, Mrs. 405
  Jennie 142
  Jeremiah 189
  Jerusha 168
  Mary (Abbott-Locke) 320
  Rhoda J. 195
  Simeon 320
  Susan 189
COLES, George 259
  Edna (Herbert) 259
COLEMAN, Abigail S. 100
  Ann 89
  Ella M. 281
  Florence B. 549
  Fred 486, 549
  Gertrude M. 549
  J. Wiley 549
  Lucy 100
  Lydia (Locke) 281
  Lyman G. 549
  Mabel 496
  Mary (Griffin) 486
  Ruth A. 549
  Tyler, Capt. 281
  William J. 281
COLLEY, Abigail W. 85

INDEX OF NAMES 611

COLLEY, Anne M. 163
  George 165
  Hannah 85
  Jane 133
  Rathiel 184, 185
  Tillie (Huston) 165
COLLINS, Mr. 186
  Abbie (Locke) 343
  Alma 349
  Arthur 343
  Arvilla 213
  Dorothy (Munsey) 431
  Elizabeth 24
  Elizabeth (Townsend) 146
  Emma, Mrs. 283
  Ezekiel 193
  Fannie 249
  Frank 343, 343
  Joseph d 343
  Lewis 213
  Lucinda (Pollard) 186
  Mary (Boyd) 193
  Rhoda 88
  Thomas 431
COLLIS, Grace A. 331
  Rebecca 210
COLOMY, Alice (Runnels) 126
  Daniel 126, 126
  Dorothy S. (Locke) 126
  Emma 126
COLPITTS, Clara (Foster) 167
  Marion 167
  Thomas E. 167
COLSON, Frank 205
  Lucia (Chittenden) 205
COLVIN, Mary (Locke-Gavitt) 80
  Miriam (Locke-Potter) 80
  Sylvester W. 80, 80
COME, Mary 435
  Mary (Walles) 435
  Peter 435
CONAN, Mary 299
CONCONNAN, Marion (Bennett), Mrs. .. 488
CONDON, Louisa 358
CONGDON, Andrew 191
  Tryphena (Churchill) 191
CONNOR. CONNORS.
  Caroline d 279
  Caroline (Woodman) 123
  Cleora (Davis) 285
  Emaline d 279
  Frank 285
  Harriet 279
  Joshua 123
  Katherine 399
  Mary 76, 399
  Mary (Connor) 279
  Pamelia 52
  Samuel 279
  William 399
CONVERSE, Mr. 49
  D. L. 559
  Frank A. 511
  Harriet (Jones) 511
  Hayden F. 559
  James M. 559
  Mary (Ledoit) 559
  Rudolph R. 559
  Sarah (Locke) 49
COOK, Adalaide 275
  Amanda (Sanborn) 361
  Ann 412
  Edward, Rev. Dr. 178
  Ellen (Locke) 187
  Emma (Watkins) 396
  Eugenie E. 187
  Francena (Locke-Davis) 285
  James 71
  Jennie 124
  Jere 187

COOK, Joel E. 509
  John L. 187
  Jose 345
  Joseph 71
  Lucy 344
  Malinda (Locke) 187
  Mark F. 285
  Mary 187, 261, 345, 371
  Mary (Davidson) 187
  Mary (Emery) 178
  Mehitable 71, 138
  Millie E. 187
  Polly 89
  Sally 246
  Sarah (Locke) 71
  Viola 187
  Wilbur F. d 345
  William 187, 187
COOKSON, Alphonzo 355
  Augusta (Leighton) 355
  John 187
  Maria (Locke) 187
COOLEDGE, John 326
  Joseph 326
  Mary 326
  Sarah B. 154
COOLEY, Eliphalet 355
  Katy (Garrott) 355
COOMS, Olive 68
COOPER, Alice 232
  Amanda (Locke) 105
  Annie (Caldwell) 394
  Arthur 394, 558
  Clara E. 232
  George 233
  Edgar F. 232
  Erastus B. 232
  Evaline 196
  Harold G. 394
  Henry d 232
  Jessie (Locke) 558
  Lizzie (Locke) 233
  Ralph C. 394
  Stanley M. 394
  Susie (Hanson) 232
  Thomas 105, 394
COPELAND, Lizzie 285
COPP, Abby (Stevens) 205
  Annie 159
  Annie Emma 376
  Carroll 205
  Charles 205
  Clara (Geer) 205
  Edith M. 376
  Edna (Rixford-Smart) 386
  Ellen 205, 376
  Emaline 205, 205
  Emaline (Locke) 95
  Flora E. 205
  Hattie B. 386
  Isaac, Prof. 376
  James W. 376
  John L. 492
  Joshua 205
  Lizzie (Locke) 492
  Malvina (Schoolcraft) 205
  Mary 205
  Moses W., Capt. 95, 376
  Oral 376
  Richard 205, 205
  Walter Fred 376
  Willard 205
CORBET, Margaret 282
CORBIN, Miriam (Locke) 456
  Paul, Rev. 456
COREY, Alfred B. 160
  Eliza (Locke) 160
  Sally 59
CORLISS, Betsey (Aldrich) 231
  John 231

INDEX OF NAMES

Corliss, Thirza 245
Cornal, Clara (Locke) 417
  O 417
Cornell, Arthur 339
  Eunice (Locke) 171
  Florence (Underwood) 339
  Frank 324, 324
  Henry 171, 339
  Lillian (Locke) 324
  Orin 339
  Wilmer F. d 324
Corser, Mary P 125
Cotton, Abigail 118
  John 117
  Mary 129
  Polly (Emery-Marston) 117
  William 2, 3
Coursey, John 470
  Margaret 295
Covell, Mr 144
  Alice 440
  Fannie 144
  Frances (Mason) 144
  Mary 299
  S 517
Covill, Esther J 337
Cowan, Ruth 58
  Viola 381
Cox, Herbert W 548
  Maude (Stevens) 548
Coyne, Edward P 326
  Elizabeth (Doty) 326
  Sarah Elizabeth 326
Cragin, Lena 421
  Nancy (Emery) 421
  Richard 421
Craig, Mary 464
Cram, Mr 94
  Miss 483
  Abigail 296
  Betsey 99
  Jane B 116
  Ruhuma (Pearsons) 94
  Patience (Leavitt) 35
  Tristram 35
Crandall, Aurilla 257
Crane, John 303
  Lucy (Locke) 303
Cranston, Catherine 274
Crawford, Aaron S 125
  Carra (Marsh) 560
  Clara 525
  Elizabeth P. (Locke) 125
  John W., Dr 560
  Lizzie (Copeland) 285
  Marion F 285
  Sarah J 285
Cressy, J. Woodman 185
  Sarah (Locke) 185
Crichett, Elvira 363
Criel, Ellen M. (Fogg) 132
  Thomas 132
Cristie, Reta 415
Crocker, Alzada (Locke) 484
  Ellen (Clark) 290
  Philip 484
Crockett, Abigail (Main) 123
  Addie (Locke) 354
  Antoinette 219
  Charles 217
  Daniel 277
  Dorcas (Welch) 354
  Eliza (Hunt) Mrs 83
  Elizabeth (Main) 277
  Ellen (Tilton) 217
  Frank N 354
  George 277
  Hezekiah, Dr 123
  John, Col 123, 277
  Jonathan 60, 277

Crockett, Lizzie (Donahue) 354
  Nathaniel 354
  Sarah (Lang) 60
Crogman, Ada (Locke) 352
  Frank 352
  Lila F 353
  Mabel (Fairfield) 353
  Mary L 353
  Samuel 353
Cronon, Minnie 358
Crosby, Amy (Locke) 450
  Gertrude (Ordway) 483
  George H 483
  Percy R 450
Cross, Aaron, Rev 330
  Augusta (Pearsons) 93
  Ellen 433
  Henry 93
  Jane H 98
  Julia A. (Pearsons) 93
  Julia (Cass) 388
  Miriam (Lowell) 330
  Otis 94, 388, 517
  Sarah (Cass) 388
  Simon H 388
  Sophia S 156
  Una E 517
Crowell, Anne 190
  E. Osborn 201
  Martha (Weeks) 201
Crowther, Clara P. (Locke) 294
  Ida 469
  Lillian 469
  William 294, 469
Cull, Mary 136
Cummings, Mr 38
  Abigail (Locke) 247
  Blanche O 247
  Charles 247
  Joseph, Dea 247
  Mary 247
  Polly (Clifford) 38
  Rosie 431
Cunningham, Agnes 189
  Bessie (Cunningham) 530
  Betsey (Woodman) 413
  Fred 530
  Gertrude 530
  Linwood 530
  M. A 413
  Minnie (Shortsheaves) 530
  Olive 530
  Willard 530
Currier, Mr 418
  Abbie (Parker) 373
  Andrew 382, 382
  Annie E. (Locke) 527
  Benjamin 294, 553
  Bessie (Drew) 553
  Carrie 224, 382
  Charles 192, 362
  Charlotte 125
  Donald L 514
  Florella G 514
  Florella (Locke) 203
  Frank 362
  Frederick M 514
  Geneva M 514
  Hannah (Locke) 192
  Harrie Locke 374
  Ida 362
  James Frederick 373
  James K 203
  John 119
  Jonathan 270
  Joshua 268
  Judith (Poor) 270
  Julia M 131
  Lillian J 374
  Lucy (Clarke) 382

INDEX OF NAMES 613

CURRIER, Mary................ 268
   Mary (Locke)............... 119
   Mary Louise............... 373
   Mattie.................... 362
   Melvina (Green)........... 418
   Ruhuma (Jewell)........... 294
   Ruth...................268, 514
   Sarah (Seavey)............. 59
   Susan..................... 268
   Timothy................... 268
   True...................... 59
   Wilfred................... 527
CURRY, Clara (Neal)............ 345
   George.................... 345
CURTIS, Ballard................ 519
   Caroline.................. 532
   Ella...................... 402
   Herman A...............519, 519
   Howard M.................. 526
   Lucretia (Bickford)........ 526
   Lydia A................... 199
   Mamie (Dana).............. 519
   Ruth, Mrs................. 112
CUSHING, Belle................. 170
CUSHMAN, Betsey (Stearns-Locke).. 45
   Samuel.................... 45
CUTHBERT, Emma................ 208
   George.................... 378
CUTLER, Edna (Herbert-Coles).... 259
   Elijah.................... 259
   Nancy..................... 365
CUTTER, Miss.................. 123
   Barbara................... 434
   Elizabeth................. 434
   George.................... 434
   Grace..................... 188
   Mabel (Mudie)............. 434
CYM, Sarah.................... 158
DAIGNEAU, Augustus............. 513
   Mary (Locke).............. 513
DAILY, Alice (O'Rourke)........ 473
   Claude.................... 230
   Grace..................... 230
   John...................... 230
   Lillian................... 230
   Mary...................... 300
   Mary (Moore).............. 230
   Paul...................... 230
   Peter..................... 473
   Susan..................... 200
DAKIN, Alice L................ 440
   Eliza..................... 101
   Irene (Hill).............. 440
   Isaac..................... 257
   Laura (Jameson)........... 257
   Robert H.................. 440
   Wilbur J.................. 440
DALRYMPLE, MT................. 69
   Charles................... 197
   Martha (Thurston)......... 197
   Octavia (Trefethern)....... 69
DALTON. DAWLTON.
   Abigail................... 127
   Ann....................... 140
   Anna L.................... 127
   Belle (Lane).............. 311
   Benjamin..............127, 127, 305
   Daniel.................127, 311
   D. Woodbury............... 311
   Deborah................... 12
   Eva....................... 343
   Lydia..................... 407
   Martha (Brown)............ 311
   Mary...................28, 127, 401
   Mary (May)................ 127
   Mercy (Philbrick)......... 57
   Michael................... 57
   Patty (Brown)............. 127
   Sally (Stickney).......... 46
   Sarah..................... 22

DALTON, Sarah (Garland)......127, 305
DAME, Abigail (Nutter)......... 275
   Almira.................... 275
   Asa....................275, 568
   Attila.................... 360
   Betsey (Locke)...........568, 569
   Elizabeth (Locke)......... 190
   Fannie.................... 360
   George.................... 275
   Hannah.................... 281
   Ina....................... 360
   Israel.................... 281
   James..................... 360
   Jerusha................... 203
   Leon...................... 360
   Mary...................... 360
   Mercy..................... 54
   Oscar..................... 360
   Peter..................... 360
   Rosamond.................. 406
   Sarah B................... 124
   Thomas.................... 190
   Timothy................568, 569
   Zebiah.................... 360
DAMON, Barley D................ 381
   Bertha (Leach-Locke)...... 381
   Edwin..................... 381
   Louisa M.................. 381
DAMREN, Betsey (Locke)......... 281
   Carrie (Page)............. 459
   Ellen..................... 459
   Emma (Dunn)............... 459
   Frank W................... 459
   Fred P.................... 459
   Gertrude.................. 459
   Herbert M................. 459
   John M.................... 459
   Lora (Goodsell)........... 459
   Mary (Mayo)............... 459
   Maurice................... 459
   Norman.................... 459
   Willard................... 281
DANA, Catherine (Neal)......... 397
   Ernest.................... 518
   Esther.................... 518
   Francis W................. 397
   Frank..................397, 518
   George.................... 518
   Mamie..................... 519
   Olive (Neal).............. 397
   Susan..................... 370
   Susie..................... 518
DANFORTH, Abigail.............. 391
   Cornelia.................. 154
   Earl...................... 336
   Emma...................... 509
   Frederick..............509, 509
   Grace (Wilcox)............ 509
   Harriet A................. 100
   Helen L................... 336
   Susie (Herrick)........... 168
   Walter.................... 168
DANIELS, Abigail............... 152
   Edw....................... 210
   Emma...................... 253
   Mary (Rollins)............ 210
DANIELSON, Hannah.............. 73
   Lydia..................... 194
DANN, Esther.................. 268
   Helen (Locke)............. 268
   Mattie.................... 268
   Trayton................... 268
DARLING, Mary................. 379
DARRAH, Betsey B............... 99
DAVIDSON, Mr................... 379
   Fannie (Davis-Locke)...... 379
   Mary...................... 187
   Patty..................... 66
   Sally (Blake)............. 139
   William................... 139

INDEX OF NAMES

DAVIS, Mr. ... 94, 135
  Miss ... 94
  Abigail ... 193, 511
  Addie E. ... 136
  Albert H. ... 136
  Alice ... 280
  Alicia ... 430
  Annah ... 247
  Bertha ... 340
  Carrie ... 220
  Catherine (Gove) ... 209
  Celestia ... 227
  Charlotte ... 220
  Cleora ... 285
  Edna E. ... 510
  Edna (Pillsbury) ... 510
  Elizabeth (Locke) ... 245
  Ephraim ... 87
  Erville (Ray) ... 297
  Eunice ... 201
  Fannie ... 208, 379
  Francena (Locke) ... 285
  George ... 285
  Hannah ... 292
  Hattie ... 297
  Hazen, Dr. ... 209
  Hiram ... 297
  J. Frank ... 285
  James C. ... 145
  John ... 279
  Lewis ... 220
  Lizzie ... 510
  Lydia (Lamprey) ... 90
  Lydia (Locke) ... 87
  Maria (Rice) ... 135
  Martha (Woodman) ... 279
  Mary ... 159, 420
  Mary A. (Locke) ... 136
  Mary (Pearsons) ... 94
  Myra (Jones) ... 510
  Nathan L. ... 136
  Nicholas ... 49
  Pearsons D. ... 94
  R. Henry ... 245
  Roxanna ... 62
  Ruth M. ... 510
  Sally ... 87
  Sally (Belnap) ... 49
  Sally (Locke) ... 87
  Samuel ... 87, 510
  Sarah d ... 145
  Sarah G. (Locke) ... 145
  Sarah (Kimball-Smith) ... 220
  Sarah (Locke) ... 568
  Selden J. ... 510
  Simon ... 90
  Walter D. ... 136
  William ... 94, 568
DAY, Adaline (Perkins) ... 325
  Albert ... 325
  Clarence ... 325
  Ebenezer ... 154
  Eliza (Locke) ... 154
  Emma ... 325
  Frederick ... 325
  Kate ... 251
  Laura ... 91
  Mary (Garrison) ... 325
  Mehitable ... 325
  Melville ... 325
  Miriam ... 73
  Stephen, Dr. ... 251
  Thomas ... 154
DEARBORN, Abigail ... 52
  Angeline (Locke) ... 282
  Anne (Breede-Mudge) ... 48
  Asa ... 47
  Capt. ... 43
  Caroline (Locke) ... 154
  Catherine d ... 101
DEARBORN, Charles W. ... 216
  Clarence ... 448
  Daniel D. ... 101
  Delia T. ... 216
  Dolly ... 266
  Dorothy ... 266
  Dominicus ... 180
  Elizabeth ... 34
  Elizabeth Spofford, Mrs. ... 303
  Elmore ... 448
  Emily (Russell) ... 280
  Emma O. (Prescott) ... 114
  Frances ... 101
  Gilbert ... 280
  Gill F. ... 280
  Gilman ... 65, 100, 216
  Hannah ... 47
  Hannah (Locke) ... 24, 144
  Helen ... 312, 312
  Irena ... 101
  Jemima (Brown) ... 47
  Jennie ... 119
  Jeremiah ... 24
  John ... 282, 346
  Julia ... 48, 101
  Katherine ... 154, 326
  Kitty (Hall) ... 216
  Leonard ... 477
  Lewis ... 144
  Lucinda (Berger) ... 101
  Lucy (Blake) ... 48
  Margaret ... 49
  Margaret (Locke) ... 180
  Marion (Lamprey) ... 448
  Martha H. ... 312
  Mary ... 29, 48, 48, 82, 101, 216
  Mary (Bachelder) ... 47
  Mary (Brown) ... 176
  Mary (Locke-Reynolds) ... 125
  Mary (Watson) ... 346
  May (Russell) ... 280
  Nathan ... 282
  Nathaniel ... 47, 48
  Ruhuma ... 101
  Ruhuma (Choate) ... 47
  Sally ... 49, 71
  Samuel ... 47, 176
  Sarah ... 48, 216
  Sarah S. (Berry) ... 65, 100
  Sherburne ... 49
  Stephen H. ... 114
  Sylvanus ... 154
  W. H. ... 125
DEBAZIN, John ... 474
DE BEVOISE, Gabriel, Rev. ... 207
  James ... 207
  Martha (Lamson) ... 207
DECKER, Elizabeth S. (Locke) ... 83
  Hannah M. ... 183
  Henry ... 83, 183
  Isaac ... 182
  Lizzie F. ... 183
  Maria (Allen) ... 183
  Mary (Mason) ... 183
  Samuel Locke ... 183
  William W. ... 183
DECOSTA, Caroline (Rollins) ... 210
  D. ... 210
DEERING, Mr. ... 116
  George ... 250
  Georgianna (Horny) ... 250
  Hattie (Chick) ... 116
  Henry ... 4
DELAMETER, Charles ... 472
  Orpha (Moody) ... 472
DELANCEY, Annie ... 448
  Curtis ... 448
DELAND, Sarah W. ... 152
DELANO, Mary ... 471
DELKIN, A. L. ... 134

INDEX OF NAMES 615

DELKIN, Hattie M. (Ladd)............ 134
DELMORE, Annie.................... 548
DEMERITT, Albert..................125, 125
  Alice L. d....................... 126
  Alice (Locke).................... 54
  Alice (Whitehouse)............... 464
  Amanda......................... 125
  Annah........................... 465
  Betsey (Locke).................. 54
  Cathleen........................ 464
  Deborah......................... 126
  Earl I........................... 464
  Ebenezer........................ 126
  Eli..........................125, 126
  Eliza (Evans)................... 125
  Elizabeth....................126, 288
  Emaline L....................... 126
  Emily........................... 125
  Emily (Perkins)................. 288
  Emma J......................... 125
  Evelyn.......................... 446
  Fannie (Joy).................... 288
  Fannie (Osgood)................. 288
  Flora W......................... 464
  Florence E...................... 465
  Francena........................ 288
  Hannah......................124, 125
  Helen........................... 464
  Isaac............................ 464
  Jacob J......................... 125
  James........................125, 288
  Jennie (Hartford)............... 288
  John W.......................... 464
  Jonathan........................ 126
  Julia M......................... 125
  Lucy d......................... 126
  Lydia d......................... 288
  Mabel A......................... 465
  Marcia d........................ 288
  Marcia H. (Fernald)............. 125
  Margaret (Gallant).............. 464
  Maria B......................... 126
  Mary........................125, 126
  Morris.......................... 465
  Moses........................54, 125
  Nancy F. d...................... 126
  Nelson.......................... 465
  Orlando......................... 288
  Philip........................... 464
  Rachel T........................ 465
  Roscoe.......................... 465
  Ruth............................ 464
  Samuel....................54, 126, 287
  Sarah (Locke)................... 287
  Sarah (Putnam).................. 125
  Seorium......................... 288
  Sophia L. d..................... 126
  Tamson.......................... 464
  Victor S......................... 464
  Walter C......................... 464
DEMICK, Charles C.................. 392
  Chloe (Aldrich)................. 392
  Leo Frances..................... 392
  Rose W.......................... 392
DENAVARRO, Estelle................. 322
DENEISE, Mr....................... 530
  Nellie (Bemis).................. 530
DENMEAD, Jessica................... 365
DENNETT, Albert.................... 155
  Alice........................... 226
  Aphia........................... 155
  Blanche E....................... 486
  Charles A....................... 155
  Cyrus........................... 155
  Eliza............................ 155
  Flora (Locke)................... 313
  George.......................313, 486
  Hannah.......................... 155
  Hannah (Locke)................. 73
  Harriet G....................... 155

DENNETT, Henry C.................. 155
  Horace.......................... 155
  John.......................3, 73, 155
  Joshua........................73, 155
  Lydia A......................... 155
  Lydia (Locke)................... 73
  Melvina......................... 155
  Martha.......................... 155
  Mary............................ 155
  Oren............................ 155
  Philip B......................... 486
  Sally............................ 155
  Sarah (Brosias)................. 87
  Simon........................... 155
  Susan........................... 122
DENNISON, Carrie................... 232
  Emery........................... 334
  John............................ 334
  Lucia........................... 334
  Phebe (Locke)................... 334
DE ROCHEMONT, Henrietta............ 447
  Louisa.......................... 159
DERRIMAN, Uldine................... 530
DEVAN, Mary (Winkley)............. 380
  William S....................... 380
DEWAR, Jennie..................... 390
DEWEL, Sarah E.................... 81
DEWEY, Alice (Covell).............. 440
  Charles.....................257, 440
  Elmer C......................... 440
  Hannah (Hurlbert).............. 440
  Julia (Jameson)................. 257
  Nettie M........................ 440
  William......................... 440
DEXTER, Alice..................... 437
  Henry........................... 437
  Lottie.......................... 429
  Mary (White).................... 437
  Sarah........................... 208
  S. S............................. 40
  Sophia S. (Farrar).............. 40
DIAMOND, Donald................... 544
  Grace (Harris).................. 544
  Louis........................... 544
  Polly............................ 50
  Robert L........................ 544
DIAZ, Alden....................... 388
  John............................ 388
  Lillie (Locke).................. 388
  Sarah........................... 388
DICKERSON, Augusta................ 315
DICKEY............................ 262
  Betsey R. (Locke).............. 85
  Olive........................... 85
  Sylvina......................... 85
  William......................85, 85
DICKINSON, Charles................ 389
  Georgeanna (Gookin)............ 475
  Harry........................... 475
  Henry........................... 475
  Roxy (Doloff-Cass)............. 389
  Sarah........................... 28
DILL, Ellen....................... 203
DIMOCK, Edward.................359, 359
  Evangeline (Locke).............. 359
  Clarence Hoyt................... 359
  Laura (Locke)................... 359
DINSMORE, Abbie (Hanscom)......... 504
  Fred............................ 504
  Helen (Pray).................... 504
  John R.......................... 504
DITSON, Sarah..................... 422
DIXON, Alice...................... 386
  Annie........................... 386
  Della (Locke)................... 504
  Eliza........................... 249
  Elsie B......................... 504
  Helen (Locke-Hartshorn)........ 399
  Janette......................... 246
  Nina (Chase).................... 399

INDEX OF NAMES

DIXON, Stephen................... 386
    William...................... 399
    William Roy.................. 504
DOCKUM, Angelina.................. 304
    Samuel....................... 479
    Sarah........................ 479
DODGE, Mr......................... 59
    Adaline...................... 212
    Almira (Moulton)............. 59
    Annie........................ 486
    Arthur M..................... 381
    Carlos A..................... 440
    Clarissa..................... 381
    Clarissa (Locke)............. 97
    Elma (Twombly).............. 258
    Emaline...................... 258
    Ephrietta (Norris)........... 443
    Francis...................... 212
    George S..................... 258
    Gertrude..................... 299
    Glenn S...................... 258
    Grace E...................... 258
    Helen d..................... 381
    Hannah P., Mrs............... 119
    Harriet...................... 381
    Harriet (Dunklee)............ 211
    Harry........................ 443
    Irene L. d.................. 440
    Jessie B..................... 381
    John.....................211, 258
    Margaret D................... 381
    Mary.....................258, 381
    Mary (Titcomb)............... 211
    Miss (Cleveland)............. 440
    Nancy (Locke)................ 115
    Nathaniel.................... 211
    Sally......................37, 211
    Salmon....................... 258
    Sarah (Merrill).............. 258
    Sarah (Philbrick)............ 212
    Richard....................97, 381
    Susan d..................... 381
    Virginia (Rose).............. 258
    William P.................... 115
DOE, James....................... 310
    Martha....................... 523
    Mary (Ladd).................. 310
DOLBEE, Catherine (Towle)........ 202
    John H....................... 202
DOLE, Belcher.................... 98
    Eliza (Gove)................. 98
    Lizzie....................... 553
    Mary (Gove).................. 98
    Nathaniel.................... 98
DOLL, Abbie A.................... 169
    Albert....................... 472
    Georgeanna (Locke)........... 472
DOLOFF, Abner F.................. 224
    Abraham...................... 49
    Abram...................105, 224, 224
    Agnes M...................... 224
    Alba O....................... 390
    Alma K....................... 231
    Almira...................105, 231
    Anna......................... 231
    Ansell G..................... 224
    Carrie (Currier)............. 224
    Clarinda (Elliot)............ 224
    Emily (Eaton-Spencer)........ 224
    Emma......................... 231
    Emma E. (Hanson)............. 105
    Frank.....................390, 390
    Gilbert B.................... 224
    Hannah....................... 224
    Harlan d.................... 231
    Harriet (Mason-Locke).....105, 225
    Helen M...................... 224
    Ida May...................... 389
    Jennie (Dewar)............... 390
    Levi.....................104, 105

DOLOFF, Levi Manson.............. 389
    Loren........................ 105
    Louis Solon.................. 390
    Lynthia d................... 231
    Lydia (Nelson)............... 105
    Mabel........................ 390
    Margaret S................... 105
    Margaret (Tilton)............ 224
    Mary......................... 105
    Mary (Vose).................. 224
    Mary (Worthley).............. 389
    Mason D...................... 105
    Maude M...................... 390
    Minnie (O'Brien)............. 390
    Myra Etta.................... 390
    Nancy (Symonds).............. 224
    Nellie (Johnson)............. 390
    Nellie (Vose)................ 390
    Nicholas................104, 105, 225
    Orrin L...................... 224
    Otis d...................... 231
    Rachel L..................... 105
    Rachel (Locke).............49, 224
    Rhoda (Aldrich).............. 105
    Roxy....................94, 388, 389
    Roxy (Locke)..............104, 105
    Sally C...................104, 105
    Sally (Clough)............... 104
    Solon........................ 224
    Susan S...................... 105
    Viola d..................... 231
    Wilbur d.................... 389
DONAHUE, Lizzie.................. 354
DONALDSON, Hannah................ 122
DORE, Alvira H................... 182
    Benjamin..................... 25
    Eliza........................ 86
    Lydia (Mason)................ 25
    Mary (Locke)................. 25
    Mehitable.................... 25
    Philip.....................25, 25
    Sarah (Locke)................ 25
DOTY, Almira..................... 136
    Elizabeth.................... 326
DOUGAN, Sarah.................... 208
DOW, Miss........................ 179
    Mr.........................59, 206
    Abby......................... 488
    Addie (Janvrin).............. 368
    Almira....................... 186
    Almira (Palmer).............. 206
    Amos......................... 383
    Angelina (Brown)............. 142
    Ann (Green).................. 252
    Annie........................ 206
    Betsey....................... 455
    Benjamin..................177, 342
    Betsey (Moulton)............. 59
    Betsey (Newman), Mrs........84, 184
    Charles.....199, 252, 342, 379, 383, 513
    Charles d................310, 342
    Chester W.................... 513
    Clara.....................309, 309
    Clara (Austin)............... 368
    Daniel W..................... 184
    Data (Drake)................. 309
    Deborah (Page)............... 84
    Doris........................ 342
    Eleanor...................... 64
    Elihu........................ 209
    Elizabeth.................184, 323
    Ella d...................... 310
    Emily........................ 383
    Emily (Gove)................. 383
    Esther....................... 21
    Ethel A...................... 512
    Flora B...................... 310
    Fred H....................... 368
    George d.................... 513
    Harvey d.................... 513

INDEX OF NAMES 617

Dow, Harriet d.................... 310
  Hattie (Weare)................ 368
  Henry......................69, 368
  Imogene B. (Dow).............. 368
  Ina (Capen)................... 342
  James..................142, 309, 516
  Jennie.....................96, 409
  John.......................... 568
  John T.....................84, 184
  Joseph........................ 474
  Josephine P................... 342
  Julia......................... 206
  Lillian (Perkins).............. 516
  Lucy.......................... 379
  Lydia......................24, 35
  Lydia (Locke)................. 209
  Martha.....................33, 184
  Martha (Fitzgerald)............ 474
  Martha (Locke)................ 568
  Martha (Perkins)............... 69
  Mary......31, 46, 53, 100, 107, 177, 419
  Mary Ann...................... 184
  Mary (Fulton)................. 342
  Merrill....................... 252
  Mima A........................ 215
  Minnie Elizabeth.............. 368
  Moses......................... 455
  Nancy......................... 458
  Nellie.....................368, 513
  Pamelia H..................... 103
  Patty L. (Rand)............... 129
  Rhoda d....................... 379
  Richard d..................... 342
  Rosa d........................ 379
  Sadie I....................... 513
  Sally......................... 184
  Sarah L....................... 512
  Sarah (Locke)...........177, 199, 568
  Simeon........................ 129
  Timothy....................... 223
  Tristram...................... 384
  Viola (Grocut)................ 513
  William....................... 568
  William Newell................ 368
Dowdell, Charlotte (Marston)..... 523
  John H........................ 523
  Muriel........................ 523
Downes. Downs.
  Mr............................ 151
  Abner......................... 56
  Adaline (Locke)............... 156
  Albert.....................156, 156
  Bertha........................ 484
  Betsey (Tucker), Mrs.......... 250
  Carrie........................ 323
  Deborah (Randall)............. 56
  Eliza......................... 191
  Ella (Goodrich)............... 484
  Hannah........................ 19
  Henrietta..................... 250
  Herbert....................... 156
  James......................... 320
  Laura......................... 156
  Mary.......................... 148
  Mary (Holmes)................. 320
  Samuel........................ 250
  Sarah (Otis).................. 151
  William....................... 484
Downing, Caleb................... 167
  Dorothy (Gray)................ 74
  Eunice (Pulsifer)............. 167
  Eva (Pulsifer)................ 167
  Ila M......................... 529
  J. J.......................... 167
  John.......................... 74
  Paul A........................ 335
  Percy G....................... 335
Dowrst. Dowst.
  Comfort....................... 23
  Edith......................... 430

Dowrst, Elizabeth (Seavey)........ 43
  Frank......................... 430
  Martha (Tallant).............. 430
  Ozem.......................... 43
  Rachel........................ 67
  Sarah......................... 129
Drake, Abigail.................... 41
  Abra A........................ 228
  Abraham....................... 145
  Adelaide (Brown).............. 145
  Anna (Doloff)................. 231
  Annie......................... 238
  Charles...............228, 392, 405
  Data.......................... 309
  Edith T....................... 443
  Edwin......................... 405
  Emalie (Pike)................. 189
  Emily......................... 145
  Frank L....................... 228
  Freeman....................... 448
  Hannah........................ 250
  Harriet (Locke)............... 104
  Harriet (Rollins)............. 228
  Helen (Weeks)................. 405
  Henry W....................228, 228
  Ida (Lukes)................... 392
  Irene......................... 228
  Irving, Dr.................... 231
  Izetta M. (Trefethern)........ 144
  Jacob......................... 228
  James......................... 431
  John.......................... 189
  Josephine..................249, 448
  J. Warren..................... 189
  Lavina (Page)..............228, 228
  Mabel (Locke-McLaughlin)...... 189
  Marcia (Clarke)............... 405
  Mary.......................... 484
  Mary (Aiken).................. 231
  Mary (Webster)................ 228
  Mercy......................... 60
  Minnie........................ 392
  Nathaniel...................5, 145
  Oliff......................... 501
  Oren.......................... 144
  Philip S...................... 104
  Polly......................... 228
  Susan (Young)................. 431
Draper, Abbie (Hart).............. 188
  Alfred........................ 188
  Cora (Wilson)................. 188
  Hattie (Russell).............. 281
  James......................... 188
  Jason......................281, 281
  Marguerite.................... 281
  Marie......................... 281
  Muriel........................ 281
Dresser, Ephraim.................. 327
  Isabella (Dudley)............. 327
Drew, Alberta (Avery)............. 392
  Amanda........................ 457
  Amasa......................... 223
  Amos.......................... 223
  Asa....................102, 227, 392
  Ater S........................ 297
  Bessie R...................... 553
  Betsey D...................... 148
  Charlotte..................... 222
  Charlotte (Babb).............. 297
  Clarence...................... 392
  Clarenda (Rand)............... 493
  Cortes.....................102, 102
  Delia (Emery)................. 392
  Dorothy....................... 223
  D. F.......................... 154
  Elizabeth (Page).............. 227
  Elmer Elsworth................ 392
  Ethel D....................... 392
  Eva........................... 521
  Finando....................... 102

INDEX OF NAMES

Drew, Franklin 392
  Fred 154
  George 102
  Grace E. 553
  Hannah W. 227
  Harvey 227
  Hattie (Davis) 297
  James 3
  John 493
  Joseph 102, 452
  Julia (Fuller) 223
  Lavinia 273
  Lewis 440
  Mary B. (Locke) 102
  Mary E. 298
  Milton 440
  Moran 553
  Nellie Eva 392
  Nettie (Dewey) 440
  Perley Asa 392
  Robert 148
  Sabrina 457
  Sarah (Wells) 227, 392
  Susie 430
  Thomas 457
  William 297, 440
  Willis 440
Drisco, Mr. 253
  Lydia (Locke) 253
Drowne, Albert I. 449
  Clarence I. 449
  Elizabeth (Locke-Barber) . 35
  Fred I. 449
  Marian (Merrick) 449
  Mary 121
  Mary (Scribner) 449
  Nancy 108, 238
  Ralph C. 449
  Samuel 35
Drummond, Major 55
Drysdale, Estelle 542
Duboise, Jacob 230
  Josephine (Moore) 230
  Methusalem 230
  Rachel 230, 230
Ducheyne, Amelia 359
Duckworth, Edward 214
  Henry 214
  S. Lucinda (Greely) 214
Dudley, Mr. 89
  Arthur D. 388
  Benjamin F. 154
  Betsey 147
  Carrie A. 388
  Clarissa d 327, 327
  Daniel 327, 327
  Delia (Lamprey) 89
  Elizabeth 251
  Fred 327, 371, 388
  George W. 222
  Gertrude (Woodhull) 388
  Hannah W. (Locke) 154
  Harriet 388
  Harriet (Towle) 371
  Hattie (Thompson) 327
  Helen S. 327
  Hubbard 50
  Isabella 327
  James S. 327
  Jennie (Pease) 201
  Lyman 201
  Mary (Moody) 119
  (Gove) Miss 327
  Sarah (Clarke) 388
  Sarah (Ingalls) 50
  Sarah (Locke) 222
  Sarah (Stevens) 327
  Susan 119
  Thomas 119
  Trueworthy 327

Dudley, William 388
Duke, Della 232
Dunbar, Abbie M. 478
  Ada 478
  Ann (Nash) 176, 176
  Annie M. 176
  Asaette d 478
  Calvin 503
  Catherine (Ladd) 62
  Charles 345
  Clara (Emery) 345
  Dellie 478
  Frank 176, 478
  George W. 176
  Harrie T. 478
  Hattie (Chick) 478
  Helen 557
  Herbert 176
  H. M. 62
  Jefferson C. 176
  Joseph 176, 304
  Josephine 478
  Lillian 478
  Lizzie (Pray) 503
  Loring 176, 176
  Mary (Palmer) 176
  Minnie D. d. 176
  Miriam (Palmer), Mrs. . 84, 176
  Nellie 176
  Norman D. 557
  Sarah 20
  Sarah (Locke) 304
  Thomas L. 478
  Ursaletta 478
  Wayne d 478
  William W. 176
Duncan, Mary 108, 239
Dunklee, Harriet 211
Dunkley, Jennie 214
Dunn, Emma 459
  John 187
  Olivia (Locke) 356
  Sarah (Locke) 187
  Walt 356
Dunnigan, Etta (Locke) 189
  P. H. 189
Duntley, J. Leighton 220
  Mary (Kimball-Miles) 220
  Wilbur J. 220
Durgan, Margaret 49
  Rhoda 215
Durgin, Addie (Locke) 569
  Almot 569
  Elizabeth (Locke-Thompson) 102
  Grace (Locke) 468
  Israel 102
  John 292
  Nancy E. 131
  Mary 457
  (James), Miss 92
  Olive 186
  Sally 248
  Susan (Goodwin) 292
  Walter 468
  Woodbury 92
Durrell, Abbie T. (Gilman) . 132
  C. F. 132
  Lydia 163
Dustin, Mary, Mrs. 52
  Nancy 531
  Nathaniel 14
  Tryphena (Hazelton) 14
Dutton, George 501
  Gertrude (Stevens) 501
  Gertrude 501
Duplaise, Elizabeth (Locke-King) 308
  William 308
Dwight, Elizabeth (Stewart) 363
  Jennie (Dyer) 363
  Sylvester 363, 363

INDEX OF NAMES

DYER, Abbie (Hoxie).................. 336
  Abigail (Fogg).................... 362
  Addie........................... 363
  Annie M......................... 181
  Betsey......................21, 170
  Edward T........................ 170
  Eliza (Locke).................... 192
  Elizabeth...................179, 338
  Elizabeth (Melcher).............. 41
  Ella (Slocum)................... 338
  Eugene.......................338, 338
  Florence (Locke)................ 499
  Fred W..................... 499, 556
  George.......................170, 556
  George P.....................170, 336
  Georgeanna...................... 170
  Harold E........................ 338
  Henry........................170, 170
  Henry A......................170, 171
  Jennie.......................... 363
  Jennie (Wilson)................. 338
  John P.......................... 170
  Lillian J........................ 338
  Lydia (Hill)..................... 170
  Mabel........................... 338
  Madeline E...................... 556
  Mary....................41, 170, 170
  Mary (Johnson)................. 170
  Melissa......................... 170
  Minnie L........................ 338
  Minnie (Locke-Brown)........... 338
  Patience........................ 170
  Phebe........................... 170
  Phebe (Locke)...............170, 171
  Phebe (Pecknam)................ 170
  Rebecca......................... 81
  Roland B........................ 338
  Sally (Locke)................... 80
  Samuel..................170, 170, 192
  Samuel, Rev..................... 362
  Sarah.......................170, 170
  Sarah Cram..................... 192
  Thelma E........................ 556
  Thomas.......................... 41
  Walter L. d..................... 338
  Warren H........................ 170
  Wilbur E........................ 338
  William......................80, 170
EAKINS, Elizabeth (Locke).......... 358
  Jean............................ 358
  Nellie.......................... 358
  Robert.......................... 358
EASTER, Clarissa (Foss)............. 278
  Samuel.......................... 278
EASTMAN, Mr........................ 543
  Augusta......................... 58
  Benjamin........................ 24
  Clarence........................ 242
  Cynthia......................... 294
  David........................... 63
  Dora............................ 415
  Eastman......................... 242
  Edward.......................... 242
  Elizabeth....................... 242
  Elizabeth (Taplin).............. 242
  Elliott.......................... 242
  F. Elizabeth (Kimball).......... 415
  Francis......................... 242
  George.......................... 384
  Grace........................... 415
  Grace (Locke)................... 543
  Huldah.......................... 58
  Inez (Locke).................... 384
  Joel............................ 58
  John L.......................... 415
  Lurancia........................ 58
  Leighton........................ 242
  Lydia (Locke)................... 24
  Mary............................ 63
  Nathan.......................... 415

EASTMAN, Orrin..................... 58
  Persis.......................... 58
  Peter........................... 63
  Priscilla....................... 58
  Sally (Moulton)................. 58
  Sarah........................... 242
  Searles......................... 58
  Sidney.......................... 242
  Susan (Locke)................... 63
EASTWOOD, Addie (Dyer)............. 363
  John............................ 363
EATON, Abigail...................... 344
  Adna P.......................... 344
  Alwilda......................... 215
  Anna............................ 438
  Annie (Kenney).................. 438
  Benjamin........................ 441
  Betsey (Brown).................. 384
  Betsey (Locke).................. 87
  Betsey (Locke-Merrill).......... 47
  Donald.......................... 438
  Dorothy......................... 438
  Elizabeth....................... 357
  Emily.......................224, 517
  Eunice.......................... 177
  Fannie.......................... 383
  Frank, Dr....................... 364
  Hannah.......................... 343
  Harriet (Locke)................. 344
  Ina (Bryant).................... 438
  Jennie.......................... 357
  Jerusha (Locke)................. 357
  Jonathan.....................87, 357
  Lawrence........................ 357
  Leonard......................... 357
  Lizzie (Hoit-Locke)............. 364
  Luke............................ 438
  Martha A........................ 177
  Maurice......................... 438
  Merriam......................... 213
  (Kenney), Miss.................. 441
  Nellie (Locke).................. 441
  Oliver.......................... 213
  Polly........................... 87
  Samuel.......................... 344
  Sarah........................... 213
  Solomon.....................438, 441
  Thomas.......................47, 384
  Winthrop........................ 343
EDDY, Charlotte.................... 414
  Harrison....................414, 414
  Minnie (Jones).................. 414
  Randolph........................ 414
  Willard T....................... 414
EDGERLY, Harriet................... 202
EDMONDS, Alice (Locke)............. 13
  Annie........................... 314
  Benjamin........................ 314
  Charles.....................314, 314
  Elizabeth J. (Mason)............ 144
  Emaline H....................... 144
  Frances A....................... 314
  Frank........................... 314
  Hannah.......................... 314
  Joseph M....................144, 314
  Lucy (Parker)................... 314
  Mary (Shute).................... 314
  Sarah E......................... 314
  Susan (Philbrick)............... 364
  Thomas.......................... 13
  William.....................314, 364
EDSON, Carrie...................... 313
  Helen........................... 503
EDWARDS, Betsey.................... 178
  Carrie.......................... 332
  Elizabeth....................... 368
  Tabitha......................... 46
EGAN, Mary (Locke-Hatch).......... 293
  Michael......................... 293
EICHER, Edith...................... 535

INDEX OF NAMES

EICHER, Ora A.................... 535
  Sarah (Locke)................. 535
  William....................... 535
EILERTSEN, Christena............. 232
ELDRIDGE, Bertha (Locke).......... 527
  Charlotte..................... 500
  Harry A....................... 560
  William...................527, 500
ELKINS, Mr...................... 159
  Betsey........................ 89
  Catherine..................111, 140
  Catherine (Marston)............ 33
  Charlotte (Locke).............. 89
  Dolly (Moulton)................ 35
  Eliza......................... 89
  Elizabeth (Taylor)............. 35
  Ella.......................... 159
  Ezekiel....................... 89
  Flora......................... 249
  Hannah........................ 89
  Hannah P. (Locke)............. 568
  Henry......................33, 111
  Irene 89, 195
  Jeremiah...................... 175
  Joanna........................ 129
  John.......................... 159
  Jonathan...................... 35
  Lovie......................... 72
  Mary.......................16, 81
  Mary (Bachelder).............. 175
  Mary (Gray)................... 159
  Mary (Lord)................... 111
  Mary (Webster)................ 111
  Moses......................... 35
  Olive (Marden).............26, 111
  Richard....................... 568
  Samuel.....................111, 111
  Sarah F....................... 103
  Walter........................ 159
ELLENWOOD, Mr................... 75
  Elizabeth (Clifford)........... 75
ELLINGWOOD, Almira (Bancroft)... 479
  Annie (Locke)................. 479
  Charles O..................... 479
  Elizabeth..................... 185
  Giles......................... 479
ELLIOTT, Albert.................. 280
  Armenia (Russell)............. 280
  Charles H..................... 455
  Clarence...................... 390
  Clarinda...................141, 224
  Daniel........................ 390
  Dorcas (Baker)................ 390
  Edwin......................... 455
  Emma (Hull)................... 455
  Eliza (Locke)................. 94
  Florence (Trefethern)......... 519
  Frank......................390, 519
  Freeman....................... 460
  George........................ 282
  Helen F....................... 568
  Joel.......................... 94
  John.......................... 130
  Leon H........................ 461
  Lila.......................... 280
  Meanie (Whicher-Colby), Mrs.... 372
  Myra (Doloff)................. 390
  Nancy......................... 191
  Orah (Locke-Thompson)......... 282
  Robert........................ 12
  Susan (Wallis)................ 130
ELLIS, Charles................... 378
  Mary.......................... 208
  Ruth (Fletcher)............... 162
EMBURY, Clarinda................. 232
  Dora H........................ 232
EMERSON, Abigail................. 446
  Betsey R. (Locke-Dickey)....... 85
  Diantha....................... 187
  Dora.......................30, 567

EMERSON, Ella (Locke)............ 490
  Ephraim W..................... 542
  Esther........................ 197
  George D...................... 512
  Hattie........................ 201
  J. E.......................... 490
  Jesse......................... 85
  Lillian....................... 542
  Lucinda (Mortimer)............ 542
  Lucinda (Straw)............... 512
  Mary.......................... 322
  Mildred E..................... 512
  Sarah......................... 105
EMERY, Abbie..................... 330
  Abbie J....................... 415
  Abbie T. (Sanderson).......... 117
  Abigail (Leavitt)............. 52
  Abby M........................ 178
  Albion........................ 117
  Ann J......................... 179
  Ann M. O. (Locke)............. 156
  Anna L........................ 415
  Annie (Tranter)............... 414
  Annis d....................... 415
  Anthony, Dr..............52, 117, 117
  Betsey (Towle)................ 117
  Blanche....................... 466
  Caleb......................... 414
  Charles W..................... 178
  Clara......................... 248
  Clara (Gilman)................ 178
  Clara Marcia.................. 345
  Clara (Sanders)............... 295
  Clayton L..................... 414
  Clinton L..................414, 415
  Comfort (Potter).............. 295
  David W....................117, 117
  Delia......................... 392
  Elbridge...................... 295
  Eliza...................101, 117, 178
  Eliza (Pepper)................ 414
  Ellen......................... 345
  Emma (Jones).................. 292
  Esther (Tay).................. 248
  Eva (Rand).................... 553
  Frank L. d.................... 415
  Frederick..................... 512
  Forest.....................559, 559
  Grace......................... 330
  George.....................119, 330
  Hannah.....................178, 178
  Hannah (Harmon).............. 178
  Hannah (Locke)................ 82
  Happy (Goodman)............... 179
  Harriet....................117, 511
  Harry......................... 242
  Inez J........................ 466
  Isaac......................... 248
  J. N.......................... 511
  John.....................82, 178, 509
  Josephine (Trafton)........... 415
  Josiah........................ 111
  Lewis T....................... 292
  Mabel......................415, 509
  Marlon........................ 559
  Martha (Hall)................. 511
  Martha V...................... 117
  Mary...................101, 117, 178, 414
  Mary (Bachelder).............. 119
  Mary (Perkins)................ 52
  Mina A........................ 86
  Nabby......................... 117
  Nancy......................... 421
  Nancy (Sanborn)............... 111
  Nathaniel..................... 52
  Peter......................... 392
  Polly......................... 117
  Ralph......................... 179
  Sally (Morse)................. 117
  Sarah......................117, 117

INDEX OF NAMES

EMERY, Sarah (Locke).............. 242
  Sarah (Perkins)................. 52
  Susan......................178, 509
  Stephen L....................... 178
  Thomas......................... 178
  Timothy........................ 295
  Walter A........................ 553
  Willard, Lieut..............117, 415
  William, Lieut.................. 52
  William S....................... 156
  Winnifred (Smith).............. 512
EMMONS, Abigail (Fuller)........... 104
  Alvira d....................... 105
  Betsey (Webster)............104, 223
  Charles.....................105, 105
  Damon Y....................... 224
  Darius......................... 224
  Edith.......................... 216
  Gilbert d...................... 105
  Grace.......................... 216
  Harry.......................... 216
  Huldah (Chandler).............. 224
  Jennie......................... 216
  Jerusha........................ 196
  Jonathan....................... 105
  Kate (Maxwell)................. 224
  Kate (Russell)................. 281
  Lavinia d...................... 105
  Leroy S........................ 105
  Lucy (Bohonon)................. 224
  Lyford......................... 224
  Marcus......................... 281
  Margaret S. (Doloff)........... 105
  Moses......................223, 224
  Paul D......................... 216
  Rose........................... 224
  Sarah (Butler)................. 216
  Sarah (Emerson), Mrs........... 105
  Sylvester M.................... 105
  Thomas R....................... 104
  W. H. H........................ 216
ERWING, Caroline................... 530
ESTERBROOK, Elizabeth (Slapp)...... 136
  Mary........................... 63
  Nehemiah....................... 136
EVANS, Mr......................186, 379
  Amy (Palmer)................... 206
  Arthur......................... 206
  Charles........................ 102
  Eliza.......................... 125
  Eunice......................... 50
  Flora.......................... 433
  Gertrude (Adams)............... 379
  Hattie (Pollard)............... 186
  Ivory.......................... 102
  Josephine...................... 273
  Mary........................... 44
  Mary (Locke)................... 102
  Oliver......................... 102
  Sarah A. C..................... 141
  Sarah (Flanders), Mrs.......... 187
  William........................ 273
EVERETT, Edwin..................... 312
  George......................... 312
  Helen (Dearborn)............... 312
  Lila (Elliott)................. 280
  Raymond........................ 280
EVERHARDT, Effie (Locke)........... 416
  Gordon G....................... 416
EVES, Hannah...................202, 372
EWOLDT, Laura...................... 387
FABER, Grace....................... 540
FAILES, Albert..................... 319
  Hannah (Caswell)............... 319
  Lizzie F....................... 319
FAIRBANKS, Sadie................... 337
FAIRCHILD, George H................ 185
  Lovina (Locke)................. 185
FAIRCLOTH.......................... 461
FAIRFIELD, Mabel P................. 353

FALL, Amanda....................... 500
  Celia.......................... 329
  Harriet........................ 271
  Mary........................... 320
  Noah........................... 500
FALLS, Missouri.................... 276
FARE, Etta......................... 346
FARLEY, Kate (Cassidy)............. 547
  Katherine...................... 547
  Philip J....................547, 547
FARMER, Charles Russell............ 313
  John...................144, 313, 313
  Martha d....................... 313
  Martha R. (Locke).............. 144
  Mary........................18, 313
  Sally (Gerrish)................ 313
FARNEST, Agnes J................... 526
  Charles........................ 403
  Hattie (Bachelder)............. 403
  Helen L........................ 526
  Mabel.......................... 526
FARNSWORTH, Addie d............... 535
  Agnes (Locke).................. 135
  Allison........................ 135
  Andrew......................... 451
  Ann............................ 423
  Blanche........................ 536
  Catherine (Pray)............... 423
  David Lovering................. 423
  Edward T....................... 536
  Elbridge G..................423, 536
  Ella J. (Locke)................ 451
  Emma E......................... 536
  Fannie L....................... 536
  Flora M........................ 536
  Florinda L..................... 423
  Frances (Carr)................. 423
  Frances (Clough)............... 423
  Frank P........................ 536
  Harold R....................... 536
  James.......................... 451
  Karl W......................... 536
  Lottie P....................... 535
  Louise (Somers)................ 423
  Lucy H......................... 536
  Mary H......................... 536
  Mary (Locke)................... 246
  Orrin E........................ 423
  Ross Elmer..................... 536
  Silas B........................ 535
  Stephen........................ 246
FARNUM, Aaron G.................... 245
  Alice d........................ 420
  Bessie......................... 530
  Edward W....................... 392
  Elizabeth (Locke-Davis)........ 245
  Harry.......................... 392
  Helen.......................... 392
  James.......................... 392
  Laura.......................... 320
  Nellie (Drew).................. 392
FARRAR, Abijah L................... 167
  Albert......................... 167
  Annie (Scribner)............... 168
  Aphia.......................... 39
  Carrie (Hondlette)............. 167
  Charles........................ 168
  David U........................ 40
  Deborah L...................... 79
  Dorothy.....................40, 79
  Dorothy (Locke)................ 21
  Eliza (Locke)...............39, 40
  Elizabeth...................... 79
  Elizabeth (Locke).............. 86
  Ellen (Hayes).................. 167
  Elthea (Bagley)................ 79
  Ephraim S...................... 79
  Eunice......................... 168
  Frederick...................... 167
  Hannah......................... 39

INDEX OF NAMES

FARRAR, Hannah (Haswell).......... 39
  George O........................ 167
  Grace M. (Hatch).............. 167
  John.................40, 40, 79, 86
  Joseph Underwood.............. 40
  Joshua......................... 79
  Josiah......................79, 167
  Julia Ann....................... 79
  Keziah......................... 86
  Mabel (Talman)................ 167
  Mary.......................86, 168
  Mary (Rollins)................. 79
  Mary (York)................... 40
  Melissa (Trim)................ 167
  Nathan......................... 21
  Nellie (Savage)................ 168
  Salome......................... 86
  Samuel, Capt.................. 86
  Sarah A. (Kelsey)............. 79
  Sewell..........39, 40, 79, 167, 168
  Sophia......................40, 40
  Sophia (Underwood)............ 40
  Washburn...................... 86
  William........................ 86
  Zerubbabel..................... 39
FARRINGTON, Eliza.................. 267
  Martha........................ 264
FARWELL, Alice.................... 531
  Charles....................... 242
  Dewitt........................ 414
  Hannah (Moore)............... 414
  Janette (Locke)............... 242
  Jennie........................ 531
  Jennie P...................... 414
FAUNCH, Mr........................ 85
  Elizabeth (Robinson)........... 85
FAVOR, Annie (Locke).............. 369
  Charles....................... 369
  Corinne....................... 516
  Cutting....................... 104
  Daniel........................ 389
  Hannah........................ 49
  Ida (Noyes)................... 365
  John A........................ 516
  Nancy......................... 224
  Nora (Griffith)............... 516
  Polly (Sleeper)............... 389
FAY, Hattie....................... 484
  Jennie........................ 153
FAYER, Edna....................... 495
  Lilla L....................... 495
FEATHERSTONE, Annie............... 184
FELCH. FELTCH.
  George E...................382, 382
  Hannah......................45, 178
  Harold........................ 384
  John W. L..................... 382
  Josephine..................... 382
  Lydia......................... 319
  Mary (Locke).................. 384
  Matilda (Janvrin)............. 98
  Nicholas...................... 45
  Rinda (Locke)................. 382
  Sarah (Gove).................. 45
FELDEN, James..................... 49
  Martha (Belnap)............... 49
FELKER, Miss...................... 75
  Addie (Garland)............... 330
  Alice......................... 289
  Charles d.................... 289
  Clarence...................... 330
  Cordelia J. (Locke)........... 157
  Deborah (Demeritt)............ 126
  Elizabeth (Paine)............. 330
  Ellery M...................... 330
  Elmer......................... 330
  Francis....................... 156
  George d..................... 330
  Hannah........................ 156
  Hannah (Varney)............... 156

FELKER, Henry.................289, 330
  Martin V. B................... 157
  Rachel........................ 156
  Samuel........................ 156
  Samuel, Gov................... 289
  Sarah M....................... 330
  William H..................... 126
FELLOWS, Albert B., Dr............ 228
  Alice A....................... 229
  Alma L. d.................... 226
  Anna.......................... 370
  Arthur........................ 469
  Benjamin...................... 228
  Caroline (Nutting)............ 226
  Charles R..................... 294
  Elizabeth (Keer).............. 228
  Ellen (Towle)................. 200
  Etta (Jeswett)................ 228
  Eva (Fling)................... 228
  Evelyn (Grant)................ 228
  Frank......................... 228
  Fred W........................ 226
  Ina........................... 370
  Jennie........................ 370
  Jonathan...................226, 226
  Joseph W...................... 226
  Leslie H...................... 228
  Loretta....................... 226
  Lottie........................ 293
  Louise (Bangs)................ 226
  Mary (Travis-Lewis), Mrs...... 226
  May........................... 293
  Milo.......................104, 228
  Miriam........................ 228
  Orra (Locke).................. 294
  Oscar F....................... 228
  Raymond....................... 228
  R. P.......................... 468
  S. B.......................... 468
  Sally D. (Locke).............. 104
  Smith D....................226, 228
  Susan D. (Locke).............. 104
  Susie M....................... 229
  Timothy G..................... 228
  Warren G...................... 226
  William....................... 200
  Willie........................ 370
  Winthrop R.................... 104
FENDERSON, Martha................. 347
  Hannah B. (Locke)............. 146
  Octavia....................... 99
  Stephen....................... 146
FENNER, Charles E................. 307
  Elizabeth (Perry)............. 307
FENNES, Elizabeth................. 171
FENNO, Anna F. (Grafton).......... 106
  John W........................ 106
FERNALD, Annie.................... 317
  Elihu......................... 240
  Elizabeth..................... 71
  Ernest W...................... 221
  Eunice........................ 76
  John.......................... 429
  Hannah (Chandler)............. 240
  Marcia H...................... 125
  Margaret...................... 474
  Martha.....................125, 287
  Martha (Smith-Locke).......... 429
  Mary (Thompson)............... 221
  Olive C....................... 108
  Ralph S....................... 221
  Wilbur F...................... 221
  William K..................... 287
FERREN, Louisa.................... 131
FERRIN, Augustus...............230, 230
  Alice (Roby).................. 230
  Sarah......................... 226
  Sarah (Roby).................. 230
FERRY, Malanton................... 278
  Miretta (Woodman)............. 278

INDEX OF NAMES

FEUNSIER, Emily (Locke)........ 426
    Henry.................... 426
    Ralph.................... 426
FIELD, Hannah................. 141
FIFIELD, Clarissa (Green)........ 252
    George................... 387
    Lillian (Chesley)............ 387
    Sherburne................. 252
FINK, Jesse.................... 385
FINNIGAN, Arthur............... 521
    Augustus.................. 521
    Clara (Moulton)............ 521
    Frederick.................. 521
FISH, Florence A. (Young)........ 524
    Frank.................... 524
    Mary J................... 515
    Sarah..................... 185
FISHER, Andrew................ 87
    Belle..................... 258
    Charles................... 441
    Cyrus.................... 296
    Edna L................... 296
    Georgeanna (Outing)........ 296
    Hannah B................. 87
    Jane..................... 229
    Joseph.................... 189
    Leo Z.................... 296
    Mary..................... 441
    Nancy (Locke)............. 87
    Nancy (Watts), Mrs......... 29
    Patience (Locke-McAlpine-Shaw).. 189
FISKE, Abbie d................. 171
    Abbie (Locke).............. 80
    Alfred L................... 80
    Amasa.................... 358
    Charles.................80, 171
    Edward................... 171
    Edwin.................... 508
    Elizabeth (Locke)........... 80
    Ellen (Locke).............. 358
    Elma..................... 436
    Frank.................... 507
    Gladys.................... 508
    Grace..................... 508
    Harry..................... 508
    Helen..................... 508
    James..................... 436
    Jean...................... 508
    Jeremiah.................. 171
    Maria d................... 171
    Marion.................... 507
    Mary E................... 171
    Mary (Smith).............. 171
    Nellie (Shiner)............. 507
    Phebe d.................. 171
    Ralph d.................. 508
    Rupert.................... 508
    Thomas d................. 171
FITCH, Mary................... 260
FITTS, Hannah (Locke).......... 91
    Laura (Day)............... 91
    Mary L................... 91
    William H................. 91
FITZGERALD, Abigail (Locke)..... 302
    Arthur W.................. 474
    Belle (Graham)............. 474
    Ezekiel, Rev............... 474
    Ezekiel................302, 474
    Georgeanna................ 474
    John d................... 474
    Louis d.................. 474
    Margaret (Fernald)......... 474
    Marie d.................. 474
    Martha A................. 474
    Martha (Holt).............. 474
    William H................. 474
FIVE, Mary.................... 216
FLAGG, Anna (Locke-Smith)...... 242
    Cassander................. 242
    Charles................... 242

FLAGG, Isaac................... 464
    Martha (Locke)............ 242
    Mary..................... 287
    Mary (Garland)............ 464
FLAKE, Nellie.................. 174
FLANDERS, Amanda (Wells)...... 226
    Ashahel................... 511
    Charles................... 226
    Clyde..................... 396
    Dyer...................... 396
    Edwin.................... 220
    Etta...................... 219
    Hannah (Drew-Page)........ 227
    Harriet.................... 230
    Harriet (Kelley)............ 230
    Hattie.................... 367
    James..................... 226
    Jennie.................... 511
    John...................... 230
    Lizzie..................... 511
    Lizzie (Locke-Clough)....... 220
    Lorenzo................... 227
    Lucy...................... 226
    Maria..................... 418
    Mary..................... 538
    Mary (Locke).............. 396
    Minnie.................... 369
    Nellie (Perkins)............ 219
    Owen L................... 226
    Samuel.................... 219
    Sarah..................... 187
    Serene.................... 396
    Stephen................... 396
FLANNIGAN, Barbara H.......... 386
    Georgine (Moses)........... 386
    Thomas................... 386
FLEEK, Grace.................. 261
    John...................... 261
    Martha (Lang)............. 261
FLEMING, Fidelia............... 268
FLETCHER, Alice................ 335
    Clara..................... 335
    Eliza (Stevens)............. 183
    Florence................232, 393
    Harriet.................... 84
    Jane...................... 162
    Jesse..................... 229
    John.................167, 335
    Joshua.................... 183
    Julia...................... 543
    Laura (Pulsifer)............ 167
    Mabel..................... 335
    Mary.................44, 229
    Patience (Hobart).......... 229
    Percy..................... 335
    Ruth...................... 162
    Thomas................... 335
FLING, Eva.................... 228
    Lewis..................... 228
    Mary (Sleeper)............. 228
FLINT, Amanda................. 365
    Dutee W.................. 509
    Emma (Wilcox)............ 509
    George H........330, 501, 509, 509
    Hannah (Locke)............ 330
    Harvey J.................. 509
    Hattie L................... 501
    Marion R. d............... 501
    Mildred E................. 501
    Thomas D................. 501
    Walter d.................. 501
FLITTER, Mary................. 376
FLOYD, Sally................... 59
FOGG, Mrs..................... 100
    Aaron H................... 223
    Abbie..................... 410
    Abigail.................... 362
    Bertha E.................. 410
    Caroline E. (Carr).......... 132
    Cyrus..................... 239

INDEX OF NAMES

FOGG, David................132, 178, 344
  Eben............................. 407
  Eliza (Hunt-Crockett), Mrs........ 83
  Eliza (Jenness).................. 380
  Elizabeth (Marston).............. 344
  Ellen M.......................... 132
  Elvin L.......................... 407
  Emma.......................132, 453
  Emma (Locke)...............237, 239
  Gertrude L....................... 407
  Hannah........................... 21
  Hannah (Hunnewell).............. 39
  Jeremiah......................... 60
  Jonathan......................... 39
  John P........................... 132
  Lodema (Tirrell)................. 223
  Lydia (Dawlton).................. 407
  Martha (Lang).................... 60
  Mary E........................... 132
  Mary (Page)...................... 132
  Oliver........................... 237
  Richard.......................... 380
  Rhoda J.......................... 178
FOLLANSBEE, David..........465, 465, 466
  Dolly (Prescott)................. 465
  Jennie (Locke-Gile).............. 466
  Mary............................. 198
  Sarah............................ 292
FOLLET, Elvira...................... 135
  George........................... 135
  Lemuel........................... 135
  Sarah (Winter)................... 135
FOLSOM, Ann......................... 14
  Dora............................. 215
  Elizabeth........................ 32
  James A.......................... 427
  Mary............................. 32
  Mary (Locke-Tilton).............. 427
  Nancy (Nutt), Mrs................ 413
  Nancy (Tash)..................... 427
  Peter............................ 32
  Sally............................ 113
  Winthrop......................... 427
FOLSTON, Gail....................... 296
  Martha (Mitchell)................ 296
  Mitchell......................... 296
FOOTE, Charles L.................... 281
  Diantha.......................... 99
  Emma (Locke)..................... 484
  Evaline G........................ 88
  Frank............................ 484
  Laura (Bickford-Munsey).......... 295
  Lewis C.......................... 484
  Loretta.......................... 308
  Maria (Locke).................... 281
  R. M............................. 295
  Sally (Green).................... 484
  Sarah............................ 459
  Thomas........................... 484
FORD, Alice......................... 370
  Arthur........................... 370
  Charles.......................... 370
  Elsie E.......................... 470
  Fred............................. 416
  Ida.............................. 370
  Issue............................ 242
  Jennie........................... 240
  Josie............................ 416
  Julia............................ 395
  Lena (Smith)..................... 470
  Mary (Towle)..................... 200
  Nelson G......................... 470
  Robert, Rev...................... 200
  Sophia (Taplin).................. 242
FORSAITH, Arthur.................... 115
  Carrie (——)..................... 115
  Carrie (Goldsmith)............... 115
  Dennis........................... 115
  Edwin............................ 115
  Emaline.......................... 115

FORSAITH, Florenda (Locke).......... 115
  Hilas............................ 115
  William.......................... 115
FOSS, Mr............................ 345
  Miss............................. 156
  Abigail.......................... 121
  Abigail (Daniels)................ 152
  Abigail (Locke).................. 27
  Abigail (Rheid).................. 64
  Ada (Smith)...................... 512
  Adaline (Locke).................. 302
  Almira P......................... 302
  Ann.............................. 181
  Benjamin......................... 302
  Carlenda......................... 278
  Caroline T....................... 121
  Carry............................ 404
  Clarissa A....................... 278
  Clement B........................ 157
  David............................ 54
  David, Dr........................ 512
  Dorcas (Shapleigh)............... 302
  Edwin............................ 558
  Eliza (Heywood).................. 121
  Elizabeth.....................54, 187
  Elizabeth (Locke)................ 54
  Elizabeth (Titcomb).............. 54
  Elizabeth (Woodman).............. 123
  Elmer M.......................... 330
  Emily............................ 552
  Emma (Locke)..................... 307
  Enoch T.......................... 157
  Ephraim.......................... 152
  Fanny............................ 83
  Frank............................ 451
  George B......................... 404
  Hannah..................64, 132, 158
  Hannah (——).................... 121
  Hannah (Donaldson), Mrs.......... 122
  Hannah (Page).................... 132
  Harriet (Spear).................. 121
  James S.......................... 64
  Jane........................18, 566
  Jennie........................... 510
  Jeremiah d....................... 64
  Job...........................54, 64
  Joel N........................... 302
  John...........5, 54, 54, 121, 132, 181, 404
  Joshua..................27, 54, 153
  Lydia............................ 34
  Lydia (Rand)..................... 153
  Lydia (Troop).................... 121
  Lucinda.......................... 121
  Mandana (Pickering).............. 404
  (Marden), Miss................... 54
  Maria M. (Locke)................. 157
  Mark............................. 307
  Martha (Spurling)................ 330
  Mary....................60, 64, 72, 121
  Mary (Berry)..................... 30
  Mary (Chamberlain)............... 451
  Mary (Drown)..................... 121
  Mary (Green)..................... 404
  Mary (Libbey).................... 64
  Mary (Tucker).................33, 345
  Mercy............................ 13
  Nathaniel........................ 33
  Olive............................ 31
  Patience......................... 64
  Patty (Berry).................... 64
  Polly d.......................... 64
  Reuben........................... 123
  Robert........................... 121
  Sally............................ 64
  Sally (Hodgdon).................. 64
  Salome (Trefethern).............. 33
  Sarah.............64, 68, 73, 129, 151
  Sarah A. (Locke)................. 157
  Sarah Ellen...................... 79
  Samuel.........33, 33, 64, 121, 316

INDEX OF NAMES

Foss, Samuel Dowst 30
   Sula (Locke) 236, 316
   Supply C........................ 33
   Wallis........................... 64
   (Tilton), Widow................. 54
   William....................... 54, 121
Foster, Mr......................... 213
   Abigail......................... 240
   Albert........................... 78
   Anna Laura..................... 167
   Betsey........................... 29
   Charlotte....................... 292
   Clara A......................... 167
   C. J............................ 466
   Elizabeth....................... 519
   Ellen............................ 422
   Francis H....................... 408
   Hannah......................... 473
   Homans......................... 408
   Ida (Sanders) 419
   James C......................... 167
   Joanna d....................... 167
   Joanna (Locke).................. 78
   Matilda (Janvrin-Feltch-Locke).... 213
   Nathaniel d.................... 167
   Rosa (Stearns).................. 408
   Stephen......................... 419
Fournier, Flora (Copp).............. 205
   James A......................... 205
   L. Samuel....................... 205
Fowle, Emma....................... 249
Fowler, Abbie...................... 255
   Abigail......................... 193
   Abigail (Davis).............. 193, 511
   Abner........................... 224
   Abraham........................ 224
   Alice............................ 461
   Ann (Locke).................... 363
   Blake........................... 389
   Dolly........................... 265
   Edward M...................... 511
   Ellen (Locke-Kennard) 247
   Elvira (Crichett)................ 363
   Etta (Bartlett).................. 511
   George.................. 226, 511, 511
   Greenleaf C..................... 247
   Hannah (Doloff)................ 224
   Hadley, Dr..................... 389
   Harriet (Emery)................ 511
   Loretta (Fellows-Pike).......... 226
   James W........................ 363
   John C.......................... 247
   Martha E....................... 511
   Mary (Beaton-Harrison), Mrs..... 511
   Mary (Nutter)................. 247
   Minot L......................... 511
   Olive (Haines).................. 511
   Ruhuma (Locke)................ 363
   Ruth (Sleeper).................. 389
   Samuel.......................... 363
   Sarah........................... 248
   Sarah (Locke).................. 389
   Winthrop................. 193, 363, 511
Fox, Harriet (Connor) 279
   Isaac........................... 279
   Katherine M.................... 162
   Patience (Gilman) 147
   Samuel.......................... 147
   Sarah T......................... 147
Frances, Carrie 436
   Fannie (Jones) 436
   George W....................... 436
Frank, Nellie 297
Frappied, John..................... 231
   Jane (Mosher)................... 231
Frauley, Mary..................... 143
Frazier, Bessie..................... 321
Freeman, Allen 357, 507
   Austin K........................ 507
   Chestina........................ 164
40

Freeman, Churchill L................ 507
   Eliza........................... 373
   Ellen........................... 507
   Ellinor (Locke)................. 357
   John............................ 334
   Mary.................... 213, 334, 507
   Mary (Bent).................... 507
   Olive (Merrill).................. 501
   Salina.......................... 506
   Willis........................... 501
Freeze, Abby S..................... 101
   Mary........................... 445
French, Mr......................... 66
   Albert.......................... 558
   Almira (Towle)................. 200
   Alonzo C........................ 284
   Andrew......................... 370
   Bertha.......................... 284
   Carl F.......................... 558
   Carrie (Bancroft)............... 377
   C. B............................ 377
   Charles......................... 558
   Christena.................... 1, 581
   Clara (Wiggin)................. 239
   Cyrus........................... 200
   Daniel.......................... 285
   David..................... 239, 410
   Dorothy........................ 307
   Elaine (Carroll)................ 558
   Emma........................... 410
   Emma (Locke).................. 284
   Etta............................ 370
   Franklin........................ 284
   French lady..................... 109
   Harry A......................... 558
   Hattie.......................... 217
   Ida (Locke)..................... 510
   Irene (Jewell).................. 410
   Irene........................... 513
   James E.................... 329, 499
   Jennie.......................... 370
   Jeremiah....................... 510
   John C.......................... 59
   Lavina.......................... 125
   Lizzie........................... 370
   Lucy...................... 270, 444
   Mabel........................... 284
   Martha.................... 108, 124
   Martha A. (Hersom)............ 499
   Martha (Hill)................... 329
   Martha (Locke)................ 284
   Mary (Tuck).................... 285
   Moses..................... 284, 284
   Newman D..................... 558
   Obadiah......................... 85
   Olive (Marden).................. 66
   Olive (Robinson-Locke).......... 85
   Orissa B........................ 249
   (Philbrick), Miss................ 59
   Rose............................ 558
   Sophronia....................... 200
   Susan........................... 293
   Sylvester....................... 558
Frenyear, Florence 479
Fretts, Emeline..................... 223
Friel, Arthur O..................... 221
   George W....................... 221
   Lucy (Thompson)............... 221
Frink, Annie 448
   Charles......................... 448
   Cyrus........................... 448
   Edith (Lamprey)................ 448
   Simes........................... 448
Frisbee, Jane (Bunker) 302
Frizzell, Anthony................... 342
   Ellen (Locke)................... 342
   Minnie.......................... 159
   Warren Eben................... 342
Froelich, Mary..................... 365
Frost, Charles, Major............... 83

INDEX OF NAMES

FROST, Charles d 197
  Elizabeth 259
  Henry 197
  Jane (White) 475
  John, Capt 475
  Lucy (Hutchins) 197
  Margaret 302
  Sarah P 83
  Sophronia D 147
FRYE, Angie B 457
  Clara (Locke) 277
  George E 457
  Hannah 456
  Ida M 457
  Joseph 277
  Leonard B 137
  Sarah W. (Berry) 137
  William 456
FULLER, Abbie (Chamberlain) 453
  Abigail 104
  Abigail (Locke) 49
  Abgiail (Locke-Smith) 274
  Clarke 104
  Comfort (Moses) 104
  Dorothy 104
  Frederick 453
  Hannah 101
  (Huckins), Miss 104
  Joanna (Seavey) 49
  John W 308
  Josiah 49, 49, 104
  Julia 223
  Levi 103
  Mable 453
  Mary (Pike) 104
  Merrill 223
  Polly 103
  Rachel 26, 103
  Russell d 104
  Sarah (Gerry-Locke) 308
  William 274
FULTON, Anna (Gemmer) 562
  Clarence D 562
  Joseph N 534
  Mary 342
  Maude O. (Locke) 534
FURBER, Joel 67
  Nabby (Locke) 67
FURBISH, Abra 73
GAFFETT, Mary J 171
  Sarah F 171
GAGE, Amanda (Lang) 262
  Benjamin F 262
  Elizabeth 210
  Lizzie 443
  Lodoiski 133
  Lydia 553
  Madella 443
  Richard 442
  Sophronia 262
  Susanna (Chandler) 442
GALE, Adela (Locke) 255
  Anna L 557
  Bethia (Blaney-Locke) 95
  Daniel, Rev 95
  Harriet E .... -557
  John 255, 503
  Mary (Mace) 503
  Roland E 557
GALLAGHER, Annie (Brogan) 477
  Augustine d 547
  Charles J 547
  Edward d 547
  Emma G 547
  Frank d 547
  George d 547
  John 477
  Nellie d 547
GALLANT, Margaret 464
GALLOWAY, Elizabeth 56

GALUSHA, Lizzie 397
GAMMON, Carrie (Locke) 369
  Danville, Rev 369
GARDNER, Annah 396
  Belle C 161
  B. Frank 396
  Ellen W 396
  Emaline (Locke) 233
  George 396
  Ida (Tucker) 396
  John 233
  Nellie (Clough) 220
  Nellie (Woodman) 458
  Sumner 220
GARLAND, Abigail 69, 238, 266
  Abigail (Perkins) 52, 238
  Addie 330
  Amos, Lieut 305
  Angenette 551
  Ann 148, 344
  Ann (Dawlton), Mrs 140
  Anna L. (Dalton) 127
  Annie (Drake) 238
  Asa 451
  Benjamin, Col 32, 117
  Benjamin 67, 128
  Caroline 140
  Betsey (Chesley) 451
  Calvin 143
  Charles 238, 489
  Clara 407
  David 266
  Edna 489
  Edna (Chesley) 410
  Eliza A 489
  Eliza (Garland) 551
  Elizabeth 17, 489, 503
  Elizabeth (Dearborn) 34
  Elizabeth (Parsons) 117
  Ella 489
  Elvira J. d 410
  Elvira Locke 238, 238
  Emma (French) 410
  Emma L 238
  Emma (Manson) 405
  Ethel (Locke) 489
  Florence 551
  Gilman 27, 28, 238
  Hannah 218, 265, 266
  Hannah (Marston) 265
  Harold 405
  Henrietta 494
  Horace 551
  James W 410
  John 34, 52, 238, 266, 410
  Joseph 238, 266
  Julia A 140, 266
  Levi 118, 250
  Lucretia (Locke) 108
  Lucy A 107
  Malvina 238
  Mary . . 60, 67, 68, 68, 266, 464, 520, 545
  Mary A. (Mowe) 143
  Mary Abby 238
  Mary (Watson) 118
  Martha 451
  Martha (Jenness) 238
  Mehitable, Mrs 52, 250
  Mehitable (Seavey) 107, 238
  Millard F 238
  Morris 405
  Moses 108, 108
  Nancy (Drown-Locke) 108, 238
  Norman d 410
  Olive (Jenness) 305
  Oliver 266
  Patty (Locke) 108
  Peter 31, 107, 238
  Polly L 107
  Polly (Perkins) 118, 250

INDEX OF NAMES

GARLAND, Polly (Philbrick) 128
  Ruel....................108, 410
  Rufus.......................... 405
  Sally (Philbrick)................ 128
  Samuel.................265, 266, 551
  Sarah A.........107, 127, 128, 250, 305
  Sarah (Jenness)................ 117
  Semira (Jenness)................ 405
  Sophia (Jenness)................ 238
  Thomas Ruel d................ 238
  Walter d..................... 238
  William....................127, 489
GARRISON, Mary..................... 325
GARROTT, Cony W.................355, 356
  Katy.......................... 355
  Margaret (Coffin)............355, 356
  Mary (Locke-Leighton).......... 187
  William....................... 187
GARVEY, B. F....................... 242
  Mary (Locke-Hatch-Egan)........ 293
  Phebe (Locke)................. 242
  Thomas....................... 293
GARVIN, Caroline.................... 201
  Ethel......................... 485
  Frank......................... 485
  Martha (Mendel).............. 485
GARWOOD, Henrietta................. 161
GATES, Charles...................... 311
  Erastus....................... 442
  Frank......................... 311
  Georgeanna.................... 442
  James......................... 311
  Lizzie (Perkins)................ 311
  Lucy (Ray).................... 442
  Mary E. (Prince)............... 40
  Mary (Locke).................. 190
  Martha (Trefethern-Green)....... 144
  Oldham....................... 190
  Ruby.......................... 311
  Samuel.....................40, 40
  Storer......................... 144
  Susie (Goodman)............... 311
  Welsley, Dea................... 190
  Woodbury..................... 311
GAVITT, Elijah...................... 80
  Mary (Locke).................. 80
GAY, Charles....................... 229
  Edna (Taft)................... 229
GEDDES, Lizzie (Gage)............... 443
  William....................... 443
GEER, Clara........................ 205
  Lucy.......................... 171
GEMMER, Anna..................... 562
GEORGE, Miss...................... 272
  Ada (Locke)................... 389
  Adoniram...................... 91
  Carolyn E..................... 517
  Charles A..................... 391
  David.....................96, 198, 517
  Edith A....................... 517
  Ellen (Wells).................. 391
  Eunice (Locke)................. 96
  Mrs. F. J...................... 391
  Frances M..................... 517
  Francis, Rev................... 389
  Helen L....................... 517
  Lloyd F....................... 517
  Loretta....................... 341
  Louisa........................ 466
  Olive d....................... 391
  Margaret...................... 391
  Mary d....................... 198
  Mary (Tyler).................. 198
  Sally (Perkins)................ 91
  Sarah......................... 198
  Sarah (Webster)............... 517
GERBER, Harriet.................... 546
  Hattie (Lyon).................. 546
  Melissa....................... 546
  William....................... 546

GERRISH, Sally...................... 313
GERRY, Annie...................... 500
  Betsey D...................... 71
  Sarah......................141, 308
GETCHELL, Fidelia (Wilson).......... 188
  Philanda (Wilson).............. 188
  Sevilla........................ 188
  Sumner....................... 188
GETMAN, Mary E................... 81
GIBBS, Delia (Bisbee)............... 258
  Ethel......................... 312
  Fanny M...................... 115
  Thomas....................... 258
GIBSON, Alice...................... 350
  Martha....................... 28
GIFFIN, Albert..................... 542
  Fannie (Colburn)............... 542
  Ida........................... 441
GIFFORD, Frances (Locke)........... 188
  Harvey C..................... 150
  Mary S. (Locke)............... 150
  Melvin........................ 188
  Oral M....................... 188
GILBERT, Mr....................... 92
  Charles....................... 361
  George........................ 361
  Harriet (Bachelder)............. 92
  Mary......................... 311
  Sarah (Tucker)................. 361
GILES. GILE.
  Alice (Bickford)................ 436
  Arthur........................ 436
  Bessie (Allen).................. 556
  Cyrus......................... 436
  Fred......................436, 466
  George........................ 364
  Jennie (Locke)................. 466
  John E.....................466, 466
  J. M.......................... 531
  Leland H...................... 556
  Leonard....................... 436
  Lillian (Pollard)................ 354
  Loren......................... 436
  Louisa (George)................ 466
  Mary (Philbrick)............... 364
  Sarah (Rand).................. 436
  Willis......................... 354
GILL, Lavinia....................... 268
GILLETT, Jennie.................... 246
  Margaret...................... 479
GILLIS, Marion..................... 549
  William....................... 549
GILMAN, Miss...................... 156
  Mr............................ 168
  Abbie T....................... 132
  Albert F....................... 132
  Carrie......................... 355
  Charles........................ 132
  Clara.......................... 178
  Daniel........................ 458
  David......................... 132
  Dudley........................ 329
  Frances....................... 114
  Horace E...................... 132
  John.......................... 97
  Julia (Prescott)................ 114
  Lavinia (Locke)................ 97
  Lizzie (Horton)................ 132
  Lydia (Hussey)................ 329
  Mary (Farrar)................. 168
  Nellie (Happiney).............. 132
  Nicholas S..................... 114
  Olive (Hussey)................ 329
  Patience....................... 147
  Samuel........................ 114
  Sula (Judkins)................. 458
  Susan......................... 104
  Tirzah (Locke)................ 132
GILMORE, Mr....................... 493
  Claude R...................... 384

INDEX OF NAMES

GILMORE, Ellen (Damren) 459
   Gertrude (Haley-Catlin) 493
   Herbert 459
   Mary 195
   Minnie (Locke) 384
   Ralph L 384
   Wilhemena (Popplar) 229
   William 384
GILPATRICK, Elizabeth 21
GILSON, Amelia 267
   Fidelia 267
   Martha 466
GIRARD of Montreal 94
   Sarah (Moses-Locke) 94
GLADDING, Freda 416
GLASCOMB, Henry 55
GLASS, John H 126
   Mary (Demeritt-Burleigh) 126
GLENN, Fannie 439
GLIDDEN, Arthur W 196
   Clara (Stevens) 196
   Josie 430
   Mary B. (Stevens) 90
   Ruth 118
   Smith 90
GLINES, Carrie 262
   Rebecca 553
GLOVER, Mary S 232
GLYNN, Florence M. (Russell) 281
   Thomas 281
GODFREY, Abigail 92
   Adaline 212
   Alida 212
   Ann (Locke) 46
   Charles 338
   Elizabeth 92
   Ethel 522
   Harriet 92
   Horace 212
   Isadora (Locke) 338
   Janette 92
   Jonathan 84
   John 46, 92, 92, 212
   Joshua 338, 338
   Marilla 92
   Mary 84, 92, 92
   Mary (Lane) 84
   Mary (Philbrick) 212
   Moses 92
   Persis 212
   Sally (Locke) 46
   Sarah 35, 212, 338
   Sarah (Godfrey) 92
   (Woodbury), Miss 92
GOFF, Julia A 96
GOLDING, Ann 306
GOLDSMITH, Miss 157
   Bernice F 561
   Carrie 115
   Charles 534
   Edna (Locke) 534
   Emaline (Forsaith) 115
   Ernest 512
   George 115
   Mary (Perkins) 512
GOODELL, Alice (West) 492
   Carrie L 492
   Charles W 492
   Elizabeth (Locke) 317
   Frank A 492
   Henry O. d 492
   Hiram S 317
   Mabel 492
   Percy H 492
GOODHUE, Abigail 264, 445
   Eva 264, 444
   James 444
GOODMAN, Charles 216
   Happy 179
   Mary (Dearborn) 216

GOODMAN, Susie 311
GOODRICH, Ella 484
   Emily (Swett) 265
   Emma 265
   James 265
   Joshua 265
   Stanley 265
GOODSELL, Lora 459
GOODWIN, Mr 62
   Abigail 139
   Clara 325
   Ella 483
   Frank 325
   G. Emma 428
   Hattie (Berry) 407
   Hattie (Locke) 451
   Helen S. (Dudley) 327
   Henry 540
   Ivory, Capt 327
   John, Col 325
   John 25
   Joseph 341
   Keziah (Tibbetts) 25
   Leonora 327
   Madeline P 198
   Mamie (Plummer) 540
   Maria 128
   Maria (Palmer) 341
   Mehitable (Day) 325
   Mehitable (Locke) 25
   Miron 198
   Nancy 274
   Octavius 325
   Sally 42
   Sarah (George) 198
   Sophia 99
   Susan 292
   Tryphena (Ladd) 62
   William H 407, 451
GOOKIN, Albert d 475
   Charles A 475
   Elizabeth (Smith) 475
   Frank 475
   Frederick 475
   Georgeanna 475
   Hannah (Locke) 302
   John S 475
   Nellie 475
   Samuel, Col 475
   William 302, 475
GORDON, Atlanta 241
   Fannie 420
   Hannah (Locke) 568
   Joseph 568
   Margaret 531
   Mary 511
   Mehitable 328
   Orrie 186
   Sarah (Tucker-Gilbert) 361
   Savory 531
   Warren 361
GOSS, Miss 60
   Abigail 66, 437
   Abigail (Locke) 107
   Ann M. (Locke) 142
   Annie 489, 552
   Arthur 316
   Clarence A 489
   Daniel 118
   Data (Mason) 140
   Elizabeth 31, 551
   Elizabeth (Brown) 31
   Elizabeth (Galloway-Randall-Jenness) 56
   Ella (Garland) 489
   Elzada 310
   Erastus L 489
   Ernest d 316
   Estelle J 489
   Florence (Garland) 551

INDEX OF NAMES

Goss, Frances (Knowles)............ 489
  Gilman P...................... 489
  Hannah (Perkins).............. 118
  Harriet D..................... 552
  Harriet (Locke)............... 316
  Isabella...................... 310
  Jonathan..................15, 31, 66
  John S................5, 236, 316, 551
  Joseph....................... 31, 66
  Laurence E.................... 489
  Leon W. d..................... 551
  Lillian (McGanty)............. 489
  Lucia......................... 203
  Marion (Bennett-Conconnan), Mrs. 488
  Martha........................ 31
  Mary.......................... 489
  Mary (Mace).................. 489
  Melvin J..................... 551
  Nathan....................... 236
  Olive A...................... 310
  Otis.......................... 142
  Patty (Davidson).............. 66
  Philip........................ 551
  Raymond...................... 551
  Richard............31, 31, 489, 551
  Richard P................316, 489
  Sally (Berry)................. 65
  Salome........................ 31
  Salome (Locke)................ 16
  Sarah B...................... 140
  Sarah (Caswell)............... 488
  Sarah (Johnson)............... 236
  Sarah (Mace).................. 118
  Sarah (Marden)............... 236
  Sarah (Seavey)................ 66
  Simon......................... 65
  Simon, Lieut.................. 235
  Stanley....................... 551
  Sula (Locke-Foss)..........236, 316
  Susan (Knowlton).............. 316
  Thomas........................ 56
  Thomas Genl.................. 107
  Wallace..................15, 33, 488
  Walter W..................... 489
  William D.................... 140
GOTHAM, Lydia.................... 354
GOULD, Arthur.................... 497
  Caroline E................325, 325
  Charles, Dr................... 281
  Ella......................497, 497
  Emma.......................... 325
  Erastus...................154, 325
  Ernest G...................... 325
  Fred E........................ 325
  George F...................... 325
  Harriet....................... 497
  Harriet B. (Locke)............ 154
  Helen (Avery)................. 325
  Jesse (Locke)................. 325
  John.......................... 187
  Kate (Russell-Emmons)......... 281
  Lucy.......................... 373
  Lydia N....................... 181
  Mary (Randall)................ 325
  Melissa (Locke)............... 187
  Melville P.................... 497
  M. (Wedgwood)................. 325
  Nellie (Brown)................ 497
  Royal C....................... 325
  Sarah (Johnson)............... 325
  Sophia........................ 76
GOVE, Miss....................... 327
  Adalaide (Rowe)............... 383
  Agnes......................... 221
  Annie......................... 321
  Betsey........................ 364
  Catherine..................... 209
  Catherine (Lawton)............ 221
  Clarissa..................212, 212
  David Locke................98, 252

GOVE, Ebenezer................... 112
  Edward....................47, 96, 209
  Edward Payson................ 213
  Edwin......................... 221
  Eleanor (Grout)............... 213
  Eliza......................... 98
  Eliza (Locke)................. 96
  Elizabeth M................... 151
  Elizabeth (Morrill)........... 221
  Elizabeth (Ring).............. 98
  Ellen.....................213, 383
  Emily.....................212, 383
  Enoch......................... 47
  Fanny (Eaton)................. 383
  Florence...................... 221
  Francis M..................... 213
  Gertrude B.................... 221
  Gertrude (Locke).............. 435
  Hannah........................ 100
  Hannah (Dearborn)............. 47
  Harriet (Boyd)................ 212
  Harriet (Lowell).............. 98
  Henry M....................... 221
  Hiram......................... 212
  Hiram Tune.................... 383
  Horace N...................... 221
  Lewis......................... 436
  (Locke-Brown), Mrs............ 98
  Louis.....................212, 383
  Lydia (Locke).............47, 102
  Luella....................198, 212
  Lurana (Boyd)................. 212
  Martha........................ 217
  Mary......................98, 209
  Mary (Dow).................... 100
  Mary (Freeman)................ 213
  Mary (Janvrin)................ 209
  Mary (Thompson)...........435, 436
  Melicent (Locke).............. 436
  Melvin L...................... 221
  Nancy L....................... 383
  Nancy (Locke).............97, 112
  Nathaniel.................97, 212
  Nellie (Lovell)............... 221
  Obadiah....................... 100
  Otis M....................221, 435, 436
  Sarah..................23, 45, 213, 252
  Stephen M..................... 102
  Walter........................ 435
  Winthrop...................... 98
  Emma G........................ 137
  James......................... 464
  Rhoda (Whittier).............. 137
  Simond........................ 137
  Susan (Johnson)............... 464
GRAFFAM, Lovina.................. 200
GRAFTON, Anna................106, 106
  Elizabeth W................... 106
  Elizabeth (Woodbridge)........ 106
  George W...................... 106
  Joseph........................ 106
  Patience (Woodbridge)......... 50
  William d..................... 106
  Woodbridge.................... 50
GRAHAM, Belle.................... 474
  Jane (Stevens)................ 90
  Thomas.....................90, 90
GRANT, Alexander................. 154
  Arthur J...................... 416
  Carrie (Yeartaw).............. 416
  Christopher................... 473
  Elsie d....................... 545
  Emily......................... 321
  Elizabeth (Tarlton)........... 240
  Elsie (Locke)................. 473
  Evelyn........................ 228
  Frazier J..................... 187
  Fred L........................ 416
  Freda (Gladding).............. 416
  Hannah........................ 111

INDEX OF NAMES

GRANT, Henrietta (Seavey)............ 228
  Henry L........................ 416
  Ida (Braman).................. 416
  Irene.......................... 416
  Jeremiah...................... 187
  Julia.......................... 473
  Lavinia (Locke)................ 187
  Levi.......................... 243
  Lucille........................ 416
  Lydia (Locke)................. 154
  Marie......................... 416
  Mary.....................108, 240
  Minnie........................ 440
  Nancy (Locke)................. 243
  Olive.......................... 83
  Richard G..................... 416
  Sarah E. d.................... 416
  Samuel........................ 240
  Timothy....................... 228
  Vernie R...................... 416
  Victor.....................416, 416
GRAVES, Elmer E................... 323
  Gertrude...................... 323
  Lester L....................... 323
  Walter E...................... 323
GRAY, Mr.......................... 83
  Abby.......................... 157
  Abigail.....................74, 158
  Alice.......................... 159
  Angelina...................... 158
  Annie......................... 159
  Annie (Copps)................. 159
  Annie (Ham).................. 159
  Barbar.....................74, 158
  Betsey.................157, 158, 158
  Caroline...................... 157
  Caroline (Wendell)............. 74
  Charles .155, 158, 158, 159, 159, 159, 159
  Clara......................... 158
  Clara (Woodman)............. 158
  Clarence S.................... 159
  C. M.......................... 483
  Cordelia...................... 286
  Dorothy..................74, 158, 158
  Dorothy (Otis)...........72, 74, 151
  Edwin......................... 159
  Eliza d....................... 159
  Elizabeth..................157, 158
  Elizabeth (Locke).............. 83
  Ella........................158, 159
  Ellen......................115, 159
  Ellen (Leach).................. 159
  Francis....................... 158
  Fred.......................... 159
  George.................158, 158, 159
  Hannah....................... 74
  Hannah (Foss)................. 158
  Hannah (Gray)..............74, 74
  Hannah J..................... 158
  Hannah (Mitchell)............. 157
  Hannah (Otis)................. 72
  Harriet........................ 158
  Hattie (Chester)............... 483
  Hattie (Pinder)................ 159
  Henry.................72, 74, 157, 158
  Hezekiah...................... 158
  Horace W..................... 159
  Ida................158, 159, 159, 308
  Jethro........................ 74
  Joanna (Hall)................. 74
  John.............72, 151, 158, 158
  Jonathan C................... 157
  Joseph..................74, 158, 279
  Josephine S................... 159
  Joshua B...................... 158
  Juliet (Woodman).............. 279
  Kate.......................... 159
  Lavinia A..................... 158
  Lavina (Perkins) 158
  Leonard S. R.................. 159

GRAY, Leonora..................... 159
  Lizzie......................... 159
  Louisa (DeRochemont).......... 159
  Lucetta....................... 68
  Lucretia (Pottle).............. 74
  Lucy.......................... 158
  Lydia.......................74, 525
  Mabel......................... 159
  Margaret P.................... 159
  Mary.......157, 158, 158, 159, 159, 159
  Mary Ann..................... 158
  Mary (Davis).................. 159
  Mary (Gray).................. 74
  Mary (Locke).................. 35
  Mary (Prime).................. 159
  Mary (Rand).................. 74
  Martha.................157, 158, 159
  Martha (Palmer).............. 159
  Minnie (Frizzell).............. 159
  Mowe......................... 159
  Oliver J....................... 159
  Otis M........................ 158
  Patty (Page)................... 73
  Ralph......................... 159
  Ruth.......................... 159
  Sadie......................... 159
  Sally.......................... 159
  Samuel........................ 159
  Sarah...............158, 158, 158, 159
  Sarah A...............158, 158, 158
  Sarah (Cym).................. 158
  Sarah (Roberts)............... 159
  Simeon L...................... 157
  Simon......................... 73
  Solomon........35, 74, 157, 158, 158
  Sophie........................ 158
  Stephen....................... 158
  Walter.....................159, 159
  Wendell....................158, 159
  Willard........................ 159
  William..................74, 74, 158
  William H................158, 159, 159
  Zerviah M..................... 159
GREELEY, Abigail................... 214
  Abigail (Smith)................ 214
  Albert........................ 383
  A. Jeremiah................... 214
  Annie......................... 166
  Charles....................... 383
  Cora d....................... 166
  Cynthia (Locke)............... 98
  Dudley d.................... 214
  Edward.....................98, 166
  Edward Nelson................ 77
  Ella.......................... 139
  Elmer G...................... 166
  Eunice B. (Noyes)............. 77
  Frank......................166, 383
  Fred E........................ 166
  George E...................... 166
  John.......................214, 214
  Helen (Huston)................ 165
  Horace W..................... 165
  Laurinda...................... 77
  Lillian (Boyd)................. 383
  Lucinda (Brown).............. 214
  Mary Ann (Noyes)............ 77
  (Merrill), Miss................ 66
  (Pitchworth), Miss............. 383
  Rensalaer..................... 77
  Sarah......................261, 384
  S. Lucinda.................... 213
  Thomas....................166, 383
GREEN, Mr......................... 416
  Abigail (Locke)............... 112
  Abigail (Sanders).............. 245
  Alonzo........................ 418
  Ann........................... 252
  Anna.......................... 249
  Annie.....................418, 494

INDEX OF NAMES

GREEN, Arthur..................271, 418
   Benjamin....................... 418
   Betsey......................... 281
   Celia (Procter)................. 386
   Charles................250, 317, 491
   Clarissa....................... 252
   Edward........................ 418
   Edwin......................... 418
   Eleanor (Locke)................ 268
   Elmer......................... 159
   Emma......................... 418
   Frank......................... 271
   Fred......................159, 491
   George....................127, 416
   Hannah (Locke)................ 416
   Hiram......................... 170
   Helen......................... 418
   James......................... 418
   John......................271, 418
   Jonathan...................... 112
   Joseph..................159, 159, 268
   Julietta........................ 127
   Lewis......................... 268
   Lucinda........................ 99
   Lucy......................397, 418
   Lucy (True).................... 271
   Margaret...................... 250
   Maria (Flanders)............... 418
   Martha........................ 327
   Martha S. (Trefethern)......... 144
   Mary....................97, 404, 545
   Mary (Lamper)................. 250
   Mary (Matteson)............... 170
   Mary A. (Parker).............. 127
   Mattie........................ 268
   Maude........................ 386
   Melinda....................... 418
   Melissa........................ 418
   Melvina....................... 418
   Meribah....................... 102
   Robert........................ 159
   Ruth (Mitchell)................ 418
   Sabrina....................... 418
   Sadie (Knowlton).............. 491
   Sally.......................... 484
   Sarah (Gray).................. 159
   Sarah Nightingale.............. 120
   Sherburn..................245, 386
   Susan (Johnson)............... 418
   Susan O. (Locke).............. 317
   Woodbury..................... 144
GREENLEAF, Abner.................. 410
   Albert H....................... 528
   Almira B...................... 411
   Almira (Locke)................ 240
   Amos.......................... 76
   Annah (Gardner-Marden)....... 396
   Etmar......................... 100
   Frank.....................411, 528
   Frederick d.................... 411
   Gardner....................... 396
   George G...................... 529
   Helen M....................... 529
   Isaac V........................ 100
   James.............240, 411, 528, 528
   Jennie (Hatfield)............... 411
   Jennie (Snyder)................ 411
   Julia (Harrie).................. 411
   Martha J...................... 529
   Mary D....................... 528
   (Mason), Miss................. 76
   Miriam (Bell).................. 410
   Myra C........................ 528
   Nancy (Page).................. 100
GREGG, Arthur, Rev................. 469
   Donald........................ 469
   Ida (Crowther)................ 469
   Marion........................ 469
GREGORY, Mary..................... 326
GRIFFIN, Ada (Lear)................ 486

GRIFFIN, Albert.................... 486
   Annie (Dodge)................. 486
   Fannie........................ 460
   George A...................... 486
   Henry......................... 486
   Ichabod G..................... 486
   James P....................... 282
   Joseph F. d................... 486
   Josephine (Locke-Lucy), Mrs.... 282
   Josiah......................... 485
   Julia (Bradford)................ 486
   Lilla M........................ 460
   Lydia (Barker)................. 485
   Lyman W...................... 486
   Mary.......................... 486
   Mary (Locke).................. 312
   Mildred A..................... 550
   Orwin.....................312, 550
   Sally.......................... 131
   Sarah......................99, 446
GRIFFITH, Ellen (Cass)............. 388
   Henry.....................267, 388
   Katherine (Moore)............. 267
   Linnie M...................... 516
   Mary Marshall, Mrs............ 516
   Nora Viola.................... 516
GRIGGS, Alice..................... 274
   Elmason...................... 274
   Miriam (Royce)................ 274
GRIMES, Attara.................... 476
GRISWOLD, Alice................... 369
   Caroline...................... 101
GROCUT, Viola.................... 513
GROSS, Charles H.................. 332
   Fannie (Locke-Young).......... 287
   Gilbert J...................... 495
   (Ingalls), Miss................. 50
   Jennie (Locke-Jones)........... 495
   William....................... 50
GROUT, Eleanor................... 213
GROVER, Alice (Pease)............. 332
   Charles....................... 287
   Dolly......................... 56
   Mary.......................... 464
GROW, Harriet E................... 133
   Lydia (Shaw).................. 133
   Peter......................... 133
GUESDON, Emilina.................. 96
GUILD, Bertha..................... 470
GUILFORD, Louisa.................. 351
GUNNISON, Pamelia................ 128
GURDY, Jacob..................... 104
   Julia (Hooper)................. 179
   Nancy......................... 49
   Stillman....................... 179
GUPTILL, Mr....................... 82
   Dr............................ 271
   Dorcas....................320, 147
   (Hooper), Miss................ 82
   Lizzie (True).................. 271
   William....................... 320
GUYON, Catherine.................. 86
GWYNNE, Mary A.................. 154
HACKETT, Mr...................... 308
   Josie (Locke-Hillsgrove)........ 308
HADCOCK, Beatrice L.............. 438
   Ceres......................... 438
   Ceres (Heywood).............. 438
   Editha........................ 438
   Edward W.................... 438
   Henry.....................256, 438
   Josephine..................... 438
   Sarah (Webster)............... 256
   Thora......................... 438
HADDAWAY, Hannah (Tate)......... 38
HADLEY, Ann..................... 274
   Carrie........................ 445
   Jane (Wallace)................ 452
   Philip......................... 452
HAINES, Abigail................... 24

INDEX OF NAMES

HAINES, Alice...... 307
  Betsey...... 76
  Emanuel...... 483
  Hannah...... 119
  Hannah (Knowles)...... 119
  Hannah (Wiggin)...... 44
  Jennie (Lamprey)...... 448
  John...... 44
  Joseph...... 33
  Mary...... 16
  Mary, Widow...... 33
  Mary (Lewis)...... 26
  Martha J...... 362
  Norman...... 448
  Olive...... 511
  Sarah...... 14
  Stephen...... 119
  William......26, 448
HALE, Elizabeth P...... 540
  Floyd O...... 539
  Frank S...... 539
  Gail (Perkins)...... 539
  Mary...... 199
  Robert L...... 540
  Sarah...... 215
HALEY, Alice...... 494
  Andrew...... 18
  Annie d...... 494
  Annie (Horn)...... 493
  Annie (Pearson)...... 496
  Charles P...... 496
  Daniel......318, 319, 494
  Deborah (Wilson)...... 18
  Dolly...... 78
  Eliza (Randall)...... 318
  Elizabeth...... 18
  Ella...... 479
  Ellen A...... 494
  Emma...... 494
  Gertrude...... 493
  Grace...... 494
  Hannah (Caswell-Failes)...... 319
  Hattie L...... 494
  Isaac M...... 78
  Isabella......395, 494
  Jacob......78, 78
  James......494, 494
  Jennie O...... 494
  Joseph B...... 494
  Josiah...... 494
  Julia (Chauncy)...... 493
  Leonora (Caswell)...... 494
  Lucy (Randall)...... 318
  Luella (Randall)...... 494
  Malinda...... 494
  Mary Ann...... 78
  Mary......73, 494, 494
  Mary (Locke)...... 41
  Mildred...... 493
  Olivia (Randall)......493, 494
  Otis...... 493
  Percy...... 493
  Richard...... 318
  Robert...... 41
  Ruth R. (Merrill)...... 78
  Samuel......479, 493, 494
  Sarah...... 479
  Thomas d...... 494
  Walter...... 494
  Wilbur J...... 496
  Willie d...... 494
HALL, Miss...... 60
  Abigail...... 552
  Almon...... 464
  Anna (Hunnewell)...... 39
  Annie (Warren)...... 386
  B...... 264
  Barbara...... 559
  Caroline...... 39
  Carrie...... 519

HALL, Charles......39, 143, 314
  Donald F...... 559
  Dorothy G...... 158
  E. E...... 264
  Ebenezer...... 39
  Edward W...... 513
  Elizabeth...... 39
  Ellen (Locke)...... 253
  Emily (Trefethern)...... 143
  Frank...... 283
  Fred...... 464
  George......25, 39, 176, 314
  Georgeanna...... 227
  Hannah J. (Gray)...... 158
  Helen F. (Locke)...... 513
  Ida...... 386
  James...... 386
  Jere, Dr...... 253
  Joanna...... 74
  John...... 158
  Kitty D...... 216
  Lizzie (Leavitt)...... 314
  Lorena...... 481
  Louisa...... 39
  Lucy S. (Rogers)...... 112
  Lydia...... 52
  Lyman...... 481
  Martha...... 511
  Martha (West)...... 276
  Mary...... 39
  Mary (Knox)...... 314
  Mertie (Young)...... 464
  Mildred...... 464
  Minnie...... 306
  Nellie (Dunbar)...... 176
  Olevia S...... 112
  Otis M...... 158
  Peter...... 39
  Rena (Tilton)...... 283
  Ruth F...... 559
  Samuel...... 112
  Sarah...... 264
  Sarah M...... 248
  Solomon H...... 158
  Stacy...... 158
  Susannah (Hunnewell)...... 39
  Susie...... 188
  Walter...... 464
HALLET, Date S...... 86
  Lucy A...... 145
HAM, Addie S...... 159
  Annie...... 159
  Augustus...... 301
  Cecelia (Salmon)...... 159
  Charles W...... 159
  Eleanor (Locke)...... 23
  Eliza...... 202
  Eva E...... 159
  Fannie (Locke)...... 301
  George H...... 159
  Hannah (Otis)...... 151
  Israel...... 272
  Jane (Otis)...... 72
  John H...... 64
  Jonathan...... 151
  Josephine (Gray)...... 159
  Lewis...... 151
  Lizzie...... 159
  Martha (Otis)...... 151
  Mary......122, 247
  Mary (Foss)...... 64
  Mehitable (Hayes)...... 272
  Nathaniel...... 72
  William...... 23
HAMILTON, Belinda...... 498
  Etta...... 321
  Ivory...... 498
  Sarah A...... 219
  Susan...... 328
HAMLIN, Maggie...... 468

INDEX OF NAMES

HAMMOND, Abbie................ 312
  Agnes (Doloff)................ 224
  Agnes M...................... 424
  Alexander.................... 190
  Anna......................... 359
  Elizabeth.................... 400
  Harris....................... 224
  Janette...................... 506
  Julia A. (Reynolds)........... 122
  Priscilla (Locke)............. 190
  Sarah........................ 396
  Theodore..................... 122
HANCOCK, Mrs.................. 303
  Franklin..................... 477
  Mary......................... 477
  Mary (Lyon).................. 477
HANCOX, Effie B. (Locke)...... 333
  John A....................... 333
HANNA, Margaret............... 450
HANNON, George............522, 522
  Eleanor...................... 522
  Helen (Locke)................ 522
HANKINS, Frank................ 447
  Zadie (Lamprey).............. 447
  Esther....................... 447
  Ralph........................ 447
HANSCOM, Abbie................ 504
  Albert W..................... 518
  Frances E. (Locke)........... 317
  Lydia........................ 73
  Mary......................... 312
  Mary (Neal).................. 518
  William...................... 317
HANSON. HANSEN.
  Andrew....................... 404
  Carmen (Mathers)............. 434
  Edward....................... 568
  Ellen d...................... 434
  Emma E....................... 105
  Enrique...................... 434
  Grace T...................... 434
  Harry....................434, 434
  Jessie....................... 321
  John......................... 155
  Martha d..................... 434
  Martha (Locke)............... 254
  Natalie...................... 434
  Nathaniel.................... 254
  Nellie (Locke)............... 568
  Philena (Pickering).......... 404
  Richard L.................... 434
  Rosanna...................... 237
  Rossina...................... 169
  Ruth......................... 510
  Sarah........................ 510
  Sarah (Runnels).............. 155
  Stacy L...................... 434
  Susie........................ 232
HAPPINEY, Nellie.............. 132
HARDING, Abiah................ 42
  Lettie....................... 356
  Lucy......................... 163
HARDY, Abby................... 514
  Arthur, Rev.................. 554
  Barbara...................... 264
  Barbara (Shirley).........265, 445
  Benjamin M................... 79
  Blanche (Talbert)............ 482
  Charles A.................... 514
  Eddie........................ 482
  Eleanor...................... 169
  Elizabeth.................... 368
  Elizabeth (Martins).......... 554
  Emma......................... 376
  George F..................... 169
  Jennie (Randall)............. 493
  Joseph....................... 265
  Louis B...................... 169
  Mary......................... 264
  Peter.....................265, 445

HARDY, Richard................ 554
  Rose......................... 323
  Sarah (Lamprey).............. 265
  Susanna Marston (Locke)...... 79
  Walter....................... 493
HARGRAVES, Howarth............ 277
  Marcy (Locke)................ 277
HARLOW, Annie................. 358
  Arabella..................... 358
  Bradford..................... 190
  Edward....................... 358
  Letitia...................... 358
  Letitia (Locke).............. 190
  Mary......................86, 358
HARMON, Carrie................ 136
  Frank........................ 136
  Hannah....................... 178
  Henry........................ 347
  Martha (Fenderson).......... 347
  Mary A. (Locke).............. 136
  Orson........................ 136
  Sarah J...................181, 181
HARRADEN, Fred................ 495
  Louisa (Randall)............. 495
HARRET, Abigail............233, 397
  Charles...................... 397
HARRIE, Julia................. 411
HARRIMAN, Mr.................. 162
  Ann (Jacobs)................. 320
  Charlotte.................... 542
  Dora (Locke)................. 320
  Eliza A. (Ladd).............. 62
  Elizabeth.................... 542
  Elizabeth (Locke)............ 568
  George....................320, 437
  Hannah (Allen-Locke)......... 45
  Helen (Clifford)............. 162
  James......................62, 283
  Jesse........................ 45
  Joel......................... 320
  Mabel (Locke)................ 437
  Mary (Locke)................. 283
  Roger L...................... 542
  Samuel....................... 568
HARRINGTON, Elizabeth (Dyer).. 338
  Fred......................... 338
HARRIS, Ephraim............... 116
  Georgeanna (Hook)............ 291
  Grace........................ 544
  Grace (Seavey)............... 469
  Honor........................ 525
  James........................ 291
  Jane......................... 189
  Jennie....................... 229
  Louisa (Locke)............... 525
  Luther R..................... 525
  Margaret A. L. (Locke)....... 116
  Mary...................264, 264, 443
  Mary (Noyes)................. 162
  Noah......................... 162
  Robert....................469, 544
  Samuel L..................... 264
  William H.................... 264
HARRISON, Frank............... 425
  Mary (Beaton), Mrs........... 511
HART, Abbie................... 188
  Abigail (Pitman)............. 240
  Albert....................... 462
  Amy.......................... 116
  Carrie (Cochran)............. 240
  George....................... 240
  John P....................... 240
  Lizzie....................... 462
  Madeline (Violette).......... 462
  Martha (Locke)............... 240
HARTFORD, Jennie.............. 288
HARTSHORN, Harry.............. 399
  Helen (Locke)................ 399
  William...................... 399
HARTWELL, Emaline (Ladd)...... 62

INDEX OF NAMES

HARTWELL, John.................... 62
HARVEY, Rhoda.................... 31
HASBROOK, Edward.............434, 434
   John V......................... 434
   Natalie (Hanson)................ 434
   Robert L....................... 434
HASKELL, ———.................... 19
   Adaline (Clarke)................ 211
   Addie M....................... 382
   Clara.......................... 164
   Edmund N..................... 382
   Jacob d....................... 382
   Jacob M....................... 211
   Marcia (Leavitt)................ 19
   Waldo C....................... 382
HASKIN, Lucy...................... 169
HASSAM, George A.................. 262
   Leonora (Babb)................. 262
HASTINGS, Edna.................... 50
   Huldah (Moulton).............. 58
   Jennett........................ 58
   Jonathan....................... 58
   Lambert A..................... 394
   Larkin......................... 58
   Luella......................... 58
   Lurancy....................... 58
   Meredith H.................... 394
   Noah.......................... 58
   Sara (Heath).................. 394
   Seraphim...................... 58
HASWELL, Hannah.................. 39
HATCH, Mr........................ 293
   Mrs........................... 163
   Abigail (Neal)................. 398
   Anderson...................... 498
   Cushing....................... 398
   David......................... 54
   Edward....................... 398
   Elizabeth...................... 142
   Elizabeth (Foss)............... 54
   Emma......................293, 498
   Grace M....................... 167
   Irving......................... 510
   Jennie (Locke)................. 510
   Lillian......................... 487
   M. M.......................... 471
   Mary (Delano)................. 471
   Mary (Locke).................. 293
   Mary (Pierce).................. 468
   Nellie......................... 398
   Ruth.......................... 298
   Samuel........................ 510
   Sarah (Hanson)................ 510
   Sarah (Lord)................... 498
   William........................ 468
HATFIELD, Jennie................... 411
HATHORNE, Carlus G................ 114
   Frances (Gilman).............. 114
   Harry......................... 390
   Mabel (Doloff)................. 390
HAUGHTON, Andrew J., Dr.......... 327
   Andrew........................ 497
   Bertha (Best).................. 498
   Charles Edward................ 497
   Dewey......................... 555
   Elizabeth (Potter).............. 497
   Estella (Bond)................. 497
   Evaline........................ 556
   Frederick L................ 497, 497
   George........................ 497
   Helen G....................... 555
   Hiram.....................497, 497
   James W...................... 498
   Jennie (Ridgway).............. 497
   Jesse P........................ 497
   Josephine...................... 497
   Laura (Lackey)................ 497
   Lewis F....................... 498
   Mary (Allen).................. 498
   Mayfair....................... 555
HAUGHTON, Nicholas J.,..........498, 498
   Pamelia (Locke)................ 327
   Surelda (Willber).............. 497
HAVEN, Clarissa.................... 251
HAWKES, Abbie.................... 166
   Ida (Merrill)................... 166
   Orrin.......................... 166
HAWKINS, Lewis.................... 227
   Lillian (Page-Adams)........... 227
HAWLEY, Della.................... 279
HAWSE. HAWES
   Amos A....................... 568
   Charles Sumner................ 437
   Ellen M........................ 113
   Emaline (Locke)................ 113
   Frances (Locke)................ 568
   Frances (Wilson)............... 437
   George E. d................... 437
   Henrietta...................... 437
   Marianna J. (Locke)........113, 255
   Mary E........................ 113
   Mary (Turner)................. 113
   William 113, 113, 255
HAYDEN, Ernest................... 413
   Harriet (Smith)................ 413
   Laura A. d.................... 413
   Minnie E....................... 413
   Thomas........................ 413
HAYES, Angelina................... 125
   Caroline....................... 234
   Elizabeth H.................... 124
   Ellen A........................ 167
   Ephraim....................... 406
   Fanny......................... 30
   Georgeanna (Locke)............. 222
   Hannah........................ 303
   Hannah (Demeritt).............. 124
   Hannah Locke)................. 34
   Joan (Winkley)................. 286
   Joshua........................ 34
   Laura......................... 237
   Lilla.......................... 347
   Lydia......................... 283
   Mary.......................... 27
   Mary (Main).................. 121
   Mehitable...................... 272
   Robert........................ 34
   Rosamond (Dame).............. 406
   Samuel........................ 124
   Sarah......................... 237
   Susan......................... 122
   Tamsen, Mrs................... 54
   Watson........................ 286
   Wentworth..................... 121
   William........................ 222
HAYNES, Abbie.................... 435
   Frances L...................... 444
   Francis G...................... 444
   Harriet (Williams).............. 444
   James M....................... 158
   Mary (Gray-Moses)............. 158
HAYWOOD, James................... 230
   Mary.......................... 230
HAZARD, Una D.................... 491
HAZELTINE, William, Rev........... 95
HAZELTON, Elizabeth (Hutchins)....... 14
   Huldah (Marston).............. 140
   James.......................14, 140
   Jessie......................... 354
   John........................14, 140
   Judith (Webster).............. 14
   Laura......................... 267
   Lucretia (Hills)................ 267
   Mary.......................... 14
   Philip......................... 14
   Ruth (Ladd)................... 14
   Susanna....................... 140
   Thomas........................ 267
   Tryphena...................... 14
HAZEN, Mr........................ 141

INDEX OF NAMES

HAZEN, Abbie (Rand).............. 141
  Bernice M...................... 512
  Edith N........................ 512
  Freeman B...................... 512
  Herman......................... 367
  Mary (Bailey).................. 512
  Mary (Merriam)................. 367
  Robert D....................... 512
  Sarah L........................ 512
HEALD, Cora....................... 331
  Phebe.......................... 199
HEALEY, Frances................... 381
  George......................... 381
  Harriet (Dodge)................ 381
  Irene G........................ 130
  Wells W........................ 381
HEATH, Albert, Dr.,............444, 444
  Clara (Locke).................. 232
  David.......................... 62
  Dorcas (Whitemore)............. 502
  Ernest......................... 482
  Hannah......................... 446
  Hiram.......................... 502
  John L......................... 394
  Kathleen L..................... 517
  Lilla M........................ 341
  Mary L......................... 394
  Mary L......................... 517
  Muriel C....................... 517
  Ray (Lamprey).................. 444
  Sara L......................... 394
  Sarah.......................... 289
  Sarah (Blood).................. 482
  Tryphena (Ladd-Goodwin)........ 62
  William........................ 232
  Winnie M. (Hill)............... 394
HEBBARD, Mabel.................... 442
HECKER, Caroline.................. 326
  George V....................... 326
  Isaac, Rev..................... 326
  Josephine (Wentworth).......... 326
HEDGES, Arthur................296, 296
  Effie. d....................... 296
  Ellen (Page)................... 296
  George......................... 296
  Harriet........................ 300
  Mabel.......................... 296
  Ross........................... 296
  Sarah A. d..................... 296
HELM, Nancy....................... 305
HEMINWAY, Alpheus................. 243
  Clarence....................... 243
  Eugenie........................ 243
  Georgeanna..................... 243
  Susan (Locke).................. 243
  Waldo.......................... 243
HENDERSON, Alba L................. 457
  Augusta A...................... 150
  Carroll C...................... 457
  Catherine (Thurston)........... 197
  Charles........................ 197
  Frank L........................ 457
  Mary E......................... 457
  Samuel......................... 277
  Samuel L....................... 457
  Sarah E........................ 457
  Sarah Izetta (Locke)........... 204
  Sarah (Locke-Richardson)....... 277
  Thomas......................... 204
HENDRICKS, Katherine.............. 227
HEPWORTH, Mary (Locke)............ 11
  Wm............................. 11
HERBERT, Augustus d............... 259
  Benjamin F..................... 115
  Carlena........................ 259
  Charles........................ 259
  Edna........................... 259
  Filenda (Locke)................ 115
  Finetta M...................... 259
  Jennie (Kimball)............... 259

HERBERT, Lena..................... 373
  Mary C......................... 94
HERKIMER, Della................... 174
  Nicholas, Genl................. 340
HERMINS, John..................... 565
  Miss........................... 565
HERRICK, Mr....................... 288
  Asenath........................ 367
  Belle (Babb)................... 288
  Daniel..................79, 168, 168
  Elizabeth (Locke).............. 79
  Fannie (Lamson)................ 168
  Frances (Plummer).............. 168
  Gladys......................... 336
  Jerusha (Cole)................. 168
  John......................168, 336
  Lincoln........................ 168
  Mary Jerusha................... 168
  Rodney....................168, 336
  Susie.......................... 168
HERSEY, Caroline (Locke).......... 185
  George T....................... 185
  Grace P........................ 353
HERSOM, Alton E................... 328
  Eunice (Locke)................. 328
  Lorenzo........................ 499
  Martha A....................... 499
  Martha (Tibbetts).............. 499
HETT, Anna (Lord-Mooney-Ackerman). 400
  Fred D......................... 522
  Gretchen A..................... 522
  Marion O....................... 522
  Valentine...................... 400
HEWETT. HEWITT.
  Caroline....................... 356
  Curtis......................... 364
  Gladys M. d.................... 378
  Judd........................... 364
  Julia (Locke).................. 364
  Katherine (Locke).............. 378
  Waterman, Prof................. 378
  Worthington.................... 364
HEWS, Lydia....................... 154
HEYWOOD, Angela (Tilton).......... 255
  Ceres.......................... 438
  Dolly (Amazeen)................ 519
  Effie.......................... 485
  Eliza.......................... 121
  Emily.......................... 390
  Eva d.......................... 519
  Ezra........................... 255
  Frances (Shapleigh-Lindsay).... 312
  Gladys......................... 519
  Harriet (Batson)............... 397
  Irving......................... 519
  Jennie (Williams).............. 519
  Thomas.....................397, 519
  Zimri.......................... 312
HIBBARD, Mr....................... 59
  Joanna (Moulton)............... 59
HICKOK, Edna...................... 425
  Ella (Rix)..................... 425
  Frank.......................... 425
  Myron.......................... 425
HICKS, Ida A...................... 141
HIDDEN, Emaline (Hovey-Locke)..... 258
  George......................... 258
HIGGINS, Edith (Tucker)........... 518
  James F........................ 518
  Martha (Magoon)................ 536
  Mehitable...................... 34
  Rosa B......................... 563
  Ruth T......................... 518
  Samuel......................... 563
  Stella......................... 563
  William....................518, 536
HIGHT, Alice...................... 256
  E.............................. 297
  Elizabeth (Watson-Kimball)..... 297
HILDEBRANT, Mary (Blood), Mrs..... 276

INDEX OF NAMES

HILL, Mr. 345
　Miss 134, 179
　Abbie 223
　Abigail (Locke) 155
　Alma G. 480
　Alma (Nelson) 480
　Alpheus (Moore) 154
　Amelia. 258
　Andrew S. 329
　Annie 347, 368
　Annie (Libby) 347
　Arianna. 329
　Benjamin 156, 195, 330
　Burleigh F. 304
　Catherine. 201
　(Chapman), Miss 329
　Charles. 305, 327
　Clara. 387
　Clarence. 233
　Daniel. 225
　Dorcas (Locke) 187
　Dorothy L. 330
　Dudley. 124
　Edith. 157
　Eliza (Freeman). 373
　Elizabeth (Hayes-Locke-Blake) ... 124
　Elizabeth. 304
　Elizabeth (Locke) 66
　Elora (True-Pecker) 304
　Enoch W. 223
　Elvira (Newbegin), Mrs. 355
　Fannie (Locke). 386
　Fannie (Smith) 329
　Fanny. 157
　Fred B. 329
　George. 154, 330
　Georgie (Smith) 223
　Grace (Emery) 330
　Hannah (Young) 225
　Hazen. 480
　Irene. 440
　John 103, 157, 187, 203
　　　　　　222, 222, 223, 373
　John Franklin. 355
　John T. 157, 157, 373
　Josiah. 66, 304
　Laura (Kimball) 222, 222
　Laura (Locke) 305
　Levi. 49
　Lucia (Locke) 203
　Lucretia. 267
　Lydia. 170
　Martha. 304, 329
　Martha (Green) 327
　Mary E. 195, 373
　Mary (Burleigh) 139
　Mary (Locke). 49, 103, 154
　Mary (Palmer) 254
　Mary (Prescott) 195
　Mary (Tucker-Foss) 345
　Mehitable (Brown) 441
　Mehitable Green 154
　Mehitable (Locke) 154
　Nellie. 463
　Olive d 329
　Patience (Meader) 49
　Peletiah. 154, 154
　Perley. 441
　Polly (Clark) 329
　Sally I. 104
　Samuel 49, 139, 347
　Sarah (Locke). 156, 233
　Sarah (Locke-Foss) 157
　Sarah M. 329
　Sarah Olive. 329
　Susan. 304
　Susan (Brown). 223
　William. 155, 329, 386
　Winnie M. 394
　Winnie (Stanton) 329

HILL, Vienna. 157
　Vienna O. (Locke) 157
HILLARD, Flora (Jewell) 488
　John C. 488
　Leon. 488
　Mildred. 488
　Pauline. 366
　Russell. 488
　Will 488
HILLSGROVE, Fred. 308
　Josephine (Locke) 308
　Susie. 308
HILTON, Harry L. 406
　Helen (Locke) 406
　Martha d 445
　Martha (Lamprey) 264
　Mary (Tilton) 445
　Myra. 445
　Nellie. 445
　William. 264
　Winthrop. 445
HINES, Addie 297
　Emma J. 164
　Mary. 249
HINKLEY, Margaret. 477
HINMAN, Ellen. 300
　Frank. 58
　Freeman. 58
　Hannah (Moulton) 58
　Hannah (Moulton-Paddleford) 58
HITCHCOCK, Lorenda. 116
HOAG, Emaline. 81
　Louisa. 212
HOAR, Anna. 117
　Julia B. 357
HOBART, Patience 229
HOBBS, Abbie. 195
　Annabel. 178
　Edwin J. 178
　Elizabeth J. 67
　Frank E. 178
　George S. 178
　Hannah (Felch) 178
　Huldah. 31
　James. 140
　Jonathan. 67, 567
　Julia M. 198
　Lucy. 31
　Mary. 69
　Mary (Berry) 67, 567
　Mary (Towle) 140
　Sarah. 30, 193
　Susan (Emery) 178
　Thomas H. 178
HODGDON, Alexander. 310
　Alton F. 500
　Augustus W. 493
　Benjamin. 473
　Charles. 329, 475, 500
　Clara (Williams-Randall) 493
　Doris. 501
　Etta (Hussey) 329
　George. 389
　Guy. 501
　Hannah. 523
　Hannah (Foster) 473
　Harriet A. 137
　Harry B. 500
　Howard. 501
　John. 500, 501
　Julia (Leary) 501
　Lavinia. 156
　Mabel. 501
　Mabel (Huntoon) 501
　Martha (Locke) 473
　May L. 483
　Oliff (Drake) 501
　Olivia A. 142
　Phineas. 137
　Raymond. 501

INDEX OF NAMES 637

HODGDON, Richard 25
    Sally........................... 64
    Sarah (Hurd).................... 137
    Sarah (Locke-Fowler)............ 389
    Sarah (Walker)................. 310
    Susanna (Locke)................. 25
    Sylvia (Mills).................. 500
    Winnie......................... 501
HODGE, Almira J. (Locke)............ 137
    Clara........................... 418
    Elias........................... 244
    Jessie.......................... 244
    John A.......................... 137
    Louisa (Chandler).............. 137
    Martha.......................... 92
    Nancy (Locke)................... 244
    Stephen......................... 137
HODGES, Andrew..................... 390
    Elizabeth....................... 225
HOFF, Andrew....................... 385
    Edith (Ormsby).................. 385
    Mary L.......................... 319
    Mary (Trefethern)............... 319
    William......................... 319
HOGAN, Sarah....................... 447
HOIRNER, Huldah H.................. 523
HOITT. HOYT, MISS................... 32
    Abigail P. (Locke).............. 122
    Alberton G...............274, 274
    Alice (Griggs).................. 274
    Ann (Hadley).................... 274
    Belle S......................... 274
    Benjamin.............191, 191, 201
    Bertha (Hussey)................. 556
    Betsey (Gove)................... 364
    Betsey J........................ 273
    Betsey (Piper).................. 273
    Blanche......................... 452
    Byron D......................... 132
    Carrie.......................... 501
    Catherine (Locke)............... 191
    Charles E....................... 209
    Charlotte....................... 201
    Emma H. (Fogg).................. 132
    Esther M........................ 556
    Eugene, Dr...................... 452
    Georgeanna...................... 274
    Gilman....................132, 209
    Gladys.......................... 274
    Goram W., Major................. 122
    Grover.......................... 556
    Hannah.................122, 123, 124
    Horace.......................... 364
    Ida B........................... 274
    Ira Gustave..................... 274
    Josephine (Hoyt)................ 191
    Julia (Burrell)................. 274
    Leander......................... 274
    Lizzie.......................... 364
    Lucy A.......................... 273
    Lydia (Buzzell)................. 124
    Mary......................202, 274
    Mary (Gove)..................... 209
    Mary A. (Jewell)................ 132
    Nancy........................... 511
    Ralph H......................... 274
    Rhoda........................... 430
    Samuel......................273, 274
    Sarah........................... 54
    Sarah (Barret).................. 452
    Stephen......................... 124
    Sylvia d........................ 274
HOLDEN, Agnes (Locke-Tryder)....... 356
    Ernest.......................... 436
    Ethel........................... 436
    Fred............................ 436
    George.......................... 356
    Hannah (Otis)................... 152
    Hattie (McMurphy)............... 436
    James G......................... 152

HOLDEN, John S..................... 419
    Lilla........................... 436
    Mabel (Sanders)................. 416
    Nancy........................... 189
    Royal D......................... 419
HOLGATE, Sarah..................... 262
HOLLAND, Catherine................. 421
HOLLAR, Emma....................... 532
HOLLISTER, Lucy.................... 278
HOLLON, Mary....................... 227
HOLMES, Miss....................... 140
    Ada P........................... 496
    Andrew.......................... 146
    Freddie......................... 320
    Hannah (Locke-Ferguson)......... 146
    Hannah (Locke-Ferguson-Holmes).. 146
    Herman.......................... 135
    James........................... 496
    Joseph.....................146, 496
    Laura (Farnum).................. 320
    Lorinda......................... 135
    Maria........................... 145
    Mary.......................320, 567
    Mehitable (Bunker) Mrs.......... 122
    Melissa (Saunders).............. 135
    Munroe.......................... 320
    Nellie.......................... 320
    Olive........................... 567
    Sadie........................... 385
    Sarah E. (Trefethern)........... 143
    Stella L........................ 496
    Susan........................... 324
    William......................143, 567
HOLRIDGE, James B.................. 300
    Mary (Chick).................... 300
HOLT, Mr........................... 457
    Abigail (Locke-Sanders)......... 131
    Hannah (Woodman)................ 278
    Henry........................... 278
    Lydia (Main).................... 457
    Marcia.......................... 477
    Martha.......................... 474
    William K....................... 131
HOMER, Elizabeth................... 280
HONDLETTE, Carrie E................ 167
HOOD, Alice........................ 368
    Captain......................... 277
    Elisha, Capt.................... 42
    Joseph E........................ 171
    Mary (Fiske).................... 171
    Miriam (Locke).................. 42
    Miribah (Main).................. 277
HOOK, Alonzo....................... 291
    Charles G....................... 131
    Edwin........................... 291
    Elbridge........................ 291
    Eliza (Locke)................... 131
    Francena........................ 131
    George.......................... 291
    Georgeanna...................... 291
    Hannah........................98, 206
    Harrison........................ 291
    Henry.......................131, 291
    H. W............................ 291
    Ida (Colby)..................... 291
    Jane........................267, 291
    Justin.......................... 291
    Levi............................ 291
    Lucy (Watts).................... 291
    Mary F.......................... 291
    Mary (Langley), Mrs............. 130
    Melissa......................... 291
    Michael......................... 291
    Parna T. (Locke)................ 131
    (Pollard), Miss................. 291
    Rachel.......................... 291
    Samuel......................291, 291
    Sarah........................... 291
    Simeon.......................... 291
    Sophie (Stowe).................. 291

INDEX OF NAMES

HOOPER, Alice M.................... 179
  Ann (Emery).................... 179
  Benjamin....................... 179
  Benjamin Hill.................. 179
  Betsey (Locke)................. 41
  Caleb.......................... 179
  Daniel O. S.................... 179
  Daniel S....................... 82
  Elizabeth (Dyer)............... 179
  (Hill), Miss................... 179
  John........................... 82
  Joseph......................41, 82
  Julia A.....................179, 179
  Mary E......................... 179
  Miriam (Locke)................. 82
  Stephen........................ 179
  Thomas......................... 179
  Tristram....................... 82
  William........................ 82
HOPKINS, Cornelia (Carlton)........ 377
  Edith (Copp)................... 376
  Helen.......................... 377
  John........................... 376
  Stephen........................ 377
HOPKINSON, Annie................... 180
HOPP, Ann (Locke).................. 55
  William........................ 55
HORN, Mr........................... 495
  Abigail (Tebbetts)............. 328
  Annie.......................... 493
  Arthur T....................... 498
  Benjamin....................155, 328
  Bertha......................... 498
  Betsey (Main).................. 123
  Camela (Horn).................. 328
  Charles H...................... 498
  Chester A...................... 498
  Edith (Berry).................. 498
  Ethel (Roberts)................ 498
  Eva M.......................... 344
  Gershom........................ 328
  Grace (Plummer)................ 498
  Guy H. d....................... 498
  Jeremiah....................... 328
  John B......................498, 498
  Jonathan....................... 123
  Lavina......................... 231
  Lydia (Parsons)................ 328
  Martha......................... 498
  Martha (Locke)................. 155
  Mary (Keir).................... 498
  Mary (Randall)................. 495
  Ralph.......................... 498
  Ruth........................498, 498
  Sarah (Meserve)................ 328
  Simon Locke.................... 328
  William........................ 328
HORNER, Charles.................... 515
  Fanny (Ballard)................ 515
HORNY, Adelaide (Webster).......... 250
  Georgianna..................... 250
  Samuel S....................... 250
  Thomas, Jr..................... 250
HORR, Alfred R..................... 442
  Amy............................ 442
  Charles W...................260, 440
  Clinton d...................... 442
  Edward......................... 442
  Elsa........................... 442
  Esther (Lang).................. 260
  Harley M....................... 442
  Mabel (Hebbard)................ 442
  Margaret (Barnard)............. 442
  Martha (Umbstaetter)........... 442
  Norton T....................... 442
  Ruth........................... 442
HORTON, Mr......................... 361
  Alfred......................... 475
  Charlotte (Locke).............. 475
  Eugene......................... 475

HORTON, Hannah (Tucker)............ 361
  Harry.......................... 361
  Henry.......................377, 377
  Lizzie......................132, 361
  Louise......................... 447
  Sarah (Noyes).................. 377
HOSKINS, Hannah.................... 58
HOTCHKISS, Mary C.................. 122
HOUGHTON, Carroll.................. 188
  Edna (Locke)................... 188
  Frank R........................ 188
HOUSTON, James B................... 329
  Sarah (Hill)................... 329
HOVEY, Albert P.................... 361
  Emaline.....................115, 258
  Mary (Kimball)................. 361
HOWARD, Abbie (Hill)............... 223
  Abigail........................ 35
  Albert O....................... 459
  Anna........................... 328
  Arthur D....................... 459
  Betsey......................... 73
  Emma (Whitney)................. 459
  Estelle........................ 428
  Esther......................... 72
  Etola A........................ 388
  Etta G......................... 459
  Frank.......................... 388
  Fred........................... 388
  John........................160, 455
  Joseph W....................... 223
  Julia (Nash)................... 383
  Hannah......................... 72
  Levi........................... 281
  Lizzie......................... 455
  Lizzie (Owen).................. 459
  Lydia.......................105, 191
  Maria (Locke-Foote)............ 281
  Marion......................... 459
  Martha......................... 455
  Mary Ann....................... 388
  Sarah.......................... 160
  Sidney W....................... 388
  Stanton B...................... 459
  William G., Prof............... 383
HOWE, Abbie........................ 215
  Adelaide....................... 428
  B. V........................... 215
  Frances (Dearborn)............. 101
  Gertrude F..................... 384
  Irena.......................... 215
  Lydia (Varnum)................. 215
  Lyman B........................ 215
  Mae L.......................... 384
  Mary (Shaw).................... 428
  Mary (Perry)................... 215
  Mary (Varnum).................. 215
  Moses, Elder................... 101
  Moses G........................ 215
  Sarah.......................... 276
  Thomas......................... 428
  William S...................... 215
HOWELL, Miss....................... 448
HOWLAND, Henrietta................. 229
  Hattie......................... 229
HOXIE, Abbie....................336, 336
  Elizabeth M.................... 337
  Ella (Whitman)................. 336
  Joseph......................171, 336
  Mary........................... 336
  Mary E. (Locke)................ 171
  M. Emma........................ 337
  Phebe (Carder)................. 336
  Warren L....................... 336
  Willard d...................... 336
  Winnifred...................... 336
HUBBARD, Addie Estey............... 349
  Alma (Collins)................. 349
  Doris A........................ 349
  George W....................... 183

INDEX OF NAMES

HUBBARD, George Walter 349
    Henry.......................... 89
    Lizzie (Decker)................. 183
    Lottie Maria.................... 349
    Mary C. (Little)................ 89
    Nellie.......................... 396
    Sarah........................... 409
HUBBS, Henry...................... 269
    Jane (Phelps)................... 269
HUCKINS, Miss..................... 104
    Abbie (Whitehouse).............. 273
    Alden........................... 452
    Alice........................... 273
    Andrew.......................... 273
    Edna T.......................... 451
    Ethel (Scruton)................. 452
    Everett......................... 452
    Hannah.......................... 273
    John....................122, 273, 452
    Laura......................452, 452
    Lucy C.......................... 273
    Maria........................... 273
    Maria (Chamberlain)............. 273
    Mary....................273, 451, 452
    Mary B. (Locke)................. 122
    Sylvester....................... 273
HUDSON, William................... 138
    Sarah (Murdock-Locke)........... 138
HUGGINS, Mehitable................ 34
HUGHES, Leonora (Goodwin)......... 327
    Matilda......................... 229
    William N....................... 327
HULL, Catherine (Locke)........... 276
    Emma A.......................... 455
    James, Capt..................... 276
HUMPHREYS, Adel C. d.............. 331
    Caroline........................ 197
    Cecil........................... 331
    Charles W....................... 331
    Clifton S....................... 331
    Cora............................ 331
    George......................159, 331
    Grace (Collis).................. 331
    Grace S......................... 331
    Julia........................... 331
    June............................ 331
    Lydia (Shannon)................. 331
    Mabel (Waldron)................. 331
    Margaret (Gray)................. 159
    Martha, Mrs..................... 162
    Mildred J....................... 331
    Philip C........................ 331
    Stewart S....................... 331
HUNDLEY, Josie H.................. 161
HUNKINS, Ada (Locke).............. 202
    Ellery D........................ 202
    Eva d........................... 202
    Harry........................... 202
    Ira A........................... 202
    Maria........................... 202
    Mark............................ 3
HUNNEWELL, Anna................... 39
    Anne (Mitchell)................. 39
    Charles......................... 39
    Edwin........................... 39
    Elijah........................21, 39
    Hannah.......................... 39
    Jerusha W. (Small).............. 39
    Lucy............................ 39
    Lucy (Barker)................... 39
    Lyman........................... 36
    Margaret (Lovett)............... 39
    Mary............................ 39
    Nathaniel....................... 39
    Patience........................ 39
    Rebecca (Locke)................. 21
    Susannah........................ 39
    William......................... 39
    Zerubbabel...................... 39
HUNT, Eliza, Mrs.................. 83

HUNT, George...................... 5
    Hannah R........................ 180
    Nellie.......................... 290
    Simon........................... 180
HUNTOON, Anna (Emery)............. 415
    Benjamin........................ 47
    Esther (Locke).................. 226
    Frank R......................... 415
    James C......................... 415
    Homer C......................... 415
    Mabel........................... 501
    Mehitable (Page)................ 47
    Warner.......................... 226
HUNTRESS, Betsey.................. 568
    Jemima.......................... 252
HURD, Miss........................ 147
    Betsey.......................... 54
    Caroline........................ 317
    Fidelia (Locke)................. 236
    John C.......................... 236
    Mary............................ 317
    Sarah........................... 137
    Webster......................... 236
    William C....................... 317
HURLBERT, Hannah.................. 440
HUSE, Mary........................ 409
HUSSEY, Mr........................ 353
    Abbie (Locke)................... 420
    Alice (Thompson)................ 328
    Alston G........................ 556
    Ann M........................... 329
    Annie (Gerry)................... 500
    Beatrice........................ 500
    Bertha L........................ 556
    Cecelia (Bernier)............... 500
    Celia (Fall).................... 329
    Celia (Preble).................. 500
    Charles.....................329, 500
    Clara (Kelley).................. 329
    Dora (Vickah)................... 353
    Etta G.......................... 329
    Edith A......................... 500
    Elmer E......................... 500
    Fanny L......................... 557
    Freeman A....................... 329
    Harriet d....................... 329
    Howard E........................ 329
    James........................... 420
    Jane............................ 72
    Jennie.......................... 501
    John.....................155, 329, 500
    John Fred....................... 353
    Julia (Perkins)................. 329
    Kirke H......................... 500
    Lela (Locke).................... 353
    Leona........................... 500
    Lydia........................... 320
    Mary A. (Locke)................. 155
    Mary (Boyle).................... 329
    Mary E......................500, 557
    Mary Ellen...................... 329
    Olive........................... 329
    Olive........................... 500
    Richard.....................328, 500
HUSTON, Mr.....................76, 296
    Abigail (Phinney)............... 76
    Dorcas A........................ 165
    Dorcas A. (Noyes)............... 77
    Harlan P........................ 165
    Helen Amelia.................... 165
    Henrietta....................... 165
    Henry F......................... 165
    Robert.......................... 77
    Tillie Crosby................... 165
    Walter P........................ 165
    Willie d........................ 165
HUTCHINS, Mr...................... 115
    Abbie........................... 495
    Abbie (Page).................... 296
    Abigail (Barrows)............... 115

640   INDEX OF NAMES

HUTCHINS, Agnes (Smith)............ 197
    Betsey.......................... 90
    Betsey (Locke).................. 44
    Caroline (Curtis)................ 532
    Clara........................... 456
    Comfort Locke................... 90
    Elizabeth....................... 14
    Esther (Barrows)................ 115
    Esther (Emerson)................ 197
    Eugene.......................... 276
    Fidelia A. (Locke).............. 138
    Fred d.......................... 197
    George.......................... 197
    Georgeanna (Locke).............. 305
    Hannah.......................... 90
    Horace F........................ 456
    Irving d........................ 197
    James........................... 260
    Jason........................... 90
    Jennie P........................ 456
    John................ 90, 197, 197, 532
    Judith.......................... 90
    Lucinda (Lang).................. 260
    Lucy............................ 197
    Lucy A. (Mills)................. 90
    Margaret........................ 90
    Margie.......................... 524
    Martha (Locke).................. 44
    Matilda......................... 90
    Mary........................197, 456
    Melvin.......................... 305
    Mercy (Locke)................... 276
    Nellie.......................... 197
    Oliver.......................... 138
    Sally Seavey.................... 90
    Sarah........................... 421
    Samuel.......................44, 90
    (Stevens), Miss................. 90
    Susan........................90, 279
    William......................... 197
HUTCHINSON, Alice................... 514
    Charles.....................191, 559
    Eliza (Downes).................. 191
    Ethel (Dow)..................... 512
    Howard A........................ 559
    Ila (Downing)................... 529
    Jonathan........................ 191
    Julia (Locke)................... 412
    Louisa I........................ 559
    Lucy (Merrill).................. 163
    Nancy (Locke)................... 191
    Nellie.......................... 529
    Neta............................ 529
    Orrin........................... 412
    Oscar........................... 512
    Samuel N........................ 163
    William, Dr..................... 529
    Winfield O...................... 559
HYDE, Lillian....................... 447
ILSLEY, Mary (Perkins).............. 91
    Peabody......................... 91
INGALLS, Miss....................... 50
    Abigail (Cleveland)............. 50
    Daniel.......................... 50
    Edna (Hastings)................. 50
    Eunice (Evans).................. 50
    Hannah.......................... 50
    James........................... 50
    Jonathan.....................26, 50
    Lizzie.......................... 510
    Lovering........................ 510
    Margaret (Jackman).............. 50
    Martha (Locke).................. 26
    Mary............................ 50
    Olive........................... 50
    Polly (Diamond)................. 50
    Ruth (Sleeper).................. 50
    Sally........................... 50
    Samuel.......................... 50
    Sarah........................... 50

INGALLS, Timothy.................... 50
INGHAM, Blanche (Wallace).......... 459
    Fred............................ 459
INGRAHAM, Harry.................... 526
    Mabel (Farnest)................. 526
INGRAM, Almon...................... 413
    Almon, Jr....................... 530
    Clara (Ryder)................... 530
    Harold G........................ 530
    Lester W........................ 530
    Mary (Smith).................... 413
    Raymond W....................... 530
    Uldine (Derryman)............... 530
    Vinthia E....................... 530
    Warren R........................ 530
IRISH, Bernice..................... 529
    Judson C........................ 529
JACKMAN, Adaline (Locke)........... 268
    Charles L....................... 217
    Edna............................ 268
    Freeman......................... 217
    Lyman, Capt..................... 217
    Margaret........................ 50
    Martha.......................... 101
    Mary............................ 268
    Noyes........................... 268
    Sarah (Tilton).................. 217
    Stillman........................ 268
JACKSON, George.................... 455
    George S........................ 542
    Ida M........................... 542
    John.......................... 2, 3
    Leslie E........................ 542
    Lillian (Emerson)............... 542
    Mamie........................... 542
    Martha (Locke).................. 455
JACOBS, Mr......................... 494
    Abigail D....................... 112
    Ann............................. 320
    Catherine (Burnes).............. 494
    Clara........................... 540
    Lyford.......................... 112
JACQUES, Mr........................ 209
    Hartley, Dr..................... 358
    Jennie (Sawyer)................. 209
    Margaret (Locke)................ 358
JAFFREYS, James.................... 26
JAMES, md Bachelder................ 92
    Abbie (Lane).................... 438
    Abigail (Godfrey)............... 92
    Anna............................ 42
    Cornelia....................444, 444
    Ebenezer........................ 444
    Edwin........................... 75
    Elizabeth (Locke)............... 75
    Ethel d......................... 444
    Frances......................... 444
    Frances (Haynes)................ 444
    Frank M......................... 444
    George P........................ 215
    Helen........................... 444
    Henry........................... 444
    Lilla J......................... 444
    Lovina.......................... 75
    Lucy............................ 444
    Lucy (French)................... 444
    Margaret....................444, 444
    Mary (Locke).................... 315
    Mehitable (Lane)................ 215
    Moses........................... 92
    Nancy (Lamprey)................. 264
    Orrin........................... 438
    Reuben.......................... 264
    Roxy............................ 75
    Sally........................... 21
    Samuel.......................92, 92
    Seth............................ 315
    Sheppard........................ 92
    Simeon C........................ 75
    William......................... 75

INDEX OF NAMES

JAMESON-JAMIESON.
Alex...........................115, 257
Annie (McSlaughlin).........257, 439
Arthur L............................ 439
Aurilla (Crandall)................ 257
Bessie d........................... 439
Caroline............................ 257
Douglas............................. 508
Dr.................................. 358
Edith............................... 508
Emaline............................. 190
Emma............................257, 439
Emma (Haley)....................... 494
Fannie (Glen)...................... 439
George.............................. 358
Gertrude............................ 508
Grace W............................. 439
Henry............................... 439
Herman.............................. 439
Horace D............................ 257
Isadore d........................... 439
Jennie (Brown)..................... 257
Julia E............................. 257
Laura M............................. 257
Lena................................ 508
Lewis............................... 508
Lucy............................257, 257
Marion (Locke)..................... 358
Mary J.........................246, 257
Mary (Thurber)..................... 439
Mary (Wilcox)...................... 257
Percy............................... 508
Rose (Sarpy)....................... 439
Sarah A............................. 257
Sarah K. (Locke)................... 115
Thomas.............................. 494
William Lov........................ 257
Zuar E.............................. 257
JANE, Sarah F......................... 466
JANVRIN, Addie........................ 368
Belinda............................. 91
Betsey.............................. 99
Clarence E.......................... 368
Denis............................... 91
Fidelia............................. 387
Gladys (Young)..................... 513
Gordon A............................ 513
James D............................. 513
John, Capt.......................... 45
John................................ 91
Joseph.............................. 214
Julia............................... 220
Mary................................ 209
Matilda............................. 98
Minnie (Dow)....................... 368
Olive G............................. 91
Philip E............................ 513
Rufus............................... 387
Sally d............................. 91
Sarah (Locke)...................... 45
Susan............................... 98
JARVIS, Maria......................... 248
JECKWORTH, Mary....................... 21
JEFFERS, Charlotte.................... 243
JEFFERSON, Hiram...................... 96
Mary (Clough)...................... 96
JEFFREYS ————.......................... 20
George.............................. 205
Anna (Philbrick)................... 205
JELLIFF, Anna M. B.................... 153
Charles E........................... 153
Edna................................ 153
Hiram, Rev......................... 153
Horatio F........................... 153
Howard.............................. 153
Jennie (Fay)....................... 153
Sarah (Locke)...................... 153
JENKINS, Alice (Richards)............ 548
Anna H.............................. 154
Ellery D............................ 548

JENKINS, Etta (Stevens)............. 196
Evelyn.............................. 548
George.............................. 229
Joseph..........................196, 478
Josephine (Dunbar)................ 478
Keziah.............................. 453
Mary................................ 543
Ralph............................... 548
Susie (Fellows).................... 229
Wayne............................... 548
Woodruff d......................... 548
JENKS, Carrie......................... 382
JENNE, Frasien........................ 194
Grace (Locke)...................... 542
Orem N.............................. 542
Polly (Perkins).................... 194
Statira............................. 88
JENNESS, Aaron.................30, 30, 30
Abbot C. d......................... 380
Abby C.............................. 238
Abigail.......................51, 107, 117
Abigail (Garland).................. 69
Abigail (Jenness).................. 107
Abigail (Locke).................... 51
Abigail (Perkins).................. 118
Amos............................108, 209
Ann (Folsom)....................... 14
Annie............................... 552
Arthur L............................ 407
Benjamin.......................117, 238
Betsey.............................. 53
Betsey (Philbrick)................. 57
Betsey (Rand)...................... 54
Byron............................... 520
Caroline............................ 380
Caroline (Polk).................... 380
Clara A............................. 408
Clara (Garland).................... 407
Clarissa............................ 408
Comfort............................. 19
Dana................................ 407
David.........................30, 107, 266
Deacon.............................. 17
Edith (Moulton).................... 520
Eliza......................128, 250, 380, 456
Elizabeth.....................14, 31, 309
Elizabeth (Galloway-Randall)..... 56
Elizabeth (Locke).................. 107
Elizabeth (Shapleigh).............. 107
Elvira (Garland)..............238, 238
Emily............................... 107
Eugene.............................. 456
Flora M............................. 409
Francis.......................5, 13, 14
Frank P............................. 380
George M............................ 409
Gertrude (Fogg-Young).............. 407
Hannah...........................11, 16
Hannah (Swaine).................... 13
Harriet (Mowe)..................... 143
Harrison............................ 456
Hezekiah............................ 14
Huldah (Perkins)...............118, 250
Hutchins............................ 456
Isabelle............................ 380
James............................... 117
Jeremiah........................30, 69
John............................56, 117
Jonathan....................51, 54, 107
Joseph, Lieut.................53, 53, 57
Joseph.......................106, 107, 250
Joseph G......................238, 238
Josephine G......................... 409
Josiah.............................. 118
Leavitt............................. 456
Levi................................ 30
Lewis W............................. 409
Martha.........................238, 238
Martha H. (Brown).................. 107
Martha (Seavey).................... 238

41

INDEX OF NAMES

JENNESS, Mary A. E. 117
  Mary (Dawlton), Mrs. 28, 28
  Mary (Dow) 31, 53, 107
  Mary (Hobbs) 69
  Mary (Hutchins) 456
  Mary (Jenness) 238
  Mary (Knowles) 53, 488
  Mary (Locke) 33, 209
  Mary (Moore-Marden) 238
  Mary (Pool) 488
  Mary (Tarlton) 120
  Mary (Wedgwood) 107
  Moses 30
  Nabby d 107
  Nancy 54, 68
  Nathaniel 107, 120
  Noah 56
  Olive 305
  Oliver Peter 107
  Patty (Locke) 117
  Polly 69, 107
  Polly L. (Garland) 107
  Polly (Philbrick) 117
  Richard 31, 380
  Reuben 53, 488
  Ruel 117
  Sally (Philbrick) 53
  Sally (Randall) 56
  Samuel 33, 69, 107, 118, 408
  Sarah 30, 53, 117, 316
  Sarah (Berry) 30
  Sarah L. (Garland) 107
  Sarah (Locke) 14, 30, 108
  S. Emaline (Locke) 316
  Sarah (Taylor) 266
  Semira 405
  Sophia 238
  Thomas 117
  Uri Harvey 107
  Wallace 488
  Wesley 143
  William 30, 30, 238
  Woodbury 316, 488
JENNINGS, Alton d 505
  Frank 490
  Gertrude M 505
  Hannah 505
  Hannah (Locke) 352
  Mary (Locke) 490
  Rufus 352, 505
JESSEMAN, Sally 538
JEWELL, Adalaide F 132
  Albert B 132
  Alice 488
  Ann M. (Locke) 316
  Asa 132, 132
  Betsey (Sherman) 295
  Charlotte 69
  DeWitt 316
  Erastus B 488
  Flora E 488
  Francis 295
  Frank O 132
  George 488
  Hannah (Marston) 488
  Irene 410
  Jefferson 295
  Levi 488
  Margaret (Robertson) 237
  Martha (Page) 295
  Mary A 132
  Nellie F 132
  Oscar 132
  Percy 488
  Ruhuma 294
  Sarah 316
  Sarah (Wiggin) 132
  Theodate (Page) 132
  Viola I 488
JEWETT, Alonzo 227

JEWETT, Annette (Locke) 227
  Arthur A 227
  Celestia (Davis-Angell), Mrs. .. 227
  Delila (Locke) 80
  Etta 228
  Henry C 227
  Jeremiah 228
  Jonah 80
  Katie B 227
  Mary 228
  Noah 176
  Sarah S. (Palmer) 176
JOCKE, Maude 472
JOHNSON, Mr. 82, 260, 346
  Almira 256
  Almira (Locke) 113
  Ann 190
  Anna 535
  Annie (Locke) 346
  Aphia 457
  Arabella 256
  Byron G 556
  Carrie 266
  Charles 177
  Charles Marc 177
  Deborah 211
  Doctor 130
  Edmund C 211
  Edna (Hickok) 425
  Edwin H 421
  Eliza 57
  Elizabeth 76, 151
  Ella (Langley) 133
  Ellen 190
  Emma J 150
  Eva (Burke) 256
  Eva (Locke) 177
  Evaline (Haughton) 556
  Fannie (Locke) 287
  Flora (Locke) 287
  Francena (Locke-Davis-Cook) 285
  Fred R 425
  Geneva (Locke) 374
  George 287
  Gilman 143
  Hannah 21
  Hattie 464
  Henry 133, 338
  (Hooper), Miss 82
  Huldah 480
  Irving 287
  James 130, 211
  John B 113
  Julius 211
  Katherine (Locke) 190
  Laura 256
  Levi 390
  Lewis 190
  Lizzie (Bishop) 421
  Mabel (Dyer) 338
  Margaret 421, 425
  Martha (Wallis) 130
  Marvin O 556
  Mary 147, 170
  Mary (Clarke) 211
  Mary (Mowe) 143
  Maude (Locke) 190, 357
  Nancy (Lang) 260
  Nellie 177, 390
  Orville B 256
  Robert 374
  Roscoe 556
  Ruth 66
  Samuel L 190
  Sarah 236, 325
  Susan 418, 464
  Walter Locke 374
  William 285
  Wynne 190, 190, 357
JONES, Abbie d 510, 510

INDEX OF NAMES 643

JONES, Addie A. 510
  Albert H. 511
  Alice M. 292
  Alice (Dennett), Mrs. 226
  Ann (Weeks) 201
  Annis (Locke) 242
  Betsey (Leavitt) 35
  Charles 341, 495
  David 174
  Della Irene 341
  Elizabeth C. 121
  Elizabeth (Locke) 239, 305
  Emma L. 292
  Eunice 121
  Fannie 436
  Flora L. 479
  Florence (Frenyear) 479
  Frank 239
  Fred Ansley 341
  Freeland 253
  Gerald Alex 341
  Hannah (Davis) 292
  Harlow 253
  Harriet F. 511
  Hayden H. d. 510
  Henry S. 201
  Huldah P. (Locke) 131
  James 131, 361, 510
  J. Edward 201
  Jennie (Flanders) 511
  Jennie (Locke) 495
  J. Green 201
  John 2, 3, 292
  Lillian (Babbett) 511
  Lizzie (Weeks) 201
  Loren M. 479
  Lydia (Whittier) 253
  Margaret 55
  Mary 195, 253, 423
  Mary Ann 341
  Mary Elizabeth 511
  Mary (Locke) 361
  Mary (Priest) 239
  Mina (Ballard) 515
  Minnie L. 414
  Myra E. 510
  Nancy 306
  Nellie (Locke) 174
  Oliver 35
  Pauline (Shea) 239
  Pearl Eliz. 341
  Peleg 253
  Raymond David 341, 341
  Ruth (Hanson) 510
  Samuel J. 305
  Sarah 34, 121
  Thomas 239
  True 239
  Warner L. 515
  Willard 242
JORDAN, Anna V. 533
JOY, Fannie 288
JOYCE, George F. 465
  Helen H. 465
  Mary 482
JUDD, Mary 279
JUDKINS, Almeda (Leighton) 355
  Almira (Doloff) 231
  Asa 355
  Charles S. 458
  Ellen A. (True) 271
  Enoch 271
  George, Rev. 231
  Hannah (Cheney) 458
  Herbert 458
  Joel 281, 458
  Mary 89
  Mary (Locke) 281
  Moses 458
  Nancy, Mrs. 568

JUDKINS, Perna 31
  Sula S. 458
JUNKINS, Arvilla 398
  Frances (Trefethern) 320
  Imogene (Tebbetts-Locke) 550
  Nathan 320
  Ormond D. 550
KATE, Patty 30
KATHEN, Warren 88
  Lydia (Locke) 88
KATHERWOOD, Mary A. 44
KAY, Amanda (Locke) 359
  Colin Campbell 359
  Colin C. C. 508
  Daniel 508
  Douglas C. M. d. 508
KEEN, Mr. 162
  Harriet 319
  Rachel (Clifford) 162
KEENEY, Marilla, Mrs. 58
KEER, Elizabeth 228
KEEZER, Ellen 388
  Frank E. 392
  George 388, 392
  Mary 392
  Minnie (Drake) 392
KEIR, Mary 498
KELLEY, Anthony 518
  Chester 518
  Clara 329
  Frances H. 516
  Freeman 329
  George F. 516
  Harriet 230
  Helen (Wingate) 518
  James 127
  John 90, 423
  Joseph 491
  Laura 317
  Mabel 387
  Mary (Locke) 324
  Phebe (Stevens) 90
  Prudentia 162
  Sadie 409
  Sarah (Burgess) 491
  Thirza 329
KELLOGG, Weltha 135
KELLUM, Caroline d. 115
  Emaline (Locke) 115
  Eugene d. 115
  George 115, 252
  George D. 252
  John C. 115
  Sarah H. D. (Locke) 115, 252
KELSEY, Phebe (Ladd) 62
  Sarah A. 79
  William 62
KEMPTON, Allen 190
  Allevia (Locke) 190
  Louisa 358
  Mary (Locke) 190
  Stephen 190
KENDALL, Mr. 417
  Anna (Pike) 541
  Charles B. 541
  Mary 437
  Mary (Straw) 417
KENDRICK, Harriet (Brown) 142
  William 142
KENNARD, Charles d. 247
  Elizabeth 312
  Ella d. 247
  Ellen (Locke) 247
  John T. 247
  Jonas B. 247
  Joseph 312
KENNEY, Miss 441
  Annie 438
KENNISTON, Mr. 92
  Aseneth 467

INDEX OF NAMES

KENNISTON, Ellen, Mrs............ 395
  Elvira (Bachelder).............. 92
  Margaret...................... 230
KENT, Ada....................... 400
  Adaline (Pennimen)............. 101
  Avice......................... 244
  Avice (Williams)................ 244
  D............................ 428
  Gilbert R...................... 244
  Harriet....................... 58
  Horace P...................... 101
  James D....................... 244
  John......................101, 101
  Mary (Warren)................. 428
  Nancy R....................... 247
  Ruhuma (Dearborn)............. 101
KENYON, Archibald................ 332
  Charles D..................332, 332
  James......................... 75
  Nathan........................ 75
  Nellie (Locke).................. 332
  Phebe......................... 75
  Thomas....................... 332
  Waity......................... 75
  Waity (Locke-Smith)............ 75
KERLEY, Jennie................... 322
KESSLER, Edith (Breed)............ 521
  Oliver......................... 521
  Verna......................... 521
KEYES, Almira (Willoughby)........ 435
  Carrie......................... 435
  Constance N................... 520
KEYS, Douglas L.................. 520
  Joseph........................ 435
  Marian (Philbrick).............. 520
KEYSER, Ellen..................... 93
  Harold........................ 538
  Harriet (Bailey)................. 538
  Roland.....................538, 538
  Winfield....................... 538
KILGORE, Mary A................. 82
KILLAM, John..................... 307
  Mark.......................... 483
  Mercy (Piper).................. 483
  Sarah (Locke-Ordway).......... 307
KIMBALL, Miss.................... 194
  Mr.......................57, 59, 159
  Abigail........................ 450
  Adaline (Wood)................ 362
  Alice (Jones)................... 292
  Alice N........................ 220
  Almira........................ 413
  Amanda G..................... 222
  Anna M. (Lang-Babb).......... 116
  Asa........................... 361
  Asa Howard................... 361
  Asenath (Herrick).............. 367
  Benjamin F.................... 362
  Betsey........................ 123
  Blanche....................... 427
  Caroline....................... 243
  Charles...................102, 220, 362
  Charlotte A.................... 361
  Charlotte (Locke).............. 102
  Clara (Walker)................. 220
  Cora d....................... 145
  Cynthia (Eastman)............. 294
  Daniel.....................261, 367
  Edward L..................... 220
  Elizabeth...................... 220
  Elizabeth (Watson)............. 297
  Ella........................... 415
  Ellen C........................ 102
  Elmer Allen.................... 362
  Emily......................145, 427
  Emma......................... 415
  Enoch......................... 192
  Ensign........................ 154
  E. (Tenney)................... 261
  Ethlyn........................ 220

KIMBALL, Eunice M............... 123
  Fred.......................... 264
  F. Elizabeth.................... 415
  Francis Locke.................. 362
  George...................145, 297, 427
  Hannah d..................... 361
  Harriet........................ 199
  Harriet (Taplin)................ 242
  Hattie S....................... 415
  Henry......................... 242
  Henry Albert................... 362
  Ida........................... 222
  Isabella....................... 319
  James......................... 222
  Jennie........................ 259
  Jennie (Peters)................. 362
  Kate (Gray)................... 159
  (Larkin), Miss................. 264
  Laura......................222, 222
  Lizzie......................... 200
  Louisa.....................199, 361
  Lucinda (Taplin)............... 242
  Lucy (Nye).................... 259
  Lulu (Randall)................. 493
  Lydia......................... 220
  Lydia (Locke)................. 247
  Lydia (Locke-Grant)........... 154
  Mabel (Emory), Mrs............ 509
  Mabel......................... 242
  Maria (Ayers).................. 427
  Martin L...................... 222
  Martha (Babb)................. 220
  Mary A........220, 340, 361, 362, 415
  Mary (Little).................. 417
  Mary (Locke)..............145, 192
  Mary (Shaw).................. 222
  Maude d..................... 242
  Miranda (Winter).............. 135
  Moody........................ 259
  Moses......................... 294
  (Moulton), Miss............... 57
  Nancy (Locke)................. 222
  Nathaniel, Capt................ 116
  Nathaniel F.................... 247
  Nellie (Stanley)................ 415
  Olivette D. d.................. 145
  Oren.......................... 297
  Orrin T....................... 427
  Phebe (Carleton)............... 361
  Priscilla....................... 92
  Reta (Cristie).................. 415
  Reuben.....................242, 415
  Rose (Swinburn)............... 292
  Sabra......................... 131
  Samuel........................ 135
  Sarah......................... 220
  Seth H........................ 222
  Solomon...................220, 220
  Stephen....................... 417
  Thomas....................... 154
  William.........242, 292, 292, 415
  Willis......................... 493
KING, Blanche (Locke)............. 451
  Edward F..................... 308
  Elizabeth (Locke).............. 308
  Emma M...................... 352
  Frederick...................... 451
  Hattie......................... 451
  Leon d....................... 451
KINGSLEY, Albert E............... 86
  Betsey (Locke)................. 86
  Hannah (Locke)................ 86
  Huldah P...................... 86
  Jeremiah...................... 86
  Sophia M...................... 86
  William.....................86, 86
KINNEAR, Ruth................... 238
KINNEY, Alonzo................... 373
  Annie (Palmer)................. 373
  Eva Alice...................... 373

INDEX OF NAMES

KINSELA, Arthur................ 547
   Charles................... 547
   Emma (Brogan)............ 477
   George.................... 547
   James..................... 477
   John d.................... 547
   Loretta................... 547
   May A..................... 547
KIRBY, Daniel................. 88
   Nancy (Locke)............ 88
KIRK, Arthur.................. 469
   Blanche................... 469
   Harold.................... 469
   Jesse..................... 469
   Lucy...................... 469
   Ora (Marden)............. 469
KIRKWOOD, Barbara............ 409
   Daniel.................... 409
   Eula M.................... 409
   Josephine (Jenness)...... 409
   Mary (Huse).............. 409
   Samuel.................... 409
KITTREDGE, Esther............ 63
   Leonard................... 456
   Samantha................. 276
KNAPP, Sally.................. 28
KNIGHT, Mr.................... 301
   Grace..................... 226
   John...................... 48
   Lilla...................... 355
   Luvia C................... 318
   Martha (Riggs)........... 301
   Mary (Locke)............. 226
   Temperance............... 48
   Thomas.................... 226
KNILANDS, Donald E. d...... 339
   Ernest.................... 173
   Grace d.................. 339
   Henry d.................. 339
   Martha E. (Locke)........ 173
   Ralph H. d............... 339
   Rhoda Gertrude........... 339
   Ruby Ann.................. 339
   Robert.................... 339
KNOWLES, Miss..............92, 119
   Mr........................ 301
   Abigail................... 18
   Amos...................... 44
   Ann (Garland)............ 344
   Betsey (Clement)......... 119
   Betsey (Palmer).......... 44
   Charles...............306, 344
   Christian................. 119
   Comfort................... 18
   Comfort (Wallace)........ 18
   Cora (Page).............. 489
   Daniel.................... 18
   David..................... 342
   Deborah................... 41
   Edith (Rand)..........301, 342
   Edwin.................306, 489
   Eleanor (Leavitt)........ 342
   Elizabeth................. 70
   Ella D.................... 306
   Esther.................52, 192
   Esther (Locke)........... 44
   Etta (Ordway)............ 306
   Frances................... 489
   Francis................192, 192
   Francis Locke............ 141
   George.............177, 306, 306
   Hannah............11, 108, 119, 119
   Hannah (Haines).......... 119
   Harriet................... 119
   Herbert Sherburne........ 342
   Isaac..................... 44
   James..................... 18
   Jemima (Austin).......... 14
   John..........13, 14, 18, 18, 18, 119
   Jonathan.................. 88

KNOWLES, Joseph.............53, 119
   Josiah.................... 192
   Lillian (Barrett)........ 306
   Lizzie.................... 344
   Lydia (Locke)............ 177
   Margaret (Locke)......... 88
   Marland Denzil........... 342
   Mary................18, 18, 53, 488
   Mary (Libbey)............ 18
   Mary (Mullen)............ 306
   Nathan.................... 18
   Nellie E.................. 306
   Nutter, Miss............. 192
   Polly..................... 119
   Sally..................... 119
   Samuel.................66, 192
   Sarah.................18, 119
   Sarah (Locke)........53, 141, 192
   Sarah (Marden).......... 66
   Sarah (Moulton).......... 18
   Simeon.................... 115
   Susannah...............18, 19
   Tryphena.................. 18
   Tryphena (Locke)......... 13
   William................... 119
   Zilpha (Thorn)........... 119
KNOWLTON, Abigail (Carter)... 316
   Ethel W................... 346
   Everett K................. 132
   Frank B................... 346
   George.................... 491
   Ida (Weeks).............. 132
   Julia (Spaulding)........ 543
   Hannah (Foss)............ 132
   Harlan.................... 543
   Henry..................... 451
   Israel.................... 316
   Laura (Locke)............ 316
   Mary...................... 316
   Mayhew.................... 132
   Sadie..................... 491
   Stella (Chamberlain).... 451
   Susan A................... 316
   Timothy................316, 316
KNOX, Adam.................... 145
   Almeda.................... 118
   Charles H................. 315
   George H.................. 314
   Inez (Bacock)............ 315
   James A................... 315
   Joseph L.................. 315
   Martha D. (Locke)........ 145
   Martha (Walton).......... 315
   Mary E.................... 314
   Mary (Adams)............. 314
   Theresa (Mowry).......... 315
KOLSETH, Betsey (Ransom-Locke)..327, 407
   Harold R.................. 497
   Harry, Dr................. 497
   Harry..................... 327
KOPP, Charles................. 541
   Mary (Tallant)........... 541
KOUGH, Myrtle................. 534
KUSE, Mary.................... 386
KYLE, Mr...................... 418
   Annie (Green)............ 418
   Jennie.................317, 318
LABAENE, Mary (Come), Mrs.... 435
LABOUNTY, Agnes............... 126
   John...................... 289
   Julia..................... 289
LACKEY, Laura................. 497
LADD, Abigail................. 62
   Adaline d................. 62
   Alonzo C.................. 134
   Amy....................... 187
   Asenath (Bachelder)..... 61
   Betsey (Rollins)......... 310
   Belinda................... 231
   Caroline.................. 310

INDEX OF NAMES

LADD, Carrie (Gilman).............. 355
   Carter d...................... 194
   Catherine..................... 62
   Charles....................62, 310
   Clara M....................... 355
   Cora B........................ 355
   Cora (Locke).................. 450
   Daniel B...................... 134
   Edwin F....................... 355
   Eleanor....................... 310
   Eleazor....................310, 310
   Elisha L...................... 61
   Emily......................... 310
   Emaline....................... 62
   Eliza A....................... 62
   Esther (Pillsbury)............ 62
   Ethan S....................... 62
   Franklin P.................... 355
   Forest D. d................... 355
   Freddie....................... 134
   Freeman....................... 310
   George P...................... 310
   Hannah (Locke)................ 29
   Hattie....................134, 310
   Henry R....................... 61
   Herbert W..................... 355
   H. H.......................... 134
   Horace........................ 62
   Idris (Williams).............. 355
   Isaac......................61, 61
   James...............29, 61, 62, 310
   John..................187, 355, 355
   Jonathan.................29, 61, 62
   Louis......................... 310
   Louisa G. (Steubner).......... 134
   Lucinda E. (Willey)........... 134
   Martha J...................... 61
   Mary.....................62, 176, 310
   Mary A. (Brown).............. 142
   Mary E. (Ladd)............... 134
   Mary S. (Locke).............. 29
   Mary D. (Melvin)............. 62
   Mehitable.................... 355
   Mehitable (Quimby)........... 355
   Mehitable (Roberts).......... 61
   Mehitable (Rogers)........... 62
   Minnie (Stanton)............. 310
   Nancy (Riggs)................ 61
   Nora A. d.................... 134
   Olive d...................... 310
   Peter........................ 450
   Phebe.....................62, 134
   Rizpah (Sprague)............. 355
   Rosella (Locke).............. 187
   Roxanna d.................... 134
   Roxana (Davis)............... 62
   Ruth......................14, 61
   Ruth (Locke)................. 194
   Samuel................62, 62, 194
   Susanna...................... 62
   Theodora..................... 62
   Theodosia.................... 61
   Timothy...................62, 341
   Tryphena..................61, 62
   William...........61, 142, 310, 355
LAKE, Jennie..................... 404
   John......................... 322
   Lovina....................149, 322
   Sarah (Moses)................ 322
LAMBAUGH, George................. 312
   Martha (Dearborn)............ 312
LAMOS, Sarah..................... 128
LAMPREY, Aaron................44, 89
   Abby......................... 196
   Abel..................89, 196, 196
   Abigail (Drake).............. 41
   Albion....................... 265
   Alma d....................... 447
   Almon d...................... 264
   Ann (Brown).................. 265

LAMPREY, Anna (White)............ 264
   Annie.....................446, 448
   Annie (Delancey)............. 448
   Austin....................89, 448
   Barbara (Hardy-Wyman)........ 264
   Benjamin..................... 196
   Betsey....................... 277
   Blanche S.................... 448
   Bridget (Phelps)............. 89
   Carrie....................... 266
   Carrie C..................... 448
   Carrie (Johnson)............. 266
   Catherine (Bachelotte)....... 265
   Charles...................265, 265
   Clara (Nudd)................. 266
   Clarence.............89, 447, 447
   Cyril........................ 89
   Daniel..................41, 89, 89
   David....................117, 266
   David C..................264, 446
   Delia.................89, 89, 89
   Dudley....................... 41
   Edgar A...................... 447
   Edith........................ 448
   Edwin M...................... 265
   Eleanor (Buzzell)............ 89
   Eliza A. (Colburn)........... 89
   Eliza (Merrill).............. 196
   Elizabeth............55, 89, 89, 90
   Elizabeth (Leavitt).......... 41
   Ellen (Bachelder)............ 266
   Elsie....................264, 447
   Ephraim...................89, 196
   Ernest....................... 266
   Ethel........................ 446
   Eva......................444, 445
   Eva (Goodhue)................ 264
   Evaline (Cooper)............. 196
   Eve d....................444, 444
   Fannie M..................... 447
   Fannie (Balch)............... 446
   Flora L...................... 196
   Florence..................... 444
   Forrest C.................... 446
   Francis...................... 447
   Fred d....................... 445
   George................89, 265, 445
   Georgie C.................... 448
   Grace........................ 265
   Hannah....................... 89
   Hannah (Garland)............. 265
   Hannah (Locke).............44, 89
   Harold....................... 266
   Hattie....................... 265
   Henry P...................... 89
   Hezekiah..................... 117
   Horace A..................... 89
   Howell....................... 448
   Irving H..................... 266
   James........................ 196
   Janette S.................... 447
   Jeannette (Roberts).......... 264
   Jennie (Tyler)............... 447
   Jennie R..................... 448
   Jerusah (Emmons)............. 196
   John............82, 82, 89, 89, 117
                 196, 264, 265, 445
   John, Lieut.................. 116
   Jonathan.............265, 265, 265
   Joseph W..................... 196
   Josephine (Drake)............ 448
   Judith.....................90, 90
   Julia (Trask)................ 196
   Lavinia...................... 196
   Leslie....................... 446
   Levi......................89, 196
   Lillian (Hyde)............... 447
   Lillian M.................... 447
   Lizzie C..................... 446
   Lois J....................... 196

INDEX OF NAMES

LAMPREY, Louis d 447
  Louisa 82
  Lucy (Arnold) 447
  Lydia 89, 90, 196
  Lydia A. (Campbell) 89
  Lydia (Locke) 82
  Madeline (Sylvestre), Mrs 448
  Mahala 196
  Maitland C 89
  Malvina 264
  Martha 264
  Marion 44, 448
  Mary 89, 250, 265, 265, 448
  Mary (Brown) 265
  Mary (Cain) 89
  Mary (Hardy) 264
  Mary (Jenness) 117
  Mary (Judkins) 89
  Mary (Nichols) 89
  Mary P. (Philbrick) 82
  Mary (Pierce) 89
  Mary (Robinson) 117
  Maud S 445
  Minerva (Signor) 446
  Miriam d 447
  Miriam (Locke) 41
  Molly (Marston) 117
  Morris 52, 89, 89, 117
  Morris J 264, 266, 446, 448
  Myra B 89
  Nancy 264
  Nancy (Locke) 52
  Norval 447
  Polly (Cook) 89
  Polly (Marston) 177
  Polly (Philbrick) 82
  Rachel 447
  Randolph 447
  Ray 444
  Reuben 171
  Rose d 447
  Ruth 177
  Sally (Marston) 117
  Sally (Stearns) 117
  Sarah 44, 264, 265, 266
  Sarah (Merchant) 196
  Sarah (Pattee) 196
  Sarah (Whittaker) 264
  Simon O 265
  Stephen 89
  Susan (Pavitt) 265
  Susan P. (Webster) 89
  Susie (Walker) 446
  Uri 117, 264, 445, 447, 448
  Wallace d 447
  Warren 89, 448
  William 264, 265, 446
  Zadie M 447
LAMSON, Asa, Rev 96
  Emilina B 207
  Fannie 168
  George O 207
  John D 207
  Joseph 207, 242
  Martha 207, 207
  Mary (Taplin) 242
  Sally D. (Locke) 96
  Samuel L 207
  Sarah 207
LANCASTER, Mr 38, 75
  Alice C 374
  Alice (Locke) 374
  Ann 30
  Archibald, Rev 374
  James Locke 374
  Mehitable (Clifford) 38
  Sally (Clifford) 75
LANE, Mrs 82
  Abbie A 438, 438
  Abigail 113, 215

LANE, Abigail (Cram) 296
  Abigail (Goss) 437
  Addie (Palmer) 341
  Adoniram J 215
  Alice L 438
  Ann (Shannon) 524
  Annie (Locke) 255
  Austice 177
  Belle 311
  Carrie 438
  Charles D 78
  Clintie W 438
  Cora 407
  David 222
  Ebenezer 117
  Eliza 311
  Erastus d 215
  George 255
  George Frederick 78
  Georgeanna 438
  Hannah O. (Locke) 142
  Hannah (Smith) 215
  Ida 401
  Isaiah 437, 438
  Jennie (Bachelder) 99
  John 142, 296, 437
  Jonathan 35
  Joshua 99
  Lilla 429
  Lizzie 386
  Lucretia L. (Merrill) 78
  Lydia 444
  Lydia (Leavitt) 35
  Mahala B 132
  Martha B 103
  Mary 78, 82, 84, 395
  Mehitable 215
  Mira (Aldrich) 215
  Miriam 199
  Nancy (Brown) 178
  Rachel 262
  Sally (Brown) 222
  Samuel 78
  Sarah 78, 180, 215, 264, 506
  Sarah (Emery) 117
  Solomon 311
  Thomas 178, 215
  Uri A 341
  Walter 437
  William 524
LANG, Abigail L 116, 259, 260
  Abigail (Locke) 52, 60
  Abrilla (Suearengen) 116
  Agnes (Smith) 263
  Albion Earle 263
  Alice (Colby) 443
  Amanda 262
  Amoret 263
  Amy (Hart) 116
  Annah 66
  Anna (Adams) 441
  Anna M 116
  Benjamin 116
  Betsey (Walker) 66
  Betsey (Williams) 260
  Bickford 29, 52, 60, 115, 116
  Burton H 261
  Carrie (Glines) 262
  Celestia (Root) 261
  Charles 260, 260, 260, 441
  Charlotte (Drew) 222
  Clara M 261
  Cyrus W 260
  Data 60
  David 116, 260, 260
  Edith (Drake) 443
  Edward R 263
  Eliza (Locke) 222
  Elizabeth 66
  Elizabeth (Rand) 66

INDEX OF NAMES

LANG, Elizabeth (Viles) 261
  Ella A 260
  Elmer L 443
  Emma A 260
  Emma (Richards) 443
  Esther 260, 443
  Eva A 441
  Fannie W 263
  Francenah M 263
  Frances 60
  Frank 263
  George 222
  George Locke.... 261, 261, 261, 443, 535
  Grace (Black) 441
  Hannah 34, 60, 66
  Hannah (Marden) 66
  Harrie 222
  Harrold 443, 443
  Helen T 263, 443
  Helen M. (Thrall) 116
  Henry B 260
  Huldah 60
  Huldah A. (Chapman) 116
  James A 260
  Jane B. (Cram) 116
  Jennie (Webster) 186
  Jesse Hart 260
  Jonathan, Dr 66
  John 60, 60, 222, 222, 259
            260, 261, 262, 443, 443
  John Locke 116
  Josephine T 562
  Josiah 116, 260
  Lilly G 263
  Lillian (Stanley) 443
  Lorenda 116
  Lorenda (Chapman) 260
  Lorenda (Hitchcock) 116
  Louisa M 260
  Lucinda 260
  Lydia 260
  Lydia (Babb) 116
  Marguerite 562
  Mark 31, 66, 66
  Martha 60, 261
  Martha (Locke) 29
  Martin V 222
  Mary 91, 260, 486
  Mary (Cook) 261
  Mary (Fitch) 260
  Mary (Locke) 222, 535
  Mary F. (Porter) 263
  Mercy (Drake) 60
  Merrill Warner 261
  Myrna L 261
  Nancy 260
  Nancy (Walker) 66
  Nicholas 259
  Olive 260
  Patience (Wentworth) 66
  Polly 60
  Richard 66
  Reuel 116, 441
  Ruth 443
  Ruthia (Boon) 260
  Salome (Goss) 31
  Samantha R 262
  Sarah 60, 116, 260, 261, 261
  Sarah (Bickford) 60
  Sarah G. (White) 116
  Sarone M 263
  Stephen K 562
  Sybil (Squire) 116
  Walter 186, 443
  Watson W 441
  William 60, 66, 66, 116, 222, 259
  Zilpha A 263
LANGDON, Abbie (Briggs) 395
  Andrew J 395
  Daisy 395

LANGDON, Ellen (Kenniston), Mrs 395
  Emaline B 395
  Frances (Beals) 395
  Hannah 395
  John W 395
  Lavinia 395
  Mary A 395
  Mary (Lane) 395
  Mary (Locke) 233
  Polly 118
  Samuel, Major 395
  William 233, 395
  Woodbury T 395
LANGILLE, Avis M 343
  John Sherburne 343
  Johnson E 343
  Mabel (Locke) 343
  Mary Ellen 343
LANGLEY, Addie (Brackett) 298
  Annie 133
  Capitola 133
  Cassandra (Woodman) 133
  Eliza McCrillis 133
  Elizabeth 133
  Elizabeth (Locke) 61
  Elizabeth (Sands) 133
  Ella 133
  Elma J. (Locke) 113
  Emerett E 298
  Gratia 298
  Hannah S 133
  Jane (Colley) 133
  John 61, 133, 298
  Josiah D 113
  Lelia (Sanborn) 298
  Lizzie 469
  Lois (Salter) 133
  Mary 130
  Minerva 298
  Moses 133
  Samuel 133
  Sherman 298
  William 133, 298, 298
LANGMAID, Miss 66
LARKIN, Mr 135
  Ann 263
  Benjamin L 264
  Josephine 264
  Lorinda (Holmes) 135
  Mary A. (Locke) 116
  Mary E 264
  Nancy 120
  Samuel 116, 263
  Sarah (Hall) 264
LARRABEE, Arthur 490, 490
  Charles F 490
  Clara (Appleton) 490
  Effie d 490
  Emma F 490
  Frances M 490
  Frank 382
  James H. d 490
  John 317, 490, 490
  Martha (Locke) 317
  Mary E. d 490
  Sarah J 63
  Sarah (Southwick-Locke) 382
LARY, George 296
  Ellen (Page) 296
LATHROP, Caroline 473
LAVERTY, Charlotte (Pulsifer) 167
  William 167
LAVERY, Sophia 323
LAWRENCE, Joseph 270
  Kate (Locke) 548
  Lucretia 162
  Stillman 548
  Susan (Locke) 270
LAWRY, Joanna 319
LAWS, William 405

INDEX OF NAMES

Laws, Mary (Whidden)............ 405
Lawton, Catherine................ 221
Lay, Jennie...................... 202
Leach, Mr....................... 268
  Caroline...................... 343
  Charles....................... 233
  Ellen S....................... 159
  Esther (Dann)................. 268
  Fred.......................... 522
  Grace (Lord).................. 522
  Hannah........................ 233
  Helen......................... 385
  Margaret...................... 233
  Martha........................ 163
  Philena........................ 80
Lear, Ada..................482, 486
  Aleck.......................... 66
  Almira (Shaw)................. 106
  Elizabeth (Brown-Goss)......... 66
  Ella (Knowles)................ 306
  George H...................... 306
  Georgeanna.................... 482
  Jessie, Mrs................... 311
  Mary.......................... 393
  Mehitable..................... 233
Leary, Julia.................... 501
Leavenworth, Edward............ 442
  Helen (Wright)................ 442
Leavitt, Abigail................. 52
  Abigail (Tuck)................. 35
  Alice d....................... 266
  Amos........................... 19
  Ann............................ 19
  Angenette..................... 245
  Annie......................... 409
  Aretus......................... 19
  Benjamin....................... 19
  Betsey......................... 35
  Brackett....................... 35
  Comfort........................ 35
  Deborah........................ 92
  Ebenezer...................... 316
  Eleanor....................... 342
  Eliza J. (Perkins)............ 118
  Elizabeth..................19, 41
  Elizabeth (Locke).............. 13
  Elizabeth (Varrell)............ 19
  Ellen d....................... 266
  Esther (Marden), Mrs.......... 108
  Esther (Towle)................. 19
  George....................212, 291
  Hannah (Melcher).............. 35
  James.....................212, 409
  Janett (Whitney).............. 109
  John..................19, 118, 266
  Jonathan...................19, 35
  Joseph.....................19, 212
  Lizzie........................ 314
  Lydia.......................... 35
  Marcia......................... 19
  Mary...........19, 106, 146, 184, 212
  Mary (Blake).................. 266
  Mary (Locke).................. 212
  Mary (Marston)................ 212
  Mary (Tilton).................. 19
  Mercy.......................... 35
  (Morse), Miss................. 118
  Mitty (Prescott)............... 35
  Moses......................... 266
  Patience....................... 35
  Rachel (Hook)................. 291
  Reuben......................... 35
  Ruth (Johnson)................. 66
  Ruth (Norris).................. 35
  Ruth (Sleeper)................. 19
  Samuel......................... 66
  Sarah......................30, 146
  Sarah (Jewell)................ 316
  Sarah (Lamprey)............... 266
  Thomas............13, 35, 35, 212

Leavitt, (Ward), Mrs.............. 35
LeBosquet, John.................. 264
  Elsie (Lamprey)............... 264
  John, Rev..................... 264
  Martha (Farrington)........... 264
Lecoy, Delia (Shortelle)......... 372
  Frank......................... 372
  Nettie........................ 372
Ledoit, Mary..................... 559
Lee, Polly........................ 72
Leedy, Carrie H. (Locke)......... 133
  Jacob M....................... 133
Leeman, Charles.................. 505
  Cora.......................... 352
  Mary.......................... 505
Legg, Elizabeth.................. 311
Leidieker, Arvilla (Locke)....... 533
  Fred.......................... 533
  Karl G........................ 533
Leigh, Fred...................... 330
  Marion........................ 330
  Sarah (Felker)................ 330
Leighton, Abbie.............165, 361
  Almeda........................ 355
  Amos........................... 77
  Andrew S...................... 446
  Anna (Whitehouse)............. 315
  Augusta....................... 355
  Charles...................315, 355
  Clarence...................... 446
  Edgar......................... 165
  Edward........................ 165
  Flavilla d................355, 355
  George W....................... 77
  Herbert G..................... 165
  Howard........................ 165
  John.......................... 361
  Lewis.....................187, 355
  Lilla (Knights)............... 355
  Lizzie (Lamprey).............. 446
  Loren C....................... 315
  Marie (Wyman)................. 165
  Mary (Locke).................. 187
  Olivette (Pigott)............. 315
  Ruth C. (Noyes)................ 77
  Sarah......................... 361
  Sarah (Griffin)............... 446
  Sarah P. (Noyes)............... 77
Leith, L. E...................... 433
Lellingham, Elizabeth............. 29
Leroy, Rachel.................... 452
Levin, Alma...................... 334
  Henry......................... 334
Lewis, Mr........................ 116
  Abbie F....................... 137
  Abigail (Berry)............... 137
  Areanna....................... 232
  Benjamin....................... 74
  Bettie........................ 243
  Charlotte A. (Locke).......... 116
  Emaline (Parker), Mrs......... 113
  Eugene Locke.................. 376
  Florence (Locke).............. 376
  Hannah......................... 74
  Izetta......................... 65
  John P........................ 376
  Joseph........................ 393
  Langley B..................... 137
  Mary........................... 26
  Mary (Cleveland).............. 74
  Mary (Lear)................... 393
  Mary (Travis)................. 226
  Minnie........................ 331
  Rhoda.......................... 75
  Vivian........................ 376
Libbey, Mr........................ 25
  Abbie B....................... 568
  Anna.......................... 155
  Annie......................... 347
  Annie (Young)................. 523

INDEX OF NAMES

LIBBEY, Ansel... 159
  Charles E... 221
  Gyrus... 221, 221
  Daniel... 523, 523
  Elizabeth... 523
  Florence E... 523
  Hannah... 526
  Ida (Gray)... 159
  Isaac... 18
  Lavinia F... 221
  Lavinia (Varney)... 221
  Lucy... 181, 181
  Mary... 18, 64
  Mary (Farmer)... 18
  Maurice Y... 523
  Sarah W... 221
  William... 523
LINCOLN, Caroline (Brett)... 481
  Helen... 481
  Lizzie (Mendel)... 485
  Samuel... 485
  William E... 481
LINDALL, John C... 446
  Lillian... 446
LINDSAY, Agnes (Snow)... 485
  Edwin P... 485
  Frances (Shapleigh)... 312
  Frederick d... 485
  Richard... 312
  Sarah... 253
LIPSETT, Ada (Bartlett)... 536
  Florinda... 536
  Walter... 536
LISKLEY, May, Mrs... 292
LITCHFIELD, Mr... 89
  Delia B. (Lamprey-Little)... 89
LITTLE, Abiah (Tewksbury)... 477
  Ada (Locke)... 299
  Alfred... 215
  Alice... 452
  (Cram), Miss... 483
  Dearborn, Dea... 452
  Delia... 89
  Delia B. (Lamprey)... 89
  Etta... 307
  Frank... 215, 483
  George... 299
  Hannah (Locke)... 225
  Horace W... 477
  James... 89, 89
  Linus... 477
  Mary... 89, 417
  Mary (Locke)... 215
  Samuel... 225
  Sarah... 402
  Sarah (Locke)... 477
  William... 477
LITTLEFIELD, Annie... 527
  Byron... 347
  Charles... 347, 347
  Emma... 347, 522
  Fannie... 287
  Frank O... 287
  George... 181, 287
  Eunice (Locke-George-Smith)... 96
  Henry... 125
  James C... 397
  John... 205
  Judith (Prescott)... 205
  Julia (Smith)... 181
  Lilla (Hayes)... 347
  Olive D... 397
  Sarah (Neal)... 397
  Sarah P. (Locke)... 125
  Stephen... 96
LIVINGSTONE, Dr... 325
LLOYD, Mr... 356
  Elizabeth... 356
  Margeret... 357
  Maria (Locke)... 356

LLOYD, Sarah... 356
LOCKE, Mr... 76, 569
  Mrs... 98
  Aaron... 139
  Aaron R... 473
  Abbie... 80, 149, 304, 308, 359
  Abbie A... 246, 282, 293
  Abbie Anna... 351
  Abbie B... 248
  Abbie (Brown)... 75
  Abbie C... 293, 428
  Abbie Florence... 343
  Abbie L... 209
  Abbie (Leighton)... 361
  Abbie (Libbey)... 568
  Abbie M... 239, 420
  Abbie M. d... 237
  Abbie (Nute), Mrs... 482
  Abbie (Palmer)... 202
  Abbie (Ware)... 200
  Abbie (White)... 253
  Abbie (Young)... 284
  Abbott A... 211
  Abiah (Harding)... 42
  Abigail... 14, 16, 23, 24, 26, 27, 31
    38, 43, 49, 49, 51, 52, 53, 60
    61, 61, 73, 86, 95, 107, 110
    112, 119, 121, 122, 131, 155
    190, 191, 244, 245, 302
  Abigail d... 24, 54, 131, 235, 281, 360
  Abigail B... 246
  Abigail (Berry)... 13
  Abigail (Blake)... 51, 284
  Abigail (Chadbourne)... 41
  Abigail W. (Colley)... 85
  Abigail (Dearborn)... 52
  Abigail (Fowler)... 193
  Abigail (Goodwin)... 139
  Abigail (Haines)... 24
  Abigail (Howard)... 35
  Abigail D. (Jacobs)... 112
  Abigail (Jenness)... 51
  Abigail (Locke)... 61, 88
  Abigail M. (Locke)... 72, 140
  Abigail M... 149
  Abigail (Mace)... 34, 72, 140
  Abigail (Marden)... 51
  Abigail (Nutter)... 49
  Abigail P... 122
  Abigail (Page)... 54
  Abigail (Perry)... 22
  Abigail (Philbrick)... 34, 56
  Abigail (Phinney-Huston)... 76
  Abigail (Pitman)... 70
  Abigail (Prescott)... 13
  Abigail S... 274
  Abigail (Saunders)... 29, 55
  Abigail (Sherburne)... 46
  Abigail T... 108
  Abigail (Towle)... 26
  Abigail (Underwood-Amazeen), Mrs... 51
  Abigail W... 247
  Abigail (Wight)... 124
  Abigail Wilkins... 134
  Abigail (Withey)... 88
  Abijah... 13, 21, 40
  Abijah, Capt... 37
  Abner... 34, 72
  Abner d... 17, 26, 34, 51, 122
  Abner D... 123
  Abner W... 81
  Abra Francis... 181
  Abra (Furbish)... 73
  Abraham, Deac... 43
  Abraham... 87
  Abraham W... 81
  Abram... 189
  Abram D... 419
  Abram Doloff... 224

INDEX OF NAMES

Locke, Abram T.................... 235
  Absolom........................ 37
  Ada............................ 449
  Ada A. C....................... 202
  Ada Blanche.................... 461
  Ada C.......................... 352
  Ada Chestina................... 299
  Ada E.......................... 259
  Ada F.......................... 294
  Ada Jennie..................... 337
  Ada Marie...................... 389
  Ada (Oare)..................... 209
  Adalaide (Cook)................ 275
  Adalaide F.................136, 315
  Adalaide (Howe)................ 428
  Adalaide L..................... 240
  Adaline..........62, 97, 135, 209, 234
                     235, 268, 302
  Adaline d...................... 150
  Adaline K...................... 293
  Adaline M..................147, 318
  Adaline P...................... 156
  Adaline (Sheppard)............. 72
  Adaline (Thompson)............. 224
  Adaline (Tibbetts)............. 71
  Addie M........................ 569
  Addie (Pearson)................ 475
  Addie R. T..................... 354
  Addie W........................ 324
  Adela.......................... 255
  Adelia......................... 81
  Adna........................... 55
  Adna P......................... 239
  Adoniram Judson................ 185
  Adre........................... 356
  Agnes......................135, 356
  Agnes (Cunningham)............. 189
  Agnes Dale..................... 350
  Agnes E........................ 170
  Agnes (Hammond)................ 424
  Agnes LaBounty................. 126
  Ai Forrest..................... 509
  Alanson........................ 86
  Alanson L...................... 187
  Alba d......................... 320
  Albert...........112, 303, 356, 358, 475
  Albert d....................... 282
  Albert C....................... 316
  Albert Edward.................. 368
  Albert Everett................. 341
  Albert G....................... 268
  Albert J....................... 552
  Albert Jones................... 321
  Albert N....................... 257
  Albert S....................... 568
  Albert S. d.................... 254
  Albert True.................... 372
  Albert Vasco................... 509
  Albert Wilbur.................. 462
  Albertina...................... 516
  Albion......................115, 252
  Albion B....................... 347
  Albion Van..................... 327
  Albro.......................... 187
  Alena.......................... 506
  Aletha Alma.................... 299
  Alexander...................... 425
  Alexander Morrill.............. 425
  Alfred.............72, 125, 244, 384
  Alfred d....................... 349
  Alfred Curtis.................. 368
  Alfred F. d.................... 150
  Alfred H....................... 284
  Alfred Nathan.................. 369
  Alice...............8, 11, 13, 54, 109
              177, 187, 244, 335, 423
  Alice d........................ 412
  Alice (Abbott-Walker), Mrs..... 491
  Alice (Baker).................. 401
  Alice (Dexter)................. 437

Locke, Alice E.................... 374
  Alice F....................288, 430
  Alice Gertrude................. 343
  Alice (Gibson)................. 350
  Alice (Griswold)............... 369
  Alice (Haines)................. 307
  Alice (Hood-Stodder), Mrs...... 368
  Alice Julia.................... 365
  Alice M........................ 549
  Alice Marion...............540, 564
  Alice Merrill.................. 513
  Alice P....................170, 246
  Alice (Pearsons)............... 46
  Alice (Strong)................. 292
  Alice (Todd)................... 357
  Allabelle d.................... 337
  Allen.......................... 506
  Allen K........................ 357
  Allen R........................ 472
  Allen Stephen.................. 349
  Allen W........................ 530
  Allevia........................ 190
  Allison N...................... 375
  Alma (Levin)................... 334
  Almeda d....................... 105
  Almeda S....................... 241
  Almer F........................ 150
  Almina......................... 187
  Almira......86, 113, 136, 137, 240, 255
  Almira d...................177, 235
  Almira (Brown).............108, 142
  Almira (Doty).................. 136
  Almira Dummer................. 328
  Almira Lydia................... 350
  Almira (Royce)................. 194
  Almira (Shaw-Lear)............. 106
  Almon Andrew................... 161
  Almon E........................ 189
  Almon Frances.................. 333
  Alonzo Stevens................. 183
  Alpheus Crosby................. 199
  Alphonzo...................276, 504
  Alphonzo d..................... 327
  Alphonzo B..................... 284
  Alton......................127, 136
  Alton d........................ 365
  Alvah H........................ 545
  Alvin H........................ 215
  Alvina (Neal).................. 204
  Alwilda (Eaton)................ 215
  Alzada......................... 484
  Amanda.....................105, 135
  Amanda (Lutz).................. 421
  Amanda Muriel.................. 359
  Amanda (Pankey)................ 246
  Amanda (Sanborn-Cook).......... 361
  Amanda (Sawtelle).............. 110
  Amanda (Squires)............... 62
  Amanda (Williams).............. 424
  Amasa.......................36, 74
  Ambrose Colby.................. 181
  Amelia (Camp).................. 275
  Amelia (Hill).................. 258
  Amelia (Shey).................. 190
  Amelia T....................... 161
  Amelia (Wardwell).............. 180
  Amos........................... 63
  Amos d......................... 63
  Amos Garland................... 305
  Amos Revilo.................... 402
  Amos S. d...................... 235
  Amos Seavey.................... 235
  Amy (Ladd)..................... 187
  Amy Luverne.................... 450
  Anagusta (Sterling)............ 287
  Ancil d........................ 357
  Andrew......................... 357
  Andrew of Michigan............. 136
  Andrew Diamond................. 361
  Andrew G....................... 479

INDEX OF NAMES

LOCKE, Andrew J. 234
  Andrew Jackson 135, 317
  Andrew Robertson 350
  Andrew W 282
  Angelina (———) 63
  Angelina (Dockum) 304
  Angelina (Hayes) 125
  Angeline M 282
  Ann 37, 46, 55, 190, 191, 477
                     505, 506, 568
  Ann Augusta (Locke) 419
  Ann (Coleman) 89
  Ann (Dawlton-Garland), Mrs 140
  Ann Eliza 173
  Ann Elizabeth 491
  Ann (Golding) 306
  Ann Isabel 286
  Ann (Lord) 302
  Ann Lydia) 363
  Ann M 142, 156, 248
  Ann M. d 178
  Ann Maria 293, 316
  Ann Merrill 199
  Ann (Pomeroy), Mrs 38
  Ann (Rose) 20
  Ann (Seager) 21
  Ann (Swain) 272
  Ann T. B 324
  Ann (Tarlton) 304
  Ann (Tewksbury) 133
  Ann (Wilkinson-Van Deryer) 21
  Anna 62, 110
  Anna d 30, 71, 207
  Anna of Montreal 95
  Anna (Balch) 287
  Annabel (Hobbs) 178
  Anna (Board) 79
  Anna D 243
  Anna (Dalton-Garland) 127
  Anna (Davis) 247
  Anna E 149
  Anna Getz 564
  Anna (Howard) 328
  Anna (James) 42
  Anna (Jenkins) 194
  Anna (Johnson) 535
  Anna (Jordan) 533
  Anna L 563
  Anna L. d 343
  Anna (Lord) 83
  Anna Lovering 115
  Anna May 173
  Anna (Merrill) 241, 256
  Anna (Pease) 218
  Anna (Perry) 126
  Anna (Prescott) 203
  Anna (Quattlebaum) 540
  Anna (Rogers) 79
  Anna S. d 248
  Anna (Towle) 51
  Anna (Trow) 401
  Anna (Wentworth) 41
  Annah 46, 52, 109
  Annah N 242
  Annah S 249
  Anne (Crowell) 190
  Annette d 423
  Annette 227
  Annie 102, 450, 477
  Annie (Amee) 241
  Annie Belle 499
  Annie (Blaisdell) 482
  Annie C. d 150
  Annie (Dixon) 386
  Annie Dora 462
  Annie (Dyer) 181
  Annie E 161, 471, 527
  Annie E. d 490
  Annie Elizabeth 369
  Annie F 322

LOCKE, Annie (Featherstone) 184
  Annie (Fernald) 317
  Annie (Florence) 460
  Annie (Hill) 347, 368
  Annie J 402, 404, 412
  Annie Jarvis 430
  Annie L 488, 490
  Annie Louise 428
  Annie Lov 255
  Annie M 375, 383, 477, 549
  Annie Maria 346, 479
  Annie (McCharles) 273
  Annie (Nute-Bradeen), Mrs 462
  Annie (Philips) 357
  Annie (Smith) 303
  Annie (Tilinghast) 161
  Annie (Whittemore) 322
  Annis 16
  Annis T 242
  Ansley A 81
  Aphia Ann 317
  Aphia Rand 144
  Arabella A 313
  Arabella (Clough) 237
  Ardelle Mary 337
  Ariadne 150
  Ariadne S 109
  Arthur 257, 461, 507
  Arthur d 240, 510
  Arthur Austin 333
  Arthur C 436
  Arthur Caverno 193
  Arthur Drinkwater 185
  Arthur F 562
  Arthur H 504
  Arthur Herbert, Rev 185
  Arthur Horton 402
  Arthur L. d 401
  Arthur L 538
  Arthur Leon 461
  Arthur M 488
  Arthur Ross 332
  Arthur True 449
  Arvilla 218, 244, 386, 533
  Arvilla (Carr) 246
  Arvilla (Collins) 213
  Arvilla P 303
  Asa 44, 67, 72, 140, 305
  Atlanta (Gordon) 241
  Atwell Edward 337
  Aubin Gale 209, 209
  Audrey Elizabeth 502
  Augusta 357, 506
  Augusta A 222
  Augusta (Henderson) 150
  Augusta (Locke) 224
  Augusta (Plummer) 492
  Augustine d 83
  Augustus 481
  Augustus d 207, 207
  Augustus B 81
  Augustus E 504
  Augustus I. d 490
  Augustus Linwood 462
  Augustus W 306
  Aurelia P. (Clarke) 81
  Aurella d 475
  Aurilla F 185
  Austice (Lane) 177
  Austin 357
  Austin P 486
  Austin Percival 359
  Barry 356
  Barzilla Shurtleff 124
  Bathia (Balch) 568
  Beatrice T 550
  Belinda 156
  Belinda (Bunker) 140
  Belle 86
  Belle Case (Gardner) 161

INDEX OF NAMES

LOCKE, Belle F. 84
  Belle (Fisher) 258
  Belle (Marshall) 292
  Belle R. 310
  Benjamin 26, 31, 37, 49, 52, 74
      75, 98, 104, 130, 130
      135, 161, 225, 227, 299
  Benjamin d 31, 255, 283
  Benjamin B. 131
  Benjamin Babb 54
  Benjamin C. 332
  Benjamin Emery 185
  Benjamin F. 116, 125, 502
  Benjamin Franklin 192
  Benjamin Harrison 340
  Benjamin Lov. 113
  Benjamin Marden 131
  Benjamin T. 126
  Benjamin Veazie 42
  Bernice E. 463
  Bernice (Irish) 529
  Bert D. 484
  Bert T. 480
  Bertha 187, 358, 506
  Bertha (Downes) 484
  Bertha E. 333
  Bertha G. 527
  Bertha I. 543
  Bertha (Leach) 381
  Bertha (Rowe) 384
  Bertram G. 568
  Bessie d 456
  Bessie (Bachelder) 309, 488
  Bessie (Frazier) 321
  Bessie J. 169
  Bessie (Whitehouse) 529
  Bethia 37, 190, 190, 356
  Bethia (Blaney) 46
  Bethia (Locke) 190
  Betsey 41, 42, 44, 47, 54, 71, 86, 87
      88, 105, 113, 122, 130, 100
      191, 281, 568, 568, 569
  Betsey of Illinois 63
  Betsey Aiken 290
  Betsey (Babb) 27, 124
  Betsey (Dyer) 21
  Betsey D. (Gerry) 71
  Betsey (Green) 281
  Betsey (Howard) 73
  Betsey (Huntress) 568
  Betsey (Hurd) 54
  Betsey J. 282
  Betsey (Janvrin-Scribner), Mrs. . . . 99
  Betsey (Locke) 568
  Betsey (Nutter) 219
  Betsey (Olds) 74
  Betsey (Patrick) 73
  Betsey (Philbrick) 110
  Betsey R. 85
  Betsey (Ransom) 327, 497
  Betsey (Starin) 185
  Betsey (Stearns) 45
  Betsey (Tucker) 67
  Betsey (Walton) 214
  Betty 97
  Betty d 97
  Bettie (Lewis) 243
  Betty (Perkins) 46
  Beulah 387
  Bilbah 37
  Bina (Wiggin) 477
  Bird 568
  Birdie 534
  Blake 47, 109, 242
  Blanche 481
  Blanche (Buzzell) 373
  Blanche L 451, 505
  Blanche (Ross) 498
  Bradbury C. 131
  Bradford 506

LOCKE, Bradley 477
  Brainard 64
  Brent (Robinson) 359
  Burness P. 372
  Burt Wallace 495
  Byron 135
  Byron G. d 460
  Byron H. 337, 337, 337
  C. A. 568
  Caleb 21, 42, 82, 181
  Calvin 156, 316
  (Campbell), Miss 115
  Candace Janette 134, 299
  Carl d 390
  Carlton d 505
  Caroline 240
  Caroline d 204
  Caroline (Barge) 276
  Caroline C. 290
  Caroline Freeman 145
  Caroline Goodwin (Garland) 140
  Caroline H. 126, 154
  Caroline (Hayes) 234
  Caroline (Hecker) 326
  Caroline (Hewitt) 356
  Caroline (Kimball) 243
  Caroline M. 185
  Caroline (Nightingale) 303
  Caroline (Nudd) 97
  Caroline (Pettingill) 185
  Caroline S. 98
  Caroline (Sperman) 337
  Caroline (Taplin) 241
  Caroline (Tebbetts) 95
  Carrie 161, 243, 243, 281, 369, 375
      378, 378, 478, 538, 540
  Carrie d 429
  Carrie (Buchanan) 173
  Carrie (Coffine) 416
  Carrie (Edson) 313
  Carrie (Edwards) 332
  Carrie (Francies) 436
  Carrie H. 133
  Carrie Macomber 246
  Carrie Maria 430
  Carrie McKitrick 337
  Carrie Newell 305
  Carrie (Paul) 411
  Carrie (Robinson) 321
  Carrie (Sawyer) 413
  Carrie (Thomas) 451
  Carrie (Varney) 568
  Carrie Wallace 490
  Carroll 563
  Carroll Dewey 350
  Catherine 189, 191, 276, 303
  Catherine (Barge) 275
  Catherine (Cranston) 274
  Catherine E. 276
  Catherine (Guyon) 86
  Catherine McKay 356
  Catherine (Newell) 218
  Catherine (Ringer) 356
  Catherine (Steadman) 75
  Catherine (Tucker) 122
  Cecil 544
  Celia A. 315
  Celia (Wiggin) 367
  Charity (Marden) 31
  Charles 86, 86, 99, 136, 241
      268, 293, 303, 307, 324
      484, 506, 516, 568
  Charles d 181, 258, 384
      427, 427, 428, 471
  Charles A. 175, 218, 237, 284, 284
      293, 308, 434, 510, 569
  Charles Arthur 353
  Charles Augustine 185
  Charles B. 74, 352
  Charles Byron 337

INDEX OF NAMES

LOCKE, Charles C............220, 243
   Charles C. d................. 243
   Charles Clarence................ 441
   Charles D...................... 274
   Charles Dennett................. 272
   Charles Dunbar................. 479
   Charles E..........153, 227, 288, 556
   Charles Edwin..........208, 332, 369
   Charles Eldad.................. 299
   Charles Elmer.................. 484
   Charles Elvin, Prof............. 406
   Charles F........161, 302, 321, 347, 369
   Charles F. d................... 150
   Charles Franklin, Dr............ 289
   Charles Fred................... 149
   Charles Fremont................ 509
   Charles Granville............... 321
   Charles H. 161, 194, 292, 292, 307, 352, 453
   Charles H. d................... 282
   Charles Henry......275, 290, 328, 360
   Charles Herbert................ 503
   Charles K...................... 417
   Charles Llewellyn............... 351
   Charles Loren.................. 549
   Charles Miller.................. 145
   Charles N...................... 315
   Charles S...................... 188
   Charles Stacy.................. 253
   Charles T...................... 214
   Charles W..........289, 343, 384, 455
   Charles W. d...............149, 395
   Charles Warren................. 368
   Charles Wesley, Rev............ 346
   Charlotte.....78, 89, 102, 284, 475, 568
   Charlotte d.................... 192
   Charlotte A..............116, 150, 207
   Charlotte (Clifford)............. 245
   Charlotte (Currier).............. 125
   Charlotte (Foster).............. 292
   Charlotte (Parker).............. 125
   Charlotte (Stevens).............. 40
   Charlotte (Wentworth).......... 72
   Chauncey E.................... 354
   Chester A...................... 354
   Chester H...................... 194
   Chestina (Freeman)............. 164
   Chloe.......................... 105
   Chloe (Woodmansee), Mrs....... 75
   Christena...................... 235
   Christena d.................... 294
   Christena B.................... 471
   Christena (French)............. 581
   Christena (Paine).............. 26
   Christena R.................... 185
   Christene L.................... 499
   Christiana (Saunders).......134, 135
   Christopher H.................. 81
   Churchill...................... 357
   Claire......................544, 561
   Clara.......................... 399
   Clara d........................ 510
   Clara A........................ 522
   Clara (Alexander).............. 421
   Clara Belle.................... 462
   Clara (Bowman)................ 435
   Clara (Crawford).............. 525
   Clara E........................ 232
   Clara Eleanor.................. 473
   Clara Ella..................... 419
   Clara (Emery).................. 248
   Clara F. d..................... 294
   Clara (Haskell)................. 164
   Clara J....................277, 417
   Clara (Jacobs)................. 540
   Clara Jos...................... 247
   Clara Louise................... 339
   Clara M........................ 539
   Clara May..................... 174
   Clara (Norton)................. 185
   Clara (Pratt).................. 183

LOCKE, Clara Prescott............... 294
   Clara S........................ 257
   Clara (Spinney)................ 343
   Clara (Struck)................. 455
   Clara T........................ 428
   Clara (Tallman)................ 434
   Clara V. d..................... 467
   Clara Victoria................. 456
   Clara (Zoeller)................. 499
   Clarence................213, 310, 379
   Clarence d........209, 471, 487, 541
   Clarence A..................... 384
   Clarence B..................... 463
   Clarence Blaine................ 502
   Clarence E..................... 492
   Clarence Edward............... 373
   Clarence H..................... 428
   Clarence P..................... 333
   Clarence Richard............... 322
   Clarence S. d.................. 150
   Clarinda (Bachelder).........120, 310
   Clarinda L. (Elliott)............ 141
   Clarissa....................... 97
   Clarissa (Tash)................ 110
   Clarissa (Wallace).............. 110
   Clayton W., Dr................. 299
   Clifford........................ 359
   Clifton......................... 340
   Clyde Earl..................... 554
   Colin.......................... 356
   Colin C........................ 508
   Colin Campbell................ 190
   Colin Campbell Stalker........ 359
   Columbus Judson.............. 185
   Comfort....................44, 88, 89
   Comfort (Dowrst)............... 23
   Cora.......................331, 366
   Cora d.....................240, 506
   Cora A......................... 450
   Cora B.....................301, 379
   Cora Belle..................... 505
   Cora (Leeman)................. 352
   Cora (Millbury)................ 435
   Cora (Pease)................... 187
   Cora (Place)................... 479
   Cora S......................... 270
   Cordelia (Gray)................ 286
   Cordelia Jane.................. 157
   Cordelia P..................... 164
   Corena Stewart................ 333
   Cornelia (Ackerly).............. 208
   Cornelia (Danforth)............ 154
   Cornelia F..................... 543
   Cornelius A.................... 124
   Cornelius E.................... 236
   Cristie[4](Bowman)............. 568
   Cynthia........................ 98
   Cynthia L...................... 127
   Cyril.......................... 506
   Cyril W. d..................... 326
   Cyrus.......................... 186
   Cyrus H. d..................... 317
   Cyrus Munroe.................. 292
   Daisy......................506, 540
   Daisy (McKeown).............. 535
   Dana A........................ 257
   Daniel 51, 122, 161, 161, 187
   Daniel d..................29, 71, 355
   Daniel B....................... 150
   Daniel Bryant.................. 483
   Daniel Evans................... 89
   Daniel L....................... 305
   Daniel Lincoln................. 364
   Daniel Moshier................ 453
   Daniel P....................245, 274
   Daniel Philbrick............... 193
   Daniel Piper................... 124
   Daniel Sherburne.............. 449
   Daniel Treadwell.............. 108
   Darius W...................... 277

INDEX OF NAMES 655

Locke, Darwin.................... 136
Date S. (Hallet)................ 86
David, Deacon................... 112
David........26, 29, 47, 51, 72, 81, 93
93, 96, 97, 109, 110, 133
177, 242, 245, 300, 565
David d...............112, 244, 357
David of Michigan................ 63
David of New York............... 63
David Abijah.................... 170
David Byron..................... 413
David E......................... 423
David J......................... 108
David Morrill...............246, 257
David Parsons................... 306
David V......................... 530
Dearborn B...................... 242
Deborah..........13, 40, 42, 80, 171
Deborah d...................21, 79
Deborah (Chase)................. 124
Deborah (Knowles)............... 41
Deborah Locke (Noyes)........... 77
Deborah (Veazey)................ 21
Deborah (Wells)................. 88
Delila........................80, 80
Deliverance.................23, 43
Deliverance (Brookin)........... 13
Della (Beard)................... 509
Della (Herkimer)................ 174
Della O......................... 504
Desdemona (Woods).............. 510
Dewitt C........................ 243
Dexter d........................ 435
Dexter H........................ 254
Diantha......................... 62
Diantha (Emerson).............. 187
Dolly........................53, 54
Dolly (Abbott).................. 85
Dolly (Bachelder-Brown)......... 46
Donnan.......................... 533
Dora Belle...................... 320
Dora (Luckey)................... 298
Dorcas.......................... 187
Dorcas (Guptil)................. 147
Dorothy........13, 13, 21, 18, 34, 37, 40
63, 63, 96, 233, 506, 548
Dorothy (Blake)................. 11
Dorothy S....................... 126
Dorothy Sargent................. 104
Dorothy (Worden)................ 37
Dow............................. 86
(Dow), Miss..................... 179
Drusilla........................ 192
Drusilla S...................... 199
Dudley of New York.............. 63
Dudley.......................97, 136
Earl M.......................... 535
Earl Russell.................... 373
Earl S.......................... 538
Eben............................ 287
Eben C.......................... 122
Eben Samuel..................... 450
Eben Sutton..................... 450
Ebenezer..38, 40, 77, 86, 189, 189, 356
Eda (Cleaves)................... 268
Edda C.......................... 354
Eddie C......................... 369
E. Donald....................... 472
Edgar H......................... 283
Edgar T......................... 326
Edgar Warren.................... 549
Edison G........................ 479
Edith.............276, 348, 461, 506
Edith d....................335, 505
Edith Badeau.................... 564
Edith (Butts)................... 299
Edith (Chamberlain)............. 185
Edith (Cogswell)................ 209
Edith F......................... 388
Edith I......................... 472

Locke, Edith J.................. 338
Edith Josephine................. 540
Edith L......................... 463
Edith M...................379, 472, 552
Edith (Staple).................. 480
Edmund Webster.................. 291
Edna........................378, 514
Edna A.......................... 534
Edna Adelle..................... 188
Edna (Bates).................... 337
Edna (Bullis)................... 276
Edna F.......................... 450
Edna (Fayer).................... 495
Edna Ulmer...................... 170
Edson B......................... 160
Edward, Rev..................... 24
Edward........8, 11, 13, 13, 21, 24, 25
41, 46, 48, 49, 114, 161
171, 171, 184, 379 568
Edward d........................ 387
Edward A.....................81, 253
Edward C....................326, 360
Edward E. d..................... 150
Edward Frank.................... 468
Edward Franklin................. 220
Edward Howard................... 164
Edward J................95, 171, 219
Edward J. d..................... 95
Edward L........................ 194
Edward Marshall................. 191
Edward Morris................... 502
Edward Oliver d................. 378
Edward P....................249, 431
Edward S....................194, 496
Edwin.........72, 136, 357, 358, 506
Edwin A., Dr.................... 465
Edwin Ansley.................... 173
Edwin Augustus.................. 248
Edwin B.....................248, 253
Edwin Cecil..................... 499
Edwin Fernald................... 288
Edwin Franklin.................. 516
Edwin H......................... 367
Edwin Howard.................... 328
Edwin J......................... 551
Edwin Merrill................... 352
Edwin N......................... 219
Edwin Norman.................... 340
Edwin R......................... 112
Edwin S., Rev................... 257
Edwin S.............150, 189, 300, 473
Edwin Wallace................... 317
Effie A......................... 492
Effie Augusta................... 450
Effie B......................... 416
Effie Blanche................... 333
Effie (Bryant), Mrs............. 308
Effie H. d...................... 490
Effie (Wallace).............130, 130
Elbreda G....................... 337
Elbridge d..................234, 399
Elbridge Gerry..............246, 361
Eleanor......23, 88, 195, 268, 268, 302
Eleanor B....................... 541
Eleanor (Berry)..............64, 139
Eleanor Dow..................... 65
Eleanor H....................... 424
Eleanor Hosmer.................. 79
Eleanor J...................269, 346
Eleanor (Payson)................ 124
Eleanor (Tucker)................ 53
Electra (Chesley)............... 222
Elenore......................... 384
Eletia.......................... 507
Eliakin d....................... 73
Elias Varney.................... 568
Elijah.....................29, 46, 60
Elijah d........................ 29
Elijah, Deacon.................. 14
Elijah Ferguson................. 171

INDEX OF NAMES

LOCKE, Elijah Frederick.............. 134
    Elijah True.................... 94
    Eliphalet...................... 102
    Eliphalet d.................... 14
    Elisha..14, 29, 29, 54, 125, 126, 136, 318
    Elisha of Ohio................. 64
    Elisha Beede................... 318
    Elisha E....................... 284
    Elisha Ferdinand............... 134
    Elisha Judson.................. 285
    Eliza...............39, 40, 81, 94, 96
               113, 131, 154, 190, 568
    Eliza A........................ 160
    Eliza B........................ 195
    Eliza (Brackett)............... 235
    Eliza (Chase).................. 99
    Eliza (Dixon).................. 249
    Eliza (Dore)................... 86
    Eliza (Hunt-Crockett-Fogg), Mrs... 83
    Eliza J....................222, 240
    Eliza M........................ 194
    Eliza (Roberts)................ 179
    Eliza (Shaw)................... 191
    Eliza (Standlick).............. 413
    Eliza (Stanton)................ 108
    Eliza T........................ 192
    Eliza (Taylor)................. 534
    Eliza (Varrell)................ 316
    Eliza (Vickers)................ 282
    Eliza (Waity).................. 172
    Elizabeth.....2, 3, 8, 11, 13, 16, 20, 23
              27, 30, 34, 35, 37, 43, 54
              61, 66, 69, 72, 79, 80, 83
              86, 96, 107, 102, 119, 122
              136, 146, 150, 153, 179
              183, 190, 191, 252, 289
              308, 317, 334, 357, 358
                    530, 566, 568
    Elizabeth d...............29, 54, 96
    Elizabeth (Allen)..............32, 34
    Elizabeth Ann.................. 141
    Elizabeth B.................... 126
    Elizabeth (Berry).............. 11
    Elizabeth (Bailey)............. 302
    Elizabeth (Bickford)........... 453
    Elizabeth (Bowl)............... 86
    Elizabeth (Bowles)............. 11
    Elizabeth (Boyd)............... 422
    Elizabeth (Braman)............. 74
    Elizabeth (Brown).............. 29
    Elizabeth (Calvin)............. 461
    Elizabeth (Chase).............. 93
    Elizabeth (Cheney)............. 130
    Elizabeth (Churchill).........190, 191
    Elizabeth (Collins)............ 24
    Elizabeth D.................... 406
    Elizabeth (Doty-Coyne), Mrs..... 326
    Elizabeth E.................... 367
    Elizabeth (Edwards)............ 368
    Elizabeth Ellen................ 343
    Elizabeth (Ellingwood)......... 185
    Elizabeth F.................... 245
    Elizabeth (Fennes)............. 171
    Elizabeth (Fernald)............ 71
    Elizabeth (Foss)............... 187
    Elizabeth G. d..............71, 305
    Elizabeth G. d................. 72
    Elizabeth (Garland)............ 17
    Elizabeth (Gilpatrick)......... 21
    Elizabeth H.................... 116
    Elizabeth (Hardy).............. 368
    Elizabeth H. (Hayes)........... 124
    Elizabeth (Hobbs).............. 67
    Elizabeth (Hodges)............. 225
    Elizabeth (Knowles)............ 70
    Elizabeth (Lellingham)......... 29
    Elizabeth (Lloyd).............. 356
    Elizabeth (Lord)............... 41
    Elizabeth M.................... 239
    Elizabeth (Mahoney)............ 284

LOCKE, Elizabeth (Marden).......... 107
    Elizabeth (McHurley)........... 569
    Elizabeth (McKay).............. 189
    Elizabeth (Meader)............. 49
    Elizabeth N.................... 502
    Elizabeth (Noble).............. 179
    Elizabeth P.................... 125
    Elizabeth (Page-Bachelder)..... 23
    Elizabeth (Parker)............. 360
    Elizabeth (Pickering).......... 568
    Elizabeth (Pillsbury).......... 84
    Elizabeth R.................... 161
    Elizabeth (Rand)............... 14
    Elizabeth (Rathburn)........... 20
    Elizabeth Ring................. 77
    Elizabeth S.................75, 83
    Elizabeth (Sanborn)............ 96
    Elizabeth (Seaver)............. 147
    Elizabeth (Smith).............. 193
    Elizabeth (Spofford) Dearborn, Mrs. 303
    Elizabeth (Stanwood-Waite), Mrs... 42
    Elizabeth Susan................ 449
    Elizabeth (Thayer)............. 153
    Elizabeth (Townsend-Collins), Mrs. 146
    Elizabeth (Waterhouse)......... 125
    Elizabeth (Webster)............ 41
    Ella.......................387, 431
    Ella d.....................468, 510
    Ella (Adams)................... 477
    Ella (Blong)................... 289
    Ella (Clark)................... 422
    Ella (Curtis).................. 402
    Ella E......................... 203
    Ella F......................... 490
    Ella (Haley)................... 479
    Ella J......................... 451
    Ella M......................283, 527
    Ella (Smith)................... 538
    Ella (Wright).................. 182
    Ellen..................187, 358, 507
    Ellen A........................ 188
    Ellen (Allen).................. 84
    Ellen Augusta.................. 247
    Ellen (Barker)................. 534
    Ellen (Chadsey)................ 190
    Ellen (Clarke)................. 240
    Ellen (Clark-Crocker), Mrs..... 290
    Ellen E........................ 232
    Ellen F........................ 306
    Ellen (Foster)................. 422
    Ellen (Hinman)................. 300
    Ellen (Kimball)................ 102
    Ellen (Locke).......149, 189, 190, 302
    Ellen M..................149, 253, 315
    Ellen (Martin)................. 399
    Ellen (Mills).................. 308
    Ellen (Morton)................. 357
    Ellen (Parker)................. 81
    Ellen R. (Pike)................ 80
    Ellen Sarah.................... 342
    Ellen (Thayer)................. 287
    Ellen (Towner)................. 358
    Ellinor........................ 357
    Elliott Hunnewell, Rev......... 37
    Elliott S...................... 243
    Elliott T...................... 416
    Elma J......................... 113
    Elmer......................241, 484
    Elmer George................... 335
    Elmira C....................... 162
    Elmore Estes................... 437
    Elroy.......................... 484
    Elsie.......................11, 538
    Elsie C........................ 473
    Elsie E........................ 294
    Elsie (Tritts)................. 41
    Elvin.......................107, 137
    Elvira......................... 233
    Elvira (Marden)............404, 489
    Elzina......................... 484

INDEX OF NAMES 657

LOCKE, Emaline..... 95, 113, 115, 233, 252
Emaline d..............175, 193, 258
Emaline (Hoag)................ 81
Emaline (Hovey)..............115, 258
Emaline (Jamieson).............. 190
Emaline (Loring)............... 132
Emaline (Nightingale)............ 303
Emaline (Parker-Lewis), Mrs...... 113
Emaline (Warring)............... 141
E. Emerett..................... 235
Emerson C..................... 526
Emery d...................... 293
Emery (Allen).................. 422
Emilie 208
Emilie Olivia................... 378
Emilina (Guesdon).............. 96
Emily..................136, 2^9, 303
Emily d....................... 71
Emily (Burton-Carrigen), Mrs..... 343
Emily F. d.................... 257
Emily J........................ 426
Emily M....................... 236
Emily (Marshall)................ 55
Emily (Milburn)................ 208
Emily (Rowell)................. 241
Emily (Sherman)................ 183
Emily W....................... 198
Emma....................307, 310
Emma d...................... 321
Emma A..............237, 239, 486
Emma Augusta................. 360
Emma (Bartlett)................ 257
Emma Caroline................. 208
Emma (Caverley)............... 455
Emma (Collins), Mrs............ 283
Emma (Cuthbert)............... 208
Emma (Daniels)................ 253
Emma E....................222, 313
Emma Elizabeth................ 342
Emma Flagg d................. 464
Emma (Fogg).................. 453
Emma (Fowle)................. 249
Emma Frances................. 352
Emma G....................... 284
Emma (Grace)................. 137
Emma H....................... 455
Emma (Hatch)..............293, 498
Emma (Hines).................. 164
Emma J...........321, 324, 454, 484
Emma J. d.................... 2u4
Emma (Johnson)............... 150
Emma (King).................. 352
Emma M....................... 145
Emma (McMillen)............... 358
Emma (Mitchell)................ 204
Emma Pearl.................... 431
Emma Perkins.................. 430
Emma (Rogers)................ 223
Emma Russell.................. 433
Emma S....................... 413
Emma S. d................... 286
Emma (Smart)................. 545
Emma (Wells).................. 289
Emmons........................ 37
Enoch.....................49, 103
Enos....................189, 190, 506
Enos C........................ 506
Ephraim, Lieut................. 23
Ephraim......44, 73, 88, 153, 192, 324
Ephraim d................... 180
Erastus B..................... 241
Eric........................... 425
Erminie d.................... 558
Ernest........................ 521
Ernest d...................399, 543
Ernest Linwood................ 350
Ernest S....................... 529
Essie (Abbott)................. 356
Estelle (Howard)............... 428
Estelle (Ordiorne).............. 321

LOCKE, Esther....................44, 268
Esther d...................... 21
Esther Annie................... 462
Esther (Bixby)................. 553
Esther (Covill)................ 337
Esther (Dow)................... 21
Esther G...................... 563
Esther (Kittredge).............. 63
Esther (Knowles)............... 52
Esther M...................... 226
Esther (Marden-Leavitt), Mrs..... 108
Esther (Nutter)................ 103
Esther (Remick)................ 140
Esther (Sanborn)............... 529
Ethan Allen................109, 240
Ethel.....................544, 548
Ethel (Knowlton)............... 346
Ethel M...................410, 533
Ethel Mae..................... 556
Ethel Maude...............391, 489
Ethel T....................... 549
Ethelyn d.................... 510
Etta.......................... 568
Etta (Little)................... 307
Etta M....................... 189
Etta (Skinner)................. 184
Eugene D..................... 299
Eugene Masters................ 359
Eugene O..................... 204
Eugene Oscar.................. 173
Eugene Parker................. 352
Eugenia....................... 386
Eugenia (Pulsiffer)............. 455
Eugenie....................... 481
Eunice.....................96, 192
Eunice d..................... 134
Eunice Belle................... 328
Eunice (Eaton)................ 177
Eunice Evelyn.................. 499
Eunice J...................... 171
Eunice (Prescott).............. 113
Eunice (Quincy)............... 106
Eunice (Rice).................. 568
Eunice (Stevens)............... 40
Eunice (Wallis)................ 72
Eunice (Wentworth)............ 155
Eustace...................243, 416
Eva...................183, 465, 507
Eva Carrie.................... 177
Eva (Kinney).................. 373
Eva L......................... 561
Eva M....................... 338
Eva (Martin).................. 495
Eva May...................... 463
Eva (Robinson)................ 372
Eva S........................ 520
Eva T. d..................... 463
Evaline G. (Foot).............. 88
Evalina d.................... 348
Evangeline.................... 359
Evelyn........................ 548
Evelyn A...................... 365
Evelyn G...................... 563
Evelyn J...................... 558
Evelyn L...................... 287
Everett...................348, 384
Everett B..................... 189
Everett H..................... 188
Everett True.................. 489
Ezekiel James, Rev............. 75
Ezra.......................... 136
Fannie................190, 287, 301
Fannie (Allison)............... 423
Fannie Augusta................ 287
Fannie B...................... 337
Fannie (Brooks)............... 427
Fannie (Davis)................ 208
Fannie E...................347, 386
Fannie (Gordon)............... 420
Fannie M..................... 160

INDEX OF NAMES

LOCKE, Fannie (Martin).............. 399
Fannie (Pye).................... 189
Fannie (Smith)................. 227
Fannie W....................... 183
Fanny (Berry) 55
Fanny (Foss)................... 83
Fanny M. (Gibbs)............... 115
Fanny S........................ 209
Fanny (Strickland)............. 86
Favor.................104, 105, 224
Fidelia d..................193, 193
Fidelia Ann.................... 138
Fidelia F...................... 236
Fidelia (Fleming)................ 268
Filenda........................ 115
Finetta d...................... 115
Finette C...................... 425
Fitz Harry..................... 525
Flavilla....................... 187
Fletcher....................... 240
Flora..............189, 331, 521, 532
Flora d........................ 510
Flora A........................ 424
Flora Albertha................. 313
Flora B........................ 568
Flora (Cobb)................... 399
Flora E...................259, 307
Flora (Elkins).................. 249
Flora Grover................... 287
Florella A...................... 203
Florence........340, 379, 441, 540, 542
Florence d.................209, 506
Florence Elizabeth............. 376
Florence Hazel................. 561
Florence June.................. 333
Florence M............359, 429, 504
Florence (Mackinnon)........... 468
Florence (Mayers).............. 534
Florence (McLean).............. 402
Florence (Perley).............. 182
Florence R..................... 499
Florence (Simmons)............. 423
Florence (Stoddard)............ 368
Florinda........95, 115, 246, 422, 539
Florinda d..................... 93
Florinda A..................... 426
Florinda J..................... 423
Florinda (Locke)............93, 110
Flossie M...................... 455
Foreste M...................... 133
Francena (Hook)................ 131
Francena M..................... 285
Frances....................23, 455
Frances d...................... 187
Frances A..............188, 520, 568
Frances (Carpenter)............ 326
Frances Ellen.................. 317
Frances L. d................... 293
Frances M...................... 108
Frances (Manson)...........234, 398
Frances (Murning).............. 534
Frances (Priest)............... 316
Francina (Rand)................ 473
Francis......13, 22, 23, 28, 43, 44, 55
          87, 88, 131, 191, 293
Francis d...................... 420
Francis C...................... 194
Francis E...................... 299
Francis K. d................... 541
Francisco H.................... 424
Frank..............137, 268, 268, 268
                 293, 356, 358, 468
Frank d...........276, 384, 384, 326
Frank A..........308, 386, 477, 568
Frank B........................ 306
Frank C........................ 529
Frank E..............183, 214, 434, 482
Frank Elmer.................... 368
Frank Hartwell................. 292
Frank I........................ 364

LOCKE, Frank Knight................ 554
Frank L...................173, 372
Frank Lovering................. 437
Frank Mortimer................. 208
Frank R........................ 387
Frank S. d..................... 541
Frank Stanwood................. 350
Frank W...................173, 538
Frank Walker................... 288
Franklin d................277, 355
Franklin D..................... 398
Franklin D. d.................. 173
Franklin P..................... 396
Franklin R..................... 455
Fred.....135,187,187, 310, 325, 417, 522
Fred A......................... 308
Fred A. d...................... 484
Fred Augustus.................. 429
Fred E..............492, 534, 560, 561
Fred Ford...................... 412
Fred Getman.................... 174
Fred Leroy..................... 390
Fred Levi...................... 292
Fred V......................... 465
Fred W......................... 137
Freddie d...................... 333
Frederick.................505, 507
Frederick A...............153, 325
Frederick Augustus............. 352
Frederick D.................... 429
Frederick Don.................. 358
Frederick G.................... 399
Frederick W.................... 203
Freeman J...................... 239
French lady.................... 109
G. Emma (Goodwin).............. 428
Gale H......................... 533
Gara C......................... 189
Garaphalia d................... 274
Gardner T...............127, 140, 266
Geneva M....................... 374
Genevieve...................... 473
George....9, 86, 130, 131, 189, 189, 276
          356, 356, 357, 478, 478, 506
George d...............285, 436, 456
George A.............412, 479, 491
George A. d.................... 326
George Andrew.................. 510
George B....................... 424
George Barr.................... 534
George E., Dr.................. 243
George E......299, 331, 387, 460, 479
George E. d.................... 194
George Edward.................. 313
George Evans................... 194
George F.................284, 337, 441
George G....................... 215
George H............171, 303, 471, 477
George H. d.................... 275
George Henry................... 200
George J....................... 190
George K..................134, 534
George M..................164, 290
George Munroe.................. 276
George Oliver.............247, 249
George P....................... 298
George R., Rev................. 420
George S....................... 203
George Scott..............292, 466
George Stanwood................ 351
George V....................... 233
George W.......274, 276, 303, 373, 463
George Washington.............. 70
George William................. 177
Georgeanna............222, 305, 359
Georgeanna M................... 472
Georgeanna (Ward).............. 345
Georgelle...................... 460
Georgetta d.................... 282
Georgie Etta................... 462

INDEX OF NAMES

LOCKE, Georgie R................. 461
  Gerry Reed..................... 510
  Gertrude...................463, 473
  Gertrude (Dodge)............... 299
  Gertrude H..................... 435
  Gertrude M..................... 487
  Gertrude (Parker).............. 462
  Gertrude (Wing)................ 484
  Giffy (Sherman)................ 37
  Gilbert E...................... 472
  Gilman......................... 96
  (Gilman) Miss.................. 156
  Gladys......................... 209
  Gladys A....................... 473
  Gladys B....................... 516
  Gladys E....................... 487
  Gladys (Reed).................. 542
  (Goldsmith), Miss.............. 157
  Goldwin d...................... 387
  Gordon H....................... 141
  Gordon R. d.................... 173
  Grace......................541, 543
  Grace A........................ 538
  Grace Amelia................... 339
  Grace E........................ 218
  Grace H. d..................... 403
  Grace M....................468, 492
  Grace Perley................... 349
  Grace W........................ 542
  Granville...................... 149
  Grover Frank d................. 466
  Guerdon........................ 506
  Guy H.......................... 533
  Guy Howard..................... 498
  Guyon.......................... 189
  H. Gertrude.................... 382
  H. W. (Putnam-Blanchard), Mrs... 214
  Hall Jackson................... 51
  Hamilton....................... 147
  Hamilton C..................... 146
  (Hancock), Mrs................. 303
  Hannah.....14, 22, 24, 27, 28, 29, 29, 31
    31, 34, 41, 43, 44, 46, 53, 54
    55, 65, 66, 71, 73, 73, 74, 77
    81, 82, 84, 86, 91, 139, 146
    155, 567, 568
  Hannah d..14, 23, 27, 63, 67, 420, 454
  Hannah A...................241, 568
  Hannah (Allen)................. 45
  Hannah B...............146, 254, 535
  Hannah Bell.................... 330
  Hannah (Berry).............30, 67
  Hannah (Blake)................. 13
  Hannah Caroline................ 352
  Hannah (Chesley)............... 97
  Hannah Clarke..............83, 185
  Hannah (Colley)................ 85
  Hannah D. d.................... 154
  Hannah (Danielson)............. 73
  Hannah (Dodge), Mrs............ 119
  Hannah (Donaldson-Foss), Mrs... 122
  Hannah Dow..................... 144
  Hannah E............181, 304, 383, 456
  Hannah (Eves)............202, 372
  Hannah F..........104, 172, 225, 416
  Hannah (Favor)................. 49
  Hannah (Felch)................. 45
  Hannah (Field)................. 141
  Hannah (Fogg).................. 21
  Hannah (Hoyt)..............123, 124
  Hannah (Hoyt) (Locke).......... 122
  Hannah (Hunt).................. 180
  Hannah J....................... 67
  Hannah (Jenness)...........11, 16
  Hannah (Knowles)...........11, 108
  Hannah (Lang)..............34, 66
  Hannah (Leach-White)........... 233
  Hannah (Lewis)................. 74
  Hannah (Locke).............45, 47
  Hannah (Lockwood).............. 171

LOCKE, Hannah (Lovering)........... 26
  Hannah M....................... 243
  Hannah (Magoon)................ 21
  Hannah Mary.................... 89
  Hannah (Moses)................. 113
  Hannah Olive................... 142
  Hannah P....................... 568
  Hannah (Philbrick)............. 11
  Hannah (Prescott).............. 52
  Hannah R....................... 302
  Hannah (Rand).................. 18
  Hannah (Randall)............... 71
  Hannah S...................83, 192
  Hannah Salter.................. 145
  Hannah (Saunders).............. 60
  Hannah (Smith)................. 213
  Hannah (Spaulding)............. 134
  Hannah (Tarlton-Beals)......... 52
  Hannah (Tate-Haddaway), Mrs.... 38
  Hannah (Tewksbury)............. 38
  Hannah (True).................. 92
  Hannah (Vittum-Berry), Mrs..... 70
  Hannah W....................... 108
  Hannah Wakefield............... 154
  Hannah (Wood)..............55, 80
  Hannah Woodmansee.............. 161
  Hannah (Young)................. 144
  Hannibal Orlando............... 422
  Harmon J....................... 413
  Harold.....................359, 544
  Harold d....................... 349
  Harold I....................... 553
  Harold Russell................. 502
  Harold S....................... 170
  Harrie......................... 475
  Harrie Francisco............... 287
  Harriet.....80, 104, 136, 269, 303, 358
  Harriet d..................113, 344
  Harriet A..................148, 367
  Harriet (Allen)................ 94
  Harriet Ann.................... 55
  Harriet (Bachelder)............ 94
  Harriet Bacon.................. 326
  Harriet (Bailey)............... 246
  Harriet (Berry)................ 463
  Harriet Bynam.................. 154
  Harriet (Carter)............... 171
  Harriet E...................... 481
  Harriet F...................... 292
  Harriet (Fletcher)............. 84
  Harriet (Grow)................. 133
  Harriet (Hedges)............... 300
  Harriet J...................... 316
  Harriet (Kimball).............. 199
  Harriet (Locke)............247, 249
  Harriet (Mason).........104, 105, 225
  Harriet Newell................. 344
  Harriet (Potter)............... 80
  Harriet R...................... 164
  Harriet S...................... 194
  Harriet (Shaw)................. 141
  Harriet Stebbins............... 134
  Harriet (Sweet)................ 318
  Harriet W..................157, 539
  Harriet (Weatherbee)........... 145
  Harriet (Young)................ 98
  Harris B....................... 94
  Harrison....................... 540
  Harry......................484, 506
  Harry d....................164, 346
  Harry Archer................... 461
  Harry B........................ 534
  Harry Fletcher................. 558
  Harry Goodwin.................. 540
  Harry Harrison................. 535
  Harry S........................ 183
  Harry (Smith).................. 83
  Harry Warren................... 335
  Harvey......................... 133
  Harvey Belnap.................. 298

INDEX OF NAMES

LOCKE, Harvey D. 81
Harvey E. 538
Harvey Morrill. 563
Hattie 307, 356, 386, 416, 451
Hattie A. 299, 466
Hattie A. d. 157
Hattie (Burnham) 181
Hattie F. 468
Hattie (Fay) 484
Hattie L. 332, 466
Hattie (Mosher) 81
Hattie (Smith) 491
Haynes 109
Hazel 337
Hazel Maria 391
Helen 240, 268, 399, 412, 533
Helen d. 284
Helen (Burbank) 538
Helen C. 406, 412
Helen E. 521, 521
Helen Elizabeth 464
Helen (Elliott) 568
Helen F. 513, 531
Helen Frances 345
Helen G. 270
Helen J. d. 496
Helen (Joyce) 465
Helen (Lincoln) 481
Helen M. 284
Helen Riley 287
Helen S. 246, 420
Helen (Scott) 175
Helen (Sears) 384
Helen (Story) 191
Helen W. 395
Helen (Woodsum) 234
Henrietta d. 254
Henrietta (Blaisdell) 328
Henrietta (Garwood) 161
Henrietta (Tilton) 367
Henry 55, 160, 190, 340, 358, 568
                                568, 569
Henry d. 69, 532, 533
Henry Allen 127
Henry B. 144, 338
Henry Brooke, Rev. 80
Henry C. 160
Henry Clay 208
Henry D. 559
Henry E., Dr. 243, 372
Henry H. 406, 455
Henry Harrison 422
Henry J. N. 162
Henry Lamott 172
Henry N. 338
Henry P. 193
Henry Peaslee 510
Henry W. 125, 175, 463
Henry Walker 421
Herbert 98, 503
Herbert d. 401
Herbert Edgar 454
Herbert H. 460
Herbert Hunt 181
Herbert L. 282
Herbert P. 301
Herbert S. 150
Herman d. 401
Herman H. 347
(Hermine), Miss 565
Hiram 97, 108, 357
Hiram d. 133
Hiram C. 240
Hiram D. 98
Hiram E. 559
Hiram Eliott 361
Hiram Ward 45
Hollis Maine 184, 350
Holly 482, 568
Homer Franklin 193, 365

LOCKE, Horace 254, 303, 307, 426
Horace d. 483
Horace A. 239
Horace B. 133, 244
Horace M. 435
Horace W. 239, 477
Horatio 153
Horatio F. d. 153
Horatio Johnson 181
Horatio Nelson 134, 135
Hosea Ballou 84
Howard 155, 357, 359, 506
Howard d. 73, 399, 558
Howard Ashton 499
Howard J. 522
Howard Milton 368
Howard R. 428
Hubbard 96
Huldah 29, 61, 85, 89
Huldah H. 141
Huldah (Hobbs) 31
Huldah P. 131
Huldah (Perkins) 14
Ichabod 86
Ida 357, 387, 396, 455, 492
Ida (Badcliff) 453
Ida Belle 510
Ida F. 292
Ida Gertrude 473
Ida (Giffen) 441
Ida (Gray) 308
Ida (Hall-Parshley), Mrs. 386
Ida I. 534
Ida L. 406
Ida (Lane) 401
Ida May 286
Ida (Miller) 382
Ida (Noyes-Favor), Mrs. 365
Ida P. L. 298
Imogene (Tebbetts) 486
Ina 357, 544
Inez 337
Inez A. 384
Ienz R. d. 333
Ingram, Dr. 506
Ira 139, 146, 568
Ira d. 273, 414
Ira A. C. 94
Ira A. 317
Ira C. 568
Ira J. 372
Ira Stephen 182
Ira W. 122, 126
Ira Washington 273
Irene 89, 357
Irene (Elkins) 195
Irene G. (Healey) 130
Irene J. 290
Irving 548
Irving Benjamin 466
Irving C. 284
Irving James 374
Irving M. 463
Isaac 73, 94, 568
Isaac d. 234
Isaac H. 290
Isaac M. 305
Isaac Stanwood 84
Isaac William 464
Isabelle (Blackburn-Chesley), Mrs.. 450
Isabel (Sprague) 171
Isabelle (Thompson) 450
Isadora N. 338
Isaiah Washington 186
Isette A. d. 302
Israel Ham 273
Ivory d. 102
Ivy d. 372
Izetta (Lewis) 65
Izetta (Plummer) 125

INDEX OF NAMES 661

LOCKE, J. Frank.................... 218
 J. W. Lamson.................. 416
 Jackson................. 207, 244
 Jacob.......... 34, 42, 70, 86, 103
     147, 189, 190, 356, 356
 Jacob d................17, 34, 71
 Jacob F........................ 218
 James.....8, 11, 13, 15, 25, 30, 30, 34, 46
  49, 64, 66, 86, 97, 102, 102,
  103, 110, 119, 136, 139, 160
  190, 189, 189, 209, 356, 552
         568, 569
 James d....75, 235, 302, 387, 484, 532
 James of Ohio.................... 63
 James A. d..................... 290
 James Adelbert.................. 491
 James Albert.................... 328
 James Andrew................... 352
 James B....................212, 436
 James B. d..................... 509
 James Brown.................... 184
 James C................133, 223, 281
 James C. d..................... 133
 James Carr..................... 124
 James Davis.................... 145
 James E........................ 127
 James Ed....................... 55
 James G........................ 304
 James Grafton.................. 185
 James H......67, 68, 140, 141, 235, 455
 James Henry.................... 455
 James I........................ 492
 James Irving................... 317
 James J........................ 302
 James Jewell................... 195
 James Jones.................... 361
 James L....................562, 568
 James Lovering................. 255
 James Lowell................... 379
 James M.......125, 147, 286, 302, 568
 James Munroe................46, 95
 James N....................141, 315
 James O........................ 222
 James Odiorne, Capt............. 97
 James P. d..................... 481
 James Pillsbury................. 350
 James R.....................85, 387
 James S........................ 516
 James T....................269, 276
 James W., Judge................ 204
 James W..............160, 248, 436
 James Wentworth............... 318
 James Wesley................... 287
 James William.................. 108
 James Wright................... 369
 Jane..........68, 146, 186, 203, 224
 Jane d......................... 357
 Jane (Bunker-Frisbee), Mrs....... 302
 Jane (Cross).................... 98
 Jane (Harris)................... 189
 Jane (McMurphy)............... 61
 Jane (Smith)................... 233
 Jane (Taggart)................. 119
 Jane (Tucker).................. 235
 Jane (Wadleigh)................ 154
 Jane (Whitet).................. 184
 Janette........................ 242
 Janette D...................... 423
 Janette (Dixon)................ 246
 Janette (Hammond)............. 506
 Janette E. R................... 244
 Janette (Levett)............... 109
 Janett (Lymburner)............. 83
 Janette Warren................. 368
 Japheth Chadbourne............ 82
 Jarvis J........................ 175
 Jemima.................14, 21, 40
 Jennie...268, 296, 300, 461, 510, 522, 568
 Jennie d....................... 465

LOCKE, Jennie B. d................ 466
 Jennie C....................... 434
 Jennie (Dow)................... 96
 Jennie Eva..................... 466
 Jennie (Ford).................. 240
 Jennie (Foss).................. 510
 Jennie Frances................. 449
 Jennie (Gillett)............... 246
 Jennie (Kyle)..............317, 318
 Jennie M....................... 559
 Jennie Martha................. 495
 Jennie (Oder).................. 161
 Jennie (Stevens)............197, 292
 Jennie (Williams).............. 305
 Jennet......................... 358
 Jeremiah...........16, 69, 70, 99, 144
     146, 147, 176, 191
 Jeremiah d.............63, 145, 384
 Jeremiah F..................... 213
 Jeremiah H..................... 47
 Jeremiah Young................ 318
 Jerome D. d................... 173
 Jerusha....................189, 357
 Jerusha (Shaw)................ 13
 Jerusha (Thornburne).......... 356
 Jesse......37, 37, 68, 73, 74, 146, 160
 Jesse Albert..........154, 326, 327, 497
 Jesse F........................ 154
 Jesse Fayette.................. 327
 Jessica (Denmead)............. 365
 Jessie B....................... 496
 Jessie C....................... 374
 Jessie Edna.................... 333
 Jessie May..................... 558
 Jethro..12, 13, 18, 35, 51, 73, 107, 144
 Jethro N....................... 222
 Jim E.......................... 382
 Joan........................... 83
 Joanna...................40, 78, 104
 Joanna (Locke)..............40, 77
 Joanna M. (Tucker)............ 119
 Job.....................34, 56, 66, 67
 Job, Capt...................... 71
 Joel.......................77, 137
 Joel Talbot.................... 80
 Joel W......................... 64
 John....5, 7, 8, 11, 12, 12, 45, 45, 47, 49
  51, 53, 54, 61, 63, 66, 68, 74, 76
  86, 88, 93, 93, 106, 109, 110, 115
  119, 122, 131, 137, 139, 139, 160
  177, 185, 189, 190, 191, 213
  233, 268, 301, 356, 356, 358, 505
  568, 568, 568, 568, 568, 569
 John d....17, 17, 20, 20, 27, 31, 40, 70
    112, 235, 241, 258, 379
 John, Capt...1, 2, 3, 4, 6, 7, 10, 11, 36
     109, 565, 581
 John, Philosopher.............. v
 John, Lieut.................... 6
 John, Dr....................... 8
 John, Rev. Dr.................. 52
 John of Florida................ 97
 John A......................... 274
 John A. d..................... 479
 John Adams.................... 454
 John Alonzo................... 455
 John B..................122, 303, 383, 529
 John Bailey.................... 474
 John Bickford................. 241
 John Buzzell.................. 124
 John C......................... 195
 John Caleb.................... 84
 John Carr..................... 422
 John D........................ 211
 John Dawlton of New York...... 96
 John Dexter.................... 208
 John E......................... 390
 John Edwin.................... 161
 John Elvin..................... 237
 John Emery.................... 293

INDEX OF NAMES

LOCKE, John Ezra............... 127
John F.............64, 171, 441, 473
John F. d...............413, 455
John Fairchild................ 180
John Forrest................... 504
John Francis...........174, 326, 365
John G........................ 124
John Goodwin.................. V
John Gould.................... 181
John H...........150, 187, 315, 568
John H. d.................... 324
John Harrison.................. 313
John Huggins................... 71
John J..................34, 241, 549
John Josiah.................... 208
John L.....................243, 535
John Langdon...............72, 235
John Lov....................... 541
John Lymburner, Rev............ 180
John M........................ 455
John Mason.................77, 164
John Morse.................... 79
John Newton................... 145
John O....................140, 304
John Oliver.................31, 208
John P....................245, 248
John Parker................... 175
John Quincy................138, 146
John R........................ 142
John Richards................. 349
John S..................154, 302, 383
John Sewell................... 236
John Shaw..................... 193
John Sherburne............177, 292
John T........................ 161
John Tash..................... 247
John W. P..................68, 71
John W...........142, 146, 212, 275
                276, 386, 516, 568
John W. F..................... 218
John W. d........122, 149, 258, 486
John Warren................... 513
John Weare.................... 42
John Webster.................. 108
John Wilkes................... 148
Johnson of New York........... 63
Jonathan....7, 7, 13, 14, 16, 20, 21, 21
        22, 26, 26, 37, 38, 41, 43, 46
        51, 52, 61, 63, 70, 81, 106
        107, 108, 112, 142, 190, 190
        246, 299, 299, 359, 508, 565
                568, 569, 569
Jonathan d................134, 176
Jonathan Dearborn............. 140
Jonathan Hobbs................ 65
Jonathan L.................... 561
Jonathan M.................... 82
Jonathan Marden............... 146
Jonathan Marston.............. 177
Jonathan Morrill...........422, 534
Jonathan Moulton.............41, 81
Joseph......7, 8, 11, 13, 16, 20, 31, 33
        37, 42, 47, 51, 65, 69, 70
        106, 108, 146, 224, 246
                533, 568
Joseph d..31, 31, 75, 110, 387, 412, 543
Joseph A...................... 453
Joseph Alfred................. 462
Joseph Alvah..............182, 349
Joseph Augustus............... 346
Joseph Berry.................. 138
Joseph Bradford............... 184
Joseph C...................... 561
Joseph E. d................... 137
Joseph H..............160, 274, 564
Joseph Hale................... 84
Joseph Ham................247, 428
Joseph Hannibal............... 422
Joseph Harrison............... 147
Joseph J., Rev................ 113

LOCKE, Joseph Jeff............. 313
Joseph L...................82, 204
Joseph Lewis.................. 343
Joseph Marden................. 318
Joseph P...................221, 254
Joseph Page d................. 274
Joseph Prentice............... 234
Joseph R...................... 269
Joseph S...................98, 98
Joseph T...................... 284
Joseph W. d................... 138
Joseph Wilbur................. 345
Josephine..........484, 505, 506, 548
Josephine (Blasier)............ 173
Josephine L................... 308
Josephine R................282, 465
Josephine S................... 429
Josephine (Trask).............. 287
Josephine (Trefethern)......... 304
Joshua.................31, 73, 154
Joshua d...................67, 73
Joshua R...................37, 75
Joshua Rochman............... 161
Joshua Smith..............157, 157
Josiah............21, 46, 79, 160, 190
Josiah d...................78, 208
Josiah Everett................ 326
Josiah Hannibal............... 246
Josiah J...................... 568
Josiah Knowles................ 110
Josiah Robert................. 185
Josiah Sanborn................ 248
Josie......................... 506
Josie (Hundley)............... 161
Josie (Searing)............... 175
Jud C......................... 354
Judith (Bishop)............... 122
Judith....................565, 565
Judith M...................... 531
Judson d...................... 357
Juley d....................... 71
Julia..................102, 147, 242
Julia A...................219, 412
Julia (Boston)................ 187
Julia (Currier)............... 131
Julia D. d.................... 198
Julia E...................294, 364
Julia F....................... 208
Julia G....................... 481
Julia (Garland)............140, 266
Julia A. (Goff)............... 96
Julia (Hoar).................. 357
Julia (Janvrin)............... 220
Julia (Parker)................ 88
Julia (Weed).................. 98
Julian Webster................ 172
Julietta (Green).............. 127
Julius F...................... 484
Justus Vinton................. 326
Kate.......................... 548
Kate Lou...................... 344
Kate (Maxwell)................ 183
Kate (Perkins)................ 137
Katherine..................... 190
Katherine B................... 399
Katherine (Connors)........... 399
Katherine (Dearborn).......154, 326
Katherine J. d................ 94
Katherine (Sullivan).......... 399
Katherine Mary................ 378
Kenneth Gilbert............... 554
Keziah (Allen)................ 87
Keziah (Chase)................ 115
(Kimball), Miss............... 194
Lafayette..................... 455
(Lane), Mrs................... 82
Langdon....................... 235
Langdon Elvin.............401, 560
Lansa W....................... 416

INDEX OF NAMES

LOCKE, Latha K. 456
　Laura 127, 384
　Laura A. 316, 402
　Laura (Cleaves) 273
　Laura Cristine 359
　Laura (Ewoldt) 387
　Laura Goodwin 305
　Laura (Hayes) 237
　Laura (Kelley) 317
　Laura (Rexford) 74
　Laurence 472
　Lavina (French) 125
　Lavina (Newton) 141
　Lavinia 97, 187
　Lavinia (Gill) 268
　Leah (Prescott) 193
　Leaman Lester 373
　Leander Moore 343
　Leander Morrison 428
　Leah 37
　Lear 38
　Lee Winfred 339
　Lela S. 353
　Lemar 37
　Lemuel 72
　Lemuel B. 140
　Lena (Clark) 413
　Lena M. 171
　Lenna (Blasier) 173
　Leonard 186, 187, 189
　Leonard Morse 79
　Leonard S. d. 456
　Leonard Standish 164
　Leroy Leslie 202
　Leroy M. 287
　Lester Herbert 344
　Lester Sargent 335
　Letitia 190, 358
　Letitia (McKillop) 86
　Lettie (Barnum) 535
　Lettie (Bradley) 424
　Lettie (Harding) 356
　Levi ... 26, 49, 52, 60, 104, 105, 131, 194
　Levi d. 29, 88
　Levi B. d. 145
　Levi D. 225, 304
　Levi F. 233
　Levi M. 227
　Levi W. d. 286
　Levina 104
　Lewis 450, 506
　Lewis Clarke 172
　Lilla d. 337, 502
　Lilla (Fayer) 495
　Lilla (Heath) 341
　Lilla Josephine 175
　Lilla (Oliver) 352
　Lillah B. 495
　Lillias 346
　Lillias (Woodman) 82
　Lillian 505, 506, 506, 535, 544
　Lillian d. 375
　Lillian A. 402
　Lillian E. 451
　Lillian F. 374
　Lillian G. 324
　Lillian May 333
　Lillian S. 472
　Lillie Beecher 368
　Lillie M. 388
　Lina B., Mrs. 568
　Linna (Buzzell) 463
　Linwood 568
　Linwood Irving 350
　Lizzie 187, 195, 220, 351
　Lizzie A. 323
　Lizzie B. 492
　Lizzie (Bean) 185
　Lizzie C. d. 150
　Lizzie (Davis) 510

LOCKE, Lizzie E. 233
　Lizzie (Hart) 462
　Lizzie (Hoit) 364
　Lizzie (Howard) 455
　Lizzie (Ingalls) 510
　Lizzie (Kimball) 200
　Lizzie M. 416
　Lizzie (Mercer) 298
　Lizzie (Moore) 164
　Lizzie (Murch) 200
　Lizzie (Nute) 461
　Lizzie (Pickering) 219
　Lizzie (Webb) 187
　Loanna (Neally) 281
　Locada 146
　Lodoiski (Gage) 133
　Lois M. 399
　Lois (Watkins) 171
　Lola G. 455
　Loraine L. 534
　Loren L. d. 202
　Loretta (Foote) 308
　Loretta J. 484
　Lottie A. 420, 468
　Lottie (Bailey) 509
　Lottie (Dexter) 429
　Lottie (Fellows) 293
　Lottie H. 254
　Lottie (Madden) 387
　Lottie (Warren) 499
　Louella J. 298
　Louis 55, 365, 507
　Louis Alden 373
　Louis Cristie 298
　Louis D. 535
　Louis Ward 339
　Louisa 86, 95, 105, 160
　Louisa d. 102, 235
　Louisa A. 203
　Louisa (Abbott) 303
　Louisa (Berry) 107, 137
　Louisa (Condon) 358
　Louisa D. 460
　Louisa (Ferren) 131
　Louisa J. 525
　Louisa (Kempton) 358
　Louisa (Kimball) 199
　Louisa (Lamprey) 82
　Louisa (Norcross) 185
　Louisa (Oke-Stewart), Mrs. 406
　Louisa (Sanborn) 47
　Louise 325
　Louise A. 374
　Louise (McKillop) 172
　Love 31
　Lovie 49, 102
　Lovie Chase 103
　Lovina 322
　Lovina D. 185
　Lovina (Graffam) 200
　Lovina (Lake) 149, 322
　Lovina (Potter) 137
　Lovinia 194
　Lowell 98
　Lowell G. 455
　Lua Catherine 289
　Lucia L. 203
　Lucia M. 365
　Lucia R. (Sanborn) 131
　Lucia (Swift) 350
　Lucilla 386
　Lucille d. 537
　Lucinda 99, 254
　Lucinda of Ohio 64
　Lucinda (Clarke) 83
　Lucinda (Green-Sanborn), Mrs. 99
　Lucretia 40, 108
　Lucretia (Brundy) 64
　Lucy 38, 42, 86, 105, 122, 209
　Lucy d. 42, 327

INDEX OF NAMES

LOCKE. Lucy A. 303
Lucy Ann 83, 303, 537
Lucy B. 82
Lucy (Beede) 146
Lucy (Bill) 22
Lucy C. 103, 277
Lucy (Cate) 54
Lucy E. 113
Lucy Ellen 449
Lucy (Geer) 171
Lucy H. d 126
Lucy (Libby) 181
Lucy M 113, 113, 243
Lucy (Marden) 70
Lucy N. 77
Lucy (Rathburn) 20
Lucy (Rogers) 137
Lucy (Smallcon) 284
Lucy T 164
Luella 384, 558
Luella M 172
Luella S. 294
Luther d 290, 352, 455
Luvia (Knight) 318
Lydia 13, 24, 31, 35, 37, 47, 73, 82
        87, 88, 95, 96, 97, 102, 115
        154, 154, 209, 276, 281
Lydia d 24, 112
Lydia A 177, 222
Lydia Ann 360
Lydia (Buzzell) 88
Lydia (Cater) 284
Lydia (Church) 317
Lydia (Curtis) 199
Lydia D. d 195
Lydia (Dow) 24
Lydia (Foss) 34
Lydia H 112, 116, 247, 253, 254
Lydia (Hall) 52
Lydia (Hanscom) 73
Lydia (Hews) 154
Lydia C. (Howard) 105, 191
Lydia M 366
Lydia (Morris) 84
Lydia (Osgood) 46
Lydia (Page) 41
Lydia (Pryor) 240
Lydia (Pendexter) 254
Lydia (Philbrick) 110
Lydia (Robinson) 269
Lydia S. 169
Lydia (Savory) 284
Lydia T. d 315
Lydia (Tebbetts) 154
Lydia (Tasker) 284
Lydia (Thompson) 221, 254
Lydia (Yeaton-Chesley), Mrs. 88
Lyman 125, 290
Lyman J. M. 424
Mabel 189, 468
Mabel d 414
Mabel B. 424
Mabel Emma 535
Mabel (Emory-Kimball), Mrs. 509
Mabel J. d 489
Mabel Jean 359
Mabel (Kelley) 387
Mabel L. 471
Mabel Louise 437
Mabel (Miller) 172
Mabel P 522
Mabel (Remick) 479
Mabel (Symonds) 402
Mabel V 379
Mabel (Wiggin) 436
Mabel Y 343
Mabel (Yearick) 534
Madeline d 541
Madeline B. 487
Madge (Hanna) 287

LOCKE, Mae (Cheney) 441
Mae Edna 334
Maggie 506, 544
Maggie (Hamblin) 468
Maggie (Mahlervin) 306
Mahala d 303
Mahala (Burgess) 186
Malinda (———) 63
Malinda 187
Malvina 473
Malvina A. 150
Mamie d 254
Mamie E. 510
Mandana C. 254
Mandana 295
Marcella 387
Marcellus d 399
Marcia 310
Marcia (Cleaves) 154
Marcia S. 292
Marcus K. 435
Marcy (Dame) 54
Margaret 23, 26, 53, 88, 109, 150
        187, 244, 304, 318, 358
        365, 513, 516, 549, 568
Margaret A. L. 116
Margaret A. 149, 245, 248
Margaret A. d 149
Margaret (Barry) 42
Margaret (Bradbury) 86
Margaret (Cleland) 359
Margaret (Dearborn) 49
Margaret (Durgan) 49
Margaret (Gillis) 479
Margaret (Hanna-Locke) 450
Margaret (Hinkley-Berry), Mrs... 477
Margaret J. L. 180
Margaret J. 560
Margaret K. 192
Margaret (Lloyd) 357
Margaret (Mullery) 150
Margaret (Pierce), Mrs. 54
Margaret (Richardson) 243
Margaret (Robinson) 359
Margaret (Roche) 186
Margaret S. 531
Margaret (Sturtevant) 185
Margaret W. 556
Margaret (Ward) 13
Margaret (Welch) 71
Margaret (Wheeler) 289
Margary (Manson) 51
Margary P. 471
Margie 522
Maria 137, 160, 187, 356
Maria d 293
Maria (———) 153
Maria A. 316
Maria (Burnham) 218
Maria H. 281
Maria (Holmes) 145
Maria (Jarvis) 248
Maria (Lord) 189
Maria M. d 195
Maria Malvina 157
Maria (Nudd) 147
Maria O. 95
Maria (Otis) 73
Maria (Stoughton) 568
Marian D. 437
Marianna J. 113, 255
Marietta (Bliss) 81
Marietta (Remick) 218
Marion 358, 387, 429
Marion B. 332
Marion C. 472
Marion Heath 502
Marjorie 516
Marjorie E. 544
Mark W. d 317

INDEX OF NAMES 665

LOCKE, Marshall A.................. 188
  Marshall E..................... 544
  Marshall Ernest................ 468
  Martha.........26, 29, 44, 88, 131, 131
                139, 302, 357, 568
  Martha d.........284, 313, 313, 328
  Martha A...............185, 240, 254
  Martha Ann............155, 235, 248
  Martha (Bradford)............... 84
  Martha (Brown)................. 211
  Martha (Chadwick).............. 292
  Martha D....................... 133
  Martha (Dow)................... 33
  Martha Dow..................... 145
  Martha E............173, 188, 345, 420
  Martha (Eaton)................. 177
  Martha F....................... 222
  Martha (Fernald)............... 125
  Martha (French)................ 108
  Martha H....................... 533
  Martha Helen................... 422
  Martha J................124, 284, 455
  Martha Jane.................... 473
  Martha Kate...............409, 410
  Martha (Lane).................. 103
  Martha (Martin)................ 249
  Martha (Mason).........107, 144, 534
  Martha O....................... 347
  Martha (Perkins)............... 306
  Martha (Rand)............106, 144
  Martha S.......177, 242, 301, 302, 317
  Martha (Seavey)................ 66
  Martha (Silver)................ 235
  Martha (Smith)......82, 124, 248, 429
  Martha (Wade).................. 422
  Martha (Webster)............... 51
  Martha (West-Hall), Mrs.......... 276
  Martha (Worthen)............... 26
  Martie L....................... 568
  Martin......................55, 268
  Martin V. D................234, 399
  Mary........8, 11, 13, 21, 16, 24, 25, 26
        27, 29, 29, 31, 31, 33, 35, 38
        40, 40, 41, 42, 43, 45, 46, 48
        49, 51, 51, 52, 60, 68, 69, 69
        70, 74, 80, 82, 86, 88, 92, 93
        94, 97, 98, 102, 107, 108,
        109, 119, 132, 154, 160, 187
        190, 190, 190, 218, 226, 233
        244, 269, 303, 356, 357, 357
                    376, 516, 568
  Mary d......17, 75, 145, 304, 412, 423
  Mary of Ohio................... 64
  Mary A.............75, 122, 136, 153
        171, 195, 242, 253, 281
        283, 284, 315, 372, 486
                    490, 535
  Mary A. d.............114, 208, 490
  Mary Abigail................... 222
  Mary A. M...................... 246
  Mary F. (Abbott)............... 147
  Mary Adelaide.................. 527
  Mary Alice..................... 428
  Mary (Allen)................... 357
  Mary (Allyn)................... 80
  Mary Ann....82, 83, 96, 103, 136, 150
        155, 194, 291, 356, 389, 462
  Mary (Ashley).................. 422
  Mary Austin.................... 116
  Mary B................102, 122, 208
  Mary B. d...................... 173
  Mary (Babb).................... 273
  Mary (Barnes).................. 161
  Mary (Beach)................... 180
  Mary (Beals)................... 112
  Mary (Bean).................... 25
  Mary Belle 169
  Mary (Bellington).............. 171
  Mary (Berry)................... 413

LOCKE, Mary (Berry-Haines).......... 16
  Mary (Bird).................... 22
  Mary (Blood-Hildebrant)........ 276
  Mary (Brockaway).............. 141
  Mary (Brown)............31, 81, 359
  Mary (Burt)..................22, 43
  Mary (Butterfield).............. 352
  Mary C....................179, 431
  Mary C. d.................150, 150
  Mary (Carey).................. 288
  Mary (Chandler)............... 64
  Mary (Clark)............136, 290
  Mary (Cleasby)................ 568
  Mary (Come-Labaene), Mrs....... 435
  Mary (Conan).................. 299
  Mary (Corser)................. 125
  Mary (Covell)................. 299
  Mary (Cull)................... 136
  Mary (Dailey)................. 300
  Mary (Dawlton)................ 401
  Mary (Dearborn)............... 82
  Mary (Dow).................46, 177
  Mary (Duncan)................. 108
  Mary (Dustin), Mrs............ 52
  Mary E.....54, 161, 171, 237, 240, 245
        254, 286, 341, 473, 496, 561
  Mary E. d.........81, 140, 199, 406
  Mary Elizabeth..........340, 361, 513
  Mary Elizabeth d.............. 360
  Mary (Elkins)...............16, 81
  Mary Ella..................... 164
  Mary Ellen.................... 179
  Mary (Ellis).................. 208
  Mary Emma.................... 176
  Mary Estella.................. 333
  Mary (Esterbrook)............. 63
  Mary (Evans).................. 44
  Mary F..........141, 150, 204, 285
                285, 290, 324, 332
  Mary F. E..................... 277
  Mary (Flagg).................. 287
  Mary (Fletcher-Nason-Shaw), Mrs. 44
  Mary (Flitter)................ 376
  Mary (Frauley)................ 143
  Mary (Gaffett)................ 171
  Mary (Getman)................. 81
  Mary (Grant)..............108, 240
  Mary (Gregory-Marshall)........ 326
  Mary (Gwynne)................. 154
  Mary K........................ 396
  Mary (Katherwood)............. 44
  Mary (Kendall)................ 437
  Mary Keziah..............422, 422
  Mary (Kilgore)................ 82
  Mary (Kimball)................ 340
  Mary L................215, 384, 516
  Mary (Lane)................... 82
  Mary (Langley-Hook), Mrs....... 130
  Mary Lizzie................... 460
  Mary (Locke) 41, 41, 68, 68
        71, 115, 146, 252
  Mary (Lombard)................ 20
  Mary Louise................... 177
  Mary H.....................161, 568
  Mary H. d..................... 161
  Mary (Haley-Staples).......... 73
  Mary (Ham).................... 122
  Mary (Harlow)................. 86
  Mary (Hayes).................. 27
  Mary (Herbert)................ 94
  Mary (Hines).................. 249
  Mary (Hurd)................... 317
  Mary J..................98, 161, 304
  Mary J. d..................... 293
  Mary (Jameson)............246, 257
  Mary Jane...............192, 209, 344
  Mary (Jeckworth).............. 21
  Mary M...............124, 137, 175, 313
  Mary M. d..................... 137
  Mary (MacFarland)............. 109

INDEX OF NAMES

LOCKE, Mary (Magoon).............. 189
Mary (Mahoney)................ 356
Mary (Marcotte)................ 498
Mary (Marston)................. 70
Mary (McCrillis)................ 242
Mary (McLeon).................. 390
Mary Emma (McSparren)........ 365
Mary (Morse)................... 40
Mary (Norton).................. 13
Mary (Nutter).................. 222
Mary O.....................212, 247
Mary O. d...................... 235
Mary Olevia.................... 190
Mary Olive............106, 206, 235
Mary (Oliver).................. 352
Mary Olivia.................... 427
Mary (Organ)................... 24
Mary (Osborn).................. 150
Mary (Otis).................... 239
Mary P......................125, 127
Mary (Page).................... 343
Mary (Palmer-Hill), Mrs......... 254
Mary Perkins................145, 284
Mary (Philbrick)............... 88
Mary (Pierce)...............84, 298
Mary (Pinkham).............102, 121
Mary (Potts)................... 315
Mary (Powers).................. 146
Mary R. d..................... 178
Mary (Rand).................... 146
Mary (Randall)................. 72
Mary (Rindge).................. 68
Mary (Roberts).............181, 195
Mary (Robinson)............269, 325
Mary (Rowell).................. 420
Mary E. (Ryder)................ 43
Mary S..................192, 293, 468
Mary S. d..................... 337
Mary (Sanborn)................. 43
Mary (Seavey).................. 125
Mary (Stubbs) 13
Mary Susan.................150, 337
Mary (Sweet)................... 37
Mary (Tanner).................. 75
Mary (Tebbetts)................ 273
Mary (Towle)................... 72
Mary (Townsend)................ 102
Mary (Vennard)................. 106
Mary W......................... 317
Mary (Wallace).............130, 130
Mary (Ward).................... 473
Mary (Warmouth)................ 81
Mary (Waterhouse).............. 284
Mary (Weare)................... 176
Mary (Weed).................... 146
Mary (Wentworth)...........146, 241
Mary (West).................... 37
Mary (Wheeler)................. 461
Mary White..................... 144
Mary (Wright).................. 200
Mary (Yeaton-Ordiorne)......... 16
Mary (Young)................... 72
Maryphosa d................... 323
Mason d....................... 194
Matilda.....................40, 76
Matilda (Janvrin-Feltch), Mrs..... 98
Matilda P...................... 80
Matthew James.................. 351
Mattie B....................... 486
Mattie E....................... 450
Mattie T....................... 542
Maude........190, 357, 427, 431, 453
Maud Emerson.................. 350
Maude G....................... 543
Maude (Green).................. 386
Maude May..................... 563
Maude Mildred.................. 561
Maude N....................... 458
Maude O....................... 534
Maude (Piper).................. 372

LOCKE, Maurice H.................. 337
May............................ 535
May (Amazeen)................. 492
May Evelyn..................... 350
May (Fellows).................. 293
May (Liskley), Mrs............. 292
Meanie (Whicher-Colby-Elliott),
    Mrs......................... 372
Mehitable.........13, 25, 46, 71, 250
Mehitable B.................... 149
Mehitable (Bickford)............ 61
Mehitable (Brown).............. 94
Mehitable(Bunker-Holmes), Mrs... 122
Mehitable D.................... 154
Mehitable Green (Hill).......... 154
Mehitable (Higgins or Huggins)... 34
Mehitable (Lear)............... 233
Mehitable (Pattee)............. 63
Mehitable (Rand)............... 69
Mehitable (Stickney)............ 29
Melicent....................... 436
Melinda (Brown)................ 86
Melinda (Williams)............. 189
Melissa........................ 187
Melville H. d.................. 326
Melvin d....................... 401
Melvin P....................... 343
Melvin Tremaine d............. 333
Mercy...................20, 37, 69, 569
Mercy A........................ 277
Mercy D........................ 123
Mercy (Dame)................... 54
Mercy (Foss)................... 13
Mercy J........................ 75
Mercy (Marshall)............... 55
Mercy (Munson)................. 88
Mercy (Nixon).................. 13
Mercy (Rand)................... 139
Mercy (Shaw)................... 61
Mercy V........................ 276
Merebeth....................27, 31
Meribah........15, 27, 31, 34, 54, 569
Meribah (Page)................. 14
Merilla........................ 187
Meta 359
Michael........................ 106
Mignon......................... 508
Mildred........................ 463
Mildred Earle.................. 335
Mildred Howard................. 334
Mildred Julia.................. 339
Mildred (Rowe)................. 384
Mildred S. d.................. 531
Miles Standish..............77, 77
Milton Hill.................... 514
Milton Putnam.................. 199
Milward........................ 359
Mima (Dow)..................... 215
Mina........................534, 537
Mina A. (Emery)................ 86
Minerva........................ 244
Minnie......................298, 507
Minnie A....................... 338
Minnie E....................... 384
Minnie (Flanders).............. 369
Minnie (Hall).................. 306
Minnie L....................... 324
Minnie Persis.................. 137
Minnie (Poston)................ 133
Minnie (Van de Sande).......... 193
Minta Anina.................... 372
Miriam...22, 35, 40, 41, 42, 80, 82, 154
Miriam (Brooke)................ 13
Miriam (Day)................73, 327
Miriam H....................... 456
Miriam Lamprey................. 82
Missouri (Falls)............... 276
Mitchell d.................... 105
Mittie......................... 300
Molly.......................37, 70

INDEX OF NAMES

LOCKE, Molly (Sanborn).............. 47
   Molly (Seavey).................. 43
   Morris......................... 177
   Morris Lamprey................. 249
   Morril Silas................... 422
   Moses........23, 24, 46, 49, 66, 87, 94
   Moses, Capt. of New York........ 95
   Moses d....................... 424
   Moshier W..................... 171
   Munroe G...................... 401
   Muriel (Palmer)................ 554
   Murray........................ 507
   Musidora (Rowantree).......... 425
   Musie......................243, 337
   Myrtle A...................... 569
   Myrtle (Kough)................ 534
   Myrtle (Rice)................. 474
   Nabby.......................67, 106
   Nabby d....................... 131
   Nahum F. d.................... 285
   Nancy........37, 52, 81, 87, 88, 97, 109
      112, 112, 115, 130, 135
      160, 191, 222, 244, 568
   Nancy A....................... 244
   Nancy Alice................... 421
   Nancy N. (Clarke)............. 247
   Nancy (Drown)............108, 238
   Nancy (Durgin)................ 131
   Nancy E...................120, 248
   Nancy (Favor)................. 224
   Nancy (Goodwin).............. 274
   Nancy (Gurdy)................. 49
   Nancy (Helm).................. 305
   Nancy (Holden)................ 189
   Nancy (Judkins), Mrs........... 568
   Nancy R. (Kent)............... 247
   Nancy M....................... 243
   Nancy (Moses)................. 86
   Nancy (Mosier)................ 274
   Nancy (Newhall).............. 124
   Nancy (Nutt-Folsom), Mrs....... 413
   Nancy (Philbrick).............. 177
   Nancy (Richardson)............ 243
   Nancy B. (Rogers)............. 141
   Nancy C. (Spare).............. 126
   Nancy (Sullivan).............. 545
   Nancy (Vanderheyden)......... 172
   Nancy W...................... 254
   Nancy (Watts-Fisher), Mrs...... 29
   Naomi......................... 93
   Naomi (Whicher).............. 568
   Natalie d..................... 473
   Nathan......................41, 63
   Nathan d...................... 233
   Nathan Smith.................. 200
   Nathan Stanwood.............. 184
   Nathan T...................... 171
   Nathan Tucker................. 80
   Nathaniel.....1, 8, 11, 12, 13, 13, 20, 20
      37, 40, 41, 43, 70, 73, 74
      87, 146, 191, 360, 565, 568
   Nathaniel d..................21, 82
   Nathaniel the Emigrant...... 565, 581
   Nathaniel C................... 77
   Nathaniel Chase............... 200
   Nanthaniel Clarke............. 83
   Nathaniel S................... 82
   Nehemiah C.................... 141
   Nellie..........307, 386, 506, 506, 568
   Nellie (———).................. 462
   Nellie d...................170, 483
   Nellie A....................287, 355
   Nellie A. M................... 321
   Nellie (Abbott)............... 372
   Nellie B...................... 332
   Nellie (Bradford)............. 424
   Nellie (Bridges).............. 164
   Nellie (Boucher).............. 398
   Nellie (Clarke)............... 173
   Nellie E...................333, 529

LOCKE, Nellie (Flake)................ 174
   Nellie H...................... 174
   Nellie (Hunt)................. 290
   Nellie Irene.................. 549
   Nellie L...................... 441
   Nellie (Philbrick)............ 449
   Nellie (Place-Colbath), Mrs..... 227
   Nellie (Plummer).............. 484
   Nellie (Ryan)................. 184
   Nellie S...................223, 417
   Nellie (Smith)................ 253
   Nellie (Stewart).............. 347
   Nellie (Varney)............... 191
   Nellie (Weed-Lovejoy)......... 192
   Nellie (Winch)................ 413
   Nellie (Woodman-Gardner), Mrs... 458
   Nelson........................ 98
   Nelson Horatio................ 62
   Neta G........................ 529
   Nettie d...................414, 450
   Nettie (Canfield)............. 243
   Nettie (Lecoy)................ 372
   Nettie M...................338, 441
   Newell........................ 92
   Nimshi, d. Rev................ 15
   Nina B........................ 502
   Nona L........................ 417
   Norman........................ 401
   Norman A...................... 341
   Norman Aldrich................ 340
   Norman Reuben................. 173
   Norman V...................... 81
   Norman Wentworth.............. 175
   Octavius d.................... 327
   Olevia (Hall)................. 112
   Olive....................44, 85, 516
   Olive d....................85, 235
   Olive Ann..................... 489
   Olive (Berry)...............65, 69
   Olive (Bickford).............44, 109
   Olive C....................... 82
   Olive (Chadbourne)............ 73
   Olive F....................... 241
   Olive (Fernald)............... 108
   Olive (Foss).................. 31
   Olive G....................... 242
   Olive (Grant)................. 83
   Olive Mae..................... 502
   Olive (Marden-Elkins)......... 26
   Olive Marion.................. 330
   Olive R....................... 234
   Olive (Rand).................. 51
   Olive (Robinson).............42, 85
   Olive S....................... 107
   Olive (Strong)................ 63
   Olive T....................... 141
   Oliver....................207, 307, 568
   Oliver Albion................. 287
   Oliver Babb................125, 317
   Oliver Elbridge............... 237
   Oliver H...................... 141
   Oliver Horton................. 235
   Oliver Luther................. 142
   Oliver Peabody................ 96
   Olivia........................ 356
   Olivia (Hodgdon).............. 142
   Ora d......................... 535
   Ora (Towle)................... 492
   Orah H........................ 282
   Oren D........................ 281
   Oretta E...................... 63
   Original G.................... 307
   Orilla H...................... 254
   Orra A........................ 294
   Orrie (Gordon)................ 186
   Orrin.....................224, 427, 533
   Orrin Wesley.................. 495
   Orsam, d. Rev................. 44
   Orson E....................... 194
   Orville G..................... 164

LOCKE, Oscar Rockwell............... 461
Osgood......................... 94
Otis L......................... 559
Pamelia........................ 116
Pamelia A...................... 137
Pamelia Ann.................... 147
Pamelia (Connor)................ 52
Pamelia (Dow).................. 103
Pamelia Prentiss 327
Pardon T....................... 161
Parna T........................ 131
Patience...........14, 26, 28, 96, 189
Patience (Churchill) 189
Patience (Perkins)............... 24
Patty...................108, 117, 131
Pauline Elizabeth................ 549
Pearl.......................268, 387
Pearl A........................ 559
Pearl B........................ 480
Pearl E........................ 504
Peggy.......................... 568
Peggy Hall..................... 112
Percy W....................... 527
Perley Whittier................. 185
Pernia T. d...............140, 140
Perry N........................ 484
———— (Pettibone).............. 62
Phebe.............62, 170, 171, 242
Phebe d....................... 207
Phebe (Abbott)................. 115
Phebe (Ames).................. 110
Phebe (Boss)................... 75
Phebe C. d.................... 315
Phebe (Chapman)............... 51
Phebe May..................... 334
Phebe (Palmer)................. 161
Phebe (Pomeroy)................ 77
Phebe (Wetherbee).............. 424
Philena F...................... 104
Philena (Leach)................. 80
Philip......................208, 383
Philip A....................... 399
Philip Aubin..................98, 365
Phineas....................... 102
Phyllis M...................... 544
Picker......................... 61
Piers.......................... 357
Polly...53, 67, 71, 74, 88, 89, 119, 160
Polly (Carleton)................ 112
Polly (Muzzey)................. 70
Polly W. (Waldron).............. 107
Portes L....................... 137
Priscilla.....................86, 190
Priscilla (McKenzie) 190
Prudence...............13, 23, 25, 44
Queen Geneva.................. 299
Rachel 13, 37, 49, 67, 68, 68, 224
                                  224
Rachel B....................72, 499
Rachel (Birdsall), Mrs............ 474
Rachel (Blake)................. 119
Rachel (Brainard)............... 29
Rachel (Fuller) 26
Rachel (Sanborn).............93, 110
Rachel (Taylor) 468
Rachel D. (Towle)............... 60
Ralph......................... 506
Ralph B....................... 560
Ralph C....................... 529
Ralph Martin................... 554
Raymond..............516, 529, 544
Raymond E.................... 559
Raymond Morris................ 184
Raymond Taylor................ 350
Rebecca........8, 11, 21, 81, 93, 96
                     127, 160, 191, 499
Rebecca (Coffin)................ 123
Rebecca (Peabody).............. 127
Rebecca (Prescott).............. 139
Rebecca (Reed)................. 87

LOCKE, Reuben..........51, 61, 87, 109
                  130, 191, 241, 256
Reuben d..................110, 241
Reuben B...................... 245
Reuben L...................... 177
Revere J. d.................... 180
Revilo V....................... 526
Rhoda d..................239, 303, 303
Rhoda A....................... 81
Rhoda Ann.................... 173
Rhoda (Cole)................... 195
Rhoda (Collins).................. 88
Rhoda (Collins-Locke)............ 88
Rhoda (Lewis).................. 75
Rhoda (Pray)................... 112
Richard........12, 17, 31, 34, 46, 67
                  70, 88, 146, 322, 569
Richard, Capt................... 71
Richard B...................... 465
Richard Dearborn............... 141
Richard Foss................... 168
Richard J...................... 551
R. Jenness..................... 309
Richard Jenness................. 488
Richard L...................53, 316
Richard Rand.................. 146
Richard Standish................ 335
Richard Van de Sande............ 365
Rinda......................... 516
Rinda C....................... 382
Robert.....................189, 235
Robert Allison.................. 537
Robert Dickson................. 423
Robert Earl.................... 169
Robert P...................120, 316
Rodney........................ 244
Rodolphus M................... 284
Rody O........................ 161
Roger......................... 508
Roger Putnam.................. 514
Rosa M........................ 386
Rosana........................ 303
Roscoe Edwin.................. 558
Roscoe J....................... 387
Rose.......................... 307
Rose (Clevett).................. 373
Rose (Perkins), Mrs.............. 284
Rosella........................ 187
Rosetta (Otto).................. 204
Rosina........................ 502
Rowena....................... 366
Rowland...................... 161
Roxbury S. (Sanborn)............ 247
Roxy......................104, 105
Roxy D........................ 227
Roy........................... 325
Roy B......................... 538
Roy D......................... 480
Roy Hamilton.................. 498
Roy Loren..................... 373
Royal......................... 372
Royal P....................... 154
Royal William.................. 326
Ruby d....................... 558
Ruel S........................ 483
Ruhuma....................... 46
Ruhuma Jane................... 363
Ruhuma P..................... 89
Ruhuma (Pearsons).............. 46
Rulenna (Slemp)................ 387
Rupert........................ 506
Russell........................ 359
Russell Y...................... 544
Ruth...............66, 387, 530, 544
Ruth d........................ 96
Ruth A........................ 194
Ruth C........................ 369
Ruth (Curtis), Mrs............... 112
Ruth E.....................533, 549
Ruth (Hatch)................... 298

INDEX OF NAMES 669

LOCKE, Ruth (Sands).................. 83
　Ruth (Wills).................... 185
　S. Helen (Chase)................ 211
　S. Emaline...................... 316
　S. M. (Sullivan)................ 568
　S. Alice........................ 468
　Sabina.......................... 566
　Sabina (Moulton)................ 246
　Sabra (Kimball)................. 131
　Sadie........................... 325
　Sadie (Fairbanks)............... 337
　Sadie Maude.................... 353
　Salina (Bickford)............... 193
　Salome......................16, 135
　Salome (White).................. 11
　Sally........74, 80, 85, 86, 87, 88, 92
　　　　　　　　97, 105, 194, 213, 568
　Sally d.....................96, 105
　Sally (Adams)................... 21
　Sally (Berry)................... 49
　Sally (Brown)................... 47
　Sally (Cass).................... 95
　Sally (Clement)................. 49
　Sally (Cook).................... 246
　Sally D......................... 104
　Sally Dalton.................... 96
　Sally (Dearborn)................ 71
　Sally (Dodge-Willis), Mrs....... 37
　Sally C. (Doloff)............104, 105
　Sally F......................... 83
　Sally (Goodwin)................. 42
　Sally (Griffin)................. 131
　Sally H......................... 140
　Sally (Hills)................... 104
　Sally (James)................... 21
　Sally (Mowe-Allen).............. 68
　Sally R......................... 85
　Sally (Stanton)..............49, 102
　Sally (Stickney-Dawlton), Mrs... 46
　Sally V......................... 131
　Sally (Wedgwood)................ 106
　Sally (Williamson).............. 153
　Sam............................. 569
　Samantha (Kittridge)............ 276
　Sampson B...................103, 123
　Samuel.......13, 13, 21, 21, 22, 23
　　　　　　　　24, 27, 41, 42, 42, 42, 44
　　　　　　　　45, 47, 53, 54, 55, 66, 82
　　　　　　　　83, 83, 85, 85, 86, 87, 88
　　　　　　　　130, 130, 177, 185, 189
　　　　　　　　190, 191, 356, 357, 507, 569
　Samuel, Col..................... 85
　Samuel of New Orleans........... 96
　Samuel Augustus................. 272
　Samuel B........................ 131
　Samuel Blake................110, 247
　Samuel Bradford................. 189
　Samuel D........................ 429
　Samuel E........................ 84
　Samuel Ed....................... 208
　Samuel Ellis.................... 283
　Samuel Hall, Capt............... 112
　Samuel Hoitt.................... 124
　Samuel J........................ 237
　Samuel Jenness.................. 107
　Samuel M........................ 245
　Samuel Merrill Ray.............. 346
　Samuel Morris................... 208
　Samuel O........................ 187
　Samuel S........................ 284
　Samuel Seavey................... 462
　Samuel Stillman................. 186
　Samuel W........................ 195
　Samuel Wesley................... 180
　Sarah...12, 14, 24, 25, 27, 30, 30, 34, 34
　　　　　　45, 49, 51, 53, 63, 66, 71, 74, 82
　　　　　　119, 122, 127, 136, 139, 153
　　　　　　178, 187, 190, 190, 191, 192, 276
　　　　　　308, 339, 389, 422, 425, 427
　　　　　　427, 429, 568, 568, 568, 569

LOCKE, Sarah d.22, 24, 26, 106, 244, 306, 364
　Sarah A.............109, 157, 185, 223
　　　　　　　　　239, 245, 258, 307, 549
　Sarah A. d...................... 136
　Sarah Abbie.................361, 369
　Sarah (Adams)................... 94
　Sarah Agnes..................... 498
　Sarah Ann..........108, 149, 177, 177
　Sarah B......................... 257
　Sarah (Bill).................357, 359
　Sarah (Bishop).................. 208
　Sarah Blake..................... 110
　Sarah (Bousley)................. 199
　Sarah (Brosias-Dennett), Mrs.... 87
　Sarah C.................... 199, 534
　Sarah (Canney).................. 123
　Sarah (Carlisle)................ 77
　Sarah (Carter-Robinson), Mrs.... 104
　Sarah (Carter).................. 161
　Sarah (Cass)................113, 245
　Sarah (Clark).................42, 307
　Sarah (Cochran)................. 113
　Sarah (Cooledge)................ 154
　Sarah Coyne..................... 326
　Sarah D.....................252, 535
　Sarah (Dame).................... 124
　Sarah (Dewel)................... 81
　Sarah (Dexter).................. 208
　Sarah (Ditson).................. 422
　Sarah (Dunbar).................. 20
　Sarah (Dyer).................... 192
　Sarah E....122, 148, 222, 233, 241, 276
　　　　　　　277, 287, 316, 324, 423, 468
　Sarah (Eaton)................... 213
　Sarah Eleanor................... 169
　Sarah Elizabeth........168, 359, 516
　Sarah (Elkins).................. 103
　Sarah Emaline................... 193
　Sarah (Evans)................... 141
　Sarah F....................242, 294, 568
　Sarah (Fish).................... 185
　Sarah (Flanders-Evans).......... 187
　Sarah (Follansbee).............. 292
　Sarah (Foss).................73, 79
　Sarah (Fox)..................... 147
　Sarah Frances................43, 94
　Sarah Frost..................... 71
　Sarah (Gaffett)................. 171
　Sarah (Gerry)................... 141
　Sarah Goss...................... 145
　Sarah H.........115, 126, 274, 304, 538
　Sarah (Haines).................. 14
　Sarah (Harmon).................. 181
　Sarah (Hayes)................... 237
　Sarah (Hobbs)................... 193
　Sarah (Hoitt).................54, 124
　Sarah (Howard).................. 160
　Sarah (Howe).................... 276
　Sarah I......................... 204
　Sarah J.....131, 194, 225, 243, 477, 479
　Sarah Jane..............161, 206, 419
　Sara (Jane)..................... 466
　Sarah (Jenness)..............53, 316
　Sarah (Jones)................... 34
　Sarah Knowles................... 115
　Sarah L......................... 237
　Sarah (Larrabee)................ 63
　Sarah (Leavitt)..............30, 146
　Sarah Lizzie.................... 477
　Sarah (Lloyd)................... 356
　Sarah (Locke)........34, 67, 248, 253
　Sarah M............150, 255, 282, 533
　Sarah Maria..................... 323
　Sarah (Mendum).................. 474
　Sarah (Moses)................46, 94
　Sarah (Moulton)................. 13
　Sarah (Mowe) (Allen), Mrs....... 140
　Sarah (Murdock)................. 138
　Sarah (Norton).................. 13

INDEX OF NAMES

LOCKE, Sarah O. D. 156
 Sarah (Osborn) 245
 Sarah P. 125, 248
 Sarah (Page) 23, 254
 Sarah (Palmer) 34
 Sarah Palmer. 146
 Sarah (Pendergast) 568
 Sarah (Pierce) 281
 Sarah (Porter) 79
 Sarah (Randall) 142, 148
 Sarah (Reed) 361
 Sarah (Remick) 15
 Sarah (Runnels) 73, 157
 Sarah (Ryer) 189
 Sarah (Sanborn) 96, 131, 569
 Sarah (Seeton) 359
 Sarah (Short) 303
 Sarah (Sleeper) 224
 Sarah (Smith) 317
 Sarah (Snell) 257
 Sarah (Southwick) 212, 382
 Sarah (Sproul) 283
 Sarah (Stanwood) 47
 Sarah (Swallow) 255
 Sarah (Thurston) 109
 Sarah (Treadwell) 247
 Sarah (Trefethern) 233, 235
 Sarah (Vennard) 235
 Sarah (Vittum), Mrs. 146
 Sarah W. 71, 102, 141, 315
 Sarah (Wallace), Mrs. 282
 Sarah (Way) 136
 Sarah (Webster) 113, 313
 Sarah (Weeks) 303
 Sarah (Willoughby) 360
 Sarah (Wilson) 160
 Sarah (Winkley) 461
 Sarah (Woods) 67
 (Sawyer), Mrs. 141
 Scott Palmer. 373
 Scott Perry 373
 Seber 74
 Selden Barney 373
 Seward D. 185
 Sherburne 82, 104
 Sherburne C. d. 467
 Sheridan P. 141
 Shirley C. 560
 Sidney 506, 543
 Silas 123
 Silas Hoyt 276
 Silas M. 192
 Silas Merrill 200, 246, 368, 424
 Simeon 51, 110, 245, 247, 428
 Simeon Gerry 424
 Simeon P. 113, 435, 568
 Simeon Young 540
 Simon 32, 34, 34, 46, 54, 71, 73, 73
 Simon d. 18, 156
 Simon, Rev. 34
 Simon J. 154, 218
 Simon Knowles 115
 Simon Lovering 246
 Simon N. d. 257
 (Smiley), Miss 132
 Smith W. 219
 (Smith), Miss 179, 292
 Sophia (———) 63
 Sophia 153, 160, 299, 302, 341, 358
 Sophia (Cross) 156
 Sophia (Lavery) 323
 Sophia (Pinkham) 54
 Sophia S. d. 150
 Sophia (Snow) 358
 Sophia (Thurston) 61
 Sophronia 97, 276
 Sophronia (French) 200
 Sophronia D. (Frost) 147
 Sophronia (Sherburne) 272
 Spanish Lady 274

LOCKE, Spaulding F. 413
 Sperry Herman. 342
 Stacy Hall. 112
 Stanley 359
 Stanley Alwood. 450
 Stanley E. 450
 Stanley Sylvanus. 340
 Statira (Jenne) 88
 Stella (Richardson) 345
 Stephanie H. 499
 Stephen 41, 41, 74, 75, 77, 83
                    130, 130, 276, 568
 Stephen Brainard. 164
 Stephen D. 562
 Stephen Decatur. 79
 Stephen F. 534
 Stephen Farnsworth 422
 Stephen H. 124
 Stephen P. 561
 Stewart Ashton. 379
 Storer Pierce. 185
 Sula 236
 Sula Ann. 316
 Sumner d. 187
 Susan 63, 243, 268, 316, 568
 Susan d. 306
 Susan Agnes. 499
 Susan (Cater) 125
 Susan (Chappel) 80
 Susan (Clarke) 73
 Susan (Cole) 189
 Susan D. 104, 302
 Susan (Dennett) 122
 Susan (Dudley) 119
 Susan (French) 293
 Susan (Gilman) 104
 Susan (Hamilton) 328
 Susan (Hayes) 122
 Susan Helen d. 453
 Susan J. 270, 317
 Susan (Janvrin) 98
 Susan (Marble) 160
 Susan Mary d. 80
 Susan (Morse-Peabody), Mrs. 177
 Susan N. 542
 Susan (Nichols) 141
 Susan Olevia. 317
 Susan P. d. 150
 Susan (Parker) 422
 Susan (Rand) 70
 Susan (Remick) 147
 Susan (Sargent) 164
 Susan (Smith) 291
 Susan (Wentworth) 155
 Susie 538
 Susie (Berry) 341
 Susie E. (Hall) 188
 Susanna 21, 25, 25, 77
 Susanna Marston. 79
 Susanna (Ring-York) 20
 Susanna W. 39
 Sybil (Secard) 188
 Sydney 506, 543
 Sylvanus Dyer. 81, 175
 Sylvester 37
 Sylvina R. 85
 Tabitha (Edwards-Ordiorne), Mrs. 46
 Tamsen (Hayes), Mrs. 54
 Tamson 102
 Tamson D. 568
 Temperance 37
 Temperance (Rose) 20
 Tennah 37
 Thaddeus 234, 521
 Thaddeus W. 399
 Thankful (Blazo) 34
 Thelma. 549
 Theodore L. 244
 Theopilus S. d. 361
 Theresa (Talbot) 172

INDEX OF NAMES

LOCKE, Thomas.........1, 1, 13, 24, 26, 41
                    72, 105, 189, 506, 581
  Thomas A...................... 561
  Thomas B. d................... 496
  Thomas D. d................... 155
  Thomas D. M................... 113
  Thomas Dennett................ 156
  Thomas Dyer................... 179
  Thomas Jefferson............... 299
  Thomas King................... 474
  Thomas L...........83, 140, 178, 304
  Thomas Oscar.................. 127
  Thomas Tanner, Deacon.......... 161
  Thomas Webster................ 80
  Thomas Y...................... 171
  Tilpah......................... 37
  Timothy......13, 21, 97, 97, 569, 569
  Timothy Blake.................. 24
  Timothy H..................... 179
  Tirzah (Martin)................. 203
  Tirzah R....................... 132
  Tony Chester................... 169
  Tristram....................41, 83
  Tristram B. d................... 126
  True.......................... 268
  True T......................119, 268
  Truman Ransom................ 364
  Tryphena.........8, 11, 13, 17, 34, 61
                    70, 135, 507
  Tryphena (Moulton)............. 14
  Tryphena (Saunders)............ 29
  Una (Hazard).................. 491
  Vander d...................... 484
  Vera (Nash).................... 342
  Veranus....................... 88
  Viss (Vernon).................. 42
  Vernon........................ 189
  Vernon B. d................... 403
  Victor......................... 359
  Victoria R...................... 243
  Vienna Olevia.................. 157
  Viola.......................... 213
  Viola L. (Chase)................ 79
  Viola (Weeks).................. 477
  Vivian M...................... 562
  Wainwright G.................. 156
  Waity......................... 75
  Waity (Brown)................. 171
  Waity (Sheldon)................ 37
  Wallace, Rev. of New York....... 62
  Walter......135, 135, 268, 461, 468, 506
  Walter A...................390, 484
  Walter E........337, 352, 404, 458, 489
  Walter Elvin................... 461
  Walter Eugene................. 333
  Walter F. d.................... 136
  Walter G...................... 136
  Walter H. d................... 331
  Walter I....................... 491
  Walter Irving................... 334
  Walter M...................... 308
  Walter Morrison................ 289
  Walter Norman................. 169
  Walter W...................... 289
  Ward....................23, 49, 533
  Ward, Rev..................... 45
  Wardswell Clifton............... 340
  Warren.....................298, 525
  Warren D...................... 484
  Warren Ellsworth............... 341
  Warren Gilman................. 164
  Warren W..................... 133
  Washington d.................. 276
  Wate E........................ 161
  Wateann....................... 161
  Wayland....................... 386
  Wayne F....................... 480
  Weare......................... 42
  Wellington J................... 127
  Weltha (Kellogg)............... 135

LOCKE, Wesley of New York.......... 63
  Widow.....................8, 12, 565
  Wilbur J....................... 401
  Wilbur T...................... 525
  Wilfred D...................... 390
  Willard C...................504, 529
  William ... v, 8, 9, 11, 14, 26, 27, 29, 29
              52, 53, 54, 55, 55, 61, 72
            96, 98, 106, 108, 109, 119
            122, 127, 131, 136, 146
            189, 193, 209, 234, 244
            268, 268, 281, 356, 357
            505, 533, 568, 568, 568
  William d..............29, 54, 244, 302
  William, Deac.................. 70
  William, Lieut.................. 14
  William of Ohio................ 63
  William A................299, 315, 487
  William A. d.................. 257
  William Arthur................. 454
  William B. A.................. 108
  William B., Rev................ 420
  William Bert................... 287
  William C..................... 411
  William D..................... 306
  William DeAlton............... 173
  William E................162, 416, 427
  William E. d.................. 287
  William Elroy, Dr.............. 413
  William F..........162, 292, 451, 568
  William Farrington............. 345
  William Floyd.................. 79
  William Giffin.................. 542
  William H......171, 194, 219, 273, 290
          300, 331, 332, 337, 472, 568
  William H. d.................281, 284
  William H., Dr................. 126
  William Hale.................. 422
  William Harvey................ 147
  William Henry..............157, 325
  William Howard............... 360
  William J...................... 124
  William Joseph................ 376
  William J. S................... 75
  William L..................... 364
  William Lov...........115, 258, 258
  William Lyman................ 482
  William M.........88, 268, 269, 406
  William Moody................ 195
  William N..................... 124
  William P..............218, 218, 350
  William Pillsbury............... 183
  William R..................... 62
  William S..................150, 323
  William Samuel, Capt........... 44
  William Sherburne, Rev......... 95
  William Stanton................ 289
  William T..........141, 149, 172, 268
  William T. d.................. 255
  William Warren................ 240
  William Watson................ 317
  Willie d....305, 399, 414, 490, 492, 530
  Willie F....................... 197
  Willie H....................... 143
  Willie M....................... 384
  Willis E....................... 147
  Willis J....................... 354
  Winfield S..................... 218
  Winfield Scott.................. 313
  Winnie.....................506, 507
  Winnie (Childs)................ 301
  Winnie (Churchill).............. 413
  Winnifred..................427, 540
  Winnifred (Wardswell).......... 340
  Winslow....................... 357
  Woodbury...............132, 142, 233
  Worthington................... 365
  Worthington Smith............. 193
  Worthy Dearborn.............. 141
  (Young), Miss................. 213

INDEX OF NAMES

LOCKE, Zilbah.......................... 37
LOCKWOOD, Elizabeth (Locke)......... 357
 Hannah T....................... 171
 Terry, Dr....................... 357
LOGAN, Herman R.................... 533
 Mary O......................... 533
 Sarah (Locke).................. 422
 Sarah (Truby).................. 533
 Stephen........................ 422
 Willis J........................ 533
LOGSDON, Amy L..................... 555
LOHNAS, Bertha (Davis).............. 340
 Charlotte...................... 340
 Clara (Locke).................. 174
 Earl J.......................... 174
 John Davis..................... 340
 Lyman Earl..................... 340
LOMBARD, Elizabeth.................. 401
 Mary........................... 20
 Ozno D......................... 477
 Sarah (Locke-Stevens).......... 477
LONGHURST, Bethia (Locke).......... 190
 Catherine...................... 190
 George......................190, 190
LONGWORTH, Hannah (Locke)......... 55
 James........................... 55
 John............................ 55
 Louisa (Apt).................... 55
LOOMIS, Alice (Dakin)................ 440
 Arthur......................... 440
LORD, Miss.......................... 314
 Abbie (Doll).................... 169
 Alice M......................... 169
 Ann............................. 302
 Anna........................83, 400
 Benjamin H..................... 169
 Charles.....................169, 169
 Clarence....................... 336
 Daniel.......................... 140
 Edward L....................... 169
 Effie............................ 502
 Eleanor d.................. 336
 Eleanor H. (Locke).............. 79
 Elizabeth....................41, 83
 Frank D.....................169, 169
 George..................234, 399, 522
 George (Mooney)................ 522
 Grace........................... 522
 Harold W....................... 169
 Irene (McQuig)................. 169
 James........................... 83
 Katherine E..................... 169
 Lavina (Varney)................. 156
 Lillian (Thaxter)................ 169
 Lottie (Riddell)................. 169
 Louis M......................... 169
 Lucy............................ 433
 Lucy (Haskin).................. 169
 Margaret (McManus)............ 400
 Maria........................... 189
 Martin.......................... 156
 Mary............................ 111
 Mary (Townsend)............... 400
 Miriam.......................... 336
 Moses........................... 399
 Norman......................400, 522
 Olive (Watson).................. 234
 Oscar W........................ 169
 Rossina (Hansen)............... 169
 R. Stanley...................... 169
 Ruth d..................... 336
 Sampson........................ 475
 Sarah.....................169, 317, 498
 Sarah B. (Goss)................. 140
 Tozar, Rev...................... 45
 William......................... 79
LORING, Emaline..................... 132
LOUGEE, Lawrence................... 408
 Richard......................... 408
 William, Dr..................... 408

LOUGEE, Winnifred (Berry).......... 408
LOVEJOY, Nellie (Weed)............. 192
LOVELACE, Mr....................... 516
 Flora........................... 516
 Flora (Perkins)................. 516
 Violet.......................... 516
LOVELL, Eliza....................... 315
 Nellie.......................... 221
LOVERING, Amos..................... 443
 Betsey.......................... 243
 D. P............................ 460
 Fannie (Moore)................. 460
 Hannah......................... 26
 John............................ 51
 Madella (Gage)................. 443
LOVETT, Margaret.................... 39
 Mary........................... 144
LOWD. LOUD.
 Annie.......................342, 502
 Ellen, Mrs...................... 216
 Florence W. (Rand)............. 139
 Henry.......................... 139
 William H...................... 139
LOWE, Annie........................ 217
 Ellen M. (Hawse)............... 113
 William......................... 113
LOWES, Mr.......................... 417
 Nona (Locke)................... 417
LOWELL, Ann (Stevens)............. 213
 Chestina (Thompson)........... 334
 Elmer........................... 334
 Harriet......................... 98
 Marion d.................. 334
 Miriam.......................... 330
 Philip........................... 334
 Stephen........................ 213
LOWRY, Arvilla L. (Barker).......... 116
 Edwin D........................ 116
LUCAS, Mr.......................... 417
 Nellie (Locke).................. 417
LUCKEY, Annie...................... 298
 Dora............................ 298
 Walter W....................... 298
LUCY, Annie........................ 460
 George.......................... 282
 George F........................ 460
 Josephine (Locke).............. 282
 J. Page......................... 460
 Orrin M......................... 460
 Thomas R....................... 460
LUKENS, L. B....................... 260
 Olive (Lang).................... 260
LUKES, Ida......................... 392
LUNT, Mary......................... 76
LUTHER, Benjamin................... 417
 Cora............................ 417
 Flora........................... 417
 James........................... 417
 Jerusah (Richardson)........... 417
 Martin.......................... 417
LUTZ, Amanda...................... 421
LYMBURNER, Janett M............... 83
 John, Capt...................... 180
LYNCH, Inez (Thompson)............ 188
 Thomas......................... 188
LYON, Asa.......................... 476
 Attara (Grimes)................. 476
 Carrie.......................... 547
 Dana............................ 303
 Edward......................... 477
 Emma........................... 547
 Harriet......................... 547
 Harriet (Locke)................. 303
 Harry........................... 547
 Hattie.......................... 546
 Herbert......................... 547
 John............................ 477
 Louise.......................... 547
 Marcia (Holt)................... 477
 Mary........................... 477

INDEX OF NAMES 673

Lyon, Melissa (Abbott).............. 477
Lytel, Samuel..................... 169
   Sarah B. (Lord)................ 169
Mace, Abigail..................... 34
   Abigail (Philbrick).............. 128
   Anna........................ 548
   Charles d..................... 503
   Edwin W. d................... 503
   Elizabeth (Garland)............. 503
   Elizabeth (Locke)............... 343
   Helen (Edson).................. 503
   Ithamar...................... 71
   John......................124, 128
   Joseph....................343, 503
   Lewis L...................... 503
   Margaret..................... 503
   Martha J. (Locke).............. 124
   Mary......................489, 503
   Robert E..................... 503
   Sarah........................ 118
MacFarland, Mary.................. 109
Mackinnon, Florence................ 468
Macomber, Carrie.................. 246
Macy, Elizabeth................... 111
Madden, Lottie.................... 387
Magoon, Alice (Andrews)............ 536
   Ann (Farnsworth).............. 423
   Cora......................... 536
   Hannah....................... 21
   Martha....................... 536
   Mary......................... 189
   Orrin E....................... 536
   Oscar S....................... 536
   Samuel....................... 423
Maguire, Arnold................... 441
   Blanche...................... 441
   George....................258, 441
   James....................441, 441
   Marie (Bucknell)................ 441
   Mary (Burrell)................. 441
   Sarah (Locke).................. 258
Mahen, Samuel.................... 263
   Helen (Lang).................. 263
Mahlervin, Jacob................... 481
   Maggie....................... 306
Mahoney......................... 461
   Elizabeth F.................... 284
   Mary......................... 356
Main, Abigail..................... 123
   Amos....................54, 123, 123
   Betsey........................ 123
   Charles.................277, 277, 457
   (Cutter), Miss.................. 123
   David........................ 123
   Edward P..................... 457
   Elizabeth..................277, 457
   Ellen (Preston)................. 277
   Esther........................ 457
   Esther (Norwood).............. 123
   Flora......................... 277
   Frank A...................... 457
   George....................277, 457
   Jacob........................ 123
   James........................ 457
   John......................... 123
   Josiah........................ 123
   Lydia.....................123, 457
   Mary......................121, 457
   Mary (Norton)................. 277
   Miribah...................123, 277
   Miribah (Locke)................ 54
   Polly......................... 123
   Susan R. (Spinney)............. 123
   William. ,.................... 123
Malcolm, Mary..................... 76
Malone, Ada E.................... 411
   John......................... 240
   Louise....................... 411
   Mary (Locke-Rhodes)........... 240
Maloney, Amanda.................. 191

Maloney, Miss..................... 191
   James........................ 191
   Sarah (Locke).................. 191
   William...................... 191
Mannent, Alice.................... 521
Manning, Martha.................. 112
Manson, Miss..................... 129
   Emma........................ 405
   Etta d....................... 405
   Frances...................234, 398
   Martha (Berry)................. 236
   Robert....................... 236
Mapes, Henry..................... 534
   Martha (Carpenter)............. 534
Marble, Susan C................... 160
March, Mary...................... 155
Marcotte, Louis.................... 498
   Mary......................498, 498
Marden, Miss...................54, 293
   Abbie........................ 404
   Abigail..................28, 51, 406
   Abigail (Brown)............111, 250
   Alfred....................... 395
   Anna (Towle).................. 64
   Annah (Gardner)............... 396
   Aphia (Locke)................. 317
   Artemesia d................... 309
   Artemesia (Brown)............. 142
   Benjamin................66, 67, 304
   Charity....................... 31
   Charles....................309, 520
   Carry (Foss)................... 404
   Clara O....................... 403
   Clara (Philbrick)............... 409
   Daniel..................142, 309, 409
   David........................ 250
   Dorcas....................... 32
   Eben......................... 64
   Edwin P...................... 317
   Eliza......................... 143
   Eliza (Parsons)................. 409
   Elizabeth W................... 107
   Elizabeth (Moulton)......55, 66, 146
   Ella d....................... 479
   Elvira G..................404, 489
   Emerett E.................... 404
   E. Emerett (Locke)............. 235
   Erven W..................... 403
   Esther....................... 108
   Francis.....................44, 91
   Fred H....................... 404
   Frederick..................... 469
   Hannah.....................66, 66
   Hannah (Berry).............30, 64
   Hannah (Locke)............304, 304
   Hannah (Wallis)................ 107
   Harriet....................... 203
   Harry........................ 469
   Herman...................395, 494
   Hollis N...................... 404
   Ida F........................ 398
   Isabelle (Haley)............395, 494
   Israel......................23, 91
   James...............66, 91, 107, 469
   Jane......................72, 469
   Jennie B..................... 469
   John...............30, 64, 65, 65, 469
   Joseph....................... 91
   Josiah........................ 64
   Keziah....................... 64
   (Langmaid), Miss.............. 66
   Levi......................309, 396
   Lizzie (Langley)................ 469
   Louisa..................308, 309, 469
   Love (Berry).................. 64
   Lowell S..................... 84
   Lucy........................ 70
   Lucy A. (Garland)............. 107
   Lyman....................... 469
   Margaret..................... 469

INDEX OF NAMES

MARDEN, Marion... 405
  (Marston), Miss... 91
  Martha... 107
  Mary... 28
  Mary (Garland), Mrs... 520
  Mary (Lang)... 91
  Mary (Langdon)... 395
  Mary (Moore)... 238
  Mary J. (Page)... 84
  Mary (Smith)... 44
  Mercy (Page)... 91
  Nancy T. (Marden)... 66
  Nathan... 293, 469, 566
  Nathaniel... 30, 55, 66, 146, 235, 235
  (Nudd), Miss... 91
  Olive... 26, 66, 107, 111, 138
  Olivia B... 143
  Ora... 469
  Patience... 91, 309
  Peter... 469
  Polly W... 403
  Polly (Jenness)... 107
  Prudence... 64, 91
  Prudence (Locke)... 23
  Rachel (Dowst)... 67
  Ralph... 409
  Reuben... 403
  Sally... 199
  Sally (Philbrick)... 56
  Samuel... 56, 65, 309, 404, 469, 469, 479
  Sarah... 44, 44, 56, 66, 66, 236, 250, 309
  Sarah (Lamprey)... 44
  Sarah (Locke)... 30
  Sarah (Saunders)... 65
  Sarah (Seavey)... 64, 293
  Simon... 91
  Susanna (Berry)... 566
  Thomas... 44, 44, 91
  Walter... 469
  William... 65, 107, 107, 319, 404
  Marietta Harvey... 263
MARR, Ethel (Gibbs)... 312
  Isabel (Shapleigh)... 312
  James... 521
  Katherine (Sullivan-Locke)... 521
  Llewellen... 312, 312
  Virginia... 312
MARSH, Carra... 560
  Lucy (Locke)... 42
  Mary (Locke-Judkins)... 281
  Nathan... 281
  Nicholas... 42
MARSHALL, Abigail (Randall)... 56
  Anderson... 466
  Belle... 292
  Ella... 322
  Ellen (Martin-Locke)... 399, 521
  Emily... 55
  Ethel (Tallant)... 430
  Frances (Perkins)... 466
  Gideon... 56
  Mary, Mrs... 516
  Mary (Gregory)... 326
  May... 256
  Mercy... 55
  Robert... 430
  Samuel... 521
  Sarah (Merrill)... 256
MARSTON, Miss... 91
  Mr... 76
  Abigail... 19, 36, 147
  Almeda V... 530
  Annie (Batson)... 400
  Bertha (Fogg)... 410
  Caroline E... 140
  Catherine... 33
  Catherine (Elkins)... 140
  Charles... 341, 531
  Charlotte P... 523
  Clarence... 237

MARSTON, David... 410, 531
  Edith L... 407
  Edwin... 341
  Eliza... 551
  Elizabeth... 344, 477
  Ella M... 341
  Georgeanna (Lear)... 482
  Georgie... 77
  Grace B... 523
  Hannah... 265, 435, 488
  Hannah (Locke)... 67
  Helen (Sanderson)... 259
  (Holmes), Miss... 140
  Huldah... 19, 140
  Ira... 530
  Irving... 410
  Jacob... 400, 523
  Jennie (Farwell)... 531
  Jeremiah... 36
  John... 67, 140, 258, 259
  Jonathan, Lieut... 36, 265
  Joseph... 176, 482
  Levi... 147
  Lucretia (Blake)... 460
  Lydia A. (Palmer)... 176
  Martha D. (Brown)... 140
  Martha (Doe)... 523
  Mary... 35, 70, 84, 140, 140, 212
  Mary (Bailey)... 341
  Mary (Smith)... 36
  Molly... 117
  Paul S... 140
  Polly... 177
  Polly (Emery)... 117
  Polly (Philbrick)... 265
  Ruhuma... 71
  Sally... 117
  Sarah... 175
  Sarah (Locke)... 237
  Sophia... 343
  Susanna (Prince)... 76
  Thomas... 117, 341
  Tryphena... 27
  Willard S... 140
  Vinthea (Ingram)... 530
  Zilpha (Lang)... 263
MARTIN, Arvilla (Locke)... 244
  Alden... 279
  Chandler... 401
  Cynthia... 132
  Elizabeth... 554
  Ella J... 244
  Ellen... 399
  Emily (Woodman)... 279
  Eva A... 495
  Fannie... 399
  Fred L... 494
  George A... 554
  Harriet (Haley)... 494
  Harriet (Vennard)... 401
  H. C... 414
  James... 522
  J. Q. A... 401
  Lizzie... 293
  Lucy... 525
  Martha... 249, 522
  Mary (Emery)... 414
  Moses... 430
  Myra (Batson)... 401
  Rhoda (Hoitt)... 430
  Tirzah... 203
  William... 244
MARVIN, Eliza (Anderson)... 476
  Cora (Wheeler)... 546
  Oliver B... 546
  Ruth A... 546
  Susan (Bent)... 546
  William... 476, 546
MASON, Miss... 76, 76, 130
  Abigail... 210

INDEX OF NAMES 675

Mason, Alice 314
  Benjamin 68, 143
  Carl 538
  Clara (Jenness) 408
  Clarence 408
  Daniel 144
  Data 140
  Edmon 128
  Elizabeth 143, 144
  Elizabeth (Norton) 144
  Elizabeth (Philbrick) 128
  Emaline H. (Edmonds) 144
  Emma 314
  Frances 144
  Fred 314
  Georgeanna (Fitzgerald) 474
  Grace A. (Locke) 538
  Harriet 104, 105, 225
  Henry 496
  Hope 474
  John 38
  Joseph 144, 496
  Joseph, Rev 474, 474
  Levi 128, 192
  Lorinda 144
  Lucy (Locke) 38
  Lydia 25
  Margary 51
  Maria 314
  Mary 144, 183, 314
  Mary (Moore) 144
  Mercy 76
  Mercy (Locke) 69
  Olive (Cooms-Mowe) 68, 143
  Olive (Philbrick) 128
  (Pickett), Miss 314
  Proprietor 5
  Rebecca 76
  Robert 144, 314
  Ruth (Philbrick) 192
  Samuel 69, 144
  Stella (Holmes) 496
  William 314
Massey, Elizabeth (Locke) 406
  Horace A 406
  Vivian I 406
Mastick, Lucretia L 155
Mathers, Carmen 434
Mathes, Belle (Hoitt) 274
  Hamilton 274
  Hamilton d 453
  Harriet 68
  John 453
  Mary Abbie 453
  Pamelia 453
  Roy W 453
  Stanley L 453
Matterson, Belle (Cushing) 170
  Esther 80
  Ida 80
  Mary A 170
  Mary (Dyer) 170
  Mary (Locke-Hoxie) 171
  Philip H 170
  Solomon 171
  Stephen 170
  William H 80
Matthews, Edith 259
  Ella (Wallace) 459
  Elsie S 459
  Finetta (Herbert) 259
  Florence 259
  Grace 259
  Henry C., Dr 259
  Herbert 259
  Jacob 94
  Jonathan 259
  Lizzie 94
  Louisa L 94
  Mary (Locke) 94

Matthews, Nancy (Bell) 259
  Thomas 459
Maureau, Alphonze 208, 208
  Mary (Locke) 208
Maurer, Abbie (Rix) 425
  Alice C 539
  Frederick 425
  Mildred 539
  Rix 539
Maxfield, Daniel 191
  Miss (Maloney) 191
Maxwell, Adre (Locke) 356
  Emma 546
  Emma (Smiley), Mrs 144
  James 356
  Kate 183, 224
  Nancy 141
May, Mary 127
Mayall, Frank 242
  Emma (Taplin) 242
Mayers, Florence 534
Maynard, Dorothy 470
  Frank W 470
  George 470
  Harrie 470
  Hattie d 470
  John W 470
  Luella (Sanders) 295
  Mary (Rand) 470
  Nancy (Cate) 470
  Roy 470
  Walter 295, 470
  Warren 470
Mayo, Mary 459
  Susie (Dana) 518
  William 518
McAllister, Abbie (Wallace) 418
  Edith 418
  James 418
  Martha 130
McAlpine, John 189
  Patience (Locke) 189
McArthur, Almira (Locke) 328
  George 328
McCaffery, Ida (Pearson) 496
  Ruth P 496
  Thomas 496
McCarthy, Eudora 557
  Eva 557
  James 503
  Henry C 557
  John W 557
  Maude 557
  Maude (Moore) 503
  William 557
McCharles, Annie 273
McClary, Arthur E 554
  Col 88
  Marie (Pickett) 554
  Regiment 46
McClure, Jane 200
McConnell, Minerva 270
McCrillis, Annette (Bickford) 414
  Eliza 133
  Evans 414
  Hannah 200
  Mary A 200, 242
McCumber, Belinda (Locke-Watson)... 156
  Cyrus 156
McCutcheon, Charlotte 437
McDermott, Charles 277
  Flora (Main) 277
McDonald, Lillian 165
McDonough, Arvilla (Locke-Martin)... 244
  George 244
McDuffie, G. W 413
  Jennie (Woodman) 413
  Phebe (Woodman) 413
McFarland, Mary 200
McFarlane, Sarah (Moulton) 28

INDEX OF NAMES

McGanty, Lillian.................... 489
McGimsey, Etta..................... 344
McGowan, Aphia.................... 446
McGrath, Ellen (Locke)............. 315
   Joseph........................... 315
   Laura............................ 495
McHurley, Elizabeth................ 569
McIndoe, Abbie d.................. 426
   Abigail (Locke).................. 246
   Clara Alice...................... 426
   Florinda......................... 426
   James............................ 426
   John............................. 426
   Lucia A. d....................... 426
   Lyman........................... 246
McIntire, Mr....................... 127
McKay, Catherine.................. 356
   Elizabeth........................ 189
McKenney, Annie (Hopkinson)...... 180
   Augusta.......................... 78
McKenzie, Anna.................... 359
   Priscilla......................... 190
McKeown, Daisy................... 535
McKessom, Georgeanna............. 241
McKillop, Captain.................. 190
   Letitia........................... 86
   Louise........................... 172
McKitrick, Carrie.................. 337
McLane, Charles.................... 166
   James............................ 166
   Jennie (Noyes)................... 166
   Nellie (Noyes)................... 166
McLaughlin, Mabel (Locke)......... 189
   Marion........................... 189
   W. H............................. 189
McLean, Christena (McRae)......... 526
   Donald........................... 526
   Florence......................... 402
McLeon, Mary...................... 390
McMann, Ruby..................... 393
   Sophia........................... 312
McManus, Margaret................ 400
   Mary............................. 234
McMartin, Esther (Locke).......... 268
   John............................. 268
McMillen, Emma................... 358
McMullen, Harriet E. (Gould)...... 497
   Martha.......................... 216
   William.......................... 497
McNeil, Alice...................... 293
McMurphy, Anna................... 436
   Carrie d......................... 436
   Emma............................ 436
   Jane............................. 61
   Hattie............................ 436
   Lucinda (Locke)................. 254
   Mary.........................97, 436
   Minot d.......................... 436
   Willie d.......................... 436
   William.......................... 254
McQuig, Irene..................... 169
McRae, Christena.................. 526
McSlaughlin, Annie............257, 439
McSparren, Mary Emma............ 365
Meader, Albert..................... 219
   Elizabeth........................ 49
   Eunice (Scruton)................. 219
   Frances.......................... 293
   Mary............................. 102
   Nathaniel........................ 102
   Patience......................... 49
Meeker, Elizabeth.................. 532
Melcher, Abbie (Vennard).......... 241
   Daniel........................... 241
   Elizabeth........................ 41
   Gershom......................... 241
   Hannah.......................... 35
   Nancy............................ 241
Melvin, Mary D.................... 62
Mendall, Abbie (Hammond)........ 312

Mendall, Elizabeth (Kennard)....... 312
   Granville........................ 312
   Martha.......................... 312
   Mary W. (Locke)................ 144
   Sophia (McMann)................ 312
   William.....................144, 312, 312
Mendel, Ford....................... 485
   Lizzie............................ 485
   Martha.......................... 485
Mendum, Charles H................ 474
   Sarah........................151, 474
Mercer, Lizzie..................... 298
Merchant, Sarah................... 196
Merriam, Ada E.................... 367
   Cornelia......................... 138
   Eleanor.......................... 138
   Frank B.......................... 367
   George........................138, 199
   Hannah (Rand).................. 138
   Mary Isadore.................... 367
   Mehitable (Cook)................ 138
   Naomi (Brackett)................ 199
   Oliver........................... 138
Merrick, Marian.................... 449
Merrill, Miss....................... 166
   Aaron............................ 35
   Abram........................... 40
   Albert........................... 361
   Albion........................... 163
   Alice (Hight).................... 256
   Anna........................109, 241
   Anna Lov........................ 256
   Anna Lov (Locke)............... 115
   Annah (Locke).................. 109
   Annie J.......................... 78
   Annie (Locke)................... 499
   Asa.............................. 256
   Augusta.......................... 78
   Augusta (McKenney)............ 78
   Benjamin F...................... 76
   Betsey (Locke).................. 47
   Capt............................. 166
   Carrie J.......................... 78
   Carrie (Hoyt).................... 501
   Charity (Totman)................ 78
   Charles..............78, 78, 163, 166
   Clara..........................99, 99
   Davis Prince..................... 78
   Clarence......................... 99
   Diantha (Foote).................. 99
   Dolly M.......................... 78
   Dorothy (Locke)................. 40
   Edward T........................ 78
   Elias........................7, 40, 40, 78
   Eliza.......................76, 78, 196
   Ella (Martin).................... 244
   Ellen............................ 78
   Esther........................256, 256
   Frank M......................... 78
   Fred............................. 501
   George W.................78, 256, 529
   George Willard.................. 78
   Hannah Elizabeth................ 256
   Harriet.......................... 256
   Henry M. d...................... 163
   Ida M............................ 166
   Isaac D.......................... 78
   Isabella (Tucker)................ 361
   James..................78, 99, 99, 499
   Jason L.......................... 499
   Jennie (Hussey)................. 501
   John..........................99, 256
   Josiah.........................78, 99
   Laura (Johnson)................. 256
   Lavonia.......................... 99
   Leon H.......................... 529
   Leonard A....................... 330
   Lizzie.........................78, 99
   Lucretia L....................... 78
   Lucy E.......................... 163

INDEX OF NAMES

MERRILL, Lydia (Durrell) 163
  Mabel S. 78
  Maria 99
  Marilla J. 501
  Marion (Works) 256
  Martha (Mason) 163
  Mary Ann 78
  Mary 78, 80, 99, 99, 163
  Mary (Locke) 40, 40
  Mercy A. d 163
  Mercy (Leavitt) 35
  Mercy (Mason) 76
  Moses 47, 99
  Nathaniel L. 80
  Nellie (Hutchinson) 529
  Octavia (Fenderson) 99
  Olevia (Stone), Mrs. 180
  Olive 501
  Olive (Locke) 330
  Paul 514
  Peter 109, 115, 256, 256
  Prudentia D. (Waters) 80
  Ralph 256
  Rhoda 76
  Richard N. 499
  Rufus S. 163
  Ruth 78, 348
  Ruth (Currier) 514
  Samuel 216, 256
  Sarah 256, 258
  Sarah H. (Chase) 78
  Sarah (Dearborn) 216
  Sarah (Griffin) 99
  Sarah (Robinson) 163
  Sarah A. (Titcomb) 78
  Sophia (Goodwin) 99
  Simon L. 501
  Sophronia (Tucker) 99
  Vesta M. 166
  William 163, 244, 256
  Winfield S. 78
  Wingate 99
MERRIMAN, Caroline 385
MERRITT, Carrie, Mrs. 324
  Virginia 542
MERROW, Joseph, Lieut. 25
  Mehitable (Dore) 25
MESERVE, Abbie 351
  Sarah J. 328
MESSERGER, Emma 217
MILBURN, Ann 379
  Emily 208
  John 379
MILES, Ada (Locke) 449
  Alice G. 220
  Annie T. 461
  Edward L. 220, 449
  Frank A. 283
  George 186
  Harrie 529
  Laban 220
  Lewis F. 461
  Mary (Kimball) 220
  Myrtle (Cate) 461
  Nellie F. 461
  Nellie (Locke) 529
  Orrie (Gordon-Locke) 186
  Sarah (Tilton) 283
MILITZ, Annie (Rix) 425
  Paul 425
MILLBURY, Charles 541
  Cora 435
  Lizzie 541
MILLER, Mr. 33, 261
  Abigail (Noyes) 267
  Charles 515
  Elvira 515
  Grace (Fleek) 261
  Ida 382
  Mabel 172

MILLER, Lucy 267
  Mary (Trefethern) 33
  Rebecca (Mason) 76
  Robert 76
  William, Capt. 267
MILLEN, Mr. 59
  Matilda (Moulton) 59
MILLING, Mary 449
MILLS, Mr. 33
  Charles 68
  Elizabeth 300
  Ellen H. 308
  Lucy Ann 90
  Mary (Brown) 68
  Mary (Trefethern) 33
  Sylvia 500
MILTON, Charlotte (Pulsifer-Laverty)... 167
  Ward V. 167
MINER, Alden 57
  Ann 57
  Ephraim 57
  Isaac 57
  John 57
  Martha 57
  Matilda (Moulton) 57
  Solomon 57
  Wesley 57
MINKLEY, Susannah 374
MINOT, Miss 57
MITCHELL, Mr. 92
  Aaron, Dr. 295
  Aaron 295
  Albert 301
  Anne 39
  C. C. 296
  Daniel C. 78
  Emma 204
  Hannah 157
  Hannah E. (Merrill) 78
  Israel 295
  Izetta 296
  James 76
  Marilla (Godfrey) 92
  Martha 296
  Mary 295
  Mary (True) 271
  (Mason), Miss 76
  Mina (Rand) 301
  Orianna 518
  Reuben 271
  Ruth 418
  Sarah (Page) 295
MIXSELL, Georgeanna (Ray) 442
  Raymond B. 442
MONSON, Polly (Emery-Marston-Cotton) 117
  Samuel 117
MONTGOMERY, A. S. 433
  Addie 463
  Annie 463
  Fannie 463
  Charles 286
  Georgie 463
  Helen (Whittier) 433
  Mary (Locke) 286
MOODY, Rev. Mr. 4
  Mr. 95
  Albert 378
  Blanche 472
  Candace (Locke) 299
  Caroline, Mrs. 210
  Charles 299
  Charles Wadsworth 378
  Charlotte (Locke) 207
  Clayton 472
  Cornelia A. (Clough) 114
  Dwight 472
  Edwin 187
  Elizabeth (Brown) 95
  Flavilla (Locke) 187
  Frank 378, 472

INDEX OF NAMES

MOODY, Fred 187, 472
  George Locke 378
  Glenn......................... 472
  Grace......................... 472
  Henry S....................... 207
  Howard, Rev................... 114
  Isabelle....................... 95
  Joseph.....................187, 472
  Mary.......................... 119
  Maude (Jocke) 472
  Murle......................... 472
  Orpha......................... 472
  Ralph Waldo................... 378
  Sargent....................... 95
  Willard....................... 187
MOONEY, Anna (Lord)............... 400
  George........................ 522
  Thomas P., Lieut 400
MOOR, George F.................... 215
  Rebecca E.....................
  Sarah (Lane).................. 215
MOORE, Abbie (Locke).............. 282
  Abbie (White-Sanborn), Mrs...... 268
  Abby (Jenness-Odiorne)......... 238
  Abigail (Locke)................. 119
  Alpheus....................... 154
  Amelia (Wardwell-Locke)........ 346
  Benjamin...................75, 268
  Calvin, Dr..................... 346
  Cephas R...................... 355
  Charles.....................53, 267
  Charles W.............272, 272, 399
  Charlotte..................... 120
  Christena (Shipman)............ 229
  Christopher................... 238
  Cora (Ladd) 355
  Dolly (Locke).................. 53
  Edward d..................... 179
  Elbridge G..................... 267
  Ellen.......................... 267
  Emma..................180, 267, 557
  Emma (Brown)................. 503
  Ethel.......................... 268
  Etta........................... 272
  Eugene.....................267, 272
  Fannie E....................... 460
  Fannie (Farnsworth)............. 536
  Franklin....................... 75
  Fred J......................... 229
  Genevieve..................... 229
  (George), Miss 272
  George.....................268, 460
  Georgeanna.................... 272
  Grace......................... 268
  Hannah..................75, 234, 414
  Harridel L..................... 557
  Harriet (Flanders)............... 230
  Harry L....................... 503
  Hattie (Howland).............. 229
  Henrietta (Howland)............ 229
  Henry..................267, 345, 557
  James.........75, 120, 120, 229, 536
  Jane R........................ 229
  Jennie (Harris)................ 229
  Jenny (Rolfe)................. 229
  John, Capt.................... 119
  John..................267, 282, 399
  Joseph.....................105, 230
  Josephine...................... 230
  Josephine (Locke)............... 429
  Josiah........................ 53
  Josie.......................... 430
  Katherine..................... 267
  Laura K. d................... 267
  Laura (Hazelton)............... 267
  Lavinia....................... 267
  Lizzie......................... 164
  Lilla Estelle................... 75
  Lois (Locke).................... 399
  Lucy.....................268, 450

MOORE, Lucy (Miller) 267
  Lulu A........................ 460
  Lurietta....................... 272
  Margaret (Locke)............... 53
  Martha (Locke)................ 345
  Mary....59, 75, 120, 144, 230, 238, 267
  Mary (Doloff).................. 105
  Mary (Locke).................. 179
  Mary (Rowell)................. 267
  Mary (Todd).................. 120
  Mary (Whittier)................ 53
  Maryanna..................... 120
  Maude W..................... 503
  Melvin B...................... 267
  Mercy J. (Locke)............... 75
  Nancy (Larkin)................ 120
  Nancy E. (Locke)...........120, 248
  Ovid D....................... 229
  Rachel L...................... 229
  Robert..............120, 229, 248, 267
  Rufus W...................... 120
  Sarah............120, 230, 399, 430, 460
  Sarah Nightingale (Green)....... 120
  Waity......................... 75
  William................179, 179, 267
  William, Capt.................53, 399
MOORS, Caroline.................... 85
  Daniel........................ 85
  Elizabeth T.................... 85
  Everard....................... 85
  Jerusha....................... 161
  Samuel........................ 85
  Sylvina....................... 85
  Sylvina R. (Locke)............. 85
  Timothy....................... 85
  True.......................... 85
MORAN, Flora...................... 548
MORDOUGH, Addie.................. 418
  John.......................... 418
  Melissa (Green)................ 418
MOREY, Betsey..................... 199
MORGAN, Ernest L.................. 426
  Fanny......................... 137
  Florinda (McIndoe)............. 426
  Stuart C...................... 427
MORRILL, ——.............31, 44, 114
  Abigail (Greely)................ 214
  Alden A....................... 386
  Alice.......................... 476
  Charles....................482, 482
  Clarence...................... 386
  Eliza A. (Prescott).............. 114
  Elizabeth...................... 221
  Emma (Larrabee).............. 490
  Ephraim...................... 196
  Frank......................... 214
  Frank, Dr..................... 490
  Hannah....................... 99
  Lizzie......................... 214
  Lizzie (Lane).................. 386
  Mahala (Lamprey)............. 196
  Rachel (Blood)................ 482
  Rosa (Locke).................. 386
  Sally.......................... 99
  Sarah (Marden)................ 44
  Thomas....................... 214
MORRIS, Miss...................... 118
  Lydia A....................... 84
MORRISON, Mr..................... 429
  Abigail (Stevens)............... 90
  Abigail (Trefethern)............ 33
  Anna......................... 280
  Augustus...................... 206
  Charles W..................... 280
  Charlotte (Russell)............. 280
  David......................... 90
  Elizabeth (Locke).............. 96
  Esther (Perkins)............... 206
  Frank......................... 280
  Frederick..................... 280

INDEX OF NAMES

MORRISON, Horace 206
  Jonathan..................96, 206
  Marion (Locke)................ 429
  Mary Esther................... 206
  Ruth.......................... 206
  Sarah......................... 341
  William....................... 33
  William Rogers................ 33
  Willis........................ 280
MORSE, Miss...................... 118
  Abbie (Locke)................. 293
  Abbie (True).................. 271
  Ada F......................... 471
  Adaline (Locke)............... 293
  Anna (Hoar)................... 117
  Benjamin...................... 117
  Charles M..................... 467
  Clara (Merrill)............... 99
  Cora......................431, 467
  Cyrus......................... 298
  Darius........................ 99
  Earl E. d..................... 471
  Edward P...................... 467
  Edwin G....................... 299
  Emma.......................... 99
  Everett....................... 271
  Fannie G...................... 471
  Gratia (Langley).............. 298
  Harriet....................... 274
  Henry......................... 293
  Lavina (Page-Drake)........... 228
  Mary Hall..................... 40
  Mary L........................ 467
  Nellie E...................... 471
  Oscar......................... 228
  Queen (Locke)................. 299
  Sally......................... 117
  Sarah M. d.................... 467
  Stephen............293, 467, 471, 471
  Susan......................... 177
  Wingate....................... 99
MORTIMER, Lucinda................ 542
MORTON, Charles.................. 506
  Ellen......................... 357
  Emily (Thurston).............. 197
  Jeremiah...................... 197
  Salina (Freeman).............. 506
MOSES, Beatrice.................. 385
  Betsey (Cate)................. 282
  Betsey (Chesley).............. 254
  Charles....................... 158
  Comfort....................... 104
  Dearborn..................124, 385
  Elizabeth..................... 405
  Frank W....................... 385
  Fred F........................ 216
  Georgine...................385, 386
  Georgine (Webster)............ 216
  Hannah P...................... 113
  Helen......................... 386
  Herbert....................... 158
  Irving........................ 158
  James......................... 254
  Joseph W...................... 131
  Julia......................... 386
  Mark.......................... 282
  Mary F. (Gray)................ 158
  Miriam (Young)................ 94
  Nancy......................... 86
  Ruth.......................... 139
  Sadie (Holmes)................ 385
  Sally (Griffin-Locke)......... 131
  Sarah...........46, 94, 282, 322, 385
  Sarah H. (Locke).............. 124
  Sylvanus...................... 94
  Wesley........................ 158
MOSHER, Betsey (Locke)........... 105
  Hattie M...................... 81
  Jane.......................... 231
  John M........................ 105

MOSHER, Levi..................... 231
  Naomi (Mosher)................ 231
  Richard....................... 231
  William....................... 231
MOSHIER, Hannah.................. 552
  Nancy......................274, 453
MOTT, Ann (Hussey)............... 329
  Perkins....................... 329
MOULTON, Abigail............28, 36, 112
  Abigail (Marston)............. 19
  Albert.....................59, 520
  Alden......................... 57
  Alice (Mannent)............... 521
  Almira........................ 59
  Alpheus....................... 57
  Alzina V., Dr................. 58
  Ann........................19, 58
  Anna (Brown).................. 36
  Annie (Way)................... 28
  Ansel......................... 58
  Arba.......................... 58
  Armenia....................... 58
  Arvista....................... 57
  Augusta....................... 58
  Barron.............58, 58, 58, 246
  Benjamin...................... 59
  Bethia........................ 22
  Betsey.....................58, 59
  Betsey (Titus)................ 59
  Byron......................... 58
  Celesta....................... 59
  Charles....................57, 58
  Clara M....................... 521
  Clara (Locke)................. 399
  Cordelia...................... 57
  Daniel.........28, 28, 29, 35, 59, 59
  Darwin........................ 58
  David..................28, 36, 58, 59
  Dolly......................... 35
  Doris......................520, 521
  Dorothy d..................... 19
  Edith......................... 520
  Elisha d..................19, 22, 35
  Eliza......................... 59
  Elizabeth...19, 19, 35, 55, 59, 66, 146
  Elizabeth (Lamprey)........... 55
  Elizabeth (Worthington)....... 19
  Ellen......................58, 58, 59
  Elsie......................... 59
  Emma (Philbrick).............. 398
  Ernest........................ 552
  Ethan......................... 59
  Ethel (Spaulding)............. 520
  Eva (Drew).................... 521
  Fannie........................ 58
  Fannie (Clough)............... 59
  Flora J....................... 57
  Florence...................... 59
  Frank......................... 58
  Gabriel....................... 58
  George.....................59, 59
  Grandison..................... 58
  Guy........................... 59
  Hannah........................ 58
  Hannah (Downes)............... 19
  Hannah (Hoskins).............. 58
  Hannah (Philbrick)............ 27
  Harriet, Mrs.................. 58
  Harriet (Goss)................ 552
  Harriet (Kent)................ 58
  Harriet (Mathes).............. 68
  Harry T....................... 520
  Helen......................... 58
  Herbert....................... 59
  Huldah.............36, 58, 59, 60, 100
  Huldah (Marston).............. 19
  Isaac......................... 57
  Jacob......................58, 398
  James......................58, 59, 59
  James Madison................. 59

INDEX OF NAMES

MOULTON, Jane 58
  Jenifer......................... 59
  Joanna......................... 59
  Job............................ 28
  John.........................28, 36
  John, Col....................... 59
  Jonathan..22, 28, 55, 55, 57, 58, 58, 58
  Joseph......................22, 22
  Josiah................19, 19, 36, 36
  Julia........................... 58
  Larkin......................... 210
  Leora I........................ 520
  Lottie.......................... 59
  Louisa.......................... 58
  Louise.......................... 58
  Lowell.......................... 59
  Lucy......................19, 55, 59
  Lucy (Titus).................... 59
  Lutheria........................ 57
  Luvia A......................... 59
  Lydia.......................... 128
  Lydia (Rollins)................. 210
  Mabel (Abbott)................. 520
  Margaret........................ 28
  Margaret (Jones)................ 55
  Marilla (Keeney), Mrs........... 58
  Martha..............57, 58, 59, 143
  Martha (Gibson)................ 28
  Martha (Moulton)............57, 58
  Mary......22, 28, 28, 35, 36, 36, 59
  Mary (Charles)................. 58
  Mary (Moore)................... 59
  Matilda......................57, 59
  Merritt......................... 59
  Millicent....................... 58
  Millicent (Wheeler)............. 28
  Mindwell....................... 57
  Minerva........................ 58
  (Minot), Miss.................. 57
  Miriam (Locke)..............22, 35
  Molly (Page).................... 35
  Moses.......................... 58
  Nabby.......................... 57
  Nancy (Bailey)................. 58
  Nathan......................... 58
  Nathaniel....................19, 36
  Noah..................14, 28, 58, 59
  (Parker), Miss.................. 58
  Patience........................ 57
  Patience (Locke)................ 14
  Pauline......................... 58
  Percy A........................ 520
  Phoebe......................... 59
  Phoebe (Philbrick).............. 29
  Priscilla........................ 58
  Priscilla (Barron)............... 28
  Polly........................... 59
  Polly (Smith)................... 28
  Rachel.......................19, 35
  Rachel (Locke)................. 13
  Reuben..................27, 59, 59
  Rinaldo........................ 58
  Robert......................... 27
  Roxanna....................... 58
  Roxanna (Moulton)..........58, 58
  Ruby........................... 57
  Ruth (Cowan).................. 58
  Sabina......................... 246
  Sabrina......................58, 58
  Sally........................... 58
  Sally (Corey)................... 59
  Sally (Floyd)................... 59
  Sally (Knapp).................. 28
  Samuel.......................58, 68
  Sarah..........13, 18, 28, 35, 143
  Sarah (Dickinson).............. 28
  Sarah (Philbrick)............... 27
  Sarah A. (Porter).............. 57
  Seth........................... 57
  Simon.......................... 61

MOULTON, Smith.................. 58
  Sophia (Walker)................ 58
  Susan (Wheelock).............. 58
  Thomas............19, 399, 521, 521
  Tryphena....................... 14
  Webster......................59, 59
  William.......13, 19, 28, 35, 58, 552
MOUNTAIN, Mary................... 424
MOWE, Dorcas (Marden)............ 32
  Elizabeth...................... 143
  Ephraim.....................68, 143
  Flora A. (Randall).............. 143
  Frances d...................... 143
  Hannah (Locke)................ 31
  Harriet........................ 143
  Jacob.......................... 143
  John........................... 143
  Mary........................... 143
  Mary Ann...................... 143
  Olive (Cooms).................. 68
  Sally........................... 68
  Samuel......................... 31
  Sarah.......................... 140
MOWRY, Theresa.................... 315
MUDGE, Anne (Breede)............. 48
MUDGET, Mr....................... 92
  (Bachelder), Miss.............. 92
MUDIE, Earl M. d................. 434
  Lydia (Locke).................. 254
  Mabel L........................ 434
  Mitchell....................... 254
MUIR, Augusta (Locke)............. 357
  William........................ 357
MULLEN, Cora (Locke)............. 270
  Edward........................ 270
  Henry B....................... 48
  Julia (Dearborn)............... 48
  Mary.......................... 306
MULLERY, Margaret................ 150
MUMPER, Susan (Sanborn).......... 251
  William........................ 251
MUNROE, Elizabeth................. 52
MUNSEL, John..................... 88
  Sally (Locke).................. 88
MUNSEY, Dorothy.................. 431
  James.......................... 295
  Laura (Bickford)............... 295
MUNSON, Bridget (Utley).......... 193
  Jared.......................... 193
  Mercy......................... 88
MURCH, Lizzie.................... 200
MURDOCK, Carrie (Locke).......... 490
  Sarah A....................... 138
  Walter......................... 490
MURNING, Frances.................. 534
MURRAY, Ada..................... 248
  Elizabeth...................... 270
  Francis, Dr.................... 447
  George......................... 159
  Jeannette...................... 447
  Lillian (Lamprey).............. 447
  Martha L. (Gray).............. 159
  Martha (Locke)................ 248
  Mattie (Dann)................. 268
  Miriam........................ 210
  T. F........................... 268
  Uri L.......................... 447
  William.....................248, 380
MUZZEY, Clara M. (Locke)........ 539
  Polly........................... 70
  Quo W......................... 539
MYER. MYERS.
  Caroline (Locke-Hersey)........ 185
  Isaac.......................... 197
  Mary (Thurston)............... 197
  Thomas.....................185, 353
NASH, Ann....................176, 176
  Edward S...................... 502
  Effie (Lord)................... 502
  Ethel Y........................ 383

INDEX OF NAMES 681

NASH, Julia L............... 383
  Mabel W. d............. 383
  Samuel............213, 383
  Vera Viola.............. 342
  Viola (Locke).......... 213
NASON, Mary (Fletcher)...... 44
NAY, Elizabeth............. 19
  George................ 128
  Martha A. (Philbrick)... 128
NEAL, Abigail........18, 398
  Abigail (Harret)....... 233
  Addie M............... 518
  Alvina................ 204
  Andrew................ 18
  Ann (Badger).......... 375
  Catherine............. 397
  Charles..........345, 518
  Clara A............... 345
  Deborah............... 18
  Elizabeth............. 18
  Elizabeth (Haley)...... 18
  Elizabeth (Locke)...... 12
  Emma.................. 518
  Eunice (Quincy)....... 233
  Frank W............... 233
  Hannah (Emery)........ 178
  Hannah (Smith)........ 18
  James.........178, 233, 397
  Jane (Foss)........... 18
  Jeremiah.............. 18
  John..............18, 375
  John Walter........... 18
  Joseph.............18, 233
  Lizzie (Galusha)...... 397
  Lucy (Green).......... 397
  Margaret (Card)....... 233
  Margaret (White)..233, 397
  Mary......18, 233, 397, 398, 518
  Nabby (Locke)......... 106
  Olive L............... 397
  Roselle (Baker)....... 345
  Samuel........12, 18, 18, 18
  Sarah..............18, 397
  Sarah (Willard)....... 233
  Walter d.............. 518
  William.......106, 233, 233, 233
  Willie................ 518
NEALLY, Miss...........93, 93
  Mr.................... 116
  Abigail (Batson)...... 397
  Andrew................ 93
  Frank d............... 397
  Fred d................ 397
  George................ 397
  Gilbert............... 59
  John.................. 457
  Loanna................ 281
  Lydia II. (Locke)..... 116
  Mary (Durgin)......... 457
  Nancy (Sanborn-Perkins). 93
  (Seavey), Miss........ 59
  Willie................ 397
NEFF, Clarence W.......... 423
  Edith................. 423
  Elbridge.............. 423
  Millard F............. 423
  Sarah (Locke)......... 423
NELSON, Alma.............. 480
  Florinda (Locke)...... 426
  Genevieve (Moore)..... 229
  Hannibal L............ 426
  Harold................ 419
  Horace................ 426
  Irene (Sanders)....... 419
  John.................. 568
  Levi.................. 231
  Lydia................. 105
  Maurice S............. 419
  Peggy (Locke)......... 568
  William............... 229

NESBIT, John, Rev.......... 456
  Latha (Locke)......... 456
  Leonard L............. 456
NETTLES, Alice (Locke)..... 540
  Henry G............... 563
  Joseph L.............. 563
  Mary E................ 563
  Thomas............540, 563
NEVENS, Anna (McMurphy).... 436
  Bertha d.............. 541
  Blanche............... 541
  Charles............... 541
  Florence L............ 541
  Freeman R............. 436
  George................ 541
NEWBEGIN, Elvira, Mrs...... 355
NEWCOMB, Almira............ 216
  Henry................. 216
  Margaret.............. 288
  Mary (Butler)......... 216
NEWELL, Anna (Tilton)...... 255
  Catherine............. 218
  Esther................ 411
  Grace................. 411
  L. D.................. 255
  Leno P., Rev.......... 411
  Louise (Malone)....... 411
  Ruth.................. 411
NEWHALL, Nancy............. 124
NEWICK, Dorothy............ 311
  George................ 311
  Nellie (Trefethern)... 311
NEWMAN, Betsey, Mrs........ 184
  Betsey, Mrs........... 84
  Louise................ 408
NEWTON, James.............. 64
  Lavina B.............. 141
  Patience (Foss)....... 64
NICHOLS, Arabella (Johnson). 256
  C., Dr................ 478
  Carrie (Locke)........ 478
  Henry................. 256
  Mary.................. 89
  Susan B............... 141
NICKERSON, Emma (Locke).... 310
  Mark.................. 310
NIGHTINGALE, Caroline...... 303
  Emaline............... 303
NILES, Emma W.............. 425
NITCHER, Hannah (Locke-Towle). 81
  Wesley................ 175
  William............... 81
NIXON, Anna................ 201
  Mercy................. 13
NOBLE, Elizabeth L......... 179
NOEL, Elijah P., Dr........ 298
  Ida (Locke)........... 298
NORCROSS, J. Cornelia...... 372
  Louisa................ 185
NORRIS, Albert L........... 443
  Allie W............... 443
  Arthur K.............. 443
  Benjamin T............ 271
  Caroline (Bartlett)... 271
  Catherine............. 485
  Comfort (Leavitt)..... 35
  Effie (Shapleigh)..... 485
  Elizabeth............. 485
  Ephraim H............. 443
  Ephrietta............. 443
  Harriet (Fall)........ 271
  John P................ 271
  Joseph................ 120
  Mary.................. 271
  Mary (Harris)....264, 264, 443
  Mary (True)........... 120
  Moses................. 35
  Ruth.................. 35
  Walter................ 485
  Welcome...........264, 443

INDEX OF NAMES

NORRIS, Willard H.................. 264
NORTHEY, Abigail................... 109
   David......................... 109
   Joshua........................ 109
   Lang.......................... 109
   Mary.......................... 109
   Mary (Locke).................. 109
NORTON, Anna....................... 56
   B. Frank...................... 136
   Betsey (Lamprey).............. 277
   Charles A..................... 300
   Clara......................... 185
   Edna.......................... 300
   Elizabeth..................... 144
   Elizabeth (Locke)............. 136
   Fred L........................ 300
   Harriet (Stewart)............. 300
   Herbert....................... 300
   Horatio....................... 260
   Kate (Norton)................. 300
   Lydia (Lang).................. 260
   Mary......................13, 277
   Mattie (Wood)................. 300
   Maude......................... 300
   Russell....................... 185
   Samuel........................ 22
   Sarah.....................13, 300
   Walter F...................... 300
   William...................277, 300
NORWOOD, Esther.................... 123
NOURSE, Calvin..................... 98
   Caroline S. (Locke)........... 98
NOWELL, Eunice G................... 111
NOYES, Mrs......................... 13
   Abigail...................76, 267
   Abigail (Locke)............... 38
   Abigail (Phinney-Huston-Locke)... 76
   Addison....................... 205
   Alexander..................... 163
   Almira (Rice)................. 163
   Almira (Royal)................ 162
   Amos W........................ 77
   Anne (Colley)................. 163
   Arthur C...................... 165
   Betsey........................ 162
   Betsey (Haines)............... 76
   Celestia (Warren)............. 162
   Charles Addison............... 377
   Charlotte (Thompson).......... 162
   Deborah Locke................. 77
   Dorcas...................76, 77, 163
   Dorcas (Noyes)................ 76
   Edward K...................... 165
   Eliza A....................... 162
   Elizabeth S................... 77
   Elizabeth (Barton)............ 77
   Emaline (Copp)................ 205
   Eunice................76, 76, 77
   George........................ 162
   Georgie (Marston)............. 77
   Gertrude...................... 163
   Harriet (Wood)................ 163
   (Hatch), Mrs.................. 163
   Helen R....................... 165
   Henry M....................... 163
   Ida........................... 365
   James...................38, 76, 163
   Jennie L...................... 166
   Joanna (Sawyer)............... 162
   John....................76, 77, 162
   Josiah, Judge................. 75
   L. (Thayer)................... 377
   Laurinda (Greely)............. 77
   Lendel........................ 163
   Lillian (McDonald)............ 165
   Lucelia (Bowie)............... 77
   Lucretia (Lawrence)........... 162
   Martha (Humphrey), Mrs........ 162
   Mary Ann...................... 77
   Mary......................162, 163

NOYES, Mary (Brackett)............. 163
   Mary (Connor)................. 76
   Mary (Locke-Prince)........... 38
   Mary (Lunt)................... 76
   Minnie A...................... 166
   Moses.................38, 76, 76, 76
   Nathaniel Locke..........76, 77, 163
   Nellie Susan.................. 166
   Reuben................39, 77, 77, 165
   Rhoda (Merrill)............... 76
   Ruth C........................ 77
   Samuel.....................77, 77
   Sarah B....................... 377
   Sarah Prince.................. 77
   Sarah (Greeley)............... 383
   Sewell........................ 383
   Sophia........................ 162
   Sophia (Gould)................ 76
   Susanna W. (Locke)............ 39
   Thomas.....................76, 162
   William...................162, 165
NUDD, Miss......................... 91
   Abigail....................... 211
   Abra (Drake).................. 228
   Andrew F...................... 228
   Caroline...................... 97
   Clara......................... 266
   David......................117, 211
   Elizabeth..................... 47
   Hannah........................ 27
   Maria S....................... 147
   Mary.......................... 56
   Mary (Johnson)................ 147
   Nabby (Emery)................. 117
   Nancy (Perkins)............... 118
   Oliver........................ 448
   Ruth.......................... 52
   Samuel........................ 118
   Sarah (Redman)................ 448
   Stacy......................... 147
NUTE, Abbie, Mrs................... 482
   Annie......................... 462
   Daniel........................ 123
   George........................ 482
   Greenleaf..................... 512
   Lizzie........................ 461
   Mary.......................... 366
   Polly (Main).................. 123
   Sarah......................... 482
   Sarah (Brock)................. 512
NUTT, Nancy........................ 413
NUTTER, Miss....................... 192
   Mr............................ 192
   Abigail.....................49, 275
   Ada........................103, 454
   Adna.......................... 143
   Almira (Dame)................. 275
   Betsey........................ 219
   Carrie........................ 454
   Charles d..................... 454
   Daniel d...................... 275
   Dora.......................... 454
   E. (Bickford), Mrs............ 275
   Eliphalet...................49, 103
   Eliza......................... 103
   Elizabeth (Locke)............. 122
   Esther........................ 103
   Esther (Knowles).............. 192
   Frank......................... 222
   Hannah F. (Otis).............. 151
   Hunking C..................... 275
   Ida (Kimball)................. 222
   Ira........................... 275
   James......................... 103
   Jerry N....................... 275
   John..............103, 103, 275, 275, 454
   Julia A....................... 454
   Lavinia....................... 454
   Lovie......................103, 103
   Lovie (Locke)................. 49

INDEX OF NAMES 683

NUTTER, Lucinda.................... 103
  Mary...........103, 103, 222, 247, 275
  Nancy.......................... 103
  Sarah.......................275, 454
  Susan.......................... 152
  Sylvia M. (Blanchard)........... 103
  William......................122, 275
  Willard........................ 151
NUTTING, Almira (Philips)........... 150
  Caroline....................... 226
  Mary F. (Locke)................ 150
  William P...................150, 150
NYE, Annie......................... 170
  Herbert........................ 170
  Irma........................... 541
  James.......................... 170
  Lilly.......................... 170
  Lucy S......................... 259
  Sarah (Dyer)................... 170
OAKS, Abigail...................... 163
  Nathan......................... 163
OARE, Ada.......................... 209
  Joseph......................... 209
  (Smith), Miss.................. 209
OBER, John A....................... 217
  Harriet (Tilton)............... 217
O'BRIEN, John..................123, 390
  Mercy D. (Locke)............... 123
  Mildred (Haley)................ 493
  Minnie......................... 390
  Richard........................ 493
O'DAY, Susan....................... 497
ODELL, George, Dr.................. 101
  Irena (Dearborn-Waldron)....... 101
ODER, Jennie....................... 161
ORDIORNE, Abby (Jenness)........... 238
  Anzoletta (Bell)............... 308
  Charles A...................... 308
  Clara E........................ 308
  Cynthia........................ 308
  Eben.......................141, 321
  Ebenezer....................... 308
  Emily (Grant).................. 321
  Estelle........................ 321
  George......................... 233
  Hannah (Rand).................. 129
  John........................... 46
  Jonathan....................... 308
  Joseph P....................... 129
  Levi d......................... 308
  Louise......................... 216
  Mary A......................... 308
  Mary S. (Brown)................ 141
  Mary (Ward-Locke).............. 473
  Mary (Yeaton).................. 16
  Moses H........................ 308
  Nathaniel......................
  Olive.......................... 129
  Ralph.......................... 308
  Ruth (Kinnear)................. 238
  Samuel......................... 129
  Simon.......................... 238
  Tabitha (Edwards).............. 46
  William........................ 473
  Winnifred (Barter)............. 308
OKE, James......................... 406
  Louisa......................... 406
  Mary E......................... 406
OLDS, Betsey....................... 74
OLIVER, Alexander.................. 504
  John........................... 504
  Julia A........................ 504
  Lavinia........................ 504
  Lilla.......................... 352
  Mary........................... 352
OLMSTEAD, Simeon................... 62
  Susanna (Ladd)................. 62
ORDWAY, Etta....................... 306
  Gertrude....................... 483
  Jennie (Marden)................ 469

ORDWAY, Lena....................... 469
  Marion......................... 469
  Perley......................... 469
  Sarah (Locke).................. 307
  Walter......................... 469
  Willard........................ 307
ORGAN, Mary........................ 24
ORMSBY, Alice H.................... 385
  Charles H...................... 339
  Edith.......................... 385
  Freddie d...................... 385
  Georgine W. d.................. 385
  Harold E....................... 339
  Helen (Leach).................. 385
  James W........................ 385
  Jesse (Fink)................... 385
  Leander.....................216, 385
  Mary (Webster)................. 216
  Rhoda (Knilands)............... 339
  Ruby (Knilands)................ 339
  William........................ 339
O'ROURKE, Alice.................... 473
ORR, Benjamin...................... 388
  Carrie (Clarke)................ 388
  Dudley W....................... 388
OSBORN, Hannah (Clough)............ 419
  Joshua......................... 419
  Mary E......................... 150
  Sarah C........................ 245
OSGOOD, Enoch F.................... 106
  Fannie......................... 288
  Henry.......................... 119
  James, Capt....................
  Jane (Tilton).................. 283
  Jennie (Dearborn).............. 119
  John S......................... 283
  Lucy (Locke-Sharrar)........... 106
  Lydia.......................... 46
  Mary........................... 50
  May E.......................... 283
  Mehitable...................... 120
  Sarah (Locke).................. 119
  Timothy........................ 119
OSMAN, Annie (Locke)............... 477
  C. Frank, Dr................... 477
OTIS, Ada (Locke).................. 461
  Ada (Perkins).................. 151
  Almira (Canney)................ 152
  Anna (Libbey).................. 155
  Carrie (Shattuck).............. 320
  Charles.....................461, 553
  Clarissa....................... 151
  David.......................... 155
  Dorothy.............72, 74, 151, 151
  Dorothy (Locke)................ 34
  Edwin.......................... 155
  Eldredge....................... 152
  Elijah......................34, 72
  Elizabeth..............152, 152, 152
  Elizabeth (Gove)............... 151
  Elizabeth (Johnson)............ 151
  Ephraim........................ 151
  Esther (Howard)................ 72
  Frank.......................... 155
  Hannah....72, 151, 151, 151, 151, 152
  Hannah (Allard)................ 72
  Hannah (Bowles)................ 72
  Hannah (Howard)................ 72
  Harriet.....................151, 152
  Harriet G. (Dennett)........... 155
  Harrold d...................... 155
  Howard L....................151, 151
  Ida (Locke).................... 492
  James..................151, 152, 320
  Jane........................... 72
  Jane (Hussey).................. 72
  Jane (Marden).................. 72
  Jane (Otis).................... 72
  Jemima (Otis)...............151, 151
  Jethro......................... 72

INDEX OF NAMES

OTIS, Joanna (Wallingford) 72
  Job............................ 157
  John........................... 72
  Jonathan C..................... 152
  Joseph Y....................... 151
  Joshua................... 72, 72, 72
  Judith (Chesley)................ 151
  Leah (Pearl)................... 72
  Lemuel......................... 72
  Lena L......................... 553
  Leon R......................... 553
  Lovie (Elkins).................. 72
  Lucy........................... 151
  Lucretia (Mastick).............. 155
  Lydia.....................151, 151
  Maria.......................... 73
  Maria (Wiggin)................. 410
  Martha..............72, 151, 151, 152
  Mary.......152, 152, 152, 152, 152, 239
  Mary (Foss).................... 72
  Maude E........................ 553
  Melinda........................ 151
  Micajah........................ 72
  Nehemiah d.................... 151
  Paul........................72, 553
  Peter.......................... 152
  Polly (Brock).................. 72
  Polly (Lee).................... 72
  Roscoe......................... 492
  Rufus.......................... 151
  Sarah.......................... 151
  Sarah (Foss)................... 151
  Sarah W. (Deland).............. 152
  Sarah (Mendum)................ 15ı
  Simeon......................... 72
  Stephen....................155, 155
  Simon.......................... 410
  Susan (Nutter)................. 152
  Thomas............72, 151, 152, 152
  Theresa........................ 152
  Willard........................ 151
  William.........72, 151, 152, 152, 152
  Winnie F....................... 553
OTTO, Rosetta...................... 204
OUTING, Foster E................... 296
  Georgeanna..................... 296
  Ida (Weeks).................... 296
  James.......................... 296
  Mary (Page).................... 296
OWEN, Emma........................ 459
OWENS, Keziah (Berry).............. 65
  Patrick........................ 65
OXFORD, Fannie.................... 371
PAARECH, Adelaide.................. 541
PACKARD, Dr....................... 420
  Mary........................... 420
PADDLEFORD, Benjamin..............58, 58
  Byron.......................... 58
  Catherine (Locke) 276
  Clayton........................ 58
  Coomer......................... 57
  Hannah (Moulton)............... 58
  Ladoska........................ 58
  Mary A......................... 57
  (Moulton), Miss................ 57
  Patience (Moulton)............. 57
  Philip......................57, 57
PADELFORD, William, Dr............. 276
PADDOCK, Gertrude d.............. 418
  James.......................... 418
  Lucy........................... 418
  Lucy (Green)................... 418
PADEN, Alfred..................... 423
  Agnes.......................... 423
  Florinda (Locke)............... 423
  Guy............................ 423
PAGE–PAIGE.
  Abbie.......................... 296
  Abigail.....................54, 132
  Abigail (Coleman).............. 100

PAGE–PAIGE
  Abigail (Locke)...............24, 61
  Albert......................... 296
  Albion L....................... 433
  Andrew J....................... 227
  Aramenta....................... 435
  Asa M.......................... 296
  August......................... 545
  Belinda (Berry)................ 132
  Belsen......................... 132
  Benjamin............47, 84, 100, 122
  Bertha (Tappan)................ 295
  Betsey......................57, 132
  Betsey (Locke)................. 42
  Betty d........................ 84
  Blanche........................ 296
  Calvin......................... 100
  Carrie.................296, 433, 459
  Catherine...................... 295
  Charles........................ 296
  Clara (Woodman), Mrs........... 435
  Clarence....................... 296
  Coffin......................42, 84
  Cora........................... 489
  Cynthia (Martin)............... 132
  D. Frank....................... 296
  Daniel......................... 122
  David............47, 84, 84, 100, 122
  Deborah........................ 84
  Dolly (Sargent)................ 47
  Dorcas......................... 227
  Dorothy (Locke)................ 104
  Dorothy (Smith)................ 132
  Edna........................... 296
  Edward......................... 205
  Elizabeth...............23, 210, 227
  Elizabeth (Akerman)............ 100
  Elizabeth (Locke).............. 252
  Ellen......................296, 296
  Elvira C. (Peaslee)............ 100
  Emily.......................... 122
  Etmar (Greenleaf).............. 100
  Etola (Howard)................. 388
  Evaline (Wyman)................ 205
  Flora (Evans).................. 433
  (Fogg), Mrs.................... 100
  Francis.....................27, 35, 84
  Fred A......................... 435
  George W....................... 295
  Georgianna (Hall).............. 227
  Glen D......................... 296
  Hannah......................100, 132
  Hannah (Bachelder)............. 47
  Hannah (Drew).................. 227
  Hannah (Lamprey)............... 89
  Hannah (Nudd).................. 27
  Hannah (Marston)............... 435
  Hannah (Walker)................ 100
  Harriet........................ 362
  Harriet A. (Danforth).......... 100
  Harry.......................... 296
  Hartley........................ 388
  Harvey......................... 433
  Horace......................... 296
  Huldah......................... 132
  Huldah (Locke)..............61, 89
  Ira............................ 176
  Izetta (Mitchell).............. 296
  James.......100, 132, 228, 252, 295
  Jane........................... 47
  Jane (Phelps).................. 100
  Jennie (Bowen)................. 296
  Jeremiah....................61, 132
  Jesse......................320, 320
  Joanna (Bohonon)............... 47
  John 35, 47, 61, 89, 100
                100, 132, 132, 227
                227, 254, 295, 362
  Jonathan....................... 122
  Joseph......................... 122

INDEX OF NAMES 685

PAGE-PAIGE
- Joshua............100, 435
- Judith (Bean).................. 47
- Katherine (Hendricks)........... 227
- Lavina J. ϶.................228, 228
- Levi L........................ 227
- Levina (Thompson)............. 227
- Lilla H........................ 362
- Lillian........................ 227
- Lillie......................... 296
- Lucy (Coleman)................ 100
- Lulu I........................ 296
- Lydia......................... 41
- Mahala B. (Lane)............... 132
- Mandana (Locke).............. 254
- Mandana (Locke).............. 295
- Martha....................295, 366
- Martin....................227, 296
- Mary.....84, 100, 132, 296, 296, 343
- Mary (Clarke)................. 84
- Mary (Elkins-Locke)............ 176
- Mary (Godfrey)................ 84
- Mary (Hollon)................. 227
- Mary (Marston)..............35, 84
- Mary (Tibbitts-Canney)......... 320
- May.......................... 296
- Mehitable..................... 47
- Mercy........................ 91
- Minnie H..................... 296
- Miribah....................... 14
- Mitchell...................... 104
- Molly......................... 35
- Moses.....................47, 100
- Munroe L..................... 296
- Nancy........................ 100
- Nancy (White)................. 295
- Nathaniel S................... 227
- Noah......................... 42
- Oliver........................ 84
- Onesephorus................24, 47, 47
- Patience...................... 47
- Patty......................... 73
- Phebe........................ 213
- Polly......................... 54
- Rachel (Moulton).............. 35
- Redman....................... 84
- Rhoda (Searles)................ 47
- Rose......................... 296
- Roy L........................ 296
- Ruth.....................132, 228
- Samuel..............47, 81, 84
- Sarah.......23, 84, 132, 132, 254, 295
- Sarah (Locke).................. 122
- Sarah (Sherburne).............. 81
- Sarah (Switzer)................ 296
- Stacy......................... 84
- Susan (Rowe).................. 84
- Thais (Tyler), Mrs.............. 100
- Theodate H.................... 132
- Vendesa...................... 132
- William...................100, 296, 296
- PAINE, Christena.................. 26
- Clara L. d..................... 393
- Elizabeth.................330, 393
- Georgeanna.................... 473
- Hattie (Tennant).............. 393
- Hilma........................ 393
- Howard....................... 393
- Isaac.....................301, 473
- Jesse.................393, 473, 473
- Joseph........................ 473
- Marion........................ 393
- Martha (Riggs-Paine)........... 301
- Mary d....................... 393
- Mary (Aldrich)................. 231
- Milton, Col.................... 473
- Rufus......................... 231
- PAINTER, Benjamin................ 535
- Carl T........................ 535
- Eva (Truxall).................. 535

- PAINTER, Roy..................... 535
- PALMER, Abbie.................... 202
- Abigail L. (Jenness)............. 107
- Abigail (Rowe)................. 566
- Ada (Nutter-Bliss).............. 454
- Addie......................... 341
- Albert........................ 206
- Alfred S...................... 176
- Allen......................... 74
- Almira........................ 206
- Amelia........................ 454
- Amos.....................454, 454
- Amy.......................... 206
- Ann........................... 566
- Annie.....................341, 373
- Benjamin..................... 435
- Betsey....................44, 342
- Catherine B................... 176
- Christopher................565, 566
- Deborah (Tuck)................ 176
- Dorothy...................... 206
- Dorothy (Locke)............... 96
- E. M.......................... 372
- Elizabeth..................... 565
- Elizabeth (Berry).............. 565
- Elizabeth (Locke).............. 566
- Ellery........................ 206
- Hannah (Avery)............... 435
- Israel........................ 100
- Jane (Foss)................... 566
- Jeremy....................... 566
- John Moore................... 176
- John......................206, 341
- Jonathan.........107, 565, 566, 566
- Joseph...........82, 176, 177, 566
- Loretta (George)............... 341
- Lottie........................ 431
- Lydia Ann.................... 176
- Maria L....................... 341
- Martha P...........159, 206, 206
- Mary K......176, 176, 206, 206, 254
- Mary (Ladd).................. 176
- Mary (Locke).................. 74
- Mary (Page)................... 100
- Mary (Palmer-Brown).......... 206
- Miriam L..................... 176
- Miriam L. (Locke)............. 82
- Miriam, Mrs................... 84
- Muriel........................ 554
- Nelson H..................... 341
- Phebe A...................... 161
- Robert d..................... 341
- Samuel....................... 566
- Sarah...................34, 176, 566
- Sarah (Willey)................. 566
- Stephen....................... 23
- W. H......................... 372
- William...........96, 566, 566, 566
- PANKEY, Abbie (Locke)........... 209
- Amanda...................... 246
- PARK, Chloe Edith................ 333
- Clare d....................... 333
- Edward....................... 209
- Herman Earl.................. 333
- John A. d..................... 333
- Joseph A...................... 161
- Roy C. d...................... 333
- Sarah J. (Locke)............... 161
- Watie Lillian.................. 333
- PARKER, Miss..................... 58
- Abbie......................... 373
- Abigail....................... 421
- Almira (Wadhams)............. 174
- Charles T..................... 127
- Charlotte..................... 125
- Christena (Locke).............. 185
- Daniel....................127, 127
- Donald....................... 380
- Elijah........................ 360
- Elizabeth..................... 360

INDEX OF NAMES

PARKER, Elizabeth (Legg)............. 311
 Ellen J........................ 81
 Emaline....................... 113
 Eva d......................... 352
 Gertrude...................... 462
 Gertrude (Benyon).............. 352
 Hannah........................ 52
 Harold P...................... 352
 Henry......................185, 380
 J. Norris...................... 311
 John........................174, 311
 Julia.......................... 88
 Levi........................58, 203
 Louisa (Locke)................. 203
 Lucy.......................... 314
 Lydia (Hayes).................. 283
 Mary A........................ 127
 Mary P. (Locke)................ 127
 Millicent (Moulton)............. 58
 Moody......................... 58
 Nathaniel..................... 283
 Nellie (Dow).................. 368
 Nellie (Trefethern-Newick)....... 311
 Priscilla (Moulton)............. 58
 Susan......................... 422
 Susan (Winkley)................ 380
 Walter Eugene.................. 352
 Wilbur........................ 368
 William H..................... 127
PARKHURST, Edith.................... 342
PARLIN, Alma....................... 467
 David......................... 467
 Mabel......................... 467
 Mina (Phenix).................. 467
PARNELL, John...................... 270
 Betsey (Worthen)............... 270
PARSHLEY, Eben..................... 220
 Elizabeth (Kimball-Tompkins).... 220
 Herman K...................... 220
 Ida (Hall).................... 386
PARSONS, Abigail.................... 93
 Abigail (Garland).............. 117
 Abigail (Philbrick)............. 128
 Albion D...................... 238
 Annie (Leavitt)................ 409
 Annie (Locke).................. 488
 Asa........................... 184
 Capt......................16, 26, 30
 Clara Ellen.................... 409
 Corinne B...................... 551
 Daniel J...................... 409
 Dorothy E..................... 528
 Eliza Anna.................... 409
 Eliza (Brown)...............409, 551
 Elizabeth..................... 117
 Elizabeth (Munroe)............. 52
 Evaline d..................... 409
 Everett....................... 262
 Frank.......................159, 409
 Hannah (Perkins)............... 52
 John.......................117, 551
 Joseph......................52, 498
 Langdon....................... 488
 Leonora (Babb-Hassam)........... 262
 Lizzie (Ham).................. 159
 Lydia......................... 328
 Martha (Jenness)............... 238
 Martha (Locke)..............409, 410
 Mary (Dow).................... 184
 Norman L...................... 409
 Samuel........................ 128
 Sarah (Hubbard)................ 409
 Thomas..............409, 409, 410, 551
PARTRIDGE, Martha (Locke)............ 422
 Samuel........................ 422
PATCH, Eliza....................... 101
PATRICK, Ada (White)................. 527
 Betsey........................ 73
 Elizabeth..................... 40
 F. B.......................... 527

PATTEE, John....................... 196
 Lavinia (Lamprey).............. 196
 Mehitable..................... 63
 Sarah......................... 196
PATTERSON, Esther (Batson).......... 400
 Flora (Locke).................. 189
 Fred.......................... 400
 Horace........................ 189
 Lester L...................... 189
 Lewis......................... 400
 Nathan........................ 400
PAUL, Carrie....................... 411
 Ella.......................... 495
PAVITT, John....................... 447
 Sarah (Bond).................. 447
 Susan......................... 265
PAYNE, John........................ 52
 Rachel........................ 52
 Sarah......................... 52
PAYSON, Clifford.................... 205
 Eleanor A..................... 124
 Mary.......................... 344
 Samuel........................ 205
 Sarah (Smith-Philbrick).......... 205
PEABODY, Eli....................... 263
 Hannah (Bachelder-Bean)........ 92
 J............................ 92
 Rebecca....................... 127
 Sarone (Lang).................. 263
 Susan (Morse).................. 177
PEARL, Hannah (Huckins)............. 273
 John.......................... 151
 Leah.......................... 72
 Melinda (Otis)................. 151
 Rufus, Dr..................... 273
PEARSON, Abigail.................... 94
 Addie......................... 475
PEARSONS, Alice..................... 46
 Annie M....................... 496
 Augusta....................... 93
 Caleb.....................46, 93, 93
 Charles....................... 496
 Clarence...................... 496
 Elizabeth..................... 496
 Ellen......................... 93
 Ellen (Keyser)................. 93
 Etta (Brown).................. 323
 Frank......................... 323
 Fred.......................... 496
 George Franklin................ 93
 Ida G......................... 496
 John G........................ 201
 Julia A....................... 93
 Mabel (Coleman)................ 496
 Martha (Sanborn)............... 201
 Mary.......................94, 94
 Mary (Locke).................. 46
 Nellie........................ 405
 Roxy (Doloff)................. 94
 Ruhuma.....................46, 94
 Ruhuma (Locke)................ 46
 Sally......................... 94
 Willie........................ 94
 Willis........................ 496
PEASE, Abigail (Weeks)............... 201
 Alice Cary.................... 332
 Anna S........................ 218
 Atumn Vine.................... 332
 Cicada Lily................... 332
 Cora.......................... 187
 George A...................... 161
 George A. d................... 332
 Henry......................... 201
 Huldah (Locke-Buzzell).......... 141
 J. H.......................... 141
 Jennie M...................... 201
 Luella d...................... 201
 Mary d........................ 201
 Minnie Marion................. 332
 Sarah (Brown)................. 332

INDEX OF NAMES

PEASE, Wateann (Locke) 161
    Winnie Winsome 332
PEASLEE, Albert 362
    Charlotte A 362
    Drusilla (Locke) 192
    Elvira C 100
    Lillian Davis (Warner) 362
    Melvin 362
    (Whittier), Miss 362
    William 192
PECK, Elvira (Follet) 135
    Otis 135
PECKER, Elora (True) 304
PECKHAM, Cyrus, Rev 389
    Earl W 389
    Edward F 389
    Mary (Cass) 389
PECKNAM, Phebe 170
PEDEN, Bessie J. (Locke) 169
    Willis 169
PEEK, Gertrude 527
    Mary (Schile) 527
    Walter 527
PEMBERTON, Annie H 344
    Edwin P 177
    Jonathan K 344
    Mary (Locke) 177
    Mary (Payson) 344
PENDERGAST, Sarah 568
PENDEXTER, Lydia 254
PENDLETON, Mr 75
    Harriet (Clifford) 75
    Kate 75
PENNIMAN, Adeline 101
PEPPER, Almeda (Smith) 413
    Eliza 414
    Lyman 413
PEPPERELL, Andrew 83
PERCIVAL, Annie (Locke) 322
    Agustus 322
PERCY, Alice 356
    Charles G 477
    Louis 187
    Merilla (Locke) 187
    Rose 477
PERKINS, Abby (Emery) 178
    Abigail 52, 118, 238, 284
    Abigail (Locke) 26
    Abigail (Tucker) 361
    Abraham 118, 128, 250
    Ada 151
    Adaline 325
    Adaline (Tasker) 267
    Addie S 219
    Alice 267
    Almeda (Knox) 118
    Amelia (Gilson) 267
    Anna 32
    Annie M 366
    Anis (Locke) 16
    Annis Prescott 32
    Benjamin 32, 45, 198, 212, 512
    Betsey (Bachelder) 52
    Betty 46
    Carolyn 512
    Charles 202, 222, 267, 383
    Christena (Philbrick) 118, 128, 250
    Christena (Robinson) 512
    Clara 516
    Clara (McIndoe) 426
    David 118, 222
    Dolly 189
    Donald 539
    Edward 118, 267, 291
    Elias 118
    Eliza J 118
    Eliza (Farrington) 267
    Elizabeth 389
    Elizabeth (Folsom) 32

PERKINS, Ellen (Trefethern) 69
    Emily 288
    Emma 219
    Ernest 222
    Esther 206
    Fannie 267
    Fidelia (Gilson) 267
    Flora 311, 516
    Frances 466
    Frank d 267
    Fred d 267
    Gail Giddings 539
    George 69, 267, 495
    Grace 267
    Hannah 52, 118, 118
    Harrie 267
    Harry 178, 267
    Hattie 267
    Henry C 197
    Herbert M 540
    Huldah 14, 52, 118, 250
    Huldah (Johnson) 480
    Huldah (Robie) 28, 32, 52
    Huldah (Seavey) 118
    James 26, 28, 32, 32, 52
        52, 118, 118, 118, 118
        129, 222, 250, 267, 267
    Jane 118
    Jane (Hook) 267, 291
    Jeremiah 118, 267
    Joanna (Elkins) 129
    John 16, 32, 52, 93, 118
        129, 219, 311
    Jonathan, Lieut 32
    Jonathan 52, 69, 118, 267
    Joseph 32, 102
    Josephine (Thurston) 197
    Josiah 52
    Julia 329
    Julia (Hobbs) 198
    Kate 137
    Katherine L 540
    Lavina 158
    Lillian 516
    Lizzie 311
    Locke McIndoe 539, 539
    Louis 118
    Louisa (Randall-Harraden) 493
    Lovie (Locke) 102
    Lucy 198
    Lucy (Prescott) 32
    Luella (Gove) 198, 212
    Margaret E 540
    Marion F 540
    Marsh O 426, 539
    Martha 69, 267, 306
    Martha (Locke) 222
    Mary 32, 52, 91, 267
        267, 284, 512
    Mary (Locke) 45, 52, 69
    Mary (Perkins) 52
    Mary (Sanborn) 202
    Mary (Stockman) 91
    Mary (Walton) 366
    Mehitable (Garland), Mrs 52, 250
    (Morris), Miss 118
    Moses 480
    Myrtie 516
    Nancy 52, 118, 118
    Nancy (Gove) 383
    Nancy (Sanborn) 93
    Nellie B 219
    Olevia d 267
    Olive 267
    Patience 24
    Phebe (Robinson) 118
    Polly 118, 194, 250
    Polly (Langdon) 118
    Rose, Mrs 284
    Ruth (Glidden) 118

INDEX OF NAMES

PERKINS, Ruth (Nudd) 52
  Ruth (Roberts) 539
  Sally 91, 219, 222
  Samuel 91, 212, 366, 366, 512
  Sarah 52, 93, 198, 247, 512
  Sarah (Rand) 129
  Susan (Carleton) 219
  William 178, 219, 267, 267, 284, 361
  Willie B. 178
PERLEY, Chester 512
  Elizabeth 512
  Florence 182
  Isabella (Tucker-Merrill) 361
  John 361
  Joseph 348
  Ruth (Merrill) 348
  Sarah (Dow) 512
  William H. 361
PERRY, Mr. 95
  Abigail 22
  Addie (Rollins) 307
  Ann (Wallingford) 95
  Anna E. 126
  Annette 307
  Caroline 95
  Charles H. 368
  Dorothy (French) 307
  Elizabeth 141, 307
  George 307, 307
  Harold 368
  Janette (Locke) 368
  Martha 370, 446
  Mary 215
  Mary (Welch) 307
  Maud 307
  Sewell A. 141
  Varnum 307
  William 307
PERRYMAN, Deborah (Locke) 80
  John 80
PERVIER, Abigail 398
PERVIERE, Abigail 56
PETERS, Jennie 262
PETTIBONE, Miss 62
PETTIGREW, Charles 397
  Clarenda (Batson-West) 397
  Ephraim 398
  Frances (Manson-Locke) 398
  Loula 519
  Mary B. 519
  Sarah 554
PETTINGILL, Caroline 185
  Merrill 351
  Rebecca 452
PEVERLY, Florence (Coleman) 549
  James H. 549
PHELPS, Bridget 89
  Charles 269
  Edmund 269
  Elizabeth (Locke) 119
  Hattie 269
  Jane 100, 269
  Jennie 269
  John 269
  Marion 512
  Randolph 119
  Salenda 299
  Sarah (Perkins) 512
  William 269
PHENIX, George d. 467
  Harriet (Locke) 292
  John 292
  Mina H. 467
PHILBRICK, Abigail 27, 34, 56, 57, 128, 192, 193
  Abigail (Brown) 68
  Abigail (Locke) 14
  Abigail (Marden) 28
  Abigail (Perviere) 56, 398
  Abigail (Williams) 128

PHILBRICK, Adaline (Locke) 97
  Alfred 308
  Almira 193
  Ann 309
  Ann (Towle) 27
  Anna 56, 205, 566
  Anna (Perkins) 32
  Annie (Jenness) 552
  Arvilla (Jenkins) 398
  Aseneth 193
  Augustus 364
  Betsey 57, 110, 193
  Betsey (Edwards) 178
  Betsey (Jenness) 53
  Betsey (Page) 57
  Betsey (Palmer) 342
  Betsey (Wells) 57
  Caleb 32
  Caroline 309
  Carrie 308
  Celia (Preble) 521
  Charles 343
  Charlotte d. 398
  Christena 118, 128, 250
  Clara 364, 409
  Clarissa (Shaw) 128
  Cynthia (Ordiorne) 308
  Daniel 28, 56, 57, 88, 128, 128, 250, 308, 364
  David 128, 178, 193, 364
  Dolly (Grover) 56
  Earl H. 343
  Edward 205, 205, 248, 271, 489
  Elias 32
  Eliza (Jenness) 128, 250
  Eliza (Jenness-Fogg) 380
  Eliza (Philbrick) 364
  Elizabeth 128, 250
  Emily 308
  Emma O. 398
  Ephraim 57, 111
  Estelle (Goss) 489
  Evelyn Arline 343
  Frank d. 178
  George 364
  Geraldine 521
  Guy 521
  Hannah 11, 27, 53, 56
  Hannah (Locke) 27, 28
  Hannah (Moshier) 552
  Hannah (White) 15
  Herbert E. 398
  Hester 552
  Huldah 129
  Ida F. 398
  Ida (Marden) 398
  Irving 308
  James 56, 178, 398
  John 97, 128, 141, 128, 212, 212, 212, 250, 309, 364
  Jonathan 28, 56, 57, 68, 250
  Joseph 27, 27, 54, 56, 57, 82, 342
  Joses 14, 54, 56, 57
  Joshua 71
  Josiah 128, 250
  Kenneth 521
  Levi 56, 59
  Lizzie (Breed) 398
  Louisa (Hoag) 212
  Lucy (Moulton) 55
  Lydia 110
  Lydia (Moulton) 128
  Madeline O. 520
  Margarite 521
  Maria A. (Goodwin) 128
  Marion C. 520
  Martha A. 128
  Mary 28, 88, 54, 128, 128, 82, 192, 212, 212, 309, 364
  Mary (Beck) 28

INDEX OF NAMES

PHILBRICK, Mary (Dawlton-Jenness), Mrs.......................... 28
  Mary (Marden)................. 28
  Mary (Nudd).................. 56
  Mary (Philbrick)............... 128
  Mary (Sanborn)................ 212
  Mary (Sherburne).............. 32
  Mary (Wedgwood), Mrs.......... 28
  Matilda....................... 271
  Mercy........................ 57
  Moses.....................128, 250
  Nancy........................ 177
  Nancy (Jenness-Woodman), Mrs... 54
  Neal B....................... 552
  Nellie........................ 449
  Newell....................... 128
  Olive......................... 128
  Olive (Locke).................. 234
  Olly......................... 129
  Page......................... 55
  Pamelia (Gunnison)............. 128
  Phoebe....................... 29
  Polly..............82, 117, 128, 265
  Polly (Locke).................. 88
  Polly (Page)................... 54
  Raymond..................... 521
  Reuben............27, 28, 53, 54, 120
  Ruth......................... 192
  Rufus........................ 552
  Sadie E....................... 520
  Sally................53, 56, 67, 128
  Sally (Brown).................. 141
  Sally (Durgin)................. 248
  Sally (Smith).................. 57
  Sally (Webster)..............57, 111
  Samuel....................128, 178
  Sarah........27, 57, 120, 212, 271, 489
  Sarah A. (Brown)........128, 128, 250
  Sarah A. (Garland)..........128, 250
  Sarah (Lamos)................. 128
  Sarah (Locke)................. 178
  Sarah (Marden).............56, 250
  Sarah (Smith)................. 205
  Sarah A. (Philbrick).........128, 250
  Sarah (Stearns)................ 193
  Sarah (Taylor)................. 343
  Sarah (Webster)............... 271
  Sarah (Wells)................. 57
  Seavey, Miss.................. 59
  Silas......................... 128
  Susan........................ 364
  Susannah (Pitman)............. 56
  Thomas............15, 128, 234, 566
  Tryphena..................... 27
  Tryphena (Marston)............ 27
  William...............128, 398, 520
  Wilmar Louise................. 343
  Woodbury.................... 380
PHILIPS, Almira................... 150
  Annie........................ 357
  Ethel L. (Bickford)............. 138
  Frank........................ 138
PHINNEY, Abigail.................. 76
  Eliza......................... 229
  Jabez........................ 229
  Jane (Fisher).................. 229
  Leroy........................ 494
  Mary (Haley).................. 494
  William...................... 494
PICKERING, Annie d............... 404
  Caleb S...................... 386
  Charles....................... 404
  Eleanor....................... 404
  Elizabeth..................... 568
  Ellen......................... 312
  Harold E..................... 528
  Ida.......................387, 476
  James....................404, 528
  Jennie (Lake).................. 404
  John.................236, 404, 404

PICKERING, Joseph................. 489
  Lizzie........................ 219
  Mandana..................... 404
  Mary......................... 404
  Mary (Berry).................. 236
  Mary (Goss)................... 489
  Olive M...................... 404
  Philena....................... 404
  Sarah........................ 405
  William d.................... 404
PICKETT, Miss..................... 314
  Addie (Randall)............... 493
  Charles....................554, 554
  Marie........................ 554
  Sarah (Pettigrew).............. 554
  William P..................... 493
PIERCE, Carrie..................... 337
  Dorothy (Locke)............... 63
  Elizabeth (Hoxie).............. 337
  George....................... 337
  James........................ 63
  Margaret, Mrs................. 54
  Mary..................84, 89, 298, 468
  Sarah........................ 281
  Willard....................... 337
PIGOTT, Alfred H...............315, 487
  Augusta (Dickerson)........... 315
  Carrie.....................315, 487
  Charles d.................... 315
  Charlotte..................... 487
  Eliza (Lovell).................. 315
  Hannah S. (Locke)............. 145
  James d..................... 315
  John J....................... 315
  Lillian (Hatch)................ 487
  Martha (Ryder)............... 315
  Olivette...................315, 487
  Richard..............145, 315, 487
PIKE, Miss........................ 391
  Alba G....................... 409
  Anna......................... 541
  Augusta (Tibbitts)............. 321
  Ellen R.....................80, 170
  Elmer........................ 226
  Emalie....................... 189
  Flora (Jenness)................ 409
  Hattie........................ 184
  James........................ 541
  Jennie (Dow)................. 409
  John, Rev.................... 6
  Loretta (Fellows).............. 226
  Louis R...................... 409
  Luther....................... 170
  Mary......................... 104
  Sadie (Kelley)................. 409
  Samuel....................... 409
  Winthrop..................... 321
PILLING, Bolinda (Jauvrin)......... 91
  Charles A.................... 198
  Edmond...................... 91
  Edward A.................... 198
  George H..................... 198
  Laura A...................... 198
  John R....................... 198
PILLSBURY, Edna.................. 510
  Elizabeth W................... 84
  Esther........................ 62
  Sally......................... 53
PINDER, Hattie.................... 159
PINKHAM, Abby (Gray)............ 157
  Ada B........................ 457
  Belle......................... 457
  Benjamin..................... 404
  Betsey (Gray)................. 158
  Clara......................... 158
  Edward R..................... 527
  Emily J....................... 158
  Elmer W...................... 527
  George................158, 158, 457
  Hattie........................ 527

INDEX OF NAMES

PINKHAM, Henry............... 158, 158
  John........................... 157
  Martha P. (Gray)............... 158
  Mary.......................102, 158
  Mary (Pickering)............... 404
  Russell W...................... 527
  Sophia.......................... 54
  Wells.......................... 158
  William H...................... 158
PIPER, Betsey.................... 273
  Charles........................ 418
  Emma (Green)................... 418
  H. L........................... 372
  Irene.......................... 391
  Mattie (Walker)................ 372
  Maude.......................... 372
  Mercy.......................... 483
  Oliver......................... 391
  Susan........................... 30
  Susanna......................... 69
  Theodore....................... 313
PITCHWORTH, Miss................. 383
PITMAN, Abigail..............70, 240
  Ann (Garland).................. 148
  Betsey (Locke).................. 71
  Elizabeth...................... 148
  Elizabeth (Locke)............... 12
  Emily.......................... 148
  Evaline........................ 148
  Hannah.....................148, 148
  Jacob L........................ 148
  James C........................ 148
  John.......................148, 148
  Joseph.......................... 71
  Mary A......................... 148
  Mary E. (Slager)............... 148
  Sarah E. (Bodwell)............. 148
  Susannah........................ 56
  William......................... 12
PLACE, Albert C.................. 434
  Cora........................... 479
  Mary (Pope).................... 434
  Nancy J........................ 227
  Nellie......................... 227
  Olive.......................... 237
  Russell........................ 434
  Smith C........................ 227
  Susan (Chesley)................ 286
PLANT, Ethel (Pollard)........... 505
  Harry.......................... 505
PLUMMER, Augusta................. 492
  B. W........................... 492
  Carrie......................... 280
  Ellen (Russell)................ 280
  Frances........................ 168
  Grace.......................... 498
  Izetta......................... 125
  John........................... 280
  Laura.......................... 492
  Margaret....................... 355
  Mamie.......................... 540
  Nellie......................... 484
  Ralph.......................... 280
POLK, Caroline................... 380
POLLARD, Miss.................... 291
  Abbie May...................... 354
  Addison........................ 186
  Almira (Bean).................. 186
  Almira (Dow)................... 186
  Arvilla Ann.................... 354
  Bernice M. d................... 354
  Charles A.................186, 354
  Dianna (Basford)............... 186
  Ellen (Bellevance)............. 505
  Emily.......................... 186
  Ethel.......................... 505
  Frank L........................ 505
  George Addison................. 354
  Hattie......................... 186
  Hiram......................186, 354

POLLARD, Isaac A................. 186
  Jessie (Hazelton).............. 354
  John............................ 85
  John Dyer...................... 354
  Lewis Osmond................... 354
  Lillian........................ 354
  Lucinda........................ 186
  Lydia (Gotham)................. 354
  Marjorie M..................... 505
  Mary B......................... 354
  Myrtle O....................... 354
  Olive (Durgin)................. 186
  Rosanna........................ 186
  Sally (Locke)................... 85
  Sarah J........................ 186
POMEROY, Ann...................... 76
  Ann, Mrs........................ 38
  Deborah......................... 77
  Joseph.......................... 77
  Phebe.......................76, 77
POOL, Albert...................... 39
  Caroline........................ 39
  Carrie......................... 519
  Edward.......................... 39
  James........................... 39
  Lucy............................ 39
  Mary........................... 488
  Monroe.......................... 39
  Patience (Hunnewell)............ 39
POOR-POORE.
  Ada............................ 271
  Almira......................... 270
  Angeline (Brown)............... 270
  Asa K.......................... 270
  Betsey (Towle)................. 270
  Carrie (Hadley)................ 445
  Darwin......................... 445
  Elizabeth (Murray)............. 270
  Ellen.......................... 271
  Gertrude....................... 445
  Joanna......................... 186
  John L......................... 270
  Judith......................... 270
  Lydia (Richards)............... 270
  Poores, Reg. Colonel............ 67
  Samuel.....................120, 270
  Sarah (True)................... 120
  Sophia (Shannon)............... 270
  Wesley......................... 270
POPE, Charles................254, 434
  Ella C......................... 197
  Irving d....................... 434
  Mary L......................... 434
  Nancy (Locke).................. 254
POPPLAR, Wilhemena............... 229
PORTER, Adelaide................. 540
  Adelbert....................... 347
  Alta........................... 347
  Fannie (Locke)................. 347
  Herman J....................... 348
  Huntington, Rev.................. 6
  Martha (Locke)................. 348
  Mary........................... 121
  Ruth........................... 180
  Sarah A......................... 57
  Verna.......................... 347
  Willis E....................... 348
POSTON, Mary (Drew).............. 298
  Minnie J....................... 133
  W. W........................... 298
POTTER, Amy...................... 418
  Augustus........................ 80
  Caleb.......................... 171
  Charles H....................... 80
  Comfort........................ 295
  Elizabeth...................... 210
  Elizabeth (Mills).........300, 497
  Georgeanna (Sanders)........... 418
  Harriet.....................80, 245
  Ida (Matterson)................. 80

INDEX OF NAMES 691

POTTER, Justice.................... 300
  Lovina......................... 137
  Miriam (Locke)................ 80
  Samuel........................ 418
  Seth........................... 418
POTTLE, Lucretia.................. 74
POTTS, Mary I..................... 315
POUND, E. C....................... 468
  George W...................... 544
  Lottie......................... 544
  Lottie (Locke)................. 468
  Olive M....................... 544
  Roy L......................... 544
POWERS, Mr....................... 28
  Betsey (Shapleigh)............. 316
  Margaret (Moulton)............ 28
  Mary.......................... 146
  Robert........................ 316
PRATT, Mr........................ 99
  Abigail........................ 63
  Clara I........................ 183
  Lavonia (Merrill).............. 99
  Letitia........................ 349
  William....................... 349
PRAY, Alice d..................... 493
  Catherine..................... 423
  Elmer O....................... 504
  Estelle........................ 504
  Ethel M. d.................... 504
  Eva A......................... 503
  Frances (Randall).............. 493
  Fred N........................ 504
  Frieda (Wetherbee)............ 504
  Hannah....................... 34
  Helen A....................... 504
  Helen (Locke)................. 345
  Isaac......................345, 493
  Levi.......................... 112
  Lizzie B....................... 503
  Lucius d...................... 503
  Marion (Thomas).............. 504
  Martha F...................... 503
  Maud Ella.................... 504
  Rhoda A...................112, 112
  Shirley....................... 504
PREBLE, Celia..................500, 521
PRESCOTT, Abbie (Hobbs).......... 195
  Abigail....................13, 247
  Abigail (Lane)................. 113
  Alfred.................114, 114, 199
  Alice.......................... 199
  Alice (Brackett)............... 199
  Alsoa d....................... 380
  Anna...................114, 203, 458
  Anna (Locke)................. 52
  Annette E. (Towle)............ 114
  Annie A....................... 114
  Benjamin L.................... 114
  Betsey (Seavey)................ 210
  Carrie......................... 458
  Carrie (Locke)................. 281
  Clara....................44, 380, 380
  Cornelia (Merriam)............ 138
  Daniel K..................116, 262
  David.....................281, 458
  DeWitt C..................... 262
  Dolly......................... 465
  Eben.......................... 254
  Edwin A............114, 114, 114, 210
  Eli S.......................... 262
  Eliza A........................ 114
  Elizabeth..................... 20
  Ellen M....................... 114
  Emma O....................... 114
  Emma (Taylor)................ 458
  Eunice........................ 113
  Florence (Bullock)............. 262
  Frances E. (Banks)............ 114
  Frank M...................... 458
  George........114, 114, 210, 380, 380

PRESCOTT, Hannah.............52, 195
  Hannah (Hayes)................ 303
  Hannah (Rundlett)............. 32
  Harriet (Madden).............. 203
  Henry d...................... 262
  Hiram A....................... 210
  Horace A...................... 138
  Increase S. D.................. 262
  Jacob......................195, 199
  James......................... 113
  John...................32, 202, 210
  Jonathan........20, 26, 114, 114, 303
  Judith........................ 205
  Julia A........................ 114
  Leah.......................... 193
  Lorenda (Lang)................ 116
  Lucy.......................32, 48
  Lydia B....................... 380
  Lydia (Locke)................. 97
  Martha E. d................... 114
  Mary......................120, 195
  Mary (Brown).................. 193
  Mary (Jones).................. 195
  Matilda (Russell).............. 114
  Miranda (Clough).............. 114
  Miriam (Murray)............... 210
  Mittie L....................... 114
  Mitty......................... 35
  Moses......................... 97
  Nancy........................ 114
  Nancy (Dow).................. 458
  Naomi (Brown)................ 254
  Octavia (Bean)................ 114
  Oscar C....................... 458
  Polly (Locke).................. 89
  Priscilla d.................... 262
  Rachel (Clifford).............. 114
  Rebecca....................... 139
  Rebecca (Collis)............... 210
  Ruth (Randall)................ 210
  Samuel..............193, 195, 262, 380
  Sarah (Holgate)................ 262
  Sarah (Ring).................. 195
  Susan A....................... 380
  Sylvester..................... 380
  Timothy....................52, 210
  Vienna........................ 202
  Walter S...................... 262
  Weare......................... 89
  William...................203, 380
  Woodbury T................... 114
PRESTON, Eben.................... 457
  Ellen.......................... 277
PRIEST, Frances................... 316
  Mary.......................... 239
PRIME, Mary O.................... 159
PRINCE, ———..................... 21
  Abigail (Oaks)................. 163
  Ann (Blanchard).............. 76
  Annette (White)............... 391
  Charles....................... 40
  Eben, Capt.................... 40
  Ebenezer...................... 76
  Ebenezer Floyd................ 40
  Edward Payson................ 40
  Eliza (Merrill)................. 76
  Elizabeth (Johnson)............ 76
  Eunice (Fernald).............. 76
  Frances M..................... 163
  Francis....................... 391
  George W..................... 40
  Julia.......................... 40
  Lucy (Harding)................ 163
  Martha........................ 163
  Martha (Leach)................ 163
  Mary Ann..................... 76
  Mary Elizabeth................ 40
  Mary (Locke)................. 38
  Mary M....................... 163
  Mary (Malcolm)............... 76

INDEX OF NAMES

PRINCE, Matilda Locke.............. 40
   Matilda (Locke)..............40, 76
   Matilda (Prince)................ 76
   Nathaniel...................... 38
   Olive.......................... 76
   Pyam.......................... 163
   Reuben........................ 76
   Susanna....................... 76
   Sylvanus....................76, 76
   Thomas R...................... 163
   Walter........................ 391
   William L. M.................. 163
PROCTOR, Celia.................... 386
PROSSER, Andrew J................. 172
   Lovicia (Ames)................. 172
PROVO, Mr......................... 362
   Ida (Currier).................. 362
PRYOR, Arnold K................... 557
   Earl F......................... 557
   Eva (Pray)..................... 503
   Fred........................... 503
   Lydia.......................... 240
PULSIFER, Charlotte E............. 167
   Charlotte (Locke).............. 78
   Elizabeth (Clarke), Mrs........ 167
   Eugenia........................ 455
   Eunice A....................... 167
   Eva............................ 167
   Isaac.......................78, 167
   Laura Alice.................... 167
   Lucinda J...................... 167
   Nathaniel M. d................. 167
   Susan Ella..................... 167
   Susan M. d..................... 167
PURINGTON, Joseph................. 184
   Sally (Dow).................... 184
PUTNAM, Miss...................... 214
   Harriet........................ 214
   Jonathan....................... 214
   Sarah.......................... 125
PUTNEY, Martha.................... 452
PYE, Fannie....................... 189
QUATTLEBAUM, Anna................. 540
QUIMBY, Elizabeth................. 56
   Jennie (Locke)................. 568
   Mehitable...................... 355
   Walter......................... 568
QUINCY, Eunice..............106, 233, 233
RAMSDELL, Annie (Littlefield)..... 527
   Blake L........................ 527
   Edna F. d...................... 527
   Edward.....................404, 527
   Emerett (Marden).............. 404
   Fred M......................... 527
RAMSEY, Lizzie.................... 493
   Ralph E........................ 527
RAND, Aaron L..................... 302
   Abbie......................141, 475
   Abigail (Berry)................ 309
   Ada d.......................... 301
   Albert.....................138, 302, 476
   Alice d........................ 301
   Alice (Morrill)................ 476
   Arthur......................... 476
   Bertha......................... 301
   Betsey......................... 54
   Bickford L..................... 129
   Billey......................... 129
   Blanche........................ 309
   Catherine (Page)............... 295
   Charles....................309, 470
   Charlotte (Bachelder).......... 129
   Clara (Dow)................309, 309
   Clara (Odiorne)................ 308
   Clarenda...................493, 493
   Cyrus d........................ 139
   Daniel....................68, 234, 318
   David.......................317, 493
   Dorothy (Seavey)............... 234
   Dowst.......................... 60

RAND, Edgar S..................... 476
   Edith......................301, 342
   Eleanor D. (Locke)............. 65
   Elizabeth...................14, 66
   Elizabeth (Stevens)............ 129
   Elvin.......................... 309
   Emily (Foss)................... 552
   Emily (Jenness)................ 107
   Emma.......................271, 301
   Emma (Ward).................... 493
   Esther (Brown)..............68, 318
   Ethel (Bickford-Phillips)...... 138
   Eunice (Carter)................ 129
   Eva............................ 553
   Francina....................... 473
   Frank.......................... 308
   Freak.......................... 357
   Fred D......................... 476
   Florence W..................... 139
   Georgette...................... 475
   Hannah....................18, 129, 138
   Hannah (Garland)............... 266
   Hannah (Lang).................. 60
   Hannah (Locke)................. 139
   Hannah (Pray).................. 34
   Harold......................... 476
   Hattie......................... 476
   Howard......................308, 309
   Ida (Blood).................... 476
   Ida (Brown).................... 493
   James....129, 158, 309, 309, 493
   Jed............................ 141
   John....................129, 129, 493, 493
   Jonathan J..................... 107
   Joseph.............65, 107, 138, 552
   Joshua......................302, 303
   Julia Ann...................... 138
   Louisa (Marden).............308, 309
   Lucinda (Brown)................ 303
   Lydia.......................... 153
   M.............................. 295
   Margaret....................... 475
   Margaret (Frost)............... 302
   Martha.................106, 303, 475
   Martha (Bachelder)............. 129
   Martha (Locke)................. 139
   Martha (Marden)................ 107
   Martha (Willey)................ 309
   Mary..............74, 138, 146, 180
                 301, 308, 470, 475
   Mary Abby...................... 143
   Mary (Brown)................... 303
   Mary (Leavitt)..............106, 146
   Mary (Locke)................141, 357
   Mary (Lovett).................. 144
   Mary (Philbrick)............... 309
   Mehitable...................... 69
   Mercy.......................60, 139
   Mina........................... 301
   Nathaniel..............106, 144, 146
   Olive.......................51, 138
   Olive (Marden)..............107, 138
   Oliver......................129, 129
   Oscar B........................ 476
   Patty L........................ 129
   Percy.......................... 493
   Polly.......................... 436
   Polly (Bean)................... 129
   Polly (Salter)................. 317
   Rachel......................... 566
   Reed........................... 266
   Roger.......................... 476
   Ruth S......................... 303
   Ruth (Seavey).................. 302
   Samuel.............64, 107, 129, 129
                138, 139, 139, 475
   Samuel Streeter................ 303
   Sarah...................129, 158, 436
   Sarah (Dowrst)................. 129
   Sarah (Foss)................64, 129

INDEX OF NAMES 693

RAND, Sarah J. (Rand).............. 138
   Serena M..................... 139
   Susan....................70, 139
   Sylvia d..................... 138
   Thomas...................... 34
   Trundy...................... 129
   William..................... 129
RANDALL, Abigail................. 56
   Abigail (Philbrick).............. 27
   Ada......................... 493
   Addie....................... 493
   Adriana...................... 493
   Alice........................ 415
   Annie....................... 319
   Annie (Wilson)................ 493
   Ariadne (Caswell).............. 318
   Arthur E..................... 553
   Augusta (Berry)............... 56
   Benjamin................148, 149, 150
   Bessie (Boardman)............. 495
   Boardman.................... 495
   Caroline (Marston-Caswell)....... 140
   Catherine.................... 318
   Clara (Wiliams)................ 493
   Daniel....................... 56
   Deborah..................... 56
   Edward...................... 56
   Eliza J....................... 318
   Elizabeth.................... 56
   Elizabeth (Galloway)............ 56
   Elizabeth G. (Locke-Caswell)..... 71
   Elizabeth (Quimby)............. 56
   Ella M....................... 553
   Eva E....................... 493
   Frances A.................... 493
   Frank B...................... 493
   Flora A...................... 143
   George W.................... 319
   Gladys M.................... 311
   Hannah..........56, 56, 71, 237, 318
   Hannah (Locke)................ 71
   Hannah O. (Locke-Lane)......... 142
   Hannah (Pitman)............148, 148
   Hannah (Randall-Becker)......... 318
   Ira.......................... 493
   James.....................7, 148
   Jane (Locke-Brown)............. 146
   Jennie L..................... 493
   Jessie (Lear), Mrs.............. 311
   Job Locke.................... 148
   John, Rev.................... 56
   John..........142, 143, 146, 318, 318
   Joseph...................318, 493, 495
   Joses......................56, 56
   Judson....................148, 494
   Lawrence d................... 493
   Levi D....................... 56
   Lincoln...................... 405
   Lizzie (Ramsey)................ 493
   Louisa B. (Caswell)............. 319
   Louisa J..................... 495
   Lucy Jane.................... 318
   Luella....................... 494
   Lulu B...................... 493
   Malinda (Haley)............... 494
   Mark..................27, 56, 56
   Mary...........72, 148, 215, 325, 495
   Mary (Caswell)............143, 318, 319
   Mary (Downes)................ 148
   Olive........................ 493
   Olivia....................... 494
   Olly......................... 56
   Parry........................ 495
   Polly (Rugg)................149, 150
   Reuben...................... 56
   Richard...................318, 319
   Ruth........................ 210
   Sally........................ 56
   Samuel...................... 56
   Sarah H...........56, 142, 148, 495

RANDALL, Sarah (Sanders)........... 148
   Sarah (Young)................. 56
   (Tibbetts), Miss................ 56
   William B.................... 71
   William..71, 140, 148, 148, 148, 495
   Willie....................... 311
RANDLETT, Charles................. 272
   Frank....................... 272
   Lucy (Reynolds)............... 272
   Mary........................ 272
RANKIN, Edna B.................... 528
   Grace E..................... 528
   Harriet L..................... 527
   Janette P..................... 527
   John........................ 404
   Mary F...................... 528
   Olive (Pickering)............... 404
   Philena M. d.................. 527
   Wellington D.................. 528
RANSOM, Asa...................... 497
   Betsey M..................327, 497
   Betsey (Clark)................. 497
   Clarence L.................... 497
   Daniel d..................... 497
   Lavant, Capt.................. 327
   Lavant...................... 497
   Lelia G...................... 497
   Lucia E...................... 497
   Mamie d.................... 497
   Miriam (Locke)................ 327
   Susan (O'Day)................. 497
RANSTEAD, George................. 69
   Polly (Trefethern).............. 69
RAPELGE, Annie.................... 197
RATHBORN. RATHBURN.
   Elizabeth.................... 20
   John........................ 37
   Lucy........................ 20
   Thomas..................... 20
RAWLINGS, Hannah................. 22
RAY, Addie (Hines)................. 297
   Banjamin F................... 406
   Emma d..................... 297
   Erville B..................... 297
   Eugene d.................... 297
   George d.................... 442
   Georgeanna (Babb)............. 262
   Herbert F.................... 406
   Hiram M..................... 297
   Ida (Locke).................. 406
   James d..................... 442
   Jennie T..................... 297
   John, Rev.................... 262
   Lucy H...................... 442
   Mary........................ 297
   Mary (Colburn)................ 297
   Mary (Locke)................. 132
   Nathaniel..................132, 297
   Nellie (Frank)................. 297
   Norman J.................... 297
   Orren C..................... 297
   Sarah....................... 406
   Sarah (Bickford)............... 297
   William d.................... 297
RECKUM, Mr....................... 94
   Mary (Pearsons)............... 94
REDDING, Elias O................... 244
   Nancy (Locke)................ 244
REDFIELD, Charles.................. 447
   Elsie (Lamprey)............... 447
REDMAN, Mary..................... 176
   Sarah....................... 448
REDMOND, Hannah (Rawlings)........ 22
   Jonathan d................... 22
   Joseph...................... 22
   Mary (Moulton)............... 22
   Tristram..................... 22
REED, Mr.......................... 538
   Addie (Bachelder).............. 403
   Annie....................... 526

INDEX OF NAMES

REED, Birdie A.................... 561
  Clyde L...................... 561
  Daisy........................ 532
  Edna (Locke-Goldsmith)........ 534
  Edward G..................... 172
  Edwin M...................... 561
  Eleazor...................... 191
  Elizabeth.................... 191
  Emma I....................... 561
  Esther E..................... 561
  Everal....................... 561
  Frank W...................... 538
  Fred Thomas.................. 532
  George....................... 403
  George B..................... 534
  Gladys....................... 542
  Harry........................ 195
  Hattie....................... 526
  Joyce A...................... 561
  Lenore E..................... 561
  Lizzie (Locke)............... 195
  Luella (Locke-Sisson)........ 172
  Margaret (Batchelder)........ 532
  Marion....................... 526
  Millard F.................... 534
  Rebecca...................... 87
  Sarah........................ 361
  Sarah (Locke)............534, 538
  Thomas....................... 532
REINHART, Sarah................... 251
REINKING, Ella.................... 202
REMICK, Albert.................... 548
  Ann (Lancaster).............. 30
  Anna (Mace).................. 548
  Esther Y..................... 140
  Hannah....................... 237
  (Hurd), Miss................. 147
  Isaac........................ 305
  Joshua....................... 30
  Lydia (Varrell).............. 305
  Mabel........................ 479
  Marietta..................... 218
  Sarah........................ 15
  Susan........................ 147
RENIE, Maud (Perry)............... 307
  Peter........................ 307
REXFORD, Anna (Blanchard)......... 160
  Edward....................... 376
  Ellen (Copp)................. 376
  Emma L....................... 376
  Laura........................ 74
  William...................... 160
REYNOLDS, Mr...................... 87
  Abel W....................... 420
  Abigail (Locke)..........121, 122
  Adaline (Smith).............. 121
  Ann (Tebbetts)............... 121
  Anna......................... 276
  Charles C.................... 122
  Elizabeth (Jones)............ 121
  Elizabeth L.................. 121
  Ephraim..................121, 125
  Ernest, Prof................. 528
  Eunice (Jones)............... 121
  George F......121, 121, 122, 122, 272
  Hannah B. (Fisher)........... 87
  Hannah (Locke)............... 54
  Horace....................... 272
  Jacob........................ 121
  Job F........................ 121
  John W........122, 272, 276, 276
  Joseph....................... 121
  Julia A...................... 122
  Louis M...................... 122
  Lucy......................... 272
  Lydia........................ 121
  Lydia (Locke)................ 276
  Margaret..................... 420
  Mary.....................272, 272
  Mary (Cass).................. 420

REYNOLDS, Mary C. (Hotchkiss)..... 122
  Mary P. (Locke).............. 125
  Mary Pinkham (Locke)......... 121
  Mary (Young)................. 272
  Mehitable (Stevens).......... 121
  Olive (Berry)................ 272
  Ruth (Caverly)............... 528
  Samuel L..................... 121
  Sarah (Jones)................ 121
  Sarah (Locke)................ 276
  Sophia....................... 272
  William...................... 121
  Winthrop.............54, 121, 272
RHEID, Abigail.................... 64
RHODES, Alice d................... 411
  David Locke.................. 411
  James W. d................... 411
  Joseph....................... 240
  Mary (Locke)................. 240
RICE, Adeline (Locke)............. 62
  Almira....................... 163
  Cornelius.................... 62
  Emma (Locke)................. 352
  Eunice....................... 568
  Frank R...................... 352
  Harvey....................... 135
  Maria........................ 135
  Maud (Lamprey)............... 445
  Myrtle....................... 474
  Rachel....................... 201
  (Thatcher), Miss............. 135
  Walter F..................... 445
RICH, Sarah, Mrs.................. 162
RICHARDS, Alice M................. 548
  David........................ 163
  Emma......................... 443
  Frances (Prince)............. 163
  Jane......................... 270
  Lydia........................ 270
RICHARDSON, Mr.................... 326
  Alice (Locke)............109, 244
  Allen....................242, 242
  Almira (Kimball)............. 413
  Anna (Alger)................. 326
  Byron d...................... 413
  Carrie (Locke)............... 243
  Emma (Locke)................. 413
  Frank d...................... 242
  Fred R....................... 413
  George....................88, 277
  Haines L..................... 417
  Ira......................109, 244
  James..............243, 307, 413
  Jerusha...................... 417
  Loren........................ 413
  Luther....................... 307
  Madge........................ 196
  Margaret..................... 243
  Mary d....................... 413
  Mary (Locke)..............88, 242
  Nancy........................ 243
  Nellie (Locke)............... 307
  Sarah E. (Locke)............. 277
  Stella....................... 345
  Wade d....................... 413
RICHER, Frank..................... 363
  Sarah (Wells)................ 363
RICHMOND, Mr...................... 119
  Harriet (Knowles)............ 119
RICHSON, Mr....................... 50
  Olive (Ingalls).............. 50
RICKE, Donald W................... 562
  Hannah (Locke)............... 535
  Jonathan L................... 562
  Otto.....................535, 562
  Margaret L................... 562
  Mary A....................... 562
  Mina J....................... 562
RICKER, Mr........................ 92
  Edwin........................ 92

INDEX OF NAMES

BICKER, Lucy (Otis).............. 151
  Marilla........................ 92
  Mary (Godfrey)................ 92
  Jeremiah...................... 151
RIDDELL, Lottie.................. 169
RIDGEWAY, Jane E................ 199
  James L....................... 198
  Jennie........................ 497
  Joseph........................ 198
  Mary A........................ 199
  Mary (Follansbee)............. 198
  Mary (Hale)................... 199
  Moses......................92, 199
  Sally (Locke).................. 92
  Sarah M....................... 199
RIGGS, Aaron..............139, 301, 302
  Angeline...................... 301
  Charles....................... 301
  Comfort....................... 301
  Martha........................ 301
  Martha (Locke)............301, 302
  Mary.......................... 301
  Nancy......................... 61
  Patience...................... 301
  Sarah......................... 301
  Sarah (Locke)................. 139
RINDGE, Mary Ann................. 68
RING, Betsey (Philbrick).......... 193
  Elizabeth..................... 98
  Sarah......................... 195
  Stephen....................... 193
  Susanna....................... 20
RINGER, Catherine................ 356
RIPLEY, Susanna.................. 441
RIX, Abbie L..................... 425
  Alice d....................... 425
  Alice (Locke)................. 246
  Annie R....................... 425
  Edward Hale................... 425
  Ella F........................ 425
  Emma W. (Niles)............... 425
  Hale.......................... 246
  Harriet Hale.................. 425
RIXFORD, Edna E.................. 386
  Mary (Locke).................. 218
  William....................... 218
ROACH–ROCHE.
  Albert F...................... 525
  Annie B....................... 525
  Arthur L...................... 525
  Bertha I...................... 525
  Fred R........................ 402
  Gladys M...................... 525
  J. P. W....................... 525
  Lillian (Locke)............... 402
  Louisa M...................... 525
  Lucy M........................ 525
  Lucy (Martin)................. 525
  Margaret...................... 186
  Martha A...................... 525
  William A..................... 525
ROBBINS–ROBINS.
  Alice......................... 523
  Florence (Lamprey)............ 444
  George........................ 444
  Jonathan...................... 16
ROBERTS, Agnes (Labounty-Locke).. 290
  Charles....................... 366
  Clinton....................... 366
  Cora (Locke).................. 366
  Edmund........................ 290
  Eliza......................... 179
  Elizabeth (Langley-Tuck-Butterfield)........................ 133
  Ethel......................... 498
  Henry......................... 225
  Howard........................ 366
  Jeannette..................... 264
  Joseph........................ 538
  Leah.......................... 237

ROBERTS, Lewis................... 347
  Louis......................... 447
  Mary J....................181, 195
  Mary (Turkin)................. 447
  Mehitable..................... 61
  Nathaniel..................... 408
  Otis G........................ 366
  Ruth.......................... 539
  Sarah......................... 159
  Sarah (Locke)................. 225
  Susan......................... 347
  Susie (Locke)................. 538
  Tryphena (Thurston)........... 408
  William W..................... 133
ROBERTSON, Margaret.............. 237
ROBIE. ROBY.
  Almira S. (Doloff)............ 105
  Francis B..................... 163
  George........................ 390
  Gustavus...................... 230
  Harriet....................... 390
  Huldah...................28, 32, 52
  John.......................... 105
  Lizzie K...................... 230
  Lowell........................ 230
  Margaret (Kenniston).......... 230
  Marion........................ 370
  Martha (Prince)............... 163
  Mary (Haywood)................ 230
  Nicholas d.................... 230
  Olive......................... 230
  Sarah.....................230, 412
ROBINSON, Mr..................... 85
  Alice E....................... 546
  Augustus...................... 372
  Brent......................... 359
  Carrie........................ 321
  Charles...................474, 546
  Chessman...................... 85
  Christena..................... 512
  Dolly (Fowler)................ 265
  Dora (Amazeen)................ 500
  Edith......................... 546
  Elizabeth..................... 85
  Elizabeth T. (Moors).......... 85
  Elizabeth (Webster)........... 225
  Ellis......................... 196
  Emaline....................... 319
  Emma (Maxwell)................ 546
  Eva........................... 372
  Frank H....................... 500
  George.....................85, 230
  Georgetta (Ball).............. 314
  Harriet....................... 85
  Hiram......................... 269
  Horace........................ 314
  J. Cornelia (Norcross)........ 072
  Squire James.................. 85
  James M....................... 85
  John, Rev..................85, 329
  Jonathan...................... 265
  Lizzie (Roby)................. 230
  Lydia......................... 269
  Lydia (Lamprey)............... 196
  Marcia (Locke)................ 292
  Margaret...................... 359
  Mary..................85, 117, 269, 325
  Mary (Hussey)................. 329
  Mary (Locke).................. 269
  Mildred....................... 546
  Mildred (Locke)............... 335
  Olive......................... 42
  Olive (Locke)................. 85
  Oscar......................... 85
  Phebe......................... 118
  Preston....................... 292
  Sadie d....................... 546
  Samuel d...................... 546
  Sarah......................... 163
  Sarah (Bazin)................. 474

INDEX OF NAMES

ROBINSON, Sarah P. (Carter), Mrs...... 104
    Washington.................... 225
    Wilfred....................... 325
    Winfield...................... 85
ROCK, Benjamin.................... 407
    Clara......................... 407
    Edith (Marston)............... 407
    Grace......................... 407
    Ida d......................... 407
ROCKFORD, Hannah.................. 331
ROGERS, Anna C.................... 79
    Catherine..................... 223
    Charles....................... 452
    Elizabeth..................... 452
    Emma.......................... 223
    Eunice........................ 243
    Florence...................... 408
    Lottie (Berry)................ 407
    Lucy E........................ 137
    Lucy Shores................... 112
    Martha (Putney)............... 452
    Mary.......................... 199
    Mehitable..................... 62
    Nancy.....................141, 308
    Nina.......................... 378
    Stacy......................... 407
    William....................... 223
ROLFE, Mr.......................... 471
    Jenny......................... 229
    Nellie (Morse)................ 471
ROLLINS, Abby..................... 210
    Abigail....................... 210
    Abigail (Mason)............... 210
    Addie......................... 307
    Anna d........................ 210
    Bartlett...................... 210
    Benjamin...................... 210
    Betsey........................ 310
    Caleb......................... 96
    Caroline...................... 210
    Caroline (Moody), Mrs......... 210
    Charles d..................... 210
    Dearborn..................210, 210
    Elizabeth (Gage).............. 210
    Elizabeth (Page).............. 210
    Elizabeth (Potter)............ 210
    Emily (Ladd).................. 310
    Fanny (Sancri)................ 210
    George W...................... 210
    Hannah........................ 225
    Harriet....................... 228
    Irene (Whipple)............... 228
    James......................... 210
    Joseph........................ 310
    Lydia......................... 210
    Lydia (Locke)................. 96
    Mary......................79, 210
    Mary E. (Willard), Mrs........ 210
    Meshack....................... 96
    S. A., Col.................... 228
    Uriah......................... 390
    Wells W....................... 210
    William....................... 210
    Winslow L..................... 210
RONAN, Mary (Locke-Little)........ 215
    Richard....................... 215
ROOT, Aaron....................... 299
    Adelle (Root)................. 299
    Almira (Locke)................ 136
    Celestia...................... 261
    Darwin........................ 136
    Emir.......................... 537
    Henry.....................299, 299
    Kate A........................ 299
    Rufus H....................... 299
    Salenda (Phelps).............. 299
    Sybil (Saulsbury)............. 299
ROSE, Ann.......................... 20
    Daniel........................ 36
    Ellen (Gardner)............... 396

ROSE, Frank....................... 396
    George........................ 396
    Georgie....................... 396
    Temperance.................... 20
    Virginia...................... 258
ROSENSTEEL, Ada................... 251
ROSS, Blanche..................... 498
    Maude......................... 433
ROSSIER, Charles.................. 535
    Lottie (Farnsworth)........... 535
ROUNDY, Alice (Aldrich)........... 394
    Oliver E...................... 394
    Ona May....................... 394
ROWANTREE, Musidora............... 425
ROWE, Abigail..................... 566
    Adelaide...................... 383
    Arvilla (Pollard)............. 354
    Bertha........................ 384
    Colonel....................... 46
    Jeremiah...................... 516
    Lewis Earle................... 354
    Mary L........................ 516
    Mildred....................... 384
    Susan......................... 84
    Thomas R., Rev................ 354
ROWELL, Charles................... 531
    Edna.......................... 378
    Emily......................... 241
    J. H.......................... 119
    J. M. (Gile).................. 531
    Martha M. (Bachelder)......... 119
    Mary......................267, 420
    Smith A....................... 267
ROYAL, Almira..................... 162
ROYCE, Almira..................... 194
    Amanda (Flint)................ 365
    Caleb......................... 365
    Miriam........................ 274
RUBLEE, Alice..................... 394
    Ona (Roundy).................. 394
    Philip S...................... 394
RUGG, Polly....................149, 150
RUGGLES, J. R..................... 507
    Minnie (Locke)................ 507
RUNDLETT, Anna (Prescott)......... 114
    Daniel........................ 114
    Edwin J....................... 114
    Elizabeth A................... 114
    Ellen (Prescott).............. 114
    Hannah........................ 32
    Mittie L. (Prescott).......... 114
    Newell A...................... 114
RUNNELS, Mr....................... 38
    Abigail (Clifford-Spatwell)... 38
    Alice......................... 126
    Daniel........................ 331
    Mary (March).................. 155
    Samuel........................ 155
    Sarah......................73, 157
    Sarah (Watson)................ 331
RUSS, (Dickey).................... 262
    Isaac......................... 262
    John.......................... 262
    Samantha (Lang)............... 262
    Sophronia (Gage).............. 262
    (Stevens)..................... 262
RUSSELL, Alice A.................. 281
    Armena H...................... 280
    Carrie (Bateman).............. 281
    Charlotte M................... 280
    Clara......................... 280
    Clarence..................280, 281
    Caroline...................... 280
    Elizabeth..................... 280
    Elizabeth (Homer)............. 280
    Ellen......................... 280
    Emily......................... 280
    Florence...................... 281
    Frank P....................... 281
    Hattie C...................... 281

INDEX OF NAMES

RUSSELL, John M. 280
  Kate E. 281
  Lavina (West) 280
  Mabel 280
  Mary A. (Woodman) 123
  Matilda 114
  Maude 280
  May M. 280
  Morris J. 280
  Pelatiah 123
  Philemon 114
  William 280
RUTLEDGE, Arthur 396
  Bradley 396
  Georgie (Rose) 396
RYAN, Clyde C. 461
  George 461
  Georgie (Locke) 461
  Margaret 461
  Martha (Locke) 357
  Nellie 184
  Stephen 461
  Thomas 357
RYDER, Clara 530
  Martha 315
  Mary E. 43
RYER, Blanche (Maguire) 441
  Doris 441
  Fletcher 441, 441
  Sarah 189
RYNES, Annie 200
SALMON, Cecelia 159
SALTER, Alexander 65
  Lois 133
  Mary (Berry) 65
  Polly 317
SANBORN, Mr. 50
  Abbie (White) 268
  Abigail (Parsons) 93, 94
  Abigail (Prescott) 247
  Ada M. 251
  Ada (Rosensteel) 251
  Albert 298, 371
  Almira 298
  Almira (True) 120
  Amanda 361
  Amelia 111
  Ann 201, 509
  Anna (Nixon) 201
  Anna (Van Horn) 251
  Annah 111
  Annah (Locke) 46
  Benjamin S. 92
  Bert 298
  Bertha 298
  Betsey 194
  Betsey (Beverly) 111
  Betty (Blake) 96
  Calvin 201
  Catherine 201
  Catherine (Hill) 201
  Charles 159, 202, 212, 214, 251
  Charlotte (Hoyt) 201
  Clara 371
  Clara (Locke) 247
  Clarissa 251, 251
  Clarissa (Haven) 251
  Clarissa (Smith) 111
  Cora (Ambrose) 371
  Cyrus 120
  Daniel 120
  David L. 111
  David, Lieut. 206
  Dearborn C. 214
  Dudley S. 97, 98
  Edward P. 370
  Eliphalet 93, 93
  Elizabeth 96, 111, 145, 145
  Elizabeth (Locke) 367
  Elizabeth (Russell) 280

SANBORN, Elizabeth (Scripture) 134
  Elizabeth (Ward) 87
  Ellen 280
  Emerett (Langley) 298
  Emily 251
  Emily (Bruce) 370
  Emily (Gove) 212
  Esther 529
  Eunice (Davis) 201
  Ezekiel 247
  Fred J., Dr. 202
  Frederick 93, 371
  George, Dr. 202, 251
  Gilman 251, 251, 251
  Hannah 93
  Hannah (Hook) 98, 206
  Hannah (Locke) 46
  Harriet A. 370, 371
  Harriet (Chesley-Bean), Mrs. 93
  Harriet (Godfrey) 92
  Harriet S. (Locke) 134
  Harvey 251
  Haven L. 251
  Henry F. 201
  Ida (Gray) 159
  James 93, 94, 96, 202, 298, 367
  Jane L. 251
  Jennie (Dunkley) 214
  Jeremiah 111, 111, 251, 509
  John W., Capt. 98
  John 93, 201, 214, 371, 371, 427
  Joseph 111, 251, 251, 251
  Josephine 280
  Josiah, Hon. 46
  Josiah 51, 93
  Kate (Day) 251
  Kendall 214
  Laura C. 251
  Lawrence A. 134
  Lelia 298
  Lena 371
  Lewis D. 202
  Lloyd D. 251
  Louisa 47
  Lucia R. 131
  Lucinda (Green), Mrs. 99
  Lucy 371
  Lucy (Sargent) 93
  Lucy T. (Tufts) 111
  Lydia (Wentworth) 93
  (Marden), Miss 293
  Margaret (Wallace) 93
  Martha 201, 251, 413
  Martha (Hodge) 92
  Mary ... 43, 111, 202, 212, 251, 251, 427
  Mary (Green) 97
  Mary (Hoitt) 202
  Mary (Ingalls) 50
  Mary J. (Locke) 98
  Mary J. (Smith) 111
  Maryanna (Moore) 120
  Miriam 504
  Molly 47
  Moody M. 134
  Moses 247
  Nancy 93, 111
  Nancy (Towle) 93
  Nina 280
  Phebe (Page) 213
  Philip A. 214
  Polly L. 111
  Quincy 251
  Rachel 93, 110, 371
  Rachel (Fuller-Locke) 49
  Rachel (Rice) 201
  Reuben 87
  Richard 213
  Roxbury S. 247
  Sally d. 93
  Sarah 96, 131, 202, 251, 569

INDEX OF NAMES

SANBORN, Sarah (Perkins)............. 247
  Sarah (Reinhart)................. 251
  Sarah (Yeaton)................... 202
  Sewell........................... 293
  Sherburne........................ 49
  Shubael.......................... 280
  Sophia........................... 202
  Susan............................ 251
  Susan (Dana)..................... 370
  Thomas W......................... 214
  Vernon........................... 298
  Vienna (Prescott)................ 202
  Walter H., L.L.D................. 370
  Willis J......................... 134
SANCRI, Fanny........................ 210
SANDERS, Mr.......................... 135
  Abigail...............29, 55, 249, 245
  Abigail (Locke)......61, 110, 131, 245
  Alice J.......................... 295
  Angenette (Leavitt).............. 245
  Anna (Locke)..................... 110
  Augusta.......................... 417
  Benjamin......................... 494
  Betsey........................... 129
  (Buzzell), Miss.................. 129
  Caroline (Colby)................. 245
  (Chapman), Miss.................. 60
  Charles..................418, 419, 419
  Charlotte........................ 135
  Christiana..................134, 135
  Christopher...................., 245
  Clara E.................249, 249, 295
  Clara (Hodge).................... 418
  Clara (Woodward)................. 419
  David.......................245, 419
  Doris............................ 419
  Elijah........................60, 129
  Eliza............................ 418
  Ella............................. 419
  Ellen (Haley).................... 494
  Emma.......................135, 245
  Etta (Tuttle).................... 432
  Frank D.......................... 419
  Frederick........................ 129
  George..................245, 245, 417
  Georgeanna....................... 418
  Gertrude......................... 419
  (Goss), Miss..................... 60
  (Hall), Miss..................... 60
  Hannah........................... 60
  Harriet (Potter)................. 245
  Henry............................ 418
  Herbert.......................... 419
  Horace W......................... 419
  Huldah (Philbrick)............... 129
  Ida M............................ 419
  Irene............................ 419
  James........................419, 419
  Jennie (Brackett)................ 249
  Job.............................. 129
  John...............27, 60, 61, 110,
                 129, 245, 417, 432
  Joseph..................245, 249, 418
  Josie............................ 432
  Luella C......................... 295
  Mabel L.......................... 419
  (Manson), Miss................... 129
  Marcy (Rand)..................... 60
  Maria............................ 135
  Mary..........60, 417, 417, 418, 418
  Mary (Berry)..................... 60
  Mary (Carr)...................... 245
  Mary (Dow)....................... 419
  Mary (Foss)...................... 60
  Mary (Locke)..................... 29
  Mary (Twombley).................. 245
  Melissa.......................... 135
  Nancy.......................245, 245
  Nancy (White).................... 417
  Nathaniel........................ 60

SANDERS, Olly........................ 55
  Olly (Philbrick)................. 129
  Orissa F......................... 249
  Orissa (French).................. 249
  Pansy (Tucker)................... 419
  Patience Locke................... 60
  Rena M........................... 432
  Reuben......................131, 245
  Robert..........29, 60, 110, 129, 432
  Sarah..........55, 65, 148, 249, 417
  Sarah (Saunders)................. 55
  Sarah (Taylor)................... 419
  Simeon L....................245, 249
  Solomon.......................... 245
  Thirza (Corliss)................. 245
  Tryphena......................... 29
  Tryphena (Philbrick)............. 27
  Victoria (Saunders).............. 135
  (Wallace), Miss.................. 129
  Walter........................... 418
  William......................55, 55
               60, 129, 249, 432
  Willis........................... 494
SANDERSON, Abbie T................... 117
  Daniel........................... 259
  Edward........................... 259
  Elizabeth (Frost)................ 259
  Flora (Locke).................... 259
  Helen L.......................... 259
  Mary............................. 429
SANDS, Elizabeth..................... 133
  Mehitable........................ 181
  Ruth............................. 83
  Samuel........................... 181
SARGENT, Abigail (Philbrick)......... 193
  Benjamin, Rev................111, 201
  Benjamin......................... 193
  Charlotte (Jeffers).............. 243
  Dolly............................ 47
  Edward M......................... 133
  Elizabeth (Sanborn).............. 111
  Ellen............................ 133
  Eunice (Rogers).................. 243
  Fred M........................... 133
  Hannah........................... 401
  Hannah (Eves-Locke).............. 372
  John............................. 372
  Lucy............................. 93
  Martha D. (Locke)................ 133
  Mary P........................... 243
  Nathaniel........................ 243
  Nellie T......................... 243
  Susan J.......................... 164
  Timothy.......................... 243
  Victoria (Locke)................. 243
SARPY, Rose.......................... 439
SAULSBURY, Sybil..................... 299
SAVAGE, Harry........................ 348
  Henry H.......................... 181
  Kirk............................. 348
  Nellie........................... 168
  Samuel, Mrs...................... 85
SAVEN, Molly......................... 43
SAVITHES, Dorothea................... 500
  Jordan........................... 500
  Leona (Hussey)................... 500
SAVORY, Lydia........................ 284
SAWTELLE, Amanda..................... 119
SAWYER, Miss......................... 75
  Mrs.............................. 141
  Adaline (Locke).................. 209
  Alice (Little)................... 452
  Andrew........................... 209
  Betsey (Hoitt)................... 273
  Carrie........................... 413
  Charles.......................... 452
  Daniel W......................... 83
  Edwin............................ 295
  Elizabeth (Rogers)............... 452
  Ella (Gray)...................... 159

INDEX OF NAMES

SAWYER, Ella M. d.............. 83
  Eugene..................... 452
  Florence M................. 83
  George..................... 159
  Gorham H................... 452
  Hannah (Locke)..........83, 181
  Hubbard H.................. 209
  Isaac...................273, 452
  Jay M...................... 295
  Jennie..................... 209
  Joanna..................... 162
  John....................... 452
  Leander.................... 452
  Lena....................... 452
  Lester..................... 452
  Lucy, Mrs.................. 216
  Lucy....................... 452
  Maggie..................... 209
  Mary (Mitchell)............ 295
  Rebecca (Pettingill)....... 452
  Roy M...................... 295
  Warren..................... 452
  Zora V..................... 295
SAXTON, H. E................... 397
  Olive (Littlefield)........ 397
SCAMMON, Charles D............. 181
  Sarah (Smith).............. 181
SCHILE, Mary................... 527
SCHNEIWINT, Hans............... 379
  Harold..................... 379
  Julia (Bloodgood).......... 379
  Max A...................... 379
  Selma...................... 379
SCHNETZER, Emma (Locke)........ 454
  Ida M...................... 454
  Wendel..................... 454
SCHOFIELD, Joseph.............. 441
  Nettie (Locke)............. 441
  Susanna (Ripley)........... 441
  William, Rev............... 441
SCHOOLCRAFT, Malvina........... 205
SCHOOLS, Francis............... 319
  Lizzie (Failes)............ 319
  Thomas..................... 319
SCHUMAN, Harriet............... 197
SCOTT, Alec J. d............... 440
  Arthur..................... 440
  Everett H.................. 440
  Florence................... 440
  Gertrude A................. 440
  Lucy (Jameson)............. 257
  Helen...................... 175
  Martha..................... 556
  Minnie (Grant)............. 440
  Orange W., Rev............. 257
SCRIBNER, Annie................ 168
  Betsey (Janvrin), Mrs...... 99
  John....................... 268
  Mary....................... 449
  Mary (Currier)............. 268
SCRIPTURE, Elizabeth........... 134
  Helen...................... 134
SCRUTON, Alice................. 219
  Arthur..................... 219
  Ethel...................... 452
  Eunice..................... 219
  John....................... 219
  Lydia (Varney)............. 219
  Mary....................... 463
SCUDDER, Charles, Dr........... 207
  Evarts, Rev................ 207
  Sarah (Lamson)............. 207
SEAGER, Ann.................... 21
  Col........................ 41
SEARING, Josie L............... 175
SEARLES, Jonathan, Rev......... 47
  Rhoda...................... 47
SEARS, Cora (Heald)............ 331
  Edwin L.................... 331
  Fannie (Locke)............. 160

SEARS, Franklin................ 331
  Hannah (Rockford).......... 331
  Helen...................... 384
  Larned..................... 331
  Leroy B.................... 331
  Lora d..................... 331
  Loren A.................... 160
  Lovisa G................... 331
  Minnie (Lewis)............. 331
  Walter J. U. S. N.......... 331
  William G.................. 331
SEAVER, Betsey (Dudley)........ 147
  Elizabeth D................ 147
  John....................... 147
SEAVEY, Abbie (Lane)........... 438
  Abigail.................... 59
  Abraham.................... 43
  Adoniram................... 202
  Alice S.................... 293
  Alice (McNeil)............. 293
  Alonzo E................... 293
  Benjamin................... 59
  Betsey..................129, 210
  Clintie (Lane)............. 438
  Dorothy.................... 234
  Ebenezer................43, 64
  Elijah..................... 59
  Elizabeth.................. 43
  Emily...................... 143
  Ernest d................... 469
  Fanny...................... 129
  Frances.................... 43
  Frances (Meader)........... 293
  Frank...................... 438
  George L................... 293
  Grace...................... 469
  Hannah..................43, 129
  Hannah (Tilton)............ 59
  Henrietta.................. 228
  Henry J.................... 43
  Huldah.............59, 118, 129
  Huldah (Locke)............. 29
  James...................30, 143
  Jeremiah................... 43
  Joanna..................... 49
  John L..................... 293
  Jonathan................... 59
  Joseph..................... 43
  Josiah..................... 129
  Letitia.................... 309
  Levi....................... 59
  Lizzie (Martin)............ 293
  Love (Blake)............... 129
  Lucy (Bassett)............. 59
  Lydia (Allen).............. 293
  Lyman W.................... 293
  Marion..................... 469
  Martha..................66, 238
  Mary...................125, 463
  Mary (Locke)............... 51
  Mary (Sanborn-Perkins)..... 202
  Mary (Trefethern).......... 143
  Mehitable..............107, 238
  Meribah.................... 129
  Molly...................... 43
  Moses.................29, 59, 129
  Patience (Berry)........... 30
  Paul....................... 66
  Peter...................... 131
  Polly...................... 129
  Prudence (Marden).......... 64
  Ruth....................... 302
  Ruth (Moses)............... 139
  Ruth (Tarlton)............. 59
  Sally (Locke).............. 131
  Sarah..........59, 64, 66, 129, 293
  Sarah F. (Locke)........... 43
  Sarah (Willis)............. 66
  Samuel..................59, 66
  (Smith), Miss.............. 43

INDEX OF NAMES

SEAVEY, William..............7, 139, 438
SEAWARD, Alice.................... 387
   Frank........................ 387
   Harry........................ 387
SEAWARDS, M. B.................. 529
   Mary (Chesley)................. 387
SECARD, Sybil..................... 188
SEDMAN, Harriet (Rankin)........... 527
   Mary......................... 527
   Oscar........................ 527
SEETON, Andrew.................. 359
   Matilda...................... 359
   Sarah........................ 359
SENTERS, Expedition................ 73
SEWARD, Ella...................... 451
SHANNON, Ann.................... 524
   Dolly (Locke-Moore), Mrs....... 53
   Edwin.....................452, 452
   Ella.......................... 452
   Lydia........................ 331
   Mary......................... 53
   Mildred...................... 452
   Myra (Berry)................. 452
   Sally (Pillsbury).............. 53
   Sophia....................... 270
   Thomas.....................53, 53
SHAPLEIGH, Aphia R. (Locke)........ 144
   Betsey....................... 316
   Dorcas....................... 302
   Effie......................... 485
   Elizabeth.................... 107
   Ellen (Pickering).............. 312
   Frances A.................... 312
   Helen........................ 485
   Isabel B...................... 312
   Isabel H...................... 485
   James A...................... 312
   Marion....................... 485
   Thomas...................144, 312
   William...................312, 485
SHARRAR, Clara B. (Stevens)......... 106
   Lucy (Locke)................. 105
   William E.................... 106
SHATFORD, Frank.................. 358
   Harriet (Locke).............. 358
SHATTUCK, Mr..................... 319
   Alonzo....................... 188
   Carrie....................... 320
   Charles....................188, 320
   Emma (Clark)................ 319
   Herbert...................... 188
   Horace....................... 135
   Martha....................... 188
   Martha (Locke).............. 188
   Mildred...................... 188
   Salome (Locke).............. 135
SHAW, Abigail (Dalton)............. 127
   Alice (Weller)................ 344
   Almira....................... 106
   Annie........................ 371
   Bathsheba................... 236
   Charles...................... 371
   Charlotte (Locke)............ 150
   Clarissa...................... 128
   Eliza.....................191, 483
   Etta (McGimsey).............. 344
   Fannie (Oxford).............. 371
   Gertrude..................... 371
   Harrie B..................... 344
   Harriet...................... 141
   Hannah (Johnson)............. 21
   Herbert G., Dr................ 344
   Herbert W.................... 344
   Henry F...................... 150
   Jerusha...................... 13
   John......................189, 202
   Joseph....................... 21
   Katherine.................... 371
   Lydia........................ 133
   Margaret L................... 344

SHAW, Mary...............222, 371, 428
   Mary (Fletcher-Nason)......... 44
   Mary (Locke-Pemberton)....... 177
   Mercy........................ 61
   Moses......................23, 127
   Nancy (Towle)................ 202
   Oliver B...................... 177
   Patience (Locke-McAlpin)...... 189
   William...................... 189
   Amelia....................... 190
SHEA, Carrie (Lamprey)............. 448
   Catherine.................... 448
   Helen........................ 448
   Richard W.................... 448
   Pauline....................... 239
   Walter....................... 448
SHEARER, Alice.................... 532
   Charles H.................... 532
   Charlotte d.................. 532
   Clara L....................... 532
   Elizabeth.................... 532
   Elizabeth (Meeker)............ 532
   Emma (Hollar)................ 532
   George....................... 532
   Grace D...................... 532
   John......................... 105
   Louise....................... 532
   Margaret L................... 532
   Mary A....................... 532
   Nancy (Locke)................ 421
   Susan........................ 532
   Theodore M...............532, 421
   Valentine d.................. 532
SHELDON, Elizabeth................. 75
SHELDRON, James.................. 75
   Waity........................ 37
SHEPPARD, Adaline................. 72
   Ann E. (Locke)............... 173
   Earl L....................... 173
   John, Rev.................... 45
   Mabel I...................... 173
SHERBURNE, Abigail................ 46
   Ann.......................... 84
   Azilla (Watson)............... 297
   Col........................... 15
   Comfort (Riggs)............... 301
   Edwin........................ 301
   Elizabeth.................... 314
   Fred......................... 314
   Henry........................ 87
   Jonathan..................... 52
   Lewis........................ 301
   Lillian....................... 314
   Manly........................ 314
   Maria (Mason)................ 314
   Mary......................... 32
   Nancy (Perkins).............. 52
   Robert....................... 314
   Samuel....................... 297
   Sarah........................ 81
   Sarah (Chesley).............. 87
   Sophronia.................... 272
   Stephen...................... 297
   Viola......................... 314
   William...................... 314
SHERMAN, Albert G................. 300
   Betsey....................... 295
   Caroline..................... 337
   Caroline (Lathrop)............ 473
   Elizabeth J. (Demeritt)........ 126
   Emily........................ 183
   Florence L.................... 473
   General W. T.................. 246
   George....................... 289
   Giffy......................... 37
   Jennie (Locke)................ 300
   Lua C. (Locke)............... 289
   Orin......................... 473
   Samuel L..................... 126
   Stanton L.................... 289

INDEX OF NAMES 701

SHINER, Nellie.................... 507
SHIPMAN, Christena............... 229
  Isaiah, Rev.................... 229
SHIRLEY, Barbara..............265, 445
SHORT, Sarah...................... 303
SHORTELLE, Delia.................. 372
SHORTSHEAVES, Minnie.............. 530
SHURTLEFF, Abigail................ 126
  Barzilla....................... 54
  Benjamin....................... 125
  Charles A...................... 126
  Dolly (Locke).................. 54
  Elisha L. d.................... 125
  Emaline (Williamson)........... 126
  Henry S........................ 126
  Hester A. (Taylor)............. 126
  Margaret (Taylor).............. 126
  Mary (Westfall)................ 126
  Priscilla B. (Brown)........... 125
  Samuel A....................... 126
  William L...................... 126
SHUTE, Mary....................... 314
SIGNOR, Minerva................... 446
SILVER, Albert.................... 280
  Martha A....................... 235
  Mary.......................280, 402
  May (Russell-Dearborn)......... 280
  Nellie......................... 280
  William........................ 402
SIMES, Joseph..................... 109
  Margaret (Locke-Childs)........ 109
SIMMONS, Clara (Jenness-Mason).... 408
  Florence....................... 423
  John........................... 408
SIMONS. SIMONDS.
  Mr............................. 184
  Albert......................... 391
  Elizabeth (Dow-Branscomb)...... 184
  Ivah........................... 374
  John R......................... 374
  Lillian........................ 391
  Susannah (Minkley)............. 374
SIMPSON, Comfort (Stevens)........ 90
  John........................... 90
  Mary........................... 90
  Samuel......................... 90
  Sarah.......................... 90
  Susan.......................... 90
  William........................ 90
SINCLAIR, Everett................. 298
  Minerva (Langley).............. 298
  Ralph.......................... 298
  William........................ 298
SISSON, Luella M. (Locke)......... 172
  Nathan A....................... 172
SKATES, Maria..................... 200
SKINNER, Etta..................... 184
SLAGER, Mary E.................... 118
SLAPP, Elizabeth.................. 136
SLEEPER, Charles.................. 195
  Daniel......................... 224
  Dorothy (Tilton)............... 224
  George.......................195, 195
  Laura (Livingston)............. 195
  Leavitt........................ 390
  Mary.......................225, 228
  Mary (Locke)................... 195
  Polly.......................... 389
  Ruth..................19, 50, 162, 389
  Sarah.......................... 224
  Sarah (Berry).................. 567
  Thomas......................... 567
SLEMP, Rulenna.................... 387
SLOCUM, Ella A.................... 338
SLOSSON, Mr....................... 135
  Elizabeth (Winter)............. 135
  Herbert........................ 135
SMALL, Jerusha W.................. 39
  Job............................ 162
  Lucy........................... 75

SMALL, Moses B.................... 198
  Sarah M. (Perkins)............. 198
SMALLCON, Lucy.................... 284
SMART, Mr.......................93, 94
  Beatrice....................... 301
  Bertha (Rand).................. 301
  Christopher.................... 301
  Edna (Rixford)................. 386
  Emma........................... 545
  Joseph......................... 386
  Mary (Garland)................. 545
  (Nealey), Miss................. 93
  Roland......................... 301
  Sally (Pearsons)............... 94
  Samuel......................... 545
SMILEY, Miss...................... 132
  Emma........................... 144
  Jessie E. (Locke).............. 333
  Mary........................... 333
  Matt........................... 333
  Robert......................... 333
SMITH, Miss.............43, 179, 209, 292
  Mr..........61, 103, 198, 267, 274
  Abbie S........................ 517
  Abigail....................13, 24, 214
  Abigail (Brackett)............. 199
  Abigail (Locke)................ 274
  Abraham........................ 42
  Ada........................321, 512
  Adaline........................ 121
  Adaline (Locke)................ 235
  Addie.......................... 181
  Addie (Brown).................. 478
  Adoniram....................... 242
  Agnes......................197, 263
  Albert G....................... 402
  Aleta (Ames)................... 517
  Alexander...................... 356
  Alice B........................ 367
  Almeda......................... 413
  Almeda S. (Locke).............. 241
  Andrew......................... 445
  Ann Maria d.................... 413
  Ann (Locke).................... 248
  Ann (Sanborn).................. 201
  Annah (Locke).................. 242
  Annette........................ 391
  Annette (Perry)................ 307
  Annie......................303, 458
  Annie (Hopkinson-McKenney).... 180
  Annie (Locke).................. 402
  Annie (Towle).................. 371
  Annis P. (Perkins)............. 32
  Arthur L....................... 180
  Arthur H. L., U. S. N.......... 525
  Arum P......................... 307
  Arvilla (Locke)................ 303
  Belle.......................... 453
  Benjamin....................... 199
  Bernice........................ 346
  Bertha (Guild)................. 470
  Catherine...................... 356
  Catherine (Locke).............. 356
  Caroline....................205, 478
  Charles..............220, 367, 525
  Charlotte (Locke-Kimball)...... 102
  Clarence O..................... 516
  Clarissa....................... 111
  Cora B......................... 483
  S. (Covell), Miss.............. 517
  Daniel..........61, 89, 235, 253, 366
  Daniel, Major.................. 366
  David..................189, 242, 356, 525
  Deborah........................ 195
  Deborah (Locke)................ 42
  Dorothy....................132, 453
  Edgar F. d..................... 525
  Edward G. d.................... 525
  Edwin......................180, 346
  Eleanor (Locke)..............88, 195

INDEX OF NAMES

SMITH, Eliza........................ 356
  Eliza (Shaw).................... 483
  Elizabeth (———)................ 63
  Elizabeth.......75, 193, 253, 470, 475
  Elizabeth (Locke)................ 449
  Elsie (Locke).................... 294
  Eunice (Locke-George).......... 96
  Ella.........................180, 538
  Ellen............................ 366
  Ellen Francis.................... 413
  Emma F.......................... 478
  Emma (Lang).................... 260
  Emma (Moore)................... 180
  Ephraim.....................241, 413
  Estelle (Drysdale)............... 542
  Ethel (Locke).................... 391
  Etta (Brown).................... 478
  Everett.......................... 401
  Frances (Atkinson).............. 445
  Francis V....................... 542
  Fannie......................227, 329
  Frank.......................478, 483
  Fred...........294, 401, 453, 483, 181
  Forrest S........................ 512
  George........63, 395, 439, 478, 483
  Georgie.......................... 223
  Grace (Jameson)................. 439
  Hannah...................18, 213, 215
  Hannah (Locke)..........83, 89, 366
  Hannah (Sargent)............... 401
  Harriet.......................... 205
  Harriet A........................ 413
  Harrison......................... 83
  Harrold L........................ 439
  Harry........................84, 483
  Hattie........................... 491
  Henry..............201, 388, 391, 413
  Hillard.......................... 303
  Hiram J......................... 439
  Ida d........................... 512
  Ida (Stewart)................... 346
  Ira A............................ 478
  Irene (Locke)................... 357
  Isabel........................... 366
  J. R............................. 371
  Jacob....................102, 356, 357
  Jane............................. 233
  Jefferson........................ 180
  Jeremiah........................ 18
  John........32, 63, 64, 228, 253, 569
  Joseph...............180, 195, 391, 366
  Josiah........................... 478
  Judson.......................... 242
  Julia Ann....................... 181
  Kate (Wright)................... 563
  Laforest......................... 542
  Laura (Pilling).................. 198
  Leland L......................... 470
  Lena F........................... 470
  Leona O......................... 470
  Leroy........................180, 346
  Lewis..................449, 542, 542
  Lillian M....................525, 542
  Linnie (Griffith)................ 516
  Louisa L......................... 367
  Loyd............................. 542
  Lucy........................180, 346
  Lucy B. (Locke)................. 82
  Lydia (Gray).................... 525
  Lydia (Gould)................... 181
  Lyle............................. 542
  M............................... 366
  Martha....................82, 124, 248
  Martha (Burns)................. 525
  Martha (Page).................. 366
  Mary.....35, 44, 111, 171, 366, 366, 413
  Mary (Coleburn)................ 291
  Mary (Gilmore)................. 195
  Mary (Howard)................. 388
  Mary (Mathes)................. 453

SMITH, Mary (Moore)................ 267
  Mary (Nute)..................... 366
  Mary (Rand).................... 180
  May (Adair)..................... 367
  May (Hodgdon)................. 483
  Mehitable....................... 75
  Mellen K........................ 367
  Moses....................83, 181, 251
  Nancy (Cutler).................. 365
  Nancy (Whittier)................ 253
  Nathan.......................96, 517
  Nellie........................... 253
  Norris........................... 75
  Olevia (Stone-Merrill), Mrs........ 180
  Olive C. (Locke)................. 82
  Oretta E. (Locke)................ 63
  Patience (Foss-Newton-Butler).... 64
  Phebe........................... 329
  Phebe (Chase).................. 61
  Phineas......................... 517
  (Pike), Miss..................... 391
  Polly............................ 28
  Polly (Fuller)................... 103
  Priscilla......................... 439
  Ransom R....................... 291
  Richard.......................82, 82
  Revere J........................ 346
  Rosa (Higgins).................. 563
  Roy............................. 516
  Ruth............................ 181
  Ruth (Porter)................... 180
  Ruth (Page).................... 228
  Sadie (Carpenter)............... 445
  Sally............................ 57
  Sally F. (Locke)................. 83
  Samuel.......................... 248
  Sarah...................181, 205, 317
  Sarah (Kimball)................. 220
  Sarah (Lane-Wentworth)........ 180
  Sarah (Lane).................... 180
  Sarah (Locke).................. 569
  Sarah (Thompson).............. 512
  Sheldon S....................... 563
  Sophia.......................... 395
  Stephen......................181, 205
  Susan.......................291, 356
  Susan (Tucker).................. 478
  Susie (Benson).................. 180
  Sylvanus........................ 445
  Theodosia (Ladd)............... 61
  Vernon.......................... 356
  Virginia (Merritt)............... 542
  Waity (Locke).................. 75
  Whitman........................ 260
  William.............329, 365, 453, 563
  Winnifred....................... 512
  Winona M....................... 346
  Winthrop.................88, 195, 366
  Zebulon......................... 401
SNELL, Abigail (Locke).............. 73
  Emily (Page).................... 122
  Samuel.......................... 73
  Sarah........................... 257
  William......................... 122
SNICKLES, Blanche (Moody).......... 472
  Henry........................... 472
SNOW, Mr......................... 89
  Agnes........................... 485
  Albert........................... 278
  Augusta (Woodman)............. 278
  Emma........................... 319
  Judith........................... 99
  Sophia.......................... 358
SNYDER, Jennie..................... 411
SOMERS, Louise.................... 423
SOULE, Betsey (Noyes).............. 162
  Clara (Prescott)................. 114
  J. K............................. 114
  Phineas......................... 162
SOUTHERD, Augusta (Locke)......... 222

INDEX OF NAMES

SOUTHERD, Nathaniel 222
SOUTHWICK, Sarah 212, 382
SPANISH LADY 274
SPARE, Nancy C. 126
SPATWELL, Mr. 38
  Betsey (Clifford) 38
SPAULDING, Benjamin J. 543
  Charles 520
  Earl E. 543
  Ethel 520
  Frank J. 462
  George E. 462
  George d 543
  Hannah 134
  Julia E. 543
  Julia (Fletcher) 543
  Mary (Jenkins) 543
  Thomas, Dr. 299
SPEAR, Abbie 546
  Abbie (Bazin) 474
  Emily 546
  Erving 546
  Harriet 121
  James S. 474, 545
  Mabel 546
  Marion 546
  Mary (Green) 545
SPEERS, Clara (Locke) 456
  James 456
  Miriam d 456
SPENCER, Betsey (Berry) 65
  Charles 517, 517
  Emily (Eaton), Mrs. 224
  Emily (Eaton) 517
  Ethel (Ames) 517
  Robert 65
SPENGLER, Josephine (Hadcock) 438
  Warren 438
SPINNEY, Abigail (Locke) 190
  Addie (Batson) 400
  Benniah 190
  Caroline (Leach) 343
  Caroline (Staples) 400
  Chandler 184
  Clara 343
  Elizabeth (Dow-Branscomb-
    Simonds) 184
  Jeremiah 400
  Nathaniel 343
  Paschal 400
  Susan R. 123
SPOFFORD, Elizabeth 303
SPOONER, Alonzo 538
  Mary (Bennett) 538
  May 538
SPRAGUE, George H. 334
  L. Isabel 171
  Mae (Locke) 334
  Rispah 355
SPROUL, Annie 371
  Sarah 283
SPURLING, Martha J. 330
SQUIRE, Sybil 116
SQUIRES, Amanda 62
STACKPOLE, George 496, 555, 555
  Louise E. 555
  Mabel (Trefethern) 496
  Mary G. 555
STACY, Mary 97
STAGE, Emma (Carpenter) 534
  Flora 534
  Leroy 534
  Levi 534
  Walter 534
STALKER, Charlotte 358
  Elizabeth 358
  Elizabeth (Locke) 190
  Fannie 358
  George 358
  Letitia 358

STALKER, Mary 358
  Susan 358
  William 190, 358
STANDLICK, Eliza 413
  Elizabeth (Trelvar) 529
  William 529
STANLEY, Albert 494
  Bernice (Breed) 521
  Carrie (Keyes) 435
  Charles 521, 521
  Herbert 435
  Jennie (Haley) 494
  Lillian 443
  Mandana (Locke-Page) 254
  Nellie 415
  Samuel 254
  Virginia 521
STANTON, Eliza 108
  Minnie 310
  Sally 49, 102
  William 218
  Winnie 329
STANWOOD, Elizabeth 42
  Sarah 47
STAPLES, Mr. 548
  Bina (Wiggin-Locke) 548
  Caroline 400
  Clara (Goodwin) 325
  Cora (Locke) 505
  Edith 480
  George 325
  Harriet (Tilton) 101
  Marshall 101
  Mary (Haley), Mrs. 73
  Sarah T. 101
  Victor 505
STARE, Burton 407
  Rosa (Berry) 407
STARIN, Betsey 185
  John 353
STARK, Mr. 135
  Abigail W. (Locke) 134
  Ambrose 134
  Helen (Scripture) 134
  (Hill), Miss. 134
  Jonathan 134
  Josephine d 134
  Maria (Saunders) 135
  Regiment 43, 46, 61, 62, 72
STEADMAN, Catherine 75
  Henry 162
  Minnie (Locke) 324
  William 324
STEARNS, Amos 237
  Betsey 45
  Edwin 314, 314
  Elizabeth (Barker) 314
  Frances (Edmonds) 314
  Harry W. 314
  John 264
  Joseph B. 314
  Josiah 45
  Lizzie L. 408
  Nath Amos 408
  Rosa F. 408
  Sally 117
  Sarah 193
  Sarah (Berry) 237
  Sarah (Lane) 264
  William B. 408
STEBBINS, Alice (Smith) 367
  Harold 367
  Luther 367
STEELE, Coyle (Wilkerson) 416
  Edward N. 416
  Laura M. 416
STEERE, G. Irving 514
  Helen 514
  Horace 374
  Lillian (Locke) 374

INDEX OF NAMES

STEERE, Louisa A. 514
  Martina 514
  Paul 514
  Tirza W. 514
STEPHENSON, Augustus W. 503
  Joseph 120, 120
  Judith (True) 120
  Lindsey 120
  Martha (Pray) 503
  Orrin 120
  Thomas 503
  Wilbur 503
STERLING, Mr. 356
  Anagusta 287
  Bethia (Locke) 356
  Eliza (Chadwick) 287
  Sumner 287
STERNBURG, Peter 339
  Rosetta 172
STERNSBEE, C. P. 444
  Marion (Lamprey-Thienes) 444
STETSON, Bradford 290
  Caroline (Locke) 290
  Jabez 290
STEUBNER, Louisa G. 134
STEVENS, Miss 90, 262
  Mr. 135
  Abbie (Emery) 330
  Abby 205
  Abby (Lamprey) 196
  Abigail 90
  Abigail (Goodhue) 264, 445
  Alice M. 501
  Ann 213
  Ann (Moulton) 58
  Artemesia (Brown) 196
  Bessie 445
  Calista 58
  Caroline (Smith) 478
  Chandler E. 90, 90
  Charlotte 40
  Clara 106, 196
  Clara (Carpenter) 445
  Clinton 445
  Comfort 90, 90
  Daniel 90, 90
  Eliza 183
  Elizabeth 129
  Elsie (Lamprey-LeBosquet) 264
  Enoch 445
  Etta 196
  Eunice 40
  Everett J. 330
  Frank 445
  Gertrude 501
  Hannah 196
  Harlton 477
  Helen M. 501
  Herod 58
  Hobart 264, 478
  Horace 445
  Ismenia (Washer) 90
  James 90, 196
  Jane M. 90
  Jennie 197, 292
  Jones 553
  Jonathan 58
  Judith (Lamprey) 90, 90
  Lena (Otis) 553
  Madge (Richardson) 196
  Maria (Rice-Davis) 135
  Mary B. 90, 197, 501
  Mary (Freeze) 445
  Maude 548
  Mehitable 121
  Molly 43
  Murilla 58
  Myra (Hilton) 445
  Olive (Locke) 44
  Olivia 58
STEVENS, Perley 196
  Phebe 90
  Philip 44
  Roy 445
  Samuel 264, 445
  Sarah 327
  Sarah (Locke) 477
  Seth d. 196
  Stella 445
  William 196, 501
STEWART, Abby (Ballard) 515
  Abby B. 560
  Asa 270
  Clara (Shearer) 532
  Edric 346
  Elizabeth 363
  Fred J. 346
  George C. 532
  Harriet 300
  Ida Marian 346
  Jeff D. 515
  Jefferson D. 560
  Lillias (Locke) 346
  Louisa (Oke) 406
  Lydia (Worthen) 270
  Nellie 347
  Rowland 346
STICKNEY, Daniel 59
  David 46
  Eleanor (Wilson) 62
  Eliza 59
  Enos 59
  James 62
  Mary Ann 59
  Mehitable 29
  Polly (Moulton) 59
  Sally 46
STILES, Clara 289
STILLINGS, Ann (Locke) 477
  Annie (Delmore) 548
  Arthur L. 548
  Charles 548
  Eugene 548
  E. Forrest 548
  Flora (Moran) 548
  Joseph 477, 548
  Katherine 548
  Medora 548
  Rita R. 548
STILPHEN, Alice (Ormsby) 385
  George 385, 386
  Julia (Moses-Chase) 386
ST. JOHN, Mr. 268
  Emilina (Lamson) 207
  Everitte 207
  Grace (Moore) 268
STOCKMAN, Mary 91
STODDARD, Carrie F. 549
  Charles L. d. 549
  Florence 368
  Frank D. 549
  Frederick 480
  Harry G. 549
  Joe M. 549
  Minnie (Willis) 480
  Willis F. 549
STODDER, Alice (Hood), Mrs. 368
STOLK, Eunice (Woodman) 278
  Henry 278
STOKER, Abigail 95
STOKES, Stella 283
STONE, Abbie (Locke) 351
  Bessie (Trefethern) 519
  Eleanor 336
  Ernest 287
  Francis 298
  Frederick 351
  Helen (Locke) 287
  James 351
  James B. 351

INDEX OF NAMES 705

STONE, Joseph..................... 184
  John C......................... 168
  Leroy.......................... 519
  Louella (Locke)................ 298
  Margaret....................... 351
  Marion......................... 336
  Martha (Dow)................... 184
  Mary (Herrick)................. 168
  Nellie (Locke)................. 287
  Olivia......................... 180
  Ortwell H...................... 298
  Robert......................... 287
  Sarah (Taylor)................. 298
STORER, Charles.................... 8
STOREY, Helen..................... 191
STOUGHTON, Maria G................ 568
STOWE, Sophie..................... 291
STOWELL, Glenna M................. 554
  Homer C........................ 554
  James.......................... 495
  Lillah (Locke)................. 495
  Myrtle L....................... 554
STRAIN, Albert E.................. 424
  Arthur......................... 424
  Cornelius...................... 424
  Flora (Locke).................. 424
  Hazel.......................... 424
STRATTON, Florence................ 217
  Fostina, Mrs................... 408
STRAW, Carrie..................... 417
  Clara (Bickford)............... 471
  Edson A........................ 512
  Ellery C....................... 511
  Fanny (Hussey)................. 557
  Frank.......................... 471
  Harry B........................ 471
  Henry F........................ 152
  James S........................ 363
  Leola M........................ 511
  Lucinda S...................... 512
  Maggie (Bernard)............... 511
  Mary........................... 417
  Mary J. (Otis)................. 152
  Mary (Wells)................... 363
  Oscar I........................ 512
  Pierce......................... 557
  Sarah (Sanders)................ 417
  William........................ 417
STRICKLAND, Fanny.................. 86
STRONG, Abigail (Pratt)............ 63
  Alice.......................... 292
  Caroline (Jameson)............. 257
  Ella (Brown)................... 439
  Fred........................... 292
  Horace W....................... 439
  Olive.......................... 63
  Warner......................... 257
  William........................ 63
STRUCK, Clara..................... 455
STRUNK, Edwin H................... 378
  Emilie (Locke)................. 378
  Katherine M.................... 378
  William, Prof.................. 378
  William O...................... 378
STRUPP, Frances, Mrs.............. 392
STUART, Miriam (Sanborn).......... 504
  Roscoe G....................... 504
STUBBS, Mary...................... 13
  Rebecca........................ 20
  Richard........................ 20
STUDLEY, Aphia (McGowan).......... 446
  Betsey (Bates)................. 446
  Dawes.......................... 446
  Edward....................264, 446
  Emily (Churchill).............. 191
  Fred M......................... 446
  Henry, Dr...................... 191
  Lillian (Lindall).............. 446
  Malvina (Lamprey).............. 264
  May L.......................... 446

STURDIVANT, Abigail (Shurtleff)........ 126
  David.......................... 126
STURTEVANT, Capt................... 77
  Hannah (Locke)................. 77
  Margaret....................... 185
SUEARENGEN, Abrilla............... 116
SULLIVAN, Genl.................... 61
  Katherine...................... 399
  Nancy.......................... 545
  S. M........................... 568
SULLOWAY, John.................... 151
  Martha (Otis).................. 151
SULTZBACK, Eva (Locke)............ 520
  Sidney......................... 520
SUMNER, Charles................... 569
  Myrtle (Locke)................. 569
SURLES, Eldora (Whidden).......... 405
  Henry.......................... 405
SWAIN, Abram...................... 192
  Ann............................ 272
  Aretus......................... 363
  Burnett........................ 450
  Carl d......................... 363
  Effie (Locke).................. 450
  Foote.......................... 372
  Hannah......................... 13
  Herbert d...................... 372
  Jesse (Burnham)................ 363
  Leslie d....................... 363
  Margaret (Locke)............192, 568
  Mary (Locke)................... 372
  Natt L......................... 372
  Richard........................ 568
  Sarah (Caswell)................ 372
  Silas L.....................363, 363
  William.....................450, 450
SWALLOW, Charlotte (McCutcheon).... 437
  John........................... 437
  Sarah.......................... 255
SWASEY, Miss...................... 277
  Evaline (Barrows).............. 115
SWASEY, John...................... 115
SWEET, Calvin..................... 105
  Caroline....................... 39
  Emily.......................... 39
  Harriet........................ 318
  Harriet (Locke)................ 80
  James.......................... 80
  John.....................39, 39, 39, 495
  Mary A.....................37, 39, 39
  Mary (Hunnewell)............... 39
  Nathaniel...................... 39
  Orrison d...................... 230
  Rachel L. (Doloff)............. 105
  Sarah.......................... 230
  Susan (Blodgett)............... 230
  Sylvanus....................... 230
  William........................ 39
SWETT, Emily...................... 265
SWIFT, Lucia...................... 350
SWINBURN, Rose.................... 292
SWITZER, Eva...................... 296
  John C......................... 296
  Mary (Page).................... 296
  Ray............................ 296
  Sarah.......................... 296
SYLVESTRE, Madeline, Mrs.......... 448
SYMONDS, Daniel................... 389
  Joseph E....................... 402
  Mabel.......................... 402
  Martha......................... 389
  Nancy.......................... 224
  Sarah (Little)................. 402
SYZE, Albert...................... 452
  Laura (Huckins)................ 452
TABOR, Edith...................... 452
  Charles........................ 452
TAFT, Alice R..................... 229
  Dennison....................... 229
  Edna M......................... 229

INDEX OF NAMES

TAFT, Rachel (Moore)............... 229
TAGGART, Jane.................... 119
TALBERT, Blanche................. 482
  Georgie d..................... 482
  John W........................ 306
  Nellie (Knowles)............... 306
TALBOT, Theresa................. 172
TALLANT, Adelaid (Paarech)......... 541
  Annah (Locke)................. 249
  Edwin F....................... 430
  Ethel......................... 430
  George M...................... 430
  Irma (Nye).................... 541
  Josie (Glidden)................ 430
  Marstin E..................... 541
  Marston....................... 249
  Martha........................ 430
  Mary S........................ 541
  Ruth L........................ 541
  Susie (Drew).................. 430
  Webster....................... 541
TALLMAN, Clara................... 434
  Hannah........................ 160
  Mabel......................... 167
TANNER, Lizzie.................... 300
  Mary H........................ 75
  Thomas B...................... 160
TAPLIN, Abbie B................... 415
  Alice (Randall)................ 415
  Almira........................ 242
  Caroline...................... 241
  Caroline (Bickford)............ 242
  Carrie....................415, 415
  Charles B..................... 415
  Elizabeth..................... 242
  Elliott....................109, 415
  Emma.......................... 242
  Emma (Campbell)............... 415
  Ethel......................... 415
  Florence...................... 415
  Harriet....................... 242
  Helen......................... 415
  James O....................... 415
  Joseph........................ 412
  Lucinda....................... 242
  Mary.......................... 242
  Nathan........................ 242
  Sarah......................... 415
  Sarah A. (Locke).............. 109
  Sarah (Robie)................. 412
  Sophia........................ 242
  Susan......................... 242
TAPPAN, Bertha.................... 295
TARBOX, Arthur................... 185
  Aurilla (Locke)............... 185
  Emery......................... 185
  Eva (Goodhue-Lamprey)......... 444
  Jasper........................ 444
TARLTON, Miss.................... 567
  Abbie C. d.................... 519
  Abigail (Ladd)................ 62
  Amos.......................... 62
  Ann........................... 304
  Carrie (Hall)................. 519
  Carrie (Poole)................ 519
  Charlotte..................... 397
  Elias...................397, 519, 519
  Elizabeth..................... 240
  Ellen......................... 400
  Evaline....................... 519
  Florence d.................... 519
  Francis d..................... 519
  Hannah.....................52, 253
  Martha (Manning).............. 112
  Mary.......................... 120
  Mary (Batson)................. 397
  Ruth.......................59, 394
  Stillman...................... 112
  Theodora (Ladd)............... 62
  William....................62, 519

TASH, Clarissa.................... 110
  John, Dea..................... 247
  Mary (Ham).................... 247
  Nancy......................... 427
TASKER, Adaline................... 267
  Eben.......................... 284
  Lydia......................... 284
TATE, Hannah...................... 38
TAY, Esther....................... 248
TAYLOR, Mr....................87, 251
  Alice (Leavitt)............... 266
  Bertha (Locke)................ 543
  Charles W..................341, 343
  Edward J...................... 343
  Edwin S....................... 343
  Eliza......................... 534
  Elizabeth..................... 35
  Elizabeth (Brown)..........341, 343
  Emma.......................... 458
  Eva (Dalton).................. 343
  Everett....................... 543
  George..................77, 543, 343
  Henry.....................266, 266
  Hester A...................... 126
  Ira J......................... 177
  James......................... 270
  Jonathan...................... 303
  Lucinda....................... 270
  Lucy N. (Locke)............... 77
  Margaret...................... 126
  Marjorie...................... 543
  Martha (Locke)................ 177
  Mary (Locke).................. 303
  Mary (Worthen)................ 270
  Mildred....................... 266
  Nellie d...................... 266
  Nellie (Bachelder)............ 343
  Polly (Eaton)................. 87
  Rachel........................ 468
  Rebecca....................... 142
  Roxanna....................... 49
  (Sanborn), Miss............... 251
  Sarah..............266, 298, 343, 419
  Sophia (Marston).............. 343
TEBBETTS, Abigail................. 328
  Ann........................... 121
  Caroline D.................... 95
  Imogene...................486, 550
  Jerusha (Dame)................ 203
  Lydia......................... 154
  Mary.......................... 273
  William....................... 203
TENNANT, Hattie................... 393
TENNER, Hezekiah D................ 360
  Lydia (Locke)................. 360
TENNEY, Achsah.................... 142
  Alice......................... 186
  Bailey........................ 102
  E............................. 261
  Edmund........................ 186
  Hannah R. (Weare)............. 102
  Joanna (Poore)................ 186
TEWKSBURY, Abiah.................. 477
  Almon......................... 270
  Ann C......................... 133
  Hannah........................ 38
  Helen (Locke)................. 270
THATCHER, Miss.................... 135
  Elizabeth..................... 429
  George........................ 429
  John......................248, 429
  Josiah P...................... 429
  Lilla (Lane).................. 429
  Margaret...................... 429
  Margaret (Locke).............. 248
  Mary (Sanderson).............. 429
  Russell....................... 429
  Ruth.......................... 429
THAXTER, Lillian G................ 169
THAYER, Miss L.................... 377

INDEX OF NAMES

THAYER, Abigail (Treat)............ 153
   Cotton....................... 153
   Elizabeth.................... 153
   Ellen........................ 287
   Frank........................ 377
   Henry........................ 287
   Mary......................... 287
   Sarah (Noyes-Horton).......... 377
THIENES, Dorothy.................. 444
   Karl.....................444, 444
   Marion (Lamprey)............. 444
THOMAS, Capt..................... 91
   Carrie....................... 451
   Cora......................... 334
   Daniel....................... 4
   Marion....................... 504
   Prudence (Marden)............ 91
THOMPKINS, Charles................ 220
   Elizabeth (Kimball).......... 220
   Isabelle..................... 220
THOMPSON, Abbie (Locke).......... 428
   Adaline...................... 224
   Adelaide (Porter)............ 540
   Alice........................ 328
   Amy.......................... 540
   Andrew E..................... 389
   Ann I. (Locke)............... 286
   Annie (Locke)................ 450
   Arthur A..................... 353
   B. A......................... 461
   Bertha L..................... 334
   Charles..................164, 334
   Charlotte.................... 162
   Chestina..................... 334
   Clara........................ 428
   Cora (Thomas)................ 334
   Cordelia (Locke)............. 164
   Dennie....................... 428
   Dora......................... 289
   Elizabeth (Locke)............ 102
   Elizabeth (Perkins).......... 389
   Ellen (Locke)................ 188
   Elmer........................ 428
   Ernest....................... 450
   Florence..................... 334
   Francis J.................... 510
   Frank........................ 282
   Fred G....................... 188
   Freddie d.................... 334
   George....................... 450
   Grace (Faber)................ 540
   Grace (Hersey)............... 353
   Harold d..................... 334
   Hattie....................... 327
   Henry F...................... 221
   Inez......................... 188
   Isaac........................ 286
   Isabelle..................... 150
   Jacob........................ 23
   J. E. V...................... 286
   Jonathan..................... 450
   Joseph....................289, 353
   Laura........................ 278
   Lawrence..................540, 540
   Levina....................... 227
   Lewis........................ 102
   Lucy.....................221, 286
   Lucy (Chesley)............... 450
   Lucy (Moore)................. 450
   Lydia M...................221, 254
   Mary.................221, 435, 436
   Nellie....................... 334
   Orah (Locke)................. 282
   Osgood....................... 188
   Phebe M. d................... 334
   Phil Sheridan................ 428
   Richard...................... 540
   Rosamond..................... 428
   Ruth......................... 100
   Samuel L..................... 540

THOMPSON, Sarah..............221, 512
   Sarah (Heath)................ 289
   Stephen C.................... 334
THOMSEN, Clara (Locke)............ 428
   Francis J.................... 428
THORN, Zilpha..................... 119
THORNBURNE, Jerusha............... 356
THORNTON, Adna.................... 58
   Betsey (Moulton)............. 58
   Hannah....................... 58
   Martha....................... 58
   Sarah........................ 58
   Sidney....................... 58
   William...................... 58
THRALL, Helen M................... 116
THURBER, Frank T.................. 415
   Mary......................... 439
   Maud......................... 415
   Sarah (Taplin)............... 415
   Thomas....................... 415
THURSTON, Annie (Rapelge)......... 197
   Benjamin d................... 52
   Betsey (Locke)............... 44
   Betsey (Lovering)............ 243
   Caroline (Humphrey).......... 197
   Catherine.................... 197
   Charles C.................... 197
   Daniel....................... 52
   Edward....................... 44
   Edwin M...................... 197
   Ella (Pope).................. 197
   Emily........................ 197
   Frank........................ 197
   Gardner, Rev................. 43
   Hannah (Parker).............. 52
   Harriet (Schuman)............ 197
   Henry S...................... 197
   Huldah (Perkins)............. 52
   John......................... 197
   Josephine.................... 197
   Leland....................... 90
   Lydia (Ball)................. 197
   Margaret (Huchins)........... 90
   Martha....................... 197
   Martha (Locke)............... 44
   Mary......................... 197
   Moses........................ 243
   Nanthaniel................... 52
   Sarah F...................... 109
   Sophia....................... 61
   Tryphena..................... 408
THYNG, J. Augusta................. 283
TIBBETTS, Miss.................... 56
   Ada (Smith).................. 321
   Adaline...................... 71
   Augusta...................... 321
   Charles...................... 219
   Etta (Hamilton).............. 321
   Gertrude..................... 400
   Herbert...................... 321
   Ida.......................... 321
   Julia (Locke)................ 219
   Keziah....................... 25
   Martha....................... 499
   Mary E....................... 320
   Matilda...................... 271
   Mehitable.................... 320
   Ora.......................... 321
   Sarah E. (Locke)............. 148
   Thomas...................148, 321
TICE, Elizabeth (Langley-Tuck-Butterfield-Roberts)................ 133
   W. W......................... 133
TIDD, Charles.................475, 475
   Nellie (Gookin).............. 475
TILE, Mr.......................... 293
   Jessie (Clarke).............. 293
TILINGHAST, Abbie................. 170
   Anna......................... 161
   Hannah....................... 170

INDEX OF NAMES

TILINGHAST, Patience (Dyer) 170
    Samuel 170
TILSON, Elma 376
TILTON, Abbie R. 217
    Abby S. (Freeze) 101
    Albert F., Rev. 101
    Albert F. 217
    Alden M. 255
    Alfaretta (Boody) 283
    Alvin H. 255
    Angela F. 255
    Ann D. d. 283
    Anna M. 255
    Annie (Lowe) 217
    Arvilla 114
    Asa d 101
    Austin V. 217
    Betsey (Locke) 113, 124
    Carey F. 217
    Caroline (Griswold), Mrs. 101
    Charles S. 427
    Cornelia (Welch) 255
    Daniel 113, 114, 255
    Deborah (Bachelder) 101
    Dorothy 224
    Eliza (Dakin) 101
    Eliza (Emery) 101
    Eliza (Patch) 101
    Ellen 217, 283
    Emma (Messerger) 217
    Florence 255
    Florence (Baytiss) 255
    Florence (Stratton) 217
    Frances d 101
    George 101, 114, 283
    Hannah 59
    Hannah (Fuller) 101
    Harriet 101, 217
    Hattie (French) 217
    Helen (Brown) 217
    Henrietta 367
    Irene 101
    Isabella 255
    Jacob 113, 124, 255
    Jane E. 283
    Janette 364
    J. Augusta (Thyng) 283
    Jeremiah, Rev. 101
    Joan F. 255
    John J. 283
    Josephine S. 255
    Josiah 48
    Josiah H., Rev. 101
    Josiah, Dr. 217
    Julia 101
    Louisa M. 217
    Lucy M. (Locke) 113
    Margaret 224
    Martha (Gove) 217
    Martha (Jackman) 101
    Martha Lucretia 217
    Mary 19, 101, 114, 217, 282, 445
    Mary (Emery) 101
    Mary (Locke) 427
    Mary (Trask) 101
    Mittie L. (Prescott-Rundlett) 114
    Oscar I. 217
    Rebecca E. (Moor) 101
    Rena M. 283
    Rinaldo 255, 255
    Royal J. 217
    Ruth 255
    Samuel 101, 101
    Sarah 101, 217, 217, 217, 283
    Sarah (Dearborn) 48
    Stella (Stokes) 283
    Widow 54
    Will F. 217
    William H. 283
TIRRILL, Adeline (Wise) 223

TIRRILL, Arvilla (Varnum) 223
    Charles 223
    Emeline (Fretts) 223
    Hazen 223
    Judith (Veasey) 223
    Lodema 223
    Melissa 223
    Nathan 103
    Rachel (Fuller) 103
    Russell P. 223
    Wooster 223
TITCOMB, Beniah 97
    Elizabeth 54
    Mary 211
    Mary (McMurphy) 97
    Mary (Stacy) 97
    Sally (Locke) 97
    Sarah A. 78
TITUS, Betsey 59
    Cordelia 211
    Lucy 59
TODD, Alice 189, 357
    Helen 189, 358
    Jerusha (Locke) 189
    Louise 189
    Mary 120
    Robert 189, 189
    Rose W. (Emmons) 224
    Susan 210
    William 224
TOMLINSON, Annette 385
    Annette (Webster) 216
    Caroline (Merriman) 385
    Henry W. 385
    John 216
TOTMAN, Charity 78
TOURTILLOT, Emma 342
    George A. 342
TOWLE, Abbie (Watson) 297
    Abigail 26
    Abigail (Moulton) 112
    Abraham 112
    Albert 200
    Almira 200
    Amos 53
    Ann 27
    Anna 51, 64
    Anna (Norton) 56
    Annette E. 114
    Annie 370, 371
    Annie (Cilley) 371
    Annie (Rynes) 200
    Annie (Shaw) 371
    Annie (Sproul) 371
    Annie (Weeks) 370
    Benjamin 93, 202, 371
    Betsey 117, 270
    Catherine 202, 202
    Charles, Rev. 202
    Charles .. 200, 200, 370, 370, 370, 372, 372
    Clara M. 202
    Collis 369
    Daniel 370
    David 369
    Dearborn 31
    Edgar 369
    Elbridge P. 175
    Eliza (Ham) 202
    Elizabeth 200, 202
    Elizabeth (Jenness) 31
    Ella 369
    Ella (Reinking) 202
    Ellen M. 200
    Esther 19
    Eugene 447
    Frank 200, 297, 370
    Fred S., Dr. 370
    George 200, 200, 369, 371, 371
    Grace S. 371
    Haley 175

INDEX OF NAMES

Towle, Hannah (Locke) 81
  Hannah (Philbrick) 53
  Hannah (Sanborn) 93
  Harrie F 371
  Harriet 371
  Harriet (Edgerly) 202
  Hattie 369
  Helen 371
  Henry 200
  Herbert 369
  Horace E 200
  Horatio 175
  Irving 553
  Isaac 93
  J. A 364
  James 200, 200
  Jane (McClure) 200
  Janette (Lamprey) 447
  Jennie (Lay) 202
  John 81, 114
  Jonathan 31, 56
  Joseph 22, 22, 175
  Kenneth 553
  Levi 31
  Lizzie 369
  Lucy 93
  Lucy (Hobbs) 31
  Lydia (Dow) 35
  Mabel 370, 371
  Maria (Skates) 200
  Marietta 372
  Marion (Roby) 370
  Martha (Perry) 370
  Mary 72, 140, 200, 200
  Mary (Locke) 31
  Mary (McCrillis) 200
  Mary (McFarland) 200
  Mary (Moulton) 22
  Mary (Moulton-Redmond) 22
  Mary (Veazey) 364
  Maude (Otis) 553
  Nancy N 202
  Nellie 372
  Nelson 372
  Ora 492
  Patrick 447
  Perna (Judkins) 31
  Philip 35
  Rachel D 60
  Ralph 372
  Rebecca (Locke) 93
  Rhoda (Harvey) 31
  Robert 175
  Rodney d 200
  Sally 305
  Sarah 130, 202
  Sarah (Dawlton) 22
  Sarah (Hogan) 447
  Sarah (Marston) 175
  Susan (Daily) 200
  Susie 369
  Willie 370, 370
  William P 200
Towner, Ellen 358
Townsend, Mr 255
  Elizabeth 146
  Isabella (Tilton) 255
  Isabelle 398
  Mary 102, 400
Tozier, Alice (Waddington) 454
  Laforeste 454
Tracy, Mr 257
  Alden 109
  Emma (Bartlett-Locke) 257
  Jennie 109
  Joseph 109
  Mary (Northey) 109
Trafton, Alfred S 143
  Emily (Trefethern-Hall) 143
  Josephine 415

Tranter, Annie 414
Trask, Ada M 523
  Joseph O 196
  Josephine 287
  Julia 196
  Lois J. (Lamprey) 196
  Mary 101
  Susie M 196
Travis, Mary 226
Treadwell, Sarah O 247, 427
Treat, Abigail 153
  Phebe 162
Tredick, Agnes 518
  Ann E 518
  Dorothy (Locke) 233
  Emma 395
  Ethan A 395
  George 395, 518
  Gertrude C 518
  Henry 233, 395
  John L 395
  Julia (Ford) 395
  Mary 395, 518
  Ruth (Tarlton) 394
  William 394
Trefethern, Abbie (Hutchins) 495
  Abigail 33, 69
  Abigail (Locke) 16
  Ada 398
  Adaline (Locke) 234
  Adna (Nutter) 143
  Albert B 143
  Alfred M 69
  Andrew J 398
  Austin 311
  Beatrice 495
  Benjamin 69, 301
  Bessie 519
  Betsey 69
  Charles 69, 320, 495
  Charlotte (Jewell) 69
  Daisy d 520
  Daniel J 69
  David 69
  Dennis H 144
  Eliza (Marden) 143
  Elizabeth (Locke) 69, 146
  Elizabeth (Mason) 143
  Elizabeth (Tucker) 33
  Ella (Paul) 495
  Ella (Smiley-Maxwell), Mrs 144
  Ellen 69
  Emma (Witherell) 320
  Emily 143, 319
  Emily (Seavey) 143
  Ethel M 496
  Florence 69, 519
  Frances 320, 398
  Frank L 495
  Fred J 495
  George L 495, 526
  Gladys 311
  Grace 311
  Hannah L. (Berry) 65, 69
  Hanson 69, 69, 69
  Harold 311
  Harriet (Keen) 319
  Helen 520
  Henry 32, 33, 69
  Hiram 234
  Hubbard 69
  Isabella (Kimball) 319
  Isabelle (Townsend) 398
  Izetta M 144
  James 319, 495
  Joanna (Lawry) 319
  John 69, 108, 144, 495
  John Ichabod 143
  Joseph 33, 33, 65, 69
  Joseph Parsons, ... 143

INDEX OF NAMES

TREFETHERN, Josephine 304
  Laura (McGrath) 495
  Levi 69, 143, 146
  Lewis 320
  Lizzie 319
  Locada (Locke) 146
  Louisa (Tretethern) 143
  Louvia 69
  Lucretia 33
  Lydia (Berry) 30, 64, 69
  Mabel S 496
  Marcellus d 311
  Margaret 33
  Martha (Moulton) 143
  Martha S 144
  Mary 32, 33, 143
  Mary (Brown) 69
  Mary (Clark) 143
  Mary (Duncan-Locke) 239
  Mary (Gilbert) 311
  Mary Jane 319
  Mary (Locke) 69, 108
  Mary (Rand) 143
  Nancy 69
  Nathaniel 69, 69
  Nellie 311
  Nellie (White) 526
  Octavia 69
  Oliver 143
  Olivia B. (Marden) 143
  Patience (Riggs) 301
  (Partridge), Miss 33
  Polly 69
  Raymond 520
  Robinson 16, 33
  Ruth 311
  Sabrina 69
  Salome 33
  Samuel A 143
  Sarah E 143, 233, 235, 404
  Sarah (Moulton) 143
  Sebastian 146
  Sebastian J. of Kansas 69
  Simon Goss 143
  Supply F 143
  Susan (Piper) 30
  Susanna (Piper) 69
  Thaddeus 398, 520
  William 30, 64, 69, 69, 143, 239, 319
  William, Capt 33, 404
TRELVAR, Elizabeth 529
TRICKEY, Betsey (Gray) 157
  John 157
TRIM, Melissa 167
TRIPP, Mr 74
  Alice M. (Fowler) 461
  Fannie (Littlefield) 287
  Grace 287
  H. F 287
  Hannah (Gray) 74
  Harold J 461
  James H 282
  Mary J 158
  Nancy 219
  Russell F 461
  Sarah (Moses) 282
  Solomon 158
  Walter H 461
TRITTS, Elsie 41
TROOP, George J 359, 508
  Lydia 121
  Mabel (Locke) 359
  Margaret 508
  Norman E 508
TROW, Anna 401
  Joseph H., Rev 294
  Julia (Locke) 294
TRUBY, Sarah 533
TRUE, Abbie J 271
  Abram 92

TRUE, Ada I 271
  Ada (Poor) 271
  Almira 120
  Arthur E 271
  Benjamin, Capt 53
  Benjamin 120, 271
  Bertha 271
  Betsey (True) 120
  Charles F 271
  Edward C 271
  Ellen A 271
  Ellen (Poor) 271
  Elora 304
  Emma (Rand) 271
  George 94, 94
  Hannah 92, 120
  Herbert A. d 271
  Horace E 271
  Jabez, Rev 92, 198
  Jane 271
  John d 271
  Judith 120
  Lizzie 271
  Lizzie (Matthews) 94
  Lucinda 271
  Lucy A 271
  Luther 271
  Lydia d 120
  Maria 94
  Mary 120, 271, 271
  Mary (Locke) 92
  Mary (Prescott) 120
  Matilda (Philbrick) 271
  Matilda (Tibbetts) 271
  Mehitable (Osgood) 120
  Nellie 271
  Olive L. d 271
  Osgood 120
  Polly (Locke) 53
  Ruth (Brown) 198
  Sarah 120, 271, 419, 420
  Sarah (Philbrick) 271
  Sarah (Worthen) 270
  Seth 270
  Willie 271
  William 120, 271
TRUXALL, Benjamin 422
  Eva S 535
  Mary (Locke) 422
TRYDER, Mr 356
  Agnes (Locke) 356
TUCK, Abigail 35
  Deborah 176
  Eliza (Bradley) 531
  Elizabeth (Langley) 133
  Emma d 133
  Grace L 531
  George 133
  Huldah (Moulton) 60
  John 35, 531
  Jonathan 60
  Josiah 60
  Mary 285
  Sarah (Godfrey) 35
  Sarah (Lang-Crockett) 60
TUCKER, Mr 21
  Abigail 53, 361
  Abigail (Locke) 53, 191
  Adaline 237
  Addie 396
  Alfred 233, 396
  Almira (Watson) 297
  Annie 297
  Betsey 67, 250
  Catherine 122
  Charles 297, 396
  Clara 297
  Cyrene 53
  Dana 361
  Edith V 518

INDEX OF NAMES

TUCKER, Eleanor............53, 179
    Eliza........................ 53
    Elizabeth................33, 99
    Elizabeth (Locke)............ 179
    Elizabeth (Lombard).......... 401
    Elizabeth (Moses)............ 405
    Elvira (Locke)............... 233
    Emma (Watkins-Cook), Mrs...... 396
    Fannie....................... 297
    Franklin P................... 396
    George A..................... 396
    Hannah....................... 361
    Ida.......................... 306
    Isabella L................... 361
    James..................53, 53, 396
    Jane......................... 235
    Joanna M..................... 119
    John.....................191, 401
    Lizzie....................... 361
    Mary......................... 30
    Mary Elizabeth............... 345
    Michael...................... 405
    Nellie (Hubbard)............. 396
    Olly (Sanders)............... 55
    Pansy........................ 419
    Roswell...................... 208
    Sarah...................361, 451
    Sarah (Dexter-Locke)......... 208
    Sophronia.................... 99
    Susan...................237, 478
    Susanna (Locke).............. 21
    William...................... 55
TUFTS, Lucy T................... 111
TURKIN, Mary.................... 447
TURNER, Arthur..............468, 544
    Betsey....................... 86
    Darius K..................... 86
    Eunice (Farrar).............. 168
    Henry........................ 168
    Herbert L.................... 544
    Lewis........................ 86
    Lydia........................ 86
    Lyman........................ 86
    Martha....................... 86
    Mary A....................... 86
    S. Alice (Locke)............. 468
    Sally (Locke)................ 86
    Samuel L..................... 86
    Sarah........................ 86
    Warren....................... 86
TUTTLE, Benjamin B.............. 427
    Daniel....................... 321
    Emily (Kimball).............. 427
    Etta......................... 432
    Ora (Tibbitts)............... 321
TWOMBLY, Abbie d................ 531
    Charles E.................... 531
    Elma......................... 258
    George W..................... 531
    Laura E...................... 531
    Mary.....................245, 531
    Mary (Sanders)............... 417
    Nathaniel.................... 417
TYLER, Jennie................... 447
    Mary......................... 198
    Thais, Mrs................... 100
ULIGGETT, Henrietta............. 394
UMBSTAETTER, Martha............. 442
UNDERWOOD, Abigail.............. 51
    Charles...................... 416
    Clarence d................... 393
    Edgar W...................... 393
    Florence..................... 339
    Fred V....................... 416
    George W..................... 75
    Harry A...................... 393
    Josie (Ford)................. 416
    Lulu d....................... 393
    Mary (Aldrich)............... 393
    Mary (Locke)................. 75

UNDERWOOD, Sophia............... 40
UPTON, Alicia (Davis)........... 430
    Harry........................ 430
    Orville...................... 430
    Sarah (Moore)................ 430
UTLEY, Anna S................... 509
    Bridget...................... 193
VAILL, Charles R................ 374
    Deborah...................... 374
    Frederick W.................. 374
    John Locke................... 374
    Louise (Locke)............... 374
VANCE, Cynthia N................ 232
VANDERHEYDEN, Nancy............. 172
VAN DERYER, Ann (Wilkinson)..... 21
VAN DE SANDE, Daniel............ 365
    Mary (Froelich).............. 365
    Minnie....................... 193
VAN HORN, Anna.................. 251
VARNEY, Albert.................. 219
    Amos......................... 102
    Annie........................ 387
    Annie (Locke)................ 102
    Antoinette (Crockett)........ 219
    Caroline H. (Locke).......... 126
    Carrie....................... 568
    Charles..................219, 321
    Clara (Appleton-Larrabee).... 490
    Clara (Hill)................. 387
    Edward d..................... 219
    Effie L...................... 387
    Elias........................ 73
    Ellen........................ 156
    Elvin K...................... 387
    Faustus...................... 219
    (Foss), Miss................. 156
    Francis...................... 490
    Freeman...................... 156
    Gladys H..................... 387
    Hannah...................156, 219
    Hannah (Locke)............... 73
    Ida (Tibbitts)............... 321
    Lavina....................... 156
    Lavinia..................156, 221
    Lavinia (Hodgdon)............ 156
    Lewis........................ 151
    Lydia L...................... 219
    Marion....................... 156
    Martha (Otis-Ham)............ 151
    Nellie....................... 191
    Obadiah...................... 102
    Parmelia H. d................ 156
    Rachel (Felker).............. 156
    Robert...................126, 126
    Rockwell..................... 156
    Rufus........................ 156
    Sarah d...................... 210
    Sarah W. (Locke)............. 102
    Shubel....................... 156
    Solomon...................... 156
    Viola G...................... 387
VARNUM, Arvilla................. 223
    Lydia........................ 215
    Mary......................... 215
VARRELL, Annie.................. 322
    Annah (Lang)................. 66
    Charles...................... 322
    Clementina................... 149
    Eliza........................ 316
    Elizabeth.................... 19
    Ella (Marshall).............. 322
    Estell (DeNevarro)........... 322
    Gilman....................... 304
    Ida.......................... 322
    Jennie (Kerley).............. 322
    J. Morrison.................. 322
    John......................... 66
    Joseph....................... 55
    Lydia........................ 305
    Lydia (Wood)................. 322

INDEX OF NAMES

VARRELL, Merton... 322
  Nancy (Berry)... 65, 250, 322
  Sadie... 322
  Sally... 149
  Sarah... 250
  Sarah (Locke)... 149
  Sarah (Sanders-Sanders)... 55
  Willie d... 322
  William... 65, 149, 250, 322
VAUGHAN LAW SUIT... 5
VEAZEY, Benjamin... 42
  Benning... 364
  Deborah... 21, 42
  Eva G... 524
  Jennette (Tilton)... 364
  Joseph H... 193
  Judith... 223
  Mary T... 364
  Sarah (Locke)... 193
VEGA, Rafaele V... 520
  Sadie (Philbrick)... 520
VENNARD, Abbie U... 241
  Andrew... 109, 241
  Ariadne S. (Locke)... 109
  Emma G... 241
  Fannie A... 241
  Frances M. (Locke)... 108
  Franklin d... 241
  Georgeanna (McKessom)... 241
  Harriet... 401
  Helen B... 241
  John, Capt... 401
  Jonathan M. T... 108
  Mary... 106
  Sarah J... 235
  William L... 241
VERNON, Viss... 42
VICKAH, Dora... 353
VICKERS, Eliza... 282
VICKERY, Grace (Hanson)... 434
  J. E... 434
VILES, Elizabeth... 261
  Dolisca... 261
  William... 261
VIOLETTE, Madeline... 462
VIRGIN, Mary... 491
VITTUM, Hannah... 70
  Sarah, Mrs... 146
VOSE, Emily (Heywood)... 390
  John... 390
  Mary... 224
  Nellie... 390
VROOMAN, Ella J... 172
  Nicholas... 172
WADDINGTON, Alice... 454
  James... 274
  Sarah (Locke)... 274
WADE, Arthur... 415
  Ella (Kimball)... 415
  Martha... 422
WADHAMS, Almira... 174
WADLEIGH, Abbie (Tilton)... 217
  Fred T... 217
  Helen A... 217
  Inez H... 217
  J. B... 217
  Jane L... 154
  Moses... 325
  Oscar S... 217
  Sarah... 325
WADSWORTH, Charles, Rev... 206, 206
  Edith... 206
  Harry... 206
  Sarah (Locke)... 206
  William S., Dr... 206
WAGNER, Cora (Magoon)... 536
  Frederick G... 536
  George... 536
WAITE, Albert... 440
  Elizabeth (Stanwood)... 42

WAITE, Eunice Hale... 83
  Gertrude (Scott)... 440
WAITY, Eliza J... 172
WALCOTT, Abigail (Brown-Marden)... 111, 250
  Catherine (Elkins)... 111
  Edward... 111, 250
WALDO, Allen... 141, 141
  Fred F... 141
  Ida A. (Hicks)... 141
  Nancy (Maxwell)... 141
  Olive (Locke)... 141
  Rolfe d... 141
WALDRON-WALDEN.
  A. D... 314
  Annie (Edmonds)... 314
  Daniel... 101
  Edna... 314
  Irena (Dearborn)... 101
  Jane... 402
  Jonathan... 235
  Mabel... 331
  Major... 235
  Polly W... 107
  William... 314
WALKER, Mr... 94, 99, 322
  Addie (Perkins)... 219
  Agnes... 219
  Albion... 219
  Albert... 380
  Alfred... 319
  Alice (Abbott), Mrs... 491
  August (Page)... 545
  Belle (Locke)... 310
  Betsey... 66
  Charles... 310, 403, 484, 484
  Clara... 220
  Clara (Marden)... 403
  Delia... 162
  Edwin... 380, 557
  Eliza A... 30, 545
  Elizabeth A... 424
  Emma E... 424
  Fannie G... 380
  Florinda (Locke)... 246
  Frank... 423, 423
  George... 220, 545
  Hannah... 100
  Helen S... 484
  Henry... 220, 246, 424
  Herbert... 423
  Irving... 423
  Isabelle (Jenness)... 380
  Jesse M... 380
  John... 319
  Joseph A... 101
  Lottie P... 220
  Louisa L. (Matthews)... 94
  Lovina (Lake-Locke)... 322
  Lydia (Kimball)... 220
  Maria M. (Merrill)... 99
  Mark, Dr... 219
  Mary (Hoff)... 319
  Mary (Hussey)... 557
  Mary (Jones)... 423
  Mattie... 372
  Nancy... 66
  Rachel R... 38
  Ruhuma (Dearborn-Kent)... 101
  Sarah... 310, 484
  Sophia... 58
  Susie... 446
  Weston... 423
  William C... 484
WALLACE, Miss... 129
  Abbie... 418
  Alexander... 459
  Alice... 537
  Alice (Locke)... 423
  Almira (Greenleaf)... 411
  Annie... 537

INDEX OF NAMES

WALLACE, Arthur C. 411
  Blanche Y. 459
  Clarissa. 110
  Comfort. 18
  Cora B. 459
  Edna J. 537
  Effie. 130, 130
  Elbridge H. 537
  Elijah. 290
  Ella E. 459
  Henry 411
  Hugh. 537
  Jane. 452
  John. 202, 245
  Joseph. 411
  Margaret. 93
  Marion d. 411
  Mary. 130
  Nancy (Sanders). 245
  Pearl. 537
  Phebe S. 123
  Polly. 290
  Robert L. 537
  Sarah N. 202
  Sarah, Mrs. 282
  Sarah (Locke). 282
  Sarah (Towle). 202
  Sophia. 459
  William. 282, 423, 537
WALLES, Mary. 435
WALLINGFORD, Abigail (Stoker). 95
  Ann. 95
  Charles. 95
  David. 95
  George. 95
  Ives. 95
  James. 95
  Joanna. 72
  Maria O. (Locke). 95
  Marion. 95
WALLIS, Abbie. 130
  Elijah. 130
  Eliza. 130
  Eunice. 72
  Hannah. 107
  John. 60
  Martha. 130
  Mary E. 130
  Mary (Locke). 60
  Nathaniel. 5
  Sarah (Towle). 130
  Susan. 130
WALTON, Betsey. 214
  Martha. 215
  Mary. 366
  Sally (Chase). 384
  Shadrack. 3
  William. 384
WALWORTH, Eliza (Whittier). 253
  H. R., Rev. 253
WARD, Mrs. 35
  Albert N. 196
  Edward. 473
  Eliza (Brown). 145
  Elizabeth. 87
  Emma. 493
  Georgeanna. 345
  Hannah (Stevens). 196
  Joseph. 145
  Julia (Grant). 473
  Lillian (Wright). 319
  Lydia. 145
  Lydia (Gage). 553
  Margaret. 13
  Mary. 473
  Sarah. 23
  Thomas. 23, 553
WARDWELL, Amelia. 180, 346
WARDSWELL, Winnifred. 340
WARE, Abbie. 200

WARE, Ebenezer. 13
  Elizabeth (Wilson). 24
  Mehit. (Wyman). 24
  Prudence (Locke). 13
  Peter. 24
WARMOUTH, Mary. 81
WARMSLEY, Emma K. 428
  Mary (Locke). 428
  Thomas. 428
WARNE, Elisha. 278
  Mary (Woodman). 278
WARNER, Agnes (Bishop). 373
  Cornelius. 373
  Lillian Davis. 33, 362
WARREN, A. K. 65
  Annie. 386
  Catherine (Palmer). 176
  Celestia. 162
  Eliza (Berry). 65
  George. 176, 242, 242
  Lottie. 499
  Martha (Scott). 556
  Mary. 428
  Susan (Taplin). 242
  Wellington. 556
  William. 242
WARRING, Emaline. 141
WASHER, Ismenia. 90
WASHINGTON, Genl. 21
WATERHOUSE, Alexander. 463
  Elizabeth A. 125
  Eva. 179
  Lucy (Cate). 463
  Mary. 284
  Nicholas V. 286
  Sarah (Locke-Webster), Mrs. 51
  Susan (Chesley-Place). 286
  Solomon. 51
WATERS, Prudentia D. 80
  Samuel. 80
WATKINS, Emma. 396
  Lois. 171
WATSON, Abbie. 297
  Abbie (Bell). 545
  Albert. 234
  Almira S. 297
  Anna. 179
  Alpha Maria. 156
  Aramenta (Page). 435
  Asa. 106, 234
  Azilla. 297
  Belinda (Locke). 156
  Benjamin D. 234
  Bertha (Watson). 545
  Charles. 414, 545
  Clara (Locke). 473
  Daniel. 207
  David L. 414
  Delila (Locke-Jewett). 80
  Edward F. 123
  Eleanor R. 545
  Eliza (Walker). 545
  Elizabeth L. 297
  Emma F. 498
  Etta (Fare). 346
  Eugene. 498
  Franklin d. 234
  George. 435
  Hannah. 297, 297
  Hannah (Langley). 133
  Hannah (Prescott). 195
  Harriet (Chick). 300
  Helen L. 234
  Henry N. 234
  Irving. 545, 545
  Isaac. 346
  James I. 473
  Jennie (Farwell). 414
  John. 80, 195, 234, 545
  Joseph. 300

INDEX OF NAMES

WATSON, Laura d.................. 545
  Lois A......................... 545
  Lucy........................... 545
  Lysander.....................156, 156
  Malinda A...................... 156
  Marion S....................... 545
  Martha (Horn).................. 498
  Mary.............118, 234, 297, 346
  Mary (Locke)................... 106
  Mary (McManus)................. 234
  Mary (Nutter).................. 275
  Miribah (Main)................. 123
  Norman......................... 234
  Olive N........................ 234
  Perley H....................... 545
  Sarah.......................... 331
  Stephen........................ 133
  Walter S....................... 156
  William..................275, 275, 300
  Zuella......................... 297
WATTS, Lucy....................... 291
  Nancy.......................... 29
WAY, Annie........................ 28
  Sarah.......................... 136
WEARE, Abigail (Young)............ 217
  Albert M....................... 217
  Caroline W..................... 102
  Caroline W. d.................. 102
  Charles D...................... 217
  Frank J........................ 217
  Hannah R....................... 102
  Hattie B....................... 368
  Irene (French)................. 513
  Jonathan....................... 513
  Mary E......................... 176
  Mary (Locke)................24, 48
  Mary (Redman).................. 176
  Meribah G...................... 217
  Meribah (Green)................ 102
  Meshcck................24, 102, 217
  Nathaniel...................24, 48
  Taylor......................... 176
WEATHERBEE, Harriet A............. 145
WEBB, Lizzie...................... 187
WEBSTER, Abbie (Locke)............ 248
  Abigail........................ 64
  Ada............................ 438
  Adelaide....................... 250
  Andrew.....................13, 24, 111
  Annette........................ 216
  Augustus F..................... 111
  Benjamin B..................... 225
  Betsey.....................104, 223
  Carrie......................... 186
  Daniel......................... 24
  David......................111, 257
  David Locke.................... 111
  Davison........................ 101
  Dorothy........................ 108
  Ebenezer....................... 24
  Elizabeth...................41, 225
  Elizabeth (Macy)............... 111
  Elizabeth (Randall)............ 56
  Emily (Pollard)................ 186
  Eunice G. (Nowell)............. 111
  Fanny.......................... 111
  Flora (Locke).................. 307
  Frances........................ 249
  Frank D........................ 216
  Georgine....................... 216
  Hannah......................... 225
  Hannah (Ayer).................. 14
  Hannah (Grant)................. 111
  Henry C........................ 216
  Jacob.......................... 104
  Jennie......................... 186
  Joanna (Callum)................ 14
  Joanna (Locke)................. 104
  John.......................11, 108, 111
  Josiah.....................111, 111

WEBSTER, Joshua................... 51
  Judith......................... 14
  Julia (Dearborn)............... 101
  Levi........................... 111
  Mark........................... 486
  Martha....................51, 68, 111
  Mary.....................111, 216, 228
  Mary (Five).................... 216
  Mary (Lang).................... 486
  Mary (Philbrick)............... 128
  Nathaniel...................... 111
  Nellie......................... 216
  Osmond......................... 186
  Porter......................... 186
  Prudence....................... 24
  Prudence (Locke-Ware).......... 13
  Rachel......................... 385
  Richard......................56, 128
  Sally........................57, 111
  Sally (Wheaton)................ 225
  Samuel......................... 248
  Sarah.....113, 256, 271, 249, 313, 517
  Sarah (Jameson)................ 257
  Sarah (Locke).................. 51
  Stephen........................ 14
  Susan P........................ 89
  Tryphena (Locke)............... 11
  William........................ 307
WEDGE, Grace (Wright)............. 260
  Utley.......................... 260
WEDGWOOD, Betsey.................. 65
  Eliza G., Mrs.................. 145
  Fannie (Batson)................ 397
  Forrest........................ 397
  Hannah (Moore)................. 234
  Jonathan....................... 234
  M. F. J........................ 325
  Mary........................... 107
  Mary, Mrs...................... 28
  Sally L........................ 106
WEED, Benjamin.................... 192
  Julia.......................... 98
  Mary........................... 146
  Nellie......................... 192
WEEKS, Abigail.................... 201
  Ann M.......................... 201
  Anna (Philbrick)............... 56
  Annie.......................... 370
  Caroline (Garvin).............. 201
  Elisha......................... 121
  Elizabeth L. (Reynolds)........ 121
  Frank B........................ 201
  George......................... 418
  Hannah (McCrillis)............. 200
  Hattie (Emerson)............... 201
  Helen.......................... 405
  Ida........................132, 296
  James.......................... 93
  John........................... 200
  Jonathan L. B.................. 201
  Joseph.....................121, 201
  Josiah......................... 56
  Lizzie C....................... 201
  Martha C....................... 201
  Mary C. d...................... 201
  Mary (Locke)................... 93
  Mary (Porter).................. 121
  Melinda (Green)................ 418
  Olive.......................... 87
  Sarah.......................... 303
  Susan.......................... 201
  Susan (Abbott)................. 200
  Viola.......................... 477
WELCH, Mr......................... 308
  Abbie (Locke).................. 308
  Cornelia....................... 255
  Dorcas......................... 354
  Margaret....................... 71
  Mary........................... 307
WELLER, Alice K................... 344

INDEX OF NAMES 715

WELLS, Mr. ... 418
  A. (Burleigh) ... 226
  Albert H. ... 208
  Albro ... 390
  Alice (Dennett-Jones), Mrs. ... 226
  Amanda W. ... 226
  Annie ... 272
  Annie (Green-Kyle) ... 418
  Beatrice ... 208
  Benjamin L. ... 225
  Betsey ... 57
  Carrie M. ... 226
  Charles ... 226, 272
  Clement ... 272
  Dalton ... 208
  Deborah ... 88
  Elizabeth (Locke-King-Duplaise) ... 308
  Ellen C. ... 391
  Elvira (Locke-Tucker) ... 233
  Emma (Locke) ... 208
  Emma ... 289
  F. J. (George), Mrs. ... 391
  Frank ... 308, 510
  Hannah (Blake) ... 226
  Hannah (Rollins) ... 225
  Hannah (Wells) ... 104
  Harriet (Robie) ... 390
  Harry D. ... 390
  Henry ... 104, 391
  Howard Elgin ... 391
  Irene (Piper) ... 391
  John ... 226, 233, 396
  Kiah ... 104
  Levina (Locke) ... 104
  Lillian (Simonds) ... 391
  Lizzie (Davis or Ingalls-Locke) ... 510
  Lois ... 111
  Lurietta (Moore) ... 272
  Lydia ... 272
  Mary E. ... 363, 390, 396
  Mary (Locke) ... 192
  Mary (Sleeper) ... 225
  Nina ... 272
  Peter ... 225, 225, 226
  Richard ... 391
  Rose (Boswell) ... 226
  Sadie ... 272
  Samuel, Capt. ... 192
  Sarah ... 57, 227, 363, 390, 392
  Sarah (Ferrin) ... 226
  Sarah (Hammond) ... 396
  Timothy ... 272
  Wilson ... 272
WENDELKEN, Carrie ... 377
WENDELL, Caroline ... 74
  Elizabeth ... 30
WENSLEY, Gertrude ... 341
WENTWORTH, Abigail (Bennett) ... 149
  Andrew ... 241, 323
  Anna ... 41
  Benjamin ... 149
  Charles ... 548
  Charlotte H. ... 72
  Dana W. ... 81
  Eliza (Locke) ... 194
  Eunice ... 155
  Evelyn (Jenkins) ... 548
  George ... 317
  John ... 194
  Josephine ... 326
  Lydia ... 93
  Lydia (Whitehouse) ... 328
  Mary ... 146, 241
  Mehitable (Gordon) ... 328
  Nathan ... 328
  Patience ... 66
  Rebecca (Dyer) ... 81
  Sarah ... 241
  Sarah (Lane) ... 180
  Sarah (Lord) ... 317

WENTWORTH, Susan W. ... 155
  Valery ... 548
WENTZELL, Elias ... 552, 552
  Hester (Philbrick) ... 552
WESLEY, John, Rev. ... 508
WEST, Alice ... 492
  Clarenda (Batson) ... 397
  Elizabeth (Foster) ... 519
  Frank ... 397, 519
  Lavina ... 280
  Martha ... 276
  Mary ... 37
  Sally ... 455
  Samuel ... 455
WESTFALL, Mary ... 126
WESTON, Alice E. ... 537
  Barret L. ... 537
  Charles ... 424, 537
  Doris ... 537
  Elizabeth (Walker) ... 424
  Emir (Root) ... 537
  Henry, Dr., U. S. A. ... 537
WETHERBEE, Frieda ... 504
  Phebe ... 424
  Sally (Jesseman) ... 538
  Smith ... 538
WETMORE, Mr. ... 358
  Sophia (Locke) ... 358
WEYGARTT, Henry J. ... 537
  Lucy (Locke) ... 537
WEYMOUTH, Gertrude (Jennings) ... 505
  J. Elmer ... 505
WHALEN, Aseneth (Kenniston) ... 467
  Cynthia L. (Locke) ... 127
  Harriet (Locke-Phenix) ... 292
  James ... 127
  John ... 292, 467
WHEATON, Sally ... 225
WHEELER, Bertha T. ... 243
  Cora I. ... 546
  Eustace A. ... 243
  Margaret ... 289
  Mary ... 461
  Millicent ... 28
  Musie (Locke) ... 243
  Robert ... 243
  Susan ... 58
WHENAL, Harry T. ... 527
  Helen ... 527
  Isabelle (White) ... 527
  Thomas ... 527
WHICHER, Benjamin ... 130
  Catherine (Cole) ... 130
  Hattie (Caswell) ... 372
  Henry ... 372
  Martin H. ... 130
  Meanie ... 372
  Nancy (Locke) ... 130
  Naomi E. ... 568
WHIDDEN, Abbie (Fowler) ... 255
  Almira (Locke) ... 255
  Carrie E. ... 405
  Charles G. ... 405
  Edith M. ... 405
  Eldora A. ... 405
  Elizabeth (Berry) ... 236
  Emily (Cole), Mrs. ... 405
  Frank L. ... 405
  Ira W. ... 405
  Joseph ... 236, 255, 405
  Marion (Marden) ... 405
  Mary O. ... 405
  Nellie (Pearson) ... 405
  Sarah (Pickering) ... 405
WHIPPLE, Irene ... 228
  Jacob ... 89
  Ruhuma P. (Locke) ... 89
WHITCOMB, E. D. ... 320
  Mary (Holmes-Downes) ... 320
WHITE, Abbie ... 253, 268

INDEX OF NAMES

WHITE, Abbot H. 527
  Abigail (Danforth) 391
  Ada E. 527
  Adelaide F. (Locke) 136
  Anna 264, 476
  Annette 391
  Benjamin 304
  Catherine (Burns) 391
  Charles J. 136, 381
  Elizabeth 32
  Erving G. 527
  Flora (Locke) 532
  Frederick G. 391
  George 227, 391, 403
  Gertrude (Peek) 527
  Grace d 304
  Hannah 15
  Hannah (Leach) 233
  Hannah (Libbey) 526
  Hannah W. (Locke) 161
  Harriet 381
  Harrison L. 136
  Henry G. d 391
  Isabelle T. 527
  Jane 475
  Jessie 381
  Joan (Bell) 446
  Joseph 32, 397
  Katherine 381
  Lillian S. 136
  Malcolm 532
  Margaret 233
  Margaret (Dodge) 381
  Margaret (White-Neal) 397
  Mary 437, 474
  Mary (Locke) 16
  Nancy 295, 417
  Nathan 32, 32
  Nathaniel 397
  Nellie M. 526
  Parkman 526
  Polly (Marden) 403
  Rollo S. 527
  Roxy (Locke) 227
  Salome 11
  Samuel H. 304
  Sarah G. 116
  Sarah (Greeley) 261
  Solomon 16, 32
  Susan (Hill) 304
  Walter H. 391
  Warren 391, 532, 532
  William 15, 161, 446, 526
  William, Major 261
WHITEHOUSE, Abbie 273
  Alice 464
  Anna 315
  Bessie 529
  Edwin 529
  Elizabeth (Dudley) 251
  John 111, 251
  Lydia 328
  M. B. (Seawards) 529
  Mary d 251
  Polly L. (Sanborn) 111
  Sarah 251
  Solomon 251
WHITET, Jane 184
WHITMAN, Ella 336
WHITNEY, Arthur 366
  Emma 459
  George 366
  Gladys 452
  Helen 452
  Irene 452
  J. W., Dr. 452
  Lucy (Berry) 452
  Mary 452
  Pauline (Hillard) 366
  Rowena (Locke) 366

WHITTAKER, Abigail (Emerson) 446
  Catherine (Holland) 421
  Edgar 421, 421
  Edith 421
  Ethel d 421
  Fred 520
  Helen (Locke) 246
  Howard 421
  James 446
  Madeline (Philbrick) 520
  Nicholas, Rev 246
  Sarah 264
WHITTEMORE, Aaron 322
  Annie 322
  Ariana (Brewster) 322
  Dorcas 502
  Fred 389, 389
  Ida (Doloff) 389
  Lena 389
  Lulu 389
  Wilfred 389
WHITTIER, Miss 362
  Mr. 148
  Adaline 253
  Almira (Poor) 270
  Angeline 253
  Angeline (Bradford) 252
  Caroline d 433
  Charles 253, 433
  Charles Henry 362
  Claire 253
  Edgar 253
  Edmund 270
  Eliza 253
  Elizabeth 433
  Emily (Pitman) 148
  Eunice (Locke) 192
  George 192, 253, 362
  Grace 362
  Helen L. 433
  Jacob H. 362
  James 85
  Jemima (Huntress) 252
  Joseph 112, 252, 433
  L. E. (Leith) 433
  Lewis 362
  Lilla (Page) 362
  Lottie 362
  Lucy 253, 433
  Lucy (Lord) 433
  Lydia 253, 253
  Martha (Haines) 362
  Mary 53
  Mary (Wood), Mrs. 433
  Matilda 85
  Maude (Ross) 433
  Nancy 253
  Nancy (Locke) 112
  Nellie 253
  Nellie (Locke) 355
  Obadiah 252
  Olive 85
  Perley 85
  Rhoda 137
  Ruth 433
  Sally (Locke) 85
  Samuel 85, 252
  Sarah (Austin) 252
  Sarah (Lindsey) 253
  Seward d 433
  Thomas P. 433
  Wilmot 355
WHITTREDGE, Annah (Locke-Tallant) . 249
  George F. 249
WIGGIN, Bina 477, 548
  Celia 367
  Clara 239
  Hannah 44
  Mabel 436
  Maria 410

INDEX OF NAMES 717

WIGGIN, Paul W. 553
  Philena F. (Locke) 104
  Samuel 276
  Sarah 132
  Sophronia (Locke) 276
  Timothy 104
  Winnie (Otis) 553
WIGHT, Abigail 124
  Andrew 282
  Margaret (Corbet) 282
WILCOX, Anna (Utley) 509
  Dutee 360
  Emma L. 509
  Emma (Locke) 360
  Grace M. 509
  Howard D. 509
  Madeline 509
  Mary 257
WILKERSON, Coyle N. 416
  John N. 416
  Lizzie (Locke) 416
WILKINSON, Ann 21
  Joseph 499
  Rachel (Locke) 499
WILLARD, Mr. 526
  Hattie (Reed) 526
  Mary E., Mrs. 210
  Sarah O. 233
WILLBER, Alice H. 555
  Amy (Logsdon) 555
  Bryan 555
  Edith 555
  George H. 555
  Josephine C. 555
  Josephine (Haughton) 497
  Karl A. 555
  Okie 555
  Parmelia F. 555
  Perry 497
  Surelda 497
WILLCUT, Sarah F. 12
WILLEY, Addie S. (Ham) 159
  Alice 194, 202
  Betsey (Sanborn) 194
  Charles 159
  Dorothy (Otis) 151
  Edith 194
  John 194, 194
  Josiah 194
  Lemuel 151
  Lucinda E. 134
  Martha 309
  Ruth 194
  Sally (Locke) 194
  Sarah 566
  Wealthy 194
WILLIAMS, Mr. 93
  Abigail 128
  Amanda 424
  Avice E. 244
  Betsey 260
  Clara 493
  Dora 307
  Dorothy L. 435
  Ernest d. 244
  Frank B. 254
  Franklin 538
  George H. 240
  Harriet 444
  Hattie (Locke) 307
  Henry A. 244
  Idris 355
  Irene (Locke) 89
  Jacob 89, 307
  Jennie 305, 519
  John H. 307
  Marguerite L. 435
  Mary (Grant-Locke) 240
  Mary (Locke) 244, 254
  Melinda 189

WILLIAMS, (Nealey), Miss 93
  Nina 378
  Sarah (Perkins) 93
  Willard 93
WILLIAMSON, Emaline 126
  Sally A. 153
WILLIS, Azro 305
  Carrie (Locke) 305
  Frances C. 480
  Locke A. 480
  Minnie L. 480
  Sally (Dodge), Mrs. 37
  Sarah 66
WILLOUGHBY, Almira 435
  Sarah 360
WILLS, John 197, 354
  Mary (Stevens) 197
  Ruth Hussey 185
WILSON, Mr. 211
  Abby (Rollins) 210
  Alanson 188
  Allen 188
  Amelia (Sanborn) 111
  Annie 493
  Cora A. 188
  Deborah 18
  Elizabeth 24
  Eleanor 62
  Emma (Bryant) 188
  Fidelia 188
  Frances 437
  Frederick 210
  Grace (Cutter) 188
  Grace (Winkley) 211
  Jennie 338
  Jesse L., Rev. 86
  Laura 321
  Lucy (Locke) 86
  Lucy (Perkins) 198
  Maria B. (Demeritt) 126
  Nathan 126
  Philanda 188
  Robert 111, 198
  Sarah A. 160
  Sumner 188
WILTH, Carrie 456
  Hannah (Locke) 456
  Joseph 456
  Silas 456
WILZIN, Arthur 385
  Rachel (Webster) 385
WINANS, Clarissa (Sanborn) ... 251
  Isaac 251
WINCH, Nellie 413
WING, Clara 484
  Frank 484
  Gertrude 484
  Jane (Locke) 186
  Matthew 186
WINGATE, Albert L. 325
  Alphonzo 325
  Arthur L. 325
  Dorothy 518
  Helen 518
  Helen (Locke) 395
  James W. 395
  Mary 187
  Orianna (Mitchell) 518
  Sadie (Locke) 325
  Samuel 518
WINKLEY, Enoch 97
  Francis J. 211
  Grace 211
  Joan 286
  John d. 380
  John Francis 210
  Mary Margaret 380
  Mary (Locke) 97
  Mary S. 210
  Mira (———) 211

INDEX OF NAMES

WINKLEY, Sarah..................210, 461
  Susan Maria................... 280
  Susan (Todd).................. 210
WINN, Arabella (Locke)............. 313
  Benjamin...................... 313
  Louis F....................... 313
  Susie......................... 445
  William....................... 445
WINSHIP, Abigail (Noyes)............ 76
  Seth.......................... 76
WINSLOW, Miss..................... 313
  John T........................ 163
  Mary (Noyes).................. 163
WINTER, Elizabeth.................. 135
  Isaac......................... 61
  Miranda....................... 135
  Sarah......................... 135
  Solomon....................... 135
  Tryphena (Locke).............. 61
WISE, Adeline...................... 223
WITHERELL, Emma L................. 320
WITHEY, Abigail.................... 88
WOLF, Genl........................ 25
WOOD-WOODS.
  Adaline....................... 362
  Channing...................... 407
  Desdemona..................... 510
  Dorcas (Noyes)................ 163
  Eliza......................... 558
  George S., U. S. N............ 557
  Hannah......................55, 80
  Harriet....................... 163
  Helen (Dunbar)................ 557
  James F....................... 558
  John L........................ 295
  Joseph.....................131, 163
  Lena A........................ 322
  Lizzie (Berry)................ 407
  Lydia......................... 322
  Martha (Locke-Bickford)....... 131
  Mary, Mrs..................... 433
  Mattie........................ 300
  Nathan........................ 322
  Peleg......................... 172
  Sarah......................... 67
WOODBRIDGE, Benjamin...........26, 50
  Elizabeth..................... 106
  Mary (Osgood)................. 50
  Patience...................... 50
  Patience (Locke).............. 26
WOODBURY, Miss.................... 92
  Charles....................... 165
  Drusilla (Locke).............. 199
  Ebenezer...................... 165
  Edith......................... 367
  Elizabeth S. (Noyes).......... 77
  Emma.......................... 165
  George W...................... 199
  Georgeanna.................... 367
  Hattie (Flanders)............. 367
  John.......................77, 367
  Josiah........................ 119
  Maud.......................... 524
  Nathaniel..................... 367
  Phebe (Locke-Garvey).......... 242
  Philander..................... 242
  Polly (Knowles)............... 119
WOODHULL, Gertrude................ 388
WOODMAN, Mr....................... 75
  Addie C....................... 124
  Alexander..................... 123
  Alice (Bartholomew)........... 279
  Alice (Davis)................. 280
  Anna (Watson)................. 179
  Annie (Smith)................. 458
  Augusta....................... 278
  Austin W...................... 124
  Betsey.....................279, 413
  Betsey (Kimball).............. 123
  Caroline...................... 123
WOODMAN, Cassandra................ 133
  Charles..................124, 124, 124
  Clara......................... 158
  Clara, Mrs.................... 435
  Clarissa d.................... 123
  Cora M........................ 124
  Corydon E..................... 124
  Della (Hawley)................ 279
  Dr............................ 92
  Eleanor (Barnard)............. 123
  Elizabeth..................... 123
  Emily C....................... 279
  Eunice A...................... 278
  Eunice M. (Kimball)........... 123
  Florenda (Bachelder).......... 92
  Freeman.................123, 278, 279
  George.....................124, 278
  Hannah.....................278, 278
  Harriet....................... 278
  Harriet (Clifford-Pendleton).. 75
  Ira........................... 123
  Ira, Rev...................... 279
  Isaac......................... 54
  Jacob A....................... 124
  James.....................278, 458
  Jemima (Avery)................ 124
  Jennie L...................... 413
  Jeremiah...................... 179
  John.......................... 280
  Joseph..................123, 278, 280
  Joshua........................ 242
  Juliet........................ 279
  Kimball F..................... 279
  Laura (Thompson).............. 278
  Lillias....................... 82
  Lucy (Hollister).............. 278
  Lydia (Burbank)............... 279
  Lyman......................124, 279
  Martha A...................... 279
  Martha (French)............... 124
  Mary......................278, 413
  Mary Ann...................... 123
  Mary (Berry).................. 279
  Mary (Judd)................... 279
  Mary (Locke).................. 54
  Miretta....................... 278
  Nancy (Jenness)............... 54
  Nathaniel..................... 123
  Nellie........................ 458
  Olive (Locke)................. 242
  Peter......................... 413
  Phebe......................... 413
  Phebe S. (Wallace)............ 123
  Roger......................... 124
  Sarah E....................... 280
  Susan (Hutchins).............. 279
WOODMANSEE, Chloe, Mrs............ 75
  Jerusha (Moors)............... 161
  John.......................... 161
  Lucy.......................... 170
WOODRUFF, Mr...................... 95
  Fred.......................... 95
  George........................ 95
  Marion (Wallingford).......... 95
WOODSUM, Helen.................... 234
  John.......................... 399
  Sarah......................... 399
WOODSWORTH, Mr.................... 314
  Sarah (Edmonds)............... 314
WOODWARD, Clara................... 419
WOODWORTH, Alice (Cooper-Clint)... 232
  Frank......................... 232
WORCESTER, Mr..................... 329
  Etta (Hussey-Hodgdon)......... 329
  George........................ 448
  Georgie (Lamprey)............. 448
  Lora.......................... 448
  Loring........................ 448
WORDEN, Dorothy................... 37
  Eliza (Babcock)............... 37

INDEX OF NAMES

WORDEN, John 37
WORKS, Marion 256
WORTHEN, Mr. 50
  Bela L. 270
  Betsey 270
  Esther 270
  George 362
  Gilman 270
  Hannah (Ingalls) 50
  Hannah (True) 120
  Isaac 120
  Jane (Richards) 270
  John D. 270
  Lotta (Whittier) 362
  Lucinda (Taylor) 270
  Lucy (French) 270
  Lydia 270
  Minerva (McConnell) 270
  Martha 26
  Mary 270
  Matthew 270
  Samuel, Lieut. 49
  Sanborn 270
  Sarah T. 270
  True W. 270
WORTHINTON, Clara (Cooper) 232
  Elizabeth 19
  Ethel M. 511
  Fred 232
  George 361, 511
  Grace B. 511
  Harvey J. d. 511
  Nancy (Hoyt) 511
  Sarah (Locke-Blanchard) 361
  Thomas 51
WORTHLEY, Albert L. 449
  Daniel 389
  Harriet L. 449
  Harriet (Locke) 269
  Henry M. 449
  Katie d 449
  Mary 389
  Mary (Milling) 449
  Sewell 269
WRIGHT, Alvira (Dore) 182
  Anna (Chambers) 442
  Charles 260, 442
  Ella P. 182
  Grace 260, 442
  Helen 442
  Jessie 442
  Kate 563
  John L. 442
  Lillian 319
  Louisa (Lang) 260
  Mary (Cook) 345
  Peter 260
  Robert 345
  Sally 94
  Sarah (Lang) 261
  Spencer 261, 442
  William H., Capt. 182
  Wilmot 260
WYMAN, Barbara (Hardy) 264
  Evaline 205
  Flora 205
  Florinda (Locke) 95
  Marie E. 165
  Mehitable 24
  Oscar 95
YEARICK, Mabel 534
YEARTAW, Carrie 416
YEATON, Alice d 431
  Anna (Green) 249
  Betsey 566
  Clarence 431
  Conrad 431
  Cora (Morse) 431
  Edna (Andrews) 432
  Elizabeth (Brown) 68

YEATON, Elmer d 431
  Fannie (Collins) 249
  Fred 431
  George W. 432, 432
  Helen 431, 432
  Ivan 431
  Joseph 68, 249
  Josephine (Drake) 249
  Lillian 432
  Lottie (Palmer) 431
  Lydia 88
  Mary 16
  Mary (Brown) 249
  Rosie (Cummings) 431
  S. Albert. 431
  Sarah 202, 431
  Sarah B. (Locke) 110
  Simeon L. 249
  William 110, 249, 249, 431
YIRRILL, Mr. 63
  Betsey (Locke) 63
YORK, Albert, Dr. 519
  Elizabeth (Dow) 323
  Joseph 38
  Mamie (Locke) 510
  Mary (Pettigrew) 519
  Omah 510
  Susanna (Ring) 20
YOUNG, Miss 213
  Mr. 260
  Abbie 284
  Abbott L. 407
  Abigail 217
  Abigail (Sanders) 249
  Ada (Trask) 523
  Addie C. d. 524
  Alice (Robbins) 523
  Angeline (Brown) 142
  Anna E. (Locke) 149
  Annie E. 523
  Arthur L. 407
  Augustine 285
  Benjamin 249
  Carroll 523
  Charles 277, 277, 464
  Clementina (Varrell) 149
  Daniel S. 400, 523, 524
  David 142
  David, Rev. 523
  Doris 464
  Elisha, Capt. 213
  Elizabeth (Batson) 400
  Emma (Perkins) 219
  Enoch 344
  Fannie (Locke) 287
  Florence 277, 534
  Francis d 523
  Frank O. 523
  Fred L. 464
  Freeman 277
  George 277, 277, 277
  Gertrude L. (Fogg) 407
  Gladys L. 513
  Hannah 144
  Hannah (Hodgdon) 523
  Harriet 98
  Herman E. 464
  Ida M. 524
  Ivory 463
  John 312
  Joseph 219
  King 287
  Leslie S. 523
  Levit 277
  Lewis E. 464
  Lucy 344
  Lucy (Cook) 344
  Lydia (Main) 123
  Margie d 524
  Marietta 172

YOUNG, Mary............72, 272, 277
   Mary (Craig).................. 464
   Mary (Hanscom)............... 312
   Mary (Locke).................. 285
   Mary (Seavey)................. 463
   Maud (Woodbury).............. 524
   May H........................ 523
   Maynard...................... 523
   Melvin S. d................... 523
   Mertie E...................... 464
   Miriam........................ 94

YOUNG, Oliver..................... 523
   Raymond...................... 523
   Sarah......................... 56
   Sarah (Lang).................. 260
   Stella (Banks)................. 464
   Stephen....................... 123
   Susan......................... 431
   (Swasey), Miss................ 277
   William P..................... 149
ZOELLER, Clara.................... 499

www.ingramcontent.com/pod-product-compliance
Lightning Source LLC
Chambersburg PA
CBHW071212290426
44108CB00013B/1166